TheStreet.com Ratings' Guide to Property and Casualty

TheStreet.com Ratings' Guide to Property and Casualty Insurers

A Quarterly Compilation of Insurance Company Ratings and Analyses

Fall 2009

GREY HOUSE PUBLISHING

TheStreet.com Ratings, Inc.
14 Wall Street, 15th Floor
New York, NY 10005
800-289-9222

Published by Grey House Publishing, Inc. located at 4919 Route 22 Amenia, NY 12501; telephone 518-789-8700. Grey House Publishing neither guarantees the accuracy of the data contained herein nor assumes any responsibility for errors, omissions or discrepancies. Grey House Publishing accepts no payment for listing; inclusion in the publication of any organization agency, institution, publication, service or individual does not imply endorsement of the publisher.

Grey House
Publishing

Edition No. 62, Fall 2009

ISBN: 978-1-59237-468-7
ISSN: 1935-5327

Contents

Terms and Conditions

Message To Insurers

All survey data received on or before August 3, 2009 has been considered or incorporated into this edition of the Directory. If you have not yet completed our survey form, call Sandy Fenton at TheStreet.com Ratings, Inc., (561) 354-4400. If there are particular circumstances which you believe could affect your rating, please use the survey sheets we have sent you or send a written request to bring it to our attention. If warranted, we will make every effort to incorporate the changes in our next edition.

Welcome to TheStreet.com Ratings'
Guide to Property and Casualty Insurers

Most people automatically assume their insurance company will survive, year after year. However, prudent consumers and professionals realize that in this world of shifting risks, the solvency of insurance companies can't be taken for granted.

If you are looking for accurate, unbiased ratings and data to help you choose property and casualty insurance for yourself, your family, your company or your clients, TheStreet.com Ratings' *Guide to Property and Casualty Insurers* gives you precisely what you need.

In fact, it's the only source that currently provides ratings and analyses on over 2,400 property and casualty insurers.

TheStreet.com Ratings' Mission Statement

TheStreet.com Ratings' mission is to empower consumers, professionals, and institutions with high quality advisory information for selecting or monitoring a financial services company or financial investment.

In doing so, TheStreet.com Ratings will adhere to the highest ethical standards by maintaining our independent, unbiased outlook and approach to advising our customers.

Why rely on TheStreet.com Ratings?

TheStreet.com Ratings provides fair, objective ratings to help professionals and consumers alike make educated purchasing decisions.

At TheStreet.com Ratings, integrity is number one. TheStreet.com Ratings never takes a penny from insurance companies for issuing a rating. We publish TheStreet.com Financial Strength Ratings without regard for insurers' preferences. However, other rating agencies like A.M. Best, Fitch, Moody's and Standard & Poor's are paid by insurance companies for their ratings and may even suppress unfavorable ratings at an insurer's request.

Our ratings are reviewed and updated more frequently than the other agencies' ratings. You can be sure that the information you receive is accurate and current, providing you with advance warning of financial vulnerability early enough to do something about it.

Other rating agencies focus primarily on a company's current claims paying ability and consider only mild economic adversity. TheStreet.com Ratings also considers these issues, but our analysis also covers a company's ability to deal with severe economic adversity and a sharp increase in claims.

Our use of more rigorous standards stems from the viewpoint that an insurance company's obligations to its policyholders should not depend on favorable business conditions. An insurer must be able to honor its policy commitments in bad times as well as good.

Our rating scale, from A to F, is easy to understand. Only a few outstanding companies receive an A (Excellent) rating, although there are many to choose from within the B (Good) category. An even larger group falls into the broad average range which receives C (Fair) ratings. Companies that demonstrate marked vulnerabilities receive either D (Weak) or E (Very Weak) ratings.

How to Use This Guide

The purpose of the *Guide to Property and Casualty Insurers* is to provide policyholders and prospective policy purchasers with a reliable source of insurance company ratings and analyses on a timely basis. We realize that the financial strength of an insurer is an important factor to consider when making the decision to purchase a policy or change companies. The ratings and analyses in this Guide can make that evaluation easier when you are considering:

- homeowners insurance
- business insurance
- auto insurance
- workers' compensation insurance
- product liability insurance
- medical malpractice and other professional liability insurance

This Guide does not include companies that strictly provide life and health insurance or annuities. For information on those companies, please refer to our *Guide to Life and Annuity Insurers.* Also, only a few of the property and casualty companies in this Guide provide any form of health insurance. For a complete listing of health insurance providers, please refer to our *Guide to Health Insurers*.

The rating for a particular company indicates our opinion regarding that company's ability to meet its commitments to the policyholder – not only under current economic conditions, but also during a declining economy or in the event of a sharp increase in claims. Such an increase in claims and related expenses may be triggered by any number of occurrences including a strong earthquake or hurricane, rising medical or legal costs, or large court awards. The safest companies, however, should be prepared to deal with harsh and unforeseen circumstances.

To use this Guide most effectively, we recommend you follow the steps outlined below:

Step 1 To ensure you evaluate the correct company, verify the company's exact name and state of domicile as it was given to you or appears on your policy. Many companies have similar names but are not related to one another, so you want to make sure the company you look up is really the one you are interested in evaluating.

Step 2 Turn to Section I, the Index of Companies, and locate the company you are evaluating. This section contains all companies analyzed by TheStreet.com Ratings including those that did not receive a Financial Strength Rating. It is sorted alphabetically by the name of the company and shows the state of domicile following the name for additional verification. Once you have located your specific company, the first column after the state of domicile shows its TheStreet.com Financial Strength Rating. Turn to *About TheStreet.com Financial Strength Ratings* on page 9 for information about what this rating means. If the rating has changed since the last issue of this Guide, a downgrade will be indicated with a down triangle ▼ to the left of the company name; an upgrade will be indicated with an up triangle ▲.

Step 3 Following TheStreet.com Financial Strength Rating are some of the various indexes that our analysts used in rating the company. Refer to the table on page 10 for an interpretation of which index values are considered strong, good, fair or weak. You can also turn to the Section I introduction beginning on page 21 to see what each of these factors measures. In most cases, lower-rated companies will have a low index value in one or more of the factors shown. Bear in mind, however, that the Financial Strength Rating is the result of a complex qualitative and quantitative analysis which cannot be reproduced using only the data provided here.

Step 4 Our analysts evaluate a great number of ratios and performance measures when assigning a rating. The right hand page of Section I shows you some of the key financial ratios we consider. Again, refer to the Section I introduction, beginning on page 21, for a description of each ratio.

Step 5 Some insurers have a bullet • preceding the company name on the right hand page of Section I. This means that more detailed information about the company is available in Section II. If the company you are evaluating is identified with a bullet, turn to Section II, the Analysis of Largest Companies, and locate it there (otherwise skip to step 8). Section II contains the largest insurers rated by TheStreet.com Ratings, regardless of rating. It too is sorted alphabetically by the name of the company.

Step 6 Once you have identified your company in Section II, you will find its Financial Strength Rating and a description of the rating immediately to the right of the company name. Then, below the company name is a description of the various rating factors that were considered in assigning the company's rating. These factors and the information below them are designed to give you a better feel for the company and its strengths and weaknesses. See the Section II introduction beginning on page 139 to get a better understanding of what each of these factors means.

Step 7 To the right, you will find a five-year summary of the company's Financial Strength Rating, capitialization and income. Look for positive or negative trends in these data. Below the five-year summary, we have included a graphic illustration of the most critical factor or factors impacting the company's rating. Again, the Section II introduction provides an overview of the content of each graph or table.

Step 8 If the company you are evaluating is not highly rated and you want to find an insurer with a higher rating, turn to the page in Section V that has your state's name at the top. This section contains those Recommended Companies (rating of A+, A, A- or B+) that are licensed to underwrite insurance in your state, sorted by rating. Then turn to the page in Section IV that shows the type of insurance you are interested in at the top. Insurers appearing on both lists will be those Recomended Companies which are licensed to sell that particular type of insurance in your state. From here you can select a company and then refer back to Sections I and II to analyze it.

Step 9 If you decide that you would like to contact one of TheStreet.com Recommended Companies about obtaining a policy or for additional information, refer to Section III. Following each company's name is its address and phone number to assist you in making contact.

Step 10 In order to use TheStreet.com Financial Strength Ratings most effectively, we strongly recommend you consult the Important Warnings and Cautions listed on page 17. These are more than just "standard disclaimers"; they are very important factors you should be aware of before using this Guide. If you have any questions regarding the precise meaning of specific terms used in the Guide, refer to the Glossary beginning on page 433.

Step 11 Page 417 in the Appendix contains information about State Guaranty Associations and the types of coverage they provide to policyholders when an insurance company fails. Keep in mind that while guaranty funds have now been established in all states, many do not cover all types of insurance. Furthermore, all of these funds have limits on their amount of coverage. Use the table to determine whether the level of coverage is applicable to your policy and the limits are adequate for your needs. You should pay particular attention to the notes regarding coverage limitations.

Step 12 If you want more information on your state's guaranty fund, call the State Commissioner's Office directly at the phone number listed on page 420.

Step 13 Keep in mind that good coverage from a state guaranty association is no substitute for dealing with a financially strong company. (See the discussion of problems with the guaranty fund system on page 417.) For that reason, TheStreet.com Ratings only recommends those companies which we feel are most able to stand on their own, without regard to what might happen in case the company does fail.

Step 14 Make sure you stay up to date with the latest information available since the publication of this Guide. For information on how to set up a rating change notification service, acquire follow-up reports, or receive a more in-depth analysis of an individual company, call 1-800-289-9222 or visit www.thestreet.ratings.com..

Data Sources: Annual and quarterly statutory statements filed with state insurance commissioners and data provided by the insurance companies being rated. The National Association of Insurance Commissioners has provided some of the raw data. Any analyses or conclusions are not provided or endorsed by the NAIC.

Date of data analyzed March 31, 2009, unless otherwise noted.

About TheStreet.com Financial Strength Ratings

TheStreet.com Financial Strength Ratings represent a completely independent, unbiased opinion of an insurance company's financial strength. The ratings are derived, for the most part, from annual and quarterly financial statements obtained from state insurance commissioners. These data are supplemented by information that we request from the insurance companies themselves. Although we seek to maintain an open line of communication with the companies being rated, we do not grant them the right to influence the ratings or stop their publication.

TheStreet.com Financial Strength Ratings are assigned by our analysts based on a complex analysis of hundreds of factors that are synthesized into five indexes: risk-adjusted capital, reserve adequacy, profitability, liquidity and stability. These indexes are then used to arrive at a letter grade rating. A good rating requires consistency across all indexes. A weak score on any one index can result in a low rating, as insolvency can be caused by any one of a number of factors, such as inadequate capital, unpredictable claims experience, poor liquidity, inadequate reserving, or operating losses.

The primary components of TheStreet.com Financial Strength Rating are as follows:

- **Risk-Adjusted Capital Indexes** gauge capital adequacy in terms of each insurer's risk profile under both *moderate* and *severe* loss scenarios.
- **Reserve Adequacy Index** measures the adequacy of the company's reserves and its ability to accurately anticipate the level of claims it will receive.
- **Profitability Index** measures the soundness of the company's operations and the contribution of profits to the company's financial strength. The profitability index is a composite of five sub-factors: 1) gain or loss on underwriting; (2) gain or loss on overall operations; 3) consistency of operating results; 4) impact of operating results on surplus; and 5) expenses in relation to industry norms for the types of policies that the company offers.
- **Liquidity Index** values a company's ability to raise the cash necessary to pay claims. We model various cash flow scenarios, applying liquidity tests to determine how the company might fare in the event of an unexpected spike in claims.
- **Stability Index** integrates a number of sub-factors that affect consistency (or lack thereof) in maintaining financial strength over time. Sub-factors include 1) risk diversification in terms of company size, group size, number of policies in force, types of policies written and use of reinsurance; 2) deterioration of operations as reported in critical asset, liability, income and expense items; 3) years in operation; 4) former problem areas where, despite recent improvement, the company has yet to establish a record of stable performance over a suitable period of time; 5) a substantial shift in the company's operations; 6) potential instabilities such as reinsurance quality, asset/liability matching, and sources of capital; and 7) relationships with holding companies and affiliates.

Each of these indexes is measured according to the following range of values.

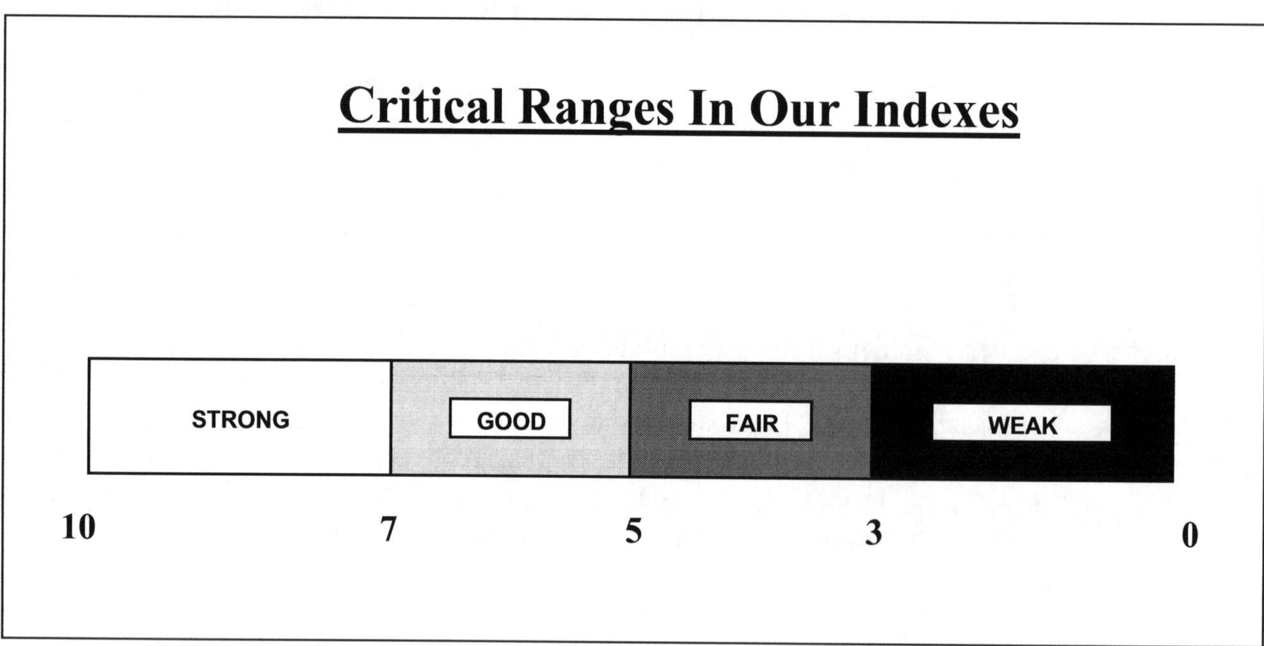

What Our Ratings Mean

A **Excellent.** The company offers excellent financial security. It has maintained a conservative stance in its investment strategies, business operations and underwriting commitments. While the financial position of any company is subject to change, we believe that this company has the resources necessary to deal with severe economic conditions.

B **Good.** The company offers good financial security and has the resources to deal with a variety of adverse economic conditions. It comfortably exceeds the minimum levels for all of our rating criteria, and is likely to remain healthy for the near future. However, in the event of a *severe* recession or major financial crisis, we feel that this assessment should be reviewed to make sure that the firm is still maintaining adequate financial strength.

C **Fair.** The company offers fair financial security and is currently stable. But during an economic downturn or other financial pressures, we feel it may encounter difficulties in maintaining its financial stability.

D **Weak.** The company currently demonstrates what we consider to be significant weaknesses which could negatively impact policyholders. In an unfavorable economic environment, these weaknesses could be magnified.

E **Very Weak.** The company currently demonstrates what we consider to be significant weaknesses and has also failed some of the basic tests that we use to identify fiscal stability. Therefore, even in a favorable economic environment, it is our opinion that policyholders could incur significant risks.

F **Failed.** The company is deemed failed if it is either 1) under supervision of an insurance regulatory authority; 2) in the process of rehabilitation; 3) in the process of liquidation; or 4) voluntarily dissolved after disciplinary or other regulatory action by an insurance regulatory authority.

\+ **The plus sign** is an indication that the company is at the upper end of the letter grade rating.

\- **The minus sign** is an indication that the company is at the lower end of the letter grade rating.

U **Unrated Companies.** The company is unrated for one or more of the following reasons: 1) total assets are less than $1 million; 2) premium income for the current year is less than $100,000; 3) the company functions almost exclusively as a holding company rather than as an underwriter; or 4) we do not have enough information to reliably issue a rating.

How Our Ratings Differ From Those of Other Services

TheStreet.com Financial Strength Ratings are conservative and consumer-oriented. We use tougher standards than other rating agencies because our system is specifically designed to inform risk-averse consumers about the financial strength of property and casualty insurers.

Our rating scale (A to F) is easy to understand by the general public. Users can intuitively understand that an A+ rating is at the top of the scale rather than in the middle like some of the other rating agencies.

Other rating agencies give top ratings more generously so that most companies receive excellent ratings.

More importantly, other rating agencies focus primarily on a company's *current* claims paying ability or consider only relatively mild economic adversity. We also consider these scenarios but extend our analyses to cover a company's ability to deal with severe economic adversity and potential liquidity problems. This stems from the viewpoint that an insurance company's obligations to its policyholders should not be contingent upon a healthy economy. The company must be capable of honoring its policy commitments in bad times as well.

Looking at the insurance industry as a whole, we note that several major rating firms have poor historical track records in identifying troubled companies. The 1980s saw a persistent decline in capital ratios, increased holdings of risky investments in the life and health industry as well as recurring long-term claims liabilities in the property and casualty industry. Despite these clear signs that insolvency risk was rising, other rating firms failed to downgrade at-risk insurance companies. Instead, they often rated companies by shades of excellence, understating the gravity of potential problems.

They have not issued clear warnings that the ordinary consumer can understand. Few, if any, companies receive "weak" or "poor" ratings. Surely, weak companies do exist. However, the other rating agencies apparently do not view themselves as consumer advocates with the responsibility of warning the public about the risks involved in doing business with such companies.

Additionally, these firms will at times agree *not* to issue a rating if a company denies them permission to do so. In short, too often insurance rating agencies work hand-in-glove with the companies they rate.

At TheStreet.com Ratings, although we seek to maintain good relationships with the firms, we owe our primary obligation to the consumer, not the industry. We reserve the right to rate companies based on publicly available data and make the necessary conservative assumptions when companies choose not to provide the additional data we request.

Comparison of Insurance Company Rating Agency Scales				
TheStreet.com Ratings [a]	Best [a,b]	S&P [c]	Moody's	Fitch[d]
A+, A, A-	A++, A+	AAA	Aaa	AAA
B+, B, B-	A, A-	AA+, AA AA-	Aa1, Aa2, Aa3	AA+, AA, AA-
C+, C, C-	B++, B+,	A+, A, A-, BBB+, BBB, BBB-	A1, A2, A3, Baa1, Baa2, Baa3	A+, A, A-, BBB+, BBB, BBB-
D+, D, D-	B, B- C++, C+, C, C-	BB+, BB, BB-, B+, B, B-	Ba1, Ba2, Ba3, B1, B2, B3	BB+, BB, BB-, B+, B, B-
E+, E, E- F	D E, F	CCC R	Caa, Ca, C	CCC+, CCC, CCC- DD

[a] TheStreet.com Ratings and Best use additional symbols to designate that they recognize an insurer's existence but do not provide a rating. These symbols are not included in this table.

[b] Best added the A++, B++ and C++ ratings in 1992. In 1994, Best classified its ratings into "secure" and "vulnerable" categories, changed the definition of its "B" and "B-" ratings from "good" to "adequate" and assigned these ratings to the "vulnerable" category. This table contains GAO's assignment of Best's ratings to bands based on our interpretation of their rating descriptions prior to 1994.

[c] S&P discontinued CCC "+" and "-" signs, CC, C and D ratings and added the R rating in 1992.

Source: 1994 GAO *Insurance Ratings* study.

[d] Duff & Phelps Credit Rating Co. merged with Fitch IBCA in 2000, and minor changes were made to the rating scale at that time. These changes were not reflected in the GAO's 1994 study, but *are* reflected in the chart.

Rate of Insurance Company Failures

TheStreet.com Ratings provides quarterly financial strength ratings for thousands of insurance companies each year. TheStreet.com Ratings strives for fairness and objectivity in its ratings and analyses, ensuring that each company receives the rating that most accurately depicts its current financial status, and more importantly, its ability to deal with severe economic adversity and a sharp increase in claims. TheStreet.com Ratings has every confidence that its financial strength ratings provide an accurate representation of a company's stability.

In order for these ratings to be of any true value, it is important that they prove accurate over time. One way to determine the accuracy of a rating is to examine those insurance companies that have failed, and their respective Financial Strength Ratings. A high percentage of failed companies with "A" ratings would indicate that TheStreet.com Ratings is not being conservative enough with its "secure" ratings, while conversely, a low percentage of failures with "vulnerable" ratings would show that TheStreet.com Ratings is overly conservative.

Over the past 20 years (1989–2008) TheStreet.com Ratings has rated 452 insurance companies, for all industries, that subsequently failed. The chart below shows the number of failed companies in each rating category, the average number of companies rated in each category per year, and the percentage of annual failures for each letter grade.

	Financial Strength Rating	Number of Failed Companies	Average Number of Companies Rated per year	Percentage of Failed Companies per year (by ratings category)*
Secure	A	1	148	0.03%
	B	2	1081	0.01%
	C	63	1642	0.19%
Vulnerable	D	208	767	1.36%
	E	178	217	4.11%

A=Excellent, B=Good, C=Fair, D=Weak, E=Very Weak

On average, only 0.08% of the companies TheStreet.com rates as "secure" fail each year. On the other hand, an average of 2.74% of the companies TheStreet.com Ratings rates as "vulnerable" fail annually. That means that a company rated by TheStreet.com Ratings as "Vulnerable" is 18 times more likely to fail than a company rated as "Secure".

When considering a TheStreet.com financial strength rating, one can be sure that they are getting the most fair, objective, and accurate financial rating available anywhere.

*Percentage of Failed Companies per year = (Number of Failed Companies) / [(Average Number of Companies Rated per year) x (years in study)]

Data as of September 2008 for Life and Annuity Insurers and Property and Casualty Insurers.
Data as of June 2008 for Health Insurers

What Does Average Mean?

At TheStreet.com Ratings, we consider the words average and fair to mean just that – average and fair. So when we assign our ratings to insurers, the largest percentage of companies receives an average C rating. That way, you can be sure that a company receiving TheStreet.com B or A rating is truly above average. Likewise, you can feel confident that companies with D or E ratings are truly below average.

Percentage for Property and Casualty Insurers in Each Rating Category

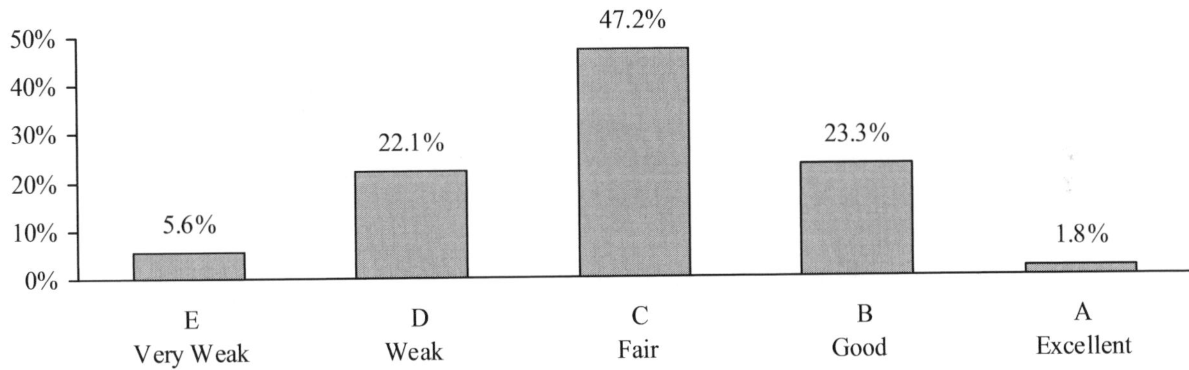

Important Warnings and Cautions

1. A rating alone cannot tell the whole story. Please read the explanatory information contained in this publication. It is provided in order to give you an understanding of our rating philosophy, as well as paint a more complete picture of how we arrive at our opinion of a company's strengths and weaknesses.

2. TheStreet.com Financial Strength Ratings represent our opinion of a company's insolvency risk. As such, a high rating means we feel that the company has less chance of running into financial difficulties. A high rating is not a guarantee of solvency nor is a low rating a prediction of insolvency. TheStreet.com Financial Strength Ratings are not deemed to be a recommendation concerning the purchase or sale of the securities of any insurance company that is publicly owned.

3. Company performance is only one factor in determining a rating. Conditions in the marketplace and overall economic conditions are additional factors that may affect the company's financial strength. Therefore, a rating upgrade or downgrade does not necessarily reflect changes in the company's profits, capital or other financial measures, but may be due to external factors. Likewise, changes in TheStreet.com indexes may reflect changes in our risk assessment of business or economic conditions as well as changes in company performance.

4. All firms that have the same Financial Strength Rating should be considered to be essentially equal in strength. This is true regardless of any differences in the underlying numbers which might appear to indicate greater strengths. TheStreet.com Financial Strength Rating already takes into account a number of lesser factors which, due to space limitations, cannot be included in this publication.

5. A good rating requires consistency. If a company is excellent on four indicators and fair on one, the company may receive a fair rating. This requirement is necessary due to the fact that fiscal problems can arise from any *one* of several causes including speculative investments, inadequate capital resources or operating losses.

6. We are an independent rating agency and do not depend on the cooperation of the companies we rate. Our data are derived, for the most part, from annual and quarterly financial statements that we obtain from federal banking regulators and state insurance commissioners. The latter may be supplemented by information insurance companies voluntarily provide upon request. Although we seek to maintain an open line of communication with the companies, we do not grant them the right to stop or influence publication of the ratings. This policy stems from the fact that this publication is designed for the protection of the consumer.

7. Affiliated companies do not automatically receive the same rating. We recognize that a troubled company may expect financial support from its parent or affiliates. TheStreet.com Financial Strength Ratings reflect our opinion of the measure of support that may become available to a subsidiary, if the subsidiary were to experience serious financial difficulties. In the case of a strong parent and a weaker subsidiary, the affiliate relationship will generally result in a higher rating for the subsidiary than it would have on a stand-alone basis. Seldom, however, would the rating be brought up to the level of the parent. This treatment is appropriate because we do not assume the parent would have either the resources or the will to "bail out" a troubled subsidiary during a severe economic crisis. Even when there is a binding legal obligation for a parent corporation to honor the policy obligations of its subsidiaries, the possibility exists that the subsidiary could be sold and lose its parental support. Therefore, it is quite common for one affiliate to have a higher rating than another. This is another reason why it is especially important that you have the precise name of the company you are evaluating.

Section I

Index of Companies

An analysis of all rated and unrated

U.S. Property and Casualty Insurers.

Companies are listed in alphabetical order.

Section I Contents

This section contains the key rating factors and performance measures for all rated and unrated insurers analyzed by TheStreet.com Ratings. An explanation of each of the footnotes and stability factors appears at the end of this section.

Left Pages

1. Insurance Company Name The legally registered name, which can sometimes differ from the name that the company uses for advertising. If you cannot find the company you are interested in, or if you have any doubts regarding the precise name, verify the information with the company before looking the name up in this Guide. Also, determine the domicile state for confirmation. (See column 2.)

2. Domicile State The state which has primary regulatory responsibility for the company. It may differ from the location of the company's corporate headquarters. You do not have to be living in the domicile state to purchase insurance from this firm, provided it is licensed to do business in your state.

Also use this column to confirm that you have located the correct company. It is possible for two unrelated companies to have the same name if they are domiciled in different states.

3. Financial Strength Rating Our rating is measured on a scale from A to F and considers a wide range of factors. Please see page 11 for specific descriptions of each letter grade. Also, refer to page 12 for information on how our ratings differ from those of other rating agencies. Most important, when using this rating, please be sure to consider the warnings beginning on page 17 regarding the ratings' limitations and the underlying assumptions. Notes in this column refer to the date of the data included in the rating evaluation and are explained on page 27.

4. Total Assets All assets admitted by state insurance regulators in millions of dollars through the most recent quarter available. This includes investments and current business assets such as receivables from agents and reinsurers.

The overall size is an important factor which affects the ability of a company to manage risk. Generally speaking, risks can be more effectively diversified by large companies. Because the insurance business is based on probability, the number of policies must be large enough so that actuarial statistics are valid. The larger the number of policyholders, the more reliable the actuarial projections will be. A large company with a correspondingly large policy base can spread its risk and minimize the effects of claims experience that exceeds actuarial expectations.

5. Capital and Surplus The company's statutory net worth in millions of dollars through the most recent quarter available. Consumers may wish to limit the size of any policy so that the policyholder's maximum potential claims do not exceed approximately 1% of the company's capital and surplus. For example, when buying a policy from a company with capital and surplus of $10,000,000, the 1% limit would be $100,000. (When performing this calculation, do not forget that figures in this column are expressed in millions of dollars.)

6. Net Premium The amount of insurance premiums received from policyholders less any premiums that have been transferred to other companies through reinsurance agreements. This figure is updated through the most recent annual report available.

Generally speaking, companies with large net premium volume generally have more predictable claims experience.

Critical Ranges In Our Indexes and Ratios

Indicators	*Strong*	*Good*	*Fair*	*Weak*
Risk-Adjusted Capital Ratio #1	—	1.0 or more	0.75 - 0.99	0.74 or less
Risk-Adjusted Capital Ratio #2	1.0 or more	0.75 - 0.99	0.5 - 0.74	0.49 or less
Capitalization Index	7 – 10	5 - 6.9	3 - 4.9	2.9 or less
Reserve Adequacy Index	7 – 10	5 - 6.9	3 - 4.9	2.9 or less
Profitability Index	7 – 10	5 - 6.9	3 - 4.9	2.9 or less
Liquidity Index	7 – 10	5 - 6.9	3 - 4.9	2.9 or less
Stability Index	7 – 10	5 - 6.9	3 - 4.9	2.9 or less

7. Net Income The company's profit for the period. Profit is defined as revenues minus expenses. In the case of an insurance company, revenues include premiums and investment income, and expenses include claims payments and underwriting expenses.

8. Capitalization Index An index that measures the adequacy of the company's capital resources to deal with a variety of business and economic scenarios. It combines Risk-Adjusted Capital Ratios #1 and #2 as well as a leverage test that examines pricing risk. (See the table above for the ranges which we believe are critical.)

9. Reserve Adequacy Index An index that uses annual and quarterly data to measure the adequacy of the company's reserves. Reserves are funds the company sets aside to cover unsettled claims it estimates each year. Included are claims that the company has already received but have not yet been settled and claims that they expect to receive, but which have not yet been reported.

If a company consistently estimates its claims accurately, that is good. Or if it errs on the side of being conservative and overestimates its claims from time to time, that is even better. Either case will cause this index to move higher.

On the other hand, some companies may have trouble accurately predicting the claims they will have to pay. Others may intentionally underestimate their claims to inflate their profits for stockholders or to make their capital appear higher than it really is. In either case, inadequate reserve levels will result in a low Reserve Adequacy Index.

If a company has chronically deficient reserves, it calls into question the company's ability to manage its policy risk effectively.

10. Profitability Index An index that uses annual and quarterly data to measure the soundness of the company's operations and the contribution of profits to the company's fiscal strength. The Profitability Index is a composite of five factors: (1) gain or loss on underwriting; (2) gain or loss on overall operations; (3) consistency of operating results; (4) impact of operating results on surplus; and (5) expenses in relation to industry averages for the types of policies that the company offers.

11. Liquidity Index An index which uses annual and quarterly data to measure the company's ability to raise the necessary cash to settle claims. Sometimes a company may appear to have the necessary resources to pay claims on paper, but in reality, it may be unable to raise the necessary cash. This can occur, for example, when a company is owed a great deal of money from its agents or reinsurers, or when it cannot sell its investments at the prices at which they are valued in the company's financial statements.

We look at various cash flow scenarios. Then we apply liquidity tests which tell us how the company might fare in each of those circumstances.

12. Stability Index An index which uses annual and quarterly data to integrate a number of factors such as: (1) risk diversification in terms of company size, number of policies in force, use of reinsurance, and single largest risk exposure; (2) deterioration of operations as reported in critical asset, liability, income, or expense items such as premium volume and/or surplus (See the table on page 22 for the levels which we believe are critical.)

13. Stability Factors Indicates those specific areas that have negatively impacted the company's Stability Index. See page 28 for explanation of these factors.

Right Pages

1. Risk-Adjusted Capital Ratio #1 This ratio examines the adequacy of the company's capital base and whether the company has sufficient capital resources to cover potential losses which might occur in an average recession or other moderate loss scenario. Specifically, the figure, calculated from annual and quarterly data, answers the question: For every dollar of capital that we feel would be needed, how many dollars in capital resources does the company actually have?

You may find that some companies have unusually high levels of capital. This often reflects special circumstances related to the small size or unusual operations of the company.

The table on page 22 shows the levels which we believe are critical. See the Appendix on page 421 for more details on how this ratio is calculated.

2. Risk-Adjusted Capital Ratio #2

This is similar to the Risk-Adjusted Capital Ratio #1. But in this case, the question relates to whether the company has enough capital cushion to withstand a *severe* recession or other severe loss scenario.

The table on page 22 shows the levels which we believe are critical. See the Appendix on page 422 for more details on how this ratio is calculated.

3. Premium to Surplus

The ratio of net premiums written compared to the company's capital and surplus level. This ratio, calculated from the company's annual report, answers the question: For every dollar of capital and surplus, how many dollars of premium does the company take in? Results of over 300% are considered perilous and could indicate that the insurer does not have adequate capital to support the volume of business that it is underwriting. A large figure could also help explain why a company has poor results on its risk-adjusted capital tests.

4. Reserves to Surplus

The ratio of reserves for expected claims compared to the company's capital and surplus level. If a company does not set aside enough reserves, it may have to withdraw capital to pay claims. This ratio, calculated from the annual report, is a rough measure of how much capital cushion the company has against claims reserves. The industry average is around 180%.

High ratios signify that reserve deficiencies would have a strong impact on capital and could help explain why a company has poor risk-adjusted capital results.

5. One-Year Reserve Development

The percentage increase or decrease in the company's annual reserve estimate compared to the previous year. If last year's estimate is below that of this year, this will result in a positive ratio meaning that the company underestimated its future claims and set aside insufficient reserves. Making this error consistently is viewed negatively because it means the company is inflating its income and capital.

6. Two-Year Reserve Development

This ratio is similar to the One-Year Reserve Development ratio. However, instead of comparing the latest estimates with those from the prior year, it compares them to the estimates from two years ago.

Again, a positive ratio means the company underestimated its reserve needs while a negative ratio indicates that reserve needs were overestimated.

7. Loss Ratio

The ratio of claims paid to premiums collected, calculated from the annual report, measures the company's underwriting profits. Needless to say, if an insurer pays out a very high percentage of what it collects, there may not be enough left over for other expenses, let alone enough to build the company's capital and financial strength over time.

8. Expense Ratio

The ratio of overhead expenses to premiums collected, calculated from the annual report, answers the question: How many cents is the company paying out in executive salaries, agents' commissions, and other administrative expenses for every dollar in premiums that it collects from policyholders? A low Expense Ratio is good for both the company and its policyholders because it means that the company is efficient and can utilize more of each premium dollar to pay claims. A high Expense Ratio is a bad sign because it signals that too much of the company's premiums are being used for things which do not directly benefit its policyholders.

9. Combined Ratio

The sum of the Loss Ratio and the Expense Ratio. The Combined Ratio shows how much the company is paying out in administrative expenses and claims for every dollar of premium collected.

Values over 100% indicate that the company is losing money on its underwriting. This is very common in the industry, but it's still a sign of possible weakness.

Underwriting losses can often be offset by income the company realizes on its investments. This is especially true for companies that issue policies on which they do not have to pay claims for several years (long-tail policies). With these policies, the premiums can be invested in order to earn income for the company until the claims are paid.

10. Cash from Underwriting

The ratio of cash received from premiums (net of reinsurance) to cash outlays for claims and underwriting expenses, compiled from the annual report. A figure under 100% indicates that the company is paying out more in claims and expenses than it is receiving in premiums, whereas a figure over 100% indicates a positive cash flow. A negative figure generally indicates that the company has sold more business to a reinsurance company than it has taken in during the current year.

When a company has a positive net cash flow from its underwriting, it can generate additional funds for investing. On the other hand, if net cash flow is negative, the company may have to rely on its investment income to make up the shortfall. And if that isn't enough, it may even have to sell assets to meet its obligations.

11. Net Premium Growth

The annual percentage change in net premiums compared to the previous year. A company can increase its premium volume by: (1) issuing more new policies; (2) raising its rates; or (3) selling less of its insurance to other insurance companies. Slow and steady growth is healthy but rapid growth is often an indicator of trouble ahead. It may mean that the company is underpricing as a means of gaining market share. Indeed, a high percentage of insurance company failures are related to rapid growth. Regulators consider a fluctuation of more than 33% as a cautionary flag.

A rapid decline in premium volume is also a negative sign. It indicates that the company is losing its customer base. However, if the decline is the result of premium redistribution among a group of affiliates, the significance of the decline is minimal.

12. Investments In Affiliates

The percentage of the company's investment portfolio from the annual report dedicated to investments in affiliates. These investments can be bonds, preferred and common stocks, as well as other vehicles which many insurance companies use to invest in – and establish a corporate link with – affiliated companies. Large investments of this type can pose problems as these investments often produce no income and can be difficult to sell.

Footnotes:

(3) Data items shown are from the company's 2008 annual statutory statement. Other more recent data may have been factored into the rating when available.

(5) Data items shown are from the company's 2007 annual statutory statement except for Risk-Adjusted Capital Indexes 1 and 2, Profitability Index, Reserve Adequacy Index, Liquidity Index and Stability Index which have been updated using the company's September 2008 quarterly statutory statement. Other more recent data may have been factored into the rating when available.

(1) Data items shown are from the company's 2007 annual statutory statement except for Risk-Adjusted Capital Indexes 1 and 2, Profitability Index, Reserve Adequacy Index, Liquidity Index and Stability Index which have been updated using the company's June 2008 quarterly statutory statement. Other more recent data may have been factored into the rating when available

(2) Data items shown are from the company's 2007 annual statutory statement except for Risk-Adjusted Capital Indexes 1 and 2, Profitability Index, Reserve Adequacy Index, Liquidity Index and Stability Index which have been updated using the company's March 2008 quarterly statutory statement. Other more recent data may have been factored into the rating when available.

(4) These companies have data items that are older than December 2008. They will be unrated (U) if they are not failed companies (F).

Stability Factors

(A) Stability Index was negatively impacted by the financial problems or weaknesses of a parent or **affiliate** company.

(C) Stability Index was negatively impacted by past results on our Risk-Adjusted **Capital** tests. In general, the Stability Index of any company can be affected by past results even if current results show improvement. While such improvement is a plus, the improved results must be maintained for a period of time to assure that the improvement is not a temporary fluctuation. During a five-year period, the impact of poor past results on the Stability Index gradually diminishes.

(D) Stability Index was negatively impacted by limited **diversification** of general business, policy, and/or investment risk. This factor especially affects smaller companies that do not issue as many policies as larger firms. It can also affect firms that specialize in only one line of business.

(E) Stability Index was negatively impacted due to a lack of operating **experience**. The company has been in operation for less than five years. Consequently, it has not been able to establish the kind of stable track record that we believe is needed to demonstrate financial permanence and strength.

(F) Stability Index was negatively impacted by negative cash **flow**. In other words, the company paid out more in claims and expenses than it received in premiums and investment income.

(G) Stability Index was negatively impacted by fast asset or premium **growth**. Fast growth can pose a serious problem for insurers. It is generally achieved by offering policies with premiums that are too low, benefits that are too costly, or agents commissions that are too high. Due to the highly competitive nature of the insurance marketplace, rapid growth has been a factor in many insurance insolvencies.

(L) Stability Index was negatively impacted by results on our **liquidity** tests. While the company may have sufficient cash flow to meet its current obligations, it could encounter difficulties under adverse scenarios, such as a dramatic increase in claims.

(O) Stability Index was negatively impacted by significant changes in the company's business **operations**. These changes can include shifts in the kinds of insurance offered by the company, a temporary or permanent freeze on the sale of new policies, or recent release from conservatorship. In these circumstances, past performance cannot be a reliable indicator of future financial strength.

(R) Stability Index was negatively impacted by concerns about the financial strength of its **reinsurers**.

(T) Stability Index was negatively impacted by significant **trends** in critical asset, liability, income or expense items. Examples include fluctuations in premium volume, changes in the types of investments the company makes, and changes in the types of policies the company writes.

(Z) This company is unrated due to data, as received by TheStreet.com Ratings, that are either incomplete in substantial ways or contains items that, in the opinion of TheStreet.com Ratings analysts, may not be reliable.

INSURANCE COMPANY NAME	DOM. STATE	RATING	TOTAL ASSETS ($MIL)	CAPITAL & SURPLUS ($MIL)	ANNUAL NET PREMIUM ($MIL)	NET INCOME ($MIL)	CAPITAL- IZATION INDEX (PTS)	RESERVE ADQ INDEX (PTS)	PROFIT- ABILITY INDEX (PTS)	LIQUIDITY INDEX (PTS)	STAB. INDEX (PTS)	STABILITY FACTORS
1ST AUTO & CASUALTY INS CO	WI	C	29.6	11.9	16.7	0.3	7.7	9.3	8.6	6.2	3.6	DFGT
1ST CHOICE AUTO INS CO	PA	C-	10.0	6.5	3.4	0.2	9.1	8.6	8.6	7.2	3.1	DGT
2-10 HOME BUYERS WARRANTY OF VA	VA	U (5)	0.0	0.0	9.7	0.0	N/A	5.3	8.0	5.5	4.5	ADGT
21ST CENTURY CASUALTY CO	CA	B	18.3	11.1	0.0	-0.1	10.0	N/A	4.7	7.0	4.6	DG
▲21ST CENTURY INS CO	CA	B	1,260.1	758.3	200.7	4.8	9.7	5.6	5.5	6.7	5.5	FT
▼21ST CENTURY INS CO OF THE SW	TX	C	5.6	3.6	0.0	0.0	10.0	N/A	6.8	7.0	3.2	DGT
A CENTRAL INS CO	NY	C	37.6	13.8	21.7	0.0	7.3	6.3	3.8	6.0	3.1	DGT
AAA MID-ATLANTIC INS CO	PA	C	24.1	9.5	10.6	0.1	8.3	7.7	4.6	6.4	3.5	DGT
AAA MIDATLANTIC INS CO OF NJ	NJ	C+	32.5	18.6	10.6	0.2	10.0	7.4	3.8	6.8	4.2	DGT
AAA SOUTHERN NEW ENGLAND INS CO	RI	C+	60.0	26.5	45.2	0.2	7.4	3.6	3.3	6.6	3.2	GT
AAA TEXAS COUNTY MUTUAL INS CO	TX	C-	62.2	7.5	0.0	0.0	7.0	N/A	7.6	6.9	2.9	DGT
ABBA INDEMNITY CO	TX	U (1)	1.7	1.6	0.0	0.0	N/A	7.9	3.8	10.0	2.1	FT
ACA FINANCIAL GUARANTY CORP	MD	D-	419.2	103.8	-17.2	6.1	10.0	5.8	0.4	5.6	0.0	FT
▲ACA HOME INS CORP	FL	C+	21.9	15.3	-4.4	0.4	10.0	4.7	3.5	10.0	3.1	DGRT
ACA INS CO	IN	C+	50.7	14.6	18.6	-0.6	6.1	6.2	4.6	1.2	3.4	DFGL
ACADEMIC HLTH PROFESSIONALS INS	NY	E	110.6	13.2	35.9	-0.9	0.0	0.1	2.8	5.5	0.3	CDGR
ACADIA INS CO	NH	C	134.6	57.8	0.0	0.2	10.0	N/A	4.1	7.0	4.1	FT
ACBG RRG INC	VT	E+	3.4	1.5	1.5	0.0	5.1	4.1	2.8	7.8	0.5	DGT
ACCC INS CO	TX	C	135.5	47.8	85.9	0.4	7.0	5.9	8.7	6.2	3.9	T
ACCEPTANCE CASUALTY INS CO	NE	C	37.3	25.2	7.3	0.4	8.1	9.3	4.6	7.0	2.7	DGRT
ACCEPTANCE INDEMNITY INS CO	NE	C	113.0	52.8	29.9	0.9	7.2	7.8	3.7	6.9	2.7	T
ACCEPTANCE INS CO	NE	F (1)	35.3	-15.9	0.0	-12.1	0.0	2.2	0.2	10.0	0.0	CDFR
▲ACCESS INS CO	TX	D+	96.8	15.6	18.1	-0.2	4.3	3.9	3.6	7.4	2.4	DGT
▲ACCIDENT FUND GENERAL INS CO	MI	C+	131.5	33.7	34.5	1.9	6.6	4.5	6.5	6.5	3.8	T
ACCIDENT FUND INS CO OF AMERICA	MI	C+	2,092.9	578.4	689.6	14.1	5.3	6.2	5.0	5.6	4.4	T
ACCIDENT FUND NATIONAL INS CO	MI	C	214.3	54.3	51.7	2.5	7.3	4.5	8.9	6.4	4.0	FT
ACCIDENT INS CO INC	SC	E	41.0	10.8	18.0	0.8	1.0	4.8	5.9	5.9	0.3	CDGR
ACCREDITED SURETY & CAS CO INC	FL	C-	28.4	20.8	10.0	0.2	7.6	6.0	7.2	7.0	2.9	DGT
▲ACE AMERICAN INS CO	PA	C+	8,025.1	1,784.2	1,029.2	39.4	6.7	5.0	7.5	7.1	4.4	T
ACE FIRE UNDERWRITERS INS CO	PA	C	112.4	61.8	5.6	1.1	10.0	6.5	8.2	9.1	3.9	T
ACE INDEMNITY INS CO	PA	C-	34.4	16.0	5.6	0.4	7.1	7.0	8.9	7.2	3.2	DGT
ACE INS CO	PR	C-	94.0	22.0	22.5	-0.5	1.7	5.0	2.9	6.4	3.3	CDT
ACE INS CO OF THE MIDWEST	IN	U (1)	51.1	50.6	0.0	0.8	N/A	4.6	7.0	10.0	6.0	T
ACE PROPERTY & CASUALTY INS CO	PA	C	5,938.4	1,426.1	978.8	-12.3	7.1	5.0	5.8	6.7	3.4	T
ACIG INS CO	IL	D+	254.2	57.4	79.5	1.1	5.5	5.0	3.7	6.8	2.2	T
ACSTAR INS CO	IL	C	81.8	31.1	7.1	0.8	8.2	4.3	6.4	9.9	4.2	DT
ACUITY A MUTUAL INS CO	WI	B	1,817.0	617.6	742.4	18.0	9.1	7.0	7.2	6.5	4.7	T
ADDISON INS CO	IL	C+	80.2	29.8	23.0	0.4	8.1	8.7	6.8	6.7	4.7	T
▲ADIRONDACK INS EXCH	NY	D	239.3	68.6	157.2	1.7	3.5	3.6	4.5	6.4	1.5	T
ADMIRAL INDEMNITY CO	DE	C	73.7	30.3	13.3	0.2	5.3	5.1	7.0	7.5	4.2	T
▼ADMIRAL INS CO	DE	C	2,494.8	1,031.7	431.0	-6.7	5.2	4.5	6.5	7.0	4.1	ACT
ADRIATIC INS CO	ND	C	65.9	57.6	8.2	0.7	10.0	9.3	8.9	9.7	4.0	DFRT
ADVANCED PHYSICIANS INS RRG INC	AZ	U (1)	0.7	0.7	0.2	0.1	N/A	4.8	6.5	8.5	0.0	T
ADVANTA INS CO	AZ	D+	18.1	17.6	4.8	0.5	10.0	4.6	7.8	9.7	2.8	DGT
▲ADVANTAGE WORKERS COMP INS CO	IN	C+	118.9	60.2	36.6	0.4	8.0	5.7	5.3	7.0	4.5	T
ADVOCATE MD INS OF THE SW INC	TX	D	74.3	30.4	22.9	1.4	4.3	6.0	4.6	9.1	1.8	GRT
AEGIS HEALTHCARE RRG INC	DC	E	3.9	1.0	0.3	0.0	4.3	5.0	6.4	6.1	0.0	DFGR
▲AEGIS SECURITY INS CO	PA	B-	67.9	36.2	45.4	-0.2	7.6	9.3	6.2	6.5	3.5	FT
AEQUICAP INS CO	FL	E+	49.9	14.5	24.2	-0.5	1.6	0.2	1.1	0.0	0.7	CDFL
AEQUICAP PROPERTY & CASUALTY INS CO	FL	D	7.1	4.0	0.0	0.0	10.0	6.8	3.8	7.0	1.9	DFGR
AETNA INS CO OF CT	CT	C	19.5	17.9	0.3	0.3	10.0	8.0	3.0	9.1	4.0	DFGR
AFFILIATED FM INS CO	RI	C	1,486.6	717.9	336.2	28.0	9.7	3.9	8.9	7.0	3.3	RT

See Page 27 for explanation of footnotes and Page 28 for explanation of stability factors.
Arrows denote recent upgrades ▲ or downgrades ▼ (see Section VII for explanations)

RISK ADJ. CAPITAL RATIO #1	RISK ADJ. CAPITAL RATIO #2	PREMIUM TO SURPLUS (%)	RESV. TO SURPLUS (%)	RESV. DEVELOP. 1 YEAR (%)	RESV. DEVELOP. 2 YEAR (%)	LOSS RATIO (%)	EXP. RATIO (%)	COMB RATIO (%)	CASH FROM UNDER-WRITING (%)	NET PREMIUM GROWTH (%)	INVEST. IN AFFIL (%)	INSURANCE COMPANY NAME
2.1	1.6	139.7	95.2	-4.4	-12.5	69.5	29.4	98.9	94.0	-1.8	0.0	1ST AUTO & CASUALTY INS CO
5.2	4.2	53.4	12.5	-5.1	-13.6	57.9	23.7	81.6	114.9	13.7	0.0	1ST CHOICE AUTO INS CO
N/A	N/A	212.3	10.6	0.6	4.6	54.9	42.2	97.1	113.2	15.9	0.0	2-10 HOME BUYERS WARRANTY OF VA
5.7	5.1	N/A	N/A	N/A	N/A	N/A	N/A	N/A	140.4	0.0	0.0	21ST CENTURY CASUALTY CO
6.7	4.7	26.9	31.3	1.5	0.3	79.6	25.1	104.7	23.0	-84.8	0.0 •	21ST CENTURY INS CO
5.0	4.5	N/A	N/A	N/A	N/A	N/A	N/A	N/A	85.4	0.0	0.0	21ST CENTURY INS CO OF THE SW
1.9	1.3	157.5	65.7	-1.8	-4.1	71.3	33.8	105.1	110.0	153.3	0.0	A CENTRAL INS CO
2.3	1.9	106.0	77.6	-4.3	-3.8	75.3	29.1	104.4	93.3	-1.6	0.0	AAA MID-ATLANTIC INS CO
4.4	3.6	56.1	41.0	-2.1	-2.0	75.3	29.1	104.4	93.3	-1.6	0.0	AAA MIDATLANTIC INS CO OF NJ
2.1	1.5	163.8	48.7	-14.7	N/A	71.5	28.9	100.4	132.2	12.4	0.0	AAA SOUTHERN NEW ENGLAND INS CO
1.0	0.9	N/A	N/A	N/A	N/A	N/A	N/A	N/A	126.2	0.0	0.0	AAA TEXAS COUNTY MUTUAL INS CO
N/A	N/A	-1.8	2.0	-2.0	-3.5	500.0	-265.5	234.5	-28.4	0.0	0.0	ABBA INDEMNITY CO
9.4	5.8	-16.9	20.7	-1.2	3.7	999 +	-31.3	999 +	-5.8	-116.3	0.2	ACA FINANCIAL GUARANTY CORP
8.5	7.7	-29.1	N/A	-7.8	-3.5	130.8	18.4	149.2	-110.0	-132.5	0.0	ACA HOME INS CORP
1.2	0.7	120.6	38.1	-8.3	-1.3	79.2	21.3	100.5	69.9	24.3	0.0	ACA INS CO
0.0	0.0	288.9	613.7	88.5	151.0	93.7	18.4	112.1	108.9	40.1	0.0	ACADEMIC HLTH PROFESSIONALS INS
7.2	6.5	N/A	N/A	N/A	N/A	N/A	N/A	N/A	-734.7	0.0	0.0	ACADIA INS CO
1.9	1.1	103.0	98.8	-5.4	-43.2	90.8	7.7	98.5	136.3	N/A	0.0	ACBG RRG INC
1.2	1.0	181.5	123.5	-13.1	-17.7	76.3	14.5	90.8	118.6	8.6	0.0	ACCC INS CO
4.1	2.3	27.3	33.3	-1.4	-7.7	67.0	34.2	101.2	92.3	-10.9	0.0	ACCEPTANCE CASUALTY INS CO
1.4	1.1	51.3	69.3	0.5	-0.8	64.9	34.2	99.1	111.2	-2.0	25.1	ACCEPTANCE INDEMNITY INS CO
-0.5	-0.3	N/A	-190.2	81.1	65.8	N/A	N/A	N/A	N/A	0.0	0.0	ACCEPTANCE INS CO
1.0	0.7	127.5	22.4	16.0	12.7	71.1	25.6	96.7	99.8	5.8	0.0	ACCESS INS CO
1.5	1.1	108.0	131.1	0.8	2.1	69.8	22.5	92.3	103.5	20.1	0.0	ACCIDENT FUND GENERAL INS CO
0.9	0.7	119.4	145.4	0.7	2.1	69.6	23.7	93.3	107.2	20.2	21.3 •	ACCIDENT FUND INS CO OF AMERICA
1.6	1.2	98.6	119.6	0.7	1.9	69.8	20.8	90.6	94.4	20.1	0.0	ACCIDENT FUND NATIONAL INS CO
0.7	0.4	255.3	118.7	10.4	5.2	51.3	24.7	76.0	121.5	97.7	0.0	ACCIDENT INS CO INC
2.4	2.1	48.9	14.7	-1.6	-2.1	7.7	79.4	87.1	94.8	-17.9	0.0	ACCREDITED SURETY & CAS CO INC
1.3	1.0	57.5	123.0	-9.8	-29.4	62.5	20.6	83.1	117.9	-19.7	15.4 •	ACE AMERICAN INS CO
9.1	6.8	9.1	19.5	-1.8	-4.9	62.5	22.8	85.3	160.2	-19.7	0.0	ACE FIRE UNDERWRITERS INS CO
2.1	1.3	35.8	76.6	-7.4	-21.3	62.5	22.8	85.3	129.9	-19.7	0.0	ACE INDEMNITY INS CO
0.5	0.4	100.8	195.1	-59.3	-72.8	25.0	51.6	76.6	115.8	8.6	0.0	ACE INS CO
N/A	N/A	N/A	0.4	0.1	N/A	60.0	816.7	876.7	7.9	-76.0	0.0	ACE INS CO OF THE MIDWEST
1.7	1.1	66.6	142.4	-9.8	-30.9	62.5	22.8	85.3	106.9	-19.7	4.0 •	ACE PROPERTY & CASUALTY INS CO
1.3	0.8	135.3	322.2	-30.6	-31.3	65.8	28.2	94.0	100.4	-2.6	0.0	ACIG INS CO
3.8	2.4	23.1	63.3	-3.6	-6.3	4.1	51.7	55.8	176.2	-22.9	0.0	ACSTAR INS CO
3.7	2.5	120.3	129.1	-3.6	-6.5	69.8	28.5	98.3	109.1	-3.1	0.1 •	ACUITY A MUTUAL INS CO
2.8	1.8	78.9	90.7	1.7	-0.9	84.6	28.4	113.0	96.7	-2.3	0.0	ADDISON INS CO
1.0	0.6	231.9	94.6	1.6	-0.8	59.5	37.1	96.6	105.5	-7.7	0.0	ADIRONDACK INS EXCH
1.6	1.0	44.4	76.4	-1.8	-4.8	63.5	16.2	79.7	260.6	-5.2	0.0	ADMIRAL INDEMNITY CO
1.1	0.7	40.8	111.6	-2.3	-5.3	62.4	25.8	88.2	111.2	-24.6	28.1 •	ADMIRAL INS CO
17.0	10.9	14.5	5.7	-4.7	-6.7	44.3	32.2	76.5	88.9	-49.9	0.0	ADRIATIC INS CO
N/A	N/A	24.8	N/A	N/A	N/A	N/A	36.4	36.4	506.1	1.3	0.0	ADVANCED PHYSICIANS INS RRG INC
3.5	3.4	28.0	0.2	-0.1	N/A	0.4	24.4	24.8	413.3	7.5	30.8	ADVANTA INS CO
3.2	2.4	61.5	74.8	-8.9	-18.8	68.2	32.2	100.4	113.2	-11.3	0.0	ADVANTAGE WORKERS COMP INS CO
0.8	0.6	78.7	96.7	32.1	-4.9	26.3	19.4	45.7	999 +	17.1	0.0	ADVOCATE MD INS OF THE SW INC
0.9	0.5	33.7	134.1	-1.8	-35.4	57.9	115.9	173.8	48.0	-65.6	0.0	AEGIS HEALTHCARE RRG INC
2.1	1.6	121.2	28.3	-15.3	-16.1	48.0	45.9	93.9	90.2	-6.3	19.0	AEGIS SECURITY INS CO
0.4	0.3	161.3	175.7	17.8	101.2	64.9	40.8	105.7	61.9	-25.0	15.2	AEQUICAP INS CO
4.1	3.6	N/A	0.2	N/A	0.6	N/A	N/A	N/A	999 +	-100.0	0.0	AEQUICAP PROPERTY & CASUALTY INS
22.9	15.8	2.0	0.8	-1.1	-1.5	-50.7	116.5	65.8	37.6	-29.7	0.0	AETNA INS CO OF CT
6.2	3.3	48.3	57.7	-9.3	-9.1	77.6	20.4	98.0	123.6	0.7	0.0 •	AFFILIATED FM INS CO

999 + Denotes number greater than 999.9%
999 - Denotes number less than -999.99%
• Bullets denote a more detailed analysis is available in Section II.

INSURANCE COMPANY NAME	DOM. STATE	RATING	TOTAL ASSETS ($MIL)	CAPITAL & SURPLUS ($MIL)	ANNUAL NET PREMIUM ($MIL)	NET INCOME ($MIL)	CAPITAL-IZATION INDEX (PTS)	RESERVE ADQ INDEX (PTS)	PROFIT-ABILITY INDEX (PTS)	LIQUIDITY INDEX (PTS)	STAB. INDEX (PTS)	STABILITY FACTORS
AFFINITY MUTUAL INS CO	OH	**C**	13.3	7.6	3.5	-0.1	9.4	7.8	2.7	7.4	2.7	DGT
▲AFFIRMATIVE INS CO	IL	**C-**	476.9	143.7	351.0	-8.1	6.8	5.8	4.0	1.9	2.9	FLT
AFFIRMATIVE INS CO OF MI	MI	**D**	16.4	9.4	0.0	0.0	10.0	N/A	5.0	9.9	1.5	DFG
AG SECURITY INS CO	OK	**C+**	42.0	25.0	13.8	0.0	9.3	6.8	5.8	6.7	4.4	DFGT
AGCS MARINE INS CO	IL	**C**	188.5	46.1	38.3	-28.8	8.4	5.8	2.8	6.7	4.2	T
AGENCY INS CO OF MARYLAND INC	MD	**C**	58.6	23.1	34.2	-0.2	7.4	5.8	7.2	6.0	3.5	DT
▲AGENT ALLIANCE INS CO	NC	**D+**	8.9	3.2	3.4	0.0	7.1	3.6	2.3	2.9	2.0	DFGL
AGENTS MUTUAL INS CO	AR	**D**	1.8	0.9	0.8	-0.1	9.1	8.1	4.5	8.2	1.0	DFGT
AGRI GENERAL INS CO	IA	**B-**	753.7	487.8	981.9	8.9	5.7	7.6	9.2	2.5	4.3	GLT
AGRI INS EXCHANGE RISK RETENTION GRP	IN	**C-**	10.1	8.1	0.4	0.1	7.5	6.0	2.5	8.3	2.7	DG
AGRICULTURAL WORKERS MUT AUTO INS	TX	**C**	54.0	22.1	34.3	-0.3	7.7	5.6	3.8	6.3	3.9	DFT
AGRINATIONAL INS CO	VT	**E**	513.6	156.7	95.0	-7.9	3.3	3.6	3.5	5.3	0.0	DT
AIG ADVANTAGE INS CO	MN	**B-**	73.2	19.2	72.9	0.8	3.0	6.8	4.0	3.9	4.8	CDGL
AIG AUTO INS CO OF NEW JERSEY	NJ	**B-**	48.4	20.7	-12.7	-0.9	10.0	4.8	4.0	6.8	3.6	DFGT
AIG CASUALTY CO	PA	**C+**	4,051.5	1,460.7	865.7	28.2	7.2	2.3	4.9	6.4	4.3	T
AIG CENTENNIAL INS CO	PA	**B**	802.9	298.6	437.6	6.4	7.4	6.6	4.3	6.2	5.4	GT
▼AIG EXCESS LIABILITY INS CO LTD	DE	**C+**	4,028.7	1,505.3	899.8	61.7	5.5	5.7	8.8	7.0	3.0	T
AIG GLOBAL TRADE & POL RISK INS CO	NJ	**C+**	369.2	175.1	82.7	0.7	9.6	7.0	6.7	7.7	4.5	T
▲AIG HAWAII INS CO INC	HI	**B**	187.5	61.0	102.5	1.8	7.5	5.6	5.5	5.2	5.4	LT
AIG INDEMNITY INS CO	PA	**B**	79.7	26.2	48.6	0.9	6.8	6.9	5.2	6.5	5.4	DGT
AIG NATIONAL INS CO INC	NY	**B-**	60.1	16.4	48.6	0.6	4.0	6.4	4.8	5.5	5.2	CDGT
AIG PREFERRED INS CO	PA	**B**	93.5	26.6	72.9	1.1	5.1	6.3	5.3	5.8	5.4	CDGT
AIG PREMIER INS CO	PA	**B-**	444.7	136.7	316.0	4.7	7.2	6.9	4.9	5.7	5.2	GT
AIMCO MUTUAL INS CO	NC	**E**	16.7	4.7	-0.4	-0.6	4.5	2.2	0.8	7.1	0.3	CDFG
AIOI INS CO OF AMERICA	NY	**C**	68.3	30.8	18.4	0.3	7.9	9.4	5.0	8.2	4.0	RT
▼AIU INS CO	NY	**C+**	2,824.7	665.9	1,175.2	7.9	7.3	4.6	2.5	5.6	3.7	FT
▼AIX SPECIALTY INS CO	DE	**B-**	21.4	21.1	18.4	1.7	5.3	3.9	4.6	6.8	3.5	CDT
ALABAMA MUNICIPAL INS CORP	AL	**C**	83.9	23.9	32.3	-0.6	7.1	4.8	5.0	7.1	3.9	T
ALAMANCE INS CO	IL	**C-**	421.7	273.6	45.1	2.7	7.3	6.0	8.7	7.0	2.6	T
▲ALASKA NATIONAL INS CO	AK	**B**	696.6	267.0	168.7	17.8	7.7	6.0	9.2	6.9	5.5	T
ALASKA TIMBER INS EXCHANGE	AK	**C**	18.0	7.4	4.7	-0.6	7.2	7.0	3.6	7.0	2.8	DFGR
ALEA NORTH AMERICA INS CO	NY	**D**	260.6	85.0	0.5	4.3	9.6	5.9	1.9	8.6	2.3	FT
ALFA ALLIANCE INS CORP	VA	**C**	34.9	17.5	6.3	-0.1	7.1	9.6	4.6	7.2	3.9	DFGT
ALFA GENERAL INS CORP	AL	**C**	119.6	55.3	-40.0	-1.2	10.0	7.9	1.9	5.5	4.0	FT
▼ALFA INS CORP	AL	**B**	111.6	50.0	-52.5	-2.2	10.0	7.9	1.9	4.8	5.6	DFLT
▼ALFA MUTUAL FIRE INS CO	AL	**B**	571.5	331.1	383.6	-1.9	6.1	6.0	2.0	2.5	4.9	CGLT
ALFA MUTUAL GENERAL INS CO	AL	**B**	77.0	45.4	40.6	-0.6	7.2	7.6	4.3	6.5	6.0	GT
▼ALFA MUTUAL INS CO	AL	**B**	1,089.8	659.4	593.5	-7.0	7.4	7.4	2.4	2.2	5.5	GLT
ALFA SPECIALTY INS CORP	AL	**B-**	34.2	18.4	21.9	-0.1	4.4	7.4	2.9	6.6	4.9	CDGT
ALFA VISION INS CORP	AL	**C**	89.3	55.4	34.4	-0.1	10.0	4.6	5.7	7.7	3.4	T
ALICOT INS CO	TX	**U** (1)	2.6	2.6	0.0	0.0	N/A	N/A	6.5	7.0	3.9	T
ALL AMERICA INS CO	OH	**B**	245.0	101.1	87.7	-0.2	10.0	5.3	6.3	6.6	5.4	T
ALLEGANY CO-OP INS CO	NY	**C+**	31.3	18.2	11.8	0.3	9.4	8.5	8.8	7.2	4.1	DGT
ALLEGHENY CASUALTY CO	PA	**C-**	22.6	17.5	33.2	0.2	2.7	N/A	8.6	5.4	3.1	CDGT
ALLEGHENY SURETY CO	PA	**D**	3.4	2.1	1.1	0.0	7.1	6.7	8.2	7.2	1.7	DFGT
ALLEGIANT INS CO INC A RRG	HI	**E**	11.2	4.9	0.9	0.1	3.3	6.0	5.6	9.3	0.0	DGOT
ALLIANCE HOME WARRANTY INC	UT	**U** (5)	0.0	0.0	7.3	0.0	N/A	N/A	2.9	0.5	2.5	DGLT
ALLIANCE INDEMNITY CO	KS	**C+**	8.9	5.7	3.1	0.1	10.0	6.4	6.3	6.9	3.6	DFGT
ALLIANCE INS CO INC	KS	**C**	22.6	9.8	12.6	0.1	8.1	6.9	5.1	6.3	3.7	DFGT
ALLIANCE MUTUAL INS CO	NC	**D+**	10.7	4.5	6.3	0.0	5.8	4.5	1.4	7.8	2.3	DFGR
ALLIANCE NATIONAL INS CO	NY	**D**	7.5	5.7	1.5	0.1	0.0	1.6	3.5	8.3	2.1	CDFG
ALLIANCE OF NONPROFITS FOR INS RRG	VT	**D**	40.4	16.9	11.0	0.2	5.7	9.4	8.5	7.6	1.9	DGT

See Page 27 for explanation of footnotes and Page 28 for explanation of stability factors.

Arrows denote recent upgrades ▲ or downgrades ▼ (see Section VII for explanations)

RISK ADJ. RATIO #1	CAPITAL RATIO #2	PREMIUM TO SURPLUS (%)	RESV. TO SURPLUS (%)	RESV. DEVELOP. 1 YEAR (%)	RESV. DEVELOP. 2 YEAR (%)	LOSS RATIO (%)	EXP. RATIO (%)	COMB RATIO (%)	CASH FROM UNDER-WRITING (%)	NET PREMIUM GROWTH (%)	INVEST. IN AFFIL (%)	INSURANCE COMPANY NAME
3.8	2.5	44.2	22.4	-5.9	-4.2	48.6	60.4	109.0	89.7	-11.9	0.0	AFFINITY MUTUAL INS CO
1.1	0.9	232.5	106.6	2.5	-1.6	74.9	31.7	106.6	89.9	-16.8	24.7	AFFIRMATIVE INS CO
4.9	4.4	N/A	N/A	N/A	N/A	N/A	N/A	N/A	-55.3	0.0	0.0	AFFIRMATIVE INS CO OF MI
4.2	2.7	55.6	31.8	-0.3	-8.7	83.5	33.3	116.8	81.8	-16.4	0.0	AG SECURITY INS CO
2.5	1.8	50.8	67.5	1.7	2.7	75.0	27.2	102.2	109.3	3.0	0.0	AGCS MARINE INS CO
1.5	1.4	147.9	71.6	-8.1	-8.8	64.0	30.7	94.7	101.6	3.7	0.0	AGENCY INS CO OF MARYLAND INC
1.7	1.2	107.2	6.0	4.0	1.0	117.3	-16.7	100.6	71.3	-35.7	0.0	AGENT ALLIANCE INS CO
2.6	2.3	77.5	0.1	-9.2	-0.1	57.1	28.9	86.0	71.9	7.5	0.0	AGENTS MUTUAL INS CO
2.1	1.3	189.5	75.4	-1.5	-1.2	82.8	2.9	85.7	133.2	97.2	0.0 ●	AGRI GENERAL INS CO
2.2	1.5	5.1	24.4	6.0	-0.7	214.1	105.9	320.0	101.1	3.7	0.0	AGRI INS EXCHANGE RISK RETENTION
1.9	1.4	147.3	26.0	-1.6	-3.9	56.3	19.5	75.8	132.8	1.4	7.3	AGRICULTURAL WORKERS MUT AUTO
0.7	0.5	57.3	149.9	-5.5	-17.0	162.4	11.1	173.5	125.5	20.0	56.1 ●	AGRINATIONAL INS CO
0.9	0.6	360.4	203.7	7.8	1.6	79.6	26.9	106.5	119.9	44.8	0.0	AIG ADVANTAGE INS CO
4.8	4.3	-61.8	N/A	N/A	N/A	N/A	26.3	N/A	-4.1	-137.9	0.0	AIG AUTO INS CO OF NEW JERSEY
1.7	1.2	59.4	120.6	-0.1	0.5	78.1	25.2	103.3	88.2	-15.4	15.6 ●	AIG CASUALTY CO
1.3	1.2	143.5	81.1	3.1	0.7	79.6	26.9	106.5	121.2	44.8	37.2 ●	AIG CENTENNIAL INS CO
1.8	1.2	62.6	126.7	-8.1	-12.8	80.5	16.7	97.2	140.9	-6.8	9.5 ●	AIG EXCESS LIABILITY INS CO LTD
3.0	2.7	48.3	46.6	-18.9	-19.2	60.0	19.9	79.9	237.0	11.4	8.1 ●	AIG GLOBAL TRADE & POL RISK INS CO
2.2	1.6	159.9	107.1	4.5	0.9	79.6	27.0	106.6	91.3	-23.7	7.8	AIG HAWAII INS CO INC
1.3	1.0	183.9	103.9	4.0	0.9	79.6	26.9	106.5	119.9	44.8	0.0	AIG INDEMNITY INS CO
1.0	0.7	280.1	158.3	6.4	1.3	79.6	26.9	106.5	119.9	44.8	0.0	AIG NATIONAL INS CO INC
1.2	0.8	259.5	146.6	6.0	1.2	79.6	26.8	106.4	120.0	44.8	0.0	AIG PREFERRED INS CO
1.6	1.2	219.8	124.2	4.7	1.0	79.6	26.9	106.5	119.8	44.8	8.5	AIG PREMIER INS CO
0.9	0.4	-9.0	246.3	13.0	20.8	999 +	-340.6	999 +	2.0	-112.2	0.0	AIMCO MUTUAL INS CO
3.2	1.9	60.0	71.0	-12.2	-31.2	50.3	48.6	98.9	139.0	-15.5	0.0	AIOI INS CO OF AMERICA
1.4	1.0	161.9	73.8	0.9	0.2	68.4	39.9	108.3	92.9	68.1	12.1 ●	AIU INS CO
3.2	1.9	90.4	99.7	3.6	-10.5	74.9	34.5	109.4	132.2	-44.0	0.0	AIX SPECIALTY INS CO
1.1	1.0	128.4	148.5	-10.8	-7.8	68.4	20.4	88.8	142.7	8.3	0.0	ALABAMA MUNICIPAL INS CORP
1.4	1.2	16.7	46.1	-3.1	-1.3	56.3	37.0	93.3	99.1	-27.7	50.2 ●	ALAMANCE INS CO
3.5	1.8	63.5	134.4	-22.0	-26.1	43.4	30.7	74.1	126.1	-4.9	0.0 ●	ALASKA NATIONAL INS CO
1.7	1.2	57.0	126.1	-11.6	-29.8	49.6	15.7	65.3	108.4	-9.4	0.0	ALASKA TIMBER INS EXCHANGE
3.9	2.0	0.4	45.9	3.1	4.6	366.9	999 +	999 +	13.1	121.7	0.0	ALEA NORTH AMERICA INS CO
2.1	1.5	35.8	47.1	-11.1	-36.0	54.8	80.2	135.0	36.1	-69.8	0.0	ALFA ALLIANCE INS CORP
7.7	7.0	-97.6	88.7	-2.3	-2.1	59.7	25.3	85.0	-28.6	-114.4	0.0	ALFA GENERAL INS CORP
7.2	6.4	-141.0	94.0	-2.5	-2.0	53.3	27.2	80.5	-58.2	-119.0	0.0	ALFA INS CORP
1.2	0.8	113.8	23.6	-1.0	-0.3	70.9	26.7	97.6	124.7	126.8	57.1 ●	ALFA MUTUAL FIRE INS CO
1.5	1.0	87.4	21.8	-1.8	-1.6	73.5	26.6	100.1	102.6	56.8	0.5	ALFA MUTUAL GENERAL INS CO
1.6	1.1	89.4	19.6	-0.4	-0.6	74.7	25.9	100.6	121.1	291.1	45.5 ●	ALFA MUTUAL INS CO
0.9	0.6	119.9	24.5	-1.0	-1.0	74.6	26.6	101.2	112.2	125.9	0.0	ALFA SPECIALTY INS CORP
7.0	5.0	61.9	20.6	-1.3	-0.7	73.5	26.1	99.6	94.1	-28.6	0.0	ALFA VISION INS CORP
N/A	N/A	N/A	N/A	N/A	N/A	N/A	N/A	N/A	N/A	0.0	0.0	ALICOT INS CO
4.2	2.9	86.7	87.7	2.5	-1.6	79.4	31.7	111.1	102.1	-1.9	0.3	ALL AMERICA INS CO
3.9	2.8	64.9	25.1	-3.7	-7.7	51.4	35.0	86.4	117.9	3.4	0.0	ALLEGANY CO-OP INS CO
0.5	0.4	191.1	0.7	N/A	N/A	0.3	96.6	96.9	103.3	11.3	0.0	ALLEGHENY CASUALTY CO
1.5	1.3	51.2	21.6	N/A	-4.2	0.1	96.2	96.3	89.0	-40.6	0.0	ALLEGHENY SURETY CO
1.4	0.7	18.0	121.2	-6.7	-32.1	55.1	65.8	120.9	106.9	-74.9	0.0	ALLEGIANT INS CO INC A RRG
N/A	N/A	478.1	28.3	N/A	N/A	63.3	27.0	90.3	122.9	30.6	0.0	ALLIANCE HOME WARRANTY INC
5.5	3.9	55.4	26.9	-3.0	-4.7	79.5	30.1	109.6	89.3	1.8	0.0	ALLIANCE INDEMNITY CO
2.4	1.7	130.1	63.1	-6.7	-10.7	79.5	30.1	109.6	89.1	1.8	0.0	ALLIANCE INS CO INC
1.4	0.9	138.8	67.3	0.2	2.6	51.7	61.2	112.9	87.4	2.7	0.0	ALLIANCE MUTUAL INS CO
0.0	0.0	27.2	758.3	-70.4	-57.7	103.7	-22.2	81.5	20.8	27.4	0.0	ALLIANCE NATIONAL INS CO
1.6	0.8	67.0	101.7	-5.5	-13.7	59.6	35.7	95.3	130.8	4.3	0.0	ALLIANCE OF NONPROFITS FOR INS RRG

999 + Denotes number greater than 999.9%
999 - Denotes number less than -999.99%
• Bullets denote a more detailed analysis is available in Section II.

INSURANCE COMPANY NAME	DOM. STATE	RATING	TOTAL ASSETS ($MIL)	CAPITAL & SURPLUS ($MIL)	ANNUAL NET PREMIUM ($MIL)	NET INCOME ($MIL)	CAPITAL-IZATION INDEX (PTS)	RESERVE ADQ INDEX (PTS)	PROFIT-ABILITY INDEX (PTS)	LIQUIDITY INDEX (PTS)	STAB. INDEX (PTS)	STABILITY FACTORS
▼ALLIANCE UNITED INS CO	CA	**D**	44.9	13.7	37.5	0.0	1.2	4.7	2.9	6.0	1.5	CDGO
ALLIANZ GLOBAL RISKS US INS CO	CA	**C+**	5,045.2	3,791.5	412.5	-32.4	7.3	6.0	5.1	6.9	4.5	GT
ALLIANZ UNDERWRITERS INS CO	CA	**C**	94.3	59.7	8.4	1.5	4.6	4.6	7.6	6.9	3.5	DGT
ALLIED EASTERN INDEMNITY CO	PA	**C**	25.3	8.5	9.0	0.2	6.2	7.0	8.0	7.4	3.9	DGT
ALLIED PROFESSIONALS INS CO RRG	AZ	**D+**	17.4	8.1	7.1	1.0	7.2	7.0	9.4	8.6	2.6	DGRT
ALLIED PROPERTY & CASUALTY INS CO	IA	**B**	120.4	59.3	0.0	1.5	10.0	N/A	2.8	0.1	5.4	FGLT
ALLIED SERVICES RRG	SC	**D-**	4.2	2.8	0.9	0.1	7.2	5.0	9.3	8.1	1.0	DGT
▲ALLIED WORLD ASR CO (US) INC	DE	**C-**	239.3	107.4	26.5	-5.9	7.8	8.7	3.8	7.3	3.0	AGT
ALLIED WORLD NATL ASR CO	NH	**C**	198.4	109.0	21.7	-5.7	8.8	8.6	3.5	7.4	4.0	AGT
ALLIED WORLD REINS CO	NJ	**C**	795.0	620.7	32.3	4.2	8.1	6.1	3.0	9.2	3.4	AGT
ALLMERICA FINANCIAL ALLIANCE INS CO	NH	**C+**	16.8	16.8	0.0	0.1	10.0	N/A	7.9	7.0	3.3	DGT
ALLMERICA FINANCIAL BENEFIT INS CO	MI	**C+**	16.3	16.3	0.0	0.1	10.0	N/A	8.2	7.0	3.2	DGT
ALLSTATE COUNTY MUTUAL INS CO	TX	**B**	14.4	14.3	0.0	0.0	10.0	N/A	7.0	7.0	4.9	DGT
ALLSTATE FIRE & CASUALTY INS CO	IL	**C**	60.4	57.7	0.0	0.4	10.0	N/A	7.8	7.0	3.9	GT
ALLSTATE FLORIDIAN INDEMNITY CORP	IL	**B**	14.6	13.7	0.0	0.1	10.0	3.9	7.3	9.0	4.9	DFG
ALLSTATE FLORIDIAN INS CO	IL	**B-**	363.6	164.1	56.4	4.3	7.2	5.8	0.8	5.9	5.2	FT
ALLSTATE INDEMNITY CO	IL	**B**	159.1	147.9	0.0	0.9	10.0	N/A	4.4	10.0	5.4	GT
ALLSTATE INS CO	IL	**B+**	39,333.3	13,090.0	24,431.4	144.6	7.7	6.5	3.2	5.1	6.4	LT
ALLSTATE NJ INS CO	IL	**B-**	2,258.5	608.3	1,132.4	-0.8	7.9	4.8	3.5	5.9	5.3	T
ALLSTATE NJ PROPERTY & CASUALTY INS	IL	**C-**	27.6	27.0	0.0	0.2	10.0	N/A	4.9	10.0	3.3	GT
ALLSTATE PROPERTY & CASUALTY INS CO	IL	**B**	164.3	156.2	0.0	1.0	10.0	N/A	7.1	10.0	6.1	GT
ALLSTATE TEXAS LLOYDS	TX	**B**	25.2	16.2	0.0	0.0	10.0	N/A	7.2	7.0	4.9	DGT
ALPHA PROPERTY & CASUALTY INS CO	WI	**B**	37.0	13.8	0.0	0.1	10.0	N/A	4.6	10.0	4.9	DG
AMALGAMATED CASUALTY INS CO	DC	**C**	39.0	31.5	4.0	0.5	10.0	8.9	8.5	7.3	3.5	DGT
AMBAC ASSURANCE CORP	WI	**D**	9,392.4	372.8	502.3	-232.2	5.8	2.6	0.6	8.4	1.4	CFT
AMCO INS CO	IA	**B**	2,453.5	416.1	0.0	3.9	10.0	N/A	4.3	9.5	5.4	GT
AMERICA FIRST INS CO	NH	**B-**	13.3	11.6	0.0	0.1	10.0	N/A	8.1	7.0	3.8	DGT
AMERICA FIRST LLOYD'S INS CO	TX	**C-**	6.2	5.8	0.0	0.0	10.0	N/A	7.4	7.0	2.9	DG
▲AMERICAN ACCESS CASUALTY CO	IL	**C**	122.6	32.8	73.9	0.2	5.5	9.9	8.3	6.2	3.6	T
▲AMERICAN AGRI BUSINESS INS CO	TX	**C+**	420.3	16.6	0.0	0.5	5.4	4.6	9.7	9.3	3.2	GT
AMERICAN AGRICULTURAL INS CO	IN	**B**	1,597.7	490.1	367.8	-4.0	8.0	6.9	5.4	6.7	5.6	T
AMERICAN ALTERNATIVE INS CORP	DE	**C**	527.0	156.1	51.1	10.3	7.0	4.3	5.8	8.3	3.4	GT
AMERICAN AMBASSADOR CASUALTY CO	IL	**U** (1)	9.5	8.2	0.0	0.2	N/A	N/A	4.1	7.0	4.8	T
AMERICAN ASSOC OF ORTHODONTIST RRG	VT	**D-**	24.2	3.2	6.1	-0.5	1.3	6.1	3.7	7.6	1.3	DGRT
AMERICAN AUTOMOBILE INS CO	MO	**C**	457.0	213.6	119.7	5.8	7.6	5.7	8.7	6.6	4.3	T
▲AMERICAN BANKERS INS CO OF FL	FL	**B-**	1,253.6	479.3	778.4	28.6	7.6	8.8	7.0	6.3	4.9	AT
AMERICAN BUILDERS INS CO RRG INC	MT	**E+**	1.6	0.8	0.0	0.0	8.7	3.6	2.0	2.6	0.7	DGLT
AMERICAN BUS & PERSONAL INS MUT INC	DE	**B**	42.5	21.9	0.2	-0.5	1.5	5.4	4.7	10.0	6.3	CDG
▲AMERICAN CAPITAL ASR CORP	FL	**C+**	108.8	65.0	44.8	1.8	7.7	3.6	7.5	7.0	3.6	DGT
AMERICAN CASUALTY CO OF READING	PA	**C**	114.2	111.0	0.0	0.5	8.9	N/A	6.3	8.9	3.8	AT
AMERICAN CENTENNIAL INS CO	DE	**U** (1)	29.0	18.5	0.0	-0.2	N/A	0.8	2.0	10.0	1.2	FT
▲AMERICAN COASTAL INS CO	FL	**D-**	130.4	62.8	78.4	1.9	6.9	3.6	5.1	7.8	1.0	DGT
AMERICAN COLONIAL INS CO INC	FL	**U** (1)	4.6	4.4	0.0	0.1	N/A	4.6	4.4	7.0	3.2	T
AMERICAN COMMERCE INS CO	OH	**B-**	340.1	138.8	139.4	2.2	10.0	8.2	7.9	6.7	4.8	T
AMERICAN COMPENSATION INS CO	MN	**C**	89.9	46.9	22.7	-2.5	5.3	9.3	5.1	5.8	3.0	FT
AMERICAN CONCEPT INS CO	RI	**U** (1)	7.3	3.9	0.0	1.1	N/A	4.7	4.5	10.0	4.2	FT
AMERICAN CONTRACTORS INDEMNITY CO	CA	**C+**	256.6	57.9	85.6	3.4	7.6	5.9	8.5	6.8	4.5	T
▲AMERICAN CONTRACTORS INS CO RISK	TX	**D**	9.6	5.6	0.0	-0.1	8.2	3.6	5.9	10.0	1.4	DGT
AMERICAN COUNTRY INS CO	IL	**D**	87.2	12.2	8.0	0.0	2.8	5.1	0.8	5.9	2.3	CDFT
▲AMERICAN EAGLE INS CO RRG	VT	**D**	9.4	2.0	3.1	0.1	1.8	2.8	2.9	8.5	1.4	CDGT
AMERICAN ECONOMY INS CO	IN	**B-**	1,774.2	430.7	747.7	11.3	7.5	6.9	2.6	5.9	4.9	AT
AMERICAN EMPIRE INS CO	OH	**C+**	44.8	23.4	6.0	0.1	8.4	9.3	3.1	8.6	4.3	DGT

See Page 27 for explanation of footnotes and Page 28 for explanation of stability factors.

Arrows denote recent upgrades ▲ or downgrades ▼ (see Section VII for explanations)

RISK ADJ. RATIO #1	CAPITAL RATIO #2	PREMIUM TO SURPLUS (%)	RESV. TO SURPLUS (%)	RESV. DEVELOP. 1 YEAR (%)	RESV. DEVELOP. 2 YEAR (%)	LOSS RATIO (%)	EXP. RATIO (%)	COMB RATIO (%)	CASH FROM UNDER-WRITING (%)	NET PREMIUM GROWTH (%)	INVEST. IN AFFIL (%)	INSURANCE COMPANY NAME
0.4	0.3	270.4	141.7	5.1	14.6	86.2	15.0	101.2	140.0	90.1	0.0	ALLIANCE UNITED INS CO
1.3	1.2	11.1	18.7	0.2	0.9	53.2	16.0	69.2	233.7	50.0	66.5 •	ALLIANZ GLOBAL RISKS US INS CO
0.9	0.6	14.4	27.1	7.9	9.0	53.2	23.3	76.5	-574.6	50.0	0.0	ALLIANZ UNDERWRITERS INS CO
1.3	0.7	87.8	65.8	-3.8	-16.6	57.4	23.5	80.9	284.5	17.6	0.0	ALLIED EASTERN INDEMNITY CO
2.4	1.8	99.5	60.2	-8.0	-14.9	30.5	44.8	75.3	165.0	6.8	0.0	ALLIED PROFESSIONALS INS CO RRG
8.1	7.3	N/A	N/A	N/A	N/A	N/A	N/A	N/A	-9.8	0.0	6.5	ALLIED PROPERTY & CASUALTY INS CO
1.9	1.1	33.6	37.1	-23.1	-39.6	-7.7	27.7	20.0	302.7	1.3	0.0	ALLIED SERVICES RRG
3.0	2.0	23.5	46.6	-6.2	-12.3	55.1	44.4	99.5	134.3	174.6	0.0	ALLIED WORLD ASR CO (US) INC
4.7	2.7	20.3	40.2	-6.8	-11.8	55.1	43.8	98.9	137.9	174.6	0.0	ALLIED WORLD NATL ASR CO
1.2	1.2	5.5	0.5	-2.7	-1.9	33.9	38.9	72.8	169.7	261.5	90.8 •	ALLIED WORLD REINS CO
116.0	56.0	N/A	N/A	N/A	N/A	N/A	N/A	N/A	N/A	0.0	0.0	ALLMERICA FINANCIAL ALLIANCE INS CO
143.0	66.2	N/A	N/A	N/A	N/A	N/A	N/A	N/A	N/A	0.0	0.0	ALLMERICA FINANCIAL BENEFIT INS CO
315.5	284.0	N/A	N/A	N/A	N/A	N/A	N/A	N/A	N/A	0.0	0.0	ALLSTATE COUNTY MUTUAL INS CO
63.7	43.1	N/A	N/A	N/A	N/A	N/A	N/A	N/A	N/A	0.0	0.0	ALLSTATE FIRE & CASUALTY INS CO
34.3	30.9	N/A	N/A	N/A	N/A	N/A	N/A	N/A	-123.8	0.0	0.0	ALLSTATE FLORIDIAN INDEMNITY CORP
1.1	0.9	34.7	43.8	7.4	15.4	158.3	81.0	239.3	32.6	65.7	10.7 •	ALLSTATE FLORIDIAN INS CO
57.8	52.0	N/A	N/A	N/A	N/A	N/A	N/A	N/A	-559.6	0.0	0.0	ALLSTATE INDEMNITY CO
1.8	1.4	187.6	114.1	1.0	0.1	74.3	24.5	98.8	103.2	-2.5	14.3 •	ALLSTATE INS CO
1.9	1.5	179.9	188.8	6.2	N/A	81.0	22.7	103.7	101.4	-0.8	3.3 •	ALLSTATE NJ INS CO
73.1	36.5	N/A	N/A	N/A	N/A	N/A	N/A	N/A	N/A	0.0	0.0	ALLSTATE NJ PROPERTY & CASUALTY
74.8	52.3	N/A	N/A	N/A	N/A	N/A	N/A	N/A	-14.0	0.0	0.0	ALLSTATE PROPERTY & CASUALTY INS
7.2	6.5	N/A	N/A	N/A	N/A	N/A	N/A	N/A	N/A	0.0	0.0	ALLSTATE TEXAS LLOYDS
3.5	3.2	N/A	N/A	N/A	N/A	N/A	N/A	N/A	-72.9	0.0	0.0	ALPHA PROPERTY & CASUALTY INS CO
14.4	9.0	12.8	24.1	-2.9	-6.2	70.3	29.7	100.0	86.6	-8.3	0.0	AMALGAMATED CASUALTY INS CO
0.6	0.2	32.3	74.6	3.4	-0.3	150.6	87.5	238.1	19.0	-35.5	2.3 •	AMBAC ASSURANCE CORP
7.9	5.7	N/A	N/A	N/A	N/A	N/A	N/A	N/A	999 +	0.0	6.4 •	AMCO INS CO
18.3	16.4	N/A	N/A	N/A	N/A	N/A	N/A	N/A	N/A	0.0	0.0	AMERICA FIRST INS CO
40.4	36.3	N/A	N/A	N/A	N/A	N/A	N/A	N/A	N/A	0.0	0.0	AMERICA FIRST LLOYD'S INS CO
1.2	0.9	204.4	131.2	-7.6	-27.7	54.0	33.0	87.0	110.5	16.5	0.0	AMERICAN ACCESS CASUALTY CO
1.4	1.2	-0.1	0.2	4.1	2.1	98.3	999 +	999 +	15.0	-100.1	0.0	AMERICAN AGRI BUSINESS INS CO
2.6	1.8	72.8	72.9	-7.7	-2.3	87.3	23.2	110.5	104.3	-20.1	0.1 •	AMERICAN AGRICULTURAL INS CO
1.8	1.1	35.0	56.9	-0.1	9.4	71.2	-31.7	39.5	-200.0	44.6	0.0	AMERICAN ALTERNATIVE INS CORP
N/A	N/A	N/A	N/A	N/A	N/A	N/A	N/A	N/A	N/A	0.0	0.0	AMERICAN AMBASSADOR CASUALTY CO
0.4	0.3	181.1	475.8	-75.5	-100.7	53.7	25.8	79.5	194.0	6.6	0.0	AMERICAN ASSOC OF ORTHODONTIST
2.1	1.6	56.3	74.9	2.0	3.4	75.0	27.7	102.7	95.9	3.0	19.8 •	AMERICAN AUTOMOBILE INS CO
2.6	1.8	173.0	29.9	-4.8	-4.6	43.9	52.0	95.9	103.5	1.0	0.6 •	AMERICAN BANKERS INS CO OF FL
2.5	2.2	3.8	16.3	-3.6	-0.1	54.3	351.5	405.8	429.9	-82.2	0.0	AMERICAN BUILDERS INS CO RRG INC
0.5	0.3	0.7	82.6	0.9	-10.7	999 +	548.8	999 +	4.5	47.4	41.3	AMERICAN BUS & PERSONAL INS MUT
2.4	1.7	71.2	12.5	-2.3	-0.1	22.2	45.0	67.2	184.6	11.5	15.8	AMERICAN CAPITAL ASR CORP
2.2	2.1	N/A	N/A	N/A	N/A	N/A	N/A	N/A	N/A	0.0	49.0	AMERICAN CASUALTY CO OF READING
N/A	N/A	N/A	195.7	1.3	8.8	N/A	N/A	N/A	N/A	-100.0	0.0	AMERICAN CENTENNIAL INS CO
1.4	1.1	131.2	20.1	-3.4	N/A	25.7	37.4	63.1	242.5	228.5	0.0	AMERICAN COASTAL INS CO
N/A	N/A	N/A	4.0	N/A	N/A	N/A	N/A	N/A	N/A	0.0	0.0	AMERICAN COLONIAL INS CO INC
4.5	3.7	100.0	49.3	-3.3	-4.1	68.0	28.0	96.0	102.8	-9.4	0.0	AMERICAN COMMERCE INS CO
1.3	0.8	48.8	61.5	-2.2	-3.4	73.9	33.6	107.5	31.7	-45.9	15.6	AMERICAN COMPENSATION INS CO
N/A	N/A	-0.4	74.5	-34.9	-37.0	999 +	-940.0	999 +	-1.6	-87.5	0.0	AMERICAN CONCEPT INS CO
1.5	1.2	126.6	41.9	N/A	-12.2	23.9	56.7	80.6	121.9	-6.3	0.0	AMERICAN CONTRACTORS INDEMNITY
4.4	4.0	N/A	N/A	N/A	N/A	N/A	N/A	N/A	40.6	0.0	0.0	AMERICAN CONTRACTORS INS CO RISK
1.6	1.2	66.1	262.0	4.6	-0.7	147.7	112.8	260.5	45.1	-33.7	0.0	AMERICAN COUNTRY INS CO
0.4	0.4	116.6	167.7	-23.8	19.3	39.6	39.8	79.4	247.3	-4.4	0.0	AMERICAN EAGLE INS CO RRG
2.6	1.8	241.9	216.5	-5.4	-5.9	67.0	31.2	98.2	101.8	-5.6	1.9 •	AMERICAN ECONOMY INS CO
2.6	2.0	25.5	74.9	-11.8	-18.8	15.5	22.4	37.9	116.8	-29.8	0.0	AMERICAN EMPIRE INS CO

999 + Denotes number greater than 999.9%
999 - Denotes number less than -999.99%
• Bullets denote a more detailed analysis is available in Section II.

INSURANCE COMPANY NAME	DOM. STATE	RATING	TOTAL ASSETS ($MIL)	CAPITAL & SURPLUS ($MIL)	ANNUAL NET PREMIUM ($MIL)	NET INCOME ($MIL)	CAPITAL-IZATION INDEX (PTS)	RESERVE ADQ INDEX (PTS)	PROFIT-ABILITY INDEX (PTS)	LIQUIDITY INDEX (PTS)	STAB. INDEX (PTS)	STABILITY FACTORS
AMERICAN EMPIRE SURPLUS LINES INS CO	DE	**C**	328.9	132.8	54.2	4.9	7.9	9.5	3.0	7.0	4.0	T
AMERICAN EQUITABLE INC	MI	**C-**	9.9	8.6	0.6	0.2	10.0	8.4	8.1	9.2	2.8	DGT
AMERICAN EQUITY INS CO	AZ	**U** (1)	104.6	102.3	0.0	5.1	N/A	4.6	8.6	7.0	6.5	T
▲AMERICAN EQUITY SPECIALTY INS CO	CT	**B**	78.5	31.0	18.1	0.8	7.7	5.7	8.7	6.7	4.6	T
AMERICAN EUROPEAN INS CO	NH	**C+**	194.2	62.1	63.0	-1.2	8.2	7.0	3.3	7.6	4.3	T
AMERICAN EXCESS INS EXCHANGE RRG	VT	**D-**	325.7	89.0	35.4	3.7	7.3	9.4	4.7	8.1	0.9	DT
AMERICAN FAMILY HOME INS CO	FL	**B+**	443.6	129.0	222.2	4.8	8.0	6.9	6.7	6.3	5.0	T
AMERICAN FAMILY INS CO	OH	**B**	55.4	12.5	0.0	0.1	8.4	N/A	8.7	5.9	4.9	D
▼AMERICAN FAMILY MUT INS CO	WI	**B-**	10,575.6	3,193.6	5,786.2	159.0	7.6	5.8	2.3	2.9	4.9	FLRT
AMERICAN FARMERS & RANCHERS INS CO	ID	**D**	24.9	10.7	0.0	-0.9	10.0	3.1	2.1	7.4	1.5	DFGR
▼AMERICAN FARMERS & RANCHERS MUTUAL	OK	**D+**	96.9	21.2	104.6	-2.9	4.4	5.8	1.3	0.2	2.5	FLT
AMERICAN FEDERATED INS CO	MS	**C**	21.9	7.0	11.0	1.6	8.5	6.3	3.7	7.1	3.0	DGT
AMERICAN FEDERATION INS CO	FL	**B**	20.1	15.5	0.0	0.1	10.0	N/A	6.7	10.0	5.1	DG
AMERICAN FEED INDUSTRY INS CO RRG	IA	**C**	14.9	8.6	2.2	0.2	8.7	9.4	8.6	9.3	2.8	DGRT
AMERICAN FELLOWSHIP MUT INS CO	MI	**D**	7.6	2.7	5.3	-0.1	2.8	3.6	1.9	6.2	1.5	DFGT
AMERICAN FIRE & CASUALTY CO	OH	**C-**	200.1	37.2	84.7	1.4	7.5	6.9	3.5	8.1	3.0	AGT
AMERICAN FOREST CASUALTY CO RRG	SC	**E+** (1)	8.7	2.0	3.1	0.0	0.8	1.1	3.8	4.8	0.8	CDFL
AMERICAN FREEDOM INS CO	IL	**D+**	28.2	12.2	10.6	0.0	8.0	10.0	7.0	7.7	2.7	DFGT
AMERICAN FUJI FIRE & MARINE INS CO	IL	**B-**	92.9	70.5	-0.5	0.1	10.0	6.0	5.0	10.0	3.9	GRT
AMERICAN GENERAL INDEMNITY CO	IL	**C+**	8.7	7.3	-0.8	0.0	10.0	5.9	1.9	7.0	3.3	DGRT
AMERICAN GENERAL PROP INS CO OF FL	FL	**U** (1)	12.9	12.5	0.0	0.5	N/A	6.1	4.7	10.0	5.0	T
AMERICAN GENERAL PROPERTY INS CO	TN	**U** (1)	56.9	40.5	0.0	0.0	N/A	5.6	3.6	10.0	5.4	T
AMERICAN GUARANTEE & LIABILITY INS	NY	**C**	212.0	155.8	0.0	0.1	10.0	N/A	7.7	7.0	3.9	T
AMERICAN GUARANTY INS CO	NC	**C**	8.5	6.5	3.3	0.5	9.2	5.5	6.1	7.2	2.7	DGT
AMERICAN HALLMARK INS CO OF TX	TX	**C-**	240.4	87.2	108.1	-0.4	5.4	4.8	5.4	6.8	3.2	T
AMERICAN HARDWARE MUTUAL INS CO	OH	**B**	334.2	95.7	117.8	-1.6	8.0	5.6	3.3	6.4	6.1	T
AMERICAN HEALTHCARE INDEMNITY CO	DE	**C-**	124.7	44.7	32.1	0.6	7.6	6.9	6.3	8.4	3.0	T
AMERICAN HEALTHCARE SPECIALTY INS CO	AR	**D+**	70.3	28.8	16.1	0.5	7.4	6.9	6.9	9.1	2.6	DT
AMERICAN HEARTLAND INS CO	IL	**E+**	13.1	2.0	10.9	0.2	0.1	0.5	1.0	1.5	0.8	CDFG
▼AMERICAN HOME ASR CO	NY	**C+**	24,768.6	5,171.0	6,846.0	2.7	5.6	1.8	4.6	5.5	4.3	FT
AMERICAN HOME SHIELD OF NV INC	NV	**U** (5)	0.0	6.6	26.1	0.0	N/A	N/A	9.5	6.4	4.2	DGT
AMERICAN HOME SHIELD OF VA INC	VA	**U** (5)	0.0	0.0	0.0	0.0	N/A	0.0	0.0	0.0	0.0	
▲AMERICAN INDEPENDENT INS CO	PA	**D+**	81.7	33.8	35.7	-0.3	7.6	6.0	6.4	2.7	2.5	LT
AMERICAN INS CO	OH	**B-**	1,425.7	382.8	550.8	17.1	5.6	5.5	3.4	5.5	4.9	T
▲AMERICAN INTEGRITY INS CO OF FL	FL	**D**	87.4	25.3	68.3	1.1	3.8	3.6	7.0	5.6	1.6	DGT
AMERICAN INTER FIDELITY EXCHANGE RRG	IN	**C**	22.4	11.3	5.7	0.1	7.3	5.2	8.5	7.5	3.2	DGT
AMERICAN INTERNATIONAL INS CO	NY	**B**	1,612.1	364.3	508.3	6.0	7.9	5.3	6.6	0.7	5.6	FGLT
AMERICAN INTERNATIONAL INS CO OF CA	CA	**B-**	74.2	20.1	72.9	0.8	3.3	5.7	3.9	5.1	4.9	CDGT
▲AMERICAN INTERNATIONAL INS CO OF DE	DE	**B-**	103.5	50.1	31.3	1.1	7.2	5.6	6.5	1.0	4.9	FLOT
AMERICAN INTERNATIONAL INS CO OF NJ	NJ	**B**	79.3	29.4	48.6	0.9	7.2	6.3	5.5	5.8	5.6	DGT
AMERICAN INTERNATIONAL PACIFIC INS	CO	**B-**	89.1	34.7	0.0	-1.1	10.0	N/A	5.1	7.0	5.3	G
AMERICAN INTERNATIONAL SOUTH INS CO	PA	**B**	44.5	38.6	0.0	0.3	10.0	N/A	8.0	7.0	5.4	DG
▲AMERICAN INTERSTATE INS CO	LA	**C+**	934.9	282.9	231.3	8.5	7.3	4.6	7.4	6.9	4.5	T
▲AMERICAN INTERSTATE INS CO OF TEXAS	TX	**C**	41.6	12.4	14.2	0.4	5.2	4.9	8.9	7.0	3.5	CDGT
AMERICAN INTL INS CO OF PR	PR	**B**	253.1	150.2	33.6	4.0	10.0	6.1	8.5	7.8	4.5	T
AMERICAN INTL SPECIALTY LINES INS CO	IL	**C**	2,497.8	754.5	198.2	21.9	2.5	2.8	4.9	6.3	4.2	CT
AMERICAN KEYSTONE INS CO	FL	**C-**	24.1	5.1	6.6	0.0	4.4	3.6	1.6	7.5	2.1	DGT
AMERICAN LIBERTY INS CO	UT	**D**	9.6	3.9	7.3	0.1	0.7	6.0	7.6	7.0	1.4	CDFG
AMERICAN LIFE INS CO	DE	**E** (1)	95.6	0.8	37.8	-10.5	0.0	4.7	0.6	7.2	0.0	CDGT
▲AMERICAN MANUFACTURERS MUTUAL INS	IL	**E+**	11.8	11.2	0.0	0.1	10.0	N/A	6.2	7.0	0.5	DGT
AMERICAN MEDICAL ASR CO	IL	**U** (1)	4.1	3.2	0.0	0.2	N/A	5.1	7.8	10.0	4.0	FRT
AMERICAN MEDICAL INS EXCHANGE	IN	**U** (1)	0.6	0.6	0.0	0.0	N/A	N/A	6.1	7.0	2.6	T

See Page 27 for explanation of footnotes and Page 28 for explanation of stability factors.
Arrows denote recent upgrades ▲ or downgrades ▼ (see Section VII for explanations)

RISK ADJ. RATIO #1	CAPITAL RATIO #2	PREMIUM TO SURPLUS (%)	RESV. TO SURPLUS (%)	RESV. DEVELOP. 1 YEAR (%)	RESV. DEVELOP. 2 YEAR (%)	LOSS RATIO (%)	EXP. RATIO (%)	COMB RATIO (%)	CASH FROM UNDER-WRITING (%)	NET PREMIUM GROWTH (%)	INVEST. IN AFFIL (%)	INSURANCE COMPANY NAME
2.2	1.7	41.1	120.9	-19.0	-27.9	15.5	22.6	38.1	94.7	-29.8	7.9	AMERICAN EMPIRE SURPLUS LINES INS
11.8	9.3	7.5	10.0	-1.2	-4.4	25.3	47.2	72.5	169.8	-15.7	0.0	AMERICAN EQUITABLE INC
N/A	N/A	N/A	N/A	N/A	N/A	N/A	N/A	N/A	N/A	100.0	29.8	AMERICAN EQUITY INS CO
2.8	1.8	60.1	123.0	-4.7	-7.7	61.5	30.3	91.8	103.9	-10.7	0.0	AMERICAN EQUITY SPECIALTY INS CO
2.3	1.7	97.3	144.6	3.0	2.3	67.7	37.8	105.5	114.3	49.3	10.3	AMERICAN EUROPEAN INS CO
2.0	1.2	37.3	219.5	-12.9	-14.3	34.3	18.4	52.7	189.2	-5.6	0.0	AMERICAN EXCESS INS EXCHANGE RRG
2.5	1.8	170.6	32.3	-3.2	-3.2	53.0	46.8	99.8	98.4	5.2	8.1 •	AMERICAN FAMILY HOME INS CO
2.1	1.8	N/A	N/A	N/A	N/A	N/A	N/A	N/A	85.6	0.0	0.0	AMERICAN FAMILY INS CO
2.0	1.4	180.9	126.1	-2.9	1.7	88.5	24.3	112.8	91.7	-2.8	8.4 •	AMERICAN FAMILY MUT INS CO
3.6	3.2	N/A	35.6	-11.2	16.5	-139.2	N/A	N/A	0.1	0.0	0.0	AMERICAN FARMERS & RANCHERS INS
0.7	0.5	386.2	114.9	-3.9	-5.2	92.1	27.0	119.1	80.2	0.0	20.2	AMERICAN FARMERS & RANCHERS
2.3	2.1	163.5	5.0	-0.8	-1.8	16.3	8.1	24.4	456.7	-3.8	0.0	AMERICAN FEDERATED INS CO
10.9	9.8	N/A	N/A	N/A	N/A	N/A	N/A	N/A	-52.2	0.0	0.0	AMERICAN FEDERATION INS CO
2.8	2.4	26.1	61.0	-6.2	-21.8	25.4	35.1	60.5	323.1	20.4	0.0	AMERICAN FEED INDUSTRY INS CO RRG
0.7	0.5	184.3	90.2	0.5	-27.1	78.4	36.7	115.1	73.2	-6.5	0.0	AMERICAN FELLOWSHIP MUT INS CO
1.8	1.2	236.8	203.0	-14.9	-24.3	63.2	24.9	88.1	-635.4	0.0	0.0	AMERICAN FIRE & CASUALTY CO
0.3	0.2	157.5	267.9	13.1	39.7	69.0	37.6	106.6	58.6	-19.2	0.0	AMERICAN FOREST CASUALTY CO RRG
2.9	2.1	85.3	88.7	-13.8	-32.0	66.0	42.1	108.1	93.9	-11.6	0.0	AMERICAN FREEDOM INS CO
10.9	6.2	-0.6	20.3	0.2	1.2	999 +	-481.5	999 +	20.5	-153.6	0.0	AMERICAN FUJI FIRE & MARINE INS CO
16.6	14.9	-10.8	1.0	-2.8	-20.4	-189.1	90.5	-98.6	162.4	-44.2	0.0	AMERICAN GENERAL INDEMNITY CO
N/A	N/A	0.1	0.5	-0.3	-0.7	418.8	-900.0	-481.2	8.2	-95.2	0.0	AMERICAN GENERAL PROP INS CO OF FL
N/A	N/A	N/A	38.5	3.2	5.8	999 +	-283.3	999 +	1.4	-98.4	23.1	AMERICAN GENERAL PROPERTY INS CO
22.1	19.9	N/A	N/A	N/A	N/A	N/A	N/A	N/A	79.9	0.0	0.0 •	AMERICAN GUARANTEE & LIABILITY INS
5.6	3.5	54.7	6.0	-0.7	-2.0	32.2	7.4	39.6	128.2	-0.4	0.0	AMERICAN GUARANTY INS CO
1.3	0.9	123.4	78.8	-2.1	-5.1	63.4	32.2	95.6	111.4	-1.4	16.1	AMERICAN HALLMARK INS CO OF TX
2.2	1.5	115.1	95.6	-2.6	-5.0	73.5	33.1	106.6	99.0	3.5	5.5	AMERICAN HARDWARE MUTUAL INS CO
2.0	1.6	72.7	155.5	-7.5	-12.0	71.9	21.6	93.5	160.2	-10.2	0.0	AMERICAN HEALTHCARE INDEMNITY CO
1.9	1.5	56.6	133.7	-4.6	-10.6	71.1	21.7	92.8	133.9	-10.2	0.0	AMERICAN HEALTHCARE SPECIALTY INS
0.1	0.1	583.3	367.1	59.6	61.3	74.7	38.6	113.3	96.8	4.8	0.0	AMERICAN HEARTLAND INS CO
1.1	0.7	120.1	233.4	-0.5	0.7	75.7	27.1	102.8	90.8	-10.6	7.4 •	AMERICAN HOME ASR CO
N/A	N/A	223.0	10.6	N/A	N/A	49.6	36.4	86.0	116.8	13.7	0.0	AMERICAN HOME SHIELD OF NV INC
N/A	N/A	N/A	N/A	N/A	N/A	N/A	N/A	N/A	N/A	0.0	0.0	AMERICAN HOME SHIELD OF VA INC
1.7	1.4	106.5	78.8	-6.5	-37.2	74.5	21.2	95.7	110.9	3.1	19.0	AMERICAN INDEPENDENT INS CO
1.1	0.8	139.6	185.6	2.7	4.5	75.0	27.4	102.4	100.7	3.0	3.9 •	AMERICAN INS CO
1.3	0.8	283.4	61.5	2.5	N/A	60.1	43.8	103.9	123.0	-35.2	0.0	AMERICAN INTEGRITY INS CO OF FL
2.0	1.4	51.8	83.8	-0.1	-4.3	66.3	29.7	96.0	143.0	-11.4	0.0	AMERICAN INTER FIDELITY EXCHANGE
2.3	1.7	136.0	84.5	3.7	0.8	79.6	27.0	106.6	72.5	-2.4	10.0 •	AMERICAN INTERNATIONAL INS CO
1.0	0.7	348.2	196.8	7.5	1.5	79.6	26.9	106.5	119.9	44.8	0.0	AMERICAN INTERNATIONAL INS CO OF
3.0	2.1	64.8	56.9	2.6	0.5	79.6	30.6	110.2	18.0	-74.4	0.0	AMERICAN INTERNATIONAL INS CO OF
1.6	1.2	162.2	91.6	3.9	0.8	79.6	26.9	106.5	128.3	44.8	0.0	AMERICAN INTERNATIONAL INS CO OF
5.0	4.5	N/A	N/A	N/A	N/A	N/A	N/A	N/A	N/A	0.0	3.4	AMERICAN INTERNATIONAL PACIFIC INS
22.9	20.6	N/A	N/A	N/A	N/A	N/A	N/A	N/A	N/A	0.0	0.0	AMERICAN INTERNATIONAL SOUTH INS
1.9	1.5	83.7	138.4	-6.6	-15.1	60.9	19.6	80.5	128.2	-6.3	7.9 •	AMERICAN INTERSTATE INS CO
1.1	0.5	118.3	151.8	-6.7	-19.5	63.2	19.8	83.0	148.5	-6.3	0.0	AMERICAN INTERSTATE INS CO OF
6.1	3.9	23.6	20.5	-5.6	-5.8	23.4	34.1	57.5	169.9	-5.1	-0.1	AMERICAN INTL INS CO OF PR
0.7	0.5	27.3	108.5	3.6	-0.2	98.5	66.2	164.7	83.5	-23.3	0.0 •	AMERICAN INTL SPECIALTY LINES INS CO
0.7	0.5	126.7	14.3	-0.8	N/A	57.2	65.6	122.8	179.6	724.0	0.0	AMERICAN KEYSTONE INS CO
0.3	0.2	199.5	108.8	-14.1	-29.6	46.3	45.6	91.9	108.4	-18.5	0.0	AMERICAN LIBERTY INS CO
0.0	0.0	999 +	67.1	-2.3	-13.3	6.7	88.9	95.6	102.0	N/A	0.0	AMERICAN LIFE INS CO
42.7	38.4	N/A	N/A	N/A	N/A	N/A	N/A	N/A	N/A	0.0	0.0	AMERICAN MANUFACTURERS MUTUAL
N/A	N/A	N/A	28.2	-7.0	-44.5	N/A	N/A	N/A	N/A	0.0	0.0	AMERICAN MEDICAL ASR CO
N/A	N/A	N/A	N/A	N/A	N/A	N/A	N/A	N/A	N/A	0.0	0.0	AMERICAN MEDICAL INS EXCHANGE

999 + Denotes number greater than 999.9%
999 - Denotes number less than -999.99%
• Bullets denote a more detailed analysis is available in Section II.

INSURANCE COMPANY NAME	DOM. STATE	RATING	TOTAL ASSETS ($MIL)	CAPITAL & SURPLUS ($MIL)	ANNUAL NET PREMIUM ($MIL)	NET INCOME ($MIL)	CAPITAL-IZATION INDEX (PTS)	RESERVE ADQ INDEX (PTS)	PROFIT-ABILITY INDEX (PTS)	LIQUIDITY INDEX (PTS)	STAB. INDEX (PTS)	STABILITY FACTORS
AMERICAN MERCHANTS CASUALTY CO	DE	**C**	61.1	57.9	0.4	0.7	10.0	N/A	6.8	9.9	2.8	DGT
AMERICAN MERCURY INS CO	OK	**B+**	334.3	108.7	196.3	1.6	8.1	6.3	4.0	5.2	6.4	FLT
AMERICAN MERCURY LLOYDS INS CO	TX	**B**	4.8	3.2	0.0	0.0	10.0	N/A	6.7	10.0	4.9	DFG
AMERICAN MILLENNIUM INS CO	NJ	**D**	10.6	4.3	2.5	0.0	8.2	5.7	4.8	7.5	2.2	DGRT
AMERICAN MILLERS INS CO	PA	**B-**	7.9	7.6	0.2	0.2	10.0	6.1	3.2	9.7	4.1	DG
AMERICAN MINING INS CO INC	AL	**C**	35.4	32.8	-1.5	0.2	10.0	4.7	8.3	1.4	3.2	FGLT
AMERICAN MODERN HOME INS CO	OH	**B+**	888.8	270.7	388.9	6.3	7.9	6.9	7.5	6.0	5.0	FT
AMERICAN MODERN INS CO OF FLORIDA	FL	**C-**	20.0	6.7	16.5	0.1	6.3	4.8	4.0	2.2	2.7	DFGL
AMERICAN MODERN LLOYDS INS CO	TX	**B**	5.4	3.7	0.0	0.0	10.0	N/A	7.5	7.0	4.0	DFG
AMERICAN MODERN SELECT INS CO	OH	**C**	120.9	23.5	41.1	0.6	7.6	6.9	8.1	7.0	3.6	DFT
▲AMERICAN MODERN SURPLUS LINES INS CO	OH	**C+**	87.4	22.0	41.1	0.6	7.3	4.7	4.6	6.8	3.5	DT
AMERICAN MOTORISTS INS CO	IL	**D**	19.7	18.9	0.0	0.2	10.0	3.6	2.8	7.0	1.4	DGT
AMERICAN MUTUAL SHARE INS CORP	OH	**C-**	184.2	167.1	1.2	0.0	10.0	7.8	3.6	10.0	1.5	DT
AMERICAN NATIONAL GENERAL INS CO	MO	**B+**	99.8	69.8	22.1	0.7	10.0	6.9	8.2	6.8	6.4	DT
AMERICAN NATIONAL LLOYDS INS CO	TX	**B**	61.8	37.3	20.3	-2.5	8.7	8.8	4.6	6.2	6.1	DFT
▼AMERICAN NATIONAL PROPERTY & CAS CO	MO	**B+**	1,068.4	357.0	563.1	-7.0	7.4	6.9	2.9	3.3	6.4	FLT
AMERICAN NATL COUNTY MUT INS CO	TX	**B-**	12.5	6.4	0.0	-0.1	9.1	N/A	2.3	7.0	3.7	DFGT
AMERICAN PACIFIC INS COMPANY	HI	**B**	24.8	10.1	-6.4	-0.3	10.0	4.9	3.1	6.2	4.2	DFGT
AMERICAN PET INS CO INC	NY	**U** (1)	10.1	10.0	0.1	-0.2	N/A	4.7	1.9	10.0	3.1	FT
AMERICAN PHYSICIANS ASR CORP	MI	**D+**	816.0	198.5	120.1	10.2	6.6	5.0	3.7	8.4	2.3	T
▲AMERICAN PHYSICIANS INS CO	TX	**D**	220.3	92.8	65.7	4.1	7.5	4.0	5.8	7.7	1.5	RT
AMERICAN PROFESSIONALS INS CO	IN	**U** (5)	--	--	--	--	N/A	--	--	--	--	Z
AMERICAN RELIABLE INS CO	AZ	**C**	316.2	100.9	175.4	1.9	5.2	1.8	2.9	3.8	3.4	FLT
AMERICAN RESOURCES INS CO INC	AL	**C-**	37.5	12.8	-9.0	0.1	5.9	2.5	2.0	8.4	2.9	DFGR
AMERICAN ROAD INS CO	MI	**C**	564.2	277.9	112.7	-26.1	10.0	7.6	2.7	7.0	4.3	T
AMERICAN SAFETY CASUALTY INS CO	OK	**D+**	156.8	74.0	18.5	0.5	2.5	3.5	3.9	6.5	2.5	CRT
AMERICAN SAFETY INDEMNITY CO	OK	**D**	243.7	57.8	65.1	0.8	0.3	5.0	5.1	6.3	1.9	CGT
AMERICAN SAFETY INS CO	GA	**C**	19.1	18.7	0.0	0.2	10.0	N/A	3.9	7.0	3.5	DG
AMERICAN SAFETY RRG INC	VT	**D**	18.3	5.2	0.9	0.1	7.0	5.8	2.8	10.0	1.9	DFGT
AMERICAN SECURITY INS CO	DE	**B**	1,854.3	850.1	1,542.7	64.9	8.7	6.3	9.4	6.8	5.2	AT
AMERICAN SELECT INS CO	OH	**B-**	160.2	48.2	82.1	-0.7	8.0	5.0	4.8	6.4	4.6	T
▲AMERICAN SENTINEL INS CO	PA	**C+**	22.9	11.0	15.1	0.1	7.7	9.3	8.3	6.8	4.3	DGT
▼AMERICAN SERVICE INS CO INC	IL	**C-**	130.3	22.0	37.8	0.7	4.9	3.7	2.6	6.2	3.2	DFRT
AMERICAN SOUTHERN HOME INS CO	FL	**B**	93.3	25.5	32.9	0.7	8.1	6.9	8.4	6.4	4.8	FT
AMERICAN SOUTHERN INS CO	KS	**C+**	89.3	34.8	36.9	1.1	7.6	9.5	7.3	7.0	4.5	T
AMERICAN SPECIAL RISK INS CO	DE	**U** (1)	5.4	3.1	0.0	-0.2	N/A	4.3	4.4	7.0	0.0	T
AMERICAN STANDARD INS CO OF OH	OH	**B**	11.3	6.3	0.0	0.0	10.0	N/A	8.2	7.0	4.9	DGT
AMERICAN STANDARD INS CO OF WI	WI	**B+**	394.2	264.8	0.0	2.0	10.0	N/A	8.2	10.0	6.4	T
AMERICAN STANDARD LLOYDS INS CO	TX	**B-**	4.5	2.0	0.0	0.0	7.9	N/A	4.9	5.6	3.9	DFGT
AMERICAN STATES INS CO	IN	**B-**	3,359.1	563.6	1,014.8	9.9	8.0	6.9	3.2	6.4	4.9	AT
AMERICAN STATES INS CO OF TX	TX	**B-**	117.4	21.6	0.0	0.2	10.0	N/A	8.1	7.0	5.1	DG
AMERICAN STATES LLOYDS INS CO	TX	**B-**	4.5	3.1	0.0	0.0	10.0	N/A	7.9	10.0	3.7	DG
AMERICAN STATES PREFERRED INS CO	IN	**B**	284.2	51.7	106.8	0.8	7.7	6.9	2.7	5.7	5.4	AT
AMERICAN STEAMSHIP O M PROT & IND AS	NY	**E**	353.0	45.8	135.2	10.4	0.0	0.1	2.7	1.5	0.1	CFLR
AMERICAN STERLING INS CO	CA	**D**	21.7	12.2	21.5	0.1	0.2	4.6	4.7	0.0	1.5	CDFG
▲AMERICAN STRATEGIC INS CO	FL	**B**	286.4	137.4	123.2	7.7	7.7	7.0	6.5	6.9	4.0	RT
AMERICAN SUMMIT INS CO	TX	**C**	39.7	25.1	20.4	0.9	7.9	6.5	7.4	7.2	4.3	DGRT
AMERICAN SURETY CO	IN	**C**	13.3	11.2	8.7	0.1	7.5	6.9	7.0	6.9	2.8	DGT
▲AMERICAN TRADITIONS INS CO	FL	**D+**	30.3	8.8	18.4	-0.1	2.7	3.6	2.9	6.6	2.3	CDGT
AMERICAN TRANSIT INS CO	NY	**E+**	396.8	67.2	150.4	0.8	0.2	0.1	4.3	2.6	0.4	CFLT
▲AMERICAN TRUCKING & TRANSP INS RRG	MT	**D-**	10.4	2.5	3.8	0.1	5.2	5.8	6.6	7.6	0.9	DGRT
AMERICAN UNDERWRITERS INS CO	AR	**D+**	6.2	5.2	2.1	0.0	7.5	4.0	6.2	2.3	2.5	DFGL

See Page 27 for explanation of footnotes and Page 28 for explanation of stability factors.

Arrows denote recent upgrades ▲ or downgrades ▼ (see Section VII for explanations)

RISK ADJ. RATIO #1	CAPITAL RATIO #2	PREMIUM TO SURPLUS (%)	RESV. TO SURPLUS (%)	RESV. DEVELOP. 1 YEAR (%)	RESV. DEVELOP. 2 YEAR (%)	LOSS RATIO (%)	EXP. RATIO (%)	COMB RATIO (%)	CASH FROM UNDER-WRITING (%)	NET PREMIUM GROWTH (%)	INVEST. IN AFFIL (%)	INSURANCE COMPANY NAME
42.0	24.3	0.6	0.5	N/A	N/A	184.4	211.0	395.4	79.2	233.8	0.0	AMERICAN MERCHANTS CASUALTY CO
2.8	1.9	182.9	58.1	4.2	5.7	83.0	28.6	111.6	86.4	-11.5	2.6 •	AMERICAN MERCURY INS CO
5.1	4.6	N/A	N/A	N/A	N/A	N/A	N/A	N/A	-97.3	0.0	0.0	AMERICAN MERCURY LLOYDS INS CO
2.4	2.2	59.2	46.2	-1.8	-14.4	61.1	35.1	96.2	109.5	104.0	0.0	AMERICAN MILLENNIUM INS CO
14.9	11.5	3.1	5.1	N/A	0.6	152.3	40.4	192.7	94.0	0.4	0.0	AMERICAN MILLERS INS CO
38.9	19.9	-4.6	N/A	N/A	N/A	N/A	N/A	N/A	-10.1	-105.1	0.0	AMERICAN MINING INS CO INC
2.2	1.7	142.6	27.1	-2.8	-2.9	53.0	47.0	100.0	96.6	3.6	22.0 •	AMERICAN MODERN HOME INS CO
1.3	0.9	251.0	47.5	-4.9	-5.5	53.0	47.8	100.8	99.6	5.2	0.0	AMERICAN MODERN INS CO OF FLORIDA
5.9	5.3	N/A	N/A	N/A	N/A	N/A	N/A	N/A	514.2	0.0	0.0	AMERICAN MODERN LLOYDS INS CO
2.4	1.6	179.8	34.0	-3.7	-4.1	53.0	45.8	98.8	97.0	5.2	0.0	AMERICAN MODERN SELECT INS CO
1.8	1.2	192.8	36.5	-3.9	-4.3	53.0	47.8	100.8	123.1	5.2	0.0	AMERICAN MODERN SURPLUS LINES INS
66.1	59.4	N/A	N/A	N/A	N/A	N/A	N/A	N/A	N/A	0.0	0.0	AMERICAN MOTORISTS INS CO
8.6	8.2	0.7	5.4	-2.6	-3.2	98.6	516.5	615.1	19.1	-17.2	11.3 •	AMERICAN MUTUAL SHARE INS CORP
6.6	4.4	32.0	18.2	-1.8	-4.3	69.6	36.8	106.4	90.6	-3.6	3.6 •	AMERICAN NATIONAL GENERAL INS CO
2.7	1.9	51.5	7.7	-2.8	-5.4	53.6	24.3	77.9	81.8	-8.2	5.6	AMERICAN NATIONAL LLOYDS INS CO
1.6	1.1	145.8	82.5	-2.9	-5.6	90.8	25.4	116.2	86.9	-1.8	14.1 •	AMERICAN NATIONAL PROPERTY & CAS
3.7	2.7	N/A	N/A	N/A	N/A	N/A	N/A	N/A	-70.2	-100.0	8.7	AMERICAN NATL COUNTY MUT INS CO
3.4	3.1	-63.0	N/A	N/A	N/A	N/A	26.3	N/A	-3.2	-137.8	0.0	AMERICAN PACIFIC INS COMPANY
N/A	N/A	0.8	0.2	N/A	N/A	120.3	503.9	624.2	18.4	0.0	0.0	AMERICAN PET INS CO INC
1.2	1.0	61.8	271.2	-14.7	-28.1	51.7	23.7	75.4	128.9	-8.2	3.4 •	AMERICAN PHYSICIANS ASR CORP
3.0	2.1	74.6	88.9	-25.4	-59.9	29.6	18.1	47.7	187.9	-3.4	0.0	AMERICAN PHYSICIANS INS CO
N/A	N/A	--	--	--	--	--	--	--	--	--	--	AMERICAN PROFESSIONALS INS CO
1.1	0.8	175.7	68.0	-3.3	-9.1	61.1	44.0	105.1	77.4	0.2	0.0	AMERICAN RELIABLE INS CO
2.2	0.9	-69.3	168.4	-10.8	19.0	47.0	-11.6	35.4	-56.9	-174.6	0.0	AMERICAN RESOURCES INS CO INC
4.8	3.7	41.6	7.6	-1.5	-2.7	71.3	1.5	72.8	116.0	-27.2	6.8 •	AMERICAN ROAD INS CO
0.4	0.4	25.3	80.3	-2.4	10.7	50.5	77.8	128.3	258.0	-14.0	32.3	AMERICAN SAFETY CASUALTY INS CO
0.1	0.1	113.4	199.9	0.7	-5.7	58.6	48.5	107.1	148.5	40.1	0.0	AMERICAN SAFETY INDEMNITY CO
45.9	19.9	N/A	N/A	N/A	N/A	N/A	N/A	N/A	N/A	0.0	0.0	AMERICAN SAFETY INS CO
1.8	1.1	16.9	108.7	-12.6	5.9	39.0	-15.4	23.6	-467.5	N/A	0.0	AMERICAN SAFETY RRG INC
4.1	2.6	196.4	18.9	-3.8	-5.2	29.5	34.7	64.2	170.3	18.0	4.9 •	AMERICAN SECURITY INS CO
2.3	1.6	154.5	127.5	-8.2	-3.8	66.7	32.6	99.3	107.2	3.0	0.0	AMERICAN SELECT INS CO
2.5	1.9	135.6	31.5	-17.8	-18.5	48.0	46.3	94.3	100.8	-6.3	0.0	AMERICAN SENTINEL INS CO
0.8	0.6	174.7	177.0	3.7	9.8	82.6	26.0	108.6	72.6	3.1	0.0	AMERICAN SERVICE INS CO INC
2.4	1.7	132.6	25.1	-2.7	-2.9	53.0	46.1	99.1	93.4	5.2	11.4	AMERICAN SOUTHERN HOME INS CO
1.6	1.3	101.2	82.5	-19.5	-25.7	46.2	48.9	95.1	101.2	2.5	21.2	AMERICAN SOUTHERN INS CO
N/A	N/A	N/A	21.4	13.3	14.3	N/A	N/A	N/A	N/A	0.0	0.0	AMERICAN SPECIAL RISK INS CO
4.1	3.7	N/A	N/A	N/A	N/A	N/A	N/A	N/A	27.2	0.0	0.0	AMERICAN STANDARD INS CO OF OH
28.5	25.7	N/A	N/A	N/A	N/A	N/A	N/A	N/A	83.5	0.0	0.0 •	AMERICAN STANDARD INS CO OF WI
2.3	2.0	N/A	N/A	N/A	N/A	N/A	N/A	N/A	-30.8	0.0	0.0	AMERICAN STANDARD LLOYDS INS CO
2.5	1.7	187.5	167.8	-5.8	-5.5	67.0	31.2	98.2	102.9	-5.6	0.0 •	AMERICAN STATES INS CO
2.4	1.4	N/A	N/A	N/A	N/A	N/A	N/A	N/A	51.0	0.0	0.0	AMERICAN STATES INS CO OF TX
5.7	5.1	N/A	N/A	N/A	N/A	N/A	N/A	N/A	-91.2	0.0	0.0	AMERICAN STATES LLOYDS INS CO
2.2	1.5	218.0	195.1	-4.0	-5.6	67.0	31.2	98.2	104.0	-5.6	0.0	AMERICAN STATES PREFERRED INS CO
0.2	0.1	371.0	616.7	12.6	100.1	60.5	23.8	84.3	95.6	13.6	0.0	AMERICAN STEAMSHIP O M PROT & IND
0.1	0.1	180.6	74.3	1.1	5.7	60.5	42.5	103.0	87.8	-28.1	34.7	AMERICAN STERLING INS CO
3.0	2.3	91.4	38.1	-6.0	-8.7	39.6	39.1	78.7	171.2	17.4	1.6	AMERICAN STRATEGIC INS CO
2.5	1.9	84.7	15.1	-1.6	-2.2	60.7	29.4	90.1	112.9	-2.4	0.0	AMERICAN SUMMIT INS CO
1.5	1.3	76.5	7.2	-6.3	-7.4	-0.8	81.4	80.6	122.6	-1.9	0.0	AMERICAN SURETY CO
0.7	0.4	208.6	29.0	1.0	-0.2	42.8	45.2	88.0	126.9	-3.2	0.0	AMERICAN TRADITIONS INS CO
0.1	0.1	225.4	305.4	78.9	153.0	94.1	22.8	116.9	69.7	-12.9	0.0	AMERICAN TRANSIT INS CO
0.9	0.5	144.2	216.2	20.0	21.5	70.1	11.4	81.5	108.0	2.4	0.0	AMERICAN TRUCKING & TRANSP INS
6.4	5.2	39.6	N/A	-0.4	-28.4	58.4	58.7	117.1	25.9	-74.0	0.0	AMERICAN UNDERWRITERS INS CO

999 + Denotes number greater than 999.9%
999 - Denotes number less than -999.99%
• Bullets denote a more detailed analysis is available in Section II.

INSURANCE COMPANY NAME	DOM. STATE	RATING	TOTAL ASSETS ($MIL)	CAPITAL & SURPLUS ($MIL)	ANNUAL NET PREMIUM ($MIL)	NET INCOME ($MIL)	CAPITAL-IZATION INDEX (PTS)	RESERVE ADQ INDEX (PTS)	PROFIT-ABILITY INDEX (PTS)	LIQUIDITY INDEX (PTS)	STAB. INDEX (PTS)	STABILITY FACTORS
AMERICAN UNION INS CO	IL	**U** (1)	122.0	121.9	0.0	-0.7	N/A	3.6	6.1	7.0	4.3	FT
AMERICAN VEHICLE INS CO	FL	**C**	72.2	24.8	25.1	-0.3	1.8	2.5	5.0	8.3	3.5	CT
AMERICAN WEST INS CO	ND	**C**	8.5	8.4	3.7	0.0	10.0	7.4	6.6	6.4	2.8	DFGT
AMERICAN WESTERN HOME INS CO	OK	**C**	196.0	41.7	74.1	1.3	8.2	6.9	7.7	6.8	3.7	T
AMERICAN ZURICH INS CO	IL	**B-**	195.0	166.6	0.0	0.2	10.0	N/A	3.6	7.0	4.9	T
AMERICAS INS CO	LA	**C**	14.7	13.0	0.9	-0.2	10.0	7.5	3.3	10.0	3.4	DFGT
AMERIGUARD RRG INC	VT	**D-**	9.8	5.3	2.8	0.0	4.7	4.4	4.8	9.1	1.2	DGT
AMERIHEALTH CASUALTY INS CO	DE	**B-**	187.2	38.7	79.6	-2.4	5.0	7.0	3.4	5.5	5.0	CT
AMERIN GUARANTY CORP	IL	**E-**	38.9	4.2	11.4	-15.7	5.0	5.2	0.5	0.0	0.1	DFLR
▲AMERISURE INS CO	MI	**B-**	647.9	179.1	167.7	2.9	8.0	5.8	8.6	7.0	4.7	T
AMERISURE MUTUAL INS CO	MI	**C+**	1,645.4	501.1	391.3	-0.2	7.6	5.7	6.7	6.9	4.5	T
AMERISURE PARTNERS INS CO	MI	**U** (1)	11.2	11.1	0.0	0.3	N/A	N/A	6.9	7.0	0.0	CT
▲AMERITRUST INS CORP	MI	**C-**	78.7	20.1	30.4	1.1	5.4	5.4	8.8	7.0	3.0	DT
AMEX ASSURANCE CO	IL	**B-**	312.6	242.1	267.2	21.9	10.0	7.0	8.1	6.6	3.8	GT
AMFED CAS INS CO	MS	**D**	2.3	1.2	0.0	0.0	9.9	N/A	3.9	7.0	1.4	DFGT
AMFED NATIONAL INS CO	MS	**E+**	37.1	6.1	13.6	0.5	0.3	6.8	4.2	5.3	0.5	CDGT
AMGUARD INS CO	PA	**C**	274.2	56.3	70.4	-0.7	6.1	4.2	5.1	6.7	4.1	T
AMICA LLOYDS OF TEXAS	TX	**B+**	70.2	57.4	8.8	0.7	10.0	8.7	7.3	6.9	6.7	DFT
AMICA MUTUAL INS CO	RI	**B**	3,433.2	1,803.0	1,321.7	9.5	8.4	8.9	5.9	6.1	6.0	T
AMICA PROPERTY & CASUALTY INS CO	RI	**C**	28.0	13.8	6.9	0.1	8.4	3.6	3.0	6.8	3.1	DGT
AMSTAR INS CO	FL	**U** (1)	6.0	5.1	0.0	0.1	N/A	6.8	5.0	10.0	4.5	FRT
ANCHOR GENERAL INS CO	CA	**C**	47.7	23.1	41.0	0.3	7.1	9.0	8.9	4.5	3.4	DGLT
ANESTHESIOLOGISTS PROF ASR CO	FL	**C**	80.8	22.9	13.2	1.0	5.0	4.6	6.1	8.2	3.7	DT
ANPAC LOUISIANA INS CO	LA	**B-**	97.0	40.7	43.7	-1.6	4.6	3.8	2.6	2.8	5.2	CFLT
ANSUR AMERICA INS CO	MI	**B-**	58.9	30.3	5.9	0.4	10.0	6.9	3.6	7.3	3.5	T
ANTHRACITE MUTUAL FIRE INS CO	PA	**C-**	2.5	2.5	0.3	0.0	10.0	6.0	7.7	8.6	3.0	DGT
ANTILLES INS CO	PR	**B**	68.7	48.4	20.6	1.8	5.4	8.1	8.6	6.3	5.6	CT
APEX LLOYDS INS CO	TX	**U** (1)	2.8	2.5	0.0	1.0	N/A	2.2	4.1	10.0	3.1	T
APOLLO CASUALTY CO	IL	**D+**	39.8	11.1	20.9	-0.5	5.8	7.0	3.0	5.3	2.7	DFGT
APOLLO CASUALTY CO OF FL	FL	**C-**	14.8	6.1	10.5	-0.1	5.6	3.6	1.8	7.5	2.6	DGOT
APOLLO MUTUAL FIRE INS CO	PA	**D** (1)	3.2	3.2	0.1	0.0	10.0	N/A	6.8	10.0	1.2	DG
▲APPALACHIAN INS CO	RI	**C**	193.2	128.4	53.7	6.5	7.6	4.2	8.9	6.6	3.3	FT
APPLIANCE MANUFACTURERS ASR CO RRG	IA	**U** (5)	0.0	0.0	0.1	0.0	N/A	3.7	1.6	10.0	1.1	CDFG
▲APPLIED MEDICO LEGAL SOLUTIONS RRG	AZ	**D**	50.9	17.1	19.6	0.2	5.2	5.7	8.8	7.1	1.5	DRT
APSPECIALTY INS CORP	MI	**U** (1)	26.8	25.9	0.0	1.3	N/A	6.5	8.2	10.0	7.0	T
AQUAGARDIAN INS CO INC	AZ	**D**	19.0	6.1	4.7	0.0	1.0	2.1	2.5	6.6	1.4	CDGT
ARA CASUALTY INS CO	FL	**U** (1)	3.7	3.4	0.0	-0.2	N/A	4.3	1.6	7.0	2.8	FT
ARAG INS CO	IA	**B-**	51.4	35.3	53.7	2.2	8.6	9.3	9.1	6.1	5.1	GT
ARBELLA INDEMNITY INS CO	MA	**C**	45.6	17.3	24.9	0.0	8.1	9.4	6.2	6.4	3.4	DGT
ARBELLA MUTUAL INS CO	MA	**C+**	920.8	429.5	430.8	-0.4	9.0	9.3	8.0	6.6	4.3	T
ARBELLA PROTECTION INS CO	MA	**C+**	268.6	97.0	148.4	0.0	9.5	9.3	7.3	6.7	4.3	T
▲ARCH EXCESS & SURPLUS INS CO	NE	**C+**	32.6	26.7	0.2	0.5	10.0	5.2	7.9	10.0	3.7	ADFG
ARCH INDEMNITY INS CO	NE	**U** (1)	21.6	21.5	0.0	0.5	N/A	N/A	6.7	7.0	5.4	RT
▲ARCH INS CO	MO	**C+**	1,680.7	598.1	298.8	14.9	5.2	6.2	7.7	6.8	3.4	AT
▲ARCH REINSURANCE CO	NE	**C**	1,212.8	791.7	83.5	6.3	7.8	6.2	7.6	8.0	2.7	ART
ARCH SPECIALTY INS CO	NE	**B+**	437.3	306.9	0.3	3.4	10.0	7.5	8.6	9.7	5.1	AFT
ARCHITECTS & ENGINEERS INS CO RRG	DE	**C-**	17.1	8.8	1.0	0.0	8.7	6.5	8.1	6.9	2.8	DGRT
ARECA INS EXCHANGE	AK	**C+**	22.3	13.8	3.6	0.5	7.8	6.9	2.6	6.9	3.5	DGT
ARGONAUT GREAT CENTRAL INS CO	IL	**C-**	143.6	79.0	0.0	-0.1	10.0	4.7	6.8	7.0	2.9	FT
ARGONAUT INS CO	IL	**C**	1,390.6	286.8	264.8	-5.8	4.2	5.5	3.1	6.9	3.3	T
ARGONAUT LIMITED RISK INS CO	IL	**U** (1)	20.0	19.3	0.0	0.6	N/A	3.6	7.7	9.7	4.6	T
ARGONAUT-MIDWEST INS CO	IL	**D+**	74.5	49.7	0.0	0.4	10.0	4.6	6.9	10.0	2.5	FT

See Page 27 for explanation of footnotes and Page 28 for explanation of stability factors.

Arrows denote recent upgrades ▲ or downgrades ▼ (see Section VII for explanations)

RISK ADJ. CAPITAL RATIO #1	RISK ADJ. CAPITAL RATIO #2	PREMIUM TO SURPLUS (%)	RESV. TO SURPLUS (%)	RESV. DEVELOP. 1 YEAR (%)	RESV. DEVELOP. 2 YEAR (%)	LOSS RATIO (%)	EXP. RATIO (%)	COMB RATIO (%)	CASH FROM UNDER-WRITING (%)	NET PREMIUM GROWTH (%)	INVEST. IN AFFIL (%)	INSURANCE COMPANY NAME
N/A	N/A	N/A	N/A	N/A	N/A	N/A	N/A	N/A	N/A	0.0	0.0	AMERICAN UNION INS CO
0.5	0.3	100.1	146.2	15.1	27.8	76.4	45.4	121.8	108.5	-25.6	0.0	AMERICAN VEHICLE INS CO
9.3	7.0	44.4	-2.0	3.8	-0.2	85.9	20.1	106.0	91.4	95.5	0.0	AMERICAN WEST INS CO
2.7	1.8	182.8	34.6	-3.8	-4.3	53.0	47.4	100.4	104.7	5.2	0.8	AMERICAN WESTERN HOME INS CO
4.3	4.2	N/A	N/A	N/A	N/A	N/A	N/A	N/A	35.3	0.0	24.0 •	AMERICAN ZURICH INS CO
5.6	3.9	7.0	4.1	0.1	-0.4	84.9	103.7	188.6	12.0	0.0	0.0	AMERICAS INS CO
1.0	0.8	52.9	70.0	-7.3	5.2	66.8	10.4	77.2	164.6	65.1	0.0	AMERIGUARD RRG INC
0.9	0.4	185.9	203.8	4.3	-3.1	73.4	26.3	99.7	121.1	5.4	0.0	AMERIHEALTH CASUALTY INS CO
0.1	0.1	58.0	236.4	51.5	2.3	999 +	-885.7	304.7	7.0	-41.0	0.0	AMERIN GUARANTY CORP
2.6	1.7	94.6	186.8	-3.6	-8.9	64.5	34.1	98.6	98.2	-7.3	0.0 •	AMERISURE INS CO
1.7	1.3	76.4	150.9	-2.3	-5.7	64.5	34.1	98.6	101.8	-7.3	14.3 •	AMERISURE MUTUAL INS CO
N/A	N/A	N/A	N/A	N/A	N/A	N/A	N/A	N/A	N/A	0.0	0.0	AMERISURE PARTNERS INS CO
1.6	1.0	158.5	196.6	-5.4	-8.3	62.0	29.4	91.4	134.3	8.5	0.0	AMERITRUST INS CORP
9.3	5.3	121.3	17.9	2.5	-7.6	30.7	16.2	46.9	208.8	226.5	0.0 •	AMEX ASSURANCE CO
2.4	2.2	N/A	N/A	N/A	N/A	N/A	N/A	N/A	-7.9	0.0	0.0	AMFED CAS INS CO
0.3	0.1	231.9	351.2	2.6	-8.4	67.1	34.8	101.9	99.7	-21.0	4.7	AMFED NATIONAL INS CO
1.2	0.8	120.4	266.1	-18.8	-23.3	53.3	29.8	83.1	118.0	1.8	1.5	AMGUARD INS CO
10.6	7.5	15.5	6.3	-0.2	-4.5	148.3	-10.6	137.7	64.4	-0.3	0.0 •	AMICA LLOYDS OF TEXAS
2.8	1.8	69.2	46.2	-3.9	-7.3	67.4	23.6	91.0	109.5	1.4	6.0 •	AMICA MUTUAL INS CO
2.1	1.8	49.5	57.1	-1.4	1.2	107.1	12.3	119.4	110.9	-2.0	0.0	AMICA PROPERTY & CASUALTY INS CO
N/A	N/A	N/A	16.1	0.1	-1.1	N/A	N/A	N/A	N/A	0.0	0.0	AMSTAR INS CO
1.5	1.2	180.0	69.2	-8.5	-3.9	64.4	29.7	94.1	109.7	14.7	23.5	ANCHOR GENERAL INS CO
1.2	0.9	59.8	177.3	N/A	-7.7	66.7	31.3	98.0	99.3	11.9	0.0	ANESTHESIOLOGISTS PROF ASR CO
0.9	0.7	100.7	58.3	10.4	8.8	89.3	32.0	121.3	75.1	-7.1	0.0	ANPAC LOUISIANA INS CO
6.8	3.3	19.9	24.6	-0.2	-9.5	97.9	36.1	134.0	96.2	589.6	0.0	ANSUR AMERICA INS CO
11.8	7.0	14.0	1.7	-0.4	-0.1	43.1	38.3	81.4	137.5	-1.5	0.0	ANTHRACITE MUTUAL FIRE INS CO
1.1	0.7	43.2	14.2	-3.2	-3.5	24.3	55.7	80.0	121.0	15.4	0.0	ANTILLES INS CO
N/A	N/A	-0.2	4.8	34.4	18.5	880.0	999 +	999 +	-2.6	-127.8	16.3	APEX LLOYDS INS CO
0.9	0.8	175.7	185.2	-0.3	-4.1	66.2	40.2	106.4	85.6	-28.9	24.3	APOLLO CASUALTY CO
0.9	0.7	170.9	51.0	-0.8	N/A	79.3	27.9	107.2	151.8	209.6	0.0	APOLLO CASUALTY CO OF FL
18.9	17.4	3.7	0.2	N/A	N/A	52.0	117.9	169.9	63.2	34.5	0.0	APOLLO MUTUAL FIRE INS CO
2.8	1.8	44.0	42.2	N/A	-8.8	77.6	21.3	98.9	62.2	-1.1	0.0	APPALACHIAN INS CO
N/A	N/A	2.3	125.1	4.2	14.3	130.2	398.1	528.3	-10.3	-81.9	0.0	APPLIANCE MANUFACTURERS ASR CO
1.3	0.8	118.9	127.3	-4.8	-9.5	63.0	28.1	91.1	134.3	8.9	0.0	APPLIED MEDICO LEGAL SOLUTIONS
N/A	N/A	N/A	2.1	-2.3	-2.8	999 +	N/A	N/A	N/A	0.0	0.0	APSPECIALTY INS CORP
0.4	0.2	77.4	166.7	-81.2	-13.7	38.4	44.5	82.9	144.0	-17.3	0.0	AQUAGARDIAN INS CO INC
N/A	N/A	N/A	8.8	2.7	14.0	N/A	N/A	N/A	N/A	0.0	0.0	ARA CASUALTY INS CO
3.5	2.3	158.7	38.4	-8.5	-12.5	53.3	30.6	83.9	123.3	9.7	0.0	ARAG INS CO
2.6	1.8	144.4	79.3	-5.2	-16.2	63.6	34.1	97.7	105.8	12.7	0.0	ARBELLA INDEMNITY INS CO
3.0	2.4	98.4	55.5	-3.8	-13.6	63.6	33.3	96.9	102.6	3.9	15.1 •	ARBELLA MUTUAL INS CO
3.5	2.5	152.8	77.5	-5.4	-17.0	63.6	34.7	98.3	120.0	49.2	0.0	ARBELLA PROTECTION INS CO
15.7	13.9	0.7	4.1	0.7	-0.4	156.8	2.2	159.0	-6.7	600.0	0.0	ARCH EXCESS & SURPLUS INS CO
N/A	N/A	N/A	N/A	N/A	N/A	N/A	N/A	N/A	N/A	0.0	0.0	ARCH INDEMNITY INS CO
0.9	0.7	51.8	89.6	-1.3	-3.5	75.0	24.3	99.3	114.6	-4.2	29.6 •	ARCH INS CO
1.6	1.6	10.9	22.7	-1.3	-1.9	74.6	39.1	113.7	98.5	-11.3	54.0 •	ARCH REINSURANCE CO
10.0	6.5	0.1	17.8	0.2	-0.1	775.9	-817.8	-41.9	-98.8	101.1	0.0 •	ARCH SPECIALTY INS CO
3.2	2.3	11.6	25.9	-4.1	-6.2	90.0	19.9	109.9	377.2	127.6	0.0	ARCHITECTS & ENGINEERS INS CO RRG
2.8	1.6	26.5	42.7	8.8	1.7	129.5	34.5	164.0	87.3	-16.6	0.0	ARECA INS EXCHANGE
10.7	9.6	N/A	N/A	N/A	N/A	N/A	N/A	N/A	433.5	100.0	1.0	ARGONAUT GREAT CENTRAL INS CO
1.0	0.7	91.7	254.7	-0.5	3.2	72.2	38.4	110.6	88.8	-11.5	18.1 •	ARGONAUT INS CO
N/A	N/A	N/A	N/A	N/A	N/A	N/A	N/A	N/A	79.3	100.0	0.0	ARGONAUT LIMITED RISK INS CO
12.4	11.1	N/A	N/A	N/A	N/A	N/A	N/A	N/A	-47.6	100.0	0.0	ARGONAUT-MIDWEST INS CO

999 + Denotes number greater than 999.9%
999 - Denotes number less than -999.99%
• Bullets denote a more detailed analysis is available in Section II.

INSURANCE COMPANY NAME	DOM. STATE	RATING	TOTAL ASSETS ($MIL)	CAPITAL & SURPLUS ($MIL)	ANNUAL NET PREMIUM ($MIL)	NET INCOME ($MIL)	CAPITAL-IZATION INDEX (PTS)	RESERVE ADQ INDEX (PTS)	PROFIT-ABILITY INDEX (PTS)	LIQUIDITY INDEX (PTS)	STAB. INDEX (PTS)	STABILITY FACTORS
ARGONAUT-SOUTHWEST INS CO	LA	**C**	16.9	15.0	0.0	0.1	10.0	6.0	6.7	9.0	2.3	DGT
ARGUS FIRE & CASUALTY INS CO	FL	**D**	47.9	6.7	16.9	-1.1	1.6	2.0	2.7	6.4	2.0	CDGT
ARI CASUALTY CO	NJ	**D+**	38.6	16.2	9.4	0.4	8.3	5.6	8.5	7.1	2.8	DGT
ARI MUTUAL INS CO	NJ	**C**	67.0	30.5	17.5	0.4	7.7	5.3	8.4	6.8	3.1	FT
ARIZONA AUTOMOBILE INS CO	AZ	**D**	6.9	3.1	1.2	0.0	5.5	7.0	8.9	7.0	1.5	DFGT
▲ARIZONA HOME INS CO	AZ	**D+**	14.7	8.8	6.2	0.3	7.2	9.3	8.7	6.7	2.4	GRT
ARMED FORCES INS EXCHANGE	KS	**C**	133.8	60.6	59.5	1.9	8.5	7.0	2.4	6.5	4.3	T
ARMOR INS CO	VT	**D-**	22.9	22.3	0.1	0.1	10.0	N/A	8.4	10.0	1.0	DGT
ARROW MUTUAL LIABILITY INS CO	MA	**C**	47.1	26.2	4.4	0.1	7.9	6.9	4.2	6.9	4.2	DFGT
ARROWOOD INDEMNITY CO	DE	**D**	2,370.5	320.8	-5.7	0.6	1.7	1.0	0.6	7.3	1.8	CFT
ARROWOOD SURPLUS LINES INS CO	DE	**U** (1)	256.5	154.3	-0.9	-12.2	N/A	3.3	1.5	7.0	2.7	T
ARTISAN & TRUCKERS CASUALTY CO	WI	**C**	82.7	22.3	15.2	0.4	9.7	6.3	5.2	6.2	3.5	DFGT
ASHLAND MUTUAL FIRE INS CO OF PA	PA	**U** (1)	0.6	0.6	0.0	0.0	N/A	4.6	3.2	10.0	1.7	FT
▲ASI ASR CORP	FL	**C+**	87.7	27.1	30.1	2.4	7.0	4.8	6.6	7.4	4.1	RT
▲ASI LLOYDS	TX	**C+**	106.1	41.9	53.5	3.7	5.1	8.9	4.9	5.6	3.6	FGRT
ASOC DE SUSCRIPCION CONJUNTA DEL	PR	**U** (1)	347.2	169.3	202.4	47.5	N/A	8.0	9.1	7.0	0.0	CD
ASPEN SPECIALTY INS CO	ND	**C**	184.1	112.7	3.0	-1.0	5.3	5.5	4.8	9.1	3.0	CDFT
ASSET PROTECTION PROGRAM RRG INC	SC	**E**	3.4	2.4	0.4	0.0	7.4	3.5	4.7	7.9	0.0	DFGT
ASSOCIATED EMPLOYERS INS CO	MA	**C**	4.4	3.8	0.0	0.0	10.0	N/A	7.9	7.0	3.3	DG
ASSOCIATED INDEMNITY CORP	CA	**C+**	181.4	75.3	47.9	1.9	7.8	5.8	8.6	6.6	4.3	FT
▲ASSOCIATED INDUSTRIES INS CO INC	FL	**C-**	174.2	45.1	-3.8	-0.5	5.1	2.2	5.7	7.0	2.9	FT
ASSOCIATED INDUSTRIES OF MA MUT INS	MA	**C**	372.1	126.0	78.3	2.8	7.8	9.5	8.8	6.8	4.0	T
▲ASSOCIATED INTERNATIONAL INS CO	IL	**C-**	206.3	83.9	28.6	-0.7	5.1	4.3	2.4	8.7	3.2	RT
ASSOCIATED LOGGERS EXCHANGE	ID	**C-**	28.0	11.2	6.1	0.2	7.3	9.6	6.8	7.1	3.0	DFGR
ASSOCIATED MUTUAL INS CO	NY	**D+**	26.9	9.2	7.6	0.1	6.3	6.1	8.4	7.1	2.6	DGT
ASSOCIATION CASUALTY INS CO	TX	**C-**	47.2	16.0	23.1	2.1	1.7	5.6	2.0	6.7	3.1	CDT
ASSOCIATION INS CO	GA	**C-**	66.1	22.7	5.8	0.4	6.2	7.0	6.1	6.9	3.1	DT
ASSURANCE COMPANY OF AMERICA	NY	**C+**	32.1	18.5	0.0	-0.1	10.0	N/A	4.1	7.0	4.6	DFGT
ASSURANCEAMERICA INS CO	SC	**E**	69.2	10.6	28.9	-0.2	2.7	6.7	5.0	0.9	0.3	DFLT
ASSURECARE RRG	DC	**U** (1)	31.1	-1.4	0.0	-4.6	N/A	2.7	0.0	7.5	-1.0	CFRT
ASSURED GUARANTY CORP	MD	**C**	1,926.3	355.7	429.4	18.4	10.0	5.8	7.2	9.0	2.0	GRT
ASSURED GUARANTY MORTGAGE INS CO	NY	**C**	50.9	14.0	0.1	-16.5	10.0	4.6	2.2	10.0	3.9	DFGR
ASTRAEA RRG INC	AZ	**E+**	3.7	0.6	0.7	0.1	0.5	4.6	0.3	8.2	0.0	CDFG
ASURE WORLDWIDE INS CO	MI	**U** (1)	12.5	12.5	0.0	0.4	N/A	N/A	6.9	7.0	5.4	T
▲ATHENA ASSURANCE CO	MN	**C+**	198.1	61.1	52.6	2.1	7.4	4.5	6.9	6.6	4.5	T
ATLANTA INTERNATIONAL INS CO	NY	**U** (1)	36.0	16.5	0.0	0.6	N/A	5.6	3.5	9.1	4.7	FRT
ATLANTIC BONDING CO	MD	**D**	9.1	8.0	0.8	0.0	8.6	8.0	2.6	9.1	0.0	DFGT
▼ATLANTIC CASUALTY INS CO	NC	**D**	174.2	58.5	51.8	1.5	1.4	2.9	8.8	6.7	2.2	CT
ATLANTIC CHARTER INS CO	MA	**C**	167.6	57.3	36.3	0.1	8.2	9.5	4.5	6.9	4.2	T
ATLANTIC EMPLOYERS INS CO	NJ	**C**	71.5	48.5	0.1	0.9	10.0	6.0	5.4	10.0	3.4	DT
ATLANTIC FLORIDIAN INS CO	OH	**U** (1)	5.5	5.5	0.0	0.1	N/A	N/A	4.9	7.0	4.5	T
ATLANTIC INS CO	TX	**U** (1)	8.7	8.7	0.0	1.2	N/A	0.5	1.9	7.0	0.8	T
ATLANTIC MUTUAL INS CO	NY	**D-**	271.8	25.0	0.4	0.2	0.0	0.8	0.5	8.0	1.1	CFT
ATLANTIC SPECIALTY INS CO	NY	**C**	66.5	50.6	10.4	0.7	10.0	6.1	6.0	8.0	3.7	DT
ATLANTIC STATES INS CO	PA	**B**	451.2	184.1	229.8	1.7	10.0	9.0	8.6	6.6	4.7	T
ATLAS RRG INC	DC	**D+**	2.3	1.6	0.5	0.0	6.8	5.0	4.7	7.9	1.4	DGT
ATRADIUS TRADE CREDIT INS CO	MD	**C**	96.4	49.1	21.1	-2.6	9.6	9.0	5.0	7.1	3.0	FRT
ATRADIUS TRADE CREDIT INS NJ	NJ	**D**	7.0	6.9	0.0	0.0	10.0	N/A	6.5	10.0	2.3	DGRT
ATRIUM INS CORP	NY	**E+**	340.9	58.6	37.9	-8.7	5.4	9.4	2.9	9.5	0.0	DT
ATTORNEYS INS MUTUAL OF ALABAMA INC	AL	**C-**	16.0	7.5	3.0	0.1	8.0	9.9	4.9	7.4	2.7	DFGR
ATTORNEYS INS MUTUAL RRG	HI	**D-**	27.8	7.7	2.2	0.1	3.2	4.8	4.4	9.9	0.4	DGRT
ATTORNEYS LIAB ASR SOCIETY INC RRG	VT	**D+**	246.2	45.6	9.8	0.7	10.0	9.3	7.0	10.0	1.9	DFRT

See Page 27 for explanation of footnotes and Page 28 for explanation of stability factors.

Arrows denote recent upgrades ▲ or downgrades ▼ (see Section VII for explanations)

RISK ADJ. CAPITAL RATIO #1	RISK ADJ. CAPITAL RATIO #2	PREMIUM TO SURPLUS (%)	RESV. TO SURPLUS (%)	RESV. DEVELOP. 1 YEAR (%)	RESV. DEVELOP. 2 YEAR (%)	LOSS RATIO (%)	EXP. RATIO (%)	COMB RATIO (%)	CASH FROM UNDER-WRITING (%)	NET PREMIUM GROWTH (%)	INVEST. IN AFFIL (%)	INSURANCE COMPANY NAME
21.3	18.2	N/A	N/A	N/A	-0.1	N/A	N/A	N/A	53.5	100.0	0.0	ARGONAUT-SOUTHWEST INS CO
0.2	0.2	213.3	68.5	-3.9	27.4	59.0	37.4	96.4	146.1	112.8	0.0	ARGUS FIRE & CASUALTY INS CO
3.8	2.3	58.5	86.2	5.2	2.5	75.7	33.3	109.0	93.7	-17.1	0.0	ARI CASUALTY CO
1.8	1.6	58.1	78.1	4.8	1.0	75.0	33.3	108.3	83.5	-17.1	28.1	ARI MUTUAL INS CO
1.8	1.4	41.0	38.6	-7.0	-23.0	92.2	-6.5	85.7	92.0	-30.9	0.0	ARIZONA AUTOMOBILE INS CO
2.4	1.7	71.9	24.6	-6.1	-14.2	50.3	33.8	84.1	115.4	0.2	0.0	ARIZONA HOME INS CO
3.0	2.2	97.0	35.6	-6.6	-11.9	68.2	34.8	103.0	94.3	3.3	7.0	ARMED FORCES INS EXCHANGE
85.1	76.6	0.5	N/A	N/A	N/A	N/A	144.1	144.1	144.7	-71.9	0.0	ARMOR INS CO
3.0	1.9	16.4	55.8	4.8	1.3	96.4	20.5	116.9	78.0	-36.5	0.0	ARROW MUTUAL LIABILITY INS CO
0.5	0.3	-1.7	303.8	14.0	59.4	999 +	999 +	999 +	-0.8	-211.0	7.3 •	ARROWOOD INDEMNITY CO
N/A	N/A	-0.6	57.8	4.0	16.5	-898.3	-254.8	999 +	-7.7	-829.4	0.0	ARROWOOD SURPLUS LINES INS CO
3.2	2.8	69.1	22.7	-2.3	-1.6	74.1	25.4	99.5	36.3	145.1	0.0	ARTISAN & TRUCKERS CASUALTY CO
N/A	N/A	0.4	0.5	N/A	N/A	250.0	999 +	999 +	4.9	-33.3	0.0	ASHLAND MUTUAL FIRE INS CO OF PA
2.0	1.3	122.5	49.2	-13.5	-9.4	39.6	33.8	73.4	119.4	-26.3	0.0	ASI ASR CORP
1.7	1.1	163.7	45.8	-12.3	-16.2	75.0	42.6	117.6	94.2	42.3	0.0	ASI LLOYDS
N/A	N/A	119.5	14.8	-1.0	-7.3	65.3	0.5	65.8	138.0	0.0	0.0	ASOC DE SUSCRIPCION CONJUNTA DEL
1.1	0.9	2.6	55.0	-8.2	-0.8	47.7	130.2	177.9	8.8	-94.7	0.0	ASPEN SPECIALTY INS CO
2.6	1.5	18.3	21.1	-0.5	6.0	11.5	123.5	135.0	55.0	-36.3	0.0	ASSET PROTECTION PROGRAM RRG INC
16.4	14.8	N/A	N/A	N/A	N/A	N/A	N/A	N/A	13.5	0.0	0.0	ASSOCIATED EMPLOYERS INS CO
2.6	1.8	63.2	84.0	2.2	3.4	75.0	28.6	103.6	89.1	3.0	0.0	ASSOCIATED INDEMNITY CORP
1.9	1.1	-8.3	271.4	-42.1	-10.9	-39.8	102.2	62.4	45.1	-108.2	0.0	ASSOCIATED INDUSTRIES INS CO INC
2.4	1.7	63.0	146.1	-11.5	-19.0	69.4	27.3	96.7	106.7	-8.2	3.1	ASSOCIATED INDUSTRIES OF MA MUT
1.3	0.8	31.3	126.4	10.6	13.0	77.2	50.7	127.9	139.4	3.4	0.0	ASSOCIATED INTERNATIONAL INS CO
1.9	1.3	54.6	146.6	-12.4	-33.7	66.4	25.7	92.1	98.6	-15.0	1.5	ASSOCIATED LOGGERS EXCHANGE
1.1	0.9	83.3	136.8	-8.4	-12.7	64.3	34.6	98.9	103.0	-12.1	0.0	ASSOCIATED MUTUAL INS CO
0.8	0.5	152.9	258.0	2.6	7.6	81.7	42.7	124.4	91.8	-7.1	0.0	ASSOCIATION CASUALTY INS CO
2.7	1.0	26.3	91.6	-8.4	-6.1	67.5	73.0	140.5	88.1	-52.0	0.0	ASSOCIATION INS CO
6.5	5.9	N/A	N/A	N/A	N/A	N/A	N/A	N/A	132.7	0.0	0.0	ASSURANCE COMPANY OF AMERICA
0.6	0.5	270.0	119.8	6.3	-6.2	82.5	21.9	104.4	88.0	1.0	0.0	ASSURANCEAMERICA INS CO
N/A	N/A	N/A	999 +	324.0	588.4	N/A	N/A	N/A	-113.6	0.0	0.0	ASSURECARE RRG
3.5	2.4	113.6	18.1	18.4	3.4	90.3	11.4	101.7	311.2	151.8	3.7 •	ASSURED GUARANTY CORP
1.3	0.9	0.4	0.3	N/A	N/A	999 +	428.5	999 +	-5.7	-69.1	0.0	ASSURED GUARANTY MORTGAGE INS
0.2	0.2	135.9	291.8	39.5	29.7	170.1	83.6	253.7	60.6	5.1	0.0	ASTRAEA RRG INC
N/A	N/A	N/A	N/A	N/A	N/A	N/A	N/A	N/A	N/A	0.0	0.0	ASURE WORLDWIDE INS CO
2.3	1.5	89.3	182.8	-6.7	-9.3	61.5	30.3	91.8	103.9	0.5	0.0	ATHENA ASSURANCE CO
N/A	N/A	0.1	35.4	-10.7	-10.2	999 +	999 +	999 +	N/A	-82.5	0.0	ATLANTA INTERNATIONAL INS CO
3.7	2.5	10.6	0.9	-1.2	-1.9	-6.2	140.7	134.5	86.2	-41.5	0.0	ATLANTIC BONDING CO
0.4	0.3	91.2	156.3	2.1	13.9	56.0	37.3	93.3	116.0	-1.5	0.0	ATLANTIC CASUALTY INS CO
2.4	1.8	66.8	146.6	-21.4	-36.9	69.1	27.6	96.7	113.0	-13.0	0.0	ATLANTIC CHARTER INS CO
12.6	11.0	0.3	11.7	-0.8	0.4	157.3	-485.8	-328.5	-49.7	-49.5	0.0	ATLANTIC EMPLOYERS INS CO
N/A	N/A	N/A	N/A	N/A	N/A	N/A	N/A	N/A	N/A	0.0	0.0	ATLANTIC FLORIDIAN INS CO
N/A	N/A	N/A	N/A	N/A	N/A	N/A	N/A	N/A	N/A	0.0	0.0	ATLANTIC INS CO
0.1	0.0	1.7	944.8	2.5	48.5	-17.2	999 +	999 +	-11.7	-97.8	8.7	ATLANTIC MUTUAL INS CO
11.1	7.3	20.7	20.6	-1.0	-2.1	60.2	34.8	95.0	102.9	6.8	0.0	ATLANTIC SPECIALTY INS CO
4.7	3.4	126.0	65.8	0.1	-5.3	63.1	29.1	92.2	116.2	21.3	0.0 •	ATLANTIC STATES INS CO
2.0	1.1	28.3	37.5	-28.6	-29.2	12.8	50.2	63.0	192.8	6.1	0.0	ATLAS RRG INC
3.3	2.5	41.2	32.4	-5.8	-10.7	50.8	50.2	101.0	94.0	3.2	9.9	ATRADIUS TRADE CREDIT INS CO
358.9	323.0	N/A	N/A	N/A	N/A	N/A	N/A	N/A	N/A	0.0	0.0	ATRADIUS TRADE CREDIT INS NJ
0.9	0.7	63.7	140.0	-39.2	-17.7	134.6	12.5	147.1	818.4	16.9	0.0	ATRIUM INS CORP
2.2	1.6	38.6	81.9	-14.1	-54.1	56.1	61.9	118.0	98.7	-3.3	0.0	ATTORNEYS INS MUTUAL OF ALABAMA
0.9	0.7	28.5	263.4	-24.2	-43.7	79.7	58.0	137.7	91.0	-57.2	0.0	ATTORNEYS INS MUTUAL RRG
4.6	3.0	22.1	64.9	7.9	-1.3	102.8	-39.7	63.1	607.3	-4.4	0.0	ATTORNEYS LIAB ASR SOCIETY INC RRG

999 + Denotes number greater than 999.9%
999 - Denotes number less than -999.99%
• Bullets denote a more detailed analysis is available in Section II.

INSURANCE COMPANY NAME	DOM. STATE	RATING	TOTAL ASSETS ($MIL)	CAPITAL & SURPLUS ($MIL)	ANNUAL NET PREMIUM ($MIL)	NET INCOME ($MIL)	CAPITAL-IZATION INDEX (PTS)	RESERVE ADQ INDEX (PTS)	PROFIT-ABILITY INDEX (PTS)	LIQUIDITY INDEX (PTS)	STAB. INDEX (PTS)	STABILITY FACTORS
▲ATTORNEYS LIAB PROTECTION SOC RRG	MT	**D**	84.4	25.4	25.8	0.1	3.0	2.0	4.6	6.7	1.5	RT
AUDUBON INDEMNITY CO	MS	**B-**	33.1	29.7	0.0	0.0	10.0	N/A	4.0	10.0	4.0	DGT
AUDUBON INS CO	LA	**C+**	76.4	43.8	0.9	0.0	7.0	2.1	3.1	7.0	4.7	DFT
AUSTIN INDEMNITY LLOYDS INS CO	TX	**F** (5)	5.5	2.5	9.5	-0.4	0.3	3.6	3.2	0.0	0.0	CDGL
AUSTIN MUTUAL INS CO	MN	**C**	144.9	61.2	85.4	1.4	7.6	6.9	3.1	5.7	4.3	RT
AUTO CLUB CASUALTY CO	TX	**B+**	2.8	2.7	0.0	0.0	10.0	N/A	7.5	7.0	5.0	DGT
AUTO CLUB FAMILY INS CO	MO	**C**	70.9	23.6	25.2	0.7	8.4	6.4	4.2	6.1	2.0	DRT
AUTO CLUB GROUP INS CO	MI	**B-**	185.6	84.0	66.3	-0.5	10.0	3.8	5.3	6.7	4.9	T
AUTO CLUB INDEMNITY CO	TX	**B+**	8.7	2.7	0.0	0.0	7.5	N/A	7.6	3.6	5.0	DFGL
AUTO CLUB INS ASSN	MI	**B**	2,905.4	1,314.2	1,193.3	-15.2	8.7	3.9	2.9	6.3	4.9	T
AUTO CLUB INS CO OF FL	FL	**C-**	23.1	11.6	5.0	-1.6	8.2	N/A	2.2	7.5	2.5	DFGT
AUTO CLUB PROPERTY & CASUALTY INS CO	IA	**C**	35.5	30.8	5.2	2.5	10.0	4.6	4.7	8.3	3.7	DGT
AUTO CLUB SOUTH INS CO	FL	**C**	71.7	32.8	34.6	0.9	8.6	9.3	8.3	6.3	4.0	T
AUTO DEALERS RRG INC	MT	**E**	1.0	0.6	0.3	0.1	1.0	3.6	0.4	5.1	0.1	CDFG
AUTO-OWNERS INS CO	MI	**A**	8,899.8	5,028.0	2,207.8	18.7	8.7	6.1	7.2	6.6	7.4	T
AUTOGLASS INS CO	NY	**U** (1)	0.3	0.0	0.1	-0.1	N/A	4.7	0.0	7.3	0.0	CFOT
AUTOMOBILE CLUB INTERINSURANCE EXCH	MO	**C+**	280.9	133.6	100.8	3.7	9.5	6.3	3.9	6.4	4.3	FRT
AUTOMOBILE INS CO OF HARTFORD CT	CT	**B**	954.1	293.7	248.5	14.3	7.7	5.0	7.0	6.7	6.0	T
AUTOMOTIVE UNDERWRITERS INS CO INC	NV	**D-**	20.7	6.4	4.2	-0.7	7.6	N/A	2.9	7.1	1.0	GRT
AUTOONE INS CO	NY	**C+**	71.3	45.1	17.3	0.8	10.0	6.2	6.1	7.7	4.3	T
AUTOONE SELECT INS CO	NY	**C**	83.4	44.2	25.9	1.2	9.8	6.3	3.6	7.6	3.9	T
▲AVEMCO INS CO	MD	**B**	120.3	72.4	42.6	2.6	8.7	8.6	4.5	6.8	4.7	T
AVERA PROPERTY INS INC	SD	**D**	1.5	0.9	0.5	0.3	6.6	10.0	7.1	9.0	0.6	DFGT
AVIVA INS CO OF CANADA (US BR)	NY	**U** (1)	18.5	5.7	0.0	-4.0	N/A	2.2	1.2	10.0	2.4	GT
AVOMARK INS CO	IN	**U** (1)	11.2	10.9	0.0	0.4	N/A	3.6	7.8	7.0	5.4	AT
AXA ART INS CORP	NY	**C**	53.9	33.0	13.7	-1.2	8.6	9.4	5.6	6.7	3.4	FRT
AXA INS CO	NY	**C-**	186.4	95.9	22.4	3.1	7.7	6.3	4.3	7.5	3.3	RT
AXA RE PROP & CAS INS CO	DE	**D+**	39.8	26.6	0.0	-0.4	10.0	6.1	1.3	7.0	2.6	DFGR
AXIS INS CO	IL	**C**	621.6	420.2	115.7	1.6	7.9	4.6	4.6	8.7	3.1	AGRT
AXIS REINS CO	NY	**C+**	2,116.6	517.5	387.6	-19.5	6.0	6.5	2.9	8.7	4.2	ART
AXIS SPECIALTY INS CO	CT	**C-**	224.1	110.8	8.8	1.9	8.1	6.0	3.6	8.3	2.9	FRT
AXIS SURPLUS INS CO	IL	**D**	405.2	156.3	-136.0	4.0	4.7	6.9	5.4	9.0	1.8	FRT
AZTEC INS CO	FL	**U** (1)	8.6	7.1	0.0	0.8	N/A	3.6	7.0	10.0	3.6	T
BADGER MUTUAL INS CO	WI	**B-**	162.4	66.1	89.2	0.5	8.7	6.9	5.6	5.8	5.3	FT
BALBOA INS CO	CA	**B**	2,605.2	1,348.2	1,517.6	115.8	8.3	6.2	9.3	6.8	5.2	T
▲BALDWIN MUTUAL INS CO	AL	**D-**	7.2	4.4	4.0	0.0	4.0	1.2	2.9	2.0	0.9	DGLT
BALTIMORE EQUITABLE SOCIETY	MD	**U** (1)	108.6	59.3	-0.7	-3.0	N/A	5.0	2.9	10.0	4.6	FRT
▼BANCINSURE INC	OK	**C-**	99.1	28.8	46.5	-1.1	5.2	4.8	1.8	5.7	3.2	FRT
BANKERS INDEPENDENT INS CO	PA	**C**	25.0	11.4	9.7	-0.1	7.8	9.5	6.7	7.1	3.7	DFGT
BANKERS INS CO	FL	**C-**	112.4	43.1	45.0	1.3	6.4	3.7	5.8	7.2	2.9	T
BANKERS STANDARD FIRE & MARINE CO	PA	**C**	155.7	55.8	25.2	1.9	7.2	5.0	8.8	7.1	4.0	T
BANKERS STANDARD INS CO	PA	**C**	349.2	126.7	58.7	3.3	6.9	5.0	8.9	6.9	3.9	T
BAR PLAN MUTUAL INS CO	MO	**C**	57.9	21.1	12.8	0.1	6.7	5.7	3.7	6.9	4.1	DT
BAR PLAN SURETY & FIDELITY CO	MO	**C**	4.2	3.4	0.3	0.0	10.0	5.6	4.2	9.7	3.2	DGO
BAR VERMONT RRG INC	VT	**D-**	16.1	11.1	2.2	-0.1	7.8	3.9	3.3	9.5	0.8	DGRT
BARNSTABLE COUNTY INS CO	MA	**C**	16.0	13.6	2.1	0.2	10.0	5.3	6.5	7.4	3.9	DGRT
BARNSTABLE COUNTY MUTUAL INS CO	MA	**B-**	71.6	50.3	19.1	0.4	7.9	7.4	5.4	7.2	5.0	T
▼BATTLE CREEK MUTUAL INS CO	NE	**D-**	5.6	1.9	4.0	-0.4	7.0	9.0	1.6	4.8	0.5	DFGL
BAY STATE INS CO	MA	**B+**	285.6	179.6	65.4	3.3	10.0	6.0	8.1	7.7	5.0	T
BCS INS CO	OH	**B-**	236.3	142.4	112.0	2.1	10.0	6.9	7.2	6.8	5.0	T
BEACON LLOYDS INS CO	TX	**C**	4.3	2.2	0.0	0.0	9.1	N/A	3.9	4.2	2.7	DFGL
BEACON MUTUAL INS CO	RI	**U** (5)	435.5	0.0	67.9	0.0	N/A	6.2	5.7	7.5	1.5	C

See Page 27 for explanation of footnotes and Page 28 for explanation of stability factors.
Arrows denote recent upgrades ▲ or downgrades ▼ (see Section VII for explanations)

RISK ADJ. RATIO #1	CAPITAL RATIO #2	PREMIUM TO SURPLUS (%)	RESV. TO SURPLUS (%)	RESV. DEVELOP. 1 YEAR (%)	RESV. DEVELOP. 2 YEAR (%)	LOSS RATIO (%)	EXP. RATIO (%)	COMB RATIO (%)	CASH FROM UNDER-WRITING (%)	NET PREMIUM GROWTH (%)	INVEST. IN AFFIL (%)	INSURANCE COMPANY NAME
0.6	0.4	100.1	166.2	-15.9	-10.2	64.4	30.0	94.4	100.1	-8.7	0.0	ATTORNEYS LIAB PROTECTION SOC
27.0	24.3	N/A	N/A	N/A	N/A	N/A	N/A	N/A	-100.6	0.0	0.0	AUDUBON INDEMNITY CO
1.5	1.4	2.4	42.2	3.3	27.5	35.0	355.7	390.7	-114.6	-24.9	43.1	AUDUBON INS CO
0.2	0.1	374.4	57.2	0.9	N/A	58.0	47.3	105.3	99.4	147.3	0.0	AUSTIN INDEMNITY LLOYDS INS CO
2.8	1.9	141.3	53.0	-6.9	-5.1	74.3	33.5	107.8	97.1	9.1	0.0	AUSTIN MUTUAL INS CO
57.2	51.4	N/A	N/A	N/A	N/A	N/A	N/A	N/A	7.5	0.0	0.0 •	AUTO CLUB CASUALTY CO
2.9	2.2	108.0	38.3	-0.3	1.5	70.0	20.9	90.9	111.6	0.6	0.0	AUTO CLUB FAMILY INS CO
4.9	3.5	77.7	62.0	-1.0	6.6	78.4	32.3	110.7	93.7	0.3	0.0	AUTO CLUB GROUP INS CO
1.5	1.3	N/A	N/A	N/A	N/A	N/A	N/A	N/A	15.8	0.0	0.0 •	AUTO CLUB INDEMNITY CO
2.7	2.1	86.7	69.3	-0.9	5.9	78.4	32.3	110.7	91.4	0.3	11.1 •	AUTO CLUB INS ASSN
1.9	1.3	45.4	4.4	N/A	N/A	62.2	91.9	154.1	89.2	N/A	0.0	AUTO CLUB INS CO OF FL
12.1	8.4	18.3	5.2	-0.2	-0.2	83.3	41.6	124.9	120.9	381.5	0.0	AUTO CLUB PROPERTY & CASUALTY INS
2.2	2.0	104.7	43.3	-7.9	-9.1	69.8	23.3	93.1	114.8	15.2	0.0	AUTO CLUB SOUTH INS CO
0.6	0.4	49.7	120.1	-5.4	N/A	238.2	146.2	384.4	-7.6	400.0	0.0	AUTO DEALERS RRG INC
2.6	2.2	42.6	49.1	-1.4	-1.5	73.4	27.0	100.4	94.1	-8.5	21.0 •	AUTO-OWNERS INS CO
N/A	N/A	444.4	11.1	-1.4	N/A	89.7	180.0	269.7	44.8	-1.2	0.0	AUTOGLASS INS CO
3.7	3.0	76.6	27.2	-0.2	1.0	70.0	21.0	91.0	96.6	0.6	11.7	AUTOMOBILE CLUB INTERINSURANCE
2.5	1.6	87.5	179.1	-6.2	-8.3	61.5	30.6	92.1	104.0	0.6	0.0 •	AUTOMOBILE INS CO OF HARTFORD CT
2.1	1.5	57.6	N/A	N/A	N/A	70.4	33.2	103.6	69.9	-45.7	0.0	AUTOMOTIVE UNDERWRITERS INS CO
6.3	4.1	37.9	37.6	-1.9	-3.8	60.2	34.8	95.0	101.9	6.8	0.0	AUTOONE INS CO
4.5	2.9	59.9	59.5	-2.7	-5.2	60.2	34.8	95.0	102.5	6.7	0.0	AUTOONE SELECT INS CO
2.6	2.2	61.0	33.2	-3.9	-7.1	53.7	23.3	77.0	126.7	-6.9	17.8	AVEMCO INS CO
2.8	1.9	89.4	89.4	-85.4	-85.2	41.0	14.6	55.6	215.1	9.4	0.0	AVERA PROPERTY INS INC
N/A	N/A	N/A	133.7	48.0	47.5	999 +	999 +	999 +	1.4	100.0	0.0	AVIVA INS CO OF CANADA (US BR)
N/A	N/A	N/A	N/A	N/A	N/A	N/A	N/A	N/A	N/A	0.0	0.0	AVOMARK INS CO
3.6	2.8	39.7	21.5	-3.4	-11.3	30.0	62.8	92.8	74.6	-60.3	0.0	AXA ART INS CORP
1.5	1.2	22.9	26.5	-5.2	-3.2	41.5	56.3	97.8	146.5	N/A	0.0	AXA INS CO
10.5	9.4	N/A	N/A	N/A	-69.0	N/A	N/A	N/A	976.3	100.0	0.0	AXA RE PROP & CAS INS CO
1.7	1.6	27.9	12.9	-0.1	N/A	80.0	21.8	101.8	455.0	236.1	45.6 •	AXIS INS CO
1.5	0.8	74.6	182.6	-2.0	-5.1	75.6	27.7	103.3	89.8	97.0	0.0 •	AXIS REINS CO
5.0	2.3	8.0	75.6	-3.8	-2.8	43.6	25.7	69.3	13.6	584.0	0.0	AXIS SPECIALTY INS CO
1.6	1.2	-88.7	58.9	-5.1	-4.2	65.7	8.0	73.7	-288.8	-349.8	0.0	AXIS SURPLUS INS CO
N/A	N/A	-0.1	0.6	N/A	N/A	25.0	999 +	999 +	-1.4	-118.2	0.0	AZTEC INS CO
3.4	2.2	136.0	84.5	-0.9	-5.5	78.4	32.6	111.0	87.9	0.4	0.0	BADGER MUTUAL INS CO
4.2	2.9	120.9	20.4	-3.0	-1.8	41.1	23.8	64.9	156.1	11.6	8.3 •	BALBOA INS CO
0.9	0.8	100.4	15.1	2.2	19.1	69.6	28.1	97.7	108.6	-3.1	13.2	BALDWIN MUTUAL INS CO
N/A	N/A	-1.1	2.4	0.3	0.3	-502.7	-292.1	-794.8	-11.6	-4.6	0.0	BALTIMORE EQUITABLE SOCIETY
1.1	0.6	160.5	149.3	7.1	-9.0	80.0	48.8	128.8	89.2	-1.9	0.0	BANCINSURE INC
2.2	1.8	86.4	64.0	-5.4	-35.8	74.5	20.5	95.0	87.3	26.1	0.0	BANKERS INDEPENDENT INS CO
1.3	0.9	109.0	89.5	-1.6	5.5	39.3	55.5	94.8	105.2	3.2	23.7	BANKERS INS CO
2.4	1.6	46.7	99.8	-9.8	-28.5	62.5	22.8	85.3	117.5	-19.7	0.0	BANKERS STANDARD FIRE & MARINE CO
1.7	1.3	47.7	102.0	-10.5	-32.8	62.5	22.8	85.3	126.2	-19.7	20.0	BANKERS STANDARD INS CO
1.1	0.9	55.0	117.9	-8.2	-19.1	65.6	34.9	100.5	93.9	-9.5	7.7	BAR PLAN MUTUAL INS CO
4.5	3.9	9.9	11.2	-0.8	-4.9	67.7	60.1	127.8	142.3	-11.9	0.0	BAR PLAN SURETY & FIDELITY CO
2.9	2.1	19.7	33.3	-3.5	-9.8	12.3	75.7	88.0	87.7	-8.4	0.0	BAR VERMONT RRG INC
6.2	3.8	15.3	3.2	0.4	-0.8	22.1	50.2	72.3	127.6	-10.1	0.0	BARNSTABLE COUNTY INS CO
2.2	1.8	37.2	9.5	N/A	-0.8	36.5	46.0	82.5	129.1	2.0	20.7	BARNSTABLE COUNTY MUTUAL INS CO
1.1	0.7	138.6	53.2	-5.7	-9.2	94.3	45.0	139.3	78.0	-12.5	0.0	BATTLE CREEK MUTUAL INS CO
6.9	4.7	36.3	29.7	0.5	0.6	59.7	36.8	96.5	116.4	-4.2	0.0 •	BAY STATE INS CO
8.0	4.5	79.7	30.4	0.6	0.4	63.3	30.1	93.4	103.6	10.3	1.9	BCS INS CO
2.8	2.5	N/A	N/A	N/A	N/A	N/A	N/A	N/A	22.0	0.0	0.0	BEACON LLOYDS INS CO
N/A	N/A	126.3	379.0	-12.2	-12.2	88.8	18.4	107.2	140.2	-29.4	0.0	BEACON MUTUAL INS CO

999 + Denotes number greater than 999.9%
999 - Denotes number less than -999.99%
• Bullets denote a more detailed analysis is available in Section II.

INSURANCE COMPANY NAME	DOM. STATE	RATING	TOTAL ASSETS ($MIL)	CAPITAL & SURPLUS ($MIL)	ANNUAL NET PREMIUM ($MIL)	NET INCOME ($MIL)	CAPITAL-IZATION INDEX (PTS)	RESERVE ADQ INDEX (PTS)	PROFIT-ABILITY INDEX (PTS)	LIQUIDITY INDEX (PTS)	STAB. INDEX (PTS)	STABILITY FACTORS
BEACON NATIONAL INS CO	TX	**C**	25.0	15.5	-0.2	0.3	10.0	4.6	5.5	2.5	3.1	DFGL
BEAR RIVER MUTUAL INS CO	UT	**B-**	140.5	67.6	79.1	0.8	9.1	9.3	7.4	6.1	5.3	T
BEAZLEY INS CO INC	CT	**C**	201.1	112.8	39.3	1.0	9.2	6.0	5.8	8.3	3.9	T
BEDFORD GRANGE MUTUAL INS CO	PA	**C-**	5.2	2.0	3.3	-0.2	7.7	6.7	3.4	6.7	1.9	DGT
BEDFORD PHYSICIANS RRG INC	VT	**D**	13.4	3.3	2.4	0.2	6.8	3.6	9.8	9.1	2.0	DGT
BELL UNITED INS CO	NV	**C**	32.2	14.3	6.3	0.1	3.7	3.6	4.2	9.1	3.5	CDGT
▲BENCHMARK INS CO	KS	**C+**	90.8	40.7	13.0	0.1	6.7	4.3	6.9	6.9	4.5	RT
▼BERKLEY INS CO	DE	**C**	6,918.5	2,000.1	1,232.3	-9.9	2.4	3.2	5.9	6.9	3.5	ACT
BERKLEY REGIONAL INS CO	DE	**B-**	2,639.6	566.8	1,276.9	5.2	6.7	4.5	3.8	6.4	5.1	AT
BERKLEY REGIONAL SPECIALTY INS CO	DE	**C**	29.3	24.7	0.0	0.1	10.0	N/A	7.8	7.0	3.7	DGRT
▼BEST AMERICAN INS CO	PR	**F** (5)	0.0	0.0	0.1	0.0	7.9	3.7	1.4	2.3	0.0	DGLT
BITUMINOUS CASUALTY CORP	IL	**A-**	725.4	227.5	211.7	2.4	8.5	4.4	4.7	6.8	6.9	T
BITUMINOUS FIRE & MARINE INS CO	IL	**A-**	463.7	106.8	133.7	3.2	7.5	5.0	6.7	6.4	6.9	T
BLOOMFIELD MUTUAL INS CO	MN	**D+**	5.9	4.4	1.9	0.2	10.0	7.4	8.8	6.9	2.2	DGT
BLOOMINGTON COMPENSATION INS CO	MN	**C**	23.3	11.3	7.1	-0.8	4.4	4.9	3.2	8.3	3.0	CDGT
BLUE CROSS BLUE SHIELD OF INDIANA (See ANTHEM INS COMPANIES INC)												
BLUE CROSS BLUE SHIELD OF OHIO (See COMMUNITY INS CO)												
BLUE RIDGE INDEMNITY CO	WI	**C**	14.0	14.0	18.1	0.2	7.3	5.7	3.6	7.5	3.5	DFGT
BLUE RIDGE INS CO	WI	**C**	46.0	44.8	54.3	-0.1	8.5	5.6	3.3	7.6	3.7	FT
BOND SAFEGUARD INS CO	IL	**C**	64.4	19.7	30.8	2.1	7.1	6.5	9.5	7.7	3.2	DGT
BREMEN FARMERS MUTUAL INS CO	KS	**C**	29.6	14.9	16.5	0.1	8.0	9.3	6.7	5.1	3.6	DFGR
BRENTWOOD NATIONAL INS CO	TN	**U** (1)	10.0	3.8	0.0	0.1	N/A	3.7	2.5	7.0	3.7	RT
BRETHREN MUTUAL INS CO	MD	**B-**	187.6	96.8	87.4	-0.1	9.6	6.0	8.3	6.7	5.1	T
BRIAR CREEK MUTUAL INS CO	PA	**C-** (1)	9.2	6.6	2.0	0.6	10.0	5.8	8.5	9.7	2.6	D
▲BRICKSTREET MUTUAL INS CO	WV	**D-**	1,529.6	484.3	420.8	8.6	5.8	4.1	9.4	7.0	1.0	T
BRIDGEFIELD CASUALTY INS CO	FL	**C**	121.9	42.0	0.0	0.2	10.0	N/A	8.5	10.0	4.3	AFT
BRIDGEFIELD EMPLOYERS INS CO	FL	**B-**	163.9	99.5	0.0	0.7	9.3	N/A	8.3	6.4	4.9	AT
BRIERFIELD INS CO	MS	**C**	9.9	7.3	0.0	0.6	10.0	6.9	6.4	7.0	3.4	DG
BRISTOL WEST CASUALTY INS CO	OH	**D**	21.6	8.6	1.9	0.1	10.0	5.9	7.8	8.5	2.0	DGT
BRISTOL WEST INS CO	OH	**C-**	188.6	38.7	22.7	3.1	6.3	1.9	3.8	6.2	2.9	FT
BRISTOL WEST PREFERRED INS CO	MI	**D-**	34.3	11.1	4.2	0.2	9.4	3.7	8.0	9.0	1.3	DGT
BRITISH AMERICAN INS CO	TX	**C+**	52.9	33.4	3.8	0.4	9.6	7.7	6.8	9.4	4.6	DT
BROOKWOOD INS CO	IA	**B-**	9.4	7.9	0.0	0.0	10.0	N/A	5.5	10.0	4.1	DFG
BROTHERHOOD MUTUAL INS CO	IN	**B**	315.2	125.8	160.5	-3.3	8.7	4.6	5.9	6.2	6.1	T
BROWARD FACTORY SERVICE INC	NV	**U** (5)	0.9	0.4	0.7	0.1	N/A	N/A	2.9	8.5	1.2	T
BUCKEYE STATE MUTUAL INS CO	OH	**C**	58.1	17.1	34.0	-0.2	7.1	9.3	2.0	1.0	3.6	DFLT
BUCKS COUNTY CONTRIBUTIONSHIP	PA	**U** (1)	5.0	4.4	0.0	-0.1	N/A	N/A	2.8	7.0	3.4	FRT
BUILDERS INS (A MUTUAL CAPTIVE CO)	GA	**C**	339.5	108.8	71.7	0.8	7.1	9.4	3.9	6.7	3.5	FT
BUILDERS INS ASSN INC RRG	SC	**D** (2)	2.2	1.6	0.6	0.2	7.0	5.0	3.6	8.8	1.3	DFGT
BUILDERS INS CO INC	NV	**D**	29.7	7.9	13.1	-0.2	2.4	7.0	2.7	3.9	2.2	CDFG
BUILDERS MUTUAL INS CO	NC	**B**	481.6	184.2	120.1	2.2	7.1	7.0	8.3	6.9	5.4	CRT
BUILDING INDUSTRY INS ASSN INC	VA	**C-**	13.2	4.4	5.0	-0.2	5.0	6.8	4.8	7.2	2.1	DGT
BUNKER HILL INS CO	MA	**C**	39.3	19.5	23.1	0.2	7.5	9.4	7.9	6.7	4.0	DGT
BURLINGTON INS CO	NC	**C-**	387.1	142.5	63.9	1.7	6.8	4.1	8.8	7.2	2.6	T
▲BUSINESS ALLIANCE INS CO	CA	**C-**	31.1	18.2	2.9	0.5	7.9	5.6	8.6	7.5	3.3	DFGT
▲BUSINESSFIRST INS CO	FL	**D**	35.5	12.3	14.1	0.1	2.7	7.0	5.4	6.6	2.0	DGT
BUTTE MUTUAL INS CO	NM	**E+**	1.0	0.9	0.2	0.0	10.0	N/A	2.0	9.1	0.5	DFGT
CALIFORNIA AUTOMOBILE INS CO	CA	**B**	216.3	109.4	177.7	2.2	8.0	6.9	8.8	3.5	5.8	LT
CALIFORNIA CAPITAL INS CO	CA	**B-**	425.3	242.4	166.4	3.0	7.9	8.1	8.7	6.2	4.7	T
CALIFORNIA CAS COMPENSATION INS CO	CA	**C+**	66.4	62.5	0.5	0.4	10.0	3.9	6.3	10.0	4.4	DFT
▲CALIFORNIA CAS GEN INS CO OF OREGON	OR	**C+**	96.0	32.8	26.5	0.2	8.8	8.1	5.8	6.7	4.5	FT
CALIFORNIA CASUALTY & FIRE INS CO	CA	**C+**	53.2	27.3	22.1	0.0	8.9	8.1	5.6	6.5	4.3	DT

RISK ADJ. RATIO #1	CAPITAL RATIO #2	PREMIUM TO SURPLUS (%)	RESV. TO SURPLUS (%)	RESV. DEVELOP. 1 YEAR (%)	RESV. DEVELOP. 2 YEAR (%)	LOSS RATIO (%)	EXP. RATIO (%)	COMB RATIO (%)	CASH FROM UNDER-WRITING (%)	NET PREMIUM GROWTH (%)	INVEST. IN AFFIL (%)	INSURANCE COMPANY NAME
6.6	6.0	-1.1	N/A	N/A	N/A	N/A	242.4	242.4	15.5	94.5	26.6	BEACON NATIONAL INS CO
3.6	2.6	111.7	41.3	-7.5	-9.8	64.6	25.3	89.9	108.3	3.2	0.0	BEAR RIVER MUTUAL INS CO
4.0	2.9	35.2	30.9	-1.2	0.8	77.8	25.5	103.3	199.4	5.3	0.0	BEAZLEY INS CO INC
1.4	1.2	142.9	19.8	-2.0	-9.0	40.7	40.9	81.6	140.5	49.4	2.9	BEDFORD GRANGE MUTUAL INS CO
1.4	1.1	77.1	66.4	-20.6	N/A	49.9	7.8	57.7	999 +	80.5	0.0	BEDFORD PHYSICIANS RRG INC
0.6	0.5	44.7	89.7	-11.3	-5.8	87.6	11.2	98.8	185.2	-1.9	0.0	BELL UNITED INS CO
1.6	0.9	32.1	51.8	-0.6	-6.0	52.5	45.3	97.8	122.4	1.5	0.0	BENCHMARK INS CO
0.6	0.4	60.5	203.9	-1.7	1.8	65.8	31.0	96.8	118.8	-19.2	17.2 •	BERKLEY INS CO
1.0	0.8	209.2	236.9	-2.4	-1.0	64.8	31.8	96.6	124.0	-2.5	18.1 •	BERKLEY REGIONAL INS CO
17.3	15.5	N/A	N/A	N/A	N/A	N/A	N/A	N/A	393.8	0.0	0.0	BERKLEY REGIONAL SPECIALTY INS CO
2.9	2.6	12.0	N/A	N/A	-1.4	N/A	267.1	267.1	129.1	0.0	0.0	BEST AMERICAN INS CO
3.1	1.9	89.2	165.2	-1.8	-0.3	66.8	27.8	94.6	106.0	-11.7	0.0 •	BITUMINOUS CASUALTY CORP
2.0	1.3	127.8	303.2	-4.1	-3.7	64.2	34.7	98.9	94.1	-20.1	0.0 •	BITUMINOUS FIRE & MARINE INS CO
7.4	6.4	48.0	4.7	-2.4	-0.7	57.2	33.7	90.9	95.9	7.6	0.0	BLOOMFIELD MUTUAL INS CO
1.0	0.7	63.0	66.2	-2.2	-11.2	74.0	28.0	102.0	-499.5	N/A	0.0	BLOOMINGTON COMPENSATION INS CO
5.7	4.7	137.4	159.2	-18.3	-13.2	52.3	33.8	86.1	73.1	-30.1	0.0	BLUE RIDGE INDEMNITY CO
5.9	4.8	125.1	145.0	-15.5	-11.0	52.3	33.8	86.1	73.1	-30.1	0.0	BLUE RIDGE INS CO
1.7	1.1	164.4	78.4	6.1	6.2	54.7	30.2	84.9	177.9	6.8	0.0	BOND SAFEGUARD INS CO
2.1	1.9	111.5	13.6	-8.6	-10.8	77.3	27.5	104.8	75.9	-1.7	0.0	BREMEN FARMERS MUTUAL INS CO
N/A	N/A	N/A	N/A	N/A	N/A	N/A	N/A	N/A	N/A	0.0	0.0	BRENTWOOD NATIONAL INS CO
5.2	3.4	87.9	39.2	-5.0	-3.0	57.1	33.2	90.3	109.0	-0.7	0.0	BRETHREN MUTUAL INS CO
4.5	3.0	29.7	11.9	-0.7	1.3	31.5	40.7	72.2	159.1	0.5	0.0	BRIAR CREEK MUTUAL INS CO
2.1	0.8	86.8	161.1	-10.3	-44.7	65.8	17.8	83.6	156.0	-40.1	0.0 •	BRICKSTREET MUTUAL INS CO
5.1	4.6	N/A	N/A	N/A	N/A	N/A	N/A	N/A	-30.8	0.0	0.0	BRIDGEFIELD CASUALTY INS CO
2.5	2.4	N/A	N/A	N/A	N/A	N/A	N/A	N/A	135.4	0.0	37.4	BRIDGEFIELD EMPLOYERS INS CO
8.5	7.6	N/A	9.7	-3.6	-8.8	N/A	N/A	N/A	65.5	0.0	0.0	BRIERFIELD INS CO
3.1	2.8	22.0	9.2	N/A	1.3	69.5	13.3	82.8	220.3	523.1	0.0	BRISTOL WEST CASUALTY INS CO
1.4	1.2	65.3	79.9	8.1	37.1	83.2	8.6	91.8	84.4	90.0	0.0	BRISTOL WEST INS CO
2.8	2.5	38.8	20.8	0.7	-1.7	79.0	10.8	89.8	123.6	47.8	0.0	BRISTOL WEST PREFERRED INS CO
5.5	2.7	11.7	56.2	-1.1	-0.5	42.7	29.7	72.4	120.5	-15.8	0.0	BRITISH AMERICAN INS CO
13.0	11.7	N/A	5.3	N/A	N/A	N/A	N/A	N/A	33.0	0.0	0.0	BROOKWOOD INS CO
2.5	2.0	122.8	51.6	-3.0	-1.8	60.9	31.5	92.4	107.7	3.7	0.0	BROTHERHOOD MUTUAL INS CO
N/A	N/A	191.3	3.2	N/A	N/A	47.9	53.9	101.8	99.9	-10.0	0.0	BROWARD FACTORY SERVICE INC
1.7	1.1	194.0	90.4	-11.9	-17.5	90.0	33.8	123.8	70.3	-30.7	7.7	BUCKEYE STATE MUTUAL INS CO
N/A	N/A	N/A	N/A	N/A	N/A	N/A	N/A	N/A	N/A	-100.0	0.0	BUCKS COUNTY CONTRIBUTIONSHIP
1.6	1.1	62.6	140.9	-9.3	-11.1	57.1	52.0	109.1	86.0	-42.3	11.8	BUILDERS INS (A MUTUAL CAPTIVE CO)
3.0	1.7	39.0	22.2	-14.6	-14.1	20.6	58.0	78.6	112.9	-44.9	0.0	BUILDERS INS ASSN INC RRG
0.7	0.3	160.5	256.2	-53.0	-60.2	55.1	52.1	107.2	73.4	-39.4	0.0	BUILDERS INS CO INC
1.6	1.0	61.5	125.3	-7.7	-22.4	45.9	36.3	82.2	113.0	-15.6	2.4 •	BUILDERS MUTUAL INS CO
1.0	0.6	100.2	37.3	11.1	5.2	58.9	40.5	99.4	158.1	858.9	0.0	BUILDING INDUSTRY INS ASSN INC
1.7	1.6	116.9	20.1	-7.9	-5.2	54.0	38.3	92.3	109.3	10.2	0.0	BUNKER HILL INS CO
1.9	1.1	45.2	126.9	-7.7	-1.8	57.5	41.9	99.4	92.5	-27.7	0.0	BURLINGTON INS CO
6.9	5.0	16.5	7.8	-20.8	-14.0	61.5	51.6	113.1	21.6	-73.8	0.0	BUSINESS ALLIANCE INS CO
1.2	0.5	116.1	113.3	-5.3	-61.6	52.2	34.3	86.5	124.4	-21.6	0.0	BUSINESSFIRST INS CO
5.8	5.4	17.3	N/A	N/A	N/A	113.2	70.1	183.3	45.2	2.4	0.0	BUTTE MUTUAL INS CO
2.4	2.1	166.1	54.2	2.2	1.0	73.2	24.9	98.1	98.6	-13.9	7.5	CALIFORNIA AUTOMOBILE INS CO
2.3	1.8	70.0	34.9	-2.3	-4.3	57.7	38.6	96.3	96.6	1.1	24.4 •	CALIFORNIA CAPITAL INS CO
8.9	5.4	0.7	50.8	-0.2	4.6	76.8	26.7	103.5	2.9	0.9	0.0	CALIFORNIA CAS COMPENSATION INS
3.8	2.6	81.4	41.6	-4.5	-4.7	76.3	25.3	101.6	84.2	-3.0	0.0	CALIFORNIA CAS GEN INS CO OF
3.9	2.7	81.1	41.4	-4.5	-4.6	76.3	25.3	101.6	105.7	-3.0	0.0	CALIFORNIA CASUALTY & FIRE INS CO

999 + Denotes number greater than 999.9%
999 - Denotes number less than -999.99%
• Bullets denote a more detailed analysis is available in Section II.

INSURANCE COMPANY NAME	DOM. STATE	RATING	TOTAL ASSETS ($MIL)	CAPITAL & SURPLUS ($MIL)	ANNUAL NET PREMIUM ($MIL)	NET INCOME ($MIL)	CAPITAL-IZATION INDEX (PTS)	RESERVE ADQ INDEX (PTS)	PROFIT-ABILITY INDEX (PTS)	LIQUIDITY INDEX (PTS)	STAB. INDEX (PTS)	STABILITY FACTORS
CALIFORNIA CASUALTY INDEMNITY EXCH	CA	**C**	539.9	303.8	154.7	1.0	8.1	7.6	5.6	6.8	4.3	T
▲CALIFORNIA CASUALTY INS CO	CA	**C+**	122.3	87.6	17.7	0.2	7.8	7.4	4.8	6.9	4.4	T
CALIFORNIA GENERAL UNDERWRITERS I C	CA	**B**	16.1	15.0	0.5	0.1	10.0	4.5	6.9	10.0	4.9	DGT
CALIFORNIA HEALTHCARE INS CO INC RRG	HI	**C**	104.2	30.0	16.4	0.3	7.5	9.5	8.9	8.3	4.1	T
▲CALIFORNIA INS CO	CA	**C+**	288.9	130.7	86.0	0.8	7.6	5.8	8.6	9.1	4.5	T
CALIFORNIA MEDICAL GROUP INS CO RRG	AZ	**C-**	14.5	5.2	5.5	-0.2	7.8	5.0	5.7	8.8	1.5	GRT
CALIFORNIA MUTUAL INS CO	CA	**D-**	12.5	8.0	3.5	0.1	7.8	9.3	5.2	6.9	1.2	DFGT
CALIFORNIA STATE AUTO ASN INTER-INS	CA	**A-**	5,291.7	2,639.8	2,357.1	-37.2	10.0	7.7	5.2	6.3	5.5	T
CALLICOON CO-OPERATIVE INS CO	NY	**C**	21.5	16.4	4.6	0.4	10.0	7.6	8.6	7.4	3.6	DGT
CAMBRIA COUNTY MUTUAL INS CO	PA	**U** (1)	0.6	0.6	0.0	0.0	N/A	N/A	3.2	10.0	1.7	FT
CAMBRIDGE MUTUAL FIRE INS CO	MA	**B**	537.4	284.9	152.7	6.7	10.0	5.9	8.5	7.7	4.8	T
CAMDEN FIRE INS ASSN CO OF NJ	NJ	**C**	66.9	63.7	0.0	0.0	10.0	N/A	3.2	7.0	3.9	T
CAMERON MUTUAL INS CO	MO	**C**	89.6	31.2	62.3	-0.9	5.1	5.7	2.4	2.0	3.9	FLT
CAMERON NATIONAL INS CO	MO	**C-**	11.4	5.7	0.9	0.1	10.0	7.4	8.6	9.3	2.6	DGT
▼CAMICO MUTUAL INS CO	CA	**C**	182.7	35.6	50.7	1.9	3.0	4.0	1.9	5.7	3.4	CRT
▲CAMPMED CAS & INDEM CO INC OF MD	MD	**D+**	36.2	10.9	8.1	0.2	2.5	3.5	7.9	7.6	2.4	DGRT
CANAL INDEMNITY CO	SC	**B**	43.5	34.1	0.0	0.2	10.0	N/A	4.5	7.0	5.5	DFGT
CANAL INS CO	SC	**B+**	1,010.6	455.9	238.2	10.0	8.0	4.3	3.6	6.7	5.8	FT
CANONSBURG MUTUAL FIRE INS CO	PA	**D**	1.7	1.1	0.5	-0.2	9.9	4.8	2.1	7.4	1.2	DGT
CAPACITY INS CO	FL	**D**	9.4	4.9	2.7	-0.1	3.6	6.9	2.4	6.8	2.1	DGT
CAPITAL ASSURANCE CO INC	FL	**U** (1)	30.6	6.2	0.0	-3.0	N/A	4.9	1.3	10.0	2.5	CFRT
▼CAPITAL CITY INS CO INC	SC	**C-**	135.5	28.8	56.2	2.9	2.9	3.8	1.7	8.6	2.9	CT
CAPITAL MARKETS ASR CORP	NY	**D+**	127.3	125.6	0.0	0.7	7.2	3.3	4.8	6.9	2.7	ACDT
CAPITOL CASUALTY CO	NE	**C**	16.9	16.2	0.9	0.0	9.5	6.4	4.2	8.8	3.9	DGT
CAPITOL COUNTY MUTUAL FIRE INS CO	TX	**C**	27.8	13.3	0.0	0.0	8.1	4.6	7.7	6.5	3.4	DFGR
CAPITOL INDEMNITY CORP	WI	**C**	379.0	149.6	124.2	0.5	7.7	4.8	4.6	6.9	4.0	T
CAPITOL INS CO	PA	**D+**	6.2	2.4	2.7	-0.2	7.7	5.9	3.6	9.0	2.0	DGRT
CAPITOL PREFERRED INS CO	FL	**E+**	30.4	11.7	10.3	1.2	0.9	2.7	2.8	5.9	0.6	CDGT
CAPITOL SPECIALTY INS CORP	WI	**C**	75.9	27.4	26.6	-0.1	6.8	5.9	3.3	6.8	4.3	T
CARDIF PROPERTY & CASUALTY INS CO	TX	**C-**	10.2	9.8	0.1	-0.5	10.0	4.6	3.1	10.0	2.9	DFGT
CARDINAL SELECT RRG INC	SC	**D-**	6.0	2.6	1.8	-0.4	7.8	3.5	2.9	9.4	0.9	DGT
▲CARE RRG INC	DC	**D-**	37.6	3.9	1.8	0.1	1.1	4.9	8.0	9.3	1.0	CDFG
CARE WEST INS CO	CA	**D-**	110.8	16.3	42.4	-3.5	0.7	4.1	2.9	7.1	1.1	CDGR
CAREGIVERS UNITED LIAB INS CO RRG	SC	**D-**	25.5	7.6	6.8	-0.2	4.2	7.1	4.8	6.9	1.3	DGRT
CARIBBEAN ALLIANCE INS CO	PR	**C+**	226.0	72.3	85.3	2.5	9.0	9.3	9.3	7.2	4.4	T
CARIBBEAN AMERICAN PROPERTY INS CO	PR	**C+**	36.2	20.1	30.8	1.8	8.4	6.5	8.0	6.6	4.8	DGT
CARING COMMUNITIES RECIP RRG	DC	**D-**	61.2	24.4	1.2	0.8	7.1	N/A	4.7	8.8	1.3	DGT
CAROLINA CASUALTY INS CO	IA	**C**	786.5	212.9	308.6	2.7	5.0	2.8	3.8	6.2	3.8	T
CAROLINA FARMERS MUTUAL INS CO	NC	**C-** (1)	8.6	7.1	2.1	-0.3	10.0	6.1	5.6	8.7	2.7	D
CASCO INDEMNITY CO	ME	**C-**	22.4	9.1	11.5	-0.5	8.0	6.9	2.4	6.1	3.0	DFGT
CASSATT RISK RETENTION GROUP INC	VT	**D-**	7.4	4.0	0.1	0.0	7.0	7.1	6.6	9.9	1.3	DGR
CASTLE HILL INS CO	RI	**U** (1)	22.6	22.4	0.0	0.5	N/A	N/A	6.8	7.0	5.3	T
CASTLEPOINT INS CO	NY	**C**	317.6	91.5	112.3	-4.5	6.1	3.6	2.8	7.2	3.2	GT
CASUALTY CORP OF AMERICA	OK	**E+**	4.4	0.8	6.4	0.1	1.0	6.1	2.8	0.0	0.4	CDFG
CASUALTY UNDERWRITERS INS CO	UT	**D**	4.1	4.0	0.0	0.0	10.0	6.6	3.8	10.0	2.0	DGRT
CATASTROPHE REINS CO	TX	**E+**	1,417.9	1,273.0	219.5	-16.8	10.0	3.6	8.0	7.8	0.0	GT
CATAWBA INS CO	SC	**D**	15.6	8.0	5.9	0.3	5.2	5.6	3.2	6.2	2.3	DFGR
CATERPILLAR INS CO	MO	**C**	327.3	111.9	113.6	3.5	8.0	8.6	5.5	7.4	4.3	GRT
CATHOLIC RELIEF INS CO OF AMERICA	NE	**C-**	79.0	24.3	22.0	-0.5	7.4	0.5	4.1	6.4	2.9	FT
CATLIN INS CO	TX	**C**	71.1	55.9	5.3	0.1	10.0	4.7	1.7	9.4	3.6	DGRT
▲CATLIN SPECIALTY INS CO	DE	**C+**	212.4	99.2	25.1	0.9	8.5	5.0	3.6	8.8	3.9	GT
CBIA COMP SERVICES INC	CT	**D**	18.3	2.7	3.4	0.0	1.9	9.3	3.4	5.9	1.7	CDFG

See Page 27 for explanation of footnotes and Page 28 for explanation of stability factors.

Arrows denote recent upgrades ▲ or downgrades ▼ (see Section VII for explanations)

RISK ADJ. RATIO #1	CAPITAL RATIO #2	PREMIUM TO SURPLUS (%)	RESV. TO SURPLUS (%)	RESV. DEVELOP. 1 YEAR (%)	RESV. DEVELOP. 2 YEAR (%)	LOSS RATIO (%)	EXP. RATIO (%)	COMB RATIO (%)	CASH FROM UNDER-WRITING (%)	NET PREMIUM GROWTH (%)	INVEST. IN AFFIL (%)	INSURANCE COMPANY NAME
1.9	1.8	50.8	25.9	-2.6	-2.7	76.3	25.3	101.6	99.3	-3.0	41.5 •	CALIFORNIA CASUALTY INDEMNITY EXCH
1.6	1.5	20.3	10.4	-1.1	-1.2	76.3	25.3	101.6	123.7	-3.0	63.2	CALIFORNIA CASUALTY INS CO
19.9	16.0	3.2	0.4	-0.4	-1.4	21.8	27.0	48.8	162.2	4.1	0.0	CALIFORNIA GENERAL UNDERWRITERS I
2.2	1.8	55.4	172.0	-32.6	-37.6	70.7	5.5	76.2	137.3	-18.2	0.2	CALIFORNIA HEALTHCARE INS CO INC
3.0	1.3	66.4	85.7	-11.8	-14.8	49.8	24.8	74.6	186.5	-17.2	0.0	CALIFORNIA INS CO
1.9	1.3	102.4	124.7	-20.0	-16.2	61.2	16.7	77.9	206.8	50.3	0.0	CALIFORNIA MEDICAL GROUP INS CO
3.3	1.9	40.8	18.7	-4.5	-6.6	48.4	58.8	107.2	71.2	-12.8	0.2	CALIFORNIA MUTUAL INS CO
4.5	3.1	86.1	35.0	-4.7	-3.1	65.6	31.4	97.0	98.1	-2.7	4.1 •	CALIFORNIA STATE AUTO ASN INTER-INS
9.6	6.8	28.6	8.8	-3.0	-2.7	40.9	37.3	78.2	132.0	4.3	0.0	CALLICOON CO-OPERATIVE INS CO
N/A	N/A	0.5	N/A	N/A	N/A	212.5	633.3	845.8	8.6	-76.9	0.0	CAMBRIA COUNTY MUTUAL INS CO
5.0	3.5	53.5	43.7	0.7	0.9	59.7	36.8	96.5	116.0	-4.2	0.0 •	CAMBRIDGE MUTUAL FIRE INS CO
38.0	19.0	N/A	N/A	N/A	N/A	N/A	N/A	N/A	N/A	0.0	0.0	CAMDEN FIRE INS ASSN CO OF NJ
1.1	0.7	193.2	85.2	-3.5	-10.8	92.8	34.5	127.3	76.6	-3.4	8.1	CAMERON MUTUAL INS CO
3.5	3.1	16.0	N/A	N/A	-1.2	N/A	-68.0	N/A	-167.2	-19.3	0.0	CAMERON NATIONAL INS CO
0.7	0.5	144.3	249.8	10.9	13.5	102.6	36.9	139.5	96.2	-11.7	0.0	CAMICO MUTUAL INS CO
0.8	0.5	74.6	166.5	-7.9	-6.0	62.2	45.5	107.7	91.9	22.6	0.0	CAMPMED CAS & INDEM CO INC OF MD
9.9	5.7	N/A	8.4	N/A	N/A	N/A	N/A	N/A	-112.6	0.0	0.0	CANAL INDEMNITY CO
2.5	1.8	51.2	95.2	4.3	9.8	76.7	30.7	107.4	68.5	-45.1	3.6 •	CANAL INS CO
2.9	2.2	41.8	7.7	2.1	3.0	113.1	23.3	136.4	88.3	60.1	0.0	CANONSBURG MUTUAL FIRE INS CO
0.8	0.6	53.3	24.8	-11.0	-18.5	3.3	115.4	118.7	125.9	-0.8	0.0	CAPACITY INS CO
N/A	N/A	N/A	368.4	N/A	N/A	N/A	N/A	N/A	N/A	100.0	0.0	CAPITAL ASSURANCE CO INC
0.7	0.5	220.1	348.5	33.4	23.5	100.1	31.4	131.5	101.4	12.4	0.0	CAPITAL CITY INS CO INC
2.6	1.1	N/A	N/A	N/A	N/A	N/A	N/A	N/A	-73.2	0.0	0.0	CAPITAL MARKETS ASR CORP
6.1	3.5	5.3	1.0	-0.4	-1.4	46.4	85.9	132.3	76.1	-10.2	0.0	CAPITOL CASUALTY CO
1.7	1.7	N/A	N/A	N/A	N/A	N/A	N/A	N/A	62.7	0.0	47.6	CAPITOL COUNTY MUTUAL FIRE INS CO
2.3	1.5	73.1	87.2	-4.2	-9.1	48.2	43.5	91.7	109.0	1.2	8.4 •	CAPITOL INDEMNITY CORP
1.8	1.5	102.8	35.3	-12.7	-5.7	58.1	39.9	98.0	67.2	5.6	0.0	CAPITOL INS CO
0.5	0.4	100.3	46.1	-22.1	-13.6	91.3	11.2	102.5	97.3	-21.7	0.0	CAPITOL PREFERRED INS CO
1.9	0.9	96.8	94.7	-5.0	-11.7	49.2	44.4	93.6	90.9	-36.4	0.0	CAPITOL SPECIALTY INS CORP
4.7	4.6	0.6	0.1	N/A	1.7	11.7	999 +	999 +	3.5	-91.8	0.0	CARDIF PROPERTY & CASUALTY INS CO
1.6	1.1	60.8	64.2	15.3	7.0	59.0	14.5	73.5	-368.1	52.1	0.0	CARDINAL SELECT RRG INC
0.3	0.2	42.7	600.0	6.4	5.7	73.9	40.9	114.8	95.1	-38.9	0.0	CARE RRG INC
0.3	0.2	213.7	282.2	-13.6	-85.5	81.8	26.2	108.0	154.6	48.5	0.0	CARE WEST INS CO
1.1	0.6	86.7	153.9	-37.8	-52.1	45.7	12.5	58.2	157.3	3.2	0.0	CAREGIVERS UNITED LIAB INS CO RRG
5.1	3.2	120.7	23.7	-4.0	-10.2	62.1	29.0	91.1	115.8	-1.2	0.0	CARIBBEAN ALLIANCE INS CO
3.5	2.0	168.4	32.8	-1.7	0.8	56.2	23.4	79.6	129.0	35.5	0.0	CARIBBEAN AMERICAN PROPERTY INS
1.7	1.2	5.1	69.9	N/A	N/A	65.0	25.4	90.4	999 +	N/A	0.0	CARING COMMUNITIES RECIP RRG
1.0	0.7	146.6	192.3	3.4	4.3	73.6	27.4	101.0	95.7	-12.1	0.0 •	CAROLINA CASUALTY INS CO
7.0	4.0	30.1	2.2	0.1	-0.1	60.1	38.7	98.8	105.4	-4.2	0.0	CAROLINA FARMERS MUTUAL INS CO
1.9	1.5	116.6	61.1	0.6	-6.9	84.8	32.1	116.9	83.6	3.9	0.0	CASCO INDEMNITY CO
1.5	1.3	2.6	27.1	-1.4	-2.1	-51.0	-1.0	-52.0	-83.9	0.0	0.0	CASSATT RISK RETENTION GROUP INC
N/A	N/A	N/A	N/A	N/A	N/A	N/A	N/A	N/A	N/A	0.0	0.0	CASTLE HILL INS CO
1.6	0.8	119.3	59.9	0.7	N/A	57.3	39.4	96.7	191.6	22.9	0.0	CASTLEPOINT INS CO
0.4	0.3	810.0	257.8	-100.1	-124.6	69.0	27.3	96.3	79.5	-8.6	0.0	CASUALTY CORP OF AMERICA
10.1	4.9	N/A	5.2	5.1	1.2	999 +	N/A	N/A	N/A	0.0	0.0	CASUALTY UNDERWRITERS INS CO
5.5	3.9	17.0	1.8	1.7	N/A	15.7	N/A	15.7	999 +	-13.1	0.0 •	CATASTROPHE REINS CO
1.3	0.8	76.1	66.0	1.6	5.7	68.2	72.5	140.7	69.9	-47.6	0.0	CATAWBA INS CO
2.4	2.0	104.3	11.5	-8.5	-12.1	60.7	9.6	70.3	220.1	32.5	0.0	CATERPILLAR INS CO
2.4	1.2	69.6	62.7	-23.0	49.9	80.1	13.5	93.6	47.8	3.4	0.0	CATHOLIC RELIEF INS CO OF AMERICA
8.8	7.1	9.5	2.0	-0.4	N/A	62.0	44.3	106.3	96.1	280.4	0.0	CATLIN INS CO
4.2	2.2	26.0	38.3	-3.2	-0.2	78.7	30.3	109.0	378.5	N/A	0.0	CATLIN SPECIALTY INS CO
0.5	0.3	108.5	485.8	-5.8	-19.4	93.0	31.0	124.0	68.4	-10.1	0.0	CBIA COMP SERVICES INC

999 + Denotes number greater than 999.9%
999 - Denotes number less than -999.99%
• Bullets denote a more detailed analysis is available in Section II.

INSURANCE COMPANY NAME	DOM. STATE	RATING	TOTAL ASSETS ($MIL)	CAPITAL & SURPLUS ($MIL)	ANNUAL NET PREMIUM ($MIL)	NET INCOME ($MIL)	CAPITAL-IZATION INDEX (PTS)	RESERVE ADQ INDEX (PTS)	PROFIT-ABILITY INDEX (PTS)	LIQUIDITY INDEX (PTS)	STAB. INDEX (PTS)	STABILITY FACTORS
CELINA MUTUAL INS CO	OH	**C**	47.8	19.3	26.0	-0.5	7.5	8.9	5.9	6.2	3.7	DGT
CEM INS CO	IL	**D-**	10.1	4.9	5.6	-0.1	3.5	7.0	3.0	6.5	1.2	DFGT
CENSTAT CASUALTY CO	NE	**D+**	13.1	11.6	1.0	0.1	10.0	5.7	8.0	9.2	2.6	DGT
CENTENNIAL CASUALTY CO	AL	**B-**	59.9	36.3	7.2	0.5	7.8	7.4	3.6	8.5	4.5	DT
CENTENNIAL INS CO	NY	**D**	94.2	11.9	0.1	-0.3	0.1	1.6	0.5	7.3	1.4	CDFT
CENTER MUTUAL INS CO	ND	**C**	32.9	16.9	20.4	0.5	8.3	9.2	8.0	6.4	4.0	DGT
CENTER VALLEY MUTUAL FIRE INS CO	PA	**D** (1)	2.2	2.1	0.1	0.1	10.0	3.6	6.5	10.0	1.7	D
CENTRAL CO-OPERATIVE INS CO	NY	**D**	9.3	4.5	4.4	0.2	8.2	9.3	8.8	6.9	1.5	DGT
CENTRAL MUTUAL INS CO	OH	**B+**	1,238.6	471.6	460.2	-7.4	8.5	5.4	5.2	6.6	6.7	T
CENTRAL NATIONAL INS CO OF OMAHA	NE	**F** (1)	31.9	12.4	0.0	1.1	5.0	6.9	5.2	10.0	0.0	DFT
▲CENTRAL PA PHYSICIANS RRG INC	SC	**D**	40.1	9.9	13.9	0.1	4.2	4.8	6.8	6.8	1.5	DGT
▼CENTRAL STATES INDEMNITY CO OF	NE	**B+**	209.1	183.4	48.5	0.9	9.1	8.1	4.8	7.4	5.3	T
CENTRE COUNTY MUTUAL FIRE INS CO	PA	**D+**	4.4	3.0	1.0	0.3	8.8	7.0	5.3	9.0	2.0	DGT
CENTRE INS CO	DE	**C**	263.2	50.5	0.0	1.1	7.2	4.7	1.9	7.6	2.2	DGRT
CENTURION CASUALTY CO	IA	**B**	394.7	370.8	36.5	7.2	10.0	6.1	9.0	9.3	4.5	T
CENTURION MEDICAL LIAB PROTECT RRG	AZ	**D-**	8.9	3.3	3.0	0.0	7.6	6.0	6.1	7.4	0.9	DGT
CENTURY CASUALTY CO	GA	**D+**	7.6	5.1	1.2	0.1	9.2	9.3	7.5	7.0	2.3	DFGT
CENTURY INDEMNITY CO	PA	**U** (1)	1,111.1	25.0	0.0	-83.5	N/A	0.1	0.9	5.9	0.0	CFRT
CENTURY REINSURANCE CO	PA	**U** (1)	104.8	92.1	0.0	4.2	N/A	6.5	7.8	10.0	7.8	T
CENTURY SURETY CO	OH	**C-**	472.3	129.1	173.7	10.0	2.6	3.5	4.4	6.1	2.9	CT
CENTURY-NATIONAL INS CO	CA	**C+**	484.5	226.7	142.3	5.3	7.4	9.7	7.1	6.4	4.4	FRT
CHARITABLE SERVICE PROVIDERS RRG	AZ	**D**	3.1	1.8	0.8	0.1	7.5	6.0	6.0	7.6	1.4	DGRT
CHARTER INDEMNITY CO	TX	**B-**	13.1	10.9	0.0	0.1	10.0	N/A	8.2	10.0	4.5	DG
▲CHARTER OAK FIRE INS CO	CT	**B**	894.8	229.1	230.4	6.3	7.3	4.6	8.1	6.6	5.4	T
CHATTAHOCHEE RRG CAPTIVE INS CO	GA	**D**	5.3	2.0	1.3	0.2	5.1	4.9	5.6	8.7	1.6	DGRT
CHAUTAUQUA PATRONS INS CO	NY	**C-**	14.9	7.2	6.2	-0.5	8.4	5.8	4.4	6.9	2.7	DGT
CHC CASUALTY RRG	VT	**E+**	29.1	7.4	9.8	-1.1	0.7	3.5	1.9	5.5	0.0	CDFG
CHEROKEE INS CO	MI	**C-**	228.0	61.7	126.2	3.8	7.2	6.9	6.3	2.3	3.3	LRT
CHERRY VALLEY COOPERATIVE INS CO	NY	**D**	1.3	1.1	0.3	0.0	9.0	6.1	3.9	9.1	1.4	DGT
CHICAGO INS CO	IL	**B-**	293.7	145.2	71.8	3.5	8.4	5.8	8.4	6.8	4.9	T
▲CHRYSLER INS CO	MI	**C**	227.3	101.9	121.3	1.4	8.5	7.0	2.9	6.9	3.5	RT
CHUBB CUSTOM INS CO	DE	**B**	306.0	108.4	44.2	3.6	8.4	6.0	8.8	7.2	5.4	T
CHUBB INDEMNITY INS CO	NY	**B**	261.0	75.4	44.2	3.3	8.1	5.6	8.9	7.2	6.0	T
CHUBB INS CO OF NEW JERSEY	NJ	**B**	42.0	27.5	0.0	0.3	10.0	N/A	8.0	7.0	5.4	DGT
CHUBB LLOYDS INS CO OF TX	TX	**B**	28.0	4.7	0.0	0.0	7.0	N/A	7.7	7.0	4.9	DG
CHUBB NATIONAL INS CO	IN	**B**	200.7	75.2	44.2	3.3	8.1	5.6	8.8	6.9	6.0	T
CHURCH INS CO	NY	**C**	49.8	18.5	-0.6	1.0	7.7	4.6	1.9	9.1	2.1	DFGT
CHURCH MUTUAL INS CO	WI	**A**	1,150.7	345.0	467.5	-0.1	8.3	9.3	6.8	6.0	7.5	T
▼CIFG ASR NORTH AMERICA INC	NY	**E-**	267.2	87.9	7.2	158.5	0.0	3.6	0.1	10.0	0.0	CFGR
CIM INS CORP	MI	**C+**	17.6	15.7	0.0	0.1	10.0	N/A	7.1	7.0	3.2	DGT
CIMARRON INS EXCH RRG	VT	**D**	6.1	1.3	1.4	0.0	3.2	4.8	3.6	7.4	1.2	DGRT
CINCINNATI CASUALTY CO	OH	**B**	297.7	240.0	0.0	11.5	10.0	N/A	4.8	10.0	5.8	T
CINCINNATI EQUITABLE INS CO	OH	**U** (1)	6.7	5.7	-0.1	-0.5	N/A	6.8	1.9	6.9	3.1	FRT
CINCINNATI INDEMNITY CO	OH	**A-**	87.6	64.0	0.0	3.5	10.0	N/A	7.0	7.0	6.2	T
CINCINNATI INS CO	OH	**A-**	8,454.0	3,105.4	2,998.5	11.0	8.0	8.8	3.1	6.3	6.9	T
CINCINNATI SPECIALTY UNDERWRITER	DE	**C+**	198.2	170.7	13.7	-4.1	10.0	N/A	2.1	9.1	4.3	DT
CIRCLE STAR INS CO RRG	VT	**D-**	5.2	1.3	0.0	0.1	10.0	N/A	7.1	10.0	1.3	DGRT
CITADEL INS CO	TX	**U** (1)	2.9	2.8	0.0	0.0	N/A	5.1	4.9	7.0	4.0	RT
CITATION INS CO	MA	**B+**	304.8	108.4	149.5	1.4	9.5	8.1	3.5	6.6	5.0	T
CITATION INS CO	CA	**U** (1)	26.5	15.2	0.0	-3.8	N/A	4.8	2.1	9.4	3.3	FRT
CITIES & VILLAGES MUTUAL INS CO	WI	**D**	39.2	21.0	10.5	-0.6	8.6	8.5	3.6	6.8	2.1	DGT
CITIZENS INS CO INC	KY	**U** (1)	2.8	2.7	0.0	0.1	N/A	3.6	6.2	7.0	4.8	RT

RISK ADJ. RATIO #1	CAPITAL RATIO #2	PREMIUM TO SURPLUS (%)	RESV. TO SURPLUS (%)	RESV. DEVELOP. 1 YEAR (%)	RESV. DEVELOP. 2 YEAR (%)	LOSS RATIO (%)	EXP. RATIO (%)	COMB RATIO (%)	CASH FROM UNDER-WRITING (%)	NET PREMIUM GROWTH (%)	INVEST. IN AFFIL (%)	INSURANCE COMPANY NAME
2.2	1.4	132.7	54.5	-6.5	-10.6	64.3	34.2	98.5	103.0	-0.6	0.0	CELINA MUTUAL INS CO
0.8	0.6	115.0	38.0	-0.9	3.9	66.8	47.2	114.0	95.0	3.9	0.0	CEM INS CO
7.9	4.6	8.6	8.6	-5.8	-4.7	59.9	26.3	86.2	171.4	33.7	0.0	CENSTAT CASUALTY CO
2.8	1.6	18.6	4.2	-0.4	-0.9	72.4	22.8	95.2	92.0	-3.8	0.0	CENTENNIAL CASUALTY CO
0.1	0.1	1.2	659.6	2.2	28.3	-17.2	999 +	999 +	-11.7	-97.8	2.9	CENTENNIAL INS CO
3.1	2.3	119.2	48.8	-6.8	-10.6	65.1	28.3	93.4	110.5	-7.5	0.0	CENTER MUTUAL INS CO
17.8	16.1	7.1	0.1	N/A	N/A	62.8	66.2	129.0	77.1	5.1	0.0	CENTER VALLEY MUTUAL FIRE INS CO
2.9	2.2	101.4	38.0	-8.3	-13.8	49.2	36.7	85.9	120.4	-0.1	0.0	CENTRAL CO-OPERATIVE INS CO
2.6	1.9	95.3	96.4	2.4	-1.6	79.4	31.5	110.9	102.1	-1.9	10.4 •	CENTRAL MUTUAL INS CO
1.0	0.5	N/A	148.7	-8.3	-10.4	999 +	N/A	N/A	N/A	0.0	0.0	CENTRAL NATIONAL INS CO OF OMAHA
0.9	0.6	140.6	194.9	-18.3	-18.3	52.1	24.1	76.2	110.5	12.2	0.0	CENTRAL PA PHYSICIANS RRG INC
4.0	2.5	25.2	5.8	-2.1	-2.9	15.8	80.7	96.5	99.7	-5.9	7.2 •	CENTRAL STATES INDEMNITY CO OF
3.8	2.5	35.1	29.0	-0.1	-29.3	62.9	35.4	98.3	95.2	8.8	0.0	CENTRE COUNTY MUTUAL FIRE INS CO
1.8	1.0	N/A	72.9	-2.3	-6.0	-798.8	999 +	999 +	72.4	-95.1	0.0	CENTRE INS CO
74.1	42.1	10.0	0.7	0.1	-0.2	11.5	8.9	20.4	519.7	26.7	0.0 •	CENTURION CASUALTY CO
2.0	1.3	88.4	96.5	-52.3	-55.8	51.3	20.4	71.7	184.2	34.1	0.0	CENTURION MEDICAL LIAB PROTECT
5.1	3.3	24.4	36.4	-3.4	-13.9	62.1	41.8	103.9	50.2	20.8	0.0	CENTURY CASUALTY CO
N/A	N/A	N/A	999 +	734.5	824.7	999 +	999 +	999 +	N/A	-97.1	12.5	CENTURY INDEMNITY CO
N/A	N/A	N/A	9.5	0.9	3.8	N/A	N/A	N/A	N/A	0.0	0.0	CENTURY REINSURANCE CO
0.8	0.5	141.3	185.7	-5.2	-3.7	64.7	36.7	101.4	102.5	-5.3	7.1	CENTURY SURETY CO
2.2	1.5	63.7	60.9	-17.1	-35.8	42.0	34.9	76.9	91.1	-12.1	0.0 •	CENTURY-NATIONAL INS CO
3.3	2.3	47.8	15.6	-11.1	0.5	11.5	46.3	57.8	167.7	-9.7	0.0	CHARITABLE SERVICE PROVIDERS RRG
13.9	12.5	N/A	N/A	N/A	N/A	N/A	N/A	N/A	75.0	0.0	0.0	CHARTER INDEMNITY CO
2.1	1.3	103.8	212.5	-7.7	-11.0	61.5	30.7	92.2	104.1	0.7	0.0 •	CHARTER OAK FIRE INS CO
1.5	1.0	69.1	101.8	-13.0	-13.6	51.9	28.5	80.4	452.5	0.0	0.0	CHATTAHOCHEE RRG CAPTIVE INS CO
2.5	1.9	76.6	36.9	-7.4	0.2	55.2	36.7	91.9	117.1	-3.6	0.0	CHAUTAUQUA PATRONS INS CO
0.1	0.1	116.8	116.6	57.1	70.4	128.7	5.6	134.3	74.2	3.3	0.0	CHC CASUALTY RRG
2.1	1.3	185.0	158.8	-9.4	1.9	73.2	9.3	82.5	106.6	-14.4	0.0	CHEROKEE INS CO
3.4	2.4	24.6	11.7	2.7	1.0	71.9	37.8	109.7	96.2	5.4	0.0	CHERRY VALLEY COOPERATIVE INS CO
3.4	2.3	49.6	66.0	1.8	2.8	75.0	27.7	102.7	109.7	3.0	0.0	CHICAGO INS CO
3.1	2.0	115.8	58.2	-17.4	-11.4	59.4	20.3	79.7	115.0	5.7	1.6	CHRYSLER INS CO
3.4	2.3	42.0	79.3	-2.2	-5.8	63.5	28.9	92.4	98.4	-2.1	0.0	CHUBB CUSTOM INS CO
3.4	2.1	61.0	109.8	-4.3	-9.3	61.3	28.7	90.0	86.7	-2.6	0.0	CHUBB INDEMNITY INS CO
9.4	8.5	N/A	N/A	N/A	N/A	N/A	N/A	N/A	N/A	0.0	0.0	CHUBB INS CO OF NEW JERSEY
1.2	1.0	N/A	N/A	N/A	N/A	N/A	N/A	N/A	N/A	0.0	0.0	CHUBB LLOYDS INS CO OF TX
3.5	2.1	61.1	110.1	-4.2	-9.3	61.3	28.7	90.0	112.3	-2.6	0.0	CHUBB NATIONAL INS CO
2.9	1.8	-3.3	110.0	2.2	-8.3	406.0	77.8	483.8	-4.2	-110.8	0.0	CHURCH INS CO
2.2	1.8	133.8	124.6	-12.6	-18.0	83.2	20.9	104.1	96.8	-1.3	0.0 •	CHURCH MUTUAL INS CO
16.3	13.9	-0.3	-16.5	126.0	N/A	999 +	475.4	999 +	9.2	-20.9	0.0	CIFG ASR NORTH AMERICA INC
22.3	20.1	N/A	N/A	N/A	N/A	N/A	N/A	N/A	30.8	0.0	0.0	CIM INS CORP
0.7	0.5	111.7	82.3	-17.8	-0.6	33.9	60.6	94.5	137.6	88.0	0.0	CIMARRON INS EXCH RRG
19.1	10.7	N/A	N/A	N/A	N/A	N/A	N/A	N/A	10.0	0.0	0.0 •	CINCINNATI CASUALTY CO
N/A	N/A	-1.0	14.1	-4.3	-5.7	77.6	-477.6	-400.0	4.8	-352.2	0.0	CINCINNATI EQUITABLE INS CO
16.4	10.8	N/A	N/A	N/A	N/A	N/A	N/A	N/A	229.1	0.0	0.0 •	CINCINNATI INDEMNITY CO
2.3	1.7	89.2	104.0	-6.7	-9.2	68.2	31.5	99.7	103.0	-3.9	11.0 •	CINCINNATI INS CO
9.8	5.5	7.9	2.6	N/A	N/A	109.5	81.1	190.6	127.8	0.0	0.0 •	CINCINNATI SPECIALTY UNDERWRITER
1.0	0.9	N/A	N/A	N/A	N/A	N/A	N/A	N/A	N/A	0.0	0.0	CIRCLE STAR INS CO RRG
N/A	N/A	N/A	N/A	N/A	-0.5	N/A	N/A	N/A	N/A	0.0	0.0	CITADEL INS CO
3.4	2.8	130.2	64.1	-3.9	-4.2	68.0	28.7	96.7	97.5	-4.0	0.0 •	CITATION INS CO
N/A	N/A	N/A	52.9	-0.7	-6.5	N/A	N/A	N/A	N/A	-100.0	18.4	CITATION INS CO
3.0	1.9	49.4	51.1	-3.2	-9.2	61.6	18.2	79.8	132.9	7.8	0.0	CITIES & VILLAGES MUTUAL INS CO
N/A	N/A	N/A	N/A	N/A	N/A	N/A	N/A	N/A	N/A	0.0	0.0	CITIZENS INS CO INC

999 + Denotes number greater than 999.9%
999 - Denotes number less than -999.99%
• Bullets denote a more detailed analysis is available in Section II.

INSURANCE COMPANY NAME	DOM. STATE	RATING	TOTAL ASSETS ($MIL)	CAPITAL & SURPLUS ($MIL)	ANNUAL NET PREMIUM ($MIL)	NET INCOME ($MIL)	CAPITAL-IZATION INDEX (PTS)	RESERVE ADQ INDEX (PTS)	PROFIT-ABILITY INDEX (PTS)	LIQUIDITY INDEX (PTS)	STAB. INDEX (PTS)	STABILITY FACTORS
CITIZENS INS CO OF AMERICA	MI	**B**	1,489.6	643.1	692.3	0.9	10.0	9.3	3.8	6.5	5.2	T
CITIZENS INS CO OF ILLINOIS	IL	**C+**	4.4	4.4	0.0	0.0	10.0	N/A	7.6	7.0	3.5	DG
CITIZENS INS CO OF OH	OH	**C**	12.4	12.4	0.0	0.1	10.0	N/A	7.8	7.0	4.1	DG
CITIZENS INS CO OF THE MIDWEST	IN	**C**	23.1	23.1	0.0	0.2	10.0	N/A	7.8	7.0	3.6	DGT
CITIZENS PROPERTY INS CORP	FL	**U** (1)	8,209.6	3,170.8	1,856.7	792.8	N/A	6.0	0.3	9.1	1.5	T
CITIZENS UNITED RECIP EXCH	NJ	**D**	78.1	18.5	37.1	-0.4	2.8	3.5	1.7	4.1	1.4	CDFL
CIVIC PROPERTY & CASUALTY CO INC	CA	**C**	218.2	72.6	117.9	0.6	7.9	4.7	7.2	6.4	3.4	T
CIVIL SERVICE EMPLOYEES INS CO	CA	**C**	181.6	98.9	69.3	3.5	8.1	7.0	8.6	6.8	4.2	T
CLAIM PROFESSIONALS LIAB INS CO RRG	VT	**D-**	3.0	1.4	0.6	-0.1	7.1	4.7	2.8	9.0	1.0	DGT
CLAREMONT LIABILITY INS CO	CA	**U** (1)	22.0	14.7	0.0	0.9	N/A	9.3	5.3	9.1	3.4	FRT
CLARENDON AMERICA INS CO	NJ	**C-**	231.5	132.7	-2.7	-0.4	6.7	2.6	1.7	7.0	2.9	T
▼CLARENDON NATIONAL INS CO	NJ	**C-**	748.2	318.8	-8.3	-23.1	5.4	5.5	1.3	7.0	2.9	FT
CLARENDON SELECT INS CO	FL	**U** (1)	17.2	14.7	0.0	-0.5	N/A	N/A	1.8	9.7	3.0	T
CLARIAN HEALTH RRG INC	SC	**E**	3.8	0.9	3.0	0.1	0.5	N/A	6.6	7.1	0.0	CDFG
CLEARFIELD CTY GRNGE MUT FIRE INS CO	PA	**C-** (1)	3.1	2.8	0.4	0.3	10.0	7.7	5.3	9.4	1.9	DT
CLEARWATER INS CO	DE	**D**	1,242.4	637.1	40.5	5.0	2.9	1.5	3.7	6.7	2.1	AFT
CLEARWATER SELECT INS CO	DE	**D-**	103.3	92.4	1.0	1.3	10.0	5.8	6.4	10.0	1.0	FT
CLERMONT INS CO	IA	**C**	24.8	23.8	0.0	0.1	10.0	N/A	6.9	10.0	3.6	DGT
CLINIC MUTUAL INS CO RRG	HI	**U** (1)	4.7	4.3	0.1	-0.3	N/A	3.7	3.1	10.0	3.3	FGRT
CLINICAL TRIALS RECIP INS CO RRG	AZ	**E+**	2.3	2.1	0.1	0.0	10.0	4.6	3.4	8.2	0.7	DGRT
CLOISTER MUTUAL CASUALTY INS CO	PA	**U** (1)	4.3	4.3	0.1	0.1	N/A	7.3	6.6	10.0	3.2	
▲CLUB INS CO	OH	**C+**	13.7	11.2	2.7	0.2	10.0	7.8	8.5	7.6	4.3	GT
CMG MORTGAGE ASR CO	WI	**B**	9.3	7.5	0.5	-0.2	10.0	5.8	2.8	9.7	4.4	DGT
▲CMG MORTGAGE INS CO	WI	**B-**	399.8	68.6	81.9	-18.1	8.1	6.0	2.9	7.4	5.1	T
CMG MORTGAGE REINS CO	WI	**D+**	38.6	2.5	12.6	-3.4	2.8	4.5	2.1	7.4	2.4	CDGT
CMI LLOYDS	TX	**B**	12.9	12.5	0.0	0.1	10.0	N/A	8.4	10.0	4.5	DGT
CNL/INS AMERICA INC	GA	**C**	29.0	19.7	14.1	0.2	8.0	5.3	4.9	6.9	4.1	DGRT
CO-OPERATIVE INS COMPANIES	VT	**B-**	81.3	38.8	45.7	0.4	8.5	8.7	7.2	6.3	5.0	T
COAST NATIONAL INS CO	CA	**D+**	559.1	360.8	2.6	2.7	10.0	4.5	8.9	7.6	2.6	FT
COASTAL CASUALTY INS CO	NC	**C-**	3.8	3.4	0.6	-0.1	10.0	4.8	1.7	7.2	2.4	DFGT
COASTAL INS RRG INC	AL	**D-**	49.4	10.7	6.5	-0.2	6.9	7.0	3.9	7.8	1.0	DGRT
COFACE NORTH AMERICA INS CO	MA	**C**	103.9	48.1	38.1	-1.2	7.3	6.0	3.7	8.0	4.0	RT
COLISEUM REINS CO	DE	**C**	430.9	248.5	-1.2	0.3	7.7	4.9	2.7	9.0	3.4	FRT
COLLEGE LIAB INS CO LTD RRG	HI	**D**	9.3	6.4	2.0	0.5	8.1	7.1	3.9	8.6	2.3	DGT
COLOGNE REINSURANCE CO OF AMERICA	CT	**C**	109.0	39.8	-0.3	0.0	5.1	0.3	3.1	10.0	3.9	CFRT
COLONIAL AMERICAN CAS & SURETY CO	MD	**C+**	25.9	23.3	0.0	0.3	10.0	N/A	6.6	7.0	4.6	DFGT
COLONIAL COOPERATIVE INS CO	NY	**E**	6.9	0.5	1.3	-0.4	2.3	6.0	0.5	2.8	0.2	DFGL
COLONIAL COUNTY MUTUAL INS CO	TX	**B**	69.9	4.9	0.0	0.0	3.4	N/A	3.9	0.0	4.5	CDFG
COLONIAL INDEMNITY INS CO	NY	**F** (5)	0.0	0.0	0.0	0.0	9.4	6.0	1.4	10.0	0.0	FT
COLONIAL LLOYDS	TX	**D**	29.6	20.5	12.5	0.0	7.9	7.0	5.5	6.6	2.0	DFGT
COLONIAL MORTGAGE INS CO	TX	**D+**	9.6	4.5	1.9	0.0	9.7	4.6	8.7	9.4	2.8	DGT
COLONIAL SURETY CO	PA	**D+**	34.5	14.0	9.2	1.4	7.1	6.0	8.8	8.9	2.5	DGT
COLONY INS CO	VA	**C**	1,390.5	394.1	150.0	-6.8	7.4	5.9	6.4	7.1	3.3	T
COLONY NATIONAL INS CO	VA	**C**	328.1	116.2	81.8	15.1	7.1	6.0	9.0	7.3	3.3	T
COLONY SPECIALTY INS CO	OH	**C-**	198.5	65.4	40.9	7.9	7.1	6.0	9.0	7.5	3.0	T
COLORADO CASUALTY INS CO	CO	**C+**	21.9	19.7	0.0	0.1	10.0	N/A	8.9	7.0	4.4	ADG
COLORADO FARM BUREAU MUTUAL INS CO	CO	**C+**	89.0	49.1	18.8	0.3	9.7	7.0	8.6	6.8	4.4	FT
COLUMBIA CASUALTY CO	IL	**C**	274.7	274.4	0.0	0.6	10.0	N/A	7.8	9.2	3.5	AT
COLUMBIA FEDERAL INS CO	DC	**D**	3.2	1.5	1.0	0.0	7.9	9.6	6.6	9.2	1.4	DFGT
▼COLUMBIA INS CO	NE	**C+**	8,967.5	6,038.8	486.5	114.7	7.2	4.3	3.8	7.7	4.5	T
▲COLUMBIA LLOYDS INS CO	TX	**C+**	32.1	24.6	5.5	-0.1	8.9	7.9	7.2	8.1	4.5	DFGT
COLUMBIA MUTUAL INS CO	MO	**B**	343.2	142.1	146.8	0.6	8.0	6.9	3.7	6.1	4.7	FT

See Page 27 for explanation of footnotes and Page 28 for explanation of stability factors.

Arrows denote recent upgrades ▲ or downgrades ▼ (see Section VII for explanations)

RISK ADJ. RATIO #1	CAPITAL RATIO #2	PREMIUM TO SURPLUS (%)	RESV. TO SURPLUS (%)	RESV. DEVELOP. 1 YEAR (%)	RESV. DEVELOP. 2 YEAR (%)	LOSS RATIO (%)	EXP. RATIO (%)	COMB RATIO (%)	CASH FROM UNDER-WRITING (%)	NET PREMIUM GROWTH (%)	INVEST. IN AFFIL (%)	INSURANCE COMPANY NAME
5.0	3.5	108.5	80.5	-7.1	-16.1	64.5	28.2	92.7	96.9	-1.1	0.2 •	CITIZENS INS CO OF AMERICA
999 +	999 +	N/A	N/A	N/A	N/A	N/A	N/A	N/A	N/A	0.0	0.0	CITIZENS INS CO OF ILLINOIS
86.0	41.0	N/A	N/A	N/A	N/A	N/A	N/A	N/A	N/A	0.0	0.0	CITIZENS INS CO OF OH
68.7	30.5	N/A	N/A	N/A	N/A	N/A	N/A	N/A	N/A	0.0	0.0	CITIZENS INS CO OF THE MIDWEST
N/A	N/A	58.6	27.2	3.8	20.9	41.3	22.3	63.6	144.9	-37.3	0.0	CITIZENS PROPERTY INS CORP
0.6	0.5	207.5	207.2	-0.6	7.6	79.8	33.3	113.1	89.4	-11.0	0.0	CITIZENS UNITED RECIP EXCH
2.6	1.7	160.0	105.0	-5.4	-6.9	74.8	30.6	105.4	103.4	-8.0	0.0	CIVIC PROPERTY & CASUALTY CO INC
2.4	2.0	73.3	44.5	-11.7	-21.5	56.1	39.0	95.1	101.7	1.3	19.3	CIVIL SERVICE EMPLOYEES INS CO
1.6	1.0	41.3	59.5	-1.9	-3.3	80.4	65.5	145.9	92.0	-27.8	0.0	CLAIM PROFESSIONALS LIAB INS CO
N/A	N/A	0.1	41.8	-12.1	-23.1	999 +	968.8	999 +	0.5	-90.1	0.0	CLAREMONT LIABILITY INS CO
1.4	1.0	-2.0	42.6	-1.2	17.9	-69.0	-45.0	-114.0	5.1	-93.2	0.0	CLARENDON AMERICA INS CO
1.2	0.7	-2.4	90.4	0.3	4.3	-186.2	-669.3	-855.5	20.3	74.7	26.5 •	CLARENDON NATIONAL INS CO
N/A	N/A	N/A	N/A	N/A	N/A	N/A	N/A	N/A	999 +	0.0	0.0	CLARENDON SELECT INS CO
0.3	0.1	354.6	N/A	N/A	N/A	N/A	90.1	90.1	80.7	-3.4	0.0	CLARIAN HEALTH RRG INC
11.8	7.9	14.5	2.1	1.4	-3.7	13.8	34.2	48.0	318.6	-7.4	0.0	CLEARFIELD CTY GRNGE MUT FIRE INS
0.8	0.5	6.4	87.4	7.2	21.8	276.1	15.9	292.0	26.0	-11.3	36.8 •	CLEARWATER INS CO
22.0	9.2	1.0	11.5	-1.4	-3.2	-121.0	33.4	-87.6	9.8	628.3	0.0	CLEARWATER SELECT INS CO
50.4	45.3	N/A	N/A	N/A	N/A	N/A	N/A	N/A	-4.0	0.0	0.0	CLERMONT INS CO
N/A	N/A	1.6	6.6	N/A	N/A	0.4	173.5	173.9	35.8	13.3	0.0	CLINIC MUTUAL INS CO RRG
7.6	6.7	2.7	5.4	N/A	0.1	65.7	270.2	335.9	77.1	-24.0	0.0	CLINICAL TRIALS RECIP INS CO RRG
N/A	N/A	1.5	0.3	-0.3	-0.4	4.7	52.4	57.1	146.5	-19.2	0.0	CLOISTER MUTUAL CASUALTY INS CO
7.9	4.8	23.0	5.2	-1.1	-2.1	34.8	35.3	70.1	148.2	4.7	0.0	CLUB INS CO
10.7	8.1	6.3	7.1	-3.1	2.3	52.1	29.6	81.7	71.6	-32.1	0.0	CMG MORTGAGE ASR CO
1.6	1.1	94.7	72.2	11.8	2.5	75.7	23.5	99.2	196.8	19.4	0.0	CMG MORTGAGE INS CO
0.2	0.1	199.1	165.7	24.9	10.6	85.2	24.3	109.5	199.1	22.5	0.0	CMG MORTGAGE REINS CO
74.0	42.0	N/A	N/A	N/A	N/A	N/A	N/A	N/A	N/A	0.0	0.0	CMI LLOYDS
2.6	2.1	72.2	6.2	-0.8	-2.1	34.7	60.3	95.0	105.6	4.2	0.0	CNL/INS AMERICA INC
2.7	1.9	113.1	37.0	-2.5	-8.1	61.7	31.0	92.7	111.2	1.9	1.9	CO-OPERATIVE INS COMPANIES
8.1	7.3	0.7	2.6	0.6	0.8	75.6	-29.9	45.7	65.5	101.5	10.9 •	COAST NATIONAL INS CO
19.5	14.0	18.6	6.1	-15.3	-7.1	54.4	33.4	87.8	68.9	-91.5	0.0	COASTAL CASUALTY INS CO
1.2	0.9	58.5	197.2	-33.0	-42.8	59.5	39.3	98.8	161.2	-8.5	0.0	COASTAL INS RRG INC
1.9	1.4	77.4	31.3	-6.0	-20.7	57.9	52.1	110.0	98.5	12.7	0.0	COFACE NORTH AMERICA INS CO
1.7	1.1	-0.3	38.4	-1.3	-2.6	999 +	999 +	373.2	36.7	-105.6	-5.3 •	COLISEUM REINS CO
3.9	2.4	31.0	41.4	-7.4	-19.3	54.5	26.0	80.5	124.8	22.8	0.0	COLLEGE LIAB INS CO LTD RRG
1.2	0.5	-0.8	174.9	5.2	148.2	-833.4	-107.9	-941.3	0.4	N/A	0.0	COLOGNE REINSURANCE CO OF
25.8	23.2	N/A	N/A	N/A	N/A	N/A	N/A	N/A	182.7	0.0	0.0	COLONIAL AMERICAN CAS & SURETY CO
0.2	0.1	136.3	157.7	20.3	7.9	126.0	-1.0	125.0	28.5	21.1	0.0	COLONIAL COOPERATIVE INS CO
0.6	0.5	N/A	N/A	N/A	N/A	N/A	N/A	N/A	22.0	0.0	0.0	COLONIAL COUNTY MUTUAL INS CO
6.2	5.6	N/A	26.2	-18.7	-28.1	999 +	999 +	999 +	-0.3	-83.3	0.0	COLONIAL INDEMNITY INS CO
1.8	1.2	60.8	9.1	-1.1	-1.3	58.2	53.2	111.4	83.0	76.4	0.0	COLONIAL LLOYDS
2.9	2.6	42.1	34.1	N/A	N/A	85.0	5.7	90.7	999 +	11.9	0.0	COLONIAL MORTGAGE INS CO
1.8	1.2	72.7	97.7	-19.2	-29.1	38.3	35.2	73.5	228.9	7.3	0.0	COLONIAL SURETY CO
1.6	1.0	39.2	97.2	-6.3	-11.5	51.9	36.0	87.9	100.8	-38.2	18.7 •	COLONY INS CO
9.8	6.7	75.4	188.5	-11.1	-23.0	54.9	33.2	88.1	111.1	-38.2	0.0	COLONY NATIONAL INS CO
7.2	6.2	64.7	162.0	-10.3	-21.7	55.4	32.8	88.2	115.1	-38.2	0.0	COLONY SPECIALTY INS CO
25.2	22.7	N/A	N/A	N/A	N/A	N/A	N/A	N/A	N/A	0.0	0.0	COLORADO CASUALTY INS CO
5.3	3.2	37.8	39.9	-10.1	-22.0	69.4	30.2	99.6	72.2	-8.3	1.0	COLORADO FARM BUREAU MUTUAL INS
232.4	116.2	N/A	N/A	N/A	N/A	N/A	N/A	N/A	N/A	0.0	0.0 •	COLUMBIA CASUALTY CO
2.6	2.3	66.1	90.4	-13.6	-22.8	74.3	22.2	96.5	93.3	-2.5	0.0	COLUMBIA FEDERAL INS CO
1.3	0.9	6.6	32.3	-1.4	-2.3	48.9	20.9	69.8	100.3	-12.9	12.1 •	COLUMBIA INS CO
3.3	2.4	24.6	3.8	-1.9	-3.6	81.5	-35.0	46.5	46.6	-4.9	14.7	COLUMBIA LLOYDS INS CO
1.8	1.5	100.3	55.0	-1.0	-4.5	84.7	27.7	112.4	89.9	1.2	26.3	COLUMBIA MUTUAL INS CO

999 + Denotes number greater than 999.9%
999 - Denotes number less than -999.99%
• Bullets denote a more detailed analysis is available in Section II.

INSURANCE COMPANY NAME	DOM. STATE	RATING	TOTAL ASSETS ($MIL)	CAPITAL & SURPLUS ($MIL)	ANNUAL NET PREMIUM ($MIL)	NET INCOME ($MIL)	CAPITAL-IZATION INDEX (PTS)	RESERVE ADQ INDEX (PTS)	PROFIT-ABILITY INDEX (PTS)	LIQUIDITY INDEX (PTS)	STAB. INDEX (PTS)	STABILITY FACTORS
COLUMBIA NATIONAL INS CO	NE	**C+**	84.7	31.4	44.4	1.2	8.3	6.9	4.7	5.9	4.5	FT
COLUMBIA NATIONAL RRG INC	VT	**D**	3.6	2.7	0.2	0.0	10.0	N/A	8.7	10.0	0.0	DG
COMBINED BENEFITS INS CO	MT	**U** (5)	0.0	0.9	0.3	0.0	N/A	5.3	1.6	7.1	2.0	DFGR
▼COMCARE PRO INS RECIPROCAL RRG	VT	**D-**	2.3	1.1	0.8	-0.2	1.5	4.7	1.4	7.5	0.6	CDFG
COMMERCE & INDUSTRY INS CO	NY	**C+**	8,533.0	2,610.1	2,023.3	31.9	7.1	2.0	6.7	6.2	4.4	T
COMMERCE INS CO	MA	**B+**	2,513.5	931.3	1,279.8	27.4	9.4	8.2	3.5	5.9	5.0	T
COMMERCE PROTECTIVE INS CO	PA	**D**	5.6	2.1	3.2	-0.1	6.3	7.0	2.7	7.5	1.8	DFGT
COMMERCE WEST INS CO	CA	**B-**	164.3	61.1	63.8	0.8	10.0	8.2	5.9	6.8	4.8	FT
COMMERCIAL ALLIANCE INS CO	TX	**C**	25.1	12.1	16.0	0.2	7.0	6.9	8.4	7.0	3.3	DGT
COMMERCIAL CASUALTY INS CO	CA	**U** (1)	182.2	66.6	0.0	2.6	N/A	2.9	3.8	9.5	4.4	FT
COMMERCIAL GUARANTY INS CO	DE	**U** (1)	34.9	34.3	0.0	1.1	N/A	3.7	8.0	7.0	5.6	T
COMMERCIAL LOAN INS CORP	WI	**U** (1)	12.1	11.6	0.0	0.6	N/A	N/A	8.3	10.0	5.4	T
COMMERCIAL MUT INS CO	GA	**F** (5)	0.0	1.9	7.9	0.0	0.0	2.3	0.1	0.0	0.0	CDFL
COMMERCIAL MUTUAL INS CO	NY	**C-**	22.3	7.7	10.4	0.0	2.7	2.7	6.9	6.7	2.7	CDGO
COMMERCIAL RISK RE-INSURANCE CO	VT	**U** (1)	36.9	21.3	0.0	-2.6	N/A	1.9	1.3	9.6	2.5	FRT
COMMONWEALTH INS CO	PA	**E+**	1.7	0.4	1.3	0.0	1.2	6.1	7.1	7.4	0.7	CDFG
COMMONWEALTH INS CO OF AMERICA	WA	**D+**	54.7	25.2	13.7	-0.2	2.7	4.9	4.2	8.2	2.7	CDRT
COMMONWEALTH MORTGAGE ASR CO OF	TX	**C**	573.8	183.2	86.7	-11.0	6.3	4.5	2.1	6.5	4.2	GT
COMMONWEALTH MUTUAL INS CO	MA	**D**	6.3	5.5	0.0	0.0	10.0	N/A	3.9	7.0	2.3	DG
COMMONWEALTH MUTUAL INS CO	MD	**E+**	1.1	0.2	2.1	-0.1	0.6	6.5	0.5	0.1	0.7	CDFG
COMMONWEALTH REINS CO	MA	**C-**	34.8	13.8	18.7	0.0	8.3	9.3	6.6	5.8	3.3	DGT
COMMUNITIES OF FAITH RRG INC	SC	**D**	9.6	6.7	2.0	0.1	8.3	7.1	7.1	9.1	1.5	DGT
COMMUNITY BLOOD CENTERS EXCHANGE	IN	**C-**	19.7	8.7	3.7	0.2	8.7	9.6	8.7	9.1	2.8	DGT
COMMUNITY HEALTH ALLIANCE RECIP RRG	VT	**D**	104.8	14.5	13.9	1.2	6.5	7.1	4.8	8.2	0.0	DRT
COMMUNITY HOSPITAL ALTERNATIVE RRG	VT	**D**	156.2	43.6	27.9	-0.4	8.0	9.6	7.5	7.2	0.6	DRT
COMMUNITY INS CORP	WI	**C**	19.9	6.1	5.0	-0.4	5.1	3.8	3.3	6.7	3.5	CDFG
COMMUNITY MUTUAL INS CO	NY	**D**	4.1	1.2	2.2	0.0	2.9	6.8	2.2	7.3	1.1	DGT
COMP OPTIONS INS CO INC	FL	**B-**	60.0	26.1	15.1	0.8	7.9	9.5	9.0	6.8	5.0	T
COMPANION COMMERCIAL INS CO	SC	**B**	13.3	8.7	0.0	0.1	10.0	N/A	7.5	6.9	4.5	DG
COMPANION INC	VI	**D** (5)	11.6	0.0	2.0	0.0	5.3	4.0	7.5	9.5	1.4	DGT
COMPANION PROPERTY & CASUALTY INS	SC	**B**	536.7	196.1	152.3	2.9	8.2	5.7	7.4	7.5	5.9	T
COMPASS INS CO	NY	**U** (1)	13.2	11.6	0.0	0.6	N/A	3.6	4.8	10.0	4.4	RT
COMPUTER INS CO	RI	**C**	44.2	42.1	5.5	0.5	10.0	7.4	8.9	10.0	4.2	DGT
COMPWEST INS CO	CA	**D**	227.8	87.8	6.6	1.6	8.1	6.0	7.5	6.2	1.5	T
CONCORD GENERAL MUTUAL INS CO	NH	**C+**	306.4	139.3	166.7	-5.0	8.0	9.3	3.7	6.7	4.5	RT
CONEMAUGH VALLEY MUTUAL INS CO	PA	**D**	4.0	2.0	1.0	0.1	8.4	4.1	5.9	8.0	1.7	DGOT
CONNECTICUT MEDICAL INS CO	CT	**C+**	404.2	138.6	37.4	6.3	8.1	9.8	8.1	8.2	4.8	RT
CONNIE LEE INS CO	WI	**U** (1)	184.2	157.0	1.4	11.2	N/A	3.0	4.7	7.0	0.6	
CONSOLIDATED INS ASN	TX	**D+**	14.2	3.4	8.2	0.0	2.2	7.9	3.9	6.6	2.6	CGT
CONSOLIDATED INS CO	IN	**C+**	24.4	22.4	0.0	0.2	10.0	N/A	3.1	7.0	4.6	DGT
CONSOLIDATED LLOYDS	TX	**D+**	2.3	1.5	0.6	0.0	7.6	7.9	2.5	8.0	2.0	DFGT
CONSORTIUM (A RRG)	VT	**U** (1)	16.4	8.5	0.1	0.5	N/A	4.4	7.8	7.7	3.3	CFT
CONSTELLATION REINSURANCE CO	NY	**U**	17.4	0.0	0.0	0.0	N/A	0.0	0.0	0.0	0.0	
CONSTITUTION INS CO	NY	**U** (1)	42.7	12.2	0.0	0.4	N/A	4.8	1.9	7.0	3.1	T
▼CONSTITUTIONAL CASUALTY CO	IL	**D-**	18.3	3.4	13.0	0.1	1.2	2.6	0.7	7.0	0.0	CDFG
▼CONSUMER FIRST INS CO	NJ	**F** (2)	10.7	2.5	5.2	-0.8	1.7	5.0	1.3	1.2	0.0	CDFG
CONSUMERS COUNTY MUTUAL INS CO	TX	**D**	117.7	2.2	0.0	0.0	0.8	N/A	3.9	0.6	2.1	CDLT
CONSUMERS INS USA INC	TN	**C**	60.6	25.7	42.1	1.0	7.6	5.3	6.8	6.6	4.1	T
CONSUMERS SPECIALTIES INS CO RRG	VT	**D**	6.9	3.4	1.0	0.0	7.3	9.3	2.8	8.3	0.9	DGT
CONTINENTAL CASUALTY CO	IL	**C**	38,541.1	7,750.5	6,135.3	-269.7	7.0	3.1	5.2	6.9	3.9	AT
CONTINENTAL DIVIDE INS CO	CO	**B**	9.3	7.2	0.0	-0.2	10.0	N/A	4.1	10.0	4.9	DFG
CONTINENTAL HERITAGE INS CO	FL	**C**	7.7	6.0	1.4	0.0	10.0	7.3	3.8	9.1	3.0	DGT

See Page 27 for explanation of footnotes and Page 28 for explanation of stability factors.

Arrows denote recent upgrades ▲ or downgrades ▼ (see Section VII for explanations)

RISK ADJ. CAPITAL RATIO #1	RATIO #2	PREMIUM TO SURPLUS (%)	RESV. TO SURPLUS (%)	RESV. DEVELOP. 1 YEAR (%)	2 YEAR (%)	LOSS RATIO (%)	EXP. RATIO (%)	COMB RATIO (%)	CASH FROM UNDER-WRITING (%)	NET PREMIUM GROWTH (%)	INVEST. IN AFFIL (%)	INSURANCE COMPANY NAME
2.6	1.7	137.8	75.6	-1.4	-6.3	84.7	25.9	110.6	93.7	1.2	0.0	COLUMBIA NATIONAL INS CO
6.0	5.4	7.9	N/A	N/A	N/A	N/A	68.1	68.1	173.0	-28.1	0.0	COLUMBIA NATIONAL RRG INC
N/A	N/A	29.1	47.6	6.3	-1.0	151.7	-55.8	95.9	21.9	-52.6	0.0	COMBINED BENEFITS INS CO
0.3	0.2	60.4	52.4	13.4	-5.1	177.8	44.8	222.6	69.7	63.3	0.0	COMCARE PRO INS RECIPROCAL RRG
1.7	1.2	75.6	150.2	-0.2	0.7	78.6	24.6	103.2	108.5	-1.1	8.1 •	COMMERCE & INDUSTRY INS CO
3.3	2.7	130.9	64.5	-3.9	-4.1	68.0	26.3	94.3	96.5	-5.7	6.3 •	COMMERCE INS CO
1.2	0.9	144.8	96.0	-13.8	-12.3	51.7	56.1	107.8	81.4	-10.9	0.0	COMMERCE PROTECTIVE INS CO
4.3	3.6	101.1	49.8	-3.3	-4.2	68.0	24.9	92.9	93.4	-9.9	0.0	COMMERCE WEST INS CO
1.1	1.0	134.3	38.6	-17.6	-27.5	18.7	67.4	86.1	204.2	33.5	0.0	COMMERCIAL ALLIANCE INS CO
N/A	N/A	N/A	178.3	9.3	-4.3	999 +	999 +	999 +	0.6	101.5	0.0	COMMERCIAL CASUALTY INS CO
N/A	N/A	N/A	N/A	N/A	N/A	N/A	N/A	N/A	N/A	0.0	0.0	COMMERCIAL GUARANTY INS CO
N/A	N/A	0.3	N/A	N/A	N/A	N/A	137.1	137.1	74.5	-32.7	0.0	COMMERCIAL LOAN INS CORP
0.0	0.0	544.6	674.2	9.5	40.7	76.4	80.1	156.5	91.3	-17.7	0.0	COMMERCIAL MUT INS CO
0.6	0.5	133.6	75.2	8.2	17.8	58.9	16.0	74.9	179.1	24.1	5.5	COMMERCIAL MUTUAL INS CO
N/A	N/A	0.1	111.1	-25.0	-5.2	999 +	999 +	999 +	N/A	103.9	0.0	COMMERCIAL RISK RE-INSURANCE CO
0.2	0.2	324.3	7.2	-3.5	-6.9	-4.3	101.5	97.2	98.2	-6.7	0.0	COMMONWEALTH INS CO
0.6	0.5	57.9	57.7	-8.4	-10.6	84.6	30.5	115.1	102.5	72.9	0.0	COMMONWEALTH INS CO OF AMERICA
1.0	0.8	44.6	153.3	13.7	5.2	291.7	21.9	313.6	41.6	86.4	0.0 •	COMMONWEALTH MORTGAGE ASR CO
17.1	15.4	N/A	N/A	N/A	N/A	N/A	N/A	N/A	N/A	0.0	0.0	COMMONWEALTH MUTUAL INS CO
0.1	0.1	528.0	29.6	-1.9	-2.6	24.6	87.0	111.6	87.3	-0.5	0.0	COMMONWEALTH MUTUAL INS CO
2.7	1.9	135.8	74.6	-4.9	-15.6	63.6	34.1	97.7	105.7	12.7	0.0	COMMONWEALTH REINS CO
5.7	3.7	28.7	15.1	-28.4	-76.2	-39.4	19.3	-20.1	412.0	5.6	0.0	COMMUNITIES OF FAITH RRG INC
3.2	2.5	42.4	87.7	-16.9	-31.3	40.5	30.6	71.1	156.3	9.1	0.0	COMMUNITY BLOOD CENTERS
1.1	0.8	69.1	187.5	-40.5	-47.5	25.1	14.1	39.2	166.6	0.1	0.0	COMMUNITY HEALTH ALLIANCE RECIP
2.1	1.4	61.2	181.5	-0.4	-19.3	83.8	13.0	96.8	119.7	13.8	0.0	COMMUNITY HOSPITAL ALTERNATIVE
1.0	0.5	77.2	179.0	-7.3	6.1	87.7	32.9	120.6	85.5	-32.7	0.0	COMMUNITY INS CORP
0.7	0.4	190.8	123.4	3.3	-3.7	74.0	34.8	108.8	109.8	4.6	1.6	COMMUNITY MUTUAL INS CO
2.9	2.4	57.7	35.4	-20.3	-22.3	10.2	51.9	62.1	136.3	-22.8	0.0	COMP OPTIONS INS CO INC
6.1	5.5	N/A	N/A	N/A	N/A	N/A	N/A	N/A	-381.3	0.0	0.0	COMPANION COMMERCIAL INS CO
2.2	1.4	30.0	40.2	-27.7	-95.8	-8.5	18.9	10.4	101.4	-10.4	0.0	COMPANION INC
3.0	2.2	84.9	99.8	-7.9	-15.0	60.7	39.0	99.7	100.1	20.6	10.8 •	COMPANION PROPERTY & CASUALTY
N/A	N/A	N/A	32.5	14.7	18.3	N/A	N/A	N/A	N/A	0.0	0.0	COMPASS INS CO
55.8	34.9	13.2	0.5	-0.5	-0.5	2.0	21.4	23.4	374.9	-14.4	0.0	COMPUTER INS CO
6.4	2.2	7.6	62.3	0.4	-21.4	73.8	20.4	94.2	131.5	-93.7	0.0	COMPWEST INS CO
2.8	1.9	109.1	55.6	-5.5	-8.7	72.3	29.7	102.0	98.2	6.7	4.9	CONCORD GENERAL MUTUAL INS CO
2.7	1.9	52.5	12.3	-1.7	-6.6	64.5	39.8	104.3	91.3	16.5	0.0	CONEMAUGH VALLEY MUTUAL INS CO
3.0	2.5	27.5	146.5	-30.0	-43.4	4.6	20.1	24.7	107.8	-3.9	0.0	CONNECTICUT MEDICAL INS CO
N/A	N/A	0.9	0.1	-0.7	-0.3	-27.1	162.2	135.1	-67.6	906.7	0.0	CONNIE LEE INS CO
0.4	0.3	240.2	11.2	0.4	-2.5	8.3	88.9	97.2	104.3	0.9	0.0	CONSOLIDATED INS ASN
30.8	27.7	N/A	N/A	N/A	N/A	N/A	N/A	N/A	N/A	0.0	0.0	CONSOLIDATED INS CO
2.2	1.6	41.0	4.4	-1.8	-3.4	35.3	73.6	108.9	80.2	14.1	0.0	CONSOLIDATED LLOYDS
N/A	N/A	0.7	69.3	2.9	6.0	106.8	689.8	796.6	N/A	-92.1	0.0	CONSORTIUM (A RRG)
N/A	N/A	N/A	N/A	N/A	N/A	N/A	N/A	N/A	N/A	0.0	0.0	CONSTELLATION REINSURANCE CO
N/A	N/A	N/A	N/A	N/A	N/A	N/A	N/A	N/A	-38.6	100.0	0.0	CONSTITUTION INS CO
0.4	0.2	364.3	259.9	2.6	25.1	59.2	46.9	106.1	93.5	-2.5	0.0	CONSTITUTIONAL CASUALTY CO
0.2	0.2	143.9	112.8	3.0	3.7	84.8	64.5	149.3	42.4	-14.1	0.0	CONSUMER FIRST INS CO
0.2	0.2	N/A	N/A	N/A	N/A	N/A	N/A	N/A	110.2	0.0	0.0	CONSUMERS COUNTY MUTUAL INS CO
2.3	1.7	170.8	57.5	N/A	1.1	74.9	20.6	95.5	96.2	1.7	0.0	CONSUMERS INS USA INC
1.6	1.2	26.6	75.9	-9.0	-3.3	56.1	69.2	125.3	113.8	-16.5	0.0	CONSUMERS SPECIALTIES INS CO RRG
1.6	1.1	78.5	255.9	-1.2	2.7	87.0	26.8	113.8	92.3	-4.9	9.9 •	CONTINENTAL CASUALTY CO
9.6	8.6	N/A	8.4	N/A	N/A	N/A	N/A	N/A	-19.2	0.0	0.0	CONTINENTAL DIVIDE INS CO
5.6	5.0	24.1	0.7	-0.4	-0.6	-0.4	76.2	75.8	124.8	-28.5	0.0	CONTINENTAL HERITAGE INS CO

999 + Denotes number greater than 999.9%
999 - Denotes number less than -999.99%
• Bullets denote a more detailed analysis is available in Section II.

INSURANCE COMPANY NAME	DOM. STATE	RATING	TOTAL ASSETS ($MIL)	CAPITAL & SURPLUS ($MIL)	ANNUAL NET PREMIUM ($MIL)	NET INCOME ($MIL)	CAPITAL-IZATION INDEX (PTS)	RESERVE ADQ INDEX (PTS)	PROFIT-ABILITY INDEX (PTS)	LIQUIDITY INDEX (PTS)	STAB. INDEX (PTS)	STABILITY FACTORS
CONTINENTAL INDEMNITY CO	IA	**C**	48.6	21.0	15.5	-0.1	5.1	5.9	6.2	9.0	3.5	CDGT
CONTINENTAL INS CO	PA	**C+**	3,668.1	1,426.5	0.0	9.8	10.0	7.3	3.5	10.0	4.5	AT
CONTINENTAL INS CO OF NJ	NJ	**C**	22.8	22.7	0.0	0.2	10.0	N/A	5.2	10.0	3.7	AGT
CONTINENTAL MUTUAL INS CO	PA	**D**	1.1	0.9	1.3	-0.1	5.8	3.6	2.3	5.3	1.4	DFGT
CONTINENTAL WESTERN INS CO	IA	**C**	252.6	89.0	0.0	0.8	10.0	N/A	8.2	7.0	3.9	T
CONTINUING CARE RRG INC	SC	**D+**	9.2	4.1	4.5	0.1	7.5	3.6	3.4	5.2	2.2	DFGR
CONTRACTORS BONDING & INS CO	WA	**B**	214.7	100.5	71.0	3.3	9.1	9.4	9.1	7.3	5.5	T
▲CONTRACTORS INS CO OF NORTH AMER	HI	**D**	39.6	14.8	5.6	0.3	1.7	5.0	7.7	10.0	1.5	CDGT
CONTRACTORS LIABILITY INS CO RRG	NV	**U** (1)	4.2	1.6	-0.2	-0.5	N/A	4.4	1.3	7.0	2.5	CT
CONTROLLED RISK INS CO OF VT RRG	VT	**C**	120.7	21.5	13.0	0.1	7.7	9.2	5.0	6.9	3.7	DGRT
CONVENTUS INTER INS EXCHANGE	NJ	**C**	79.3	23.9	15.8	0.6	4.7	6.9	6.2	8.3	3.5	CDRT
COOPERATIVA D SEGUROS MULTIPLES D	PR	**A-**	455.9	205.3	151.2	-4.1	8.3	6.2	3.5	6.7	6.8	FT
COOPERATIVE MUTUAL INS CO	NE	**C**	27.8	6.1	16.4	-1.1	5.4	7.0	2.0	2.8	2.7	DFGL
COPIC INS CO	CO	**B+**	435.6	121.5	100.9	-11.1	7.3	7.0	3.0	7.1	6.4	T
▼CORAL INS CO	FL	**F** (2)	13.9	6.4	0.7	-0.6	3.7	4.6	2.5	9.1	0.5	DFGT
CORNERSTONE MUTUAL INS CO	GA	**U** (5)	0.0	3.1	7.9	0.0	N/A	3.2	0.8	0.1	0.3	CDFL
CORNERSTONE NATIONAL INS CO	MO	**C-**	56.2	13.6	29.6	0.6	3.6	8.9	1.9	1.9	3.3	DFLT
CORNHUSKER CASUALTY CO	NE	**B+**	533.2	370.9	102.5	6.4	8.7	7.5	4.6	8.6	5.3	T
COTTON STATES MUTUAL INS CO	GA	**C**	245.5	51.7	89.9	-1.4	7.3	4.6	2.8	3.3	4.2	FLT
COUNTRY CASUALTY INS CO	IL	**B+**	75.7	61.1	0.0	0.3	10.0	N/A	7.4	7.0	6.3	
COUNTRY MUTUAL INS CO	IL	**A**	3,364.1	1,375.3	1,802.4	5.2	9.5	7.5	5.9	5.7	7.6	T
COUNTRY PREFERRED INS CO	IL	**B**	97.2	16.1	0.0	0.1	8.3	N/A	7.8	9.4	6.0	FT
COUNTRYWAY INS CO	NY	**C**	58.2	16.7	33.3	-2.9	7.1	4.9	1.9	5.1	3.5	DFT
▲COUNTRYWIDE INS CO	NY	**D-**	135.9	32.3	50.7	0.3	3.4	0.9	6.9	7.2	0.9	RT
COURTESY INS CO	FL	**B-**	421.8	126.2	108.5	-1.8	10.0	7.5	6.9	7.4	5.1	T
COVENANT INS CO	CT	**C**	66.6	25.4	30.3	0.1	8.6	8.6	6.9	6.7	3.6	T
COVENTRY INSURANCE CO	RI	**U** (1)	1.5	1.5	0.0	0.1	N/A	N/A	3.7	7.0	0.0	T
CPA INS CO	MI	**C**	19.8	19.1	2.1	0.2	10.0	6.3	4.4	8.6	3.9	DFGT
CPA MUTUAL INS CO OF AMERICA RRG	VT	**C-**	22.2	9.4	5.9	-0.2	5.4	3.5	3.7	6.5	2.9	DGT
CRANBROOK INS CO	TX	**D-**	31.6	17.1	4.8	0.3	1.0	4.6	8.9	6.7	1.1	CDGT
CRESTBROOK INS CO	OH	**U** (1)	90.4	90.4	0.0	7.7	N/A	N/A	2.7	7.0	3.9	T
CROWN CAPTIVE INS CO	GA	**U** (1)	0.8	0.7	0.2	0.1	N/A	3.7	4.8	9.9	1.8	T
CROWN CAPTIVE INS CO INC	DC	**E+**	3.5	1.2	2.6	0.0	5.0	6.0	7.1	4.2	0.5	DFGL
CRUDEN BAY RRG INC	VT	**E+**	11.1	2.3	2.5	-0.1	0.3	5.1	4.4	9.4	0.8	CDGT
CRUM & FORSTER INDEMNITY CO	DE	**D+**	37.5	13.1	7.6	0.2	5.3	5.9	6.9	9.2	2.7	DFGT
CRUM & FORSTER INS CO	NJ	**C-**	37.6	13.2	7.6	0.1	5.3	5.9	6.9	9.3	2.9	DFGT
CRUM & FORSTER SPECIALTY INS CO	AZ	**C**	88.2	32.9	14.0	0.5	5.1	6.1	8.3	7.5	3.4	CFT
▲CRUSADER INS CO	CA	**C+**	147.9	65.9	31.2	1.1	7.9	6.0	8.8	7.5	4.5	FT
CSE SAFEGUARD INS CO	CA	**C**	73.1	32.2	34.7	1.1	7.2	7.0	8.0	6.7	4.3	T
CTLIC RRG INC	DC	**E** (5)	0.0	0.8	0.3	0.0	0.8	N/A	2.5	9.2	0.1	CDGT
CUMBERLAND CASUALTY & SURETY CO	FL	**F** (1)	5.7	-3.7	0.0	0.2	0.0	5.1	0.6	7.0	0.0	CDFR
CUMBERLAND INS CO INC	NJ	**C-**	86.1	20.3	26.8	-0.2	5.1	2.0	2.2	7.0	2.9	CDT
CUMBERLAND MUTUAL FIRE INS CO	NJ	**B+**	245.0	132.9	84.3	-5.2	9.1	6.1	4.3	6.8	5.2	FT
CUMIS INS SOCIETY INC	IA	**B+**	1,228.8	413.8	850.5	-28.6	7.4	9.3	4.6	3.3	6.2	LT
▼CYPRESS INS CO	CA	**B-**	582.9	208.6	196.7	-3.9	7.5	8.7	5.5	9.0	5.3	GT
▲CYPRESS PROPERTY & CASUALTY INS CO	FL	**D**	97.1	52.3	27.0	0.2	4.6	2.5	2.9	6.7	1.5	FRT
▲CYPRESS TEXAS LLOYDS	TX	**D-**	47.6	17.2	25.3	0.2	5.1	6.1	2.8	4.9	0.9	DFGL
DAILY UNDERWRITERS OF AMERICA	PA	**C**	29.4	18.1	13.8	0.8	9.4	5.9	7.4	6.9	3.8	GT
DAIRYLAND COUNTY MUTUAL INS CO OF TX	TX	**B**	16.5	11.6	0.0	0.0	10.0	N/A	5.2	7.0	4.9	DFG
▲DAIRYLAND INS CO	WI	**A+**	1,222.3	474.5	312.6	2.4	10.0	9.3	6.8	6.7	7.4	T
DAKOTA FIRE INS CO	ND	**C**	174.6	43.3	67.8	1.0	7.6	4.9	4.5	6.7	4.2	T
DAKOTA TRUCK UNDERWRITERS	SD	**C**	77.7	21.2	30.2	0.1	4.5	4.6	8.0	6.0	3.7	CDRT

See Page 27 for explanation of footnotes and Page 28 for explanation of stability factors.
Arrows denote recent upgrades ▲ or downgrades ▼ (see Section VII for explanations)

RISK ADJ. CAPITAL RATIO #1	RISK ADJ. CAPITAL RATIO #2	PREMIUM TO SURPLUS (%)	RESV. TO SURPLUS (%)	RESV. DEVELOP. 1 YEAR (%)	RESV. DEVELOP. 2 YEAR (%)	LOSS RATIO (%)	EXP. RATIO (%)	COMB RATIO (%)	CASH FROM UNDER-WRITING (%)	NET PREMIUM GROWTH (%)	INVEST. IN AFFIL (%)	INSURANCE COMPANY NAME
1.0	0.6	74.6	91.7	-13.9	-15.8	52.1	24.4	76.5	167.5	-14.8	0.0	CONTINENTAL INDEMNITY CO
5.5	4.3	N/A	0.7	0.1	-0.3	N/A	N/A	N/A	131.2	0.0	6.6 •	CONTINENTAL INS CO
112.8	56.4	N/A	N/A	N/A	N/A	N/A	N/A	N/A	N/A	0.0	0.0	CONTINENTAL INS CO OF NJ
0.8	0.7	139.4	3.2	-0.7	N/A	29.2	76.9	106.1	94.3	3.1	0.0	CONTINENTAL MUTUAL INS CO
9.3	8.3	N/A	N/A	N/A	N/A	N/A	N/A	N/A	78.3	0.0	0.0	CONTINENTAL WESTERN INS CO
1.8	1.3	113.2	0.3	-4.9	0.1	78.2	42.8	121.0	68.6	-37.9	0.0	CONTINUING CARE RRG INC
4.3	3.3	72.3	59.5	-3.4	-9.4	27.8	54.5	82.3	119.6	-11.6	0.0	CONTRACTORS BONDING & INS CO
1.1	0.5	38.7	155.6	-0.5	N/A	41.3	23.9	65.2	220.1	-57.7	0.0	CONTRACTORS INS CO OF NORTH AMER
N/A	N/A	-13.7	151.2	-5.4	2.4	38.4	-258.1	-219.7	22.5	20.1	0.0	CONTRACTORS LIABILITY INS CO RRG
1.6	1.3	60.5	87.6	-4.2	-4.6	37.9	60.2	98.1	90.3	7.5	0.0	CONTROLLED RISK INS CO OF VT RRG
0.8	0.6	66.5	130.1	-19.5	-14.0	67.1	30.5	97.6	144.1	-15.4	0.0	CONVENTUS INTER INS EXCHANGE
2.2	1.8	70.6	18.3	-0.4	-0.8	63.1	41.5	104.6	81.7	-8.9	16.2 •	COOPERATIVA D SEGUROS MULTIPLES
1.0	0.6	215.6	131.9	-14.1	-32.0	72.1	25.9	98.0	92.4	39.7	0.0	COOPERATIVE MUTUAL INS CO
1.5	1.1	76.0	151.6	-24.6	-23.5	51.4	26.5	77.9	132.5	0.1	0.0 •	COPIC INS CO
1.4	1.0	10.4	33.7	4.5	0.5	43.7	999 +	999 +	-3.5	-94.8	0.0	CORAL INS CO
N/A	N/A	172.5	213.5	6.7	29.5	76.4	86.4	162.8	67.9	-17.7	0.0	CORNERSTONE MUTUAL INS CO
1.1	0.9	229.2	117.3	-7.2	-8.1	83.3	21.6	104.9	88.2	-27.8	0.0	CORNERSTONE NATIONAL INS CO
3.7	2.0	16.8	19.6	-2.3	-2.5	58.9	32.7	91.6	138.4	1.8	0.0 •	CORNHUSKER CASUALTY CO
1.4	1.1	166.0	92.2	-2.3	-2.7	75.7	31.3	107.0	86.2	2.2	14.1	COTTON STATES MUTUAL INS CO
20.9	18.8	N/A	N/A	N/A	N/A	N/A	N/A	N/A	999 +	0.0	0.0 •	COUNTRY CASUALTY INS CO
3.6	2.6	127.3	70.8	-2.9	-2.9	75.4	30.3	105.7	95.4	2.2	3.9 •	COUNTRY MUTUAL INS CO
1.9	1.7	N/A	N/A	N/A	N/A	N/A	N/A	N/A	21.0	0.0	0.0	COUNTRY PREFERRED INS CO
1.3	0.8	165.7	96.9	-15.0	-19.8	77.3	37.5	114.8	78.3	-4.4	0.0	COUNTRYWAY INS CO
0.8	0.7	157.3	174.7	33.4	49.6	80.4	20.8	101.2	115.0	11.2	1.3	COUNTRYWIDE INS CO
8.1	4.4	84.5	9.6	-0.2	-0.4	60.0	20.4	80.4	125.3	-9.9	0.0	COURTESY INS CO
2.6	2.0	120.0	68.0	-6.2	-8.0	58.3	31.8	90.1	111.0	17.1	0.0	COVENANT INS CO
N/A	N/A	N/A	N/A	N/A	N/A	N/A	N/A	N/A	N/A	0.0	0.0	COVENTRY INSURANCE CO
9.5	6.7	12.2	3.3	-1.2	-2.1	61.2	69.8	131.0	77.7	27.8	0.0	CPA INS CO
1.0	0.7	61.6	90.7	5.7	4.2	77.2	18.1	95.3	126.9	73.5	0.0	CPA MUTUAL INS CO OF AMERICA RRG
0.3	0.2	28.7	62.6	-10.7	-7.9	64.2	11.8	76.0	224.8	-0.5	0.0	CRANBROOK INS CO
N/A	N/A	N/A	N/A	N/A	N/A	N/A	N/A	N/A	N/A	0.0	0.0	CRESTBROOK INS CO
N/A	N/A	24.6	14.4	-13.0	-2.7	18.6	55.6	74.2	169.5	8.0	0.0	CROWN CAPTIVE INS CO
1.1	0.6	230.5	124.7	5.3	-44.9	60.2	34.8	95.0	92.9	15.6	0.0	CROWN CAPTIVE INS CO INC
0.1	0.1	105.7	249.9	-97.7	-132.9	97.0	8.1	105.1	327.0	15.5	0.0	CRUDEN BAY RRG INC
1.4	0.8	59.1	169.4	-5.2	-9.2	78.2	50.5	128.7	81.2	-22.0	0.0	CRUM & FORSTER INDEMNITY CO
1.4	0.8	57.9	166.1	-5.3	-9.2	78.2	50.5	128.7	81.2	-22.0	0.0	CRUM & FORSTER INS CO
1.2	0.6	42.9	149.6	-2.3	0.5	86.5	15.8	102.3	35.6	-33.8	0.0	CRUM & FORSTER SPECIALTY INS CO
3.3	2.5	48.2	90.9	-6.2	-18.1	60.3	28.4	88.7	87.1	-6.7	0.0	CRUSADER INS CO
1.6	1.2	111.6	67.7	-17.0	-30.8	56.1	39.0	95.1	101.2	1.3	0.0	CSE SAFEGUARD INS CO
0.3	0.2	40.8	336.8	N/A	N/A	70.2	-3.0	67.2	-127.4	0.0	0.0	CTLIC RRG INC
-0.6	-0.5	-0.1	-162.8	51.0	-172.2	999 +	999 +	999 +	17.9	-89.5	0.0	CUMBERLAND CASUALTY & SURETY CO
1.0	0.5	127.3	213.8	-24.4	45.6	50.3	39.5	89.8	103.9	-33.5	0.0	CUMBERLAND INS CO INC
3.4	2.5	60.1	39.1	-2.3	-0.9	64.4	34.6	99.0	93.8	-1.5	9.1 •	CUMBERLAND MUTUAL FIRE INS CO
1.9	1.2	189.5	84.7	-13.2	-16.0	65.1	36.3	101.4	99.3	19.7	5.1 •	CUMIS INS SOCIETY INC
1.5	1.0	82.3	117.7	-0.2	-6.2	80.6	27.0	107.6	180.5	108.9	0.0 •	CYPRESS INS CO
1.9	1.3	51.4	22.5	-1.8	-8.1	54.7	65.3	120.0	89.7	-53.5	0.0	CYPRESS PROPERTY & CASUALTY INS
1.1	0.7	150.4	29.2	-4.2	-8.3	81.1	57.4	138.5	67.9	-44.2	0.0	CYPRESS TEXAS LLOYDS
4.3	2.6	73.8	26.1	3.2	4.4	40.6	27.2	67.8	153.7	13.3	0.0	DAILY UNDERWRITERS OF AMERICA
7.7	6.9	N/A	N/A	N/A	N/A	N/A	N/A	N/A	21.9	0.0	0.0	DAIRYLAND COUNTY MUTUAL INS CO OF
4.9	3.3	66.2	106.9	-5.7	-12.5	74.5	26.8	101.3	95.2	1.0	0.0 •	DAIRYLAND INS CO
2.1	1.3	159.4	201.3	-7.0	-15.7	73.9	33.1	107.0	97.9	-3.5	0.0	DAKOTA FIRE INS CO
0.9	0.5	143.6	173.6	5.7	-1.0	76.3	27.4	103.7	109.7	-5.7	6.9	DAKOTA TRUCK UNDERWRITERS

999 + Denotes number greater than 999.9%

999 - Denotes number less than -999.99%

• Bullets denote a more detailed analysis is available in Section II.

INSURANCE COMPANY NAME	DOM. STATE	RATING	TOTAL ASSETS ($MIL)	CAPITAL & SURPLUS ($MIL)	ANNUAL NET PREMIUM ($MIL)	NET INCOME ($MIL)	CAPITAL-IZATION INDEX (PTS)	RESERVE ADQ INDEX (PTS)	PROFIT-ABILITY INDEX (PTS)	LIQUIDITY INDEX (PTS)	STAB. INDEX (PTS)	STABILITY FACTORS
DALLAS NATIONAL INS CO	TX	**C-**	262.6	86.1	78.7	1.2	4.3	6.8	7.5	8.1	3.2	CRT
DANBURY INS CO	MA	**C+**	16.5	6.9	12.4	-0.7	7.4	4.6	1.9	7.0	2.9	DGT
DANIELSON INS CO	CA	**D+**	8.5	5.7	5.2	-0.1	2.4	4.8	2.2	0.9	2.7	CDFG
DANIELSON NATIONAL INS CO	CA	**C-**	15.2	8.0	6.4	0.0	8.1	4.9	2.3	7.4	3.0	DGT
DARWIN NATIONAL ASR CO	DE	**C**	687.3	266.4	190.1	16.1	6.7	6.9	5.5	7.1	4.2	RT
DARWIN SELECT INS CO	AR	**C**	92.7	50.0	13.6	0.8	8.9	4.8	7.7	7.0	3.4	T
DE SMET FARM MUTUAL INS CO OF SD	SD	**C**	30.5	19.2	16.7	0.6	7.7	6.2	8.8	6.4	3.7	DGT
DE SMET INS CO OF SD	SD	**C-**	11.1	8.3	2.5	0.2	10.0	9.3	9.3	7.1	3.0	DGT
DEALERS ASR CO	OH	**C**	57.8	33.5	2.8	0.8	10.0	4.6	8.7	9.3	3.2	FRT
▲DEERBROOK INS CO	IL	**B**	22.2	22.0	0.0	0.2	10.0	N/A	3.1	7.0	4.2	DGT
DEERFIELD INS CO	IL	**C-**	53.8	38.2	2.9	-0.7	8.0	7.0	3.4	9.1	2.9	DRT
DELAWARE GRANGE MUTUAL FIRE INS CO	DE	**D**	1.1	0.9	0.2	-0.1	10.0	6.0	4.0	9.3	1.0	DGT
DELAWARE PROFESSIONAL INS CO	DE	**D-**	9.4	2.6	2.5	0.1	3.1	4.6	6.4	6.0	1.3	DFGT
▼DELOS INS CO	DE	**D+**	568.2	197.5	262.8	1.9	1.2	6.1	6.9	2.6	2.4	CGLT
▲DELPHI CASUALTY CO	IL	**D**	9.0	2.9	4.7	0.0	7.2	5.5	3.4	8.1	1.4	DGT
DELTA FIRE & CAS INS CO	GA	**C-**	7.8	6.1	2.2	-0.1	7.9	7.7	2.2	8.5	2.9	GT
DELTA LLOYDS INS CO OF HOUSTON	TX	**D**	8.2	6.3	1.5	0.0	8.8	6.4	2.4	6.2	1.7	DFGT
DENTISTS BENEFITS INS CO	OR	**C-**	15.3	10.6	4.6	0.0	9.4	6.6	4.5	6.9	3.3	DGT
DENTISTS INS CO	CA	**B-**	204.0	125.7	38.1	0.8	10.0	9.3	5.5	7.8	5.3	T
DEPOSITORS INS CO	IA	**B-**	66.6	33.0	0.0	0.9	10.0	N/A	3.0	0.9	4.9	FGLT
DEVELOPERS SURETY & INDEMNITY CO	IA	**C+**	128.0	71.9	55.6	1.3	8.0	9.4	8.6	7.0	4.4	T
▼DIAMOND INS CO	IL	**E**	47.4	3.1	19.3	-0.2	0.1	1.9	0.6	5.9	0.2	CDFR
DIAMOND STATE INS CO	IN	**B-**	188.6	112.6	7.5	-0.7	7.5	6.1	4.9	7.9	5.0	T
DIRECT GENERAL INS CO	IN	**C+**	425.1	138.9	271.1	0.7	7.6	5.4	7.0	4.3	4.2	LT
DIRECT GENERAL INS CO OF LA	LA	**C-**	44.1	11.5	29.9	-0.2	6.2	4.1	4.2	4.6	3.3	DGLR
DIRECT GENERAL INS CO OF MS	MS	**C**	50.9	13.0	35.0	-0.4	6.0	5.3	5.6	5.6	3.4	DGT
DIRECT INS CO	TN	**C**	81.0	25.5	53.2	-0.5	7.4	4.6	5.2	5.0	4.0	T
DIRECT NATIONAL INS CO	AR	**C+**	23.8	6.6	13.9	-0.3	6.8	4.7	4.8	6.1	3.4	DGRT
DISCOVER PROPERTY & CASUALTY INS CO	IL	**C+**	175.0	52.5	25.4	1.2	8.6	4.5	7.6	7.0	4.7	T
DISCOVER SPECIALTY INS CO	IL	**C+**	110.8	37.5	25.4	1.2	7.8	4.4	7.5	6.7	4.7	T
DISCOVERY INS CO	NC	**D**	29.4	8.5	10.4	-0.7	5.4	9.8	3.3	5.5	1.4	DGT
DISTRIBUTORS INS CO	TN	**C-**	16.4	9.8	2.4	-0.4	7.1	5.6	4.0	7.1	3.0	DGT
DISTRICTS MUTUAL INS	WI	**E+**	12.9	7.1	3.6	0.1	7.7	6.1	7.0	9.4	0.7	DGT
DOCTORS CO AN INTERINSURANCE EXCH	CA	**B-**	2,076.4	791.6	500.5	8.9	6.9	4.9	8.4	6.9	4.7	T
DOCTORS DIRECT INS INC	IL	**C**	7.7	5.1	1.8	0.0	9.2	3.6	3.4	9.6	2.1	DGT
▼DONEGAL MUTUAL INS CO	PA	**C+**	302.1	158.4	51.5	-0.3	5.7	8.2	8.4	5.7	4.3	CFT
▲DONGBU INS CO LTD	HI	**D-**	28.7	17.4	10.9	1.3	7.7	3.8	5.2	9.0	1.1	DGT
DORCHESTER INS CO LTD	VI	**C**	19.9	8.0	3.9	0.1	8.0	9.4	3.8	7.4	3.5	DGRT
DORCHESTER MUTUAL INS CO	MA	**C**	47.8	24.1	18.0	0.9	8.2	8.4	7.4	6.8	3.9	DGT
DORINCO REINSURANCE CO	MI	**D**	1,545.7	535.0	174.2	11.2	2.0	9.4	6.1	6.6	1.8	CFGR
DRIVE NEW JERSEY INS CO	NJ	**C+**	115.4	27.6	15.7	0.5	10.0	7.1	5.3	6.4	3.7	GT
DRIVERS INS CO	NY	**D+**	7.1	2.3	3.1	0.0	6.3	9.8	3.7	6.6	2.5	DGOT
DRIVERS INS CO	OK	**C-**	16.1	5.6	17.9	0.2	1.2	N/A	2.5	5.9	3.2	CDGT
DRYDEN MUTUAL INS CO	NY	**C+**	104.9	56.8	39.6	2.4	9.0	6.4	8.7	6.9	4.4	T
DTRIC INS CO LTD	HI	**C** (1)	79.2	28.6	32.1	0.7	5.7	5.8	6.4	6.6	3.9	R
DTRIC INS UNDERWRITERS LTD	HI	**C-** (1)	6.2	3.9	0.0	0.0	10.0	N/A	5.2	8.8	2.5	DGT
DUBOIS MEDICAL RRG	DC	**D**	3.9	1.8	1.1	0.1	4.7	3.7	2.9	8.0	0.1	DGT
EAGLE WEST INS CO	CA	**B**	85.7	38.4	43.7	0.8	7.0	8.4	8.7	5.6	4.7	T
▼EASTERN ALLIANCE INS CO	PA	**D**	133.3	31.1	49.1	0.8	6.9	6.0	5.9	6.8	1.9	RT
EASTERN AMERICA INS CO	PR	**B-**	109.0	32.8	30.0	1.3	9.5	9.0	9.1	7.6	4.7	RT
▲EASTERN ATLANTIC INS CO	PA	**C-**	45.1	27.3	2.4	0.0	7.9	5.0	5.6	9.5	3.1	DFGT
EASTERN CASUALTY INS CO	MA	**U** (1)	28.2	2.6	0.0	-11.1	N/A	5.6	0.0	9.6	0.8	CFRT

See Page 27 for explanation of footnotes and Page 28 for explanation of stability factors.
Arrows denote recent upgrades ▲ or downgrades ▼ (see Section VII for explanations)

RISK ADJ. RATIO #1	CAPITAL RATIO #2	PREMIUM TO SURPLUS (%)	RESV. TO SURPLUS (%)	RESV. DEVELOP. 1 YEAR (%)	RESV. DEVELOP. 2 YEAR (%)	LOSS RATIO (%)	EXP. RATIO (%)	COMB RATIO (%)	CASH FROM UNDER-WRITING (%)	NET PREMIUM GROWTH (%)	INVEST. IN AFFIL (%)	INSURANCE COMPANY NAME
1.0	0.6	93.1	109.4	-0.3	-7.1	55.7	31.1	86.8	122.1	-16.9	0.0	DALLAS NATIONAL INS CO
1.3	1.2	163.1	45.3	0.3	N/A	73.8	35.6	109.4	128.0	425.1	11.2	DANBURY INS CO
0.4	0.3	87.6	31.2	-1.9	-1.3	58.5	46.5	105.0	87.6	36.8	0.0	DANIELSON INS CO
2.2	1.5	79.5	31.8	-1.6	-1.5	60.6	45.9	106.5	95.3	36.8	0.0	DANIELSON NATIONAL INS CO
2.1	1.2	74.4	113.4	-19.0	-24.3	40.0	40.3	80.3	212.3	0.8	8.6 •	DARWIN NATIONAL ASR CO
4.5	2.9	27.8	28.0	-3.8	-4.3	47.7	26.6	74.3	103.0	21.9	0.0	DARWIN SELECT INS CO
1.8	1.6	90.7	14.1	1.8	2.1	69.4	27.9	97.3	110.2	0.3	29.6	DE SMET FARM MUTUAL INS CO OF SD
9.0	8.1	30.4	13.8	-4.9	-8.7	72.3	-26.3	46.0	158.9	6.7	0.0	DE SMET INS CO OF SD
8.4	7.5	8.5	0.1	-0.3	N/A	19.5	79.1	98.6	65.1	-82.7	0.0	DEALERS ASR CO
96.2	46.5	N/A	N/A	N/A	N/A	N/A	N/A	N/A	N/A	0.0	0.0	DEERBROOK INS CO
1.9	1.4	7.5	27.1	-2.0	-1.0	162.3	71.1	233.4	132.1	279.8	0.0	DEERFIELD INS CO
7.5	5.1	24.5	4.3	0.1	0.3	42.5	37.7	80.2	246.7	2.5	0.0	DELAWARE GRANGE MUTUAL FIRE INS
1.0	0.9	96.9	196.8	-27.8	-44.0	75.9	20.4	96.3	96.2	-11.6	0.0	DELAWARE PROFESSIONAL INS CO
0.3	0.2	131.1	97.6	-2.0	-5.9	65.1	29.0	94.1	134.4	41.1	4.6 •	DELOS INS CO
1.7	1.0	165.4	113.1	-12.6	-1.7	45.1	42.8	87.9	129.1	-23.9	0.0	DELPHI CASUALTY CO
2.6	2.2	33.0	6.7	-2.6	-2.2	30.6	89.6	120.2	86.1	-3.0	11.0	DELTA FIRE & CAS INS CO
4.6	2.8	24.2	11.8	-3.8	-3.4	60.7	54.5	115.2	37.9	-11.4	0.0	DELTA LLOYDS INS CO OF HOUSTON
5.6	4.2	41.4	22.4	-2.0	-1.2	56.6	39.3	95.9	130.0	3.7	0.0	DENTISTS BENEFITS INS CO
6.2	4.0	29.7	35.9	-5.4	-7.5	61.4	27.2	88.6	113.0	5.2	0.0	DENTISTS INS CO
6.6	5.9	N/A	N/A	N/A	N/A	N/A	N/A	N/A	558.6	0.0	5.8	DEPOSITORS INS CO
2.3	2.0	78.0	31.6	-11.4	-19.4	13.3	65.2	78.5	120.7	2.8	10.9	DEVELOPERS SURETY & INDEMNITY CO
0.1	0.0	418.7	846.7	34.2	17.1	116.5	23.3	139.8	75.4	-5.1	0.0	DIAMOND INS CO
1.4	1.3	6.7	24.7	2.3	0.2	100.9	37.1	138.0	134.8	-45.7	59.4	DIAMOND STATE INS CO
1.5	1.4	194.7	60.6	-2.4	-0.2	77.9	20.0	97.9	97.1	-6.6	13.6	DIRECT GENERAL INS CO
0.9	0.8	247.1	99.7	-2.0	7.3	85.8	15.4	101.2	100.0	4.9	0.0	DIRECT GENERAL INS CO OF LA
0.9	0.8	247.3	94.9	9.1	1.9	83.3	20.0	103.3	100.1	-4.9	0.0	DIRECT GENERAL INS CO OF MS
1.4	1.3	204.5	82.4	7.3	0.5	79.3	19.2	98.5	94.9	-4.7	0.0	DIRECT INS CO
1.0	0.9	202.6	71.9	9.0	0.3	84.3	15.0	99.3	100.8	23.8	0.0	DIRECT NATIONAL INS CO
4.0	2.6	49.5	101.4	-4.2	-5.9	61.5	31.6	93.1	104.1	2.1	0.0	DISCOVER PROPERTY & CASUALTY INS
2.7	1.8	70.0	143.3	-5.4	-7.2	61.5	30.4	91.9	103.9	2.1	0.0	DISCOVER SPECIALTY INS CO
1.4	0.8	109.3	160.5	-13.8	-36.5	88.2	13.1	101.3	95.7	-20.5	0.0	DISCOVERY INS CO
1.6	0.9	23.3	45.4	-5.4	-9.6	31.8	38.6	70.4	121.4	-10.1	0.0	DISTRIBUTORS INS CO
3.4	1.4	50.9	58.7	-14.8	-21.5	63.9	19.5	83.4	152.9	18.9	0.0	DISTRICTS MUTUAL INS
1.3	1.1	63.7	109.7	-9.6	-19.4	47.8	20.2	68.0	152.6	-3.1	30.3 •	DOCTORS CO AN INTERINSURANCE
4.3	2.8	33.1	22.0	-2.6	N/A	72.4	31.0	103.4	271.0	188.0	0.0	DOCTORS DIRECT INS INC
0.9	0.8	32.6	30.6	0.3	-3.0	72.1	33.5	105.6	74.0	-40.7	74.5 •	DONEGAL MUTUAL INS CO
3.5	2.2	66.3	10.8	-3.4	-6.9	35.6	39.1	74.7	244.8	35.7	0.0	DONGBU INS CO LTD
2.7	1.7	46.5	72.0	-13.4	-26.9	42.8	54.3	97.1	90.3	-1.0	0.0	DORCHESTER INS CO LTD
2.9	2.0	75.2	46.1	-1.8	-1.3	53.4	39.3	92.7	108.0	2.2	7.1	DORCHESTER MUTUAL INS CO
0.5	0.3	32.8	153.2	-9.7	-22.2	59.4	14.0	73.4	87.1	59.4	0.0 •	DORINCO REINSURANCE CO
3.3	2.7	57.9	28.5	4.6	1.8	81.9	19.5	101.4	101.5	36.2	0.0	DRIVE NEW JERSEY INS CO
1.2	0.9	135.8	134.3	-18.7	-36.5	87.7	22.8	110.5	97.2	9.5	0.0	DRIVERS INS CO
0.4	0.3	348.9	62.6	N/A	N/A	56.8	36.8	93.6	99.6	0.0	0.0	DRIVERS INS CO
4.3	3.1	72.5	41.2	-2.1	-2.2	41.8	38.2	80.0	133.7	2.2	0.0	DRYDEN MUTUAL INS CO
1.5	0.9	112.5	99.0	10.3	4.4	62.4	45.9	108.3	100.1	-13.6	6.5	DTRIC INS CO LTD
4.9	4.4	N/A	N/A	N/A	N/A	N/A	N/A	N/A	999 +	0.0	0.0	DTRIC INS UNDERWRITERS LTD
0.9	0.6	58.6	86.7	5.0	1.4	55.4	17.9	73.3	205.3	5.0	0.0	DUBOIS MEDICAL RRG
1.9	1.1	116.1	57.9	-3.9	-7.2	57.7	38.6	96.3	96.6	1.1	0.0	EAGLE WEST INS CO
1.0	0.7	117.8	100.7	-4.7	-17.9	55.2	23.5	78.7	117.3	-5.6	0.0	EASTERN ALLIANCE INS CO
4.1	3.7	94.9	10.5	-3.5	-4.6	69.3	29.4	98.7	87.3	-4.4	0.0	EASTERN AMERICA INS CO
2.9	2.1	8.6	45.7	N/A	-0.3	64.3	71.6	135.9	57.6	-64.5	0.0	EASTERN ATLANTIC INS CO
N/A	N/A	N/A	544.8	-2.7	4.0	N/A	N/A	N/A	N/A	0.0	0.0	EASTERN CASUALTY INS CO

999 + Denotes number greater than 999.9%
999 - Denotes number less than -999.99%
• Bullets denote a more detailed analysis is available in Section II.

INSURANCE COMPANY NAME	DOM. STATE	RATING	TOTAL ASSETS ($MIL)	CAPITAL & SURPLUS ($MIL)	ANNUAL NET PREMIUM ($MIL)	NET INCOME ($MIL)	CAPITAL-IZATION INDEX (PTS)	RESERVE ADQ INDEX (PTS)	PROFIT-ABILITY INDEX (PTS)	LIQUIDITY INDEX (PTS)	STAB. INDEX (PTS)	STABILITY FACTORS
▲EASTERN DENTISTS INS CO RRG	VT	**D+**	36.8	9.3	7.9	0.2	3.2	9.6	7.1	7.4	2.5	DGT
EASTERN MUTUAL INS CO	NY	**C**	15.8	8.0	5.1	0.2	9.3	9.4	8.8	7.0	3.9	DGT
▲EASTGUARD INS CO	PA	**C+**	102.0	20.4	20.1	0.4	5.2	4.6	7.6	7.2	4.3	DT
ECHELON PROP & CAS INS CO	IL	**E+**	5.7	2.6	0.5	-0.1	2.5	2.7	0.1	9.0	0.8	DFGT
ECONOMY FIRE & CAS CO	IL	**B-**	388.6	367.1	0.0	4.5	10.0	N/A	8.0	7.0	5.1	T
ECONOMY PREFERRED INS CO	IL	**B**	8.8	8.6	0.0	0.1	10.0	N/A	7.2	7.0	4.9	DGT
ECONOMY PREMIER ASR CO	IL	**B**	35.9	35.6	0.0	0.4	10.0	N/A	7.5	7.0	5.7	DGT
EDISON INS CO	FL	**E+**	28.8	7.0	10.0	-0.3	2.0	3.7	1.4	6.8	0.7	DFGT
ELDERCARE MUTUAL CO RRG INC	AZ	**D**	1.8	1.2	0.2	0.0	7.9	6.0	2.3	7.1	1.2	DFGR
ELECTRIC INS CO	MA	**C+**	1,423.1	344.4	370.1	3.1	5.5	2.9	6.6	6.3	3.4	CRT
ELECTRIC LLOYDS OF TX	TX	**C**	2.8	2.8	0.0	0.0	10.0	N/A	7.8	10.0	3.0	DGT
ELITE TRANSPORTATION RRG INC	AZ	**D**	12.7	1.6	0.7	0.0	1.9	4.9	7.0	5.4	1.3	CDGT
ELLINGTON MUTUAL INS CO	WI	**C-**	5.4	3.8	1.4	0.0	8.4	7.3	6.8	6.9	2.2	DGT
EMC PROPERTY & CASUALTY CO	IA	**B**	130.8	59.9	36.5	1.1	10.0	5.8	7.2	7.3	4.8	T
EMC REINSURANCE CO	IA	**C+**	251.7	84.1	73.6	0.0	7.2	7.0	4.9	6.9	4.5	T
EMCASCO INS CO	IA	**B-**	360.1	87.4	140.8	2.8	7.6	4.9	5.0	6.8	4.6	T
EMERGENCY MEDICINE PROFESSIONAL	NV	**D-**	13.6	3.7	3.8	-0.2	4.8	6.0	2.9	6.7	1.3	DGRT
EMERGENCY MEDICINE RRG INC	SC	**E+**	29.5	7.8	6.3	-0.2	6.4	6.1	5.3	7.4	0.0	DGRT
▲EMERGENCY PHYSICIANS INS CO RRG	NV	**D-**	31.7	8.0	15.2	-0.3	1.4	5.0	2.9	7.0	1.3	DGRT
EMPIRE FIRE & MARINE INS CO	NE	**C**	121.1	55.7	0.0	0.8	10.0	N/A	2.4	7.2	3.6	FT
EMPIRE INDEMNITY INS CO	OK	**C+**	16.0	16.0	0.0	0.1	10.0	N/A	2.9	6.4	4.5	DG
EMPIRE INS CO	NY	**F** (1)	70.6	32.3	0.2	12.8	5.6	5.1	2.9	10.0	0.0	RT
EMPLOYERS ASSURANCE CO	FL	**C**	450.9	92.0	43.9	2.2	7.8	9.5	5.9	6.5	3.3	GT
▲EMPLOYERS COMPENSATION INS CO	CA	**B-**	1,296.7	343.7	146.6	6.5	8.0	9.5	8.8	6.7	5.0	T
EMPLOYERS DIRECT INS CO	CA	**C+**	366.4	138.7	69.8	-3.8	6.8	7.0	3.7	7.3	4.5	CFT
EMPLOYERS FIRE INS CO	MA	**C**	91.2	52.3	25.9	-0.2	9.4	6.2	3.7	7.7	3.7	T
EMPLOYERS INS CO OF NEVADA INC	NV	**C**	1,999.2	410.0	223.2	10.0	6.8	9.4	3.2	10.0	4.1	T
EMPLOYERS INS OF WAUSAU	WI	**B-**	4,009.7	912.5	1,070.7	8.5	7.1	3.1	3.6	5.8	4.9	AT
EMPLOYERS MUTUAL CAS CO	IA	**B-**	2,009.8	711.5	651.7	0.2	7.5	5.8	4.2	6.6	4.8	FT
EMPLOYERS PREFERRED INS CO	FL	**C**	442.9	178.4	56.7	1.5	7.5	9.4	6.0	4.0	3.3	FLT
▲EMPLOYERS SECURITY INS CO	IN	**D-**	29.7	8.0	9.3	0.1	4.5	9.5	9.1	6.9	1.0	DGT
ENCOMPASS FLORIDIAN INDEMNITY CO	IL	**C-**	5.9	5.7	0.0	0.0	10.0	N/A	7.6	7.0	2.9	DGT
ENCOMPASS FLORIDIAN INS CO	IL	**C-**	6.2	5.7	0.0	0.0	10.0	N/A	7.6	7.0	2.9	DGT
ENCOMPASS HOME & AUTO INS CO	IL	**B-**	6.6	6.3	0.0	0.0	10.0	N/A	7.6	10.0	3.5	DGT
ENCOMPASS INDEMNITY CO	IL	**B**	23.8	22.4	0.0	0.1	10.0	N/A	7.9	10.0	5.5	DG
ENCOMPASS INDEPENDENT INS CO	IL	**B-**	6.6	6.6	0.0	0.0	10.0	N/A	7.6	7.0	3.8	DGT
ENCOMPASS INS CO	IL	**C**	24.6	14.2	9.6	0.5	9.4	4.8	8.8	6.3	3.1	DGT
ENCOMPASS INS CO OF AMERICA	IL	**C**	22.7	21.8	0.0	0.2	10.0	N/A	3.6	7.0	3.4	DG
▲ENCOMPASS INS CO OF MA	MA	**C-**	6.2	6.1	0.0	0.0	10.0	N/A	7.3	7.0	2.9	DGT
ENCOMPASS INS CO OF NJ	IL	**C**	26.9	26.1	0.0	0.2	10.0	3.6	8.7	7.0	4.2	G
ENCOMPASS PROPERTY & CASUALTY CO	IL	**C**	12.0	11.2	0.0	0.1	10.0	N/A	3.6	10.0	4.1	DG
ENDEAVOUR INS CO	MA	**C**	4.8	4.7	0.0	0.0	10.0	N/A	7.9	7.0	3.5	DG
ENDURANCE AMERICAN INS CO	DE	**C**	162.9	146.7	1.0	-0.2	8.7	3.6	3.8	7.6	4.1	DFT
ENDURANCE AMERICAN SPECIALTY INS CO	DE	**C**	149.4	72.8	10.9	-1.1	8.7	4.8	2.5	6.7	3.5	GT
ENDURANCE REINS CORP OF AMERICA	DE	**C+**	1,884.9	605.1	445.5	13.1	5.6	6.6	5.1	6.8	4.4	RT
ENUMCLAW PROP & CAS INS CO	WA	**C-**	7.7	7.2	0.0	0.0	10.0	N/A	7.3	10.0	2.2	DFG
▲EQUITIBLE LIABILITY INS CO	DC	**D-**	4.7	1.3	1.6	0.0	4.0	9.7	2.9	7.8	1.0	DGT
EQUITY INS CO	TX	**C+**	57.9	28.9	21.1	0.5	8.0	8.4	5.9	6.6	3.2	T
ERIE & NIAGARA INS ASSOC	NY	**C**	104.4	59.9	46.5	1.7	10.0	6.1	8.8	6.8	3.4	T
ERIE INS CO	PA	**B**	601.5	200.6	189.4	-2.7	9.7	7.0	5.9	6.7	5.1	T
▲ERIE INS CO OF NY	NY	**B+**	58.4	19.8	18.9	0.0	8.3	7.0	8.3	6.8	5.1	DT
ERIE INS EXCHANGE	PA	**B**	8,719.4	3,618.3	3,579.4	-248.9	9.4	7.0	3.9	6.6	5.1	T

Arrows denote recent upgrades ▲ or downgrades ▼ (see Section VII for explanations)

RISK ADJ. RATIO #1	CAPITAL RATIO #2	PREMIUM TO SURPLUS (%)	RESV. TO SURPLUS (%)	RESV. DEVELOP. 1 YEAR (%)	RESV. DEVELOP. 2 YEAR (%)	LOSS RATIO (%)	EXP. RATIO (%)	COMB RATIO (%)	CASH FROM UNDER-WRITING (%)	NET PREMIUM GROWTH (%)	INVEST. IN AFFIL (%)	INSURANCE COMPANY NAME
0.7	0.6	89.1	216.3	-16.5	-36.0	54.7	37.7	92.4	121.3	-1.4	0.0	EASTERN DENTISTS INS CO RRG
3.5	2.7	64.5	47.4	-6.5	-17.0	63.7	29.0	92.7	113.7	-1.9	0.5	EASTERN MUTUAL INS CO
1.1	0.8	100.8	209.0	-16.9	-20.3	53.5	29.6	83.1	169.4	1.5	1.4	EASTGUARD INS CO
1.1	0.6	21.2	112.6	120.4	38.7	140.9	244.6	385.5	19.0	-68.6	3.4	ECHELON PROP & CAS INS CO
8.3	7.4	N/A	N/A	N/A	N/A	N/A	N/A	N/A	N/A	0.0	11.8 •	ECONOMY FIRE & CAS CO
78.3	39.5	N/A	N/A	N/A	N/A	N/A	N/A	N/A	N/A	0.0	0.0	ECONOMY PREFERRED INS CO
64.3	30.5	N/A	N/A	N/A	N/A	N/A	N/A	N/A	N/A	0.0	0.0	ECONOMY PREMIER ASR CO
0.7	0.5	135.7	25.1	0.9	-3.3	56.3	63.5	119.8	87.5	12.1	0.0	EDISON INS CO
2.0	1.8	18.9	35.4	-8.7	-17.7	155.5	119.2	274.7	44.7	-33.9	0.0	ELDERCARE MUTUAL CO RRG INC
1.2	0.6	105.7	220.4	6.4	5.8	87.1	17.0	104.1	92.0	0.6	4.1 •	ELECTRIC INS CO
75.0	44.5	N/A	N/A	N/A	N/A	N/A	N/A	N/A	N/A	0.0	0.0	ELECTRIC LLOYDS OF TX
0.7	0.5	50.8	305.0	-69.6	-11.1	46.1	104.5	150.6	101.6	-87.1	0.0	ELITE TRANSPORTATION RRG INC
3.4	2.1	38.3	10.6	-0.5	-0.1	60.9	39.5	100.4	105.2	1.8	0.0	ELLINGTON MUTUAL INS CO
5.5	3.5	62.6	79.0	-3.6	-7.7	73.9	33.1	107.0	97.9	-3.5	0.0	EMC PROPERTY & CASUALTY CO
1.6	1.0	87.8	172.3	-14.0	-13.8	83.8	24.0	107.8	98.7	3.7	0.0	EMC REINSURANCE CO
2.1	1.3	154.3	194.8	-7.4	-16.4	73.9	33.1	107.0	97.9	-3.5	0.0	EMCASCO INS CO
0.8	0.6	100.8	138.3	-7.1	-11.6	46.4	58.3	104.7	109.3	-22.7	0.0	EMERGENCY MEDICINE PROFESSIONAL
1.3	0.9	77.2	212.9	-44.6	-87.9	39.2	24.7	63.9	271.6	-8.6	0.0	EMERGENCY MEDICINE RRG INC
0.4	0.3	185.9	155.2	-47.7	-46.3	42.5	42.0	84.5	96.3	31.5	0.0	EMERGENCY PHYSICIANS INS CO RRG
7.4	6.7	N/A	N/A	N/A	N/A	N/A	N/A	N/A	-66.9	0.0	2.7	EMPIRE FIRE & MARINE INS CO
398.4	258.3	N/A	N/A	N/A	N/A	N/A	N/A	N/A	N/A	0.0	0.0	EMPIRE INDEMNITY INS CO
1.4	0.8	0.6	98.9	-10.7	-13.4	999 +	959.6	999 +	41.7	-48.9	0.0	EMPIRE INS CO
2.6	1.6	46.0	149.9	-8.7	-19.4	59.1	53.7	112.8	607.6	-46.4	0.0	EMPLOYERS ASSURANCE CO
3.3	2.4	43.5	114.4	-7.2	-14.2	46.2	34.1	80.3	86.0	-7.9	0.0 •	EMPLOYERS COMPENSATION INS CO
2.4	0.8	49.6	148.0	13.1	-3.3	136.5	41.9	178.4	72.6	-35.7	0.0	EMPLOYERS DIRECT INS CO
3.8	2.8	48.8	48.5	-2.2	-4.2	60.2	34.8	95.0	100.5	6.7	10.3	EMPLOYERS FIRE INS CO
1.1	0.9	55.8	189.3	-6.7	-13.7	48.0	32.1	80.1	131.8	24.4	30.8 •	EMPLOYERS INS CO OF NEVADA INC
1.5	1.1	112.8	209.1	-2.6	2.0	83.5	24.1	107.6	93.2	9.2	12.8 •	EMPLOYERS INS OF WAUSAU
1.8	1.3	90.0	119.0	-4.1	-9.0	74.9	32.8	107.7	94.1	-5.3	18.4 •	EMPLOYERS MUTUAL CAS CO
1.9	1.6	32.0	80.6	-5.0	-10.6	59.1	61.0	120.1	81.9	-59.3	35.7 •	EMPLOYERS PREFERRED INS CO
1.1	0.9	115.9	92.4	-14.4	-24.5	45.9	29.8	75.7	107.4	-2.8	0.0	EMPLOYERS SECURITY INS CO
54.0	48.6	N/A	N/A	N/A	N/A	N/A	N/A	N/A	N/A	0.0	0.0	ENCOMPASS FLORIDIAN INDEMNITY CO
25.0	22.5	N/A	N/A	N/A	N/A	N/A	N/A	N/A	N/A	0.0	0.0	ENCOMPASS FLORIDIAN INS CO
54.1	48.7	N/A	N/A	N/A	N/A	N/A	N/A	N/A	N/A	0.0	0.0	ENCOMPASS HOME & AUTO INS CO
40.0	34.6	N/A	N/A	N/A	N/A	N/A	N/A	N/A	-292.9	0.0	0.0	ENCOMPASS INDEMNITY CO
163.8	147.4	N/A	N/A	N/A	N/A	N/A	N/A	N/A	N/A	0.0	0.0	ENCOMPASS INDEPENDENT INS CO
4.3	2.8	70.6	35.4	-0.3	-9.1	56.7	28.4	85.1	105.2	-16.0	0.0	ENCOMPASS INS CO
51.7	36.6	N/A	N/A	N/A	N/A	N/A	N/A	N/A	N/A	0.0	0.0	ENCOMPASS INS CO OF AMERICA
89.2	80.2	N/A	N/A	N/A	N/A	N/A	N/A	N/A	N/A	0.0	0.0	ENCOMPASS INS CO OF MA
72.5	36.3	N/A	N/A	N/A	N/A	N/A	N/A	N/A	N/A	0.0	0.0	ENCOMPASS INS CO OF NJ
34.2	30.7	N/A	N/A	N/A	N/A	N/A	N/A	N/A	-5.1	0.0	0.0	ENCOMPASS PROPERTY & CASUALTY
80.4	39.3	N/A	N/A	N/A	N/A	N/A	N/A	N/A	N/A	0.0	0.0	ENDEAVOUR INS CO
2.0	2.0	0.7	1.0	0.3	N/A	231.1	999 +	999 +	60.1	774.2	49.4	ENDURANCE AMERICAN INS CO
2.5	1.6	14.0	15.9	-0.8	-0.4	79.4	267.3	346.7	133.0	567.8	0.0	ENDURANCE AMERICAN SPECIALTY INS
1.6	1.0	75.2	101.3	-6.5	-6.1	74.2	23.6	97.8	102.5	21.7	19.7 •	ENDURANCE REINS CORP OF AMERICA
32.8	29.5	N/A	N/A	N/A	N/A	N/A	N/A	N/A	999 +	0.0	0.0	ENUMCLAW PROP & CAS INS CO
0.8	0.7	120.9	244.8	-122.3	-60.1	34.6	25.6	60.2	106.2	-14.4	0.0	EQUITIBLE LIABILITY INS CO
2.2	1.8	74.2	35.3	-2.9	-8.6	87.4	17.2	104.6	88.7	-4.4	0.0	EQUITY INS CO
5.2	3.9	78.7	24.7	0.3	-2.9	49.3	38.7	88.0	115.6	2.2	0.1	ERIE & NIAGARA INS ASSOC
4.2	2.7	90.4	83.9	-6.3	-11.9	66.0	27.5	93.5	104.2	0.3	4.8 •	ERIE INS CO
3.3	2.0	95.0	90.7	-7.3	-14.0	66.0	27.5	93.5	103.5	0.3	0.0 •	ERIE INS CO OF NY
4.3	2.6	88.5	82.1	-5.4	-10.3	66.0	27.5	93.5	104.8	0.3	1.3 •	ERIE INS EXCHANGE

999 + Denotes number greater than 999.9%
999 - Denotes number less than -999.99%
• Bullets denote a more detailed analysis is available in Section II.

INSURANCE COMPANY NAME	DOM. STATE	RATING	TOTAL ASSETS ($MIL)	CAPITAL & SURPLUS ($MIL)	ANNUAL NET PREMIUM ($MIL)	NET INCOME ($MIL)	CAPITAL-IZATION INDEX (PTS)	RESERVE ADQ INDEX (PTS)	PROFIT-ABILITY INDEX (PTS)	LIQUIDITY INDEX (PTS)	STAB. INDEX (PTS)	STABILITY FACTORS
ERIE INS PROPERTY & CASUALTY CO	PA	**B**	59.2	9.9	0.0	0.1	7.4	N/A	7.8	7.0	5.1	
ESSENTIA INS CO	MO	**C**	48.6	38.3	10.5	0.0	10.0	N/A	3.5	9.1	3.9	GT
ESSENTIAL RRG INC	SC	**E+**	8.8	4.4	0.4	-0.2	6.8	6.1	2.9	7.5	0.5	DGT
ESSEX BENEFITS INS CO INC	MO	**D**	2.7	2.6	1.2	0.0	8.8	3.6	2.5	7.3	1.9	DFGT
▲ESSEX INS CO	DE	**C**	1,033.7	277.7	304.3	2.2	5.1	4.8	6.2	6.8	3.4	AT
ESURANCE INS CO	WI	**C**	445.1	125.0	125.0	0.5	7.9	4.3	4.0	6.7	3.8	T
ESURANCE INS CO OF NEW JERSEY	WI	**C**	21.1	9.3	0.1	0.0	10.0	N/A	3.0	9.2	2.9	DGT
ESURANCE PROP & CAS INS CO	CA	**C**	106.5	33.8	22.5	1.3	10.0	6.1	5.9	8.4	3.8	T
ETHIO AMERICAN INS CO	GA	**E+**	6.9	3.0	4.6	0.0	4.4	3.8	1.8	7.2	0.8	DFGT
EULER HERMES AMERICAN CREDIT IND CO	MD	**B-**	444.7	159.6	123.9	-2.4	10.0	8.0	6.3	7.0	4.2	T
EVANSTON INS CO	IL	**C**	2,108.9	370.5	597.6	7.4	3.6	7.1	2.7	7.1	3.6	ACT
EVER-GREENE MUTUAL INS CO	PA	**C**	3.4	3.0	0.4	-0.1	10.0	7.6	6.3	9.1	2.1	DG
▲EVEREADY INS CO	NY	**C-**	20.4	7.5	12.5	0.0	3.0	4.8	3.1	5.6	2.7	CDFG
EVEREST INDEMNITY INS CO	DE	**C**	173.7	66.0	12.1	1.5	7.3	8.0	8.8	10.0	3.9	FT
EVEREST NATIONAL INS CO	DE	**C**	467.9	186.4	78.1	0.8	7.3	5.1	8.7	7.7	4.3	T
EVEREST REINSURANCE CO	DE	**C-**	8,311.4	2,422.4	838.8	65.8	4.4	3.7	4.1	6.5	2.9	CFT
EVEREST SECURITY INS CO	GA	**C**	33.4	28.0	3.3	0.1	10.0	4.6	6.3	9.0	3.7	DGT
EVERETT CASH MUTUAL INS CO	PA	**C**	59.3	24.6	28.9	-0.8	7.5	4.6	5.6	6.7	4.0	T
EVERGREEN NATIONAL INDEMNITY CO	OH	**C**	46.0	31.1	11.2	0.6	9.2	8.0	6.5	8.7	3.7	T
EVERGREEN USA RRG INC	VT	**D+**	12.1	5.2	3.3	-0.1	5.2	9.6	4.7	6.8	2.4	DFGT
EXACT PROPERTY & CASUALTY CO INC	CA	**C+**	211.8	71.8	117.9	0.6	7.9	4.7	7.0	6.3	4.6	T
EXCELSIOR INS CO	NH	**B-**	52.4	44.2	0.0	0.4	10.0	N/A	3.9	7.0	4.9	
EXCESS SHARE INS CORP	OH	**C**	63.6	19.9	3.2	0.0	9.5	8.4	8.2	10.0	2.8	DT
EXECUTIVE INS CO	NY	**C-**	4.3	4.2	0.3	0.0	10.0	7.8	2.9	10.0	2.2	DFGT
EXECUTIVE RISK INDEMNITY INC	DE	**B**	2,691.1	936.7	707.5	45.9	7.8	5.6	9.1	6.7	6.0	T
EXECUTIVE RISK SPECIALTY INS CO	CT	**B-**	203.1	83.9	44.2	3.5	8.1	5.6	8.9	6.9	5.0	T
EXPLORER INS CO	CA	**C-**	163.1	40.2	49.9	0.6	3.0	4.8	7.6	5.5	2.8	CDFT
EZ AUTO INC CO	UT	**D** (1)	3.4	1.1	2.6	-0.1	1.9	4.6	2.4	1.0	1.6	CDGL
FACILITY INS CORP	TX	**C-**	191.4	75.2	0.2	-0.9	6.8	N/A	5.7	9.2	3.0	DFGR
FACTORY MUTUAL INS CO	RI	**C**	8,433.0	4,667.6	2,262.5	189.2	7.8	5.5	5.6	6.6	4.1	T
FAIRFIELD INS CO	CT	**U** (1)	26.4	19.1	0.0	-0.6	N/A	5.7	3.4	10.0	4.6	FT
FAIRMONT FARMERS MUTUAL INS CO	MN	**B-**	16.1	9.7	7.9	0.6	10.0	8.3	8.8	7.4	3.5	DGT
FAIRMONT INS CO	CA	**D+**	38.2	25.5	-0.2	0.0	10.0	4.5	8.1	10.0	2.7	DFGT
FAIRMONT PREMIER INS CO	CA	**C-**	209.7	186.7	-0.2	-0.1	7.4	4.0	7.2	10.0	3.1	FT
FAIRMONT SPECIALTY INS CO	CA	**D+**	210.0	133.1	-0.8	1.0	10.0	6.0	7.9	10.0	2.7	DFT
▼FAIRWAY PHYSICIANS INS CO RRG	DC	**E+**	17.4	3.4	7.5	-0.2	0.4	2.5	2.9	7.6	0.6	CDGR
FAITH AFFILIATED RRG INC	SC	**E+**	6.6	4.9	0.6	0.0	5.2	3.9	4.8	7.2	0.8	DGT
FARM BU TOWN & COUNTRY INS CO OF MO	MO	**B**	223.4	94.0	120.9	-0.5	9.8	8.2	5.4	5.5	5.5	T
FARM BUREAU CNTY MUTUAL INS CO OF TX	TX	**C**	17.3	2.2	0.0	0.0	4.7	N/A	3.6	7.0	2.9	CDFG
FARM BUREAU GENERAL INS CO OF MI	MI	**B**	312.6	118.9	115.6	-0.3	10.0	6.2	5.8	5.9	5.5	T
FARM BUREAU INS OF NC INC	NC	**B**	9.2	8.2	0.0	0.0	10.0	N/A	7.7	7.0	4.7	DGT
FARM BUREAU MUTUAL INS CO	IA	**A-**	1,586.9	560.9	908.8	13.2	8.4	7.0	5.2	5.6	7.0	FT
FARM BUREAU MUTUAL INS CO OF AR	AR	**C**	257.8	119.2	167.8	0.7	7.8	6.4	2.6	1.9	4.3	FLT
FARM BUREAU MUTUAL INS CO OF ID	ID	**B+**	346.7	190.9	132.7	1.7	9.4	8.0	8.0	6.4	5.0	T
FARM BUREAU MUTUAL INS CO OF MI	MI	**B-**	559.9	217.2	311.3	-4.6	9.0	6.5	3.6	5.3	4.9	T
FARM BUREAU NEW HORIZONS INS CO MO	MO	**D+**	7.5	5.9	1.0	-0.2	10.0	3.6	3.6	9.4	2.5	DFGT
FARM CREDIT SYS ASSOC CAPTIVE INS CO	CO	**C+**	89.1	65.4	12.5	3.6	10.0	9.4	8.9	8.2	4.1	DT
FARM FAMILY CASUALTY INS CO	NY	**B**	954.1	273.4	367.2	-2.0	8.7	7.0	6.9	6.3	5.5	T
FARMERS & MECH MU I ASN OF CECIL CTY	MD	**D+**	1.3	0.8	0.5	-0.1	7.2	6.2	3.2	6.9	1.2	DFGT
FARMERS & MECH MUTUAL INS CO	PA	**B**	3.0	2.2	0.3	0.0	8.9	5.0	4.4	8.1	4.5	ADG
FARMERS & MECHANICS FIRE & CAS INS	WV	**D**	3.6	2.4	1.3	0.0	10.0	3.7	3.4	6.8	1.4	DFGO
▲FARMERS & MECHANICS MUTUAL IC OF WV	WV	**B-**	35.4	22.4	17.9	0.4	8.7	5.9	9.0	6.7	4.9	GRT

See Page 27 for explanation of footnotes and Page 28 for explanation of stability factors.

Arrows denote recent upgrades ▲ or downgrades ▼ (see Section VII for explanations)

RISK ADJ. CAPITAL RATIO #1	RISK ADJ. CAPITAL RATIO #2	PREMIUM TO SURPLUS (%)	RESV. TO SURPLUS (%)	RESV. DEVELOP. 1 YEAR (%)	RESV. DEVELOP. 2 YEAR (%)	LOSS RATIO (%)	EXP. RATIO (%)	COMB RATIO (%)	CASH FROM UNDER-WRITING (%)	NET PREMIUM GROWTH (%)	INVEST. IN AFFIL (%)	INSURANCE COMPANY NAME
1.4	1.3	N/A	N/A	N/A	N/A	N/A	N/A	N/A	N/A	0.0	0.0	ERIE INS PROPERTY & CASUALTY CO
7.2	5.3	27.0	3.8	N/A	N/A	81.0	39.7	120.7	275.1	0.0	0.0	ESSENTIA INS CO
2.6	1.9	9.1	95.4	-0.3	-279.7	136.4	33.9	170.3	273.1	-78.3	0.0	ESSENTIAL RRG INC
3.2	2.4	46.0	3.7	N/A	1.6	76.1	37.7	113.8	87.8	62.6	0.0	ESSEX BENEFITS INS CO INC
1.1	0.7	102.8	213.7	-7.5	-15.2	53.4	41.0	94.4	109.0	-13.0	0.0 •	ESSEX INS CO
1.9	1.6	100.3	50.5	1.3	9.4	76.2	27.8	104.0	87.8	2.7	16.0	ESURANCE INS CO
3.5	3.1	1.0	N/A	N/A	N/A	N/A	-468.1	-468.1	647.6	N/A	0.0	ESURANCE INS CO OF NEW JERSEY
4.3	3.7	68.6	20.5	-1.3	1.2	61.7	-6.0	55.7	132.3	12.4	0.0	ESURANCE PROP & CAS INS CO
0.9	0.7	157.3	91.5	42.4	30.5	98.8	33.5	132.3	82.0	12.8	0.0	ETHIO AMERICAN INS CO
5.0	3.2	73.6	34.5	5.5	-1.3	82.0	24.0	106.0	103.5	10.3	0.0 •	EULER HERMES AMERICAN CREDIT IND
0.8	0.5	161.6	372.7	-14.5	-35.2	58.1	40.2	98.3	121.6	-13.3	0.0 •	EVANSTON INS CO
18.2	16.4	12.8	1.5	-1.2	-1.5	12.2	34.9	47.1	203.2	-7.3	0.0	EVER-GREENE MUTUAL INS CO
0.7	0.6	167.1	98.2	-12.7	-23.0	59.0	47.4	106.4	70.9	-6.4	0.0	EVEREADY INS CO
1.6	1.2	19.3	76.2	-4.9	-1.4	49.4	57.9	107.3	-402.5	-40.4	0.0	EVEREST INDEMNITY INS CO
2.1	1.1	42.3	86.7	-0.3	4.7	72.9	32.3	105.2	127.4	-1.3	0.0 •	EVEREST NATIONAL INS CO
1.0	0.6	35.8	180.7	4.0	12.1	61.7	56.4	118.1	46.3	-57.6	9.2 •	EVEREST REINSURANCE CO
16.9	13.0	11.9	6.3	-0.1	N/A	72.4	33.5	105.9	72.3	-8.6	0.0	EVEREST SECURITY INS CO
1.9	1.5	112.3	53.4	-9.4	-6.5	52.3	28.2	80.5	124.9	3.1	12.5	EVERETT CASH MUTUAL INS CO
3.1	2.6	35.2	12.9	-3.9	-2.4	5.6	70.3	75.9	197.9	-0.5	13.8	EVERGREEN NATIONAL INDEMNITY CO
1.3	0.9	63.0	95.3	-4.9	-24.2	53.6	51.6	105.2	72.9	-7.4	0.0	EVERGREEN USA RRG INC
2.6	1.6	161.3	105.8	-5.4	-6.9	74.8	30.6	105.4	102.3	-8.0	0.0	EXACT PROPERTY & CASUALTY CO INC
21.0	18.9	N/A	N/A	N/A	N/A	N/A	N/A	N/A	N/A	0.0	0.0	EXCELSIOR INS CO
3.3	3.0	16.1	5.6	-3.6	-5.4	0.9	62.9	63.8	184.3	0.6	0.0	EXCESS SHARE INS CORP
15.5	13.7	8.0	1.0	0.9	-0.8	50.7	82.6	133.3	62.9	24.1	0.0	EXECUTIVE INS CO
2.7	1.8	76.8	138.2	-5.3	-9.9	61.3	28.7	90.0	114.7	-2.6	3.3 •	EXECUTIVE RISK INDEMNITY INC
3.0	2.0	55.2	99.3	-3.9	-8.5	61.3	28.7	90.0	112.1	-2.6	0.0	EXECUTIVE RISK SPECIALTY INS CO
0.9	0.5	119.4	115.2	-14.0	-18.2	50.0	46.7	96.7	109.7	-4.0	0.0	EXPLORER INS CO
0.4	0.3	246.8	78.1	2.3	3.9	74.0	30.7	104.7	100.4	31.3	0.0	EZ AUTO INC CO
3.9	0.9	0.2	170.7	N/A	N/A	122.9	999 +	999 +	0.6	-20.8	0.0	FACILITY INS CORP
2.0	1.6	47.8	44.6	-6.5	-5.7	77.6	21.6	99.2	114.6	-5.1	23.1 •	FACTORY MUTUAL INS CO
N/A	N/A	N/A	28.3	-2.3	-3.0	N/A	N/A	N/A	-20.1	0.0	0.0	FAIRFIELD INS CO
5.1	3.3	87.0	13.6	-5.4	-5.7	33.9	35.0	68.9	158.6	-3.5	0.0	FAIRMONT FARMERS MUTUAL INS CO
8.9	5.6	-0.6	48.7	0.3	-16.3	-50.4	-514.5	-564.9	8.5	-353.3	1.8	FAIRMONT INS CO
1.2	1.2	-0.1	10.1	0.1	-3.7	-50.5	-527.0	-577.5	8.8	-353.3	77.6 •	FAIRMONT PREMIER INS CO
7.3	4.9	-0.6	47.5	0.3	-17.9	-50.7	-551.3	-602.0	11.3	-351.9	5.5	FAIRMONT SPECIALTY INS CO
0.2	0.1	225.1	261.2	20.7	58.5	83.2	30.7	113.9	118.2	-7.3	0.0	FAIRWAY PHYSICIANS INS CO RRG
1.0	0.7	12.7	28.3	1.1	-1.6	73.6	41.0	114.6	195.6	-1.7	0.0	FAITH AFFILIATED RRG INC
3.9	2.7	126.1	50.0	-2.4	-5.5	83.9	21.5	105.4	98.2	15.7	1.1	FARM BU TOWN & COUNTRY INS CO OF
0.7	0.6	N/A	N/A	N/A	N/A	N/A	N/A	N/A	N/A	0.0	0.0	FARM BUREAU CNTY MUTUAL INS CO OF
5.2	3.3	94.7	51.7	2.1	0.9	84.8	23.5	108.3	93.0	-4.4	0.0	FARM BUREAU GENERAL INS CO OF MI
17.8	16.0	N/A	N/A	N/A	N/A	N/A	N/A	N/A	N/A	0.0	0.0	FARM BUREAU INS OF NC INC
2.7	1.9	158.2	86.6	-2.3	-9.3	85.1	24.7	109.8	95.8	18.9	6.3 •	FARM BUREAU MUTUAL INS CO
2.1	1.5	139.9	23.0	-1.8	0.2	105.5	21.2	126.7	79.9	5.9	0.4	FARM BUREAU MUTUAL INS CO OF AR
3.7	2.8	68.6	36.1	-1.8	-5.3	72.6	25.3	97.9	101.8	-6.1	12.5 •	FARM BUREAU MUTUAL INS CO OF ID
3.2	2.2	138.1	78.5	3.8	1.9	84.4	30.1	114.5	94.4	5.9	0.0 •	FARM BUREAU MUTUAL INS CO OF MI
8.3	5.1	16.4	5.6	N/A	-1.1	104.3	38.0	142.3	79.3	33.8	0.0	FARM BUREAU NEW HORIZONS INS CO
14.8	9.4	20.3	28.5	-6.9	-14.0	47.6	6.7	54.3	261.7	10.1	0.0	FARM CREDIT SYS ASSOC CAPTIVE INS
3.3	2.2	134.9	168.1	-7.8	-21.3	76.4	26.2	102.6	99.3	-2.8	0.0 •	FARM FAMILY CASUALTY INS CO
1.4	1.0	54.7	10.3	-1.0	-2.2	69.6	53.7	123.3	85.4	-7.3	0.0	FARMERS & MECH MU I ASN OF CECIL
4.5	2.6	12.1	7.5	-1.3	-0.3	69.8	21.3	91.1	81.6	-4.9	0.0	FARMERS & MECH MUTUAL INS CO
4.1	3.1	55.0	11.2	N/A	-2.0	64.7	46.5	111.2	77.0	13.8	0.0	FARMERS & MECHANICS FIRE & CAS INS
3.0	2.4	78.3	10.8	2.4	-1.8	48.8	31.2	80.0	123.1	-0.6	7.5	FARMERS & MECHANICS MUTUAL IC OF

999 + Denotes number greater than 999.9%
999 - Denotes number less than -999.99%
• Bullets denote a more detailed analysis is available in Section II.

INSURANCE COMPANY NAME	DOM. STATE	RATING	TOTAL ASSETS ($MIL)	CAPITAL & SURPLUS ($MIL)	ANNUAL NET PREMIUM ($MIL)	NET INCOME ($MIL)	CAPITAL-IZATION INDEX (PTS)	RESERVE ADQ INDEX (PTS)	PROFIT-ABILITY INDEX (PTS)	LIQUIDITY INDEX (PTS)	STAB. INDEX (PTS)	STABILITY FACTORS
FARMERS & MERCHANTS MUTUAL FIRE I C	MI	**C**	19.1	15.4	3.6	-0.1	10.0	7.3	4.2	7.4	3.8	DGRT
FARMERS ALLIANCE MUTUAL INS CO	KS	**C**	286.0	143.0	110.1	2.7	10.0	6.5	5.6	6.6	4.3	FT
FARMERS AUTOMOBILE INS ASN	IL	**B+**	852.7	369.7	318.7	-1.2	8.5	9.3	4.5	6.2	6.0	T
FARMERS CASUALTY INS CO	IA	**C**	85.1	29.8	43.5	-0.4	7.6	7.0	4.7	6.3	3.5	AT
FARMERS FIRE INS CO	PA	**C+**	25.1	13.4	11.4	-0.4	7.4	5.9	2.6	6.7	3.6	DGT
FARMERS INS CO INC	KS	**C+**	322.3	94.9	88.4	0.8	9.8	4.6	6.8	6.7	4.6	FT
FARMERS INS CO OF AZ	AZ	**C+**	70.7	4.9	0.0	0.0	4.0	N/A	4.3	4.6	3.5	CDL
FARMERS INS CO OF FLEMINGTON	NJ	**C**	52.9	14.1	22.0	-0.6	5.6	3.7	2.0	7.1	2.6	DT
FARMERS INS CO OF ID	ID	**C+**	169.6	61.8	88.4	0.6	8.2	4.8	7.2	6.6	4.5	T
FARMERS INS CO OF OR	OR	**B-**	1,505.0	524.6	825.2	5.1	8.1	4.4	6.8	6.3	4.9	T
FARMERS INS CO OF WA	WA	**C+**	501.2	165.6	235.8	1.9	8.3	4.7	7.2	6.5	4.7	T
FARMERS INS EXCHANGE	CA	**C**	13,763.9	3,253.9	6,100.5	-5.2	7.1	3.7	5.3	5.9	3.4	FT
FARMERS INS OF COLUMBUS INC	OH	**C+**	231.6	85.1	117.9	1.0	8.2	4.8	7.4	6.5	4.6	T
▲FARMERS MUTUAL F I C OF BRANCH CTY	MI	**D**	1.7	1.1	0.7	-0.1	6.0	7.9	1.6	5.6	1.2	DFGT
FARMERS MUTUAL F I C OF DUG HILL	MD	**D**	3.6	1.6	2.4	0.2	3.9	6.8	3.2	6.1	1.2	DFGT
FARMERS MUTUAL F I C OF MCCANDLESS	PA	**C-**	5.5	1.9	3.7	-0.2	5.1	4.0	3.3	6.6	1.5	DGT
FARMERS MUTUAL F I C OF OKARCHE OK	OK	**C**	12.4	9.3	5.0	0.1	9.8	5.2	3.8	6.5	2.9	DFGT
FARMERS MUTUAL F I C OF SALEM CTY	NJ	**C**	86.3	31.6	28.8	1.2	7.4	4.6	8.1	7.0	4.0	T
FARMERS MUTUAL FIRE INS CO OF MARBLE	PA	**C-**	15.0	6.8	7.8	-0.1	7.4	9.4	5.8	6.3	2.6	DGT
▲FARMERS MUTUAL HAIL INS CO OF IA	IA	**C+**	497.8	234.6	384.9	-27.8	5.3	6.0	3.1	1.3	4.0	GLT
FARMERS MUTUAL INS CO	PA	**D**	4.0	0.6	3.2	-0.6	2.0	6.8	0.8	6.8	1.4	CDGT
FARMERS MUTUAL INS CO	MI	**D+**	2.7	1.8	0.6	-0.1	8.3	5.3	1.5	7.0	1.7	DFGT
FARMERS MUTUAL INS CO	WV	**F** (1)	9.0	5.4	4.7	0.3	8.0	4.6	8.5	6.9	0.0	DFR
FARMERS MUTUAL INS CO OF ELLINWOOD	KS	**D+**	5.7	2.0	4.1	0.0	7.2	8.2	2.0	1.5	2.0	DFGL
FARMERS MUTUAL INS CO OF NE	NE	**B-**	431.3	249.5	185.9	6.9	10.0	8.2	8.2	6.8	5.3	FT
FARMERS MUTUAL OF TENNESSEE	TN	**C** (1)	18.7	13.3	6.2	0.1	10.0	6.1	7.9	7.3	3.5	DR
▲FARMERS NEW CENTURY INS CO	IL	**C+**	173.7	61.1	88.4	1.4	8.1	4.8	7.2	6.6	4.5	T
FARMERS REINS CO	CA	**C+**	1,536.5	971.9	676.2	-12.6	10.0	5.3	4.4	6.9	4.5	T
FARMERS TEXAS COUNTY MUTUAL INS CO	TX	**C+**	157.6	29.9	0.0	0.7	10.0	N/A	8.9	2.3	4.6	LT
FARMERS UNION COOPERATIVE INS CO	IA	**C**	8.0	6.8	0.0	0.0	10.0	4.9	6.8	10.0	3.6	DG
FARMERS UNION MUTUAL INS CO	MT	**C**	44.8	25.2	18.4	1.0	8.2	5.1	9.1	6.7	4.3	DGT
FARMERS UNION MUTUAL INS CO	ND	**C**	62.7	32.5	36.9	0.9	8.8	8.5	8.8	6.0	4.1	T
▼FARMERS UNION MUTUAL INS CO	AR	**D+**(1)	8.7	4.3	5.0	-2.2	5.2	6.2	1.2	2.3	2.4	DFL
▲FARMINGTON CASUALTY CO	CT	**B**	976.9	277.4	268.5	11.0	7.3	4.6	8.4	6.6	5.4	T
FARMINGTON MUTUAL INS CO	WI	**D**	5.9	4.5	1.3	0.0	8.8	5.9	4.3	6.0	0.0	DFGT
FARMLAND MUTUAL INS CO	IA	**B+**	371.1	154.3	152.7	2.2	10.0	6.2	7.9	6.0	6.4	FT
FB INS CO	KY	**B-**	41.5	36.8	5.2	0.1	10.0	7.8	7.6	7.0	4.8	DGT
FCCI ADVANTAGE INS CO	FL	**C+**	5.8	5.5	0.0	0.0	10.0	N/A	4.9	10.0	3.2	DGT
FCCI COMMERCIAL INS CO	FL	**C-**	12.6	15.4	0.0	0.1	10.0	3.9	4.4	6.9	3.2	DFGT
▲FCCI INS CO	FL	**C+**	1,450.2	360.9	474.9	-3.5	7.0	9.4	4.8	6.2	4.2	T
FEDERAL INS CO	IN	**B+**	28,842.9	12,301.0	6,660.6	397.5	7.5	5.6	7.7	6.8	6.8	T
FEDERAL MOTOR CARRIERS RRG INC	DE	**E**	25.1	3.3	6.2	0.3	1.1	3.6	4.6	7.9	0.0	CDGT
▲FEDERATED MUTUAL INS CO	MN	**A-**	3,817.8	1,812.7	929.8	27.1	9.2	7.0	8.6	6.8	5.5	T
▲FEDERATED NATIONAL INS CO	FL	**D-**	79.1	29.3	30.3	-3.0	1.7	0.9	2.8	7.3	1.1	FT
▲FEDERATED RURAL ELECTRIC INS EXCH	KS	**C**	339.0	96.7	106.8	2.1	7.8	4.3	8.7	6.7	3.5	T
▲FEDERATED SERVICE INS CO	MN	**B+**	358.9	137.2	103.3	3.3	9.0	7.0	8.5	6.7	5.4	T
FFG INS CO	TX	**C**	140.2	39.7	0.4	0.9	2.5	0.6	3.1	9.5	3.4	CDFT
FFVA MUTUAL INS CO	FL	**B-**	276.7	100.9	111.4	-4.3	8.0	8.7	5.4	6.5	5.3	T
FIDELITY & DEPOSIT CO OF MARYLAND	MD	**C+**	229.1	180.5	0.0	2.0	10.0	N/A	3.9	7.0	4.6	FT
FIDELITY & GUARANTY INS CO	IA	**C+**	23.2	19.7	0.0	0.1	10.0	N/A	7.9	7.0	4.0	DGT
FIDELITY & GUARANTY INS UDWRS INC	WI	**C+**	83.4	36.0	18.1	0.9	8.7	5.3	8.6	6.9	3.8	DT
FIDELITY FIRE & CASUALTY CO	FL	**C**	25.8	11.0	8.2	-0.4	7.1	3.6	4.7	8.0	2.7	DGT

See Page 27 for explanation of footnotes and Page 28 for explanation of stability factors.

Arrows denote recent upgrades ▲ or downgrades ▼ (see Section VII for explanations)

RISK ADJ. RATIO #1	CAPITAL RATIO #2	PREMIUM TO SURPLUS (%)	RESV. TO SURPLUS (%)	RESV. DEVELOP. 1 YEAR (%)	RESV. DEVELOP. 2 YEAR (%)	LOSS RATIO (%)	EXP. RATIO (%)	COMB RATIO (%)	CASH FROM UNDER-WRITING (%)	NET PREMIUM GROWTH (%)	INVEST. IN AFFIL (%)	INSURANCE COMPANY NAME
6.0	3.9	22.8	5.6	N/A	-0.5	60.7	45.8	106.5	95.2	-1.9	0.0	FARMERS & MERCHANTS MUTUAL FIRE I
4.8	3.4	76.9	37.3	-3.7	-6.7	79.5	30.1	109.6	87.5	1.8	6.4	FARMERS ALLIANCE MUTUAL INS CO
2.2	1.9	84.8	78.6	-3.0	-6.9	89.9	25.6	115.5	95.0	-0.3	21.3 •	FARMERS AUTOMOBILE INS ASN
2.0	1.3	142.7	92.3	-1.5	-5.4	75.0	33.3	108.3	111.0	19.4	0.0	FARMERS CASUALTY INS CO
1.9	1.2	79.5	22.4	-0.3	-0.6	63.7	40.5	104.2	92.9	-4.6	0.0	FARMERS FIRE INS CO
4.6	3.0	94.0	64.0	-2.5	-1.2	75.7	30.8	106.5	80.4	-8.0	0.0	FARMERS INS CO INC
0.6	0.5	N/A	N/A	N/A	N/A	N/A	N/A	N/A	72.3	0.0	0.0	FARMERS INS CO OF AZ
1.1	0.6	145.0	157.8	1.1	8.6	57.9	37.0	94.9	113.6	0.0	0.0	FARMERS INS CO OF FLEMINGTON
3.2	2.1	144.0	94.5	-5.2	-6.6	74.8	30.7	105.5	103.2	-8.0	0.0	FARMERS INS CO OF ID
2.9	1.9	158.6	107.3	-4.4	-2.9	75.5	30.7	106.2	102.2	-8.0	0.0 •	FARMERS INS CO OF OR
3.2	2.1	143.5	94.7	-5.0	-6.1	74.9	30.7	105.6	104.1	-8.0	0.0 •	FARMERS INS CO OF WA
1.4	1.1	187.5	130.2	-3.8	1.0	76.2	31.0	107.2	89.1	-8.0	20.7 •	FARMERS INS EXCHANGE
3.3	2.1	139.9	91.7	-5.0	-6.3	74.8	30.6	105.4	101.2	-8.0	0.0	FARMERS INS OF COLUMBUS INC
1.0	0.7	53.8	6.0	-8.3	-3.9	51.1	63.0	114.1	84.6	-1.6	0.0	FARMERS MUTUAL F I C OF BRANCH CTY
1.2	0.8	176.0	30.9	-6.3	0.9	58.5	52.1	110.6	92.3	4.1	0.0	FARMERS MUTUAL F I C OF DUG HILL
1.0	0.6	190.4	58.3	-12.2	-3.2	58.8	31.5	90.3	111.6	-3.5	0.0	FARMERS MUTUAL F I C OF
5.0	3.2	53.7	3.2	-1.0	-0.5	71.4	47.8	119.2	77.5	-2.2	0.0	FARMERS MUTUAL F I C OF OKARCHE OK
2.2	1.4	89.5	108.8	-9.7	-5.9	54.9	35.8	90.7	111.8	-7.9	0.1	FARMERS MUTUAL F I C OF SALEM CTY
2.0	1.3	116.5	37.6	-12.1	-19.4	45.8	35.7	81.5	119.4	11.5	0.0	FARMERS MUTUAL FIRE INS CO OF
2.6	1.5	148.1	85.3	-1.2	0.2	85.2	13.1	98.3	101.8	67.4	2.6 •	FARMERS MUTUAL HAIL INS CO OF IA
0.4	0.2	329.9	78.1	-20.1	-12.1	45.8	53.2	99.0	105.7	4.5	0.0	FARMERS MUTUAL INS CO
2.5	1.7	30.6	15.9	-3.4	-1.6	95.7	68.6	164.3	63.4	-17.1	0.0	FARMERS MUTUAL INS CO
3.5	2.2	86.7	6.2	7.4	8.3	50.5	43.6	94.1	94.9	-1.4	0.0	FARMERS MUTUAL INS CO
1.2	0.8	165.3	3.0	-6.3	-3.7	68.3	48.9	117.2	75.5	1.8	0.0	FARMERS MUTUAL INS CO OF
6.0	4.6	74.4	27.1	-2.8	-4.9	79.9	24.2	104.1	91.8	-4.2	0.0 •	FARMERS MUTUAL INS CO OF NE
5.5	4.0	47.0	10.5	-0.7	-2.4	60.0	34.9	94.9	104.0	1.4	0.3	FARMERS MUTUAL OF TENNESSEE
3.1	2.0	147.5	96.7	-5.3	-6.6	74.8	30.5	105.3	105.2	-8.0	0.0	FARMERS NEW CENTURY INS CO
7.6	4.7	68.6	17.0	-0.7	-1.2	68.2	28.0	96.2	96.5	95.3	0.0 •	FARMERS REINS CO
3.2	2.9	N/A	N/A	N/A	N/A	N/A	N/A	N/A	588.8	0.0	0.0	FARMERS TEXAS COUNTY MUTUAL INS
13.8	12.4	N/A	N/A	N/A	N/A	N/A	N/A	N/A	-111.2	0.0	0.0	FARMERS UNION COOPERATIVE INS CO
2.9	1.9	76.3	33.7	-0.7	0.9	50.9	34.0	84.9	109.9	-2.2	4.2	FARMERS UNION MUTUAL INS CO
2.7	2.3	116.4	25.2	-4.0	-5.1	62.1	27.2	89.3	126.8	16.2	0.0	FARMERS UNION MUTUAL INS CO
1.1	0.7	115.7	15.9	-2.7	-1.3	99.9	50.1	150.0	72.0	0.8	0.0	FARMERS UNION MUTUAL INS CO
2.1	1.4	100.0	204.8	-7.5	-10.6	61.5	30.4	91.9	104.1	0.8	1.8 •	FARMINGTON CASUALTY CO
3.9	2.5	28.0	0.9	-2.3	-3.7	77.1	31.6	108.7	54.0	15.6	0.0	FARMINGTON MUTUAL INS CO
4.4	3.2	100.4	66.6	0.5	-0.1	74.7	30.9	105.6	92.6	-1.7	0.0 •	FARMLAND MUTUAL INS CO
8.1	5.2	13.7	8.0	-0.5	-1.4	70.8	24.4	95.2	98.0	-22.5	0.0	FB INS CO
38.1	34.3	N/A	N/A	N/A	N/A	N/A	N/A	N/A	43.5	0.0	0.0	FCCI ADVANTAGE INS CO
125.7	63.1	N/A	N/A	N/A	N/A	N/A	N/A	N/A	28.7	0.0	0.0	FCCI COMMERCIAL INS CO
1.2	0.9	126.0	188.1	-11.0	-13.7	69.7	34.1	103.8	101.5	-6.6	8.9 •	FCCI INS CO
1.4	1.3	54.9	97.1	-3.7	-8.1	59.0	29.1	88.1	116.3	-2.3	31.9 •	FEDERAL INS CO
0.4	0.3	257.7	116.2	11.9	N/A	48.4	25.9	74.3	999 +	N/A	0.0	FEDERAL MOTOR CARRIERS RRG INC
3.3	2.6	51.4	80.0	-8.1	-12.9	66.7	31.2	97.9	99.1	-9.2	12.5 •	FEDERATED MUTUAL INS CO
0.7	0.5	96.3	49.8	4.6	26.7	63.3	41.6	104.9	75.8	-46.1	0.0	FEDERATED NATIONAL INS CO
2.3	1.4	108.4	171.6	0.6	-1.0	84.9	13.4	98.3	111.8	3.8	0.0	FEDERATED RURAL ELECTRIC INS EXCH
4.5	2.8	76.9	119.8	-13.2	-21.4	66.7	31.3	98.0	97.0	-9.2	0.0 •	FEDERATED SERVICE INS CO
0.9	0.5	1.0	229.1	-9.8	4.5	-864.9	999 +	999 +	1.1	-83.9	0.0	FFG INS CO
1.9	1.5	104.8	93.9	0.7	-6.6	56.7	25.5	82.2	126.0	13.3	0.0	FFVA MUTUAL INS CO
8.0	7.5	N/A	N/A	N/A	N/A	N/A	N/A	N/A	258.1	0.0	12.5 •	FIDELITY & DEPOSIT CO OF MARYLAND
17.4	15.7	N/A	N/A	N/A	N/A	N/A	N/A	N/A	N/A	0.0	0.0	FIDELITY & GUARANTY INS CO
3.3	2.1	51.7	105.8	-4.3	-5.5	61.5	29.8	91.3	104.6	-29.4	0.0	FIDELITY & GUARANTY INS UDWRS INC
1.8	1.4	71.7	12.0	-3.6	N/A	55.5	32.7	88.2	123.7	19.4	0.0	FIDELITY FIRE & CASUALTY CO

999 + Denotes number greater than 999.9%
999 - Denotes number less than -999.99%
• Bullets denote a more detailed analysis is available in Section II.

INSURANCE COMPANY NAME	DOM. STATE	RATING	TOTAL ASSETS ($MIL)	CAPITAL & SURPLUS ($MIL)	ANNUAL NET PREMIUM ($MIL)	NET INCOME ($MIL)	CAPITAL-IZATION INDEX (PTS)	RESERVE ADQ INDEX (PTS)	PROFIT-ABILITY INDEX (PTS)	LIQUIDITY INDEX (PTS)	STAB. INDEX (PTS)	STABILITY FACTORS
FIDELITY FIRST INS CO	TX	**U** (1)	7.6	7.4	0.0	0.1	N/A	4.9	4.8	10.0	4.9	RT
FIDELITY MOHAWK INS CO	NJ	**C+**	11.3	10.8	0.0	0.0	10.0	N/A	3.6	7.0	4.5	DG
▲FIDELITY NATIONAL INDEMNITY INS CO	TX	**C-**	20.3	18.4	0.9	0.3	10.0	N/A	8.6	7.9	2.9	DGT
FIDELITY NATIONAL INS CO	CA	**C**	258.7	141.0	127.8	1.6	6.5	6.9	4.4	3.2	4.3	FLT
FIDELITY NATIONAL PROP & CAS INS	NY	**C**	153.6	85.0	6.2	2.7	10.0	6.4	9.6	10.0	4.1	GT
FIDUCIARY INS CO OF AMERICA	NY	**E+**	64.1	5.7	19.7	0.4	0.3	4.6	5.1	6.7	0.4	CDGT
FINANCIAL ADVISORS ASR SELECT RRG	NV	**D**	1.4	0.7	0.3	-0.1	4.3	3.6	1.1	9.2	1.2	DFGT
FINANCIAL BENEFITS INS CO	IL	**U** (1)	5.1	5.0	0.0	0.0	N/A	6.0	3.1	10.0	4.3	T
FINANCIAL CASUALTY & SURETY INC	TX	**C-**	18.8	10.6	8.1	0.2	5.2	7.0	7.8	6.9	2.4	DFGT
FINANCIAL GUARANTY INS CO	NY	**D-** (2)	3,301.3	350.2	311.2	-287.6	0.2	2.6	0.3	6.7	0.9	CT
FINANCIAL INDEMNITY CO	CA	**B**	143.5	31.3	33.3	0.4	8.7	7.0	4.4	6.7	5.5	DT
FINANCIAL INSTITUTIONS RESERVE RRG	VT	**U** (1)	36.9	36.8	0.0	0.3	N/A	5.0	7.5	7.0	0.0	T
FINANCIAL PACIFIC INS CO	CA	**C**	226.8	64.3	58.9	0.8	4.7	2.5	8.8	7.1	3.4	T
▼FINANCIAL SECURITY ASR INC	NY	**D+**	4,298.5	843.7	528.2	-11.3	2.5	3.0	0.9	8.3	2.4	CT
FINGER LAKES FIRE & CASUALTY CO	NY	**C**	21.6	12.5	7.5	0.2	9.1	8.0	8.2	6.9	3.4	DGT
FINIAL REINS CO	CT	**D**	1,278.3	459.8	-1.0	11.8	5.7	3.9	2.9	10.0	2.3	FT
FIRE DISTRICTS OF NY MUT INS CO INC	NY	**C-**	47.4	8.8	11.8	0.0	3.4	4.6	4.7	7.0	2.9	CDGT
FIRE INS EXCHANGE	CA	**C**	2,315.5	530.2	884.1	-4.3	5.7	3.9	5.4	5.5	3.4	T
FIREMANS FUND COUNTY MUTUAL INS CO	TX	**B-**	3.0	2.0	0.0	0.0	10.0	N/A	5.9	7.0	3.6	DGT
FIREMANS FUND INDEMNITY CORP	NJ	**B-**	15.5	13.5	0.0	0.1	10.0	N/A	8.0	7.0	4.8	DG
FIREMANS FUND INS CO	CA	**C**	9,398.7	2,958.3	3,592.2	75.8	5.7	5.6	5.0	5.4	3.4	T
FIREMANS FUND INS CO OF HI INC	HI	**B-**	10.5	8.0	0.0	0.1	10.0	N/A	8.7	6.9	4.1	DFG
FIREMANS FUND INS CO OF LA	LA	**C+**	6.3	5.7	0.0	0.0	10.0	N/A	8.0	7.0	3.6	DFG
FIREMANS FUND INS CO OF OH	OH	**B-**	57.1	34.3	9.6	0.4	8.9	5.9	8.4	7.2	4.9	T
FIREMENS INS CO OF WASHINGTON DC	DE	**C**	102.3	34.1	0.0	0.1	10.0	N/A	6.3	7.0	4.3	FT
FIRST ACCEPTANCE INS CO INC	TX	**D**	224.0	109.5	149.2	1.4	5.6	4.4	4.1	5.0	1.6	FRT
▼FIRST ACCEPTANCE INS CO OF GEORGIA	GA	**D**	72.0	22.0	70.0	1.1	1.3	4.3	2.4	1.9	1.6	CDFL
▼FIRST ACCEPTANCE INS CO OF TN INC	TN	**C-**	21.9	8.2	22.9	0.0	2.3	3.6	3.9	3.8	2.8	CDGL
FIRST AMERICAN HOME BUYERS PRO CORP	CA	**U** (5)	0.0	129.8	179.3	0.0	N/A	N/A	8.9	0.9	5.4	L
FIRST AMERICAN PROP & CAS INS CO	CA	**C**	74.1	39.6	40.2	2.4	4.5	5.0	7.0	5.6	3.5	CT
FIRST AMERICAN SPECIALTY INS CO	CA	**C**	98.3	31.6	70.6	1.4	5.2	3.4	7.9	4.2	3.6	LT
FIRST AUTOMOTIVE INS RRG INC	HI	**U** (1)	5.5	2.1	0.0	0.3	N/A	4.7	8.4	7.0	2.6	FT
FIRST CHICAGO INS CO	IL	**D**	21.5	4.4	12.7	-0.3	1.2	1.0	2.5	5.7	1.5	CDGT
▼FIRST COLONIAL INS CO	FL	**B-**	363.8	104.2	117.6	1.6	6.0	4.4	2.9	6.0	5.3	CFT
▼FIRST COMMERCIAL INS CO	FL	**F**	79.7	19.5	41.4	1.0	1.0	2.1	3.0	0.0	0.0	CDFL
▼FIRST COMMERCIAL TRANSPORTATION	FL	**F**	18.5	6.5	8.6	0.1	2.6	0.7	2.7	7.2	0.0	CDFG
FIRST COMMUNITY INS CO	FL	**C**	59.8	19.0	22.0	1.4	6.2	9.3	2.9	7.1	3.4	DT
FIRST DAKOTA INDEMNITY CO	SD	**C-**	32.9	7.3	12.3	0.0	2.6	4.6	8.1	6.2	3.0	CDGT
FIRST FINANCIAL INS CO	IL	**C-**	492.2	311.6	33.8	2.2	7.1	3.3	4.8	7.3	2.6	T
FIRST FIRE & CASUALTY INS OF HI INC	HI	**C**	6.4	6.4	0.0	0.0	10.0	N/A	4.6	7.0	2.5	DG
▲FIRST FLORIDIAN AUTO & HOME INS CO	FL	**B**	410.3	253.4	144.3	17.9	10.0	9.4	6.0	6.8	5.4	T
FIRST FOUNDERS ASR CO	NJ	**D**	2.6	2.4	0.3	0.0	10.0	N/A	4.2	8.1	1.9	DGT
FIRST GUARD INS CO	AZ	**C-**	13.6	12.6	8.1	0.5	10.0	7.6	8.9	6.8	3.3	DGT
FIRST HOME INS CO	FL	**D+**	73.7	42.4	23.9	-0.9	7.4	4.8	2.7	6.9	2.4	GT
FIRST INDEMNITY INS OF HI INC	HI	**C**	6.6	6.6	0.0	0.0	10.0	N/A	7.4	7.0	2.5	DG
FIRST INDEMNITY OF AMERICA INS CO	NJ	**D-**	4.9	4.0	3.1	0.0	7.5	1.1	1.6	6.8	1.3	DFGT
FIRST INS CO OF HI LTD	HI	**C+**	602.2	198.4	146.6	3.7	8.5	8.8	8.2	7.3	4.3	RT
▲FIRST JERSEY CASUALTY INS CO INC	NJ	**D**	12.9	5.3	1.5	-0.4	1.8	1.7	2.5	5.6	1.5	CDFG
▲FIRST KEYSTONE RRG INC	SC	**D**	18.3	4.3	9.7	0.0	2.3	7.0	4.6	7.0	1.7	DGT
FIRST LIBERTY INS CORP	IA	**B**	51.7	22.0	10.7	0.3	7.9	4.5	6.3	7.3	5.3	ADGT
FIRST MARINE INS CO	MO	**B-**	9.6	5.1	5.6	0.1	9.5	7.4	3.3	7.4	3.9	DFGT
FIRST MEDICAL INS CO RRG	VT	**D**	66.6	22.0	13.3	0.9	2.5	5.1	9.3	6.6	2.1	DT

Arrows denote recent upgrades ▲ or downgrades ▼ (see Section VII for explanations)

RISK ADJ. CAPITAL RATIO #1	RATIO #2	PREMIUM TO SURPLUS (%)	RESV. TO SURPLUS (%)	RESV. DEVELOP. 1 YEAR (%)	2 YEAR (%)	LOSS RATIO (%)	EXP. RATIO (%)	COMB RATIO (%)	CASH FROM UNDER-WRITING (%)	NET PREMIUM GROWTH (%)	INVEST. IN AFFIL (%)	INSURANCE COMPANY NAME
N/A	N/A	N/A	2.1	0.9	0.5	N/A	N/A	N/A	N/A	0.0	0.0	FIDELITY FIRST INS CO
6.8	4.0	N/A	N/A	N/A	N/A	N/A	N/A	N/A	N/A	0.0	0.0	FIDELITY MOHAWK INS CO
27.1	24.4	5.1	N/A	N/A	N/A	N/A	42.8	42.8	79.9	-11.3	0.0	FIDELITY NATIONAL INDEMNITY INS CO
1.3	1.1	93.6	39.4	-7.2	-10.3	80.8	33.1	113.9	76.2	-14.8	42.2	FIDELITY NATIONAL INS CO
11.2	10.1	7.5	4.0	-3.2	-3.3	56.8	-199.6	-142.8	-74.9	36.6	0.0	FIDELITY NATIONAL PROP & CAS INS
0.3	0.1	368.5	371.9	12.9	-1.1	64.4	32.0	96.4	181.9	50.1	0.0	FIDUCIARY INS CO OF AMERICA
0.7	0.6	38.1	36.2	-1.1	N/A	116.3	130.2	246.5	53.9	126.5	0.0	FINANCIAL ADVISORS ASR SELECT RRG
N/A	N/A	0.5	N/A	N/A	2.5	N/A	708.3	708.3	6.4	166.7	0.0	FINANCIAL BENEFITS INS CO
1.1	0.8	75.5	33.8	-9.4	-12.6	53.4	48.1	101.5	88.8	31.8	0.0	FINANCIAL CASUALTY & SURETY INC
0.2	0.1	119.3	748.7	-0.5	-1.0	772.1	25.1	797.2	413.5	-11.7	-0.3 •	FINANCIAL GUARANTY INS CO
2.5	2.0	108.1	55.5	-2.7	-7.0	76.0	21.2	97.2	112.8	25.9	0.0	FINANCIAL INDEMNITY CO
N/A	N/A	N/A	N/A	N/A	N/A	N/A	N/A	N/A	N/A	0.0	0.0	FINANCIAL INSTITUTIONS RESERVE RRG
1.2	0.8	92.0	136.1	2.6	10.0	62.4	33.4	95.8	111.8	-7.7	0.0	FINANCIAL PACIFIC INS CO
0.9	0.5	85.2	178.1	44.7	-0.1	477.0	2.7	479.7	82.5	33.7	10.5 •	FINANCIAL SECURITY ASR INC
3.5	2.6	58.9	27.3	-6.2	-3.8	42.4	34.6	77.0	130.8	-0.2	0.0	FINGER LAKES FIRE & CASUALTY CO
2.5	1.3	-0.2	166.2	-3.1	4.8	143.0	999 +	999 +	-1.4	-186.9	0.0 •	FINIAL REINS CO
0.7	0.5	128.9	287.3	1.1	11.4	94.9	16.7	111.6	133.3	2.7	0.0	FIRE DISTRICTS OF NY MUT INS CO INC
0.9	0.8	162.0	112.2	-3.3	0.5	76.1	30.6	106.7	115.4	-8.0	31.5 •	FIRE INS EXCHANGE
4.5	4.1	N/A	N/A	N/A	N/A	N/A	N/A	N/A	9.6	0.0	0.0	FIREMANS FUND COUNTY MUTUAL INS
18.9	17.0	N/A	N/A	N/A	N/A	N/A	N/A	N/A	-15.3	0.0	0.0	FIREMANS FUND INDEMNITY CORP
1.2	0.9	125.5	166.8	4.1	5.4	75.0	28.5	103.5	101.0	3.0	18.4 •	FIREMANS FUND INS CO
9.2	8.3	N/A	N/A	N/A	N/A	N/A	N/A	N/A	-36.2	0.0	0.0	FIREMANS FUND INS CO OF HI INC
19.5	17.5	N/A	N/A	N/A	N/A	N/A	N/A	N/A	-53.2	0.0	0.0	FIREMANS FUND INS CO OF LA
3.9	2.7	28.3	37.6	1.0	1.5	75.0	27.2	102.2	239.1	3.0	0.0	FIREMANS FUND INS CO OF OH
4.5	4.0	N/A	N/A	N/A	N/A	N/A	N/A	N/A	-20.3	0.0	0.0	FIREMENS INS CO OF WASHINGTON DC
1.6	1.3	135.2	56.0	1.7	11.8	72.6	29.9	102.5	84.3	-27.9	16.9	FIRST ACCEPTANCE INS CO INC
0.5	0.3	326.9	113.8	-1.5	19.8	74.7	38.3	113.0	86.9	11.4	0.0	FIRST ACCEPTANCE INS CO OF
0.7	0.5	278.0	91.2	-4.9	N/A	76.8	23.7	100.5	107.3	-18.5	0.0	FIRST ACCEPTANCE INS CO OF TN INC
N/A	N/A	138.2	6.8	N/A	N/A	61.4	26.4	87.8	116.2	17.7	0.0	FIRST AMERICAN HOME BUYERS PRO
0.8	0.5	95.6	22.4	2.0	-2.9	52.3	33.8	86.1	119.7	-0.1	0.0	FIRST AMERICAN PROP & CAS INS CO
0.8	0.5	182.7	64.5	-2.8	0.2	55.5	33.2	88.7	111.3	-8.7	0.0	FIRST AMERICAN SPECIALTY INS CO
N/A	N/A	N/A	N/A	N/A	-1.9	N/A	N/A	N/A	N/A	100.0	0.0	FIRST AUTOMOTIVE INS RRG INC
0.3	0.2	268.0	141.7	15.6	36.0	69.3	41.1	110.4	103.2	22.1	0.0	FIRST CHICAGO INS CO
1.1	0.7	110.6	29.8	-0.9	-4.4	120.5	19.5	140.0	78.2	-18.7	0.0	FIRST COLONIAL INS CO
0.5	0.2	204.7	173.3	55.2	41.1	85.3	41.6	126.9	60.1	-27.0	14.2	FIRST COMMERCIAL INS CO
0.4	0.4	130.0	71.2	-14.6	11.6	56.5	31.3	87.8	100.6	-0.7	0.0	FIRST COMMERCIAL TRANSPORTATION
1.7	1.1	120.3	30.9	-12.0	-14.1	38.5	39.0	77.5	117.3	-15.2	3.7	FIRST COMMUNITY INS CO
0.7	0.4	171.3	207.2	7.1	-1.3	76.3	26.5	102.8	114.1	-5.7	0.0	FIRST DAKOTA INDEMNITY CO
1.2	1.1	11.0	39.3	0.7	4.7	83.7	40.4	124.1	76.0	-27.7	62.1 •	FIRST FINANCIAL INS CO
619.9	311.9	N/A	N/A	N/A	N/A	N/A	N/A	N/A	N/A	0.0	0.0	FIRST FIRE & CASUALTY INS OF HI INC
7.3	5.6	61.3	42.0	-14.9	-14.1	39.5	21.2	60.7	105.0	-26.0	0.0 •	FIRST FLORIDIAN AUTO & HOME INS CO
8.0	5.2	10.7	3.1	N/A	N/A	19.3	63.9	83.2	142.9	8.1	0.0	FIRST FOUNDERS ASR CO
14.6	7.9	67.0	1.8	-0.4	-2.1	61.1	13.0	74.1	128.6	0.0	0.0	FIRST GUARD INS CO
2.2	1.5	53.9	18.6	-0.4	-3.7	67.6	59.1	126.7	101.5	36.7	0.0	FIRST HOME INS CO
534.8	268.6	N/A	N/A	N/A	N/A	N/A	N/A	N/A	N/A	0.0	0.0	FIRST INDEMNITY INS OF HI INC
1.3	1.2	77.9	-39.2	1.1	31.7	40.8	80.8	121.6	74.8	5.2	0.0	FIRST INDEMNITY OF AMERICA INS CO
3.4	2.2	77.2	151.5	-7.5	-11.8	58.4	29.8	88.2	127.1	-6.1	3.4 •	FIRST INS CO OF HI LTD
0.4	0.4	23.9	102.7	1.5	28.0	40.1	27.6	67.7	36.8	-49.2	0.0	FIRST JERSEY CASUALTY INS CO INC
1.1	0.6	237.0	227.7	11.5	-24.7	71.9	34.4	106.3	100.4	8.1	0.0	FIRST KEYSTONE RRG INC
2.8	1.7	49.4	91.6	-1.5	1.1	83.5	24.1	107.6	93.0	-11.9	0.0	FIRST LIBERTY INS CORP
3.7	2.7	111.5	15.6	-1.2	-1.3	53.2	40.8	94.0	155.2	543.1	0.0	FIRST MARINE INS CO
0.7	0.4	58.2	168.4	-12.5	-48.3	69.0	3.9	72.9	259.5	5.6	0.0	FIRST MEDICAL INS CO RRG

999 + Denotes number greater than 999.9%
999 - Denotes number less than -999.99%
• Bullets denote a more detailed analysis is available in Section II.

INSURANCE COMPANY NAME	DOM. STATE	RATING	TOTAL ASSETS ($MIL)	CAPITAL & SURPLUS ($MIL)	ANNUAL NET PREMIUM ($MIL)	NET INCOME ($MIL)	CAPITAL-IZATION INDEX (PTS)	RESERVE ADQ INDEX (PTS)	PROFIT-ABILITY INDEX (PTS)	LIQUIDITY INDEX (PTS)	STAB. INDEX (PTS)	STABILITY FACTORS
▲FIRST MERCURY CASUALTY CO	MN	**C-**	69.8	32.7	21.9	0.9	2.9	3.9	8.8	6.7	3.0	CDT
▲FIRST MERCURY INS CO	IL	**D+**	579.6	184.2	196.7	7.4	3.3	2.0	8.8	6.6	2.5	T
FIRST MUTUAL INS CO	NC	**D**	4.2	3.0	1.3	0.1	10.0	8.1	9.6	9.0	1.5	DGT
FIRST NATIONAL INS CO OF AMERICA	WA	**B**	658.5	70.3	106.8	1.5	8.2	6.9	4.0	6.6	4.2	AT
FIRST NET INS CO	GU	**D-**	11.3	6.6	4.4	0.3	8.2	6.3	8.7	6.9	0.9	DGT
▲FIRST NONPROFIT INS CO	IL	**C**	126.2	52.5	36.6	-1.0	7.3	4.0	4.6	7.0	3.5	T
▲FIRST PROFESSIONALS INS CO INC	FL	**C+**	615.6	213.7	116.1	3.6	7.7	7.0	7.5	7.4	4.2	T
FIRST PROTECTIVE INS CO	FL	**D-**	67.4	16.9	53.0	1.1	1.6	1.3	2.9	7.1	0.9	CDGT
FIRST SEALORD SURETY INC	PA	**C**	13.4	11.5	17.3	0.0	5.0	2.7	8.6	6.6	3.2	DGT
FIRST SECURITY INS OF HI INC	HI	**C**	5.0	5.0	0.0	0.0	10.0	N/A	7.5	7.0	2.5	DG
FIRST SPECIALTY INS CORP	MO	**C**	183.0	83.9	12.8	-2.2	3.0	4.2	3.5	9.8	4.1	CT
FIRST STATE INS CO	CT	**U** (1)	914.7	27.1	0.0	-9.7	N/A	0.1	1.3	5.6	0.0	CFT
FIRST SURETY CORP	WV	**D+**	6.3	5.4	0.7	0.1	10.0	3.6	5.3	9.3	2.4	DGT
FIRST TRENTON INDEMNITY CO	NJ	**B-**	862.1	277.5	385.0	-9.8	8.3	8.2	4.4	6.2	5.3	FT
FIRST WASHINGTON INS CO INC	DC	**U** (1)	3.7	3.3	0.0	0.3	N/A	9.9	3.1	9.5	3.3	FT
▲FIRSTCOMP INS CO	NE	**C**	248.8	59.3	98.8	0.5	4.0	4.9	8.0	5.4	3.6	FT
▲FIRSTLINE NATIONAL INS CO	MD	**C+**	59.3	28.0	22.9	-0.2	7.8	6.0	7.2	6.8	4.5	T
FITCHBURG MUTUAL INS CO	MA	**C**	68.0	33.5	27.8	1.1	8.2	6.9	7.2	6.8	4.1	T
FLAGSHIP CITY INS CO	PA	**B**	22.0	10.1	0.0	0.1	10.0	N/A	7.8	7.0	4.4	DG
FLEET INS CO	AZ	**U** (1)	63.1	61.3	0.0	0.9	N/A	N/A	6.4	7.0	5.4	T
▼FLORIDA DOCTORS INS CO	FL	**D+**	46.7	13.4	19.6	0.7	2.4	4.7	5.6	7.2	2.5	CDGT
FLORIDA FAMILY INS CO	FL	**C-**	65.1	20.8	24.2	2.2	7.4	3.6	2.9	6.4	3.1	DT
FLORIDA FARM BU CASUALTY INS CO	FL	**B-**	424.6	198.9	172.1	2.5	8.4	9.3	4.9	6.6	4.8	T
FLORIDA FARM BUREAU GENERAL INS CO	FL	**B**	5.4	5.4	0.0	0.0	10.0	N/A	6.9	10.0	4.9	DG
▲FLORIDA HOSPITALITY MUTUAL INS CO	FL	**C+**	123.5	52.8	36.7	0.9	8.0	9.5	8.6	7.0	4.3	DT
FLORIDA LAWYERS MUTUAL INS CO	FL	**C**	53.9	19.0	11.4	-0.1	8.0	9.6	4.8	8.1	3.7	DT
FLORIDA PENINSULA INS CO	FL	**C-**	193.0	68.9	120.8	3.8	4.0	4.4	2.9	8.1	3.2	GRT
FLORIDA SELECT INS CO	FL	**F** (1)	11.8	-11.3	-0.3	-0.6	0.0	5.0	1.9	7.0	0.0	CDFT
FLORISTS INS CO	IL	**C**	11.8	8.5	0.7	0.0	8.0	8.9	5.8	9.3	3.2	DGT
▲FLORISTS MUTUAL INS CO	IL	**C+**	154.2	50.7	47.2	0.3	7.5	5.9	6.3	6.4	4.5	FT
FMI INS CO	NJ	**C**	18.7	16.2	0.0	0.1	7.9	N/A	3.1	7.0	4.3	DGT
FOREMOST COUNTY MUTUAL INS CO	TX	**C**	44.2	2.5	0.0	0.0	2.0	N/A	1.9	0.0	3.0	CDFG
FOREMOST INS CO	MI	**B+**	2,024.3	584.2	1,325.7	3.4	7.9	6.0	5.7	4.3	5.6	FLT
FOREMOST LLOYDS OF TEXAS	TX	**C+**	39.5	3.3	0.0	0.1	3.2	N/A	3.9	0.0	3.2	CDFG
FOREMOST PROPERTY & CASUALTY INS CO	MI	**C**	47.1	16.0	0.0	0.0	10.0	N/A	5.8	7.5	4.0	DG
FOREMOST SIGNATURE INS CO	MI	**C+**	57.0	18.4	0.0	0.1	10.0	N/A	4.9	8.5	4.6	D
▲FORESTRY MUTUAL INS CO	NC	**C-**	50.3	9.7	13.7	-0.3	2.9	9.7	4.0	6.5	3.0	CDFG
FORT WAYNE MEDICAL ASR CO RRG	AZ	**D**	2.2	1.2	1.1	0.1	7.4	3.6	6.1	8.7	1.1	DGT
FORTRESS INS CO	IL	**C**	47.4	20.7	3.0	0.3	6.7	5.8	4.6	7.9	4.2	DT
FORTUITY INS CO	MI	**U** (1)	13.3	13.3	0.0	0.3	N/A	N/A	6.9	7.0	5.4	RT
▲FOUNDATION RESERVE INS CO INC	NM	**C-**	17.3	12.8	0.0	0.2	10.0	9.2	8.7	9.3	3.2	DG
FOUNDERS INS CO	NJ	**C**	6.7	6.6	0.0	0.0	10.0	N/A	6.2	7.0	3.8	DG
FOUNDERS INS CO	IL	**C**	209.8	64.2	111.1	-1.4	7.9	7.0	6.3	6.8	4.2	T
FOUNDERS INS CO OF MICHIGAN	MI	**U** (1)	6.9	5.8	0.0	0.4	N/A	6.1	5.8	10.0	4.7	T
FRANDISCO PROPERTY & CAS INS CO	GA	**C**	55.3	35.0	25.0	1.6	8.3	7.3	3.9	6.9	4.1	DT
FRANK WINSTON CRUM INS INC	FL	**D-**	74.0	12.6	0.5	-0.1	1.0	1.7	5.6	10.0	0.9	CDFT
FRANKENMUTH MUTUAL INS CO	MI	**A**	955.3	319.9	415.9	5.2	8.7	9.4	4.5	6.6	7.6	FT
▼FRANKLIN CASUALTY INS CO RRG	VT	**E**	24.2	1.5	2.8	0.2	0.1	3.4	1.3	0.0	0.2	CDFG
FRANKLIN HOMEOWNERS ASR CO	PA	**C**	13.7	12.7	0.4	0.2	10.0	7.4	4.9	9.4	3.0	DGT
FRANKLIN INS CO	PA	**C**	28.0	9.5	7.4	0.3	3.1	3.8	8.7	6.7	3.4	CDGT
FRANKLIN MUTUAL INS CO	NJ	**B**	462.1	251.7	102.1	2.8	7.9	6.5	6.2	8.8	5.6	T
FREDERICK MUTUAL INS CO	MD	**B**	43.4	23.8	17.2	-0.7	8.2	6.5	4.6	6.8	5.0	DGT

See Page 27 for explanation of footnotes and Page 28 for explanation of stability factors.

Arrows denote recent upgrades ▲ or downgrades ▼ (see Section VII for explanations)

RISK ADJ. RATIO #1	CAPITAL RATIO #2	PREMIUM TO SURPLUS (%)	RESV. TO SURPLUS (%)	RESV. DEVELOP. 1 YEAR (%)	RESV. DEVELOP. 2 YEAR (%)	LOSS RATIO (%)	EXP. RATIO (%)	COMB RATIO (%)	CASH FROM UNDER-WRITING (%)	NET PREMIUM GROWTH (%)	INVEST. IN AFFIL (%)	INSURANCE COMPANY NAME
0.9	0.6	68.7	76.8	-1.7	2.5	55.8	26.0	81.8	209.7	37.8	0.0	FIRST MERCURY CASUALTY CO
0.8	0.5	111.0	124.0	-2.8	2.6	55.8	25.8	81.6	204.8	41.3	0.0 •	FIRST MERCURY INS CO
6.1	5.5	45.5	4.8	-3.8	-4.1	35.2	6.0	41.2	181.3	-12.1	0.0	FIRST MUTUAL INS CO
2.2	1.3	153.0	137.0	-4.2	-5.8	67.0	31.2	98.2	99.1	-5.6	0.0	FIRST NATIONAL INS CO OF AMERICA
3.2	2.0	69.8	18.2	0.1	3.5	41.6	42.5	84.1	107.0	6.8	0.0	FIRST NET INS CO
1.4	1.1	70.0	68.5	-0.7	-2.0	59.0	39.7	98.7	143.7	-29.3	33.4	FIRST NONPROFIT INS CO
2.1	1.7	52.6	136.9	-5.5	-15.7	57.6	30.8	88.4	95.4	25.6	11.4 •	FIRST PROFESSIONALS INS CO INC
0.3	0.3	333.2	59.2	-13.8	-7.4	61.5	7.6	69.1	139.4	317.9	0.0	FIRST PROTECTIVE INS CO
0.9	0.8	151.4	-6.6	20.4	31.1	23.3	74.7	98.0	105.9	7.1	0.0	FIRST SEALORD SURETY INC
215.8	108.0	N/A	N/A	N/A	N/A	N/A	N/A	N/A	N/A	0.0	0.0	FIRST SECURITY INS OF HI INC
0.5	0.4	15.0	79.8	-10.4	-7.7	61.1	73.5	134.6	-651.0	-34.2	0.0	FIRST SPECIALTY INS CORP
N/A	N/A	0.1	999 +	73.5	258.8	999 +	999 +	999 +	0.1	-92.7	50.6	FIRST STATE INS CO
11.0	8.6	12.7	6.7	N/A	N/A	30.0	55.0	85.0	205.4	18.8	0.0	FIRST SURETY CORP
2.2	1.7	133.7	123.1	5.3	-5.4	81.6	28.0	109.6	84.9	-0.3	6.2 •	FIRST TRENTON INDEMNITY CO
N/A	N/A	N/A	8.4	-12.0	-54.7	N/A	N/A	N/A	N/A	0.0	0.0	FIRST WASHINGTON INS CO INC
1.1	0.8	165.3	201.5	18.0	19.0	74.0	35.4	109.4	95.8	-21.4	0.0	FIRSTCOMP INS CO
2.6	1.7	79.3	100.3	-17.5	-30.7	52.4	37.1	89.5	107.5	-2.7	0.0	FIRSTLINE NATIONAL INS CO
2.7	1.8	82.5	47.8	-2.9	0.1	53.4	39.2	92.6	118.0	20.8	5.9	FITCHBURG MUTUAL INS CO
3.8	3.4	N/A	N/A	N/A	N/A	N/A	N/A	N/A	N/A	0.0	0.0	FLAGSHIP CITY INS CO
N/A	N/A	N/A	N/A	N/A	N/A	N/A	N/A	N/A	N/A	0.0	0.0	FLEET INS CO
0.7	0.5	154.9	101.3	-5.2	-5.0	51.6	32.5	84.1	199.2	51.0	0.0	FLORIDA DOCTORS INS CO
2.0	1.7	127.4	18.9	-1.0	-0.5	35.0	37.3	72.3	164.4	11.8	0.0	FLORIDA FAMILY INS CO
3.3	2.2	87.0	47.7	-3.9	-6.0	74.5	22.0	96.5	100.6	1.6	1.5 •	FLORIDA FARM BU CASUALTY INS CO
49.5	24.7	N/A	N/A	N/A	N/A	N/A	N/A	N/A	N/A	0.0	0.0	FLORIDA FARM BUREAU GENERAL INS
2.6	2.0	69.1	120.7	-10.6	-16.8	58.7	30.9	89.6	95.4	-4.7	0.0	FLORIDA HOSPITALITY MUTUAL INS CO
2.4	1.6	59.5	109.2	-19.1	-23.6	65.2	18.1	83.3	145.6	6.8	0.0	FLORIDA LAWYERS MUTUAL INS CO
1.3	1.0	185.0	32.4	-2.4	-1.5	42.7	32.6	75.3	151.5	58.5	0.0	FLORIDA PENINSULA INS CO
-1.9	-1.7	2.3	-16.5	8.4	0.3	537.6	-780.2	-242.6	28.4	0.0	0.0	FLORIDA SELECT INS CO
4.9	2.7	8.9	25.4	-0.7	-5.9	23.6	35.6	59.2	143.4	-32.6	0.0	FLORISTS INS CO
2.6	1.5	91.6	119.1	-6.4	-16.3	67.0	36.4	103.4	82.1	3.7	8.0	FLORISTS MUTUAL INS CO
2.5	1.5	N/A	N/A	N/A	N/A	N/A	N/A	N/A	N/A	0.0	0.0	FMI INS CO
0.4	0.3	N/A	N/A	N/A	N/A	N/A	N/A	N/A	20.5	0.0	0.0	FOREMOST COUNTY MUTUAL INS CO
1.9	1.6	227.2	44.5	-0.8	0.7	64.2	41.4	105.6	91.3	-0.6	3.9 •	FOREMOST INS CO
0.6	0.5	N/A	N/A	N/A	N/A	N/A	N/A	N/A	42.3	0.0	0.0	FOREMOST LLOYDS OF TEXAS
3.4	3.0	N/A	N/A	N/A	N/A	N/A	N/A	N/A	168.6	0.0	0.0	FOREMOST PROPERTY & CASUALTY INS
3.3	3.0	N/A	N/A	N/A	N/A	N/A	N/A	N/A	53.5	0.0	0.0	FOREMOST SIGNATURE INS CO
0.8	0.5	138.3	308.5	-35.1	-55.6	64.1	31.7	95.8	87.5	-6.0	0.6	FORESTRY MUTUAL INS CO
1.7	1.3	93.1	60.3	11.0	N/A	42.3	48.6	90.9	187.1	9.9	0.0	FORT WAYNE MEDICAL ASR CO RRG
1.2	0.9	14.7	28.7	0.5	-0.1	75.6	36.7	112.3	101.3	6.4	0.0	FORTRESS INS CO
N/A	N/A	N/A	N/A	N/A	N/A	N/A	N/A	N/A	N/A	0.0	0.0	FORTUITY INS CO
9.3	5.8	N/A	20.1	0.1	-1.1	N/A	N/A	N/A	-23.4	0.0	0.0	FOUNDATION RESERVE INS CO INC
114.4	55.3	N/A	N/A	N/A	N/A	N/A	N/A	N/A	N/A	0.0	0.0	FOUNDERS INS CO
1.8	1.4	170.2	135.2	-10.3	-14.8	64.5	31.0	95.5	112.4	13.3	3.6	FOUNDERS INS CO
N/A	N/A	N/A	14.9	-8.6	-10.9	N/A	N/A	N/A	N/A	0.0	0.0	FOUNDERS INS CO OF MICHIGAN
2.2	1.9	74.6	2.0	0.4	-0.4	13.6	68.2	81.8	123.8	-1.1	0.0	FRANDISCO PROPERTY & CAS INS CO
0.4	0.2	3.8	134.0	-6.8	-1.9	267.7	537.2	804.9	-64.5	-91.1	0.0	FRANK WINSTON CRUM INS INC
2.7	2.0	132.4	112.3	-0.5	-18.2	84.1	28.5	112.6	93.6	3.0	10.8 •	FRANKENMUTH MUTUAL INS CO
0.2	0.1	280.1	525.5	19.9	9.0	73.8	37.6	111.4	56.8	11.4	0.0	FRANKLIN CASUALTY INS CO RRG
11.2	10.5	3.1	N/A	-0.5	-1.0	8.6	171.4	180.0	49.9	37.1	0.0	FRANKLIN HOMEOWNERS ASR CO
0.7	0.5	79.0	116.9	0.1	6.5	62.4	34.7	97.1	120.9	-7.7	0.0	FRANKLIN INS CO
2.7	1.8	38.0	50.8	-6.8	-9.0	40.3	27.5	67.8	128.8	0.2	6.7 •	FRANKLIN MUTUAL INS CO
3.2	2.0	68.3	30.9	-1.8	-2.5	53.7	42.6	96.3	102.9	-4.3	0.0	FREDERICK MUTUAL INS CO

999 + Denotes number greater than 999.9%
999 - Denotes number less than -999.99%
• Bullets denote a more detailed analysis is available in Section II.

INSURANCE COMPANY NAME	DOM. STATE	RATING	TOTAL ASSETS ($MIL)	CAPITAL & SURPLUS ($MIL)	ANNUAL NET PREMIUM ($MIL)	NET INCOME ($MIL)	CAPITAL-IZATION INDEX (PTS)	RESERVE ADQ INDEX (PTS)	PROFIT-ABILITY INDEX (PTS)	LIQUIDITY INDEX (PTS)	STAB. INDEX (PTS)	STABILITY FACTORS
FREDERICKSBURG PROFESSIONAL RISK	VT	**D**	25.3	11.9	4.9	0.1	7.8	6.0	7.1	7.8	1.5	DGT
FREEDOM ADVANTAGE INS CO	PA	**D**	10.8	3.4	4.4	-0.1	3.6	6.0	2.9	4.8	2.1	CDGL
FREMONT INS CO	MI	**D+**	78.7	33.1	50.0	0.3	8.0	7.0	7.2	6.6	2.5	T
FRIENDS COVE MUTUAL INS CO	PA	**C-** (1)	6.1	3.4	2.7	-0.1	7.9	6.4	4.0	7.1	2.2	D
FRONTIER INS CO	NY	**F** (1)	95.9	-90.6	-2.8	3.5	0.0	3.5	0.9	8.7	0.0	CFRT
▼FSA INS CO	OK	**D**	2,034.9	423.1	251.8	-3.6	4.9	6.1	1.3	8.4	0.8	T
FULMONT MUTUAL INS CO	NY	**D**	4.8	1.8	3.2	0.0	7.4	6.2	3.4	6.9	1.5	DGT
GA TIMBER HARVESTERS MUTL CAPTIVE IC	GA	**U** (1)	1.2	0.5	0.1	-0.3	N/A	2.5	0.7	9.1	0.0	FT
GALEN INS CO	MO	**D-**	6.2	3.2	2.0	0.1	8.8	4.0	7.0	7.3	1.3	DGT
GARDEN STATE INDEMNITY CO INC	NJ	**U** (1)	2.7	2.7	0.0	-0.4	N/A	6.6	1.7	10.0	2.9	FRT
GARRISON PROPERTY & CASUALTY INS CO	TX	**B**	215.0	68.7	140.5	-1.0	8.0	3.3	4.6	6.6	4.9	GT
GATEWAY INS CO	MO	**C-**	36.4	15.6	14.7	0.2	7.3	5.0	7.0	6.7	3.2	DGT
▼GEICO CASUALTY CO	MD	**B**	283.4	131.8	50.3	1.6	10.0	8.5	8.9	7.6	5.3	T
GEICO GENERAL INS CO	MD	**B+**	175.2	90.1	0.0	1.0	10.0	N/A	8.8	7.0	5.3	T
GEICO INDEMNITY CO	MD	**B+**	5,117.3	1,687.4	3,736.7	11.0	7.8	9.3	6.0	4.9	5.3	LT
GEISINGER INS CORP RRG	VT	**E**	14.8	11.7	0.4	0.0	10.0	N/A	7.3	9.5	0.3	DGRT
GEM STATE INS CO	ID	**C-**	6.0	4.2	2.5	0.0	10.0	6.5	5.5	6.9	2.0	DGT
GEMINI INS CO	DE	**C**	81.7	54.6	0.0	0.4	10.0	N/A	7.3	7.0	3.9	T
GENERAL CASUALTY CO OF IL	WI	**B-**	154.7	46.0	63.4	-0.8	8.3	5.7	3.1	7.5	4.5	FT
GENERAL CASUALTY CO OF WI	WI	**B-**	1,150.7	515.1	370.7	-6.4	7.3	5.2	3.4	7.4	4.5	T
GENERAL EASTERN SKI INS RRG INC	VT	**D+**	4.9	3.8	0.3	-0.1	7.8	6.3	3.3	9.2	2.2	DG
GENERAL FIDELITY INS CO	SC	**B-**	699.3	357.7	218.0	0.1	7.1	5.9	4.6	6.9	4.0	RT
GENERAL INS CO OF AMERICA	WA	**B-**	3,068.0	454.7	1,228.4	11.1	7.3	6.9	2.4	5.7	4.9	AT
GENERAL REINSURANCE CORP	DE	**B-**	13,285.1	7,921.8	625.6	143.2	7.3	5.0	6.6	7.4	5.0	T
GENERAL SECURITY IND CO OF AZ	AZ	**D+**	86.2	33.6	13.1	0.5	6.8	6.0	4.9	8.2	2.7	GT
▲GENERAL SECURITY NATIONAL INS CO	NY	**D**	291.5	95.3	0.0	-2.2	5.2	1.9	2.9	10.0	1.5	FGT
GENERAL STAR INDEMNITY CO	CT	**B**	888.7	623.6	57.9	7.8	10.0	7.1	7.7	7.0	5.3	T
GENERAL STAR NATIONAL INS CO	OH	**A-**	340.1	232.9	27.7	-1.6	10.0	7.0	6.0	10.0	5.5	T
GENERALI - US BRANCH	NY	**C-**	56.7	29.0	0.5	-0.5	7.5	4.6	1.6	8.3	3.1	DFRT
GENESEE PATRONS COOP INS	NY	**D-**	6.7	3.1	3.0	-0.1	7.7	6.9	2.9	6.7	1.0	DFGT
GENESIS INDEMNITY INS CO	ND	**B**	60.5	52.1	1.0	0.3	8.0	6.9	6.5	10.0	4.0	DT
GENESIS INS CO	CT	**C**	203.2	118.9	12.6	2.8	5.7	6.1	6.4	9.1	2.6	DFT
GENEVA INS CO	IN	**D+**	4.1	2.1	2.5	0.1	7.6	5.8	3.9	7.4	1.8	DGT
▼GENWORTH FINANCIAL ASR CORP	NC	**C**	24.4	5.4	5.0	-5.8	1.8	3.6	0.4	7.3	2.7	CDGT
GENWORTH HOME EQUITY INS CORP	NC	**C-**	12.4	11.6	0.1	-0.2	10.0	3.6	3.9	9.1	3.0	DGT
GENWORTH MORTGAGE INS CORP	NC	**C**	3,060.0	212.7	657.0	-180.8	0.9	6.0	2.8	3.5	4.0	CLT
GENWORTH MORTGAGE REINS CORP	NC	**U** (1)	1.5	1.5	0.0	0.0	N/A	N/A	3.7	7.0	0.0	ACT
GENWORTH MTG INS CORP OF NC	NC	**C+**	601.6	269.4	99.5	-40.4	6.4	9.4	2.9	7.2	4.3	CGT
GENWORTH RESIDENTIAL MTG INS CORP	NC	**B-**	230.6	104.0	21.1	-35.9	8.4	8.0	2.9	9.1	3.9	GT
GEORGIA CASUALTY & SURETY CO	GA	**D+**	36.7	14.4	7.1	0.4	2.5	1.6	1.4	7.0	2.8	CDFT
GEORGIA FARM BUREAU CASUALTY INS CO	GA	**B**	4.6	4.2	0.0	0.1	10.0	N/A	7.6	9.0	4.9	DG
▼GEORGIA FARM BUREAU MUTUAL INS CO	GA	**B**	743.0	282.0	521.3	-24.3	8.0	4.7	2.2	4.8	4.8	FLT
GEORGIA MUTUAL INS CO	GA	**C-**	8.6	3.8	5.2	0.1	3.2	4.4	3.9	5.2	2.0	CDGR
GEORGIA REST MUTUAL CAPTIVE INS CO	GA	**E** (2)	2.5	0.5	3.1	-0.2	0.1	2.5	0.6	2.8	0.3	CDFG
GEORGIA TRANSPORTATION CAPTIVE INS	GA	**D**	1.4	0.6	0.6	0.1	5.6	3.6	2.9	7.8	0.8	DGT
GEOVERA INS CO	CA	**C**	96.8	34.7	25.9	1.8	1.7	4.6	3.3	6.3	3.5	CT
GEOVERA SPECIALTY INS CO	CA	**C**	65.0	23.6	12.1	0.9	2.4	5.0	7.6	1.8	3.8	CDFL
GERLING AMERICA INS CO	NY	**D**	201.5	90.1	4.9	0.9	2.8	3.9	5.6	7.5	2.3	GRT
GERMAN MUTUAL INS CO	OH	**C**	31.0	12.9	21.8	-1.7	7.6	6.5	2.9	6.1	3.7	DFGT
GERMANIA FARM MUTUAL INS ASN	TX	**B**	312.7	193.3	152.0	-3.3	8.0	7.5	4.4	6.0	4.9	RT
▼GERMANIA FIRE & CASUALTY CO	TX	**C+**	20.3	7.9	13.6	-0.1	7.9	3.6	2.4	7.5	4.1	DGT
GERMANIA INS CO	TX	**C-**	56.8	27.9	24.0	1.3	8.2	6.5	1.9	1.9	3.1	FLRT

See Page 27 for explanation of footnotes and Page 28 for explanation of stability factors.

Arrows denote recent upgrades ▲ or downgrades ▼ (see Section VII for explanations)

RISK ADJ. CAPITAL RATIO #1	RATIO #2	PREMIUM TO SURPLUS (%)	RESV. TO SURPLUS (%)	RESV. DEVELOP. 1 YEAR (%)	2 YEAR (%)	LOSS RATIO (%)	EXP. RATIO (%)	COMB RATIO (%)	CASH FROM UNDER-WRITING (%)	NET PREMIUM GROWTH (%)	INVEST. IN AFFIL (%)	INSURANCE COMPANY NAME
3.2	2.4	41.9	67.8	-6.1	-24.7	59.7	17.2	76.9	179.2	1.4	0.0	FREDERICKSBURG PROFESSIONAL RISK
0.9	0.3	125.4	178.8	-18.6	-26.1	70.9	29.2	100.1	130.0	-1.4	0.0	FREEDOM ADVANTAGE INS CO
2.6	1.8	150.8	46.0	-8.0	-15.4	61.0	30.6	91.6	119.1	13.7	0.0	FREMONT INS CO
2.4	1.6	80.2	13.2	-3.8	-2.8	47.8	44.3	92.1	109.8	-16.5	0.0	FRIENDS COVE MUTUAL INS CO
-1.0	-0.5	3.1	-142.3	17.6	24.3	585.0	-38.2	546.8	12.4	-575.6	0.0	FRONTIER INS CO
0.8	0.6	56.7	113.6	39.4	-0.1	522.2	28.8	551.0	148.5	38.2	14.4 •	FSA INS CO
1.6	1.2	182.1	26.4	-4.5	-1.1	42.8	51.7	94.5	98.7	14.8	3.2	FULMONT MUTUAL INS CO
N/A	N/A	12.1	11.7	21.9	9.7	377.8	296.8	674.6	-37.2	-79.0	0.0	GA TIMBER HARVESTERS MUTL CAPTIVE
3.2	2.1	63.6	59.7	-15.2	-20.4	43.0	28.9	71.9	287.8	15.4	0.0	GALEN INS CO
N/A	N/A	N/A	2.2	-2.6	-3.6	N/A	N/A	N/A	N/A	0.0	0.0	GARDEN STATE INDEMNITY CO INC
1.8	1.4	203.8	94.9	13.7	14.6	84.4	13.5	97.9	164.7	71.3	0.0	GARRISON PROPERTY & CASUALTY INS
1.7	1.1	92.6	61.8	-4.4	-4.7	50.6	39.0	89.6	102.2	15.9	0.0	GATEWAY INS CO
8.0	5.8	39.5	20.8	-2.4	-3.9	67.0	19.0	86.0	121.3	-9.4	0.0	GEICO CASUALTY CO
10.8	9.7	N/A	N/A	N/A	N/A	N/A	N/A	N/A	999 +	0.0	0.0 •	GEICO GENERAL INS CO
1.6	1.3	210.6	108.4	-7.6	-11.6	78.4	20.4	98.8	109.1	12.7	3.2 •	GEICO INDEMNITY CO
11.4	6.7	3.7	N/A	N/A	N/A	N/A	105.4	105.4	86.8	-9.7	0.0	GEISINGER INS CORP RRG
3.7	3.2	57.9	12.5	1.3	-1.4	76.7	30.8	107.5	104.7	3.4	0.0	GEM STATE INS CO
12.7	11.5	N/A	N/A	N/A	N/A	N/A	N/A	N/A	84.4	0.0	0.0	GEMINI INS CO
3.3	2.3	137.2	159.0	-16.9	-11.7	52.3	33.8	86.1	73.1	-30.1	0.0	GENERAL CASUALTY CO OF IL
1.2	1.1	68.9	76.1	-8.0	-5.6	52.3	32.2	84.5	81.7	-20.5	44.3 •	GENERAL CASUALTY CO OF WI
2.0	1.3	7.7	21.9	6.1	5.6	81.4	29.1	110.5	74.3	-9.8	0.0	GENERAL EASTERN SKI INS RRG INC
1.8	1.2	57.1	61.3	3.3	3.9	65.4	47.1	112.5	108.8	-15.7	0.0 •	GENERAL FIDELITY INS CO
1.7	1.1	274.4	245.7	-6.0	-5.9	67.0	31.2	98.2	102.3	-5.6	0.7 •	GENERAL INS CO OF AMERICA
1.2	1.1	7.0	43.1	-1.6	-2.4	60.8	48.0	108.8	74.6	-11.6	44.6 •	GENERAL REINSURANCE CORP
1.8	1.2	39.6	62.5	8.3	0.2	101.4	21.4	122.8	117.5	34.4	0.0	GENERAL SECURITY IND CO OF AZ
1.4	0.8	N/A	167.7	-1.3	-11.0	999 +	N/A	N/A	-15.1	100.0	0.0	GENERAL SECURITY NATIONAL INS CO
6.5	4.7	8.1	30.9	-7.6	-14.8	8.1	56.5	64.6	-64.4	-41.1	2.2 •	GENERAL STAR INDEMNITY CO
5.8	4.4	11.4	34.3	-5.5	-16.6	42.7	41.5	84.2	-163.9	60.0	0.0 •	GENERAL STAR NATIONAL INS CO
2.3	1.5	1.7	65.4	-2.4	-1.4	28.0	799.4	827.4	8.9	-36.5	0.1	GENERALI - US BRANCH
2.1	1.4	89.8	33.9	-6.7	-12.0	81.9	29.3	111.2	91.4	-6.6	0.1	GENESEE PATRONS COOP INS
1.9	1.5	1.8	13.7	-1.8	2.9	20.0	17.5	37.5	253.6	-24.6	0.0	GENESIS INDEMNITY INS CO
1.5	1.0	10.1	61.9	-6.1	-14.2	56.2	28.8	85.0	31.4	-13.8	0.0	GENESIS INS CO
1.5	1.4	116.3	44.9	1.3	0.6	67.7	35.0	102.7	99.6	22.9	0.0	GENEVA INS CO
0.3	0.2	79.6	208.3	10.1	N/A	267.2	25.8	293.0	228.6	76.1	0.0	GENWORTH FINANCIAL ASR CORP
19.8	15.5	1.0	3.5	1.6	N/A	561.9	118.6	680.5	36.5	453.1	0.0	GENWORTH HOME EQUITY INS CORP
0.2	0.1	237.3	316.2	84.2	10.8	144.6	23.1	167.7	117.4	15.1	0.0 •	GENWORTH MORTGAGE INS CORP
N/A	N/A	N/A	N/A	N/A	N/A	N/A	N/A	N/A	N/A	0.0	0.0	GENWORTH MORTGAGE REINS CORP
1.6	1.1	50.7	133.4	81.9	-8.4	257.0	0.2	257.2	234.1	13.5	0.0 •	GENWORTH MTG INS CORP OF NC
1.8	1.4	15.2	44.7	-7.9	-2.7	248.0	31.4	279.4	133.4	-4.1	5.7	GENWORTH RESIDENTIAL MTG INS
1.2	0.7	47.4	216.2	3.8	40.6	79.3	43.6	122.9	54.4	-25.9	0.0	GEORGIA CASUALTY & SURETY CO
22.4	20.2	N/A	N/A	N/A	N/A	N/A	N/A	N/A	N/A	0.0	0.0	GEORGIA FARM BUREAU CASUALTY INS
2.3	1.5	169.8	63.7	-4.1	1.6	89.3	25.5	114.8	85.2	-5.7	1.3 •	GEORGIA FARM BUREAU MUTUAL INS CO
0.8	0.6	140.4	28.1	1.4	-0.7	61.7	38.6	100.3	87.5	27.6	0.0	GEORGIA MUTUAL INS CO
0.4	0.2	552.3	541.5	36.6	27.4	86.2	35.4	121.6	88.2	-17.2	0.0	GEORGIA REST MUTUAL CAPTIVE INS CO
1.5	1.0	120.1	112.0	-0.1	N/A	75.2	19.3	94.5	205.0	0.6	0.0	GEORGIA TRANSPORTATION CAPTIVE
0.4	0.3	77.8	20.0	0.4	0.9	50.3	23.5	73.8	154.9	41.4	0.0	GEOVERA INS CO
0.6	0.4	53.1	13.7	0.4	0.4	50.3	23.5	73.8	53.6	41.4	0.0	GEOVERA SPECIALTY INS CO
0.7	0.5	5.5	69.0	12.1	3.7	321.7	-137.1	184.6	999 +	153.6	6.0	GERLING AMERICA INS CO
1.7	1.1	141.6	40.0	-4.7	-1.2	62.1	36.5	98.6	92.9	0.8	0.0	GERMAN MUTUAL INS CO
1.6	1.5	77.2	6.4	-0.6	-1.2	95.2	30.8	126.0	81.8	6.2	44.2 •	GERMANIA FARM MUTUAL INS ASN
1.5	1.3	169.8	56.0	-1.5	-0.6	71.3	23.8	95.1	189.6	0.0	0.0	GERMANIA FIRE & CASUALTY CO
3.0	2.3	90.8	38.0	-4.6	-2.4	61.2	49.8	111.0	85.7	-75.7	0.0	GERMANIA INS CO

999 + Denotes number greater than 999.9%
999 - Denotes number less than -999.99%
• Bullets denote a more detailed analysis is available in Section II.

INSURANCE COMPANY NAME	DOM. STATE	RATING	TOTAL ASSETS ($MIL)	CAPITAL & SURPLUS ($MIL)	ANNUAL NET PREMIUM ($MIL)	NET INCOME ($MIL)	CAPITAL-IZATION INDEX (PTS)	RESERVE ADQ INDEX (PTS)	PROFIT-ABILITY INDEX (PTS)	LIQUIDITY INDEX (PTS)	STAB. INDEX (PTS)	STABILITY FACTORS
GERMANIA SELECT INS CO	TX	**C**	111.4	46.3	80.7	1.2	7.6	3.3	5.8	6.9	3.4	GT
GERMANTOWN INS CO	PA	**C+**	75.1	36.4	27.7	0.6	7.4	4.4	7.4	6.6	4.6	T
GERMANTOWN MUTUAL INS CO	WI	**C+**	62.8	29.5	28.4	0.0	8.8	6.9	6.1	5.9	4.7	T
▼GHS PROPERTY & CASUALTY INS CO	OK	**C**	44.5	20.5	32.3	-0.1	5.0	9.6	3.7	6.2	2.9	DFGR
GIBRALTAR NATIONAL INS CO	AR	**E+**	5.4	1.7	3.2	-0.1	0.8	0.3	1.1	0.0	0.4	CDFG
▲GLOBAL HAWK INS CO RRG	VT	**D**	4.9	3.0	0.8	0.0	3.4	1.3	3.0	7.0	1.5	CDFG
GLOBAL INS CO	GA	**U** (1)	3.1	3.0	0.0	-0.4	N/A	3.6	2.5	10.0	3.7	GORT
GLOBAL INTL INS CO RRG	DC	**D+**	16.7	15.6	0.9	0.2	10.0	N/A	8.5	9.5	2.4	DGRT
▲GLOBAL LIBERTY INS CO OF NY	NY	**D-**	44.1	9.1	15.6	-0.1	2.7	7.1	6.8	7.0	1.2	DFGT
GLOBAL REINS CORP OF AMERICA	NY	**D-**	504.8	134.6	0.2	7.5	2.7	4.9	2.9	8.2	1.3	FGT
GLOBAL REINSURANCE CORP	NY	**U** (1)	266.6	45.0	-0.4	0.8	N/A	1.5	2.9	10.0	1.5	CFRT
GLOBAL SURETY & INS CO	NE	**U** (1)	74.2	73.2	0.0	2.3	N/A	6.0	7.2	10.0	5.3	T
GLOBE AMERICAN CAS CO	OH	**B**	8.8	8.5	0.0	0.1	10.0	N/A	5.3	7.0	4.0	DGT
GMAC INS CO ONLINE INC	MO	**C**	13.7	10.0	1.2	0.0	10.0	6.2	3.3	8.5	2.9	DGT
GNY CUSTOM INS CO	AZ	**B**	48.7	43.3	2.2	0.4	10.0	3.6	5.0	9.2	5.5	DGT
GOLDEN BEAR INS CO	CA	**D**	96.8	31.7	10.1	0.9	3.5	5.8	8.8	9.5	1.5	CT
GOLDEN EAGLE INS CORP	CA	**C+**	975.7	187.9	372.8	7.0	7.3	7.0	2.8	5.8	2.9	ADT
GOLDSTREET INS CO	NY	**U** (1)	18.4	9.1	0.0	0.5	N/A	4.0	4.7	10.0	3.8	RT
GOOD SHEPHERD RECIPROCAL RRG	SC	**D-**	2.7	1.9	0.6	0.0	10.0	N/A	9.0	9.8	1.2	DGT
GOODVILLE MUTUAL CAS CO	PA	**C+**	119.6	68.3	58.8	0.1	10.0	9.0	7.9	6.8	4.5	RT
GOTHAM INS CO	NY	**B**	117.8	56.1	24.1	-0.2	9.3	9.0	3.7	8.0	4.7	T
GOVERNMENT EMPLOYEES INS CO	MD	**B+**	12,473.2	3,968.3	8,763.3	-172.8	7.4	9.3	3.5	2.6	5.3	LT
GOVERNMENT ENTITIES MUTUAL INC	DC	**D-**	45.6	18.8	7.9	0.6	4.5	5.5	6.4	7.7	1.2	DGT
GOVERNMENTAL INTERINSURANCE	IL	**B-**	64.3	43.2	6.0	0.2	10.0	8.6	4.8	7.0	4.9	DT
GRACO RRG INC	SC	**D**	1.7	0.5	0.1	0.0	8.0	3.3	5.3	7.0	0.8	DFGO
▼GRAIN DEALERS MUTUAL INS CO	IN	**C-**	49.1	8.5	27.0	-1.3	4.3	6.6	1.3	4.3	2.9	CDFL
GRAMERCY INS CO	TX	**C-**	30.5	14.6	10.0	0.1	8.4	8.9	7.8	6.7	3.2	DFGT
▼GRANADA INS CO	FL	**E+**	28.1	9.1	13.3	0.3	0.4	2.1	3.3	2.3	0.6	CDFG
GRANGE INDEMNITY INS CO	OH	**B-**	72.3	32.6	42.8	-0.3	8.2	8.1	6.5	6.1	4.9	FT
▲GRANGE INS ASN	WA	**C+**	203.0	104.5	105.9	2.1	9.3	5.6	8.6	6.4	4.5	T
GRANGE INS CO OF MI	OH	**C**	49.6	24.1	26.8	0.1	8.2	8.1	7.1	6.3	4.2	DT
GRANGE MUTUAL CAS CO	OH	**A-**	1,525.7	682.0	899.0	-14.0	8.3	8.1	5.5	5.5	5.5	FT
GRANGE MUTUAL FIRE INS CO	PA	**D+**	2.9	2.0	0.8	0.1	7.8	8.4	5.2	7.9	1.7	DGT
▲GRANGE PROPERTY & CASUALTY INS CO	OH	**C**	37.2	16.7	21.4	0.0	8.0	5.8	4.5	6.3	3.0	DFGT
GRANITE MUTUAL INS CO	VT	**C+**	4.0	4.0	0.0	0.1	10.0	N/A	6.9	7.0	3.4	DG
GRANITE RE INC	OK	**C-**	26.3	13.2	19.0	0.2	3.8	10.0	8.6	6.9	2.9	DGT
GRANITE STATE INS CO	PA	**B-**	38.6	35.2	0.0	0.3	10.0	N/A	8.0	7.0	5.3	GT
GRAPHIC ARTS MUTUAL INS CO	NY	**C+**	124.0	45.8	30.4	0.4	9.3	6.2	7.7	7.0	4.4	T
GRAY CASUALTY & SURETY CO	LA	**C-**	17.2	14.5	2.1	0.1	10.0	N/A	8.5	10.0	2.5	DGT
GRAY INS CO	LA	**B-**	328.3	88.7	84.6	2.6	5.1	3.7	7.7	8.7	4.7	CRT
GREAT AMERICAN ALLIANCE INS CO	OH	**C**	27.7	27.6	0.0	0.2	10.0	N/A	7.4	7.0	4.3	AG
GREAT AMERICAN ASR CO	OH	**C+**	16.9	16.9	0.0	0.1	10.0	N/A	7.7	7.0	4.4	ADG
GREAT AMERICAN CASUALTY INS CO	OH	**U** (1)	11.8	11.8	0.0	0.4	N/A	N/A	4.0	7.0	5.2	AT
GREAT AMERICAN CONTEMPORARY INS CO	OH	**C+**	10.5	10.5	0.0	-0.1	10.0	N/A	4.7	7.0	4.4	ADG
GREAT AMERICAN E & S INS CO	DE	**C**	26.1	25.8	0.0	0.4	10.0	N/A	7.0	7.0	4.0	AG
GREAT AMERICAN FIDELITY INS CO	DE	**C**	25.9	25.3	0.0	0.3	10.0	N/A	6.7	7.0	3.7	ADGT
▲GREAT AMERICAN INS CO	OH	**C**	5,206.4	1,289.6	1,952.7	60.8	5.3	3.3	3.6	6.5	3.5	AT
GREAT AMERICAN INS CO OF NEW YORK	NY	**C**	58.9	58.2	0.0	0.4	10.0	N/A	7.1	7.0	4.3	AT
GREAT AMERICAN LLOYDS INS CO	TX	**C**	1.4	1.4	0.0	0.0	10.0	N/A	7.6	10.0	2.9	DGT
GREAT AMERICAN PROTECTION INS CO	OH	**U** (1)	24.5	24.5	0.0	0.5	N/A	N/A	6.7	7.0	5.4	ADRT
GREAT AMERICAN SECURITY INS CO	OH	**C**	18.2	17.4	0.0	-0.1	10.0	N/A	4.8	7.0	3.3	ADGT
GREAT AMERICAN SPIRIT INS CO	OH	**C+**	20.2	19.2	0.0	0.1	10.0	N/A	7.0	7.0	3.4	ADGT

See Page 27 for explanation of footnotes and Page 28 for explanation of stability factors.

Arrows denote recent upgrades ▲ or downgrades ▼ (see Section VII for explanations)

RISK ADJ. RATIO #1	CAPITAL RATIO #2	PREMIUM TO SURPLUS (%)	RESV. TO SURPLUS (%)	RESV. DEVELOP. 1 YEAR (%)	RESV. DEVELOP. 2 YEAR (%)	LOSS RATIO (%)	EXP. RATIO (%)	COMB RATIO (%)	CASH FROM UNDER-WRITING (%)	NET PREMIUM GROWTH (%)	INVEST. IN AFFIL (%)	INSURANCE COMPANY NAME
1.8	1.5	179.8	38.2	20.3	9.6	65.4	22.6	88.0	161.5	0.0	1.3	GERMANIA SELECT INS CO
2.3	1.6	75.3	49.6	-10.8	-5.2	56.1	23.3	79.4	110.2	-1.2	0.0	GERMANTOWN INS CO
3.5	2.3	94.0	52.2	-8.0	-8.6	70.4	31.3	101.7	93.6	-2.4	0.0	GERMANTOWN MUTUAL INS CO
1.2	0.8	152.1	58.3	1.8	-17.6	78.2	40.5	118.7	83.4	16.0	0.0	GHS PROPERTY & CASUALTY INS CO
0.2	0.2	189.4	193.1	43.2	63.6	113.4	29.1	142.5	95.3	41.6	0.0	GIBRALTAR NATIONAL INS CO
0.7	0.5	38.5	112.1	8.3	55.6	50.0	200.4	250.4	25.7	-79.4	0.0	GLOBAL HAWK INS CO RRG
N/A	N/A	0.4	N/A	N/A	N/A	N/A	608.3	608.3	15.1	140.0	0.0	GLOBAL INS CO
32.1	28.9	5.5	N/A	N/A	N/A	N/A	30.8	30.8	344.8	-12.5	0.0	GLOBAL INTL INS CO RRG
1.0	0.6	172.6	210.5	-46.8	-61.7	54.3	25.6	79.9	100.7	-10.7	0.0	GLOBAL LIBERTY INS CO OF NY
1.2	0.8	0.1	248.0	11.2	9.4	999 +	999 +	999 +	2.5	78.4	2.5	GLOBAL REINS CORP OF AMERICA
N/A	N/A	-0.8	432.9	16.6	28.0	999 +	-882.3	999 +	-0.9	N/A	0.0	GLOBAL REINSURANCE CORP
N/A	N/A	N/A	0.8	0.1	0.2	3.8	N/A	N/A	N/A	100.0	0.0	GLOBAL SURETY & INS CO
52.5	47.2	N/A	N/A	N/A	N/A	N/A	N/A	N/A	N/A	0.0	0.0	GLOBE AMERICAN CAS CO
8.4	7.6	12.0	4.1	N/A	-0.3	106.6	25.1	131.7	131.5	N/A	0.0	GMAC INS CO ONLINE INC
24.4	18.4	5.0	9.0	-0.2	-0.3	62.5	32.7	95.2	100.8	0.0	0.0	GNY CUSTOM INS CO
0.7	0.5	30.9	172.5	-3.0	-4.0	56.7	35.8	92.5	103.5	-37.9	0.0	GOLDEN BEAR INS CO
2.1	1.4	206.2	281.1	-11.9	-23.0	63.2	39.5	102.7	100.5	-24.2	0.0 •	GOLDEN EAGLE INS CORP
N/A	N/A	N/A	96.1	-0.6	1.4	N/A	N/A	N/A	N/A	100.0	0.0	GOLDSTREET INS CO
5.1	4.5	30.5	12.8	N/A	N/A	-16.1	35.5	19.4	294.4	31.1	0.0	GOOD SHEPHERD RECIPROCAL RRG
5.9	4.2	84.8	27.0	-4.2	-6.5	53.5	29.2	82.7	114.5	1.8	0.0	GOODVILLE MUTUAL CAS CO
3.7	2.5	43.2	75.8	-5.3	-10.1	54.3	33.4	87.7	119.6	-3.8	0.0	GOTHAM INS CO
1.6	1.2	212.1	132.9	-6.8	-12.3	75.5	15.7	91.2	116.3	4.5	3.6 •	GOVERNMENT EMPLOYEES INS CO
1.1	0.5	43.0	121.7	-3.9	-2.4	62.9	18.3	81.2	119.4	-0.4	0.0	GOVERNMENT ENTITIES MUTUAL INC
5.1	3.7	14.0	36.4	-2.0	-6.9	110.5	40.6	151.1	64.8	-14.2	0.0	GOVERNMENTAL INTERINSURANCE
0.9	0.8	29.0	N/A	N/A	N/A	N/A	113.0	113.0	-5.3	5.0	0.0	GRACO RRG INC
0.8	0.5	285.1	142.0	-4.4	-14.2	79.0	36.5	115.5	82.3	2.0	0.6	GRAIN DEALERS MUTUAL INS CO
4.1	2.9	68.8	15.5	-3.9	-7.1	69.1	43.5	112.6	63.0	-4.3	0.0	GRAMERCY INS CO
0.1	0.1	147.3	125.0	19.5	34.5	58.9	63.0	121.9	81.2	-26.9	0.0	GRANADA INS CO
2.8	1.7	129.4	62.0	-3.6	-8.1	67.8	28.1	95.9	95.4	-17.5	0.0	GRANGE INDEMNITY INS CO
4.2	3.3	101.8	43.4	-2.6	-8.8	65.5	29.7	95.2	99.0	1.9	7.6	GRANGE INS ASN
3.0	1.9	109.3	52.4	-3.1	-7.4	67.8	24.1	91.9	94.4	-9.2	0.0	GRANGE INS CO OF MI
2.7	1.8	126.1	60.4	-2.9	-6.7	67.8	30.8	98.6	94.3	-1.0	10.1 •	GRANGE MUTUAL CAS CO
2.4	1.7	37.6	8.3	-2.2	-3.7	42.8	42.5	85.3	133.7	-1.0	0.0	GRANGE MUTUAL FIRE INS CO
2.6	1.6	127.2	60.9	-5.1	-10.7	67.8	29.8	97.6	95.4	-28.4	0.0	GRANGE PROPERTY & CASUALTY INS CO
136.7	71.1	N/A	N/A	N/A	N/A	N/A	N/A	N/A	N/A	0.0	0.0	GRANITE MUTUAL INS CO
0.7	0.6	146.0	87.4	-38.8	-57.1	23.3	68.8	92.1	134.8	13.0	0.0	GRANITE RE INC
23.4	18.4	N/A	N/A	N/A	N/A	N/A	N/A	N/A	N/A	0.0	3.5	GRANITE STATE INS CO
4.1	2.7	65.4	122.6	-1.2	-3.1	61.7	35.3	97.0	99.3	0.2	2.2	GRAPHIC ARTS MUTUAL INS CO
15.7	11.1	14.6	7.0	N/A	N/A	4.7	34.9	39.6	280.8	30.2	0.0	GRAY CASUALTY & SURETY CO
0.9	0.6	87.3	224.4	-1.0	8.7	69.0	31.5	100.5	112.9	-12.4	4.9	GRAY INS CO
297.1	149.2	N/A	N/A	N/A	N/A	N/A	N/A	N/A	N/A	0.0	0.0	GREAT AMERICAN ALLIANCE INS CO
586.0	448.6	N/A	N/A	N/A	N/A	N/A	N/A	N/A	N/A	0.0	0.0	GREAT AMERICAN ASR CO
N/A	N/A	N/A	N/A	N/A	N/A	N/A	N/A	N/A	N/A	0.0	0.0	GREAT AMERICAN CASUALTY INS CO
152.9	69.2	N/A	N/A	N/A	N/A	N/A	N/A	N/A	N/A	0.0	0.0	GREAT AMERICAN CONTEMPORARY INS
97.8	42.4	N/A	N/A	N/A	N/A	N/A	N/A	N/A	N/A	0.0	0.0	GREAT AMERICAN E & S INS CO
77.2	34.9	N/A	N/A	N/A	N/A	N/A	N/A	N/A	N/A	0.0	0.0	GREAT AMERICAN FIDELITY INS CO
1.3	0.8	151.8	214.4	-11.1	-2.2	62.6	34.0	96.6	104.5	8.1	9.4 •	GREAT AMERICAN INS CO
74.3	39.0	N/A	N/A	N/A	N/A	N/A	N/A	N/A	N/A	0.0	0.0	GREAT AMERICAN INS CO OF NEW YORK
240.8	120.4	N/A	N/A	N/A	N/A	N/A	N/A	N/A	N/A	0.0	0.0	GREAT AMERICAN LLOYDS INS CO
N/A	N/A	N/A	N/A	N/A	N/A	N/A	N/A	N/A	N/A	0.0	0.0	GREAT AMERICAN PROTECTION INS CO
49.1	44.2	N/A	N/A	N/A	N/A	N/A	N/A	N/A	N/A	0.0	0.0	GREAT AMERICAN SECURITY INS CO
44.1	39.7	N/A	N/A	N/A	N/A	N/A	N/A	N/A	N/A	0.0	0.0	GREAT AMERICAN SPIRIT INS CO

999 + Denotes number greater than 999.9%
999 - Denotes number less than -999.99%
• Bullets denote a more detailed analysis is available in Section II.

INSURANCE COMPANY NAME	DOM. STATE	RATING	TOTAL ASSETS ($MIL)	CAPITAL & SURPLUS ($MIL)	ANNUAL NET PREMIUM ($MIL)	NET INCOME ($MIL)	CAPITAL-IZATION INDEX (PTS)	RESERVE ADQ INDEX (PTS)	PROFIT-ABILITY INDEX (PTS)	LIQUIDITY INDEX (PTS)	STAB. INDEX (PTS)	STABILITY FACTORS
GREAT CENTRAL FIRE INS CO	LA	**D+**	3.4	2.5	3.5	0.1	5.4	6.7	3.7	7.0	2.4	DGT
GREAT DIVIDE INS CO	ND	**C**	157.5	70.1	24.7	0.8	10.0	8.6	8.9	7.1	4.3	T
▲GREAT LAKES CASUALTY INS CO	MI	**C-**	12.8	12.7	2.9	0.3	8.7	3.2	2.8	6.7	3.2	DFGT
GREAT LAKES MUTUAL INS CO	MI	**D**	4.0	2.2	2.2	0.0	8.1	7.7	5.3	6.3	1.8	DGOT
GREAT MIDWEST INS CO	MI	**C**	44.5	33.0	3.3	0.2	8.7	9.4	8.4	8.4	4.3	DFGT
GREAT NORTHERN INS CO	IN	**B+**	1,518.9	400.5	353.8	23.2	7.6	5.6	9.3	6.7	5.8	T
▼GREAT NORTHWEST INS CO	IN	**D**	25.8	7.9	15.0	0.4	1.2	5.0	1.6	0.7	1.9	CDFG
GREAT WEST CASUALTY CO	NE	**A-**	1,460.5	375.0	572.5	15.0	9.1	9.4	3.8	6.4	6.9	T
GREATER NEW YORK MUTUAL INS CO	NY	**B**	810.8	364.7	181.1	6.6	8.3	4.8	8.7	7.0	4.9	T
GREEN HILLS INS CO RRG	VT	**D-**	14.3	7.4	4.9	0.5	9.1	5.9	9.5	6.7	0.0	DGT
GREEN MOUNTAIN INS CO INC	VT	**B**	9.3	8.8	0.0	0.1	10.0	3.6	1.9	7.0	4.0	DGT
GREEN TREE PERPETUAL ASR CO	PA	**U** (1)	1.2	1.2	0.0	0.6	N/A	6.3	2.9	10.0	0.0	CFGT
GREENVILLE CASUALTY INS CO INC	SC	**D-**	11.9	7.7	3.3	0.2	9.0	9.3	8.6	7.6	1.0	DGT
▲GREENWICH INS CO	DE	**D+**	919.6	419.8	215.3	19.4	4.5	4.0	7.8	6.8	2.8	AGT
GRINNELL MUTUAL REINSURANCE CO	IA	**B-**	725.2	289.6	303.3	6.6	8.2	6.9	6.0	6.3	4.7	FT
GRINNELL SELECT INS CO	IA	**B**	87.6	29.4	54.2	2.2	7.7	7.0	4.5	5.7	4.7	T
GROWERS AUTOMOBILE INS ASN	IN	**C-** (2)	4.3	2.5	0.2	0.2	7.1	6.7	3.5	9.4	2.0	DG
GSA INS CO	NJ	**U** (5)	0.0	0.0	-1.2	0.0	N/A	5.0	1.5	8.2	1.0	FRT
GUARANTEE CO OF NORTH AMERICA USA	MI	**C**	179.8	114.6	17.5	2.2	10.0	6.0	4.0	9.7	4.0	T
GUARANTEE INS CO	FL	**D+**	139.2	17.1	46.5	-2.8	1.0	5.0	3.9	6.1	2.4	CDGR
GUARDIAN INS CO INC	VI	**C+**(1)	26.5	13.2	14.9	2.0	8.1	5.8	8.8	6.5	3.0	DT
GUARDIAN RRG INC	MT	**E+**	4.9	1.8	1.1	0.0	2.5	3.7	2.1	7.1	0.0	DGT
GUIDEONE AMERICA INS CO	IA	**B-**	14.0	9.2	0.0	0.1	10.0	N/A	8.0	7.0	5.3	G
GUIDEONE ELITE INS CO	IA	**C+**	27.6	18.3	0.0	0.1	10.0	N/A	7.3	8.4	4.4	FG
GUIDEONE LLOYDS INS CO	TX	**B-**	3.6	2.9	0.0	0.0	10.0	N/A	7.7	9.3	3.9	DFG
▲GUIDEONE MUTUAL INS CO	IA	**C+**	1,000.8	362.0	298.1	4.1	7.7	5.8	8.5	6.6	4.5	FT
▲GUIDEONE PROPERTY & CASUALTY INS CO	IA	**B**	376.0	195.1	93.2	2.1	10.0	6.7	8.5	6.9	5.5	FT
▲GUIDEONE SPECIALTY MUTUAL INS CO	IA	**C+**	222.1	70.5	74.5	0.8	7.8	5.8	8.3	6.6	4.5	T
GUILDERLAND REINSURANCE CO	NY	**U** (1)	13.7	12.7	0.0	0.1	N/A	6.0	3.5	7.0	4.7	T
▲GUILFORD INS CO	IL	**C-**	356.4	208.0	45.1	2.4	7.2	5.9	8.8	7.0	2.6	T
GULF BUILDERS RRG INC	SC	**U** (1)	0.9	0.4	0.1	-0.1	N/A	3.6	1.3	2.7	1.2	GLT
GULF GUARANTY INS CO	MS	**C**	4.9	3.8	1.5	0.0	9.3	7.5	3.5	6.9	2.7	DFGT
GULF UNDERWRITERS INS CO	CT	**U** (1)	60.7	52.0	0.0	1.6	N/A	0.5	8.0	7.0	0.8	T
GULFSTREAM PROP & CAS INS CO	FL	**D+**	55.5	24.7	19.5	7.6	5.5	5.0	3.4	7.7	2.4	DOT
GUTHRIE RRG	SC	**D**	32.7	4.2	6.6	-0.2	1.9	6.1	1.9	6.6	1.5	CDGT
HALIFAX MUTUAL INS CO	NC	**D+**	5.0	2.1	2.5	0.0	7.6	4.6	4.5	6.5	1.8	DFGR
HALLMARK INS CO	AZ	**D**	163.7	51.1	80.0	0.9	5.4	4.9	8.3	6.9	2.2	T
HALLMARK SPECIALTY INS CO	OK	**D**	90.1	28.7	46.8	0.1	1.6	7.1	7.3	6.6	2.1	CT
HAMILTON MUTUAL INS CO	IA	**C**	63.9	23.7	20.9	0.6	7.9	5.8	3.6	6.9	3.9	DT
HANNAHSTOWN MUTUAL INS CO	PA	**D**	2.2	1.2	1.1	-0.2	8.2	6.8	2.9	7.0	1.3	DFGT
HANOVER AMERICAN INS CO	NH	**C+**	16.2	16.2	0.0	0.1	10.0	N/A	7.3	7.0	3.2	DGT
HANOVER FIRE & CASUALTY INS CO	PA	**D+**	3.4	2.6	4.4	0.0	4.0	6.0	1.8	5.4	2.5	DFGT
HANOVER INS CO	NH	**B-**	4,742.8	1,519.8	1,782.4	18.8	7.7	7.0	5.9	6.5	5.1	AT
HANOVER LLOYDS INS CO	TX	**C+**	5.0	5.0	0.0	0.0	10.0	N/A	8.1	7.0	3.0	DGT
HANOVER NJ INS CO	NH	**C**	26.2	26.1	0.0	0.2	10.0	N/A	6.8	7.0	3.8	GT
HANYS MEMBER HOSP SELF INS TRUST	NY	**C**	62.0	55.7	0.0	0.3	7.9	6.3	2.6	10.0	3.7	DT
HARBOR INS CO	OK	**D+**	12.8	4.2	4.0	0.0	7.9	9.3	7.6	8.5	2.2	DGRT
HARBOR POINT REINS US INC	CT	**B**	793.7	515.4	64.8	0.0	10.0	4.5	6.1	9.2	4.1	GT
HARBOR SPECIALTY INS CO	NJ	**U** (1)	131.8	28.5	-0.1	5.7	N/A	6.0	2.6	10.0	4.0	RT
HARCO NATIONAL INS CO	IL	**B**	301.2	116.7	66.4	1.9	8.0	6.4	2.8	6.9	4.7	T
HARFORD MUTUAL INS CO	MD	**B-**	271.9	117.6	67.9	-0.8	8.5	6.0	6.6	7.0	4.7	T
HARLEYSVILLE INS CO	PA	**C**	133.8	30.1	50.9	0.8	7.5	4.7	6.7	7.4	4.0	AT

See Page 27 for explanation of footnotes and Page 28 for explanation of stability factors.
Arrows denote recent upgrades ▲ or downgrades ▼ (see Section VII for explanations)

RISK ADJ. RATIO #1	CAPITAL RATIO #2	PREMIUM TO SURPLUS (%)	RESV. TO SURPLUS (%)	RESV. DEVELOP. 1 YEAR (%)	RESV. DEVELOP. 2 YEAR (%)	LOSS RATIO (%)	EXP. RATIO (%)	COMB RATIO (%)	CASH FROM UNDER-WRITING (%)	NET PREMIUM GROWTH (%)	INVEST. IN AFFIL (%)	INSURANCE COMPANY NAME
0.9	0.8	146.2	11.1	-2.6	-6.3	24.9	75.3	100.2	100.3	-7.6	0.0	GREAT CENTRAL FIRE INS CO
6.3	3.6	35.8	54.7	-3.8	-7.1	54.1	24.4	78.5	136.5	1.8	0.0	GREAT DIVIDE INS CO
8.4	6.8	23.3	N/A	42.8	49.3	100.3	60.7	161.0	36.9	-59.6	0.0	GREAT LAKES CASUALTY INS CO
2.8	1.7	98.6	17.0	-6.0	-2.4	57.0	33.5	90.5	119.6	28.2	0.0	GREAT LAKES MUTUAL INS CO
2.0	2.0	9.8	14.8	-9.4	-18.5	45.8	38.1	83.9	81.2	-52.2	41.0	GREAT MIDWEST INS CO
2.3	1.5	91.7	165.1	-5.9	-11.4	61.3	28.7	90.0	111.8	-2.6	0.0 •	GREAT NORTHERN INS CO
0.4	0.3	224.1	89.1	1.2	2.0	91.0	33.4	124.4	84.5	-1.0	0.0	GREAT NORTHWEST INS CO
3.7	2.3	153.8	182.6	-8.4	-15.2	73.2	23.2	96.4	101.9	-3.9	0.0 •	GREAT WEST CASUALTY CO
2.5	2.1	50.7	91.0	-2.4	-3.1	62.5	32.7	95.2	100.8	-7.1	15.2 •	GREATER NEW YORK MUTUAL INS CO
3.9	2.5	71.0	61.9	-10.3	-18.1	19.8	21.2	41.0	494.8	20.6	0.0	GREEN HILLS INS CO RRG
39.9	35.9	N/A	N/A	N/A	N/A	N/A	N/A	N/A	N/A	0.0	0.0	GREEN MOUNTAIN INS CO INC
N/A	N/A	N/A	1.3	0.1	-3.0	N/A	N/A	N/A	N/A	0.0	0.0	GREEN TREE PERPETUAL ASR CO
4.0	2.9	43.6	20.3	-15.0	-17.2	42.3	41.9	84.2	109.0	10.1	0.0	GREENVILLE CASUALTY INS CO INC
1.0	0.7	48.4	70.0	-7.1	-5.3	60.4	23.0	83.4	185.7	128.2	31.5 •	GREENWICH INS CO
2.4	1.7	106.3	77.7	-3.5	-10.9	78.3	32.8	111.1	89.9	-2.0	5.2 •	GRINNELL MUTUAL REINSURANCE CO
3.2	2.6	189.4	99.4	-6.7	-14.7	87.0	22.9	109.9	105.7	15.9	0.0	GRINNELL SELECT INS CO
1.8	1.1	8.8	0.7	-0.3	-1.0	98.9	53.4	152.3	80.1	-5.6	0.0	GROWERS AUTOMOBILE INS ASN
N/A	N/A	-7.6	56.1	14.5	22.4	-254.6	13.1	-241.5	-6.3	0.0	0.0	GSA INS CO
5.3	4.6	15.5	2.9	0.1	1.7	28.4	75.1	103.5	109.3	17.2	0.0	GUARANTEE CO OF NORTH AMERICA
0.4	0.2	254.4	205.4	17.3	-66.3	72.5	26.8	99.3	115.4	57.6	0.0	GUARANTEE INS CO
2.6	2.2	112.6	31.4	-8.6	-13.0	47.8	41.7	89.5	103.0	-9.6	0.0	GUARDIAN INS CO INC
0.5	0.4	59.4	123.9	27.9	9.9	159.9	14.2	174.1	149.4	-4.6	0.0	GUARDIAN RRG INC
6.2	5.6	N/A	N/A	N/A	N/A	N/A	N/A	N/A	-54.0	0.0	0.0	GUIDEONE AMERICA INS CO
7.9	7.1	N/A	N/A	N/A	N/A	N/A	N/A	N/A	-27.7	0.0	0.0	GUIDEONE ELITE INS CO
10.4	9.4	N/A	N/A	N/A	N/A	N/A	N/A	N/A	6.2	0.0	0.0	GUIDEONE LLOYDS INS CO
1.8	1.5	82.8	103.8	-9.1	-15.0	70.7	32.8	103.5	91.0	-4.7	21.0 •	GUIDEONE MUTUAL INS CO
4.6	3.4	48.0	60.2	-5.3	-7.7	70.7	30.8	101.5	93.2	-4.7	9.1 •	GUIDEONE PROPERTY & CASUALTY INS
2.6	1.8	105.7	138.7	-11.3	-21.0	71.1	30.8	101.9	92.7	-4.7	7.2	GUIDEONE SPECIALTY MUTUAL INS CO
N/A	N/A	N/A	5.9	-2.1	-2.4	N/A	N/A	N/A	-27.9	100.0	0.0	GUILDERLAND REINSURANCE CO
1.5	1.2	21.9	60.5	-4.0	-1.7	56.3	37.0	93.3	99.5	-27.7	40.9 •	GUILFORD INS CO
N/A	N/A	32.2	2.1	0.4	N/A	23.1	110.1	133.2	228.5	-8.6	0.0	GULF BUILDERS RRG INC
3.3	2.9	40.1	4.1	-1.3	-1.9	38.5	74.0	112.5	87.6	-7.7	1.9	GULF GUARANTY INS CO
N/A	N/A	N/A	N/A	N/A	N/A	N/A	N/A	N/A	N/A	0.0	0.0	GULF UNDERWRITERS INS CO
1.8	1.1	111.9	50.7	-3.9	-22.7	61.5	58.9	120.4	95.2	-3.7	0.0	GULFSTREAM PROP & CAS INS CO
0.4	0.3	147.8	573.7	-40.5	-61.7	114.3	7.4	121.7	227.5	1.1	0.0	GUTHRIE RRG
2.0	1.5	114.2	12.7	0.6	-2.3	72.8	27.9	100.7	87.7	9.4	0.0	HALIFAX MUTUAL INS CO
1.4	1.0	158.2	101.1	-2.9	-7.4	63.4	26.2	89.6	120.1	-1.4	0.0	HALLMARK INS CO
0.4	0.3	163.4	104.3	-3.1	-7.4	63.4	29.0	92.4	128.0	-1.4	0.0	HALLMARK SPECIALTY INS CO
2.8	1.8	89.5	113.0	-4.7	-7.8	73.7	33.1	106.8	98.1	167.5	0.0	HAMILTON MUTUAL INS CO
2.6	1.6	71.1	12.5	-4.0	-1.3	44.0	44.0	88.0	101.1	1.7	0.0	HANNAHSTOWN MUTUAL INS CO
70.1	30.7	N/A	N/A	N/A	N/A	N/A	N/A	N/A	N/A	0.0	0.0	HANOVER AMERICAN INS CO
0.6	0.5	166.6	7.2	-0.9	0.2	21.9	85.0	106.9	86.8	174.5	0.0	HANOVER FIRE & CASUALTY INS CO
1.6	1.4	115.9	104.0	-6.4	-10.4	65.6	35.1	100.7	107.2	4.1	23.3 •	HANOVER INS CO
68.2	32.5	N/A	N/A	N/A	N/A	N/A	N/A	N/A	N/A	0.0	0.0	HANOVER LLOYDS INS CO
72.2	32.4	N/A	N/A	N/A	N/A	N/A	N/A	N/A	N/A	0.0	0.0	HANOVER NJ INS CO
1.9	1.6	N/A	N/A	-0.6	-2.5	N/A	N/A	N/A	N/A	0.0	53.3	HANYS MEMBER HOSP SELF INS TRUST
1.9	1.7	93.8	41.3	-4.4	-16.4	78.2	15.0	93.2	104.6	-3.8	0.0	HARBOR INS CO
17.0	9.9	12.6	3.4	N/A	N/A	76.8	28.6	105.4	279.8	N/A	0.0 •	HARBOR POINT REINS US INC
N/A	N/A	-0.3	42.5	-11.4	-17.8	999 +	-862.2	999 +	30.1	95.5	0.0	HARBOR SPECIALTY INS CO
2.9	1.7	51.0	116.0	0.4	-1.9	84.4	30.3	114.7	51.7	-23.7	0.0	HARCO NATIONAL INS CO
2.8	2.1	55.7	71.4	-12.3	-21.3	52.4	37.9	90.3	112.4	-1.6	12.2	HARFORD MUTUAL INS CO
2.0	1.3	174.8	267.4	-5.0	-9.0	66.5	32.8	99.3	183.2	45.9	0.0	HARLEYSVILLE INS CO

999 + Denotes number greater than 999.9%
999 - Denotes number less than -999.99%
• Bullets denote a more detailed analysis is available in Section II.

INSURANCE COMPANY NAME	DOM. STATE	RATING	TOTAL ASSETS ($MIL)	CAPITAL & SURPLUS ($MIL)	ANNUAL NET PREMIUM ($MIL)	NET INCOME ($MIL)	CAPITAL-IZATION INDEX (PTS)	RESERVE ADQ INDEX (PTS)	PROFIT-ABILITY INDEX (PTS)	LIQUIDITY INDEX (PTS)	STAB. INDEX (PTS)	STABILITY FACTORS
HARLEYSVILLE INS CO OF NEW YORK	NY	**C+**	80.0	19.9	22.6	0.2	7.2	4.7	7.0	7.0	4.4	ADFT
HARLEYSVILLE INS CO OF NJ	NJ	**B-**	696.3	151.5	248.8	3.7	7.5	4.7	4.5	7.0	4.8	AT
HARLEYSVILLE INS CO OF OHIO	OH	**B-**	38.5	11.8	11.3	0.3	7.5	4.7	7.0	7.0	4.6	ADGT
HARLEYSVILLE LAKE STATES INS CO	MI	**C+**	295.5	64.9	107.5	1.4	7.5	4.7	5.6	6.8	4.5	AT
HARLEYSVILLE MUTUAL INS CO	PA	**B-**	1,296.4	741.0	140.9	0.4	7.8	4.9	6.8	6.9	4.8	AFT
HARLEYSVILLE PENNLAND INS CO	PA	**C+**	184.6	80.0	39.5	0.3	9.8	5.3	8.2	6.7	4.4	AFT
HARLEYSVILLE PREFERRED INS CO	PA	**B-**	693.3	147.4	254.6	4.7	7.4	4.7	3.7	7.1	4.8	AT
▲HARLEYSVILLE WORCESTER INS CO	PA	**C+**	535.2	121.7	180.9	2.8	7.7	4.7	5.6	6.8	4.5	AT
HARLEYSVILLE-ATLANTIC INS CO	GA	**B**	204.9	49.0	73.5	1.4	7.7	4.7	6.5	7.1	4.8	AT
HARTFORD ACCIDENT & INDEMNITY CO	CT	**C+**	10,829.4	2,765.0	3,337.5	-44.7	7.8	4.3	3.5	6.8	4.3	T
HARTFORD CASUALTY INS CO	IN	**B**	2,124.5	847.0	561.5	-60.5	9.7	4.7	4.6	6.9	5.9	T
HARTFORD FIRE INS CO	CT	**B+**	23,864.9	12,364.8	4,237.0	95.1	8.7	4.8	6.9	6.9	6.4	T
▲HARTFORD INS CO OF IL	IL	**B**	3,683.3	1,324.3	1,031.2	8.4	9.3	4.5	5.0	6.9	5.4	T
HARTFORD INS CO OF THE MIDWEST	IN	**B+**	359.6	244.2	51.0	4.6	10.0	4.9	8.9	7.0	6.4	T
HARTFORD INS CO OF THE SOUTHEAST	CT	**B**	170.0	55.9	51.0	2.9	8.6	4.5	3.2	6.7	5.4	T
HARTFORD LLOYDS INS CO	TX	**B**	55.1	52.5	1.0	0.7	10.0	6.0	8.4	10.0	6.2	T
▼HARTFORD SM BOIL INSPECTION & INS	CT	**B-**	1,164.7	466.6	643.4	10.6	8.0	9.3	3.1	6.7	4.9	T
HARTFORD SM BOIL INSPECTION IC OF CT	CT	**B**	101.1	50.7	30.8	3.6	10.0	9.3	9.4	7.5	5.6	T
HARTFORD UNDERWRITERS INS CO	CT	**B+**	1,564.1	645.7	408.4	-18.9	9.7	4.7	5.8	6.8	6.4	T
HARTLAND MUT INS CO	ND	**C-**	7.3	4.3	3.6	0.2	7.5	6.2	2.2	6.5	2.2	DFGT
HASTINGS MUTUAL INS CO	MI	**A+**	591.7	289.3	266.8	-0.4	10.0	9.3	8.4	6.6	7.4	FT
HAULERS INS CO INC	TN	**C**	50.8	33.2	25.3	0.4	10.0	7.0	8.6	6.7	4.3	T
HAWAII EMPLOYERS MUTUAL INS CO	HI	**D+**	258.9	135.3	44.7	2.0	7.4	6.1	9.4	7.1	2.8	RT
▲HAWAIIAN INS & GUARANTY CO LTD	HI	**C**	24.8	10.1	9.8	0.2	6.6	3.6	3.2	7.1	2.6	DGT
HAWKEYE-SECURITY INS CO	WI	**C+**	12.8	11.9	0.0	0.1	10.0	N/A	3.3	7.0	4.4	DG
HAY CREEK MUTUAL INS CO	MN	**E+**	3.5	1.6	2.8	0.1	7.6	6.0	2.8	2.8	0.4	DFGL
HCC INS CO	IN	**C+**	29.0	28.7	0.0	0.2	10.0	6.1	6.8	10.0	3.7	DFGR
HCC SPECIALTY INS CO	OK	**C**	22.4	18.9	0.0	0.1	10.0	N/A	6.4	10.0	3.9	DG
HEALTH CARE CASUALTY RRG INC	DC	**E**	31.3	1.3	2.1	0.0	0.0	4.8	5.0	9.1	0.3	CDGR
HEALTH CARE INDEMNITY INC	CO	**C**	1,637.6	775.9	32.9	19.5	8.1	9.9	7.0	9.1	4.3	FRT
▼HEALTH CARE INDUSTRY LIAB RECIP INS	DC	**E**	130.0	5.7	3.0	0.2	0.0	3.5	9.8	9.2	0.1	CDRT
HEALTH CARE INS RECIPROCAL	MN	**D**	21.5	7.3	4.7	0.1	3.9	5.2	8.9	6.7	1.7	CDGT
▲HEALTH CARE MUT CAPTIVE INS CO	GA	**D**	10.7	2.5	4.4	0.0	2.4	3.8	4.1	6.7	1.5	CDGT
▼HEALTH FACILITIES OF CA MUT I C RRG	NV	**D-**	5.6	1.0	2.3	-0.2	1.1	4.2	0.7	7.1	0.0	CDFG
HEALTH FUTURE INS EXCHANGE RRG	NV	**E**	3.2	1.2	1.5	0.1	0.9	0.5	1.7	6.9	0.3	CDFG
HEALTH NETWORK PROVIDERS MUT INS CO	DC	**D**	8.0	2.5	2.0	0.0	5.4	6.0	7.0	8.3	2.0	FGRT
▼HEALTH PROVIDERS INS RECIPROCAL RRG	HI	**C-**	60.7	24.9	14.1	-1.8	3.7	4.6	1.8	6.9	3.3	DT
HEALTHCARE PROFESSIONAL INS CO INC	NY	**E**	177.4	23.1	38.6	0.6	0.1	3.5	3.0	6.4	0.2	CDT
HEALTHCARE PROVIDERS INS CO RRG	SC	**D**	52.1	23.8	11.0	0.6	7.9	7.0	9.1	7.6	2.0	RT
▲HEALTHCARE PROVIDERS INS EXCH	PA	**C-**	99.8	32.0	25.8	0.1	5.0	7.0	5.9	7.9	2.9	GT
HEALTHCARE UNDERWRITERS GROUP OF	KY	**D+**	28.0	8.6	6.6	-0.1	6.5	5.8	4.7	7.8	2.8	DGRT
HEALTHCARE UNDERWRITERS GRP MUT	OH	**D+**	21.0	10.3	6.4	0.1	8.5	5.0	6.2	8.0	2.7	DGRT
HEALTHCARE UNDERWRITERS GRP OF FL	FL	**D**	40.9	16.7	9.2	0.1	7.6	4.9	5.4	7.9	1.5	DGRT
HEARTLAND HEALTHCARE RECIPROCAL	VT	**E+**	14.0	5.1	3.5	-0.4	6.6	6.1	4.2	8.2	0.0	DGT
HEARTLAND LLOYDS INS CO	TX	**U** (1)	7.3	7.3	0.0	0.2	N/A	5.0	7.8	7.0	4.8	RT
HEARTLAND MUTUAL INS CO	MN	**D+**	3.4	2.1	1.9	0.1	7.4	4.3	2.3	6.5	1.6	DGT
HEREFORD INS CO	NY	**D**	124.2	20.6	32.7	-0.7	5.0	7.0	5.6	7.9	2.3	DT
HERITAGE CASUALTY INS CO	IL	**B-**	113.3	51.8	41.7	9.3	7.3	7.0	2.6	1.8	4.9	LT
▲HERITAGE INDEMNITY CO	CA	**C+**	182.1	72.4	56.7	0.5	10.0	7.3	3.5	6.8	4.5	RT
HERITAGE WARRANTY INS RRG INC	SC	**E+**	4.4	2.0	0.9	0.1	7.2	7.1	1.9	9.0	0.8	FGT
HERMITAGE INS CO	NY	**C**	188.1	76.4	66.2	0.9	7.5	10.0	4.4	8.2	4.2	T
HIG LTD	HI	**F** (5)	0.0	0.0	0.0	0.0	10.0	N/A	2.9	10.0	0.9	DFT

See Page 27 for explanation of footnotes and Page 28 for explanation of stability factors.

Arrows denote recent upgrades ▲ or downgrades ▼ (see Section VII for explanations)

RISK ADJ. RATIO #1	CAPITAL RATIO #2	PREMIUM TO SURPLUS (%)	RESV. TO SURPLUS (%)	RESV. DEVELOP. 1 YEAR (%)	RESV. DEVELOP. 2 YEAR (%)	LOSS RATIO (%)	EXP. RATIO (%)	COMB RATIO (%)	CASH FROM UNDER-WRITING (%)	NET PREMIUM GROWTH (%)	INVEST. IN AFFIL (%)	INSURANCE COMPANY NAME
1.9	1.2	116.5	200.7	-4.6	-9.0	66.5	32.5	99.0	79.5	-2.9	0.0	HARLEYSVILLE INS CO OF NEW YORK
2.0	1.3	166.0	272.9	-4.8	-8.9	66.5	33.6	100.1	119.7	12.5	0.0	HARLEYSVILLE INS CO OF NJ
2.3	1.4	97.9	168.6	-3.9	-7.5	66.5	34.0	100.5	100.6	-2.9	0.0	HARLEYSVILLE INS CO OF OHIO
2.0	1.3	165.3	269.7	-4.9	-9.1	66.5	33.5	100.0	130.3	15.4	0.0	HARLEYSVILLE LAKE STATES INS CO
1.9	1.8	19.0	49.7	-0.3	-1.1	69.3	40.9	110.2	47.5	-47.4	35.4 •	HARLEYSVILLE MUTUAL INS CO
5.8	3.7	49.6	97.7	-2.2	-5.0	66.5	35.4	101.9	65.0	-32.1	0.0	HARLEYSVILLE PENNLAND INS CO
1.9	1.2	175.8	282.5	-4.8	-8.3	66.5	33.2	99.7	146.7	21.5	0.0	HARLEYSVILLE PREFERRED INS CO
2.2	1.4	149.1	256.9	-4.8	-8.8	66.5	33.8	100.3	104.6	-2.9	0.0	HARLEYSVILLE WORCESTER INS CO
2.2	1.4	153.9	244.6	-4.7	-8.4	66.5	33.4	99.9	147.3	26.4	0.0	HARLEYSVILLE-ATLANTIC INS CO
2.0	1.4	117.7	194.6	-3.3	-5.4	64.1	28.1	92.2	110.9	-2.2	8.4 •	HARTFORD ACCIDENT & INDEMNITY CO
4.7	3.0	67.1	110.9	-2.4	-3.8	64.1	24.7	88.8	110.9	-2.2	0.0 •	HARTFORD CASUALTY INS CO
2.4	2.2	33.9	56.1	-1.1	-2.0	64.1	33.3	97.4	110.1	-2.2	25.7 •	HARTFORD FIRE INS CO
4.1	2.6	78.5	129.8	-2.8	-4.4	64.1	27.7	91.8	110.9	-2.2	0.0 •	HARTFORD INS CO OF IL
14.1	8.9	21.3	35.1	-0.9	-1.6	64.1	4.9	69.0	110.9	-2.2	0.0 •	HARTFORD INS CO OF THE MIDWEST
3.3	2.1	96.3	159.2	-2.6	-4.1	64.1	26.6	90.7	110.9	-2.2	0.0	HARTFORD INS CO OF THE SOUTHEAST
60.4	32.4	2.0	3.3	-0.1	-0.1	64.1	-78.2	-14.1	110.9	-2.2	0.0	HARTFORD LLOYDS INS CO
1.9	1.7	145.4	46.6	-9.0	-11.6	27.4	50.1	77.5	126.1	4.0	13.1 •	HARTFORD SM BOIL INSPECTION & INS
3.8	3.4	66.4	16.8	-5.0	-6.6	27.2	18.0	45.2	244.6	3.4	6.6	HARTFORD SM BOIL INSPECTION IC OF
4.8	3.1	64.4	106.5	-2.4	-3.8	64.1	23.9	88.0	110.9	-2.2	0.0 •	HARTFORD UNDERWRITERS INS CO
1.7	1.3	86.4	12.4	0.8	-0.7	93.7	36.4	130.1	79.1	-3.5	8.9	HARTLAND MUT INS CO
6.0	4.2	91.3	51.3	-5.0	-6.7	64.3	30.2	94.5	94.1	0.5	0.0 •	HASTINGS MUTUAL INS CO
4.7	3.9	77.1	24.4	-1.3	-9.3	68.5	26.2	94.7	96.6	-4.6	0.0	HAULERS INS CO INC
4.0	2.2	32.9	69.6	-16.3	-29.8	42.9	23.5	66.4	130.9	-24.7	0.1	HAWAII EMPLOYERS MUTUAL INS CO
1.7	1.1	97.2	20.8	3.2	0.3	34.8	57.8	92.6	113.2	-12.2	0.0	HAWAIIAN INS & GUARANTY CO LTD
31.7	28.5	N/A	N/A	N/A	N/A	N/A	N/A	N/A	N/A	0.0	0.0	HAWKEYE-SECURITY INS CO
1.6	1.2	182.9	0.3	1.9	-5.8	61.9	33.3	95.2	80.3	25.7	0.0	HAY CREEK MUTUAL INS CO
45.6	21.3	N/A	4.8	1.9	1.5	999 +	999 +	999 +	-168.9	0.0	0.0	HCC INS CO
16.9	15.2	N/A	N/A	N/A	N/A	N/A	N/A	N/A	106.8	0.0	0.0	HCC SPECIALTY INS CO
0.1	0.0	169.4	999 +	-16.9	-17.5	74.2	32.5	106.7	262.9	15.7	0.0	HEALTH CARE CASUALTY RRG INC
2.8	2.5	3.8	96.1	-3.8	-43.0	16.9	-30.0	-13.1	12.2	-29.1	0.0 •	HEALTH CARE INDEMNITY INC
0.1	0.0	53.8	999 +	5.1	6.6	75.9	-26.5	49.4	-526.5	-15.9	0.0	HEALTH CARE INDUSTRY LIAB RECIP INS
1.2	0.4	64.0	139.6	-15.0	-16.2	59.6	29.1	88.7	98.5	-23.7	0.0	HEALTH CARE INS RECIPROCAL
0.7	0.3	160.6	169.6	-2.4	-22.1	66.9	33.9	100.8	99.3	-5.1	0.0	HEALTH CARE MUT CAPTIVE INS CO
0.3	0.2	213.2	232.6	43.3	8.5	88.4	44.1	132.5	76.8	-12.7	0.0	HEALTH FACILITIES OF CA MUT I C RRG
0.3	0.2	131.4	146.8	-43.8	32.7	35.6	41.2	76.8	57.4	7.2	0.0	HEALTH FUTURE INS EXCHANGE RRG
1.6	1.3	80.3	154.9	-11.9	-42.0	59.4	21.1	80.5	100.0	-11.7	0.0	HEALTH NETWORK PROVIDERS MUT INS
0.6	0.5	51.6	95.3	-2.2	9.7	61.7	28.9	90.6	94.4	-4.5	0.0	HEALTH PROVIDERS INS RECIPROCAL
0.2	0.1	174.2	494.6	-54.6	7.7	78.5	5.5	84.0	900.9	-20.6	0.0	HEALTHCARE PROFESSIONAL INS CO
2.9	1.9	46.5	81.1	-27.6	-44.7	13.4	29.4	42.8	239.9	-18.1	0.0	HEALTHCARE PROVIDERS INS CO RRG
1.5	1.0	79.4	130.8	0.7	-22.3	49.7	42.4	92.1	182.4	15.5	0.0	HEALTHCARE PROVIDERS INS EXCH
1.4	1.0	71.8	150.1	-8.2	-7.3	74.3	37.3	111.6	110.5	2.5	0.0	HEALTHCARE UNDERWRITERS GROUP
2.7	1.9	61.8	64.2	-13.9	-21.4	39.8	42.8	82.6	175.4	2.0	0.0	HEALTHCARE UNDERWRITERS GRP MUT
2.3	1.6	55.7	105.0	-11.6	-16.7	63.5	33.1	96.6	158.5	2.1	0.0	HEALTHCARE UNDERWRITERS GRP OF
2.1	1.3	64.4	102.3	-25.1	-98.8	39.6	21.0	60.6	277.5	5.5	0.0	HEARTLAND HEALTHCARE RECIPROCAL
N/A	N/A	N/A	N/A	N/A	N/A	N/A	N/A	N/A	N/A	0.0	0.0	HEARTLAND LLOYDS INS CO
2.4	1.7	97.1	7.4	-1.8	5.4	62.4	42.1	104.5	97.9	-5.8	0.0	HEARTLAND MUTUAL INS CO
1.3	0.8	158.0	198.2	2.6	-29.1	91.3	-5.2	86.1	142.9	6.2	0.0	HEREFORD INS CO
1.8	1.4	101.4	36.2	-14.7	-18.1	96.5	16.0	112.5	115.5	-41.5	0.0	HERITAGE CASUALTY INS CO
8.0	7.0	79.7	2.4	-0.6	-0.4	67.9	19.8	87.7	118.5	-13.0	0.0	HERITAGE INDEMNITY CO
2.0	1.7	48.6	39.6	-3.0	-9.8	56.9	105.9	162.8	18.5	163.5	0.0	HERITAGE WARRANTY INS RRG INC
2.2	1.8	86.0	88.2	11.5	-296.1	55.0	43.0	98.0	112.1	12.6	8.9	HERMITAGE INS CO
4.6	4.1	N/A	N/A	N/A	N/A	N/A	N/A	N/A	-22.4	0.0	0.0	HIG LTD

999 + Denotes number greater than 999.9%
999 - Denotes number less than -999.99%
• Bullets denote a more detailed analysis is available in Section II.

INSURANCE COMPANY NAME	DOM. STATE	RATING	TOTAL ASSETS ($MIL)	CAPITAL & SURPLUS ($MIL)	ANNUAL NET PREMIUM ($MIL)	NET INCOME ($MIL)	CAPITAL-IZATION INDEX (PTS)	RESERVE ADQ INDEX (PTS)	PROFIT-ABILITY INDEX (PTS)	LIQUIDITY INDEX (PTS)	STAB. INDEX (PTS)	STABILITY FACTORS
HIGH POINT PREFERRED INS CO	NJ	**C+**	866.7	221.2	497.3	3.1	6.1	9.5	5.6	6.1	4.4	T
HIGH POINT PROPERTY & CASUALTY INS	NJ	**B-**	36.0	24.4	0.0	0.2	10.0	N/A	6.5	7.0	4.9	DG
HIGH POINT SAFETY & INS CO	NJ	**C+**	56.4	39.4	0.0	0.3	10.0	N/A	6.6	10.0	4.6	
HIGH TECH SERVICES RRG INC	VT	**D** (1)	33.6	6.0	20.8	-0.9	0.1	3.6	2.0	9.0	1.4	CDGT
▲HIGHMARK CASUALTY INS CO	PA	**C**	221.7	99.0	79.1	2.1	2.6	4.7	7.8	5.6	3.4	CDT
▲HILLCREST INS CO	FL	**C-**	24.3	9.4	15.5	0.3	4.0	3.7	3.6	6.9	2.3	CDGT
HILLSTAR INS CO	IN	**C**	6.8	5.8	0.9	0.1	10.0	7.4	4.8	9.2	3.6	DGT
HINGHAM MUTUAL FIRE INS CO	MA	**C**	90.3	34.2	35.1	-2.3	7.1	4.8	2.1	5.3	4.1	FRT
HISCOX INS CO INC	IL	**B-**	57.7	51.5	8.6	0.4	9.2	7.6	6.4	8.9	4.7	DT
HOCHHEIM PRAIRIE CASUALTY INS CO	TX	**C-**	43.0	14.3	30.4	-0.2	7.3	8.6	4.4	5.5	3.1	DGRT
HOCHHEIM PRAIRIE FARM MUT INS ASN	TX	**C**	139.3	77.1	73.4	0.5	8.5	6.1	5.8	6.2	3.5	FT
HOLYOKE MUTUAL INS CO IN SALEM	MA	**B**	183.4	73.0	81.5	-0.2	9.9	7.5	5.8	6.1	5.6	FT
HOME & FARM INS CO	IN	**C-**	4.0	3.1	0.7	0.0	10.0	7.8	5.8	6.8	3.2	DFGT
HOME CONSTRUCTION INS CO RRG	NV	**D-**	5.9	2.0	0.1	0.0	3.8	5.0	3.7	10.0	1.0	DFGR
HOME STATE COUNTY MUTUAL INS CO	TX	**D**	131.1	4.6	3.1	0.2	1.7	3.2	2.9	8.2	1.7	CDFT
HOME-OWNERS INS CO	MI	**A**	1,353.2	451.9	770.2	11.1	8.4	8.3	5.5	4.7	7.4	LT
HOMELAND INS CO OF NEW YORK	NY	**C**	464.7	205.2	172.8	6.3	8.7	5.6	4.3	7.1	4.3	T
HOMEOWNERS CHOICE PROP & CAS INS	FL	**D+**	138.0	25.5	93.6	0.4	1.7	3.6	3.5	8.0	2.4	CGT
HOMEOWNERS OF AMERICA INS CO	TX	**D-**	7.7	3.6	4.0	-0.2	5.3	3.6	3.3	7.7	0.9	DGT
HOMESHIELD FIRE & CASUALTY INS CO	OK	**U** (1)	0.9	0.9	0.0	0.0	N/A	N/A	3.6	7.0	0.0	T
HOMESITE INDEMNITY CO	KS	**C-**	58.8	21.5	33.0	-0.2	2.4	4.1	4.5	6.0	2.9	DT
▲HOMESITE INS CO	CT	**C-**	133.8	47.1	73.5	-0.7	4.2	4.0	4.3	6.2	2.9	T
HOMESITE INS CO OF CA	CA	**D+**	71.0	27.6	44.0	-0.3	2.8	4.1	4.2	6.1	2.7	T
HOMESITE INS CO OF FL	FL	**C**	11.9	9.7	1.9	0.2	10.0	4.3	3.8	7.2	2.3	DFGT
HOMESITE INS CO OF IL	IL	**C**	20.3	5.1	7.6	-0.1	5.1	5.9	3.1	6.7	2.6	DGT
HOMESITE INS CO OF NY	NY	**C**	27.1	11.4	15.0	-0.1	4.9	6.0	5.5	6.5	3.0	DGT
HOMESITE INS CO OF PA	PA	**C**	14.8	7.3	2.9	0.0	3.0	4.1	5.1	6.2	3.5	DFGT
HOMESITE INS CO OF THE MIDWEST	ND	**D+**	148.4	48.0	69.0	-0.7	3.9	4.1	4.7	6.1	2.6	T
▼HOMESITE LLOYDS OF TEXAS	TX	**D**	16.0	3.8	10.6	-1.1	3.9	6.5	2.6	6.3	0.4	DFGT
HOMESTEAD INS CO	PA	**U** (1)	6.4	2.4	0.0	-0.6	N/A	7.0	1.0	9.5	2.2	FRT
HOMESURE OF VIRGINIA INC	VA	**U** (5)	0.0	0.0	13.6	0.0	N/A	9.3	4.3	7.0	3.7	DGT
HOMEWISE INS CO	FL	**C**	11.8	8.5	1.2	0.1	7.5	3.6	2.0	10.0	2.0	DFGT
HOMEWISE PREFERRED INS CO	FL	**D**	85.0	21.9	37.6	-1.0	1.7	3.6	2.8	1.2	1.5	CDFG
HOOSIER INS CO	IN	**C**	99.7	27.8	36.2	-0.8	8.2	5.6	3.3	7.5	3.6	FT
HOOSIER MOTOR MUTUAL INS CO	IN	**C+**	12.4	11.4	1.1	0.1	9.7	5.1	3.2	9.1	3.2	DFGT
HORACE MANN INS CO	IL	**B**	362.0	129.1	224.6	-1.8	7.3	4.7	3.5	4.2	5.4	ALRT
HORACE MANN LLOYDS	TX	**C**	3.0	2.5	0.0	0.0	10.0	N/A	7.5	10.0	3.0	DGT
▲HORACE MANN PROP & CAS INS CO	CA	**B**	171.8	61.7	121.2	5.5	7.5	4.9	8.6	5.1	5.4	ALRT
HOSPITAL UNDERWRITING GROUP INC	TN	**U** (1)	34.5	29.1	0.0	1.2	N/A	4.7	6.7	10.0	5.2	GT
HOSPITALITY MUT CAPT INS CO	GA	**U** (5)	0.0	0.0	2.5	0.0	N/A	5.8	2.5	0.0	0.0	CDFG
▼HOSPITALS INS CO INC	NY	**E**	800.3	65.9	140.9	3.0	0.0	3.6	1.1	3.0	0.0	CDLT
HOUSING & REDEVELOPMENT INS EXCH	PA	**D**	38.7	7.6	10.0	-2.4	2.1	5.3	2.9	6.5	2.1	CDFG
HOUSING AUTHORITY PROP A MUTUAL CO	VT	**C+**	157.1	93.3	39.1	3.8	9.6	7.1	9.0	7.5	4.5	T
HOUSING AUTHORITY RISK RET GROUP INC	VT	**C**	275.4	106.2	32.1	1.1	7.4	6.0	8.2	8.1	4.0	T
▼HOUSING ENTERPRISE INS CO	VT	**B+**	36.4	26.6	4.5	0.2	7.8	9.4	5.2	7.3	5.0	DGT
HOUSTON CASUALTY CO	TX	**B-**	2,917.5	1,411.9	372.0	22.0	7.6	5.0	8.5	7.5	4.9	RT
HOUSTON GENERAL INS CO	TX	**C**	27.2	17.5	-5.8	0.2	10.0	3.6	2.1	8.7	3.3	FGT
▲HOUSTON GENERAL INS EXCH	TX	**C**	24.0	20.6	-0.6	0.0	7.3	3.6	3.9	8.4	3.5	DFGT
HOW INS CO A RRG	VA	**U** (1)	131.2	101.9	0.0	-6.3	N/A	6.1	6.9	10.0	5.3	FT
HSBC INS CO OF DELAWARE	DE	**C**	370.0	276.2	92.1	-11.3	10.0	9.2	4.9	7.4	4.2	T
▼HUDSON INS CO	DE	**D**	431.0	135.6	115.4	3.3	1.5	5.6	6.9	4.7	1.4	CLT
HUDSON SPECIALTY INS CO	NY	**D+**	189.6	106.9	25.9	3.3	10.0	6.4	8.9	8.4	2.6	T

See Page 27 for explanation of footnotes and Page 28 for explanation of stability factors.
Arrows denote recent upgrades ▲ or downgrades ▼ (see Section VII for explanations)

RISK ADJ. RATIO #1	CAPITAL RATIO #2	PREMIUM TO SURPLUS (%)	RESV. TO SURPLUS (%)	RESV. DEVELOP. 1 YEAR (%)	RESV. DEVELOP. 2 YEAR (%)	LOSS RATIO (%)	EXP. RATIO (%)	COMB RATIO (%)	CASH FROM UNDER-WRITING (%)	NET PREMIUM GROWTH (%)	INVEST. IN AFFIL (%)	INSURANCE COMPANY NAME
1.2	0.8	221.0	189.8	-4.0	-21.1	72.1	24.7	96.8	109.8	34.2	10.8 •	HIGH POINT PREFERRED INS CO
9.3	8.4	N/A	N/A	N/A	N/A	N/A	N/A	N/A	N/A	0.0	0.0	HIGH POINT PROPERTY & CASUALTY INS
12.3	10.0	N/A	N/A	N/A	N/A	N/A	N/A	N/A	N/A	0.0	0.0	HIGH POINT SAFETY & INS CO
0.1	0.1	347.8	283.9	10.5	-20.9	97.4	3.8	101.2	999 +	N/A	0.0	HIGH TECH SERVICES RRG INC
0.9	0.5	81.6	85.7	-11.8	-14.1	54.6	15.8	70.4	120.0	-22.4	0.0	HIGHMARK CASUALTY INS CO
0.9	0.6	172.7	35.8	1.4	-1.6	41.9	48.6	90.5	127.5	-8.5	0.0	HILLCREST INS CO
12.8	11.5	15.5	9.1	-0.4	-0.9	70.4	22.9	93.3	92.3	-12.0	0.0	HILLSTAR INS CO
1.2	0.9	88.0	56.7	1.0	N/A	74.1	45.2	119.3	90.8	-22.1	15.2	HINGHAM MUTUAL FIRE INS CO
2.6	2.5	16.8	3.8	0.1	-1.1	46.7	50.7	97.4	101.5	-23.2	30.5	HISCOX INS CO INC
1.4	1.1	199.9	75.9	-4.0	-3.8	74.7	22.1	96.8	111.1	18.0	0.9	HOCHHEIM PRAIRIE CASUALTY INS CO
2.8	2.3	93.6	12.2	-2.1	-1.9	79.8	27.7	107.5	91.1	-3.8	19.4	HOCHHEIM PRAIRIE FARM MUT INS ASN
4.2	2.9	108.5	60.2	-2.6	-2.6	75.4	30.2	105.6	93.0	2.2	0.4	HOLYOKE MUTUAL INS CO IN SALEM
7.1	6.4	22.8	10.6	-1.9	-2.7	89.9	34.8	124.7	72.4	-30.8	0.3	HOME & FARM INS CO
1.1	0.5	5.1	173.0	-17.2	-24.0	83.2	437.5	520.7	22.5	-93.4	0.0	HOME CONSTRUCTION INS CO RRG
0.5	0.4	69.6	71.3	-61.4	-63.4	6.4	62.8	69.2	94.0	-14.9	0.0	HOME STATE COUNTY MUTUAL INS CO
2.9	1.9	171.4	88.2	-2.0	-3.0	90.8	21.9	112.7	99.8	11.6	0.0 •	HOME-OWNERS INS CO
3.9	2.5	86.1	85.5	-3.5	-7.6	60.2	34.8	95.0	101.6	6.8	0.0 •	HOMELAND INS CO OF NEW YORK
0.4	0.3	378.1	59.6	3.3	N/A	52.2	14.2	66.4	370.6	248.8	0.0	HOMEOWNERS CHOICE PROP & CAS INS
1.1	0.8	104.3	7.3	-1.9	-0.7	47.0	50.8	97.8	105.8	68.7	0.0	HOMEOWNERS OF AMERICA INS CO
N/A	N/A	N/A	N/A	N/A	N/A	N/A	N/A	N/A	N/A	0.0	0.0	HOMESHIELD FIRE & CASUALTY INS CO
1.0	0.6	153.4	44.5	-0.3	1.3	67.5	27.6	95.1	121.2	35.1	0.0	HOMESITE INDEMNITY CO
1.4	0.9	155.4	45.1	-0.3	1.3	67.5	27.7	95.2	120.3	33.8	0.0	HOMESITE INS CO
1.0	0.6	157.3	44.7	-0.3	1.3	67.5	27.9	95.4	126.8	52.5	0.0	HOMESITE INS CO OF CA
7.7	5.3	19.5	7.8	3.3	10.3	81.5	47.9	129.4	56.3	158.5	0.0	HOMESITE INS CO OF FL
1.0	0.6	145.7	42.5	-0.3	2.0	67.5	27.4	94.9	109.3	37.9	0.0	HOMESITE INS CO OF IL
1.2	0.8	130.6	38.5	-0.2	1.2	67.5	28.4	95.9	122.1	33.4	0.0	HOMESITE INS CO OF NY
1.6	1.0	38.5	29.9	-0.2	0.9	67.5	75.5	143.0	33.5	-78.4	0.0	HOMESITE INS CO OF PA
1.5	1.0	142.2	44.0	-0.3	1.2	67.5	29.5	97.0	105.2	8.3	0.0	HOMESITE INS CO OF THE MIDWEST
0.5	0.4	218.1	45.3	1.0	-10.2	105.5	29.5	135.0	85.4	40.0	0.0	HOMESITE LLOYDS OF TEXAS
N/A	N/A	N/A	160.0	-16.5	-1.5	N/A	N/A	N/A	N/A	0.0	0.0	HOMESTEAD INS CO
N/A	N/A	167.2	16.9	N/A	-7.9	55.2	41.8	97.0	104.3	0.4	0.0	HOMESURE OF VIRGINIA INC
1.5	1.3	14.5	2.5	-0.3	-1.0	17.8	266.8	284.6	-2.6	-9.9	0.0	HOMEWISE INS CO
0.6	0.4	164.1	86.7	3.4	-0.2	68.5	40.7	109.2	62.5	68.0	0.0	HOMEWISE PREFERRED INS CO
2.6	1.8	127.6	147.9	-16.1	-11.3	52.3	33.8	86.1	73.1	-30.1	0.0	HOOSIER INS CO
5.6	3.0	9.8	3.1	1.3	-0.7	54.0	38.1	92.1	109.9	0.0	0.0	HOOSIER MOTOR MUTUAL INS CO
1.9	1.2	175.8	101.5	-8.3	-9.6	76.9	23.9	100.8	92.8	-1.5	0.0	HORACE MANN INS CO
12.9	11.6	N/A	N/A	N/A	N/A	N/A	N/A	N/A	133.3	0.0	0.0	HORACE MANN LLOYDS
2.0	1.3	195.6	91.5	1.0	1.5	79.2	19.1	98.3	112.5	17.4	0.0	HORACE MANN PROP & CAS INS CO
N/A	N/A	0.1	12.9	-0.9	-1.2	999 +	539.1	-547.9	23.0	0.0	8.2	HOSPITAL UNDERWRITING GROUP INC
N/A	N/A	408.3	213.6	77.4	0.4	85.4	54.4	139.8	89.5	84.7	0.0	HOSPITALITY MUT CAPT INS CO
0.1	0.1	219.2	995.9	28.0	35.1	121.5	4.6	126.1	113.5	11.7	0.0	HOSPITALS INS CO INC
0.4	0.3	100.3	212.7	-33.2	-6.5	78.4	24.4	102.8	78.3	-16.6	0.0	HOUSING & REDEVELOPMENT INS EXCH
4.8	3.9	44.0	32.3	-15.5	-25.8	41.4	22.4	63.8	145.8	9.5	11.6	HOUSING AUTHORITY PROP A MUTUAL
2.2	1.7	30.3	134.4	-35.3	-67.1	32.7	18.6	51.3	114.2	-15.2	6.4	HOUSING AUTHORITY RISK RET GROUP
3.5	2.0	17.1	21.4	-4.2	-12.6	36.0	65.0	101.0	80.6	2.0	0.0 •	HOUSING ENTERPRISE INS CO
1.9	1.7	27.7	83.1	-5.3	-11.0	48.0	27.9	75.9	124.4	-12.4	26.5 •	HOUSTON CASUALTY CO
7.4	6.6	-33.3	9.9	-2.3	N/A	138.9	17.0	155.9	-91.0	-142.4	0.0	HOUSTON GENERAL INS CO
1.2	1.2	-3.1	0.9	-0.2	N/A	137.9	18.1	156.0	-69.0	-142.4	81.0	HOUSTON GENERAL INS EXCH
N/A	N/A	N/A	4.8	22.1	-32.4	N/A	N/A	N/A	N/A	0.0	0.0	HOW INS CO A RRG
13.7	8.4	32.8	16.8	0.7	-0.6	29.8	19.5	49.3	164.5	-13.8	0.0 •	HSBC INS CO OF DELAWARE
0.4	0.3	85.4	127.6	-0.3	-4.9	73.4	35.0	108.4	106.1	-40.0	0.0	HUDSON INS CO
11.5	6.0	25.1	34.3	-3.3	-5.6	53.9	-11.0	42.9	400.3	36.6	0.0	HUDSON SPECIALTY INS CO

999 + Denotes number greater than 999.9%
999 - Denotes number less than -999.99%
• Bullets denote a more detailed analysis is available in Section II.

INSURANCE COMPANY NAME	DOM. STATE	RATING	TOTAL ASSETS ($MIL)	CAPITAL & SURPLUS ($MIL)	ANNUAL NET PREMIUM ($MIL)	NET INCOME ($MIL)	CAPITAL-IZATION INDEX (PTS)	RESERVE ADQ INDEX (PTS)	PROFIT-ABILITY INDEX (PTS)	LIQUIDITY INDEX (PTS)	STAB. INDEX (PTS)	STABILITY FACTORS
HYUNDAI MARINE & FIRE INS CO LTD	CA	**B-**	29.1	13.5	6.0	0.2	6.8	6.4	4.8	7.5	3.7	DGRT
▲ICAT SPECIALTY INS CO	FL	**D**	20.0	14.0	-1.4	-0.1	10.0	N/A	2.7	10.0	1.4	DGT
ICM INS CO	NY	**D**	10.9	5.0	5.1	-0.1	1.2	2.3	1.1	6.9	1.5	CDFG
ID COUNTIES RISK MGMT PROGRAM UNDW	ID	**D**	45.3	18.1	15.5	0.4	7.3	7.0	6.6	6.9	2.3	DGT
IDS PROPERTY CASUALTY INS CO	WI	**B-**	972.4	450.2	619.0	13.8	8.9	7.0	5.8	5.1	5.2	T
IFA INS CO	NJ	**C**	88.7	23.4	33.8	0.0	6.7	5.6	3.3	7.3	3.6	DFT
IL STATE BAR ASSOC MUTUAL INS CO	IL	**C+**	56.0	24.7	11.0	0.2	8.0	9.6	8.8	7.9	4.5	DT
ILLINOIS CASUALTY CO	IL	**C-**	78.9	19.0	27.8	0.4	2.5	3.8	2.2	6.5	2.9	CDT
ILLINOIS EMCASCO INS CO	IA	**C+**	268.8	66.9	104.3	1.1	7.6	4.9	4.7	6.7	4.5	T
ILLINOIS FARMERS INS CO	IL	**C+**	253.4	78.3	88.4	0.4	7.2	4.4	6.8	6.5	4.6	T
ILLINOIS NATIONAL INS CO	IL	**B-**	66.9	60.3	0.0	0.5	10.0	N/A	8.7	7.0	5.3	
ILLINOIS UNION INS CO	IL	**C**	393.3	132.8	0.0	1.9	10.0	N/A	7.8	6.9	3.5	FT
▲IMPERIAL CASUALTY & INDEMNITY CO	OK	**C-**	39.6	12.8	7.7	1.0	4.9	4.0	6.5	6.8	2.9	CDGT
IMPERIAL FIRE & CASUALTY INS CO	LA	**C**	71.8	29.3	60.6	-0.5	7.2	6.0	5.1	2.3	3.9	FLT
IMT INS CO	IA	**B-**	212.4	102.0	104.5	3.3	10.0	8.5	7.9	6.6	5.3	T
INDEMNITY CO OF CA	CA	**C**	22.5	13.0	8.3	0.6	7.9	9.3	8.6	7.4	3.3	DGT
INDEMNITY INS CO OF NORTH AMERICA	PA	**C**	409.2	124.1	55.9	3.1	7.1	5.0	8.8	6.9	4.0	T
INDEMNITY INS CORP OF DC RRG	DC	**E**	15.9	1.3	1.0	0.6	1.8	3.6	0.5	2.2	0.0	DGLT
INDEMNITY NATIONAL INS CO	MS	**C**	13.0	10.4	2.0	0.3	10.0	3.6	2.8	8.0	2.7	DGT
INDEPENDENCE AMERICAN INS CO	DE	**C**	74.1	41.7	96.9	1.5	6.7	5.2	6.2	1.3	4.1	LT
INDEPENDENCE CASUALTY & SURETY CO	TX	**C+**	28.2	21.3	5.0	-0.2	8.0	6.2	3.8	6.7	3.7	DGT
INDEPENDENCE CASUALTY INS CO	MA	**E+**	3.7	3.6	0.0	0.0	10.0	N/A	7.9	7.0	0.8	DGT
INDEPENDENT MUTUAL FIRE INS CO	IL	**C+**	25.3	23.3	6.0	0.1	9.1	6.0	4.6	7.5	4.6	DGT
INDEPENDENT NEVADA DOCTORS INS	NV	**E**	44.3	11.0	13.6	0.0	0.1	4.1	2.9	7.1	0.0	CFGT
▲INDIAN HARBOR INS CO	ND	**C-**	201.0	54.1	35.9	-0.4	3.0	3.9	6.6	7.7	2.9	AGT
INDIANA FARMERS MUTUAL INS CO	IN	**B**	246.6	81.3	157.8	-3.7	7.9	7.6	2.2	2.5	5.4	FLT
INDIANA HEALTHCARE RECIPROCAL RRG	VT	**E+**	18.6	2.7	5.1	0.2	1.5	4.9	6.3	7.1	0.0	DGT
INDIANA INS CO	IN	**C+**	1,264.7	284.8	474.2	10.8	7.8	7.0	4.0	6.7	2.9	T
INDIANA LUMBERMENS MUTUAL INS CO	IN	**C**	108.0	32.7	42.1	-0.1	5.7	5.8	2.3	6.3	4.1	FRT
INDIANA OLD NATIONAL INS CO	VT	**D**	1,597.5	1,571.1	1.2	15.9	10.0	4.6	3.4	10.0	2.0	FT
INFINITY ASSURANCE INS CO	OH	**C**	6.9	5.8	0.9	0.0	10.0	6.1	4.9	9.1	3.6	DGT
INFINITY AUTO INS CO	OH	**C**	12.3	10.7	0.9	0.1	10.0	4.5	3.1	9.3	3.9	DGT
▲INFINITY CASUALTY INS CO	OH	**C**	8.5	7.5	0.9	0.0	10.0	6.1	2.8	7.0	3.8	DGT
INFINITY COUNTY MUTUAL INS CO	TX	**C**	30.7	3.5	0.0	0.0	5.1	N/A	6.1	10.0	3.2	DG
INFINITY GENERAL INS CO	OH	**C**	5.1	4.1	0.9	0.0	10.0	6.1	4.4	8.1	2.8	DGT
INFINITY INDEMNITY INS CO	IN	**C**	7.1	6.1	0.9	0.0	10.0	6.1	5.9	9.1	3.8	DGT
INFINITY INS CO	IN	**B-**	1,411.6	433.4	879.6	8.6	7.7	9.1	4.8	5.0	4.9	T
INFINITY PREFERRED INS CO	OH	**C**	5.5	4.5	0.9	0.0	10.0	6.1	5.8	9.0	3.5	DGT
INFINITY PREMIER INS CO	IN	**C**	7.1	6.1	0.9	0.1	10.0	6.2	6.2	9.2	3.8	DGT
INFINITY RESERVE INS CO	OH	**C**	4.9	3.9	0.9	0.0	10.0	6.3	3.8	7.4	2.9	DGT
INFINITY SAFEGUARD INS CO	OH	**C**	7.2	6.2	0.9	0.1	10.0	5.7	4.3	8.3	2.7	DGT
INFINITY SECURITY INS CO	IN	**C**	8.1	7.1	0.9	0.1	10.0	4.8	4.0	7.5	3.9	DGT
INFINITY SELECT INS CO	IN	**C**	7.2	6.2	0.9	0.1	10.0	7.4	3.9	7.8	3.8	DGT
INFINITY SPECIALTY INS CO	OH	**C**	10.1	9.1	0.9	0.1	10.0	5.2	3.9	9.5	3.5	DGT
INFINITY STANDARD INS CO	IN	**C**	11.6	9.8	0.9	0.1	10.0	4.5	2.9	7.7	3.9	DGT
INLAND INS CO	NE	**C**	132.9	104.6	0.9	-0.4	8.0	6.1	4.8	10.0	2.3	DT
INLAND MUTUAL INS CO	WV	**C-**	5.3	4.9	0.2	0.1	10.0	6.0	4.7	9.6	2.3	DGR
INNOVATIVE PHYSICIAN SOLUTIONS RRG	AZ	**D**	4.0	1.9	1.2	0.1	8.9	4.0	7.6	9.2	1.5	DGT
INS CO OF GREATER NY	NY	**B+**	101.2	48.5	21.6	0.9	9.0	5.4	8.7	7.1	5.0	T
INS CO OF ILLINOIS	IL	**C+**	37.3	32.8	0.0	0.2	10.0	N/A	8.1	10.0	4.0	ADGT
INS CO OF NORTH AMERICA	PA	**C**	764.4	249.3	139.8	5.4	6.5	5.0	9.0	6.7	4.3	T
▲INS CO OF THE AMERICAS	FL	**E+**	38.9	10.1	1.3	0.4	1.0	1.1	2.4	7.6	0.5	CDFG

See Page 27 for explanation of footnotes and Page 28 for explanation of stability factors.
Arrows denote recent upgrades ▲ or downgrades ▼ (see Section VII for explanations)

RISK ADJ. RATIO #1	CAPITAL RATIO #2	PREMIUM TO SURPLUS (%)	RESV. TO SURPLUS (%)	RESV. DEVELOP. 1 YEAR (%)	RESV. DEVELOP. 2 YEAR (%)	LOSS RATIO (%)	EXP. RATIO (%)	COMB RATIO (%)	CASH FROM UNDER-WRITING (%)	NET PREMIUM GROWTH (%)	INVEST. IN AFFIL (%)	INSURANCE COMPANY NAME
1.8	1.0	43.9	54.2	1.1	3.7	65.7	30.7	96.4	145.7	17.6	0.0	HYUNDAI MARINE & FIRE INS CO LTD
8.1	7.3	-10.1	N/A	N/A	N/A	52.0	-25.6	26.4	-89.0	-126.6	0.0	ICAT SPECIALTY INS CO
0.5	0.3	99.2	239.9	-5.0	21.1	94.3	34.4	128.7	50.9	-15.4	0.0	ICM INS CO
1.4	1.3	87.9	98.2	-24.4	-25.8	48.1	26.0	74.1	115.4	10.7	0.0	ID COUNTIES RISK MGMT PROGRAM
3.2	2.6	141.9	70.5	-15.1	-19.3	77.2	17.6	94.8	99.2	5.6	5.4 •	IDS PROPERTY CASUALTY INS CO
1.2	0.9	144.0	191.2	-0.5	-0.1	88.9	22.1	111.0	87.8	1.0	0.0	IFA INS CO
2.9	1.9	44.7	97.3	-7.8	-19.2	64.5	26.0	90.5	129.9	-0.5	0.0	IL STATE BAR ASSOC MUTUAL INS CO
0.6	0.4	143.5	206.7	-4.2	3.6	76.8	31.5	108.3	100.6	-2.2	0.0	ILLINOIS CASUALTY CO
2.1	1.3	156.2	197.2	-7.1	-15.9	73.9	33.1	107.0	97.9	-3.5	0.0	ILLINOIS EMCASCO INS CO
1.3	1.2	115.3	78.3	-3.1	-1.7	75.6	31.0	106.6	99.3	-8.0	35.9	ILLINOIS FARMERS INS CO
29.3	21.4	N/A	N/A	N/A	N/A	N/A	N/A	N/A	N/A	0.0	2.5	ILLINOIS NATIONAL INS CO
9.7	4.2	N/A	45.5	N/A	N/A	N/A	N/A	N/A	57.0	0.0	0.0	ILLINOIS UNION INS CO
2.1	1.4	64.3	155.9	-9.8	6.5	47.1	54.9	102.0	122.2	-33.7	0.0	IMPERIAL CASUALTY & INDEMNITY CO
1.4	1.2	203.2	87.8	-6.3	-18.5	77.5	26.5	104.0	94.1	-9.5	0.0	IMPERIAL FIRE & CASUALTY INS CO
5.1	3.4	102.9	38.8	-3.8	-4.9	62.2	31.7	93.9	102.3	4.6	0.0	IMT INS CO
2.0	1.7	64.6	30.3	-5.5	-8.4	30.0	63.4	93.4	124.4	-8.4	0.0	INDEMNITY CO OF CA
2.1	1.4	46.3	98.8	-9.2	-28.7	62.6	23.7	86.3	128.6	-19.7	6.0	INDEMNITY INS CO OF NORTH AMERICA
0.4	0.3	39.9	63.4	38.6	-66.8	28.9	-70.7	-41.8	206.3	-30.4	0.0	INDEMNITY INS CORP OF DC RRG
5.6	3.6	18.7	10.0	-3.2	-0.6	19.6	39.3	58.9	331.0	24.2	0.0	INDEMNITY NATIONAL INS CO
1.9	1.1	240.2	71.4	-0.3	7.0	72.3	27.5	99.8	97.5	-8.7	0.0	INDEPENDENCE AMERICAN INS CO
3.2	1.8	22.8	22.0	-2.5	-2.7	50.0	46.7	96.7	115.5	-3.9	0.0	INDEPENDENCE CASUALTY & SURETY
85.7	42.8	N/A	N/A	N/A	N/A	N/A	N/A	N/A	N/A	0.0	0.0	INDEPENDENCE CASUALTY INS CO
4.5	3.0	24.7	1.2	-0.2	-0.1	31.3	62.3	93.6	102.9	-4.8	0.0	INDEPENDENT MUTUAL FIRE INS CO
0.1	0.1	124.1	246.4	-29.2	-97.5	53.8	26.7	80.5	104.6	2.1	0.0	INDEPENDENT NEVADA DOCTORS INS
0.9	0.5	65.1	94.1	-10.4	-7.7	60.4	27.0	87.4	185.7	128.2	0.0	INDIAN HARBOR INS CO
2.1	1.4	173.8	72.0	-1.5	-3.1	90.0	28.2	118.2	87.4	2.3	0.0	INDIANA FARMERS MUTUAL INS CO
0.5	0.3	174.2	380.2	-3.4	-0.5	81.8	18.6	100.4	168.1	8.2	0.0	INDIANA HEALTHCARE RECIPROCAL
2.2	1.5	170.8	209.3	-14.1	-27.4	63.2	35.5	98.7	139.7	4.2	2.2 •	INDIANA INS CO
1.4	0.8	127.5	148.3	-2.1	8.2	65.9	49.3	115.2	86.6	-8.3	6.2	INDIANA LUMBERMENS MUTUAL INS CO
57.3	23.7	0.1	N/A	N/A	N/A	12.4	33.7	46.1	114.3	-17.0	0.0 •	INDIANA OLD NATIONAL INS CO
12.7	11.5	15.4	9.0	-0.4	-0.9	70.4	22.9	93.3	92.3	-12.0	0.0	INFINITY ASSURANCE INS CO
17.2	15.5	8.5	5.0	-0.2	-0.5	70.4	22.9	93.3	92.3	-12.0	0.0	INFINITY AUTO INS CO
16.1	14.5	12.0	7.1	-0.3	-0.6	70.4	22.9	93.3	92.3	-12.0	0.0	INFINITY CASUALTY INS CO
0.8	0.7	N/A	N/A	N/A	N/A	N/A	N/A	N/A	N/A	0.0	0.0	INFINITY COUNTY MUTUAL INS CO
9.0	8.1	21.8	12.8	-0.5	-1.3	70.4	22.9	93.3	92.3	-12.0	0.0	INFINITY GENERAL INS CO
13.3	11.9	14.8	8.7	-0.4	-0.9	70.4	22.9	93.3	92.3	-12.0	0.0	INFINITY INDEMNITY INS CO
1.7	1.5	206.9	121.5	-4.6	-9.2	70.3	22.9	93.2	95.1	-12.0	8.6 •	INFINITY INS CO
9.9	8.9	20.0	11.7	-0.5	-1.2	70.4	22.9	93.3	92.3	-12.0	0.0	INFINITY PREFERRED INS CO
13.4	12.0	14.8	8.7	-0.4	-0.9	70.4	22.9	93.3	92.3	-12.0	0.0	INFINITY PREMIER INS CO
8.7	7.8	22.9	13.5	-0.6	-1.3	70.4	22.9	93.3	92.3	-12.0	0.0	INFINITY RESERVE INS CO
13.5	12.2	14.5	8.5	-0.4	-0.9	70.4	22.9	93.3	92.3	-12.0	0.0	INFINITY SAFEGUARD INS CO
15.2	13.6	12.7	7.5	-0.3	-0.7	70.4	22.9	93.3	92.3	-12.0	0.0	INFINITY SECURITY INS CO
13.5	12.2	14.6	8.6	-0.4	-0.9	70.4	22.9	93.3	92.3	-12.0	0.0	INFINITY SELECT INS CO
20.0	18.0	9.9	5.8	-0.2	-0.6	70.4	22.9	93.3	92.3	-12.0	0.0	INFINITY SPECIALTY INS CO
14.3	12.9	9.2	5.4	-0.2	-0.5	70.4	30.0	100.4	92.3	-12.0	0.0	INFINITY STANDARD INS CO
3.1	1.8	0.7	2.3	0.1	0.1	49.8	44.9	94.7	259.1	-0.2	0.0	INLAND INS CO
8.7	5.0	4.3	7.0	-0.4	-1.6	66.5	63.6	130.1	65.0	-5.9	0.0	INLAND MUTUAL INS CO
3.1	2.2	66.9	86.4	-78.4	-29.2	33.4	35.6	69.0	286.4	-4.2	0.0	INNOVATIVE PHYSICIAN SOLUTIONS RRG
3.8	2.8	45.2	81.2	-2.1	-2.6	62.5	32.7	95.2	100.8	-6.0	0.0 •	INS CO OF GREATER NY
23.4	21.1	N/A	N/A	N/A	N/A	N/A	N/A	N/A	-115.5	0.0	0.0	INS CO OF ILLINOIS
1.9	1.3	56.5	120.7	-11.3	-38.6	62.5	22.8	85.3	97.7	-19.7	0.0 •	INS CO OF NORTH AMERICA
0.4	0.2	11.5	260.0	-19.8	33.9	-123.9	261.1	137.2	16.4	23.0	0.0	INS CO OF THE AMERICAS

999 + Denotes number greater than 999.9%
999 - Denotes number less than -999.99%
• Bullets denote a more detailed analysis is available in Section II.

INSURANCE COMPANY NAME	DOM. STATE	RATING	TOTAL ASSETS ($MIL)	CAPITAL & SURPLUS ($MIL)	ANNUAL NET PREMIUM ($MIL)	NET INCOME ($MIL)	CAPITAL-IZATION INDEX (PTS)	RESERVE ADQ INDEX (PTS)	PROFIT-ABILITY INDEX (PTS)	LIQUIDITY INDEX (PTS)	STAB. INDEX (PTS)	STABILITY FACTORS
INS CO OF THE STATE OF PA	PA	**C+**	4,578.1	1,986.1	865.7	52.6	7.2	2.8	7.0	6.7	4.4	T
INS CO OF THE WEST	CA	**C**	801.8	347.0	277.6	6.1	5.6	5.6	4.7	6.1	3.7	FT
INSURA PROPERTY & CAS INS CO INC	IL	**C-**	35.4	26.1	0.0	0.1	10.0	N/A	6.9	7.0	3.3	DGT
INSURANCE CORP OF AMERICA	MI	**U** (1)	33.0	10.7	0.0	-0.2	N/A	1.0	1.6	9.2	0.5	CFT
INSURANCE CORP OF NY	NY	**F** (1)	62.2	-113.5	-1.7	-24.7	0.0	4.0	0.9	7.0	0.0	CFT
INSUREMAX INS CO	IN	**D+**	17.0	8.5	9.6	0.1	7.4	4.4	2.2	6.3	2.6	DFGT
INSURORS INDEMNITY CO	TX	**D**	14.5	8.3	4.3	0.1	8.0	9.4	8.6	8.5	2.0	DGT
INSURORS INDEMNITY LLOYDS	TX	**D**	3.3	2.6	0.0	0.0	10.0	N/A	5.7	10.0	2.0	DFGT
INTEGON CASUALTY INS CO	NC	**C+**	44.2	12.5	0.0	0.0	9.1	N/A	3.9	7.0	4.3	DGT
INTEGON GENERAL INS CORP	NC	**C+**	46.2	37.6	0.0	0.1	10.0	N/A	3.9	7.0	4.3	GT
INTEGON INDEMNITY CORP	NC	**C+**	98.8	47.4	0.0	5.0	10.0	N/A	6.3	9.9	4.3	T
INTEGON NATIONAL INS CO	NC	**C+**	186.6	55.9	0.0	0.8	10.0	N/A	3.0	7.0	4.3	T
INTEGON PREFERRED INS CO	NC	**C+**	30.1	12.1	0.0	0.1	10.0	N/A	3.8	7.0	4.3	DG
INTEGON SPECIALTY INS	NC	**C**	54.8	27.7	5.2	0.6	10.0	5.7	6.2	7.0	3.5	T
INTEGRA INS INC	MN	**D**	1.8	1.7	3.4	0.0	3.0	N/A	5.7	6.0	1.6	CDGT
INTEGRAND ASR CO	PR	**C**	137.7	60.6	37.3	1.4	7.2	5.9	5.4	6.1	3.6	FRT
INTEGRITY MUTUAL INS CO	WI	**B-**	63.3	30.4	35.3	-0.4	7.6	8.2	6.3	5.9	5.0	FT
INTEGRITY PROP & CAS INS CO	WI	**D+**	13.2	6.3	7.5	-0.1	7.8	3.6	4.2	5.7	1.1	DFGT
INTERBORO MUTUAL INDEMNITY INS CO	NY	**F** (1)	67.8	14.1	24.4	2.2	1.7	0.1	0.1	8.0	0.0	CDFR
INTERINS EXCH OF THE AUTOMOBILE CLUB	CA	**A+**	5,434.9	3,146.8	2,393.7	78.2	10.0	6.5	7.9	6.5	6.5	T
INTERLEX INS CO	MO	**C-**	35.4	14.0	6.3	0.4	6.9	6.8	8.7	8.1	3.2	DGT
INTERMED INS CO	MO	**C**	139.1	63.9	26.8	1.5	8.2	5.9	7.0	7.7	4.2	T
INTERMODAL INS CO RRG	DC	**D-**	7.5	2.6	3.1	0.1	6.6	6.0	5.7	7.1	1.3	DFGR
INTERNATIONAL CREDIT OF N AMER REIN	NY	**D**	2.3	2.0	0.4	-0.1	8.3	7.0	3.0	9.2	1.7	DFGT
INTERNATIONAL FIDELITY INS CO	NJ	**C+**	200.1	92.9	96.9	3.0	7.8	9.2	8.6	7.7	3.4	T
INTERSTATE AUTO INS CO	MD	**D**	5.5	1.6	3.9	0.0	4.5	9.3	1.4	3.8	1.4	DFGL
INTERSTATE BANKERS CASUALTY CO	IL	**C**	18.3	7.2	11.7	-0.7	7.3	9.4	2.6	5.7	2.8	DGT
INTERSTATE FIRE & CAS CO	IL	**C**	612.2	279.0	167.6	5.8	7.4	5.8	7.3	6.7	4.3	T
▲INTREPID INS CO	MI	**B-**	38.6	24.1	0.2	0.9	10.0	6.3	5.9	10.0	4.9	DGRT
INVERNESS INS CO	AZ	**U** (1)	1.7	1.7	0.0	0.0	N/A	N/A	6.7	7.0	3.1	T
IOWA AMERICAN INS CO	IA	**B-**	14.3	6.7	3.2	0.0	9.7	6.1	6.8	7.3	3.9	DGT
IOWA MUTUAL INS CO	IA	**B**	80.8	25.5	22.3	-0.8	7.5	5.2	3.8	6.7	5.4	T
IRONSHORE INDEMNITY INC	MN	**B**	76.4	58.8	2.4	-0.1	10.0	4.8	3.8	8.6	4.5	DGRT
IRONSHORE SPECIALTY INS CO	AZ	**C**	128.3	55.2	8.4	-3.4	10.0	N/A	3.4	7.5	2.7	GT
ISLAND INS CO LTD	HI	**B-**	313.0	101.1	109.5	-0.1	8.5	9.6	5.4	7.2	4.8	T
ISLAND PREMIER INS CO LTD	HI	**C-**	7.1	3.9	0.0	0.1	8.4	N/A	6.2	7.9	3.0	DG
ISMIE INDEMNITY CO	IL	**U** (1)	16.5	16.1	0.0	0.1	N/A	N/A	6.8	7.0	4.0	T
▲ISMIE MUTUAL INS CO	IL	**C+**	1,396.5	362.3	233.0	4.4	7.1	4.8	6.9	7.7	4.5	T
JAMES RIVER INS CO	OH	**C**	471.3	181.3	-5.1	-1.7	8.1	6.7	7.0	7.0	4.0	T
JAMESTOWN INS CO RRG	SC	**D-**	7.4	2.7	3.3	0.1	4.8	4.5	6.7	6.8	1.3	DGT
JEFFERSON INS CO	NY	**C**	66.2	9.3	8.9	-1.1	4.7	4.9	1.3	2.3	2.9	CDGL
JEWELERS MUTUAL INS CO	WI	**A-**	186.8	108.9	108.9	-1.3	10.0	7.5	6.1	6.6	5.9	T
JM WOODWORTH RRG INC	NV	**D-**	9.0	5.0	3.2	-0.2	7.7	3.6	3.0	7.0	1.3	DGT
JOLIET AREA RRG CAPTIVE INS CO	GA	**D-**	8.6	1.9	1.9	0.5	4.1	6.1	3.7	8.7	1.3	DGRT
JUNIATA MUTUAL INS CO	PA	**D+**(1)	6.4	2.8	3.8	-0.1	7.5	4.1	3.7	6.3	2.1	DF
KANSAS BANKERS SURETY CO	KS	**B**	156.2	134.8	17.9	0.5	10.0	6.2	8.2	9.7	4.0	DFT
KANSAS MEDICAL MUTUAL INS CO	KS	**C+**	177.6	64.7	34.5	-0.3	9.0	10.0	6.8	7.6	4.6	RT
KANSAS MUTUAL INS CO	KS	**C-** (1)	9.7	6.5	3.5	0.6	10.0	6.6	7.7	6.2	2.4	DF
KEMPER CASUALTY INS CO	IL	**D-**	20.2	10.9	-0.1	0.5	8.9	7.0	1.9	7.0	1.0	DGT
KEMPER INDEPENDENCE INS CO	IL	**B-**	129.6	21.4	28.3	0.2	2.0	6.9	6.0	4.2	5.2	CDLT
KEMPER INS CO OF TEXAS	TX	**U** (1)	2.8	2.7	0.0	0.1	N/A	N/A	1.9	7.0	3.1	FT
KENSINGTON INS CO	NY	**D-**	12.7	3.9	5.0	-0.2	0.6	4.3	3.4	7.7	0.9	CDGT

See Page 27 for explanation of footnotes and Page 28 for explanation of stability factors.

Arrows denote recent upgrades ▲ or downgrades ▼ (see Section VII for explanations)

RISK ADJ. CAPITAL RATIO #1	RISK ADJ. CAPITAL RATIO #2	PREMIUM TO SURPLUS (%)	RESV. TO SURPLUS (%)	RESV. DEVELOP. 1 YEAR (%)	RESV. DEVELOP. 2 YEAR (%)	LOSS RATIO (%)	EXP. RATIO (%)	COMB RATIO (%)	CASH FROM UNDER-WRITING (%)	NET PREMIUM GROWTH (%)	INVEST. IN AFFIL (%)	INSURANCE COMPANY NAME
1.4	1.2	43.0	87.3	-0.1	0.4	78.1	25.2	103.3	88.2	-15.4	35.7 •	INS CO OF THE STATE OF PA
1.3	0.7	74.1	71.5	-7.3	-8.0	50.0	46.9	96.9	104.5	-4.0	11.6 •	INS CO OF THE WEST
11.3	10.1	N/A	N/A	N/A	N/A	N/A	N/A	N/A	2.5	0.0	0.0	INSURA PROPERTY & CAS INS CO INC
N/A	N/A	-0.1	208.7	20.6	33.7	999 +	-385.7	999 +	-2.0	-216.7	0.0	INSURANCE CORP OF AMERICA
-0.2	-0.1	1.5	-133.9	-23.1	-11.1	999 +	-94.0	999 +	-2.8	-961.3	0.0	INSURANCE CORP OF NY
1.8	1.6	115.0	48.8	-5.0	11.9	62.7	39.9	102.6	75.9	-29.0	0.0	INSUREMAX INS CO
2.7	1.9	52.0	31.1	-10.4	-11.5	38.7	46.7	85.4	109.9	10.9	19.3	INSURORS INDEMNITY CO
8.5	7.6	N/A	N/A	N/A	N/A	N/A	N/A	N/A	36.4	0.0	0.0	INSURORS INDEMNITY LLOYDS
2.6	2.3	N/A	N/A	N/A	N/A	N/A	N/A	N/A	54.0	0.0	0.0	INTEGON CASUALTY INS CO
17.2	15.5	N/A	N/A	N/A	N/A	N/A	N/A	N/A	57.1	0.0	0.0	INTEGON GENERAL INS CORP
6.9	6.2	N/A	N/A	N/A	N/A	N/A	N/A	N/A	-344.9	0.0	0.0	INTEGON INDEMNITY CORP
6.0	5.4	N/A	N/A	N/A	N/A	N/A	N/A	N/A	99.8	0.0	0.0	INTEGON NATIONAL INS CO
3.6	3.3	N/A	N/A	N/A	N/A	N/A	N/A	N/A	25.2	0.0	0.0	INTEGON PREFERRED INS CO
6.4	5.8	19.2	1.3	-0.3	-0.6	53.4	16.7	70.1	-41.2	-22.7	0.0	INTEGON SPECIALTY INS
0.5	0.5	171.9	N/A	N/A	N/A	N/A	92.3	92.3	110.0	-20.9	0.0	INTEGRA INS INC
2.2	1.4	59.6	57.6	-4.4	-6.8	59.1	46.4	105.5	85.3	-25.0	0.4	INTEGRAND ASR CO
1.8	1.4	113.6	54.4	-3.0	-7.0	67.8	29.5	97.3	94.0	5.3	25.1	INTEGRITY MUTUAL INS CO
2.8	1.7	118.7	56.8	-3.2	N/A	67.8	32.5	100.3	95.7	-28.4	0.0	INTEGRITY PROP & CAS INS CO
0.8	0.6	173.4	236.6	-59.9	999 +	34.7	42.5	77.2	85.8	25.3	0.0	INTERBORO MUTUAL INDEMNITY INS CO
6.0	4.2	75.7	26.8	-0.3	1.1	70.0	21.0	91.0	110.5	0.6	0.7 •	INTERINS EXCH OF THE AUTOMOBILE
1.7	1.3	45.9	125.1	0.4	-9.2	66.1	30.8	96.9	86.4	35.9	0.0	INTERLEX INS CO
2.7	2.2	43.2	99.4	-7.8	-19.8	51.8	30.5	82.3	116.7	40.0	10.7	INTERMED INS CO
1.7	1.3	124.7	140.3	-17.5	-30.4	75.2	4.0	79.2	97.9	38.3	0.0	INTERMODAL INS CO RRG
1.6	1.5	21.3	N/A	N/A	2.4	N/A	163.1	163.1	60.3	0.0	0.0	INTERNATIONAL CREDIT OF N AMER
1.9	1.6	104.7	21.4	-6.4	-12.3	10.7	68.3	79.0	128.2	2.9	0.0	INTERNATIONAL FIDELITY INS CO
0.7	0.6	241.5	96.9	-14.7	-9.2	65.6	43.9	109.5	87.1	27.5	0.0	INTERSTATE AUTO INS CO
1.4	1.0	153.1	46.5	-3.2	-14.2	62.0	39.3	101.3	125.5	48.2	0.0	INTERSTATE BANKERS CASUALTY CO
1.2	1.0	47.3	62.9	1.7	2.7	75.0	27.2	102.2	106.2	3.0	35.5 •	INTERSTATE FIRE & CAS CO
8.4	7.5	0.9	0.1	-3.2	-7.6	202.8	86.7	289.5	-128.3	-98.6	0.0	INTREPID INS CO
N/A	N/A	N/A	N/A	N/A	N/A	N/A	N/A	N/A	N/A	0.0	0.0	INVERNESS INS CO
3.3	2.7	47.2	39.2	-1.3	-2.5	73.5	33.0	106.5	96.7	3.5	0.0	IOWA AMERICAN INS CO
1.8	1.2	83.0	69.0	-2.0	-3.7	73.5	33.0	106.5	98.7	3.5	13.2	IOWA MUTUAL INS CO
11.9	9.8	4.1	2.0	N/A	N/A	133.5	58.1	191.6	867.1	N/A	0.0	IRONSHORE INDEMNITY INC
6.3	4.4	14.3	5.0	N/A	N/A	113.7	75.6	189.3	381.1	0.0	0.0	IRONSHORE SPECIALTY INS CO
3.0	2.1	96.2	116.9	-10.8	-24.0	46.4	30.8	77.2	132.9	-4.9	4.0	ISLAND INS CO LTD
3.7	3.3	N/A	N/A	N/A	N/A	N/A	N/A	N/A	N/A	0.0	0.0	ISLAND PREMIER INS CO LTD
N/A	N/A	N/A	N/A	N/A	N/A	N/A	N/A	N/A	N/A	0.0	0.0	ISMIE INDEMNITY CO
1.5	1.3	64.7	233.4	-9.1	-19.7	70.1	17.9	88.0	121.8	-9.0	2.1 •	ISMIE MUTUAL INS CO
3.8	2.0	-2.8	126.9	-3.5	-7.0	65.3	-17.5	47.8	133.6	-102.5	0.0 •	JAMES RIVER INS CO
1.3	0.7	125.6	92.4	-21.6	-3.9	41.0	48.3	89.3	120.6	0.1	0.0	JAMESTOWN INS CO RRG
0.5	0.5	85.2	15.8	-1.0	-12.5	50.4	48.3	98.7	155.3	192.9	0.0	JEFFERSON INS CO
5.5	3.4	97.2	16.9	-1.6	-2.2	51.1	38.3	89.4	113.4	8.9	0.3 •	JEWELERS MUTUAL INS CO
2.3	1.6	62.1	19.2	7.4	-1.0	48.1	42.9	91.0	256.6	290.0	0.0	JM WOODWORTH RRG INC
1.0	0.6	129.1	307.0	-31.2	-57.3	45.2	25.1	70.3	205.3	0.0	0.0	JOLIET AREA RRG CAPTIVE INS CO
1.8	1.3	136.5	21.1	-1.2	5.4	52.4	51.1	103.5	99.8	-4.0	0.0	JUNIATA MUTUAL INS CO
22.0	13.8	12.7	10.5	0.3	-2.1	82.1	31.6	113.7	67.2	-8.4	0.0	KANSAS BANKERS SURETY CO
4.3	3.3	54.2	100.0	-35.2	-72.6	30.0	17.5	47.5	125.0	-5.2	0.0	KANSAS MEDICAL MUTUAL INS CO
5.2	4.5	53.1	2.5	-4.8	-2.7	70.3	14.6	84.9	66.7	-13.3	0.0	KANSAS MUTUAL INS CO
4.4	2.8	-0.7	50.9	-8.2	-10.8	999 +	-353.2	999 +	13.8	-153.4	0.0	KEMPER CASUALTY INS CO
0.5	0.4	157.1	64.3	-4.1	-4.4	60.9	32.0	92.9	133.8	7.3	0.0	KEMPER INDEPENDENCE INS CO
N/A	N/A	N/A	N/A	N/A	N/A	N/A	N/A	N/A	N/A	0.0	0.0	KEMPER INS CO OF TEXAS
0.3	0.2	128.1	136.4	-9.6	8.1	65.9	49.9	115.8	125.8	9.1	0.0	KENSINGTON INS CO

999 + Denotes number greater than 999.9%
999 - Denotes number less than -999.99%
• Bullets denote a more detailed analysis is available in Section II.

INSURANCE COMPANY NAME	DOM. STATE	RATING	TOTAL ASSETS ($MIL)	CAPITAL & SURPLUS ($MIL)	ANNUAL NET PREMIUM ($MIL)	NET INCOME ($MIL)	CAPITAL-IZATION INDEX (PTS)	RESERVE ADQ INDEX (PTS)	PROFIT-ABILITY INDEX (PTS)	LIQUIDITY INDEX (PTS)	STAB. INDEX (PTS)	STABILITY FACTORS
KENTUCKIANA MEDICAL RRG & INS CO INC	KY	**D**	41.6	14.6	7.9	0.3	7.1	6.0	8.3	7.0	1.7	DGT
KENTUCKY EMPLOYERS MUTUAL INS	KY	**C**	626.3	135.9	107.0	5.8	5.3	2.2	8.9	7.1	4.3	CT
KENTUCKY FARM BUREAU MUTUAL INS CO	KY	**A**	1,580.7	814.5	719.4	-51.3	10.0	7.8	4.2	5.7	6.0	FT
KENTUCKY HOSPITAL INS CO RRG	KY	**E+**	23.7	8.2	5.4	1.1	7.2	7.1	9.5	9.2	0.7	DGRT
KENTUCKY NATIONAL INS CO	KY	**D+**	6.4	5.0	1.1	-0.6	7.7	4.0	2.9	7.0	2.1	DFGO
KEY RISK INS CO	NC	**C**	74.8	23.6	0.0	0.4	10.0	N/A	5.9	8.6	4.2	DF
KEYSTONE INS CO	PA	**C+**	372.4	110.6	190.7	0.8	7.9	7.9	3.1	6.0	4.2	T
KEYSTONE NATIONAL INS CO	PA	**C**	5.7	2.9	2.3	-0.1	7.7	4.6	1.8	6.9	2.4	DGT
KNIGHTBROOK INS CO	DE	**B-**	29.6	23.4	0.8	-0.4	7.3	8.3	2.7	9.2	4.6	DFG
KODIAK INS CO	NJ	**C**	40.8	14.6	27.9	-0.2	5.1	9.4	6.3	7.7	3.2	DGT
▲LA MEDICAL MUTUAL INS CO	LA	**C+**	325.9	112.2	47.6	2.4	7.5	9.7	8.1	9.0	4.5	T
LACKAWANNA AMERICAN INS CO	PA	**C**	53.6	21.8	12.5	0.4	6.0	7.0	8.9	7.1	4.3	DT
LACKAWANNA CASUALTY CO	PA	**B-**	190.3	86.1	44.0	-0.3	7.3	7.0	6.1	6.7	4.5	T
LACKAWANNA NATIONAL INS CO	PA	**C**	16.7	7.0	6.3	0.1	5.9	4.6	8.7	6.5	2.7	DGT
LAFAYETTE INS CO	LA	**B-**	134.1	59.9	36.8	0.5	9.9	8.3	7.2	7.4	4.9	T
LAKE STREET RRG INC	VT	**D-**	2.8	1.5	0.2	0.0	10.0	6.1	1.9	9.7	1.0	DGT
LANCER INS CO	IL	**C+**	623.9	139.0	173.0	8.6	9.0	9.3	9.0	7.4	4.5	T
LANDCAR CASUALTY CO	UT	**C-**	8.9	1.9	2.5	0.0	6.5	8.1	3.0	5.2	3.0	DGT
LANDMARK AMERICAN INS CO	OK	**C**	344.4	145.9	40.1	1.8	9.7	6.1	5.8	7.2	4.1	T
LANDMARK INS CO	CA	**B**	449.5	163.1	100.0	7.5	6.4	5.7	8.8	7.0	4.0	CT
▼LANDMARK ONE INS CO	FL	**D+**	29.7	7.9	14.1	-1.0	1.8	N/A	2.8	4.1	2.4	CDGL
LAUNDRY OWNERS MUTUAL LIAB INS ASN	PA	**C-**	10.5	4.4	4.9	0.1	5.7	3.6	2.0	7.3	2.2	DGRT
LAURIER INDEMNITY CO	WI	**D+**	24.6	14.3	2.7	0.2	2.8	4.7	4.4	7.3	1.5	CDGT
LAWYERS MUTUAL INS CO	CA	**C**	242.7	110.5	41.6	1.7	9.5	9.7	7.9	7.8	4.0	RT
LAWYERS MUTUAL INS CO OF KENTUCKY	KY	**C**	21.6	6.7	4.0	0.1	4.5	5.4	5.0	6.7	2.5	DFGR
LAWYERS MUTUAL LIAB INS CO OF NC	NC	**C** (1)	72.6	39.4	13.5	-1.9	8.0	6.3	3.0	7.0	4.3	D
LE MARS INS CO	IA	**C**	51.4	28.0	23.0	0.0	10.0	9.5	8.2	6.8	4.3	T
LEADING INS GROUP INS CO LTD US BR	NY	**C**	58.4	19.0	23.4	-0.4	4.9	8.2	4.1	6.9	2.9	DT
LEAGUE OF WI MUNICIPALITIES MUT INS	WI	**C-**	44.9	10.9	15.2	-4.2	5.4	9.4	2.9	6.8	3.1	DGT
LEATHERSTOCKING COOP INS CO	NY	**D+**	11.5	6.0	5.0	0.1	8.4	6.9	8.6	7.1	2.4	DGT
LEBANON MUTUAL INS CO	PA	**C**	23.7	11.4	7.9	-0.4	8.5	5.8	5.7	6.9	3.2	DGT
LEGAL MUTUAL LIAB INS SOCIETY OF MD	MD	**D-**	3.6	0.9	-0.2	-0.2	4.7	4.5	1.8	7.2	1.1	DFGR
LEMIC INS CO	LA	**D**	68.8	22.4	24.4	0.2	5.6	4.3	4.3	6.9	2.1	DT
LENDERS PROTECTION ASR CO RRG	NE	**D**	2.5	2.3	0.0	0.0	10.0	N/A	6.0	10.0	1.9	DGOT
LEWIS & CLARK LTC RRG INC	NV	**E+**	16.4	3.9	6.4	0.6	3.2	6.1	2.9	6.8	0.5	DGRT
LEXINGTON INS CO	DE	**C+**	15,208.1	4,379.3	3,999.3	174.9	5.3	5.8	7.4	6.8	2.9	T
LEXINGTON NATIONAL INS CORP	MD	**C**	54.0	17.3	12.4	1.5	7.7	6.2	9.3	7.5	2.0	DT
LEXON INS CO	TX	**C**	92.7	43.1	57.4	4.5	7.5	8.9	9.4	7.1	3.7	T
▲LIBERTY AMERICAN INS CO	FL	**C**	32.0	27.3	2.8	0.7	10.0	3.9	4.0	8.0	3.4	DFGT
▲LIBERTY AMERICAN SELECT INS CO	FL	**C**	29.2	24.8	2.8	0.6	10.0	3.9	3.9	7.9	3.4	DGT
LIBERTY COUNTY MUTUAL INS CO	TX	**C-**	13.5	13.2	0.0	0.0	10.0	N/A	8.2	10.0	2.9	DG
▲LIBERTY FIRST RRG INS CO	UT	**C-**	2.4	1.2	1.3	0.1	5.1	4.0	6.6	7.5	1.5	DGT
LIBERTY INS CO OF AMERICA	IL	**C+**	12.2	11.6	0.0	0.1	10.0	N/A	3.6	7.0	3.3	ADGT
LIBERTY INS CORP	IL	**C**	1,101.9	256.1	321.2	4.9	6.1	2.7	3.5	6.2	3.8	AT
LIBERTY INS UNDERWRITERS INC	NY	**C**	154.8	90.4	0.0	1.3	10.0	N/A	8.5	7.0	3.9	AT
LIBERTY LLOYDS OF TX INS CO	TX	**B**	6.4	6.0	0.0	0.0	10.0	N/A	7.1	7.0	4.4	DGT
LIBERTY MUTUAL FIRE INS CO	WI	**B-**	4,524.1	947.5	1,070.7	11.5	7.0	3.2	6.2	5.9	4.9	AT
LIBERTY MUTUAL INS CO	MA	**B-**	33,672.9	10,223.6	8,126.3	26.6	7.1	3.6	6.2	6.3	4.9	AT
LIBERTY MUTUAL MID ATLANTIC INS CO	PA	**C**	20.3	15.0	0.0	0.2	10.0	N/A	8.2	7.0	3.1	ADGT
LIBERTY NORTHWEST INS CORP	OR	**C**	185.1	85.9	0.0	1.0	10.0	1.8	3.0	7.0	3.4	FRT
LIBERTY PERSONAL INS CO	MI	**U** (1)	22.4	21.7	0.0	0.6	N/A	N/A	3.7	7.0	4.9	AT
▲LIBERTY SURPLUS INS CORP	NH	**C**	114.1	72.4	0.0	0.5	10.0	N/A	7.9	9.2	3.5	AFT

See Page 27 for explanation of footnotes and Page 28 for explanation of stability factors.

Arrows denote recent upgrades ▲ or downgrades ▼ (see Section VII for explanations)

RISK ADJ. RATIO #1	CAPITAL RATIO #2	PREMIUM TO SURPLUS (%)	RESV. TO SURPLUS (%)	RESV. DEVELOP. 1 YEAR (%)	RESV. DEVELOP. 2 YEAR (%)	LOSS RATIO (%)	EXP. RATIO (%)	COMB RATIO (%)	CASH FROM UNDER-WRITING (%)	NET PREMIUM GROWTH (%)	INVEST. IN AFFIL (%)	INSURANCE COMPANY NAME
2.0	1.3	54.7	142.2	-4.7	-18.1	93.3	8.0	101.3	274.5	3.4	0.0	KENTUCKIANA MEDICAL RRG & INS CO
1.2	0.6	81.2	263.9	-4.5	4.9	79.8	15.9	95.7	173.6	-0.8	0.0	KENTUCKY EMPLOYERS MUTUAL INS
4.5	3.0	80.8	32.3	-0.9	-1.6	91.2	26.7	117.9	88.4	1.3	2.6 •	KENTUCKY FARM BUREAU MUTUAL INS
2.7	1.7	75.4	141.3	-17.8	-47.2	49.8	16.2	66.0	116.5	42.5	0.0	KENTUCKY HOSPITAL INS CO RRG
1.6	1.1	19.5	25.7	-3.4	-42.0	68.1	138.4	206.5	27.3	N/A	0.0	KENTUCKY NATIONAL INS CO
3.4	3.1	N/A	N/A	N/A	N/A	N/A	N/A	N/A	-272.0	0.0	0.0	KEY RISK INS CO
1.9	1.5	170.6	124.9	-6.1	-5.5	75.3	29.1	104.4	92.8	-1.6	9.3	KEYSTONE INS CO
2.0	1.2	75.7	19.6	-1.4	-0.3	67.3	51.0	118.3	89.9	28.5	0.0	KEYSTONE NATIONAL INS CO
1.5	1.2	3.2	10.2	-2.1	-3.4	-87.2	298.0	210.8	28.7	0.0	43.7	KNIGHTBROOK INS CO
1.2	0.8	185.5	72.0	0.9	-19.3	65.9	29.0	94.9	260.4	881.8	0.0	KODIAK INS CO
2.5	2.1	43.0	156.3	-20.4	-48.4	27.3	19.0	46.3	107.0	-5.8	0.1	LA MEDICAL MUTUAL INS CO
2.1	0.9	58.4	80.4	-10.9	-36.3	53.5	17.8	71.3	141.8	4.8	0.0	LACKAWANNA AMERICAN INS CO
1.7	1.3	50.3	82.4	-6.2	-18.9	55.9	16.5	72.4	139.6	5.3	18.4	LACKAWANNA CASUALTY CO
1.5	0.8	92.2	80.7	0.4	0.6	65.7	16.8	82.5	151.7	4.8	0.0	LACKAWANNA NATIONAL INS CO
4.7	3.1	61.7	70.8	1.3	-0.7	84.6	28.2	112.8	100.3	-2.3	0.0	LAFAYETTE INS CO
3.5	3.0	15.1	61.0	-10.1	-88.4	85.0	42.7	127.7	367.5	-56.2	0.0	LAKE STREET RRG INC
3.8	2.2	130.1	115.8	-9.7	-19.9	60.9	15.4	76.3	145.8	44.4	0.0	LANCER INS CO
0.9	0.8	102.8	40.1	-7.9	-6.8	114.5	6.5	121.0	92.7	-21.5	0.0	LANDCAR CASUALTY CO
6.1	3.2	27.9	46.9	-3.1	-5.2	57.6	26.9	84.5	135.2	-8.4	0.0	LANDMARK AMERICAN INS CO
1.8	1.1	64.2	129.9	-7.7	-11.9	80.5	16.9	97.4	140.9	-6.8	0.0	LANDMARK INS CO
0.5	0.3	144.9	29.0	N/A	N/A	42.6	63.7	106.3	201.8	11.4	0.0	LANDMARK ONE INS CO
1.2	0.8	113.2	79.2	22.1	19.4	73.4	39.0	112.4	98.9	44.7	0.0	LAUNDRY OWNERS MUTUAL LIAB INS
0.7	0.5	18.8	60.3	8.4	13.0	114.6	23.7	138.3	107.9	-0.9	0.0	LAURIER INDEMNITY CO
4.5	3.0	37.5	89.4	-11.6	-29.2	73.7	14.0	87.7	120.7	-1.6	0.0	LAWYERS MUTUAL INS CO
1.2	0.9	60.6	147.8	-8.5	-10.5	97.4	8.8	106.2	72.1	-9.9	0.0	LAWYERS MUTUAL INS CO OF
2.3	1.6	34.2	56.3	2.3	-1.8	110.2	20.7	130.9	93.5	3.9	7.6	LAWYERS MUTUAL LIAB INS CO OF NC
4.8	3.2	82.5	27.4	-6.2	-14.4	59.8	35.2	95.0	111.6	13.9	0.0	LE MARS INS CO
0.8	0.6	120.4	97.5	-9.0	-3.6	41.7	51.5	93.2	120.6	45.0	0.0	LEADING INS GROUP INS CO LTD US BR
1.1	0.5	100.3	120.1	-29.6	-35.6	59.2	17.4	76.6	126.0	7.9	0.0	LEAGUE OF WI MUNICIPALITIES MUT INS
3.0	2.3	81.6	36.7	-14.0	-3.8	38.9	31.6	70.5	129.1	4.0	0.0	LEATHERSTOCKING COOP INS CO
3.7	2.3	67.7	38.1	-2.4	-2.0	48.1	49.8	97.9	94.9	-18.0	0.0	LEBANON MUTUAL INS CO
1.0	0.9	-16.3	107.2	-18.8	19.3	65.3	11.2	76.5	-26.9	20.5	0.0	LEGAL MUTUAL LIAB INS SOCIETY OF MD
1.1	0.9	109.8	158.1	-2.3	-10.0	65.3	35.3	100.6	101.7	-7.7	0.0	LEMIC INS CO
25.4	22.8	N/A	N/A	N/A	N/A	N/A	N/A	N/A	550.0	0.0	0.0	LENDERS PROTECTION ASR CO RRG
1.0	0.6	181.7	111.3	-8.5	-87.5	32.4	45.5	77.9	147.5	25.9	0.0	LEWIS & CLARK LTC RRG INC
1.3	0.8	93.8	189.9	-9.9	-15.4	80.5	16.7	97.2	140.9	-6.8	3.2 •	LEXINGTON INS CO
2.8	1.9	77.7	1.6	3.0	-2.3	0.7	54.9	55.6	177.0	-3.9	0.0	LEXINGTON NATIONAL INS CORP
2.5	1.8	146.3	27.0	-14.5	-9.7	9.6	42.8	52.4	199.5	6.1	0.0	LEXON INS CO
7.4	5.2	10.7	16.7	0.5	0.3	88.2	54.9	143.1	13.0	176.7	0.0	LIBERTY AMERICAN INS CO
7.0	4.9	11.7	18.3	0.5	0.3	88.2	54.7	142.9	83.9	176.7	0.0	LIBERTY AMERICAN SELECT INS CO
63.0	31.5	N/A	N/A	N/A	N/A	N/A	N/A	N/A	N/A	0.0	0.0	LIBERTY COUNTY MUTUAL INS CO
1.4	0.8	114.0	85.6	-20.3	-18.0	43.8	16.7	60.5	215.8	1.3	0.0	LIBERTY FIRST RRG INS CO
39.6	35.7	N/A	N/A	N/A	N/A	N/A	N/A	N/A	N/A	0.0	0.0	LIBERTY INS CO OF AMERICA
1.5	0.9	125.8	233.2	-2.7	2.2	83.5	24.1	107.6	93.0	30.0	0.0 •	LIBERTY INS CORP
12.2	11.0	N/A	N/A	N/A	N/A	N/A	N/A	N/A	2.2	0.0	0.0	LIBERTY INS UNDERWRITERS INC
34.0	30.6	N/A	N/A	N/A	N/A	N/A	N/A	N/A	N/A	0.0	0.0	LIBERTY LLOYDS OF TX INS CO
1.3	0.9	110.6	205.1	-3.5	2.6	83.5	24.1	107.6	93.0	-11.9	10.8 •	LIBERTY MUTUAL FIRE INS CO
1.2	1.0	78.6	145.8	-2.1	1.8	83.5	24.5	108.0	91.0	-15.3	28.3 •	LIBERTY MUTUAL INS CO
9.3	8.4	N/A	N/A	N/A	N/A	N/A	N/A	N/A	N/A	0.0	0.0	LIBERTY MUTUAL MID ATLANTIC INS CO
4.7	4.3	N/A	N/A	N/A	N/A	N/A	N/A	N/A	-1.7	0.0	16.4	LIBERTY NORTHWEST INS CORP
N/A	N/A	N/A	N/A	N/A	N/A	N/A	N/A	N/A	N/A	0.0	0.0	LIBERTY PERSONAL INS CO
12.3	11.1	N/A	N/A	N/A	N/A	N/A	N/A	N/A	-248.9	0.0	0.0	LIBERTY SURPLUS INS CORP

999 + Denotes number greater than 999.9%
999 - Denotes number less than -999.99%
• Bullets denote a more detailed analysis is available in Section II.

INSURANCE COMPANY NAME	DOM. STATE	RATING	TOTAL ASSETS ($MIL)	CAPITAL & SURPLUS ($MIL)	ANNUAL NET PREMIUM ($MIL)	NET INCOME ($MIL)	CAPITAL-IZATION INDEX (PTS)	RESERVE ADQ INDEX (PTS)	PROFIT-ABILITY INDEX (PTS)	LIQUIDITY INDEX (PTS)	STAB. INDEX (PTS)	STABILITY FACTORS
LIFE SERVICES NETWORK RECIP INS RRG	DC	**D**	7.6	4.4	2.0	0.1	9.4	6.0	9.4	7.8	1.4	DGRT
LIGHTNING ROD MUTUAL INS CO	OH	**B-**	189.3	111.7	77.1	-1.5	10.0	8.6	3.8	6.8	4.7	T
LILLIAN ASR GROUP INC	FL	**U** (1)	5.6	5.2	0.0	0.0	N/A	N/A	3.1	7.0	3.4	T
▼LINCOLN GENERAL INS CO	PA	**D** (1)	386.7	79.2	185.8	-110.7	2.0	5.0	0.4	1.2	1.6	CGLR
▼LINCOLN MUTUAL INS CO	NC	**D+**	3.0	1.9	1.0	-0.3	7.7	6.0	1.4	7.2	1.8	DFGT
LION INS CO	NY	**F** (5)	0.0	0.0	0.0	0.0	10.0	5.7	2.9	10.0	0.0	FRT
LION INS CO	FL	**C**	362.7	57.0	9.2	0.5	7.6	3.6	8.3	10.0	4.0	T
LITCHFIELD MUTUAL FIRE INS CO	CT	**C-**	7.0	4.3	-0.5	0.0	9.1	5.2	3.7	6.9	2.5	DFGT
LITITZ MUTUAL INS CO	PA	**B**	168.8	107.7	58.1	-0.7	7.9	5.1	3.5	6.0	4.7	AFT
LITTLE BLACK MUTUAL INS CO	WI	**D-**	4.9	2.9	2.3	0.1	7.3	8.0	6.7	7.0	1.3	DGOT
LIVINGSTON MUTUAL INS CO	PA	**B-**	2.8	1.7	0.6	0.0	9.3	6.4	3.0	6.7	3.5	DGT
LM GENERAL INS CO	DE	**U** (1)	9.6	6.9	0.0	0.2	N/A	4.7	4.9	7.0	4.7	FT
LM INS CORP	IA	**C**	77.2	20.9	21.4	0.5	5.4	3.4	6.3	6.7	4.3	ADT
LM PERSONAL INS CO	DE	**U** (1)	8.0	6.9	0.0	0.2	N/A	N/A	3.8	7.0	5.0	T
LM PROPERTY & CASUALTY INS CO	IN	**U** (1)	128.8	66.4	0.0	4.7	N/A	6.1	1.9	7.0	3.1	AFT
LOCUST MUTUAL FIRE INS CO	PA	**U** (1)	1.4	1.4	0.0	0.0	N/A	N/A	6.8	10.0	1.8	GT
LONE STAR NATIONAL INS CO	IN	**D-**	3.7	2.8	0.1	0.0	10.0	6.1	6.8	10.0	1.0	DFGT
LONE STAR RRG INC	TX	**U** (1)	2.7	2.1	0.0	0.0	N/A	4.9	3.8	10.0	2.6	FT
LONG ISLAND INS CO	NY	**E**	6.3	1.2	8.3	0.0	0.0	0.8	1.6	0.0	0.3	CDGL
LOUISIANA FARM BUREAU CAS INS CO	LA	**B**	8.8	8.8	0.0	0.1	10.0	N/A	7.9	10.0	4.8	DG
LOUISIANA FARM BUREAU MUTUAL INS CO	LA	**B-**	139.7	59.1	65.8	0.7	8.0	7.7	2.9	5.6	4.9	FT
▲LOUISIANA PEST CONTROL INS CO	LA	**D**	3.2	3.0	0.4	0.0	9.4	2.9	3.3	9.6	1.4	DGT
LOUISIANA RETAILERS MUTUAL INS CO	LA	**D**	53.5	23.4	19.3	0.5	7.3	5.0	8.5	7.0	1.7	DT
LOUISIANA WORKERS COMPENSATION	LA	**U** (5)	1,269.3	511.0	182.3	0.0	N/A	4.8	2.9	6.9	1.5	CT
LOYA CASUALTY INS CO	CA	**D-**	38.4	19.5	38.1	-1.1	4.0	3.6	3.6	5.9	1.3	DGT
▲LOYA INS CO	TX	**D**	226.6	126.5	273.0	1.5	5.8	6.3	6.0	2.1	1.4	LT
LR INS INC	DE	**U** (1)	2.6	2.6	0.0	0.8	N/A	N/A	5.7	7.0	3.1	T
LUBA CASUALTY INS CO	LA	**B-**	190.7	53.0	68.0	1.2	7.3	3.8	9.1	6.7	3.9	T
LUMBER MUTUAL INS CO	MA	**F** (1)	38.5	4.7	0.0	-0.5	0.3	2.4	1.8	9.1	0.0	CFGR
LUMBERMENS MUTUAL CAS CO	IL	**E**	1,346.1	104.0	6.1	-10.3	0.0	6.6	0.7	9.1	0.0	CFT
LUMBERMENS UNDERWRITERS	TX	**U** (1)	0.7	0.4	0.2	0.0	N/A	N/A	2.3	6.3	2.3	FT
LUMBERMENS UNDERWRITING ALLIANCE	MO	**C**	331.7	85.1	89.3	-6.1	5.8	4.7	3.4	6.8	4.0	FRT
LUTHERAN MUTUAL FIRE INS CO	IL	**C**	9.0	8.8	0.3	0.0	10.0	6.0	5.3	8.5	2.8	DG
LVHN RRG	SC	**U** (1)	30.2	7.0	0.0	0.0	N/A	N/A	4.9	4.7	0.0	FLT
▲LYNDON PROPERTY INS CO	MO	**C+**	422.9	145.8	74.5	-18.3	10.0	5.8	3.9	7.0	4.5	T
▼LYNDON SOUTHERN INS CO	LA	**C**	22.7	11.3	20.4	-0.1	3.8	6.0	5.8	7.0	3.0	CDGT
MACHINERY INS INC AN ASSESSABLE MUT	FL	**D-**	2.2	1.9	0.2	0.0	10.0	N/A	8.6	10.0	0.0	DGT
MADA INS EXCHANGE	MN	**U** (1)	1.0	0.0	0.0	0.0	N/A	0.4	0.6	9.6	0.0	CFRT
MADISON INS CO	GA	**U** (1)	9.1	9.0	0.0	0.0	N/A	9.4	1.9	10.0	0.0	FGT
MADISON MUTUAL INS CO	IL	**C**	60.6	39.5	28.3	-0.2	9.0	5.9	2.6	6.0	4.3	FT
MADISON MUTUAL INS CO	NY	**C+**	11.1	7.1	3.2	-0.1	9.4	6.0	5.9	7.1	3.0	DGT
MAG MUTUAL INS CO	GA	**B-**	1,367.0	356.2	225.7	7.2	7.6	9.7	8.5	7.8	4.7	T
MAIDEN REINS CO	MO	**U** (1)	8.3	8.3	0.0	0.2	N/A	N/A	4.2	7.0	5.2	T
MAIN STREET AMERICA ASR CO	FL	**B-**	118.3	100.1	0.0	1.4	10.0	3.1	2.4	7.0	4.3	T
MAINE BONDING & CAS CO	ME	**U** (1)	6.5	6.4	0.0	0.3	N/A	N/A	1.9	7.0	3.1	T
MAINE EMPLOYERS MUTUAL INS CO	ME	**U** (5)	649.5	212.6	64.3	0.0	N/A	4.1	0.9	7.0	2.1	RT
MAINLAND INS CO	PA	**U** (1)	4.9	4.8	0.0	0.1	N/A	7.5	7.6	7.0	4.5	RT
MAJESTIC INS CO	CA	**D+**	326.6	99.8	92.5	-1.7	5.0	4.5	6.7	7.0	2.4	CRT
MAKE TRANSPORTATION INS INC RRG	DE	**E+**	3.6	1.3	1.4	0.0	7.2	3.4	6.9	9.0	0.7	DGT
MANHATTAN RE-INS CO	DE	**U** (5)	0.0	0.0	0.0	0.0	N/A	9.8	0.8	9.2	2.0	FRT
MANITOWOC MUTUAL INS CO	WI	**D-**	5.9	2.6	3.1	-0.1	6.9	6.3	1.6	5.1	1.3	DFGT
MANUFACTURERS ALLIANCE INS CO	PA	**C**	207.0	63.3	81.4	1.9	7.6	4.9	6.6	6.3	3.6	AT

See Page 27 for explanation of footnotes and Page 28 for explanation of stability factors.

Arrows denote recent upgrades ▲ or downgrades ▼ (see Section VII for explanations)

RISK ADJ. RATIO #1	CAPITAL RATIO #2	PREMIUM TO SURPLUS (%)	RESV. TO SURPLUS (%)	RESV. DEVELOP. 1 YEAR (%)	RESV. DEVELOP. 2 YEAR (%)	LOSS RATIO (%)	EXP. RATIO (%)	COMB RATIO (%)	CASH FROM UNDER-WRITING (%)	NET PREMIUM GROWTH (%)	INVEST. IN AFFIL (%)	INSURANCE COMPANY NAME
4.4	4.0	46.9	27.1	-1.6	-17.2	18.3	32.1	50.4	167.3	18.1	0.0	LIFE SERVICES NETWORK RECIP INS
5.4	3.4	66.0	25.2	-1.7	-2.6	73.3	32.0	105.3	94.1	-0.4	0.1	LIGHTNING ROD MUTUAL INS CO
N/A	N/A	N/A	N/A	N/A	N/A	N/A	N/A	N/A	N/A	0.0	0.0	LILLIAN ASR GROUP INC
0.5	0.3	234.5	237.3	7.7	-89.0	92.2	67.4	159.6	107.9	74.3	0.0	LINCOLN GENERAL INS CO
1.7	1.1	46.0	6.8	0.6	1.0	104.3	56.7	161.0	75.0	2.4	0.0	LINCOLN MUTUAL INS CO
6.9	6.2	N/A	30.4	-8.2	-0.5	999 +	N/A	N/A	8.2	100.0	0.0	LION INS CO
2.0	1.3	16.3	34.5	0.2	1.7	62.6	29.2	91.8	160.8	-28.9	0.0	LION INS CO
4.6	4.2	-10.5	21.5	-0.4	-1.2	75.5	2.6	78.1	12.9	-347.3	0.0	LITCHFIELD MUTUAL FIRE INS CO
2.9	1.8	48.7	14.4	-0.7	-0.8	70.9	36.4	107.3	89.1	-8.5	0.0	LITITZ MUTUAL INS CO
1.9	1.2	80.7	11.9	1.0	-2.3	59.9	35.2	95.1	113.4	18.5	0.0	LITTLE BLACK MUTUAL INS CO
3.3	2.7	32.3	11.5	-3.2	-2.7	71.4	26.5	97.9	89.6	-2.7	0.0	LIVINGSTON MUTUAL INS CO
N/A	N/A	N/A	10.9	0.3	0.4	N/A	N/A	N/A	3.1	0.0	0.0	LM GENERAL INS CO
1.4	0.9	105.1	194.9	-3.4	2.5	83.6	24.1	107.7	93.0	-11.9	0.0	LM INS CORP
N/A	N/A	N/A	N/A	N/A	N/A	N/A	N/A	N/A	-2.0	0.0	0.0	LM PERSONAL INS CO
N/A	N/A	0.1	66.3	-0.8	-1.2	999 +	999 +	-116.2	-6.5	N/A	0.0	LM PROPERTY & CASUALTY INS CO
N/A	N/A	2.4	N/A	N/A	N/A	15.2	115.2	130.4	70.2	83.3	0.0	LOCUST MUTUAL FIRE INS CO
7.1	6.3	1.8	4.8	0.6	-0.2	112.7	84.3	197.0	-23.8	-17.7	0.0	LONE STAR NATIONAL INS CO
N/A	N/A	N/A	32.2	-18.7	-15.4	84.1	N/A	N/A	29.7	-100.0	0.0	LONE STAR RRG INC
0.0	0.0	696.2	203.2	64.6	85.0	74.8	26.0	100.8	91.8	33.5	0.0	LONG ISLAND INS CO
52.6	26.7	N/A	N/A	N/A	N/A	N/A	N/A	N/A	N/A	0.0	0.0	LOUISIANA FARM BUREAU CAS INS CO
2.9	2.0	112.6	9.1	-3.6	-0.5	72.0	27.7	99.7	88.4	18.0	1.4	LOUISIANA FARM BUREAU MUTUAL INS
13.7	5.9	11.9	6.2	0.6	6.9	4.2	48.3	52.5	84.5	130.0	0.0	LOUISIANA PEST CONTROL INS CO
1.5	1.1	84.6	88.8	2.7	8.6	64.8	34.1	98.9	128.7	19.0	0.0	LOUISIANA RETAILERS MUTUAL INS CO
N/A	N/A	190.5	376.1	-19.0	-23.0	76.3	28.1	104.4	141.4	-14.1	0.0	LOUISIANA WORKERS COMPENSATION
0.8	0.6	246.3	59.6	3.2	0.3	62.7	36.7	99.4	122.6	106.0	0.0	LOYA CASUALTY INS CO
1.3	1.0	216.7	58.4	-1.4	-2.8	64.2	38.6	102.8	101.3	2.5	10.4	LOYA INS CO
N/A	N/A	N/A	N/A	N/A	N/A	N/A	N/A	N/A	N/A	0.0	0.0	LR INS INC
1.6	1.3	129.4	138.6	-24.2	-7.2	46.3	35.3	81.6	121.6	-6.0	0.0	LUBA CASUALTY INS CO
0.1	0.1	0.7	407.0	33.1	32.6	999 +	999 +	999 +	0.4	146.2	54.4	LUMBER MUTUAL INS CO
0.1	0.0	5.4	919.3	15.3	6.6	999 +	995.3	999 +	8.9	-36.9	5.8	LUMBERMENS MUTUAL CAS CO
N/A	N/A	36.1	N/A	N/A	N/A	61.4	81.4	142.8	48.7	-30.6	0.0	LUMBERMENS UNDERWRITERS
1.6	0.8	95.2	135.2	-5.7	-4.5	61.6	35.8	97.4	88.5	-0.6	0.0	LUMBERMENS UNDERWRITING
26.8	19.6	3.1	0.4	-0.1	0.1	78.2	88.4	166.6	52.2	1.9	0.0	LUTHERAN MUTUAL FIRE INS CO
N/A	N/A	N/A	N/A	N/A	N/A	N/A	N/A	N/A	361.0	0.0	0.0	LVHN RRG
6.8	4.0	52.0	14.0	1.8	1.3	86.1	16.3	102.4	87.2	-30.1	0.0	LYNDON PROPERTY INS CO
0.7	0.6	155.4	6.1	-1.7	3.0	23.2	59.2	82.4	139.6	41.4	0.0	LYNDON SOUTHERN INS CO
10.1	7.8	12.3	5.0	N/A	N/A	-8.0	68.4	60.4	159.6	-44.2	0.0	MACHINERY INS INC AN ASSESSABLE
N/A	N/A	N/A	999 +	65.2	825.5	N/A	N/A	N/A	N/A	0.0	0.0	MADA INS EXCHANGE
N/A	N/A	N/A	1.7	2.3	-24.3	N/A	N/A	N/A	N/A	-100.0	0.0	MADISON INS CO
3.3	2.2	71.2	29.2	-0.3	3.0	90.2	23.1	113.3	89.5	-2.9	0.0	MADISON MUTUAL INS CO
4.0	2.8	44.8	20.7	-3.4	-1.2	50.6	36.8	87.4	112.8	0.7	0.0	MADISON MUTUAL INS CO
2.2	1.8	63.2	179.2	-29.8	-60.1	53.2	18.9	72.1	135.2	-10.8	1.8 •	MAG MUTUAL INS CO
N/A	N/A	N/A	N/A	N/A	N/A	N/A	N/A	N/A	28.1	0.0	0.0	MAIDEN REINS CO
29.1	26.2	N/A	N/A	N/A	N/A	N/A	N/A	N/A	N/A	100.0	0.0	MAIN STREET AMERICA ASR CO
N/A	N/A	N/A	N/A	N/A	N/A	N/A	N/A	N/A	0.1	0.0	0.0	MAINE BONDING & CAS CO
N/A	N/A	63.7	186.1	-34.3	-163.2	31.2	20.8	52.0	113.9	-2.6	0.0	MAINE EMPLOYERS MUTUAL INS CO
N/A	N/A	N/A	N/A	N/A	-0.1	N/A	N/A	N/A	N/A	0.0	0.0	MAINLAND INS CO
1.3	0.7	91.1	154.4	-3.3	-17.6	73.4	33.9	107.3	118.8	-1.1	0.0	MAJESTIC INS CO
1.6	1.2	110.1	139.5	-5.6	8.5	75.2	18.5	93.7	163.4	-15.7	0.0	MAKE TRANSPORTATION INS INC RRG
N/A	N/A	-0.2	102.5	-76.7	-71.0	999 +	999 +	999 +	0.9	-120.0	0.0	MANHATTAN RE-INS CO
1.3	0.9	110.9	1.5	0.1	-1.9	81.7	40.9	122.6	79.5	-13.4	0.0	MANITOWOC MUTUAL INS CO
1.6	1.3	133.9	139.4	-2.0	-0.2	69.0	25.6	94.6	105.1	5.3	2.9	MANUFACTURERS ALLIANCE INS CO

999 + Denotes number greater than 999.9%
999 - Denotes number less than -999.99%
• Bullets denote a more detailed analysis is available in Section II.

INSURANCE COMPANY NAME	DOM. STATE	RATING	TOTAL ASSETS ($MIL)	CAPITAL & SURPLUS ($MIL)	ANNUAL NET PREMIUM ($MIL)	NET INCOME ($MIL)	CAPITAL-IZATION INDEX (PTS)	RESERVE ADQ INDEX (PTS)	PROFIT-ABILITY INDEX (PTS)	LIQUIDITY INDEX (PTS)	STAB. INDEX (PTS)	STABILITY FACTORS
MANUFACTURING TECHNOLOGY MUT INS	MI	**C-**	28.2	8.9	10.8	-0.3	3.8	3.6	2.0	6.9	2.3	CDGT
MAPFRE INS CO OF FLORIDA	FL	**C-**	45.4	21.6	14.8	-0.4	8.3	5.6	4.6	7.1	3.1	DGT
MAPFRE INSURANCE CO	NJ	**U** (1)	38.4	29.7	0.0	3.3	N/A	6.0	1.9	10.0	3.1	RT
MAPFRE PAN AMERICAN INS CO	PR	**C+**	23.7	13.9	1.5	0.2	10.0	7.7	1.9	9.4	4.3	DGT
MAPFRE PRAICO INS CO	PR	**B**	444.6	183.4	169.4	4.9	7.1	8.2	8.6	5.9	4.8	T
MAPFRE PREFERRED RISK INS CO	PR	**B-**	102.2	33.8	10.1	1.3	10.0	8.1	6.7	7.9	4.8	T
▲MAPLE VALLEY MUTUAL INS CO	WI	**B-**	9.1	5.9	3.7	0.2	9.1	5.8	7.8	7.4	3.6	DGT
MARATHON FINANCIAL INS INC RRG	SC	**D**	12.4	2.4	1.8	0.2	5.1	3.6	1.6	2.1	1.8	DFGL
MARKEL AMERICAN INS CO	VA	**C**	448.8	88.0	187.7	1.5	5.1	7.1	5.3	7.0	3.8	ACGT
MARKEL INS CO	IL	**C-**	643.9	121.0	228.6	-6.4	4.3	5.8	1.9	6.2	3.3	AT
MARTINGALE NATIONAL INS CO	IL	**U** (1)	3.1	3.0	0.0	0.0	N/A	3.6	1.9	7.0	3.1	FT
MARYLAND CASUALTY CO	MD	**C+**	384.6	434.7	0.0	1.5	10.0	N/A	8.5	7.0	4.4	FT
MARYLAND INS CO	TX	**U** (1)	18.9	18.4	0.0	0.6	N/A	N/A	3.3	10.0	4.5	T
MARYSVILLE MUTUAL INS CO	KS	**C**	23.9	13.6	12.5	-0.2	8.8	7.8	6.6	6.0	3.5	DFGR
MASSACHUSETTS BAY INS CO	NH	**C+**	46.9	46.7	0.0	0.4	10.0	N/A	7.8	7.0	4.7	G
MASSACHUSETTS EMPLOYERS INS CO	MA	**C**	4.0	3.3	0.0	0.0	10.0	N/A	5.0	9.3	3.2	DGT
MASSACHUSETTS HOMELAND INS CO	MA	**B**	9.1	8.9	0.0	0.4	10.0	N/A	3.6	7.0	4.2	DGT
MAX AMERICA INS CO	IN	**U** (1)	20.0	20.0	0.0	2.1	N/A	4.9	1.9	7.0	3.1	FT
MAX SPECIALTY INS CO	DE	**C**	199.0	124.3	15.1	0.1	9.5	6.6	3.5	6.9	3.3	GT
MAXUM CASUALTY INS CO	DE	**D**	11.5	9.7	0.0	0.1	10.0	N/A	7.6	9.2	1.5	DGT
MAXUM INDEMNITY CO	DE	**C**	173.3	63.3	45.9	0.5	7.0	6.5	6.8	7.5	4.1	T
MAYA ASR CO	NY	**D-**	19.9	2.6	3.2	-0.2	3.7	3.7	3.1	7.6	1.3	DGT
MBIA INS CORP	NY	**D+**	6,123.8	2,515.5	1,429.4	-17.9	6.0	3.2	2.2	8.5	2.6	ACFT
MCIC VERMONT INC RRG	VT	**D-**	236.1	10.0	38.0	0.0	2.2	N/A	3.3	1.8	1.3	DGLR
MCMILLAN WARNER MUTUAL INS CO	WI	**C**	12.2	7.6	5.7	0.0	9.0	6.0	6.7	7.4	2.7	DGT
MD RRG INC	MT	**D-**	8.4	4.7	3.9	0.4	8.0	4.1	9.6	8.9	1.3	DGT
▲MDADVANTAGE INS CO OF NJ	NJ	**C-**	301.1	76.6	41.0	1.8	3.5	5.9	6.4	6.9	3.1	CT
MEDAMERICA MUTUAL RRG INC	HI	**C**	54.4	17.7	12.9	0.9	7.6	5.9	8.9	7.3	3.5	DGRT
MEDICAL ALLIANCE INS CO	IL	**D**	37.2	3.8	2.4	0.0	4.6	N/A	8.5	10.0	2.1	DGRT
MEDICAL INS EXCHANGE OF CALIFORNIA	CA	**B-**	371.4	126.1	65.7	4.4	7.4	6.0	5.8	7.3	4.7	RT
MEDICAL INS UNDERWRITERS RRG INC	AZ	**D**	0.9	0.5	0.4	0.0	7.1	N/A	3.7	10.0	0.9	DFGT
MEDICAL LIABILITY ALLIANCE	MO	**C**	41.8	23.9	8.7	2.0	7.4	9.4	8.8	8.7	2.7	DGT
MEDICAL LIABILITY MUTUAL INS CO	NY	**D+**	4,915.9	287.6	643.7	-2.7	0.2	5.1	2.6	5.6	2.4	CRT
▲MEDICAL MUTUAL INS CO OF MAINE	ME	**C+**	212.6	79.3	40.6	1.2	7.9	4.9	5.3	6.9	4.5	T
MEDICAL MUTUAL INS CO OF NC	NC	**B-**	445.8	160.3	85.7	2.9	8.4	7.0	8.9	7.5	4.5	T
MEDICAL MUTUAL LIAB INS SOC OF MD	MD	**B-**	787.8	252.8	138.9	-1.1	7.8	9.9	6.5	7.4	4.6	RT
▲MEDICAL PROFESSIONAL MUTUAL INS CO	MA	**C+**	2,198.8	585.0	297.5	-2.3	5.7	9.6	6.7	6.9	4.5	RT
MEDICAL PROTECTIVE CO	IN	**B**	1,922.5	554.5	343.2	10.1	7.5	6.0	7.0	7.7	5.6	T
MEDICAL SECURITY INS CO	NC	**C+**	8.1	4.1	1.5	0.2	10.0	9.4	5.7	8.7	3.4	DGT
MEDICUS INS CO	TX	**D-**	59.7	17.6	27.0	-1.0	3.2	3.6	2.8	7.6	1.0	DGT
MEDILINK RRG INC	SC	**U** (1)	0.8	0.6	0.0	-0.2	N/A	4.1	2.3	7.0	1.5	FRT
MEDMARC CASUALTY INS CO	VT	**C**	110.2	33.9	13.0	0.4	5.1	6.1	3.5	7.2	4.0	T
MEDMARC MUTUAL INS CO	VT	**C+**	238.3	111.0	26.0	0.3	7.1	6.1	5.4	7.8	4.3	T
MEDSTAR LIABILITY LTD INS CO INC RRG	DC	**D-**	5.1	0.7	0.9	0.1	0.9	5.0	4.4	7.6	0.5	CDGT
MEEMIC INS CO	MI	**C+**	118.0	83.6	0.0	0.9	10.0	4.8	3.0	7.0	4.3	T
MEMBERS INS CO	NC	**E+**	5.9	4.0	1.5	-0.2	7.2	3.6	1.7	7.7	0.4	DFGT
MEMBERSELECT INS CO	MI	**B**	215.0	128.6	66.3	-0.3	10.0	5.3	5.4	6.8	4.9	T
▲MEMIC INDEMNITY CO	NH	**C**	149.2	56.9	45.1	-0.9	7.0	7.0	5.9	6.7	3.2	T
MENDAKOTA INS CO	MN	**B**	12.3	9.2	-21.1	0.0	9.6	6.1	5.0	7.0	4.4	DFGT
MENDOTA INS CO	MN	**B-**	68.9	29.3	54.6	-0.5	0.3	6.0	2.2	0.0	4.9	CGLT
MENNONITE MUTUAL INS CO	OH	**C-**	16.2	7.6	9.5	-0.8	8.0	9.3	3.4	6.7	2.8	DGT
MENTAL HEALTH RISK RETENTION GROUP	VT	**C-**	19.8	6.5	3.3	0.3	7.4	9.5	8.9	8.2	2.5	DGT

See Page 27 for explanation of footnotes and Page 28 for explanation of stability factors.

Arrows denote recent upgrades ▲ or downgrades ▼ (see Section VII for explanations)

RISK ADJ. RATIO #1	CAPITAL RATIO #2	PREMIUM TO SURPLUS (%)	RESV. TO SURPLUS (%)	RESV. DEVELOP. 1 YEAR (%)	RESV. DEVELOP. 2 YEAR (%)	LOSS RATIO (%)	EXP. RATIO (%)	COMB RATIO (%)	CASH FROM UNDER-WRITING (%)	NET PREMIUM GROWTH (%)	INVEST. IN AFFIL (%)	INSURANCE COMPANY NAME
0.8	0.3	112.4	158.6	8.2	N/A	116.8	12.3	129.1	118.4	-34.2	0.0	MANUFACTURING TECHNOLOGY MUT
2.6	1.7	67.6	53.1	-1.1	-0.5	50.4	47.0	97.4	90.2	21.6	0.0	MAPFRE INS CO OF FLORIDA
N/A	N/A	0.1	18.4	-9.1	-5.2	999 +	999 +	999 +	21.7	109.7	0.0	MAPFRE INSURANCE CO
5.8	5.3	10.1	3.2	-4.4	-3.0	-1.3	-1.1	-2.4	999 +	36.0	0.0	MAPFRE PAN AMERICAN INS CO
1.6	1.1	95.2	55.9	-5.3	-3.3	60.9	36.2	97.1	108.1	1.2	7.9 •	MAPFRE PRAICO INS CO
4.5	4.0	30.9	6.3	-0.9	-3.0	52.5	23.8	76.3	105.7	0.9	0.0	MAPFRE PREFERRED RISK INS CO
3.5	2.7	64.9	15.8	1.2	4.7	53.8	33.8	87.6	119.5	-3.4	0.0	MAPLE VALLEY MUTUAL INS CO
1.0	0.6	82.0	14.0	-25.6	N/A	48.9	91.1	140.0	43.7	8.3	0.0	MARATHON FINANCIAL INS INC RRG
0.9	0.6	192.7	240.8	-14.8	-38.5	56.6	37.9	94.5	116.3	74.8	0.0	MARKEL AMERICAN INS CO
1.1	0.8	248.6	429.0	18.0	17.9	73.3	39.4	112.7	112.6	-13.7	0.0	MARKEL INS CO
N/A	N/A	N/A	N/A	N/A	N/A	N/A	N/A	N/A	N/A	0.0	0.0	MARTINGALE NATIONAL INS CO
5.6	5.1	N/A	N/A	N/A	N/A	N/A	N/A	N/A	128.2	0.0	18.2 •	MARYLAND CASUALTY CO
N/A	N/A	N/A	N/A	N/A	N/A	N/A	N/A	N/A	N/A	0.0	0.0	MARYLAND INS CO
2.8	2.4	88.8	2.9	-2.6	-1.9	73.9	27.1	101.0	89.5	1.3	0.0	MARYSVILLE MUTUAL INS CO
71.1	31.9	N/A	N/A	N/A	N/A	N/A	N/A	N/A	N/A	0.0	0.0	MASSACHUSETTS BAY INS CO
9.7	8.7	N/A	N/A	N/A	N/A	N/A	N/A	N/A	N/A	0.0	0.0	MASSACHUSETTS EMPLOYERS INS CO
72.1	64.9	N/A	N/A	N/A	N/A	N/A	N/A	N/A	N/A	0.0	0.0	MASSACHUSETTS HOMELAND INS CO
N/A	N/A	N/A	N/A	N/A	N/A	N/A	N/A	N/A	N/A	-100.0	0.0	MAX AMERICA INS CO
2.4	2.0	11.9	3.6	N/A	-17.9	59.0	138.1	197.1	93.7	455.0	20.4	MAX SPECIALTY INS CO
14.4	13.0	N/A	N/A	N/A	N/A	N/A	N/A	N/A	-227.1	0.0	0.0	MAXUM CASUALTY INS CO
1.8	0.9	72.0	108.4	-8.7	-12.5	60.3	36.7	97.0	150.6	42.3	6.7	MAXUM INDEMNITY CO
0.8	0.6	122.6	120.1	-4.8	-1.7	79.0	10.4	89.4	198.8	73.6	0.0	MAYA ASR CO
1.2	0.5	40.8	53.4	23.3	1.0	339.0	17.7	356.7	54.2	86.9	5.5 •	MBIA INS CORP
0.4	0.3	373.1	169.3	N/A	N/A	47.6	54.5	102.1	109.7	12.4	0.0	MCIC VERMONT INC RRG
2.6	2.4	72.9	7.6	-0.7	-1.8	66.9	33.2	100.1	101.2	14.6	0.0	MCMILLAN WARNER MUTUAL INS CO
4.6	2.9	95.0	61.1	-85.1	-168.0	-0.6	8.9	8.3	207.2	87.9	0.0	MD RRG INC
1.1	0.7	55.2	192.6	-5.3	-14.9	50.9	30.7	81.6	101.5	-14.5	0.0	MDADVANTAGE INS CO OF NJ
1.7	1.3	75.9	104.9	-2.4	-16.9	71.8	11.5	83.3	161.7	0.8	0.4	MEDAMERICA MUTUAL RRG INC
0.7	0.6	63.8	N/A	N/A	N/A	15.2	72.1	87.3	183.1	9.4	0.0	MEDICAL ALLIANCE INS CO
2.7	1.8	53.1	108.1	-20.6	-36.0	38.1	13.6	51.7	143.1	-4.7	5.0	MEDICAL INS EXCHANGE OF CALIFORNIA
3.2	2.8	75.8	N/A	N/A	N/A	63.8	37.4	101.2	-123.4	123.8	0.0	MEDICAL INS UNDERWRITERS RRG INC
3.7	2.4	39.7	64.4	-3.7	-22.8	72.0	17.2	89.2	222.6	3.5	0.0	MEDICAL LIABILITY ALLIANCE
0.2	0.1	223.9	999 +	-75.1	-189.5	91.8	12.1	103.9	79.7	-9.4	4.9 •	MEDICAL LIABILITY MUTUAL INS CO
2.0	1.7	50.9	119.0	-5.0	-16.5	66.5	24.3	90.8	123.5	-3.8	0.0	MEDICAL MUTUAL INS CO OF MAINE
3.1	2.4	54.6	108.5	-17.7	-26.7	53.9	10.4	64.3	175.7	-9.3	3.9 •	MEDICAL MUTUAL INS CO OF NC
2.0	1.8	54.9	124.8	-22.6	-52.9	45.4	15.2	60.6	170.1	-7.8	7.1 •	MEDICAL MUTUAL LIAB INS SOC OF MD
1.2	1.0	48.6	217.1	-22.2	-40.7	55.4	18.7	74.1	124.1	-5.9	1.7 •	MEDICAL PROFESSIONAL MUTUAL INS
1.4	1.1	54.3	165.1	-6.0	-5.2	74.0	14.1	88.1	220.2	0.0	0.0 •	MEDICAL PROTECTIVE CO
3.4	3.1	37.5	58.3	-8.9	-17.4	53.3	27.3	80.6	132.2	-15.9	0.0	MEDICAL SECURITY INS CO
0.8	0.5	148.2	90.8	N/A	-0.6	59.0	38.7	97.7	255.8	76.0	0.0	MEDICUS INS CO
N/A	N/A	N/A	N/A	N/A	N/A	N/A	N/A	N/A	N/A	0.0	0.0	MEDILINK RRG INC
0.9	0.7	38.7	142.0	-2.2	-7.3	89.8	30.4	120.2	89.1	-11.0	0.0	MEDMARC CASUALTY INS CO
1.2	1.0	23.0	84.5	-1.6	-5.0	89.8	30.4	120.2	100.7	-11.0	30.3	MEDMARC MUTUAL INS CO
0.4	0.3	126.2	327.0	-41.8	-39.6	60.2	50.2	110.4	187.2	-7.2	0.0	MEDSTAR LIABILITY LTD INS CO INC RRG
16.7	12.0	N/A	N/A	N/A	N/A	N/A	N/A	N/A	-37.4	0.0	0.0	MEEMIC INS CO
1.5	1.1	36.0	9.0	0.1	N/A	71.9	50.9	122.8	67.5	37.0	0.0	MEMBERS INS CO
7.3	5.0	50.4	40.3	-0.6	4.1	78.4	32.5	110.9	94.6	0.3	0.0	MEMBERSELECT INS CO
2.0	0.9	78.2	100.0	-12.1	-21.1	65.2	29.6	94.8	118.5	23.0	0.0	MEMIC INDEMNITY CO
11.3	10.1	-230.1	N/A	-192.3	-112.5	100.1	-0.7	99.4	141.0	-337.4	0.0	MENDAKOTA INS CO
0.1	0.1	188.8	44.1	68.0	-42.0	70.5	23.9	94.4	98.6	235.4	29.5	MENDOTA INS CO
2.3	1.7	111.5	16.9	-6.3	-12.3	45.3	40.4	85.7	109.4	0.9	0.0	MENNONITE MUTUAL INS CO
1.8	1.2	52.6	149.7	-7.3	-15.9	75.0	8.3	83.3	247.5	7.9	0.0	MENTAL HEALTH RISK RETENTION

999 + Denotes number greater than 999.9%
999 - Denotes number less than -999.99%
• Bullets denote a more detailed analysis is available in Section II.

INSURANCE COMPANY NAME	DOM. STATE	RATING	TOTAL ASSETS ($MIL)	CAPITAL & SURPLUS ($MIL)	ANNUAL NET PREMIUM ($MIL)	NET INCOME ($MIL)	CAPITAL-IZATION INDEX (PTS)	RESERVE ADQ INDEX (PTS)	PROFIT-ABILITY INDEX (PTS)	LIQUIDITY INDEX (PTS)	STAB. INDEX (PTS)	STABILITY FACTORS
▲MERASTAR INS CO	IN	**C+**	32.8	12.8	0.0	0.1	10.0	5.1	3.1	7.0	3.1	DGRT
MERCED MUTUAL INS CO	CA	**C**	17.6	12.0	5.2	0.2	8.0	6.9	4.3	8.1	3.3	DFGT
MERCER INS CO	PA	**C-**	227.0	56.4	61.9	1.6	3.6	3.6	4.8	6.4	3.0	CT
MERCER INS CO OF NJ INC	NJ	**C**	72.8	19.6	19.2	0.4	3.4	3.7	8.6	6.8	4.0	CDT
MERCHANTS BONDING CO (MUTUAL)	IA	**C+**	80.2	54.2	29.3	1.3	8.3	7.9	8.6	8.2	3.9	T
MERCHANTS MUTUAL INS CO	NY	**C+**	351.7	123.3	89.9	0.1	8.3	7.0	7.8	6.8	4.5	T
MERCHANTS NATIONAL INS CO	NH	**C**	59.3	23.7	25.7	-0.6	7.3	3.6	2.0	6.7	3.1	DT
MERCHANTS PREFERRED INS CO	NY	**C**	33.7	12.8	12.8	-0.1	7.2	3.6	2.4	6.7	2.5	DGT
MERCHANTS PROPERTY INS CO OF IN	IN	**U** (1)	43.4	35.8	0.0	3.6	N/A	3.6	3.9	10.0	5.3	FT
MERCURY CASUALTY CO	CA	**A-**	2,212.7	1,056.6	1,042.5	-0.9	7.7	5.9	3.5	6.2	6.9	T
MERCURY COUNTY MUTUAL INS CO	TX	**C**	10.1	3.8	0.0	0.0	8.3	N/A	3.5	9.3	3.3	DFG
MERCURY INDEMNITY CO OF AMERICA	FL	**D-**	46.6	32.5	0.0	0.2	10.0	3.7	5.3	7.0	1.0	FGT
▲MERCURY INDEMNITY CO OF GEORGIA	GA	**B**	9.6	9.0	0.2	0.1	10.0	6.1	8.5	7.5	4.4	DFGT
▼MERCURY INS CO	CA	**A-**	1,373.9	582.4	1,304.2	13.4	7.9	6.0	3.3	3.0	6.9	LT
MERCURY INS CO OF FL	FL	**C-**	63.2	36.9	0.0	0.2	10.0	N/A	6.8	9.8	3.3	T
MERCURY INS CO OF GA	GA	**B**	14.4	13.7	0.3	0.1	10.0	5.1	7.8	7.0	4.9	DFGT
MERCURY INS CO OF IL	IL	**B**	28.3	25.6	5.1	0.1	7.6	4.7	5.0	2.6	5.7	DFGL
MERCURY NATIONAL INS CO	IL	**B**	13.2	12.6	0.0	0.1	10.0	4.8	8.0	10.0	4.9	DG
MERIDIAN CITIZENS MUTUAL INS CO	IN	**C**	24.4	8.2	7.2	-0.1	8.7	7.9	2.9	6.4	3.4	DGT
MERIDIAN SECURITY INS CO	IN	**C**	64.8	30.4	-0.6	-0.1	10.0	3.8	1.9	6.5	3.4	T
MERITPLAN INS CO	CA	**B-**	195.3	87.8	66.0	5.7	10.0	6.3	8.5	6.9	5.1	GT
▲MERRIMACK MUTUAL FIRE INS CO	MA	**A**	883.0	520.3	218.2	11.7	9.1	6.0	8.3	7.6	6.0	T
METROPOLITAN CASUALTY INS CO	RI	**B**	51.0	50.4	0.0	0.5	10.0	N/A	8.5	7.0	5.6	
METROPOLITAN DIRECT PROP & CAS INS	RI	**B**	26.6	25.9	0.0	0.3	10.0	N/A	8.1	7.0	5.9	DG
METROPOLITAN GENERAL INS CO	RI	**B**	33.0	32.2	0.0	0.4	10.0	N/A	8.2	7.0	5.8	DGT
▲METROPOLITAN GROUP PROP & CAS INS	RI	**B**	414.3	305.1	0.0	3.7	10.0	5.3	6.8	9.2	5.5	FT
METROPOLITAN LLOYDS INS CO TEXAS	TX	**B**	14.0	14.0	0.0	0.1	10.0	N/A	7.9	7.0	4.9	DGT
METROPOLITAN PROPERTY & CAS INS CO	RI	**B+**	4,771.4	1,769.8	2,962.5	65.5	7.6	7.0	4.6	3.5	6.4	LT
MFS MUTUAL INS CO	IA	**C-**	3.6	3.3	0.5	0.0	9.4	6.2	2.3	7.4	2.1	DFGT
▲MGA INS CO INC	TX	**C-**	219.5	88.3	180.6	1.9	4.5	1.5	4.9	6.0	2.9	GT
MGIC ASSURANCE CORP	WI	**U** (1)	9.8	9.7	0.3	0.3	N/A	N/A	6.8	10.0	3.9	DGT
MGIC CREDIT ASR CORP	WI	**C-**	44.3	41.1	0.7	-0.2	10.0	7.0	5.1	9.3	2.9	DGT
MGIC INDEMNITY CORP	WI	**U** (1)	24.3	23.8	0.0	0.8	N/A	3.6	6.8	7.0	0.0	CDT
MGIC MORTGAGE REINSURANCE CORP	WI	**C+**	32.8	18.8	1.2	0.2	8.4	6.4	6.9	9.2	4.3	DGT
MGIC REINSURANCE CORP	WI	**C-**	384.4	104.0	68.9	-4.8	3.5	1.9	2.1	6.0	2.9	CFT
▼MGIC REINSURANCE CORP OF WI	WI	**D**	982.7	178.0	144.0	-90.5	2.3	4.1	0.5	7.7	1.4	CGT
MGIC RESIDENTIAL REINSURANCE CORP	WI	**C+**	32.1	18.1	1.2	0.1	8.3	6.4	6.9	8.6	4.3	DGT
MHA INS CO	MI	**B**	427.5	138.0	63.4	5.5	8.3	9.9	8.9	7.6	5.4	T
MIAMI MUTUAL INS CO	OH	**C**	25.6	9.8	13.0	-0.3	7.5	7.0	5.7	5.9	4.2	DGRT
MIC GENERAL INS CORP	MI	**C+**	38.1	13.4	0.0	0.1	10.0	N/A	4.1	7.0	4.3	DG
MIC PROPERTY & CASUALTY INS CORP	MI	**C**	133.5	52.8	0.0	0.3	10.0	N/A	6.8	9.4	3.8	FT
▲MICHIGAN COMMERCIAL INS MUTUAL	MI	**C-**	118.8	38.1	44.1	-2.8	6.2	9.5	3.5	5.9	2.9	DFT
MICHIGAN INS CO	MI	**B-**	94.7	28.6	28.7	-0.2	7.0	7.7	5.2	6.5	4.7	T
▼MICHIGAN MILLERS MUTUAL INS CO	MI	**B-**	285.9	83.2	141.3	-8.6	8.1	4.8	1.9	6.2	4.9	FT
MICHIGAN PROFESSIONAL INS EXCHANGE	MI	**C**	103.0	25.1	15.9	3.1	5.5	7.0	5.7	7.3	4.3	DT
MICO INS CO	OH	**B-**	18.8	14.6	5.2	0.1	10.0	8.0	3.1	7.0	5.0	FGT
MID AMERICAN FIRE & CAS CO	OH	**B**	8.1	7.5	0.0	0.1	10.0	N/A	5.8	7.0	4.1	DG
MID-ATLANTIC INS CORP	VA	**D** (5)	0.0	3.1	0.7	0.0	8.0	8.9	6.6	7.7	2.0	DGT
MID-CENTURY INS CO	CA	**C-**	3,285.3	616.9	1,886.1	23.7	2.6	1.6	3.9	4.2	3.2	LT
MID-CENTURY INS CO OF TEXAS	TX	**B-**	54.2	30.1	0.0	0.2	10.0	N/A	8.8	7.0	4.3	T
MID-CONTINENT CAS CO	OH	**C-**	696.5	217.8	206.0	16.8	3.6	5.0	3.7	7.1	3.2	T
▼MID-CONTINENT INS CO	PA	**D+**	41.2	11.6	15.0	-1.0	1.7	2.5	1.4	5.8	2.4	CDFG

See Page 27 for explanation of footnotes and Page 28 for explanation of stability factors.
Arrows denote recent upgrades ▲ or downgrades ▼ (see Section VII for explanations)

RISK ADJ. RATIO #1	CAPITAL RATIO #2	PREMIUM TO SURPLUS (%)	RESV. TO SURPLUS (%)	RESV. DEVELOP. 1 YEAR (%)	RESV. DEVELOP. 2 YEAR (%)	LOSS RATIO (%)	EXP. RATIO (%)	COMB RATIO (%)	CASH FROM UNDER-WRITING (%)	NET PREMIUM GROWTH (%)	INVEST. IN AFFIL (%)	INSURANCE COMPANY NAME
4.5	4.0	N/A	N/A	N/A	-46.7	N/A	N/A	N/A	36.6	-100.0	0.0	MERASTAR INS CO
3.0	1.8	41.3	19.7	-3.8	-8.7	64.2	47.0	111.2	95.8	-12.0	0.0	MERCED MUTUAL INS CO
0.8	0.5	108.6	160.7	2.4	9.8	62.4	36.0	98.4	130.1	-7.7	13.2	MERCER INS CO
0.8	0.5	98.9	146.4	0.7	8.0	62.4	36.3	98.7	106.9	-7.7	0.0	MERCER INS CO OF NJ INC
3.3	2.2	54.7	22.0	-2.2	-2.9	17.8	52.7	70.5	140.7	-7.0	4.5	MERCHANTS BONDING CO (MUTUAL)
2.8	2.0	72.0	124.2	-2.8	-13.8	59.8	36.2	96.0	100.3	30.4	8.6	MERCHANTS MUTUAL INS CO
1.5	1.1	104.8	75.1	-1.9	N/A	64.7	39.6	104.3	132.9	-32.9	27.3	MERCHANTS NATIONAL INS CO
2.6	1.3	98.1	70.3	-1.8	N/A	64.7	39.6	104.3	199.5	-32.9	0.0	MERCHANTS PREFERRED INS CO
N/A	N/A	N/A	0.1	-0.1	N/A	N/A	N/A	N/A	N/A	0.0	0.0	MERCHANTS PROPERTY INS CO OF IN
1.6	1.4	99.3	56.3	3.2	2.7	74.7	29.0	103.7	98.2	-8.2	31.1 •	MERCURY CASUALTY CO
2.1	1.9	N/A	N/A	N/A	N/A	N/A	N/A	N/A	18.3	0.0	0.0	MERCURY COUNTY MUTUAL INS CO
11.4	10.2	N/A	N/A	N/A	N/A	N/A	N/A	N/A	-100.0	0.0	0.0	MERCURY INDEMNITY CO OF AMERICA
31.8	21.6	2.7	N/A	1.3	0.1	64.4	166.0	230.4	28.8	-89.2	0.0	MERCURY INDEMNITY CO OF GEORGIA
1.8	1.6	231.6	73.9	4.8	4.7	71.0	27.9	98.9	102.5	-4.1	0.0 •	MERCURY INS CO
8.8	7.9	N/A	N/A	N/A	N/A	N/A	N/A	N/A	-208.0	0.0	0.0	MERCURY INS CO OF FL
29.0	19.7	2.2	N/A	0.8	-0.4	87.0	221.8	308.8	49.4	-91.2	0.0	MERCURY INS CO OF GA
2.0	1.9	20.0	N/A	-0.6	9.0	65.5	81.6	147.1	37.6	-80.5	47.8	MERCURY INS CO OF IL
34.4	19.7	N/A	1.5	0.3	0.9	N/A	N/A	N/A	250.0	0.0	0.0	MERCURY NATIONAL INS CO
3.0	1.9	83.5	54.7	-1.0	-2.4	76.0	33.7	109.7	108.4	21.8	0.0	MERIDIAN CITIZENS MUTUAL INS CO
6.9	6.2	-1.9	N/A	N/A	N/A	N/A	22.3	22.3	107.0	-307.3	0.0	MERIDIAN SECURITY INS CO
8.2	4.9	77.8	13.1	-1.7	-0.9	41.1	24.5	65.6	228.4	11.6	0.0	MERITPLAN INS CO
2.7	2.4	41.4	33.9	0.6	0.7	59.7	36.8	96.5	119.2	-4.2	21.1 •	MERRIMACK MUTUAL FIRE INS CO
69.4	31.5	N/A	N/A	N/A	N/A	N/A	N/A	N/A	N/A	0.0	0.0	METROPOLITAN CASUALTY INS CO
69.1	31.5	N/A	N/A	N/A	N/A	N/A	N/A	N/A	N/A	0.0	0.0	METROPOLITAN DIRECT PROP & CAS INS
48.7	22.5	N/A	N/A	N/A	N/A	N/A	N/A	N/A	N/A	0.0	0.0	METROPOLITAN GENERAL INS CO
11.1	8.2	N/A	32.3	-0.9	-1.0	N/A	N/A	N/A	-0.3	0.0	2.2 •	METROPOLITAN GROUP PROP & CAS INS
97.7	47.5	N/A	N/A	N/A	N/A	N/A	N/A	N/A	N/A	0.0	0.0	METROPOLITAN LLOYDS INS CO TEXAS
1.8	1.4	168.1	95.1	-9.3	-15.1	64.3	26.8	91.1	103.8	-0.9	20.9 •	METROPOLITAN PROPERTY & CAS INS
4.8	3.1	14.2	1.7	-0.9	-1.8	98.2	87.9	186.1	54.4	-1.0	1.1	MFS MUTUAL INS CO
1.3	1.1	201.1	81.1	1.1	69.9	73.2	26.7	99.9	102.3	89.5	0.0	MGA INS CO INC
N/A	N/A	2.7	1.0	N/A	N/A	28.1	83.1	111.2	117.9	282.4	0.0	MGIC ASSURANCE CORP
23.8	16.8	1.7	8.4	-3.9	-10.6	207.3	-12.6	194.7	26.3	-28.8	0.0	MGIC CREDIT ASR CORP
N/A	N/A	N/A	1.9	N/A	N/A	-100.0	999 +	999 +	N/A	0.0	0.0	MGIC INDEMNITY CORP
2.5	1.9	6.2	58.6	-1.7	-1.5	12.0	119.9	131.9	264.1	-19.5	0.0	MGIC MORTGAGE REINSURANCE CORP
1.0	0.7	63.4	237.2	65.8	106.0	385.4	-54.1	331.3	35.9	-10.1	0.0	MGIC REINSURANCE CORP
0.4	0.3	78.7	344.5	18.1	17.8	331.1	15.7	346.8	103.6	49.5	0.0 •	MGIC REINSURANCE CORP OF WI
2.4	1.8	6.4	60.3	-1.8	-1.6	12.0	119.9	131.9	264.1	-19.5	0.0	MGIC RESIDENTIAL REINSURANCE CORP
2.6	2.2	46.5	172.1	-32.7	-55.0	55.4	17.9	73.3	155.0	-4.5	0.0	MHA INS CO
2.2	1.4	129.8	53.3	-6.4	-10.0	64.3	34.2	98.5	99.6	5.3	0.0	MIAMI MUTUAL INS CO
3.3	3.0	N/A	N/A	N/A	N/A	N/A	N/A	N/A	319.1	0.0	0.0	MIC GENERAL INS CORP
6.4	5.8	N/A	N/A	N/A	N/A	N/A	N/A	N/A	-159.8	0.0	0.0	MIC PROPERTY & CASUALTY INS CORP
1.6	0.7	106.4	123.4	-12.8	-21.9	61.1	45.2	106.3	87.9	4.6	0.0	MICHIGAN COMMERCIAL INS MUTUAL
1.5	0.9	96.2	82.0	-1.3	-0.8	68.8	28.6	97.4	106.1	24.5	0.0	MICHIGAN INS CO
2.4	1.4	148.1	102.0	-1.9	-1.2	87.1	35.0	122.1	86.1	-5.1	0.0	MICHIGAN MILLERS MUTUAL INS CO
1.1	0.9	67.5	202.5	-7.5	-24.4	84.1	13.8	97.9	131.2	-8.4	0.0	MICHIGAN PROFESSIONAL INS
5.1	3.7	34.8	18.5	-3.1	-5.5	51.1	39.2	90.3	93.4	-19.6	0.0	MICO INS CO
25.5	23.0	N/A	N/A	N/A	N/A	N/A	N/A	N/A	N/A	0.0	0.0	MID AMERICAN FIRE & CAS CO
2.4	2.1	28.5	16.8	-6.1	-8.1	24.0	75.7	99.7	104.7	-9.7	0.0	MID-ATLANTIC INS CORP
1.1	0.7	312.5	262.5	-0.6	-0.5	78.4	30.7	109.1	98.9	-8.0	9.7 •	MID-CENTURY INS CO
7.6	6.8	N/A	N/A	N/A	N/A	N/A	N/A	N/A	-6.5	0.0	0.0	MID-CENTURY INS CO OF TEXAS
0.8	0.6	98.3	187.6	-11.8	-30.6	28.0	31.7	59.7	130.2	-22.7	4.6 •	MID-CONTINENT CAS CO
0.4	0.2	109.3	136.4	16.1	30.0	99.2	43.1	142.3	90.1	-16.1	0.0	MID-CONTINENT INS CO

999 + Denotes number greater than 999.9%
999 - Denotes number less than -999.99%
• Bullets denote a more detailed analysis is available in Section II.

INSURANCE COMPANY NAME	DOM. STATE	RATING	TOTAL ASSETS ($MIL)	CAPITAL & SURPLUS ($MIL)	ANNUAL NET PREMIUM ($MIL)	NET INCOME ($MIL)	CAPITAL-IZATION INDEX (PTS)	RESERVE ADQ INDEX (PTS)	PROFIT-ABILITY INDEX (PTS)	LIQUIDITY INDEX (PTS)	STAB. INDEX (PTS)	STABILITY FACTORS
MID-CONTINENT INS CO	OH	**C**	32.1	16.7	6.6	0.7	5.4	6.0	9.0	7.6	4.3	CDGT
▲MID-HUDSON CO-OPERTIVE INS CO	NY	**C**	12.6	6.5	4.8	0.0	8.2	6.7	6.4	6.9	2.5	DGT
MIDDLE GEORGIA MUTUAL INS CO	GA	**C**	14.8	9.5	5.9	-0.6	8.2	6.2	1.6	6.1	3.4	DFGT
MIDDLE STATES INS CO INC	OK	**D+**	5.3	4.3	2.0	0.0	10.0	6.4	8.1	7.6	2.2	DGT
MIDDLESEX INS CO	WI	**B**	660.8	241.1	178.6	2.5	9.5	9.3	6.7	6.7	6.3	T
MIDDLESEX MUTUAL ASR CO	CT	**B-**	238.2	55.8	93.4	-1.0	7.3	7.6	3.7	4.9	5.3	FLT
MIDROX INS CO	NY	**D+**	5.6	2.2	2.4	-0.2	7.5	5.5	2.9	6.9	1.9	DGT
MIDSTATE MUTUAL INS CO	NY	**C**	32.3	20.1	10.0	0.4	9.7	6.3	5.5	6.8	4.1	DFGT
MIDSTATES REINSURANCE CORP	IL	**U** (1)	140.6	59.6	0.0	-1.7	N/A	9.1	3.5	10.0	5.6	FT
MIDWEST EMPLOYERS CAS CO	DE	**C-**	371.2	124.4	28.3	0.1	3.3	3.9	6.3	6.8	2.9	CT
MIDWEST FAMILY MUTUAL INS CO	MN	**C**	109.5	34.0	62.9	0.7	7.0	5.9	8.8	6.1	4.0	T
MIDWEST INS CO	IL	**C-**	53.9	13.3	14.2	-0.3	4.9	7.0	6.3	7.0	3.3	DFT
MIDWEST INS GROUP INC RRG	AZ	**E**	10.6	1.3	3.0	0.0	0.5	1.9	4.7	6.8	0.3	CDGR
▲MIDWEST MEDICAL INS CO	MN	**B+**	490.6	154.1	116.1	1.0	8.0	5.8	6.9	6.9	6.4	T
MIDWEST PROVIDER INS CO RRG INC	AZ	**D** (2)	9.7	1.1	2.2	0.1	1.3	5.1	5.9	7.7	0.9	CDGT
MIDWEST TRUCKERS INS EXCHANGE	IN	**U** (5)	0.0	1.4	0.1	0.0	N/A	4.8	5.6	10.0	1.5	RT
MIDWESTERN EQUITY TITLE INS CO	IN	**D+**	2.8	2.2	0.2	0.0	10.0	3.6	8.0	10.0	2.0	DGT
MIDWESTERN INDEMNITY CO	OH	**C**	16.4	16.0	0.0	0.1	9.0	N/A	3.6	7.0	4.3	DG
MILBANK INS CO	SD	**B-**	461.0	141.6	246.6	-2.0	7.7	7.0	4.3	6.4	4.3	AT
▲MILLERS CAPITAL INS CO	PA	**C+**	119.6	40.2	39.6	-0.1	7.9	4.8	5.5	6.6	4.5	T
MILLERS CLASSIFIED INS CO	WI	**C**	23.0	11.3	11.8	-0.1	7.2	8.8	5.9	6.5	3.4	DFGR
MILLERS FIRST INS CO	IL	**D+**	37.4	17.7	9.0	0.6	7.0	5.7	2.4	6.5	2.7	DFGR
MILLVILLE MUTUAL INS CO	PA	**C**	42.7	20.2	20.2	0.0	8.3	6.9	7.9	6.8	4.1	DGT
MILWAUKEE CASUALTY INS CO	WI	**B**	26.9	10.7	1.4	0.2	10.0	N/A	5.2	10.0	4.5	DFG
MILWAUKEE INS CO	WI	**B-**	40.4	32.5	0.0	0.2	10.0	6.3	3.7	10.0	3.7	DFGT
MINNESOTA LAWYERS MUTUAL INS CO	MN	**C+**	108.5	39.8	30.5	-2.0	8.1	7.0	2.7	6.8	4.5	RT
MINNESOTA SURETY & TRUST CO	MN	**D**	2.4	1.5	0.6	0.0	8.5	7.4	2.4	7.0	0.0	DFGT
MISSISSIPPI FARM BU MUTUAL INS CO	MS	**U** (1)	25.5	0.5	0.0	-1.4	N/A	1.6	0.0	0.0	0.0	CFLT
MISSISSIPPI FARM BUREAU CAS INS CO	MS	**B**	293.8	178.1	124.9	3.6	10.0	4.6	6.4	6.7	4.8	T
MISSOURI DOCTORS MUTUAL INS CO	MO	**E**	6.2	0.1	5.2	0.1	0.0	1.2	0.1	7.7	0.0	CDFG
MISSOURI HOSPITAL PLAN	MO	**C+**	137.2	93.4	17.9	-10.6	10.0	7.0	3.2	8.0	4.5	T
MISSOURI PHYSICIANS ASSOCIATES	MO	**U** (1)	3.4	2.3	0.0	0.1	N/A	8.3	1.9	7.0	0.0	FRT
▲MISSOURI PROFESSIONALS MUTUAL INS CO	MO	**E+**	76.1	15.3	40.7	1.5	1.1	1.1	9.4	7.0	0.5	DRT
MISSOURI VALLEY MUTUAL INS CO	SD	**D+**	6.0	2.9	3.3	0.1	8.3	6.7	5.2	6.8	2.0	DGT
▲MITSUI SUMITOMO INS CO OF AMER	NY	**B**	712.3	231.6	141.4	1.5	7.5	5.0	6.5	6.9	5.5	T
▲MITSUI SUMITOMO INS USA INC	NY	**C+**	105.6	53.5	15.7	0.1	9.4	6.1	6.8	9.1	4.3	T
MLBA MUTUAL INS CO	MI	**C**	12.0	8.2	1.6	0.0	9.9	9.4	5.4	8.4	2.8	DFGT
MMG INS CO	ME	**C+**	161.7	53.5	85.6	-2.9	9.3	7.0	4.5	6.0	4.4	T
▲MO EMPLOYERS MUTUAL INS CO	MO	**C**	335.4	134.8	126.8	1.5	7.5	5.9	8.5	6.8	3.5	T
MODERN SERVICE INS CO	IL	**B**	26.4	24.1	0.0	0.1	10.0	6.1	6.1	10.0	4.3	DGT
MODERN USA INS CO	FL	**C**	24.7	11.4	12.3	-0.6	5.0	3.6	1.9	7.1	2.4	CDGT
MONROE GUARANTY INS CO	IN	**C**	28.3	44.5	0.0	1.3	10.0	4.0	8.4	7.3	3.4	DG
MONTEREY INS CO	CA	**C+**	61.4	26.9	30.0	0.6	5.8	8.6	8.8	5.5	4.4	T
MONTGOMERY MUTUAL INS CO	MD	**C**	48.8	42.6	0.0	0.4	10.0	3.5	4.4	7.0	4.3	A
MONTOUR MUTUAL INS CO	PA	**D** (1)	1.0	0.7	0.2	-0.1	7.7	8.3	2.6	7.0	1.4	DT
MONTPELIER US INS CO	OK	**D**	57.2	49.1	1.4	-0.8	10.0	7.0	2.2	10.0	2.0	DFT
▼MORTGAGE GUARANTY INS CORP	WI	**D**	7,527.3	1,350.0	1,237.7	-88.0	3.4	4.4	4.7	7.5	1.4	T
MOTORISTS MUTUAL INS CO	OH	**B+**	1,212.1	388.4	474.2	-8.9	7.9	5.7	3.2	6.3	6.4	T
MOTORS INS CORP	MI	**C+**	5,444.4	1,681.2	2,186.0	-14.4	7.8	5.2	3.0	6.1	4.3	FRT
MOUND PRAIRIE MUTUAL INS CO	MN	**D**	3.7	2.3	2.2	0.1	8.9	7.5	4.9	7.0	1.8	DFGT
MOUNT CARROLL MUTUAL FIRE INS CO	IL	**D**	3.2	2.5	1.0	-0.1	10.0	6.1	6.3	6.8	1.8	DFGT
MOUNT VERNON FIRE INS CO	PA	**B-**	283.4	116.3	68.6	2.7	7.9	9.5	3.2	9.1	4.6	T

See Page 27 for explanation of footnotes and Page 28 for explanation of stability factors.
Arrows denote recent upgrades ▲ or downgrades ▼ (see Section VII for explanations)

RISK ADJ. RATIO #1	CAPITAL RATIO #2	PREMIUM TO SURPLUS (%)	RESV. TO SURPLUS (%)	RESV. DEVELOP. 1 YEAR (%)	RESV. DEVELOP. 2 YEAR (%)	LOSS RATIO (%)	EXP. RATIO (%)	COMB RATIO (%)	CASH FROM UNDER-WRITING (%)	NET PREMIUM GROWTH (%)	INVEST. IN AFFIL (%)	INSURANCE COMPANY NAME
1.3	0.9	40.9	77.9	-9.3	-23.6	28.0	30.9	58.9	126.8	-22.6	0.0	MID-CONTINENT INS CO
2.7	1.7	73.0	35.5	-9.0	-9.1	48.5	33.3	81.8	107.5	0.6	0.0	MID-HUDSON CO-OPERTIVE INS CO
2.2	1.8	58.6	7.4	0.6	-2.5	102.2	37.4	139.6	69.9	0.0	22.9	MIDDLE GEORGIA MUTUAL INS CO
4.6	4.1	47.6	8.4	-1.1	0.9	69.3	24.1	93.4	98.5	-5.8	0.0	MIDDLE STATES INS CO INC
4.0	2.8	75.1	121.2	-6.5	-14.3	74.5	26.8	101.3	96.2	-5.6	4.0 •	MIDDLESEX INS CO
1.4	1.2	167.1	89.7	-3.3	-3.3	75.6	30.4	106.0	96.8	2.2	24.9	MIDDLESEX MUTUAL ASR CO
1.9	1.2	101.2	55.7	1.2	-1.8	60.9	38.6	99.5	100.3	5.7	0.2	MIDROX INS CO
4.1	3.2	49.9	28.0	-1.2	-3.6	75.3	38.8	114.1	91.7	-1.9	0.0	MIDSTATE MUTUAL INS CO
N/A	N/A	N/A	115.7	-1.8	-3.4	999 +	999 +	999 +	N/A	0.0	0.0	MIDSTATES REINSURANCE CORP
0.7	0.5	22.6	107.2	2.6	6.2	82.5	22.8	105.3	148.4	-12.9	19.7	MIDWEST EMPLOYERS CAS CO
1.6	0.9	185.8	108.0	-7.3	-14.3	72.8	25.6	98.4	117.9	8.5	0.0	MIDWEST FAMILY MUTUAL INS CO
1.0	0.8	104.8	129.6	-10.9	-27.0	48.2	34.5	82.7	84.8	24.1	0.0	MIDWEST INS CO
0.4	0.2	210.4	467.6	-19.6	-7.8	69.6	36.7	106.3	109.1	-6.8	0.0	MIDWEST INS GROUP INC RRG
2.3	1.7	73.7	151.3	-17.0	-21.5	69.5	14.3	83.8	109.2	-5.7	0.0 •	MIDWEST MEDICAL INS CO
0.5	0.3	207.3	146.8	-72.6	-123.8	30.8	56.0	86.8	159.4	0.0	0.0	MIDWEST PROVIDER INS CO RRG INC
N/A	N/A	6.4	0.3	-0.9	N/A	38.1	61.4	99.5	114.6	-52.6	0.0	MIDWEST TRUCKERS INS EXCHANGE
8.1	7.3	7.4	N/A	N/A	N/A	3.9	21.5	25.4	411.4	-9.5	0.0	MIDWESTERN EQUITY TITLE INS CO
2.3	2.3	N/A	N/A	N/A	N/A	N/A	N/A	N/A	N/A	0.0	46.2	MIDWESTERN INDEMNITY CO
2.2	1.3	170.1	110.0	-1.7	-6.1	75.0	33.3	108.3	111.6	19.3	0.0	MILBANK INS CO
2.1	1.8	95.6	112.3	-17.1	-29.3	59.8	39.3	99.1	105.2	-5.0	0.0	MILLERS CAPITAL INS CO
2.0	1.2	103.4	52.4	-5.5	-5.5	71.1	31.8	102.9	87.5	-7.6	0.0	MILLERS CLASSIFIED INS CO
1.3	1.0	51.9	73.2	-0.1	-1.6	87.3	36.2	123.5	72.8	-7.2	33.1	MILLERS FIRST INS CO
2.7	2.1	97.2	36.1	-4.2	-8.0	56.2	26.9	83.1	117.7	1.3	0.0	MILLVILLE MUTUAL INS CO
3.4	3.1	13.3	3.5	N/A	N/A	116.2	20.6	136.8	999 +	0.0	0.0	MILWAUKEE CASUALTY INS CO
5.9	4.2	N/A	5.5	-1.2	-2.2	N/A	N/A	N/A	-7.0	100.0	7.3	MILWAUKEE INS CO
2.1	1.5	71.0	97.8	5.1	0.9	94.5	26.2	120.7	138.0	5.7	0.0	MINNESOTA LAWYERS MUTUAL INS CO
2.3	2.1	38.2	9.8	-8.3	-1.3	7.5	94.9	102.4	64.1	6.8	0.0	MINNESOTA SURETY & TRUST CO
N/A	N/A	1.0	999 +	28.4	13.4	999 +	999 +	999 +	1.7	-64.3	0.0	MISSISSIPPI FARM BU MUTUAL INS CO
5.4	4.4	71.5	11.2	-1.6	-0.1	72.4	20.5	92.9	110.1	0.5	0.0 •	MISSISSIPPI FARM BUREAU CAS INS CO
0.0	0.0	999 +	999 +	999 +	30.3	47.1	47.0	94.1	96.6	13.2	0.0	MISSOURI DOCTORS MUTUAL INS CO
3.9	3.3	17.3	21.5	-5.1	-9.7	20.0	4.6	24.6	182.5	-2.0	15.7	MISSOURI HOSPITAL PLAN
N/A	N/A	N/A	23.6	N/A	-2.2	N/A	N/A	N/A	N/A	0.0	0.0	MISSOURI PHYSICIANS ASSOCIATES
0.5	0.3	296.5	285.8	19.2	-0.8	53.8	33.5	87.3	126.2	5.9	0.1	MISSOURI PROFESSIONALS MUTUAL INS
2.8	1.8	115.5	30.4	-6.8	-7.2	57.2	36.4	93.6	102.1	4.9	0.0	MISSOURI VALLEY MUTUAL INS CO
2.8	1.5	61.6	153.9	-7.9	-14.7	61.4	31.7	93.1	100.0	4.6	0.0 •	MITSUI SUMITOMO INS CO OF AMER
5.3	2.9	29.5	73.7	-3.7	-6.6	61.4	31.7	93.1	100.0	4.6	0.0	MITSUI SUMITOMO INS USA INC
5.1	3.1	19.8	27.3	-4.3	-12.8	32.6	64.3	96.9	91.7	-10.5	0.2	MLBA MUTUAL INS CO
3.5	2.3	147.7	67.7	-10.0	-13.9	71.1	31.6	102.7	97.9	2.2	0.0	MMG INS CO
2.1	1.6	94.1	115.0	-16.2	-21.7	61.6	36.5	98.1	104.1	-7.7	0.1	MO EMPLOYERS MUTUAL INS CO
29.6	24.4	N/A	0.1	-0.1	-0.1	N/A	N/A	N/A	-1.1	0.0	0.0	MODERN SERVICE INS CO
0.9	0.6	104.7	10.0	0.2	N/A	45.2	47.6	92.8	127.1	393.9	0.0	MODERN USA INS CO
615.3	283.7	N/A	N/A	N/A	N/A	N/A	N/A	N/A	140.9	0.0	0.0	MONROE GUARANTY INS CO
1.7	1.0	114.1	56.9	-3.9	-7.1	57.7	38.6	96.3	96.7	1.1	0.0	MONTEREY INS CO
24.0	21.6	N/A	N/A	N/A	N/A	N/A	N/A	N/A	N/A	0.0	0.0	MONTGOMERY MUTUAL INS CO
2.4	1.4	27.8	10.2	0.7	-6.5	68.3	85.8	154.1	100.0	-6.2	0.0	MONTOUR MUTUAL INS CO
7.3	4.9	2.8	0.7	N/A	-1.9	96.9	359.4	456.3	8.2	-98.4	0.0	MONTPELIER US INS CO
0.6	0.4	80.9	373.3	19.9	19.0	195.7	-93.1	102.6	123.2	5.6	5.1 •	MORTGAGE GUARANTY INS CORP
2.2	1.5	115.9	96.3	-2.5	-4.8	73.5	33.0	106.5	97.3	3.5	4.9 •	MOTORISTS MUTUAL INS CO
2.5	1.8	129.2	82.6	-3.1	-5.4	63.5	32.3	95.8	87.9	-16.2	7.4 •	MOTORS INS CORP
4.1	3.0	101.6	17.5	1.3	-0.1	77.5	35.9	113.4	98.7	3.9	0.0	MOUND PRAIRIE MUTUAL INS CO
6.8	3.7	38.0	-1.1	-0.7	-0.2	76.6	29.0	105.6	80.3	6.9	0.8	MOUNT CARROLL MUTUAL FIRE INS CO
1.4	1.1	31.8	54.7	-9.5	-40.1	31.4	37.8	69.2	135.4	188.3	15.6 •	MOUNT VERNON FIRE INS CO

999 + Denotes number greater than 999.9%
999 - Denotes number less than -999.99%
• Bullets denote a more detailed analysis is available in Section II.

INSURANCE COMPANY NAME	DOM. STATE	RATING	TOTAL ASSETS ($MIL)	CAPITAL & SURPLUS ($MIL)	ANNUAL NET PREMIUM ($MIL)	NET INCOME ($MIL)	CAPITAL-IZATION INDEX (PTS)	RESERVE ADQ INDEX (PTS)	PROFIT-ABILITY INDEX (PTS)	LIQUIDITY INDEX (PTS)	STAB. INDEX (PTS)	STABILITY FACTORS
MOUNTAIN LAUREL ASR CO	OH	**C**	94.1	35.0	93.5	3.3	6.4	4.6	3.9	2.4	3.5	LT
MOUNTAIN LAUREL RRG INC	VT	**E**	15.6	4.6	5.3	0.1	1.3	2.2	1.3	8.2	0.0	CDGR
MOUNTAIN STATES HEALTHCARE RECIP	MT	**E**	64.8	16.3	19.5	0.9	3.2	7.1	8.9	7.4	0.0	DT
MOUNTAIN STATES INDEMNITY CO	NM	**C**	66.2	30.2	17.8	0.5	7.5	4.3	6.0	6.9	4.0	DRT
MOUNTAIN STATES MUTUAL CAS CO	NM	**C+**	152.7	66.1	36.3	-0.2	7.3	3.8	4.5	6.9	4.5	RT
MOUNTAIN VALLEY INDEMNITY CO	NH	**D+**	36.9	12.7	11.3	-0.6	3.6	3.6	5.0	0.4	2.4	DFGL
▲MOUNTAIN WEST FARM BU MUTUAL INS CO	WY	**A**	339.7	173.3	118.8	2.3	10.0	9.2	7.5	6.7	7.2	T
MOUNTAINEER FREEDOM RRG INC	WV	**E**	18.1	5.7	3.9	-0.2	5.2	3.9	4.3	9.6	0.0	DGT
MOWER COUNTY FARMERS MUT INS CO	MN	**D**	2.8	1.9	1.2	0.1	8.4	4.6	8.4	7.5	1.6	DGT
MSA INS CO	SC	**B-**	5.7	5.6	0.0	0.1	10.0	N/A	4.9	7.0	3.5	DGT
MSI PREFERRED INS CO	IL	**U** (1)	22.7	22.0	0.0	0.4	N/A	N/A	7.7	7.0	5.4	T
▲MT HAWLEY INS CO	IL	**C+**	1,050.6	471.7	238.6	15.3	7.3	9.5	8.7	6.9	4.3	AT
MT MCKINLEY INS CO	DE	**U** (1)	49.9	20.9	0.0	0.8	N/A	N/A	5.3	7.0	5.4	RT
MT MORRIS MUTUAL INS CO	WI	**D+**	15.3	5.6	11.2	-0.5	7.2	4.6	2.6	2.5	2.5	DFGL
MT WASHINGTON ASR CORP	NH	**C**	5.1	2.8	0.0	0.0	10.0	3.6	7.7	10.0	3.0	DG
MUNICH REINSURANCE AMERICA INC	DE	**C**	15,783.4	3,299.2	2,290.0	-176.5	7.5	5.0	2.9	7.3	3.7	RT
MUNICIPAL MUTUAL INS CO	WV	**C**	22.9	14.6	12.3	-0.6	8.2	4.9	5.4	6.6	3.8	DGT
MUTUAL BENEFIT INS CO	PA	**B-**	166.4	52.1	78.8	-2.7	8.2	6.9	4.6	6.4	4.7	T
MUTUAL FIRE INS CO OF S BEND TOWNSHP	PA	**D+**(1)	2.8	2.8	0.1	0.1	10.0	N/A	8.3	10.0	2.0	D
MUTUAL FIRE MARINE & INLAND INS CO	PA	**C** (1)	127.3	119.7	0.1	5.1	9.1	7.2	4.2	10.0	4.2	D
▲MUTUAL INS CO OF AZ	AZ	**A-**	891.6	356.2	149.2	8.1	8.7	7.1	8.0	7.5	7.0	T
MUTUAL INS CO OF LEHIGH CTY	PA	**D** (1)	3.8	1.7	2.0	-0.2	7.4	4.0	2.6	6.5	1.7	DFRT
▲MUTUAL OF ENUMCLAW INS CO	WA	**B**	533.6	207.5	311.3	4.6	7.9	4.5	8.0	6.2	5.4	T
MUTUAL SAVINGS FIRE INS CO	AL	**D**	6.1	4.9	3.6	0.1	8.2	6.2	2.9	6.7	2.2	DGT
MUTUALAID EXCHANGE	KS	**C**	30.0	16.3	13.5	-0.9	7.3	8.0	2.4	5.9	3.9	DFGT
N A D A INDEMNITY INC	CO	**E**	1.2	1.1	1.1	-0.1	8.0	3.6	3.9	6.8	0.3	DGT
NAMIC INS CO INC	IN	**C+**	43.8	17.0	2.5	-0.3	8.3	5.8	3.2	9.1	4.0	DFGT
NARRAGANSETT BAY INS CO	RI	**C-**	33.4	21.9	9.4	-2.0	7.4	3.8	2.6	6.7	2.9	DGRT
▲NATIONAL AMERICAN INS CO	OK	**D+**	146.3	52.1	62.3	1.3	7.3	2.2	5.1	6.8	2.4	T
NATIONAL AMERICAN INS CO OF CA	CA	**D**	38.5	14.8	1.3	-0.3	2.1	3.3	1.8	8.2	2.0	CDFG
NATIONAL ASSISTED LIVING RRG INC	DC	**D**	5.9	2.4	1.8	-0.1	4.6	7.0	5.4	7.1	1.4	DGT
NATIONAL AUTOMOTIVE INS	LA	**D**	19.5	6.9	17.6	-0.1	7.0	6.0	4.1	3.2	1.5	DGLT
NATIONAL BUILDERS & CONTRACTORS INS	NV	**D+**	6.3	3.7	1.4	0.1	6.0	4.0	8.7	5.2	2.2	DGRT
NATIONAL BUILDING MATERIAL ASR CO	IN	**C**	3.1	2.7	0.0	0.0	10.0	3.6	6.1	9.6	2.6	DGT
NATIONAL CASUALTY CO	WI	**B+**	144.3	107.5	0.0	1.4	10.0	5.0	6.9	10.0	6.4	FT
NATIONAL CATHOLIC RRG	VT	**E+**	54.1	6.1	9.1	-1.7	0.0	2.2	0.9	4.9	0.0	CDFL
NATIONAL CONSUMER INS CO	NJ	**U** (5)	0.0	0.0	-1.1	0.0	N/A	4.2	0.2	7.0	0.0	FRT
NATIONAL CONTINENTAL INS CO	NY	**D+**	243.4	53.2	119.0	1.0	3.2	6.6	4.0	5.4	2.4	CGT
NATIONAL CONTRACTORS INS CO INC RRG	MT	**E+**	21.6	3.9	2.0	0.0	0.3	4.0	4.0	10.0	0.0	CDFG
NATIONAL FARMERS UNION PROP & CAS CO	CO	**B-**	319.7	95.1	118.8	-0.7	8.9	5.8	3.8	7.1	4.9	FT
NATIONAL FIRE & CASUALTY CO	IL	**C-**	7.8	4.8	1.5	0.0	7.4	8.2	2.4	7.0	2.4	DFGT
NATIONAL FIRE & INDEMNITY EXCHANGE	MO	**C-**	10.7	4.6	4.1	-0.3	7.9	4.1	2.0	7.2	2.3	DFGT
NATIONAL FIRE & MARINE INS CO	NE	**C**	3,829.2	2,488.0	282.8	-48.4	8.6	7.5	4.0	7.6	4.1	T
NATIONAL FIRE INS CO OF HARTFORD	IL	**C**	138.7	108.7	0.0	1.8	10.0	N/A	2.8	9.3	3.8	AT
NATIONAL GENERAL ASR CO	MO	**C+**	39.8	19.4	0.0	0.3	10.0	N/A	7.1	7.1	4.4	DG
NATIONAL GENERAL INS CO	MO	**B-**	99.9	37.9	24.9	2.5	10.0	5.1	3.8	7.9	4.7	T
NATIONAL GROUP INS CO	FL	**D+**	9.5	6.1	0.1	0.4	10.0	N/A	7.1	10.0	2.4	DFGT
NATIONAL GUARANTY INS CO	AZ	**D-**	11.0	7.1	5.2	0.0	4.5	3.7	3.8	5.1	1.3	DGT
▼NATIONAL GUARDIAN RRG INC	HI	**E**	20.8	3.2	4.0	-0.2	0.1	7.1	4.0	5.7	0.2	CDGR
NATIONAL HERITAGE INS CO	IL	**D+**	6.3	3.9	3.6	-0.1	8.6	4.6	6.4	6.5	2.2	DFGT
NATIONAL HOME INS CO RRG	CO	**C-**	72.6	18.4	2.2	0.1	8.9	6.9	5.6	10.0	3.0	DFT
NATIONAL HOME WARRANTY INC	NV	**D**	3.5	1.5	3.6	0.1	7.7	N/A	3.8	3.5	1.4	DGLT

See Page 27 for explanation of footnotes and Page 28 for explanation of stability factors.
Arrows denote recent upgrades ▲ or downgrades ▼ (see Section VII for explanations)

RISK ADJ. RATIO #1	CAPITAL RATIO #2	PREMIUM TO SURPLUS (%)	RESV. TO SURPLUS (%)	RESV. DEVELOP. 1 YEAR (%)	RESV. DEVELOP. 2 YEAR (%)	LOSS RATIO (%)	EXP. RATIO (%)	COMB RATIO (%)	CASH FROM UNDER-WRITING (%)	NET PREMIUM GROWTH (%)	INVEST. IN AFFIL (%)	INSURANCE COMPANY NAME
1.2	1.0	296.7	89.4	1.7	-1.1	67.9	19.7	87.6	115.5	-9.3	0.0	MOUNTAIN LAUREL ASR CO
0.7	0.3	116.0	165.2	-121.4	38.9	39.8	47.7	87.5	165.0	11.7	0.0	MOUNTAIN LAUREL RRG INC
0.8	0.6	111.4	189.5	-84.2	-62.4	19.8	35.7	55.5	133.5	-2.6	0.0	MOUNTAIN STATES HEALTHCARE RECIP
2.7	1.3	59.4	93.3	7.8	-5.9	90.1	33.5	123.6	102.6	-11.2	0.0	MOUNTAIN STATES INDEMNITY CO
1.5	1.1	53.0	95.1	8.9	9.9	84.5	35.9	120.4	106.2	-4.3	22.4	MOUNTAIN STATES MUTUAL CAS CO
0.8	0.6	89.0	73.8	-2.6	-1.2	51.7	29.1	80.8	31.9	22.0	0.0	MOUNTAIN VALLEY INDEMNITY CO
5.4	3.7	67.4	51.3	-14.2	-13.5	80.3	23.5	103.8	102.0	6.3	0.0 •	MOUNTAIN WEST FARM BU MUTUAL INS
1.2	0.8	66.7	87.7	11.7	-9.3	84.5	22.6	107.1	440.5	97.4	0.0	MOUNTAINEER FREEDOM RRG INC
3.2	2.3	63.0	3.9	-0.2	0.1	36.6	45.2	81.8	121.3	-26.9	0.0	MOWER COUNTY FARMERS MUT INS CO
82.1	39.4	N/A	N/A	N/A	N/A	N/A	N/A	N/A	N/A	0.0	0.0	MSA INS CO
N/A	N/A	N/A	N/A	N/A	N/A	N/A	N/A	N/A	999 +	0.0	0.0	MSI PREFERRED INS CO
2.2	1.5	50.8	97.5	-9.2	-27.7	49.2	33.7	82.9	132.1	-16.3	7.1 •	MT HAWLEY INS CO
N/A	N/A	N/A	N/A	N/A	N/A	N/A	N/A	N/A	N/A	0.0	0.0	MT MCKINLEY INS CO
1.2	0.9	172.5	33.7	1.2	-5.4	74.6	28.7	103.3	82.9	-12.2	0.1	MT MORRIS MUTUAL INS CO
3.5	3.2	N/A	N/A	N/A	N/A	N/A	N/A	N/A	73.1	0.0	0.0	MT WASHINGTON ASR CORP
1.8	1.1	64.6	106.3	-1.6	-3.8	78.6	50.5	129.1	121.8	-0.4	0.2 •	MUNICH REINSURANCE AMERICA INC
2.4	1.8	76.7	16.9	-2.5	-2.3	56.9	29.4	86.3	113.9	-3.7	0.0	MUNICIPAL MUTUAL INS CO
2.5	1.8	143.8	106.8	-4.5	-10.2	63.2	34.8	98.0	101.4	3.9	7.0	MUTUAL BENEFIT INS CO
103.2	77.4	4.0	0.1	N/A	N/A	43.6	36.9	80.5	123.3	8.8	0.0	MUTUAL FIRE INS CO OF S BEND
3.1	2.6	0.1	0.2	-0.1	-0.2	569.0	999 +	999 +	5.2	5.3	22.4	MUTUAL FIRE MARINE & INLAND INS CO
3.4	2.8	42.4	105.0	-26.7	-43.3	29.6	10.8	40.4	155.0	-8.2	0.0 •	MUTUAL INS CO OF AZ
2.1	1.3	117.9	30.0	0.5	4.2	63.6	43.0	106.6	84.7	-2.5	0.8	MUTUAL INS CO OF LEHIGH CTY
2.8	1.9	152.0	88.6	-5.7	-5.6	64.9	30.9	95.8	99.9	2.5	1.6 •	MUTUAL OF ENUMCLAW INS CO
3.3	2.9	73.6	5.3	0.8	0.1	54.4	36.7	91.1	110.5	-3.8	0.0	MUTUAL SAVINGS FIRE INS CO
1.4	1.1	76.6	19.5	-3.4	-2.5	89.2	45.9	135.1	72.1	3.2	33.2	MUTUALAID EXCHANGE
1.8	1.7	91.4	0.1	N/A	-0.3	30.1	64.8	94.9	102.0	1.5	0.0	N A D A INDEMNITY INC
2.9	2.0	13.8	26.6	-7.0	-12.6	39.4	44.5	83.9	79.6	-1.2	0.0	NAMIC INS CO INC
1.5	1.0	39.1	4.0	-0.5	-4.3	28.2	107.5	135.7	111.9	126.0	1.3	NARRAGANSETT BAY INS CO
2.5	1.4	122.0	96.1	4.0	6.0	64.4	36.1	100.5	107.4	-3.3	0.0	NATIONAL AMERICAN INS CO
0.5	0.4	8.4	90.7	13.6	17.6	213.2	98.8	312.0	18.2	36.8	39.2	NATIONAL AMERICAN INS CO OF CA
1.0	0.5	69.6	95.6	-19.5	-9.7	43.9	46.1	90.0	158.6	-4.2	0.0	NATIONAL ASSISTED LIVING RRG INC
1.0	0.9	250.2	80.4	-9.1	-23.3	77.9	25.5	103.4	92.4	28.6	0.0	NATIONAL AUTOMOTIVE INS
2.0	1.0	39.1	46.6	-9.6	-21.0	21.7	48.5	70.2	215.1	-36.6	0.0	NATIONAL BUILDERS & CONTRACTORS
16.4	14.7	1.0	0.9	-0.1	N/A	96.0	61.5	157.5	566.7	73.3	0.0	NATIONAL BUILDING MATERIAL ASR CO
20.1	18.1	N/A	0.3	-0.6	-0.3	N/A	N/A	N/A	-969.5	0.0	0.0 •	NATIONAL CASUALTY CO
0.0	0.0	94.6	449.7	-1.9	33.5	124.3	34.4	158.7	53.3	4.1	0.0	NATIONAL CATHOLIC RRG
N/A	N/A	-16.3	9.9	1.2	6.1	-69.4	-166.4	-235.8	75.7	90.1	0.0	NATIONAL CONSUMER INS CO
0.5	0.5	228.5	203.1	16.1	1.4	85.9	16.8	102.7	155.6	5.3	0.0	NATIONAL CONTINENTAL INS CO
0.3	0.2	70.4	384.1	-13.9	-14.4	53.1	59.8	112.9	-22.1	-27.4	0.0	NATIONAL CONTRACTORS INS CO INC
3.0	2.1	124.2	60.1	-1.5	-8.4	65.2	34.5	99.7	85.8	-26.3	6.0	NATIONAL FARMERS UNION PROP & CAS
2.1	1.3	29.4	32.8	-0.4	-4.3	63.2	43.5	106.7	90.5	9.1	0.0	NATIONAL FIRE & CASUALTY CO
1.6	1.4	82.1	58.8	10.2	9.3	64.0	56.1	120.1	87.3	-12.4	0.0	NATIONAL FIRE & INDEMNITY EXCHANGE
2.4	1.6	9.1	32.8	-0.1	-1.2	70.1	22.8	92.9	150.0	-43.8	8.1 •	NATIONAL FIRE & MARINE INS CO
23.6	21.3	N/A	N/A	N/A	N/A	N/A	N/A	N/A	N/A	0.0	0.0	NATIONAL FIRE INS CO OF HARTFORD
5.4	4.9	N/A	N/A	N/A	N/A	N/A	N/A	N/A	229.8	0.0	0.0	NATIONAL GENERAL ASR CO
5.1	4.2	70.3	30.0	2.5	-2.2	67.3	29.4	96.7	128.5	-13.8	0.0	NATIONAL GENERAL INS CO
5.6	5.1	1.9	N/A	N/A	N/A	N/A	120.0	120.0	-107.5	0.0	0.0	NATIONAL GROUP INS CO
0.9	0.8	75.3	32.6	15.7	14.4	87.7	10.3	98.0	115.2	-17.4	67.3	NATIONAL GUARANTY INS CO
0.1	0.1	114.1	374.5	-47.5	-36.2	91.5	7.4	98.9	170.7	-27.8	0.0	NATIONAL GUARDIAN RRG INC
3.3	2.6	91.8	6.6	1.8	2.9	55.8	46.3	102.1	91.4	-19.4	0.0	NATIONAL HERITAGE INS CO
2.6	2.4	12.1	33.2	-6.0	-8.3	150.5	10.9	161.4	12.1	-40.0	0.0	NATIONAL HOME INS CO RRG
2.1	1.6	230.2	9.8	N/A	N/A	58.0	23.3	81.3	123.3	-3.0	0.0	NATIONAL HOME WARRANTY INC

999 + Denotes number greater than 999.9%

999 - Denotes number less than -999.99%

• Bullets denote a more detailed analysis is available in Section II.

INSURANCE COMPANY NAME	DOM. STATE	RATING	TOTAL ASSETS ($MIL)	CAPITAL & SURPLUS ($MIL)	ANNUAL NET PREMIUM ($MIL)	NET INCOME ($MIL)	CAPITAL-IZATION INDEX (PTS)	RESERVE ADQ INDEX (PTS)	PROFIT-ABILITY INDEX (PTS)	LIQUIDITY INDEX (PTS)	STAB. INDEX (PTS)	STABILITY FACTORS
▼NATIONAL INDEMNITY CO	NE	**C+**	59,159.5	24,111.0	5,171.8	-2,172.9	3.5	3.9	3.7	6.8	4.3	CT
▼NATIONAL INDEMNITY CO OF MID-AMERICA	IA	**B-**	125.3	82.5	9.6	2.0	8.7	6.4	7.3	9.2	3.8	GT
NATIONAL INDEMNITY CO OF THE SOUTH	FL	**B-**	169.8	100.9	21.3	3.5	8.6	7.0	7.8	9.4	4.9	FT
NATIONAL INDEPENDENT TRUCKERS IC	SC	**D+**	7.8	4.3	1.8	-0.1	8.0	7.0	4.1	6.8	2.2	DGRT
NATIONAL INS ASN	IN	**U** (1)	11.5	11.4	0.0	0.5	N/A	N/A	8.4	7.0	4.9	T
NATIONAL INS CO	PR	**C**	130.0	50.8	44.3	0.7	5.3	3.1	2.1	6.4	3.4	FT
NATIONAL INS CO OF WISCONSIN INC	WI	**C**	44.9	14.9	12.7	0.3	5.2	9.3	5.5	6.7	2.6	DGT
NATIONAL INTERSTATE INS CO	OH	**C+**	740.4	186.6	217.9	7.2	9.0	8.2	8.8	7.3	4.7	T
NATIONAL INTERSTATE INS CO OF HAWAII	OH	**D-**	28.8	10.5	4.0	0.2	10.0	4.6	8.5	9.2	1.1	DGT
NATIONAL LIABILITY & FIRE INS CO	CT	**A-**	1,040.7	499.0	190.4	2.4	8.9	9.3	6.9	9.0	5.5	T
NATIONAL LLOYDS INS CO	TX	**B-**	166.0	87.3	92.8	2.7	10.0	6.9	6.3	6.5	4.8	FRT
NATIONAL MEDICAL PROFESSIONAL RRG	SC	**D**	7.3	2.3	0.8	0.0	7.8	N/A	3.3	6.3	1.9	DGT
NATIONAL MERIT INS CO	WA	**C**	33.4	12.7	19.8	-1.1	7.3	7.8	2.1	6.1	3.5	DFGT
NATIONAL MUTUAL INS CO	OH	**C**	51.6	18.2	24.5	-0.5	7.4	8.9	5.9	6.1	3.4	DT
NATIONAL PUBLIC FINANCE GUAR CORP	IL	**U** (1)	187.4	185.1	0.0	6.6	N/A	N/A	6.4	7.0	5.4	AT
NATIONAL REINSURANCE CORP	DE	**U** (1)	699.9	541.6	0.1	18.2	N/A	7.0	3.3	10.0	5.1	T
NATIONAL SECURITY FIRE & CAS CO	AL	**C**	68.2	27.5	53.1	1.4	7.0	6.2	2.7	2.1	3.7	FLRT
NATIONAL SERVICE CONTRACT INS CO RRG	DC	**C**	16.2	14.2	0.5	0.0	10.0	8.5	7.8	9.2	2.8	DFGR
NATIONAL SPECIALTY INS CO	TX	**C**	29.0	16.5	8.8	0.3	9.8	6.0	8.5	7.1	4.2	DFGT
NATIONAL STANDARD INS CO	TX	**U** (1)	7.8	7.5	0.0	0.4	N/A	N/A	2.8	7.0	4.0	T
NATIONAL SURETY CORP	IL	**C**	624.0	231.1	191.6	6.9	7.2	5.5	8.6	6.4	4.3	T
NATIONAL TRUST INS CO	TN	**C-**	25.7	31.2	0.0	0.2	10.0	3.6	4.2	6.9	3.3	GT
NATIONAL UNION FIRE INS CO OF LA	LA	**B**	6.8	7.2	0.0	0.0	10.0	N/A	1.9	7.0	4.2	DGT
NATIONAL UNION FIRE INS CO OF PITTSB	PA	**B**	33,210.5	11,993.7	6,579.2	164.6	7.0	2.9	7.1	6.6	5.4	CT
NATIONAL UNITY INS CO	TX	**C-**	37.4	15.2	24.4	1.2	7.1	9.6	8.7	5.9	3.3	DGT
NATIONS BONDING CO	TX	**D**	3.4	3.3	0.0	0.0	10.0	N/A	8.5	10.0	1.5	DGT
▲NATIONSBUILDERS INS CO	DC	**D**	153.7	41.7	21.6	1.7	3.9	6.8	5.8	6.9	1.5	CDOT
▲NATIONWELD RRG INC	DC	**D+**	1.7	1.1	0.1	0.0	9.5	3.8	5.9	8.7	1.0	DFGT
NATIONWIDE AFFINITY INS CO OF AMER	OH	**B-**	45.5	10.7	13.0	-0.2	7.6	4.9	2.3	0.4	3.5	DFGL
NATIONWIDE AGRIBUSINESS INS CO	IA	**B-**	168.9	42.1	0.0	0.7	10.0	N/A	3.4	6.0	5.1	FGT
NATIONWIDE ASR CO	WI	**B-**	62.4	56.3	0.0	0.9	10.0	N/A	3.3	10.0	5.2	T
NATIONWIDE GENERAL INS CO	OH	**B-**	54.2	20.7	0.0	0.1	10.0	N/A	3.8	1.9	3.9	DLT
NATIONWIDE INDEMNITY CO	OH	**C+**	3,670.8	850.1	1.4	50.9	0.2	0.5	3.9	9.5	4.5	CFT
NATIONWIDE INS CO OF AMERICA	WI	**B-**	189.5	92.6	0.0	2.6	10.0	N/A	8.6	7.9	4.4	FGT
NATIONWIDE INS CO OF FLORIDA	OH	**C+**	436.1	263.0	104.7	10.1	4.3	4.2	2.8	6.7	4.5	FT
NATIONWIDE LLOYDS	TX	**B**	41.0	25.9	0.0	0.1	10.0	4.0	7.8	10.0	5.4	DFGT
NATIONWIDE MUTUAL FIRE INS CO	OH	**B+**	4,143.4	1,986.0	1,725.8	30.3	10.0	6.2	7.8	6.3	6.4	T
NATIONWIDE MUTUAL INS CO	OH	**B**	25,410.2	7,633.1	12,783.2	85.9	7.5	6.3	6.2	5.8	5.4	T
NATIONWIDE PROPERTY & CAS INS CO	OH	**B-**	152.8	38.9	0.0	0.2	10.0	N/A	7.8	0.9	5.2	FGLT
▼NAU COUNTRY INS CO	MN	**C-**	447.1	188.1	555.3	-8.4	3.2	3.6	5.3	0.9	2.9	CGLT
NAUTILUS INS CO	AZ	**C+**	1,408.7	471.0	423.8	23.5	7.4	5.9	8.6	7.1	4.3	T
NAVIGATORS INS CO	NY	**B**	1,680.3	568.0	472.7	-0.8	7.9	4.9	8.6	7.1	5.6	AT
NAVIGATORS SPECIALTY INS CO	NY	**C+**	125.9	111.7	0.0	-0.7	10.0	N/A	4.8	7.0	4.5	AT
▼NAZARETH MUTUAL INS CO	PA	**D+**	10.1	2.5	5.6	-0.5	4.1	4.4	1.6	6.6	2.1	DGT
NCMIC INS CO	IA	**C+**	467.3	136.1	81.8	-2.5	7.0	7.0	4.2	7.1	4.4	T
NEIGHBORHOOD SPIRIT PROP & CAS CO	CA	**C+**	211.1	73.6	117.9	0.4	7.9	4.7	7.1	6.4	4.6	T
NETHERLANDS INS CO	NH	**B-**	488.3	123.9	199.8	4.7	7.7	6.0	8.7	7.1	3.5	GT
NEVADA CAPITAL INS CO	NV	**C**	65.3	29.8	32.7	0.6	6.4	8.6	8.8	5.7	3.9	T
NEVADA CONTRACTORS INS CO INC	NV	**D+**(1)	47.4	10.3	12.4	-0.7	2.5	9.6	2.4	6.2	2.4	ACDF
NEVADA DIRECT INS CO	NV	**D**	3.5	1.8	2.7	0.0	3.0	3.4	2.9	4.5	1.5	DGLO
NEVADA DOCS MEDICAL RRG INC	NV	**E+**	3.6	1.0	1.3	0.0	5.5	3.8	3.7	9.8	0.4	GT
NEVADA GENERAL INS CO	NV	**C**	28.0	17.6	15.7	0.4	8.1	5.5	8.0	6.8	3.9	DGT

RISK ADJ. RATIO #1	CAPITAL RATIO #2	PREMIUM TO SURPLUS (%)	RESV. TO SURPLUS (%)	RESV. DEVELOP. 1 YEAR (%)	RESV. DEVELOP. 2 YEAR (%)	LOSS RATIO (%)	EXP. RATIO (%)	COMB RATIO (%)	CASH FROM UNDER-WRITING (%)	NET PREMIUM GROWTH (%)	INVEST. IN AFFIL (%)	INSURANCE COMPANY NAME
0.6	0.4	18.7	42.9	-1.1	-0.3	64.1	31.4	95.5	131.2	22.1	30.6 •	NATIONAL INDEMNITY CO
4.2	2.3	11.7	27.6	1.0	2.4	36.1	8.6	44.7	536.6	146.1	0.0	NATIONAL INDEMNITY CO OF
4.6	3.0	20.6	46.1	-0.1	-0.7	53.9	33.8	87.7	85.1	-26.8	0.0	NATIONAL INDEMNITY CO OF THE SOUTH
2.8	1.9	40.7	46.4	-10.2	-38.5	32.6	73.8	106.4	98.8	2.5	0.0	NATIONAL INDEPENDENT TRUCKERS IC
N/A	N/A	N/A	N/A	N/A	N/A	N/A	N/A	N/A	N/A	0.0	0.0	NATIONAL INS ASN
1.3	0.8	88.0	76.5	-5.2	8.8	59.4	69.3	128.7	54.2	9.3	11.5	NATIONAL INS CO
1.1	0.7	87.0	187.4	-8.4	-24.2	72.9	22.6	95.5	131.9	-7.2	0.0	NATIONAL INS CO OF WISCONSIN INC
3.8	2.5	114.6	88.5	-0.3	-3.6	59.3	29.7	89.0	127.7	7.0	4.2 •	NATIONAL INTERSTATE INS CO
3.1	2.8	38.6	33.7	-0.1	-1.3	59.4	32.4	91.8	155.0	-16.5	0.0	NATIONAL INTERSTATE INS CO OF
5.0	2.2	34.8	65.2	-7.8	-14.9	43.3	25.0	68.3	108.1	-33.5	0.0 •	NATIONAL LIABILITY & FIRE INS CO
4.6	3.8	108.8	18.5	0.2	-2.0	71.3	36.4	107.7	89.1	-11.0	0.0	NATIONAL LLOYDS INS CO
1.5	1.3	35.2	N/A	N/A	N/A	N/A	89.8	89.8	245.9	54.4	0.0	NATIONAL MEDICAL PROFESSIONAL RRG
1.5	1.2	146.7	88.6	3.2	-2.3	83.9	32.1	116.0	84.5	5.8	0.0	NATIONAL MERIT INS CO
2.1	1.3	132.6	54.4	-6.5	-10.5	64.3	34.2	98.5	98.2	-3.3	0.3	NATIONAL MUTUAL INS CO
N/A	N/A	N/A	N/A	N/A	N/A	N/A	N/A	N/A	N/A	0.0	0.0	NATIONAL PUBLIC FINANCE GUAR CORP
N/A	N/A	N/A	26.9	-1.3	-0.9	999 +	999 +	-553.9	12.3	100.5	2.8	NATIONAL REINSURANCE CORP
1.6	1.0	198.4	41.9	-6.2	2.0	82.3	34.1	116.4	89.7	-7.7	10.6	NATIONAL SECURITY FIRE & CAS CO
12.4	7.6	3.6	3.7	-1.6	-4.4	63.0	201.0	264.0	23.0	-65.3	0.0	NATIONAL SERVICE CONTRACT INS CO
5.3	3.9	54.5	9.0	-0.3	-0.4	49.0	45.4	94.4	101.4	-14.6	0.0	NATIONAL SPECIALTY INS CO
N/A	N/A	N/A	N/A	N/A	N/A	N/A	N/A	N/A	N/A	0.0	0.0	NATIONAL STANDARD INS CO
2.0	1.4	82.5	109.6	2.9	4.6	75.0	27.7	102.7	103.4	3.0	0.0 •	NATIONAL SURETY CORP
390.3	195.4	N/A	N/A	N/A	N/A	N/A	N/A	N/A	84.7	0.0	0.0	NATIONAL TRUST INS CO
92.6	46.3	N/A	N/A	N/A	N/A	N/A	N/A	N/A	-28.0	0.0	0.0	NATIONAL UNION FIRE INS CO OF LA
1.2	1.0	55.6	112.9	-0.1	0.4	78.1	25.2	103.3	88.2	-15.4	31.5 •	NATIONAL UNION FIRE INS CO OF PITTSB
1.2	1.1	170.9	75.2	-14.9	-26.3	34.4	49.5	83.9	121.2	19.1	4.7	NATIONAL UNITY INS CO
45.1	40.6	N/A	N/A	N/A	N/A	N/A	N/A	N/A	43.6	0.0	0.0	NATIONS BONDING CO
1.2	0.6	52.8	214.9	N/A	1.1	69.8	35.5	105.3	104.4	-44.6	0.0	NATIONSBUILDERS INS CO
3.5	2.4	10.4	18.1	-7.8	-7.2	11.3	167.8	179.1	67.6	-62.8	0.0	NATIONWELD RRG INC
1.5	1.1	118.0	30.8	-0.5	2.0	83.7	30.2	113.9	125.1	98.9	0.0	NATIONWIDE AFFINITY INS CO OF AMER
4.5	4.1	N/A	N/A	N/A	N/A	N/A	N/A	N/A	51.5	0.0	0.0	NATIONWIDE AGRIBUSINESS INS CO
32.7	29.4	N/A	N/A	N/A	N/A	N/A	N/A	N/A	-65.3	0.0	0.0	NATIONWIDE ASR CO
4.1	3.7	N/A	N/A	N/A	N/A	N/A	N/A	N/A	398.9	0.0	0.0	NATIONWIDE GENERAL INS CO
0.2	0.1	0.2	332.8	3.5	24.9	999 +	157.8	999 +	0.7	-39.8	0.0 •	NATIONWIDE INDEMNITY CO
10.4	9.4	N/A	N/A	N/A	N/A	N/A	N/A	N/A	131.3	0.0	0.0	NATIONWIDE INS CO OF AMERICA
1.6	1.1	42.0	37.8	12.4	11.9	92.9	27.9	120.8	13.4	-20.5	0.0 •	NATIONWIDE INS CO OF FLORIDA
8.7	7.8	N/A	N/A	N/A	N/A	N/A	N/A	N/A	-277.4	0.0	0.0	NATIONWIDE LLOYDS
4.8	3.5	81.8	54.3	0.5	-0.1	74.7	30.9	105.6	103.2	-1.7	4.8 •	NATIONWIDE MUTUAL FIRE INS CO
1.1	1.0	117.4	77.9	0.4	-0.5	74.7	30.9	105.6	96.3	-2.1	27.4 •	NATIONWIDE MUTUAL INS CO
4.2	3.8	N/A	N/A	N/A	N/A	N/A	N/A	N/A	127.3	0.0	0.0	NATIONWIDE PROPERTY & CAS INS CO
1.0	0.6	239.8	111.7	11.7	1.7	94.2	-5.8	88.4	240.3	68.2	0.0 •	NAU COUNTRY INS CO
1.9	1.4	93.5	150.6	-13.6	-21.5	44.8	36.6	81.4	135.6	-10.5	6.7 •	NAUTILUS INS CO
2.2	1.7	81.3	128.9	-7.4	-15.3	59.5	31.2	90.7	152.4	-1.1	7.4 •	NAVIGATORS INS CO
38.7	34.8	N/A	N/A	N/A	N/A	N/A	N/A	N/A	N/A	0.0	0.0	NAVIGATORS SPECIALTY INS CO
0.6	0.4	176.7	66.7	-1.5	-5.8	44.3	47.6	91.9	108.5	-2.7	0.0	NAZARETH MUTUAL INS CO
1.4	1.0	60.6	149.3	-9.6	-33.7	47.8	21.3	69.1	137.0	-1.1	2.2	NCMIC INS CO
2.7	1.7	157.4	103.2	-5.3	-6.7	74.8	30.6	105.4	102.8	-8.0	0.0	NEIGHBORHOOD SPIRIT PROP & CAS CO
2.4	1.6	166.2	181.3	-24.8	-48.9	63.2	31.6	94.8	255.7	64.5	0.0	NETHERLANDS INS CO
1.7	1.0	111.9	55.8	-3.8	-6.8	57.7	38.6	96.3	96.7	1.1	0.0	NEVADA CAPITAL INS CO
0.6	0.4	119.8	280.8	-14.1	-7.8	81.6	37.7	119.3	78.7	-33.5	24.2	NEVADA CONTRACTORS INS CO INC
1.0	0.7	151.1	77.0	38.4	19.1	84.1	-4.7	79.4	73.4	-11.6	0.0	NEVADA DIRECT INS CO
1.0	0.7	126.0	184.5	20.3	-3.9	92.3	22.7	115.0	190.7	143.9	0.0	NEVADA DOCS MEDICAL RRG INC
2.3	2.1	92.0	50.3	4.8	7.0	59.8	35.6	95.4	105.3	-3.0	0.0	NEVADA GENERAL INS CO

999 + Denotes number greater than 999.9%
999 - Denotes number less than -999.99%
• Bullets denote a more detailed analysis is available in Section II.

INSURANCE COMPANY NAME	DOM. STATE	RATING	TOTAL ASSETS ($MIL)	CAPITAL & SURPLUS ($MIL)	ANNUAL NET PREMIUM ($MIL)	NET INCOME ($MIL)	CAPITAL-IZATION INDEX (PTS)	RESERVE ADQ INDEX (PTS)	PROFIT-ABILITY INDEX (PTS)	LIQUIDITY INDEX (PTS)	STAB. INDEX (PTS)	STABILITY FACTORS
NEVADA MUTUAL INS CO INC	NV	**C-**	55.0	13.7	16.0	-0.3	3.8	5.0	4.5	7.3	3.3	CDFT
NEW AMERICA INS CO INC	FL	**F** (1)	0.7	0.4	0.0	-0.1	8.3	3.5	0.3	7.0	0.0	DFRT
NEW CENTURY INS CO	TX	**C**	3.6	3.2	0.2	0.0	10.0	8.3	5.0	10.0	3.2	DFGR
NEW ENGLAND GUARANTY INS CO INC	VT	**C**	32.2	31.9	0.0	0.1	10.0	4.9	8.4	6.9	3.6	FGT
NEW ENGLAND INS CO	CT	**U** (1)	298.9	286.7	0.0	6.7	N/A	6.0	6.9	10.0	6.6	T
▲NEW ENGLAND MUTUAL INS CO	MA	**B-**	27.7	20.5	6.5	0.1	10.0	N/A	4.1	6.9	3.5	DGT
NEW ENGLAND REINSURANCE CORP	CT	**U** (1)	137.6	125.8	0.0	4.4	N/A	5.9	6.9	10.0	6.5	T
NEW HAMPSHIRE INDEMNITY CO INC	PA	**B**	343.0	142.6	138.4	2.9	8.0	5.4	6.6	6.0	5.6	FT
NEW HAMPSHIRE INS CO	PA	**C+**	4,181.7	1,511.2	865.7	9.1	6.9	2.5	7.1	6.7	4.4	FT
NEW JERSEY CAR RRG	DC	**U** (1)	0.8	0.4	0.1	0.0	N/A	N/A	4.9	10.0	1.2	T
▲NEW JERSEY CASUALTY INS CO	NJ	**C+**	236.1	81.4	64.6	0.4	6.2	7.0	7.8	6.7	4.3	T
NEW JERSEY HEALTHCARE PROVIDERS INS	NJ	**C-** (2)	14.6	6.2	4.1	-0.5	6.7	N/A	2.8	7.4	2.1	DGRT
NEW JERSEY INDEMNITY INS CO	NJ	**C+**	101.9	85.4	2.1	0.4	10.0	7.9	8.1	9.2	4.3	FT
NEW JERSEY MANUFACTURERS INS CO	NJ	**B**	4,941.6	2,108.6	1,266.3	-16.9	8.3	8.6	4.8	6.9	5.7	T
▲NEW JERSEY PHYS UNITED RECIP EXCH	NJ	**C-**	43.0	12.8	11.1	0.5	4.0	3.0	3.7	6.7	2.9	CDFG
NEW JERSEY RE-INS CO	NJ	**B**	1,506.3	710.5	102.4	7.2	8.1	5.6	5.7	8.2	5.5	T
NEW JERSEY SKYLANDS INS ASSN	NJ	**C**	86.4	23.7	34.1	-0.4	6.3	7.0	4.4	6.8	4.0	FT
▲NEW JERSEY SKYLANDS INS CO	NJ	**C-**	44.6	14.4	18.4	-0.2	6.5	7.0	5.6	6.8	3.0	DGT
▲NEW LONDON COUNTY MUTUAL INS CO	CT	**B-**	115.0	55.9	41.7	0.3	8.1	4.4	4.4	6.8	4.7	FT
NEW MEXICO MUTUAL CASUALTY CO	NM	**C**	253.6	71.8	74.7	0.4	6.8	4.5	4.8	6.8	3.9	T
NEW MEXICO PROPERTY & CASUALTY CO	NM	**E**	5.3	1.1	1.7	0.2	0.1	3.8	0.8	5.8	0.2	CDFG
NEW SOUTH INS CO	NC	**C+**	71.5	28.3	0.0	0.1	10.0	N/A	3.8	7.0	4.3	
NEW STAR RRG INC	SC	**D-**	5.4	4.7	0.8	0.0	10.0	N/A	4.7	10.0	1.0	DGT
▲NEW YORK CENTRAL MUTUAL FIRE INS CO	NY	**B-**	915.1	365.1	410.8	2.3	8.9	5.8	8.7	6.3	4.7	T
NEW YORK HEALTHCARE INS CO INC RRG	DC	**D**	10.4	2.6	3.5	0.0	2.1	5.0	3.8	9.1	1.9	CDGR
▼NEW YORK MARINE & GENERAL INS CO	NY	**B**	598.4	176.4	129.3	-2.5	7.3	9.4	4.0	7.0	4.9	RT
NEW YORK MUNICIPAL INS RECIPROCAL	NY	**C**	120.4	43.9	31.2	2.3	7.4	9.4	9.2	7.5	3.5	T
NEW YORK SCHOOLS INS RECIPROCAL	NY	**B-**	205.9	89.2	55.5	-0.5	8.0	6.8	7.1	7.3	4.8	T
NEW YORK TRANSPORTATION INS CORP	NY	**D** (5)	3.5	0.0	0.9	0.0	7.9	N/A	2.9	9.9	1.5	DGT
NEWARK INS CO	NJ	**F** (5)	0.0	0.0	0.0	0.0	0.1	4.3	0.1	2.0	0.0	CDFL
NEWPORT BONDING & SURETY CO	PR	**U** (5)	6.6	0.0	3.2	0.0	N/A	1.2	7.2	5.0	1.8	CDG
NEWPORT E&S INS CO	TX	**D-**	30.8	30.2	0.2	0.3	10.0	5.9	8.0	9.8	1.2	DFGT
NEWPORT INS CO	AZ	**B-**	120.5	62.9	66.0	5.7	8.3	6.1	9.3	6.5	4.1	T
NEWPORT MUT INS RRG INC	HI	**U** (1)	0.7	0.2	0.0	-0.1	N/A	3.6	0.2	10.0	0.9	FGT
NEWSTEAD INS CO	DE	**U** (1)	1.3	1.3	0.0	0.0	N/A	N/A	6.9	7.0	2.7	T
NGM INS CO	FL	**B-**	1,790.2	617.8	806.4	11.0	7.7	5.6	7.9	6.3	4.6	T
NHRMA MUTUAL INS CO	IL	**D-**	23.9	4.4	11.5	0.4	1.4	3.3	3.6	2.0	1.2	DFGL
▲NIPPONKOA INS CO LTD US BR	NY	**B**	241.9	79.9	54.9	0.6	6.3	7.0	6.7	7.9	5.4	CT
NISSAY DOWA GENERAL INS CO LTD US BR	NY	**U** (1)	18.7	18.5	0.0	0.3	N/A	6.5	6.3	10.0	4.9	T
▲NLC MUTUAL INS CO	VT	**C-**	235.6	65.3	9.0	3.0	3.1	2.4	4.9	7.9	2.9	CDT
NODAK MUTUAL INS CO	ND	**C+**	122.6	62.6	77.4	-1.2	8.9	7.0	6.4	5.5	4.4	T
NOETIC SPECIALTY INS CO	IL	**C**	95.6	29.6	13.0	0.4	4.2	5.9	3.7	6.8	4.0	CFT
NORCAL MUTUAL INS CO	CA	**B-**	1,142.9	366.2	182.2	-11.0	7.3	9.5	4.6	7.1	4.6	T
NORFOLK & DEDHAM MUTUAL FIRE INS CO	MA	**C**	244.0	118.9	92.5	5.2	9.6	8.0	6.3	6.7	4.0	T
▲NORGUARD INS CO	PA	**B-**	387.1	92.7	100.3	-0.2	6.9	4.6	7.5	6.8	4.4	T
NORTH AMERICAN CAPACITY INS CO	NH	**C**	66.1	44.9	0.0	0.2	10.0	N/A	6.3	8.9	4.0	FT
NORTH AMERICAN ELITE INS CO	NH	**C**	42.3	33.1	0.0	0.3	10.0	N/A	5.4	10.0	3.7	DGT
NORTH AMERICAN FIRE & CAS INS CO	LA	**U** (1)	3.1	3.0	0.0	0.0	N/A	5.0	2.2	7.0	3.4	T
NORTH AMERICAN INDEMNITY CO	TN	**U** (1)	1.3	1.3	0.0	0.0	N/A	9.7	3.2	7.0	0.0	FT
NORTH AMERICAN SPECIALTY INS CO	NH	**C**	541.9	282.9	10.9	9.9	10.0	7.0	6.4	9.6	3.6	T
▲NORTH CAROLINA FARM BU MUTUAL INS CO	NC	**A**	1,627.5	898.2	691.3	2.4	10.0	6.1	8.3	6.4	6.0	T
NORTH CAROLINA GRANGE MUTUAL INS CO	NC	**C-**	17.9	6.4	11.9	-0.2	6.8	8.9	3.1	2.9	2.6	DFGL

See Page 27 for explanation of footnotes and Page 28 for explanation of stability factors.

Arrows denote recent upgrades ▲ or downgrades ▼ (see Section VII for explanations)

RISK ADJ. CAPITAL RATIO #1	RISK ADJ. CAPITAL RATIO #2	PREMIUM TO SURPLUS (%)	RESV. TO SURPLUS (%)	RESV. DEVELOP. 1 YEAR (%)	RESV. DEVELOP. 2 YEAR (%)	LOSS RATIO (%)	EXP. RATIO (%)	COMB RATIO (%)	CASH FROM UNDER-WRITING (%)	NET PREMIUM GROWTH (%)	INVEST. IN AFFIL (%)	INSURANCE COMPANY NAME
0.8	0.6	113.8	258.4	-25.6	-25.5	91.1	35.5	126.6	80.3	-20.7	0.0	NEVADA MUTUAL INS CO INC
2.8	1.8	N/A	56.3	-6.0	-454.6	N/A	N/A	N/A	N/A	0.0	0.0	NEW AMERICA INS CO INC
13.0	7.9	6.2	5.4	-3.2	-4.2	72.5	50.5	123.0	57.2	-24.6	0.0	NEW CENTURY INS CO
119.1	57.7	N/A	N/A	N/A	N/A	N/A	N/A	N/A	-81.1	-100.0	0.0	NEW ENGLAND GUARANTY INS CO INC
N/A	N/A	N/A	3.1	0.1	0.3	N/A	N/A	N/A	N/A	-100.0	0.0	NEW ENGLAND INS CO
8.5	5.3	32.1	10.3	N/A	N/A	66.2	38.6	104.8	128.7	-0.3	0.0	NEW ENGLAND MUTUAL INS CO
N/A	N/A	N/A	7.1	0.2	0.6	N/A	N/A	N/A	N/A	-100.0	0.0	NEW ENGLAND REINSURANCE CORP
3.3	2.5	99.0	68.8	4.0	0.8	79.6	27.0	106.6	87.4	-31.3	8.9	NEW HAMPSHIRE INDEMNITY CO INC
1.1	1.0	52.4	106.4	-0.2	0.6	78.1	25.2	103.3	88.2	-15.4	30.9 •	NEW HAMPSHIRE INS CO
N/A	N/A	20.0	N/A	N/A	N/A	16.7	94.0	110.7	145.2	-11.6	0.0	NEW JERSEY CAR RRG
1.8	1.2	78.1	157.6	8.2	5.6	85.4	15.7	101.1	103.4	-11.3	0.0	NEW JERSEY CASUALTY INS CO
1.2	0.8	64.5	42.5	N/A	N/A	73.3	48.0	121.3	121.7	82.0	0.0	NEW JERSEY HEALTHCARE PROVIDERS
27.5	21.7	2.5	19.9	-0.7	-1.2	77.9	94.6	172.5	23.3	-70.9	0.0	NEW JERSEY INDEMNITY INS CO
2.1	1.7	59.2	100.3	-1.6	-4.1	80.1	11.8	91.9	122.0	-1.3	20.1 •	NEW JERSEY MANUFACTURERS INS CO
0.1	0.1	93.8	188.4	7.6	19.3	61.9	42.7	104.6	89.9	14.7	0.0	NEW JERSEY PHYS UNITED RECIP EXCH
2.7	1.8	14.5	108.6	N/A	0.2	98.5	11.3	109.8	76.4	-15.4	0.0 •	NEW JERSEY RE-INS CO
1.1	0.8	127.1	112.7	0.1	-13.7	70.6	31.2	101.8	76.0	46.6	22.0	NEW JERSEY SKYLANDS INS ASSN
1.3	0.9	126.1	111.8	0.1	-13.5	70.6	31.2	101.8	121.4	46.6	0.0	NEW JERSEY SKYLANDS INS CO
2.4	1.8	72.9	52.5	-3.1	-4.1	53.3	44.4	97.7	92.5	-4.9	14.1	NEW LONDON COUNTY MUTUAL INS CO
1.2	0.9	102.6	216.8	7.3	10.1	77.4	32.4	109.8	113.4	0.0	10.6	NEW MEXICO MUTUAL CASUALTY CO
0.3	0.1	174.3	331.4	71.0	22.3	78.7	42.3	121.0	85.5	-55.0	0.0	NEW MEXICO PROPERTY & CASUALTY
4.7	4.2	N/A	N/A	N/A	N/A	N/A	N/A	N/A	-36.0	0.0	0.0	NEW SOUTH INS CO
13.7	10.3	18.0	0.3	N/A	N/A	0.6	45.4	46.0	224.4	456.0	0.0	NEW STAR RRG INC
3.5	2.6	112.3	89.9	-2.8	-5.9	68.1	30.5	98.6	94.8	-2.3	2.0 •	NEW YORK CENTRAL MUTUAL FIRE INS
0.7	0.4	143.7	196.6	-24.8	-24.2	66.2	34.6	100.8	223.6	17.0	0.0	NEW YORK HEALTHCARE INS CO INC
1.6	1.2	73.7	145.8	-8.3	-17.6	55.0	47.5	102.5	122.9	-4.4	13.8 •	NEW YORK MARINE & GENERAL INS CO
2.3	1.9	73.4	124.9	-12.4	-25.8	55.6	30.2	85.8	126.0	3.5	0.0	NEW YORK MUNICIPAL INS RECIPROCAL
2.5	2.0	61.9	105.7	-4.6	-9.4	73.1	17.2	90.3	121.8	-2.1	0.0	NEW YORK SCHOOLS INS RECIPROCAL
1.7	1.2	51.5	9.8	N/A	N/A	87.7	27.9	115.6	569.2	0.0	0.0	NEW YORK TRANSPORTATION INS CORP
0.1	0.1	0.5	475.6	19.6	-2.4	999 +	999 +	642.1	-28.4	0.0	68.2	NEWARK INS CO
N/A	N/A	105.0	106.3	-11.9	65.9	26.9	74.8	101.7	93.0	0.0	0.0	NEWPORT BONDING & SURETY CO
26.6	22.7	0.6	0.5	-1.3	-1.4	107.0	102.2	209.2	12.5	-73.9	0.0	NEWPORT E&S INS CO
5.2	3.0	111.0	18.8	-2.8	-1.6	41.1	23.9	65.0	152.2	11.6	0.0	NEWPORT INS CO
N/A	N/A	-17.9	1.1	N/A	N/A	95.9	-478.8	-382.9	-6.6	-450.0	0.0	NEWPORT MUT INS RRG INC
N/A	N/A	N/A	N/A	N/A	N/A	N/A	N/A	N/A	N/A	0.0	0.0	NEWSTEAD INS CO
2.1	1.5	132.7	108.8	-4.1	-1.1	62.8	31.7	94.5	109.0	-25.7	13.1 •	NGM INS CO
0.5	0.3	282.8	334.5	-59.8	-37.3	90.1	6.8	96.9	92.4	13.3	4.0	NHRMA MUTUAL INS CO
1.9	1.0	69.1	155.3	-22.7	-49.2	43.4	45.8	89.2	101.5	-0.9	0.0	NIPPONKOA INS CO LTD US BR
N/A	N/A	N/A	1.0	-0.8	-2.0	N/A	N/A	N/A	N/A	0.0	0.0	NISSAY DOWA GENERAL INS CO LTD US
0.9	0.6	14.2	247.7	-1.9	5.1	92.0	26.2	118.2	75.7	3.9	0.0	NLC MUTUAL INS CO
3.9	2.9	122.6	44.9	-9.7	-18.4	75.5	17.0	92.5	106.7	11.4	8.7	NODAK MUTUAL INS CO
0.8	0.6	44.0	161.4	-2.6	-8.7	89.8	28.8	118.6	51.8	-11.0	0.0	NOETIC SPECIALTY INS CO
1.5	1.2	46.9	128.4	-18.7	-28.0	54.9	22.5	77.4	107.5	-2.4	17.2 •	NORCAL MUTUAL INS CO
4.6	3.0	80.8	50.3	-2.0	-0.3	53.4	39.1	92.5	109.0	-2.3	1.4	NORFOLK & DEDHAM MUTUAL FIRE INS
1.4	1.1	108.4	211.6	-17.8	-22.7	53.7	29.6	83.3	133.1	1.5	1.4	NORGUARD INS CO
12.3	11.0	N/A	N/A	N/A	N/A	N/A	N/A	N/A	44.3	0.0	0.0	NORTH AMERICAN CAPACITY INS CO
14.4	13.0	N/A	N/A	N/A	N/A	N/A	N/A	N/A	52.3	0.0	0.0	NORTH AMERICAN ELITE INS CO
N/A	N/A	N/A	0.2	-0.3	-0.8	-100.0	N/A	N/A	0.8	-100.0	0.0	NORTH AMERICAN FIRE & CAS INS CO
N/A	N/A	N/A	N/A	N/A	-34.8	N/A	N/A	N/A	N/A	0.0	0.0	NORTH AMERICAN INDEMNITY CO
4.3	3.9	4.0	31.8	-12.0	-15.8	-138.7	-36.2	-174.9	262.5	220.2	16.0 •	NORTH AMERICAN SPECIALTY INS CO
6.5	4.9	76.2	38.7	-1.0	-0.2	75.3	23.9	99.2	100.4	1.5	0.6 •	NORTH CAROLINA FARM BU MUTUAL INS
1.3	0.9	162.6	29.6	-9.5	-6.0	86.8	24.8	111.6	90.5	2.0	0.0	NORTH CAROLINA GRANGE MUTUAL INS

999 + Denotes number greater than 999.9%
999 - Denotes number less than -999.99%
• Bullets denote a more detailed analysis is available in Section II.

INSURANCE COMPANY NAME	DOM. STATE	RATING	TOTAL ASSETS ($MIL)	CAPITAL & SURPLUS ($MIL)	ANNUAL NET PREMIUM ($MIL)	NET INCOME ($MIL)	CAPITAL-IZATION INDEX (PTS)	RESERVE ADQ INDEX (PTS)	PROFIT-ABILITY INDEX (PTS)	LIQUIDITY INDEX (PTS)	STAB. INDEX (PTS)	STABILITY FACTORS
NORTH COUNTRY INS CO	NY	**C-**	19.0	9.4	7.7	0.4	8.1	7.9	8.6	6.8	2.9	DGT
NORTH EAST INS CO	ME	**D**	62.7	20.6	17.2	-0.5	4.9	5.5	6.1	6.9	2.0	DGT
NORTH PACIFIC INS CO	OR	**C+**	62.9	7.2	0.0	0.0	7.9	N/A	8.4	7.0	3.9	DFGT
NORTH POINTE CASUALTY INS CO	FL	**C-**	44.8	20.0	16.4	0.4	6.2	5.2	2.9	8.4	3.2	DGT
▼NORTH POINTE INS CO	MI	**C-**	111.8	35.1	62.8	2.5	5.6	6.9	1.8	7.9	3.3	T
NORTH RIVER INS CO	NJ	**C**	1,011.9	393.8	167.7	36.8	7.4	5.8	6.6	7.8	3.5	AFT
NORTH SEA INS CO	NY	**C-**	11.9	6.0	4.1	-0.2	7.2	9.5	4.3	8.3	2.5	DGT
NORTH STAR GENERAL INS CO	MN	**U** (1)	4.5	4.2	0.0	0.2	N/A	N/A	6.5	7.0	4.8	T
NORTH STAR MUTUAL INS CO	MN	**B+**	340.1	197.6	151.6	8.5	10.0	7.5	8.3	6.7	5.0	T
NORTH STAR REINSURANCE CORP	DE	**U** (1)	22.4	19.5	0.0	0.5	N/A	N/A	7.5	7.0	5.4	T
NORTHBROOK INDEMNITY CO	IL	**B-**	39.6	39.3	0.0	0.4	10.0	N/A	3.5	7.0	3.9	GT
NORTHEAST PHYSICIANS RRG INC	SC	**E+**	8.2	1.7	2.3	-0.2	1.2	4.4	2.0	6.2	0.0	CDGT
NORTHERN ASR CO OF AMERICA	MA	**C**	281.5	151.7	86.4	-0.1	9.5	6.2	3.5	7.5	4.0	T
▲NORTHERN CAPITAL INS CO	FL	**E+**	68.6	17.1	46.6	-1.0	1.2	3.7	3.8	5.9	0.5	CDGT
NORTHERN CASUALTY CO (MUTUAL)	IA	**D+**	2.4	2.0	0.4	0.0	8.8	7.3	3.3	9.0	2.6	DGT
NORTHERN INS CO OF NY	NY	**C+**	31.6	29.2	0.0	0.2	10.0	N/A	5.0	7.0	4.6	FGT
NORTHERN MUTUAL INS CO	MI	**C**	21.7	14.4	8.1	-0.2	9.4	7.6	4.0	6.8	3.7	DGT
NORTHERN SECURITY INS CO INC	VT	**C**	7.5	7.4	0.0	0.1	10.0	N/A	8.0	7.0	3.7	DG
NORTHFIELD INS CO	IA	**C+**	373.0	122.7	94.3	4.4	7.2	4.7	7.3	6.8	4.8	T
NORTHLAND CASUALTY CO	MN	**B**	101.0	33.6	25.4	1.1	7.3	4.7	8.1	6.8	5.0	T
NORTHLAND INS CO	MN	**B**	1,176.4	578.3	221.3	10.9	8.6	5.5	7.4	6.9	5.9	T
NORTHWEST DENTISTS INS CO	WA	**C**	16.9	6.7	5.1	0.2	7.5	7.0	4.0	6.9	3.5	DFGT
NORTHWEST GF MUTUAL INS CO	SD	**D**	9.7	5.2	5.6	0.2	7.6	6.6	3.1	5.7	1.5	DFGT
NORTHWEST PHYSICIANS INS CO	OR	**C**	129.5	32.7	1.7	1.7	10.0	5.1	7.6	9.8	3.8	FT
NORTHWESTERN NATL INS CO SEG ACCNT	WI	**E+**	57.5	4.3	0.8	0.0	0.3	N/A	1.0	9.6	0.5	CDFT
NORTHWESTERN NTL INS CO MILWAUKEE	WI	**F** (1)	60.1	4.5	0.0	8.9	3.6	N/A	0.2	6.6	0.0	DFRT
NORTHWESTERN PACIFIC INDEMNITY CO	OR	**B**	15.6	14.3	0.0	0.1	10.0	N/A	3.9	7.0	5.0	DG
▲NOVA CASUALTY CO	NY	**C-**	96.9	86.0	45.4	4.7	5.6	5.6	4.4	6.5	2.9	GT
▼NOVUS INS CO RRG	SC	**E+**	17.5	3.6	5.8	-0.6	0.7	5.0	2.3	6.7	0.0	CDGT
▼NSA RRG INC	VT	**F**	19.6	-0.5	5.8	0.0	0.0	0.8	0.3	7.0	0.0	CDGR
NUCLEAR ELECTRIC INS LTD	DE	**E+** (1)	3,950.3	2,988.6	211.4	-635.7	9.9	6.0	2.6	7.0	0.0	FT
NUTMEG INS CO	CT	**B-**	349.9	184.5	71.5	-7.0	8.2	4.9	3.4	7.0	5.2	T
OAK BROOK COUNTY MUTUAL INS CO	TX	**C**	8.6	2.9	0.0	0.0	8.1	N/A	7.7	10.0	3.2	DGT
OAK RIVER INS CO	NE	**B-**	286.1	112.5	68.5	1.0	7.9	7.9	5.0	8.6	4.5	T
▲OBSTETRICIANS & GYNECOLOGISTS RRG	MT	**E+**	2.8	1.0	1.3	0.0	7.1	3.6	5.9	8.0	0.5	DGT
OCCIDENTAL FIRE & CAS CO OF NC	NC	**C-**	191.1	88.0	67.0	-0.3	7.3	5.4	2.3	5.5	2.7	RT
OCEAN HARBOR CASUALTY INS CO	FL	**C-**	101.6	27.2	74.4	-1.2	6.4	9.7	5.4	5.8	3.3	T
OCEAN MARINE INDEMNITY INS CO	LA	**C-**	13.4	7.8	1.7	0.0	9.4	4.8	6.5	7.0	2.7	DGT
OCEAN RRG INC	DC	**E**	16.6	1.0	7.3	0.0	0.0	0.4	0.1	7.6	0.0	CDGT
OCEANUS INS CO A RRG	SC	**C**	37.7	12.0	15.4	-0.1	3.0	5.0	5.7	6.9	2.4	CDGR
ODYSSEY AMERICA REINSURANCE CO	CT	**C**	6,880.8	2,671.1	1,702.4	-21.6	6.1	4.0	6.0	7.1	3.7	AT
OHA INS SOLUTIONS	OH	**D+**	44.5	20.8	7.6	-0.2	8.5	5.8	5.9	9.0	2.2	DGT
▲OHIC INS CO	OH	**C-**	231.0	94.0	-1.4	1.5	3.0	3.6	4.7	8.3	3.0	CDRT
OHIO BAR LIABILITY INS CO	OH	**C+**	35.5	24.7	4.2	0.0	10.0	8.1	3.8	9.1	4.6	DGT
OHIO CASUALTY INS CO	OH	**C+**	5,328.1	1,072.8	2,272.1	34.4	7.3	7.0	6.0	6.6	2.9	AGT
OHIO CASUALTY OF NEW JERSEY INC	OH	**U** (1)	76.3	72.7	0.0	6.4	N/A	4.8	5.3	6.8	6.6	FT
OHIO FARMERS INS CO	OH	**B**	1,314.5	1,029.7	147.7	21.2	7.3	5.0	5.7	7.0	4.6	FT
OHIO INDEMNITY CO	OH	**C**	99.1	43.6	40.4	-2.3	7.5	6.7	2.9	6.7	4.2	T
OHIO MUTUAL INS ASSOC	OH	**B-**	159.9	122.6	34.9	-0.2	7.6	8.1	7.3	6.9	4.7	T
OHIO SECURITY INS CO	OH	**C-**	20.5	13.8	0.0	0.2	10.0	3.6	3.7	7.8	3.1	ADFG
OKLAHOMA ATTORNEYS MUTUAL INS CO	OK	**C+**	44.4	29.9	4.8	0.3	10.0	6.5	3.0	8.9	4.8	DFGT
OKLAHOMA FARM BUREAU MUTUAL INS CO	OK	**B-**	297.9	96.7	190.9	-11.6	7.5	9.1	2.5	0.9	4.7	FLT

See Page 27 for explanation of footnotes and Page 28 for explanation of stability factors.

Arrows denote recent upgrades ▲ or downgrades ▼ (see Section VII for explanations)

RISK ADJ. RATIO #1	CAPITAL RATIO #2	PREMIUM TO SURPLUS (%)	RESV. TO SURPLUS (%)	RESV. DEVELOP. 1 YEAR (%)	RESV. DEVELOP. 2 YEAR (%)	LOSS RATIO (%)	EXP. RATIO (%)	COMB RATIO (%)	CASH FROM UNDER-WRITING (%)	NET PREMIUM GROWTH (%)	INVEST. IN AFFIL (%)	INSURANCE COMPANY NAME
2.8	2.3	84.5	56.9	-3.5	-1.4	54.9	38.3	93.2	102.0	-0.7	4.4	NORTH COUNTRY INS CO
0.8	0.6	83.4	75.9	-2.9	-1.3	51.7	32.0	83.7	143.3	19.6	0.3	NORTH EAST INS CO
1.0	0.9	N/A	N/A	N/A	N/A	N/A	N/A	N/A	635.5	0.0	0.0	NORTH PACIFIC INS CO
1.7	1.1	83.7	89.6	6.4	0.9	60.7	50.3	111.0	103.5	-31.9	0.0	NORTH POINTE CASUALTY INS CO
1.4	0.9	194.2	143.9	6.5	8.7	65.0	50.7	115.7	102.4	16.3	0.0	NORTH POINTE INS CO
1.5	1.0	38.0	109.0	-3.1	-5.5	78.2	50.4	128.6	81.2	-22.0	15.9 •	NORTH RIVER INS CO
2.2	1.9	66.6	69.3	-22.3	-35.7	26.8	42.1	68.9	105.8	25.6	0.0	NORTH SEA INS CO
N/A	N/A	N/A	N/A	N/A	N/A	N/A	N/A	N/A	N/A	0.0	0.0	NORTH STAR GENERAL INS CO
6.9	4.7	79.0	27.3	-0.3	-0.8	69.1	28.0	97.1	105.0	6.9	1.4 •	NORTH STAR MUTUAL INS CO
N/A	N/A	N/A	N/A	N/A	N/A	N/A	N/A	N/A	N/A	0.0	0.0	NORTH STAR REINSURANCE CORP
76.9	35.6	N/A	N/A	N/A	N/A	N/A	N/A	N/A	N/A	0.0	0.0	NORTHBROOK INDEMNITY CO
0.4	0.3	128.3	251.3	-10.0	0.5	85.5	22.0	107.5	117.7	17.8	0.0	NORTHEAST PHYSICIANS RRG INC
4.3	3.1	56.9	56.5	-2.4	-4.5	60.2	34.8	95.0	101.7	6.8	8.6	NORTHERN ASR CO OF AMERICA
0.4	0.3	255.2	30.8	1.1	-3.6	42.5	40.9	83.4	135.9	68.5	0.0	NORTHERN CAPITAL INS CO
3.9	2.7	18.6	2.0	-0.7	-0.6	7.4	82.6	90.0	114.8	-1.8	0.0	NORTHERN CASUALTY CO (MUTUAL)
34.5	31.0	N/A	N/A	N/A	N/A	N/A	N/A	N/A	182.4	0.0	0.0	NORTHERN INS CO OF NY
4.5	3.0	54.2	11.9	-0.7	-1.8	64.8	37.5	102.3	97.5	2.0	0.0	NORTHERN MUTUAL INS CO
101.8	61.5	N/A	N/A	N/A	N/A	N/A	N/A	N/A	N/A	0.0	0.0	NORTHERN SECURITY INS CO INC
2.3	1.5	79.7	163.3	-5.9	-7.5	61.5	32.1	93.6	103.9	23.9	0.0	NORTHFIELD INS CO
2.5	1.6	78.4	160.5	-5.8	-7.6	61.5	32.2	93.7	103.9	24.5	0.0	NORTHLAND CASUALTY CO
3.2	2.5	39.5	80.8	-2.8	-3.7	61.5	28.2	89.7	103.8	26.2	14.2 •	NORTHLAND INS CO
1.7	1.3	75.0	79.6	-14.5	-26.7	60.0	32.7	92.7	97.4	22.4	0.0	NORTHWEST DENTISTS INS CO
2.1	1.6	113.1	20.6	-2.1	-2.8	75.5	37.4	112.9	92.0	8.9	0.0	NORTHWEST GF MUTUAL INS CO
3.8	3.3	5.4	43.7	0.3	-26.5	104.7	37.4	142.1	44.1	-43.7	0.4	NORTHWEST PHYSICIANS INS CO
0.1	0.1	17.7	964.7	N/A	N/A	408.7	229.4	638.1	16.5	-2.7	21.4	NORTHWESTERN NATL INS CO SEG
0.6	0.5	N/A	N/A	N/A	N/A	N/A	N/A	N/A	N/A	0.0	0.0	NORTHWESTERN NTL INS CO
25.9	23.3	N/A	N/A	N/A	N/A	N/A	N/A	N/A	N/A	0.0	0.0	NORTHWESTERN PACIFIC INDEMNITY
3.5	2.6	77.4	85.3	3.0	-7.7	75.3	35.3	110.6	125.3	220.0	18.8	NOVA CASUALTY CO
0.3	0.2	126.4	252.1	16.2	-22.8	94.7	27.1	121.8	142.4	17.9	0.0	NOVUS INS CO RRG
0.0	0.0	-312.0	999 +	323.4	175.5	161.9	26.0	187.9	90.8	-7.2	0.0	NSA RRG INC
5.1	3.2	7.1	18.5	0.1	0.8	207.5	11.4	218.9	119.1	2.5	0.3 •	NUCLEAR ELECTRIC INS LTD
3.1	2.2	50.0	82.7	-1.8	-2.3	64.1	27.8	91.9	110.9	-2.2	7.6	NUTMEG INS CO
1.7	1.5	N/A	N/A	N/A	N/A	N/A	N/A	N/A	N/A	0.0	0.0	OAK BROOK COUNTY MUTUAL INS CO
3.2	1.9	61.5	109.0	-6.3	-4.6	73.5	20.1	93.6	141.7	-56.0	0.0	OAK RIVER INS CO
1.9	1.4	124.9	74.0	-27.7	N/A	45.3	40.2	85.5	286.0	35.9	0.0	OBSTETRICIANS & GYNECOLOGISTS
1.1	1.0	65.6	56.7	N/A	-0.6	87.8	34.2	122.0	99.4	47.0	43.0	OCCIDENTAL FIRE & CAS CO OF NC
0.9	0.8	260.3	115.0	-19.3	-31.2	65.4	34.0	99.4	100.8	0.8	9.5	OCEAN HARBOR CASUALTY INS CO
4.8	3.5	21.7	53.6	-9.3	-17.6	58.9	32.9	91.8	78.6	-13.2	0.0	OCEAN MARINE INDEMNITY INS CO
0.0	0.0	829.6	999 +	135.6	124.2	89.8	39.6	129.4	110.1	-17.7	0.0	OCEAN RRG INC
0.9	0.6	133.3	112.8	-16.0	-20.5	58.3	34.8	93.1	217.3	74.9	0.0	OCEANUS INS CO A RRG
1.2	0.8	57.7	109.6	-1.5	-1.0	68.8	28.2	97.0	115.7	0.6	14.3 •	ODYSSEY AMERICA REINSURANCE CO
4.1	2.7	35.9	59.4	-6.4	-8.1	55.6	29.0	84.6	206.8	11.1	0.0	OHA INS SOLUTIONS
1.1	0.7	-1.5	106.6	-14.4	12.1	-357.8	-162.7	-520.5	32.1	70.4	0.0	OHIC INS CO
5.1	3.5	16.6	27.3	-3.8	-3.9	59.3	29.1	88.4	92.7	1.4	6.9	OHIO BAR LIABILITY INS CO
1.7	1.2	219.4	238.5	-13.3	-28.9	63.2	31.2	94.4	132.4	70.2	8.4 •	OHIO CASUALTY INS CO
N/A	N/A	N/A	N/A	N/A	N/A	N/A	N/A	N/A	N/A	-100.0	0.0	OHIO CASUALTY OF NEW JERSEY INC
1.2	1.1	13.7	11.3	-0.7	-0.3	66.7	36.2	102.9	105.6	3.0	73.1 •	OHIO FARMERS INS CO
1.7	1.3	89.5	35.3	-3.0	0.1	55.1	43.0	98.1	100.3	-11.7	0.0	OHIO INDEMNITY CO
1.4	1.3	28.2	13.5	-3.8	-5.3	60.2	31.3	91.5	111.9	6.4	64.0	OHIO MUTUAL INS ASSOC
7.7	6.9	N/A	N/A	N/A	N/A	N/A	N/A	N/A	54.3	0.0	0.0	OHIO SECURITY INS CO
4.5	3.3	15.9	27.0	2.1	0.4	113.2	24.1	137.3	90.3	5.1	0.0	OKLAHOMA ATTORNEYS MUTUAL INS CO
1.7	1.2	172.8	70.0	2.2	-2.7	110.7	19.8	130.5	69.0	-17.3	10.4	OKLAHOMA FARM BUREAU MUTUAL INS

999 + Denotes number greater than 999.9%
999 - Denotes number less than -999.99%
• Bullets denote a more detailed analysis is available in Section II.

INSURANCE COMPANY NAME	DOM. STATE	RATING	TOTAL ASSETS ($MIL)	CAPITAL & SURPLUS ($MIL)	ANNUAL NET PREMIUM ($MIL)	NET INCOME ($MIL)	CAPITAL-IZATION INDEX (PTS)	RESERVE ADQ INDEX (PTS)	PROFIT-ABILITY INDEX (PTS)	LIQUIDITY INDEX (PTS)	STAB. INDEX (PTS)	STABILITY FACTORS
OKLAHOMA PROPERTY & CAS INS CO	OK	**E+** (1)	4.4	2.6	0.6	0.0	8.2	10.0	6.7	7.9	0.6	DFT
OKLAHOMA SURETY CO	OH	**C**	28.9	13.6	6.6	0.7	4.9	6.0	9.3	7.5	4.3	CDGT
OKLAHOMA TRANSIT INS CO	OK	**U** (1)	1.0	1.0	0.0	0.0	N/A	N/A	2.8	7.0	0.0	FT
OLD AMERICAN CTY MUTUAL FIRE INS CO	TX	**E+**	86.9	5.0	56.7	0.0	0.0	1.3	5.6	0.0	0.7	CDFL
OLD DOMINION INS CO	FL	**B-**	28.0	26.6	0.0	0.4	10.0	3.1	6.0	7.0	3.7	GT
OLD ELIZABETH MUTUAL FIRE INS CO	PA	**U** (1)	0.7	0.7	0.0	0.0	N/A	4.6	3.3	10.0	2.1	FT
OLD GLORY INS CO	TX	**D**	11.6	6.3	5.4	0.0	6.7	7.0	3.6	7.0	1.4	DGT
OLD GUARD INS CO	OH	**C**	289.3	88.1	147.7	-0.3	8.2	5.0	5.2	6.3	3.4	T
OLD LYME INS CO OF RI INC	RI	**U** (1)	27.3	25.3	0.0	1.6	N/A	4.1	2.6	7.0	3.8	RT
OLD RELIABLE CAS CO	MO	**C-**	10.7	8.0	0.0	0.0	10.0	4.6	5.8	10.0	3.3	DGR
OLD REPUBLIC GENERAL INS CORP	IL	**A-**	985.4	254.9	220.0	4.9	7.1	9.3	6.9	6.7	6.6	CT
OLD REPUBLIC INS CO	PA	**A-**	2,301.6	793.7	388.1	18.5	8.3	8.5	6.3	7.5	7.3	T
OLD REPUBLIC LLOYDS OF TX	TX	**B**	2.2	0.6	0.3	0.0	7.0	3.6	2.1	10.0	4.9	DGT
OLD REPUBLIC MERCANTILE INS CO	IL	**U** (1)	3.2	3.2	0.0	-0.2	N/A	3.6	3.0	7.0	4.2	T
OLD REPUBLIC SECURITY ASR CO	AZ	**B**	107.3	57.4	49.6	-1.4	7.8	7.0	4.3	5.7	4.9	T
OLD REPUBLIC SURETY CO	WI	**A-**	94.2	42.1	40.0	0.2	7.6	9.3	6.4	6.9	6.0	T
OLD REPUBLIC UNION INS CO	IL	**B**	24.6	19.4	0.0	0.2	10.0	6.0	3.1	10.0	4.9	DGT
OLD UNITED CAS CO	KS	**B-**	376.9	166.5	71.9	8.8	10.0	5.3	9.3	7.6	4.7	RT
▼OLYMPUS INS CO	FL	**C-**	65.7	31.0	25.9	-3.7	5.2	3.6	1.3	6.5	2.9	FGT
OMAHA INDEMNITY CO	WI	**U** (1)	20.9	13.1	0.0	0.4	N/A	3.1	3.1	10.0	4.3	FT
▲OMEGA INS CO	FL	**D-**	23.5	10.0	9.1	-0.4	1.8	6.3	3.1	1.5	1.3	CDGL
OMEGA ONE INS CO	AL	**C**	10.6	9.0	1.5	0.2	10.0	8.3	5.5	6.9	3.6	DFGT
OMNI INDEMNITY CO	IL	**C**	73.7	30.1	32.4	-0.2	7.7	6.0	5.3	6.3	3.6	FT
▲OMNI INS CO	IL	**B**	190.5	83.9	64.8	0.0	7.7	6.0	3.3	6.5	5.4	FT
▲OMS NATIONAL INS CO RRG	IL	**C+**	286.1	87.6	74.5	2.4	7.3	4.7	8.7	7.6	4.5	RT
ONEBEACON AMERICA INS CO	MA	**C**	722.9	296.7	283.4	12.0	8.6	6.3	2.4	7.0	3.5	T
ONEBEACON INS CO	PA	**B-**	2,859.8	1,173.5	933.2	40.7	7.3	6.4	3.2	6.9	4.9	FT
ONEBEACON LLOYDS OF TEXAS	TX	**B**	17.8	17.8	0.0	0.6	10.0	N/A	8.1	10.0	4.9	DG
ONEBEACON MIDWEST INS CO	WI	**C**	21.8	21.8	0.0	0.4	10.0	N/A	2.6	7.0	3.6	DGT
ONECIS INS CO	IL	**U** (1)	10.2	8.6	0.0	2.3	N/A	N/A	3.6	7.0	3.2	GT
ONTARIO INS CO	NY	**C-**	12.3	7.5	3.8	-0.1	10.0	6.5	6.8	7.4	2.7	DGT
ONTARIO REINS CO LTD	GA	**D-**	14.2	10.5	0.6	0.0	7.1	5.9	3.3	6.9	1.3	DFGT
OOIDA RISK RETENTION GROUP INC	VT	**D**	61.0	15.5	7.5	0.3	3.2	7.1	8.5	9.2	2.3	DFRT
OPHTHALMIC MUTUAL INS CO RRG	VT	**B**	195.1	93.2	38.0	2.1	10.0	9.7	9.5	8.2	5.6	T
▲OPTIMA INS CO	PR	**D**	33.2	10.3	13.5	0.3	4.6	4.6	3.9	7.6	1.9	DGOT
OPTIMUM PROPERTY & CASUALTY INS CO	TX	**C**	3.5	2.9	0.4	0.0	10.0	7.3	6.4	9.5	2.6	DGT
▲ORANGE COUNTY MEDICAL RECIP INS RRG	AZ	**D-**	3.4	1.4	1.2	0.0	5.1	5.4	5.1	6.9	1.1	DGT
ORDINARY MUTUAL A RRG CORP	VT	**D**	38.8	15.0	12.2	0.3	2.8	5.0	3.5	6.8	2.3	DGT
OREGON AUTOMOBILE INS CO	OR	**C**	26.6	7.0	0.0	0.1	10.0	N/A	7.9	7.0	3.9	DGT
▲OREGON MUTUAL INS CO	OR	**B-**	199.6	73.5	112.1	-0.3	7.5	7.0	6.2	5.9	4.5	T
▲ORISKA INS CO	NY	**D-**	9.8	2.4	0.7	0.0	1.4	9.9	3.3	0.8	1.0	CFGL
OSWEGO COUNTY MUTUAL INS CO	NY	**C-**	14.2	8.0	4.9	0.5	8.6	9.3	8.6	6.9	2.7	DGT
OTSEGO COUNTY PATRONS CO-OP F R ASN	NY	**D**	1.8	0.7	0.4	0.1	7.0	6.9	8.5	9.1	1.1	DGT
▲OTSEGO MUTUAL FIRE INS CO	NY	**A-**	70.8	62.1	4.3	0.2	10.0	7.5	7.4	7.1	6.2	T
OWNERS INS CO	OH	**A-**	2,535.6	781.0	1,086.7	1.4	8.4	5.8	6.6	5.5	7.0	T
PACE RRG INC	VT	**E+**	22.2	2.3	4.9	-0.2	1.8	2.8	3.3	9.0	0.0	CDFG
▲PACIFIC EMPLOYERS INS CO	PA	**C+**	2,554.7	809.4	497.8	22.5	6.0	5.0	8.8	6.8	4.4	T
▲PACIFIC INDEMNITY CO	WI	**B+**	5,651.8	1,862.6	1,523.2	84.6	8.0	5.6	9.0	6.7	6.0	T
PACIFIC INDEMNITY INS CO	GU	**D+** (1)	15.2	6.8	8.2	2.0	7.2	6.8	4.3	7.2	2.4	D
PACIFIC INS CO LTD	CT	**B**	622.5	227.7	173.6	5.5	9.3	4.8	3.3	7.0	5.4	T
PACIFIC PIONEER INSURANCE CO	CA	**D+**	23.1	11.8	3.4	0.1	7.3	7.0	8.5	8.3	2.6	DGT
PACIFIC PROPERTY & CASUALTY CO	CA	**B**	45.0	24.2	22.3	1.0	7.2	9.3	8.8	5.8	5.6	DFGT

See Page 27 for explanation of footnotes and Page 28 for explanation of stability factors.

Arrows denote recent upgrades ▲ or downgrades ▼ (see Section VII for explanations)

RISK ADJ. RATIO #1	CAPITAL RATIO #2	PREMIUM TO SURPLUS (%)	RESV. TO SURPLUS (%)	RESV. DEVELOP. 1 YEAR (%)	RESV. DEVELOP. 2 YEAR (%)	LOSS RATIO (%)	EXP. RATIO (%)	COMB RATIO (%)	CASH FROM UNDER-WRITING (%)	NET PREMIUM GROWTH (%)	INVEST. IN AFFIL (%)	INSURANCE COMPANY NAME
2.1	1.8	24.2	66.0	-35.5	-44.5	6.3	127.6	133.9	47.1	-17.1	0.0	OKLAHOMA PROPERTY & CAS INS CO
1.1	0.7	51.9	98.9	-10.2	-26.6	28.0	30.9	58.9	126.8	-22.6	0.0	OKLAHOMA SURETY CO
N/A	N/A	N/A	N/A	N/A	N/A	N/A	N/A	N/A	N/A	0.0	0.0	OKLAHOMA TRANSIT INS CO
0.0	0.0	999 +	18.4	-4.2	-20.5	0.5	99.6	100.1	94.5	-2.3	0.0	OLD AMERICAN CTY MUTUAL FIRE INS
46.9	42.2	N/A	N/A	N/A	N/A	N/A	N/A	N/A	N/A	100.0	0.0	OLD DOMINION INS CO
N/A	N/A	6.1	0.3	N/A	N/A	15.9	154.5	170.4	57.9	12.8	0.0	OLD ELIZABETH MUTUAL FIRE INS CO
1.4	0.8	85.5	33.2	-3.1	-17.3	41.3	50.0	91.3	120.6	131.2	0.0	OLD GLORY INS CO
2.3	1.6	153.1	126.3	-8.4	-3.8	66.7	33.0	99.7	107.2	3.0	0.0	OLD GUARD INS CO
N/A	N/A	N/A	N/A	N/A	N/A	N/A	N/A	N/A	N/A	0.0	0.0	OLD LYME INS CO OF RI INC
8.6	7.7	N/A	N/A	N/A	N/A	N/A	N/A	N/A	145.0	0.0	0.0	OLD RELIABLE CAS CO
2.0	1.0	86.2	206.7	-3.9	-6.8	92.3	5.8	98.1	114.2	-17.7	0.0 •	OLD REPUBLIC GENERAL INS CORP
4.0	2.0	48.2	98.8	-3.1	-9.4	55.7	27.5	83.2	133.4	-19.5	0.7 •	OLD REPUBLIC INS CO
1.0	0.8	50.9	132.0	-0.2	-0.4	60.4	47.1	107.5	-120.9	0.0	0.0	OLD REPUBLIC LLOYDS OF TX
N/A	N/A	N/A	N/A	N/A	N/A	N/A	N/A	N/A	N/A	0.0	0.0	OLD REPUBLIC MERCANTILE INS CO
2.1	1.6	84.8	57.5	2.2	-19.6	118.8	13.9	132.7	102.7	217.7	0.0	OLD REPUBLIC SECURITY ASR CO
1.5	1.3	93.5	37.4	-8.7	-12.1	14.3	73.1	87.4	115.4	-1.6	0.2 •	OLD REPUBLIC SURETY CO
10.4	6.0	0.2	24.5	-0.6	-0.1	-204.5	793.0	588.5	15.2	-37.7	0.0	OLD REPUBLIC UNION INS CO
11.3	5.6	45.5	5.7	-0.4	-0.7	51.2	16.5	67.7	137.2	-15.7	0.0 •	OLD UNITED CAS CO
1.2	0.8	74.7	19.4	-0.6	N/A	69.7	65.9	135.6	97.2	2.0	0.0	OLYMPUS INS CO
N/A	N/A	N/A	58.1	-1.4	-2.6	N/A	N/A	N/A	0.8	100.0	0.0	OMAHA INDEMNITY CO
0.5	0.3	74.8	15.9	-1.7	5.4	38.6	65.7	104.3	114.4	-45.7	0.0	OMEGA INS CO
6.5	4.3	16.5	8.9	-5.1	-5.0	103.8	39.2	143.0	51.6	-32.7	0.0	OMEGA ONE INS CO
1.9	1.6	108.9	80.6	-6.4	-39.3	74.5	20.5	95.0	89.3	-23.0	0.0	OMNI INDEMNITY CO
2.1	1.8	81.6	60.4	-5.0	-35.8	74.9	20.5	95.4	82.9	-4.4	23.2	OMNI INS CO
1.7	1.4	84.3	168.2	-19.2	-24.9	54.0	25.0	79.0	151.0	3.1	8.3	OMS NATIONAL INS CO RRG
3.3	2.1	95.7	95.0	-3.3	-5.4	60.2	34.8	95.0	101.6	6.8	2.6 •	ONEBEACON AMERICA INS CO
1.3	1.2	80.2	79.6	-2.9	-5.5	60.2	36.4	96.6	93.3	6.8	35.8 •	ONEBEACON INS CO
229.4	114.7	N/A	N/A	N/A	N/A	N/A	N/A	N/A	N/A	0.0	0.0	ONEBEACON LLOYDS OF TEXAS
156.8	78.4	N/A	N/A	N/A	N/A	N/A	N/A	N/A	N/A	0.0	0.0	ONEBEACON MIDWEST INS CO
N/A	N/A	N/A	N/A	N/A	N/A	N/A	N/A	N/A	N/A	0.0	0.0	ONECIS INS CO
5.0	3.2	49.4	22.1	-3.4	-4.6	43.2	30.6	73.8	128.0	13.1	0.0	ONTARIO INS CO
1.8	1.1	5.6	9.5	-2.2	-4.4	76.0	40.0	116.0	87.3	9.4	0.0	ONTARIO REINS CO LTD
1.3	0.9	49.2	177.2	-7.6	-57.6	79.7	23.6	103.3	83.5	-15.7	0.0	OOIDA RISK RETENTION GROUP INC
6.1	4.7	41.3	67.5	-20.4	-37.9	19.7	19.0	38.7	177.2	-2.9	0.0	OPHTHALMIC MUTUAL INS CO RRG
1.0	0.7	131.7	14.1	-0.2	-1.6	56.5	32.8	89.3	162.4	80.7	0.0	OPTIMA INS CO
9.7	5.2	14.5	16.1	-0.7	-0.2	80.0	19.0	99.0	107.6	0.0	0.0	OPTIMUM PROPERTY & CASUALTY INS
1.4	1.0	87.9	111.0	3.9	17.6	57.2	11.1	68.3	160.1	27.9	0.0	ORANGE COUNTY MEDICAL RECIP INS
0.6	0.4	82.5	144.9	-12.5	8.9	64.2	15.7	79.9	117.1	9.1	0.0	ORDINARY MUTUAL A RRG CORP
2.0	1.8	N/A	N/A	N/A	N/A	N/A	N/A	N/A	83.1	0.0	0.0	OREGON AUTOMOBILE INS CO
2.5	1.7	149.8	85.7	-3.1	-9.8	64.7	32.8	97.5	95.6	-5.5	5.1	OREGON MUTUAL INS CO
0.6	0.4	17.4	195.3	-54.9	-85.1	-1.3	542.4	541.1	79.5	-86.6	0.0	ORISKA INS CO
3.5	2.3	64.9	43.3	-12.4	-14.9	54.9	37.2	92.1	110.5	0.3	0.0	OSWEGO COUNTY MUTUAL INS CO
1.3	1.2	63.7	23.4	-3.6	-6.5	107.2	-8.1	99.1	242.9	-28.8	0.0	OTSEGO COUNTY PATRONS CO-OP F R
6.1	3.6	6.7	6.9	-0.1	-0.9	48.7	-23.8	24.9	284.7	-1.3	0.0 •	OTSEGO MUTUAL FIRE INS CO
2.8	1.7	136.9	118.9	-6.0	-10.2	82.8	24.2	107.0	106.0	4.1	0.0 •	OWNERS INS CO
0.5	0.3	41.7	142.4	10.0	24.7	92.2	29.3	121.5	80.0	-10.3	0.0	PACE RRG INC
1.7	1.2	62.1	132.8	-13.5	-41.9	62.5	22.8	85.3	111.9	-19.7	6.8 •	PACIFIC EMPLOYERS INS CO
2.8	1.8	83.2	151.2	-4.3	-9.6	62.4	28.3	90.7	118.2	-1.4	0.4 •	PACIFIC INDEMNITY CO
2.1	1.4	120.3	32.1	-5.4	-6.2	35.1	43.3	78.4	137.7	2.8	0.0	PACIFIC INDEMNITY INS CO
3.9	2.5	78.1	129.2	-2.3	-3.5	64.1	27.7	91.8	110.9	-2.2	0.0 •	PACIFIC INS CO LTD
2.5	1.6	29.3	54.5	-8.7	-11.4	53.8	45.7	99.5	88.0	-29.4	0.0	PACIFIC PIONEER INSURANCE CO
1.9	1.1	96.2	43.1	7.5	-4.2	70.3	21.7	92.0	90.6	-3.3	0.0	PACIFIC PROPERTY & CASUALTY CO

999 + Denotes number greater than 999.9%
999 - Denotes number less than -999.99%
• Bullets denote a more detailed analysis is available in Section II.

INSURANCE COMPANY NAME	DOM. STATE	RATING	TOTAL ASSETS ($MIL)	CAPITAL & SURPLUS ($MIL)	ANNUAL NET PREMIUM ($MIL)	NET INCOME ($MIL)	CAPITAL-IZATION INDEX (PTS)	RESERVE ADQ INDEX (PTS)	PROFIT-ABILITY INDEX (PTS)	LIQUIDITY INDEX (PTS)	STAB. INDEX (PTS)	STABILITY FACTORS
PACIFIC SELECT PROPERTY INS CO	CA	**C**	109.7	44.3	33.0	3.0	1.7	4.6	3.9	6.2	3.5	CT
PACIFIC SPECIALTY INS CO	CA	**C**	227.0	122.4	127.6	4.9	5.2	7.0	6.2	1.7	4.1	LT
▲PACIFIC SPECIALTY PROPERTY & CAS CO	TX	**D+**	3.3	3.2	0.2	0.0	10.0	3.6	7.3	9.1	2.4	DGT
PACIFIC STAR INS CO	WI	**C**	8.4	7.3	0.5	0.0	10.0	N/A	3.5	10.0	3.5	DGT
PACO ASR CO INC	IL	**C**	46.7	20.9	12.5	0.2	7.1	6.9	4.3	7.8	3.9	DGT
PADDINGTON LIABILITY RRG	NV	**U** (1)	1.3	1.3	0.0	-0.1	N/A	5.0	6.3	7.0	2.0	FT
PALADIN REINSURANCE CORP	NY	**U** (1)	8.4	0.5	0.3	-0.1	N/A	0.9	0.1	8.1	0.6	CFGT
PALISADES INS CO	NJ	**D+**	25.9	11.6	0.0	0.1	10.0	6.1	3.4	7.0	2.5	DGT
PALISADES PROPERTY & CASUALTY INS	NJ	**D**	103.0	41.9	-165.3	0.0	9.0	4.3	0.9	0.0	1.7	FLT
PALISADES SAFETY & INS ASSOC	NJ	**C**	754.6	287.3	382.2	3.8	5.0	4.5	4.8	6.8	3.5	CGT
PALMETTO CASUALTY INS CO	SC	**C**	6.0	5.9	0.0	0.0	10.0	N/A	7.7	7.0	3.6	DG
PANHANDLE FARMERS MUT INS CO OF WV	WV	**D+**	3.8	2.1	2.1	0.1	8.3	4.1	8.6	7.3	1.7	DGT
PARAMOUNT INS CO	MD	**E+**	7.5	2.1	6.0	0.0	0.0	3.7	4.8	0.0	0.4	CDGL
PARAMOUNT INS CO	NY	**C**	62.5	26.5	15.6	0.2	7.7	6.1	6.9	7.0	4.1	FT
PARATRANSIT INS CO A MUTUAL RRG	TN	**D**	19.9	6.6	2.8	0.0	6.6	9.9	5.1	7.3	2.2	DFGT
PARIS RE AMERICA INS CO	DE	**C**	305.2	152.3	28.9	-1.2	10.0	7.8	4.3	7.8	3.8	GT
▼PARTNER REINSURANCE CO OF THE US	NY	**D**	3,410.2	596.9	757.9	-13.7	0.9	5.8	3.5	6.3	1.4	CRT
PARTNERRE INS CO OF NEW YORK	NY	**C**	117.1	104.8	2.8	1.1	8.0	2.7	5.9	9.0	3.7	DGT
PARTNERS MUTUAL INS CO	WI	**C**	39.5	13.0	30.3	-0.5	7.3	6.9	2.9	5.3	3.5	DFGT
PASSPORT INS CO	ND	**U** (1)	2.0	1.6	0.0	0.0	N/A	N/A	7.1	7.0	0.0	T
PATHFINDER INS CO	CO	**U** (1)	8.8	7.8	0.0	0.4	N/A	9.6	6.3	7.0	3.8	FT
PATRIOT GENERAL INS CO	WI	**B**	25.8	22.1	0.0	0.2	10.0	N/A	7.9	8.6	4.9	DG
PATRIOT INS CO	ME	**C**	59.0	24.1	0.0	-0.1	10.0	4.8	5.6	9.9	2.7	DFT
PATRONS MUTUAL FIRE ASSOC OF NW PA	PA	**D**	1.2	1.0	0.2	0.0	10.0	6.0	2.8	6.9	1.5	DFGT
PATRONS MUTUAL FIRE INS CO OF IN PA	PA	**D+**(1)	2.6	2.3	0.4	0.0	10.0	8.1	5.0	9.1	1.8	DT
PATRONS MUTUAL INS CO OF CT	CT	**C**	39.9	18.5	-14.1	-0.1	9.1	6.0	4.9	3.0	3.6	DFGL
PATRONS-OXFORD INS CO	ME	**C**	15.5	7.1	2.2	0.0	9.7	7.8	8.0	7.0	3.9	DGT
PAWTUCKET INS CO	RI	**F** (1)	12.0	2.3	0.0	-0.1	6.8	9.8	0.9	8.8	0.0	DFRT
PCH MUTUAL INS CO INC RRG	DC	**D-**	10.3	3.2	3.7	0.1	2.1	6.0	7.5	6.9	1.0	DGRT
PEACE CHURCH RRG INC	VT	**D-**	19.2	9.1	3.5	0.2	8.5	6.1	9.1	9.1	0.9	DGRT
PEACHTREE CASUALTY INS CO	FL	**C-**	12.4	6.2	4.8	-0.2	8.6	9.3	4.8	6.7	2.5	DGT
▲PEAK PROP & CAS INS CORP	WI	**B**	38.0	17.1	0.0	0.8	10.0	N/A	9.1	6.7	4.0	DGT
PEDIATRICIANS INS RRG OF AMERICA	DC	**D-**	2.8	1.3	1.1	-0.1	5.6	5.8	2.4	4.5	1.0	DFGL
PEERLESS INDEMNITY INS CO	IL	**C**	789.6	186.5	418.7	7.2	7.5	5.0	2.9	8.7	2.7	GT
PEERLESS INS CO	NH	**C+**	12,656.5	2,012.8	2,379.5	58.4	7.5	5.0	8.5	6.5	3.3	T
PEGASUS INS CO	OK	**C-**	10.7	7.6	4.9	0.0	7.1	5.9	3.3	7.6	2.2	DFGR
PEKIN INS CO	IL	**B+**	195.5	84.7	79.7	0.3	10.0	9.3	5.3	6.2	6.0	T
PELICAN INS RRG	VT	**D-**	16.6	9.7	3.5	0.1	8.8	6.9	7.9	8.1	1.2	DGRT
PEMCO INS CO	WA	**B-**	132.6	50.4	70.4	0.0	8.7	7.0	2.9	6.2	4.7	FT
PEMCO MUTUAL INS CO	WA	**B**	492.9	212.6	234.0	-0.8	8.2	6.9	4.7	6.5	4.7	RT
PENINSULA INDEMNITY CO	MD	**C**	9.6	9.0	0.0	0.1	10.0	4.6	8.3	10.0	3.9	DFGT
PENINSULA INS CO	MD	**C**	72.9	39.7	37.1	0.1	8.7	6.3	8.7	6.4	4.2	T
PENN CHARTER MUTUAL INS CO	PA	**C**	6.1	5.6	0.0	0.0	7.5	6.1	2.5	10.0	3.7	DGT
PENN MILLERS INS CO	PA	**B-**	183.6	43.5	77.1	1.7	7.4	5.5	2.8	6.4	4.7	T
▲PENN NATIONAL SECURITY INS CO	PA	**C+**	659.6	213.9	222.4	1.9	8.6	5.8	8.4	6.6	4.5	T
PENN PATRIOT INS CO	VA	**C**	69.0	30.3	11.6	1.1	7.7	4.9	8.7	7.8	4.1	DFT
PENN-AMERICA INS CO	PA	**B-**	350.9	191.8	38.7	1.4	8.1	5.0	7.8	7.3	4.7	FT
▲PENN-STAR INS CO	PA	**B-**	167.4	71.9	27.1	1.9	8.6	5.1	8.8	7.2	4.7	FT
PENNSYLVANIA GENERAL INS CO	PA	**C**	387.4	127.8	172.8	3.2	7.5	5.6	2.5	7.0	4.1	T
PENNSYLVANIA LUMBERMENS MUTUAL INS	PA	**B-**	300.3	82.1	116.2	-4.3	7.7	4.3	3.3	6.8	5.3	T
PENNSYLVANIA MANUFACTURERS ASN INS	PA	**C**	717.6	202.1	244.1	4.9	7.8	5.1	6.2	6.4	3.5	AT
PENNSYLVANIA MANUFACTURERS IND CO	PA	**C**	217.5	72.1	81.4	2.4	7.9	4.9	7.8	6.4	3.6	AT

RISK ADJ. RATIO #1	CAPITAL RATIO #2	PREMIUM TO SURPLUS (%)	RESV. TO SURPLUS (%)	RESV. DEVELOP. 1 YEAR (%)	RESV. DEVELOP. 2 YEAR (%)	LOSS RATIO (%)	EXP. RATIO (%)	COMB RATIO (%)	CASH FROM UNDER-WRITING (%)	NET PREMIUM GROWTH (%)	INVEST. IN AFFIL (%)	INSURANCE COMPANY NAME
0.5	0.3	77.9	20.1	0.5	0.5	50.3	23.5	73.8	153.0	41.4	18.2	PACIFIC SELECT PROPERTY INS CO
1.0	0.7	106.1	27.9	-4.2	-4.6	56.5	41.3	97.8	96.6	9.5	1.5	PACIFIC SPECIALTY INS CO
31.3	20.9	5.3	0.9	-1.2	N/A	36.7	64.7	101.4	144.7	-65.5	0.0	PACIFIC SPECIALTY PROPERTY & CAS
15.3	13.8	6.7	1.3	N/A	N/A	79.5	43.4	122.9	81.6	0.0	0.0	PACIFIC STAR INS CO
1.6	1.0	60.5	82.2	-2.5	-14.8	87.7	33.6	121.3	130.0	32.1	0.0	PACO ASR CO INC
N/A	N/A	N/A	N/A	-12.4	-28.5	-181.9	N/A	N/A	N/A	-100.0	0.0	PADDINGTON LIABILITY RRG
N/A	N/A	52.2	284.0	38.8	27.8	76.5	93.7	170.2	6.7	N/A	0.0	PALADIN REINSURANCE CORP
5.3	4.8	N/A	N/A	-114.5	-117.5	N/A	N/A	N/A	99.1	0.0	0.0	PALISADES INS CO
6.3	5.6	-381.3	N/A	-85.1	-32.6	89.9	-33.5	56.4	-49.8	-199.4	4.8	PALISADES PROPERTY & CASUALTY INS
0.8	0.7	132.7	98.2	43.6	31.6	89.2	12.3	101.5	218.9	133.5	39.3 •	PALISADES SAFETY & INS ASSOC
134.3	100.6	N/A	N/A	N/A	N/A	N/A	N/A	N/A	N/A	0.0	0.0	PALMETTO CASUALTY INS CO
2.7	2.0	98.6	11.1	-1.2	2.9	44.6	41.9	86.5	117.1	6.6	0.0	PANHANDLE FARMERS MUT INS CO OF
0.1	0.0	290.0	92.6	-4.0	6.4	68.4	28.6	97.0	110.2	24.0	0.0	PARAMOUNT INS CO
3.0	1.7	59.3	92.8	-1.6	-2.1	65.3	36.3	101.6	87.4	-3.7	0.0	PARAMOUNT INS CO
1.2	0.9	43.8	161.1	-12.2	-36.3	40.4	37.0	77.4	104.6	6.3	0.0	PARATRANSIT INS CO A MUTUAL RRG
6.6	4.5	18.9	6.2	N/A	-0.1	56.4	51.4	107.8	270.8	N/A	0.0	PARIS RE AMERICA INS CO
0.3	0.2	124.6	343.1	-11.3	-16.4	75.0	32.3	107.3	101.6	6.6	4.2 •	PARTNER REINSURANCE CO OF THE US
2.9	1.9	2.7	100.7	10.7	11.6	436.7	-347.0	89.7	24.2	453.4	0.0	PARTNERRE INS CO OF NEW YORK
1.8	1.2	224.0	92.1	-3.9	-4.3	70.5	34.1	104.6	89.8	5.3	0.0	PARTNERS MUTUAL INS CO
N/A	N/A	N/A	N/A	N/A	N/A	N/A	N/A	N/A	N/A	0.0	0.0	PASSPORT INS CO
N/A	N/A	N/A	11.3	-6.1	-23.0	N/A	N/A	N/A	N/A	-100.0	0.0	PATHFINDER INS CO
18.7	16.8	N/A	N/A	N/A	N/A	N/A	N/A	N/A	-504.6	0.0	0.0	PATRIOT GENERAL INS CO
3.7	3.4	N/A	N/A	N/A	N/A	N/A	N/A	N/A	-56.1	100.0	15.7	PATRIOT INS CO
6.7	4.3	23.9	2.0	-1.8	-0.7	49.8	61.7	111.5	80.8	-7.3	0.0	PATRONS MUTUAL FIRE ASSOC OF NW
6.8	4.8	18.2	8.5	5.8	-1.9	72.0	38.0	110.0	97.6	-4.1	0.0	PATRONS MUTUAL FIRE INS CO OF IN PA
5.0	4.5	-75.4	20.1	-0.4	-1.3	77.5	22.4	99.9	-20.0	-132.7	0.0	PATRONS MUTUAL INS CO OF CT
3.3	3.0	30.6	14.2	0.1	-0.2	66.0	22.8	88.8	100.3	-0.3	0.0	PATRONS-OXFORD INS CO
1.0	0.9	N/A	193.8	10.6	-24.5	N/A	N/A	N/A	N/A	0.0	0.0	PAWTUCKET INS CO
0.9	0.6	122.7	120.1	30.5	-4.5	46.6	53.8	100.4	145.4	-8.7	0.0	PCH MUTUAL INS CO INC RRG
4.0	2.7	38.5	73.0	-14.3	-76.5	33.5	12.8	46.3	244.7	-6.2	0.0	PEACE CHURCH RRG INC
2.4	2.2	74.4	34.5	-9.4	-14.0	61.5	39.6	101.1	98.9	21.4	0.0	PEACHTREE CASUALTY INS CO
4.7	4.2	N/A	N/A	N/A	N/A	N/A	N/A	N/A	-432.8	0.0	0.0	PEAK PROP & CAS INS CORP
1.0	0.9	78.5	90.7	-2.9	-0.1	105.9	64.3	170.2	46.1	38.0	0.0	PEDIATRICIANS INS RRG OF AMERICA
1.9	1.3	232.7	201.8	-16.0	-27.4	63.2	25.1	88.3	-325.7	N/A	0.0 •	PEERLESS INDEMNITY INS CO
1.7	1.4	117.9	151.1	-15.2	-31.7	63.2	36.9	100.1	116.0	-9.7	16.6 •	PEERLESS INS CO
2.1	1.1	64.6	44.4	-12.9	-17.5	33.0	56.9	89.9	79.0	-18.1	0.0	PEGASUS INS CO
4.1	2.9	93.7	86.9	-3.4	-7.9	89.9	25.5	115.4	94.6	-0.3	5.0 •	PEKIN INS CO
4.5	2.8	33.2	29.7	-20.5	-20.3	-15.5	36.6	21.1	194.7	29.0	0.0	PELICAN INS RRG
2.4	2.1	138.8	81.4	-2.8	-11.5	74.2	32.0	106.2	91.2	-0.6	0.2	PEMCO INS CO
2.3	2.0	110.1	50.8	-2.5	-7.0	69.9	34.3	104.2	95.3	2.1	20.0 •	PEMCO MUTUAL INS CO
15.8	9.0	0.3	N/A	N/A	N/A	36.1	-545.2	-509.1	999 +	-34.0	0.0	PENINSULA INDEMNITY CO
2.8	2.2	94.9	37.6	-2.4	-5.0	64.5	28.1	92.6	108.7	-1.1	14.5	PENINSULA INS CO
2.9	1.7	0.6	0.5	-0.2	-0.2	53.8	15.8	69.6	-135.7	121.1	0.0	PENN CHARTER MUTUAL INS CO
2.1	1.2	180.1	198.6	-8.4	-7.9	72.7	32.7	105.4	99.6	4.4	5.6	PENN MILLERS INS CO
3.5	2.2	104.2	125.0	-3.0	-4.1	64.3	34.5	98.8	103.2	-6.2	0.0 •	PENN NATIONAL SECURITY INS CO
3.4	2.6	39.4	113.5	-11.1	-14.6	60.8	34.8	95.6	82.7	-18.3	0.0	PENN PATRIOT INS CO
1.9	1.8	20.5	59.2	-5.1	-6.7	60.8	34.5	95.3	63.5	-18.3	32.3 •	PENN-AMERICA INS CO
5.1	3.9	38.3	110.3	-10.1	-13.3	60.8	34.7	95.5	76.4	-18.3	0.0	PENN-STAR INS CO
1.9	1.4	134.9	133.9	-4.6	-7.7	60.2	34.8	95.0	101.5	6.8	11.9	PENNSYLVANIA GENERAL INS CO
2.1	1.2	130.7	123.6	3.8	3.7	69.1	33.2	102.3	96.4	1.6	0.0	PENNSYLVANIA LUMBERMENS MUTUAL
1.8	1.4	120.9	125.9	-1.7	-0.1	69.0	26.5	95.5	105.4	5.3	0.0 •	PENNSYLVANIA MANUFACTURERS ASN
1.9	1.5	115.9	120.7	-1.8	-0.1	69.0	25.6	94.6	104.1	5.3	0.0	PENNSYLVANIA MANUFACTURERS IND

999 + Denotes number greater than 999.9%
999 - Denotes number less than -999.99%
• Bullets denote a more detailed analysis is available in Section II.

INSURANCE COMPANY NAME	DOM. STATE	RATING	TOTAL ASSETS ($MIL)	CAPITAL & SURPLUS ($MIL)	ANNUAL NET PREMIUM ($MIL)	NET INCOME ($MIL)	CAPITAL-IZATION INDEX (PTS)	RESERVE ADQ INDEX (PTS)	PROFIT-ABILITY INDEX (PTS)	LIQUIDITY INDEX (PTS)	STAB. INDEX (PTS)	STABILITY FACTORS
▲PENNSYLVANIA NTL MUTUAL CAS INS CO	PA	**B-**	1,025.3	425.1	284.3	2.0	7.7	4.2	6.9	6.6	4.7	T
PENNSYLVANIA PHYSICIANS RECIP INS	PA	**E+**	57.2	6.2	0.0	0.3	5.4	N/A	8.2	9.4	0.0	D
PENNSYLVANIA SURFACE COAL MIN INS EX	PA	**D**	3.0	1.9	0.1	0.0	5.8	8.1	2.7	7.7	1.6	DGT
PEOPLES TRUST INS CO	FL	**E**	38.0	7.1	0.0	-0.6	0.0	N/A	2.8	7.6	0.0	CGT
PERMANENT GEN ASR CORP OF OHIO	OH	**C**	96.5	40.4	60.6	0.1	7.7	6.8	6.6	5.7	3.7	T
PERMANENT GENERAL ASR CORP	TN	**C**	212.4	75.5	155.9	-1.1	8.0	6.7	6.3	3.4	3.7	FLT
▲PERSONAL EXPRESS INS CO	CA	**C**	20.9	9.5	14.4	0.3	5.2	3.6	2.9	5.9	2.7	DGT
▲PERSONAL SERVICE INS CO	PA	**C+**	44.2	19.5	19.5	-0.1	7.8	9.6	7.0	6.4	4.5	DGT
PETROLEUM CAS CO	TX	**C-**	24.3	16.3	4.7	0.8	4.8	4.2	8.3	9.1	3.3	DGT
PETROLEUM MARKETERS MGMT INS CO	IA	**D**	20.9	11.9	3.2	0.3	7.2	9.3	3.0	7.9	2.0	DGT
PHARMACISTS MUTUAL INS CO	IA	**B**	183.9	52.8	88.4	1.1	7.5	4.2	3.8	5.7	5.2	T
▼PHENIX MUTUAL FIRE INS CO	NH	**C-**	43.3	15.9	22.2	-1.8	6.0	8.3	1.8	5.5	3.2	DFGT
PHILADELPHIA CBSP FOR INS OF HOUSES	PA	**B**	235.6	169.9	33.3	0.5	7.0	5.1	4.5	6.7	4.1	GRT
PHILADELPHIA CONTRIBUTIONSHIP INS CO	PA	**B**	138.5	65.8	49.9	-0.2	7.5	4.4	6.7	6.8	4.7	T
▲PHILADELPHIA INDEMNITY INS CO	PA	**B**	3,975.6	1,229.8	1,604.5	3.5	8.2	5.9	9.0	6.6	4.6	T
▲PHILADELPHIA INS CO	PA	**C+**	243.6	85.5	84.4	0.1	8.8	4.7	8.8	6.9	4.3	T
PHILADELPHIA REINSURANCE CORP	PA	**U** (1)	151.3	78.0	0.0	3.2	N/A	6.9	2.9	10.0	4.2	RT
PHILADELPHIA UNITED FIRE INS CO	PA	**U** (1)	0.9	0.9	0.1	0.0	N/A	8.1	6.9	8.3	3.3	RT
PHOEBE RECIPROCAL RRG	SC	**D-**	3.6	2.0	0.7	0.0	8.3	6.0	6.9	9.1	1.3	DGT
▲PHOENIX INS CO	CT	**B**	3,614.1	1,206.6	907.0	31.0	7.5	4.9	8.2	6.7	5.5	T
PHP RRG LTD	AZ	**C-**	10.1	6.9	3.9	0.6	8.4	N/A	9.8	9.0	2.1	DGT
PHYSICIANS IND RRG INC	NV	**E**	6.8	1.7	3.3	-0.5	1.2	3.6	3.6	9.1	0.0	CDGT
▲PHYSICIANS INS A MUTUAL CO	WA	**B-**	406.6	140.3	71.3	4.5	8.0	9.6	8.9	7.3	4.7	T
PHYSICIANS INS CO	FL	**D**	17.1	7.0	3.7	-0.1	7.3	7.1	6.5	8.1	1.5	DFGR
PHYSICIANS INS CO OF OHIO	OH	**U** (1)	55.6	43.7	0.0	-6.3	N/A	8.8	3.4	10.0	5.3	FT
▼PHYSICIANS INS PROGRAM RECIP EXCH	PA	**D**	23.5	5.9	6.0	-0.8	1.4	5.0	2.9	8.4	1.7	CDGR
PHYSICIANS LIABILITY INS CO	OK	**E**	176.2	19.6	-3.6	-0.1	0.0	0.3	1.9	7.2	0.1	CDFR
▲PHYSICIANS PREFERRED INS	FL	**D**	42.4	10.4	17.1	-0.1	3.2	5.6	4.5	7.1	1.5	DGT
▲PHYSICIANS PROACTIVE PROTECTION INC	SC	**D**	29.9	3.8	7.2	-0.2	1.4	4.0	4.9	7.2	1.3	CDGT
PHYSICIANS PROFESSIONAL IND ASSN	MO	**E**	17.2	1.8	7.2	0.0	0.2	0.3	2.9	7.0	0.3	CDGO
PHYSICIANS PROFESSIONAL LIABILTY RRG	VT	**C**	40.3	13.7	7.4	0.3	7.2	4.8	6.4	7.8	3.5	DGRT
PHYSICIANS RECIPROCAL INSURERS	NY	**E-**	1,423.9	-43.2	391.2	-10.5	0.0	0.3	0.3	7.0	0.0	CT
PHYSICIANS REIMBURSEMENT FUND RRG	VT	**D-**	24.4	6.7	3.7	-0.5	3.0	6.0	4.2	7.6	0.0	DGT
PHYSICIANS SPECIALTY LTD RRG	SC	**D-**	8.1	4.4	2.6	0.0	7.0	7.1	4.9	9.2	1.0	DGT
PIEDMONT MUTUAL INS CO	NC	**D**	2.7	1.7	1.1	-0.2	7.6	9.3	2.9	6.6	1.6	DGT
PILGRIM INS CO	MA	**C**	30.5	9.0	0.0	-0.1	8.8	N/A	3.7	7.0	3.7	DGT
PINE TREE INS RECIPROCAL RRG	VT	**E**	16.1	6.9	3.3	0.1	8.0	1.2	8.0	6.7	0.0	DFGT
PINELANDS INS CO RRG INC	DC	**E+**	9.0	0.8	1.5	0.0	1.0	6.0	1.9	7.7	0.8	CDFG
PINNACLE CONSORTIUM OF HIGHER ED	VT	**D**	5.3	3.9	0.9	0.0	8.4	5.6	5.7	9.8	1.4	DGRT
PINNACLE RRG INC	DC	**D**	2.1	1.3	0.4	0.0	6.6	4.0	2.9	9.3	1.2	DGT
PIONEER GENERAL INS CO	CO	**C+**	11.6	6.8	5.9	0.1	5.4	8.6	8.6	8.2	2.9	CDGT
PIONEER SPECIALTY INS CO	MN	**C-**	33.7	17.1	10.3	0.4	7.2	6.7	8.5	6.8	3.2	DGT
PIONEER STATE MUTUAL INS CO	MI	**A**	294.4	169.9	127.7	0.3	10.0	8.9	6.6	6.6	7.0	T
▲PLANS LIABILITY INS CO	OH	**C+**	89.5	49.7	5.4	-0.5	9.1	6.7	5.0	9.2	4.5	DT
PLATEAU CASUALTY INS CO	TN	**C**	19.8	13.2	7.3	0.3	8.0	7.8	6.5	8.2	3.8	DFGR
PLATINUM UNDERWRITERS REINS CO	MD	**C**	1,770.8	575.2	566.0	5.8	5.6	8.8	6.4	7.5	3.5	GRT
PLATTE RIVER INS CO	NE	**C-**	155.2	28.9	26.6	-0.6	7.0	8.7	3.3	7.7	3.3	T
PLAZA INS CO	MO	**C-**	32.7	10.4	6.7	-0.5	4.4	5.9	1.5	8.7	2.7	DGRT
PLYMOUTH ROCK ASR CORP	MA	**C**	385.3	105.1	227.2	-2.1	7.6	4.4	5.3	5.9	4.2	T
PMA CAPITAL INS CO	PA	**D+**(1)	276.4	34.5	1.5	-26.8	1.1	4.4	0.5	9.4	2.6	CFRT
PMI INS CO	AZ	**D**	524.4	37.2	88.5	-25.5	1.1	2.0	0.8	3.7	1.5	ACFL
PMI MORTGAGE GUARANTY COMPANY	AZ	**D+**	14.8	4.9	1.0	-0.7	8.5	3.6	2.6	7.1	2.4	DGT

RISK ADJ. RATIO #1	CAPITAL RATIO #2	PREMIUM TO SURPLUS (%)	RESV. TO SURPLUS (%)	RESV. DEVELOP. 1 YEAR (%)	RESV. DEVELOP. 2 YEAR (%)	LOSS RATIO (%)	EXP. RATIO (%)	COMB RATIO (%)	CASH FROM UNDER-WRITING (%)	NET PREMIUM GROWTH (%)	INVEST. IN AFFIL (%)	INSURANCE COMPANY NAME
1.6	1.5	66.6	85.0	-1.8	-0.3	65.6	33.2	98.8	101.0	-5.1	29.8 •	PENNSYLVANIA NTL MUTUAL CAS INS CO
0.9	0.8	N/A	N/A	N/A	N/A	N/A	N/A	N/A	522.4	0.0	0.0	PENNSYLVANIA PHYSICIANS RECIP INS
1.6	0.9	7.4	64.1	-1.7	-4.3	44.5	45.3	89.8	195.5	20.2	0.0	PENNSYLVANIA SURFACE COAL MIN INS
0.4	0.3	N/A	N/A	N/A	N/A	N/A	N/A	N/A	N/A	0.0	0.0	PEOPLES TRUST INS CO
1.8	1.6	150.5	42.5	-0.8	-3.9	66.2	31.5	97.7	101.7	-4.2	0.0	PERMANENT GEN ASR CORP OF OHIO
1.8	1.6	198.3	56.0	-1.2	-3.8	66.2	31.6	97.8	93.1	-4.2	0.9	PERMANENT GENERAL ASR CORP
1.3	0.7	153.6	21.8	-1.1	N/A	60.8	29.5	90.3	108.4	-0.9	0.0	PERSONAL EXPRESS INS CO
1.9	1.6	101.3	75.0	-5.9	-38.6	74.5	20.4	94.9	114.3	7.3	0.0	PERSONAL SERVICE INS CO
1.0	0.6	32.5	44.8	3.8	-3.6	40.2	28.6	68.8	99.9	5.6	0.0	PETROLEUM CAS CO
2.3	1.4	25.7	57.8	-10.3	-16.5	14.6	33.9	48.5	215.0	6.3	0.0	PETROLEUM MARKETERS MGMT INS CO
2.1	1.3	162.9	133.7	-1.9	2.8	70.7	29.0	99.7	109.1	-1.8	5.4	PHARMACISTS MUTUAL INS CO
1.0	0.7	114.6	63.5	-4.2	-4.9	79.4	41.5	120.9	84.1	-3.2	16.5	PHENIX MUTUAL FIRE INS CO
1.0	0.9	17.6	12.6	-2.8	-1.9	51.2	29.2	80.4	106.3	-7.6	58.1 •	PHILADELPHIA CBSP FOR INS OF
2.5	1.6	69.3	45.6	-7.9	-3.9	56.1	23.2	79.3	149.3	2.9	0.0	PHILADELPHIA CONTRIBUTIONSHIP INS
2.4	1.9	133.2	118.7	-1.8	-12.4	55.0	32.8	87.8	138.2	15.1	0.0 •	PHILADELPHIA INDEMNITY INS CO
2.8	2.2	100.4	89.5	-1.4	-9.1	55.0	32.7	87.7	148.4	15.1	0.0	PHILADELPHIA INS CO
N/A	N/A	N/A	93.3	0.5	2.7	N/A	N/A	N/A	0.6	0.0	0.0	PHILADELPHIA REINSURANCE CORP
N/A	N/A	6.2	3.0	-3.1	-3.9	33.3	77.4	110.7	86.9	-11.7	0.0	PHILADELPHIA UNITED FIRE INS CO
3.4	1.7	32.9	60.0	-15.8	-27.7	33.9	18.2	52.1	999 +	16.4	0.0	PHOEBE RECIPROCAL RRG
1.7	1.4	77.5	158.7	-5.9	-7.5	61.5	30.4	91.9	104.0	0.7	18.0 •	PHOENIX INS CO
4.8	3.0	72.3	9.2	N/A	N/A	19.3	7.3	26.6	999 +	150.0	0.0	PHP RRG LTD
0.2	0.2	158.3	80.5	8.9	N/A	58.2	31.8	90.0	316.3	88.3	0.0	PHYSICIANS IND RRG INC
2.9	2.3	51.6	132.4	-24.5	-42.6	51.0	14.1	65.1	140.5	-7.4	3.6	PHYSICIANS INS A MUTUAL CO
1.6	1.3	52.3	94.8	-43.0	-72.0	26.9	75.1	102.0	82.4	-40.1	0.0	PHYSICIANS INS CO
N/A	N/A	N/A	8.8	-3.0	-6.8	N/A	N/A	N/A	N/A	0.0	0.0	PHYSICIANS INS CO OF OHIO
0.4	0.3	98.9	169.3	21.7	-28.4	87.0	33.4	120.4	223.8	4.4	0.0	PHYSICIANS INS PROGRAM RECIP EXCH
0.1	0.1	-18.7	368.3	-713.7	635.8	329.8	-163.6	166.2	-14.1	-108.1	1.9	PHYSICIANS LIABILITY INS CO
1.1	0.7	163.2	200.1	1.1	-0.4	74.0	28.5	102.5	169.4	15.9	0.0	PHYSICIANS PREFERRED INS
0.4	0.3	179.9	241.9	-29.5	-16.0	71.8	6.0	77.8	999 +	60.0	0.0	PHYSICIANS PROACTIVE PROTECTION
0.3	0.2	407.5	633.4	38.3	302.7	66.7	23.9	90.6	90.6	2.3	0.0	PHYSICIANS PROFESSIONAL IND ASSN
1.7	1.2	53.2	129.9	-38.2	-40.8	30.0	39.3	69.3	132.5	2.0	0.0	PHYSICIANS PROFESSIONAL LIABILTY
-0.0	-0.0	-891.9	999 +	-57.1	960.8	87.0	12.7	99.7	111.0	-15.7	0.1	PHYSICIANS RECIPROCAL INSURERS
0.5	0.4	51.8	195.5	-22.8	-39.2	11.3	41.2	52.5	135.3	-1.0	0.0	PHYSICIANS REIMBURSEMENT FUND
1.8	1.2	58.2	72.3	-16.3	-15.5	22.4	25.1	47.5	219.9	81.7	0.0	PHYSICIANS SPECIALTY LTD RRG
2.4	1.7	60.7	9.5	-9.8	-19.1	32.6	55.5	88.1	112.6	28.9	0.0	PIEDMONT MUTUAL INS CO
2.4	2.1	N/A	20.3	N/A	N/A	N/A	N/A	N/A	-35.5	0.0	0.0	PILGRIM INS CO
2.4	1.8	40.0	66.7	-5.7	1.7	57.0	17.8	74.8	17.7	-4.5	0.0	PINE TREE INS RECIPROCAL RRG
0.3	0.2	172.0	440.0	19.0	-12.6	123.8	14.7	138.5	94.9	2.7	0.0	PINELANDS INS CO RRG INC
3.3	1.8	21.8	26.4	-4.5	-3.7	37.0	47.9	84.9	169.2	5.1	0.0	PINNACLE CONSORTIUM OF HIGHER ED
2.0	1.1	28.5	54.6	-38.5	-25.7	-39.3	69.1	29.8	156.9	-46.4	0.0	PINNACLE RRG INC
1.1	1.0	88.3	18.0	N/A	-6.8	8.8	90.3	99.1	103.9	-32.5	0.0	PIONEER GENERAL INS CO
1.8	1.1	61.6	62.1	-2.9	-5.2	69.3	27.3	96.6	113.3	-3.0	0.0	PIONEER SPECIALTY INS CO
5.3	3.6	72.4	35.3	-3.2	-8.2	77.7	26.4	104.1	93.8	1.6	0.0 •	PIONEER STATE MUTUAL INS CO
3.8	2.9	10.6	68.5	-7.8	-0.5	8.5	97.2	105.7	64.3	-48.3	0.0	PLANS LIABILITY INS CO
1.9	1.8	56.2	4.0	-1.6	-1.7	36.0	55.4	91.4	90.0	-5.1	34.9	PLATEAU CASUALTY INS CO
1.3	0.6	98.6	143.4	-6.6	-9.7	72.2	27.9	100.1	140.5	54.7	0.0 •	PLATINUM UNDERWRITERS REINS CO
1.7	0.9	89.5	87.6	-4.0	-10.5	49.2	49.4	98.6	104.9	-23.2	0.0	PLATTE RIVER INS CO
1.0	0.7	66.0	62.0	-2.2	-1.7	73.9	25.0	98.9	-416.5	0.0	0.0	PLAZA INS CO
1.6	1.3	210.1	109.7	-3.1	4.5	74.8	24.6	99.4	100.7	7.9	0.0	PLYMOUTH ROCK ASR CORP
0.3	0.2	4.3	318.2	33.3	18.4	999 +	999 +	999 +	-2.7	115.8	0.0	PMA CAPITAL INS CO
0.1	0.1	139.8	433.1	24.2	41.4	249.0	29.1	278.1	70.3	-30.4	0.0	PMI INS CO
1.8	1.3	17.8	43.3	16.3	14.7	260.0	3.4	263.4	64.7	-27.1	0.0	PMI MORTGAGE GUARANTY COMPANY

999 + Denotes number greater than 999.9%
999 - Denotes number less than -999.99%
• Bullets denote a more detailed analysis is available in Section II.

INSURANCE COMPANY NAME	DOM. STATE	RATING	TOTAL ASSETS ($MIL)	CAPITAL & SURPLUS ($MIL)	ANNUAL NET PREMIUM ($MIL)	NET INCOME ($MIL)	CAPITAL-IZATION INDEX (PTS)	RESERVE ADQ INDEX (PTS)	PROFIT-ABILITY INDEX (PTS)	LIQUIDITY INDEX (PTS)	STAB. INDEX (PTS)	STABILITY FACTORS
PMI MORTGAGE INS CO	AZ	**D-**	3,434.9	379.3	653.8	-181.1	1.4	3.3	1.3	7.1	1.1	ACFT
▲PMSLIC INS CO	PA	**C+**	482.4	162.7	67.4	-1.4	8.1	4.9	6.8	7.8	4.3	T
PODIATRY INS CO OF AMERICA A MUT CO	IL	**C**	262.4	80.7	81.1	2.6	7.6	5.8	7.7	6.8	3.7	T
POLICYHOLDERS MUTUAL INS CO	WI	**U** (1)	0.2	0.2	0.0	0.0	N/A	N/A	4.9	10.0	0.6	FRT
PONCE DE LEON LTC RRG INC	FL	**D**	17.9	7.9	5.2	0.1	7.5	6.5	4.8	6.7	1.4	DFGR
POSITIVE PHYSICIANS INS EXCHANGE	PA	**E+**	31.0	8.5	6.4	0.0	1.3	5.3	2.9	6.9	0.8	CDGR
POTOMAC INS CO	PA	**U** (1)	10.3	10.3	0.0	0.3	N/A	0.1	1.9	7.3	0.0	CFGR
PRAETORIAN INS CO	IL	**C+**	934.9	334.3	248.0	-5.7	5.9	6.9	4.6	8.0	4.5	CFRT
PRE-PAID LEGAL CAS INC	OK	**C-**	23.0	18.7	54.2	1.9	6.4	7.3	3.2	0.9	3.3	DGLT
PREFERRED AUTO INS CO INC	TN	**D-**	7.6	2.7	2.2	0.1	8.3	7.0	3.7	8.2	0.9	DGT
PREFERRED CONTRACTORS INS CO RRG	MT	**E+**	29.3	6.0	1.3	0.0	4.5	3.7	3.2	7.0	0.5	DGT
PREFERRED EMPLOYERS INS CO	CA	**C**	95.4	44.5	6.5	1.4	4.6	7.0	9.3	7.2	3.7	CT
PREFERRED MANAGED RISK LTD	DC	**U** (5)	0.0	0.0	9.4	0.0	N/A	3.6	8.9	5.6	0.0	CDT
▲PREFERRED MUTUAL INS CO	NY	**C+**	367.2	136.4	142.6	4.2	9.1	4.9	8.6	6.8	4.5	T
▲PREFERRED PHYSICIANS MEDICAL RRG	MO	**B-**	147.4	52.8	32.2	0.9	9.0	10.0	8.8	8.3	4.9	T
PREFERRED PROFESSIONAL INS CO	NE	**C+**	320.0	119.4	61.5	1.6	8.6	6.0	8.2	7.8	4.7	T
PREMIER GROUP INS CO INC	TN	**C-**	61.0	30.1	14.4	1.0	7.6	9.5	8.8	9.3	3.2	DT
PREMIER INS CO OF MASSACHUSETTS	MA	**B-**	447.7	208.6	231.1	1.6	9.8	9.4	3.7	6.4	5.3	T
PREMIER INS EXCHANGE RRG	VT	**U** (1)	24.4	19.2	0.0	0.2	N/A	4.7	3.2	7.0	4.4	T
▲PREMIER PHYSICIANS INS CO INC A RRG	NV	**D-**	9.3	3.5	5.7	0.4	3.6	N/A	6.3	8.8	1.0	DGT
PRESERVER INS CO	NJ	**D+**	114.1	36.0	30.0	-1.7	4.5	3.8	4.5	1.9	2.6	FLT
PRIDE NATIONAL INS CO	OK	**U** (1)	6.7	6.6	0.0	0.2	N/A	N/A	3.0	7.0	4.2	RT
▲PRIME INS CO	IL	**D**	35.3	27.7	3.5	0.1	8.8	3.6	3.1	9.3	1.4	DGT
PRIME INS SYNDICATE INC	IL	**D+**	23.0	10.9	3.7	0.0	5.7	1.4	2.6	6.8	2.4	DFGT
▲PRIMERO INS CO	NV	**D-**	16.8	6.8	16.1	0.2	3.7	2.5	3.6	3.2	1.0	DGLT
PRINCETON EXCESS & SURPLUS LINES INS	DE	**C+**	206.8	57.3	25.8	2.5	7.5	6.4	9.3	6.7	3.5	GT
PRINCETON INS CO	NJ	**D+**	976.8	266.3	164.6	14.1	4.1	0.6	7.5	6.7	2.6	T
PRIORITY ONE INS CO	TX	**C+**	17.7	11.0	6.4	-0.8	9.2	8.5	4.0	6.7	4.3	DFGT
PRIVILEGE UNDERWRITERS RECIP EXCH	FL	**B-**	65.9	48.2	6.8	-0.4	10.0	3.6	2.7	7.4	3.5	FGT
▲PROASSURANCE CASUALTY CO	MI	**C+**	1,108.5	299.7	126.0	13.5	5.9	5.6	6.8	7.0	4.5	FRT
▲PROASSURANCE INDEMNTIY CO INC	AL	**B**	1,822.2	584.9	228.8	21.8	7.9	7.1	9.0	7.8	4.6	RT
▲PROASSURANCE NATIONAL CAPITAL INS	DC	**C**	258.2	86.0	17.1	-0.1	5.2	4.1	2.9	10.0	3.4	RT
▲PROASSURANCE SPECIALTY INS CO INC	AL	**C+**	33.7	25.4	0.0	0.0	10.0	N/A	6.8	7.0	4.3	DT
PROASSURANCE WISCONSIN INS CO	WI	**C**	364.5	80.3	56.0	-0.9	3.8	3.3	3.3	7.5	3.9	CRT
▼PROBUILDERS SPECIALTY INS CO RRG	DC	**E**	208.2	25.7	3.5	0.3	0.0	2.8	3.5	7.0	0.1	CDFO
PROCENTURY INS CO	TX	**C+**	130.4	31.6	19.3	-0.7	7.5	5.8	4.6	6.2	3.7	FRT
PRODUCERS AGRICULTURE INS CO	TX	**C**	153.0	38.5	107.6	1.3	3.6	4.6	9.1	0.0	3.3	CFGL
PRODUCERS LLOYDS INS CO	TX	**C**	4.1	3.9	0.0	0.0	10.0	3.6	7.4	10.0	3.3	DG
PROFESSIONAL CASUALTY ASSN	PA	**D**	52.5	9.8	15.7	-0.2	2.3	7.0	5.0	7.3	1.8	CDRT
PROFESSIONAL INS EXCHANGE	UT	**D-**	6.4	5.0	1.0	0.0	7.4	4.1	2.9	8.8	0.0	DGT
▼PROFESSIONAL LIAB INS CO OF AMERICA	NY	**D-**	40.9	15.1	16.5	-0.2	2.1	2.3	4.1	6.9	0.7	CDFG
PROFESSIONAL LIABILITY INS CO	TN	**U** (1)	3.7	3.0	0.0	0.2	N/A	0.5	3.7	10.0	0.8	FGRT
PROFESSIONAL MEDICAL INS RRG	HI	**U** (1)	0.3	0.3	0.0	-0.1	N/A	N/A	2.5	7.0	1.1	FRT
PROFESSIONAL QUALITY LIABILITY INS	VT	**D**	1.5	1.1	0.0	0.0	7.3	3.6	6.1	9.1	1.1	DGT
▲PROFESSIONAL SECURITY INS CO	AZ	**C**	19.0	18.3	0.0	0.2	10.0	4.6	6.2	10.0	3.5	DGT
PROFESSIONAL SOLUTIONS INS CO	IA	**D**	12.3	9.6	0.0	0.1	10.0	5.8	4.9	10.0	1.4	DGT
PROFESSIONAL UNDRWTRS LIAB INS CO	UT	**C+**	96.1	63.3	0.5	1.1	10.0	5.7	2.8	10.0	4.3	T
PROFESSIONALS ADVOCATE INS CO	MD	**B-**	103.4	52.1	8.9	0.7	9.8	9.6	8.5	9.2	4.6	T
PROFESSIONALS DIRECT INS CO	MI	**C-**	20.7	18.3	24.7	2.0	5.2	1.9	4.2	7.1	3.0	DGRT
PROGRESSIVE ADVANCED INS CO	OH	**C**	177.5	58.6	151.1	3.0	7.1	8.3	8.0	2.0	3.6	LT
PROGRESSIVE AMERICAN INS CO	FL	**B-**	323.6	126.8	161.3	3.9	9.7	6.4	5.7	5.9	4.5	T
PROGRESSIVE BAYSIDE INS CO	FL	**B-**	101.0	34.0	80.7	2.2	7.6	6.5	5.4	5.6	4.5	T

See Page 27 for explanation of footnotes and Page 28 for explanation of stability factors.
Arrows denote recent upgrades ▲ or downgrades ▼ (see Section VII for explanations)

RISK ADJ. RATIO #1	CAPITAL RATIO #2	PREMIUM TO SURPLUS (%)	RESV. TO SURPLUS (%)	RESV. DEVELOP. 1 YEAR (%)	RESV. DEVELOP. 2 YEAR (%)	LOSS RATIO (%)	EXP. RATIO (%)	COMB RATIO (%)	CASH FROM UNDER-WRITING (%)	NET PREMIUM GROWTH (%)	INVEST. IN AFFIL (%)	INSURANCE COMPANY NAME
0.2	0.2	141.5	401.2	24.0	30.9	239.6	25.6	265.2	74.4	-2.5	5.7 •	PMI MORTGAGE INS CO
3.1	2.5	40.8	111.7	-19.7	-28.3	54.9	19.9	74.8	123.2	-12.7	0.0 •	PMSLIC INS CO
1.9	1.5	108.1	178.3	0.3	2.9	76.2	15.6	91.8	127.0	-14.4	8.8	PODIATRY INS CO OF AMERICA A MUT
N/A	N/A	5.3	N/A	N/A	N/A	N/A	100.0	100.0	18.2	0.0	0.0	POLICYHOLDERS MUTUAL INS CO
2.8	1.8	67.2	80.5	-13.3	-25.8	52.5	41.3	93.8	82.8	-12.7	0.0	PONCE DE LEON LTC RRG INC
0.4	0.3	74.9	203.3	10.2	5.1	71.8	36.1	107.9	150.7	-23.8	0.0	POSITIVE PHYSICIANS INS EXCHANGE
N/A	N/A	0.1	999 +	839.7	862.4	999 +	999 +	-700.0	N/A	400.0	0.0	POTOMAC INS CO
1.2	0.8	70.9	108.9	-6.1	-4.7	59.5	50.6	110.1	84.6	-38.2	5.7 •	PRAETORIAN INS CO
1.2	0.9	309.0	0.6	-0.4	-0.6	33.5	46.6	80.1	124.8	4.5	28.8	PRE-PAID LEGAL CAS INC
1.8	1.6	85.5	50.3	-6.6	-13.9	83.7	25.4	109.1	84.6	-13.1	0.0	PREFERRED AUTO INS CO INC
1.2	0.7	22.2	137.6	5.4	-3.6	66.8	46.7	113.5	-44.3	-55.8	0.0	PREFERRED CONTRACTORS INS CO
1.5	0.9	15.1	43.7	-8.9	-24.5	8.5	32.3	40.8	202.2	-31.9	0.0	PREFERRED EMPLOYERS INS CO
N/A	N/A	577.4	347.5	-19.0	N/A	62.0	25.8	87.8	238.6	0.0	0.0	PREFERRED MANAGED RISK LTD
4.0	2.8	104.8	95.7	-15.1	-11.8	62.3	30.9	93.2	112.0	-2.3	0.1	PREFERRED MUTUAL INS CO
3.4	2.8	61.5	120.8	-8.1	-52.1	48.5	15.6	64.1	193.6	9.3	0.0	PREFERRED PHYSICIANS MEDICAL RRG
4.1	2.9	51.5	106.8	-5.1	-23.8	68.3	-13.8	54.5	273.0	-1.3	0.4	PREFERRED PROFESSIONAL INS CO
2.7	2.0	49.4	68.3	-11.5	-17.8	39.4	22.7	62.1	144.5	22.1	0.0	PREMIER GROUP INS CO INC
3.6	3.2	111.1	56.2	-3.1	-4.8	70.3	26.6	96.9	94.8	-12.0	0.0 •	PREMIER INS CO OF MASSACHUSETTS
N/A	N/A	N/A	26.1	-3.2	-10.0	N/A	N/A	N/A	N/A	0.0	0.0	PREMIER INS EXCHANGE RRG
1.0	0.8	157.1	70.5	N/A	N/A	42.6	52.1	94.7	163.7	13.9	0.0	PREMIER PHYSICIANS INS CO INC A RRG
0.7	0.5	82.1	77.2	-2.6	-0.9	51.7	33.1	84.8	35.4	7.6	0.0	PRESERVER INS CO
N/A	N/A	N/A	N/A	N/A	N/A	N/A	N/A	N/A	N/A	0.0	0.0	PRIDE NATIONAL INS CO
2.5	2.4	12.3	13.7	-1.7	-0.4	69.7	20.1	89.8	122.9	19.8	36.3	PRIME INS CO
0.9	0.7	31.6	64.7	14.8	23.4	122.2	18.8	141.0	37.9	-25.9	0.0	PRIME INS SYNDICATE INC
0.7	0.6	244.0	100.9	2.4	-10.3	70.7	25.4	96.1	101.1	6.6	0.0	PRIMERO INS CO
1.6	1.1	46.0	57.2	-1.8	1.9	59.1	-22.7	36.4	999 +	49.4	0.0	PRINCETON EXCESS & SURPLUS LINES
1.1	0.8	63.4	196.3	18.1	33.9	77.8	18.3	96.1	105.2	-12.6	0.0 •	PRINCETON INS CO
3.0	2.1	55.1	20.8	-3.1	-4.3	63.3	52.8	116.1	74.8	-4.5	6.6	PRIORITY ONE INS CO
6.2	4.1	14.2	5.1	-0.2	N/A	51.3	93.1	144.4	35.8	20.7	0.0	PRIVILEGE UNDERWRITERS RECIP EXCH
1.5	1.1	40.4	228.3	-19.8	-13.1	53.5	21.6	75.1	72.5	-17.2	0.0 •	PROASSURANCE CASUALTY CO
2.4	2.0	40.4	175.6	-21.6	-53.1	30.8	19.0	49.8	134.6	-12.0	0.2 •	PROASSURANCE INDEMNTIY CO INC
1.5	1.0	18.3	144.9	-12.6	-23.3	22.6	18.5	41.1	-442.0	-10.3	0.0	PROASSURANCE NATIONAL CAPITAL INS
11.9	10.7	N/A	3.5	N/A	N/A	N/A	N/A	N/A	211.6	0.0	0.0	PROASSURANCE SPECIALTY INS CO INC
0.7	0.5	64.6	261.7	6.6	10.3	96.9	23.5	120.4	110.5	-9.3	0.0	PROASSURANCE WISCONSIN INS CO
0.3	0.2	24.2	999 +	31.7	53.2	70.3	107.2	177.5	-322.5	-59.2	0.0	PROBUILDERS SPECIALTY INS CO RRG
1.5	0.8	61.8	62.9	-5.0	-10.0	62.1	36.5	98.6	94.5	-5.3	0.0	PROCENTURY INS CO
1.2	0.7	291.8	12.4	6.5	-1.5	85.7	7.0	92.7	74.9	89.8	11.6	PRODUCERS AGRICULTURE INS CO
55.5	49.9	N/A	N/A	N/A	N/A	N/A	N/A	N/A	N/A	0.0	0.0	PRODUCERS LLOYDS INS CO
0.5	0.3	153.2	270.1	-28.6	-58.3	77.6	38.3	115.9	110.1	-4.7	0.0	PROFESSIONAL CASUALTY ASSN
2.5	1.5	20.9	19.2	2.5	4.1	60.6	36.5	97.1	102.1	9.6	0.0	PROFESSIONAL INS EXCHANGE
0.4	0.4	104.3	101.5	41.5	40.4	78.1	69.7	147.8	89.3	-22.0	0.0	PROFESSIONAL LIAB INS CO OF
N/A	N/A	0.1	12.3	-11.1	N/A	999 +	999 +	999 +	0.5	0.0	0.0	PROFESSIONAL LIABILITY INS CO
N/A	N/A	N/A	N/A	N/A	N/A	N/A	N/A	N/A	N/A	0.0	0.0	PROFESSIONAL MEDICAL INS RRG
1.8	1.1	3.7	2.8	-1.7	N/A	6.8	-104.9	-98.1	-141.4	-8.9	0.0	PROFESSIONAL QUALITY LIABILITY INS
56.6	51.0	N/A	0.4	-0.1	-0.3	N/A	N/A	N/A	32.9	0.0	0.0	PROFESSIONAL SECURITY INS CO
10.3	9.3	N/A	11.1	-0.5	-9.2	-262.5	N/A	N/A	100.3	100.0	0.0	PROFESSIONAL SOLUTIONS INS CO
10.4	8.7	0.8	10.5	-0.9	-2.8	36.5	913.9	950.4	87.8	139.0	0.0	PROFESSIONAL UNDRWTRS LIAB INS CO
5.7	4.7	17.3	58.2	-10.6	-27.8	17.2	-11.6	5.6	294.8	-1.9	0.0	PROFESSIONALS ADVOCATE INS CO
2.6	2.1	132.1	140.0	31.0	33.0	100.4	22.0	122.4	121.1	36.2	0.0	PROFESSIONALS DIRECT INS CO
1.2	1.1	272.8	102.4	-0.8	-0.4	73.7	20.9	94.6	104.0	6.1	0.0	PROGRESSIVE ADVANCED INS CO
3.4	3.0	130.9	55.7	0.3	1.1	73.5	21.2	94.7	104.1	-3.6	0.0	PROGRESSIVE AMERICAN INS CO
1.6	1.4	253.2	107.8	0.6	2.4	73.5	21.5	95.0	110.6	-3.6	0.0	PROGRESSIVE BAYSIDE INS CO

999 + Denotes number greater than 999.9%
999 - Denotes number less than -999.99%
• Bullets denote a more detailed analysis is available in Section II.

INSURANCE COMPANY NAME	DOM. STATE	RATING	TOTAL ASSETS ($MIL)	CAPITAL & SURPLUS ($MIL)	ANNUAL NET PREMIUM ($MIL)	NET INCOME ($MIL)	CAPITAL-IZATION INDEX (PTS)	RESERVE ADQ INDEX (PTS)	PROFIT-ABILITY INDEX (PTS)	LIQUIDITY INDEX (PTS)	STAB. INDEX (PTS)	STABILITY FACTORS
PROGRESSIVE CASUALTY INS CO	OH	**C**	5,072.6	1,271.5	3,952.4	80.2	5.0	6.5	3.2	1.1	4.1	LT
PROGRESSIVE CHOICE INS CO	OH	**C**	195.8	49.8	42.0	1.0	10.0	6.1	7.2	6.8	3.6	T
PROGRESSIVE CLASSIC INS CO	WI	**C+**	301.0	86.5	242.0	7.7	7.4	6.5	3.6	4.5	4.5	LT
PROGRESSIVE COMMERCIAL CASUALTY CO	OH	**U** (1)	8.4	0.0	0.0	0.7	N/A	N/A	2.6	7.0	0.0	T
PROGRESSIVE COUNTY MUTUAL INS CO	TX	**C**	310.1	1.0	0.0	0.0	0.3	N/A	3.9	7.3	2.1	CT
PROGRESSIVE DIRECT INS CO	OH	**C-**	3,169.5	948.4	2,926.7	47.8	7.1	8.3	7.7	2.0	2.9	LT
PROGRESSIVE EXPRESS INS CO	FL	**C**	250.7	74.9	46.7	1.4	10.0	5.8	3.4	7.1	3.7	T
PROGRESSIVE FREEDOM INS CO	NJ	**C**	20.5	6.5	3.3	0.2	8.3	4.6	4.8	7.4	2.7	DFGT
▲PROGRESSIVE GARDEN STATE INS CO	NJ	**C**	73.1	16.6	9.5	0.3	8.9	4.6	4.4	6.1	3.2	DGT
PROGRESSIVE GULF INS CO	OH	**B**	340.1	196.3	161.3	5.9	10.0	6.4	8.9	6.5	4.5	T
PROGRESSIVE HAWAII INS CORP	OH	**C**	101.5	34.1	89.6	3.0	7.1	4.6	8.4	5.1	3.5	T
PROGRESSIVE MARATHON INS CO	MI	**C**	248.1	84.7	226.6	5.2	7.4	8.6	9.4	4.7	3.6	LT
PROGRESSIVE MAX INS CO	OH	**C+**	252.9	83.1	226.6	8.0	7.2	7.9	9.6	4.3	4.5	LT
PROGRESSIVE MICHIGAN INS CO	MI	**C**	390.7	124.5	322.6	10.3	7.6	6.2	6.9	4.3	3.8	LT
PROGRESSIVE MOUNTAIN INS CO	OH	**B**	176.0	50.5	80.7	2.2	8.3	6.5	8.0	6.1	4.0	FT
▲PROGRESSIVE NORTHEASTERN INS CO	NY	**C+**	183.1	57.5	29.4	1.4	10.0	6.3	3.3	9.3	4.3	T
PROGRESSIVE NORTHERN INS CO	WI	**C+**	1,147.5	322.1	967.9	25.1	7.2	6.5	3.3	3.2	4.4	LT
PROGRESSIVE NORTHWESTERN INS CO	OH	**C+**	1,118.3	332.7	967.9	29.5	7.1	6.5	3.3	3.9	4.5	LT
PROGRESSIVE PALOVERDE INS CO	IN	**C**	66.2	21.3	18.9	0.6	8.7	7.4	7.1	7.0	3.5	DFT
PROGRESSIVE PREFERRED INS CO	OH	**C**	604.6	182.3	484.0	17.1	7.4	6.5	3.9	4.3	4.0	LT
PROGRESSIVE PREMIER INS CO OF IL	OH	**B-**	126.6	29.8	75.5	1.3	6.4	7.9	9.4	5.8	4.2	T
▲PROGRESSIVE SECURITY INS CO	LA	**C+**	192.5	36.6	30.7	1.1	10.0	6.4	4.6	6.7	4.3	FT
PROGRESSIVE SELECT INS CO	FL	**C**	256.3	66.0	51.6	1.3	9.2	6.0	7.3	6.5	3.6	T
PROGRESSIVE SOUTHEASTERN INS CO	IN	**B-**	128.4	45.8	80.7	2.3	7.5	6.5	9.3	5.1	4.5	T
PROGRESSIVE SPECIALTY INS CO	OH	**B**	1,061.2	594.4	564.6	16.5	10.0	6.4	5.9	6.5	4.5	T
PROGRESSIVE UNIVERSAL INS CO	WI	**C+**	172.4	51.1	151.1	2.8	7.0	8.0	8.6	1.4	4.4	LT
PROGRESSIVE WEST INS CO	OH	**B-**	138.3	41.6	31.1	1.8	10.0	6.0	5.3	6.8	4.5	T
▲PROPERTY & CASUALTY I CO OF HARTFORD	IN	**B**	226.5	111.5	51.0	4.9	10.0	4.5	8.9	7.1	5.5	T
▲PROPERTY-OWNERS INS CO	IN	**A-**	147.1	67.7	60.5	-1.8	7.2	7.0	5.8	5.6	6.9	T
PROSELECT INS CO	MA	**C**	72.1	21.4	0.0	0.2	9.3	3.4	6.0	10.0	4.2	DF
PROSELECT NATIONAL INS CO INC	AZ	**U** (1)	11.8	11.7	0.0	0.3	N/A	N/A	6.4	7.0	5.2	T
PROTECTION MUT INS CO OF	PA	**U** (1)	0.7	0.6	0.0	-0.1	N/A	7.4	2.2	10.0	2.0	FRT
▼PROTECTIVE INS CO	IN	**A**	529.3	310.0	148.6	4.4	7.7	9.1	3.9	6.8	7.3	FT
PROVIDENCE MUTUAL FIRE INS CO	RI	**B-**	153.4	84.4	54.1	1.3	8.7	5.9	3.1	6.9	4.7	T
PROVIDENCE PLANTATIONS INS CO	RI	**U** (1)	1.3	1.3	0.0	0.0	N/A	N/A	5.5	7.0	0.0	CFT
PROVIDENCE PROPERTY & CAS INS CO	OK	**C-** (1)	92.0	16.4	11.5	1.7	2.9	4.2	4.3	7.3	3.2	CDT
PROVIDENCE WASHINGTON INS CO	RI	**U** (1)	165.4	65.9	-0.4	28.2	N/A	4.0	3.9	9.7	4.8	CFT
▲PUBLIC SERVICE MUTUAL INS CO	NY	**C+**	639.5	274.3	140.4	1.3	7.8	4.6	7.7	7.0	4.4	FT
PUBLIC UTILITY MUTUAL INS CO RRG	VT	**E**	4.9	3.2	1.0	0.0	9.9	9.9	8.3	9.5	0.1	DGT
PUTNAM REINSURANCE CO	NY	**C**	623.2	172.8	183.6	7.2	3.9	2.5	7.0	6.2	4.2	CT
PXRE REINSURANCE CO	CT	**D**	200.9	65.5	-1.5	1.0	2.8	3.8	1.1	7.0	0.0	DRT
PYMATUNING MUTUAL FIRE INS CO	PA	**D+**(1)	3.3	3.2	0.1	0.1	10.0	3.6	6.9	10.0	2.1	DG
QBE INS CORP	PA	**B-**	844.5	256.2	131.6	-25.5	7.3	4.3	3.5	8.8	5.2	T
QBE REINSURANCE CORP	PA	**B-**	1,129.0	547.7	667.6	37.7	7.1	3.3	4.7	7.5	5.0	T
QBE SPECIALTY INS CO	ND	**D-**	318.7	126.6	31.1	-15.2	10.0	4.9	2.9	10.0	1.3	GT
QUALITY CASUALTY INS CO INC	AL	**E**	2.8	0.9	1.0	0.0	7.4	6.9	1.5	6.9	0.3	DGT
QUANTA INDEMNITY CO	CO	**C-**	173.8	74.7	-0.2	1.1	7.5	5.0	2.9	7.0	2.9	DFT
QUANTA SPECIALTY LINES INS CO	IN	**C-**	89.5	25.2	-2.0	0.6	7.4	6.0	1.5	10.0	3.0	DFRT
QUINCY MUTUAL FIRE INS CO	MA	**B**	997.9	584.9	261.5	3.6	8.8	7.4	3.9	6.9	4.7	T
R&Q REINS CO	PA	**E**	265.6	38.3	0.7	1.3	0.3	4.1	2.4	7.0	0.2	CT
RADIAN ASSET ASR CO	NY	**B**	2,309.6	997.3	79.6	11.0	10.0	5.0	4.5	9.1	4.5	FT
RADIAN GUARANTY INC	PA	**D**	4,318.0	399.2	688.5	-55.6	0.7	5.8	0.3	5.5	1.9	CFT

See Page 27 for explanation of footnotes and Page 28 for explanation of stability factors.

Arrows denote recent upgrades ▲ or downgrades ▼ (see Section VII for explanations)

RISK ADJ. CAPITAL RATIO #1	RISK ADJ. CAPITAL RATIO #2	PREMIUM TO SURPLUS (%)	RESV. TO SURPLUS (%)	RESV. DEVELOP. 1 YEAR (%)	RESV. DEVELOP. 2 YEAR (%)	LOSS RATIO (%)	EXP. RATIO (%)	COMB RATIO (%)	CASH FROM UNDER-WRITING (%)	NET PREMIUM GROWTH (%)	INVEST. IN AFFIL (%)	INSURANCE COMPANY NAME
0.9	0.8	325.4	138.6	0.8	2.2	73.5	22.2	95.7	102.4	-1.1	28.6 •	PROGRESSIVE CASUALTY INS CO
4.2	3.5	85.5	27.2	-0.1	1.3	71.5	18.7	90.2	124.5	1.9	0.0	PROGRESSIVE CHOICE INS CO
1.5	1.3	305.3	130.0	0.8	2.5	73.5	20.2	93.7	109.2	-3.6	0.0	PROGRESSIVE CLASSIC INS CO
N/A	N/A	N/A	N/A	N/A	N/A	N/A	N/A	N/A	-40.0	0.0	0.0	PROGRESSIVE COMMERCIAL CASUALTY
0.1	0.1	N/A	N/A	N/A	N/A	N/A	N/A	N/A	62.7	0.0	0.0	PROGRESSIVE COUNTY MUTUAL INS CO
1.3	1.1	331.1	124.3	-0.8	-0.4	73.7	20.4	94.1	111.0	6.1	0.0 •	PROGRESSIVE DIRECT INS CO
6.8	4.6	63.4	43.6	0.5	5.8	72.9	19.2	92.1	241.2	-16.8	0.0	PROGRESSIVE EXPRESS INS CO
2.2	2.0	52.7	35.8	-0.1	1.4	62.4	21.6	84.0	0.3	-37.0	0.0	PROGRESSIVE FREEDOM INS CO
2.3	2.1	58.0	25.6	0.2	-0.5	83.4	17.3	100.7	126.6	121.0	0.0	PROGRESSIVE GARDEN STATE INS CO
5.3	4.6	84.9	36.2	0.2	0.9	73.5	20.6	94.1	103.6	-3.6	0.0 •	PROGRESSIVE GULF INS CO
1.6	1.2	298.0	94.9	0.3	1.8	63.9	20.8	84.7	125.7	-2.1	0.0	PROGRESSIVE HAWAII INS CORP
1.4	1.3	280.1	105.1	-0.7	-0.4	73.7	20.7	94.4	109.1	6.1	0.0	PROGRESSIVE MARATHON INS CO
1.4	1.3	303.0	114.5	-0.8	-0.4	73.7	20.6	94.3	114.3	6.1	0.0	PROGRESSIVE MAX INS CO
1.6	1.4	269.6	114.8	0.6	5.1	73.5	21.3	94.8	102.4	-24.7	0.0	PROGRESSIVE MICHIGAN INS CO
2.7	2.3	167.1	71.1	0.4	2.5	73.5	23.9	97.4	93.3	-3.6	0.0	PROGRESSIVE MOUNTAIN INS CO
5.7	4.8	52.2	45.7	-3.0	1.9	69.3	21.0	90.3	77.5	-31.8	0.0	PROGRESSIVE NORTHEASTERN INS CO
1.4	1.2	324.2	138.0	0.8	2.4	73.5	20.6	94.1	106.0	-3.6	0.0 •	PROGRESSIVE NORTHERN INS CO
1.5	1.3	325.6	138.7	0.8	2.4	73.5	21.5	95.0	105.4	-3.6	0.0 •	PROGRESSIVE NORTHWESTERN INS CO
2.8	2.4	91.0	34.2	-0.2	-0.2	73.7	18.7	92.4	93.4	6.1	0.0	PROGRESSIVE PALOVERDE INS CO
1.6	1.4	292.8	124.7	0.8	2.5	73.5	20.8	94.3	104.1	-3.6	0.0 •	PROGRESSIVE PREFERRED INS CO
1.3	1.1	265.4	99.6	-0.7	-0.4	73.7	19.7	93.4	99.7	6.1	0.0	PROGRESSIVE PREMIER INS CO OF IL
4.0	3.0	86.4	32.0	1.2	-0.8	75.4	17.4	92.8	71.0	1.6	0.0	PROGRESSIVE SECURITY INS CO
2.8	2.2	79.4	36.9	-0.2	1.0	79.2	16.2	95.4	121.4	3.4	0.0	PROGRESSIVE SELECT INS CO
1.7	1.5	184.7	78.6	0.5	2.2	73.5	19.9	93.4	116.6	-3.6	0.0	PROGRESSIVE SOUTHEASTERN INS CO
4.6	4.0	95.8	40.8	0.2	0.8	73.5	21.2	94.7	105.2	-3.6	0.0 •	PROGRESSIVE SPECIALTY INS CO
1.2	1.0	312.2	117.2	-0.8	-0.4	73.7	19.7	93.4	111.8	6.1	0.0	PROGRESSIVE UNIVERSAL INS CO
4.4	3.7	78.0	27.5	-0.1	1.3	70.4	21.0	91.4	102.3	-18.0	0.0	PROGRESSIVE WEST INS CO
6.5	4.2	47.8	79.1	-2.0	-3.4	64.1	6.8	70.9	110.9	-2.2	0.0	PROPERTY & CASUALTY I CO OF
2.3	1.3	86.0	44.5	-3.8	-3.2	61.3	24.6	85.9	120.9	-8.1	0.0 •	PROPERTY-OWNERS INS CO
2.9	2.6	N/A	N/A	N/A	N/A	N/A	N/A	N/A	-52.7	0.0	0.0	PROSELECT INS CO
N/A	N/A	N/A	N/A	N/A	N/A	N/A	N/A	N/A	N/A	0.0	0.0	PROSELECT NATIONAL INS CO INC
N/A	N/A	-2.2	3.9	-0.8	-1.4	-566.7	-415.4	-982.1	38.7	-230.0	0.0	PROTECTION MUT INS CO OF
1.7	1.4	47.3	68.3	-4.8	-11.9	63.2	28.8	92.0	95.6	13.6	26.5 •	PROTECTIVE INS CO
3.7	2.4	59.9	38.5	0.2	1.2	63.1	41.5	104.6	99.4	1.6	0.9	PROVIDENCE MUTUAL FIRE INS CO
N/A	N/A	N/A	N/A	N/A	N/A	N/A	N/A	N/A	N/A	0.0	0.0	PROVIDENCE PLANTATIONS INS CO
0.8	0.4	70.3	238.2	-15.0	5.4	47.2	54.8	102.0	132.4	-33.2	13.3	PROVIDENCE PROPERTY & CAS INS CO
N/A	N/A	-0.6	124.9	-79.0	-94.3	999 +	-935.2	999 +	1.5	-99.1	8.7	PROVIDENCE WASHINGTON INS CO
2.9	2.0	51.6	97.6	-1.2	-4.4	65.3	25.7	91.0	82.3	-3.8	10.4 •	PUBLIC SERVICE MUTUAL INS CO
4.1	2.9	30.7	28.5	-4.0	-22.7	33.6	44.1	77.7	125.4	27.3	0.0	PUBLIC UTILITY MUTUAL INS CO RRG
0.9	0.6	110.7	210.2	N/A	6.8	71.1	28.4	99.5	129.9	1.7	0.0 •	PUTNAM REINSURANCE CO
0.7	0.5	-2.4	142.9	12.6	14.6	999 +	735.6	-471.3	-27.7	-162.4	0.0	PXRE REINSURANCE CO
55.1	47.7	2.0	N/A	N/A	N/A	59.1	72.6	131.7	39.7	19.2	0.0	PYMATUNING MUTUAL FIRE INS CO
1.2	0.9	48.3	36.0	7.8	5.9	72.5	39.7	112.2	182.8	21.4	41.3 •	QBE INS CORP
1.6	1.3	123.9	104.8	10.2	17.9	74.9	33.6	108.5	108.0	38.4	26.4 •	QBE REINSURANCE CORP
8.0	4.6	22.5	7.1	2.0	1.0	47.4	33.2	80.6	110.1	531.2	0.0	QBE SPECIALTY INS CO
1.2	1.1	111.6	39.4	3.1	6.0	72.6	38.7	111.3	97.5	-7.3	0.0	QUALITY CASUALTY INS CO INC
1.6	1.5	-0.3	35.6	-5.3	-3.9	-239.6	999 +	999 +	-26.8	-111.3	27.3	QUANTA INDEMNITY CO
3.0	1.5	-7.8	87.3	-6.4	-25.5	844.8	-534.0	310.8	-1.1	68.0	0.0	QUANTA SPECIALTY LINES INS CO
3.8	2.4	42.2	34.0	-1.6	-1.9	60.6	36.6	97.2	94.6	-2.7	2.8 •	QUINCY MUTUAL FIRE INS CO
0.2	0.1	1.9	588.1	-40.3	-25.8	-1.0	533.3	532.3	18.4	-54.1	0.0	R&Q REINS CO
5.5	4.7	8.2	7.8	N/A	-0.6	73.0	168.1	241.1	35.5	-69.3	4.4 •	RADIAN ASSET ASR CO
0.2	0.2	169.3	500.6	3.2	13.7	238.9	28.6	267.5	91.7	-11.8	29.3 •	RADIAN GUARANTY INC

999 + Denotes number greater than 999.9%
999 - Denotes number less than -999.99%
• Bullets denote a more detailed analysis is available in Section II.

INSURANCE COMPANY NAME	DOM. STATE	RATING	TOTAL ASSETS ($MIL)	CAPITAL & SURPLUS ($MIL)	ANNUAL NET PREMIUM ($MIL)	NET INCOME ($MIL)	CAPITAL-IZATION INDEX (PTS)	RESERVE ADQ INDEX (PTS)	PROFIT-ABILITY INDEX (PTS)	LIQUIDITY INDEX (PTS)	STAB. INDEX (PTS)	STABILITY FACTORS
▼RADIAN INS INC	PA	**C-**	769.7	90.3	7.7	-22.8	2.7	9.2	0.5	7.6	2.9	CFT
▼RADIAN MORTGAGE INS INC	AZ	**C+**	65.2	22.4	1.1	-3.6	8.8	7.0	2.9	9.2	3.7	DT
RAINIER INS CO	AZ	**C+**	27.9	19.3	4.9	0.1	8.1	5.1	7.0	9.1	4.4	DGT
RAM MUTUAL INS CO	MN	**C**	64.0	33.6	26.0	1.7	8.4	5.9	6.6	6.7	4.3	T
RAMPART INS CO	NY	**U** (1)	77.9	25.2	0.0	-5.3	N/A	2.0	1.8	7.0	3.0	FT
RANCHERS & FARMERS INS CO	TX	**D+**	8.5	5.2	2.8	0.1	7.7	4.5	3.0	6.2	2.7	DFGR
RANCHERS & FARMERS MUTUAL INS CO	TX	**D+**	9.1	2.1	0.5	0.1	3.7	2.7	2.9	5.4	2.4	CDGT
REAL LEGACY ASR CO INC	PR	**C**	143.3	61.6	38.8	1.3	8.1	8.8	7.5	6.7	3.8	RT
REAMSTOWN MUTUAL INS CO	PA	**D**	5.5	2.2	3.8	0.0	7.3	6.3	4.6	6.4	1.9	DGT
RED SHIELD INS CO	WA	**B-**	41.4	20.7	9.5	0.1	7.4	4.7	3.9	9.0	4.9	DGT
RED VIKING INS CO	CA	**U** (1)	10.1	10.1	0.0	-0.3	N/A	N/A	4.2	7.0	0.0	FT
▲REDLAND INS CO	NJ	**C**	163.3	64.4	41.4	-0.1	5.7	5.8	5.7	7.0	3.5	FT
REDWOOD FIRE & CAS INS CO	NE	**B**	863.5	378.6	121.0	8.0	6.0	7.0	7.8	8.4	5.3	CFT
REGENT INS CO	WI	**B-**	228.2	62.6	81.5	-1.9	8.5	6.3	3.3	7.5	4.5	FT
REGIONAL HEALTH INS CO RRG	DC	**E+**	3.8	0.8	0.1	-0.1	1.9	5.0	1.7	7.9	0.0	CDFG
REGIS INS CO	PA	**C-**	16.9	7.3	5.8	-0.3	4.3	7.0	4.7	7.7	2.7	GT
REINSURANCE CO OF AMERICA INC	IL	**D+**	14.6	4.1	3.9	-0.8	1.7	3.5	0.9	0.5	1.1	CDFG
RELIABLE LLOYDS INS CO	TX	**D+**	8.7	6.4	0.0	0.4	10.0	4.6	8.2	9.3	2.7	DFGT
RELIAMAX INS CO	SD	**E**	6.4	2.1	5.1	0.1	0.6	3.6	3.5	7.1	0.3	CDGT
REPUBLIC FIRE & CASUALTY INS CO	OK	**C+**	5.7	5.4	0.0	0.1	10.0	N/A	7.2	7.6	3.0	DGT
REPUBLIC INDEMNITY CO OF AMERICA	CA	**B-**	862.6	294.2	206.7	4.5	7.4	5.9	5.3	6.9	4.9	AT
REPUBLIC INDEMNITY OF CA	CA	**C**	42.5	23.9	6.4	0.2	8.4	5.8	8.8	6.8	4.3	DGT
REPUBLIC LLOYDS	TX	**C**	7.0	6.5	0.0	0.3	10.0	N/A	4.4	10.0	3.5	DFG
REPUBLIC MORTGAGE INS CO	NC	**D**	1,998.0	180.4	484.7	-109.9	0.1	1.9	0.9	7.1	1.4	CT
REPUBLIC MORTGAGE INS CO OF FLORIDA	FL	**C**	49.3	13.4	8.3	-2.9	0.7	4.5	0.8	7.7	3.4	CDT
REPUBLIC MORTGAGE INS CO OF NC	NC	**C**	687.3	142.7	109.0	-31.6	2.0	3.8	2.3	7.1	3.4	CT
REPUBLIC MUTUAL INS CO	OH	**D+**	15.3	6.3	8.7	-0.2	7.4	8.9	5.9	6.3	2.6	DGT
▲REPUBLIC RRG	SC	**C-**	2.4	2.2	0.2	0.0	10.0	6.0	7.4	9.3	1.8	DGT
REPUBLIC UNDERWRITERS INS CO	TX	**B-**	694.4	242.3	409.8	4.4	7.4	5.9	4.7	6.1	4.5	FT
REPUBLIC VANGUARD INS CO	AZ	**B-**	22.1	21.6	0.0	0.3	10.0	N/A	7.4	10.0	4.5	DG
▲REPUBLIC WESTERN INS CO	AZ	**C-**	232.2	106.6	27.4	1.4	3.6	1.8	5.2	9.1	2.9	FRT
REPUBLIC-FRANKLIN INS CO	OH	**C+**	84.2	37.1	18.2	0.5	9.7	6.2	7.8	7.0	4.3	T
▲RESIDENCE MUTUAL INS CO	CA	**C**	69.1	43.4	27.3	1.4	7.6	8.8	8.8	6.6	2.7	RT
RESIDENTIAL INS CO	AZ	**D+**	8.5	5.6	0.3	-0.2	10.0	6.0	5.7	10.0	2.4	DGT
RESIDENTIAL INS CO INC RRG	HI	**C-**	3.2	1.5	0.1	0.0	8.8	6.2	1.7	7.2	1.5	DFGT
RESPONSE INDEMNITY CO	NY	**U** (1)	4.1	3.8	0.0	0.1	N/A	6.5	1.9	10.0	3.1	FT
RESPONSE INDEMNITY CO OF CA	CA	**C-**	7.9	6.3	1.9	0.1	10.0	6.2	4.6	6.9	2.7	DGT
RESPONSE INS CO	CT	**C**	80.3	47.8	22.8	-1.4	7.2	7.3	2.5	6.9	3.5	T
RESPONSE WORLDWIDE DIRECT AUTO INS	CT	**C**	45.5	9.2	33.5	-1.6	2.5	8.1	1.3	2.9	3.9	CDFG
RESPONSE WORLDWIDE INS CO	CT	**C**	86.3	17.9	67.0	-3.7	3.2	8.7	1.1	2.6	3.4	CDFG
RESTORATION RRG INC	AZ	**C-**	25.9	10.0	8.4	0.9	5.2	4.9	9.6	9.1	2.9	CDGR
RETAILERS MUTUAL INS CO	MI	**D-**	14.1	8.3	2.5	-0.2	7.9	3.8	3.4	9.1	1.0	DGT
RICHPORT INS CO	PR	**U** (1)	2.5	2.4	0.0	0.1	N/A	N/A	6.7	7.0	0.0	T
RIDER INS CO	NJ	**C**	39.7	19.7	25.1	-1.0	7.4	4.9	5.2	5.8	4.2	DGT
RISK MGMT INDEMNITY INC	DE	**U** (5)	0.0	5.3	4.8	0.0	N/A	6.0	6.2	8.9	3.4	DT
RIVERPORT INS CO	MN	**C+**	84.7	39.7	9.2	0.7	5.6	5.2	8.8	7.6	4.8	CT
▲RLI INDEMNITY CO	IL	**B-**	41.0	38.7	0.4	0.3	10.0	4.6	8.1	10.0	3.9	ADFG
RLI INS CO	IL	**B**	1,266.2	663.1	274.4	-11.4	7.3	8.0	4.7	7.0	5.4	AT
ROAD CONTRACTORS MUTUAL INS CO	TN	**C-**	11.1	3.5	2.7	-0.1	5.7	3.6	4.4	6.8	2.0	DFGT
ROCHDALE INS CO OF NEW YORK NY	NY	**D**	174.9	30.2	41.3	1.5	4.4	6.5	8.8	6.8	2.3	T
ROCHE SURETY & CASUALTY INC	FL	**D+**	16.8	6.6	2.3	0.1	9.1	4.6	8.6	9.2	2.5	DGT
ROCKFORD MUTUAL INS CO	IL	**C**	63.8	29.5	34.1	0.8	6.4	7.0	8.3	6.1	3.9	T

See Page 27 for explanation of footnotes and Page 28 for explanation of stability factors.
Arrows denote recent upgrades ▲ or downgrades ▼ (see Section VII for explanations)

RISK ADJ. RATIO #1	CAPITAL RATIO #2	PREMIUM TO SURPLUS (%)	RESV. TO SURPLUS (%)	RESV. DEVELOP. 1 YEAR (%)	RESV. DEVELOP. 2 YEAR (%)	LOSS RATIO (%)	EXP. RATIO (%)	COMB RATIO (%)	CASH FROM UNDER-WRITING (%)	NET PREMIUM GROWTH (%)	INVEST. IN AFFIL (%)	INSURANCE COMPANY NAME
0.4	0.3	6.9	479.7	-8.5	-0.8	804.2	-222.6	581.6	13.4	-92.5	0.0	RADIAN INS INC
2.0	1.4	4.1	63.4	-11.5	-15.4	215.0	17.8	232.8	57.6	0.0	0.0	RADIAN MORTGAGE INS INC
3.1	1.9	25.5	30.1	-1.8	2.5	29.3	46.1	75.4	123.1	-26.6	0.0	RAINIER INS CO
3.5	2.3	80.9	59.1	-6.3	-9.6	73.3	32.2	105.5	95.8	-1.1	0.0	RAM MUTUAL INS CO
N/A	N/A	N/A	172.9	20.4	30.5	999 +	999 +	999 +	-1.5	-125.0	0.0	RAMPART INS CO
2.3	1.6	54.9	12.8	-0.2	1.1	97.4	53.9	151.3	85.4	-24.1	0.0	RANCHERS & FARMERS INS CO
1.0	0.9	25.7	10.7	4.8	26.1	67.0	-36.1	30.9	112.3	-42.9	0.0	RANCHERS & FARMERS MUTUAL INS CO
3.8	2.5	65.2	52.1	1.1	-3.4	43.4	56.1	99.5	102.8	0.0	1.4	REAL LEGACY ASR CO INC
1.8	1.4	167.2	35.5	-3.9	-5.7	57.5	38.0	95.5	102.5	-2.0	0.0	REAMSTOWN MUTUAL INS CO
2.1	1.3	46.1	39.2	-0.7	3.0	35.3	52.6	87.9	119.0	6.7	0.0	RED SHIELD INS CO
N/A	N/A	N/A	N/A	N/A	N/A	N/A	N/A	N/A	N/A	0.0	0.0	RED VIKING INS CO
1.6	0.9	65.9	87.1	-8.9	-13.9	49.6	42.8	92.4	57.7	5.7	0.0	REDLAND INS CO
2.5	1.3	32.5	123.8	-6.5	-15.7	60.6	29.8	90.4	87.7	-49.3	0.0 •	REDWOOD FIRE & CAS INS CO
3.2	2.2	128.5	148.9	-16.0	-11.3	52.3	33.8	86.1	73.1	-30.1	0.0	REGENT INS CO
0.4	0.3	15.0	368.6	-2.6	-19.5	52.3	255.4	307.7	-63.8	-42.9	0.0	REGIONAL HEALTH INS CO RRG
1.0	0.7	72.8	77.5	-6.3	-19.1	51.2	48.9	100.1	101.9	14.2	0.0	REGIS INS CO
0.4	0.3	77.1	155.4	19.8	24.8	84.7	68.8	153.5	47.8	-84.3	39.4	REINSURANCE CO OF AMERICA INC
7.7	7.0	N/A	N/A	N/A	N/A	N/A	N/A	N/A	128.1	-100.0	0.0	RELIABLE LLOYDS INS CO
0.3	0.2	263.2	137.8	60.4	0.5	67.3	34.5	101.8	123.4	39.0	24.7	RELIAMAX INS CO
37.4	33.6	N/A	N/A	N/A	N/A	N/A	N/A	N/A	-79.4	0.0	0.0	REPUBLIC FIRE & CASUALTY INS CO
2.1	1.4	70.6	184.1	-8.6	-19.7	47.0	33.5	80.5	109.5	-8.6	3.0 •	REPUBLIC INDEMNITY CO OF AMERICA
3.7	2.4	26.8	69.9	-3.8	-9.5	47.0	33.5	80.5	108.3	-8.6	0.0	REPUBLIC INDEMNITY OF CA
26.1	23.4	N/A	N/A	N/A	N/A	N/A	N/A	N/A	-33.0	0.0	0.0	REPUBLIC LLOYDS
0.2	0.2	495.9	999 +	-11.9	57.6	191.0	12.1	203.1	113.1	20.5	0.0	REPUBLIC MORTGAGE INS CO
0.7	0.5	178.1	386.2	-2.8	9.2	191.0	13.0	204.0	137.6	20.5	0.0	REPUBLIC MORTGAGE INS CO OF
0.7	0.5	118.6	336.5	-4.3	13.7	232.4	25.7	258.1	114.1	-18.5	0.0	REPUBLIC MORTGAGE INS CO OF NC
2.1	1.3	134.8	55.3	-6.5	-10.5	64.3	34.2	98.5	100.5	-0.6	0.0	REPUBLIC MUTUAL INS CO
9.7	5.5	9.2	4.5	-3.5	-23.0	-13.8	55.0	41.2	147.1	-50.0	0.0	REPUBLIC RRG
1.8	1.3	174.0	76.3	-1.6	-8.3	70.0	42.2	112.2	90.9	-1.3	13.4 •	REPUBLIC UNDERWRITERS INS CO
99.6	53.5	N/A	N/A	N/A	N/A	N/A	N/A	N/A	N/A	0.0	0.0	REPUBLIC VANGUARD INS CO
0.9	0.6	26.4	109.9	5.1	12.4	66.3	42.7	109.0	57.1	-3.3	1.4	REPUBLIC WESTERN INS CO
4.7	3.0	49.1	92.0	-0.9	-2.3	61.7	34.7	96.4	99.3	0.2	0.0	REPUBLIC-FRANKLIN INS CO
2.7	1.9	64.4	22.1	-5.5	-12.8	50.4	33.4	83.8	115.2	0.2	8.1	RESIDENCE MUTUAL INS CO
5.7	5.0	4.9	13.6	0.6	1.0	229.4	4.7	234.1	243.2	-13.2	0.0	RESIDENTIAL INS CO
2.4	2.2	4.9	22.7	-0.9	-0.1	-367.3	170.7	-196.6	9.5	-30.6	0.0	RESIDENTIAL INS CO INC RRG
N/A	N/A	N/A	4.9	N/A	0.2	N/A	N/A	N/A	N/A	0.0	0.0	RESPONSE INDEMNITY CO
4.4	3.5	30.3	16.5	-0.9	-2.1	86.2	25.6	111.8	103.8	22.4	0.0	RESPONSE INDEMNITY CO OF CA
1.1	1.1	43.2	26.1	0.9	-0.6	83.9	31.5	115.4	105.7	5.8	63.7	RESPONSE INS CO
0.4	0.3	316.9	191.5	6.1	-4.2	83.9	31.6	115.5	87.9	5.8	0.0	RESPONSE WORLDWIDE DIRECT AUTO
0.5	0.4	316.4	191.2	5.8	-4.0	83.9	32.2	116.1	89.4	45.5	0.4	RESPONSE WORLDWIDE INS CO
1.1	0.6	91.9	117.4	-7.7	-12.1	47.2	20.8	68.0	322.0	8.3	0.0	RESTORATION RRG INC
3.9	1.5	28.8	44.7	-5.9	-5.1	68.6	36.9	105.5	102.9	-12.3	0.0	RETAILERS MUTUAL INS CO
N/A	N/A	N/A	N/A	N/A	N/A	N/A	N/A	N/A	N/A	0.0	0.0	RICHPORT INS CO
1.7	1.2	123.4	43.8	-5.0	N/A	51.4	47.6	99.0	103.9	-6.2	0.0	RIDER INS CO
N/A	N/A	90.1	165.5	7.4	14.9	103.7	5.7	109.4	118.1	3.6	0.0	RISK MGMT INDEMNITY INC
1.5	0.9	23.6	62.7	-6.0	-9.3	56.7	14.4	71.1	173.6	-6.8	0.0	RIVERPORT INS CO
49.6	38.0	1.2	1.1	-0.4	-0.5	20.8	46.5	67.3	-154.3	-20.6	0.0	RLI INDEMNITY CO
1.3	1.1	40.5	51.7	-2.2	-5.4	44.4	43.4	87.8	118.5	8.3	39.6 •	RLI INS CO
1.6	0.8	74.7	82.3	2.3	N/A	93.3	13.0	106.3	94.3	-10.0	0.0	ROAD CONTRACTORS MUTUAL INS CO
1.3	0.7	134.5	125.3	-20.3	-16.0	56.1	20.4	76.5	103.8	1.6	0.0	ROCHDALE INS CO OF NEW YORK NY
2.7	2.4	35.6	N/A	N/A	N/A	N/A	68.3	68.3	146.9	-2.8	0.0	ROCHE SURETY & CASUALTY INC
1.7	1.0	106.4	46.2	-5.0	-7.0	54.8	34.8	89.6	102.5	3.0	0.3	ROCKFORD MUTUAL INS CO

999 + Denotes number greater than 999.9%
999 - Denotes number less than -999.99%
• Bullets denote a more detailed analysis is available in Section II.

INSURANCE COMPANY NAME	DOM. STATE	RATING	TOTAL ASSETS ($MIL)	CAPITAL & SURPLUS ($MIL)	ANNUAL NET PREMIUM ($MIL)	NET INCOME ($MIL)	CAPITAL-IZATION INDEX (PTS)	RESERVE ADQ INDEX (PTS)	PROFIT-ABILITY INDEX (PTS)	LIQUIDITY INDEX (PTS)	STAB. INDEX (PTS)	STABILITY FACTORS
ROCKHILL INS CO	AZ	**C**	206.4	73.2	46.1	-6.7	5.0	6.0	2.3	8.9	2.1	DT
ROCKINGHAM CASUALTY CO	VA	**C**	42.0	22.4	13.9	0.4	9.8	7.0	8.8	6.7	3.9	DFGT
ROCKINGHAM MUTUAL INS CO	VA	**C**	57.8	41.6	17.8	0.3	7.6	6.6	7.8	6.8	4.3	DT
ROCKWOOD CASUALTY INS CO	PA	**C-**	256.8	91.3	46.5	1.9	6.7	7.0	7.5	7.3	3.2	T
ROCKY MOUNTAIN FIRE & CAS CO	WA	**C**	25.5	14.4	12.5	0.5	9.9	6.9	3.4	6.6	3.9	DGT
ROYAL PALM INS CO	FL	**E+**	180.2	55.1	104.8	3.3	5.3	3.6	1.0	6.4	0.7	FT
RSUI INDEMNITY CO	NH	**C**	2,480.2	984.4	610.7	18.0	7.5	6.3	6.1	7.0	3.5	T
▲RURAL COMMUNITY INS CO	MN	**B-**	856.9	339.5	318.6	19.4	7.1	10.0	8.9	1.8	4.9	FGLT
RURAL MUTUAL INS CO	WI	**C+**	259.6	111.5	118.0	2.8	10.0	7.0	8.8	6.4	4.5	T
RUTGERS CASUALTY INS CO	NJ	**D+**	52.6	14.4	12.9	-0.4	5.1	2.5	1.5	7.2	2.7	DFT
RUTGERS ENHANCED INS CO	NJ	**U** (1)	3.7	3.7	0.0	0.5	N/A	1.5	4.0	1.3	2.3	FLT
▲RVI AMERICA INS CO	CT	**B-**	54.4	29.5	4.2	0.9	10.0	5.8	6.7	6.8	5.0	FGT
RVI NATIONAL INS CO	CT	**D+**	13.6	12.8	0.1	0.1	10.0	3.6	3.7	10.0	2.4	DFGT
RVOS FARM MUTUAL INS CO	TX	**C+**	73.1	35.0	40.1	0.0	7.3	6.2	2.0	4.9	4.3	FLRT
SAFE AUTO INS CO	OH	**C**	442.1	151.4	321.5	-3.3	7.5	6.0	5.2	4.9	4.2	LT
▲SAFE HARBOR INS CO	FL	**D+**	15.6	8.0	6.4	0.2	7.5	3.7	7.3	8.3	2.4	DGT
SAFE INS CO	WV	**D-**	6.6	4.2	2.9	0.1	9.2	9.3	8.7	7.1	1.0	DGT
SAFECARD SERVICE INS CO	ND	**D** (1)	2.1	1.9	0.2	0.2	10.0	7.6	8.4	10.0	1.6	DT
SAFECO INS CO OF AMERICA	WA	**B-**	7,272.4	955.7	1,762.5	20.1	7.5	6.9	3.0	5.7	4.9	AT
SAFECO INS CO OF ILLINOIS	IL	**B**	1,767.4	155.0	267.0	2.3	7.7	6.9	3.7	6.7	5.6	AT
SAFECO INS CO OF INDIANA	IN	**B-**	140.5	13.1	0.0	0.1	10.0	N/A	7.8	6.7	4.8	DFG
SAFECO INS CO OF OREGON	OR	**B**	205.9	7.9	0.0	0.1	9.3	N/A	8.0	7.0	4.1	DG
SAFECO LLOYDS INS CO	TX	**B**	103.6	10.5	0.0	0.1	10.0	N/A	8.2	7.0	4.5	DFG
SAFECO NATIONAL INS CO	MO	**B**	188.1	57.2	106.8	0.1	7.8	6.9	3.0	6.3	5.4	AT
SAFECO SURPLUS LINES INS CO	WA	**B**	46.0	30.6	0.0	0.2	10.0	N/A	8.0	7.0	5.4	DFG
SAFETY FIRST INS CO	IL	**C**	15.8	12.5	0.9	0.0	10.0	6.2	5.0	9.7	4.0	DGT
SAFETY INDEMNITY INS CO	MA	**B-**	93.9	39.8	38.7	0.8	9.0	7.0	8.9	7.2	4.7	T
SAFETY INS CO	MA	**B+**	1,190.4	550.8	497.6	10.7	10.0	7.0	8.7	6.7	5.0	T
SAFETY NATIONAL CASUALTY CORP	MO	**C**	1,969.0	529.8	302.0	-1.9	5.2	1.5	6.7	7.0	4.3	ACRT
SAFETY PROPERTY & CASUALTY INS CO	MA	**C**	33.7	12.9	16.6	0.3	7.8	4.0	8.8	6.6	2.3	DFGT
SAFEWAY DIRECT INS CO	CA	**C**	15.0	8.9	7.8	0.1	7.2	6.1	8.6	6.2	2.8	DGT
SAFEWAY INS CO	IL	**B-**	334.5	243.3	141.1	1.5	7.8	4.9	5.7	6.6	4.5	T
SAFEWAY INS CO OF AL	IL	**C+**	51.1	28.5	31.3	0.1	7.9	6.0	6.4	6.6	4.3	T
SAFEWAY INS CO OF GEORGIA	GA	**C**	53.1	29.7	31.3	0.1	8.0	6.4	7.6	6.6	4.0	T
SAFEWAY INS CO OF LA	LA	**C+**	92.8	52.3	49.6	0.3	8.8	8.0	8.6	6.7	4.5	T
SAFEWAY PROPERTY INS CO	NE	**C**	34.9	18.9	14.1	0.8	6.0	7.4	3.9	7.7	3.7	DGT
SAGAMORE INS CO	IN	**B**	148.6	109.4	25.1	0.9	10.0	7.8	8.4	7.7	4.7	T
SAIF CORP	OR	**U** (5)	3,879.9	871.8	252.9	0.0	N/A	9.9	4.0	7.3	3.5	
SAINT LUKES HEALTH SYSTEM RRG	SC	**D**	14.6	7.8	3.3	0.2	7.7	9.5	9.5	7.0	1.6	DGT
SALEM COUNTY MUTUAL FIRE INS CO	NJ	**U** (1)	2.2	2.2	0.0	0.0	N/A	N/A	2.8	10.0	2.9	T
▲SAMARITAN RRG INC	SC	**D**	14.5	5.7	4.6	-0.1	6.1	3.7	4.0	8.0	1.4	DGT
▲SAMSUNG FIRE & MARINE INS CO LTD US	NY	**B+**	69.7	36.1	13.5	0.2	8.0	9.5	8.1	7.0	5.7	DT
SAN ANTONIO INDEMNITY CO	TX	**D+**	2.8	2.1	0.8	0.1	8.7	5.6	2.1	5.8	1.7	DFGT
SAN DIEGO INS CO	CA	**U** (1)	75.1	59.2	0.0	2.0	N/A	N/A	6.1	7.0	0.0	T
SAN FRANCISCO REINSURANCE CO	CA	**U** (1)	107.8	91.7	0.0	14.1	N/A	6.9	3.9	9.5	6.4	T
SANILAC MUTUAL INS CO	MI	**D** (1)	1.1	0.8	0.4	-0.1	7.2	6.4	2.1	7.2	1.3	DFT
SANTA FE AUTO INS CO	TX	**D+**	20.5	12.8	30.0	0.8	1.9	3.6	5.5	0.2	2.5	CDFG
SAUCON MUTUAL INS CO	PA	**U** (1)	14.1	11.2	-0.1	0.0	N/A	5.0	3.1	10.0	4.3	T
SAUQUOIT VALLEY INS CO	NY	**C-**	3.5	2.8	0.7	0.0	8.3	8.0	3.3	7.7	1.9	DGRT
SAVERS PROPERTY & CASUALTY INS CO	MO	**C**	179.2	44.1	66.9	2.4	6.9	5.6	6.9	6.7	3.6	T
▲SCAFFOLD INDUSTRY INS CO RRG INC	DC	**E+**	3.3	0.5	0.2	0.0	0.9	3.7	2.0	1.4	0.5	CDFG
SCF PREMIER INS CO	AZ	**C**	15.1	6.4	3.0	0.1	6.4	3.6	4.7	9.3	2.7	DGT

See Page 27 for explanation of footnotes and Page 28 for explanation of stability factors.

Arrows denote recent upgrades ▲ or downgrades ▼ (see Section VII for explanations)

RISK ADJ. RATIO #1	CAPITAL RATIO #2	PREMIUM TO SURPLUS (%)	RESV. TO SURPLUS (%)	RESV. DEVELOP. 1 YEAR (%)	RESV. DEVELOP. 2 YEAR (%)	LOSS RATIO (%)	EXP. RATIO (%)	COMB RATIO (%)	CASH FROM UNDER-WRITING (%)	NET PREMIUM GROWTH (%)	INVEST. IN AFFIL (%)	INSURANCE COMPANY NAME
1.0	0.7	61.7	92.1	-2.2	-3.1	73.9	39.8	113.7	463.7	15.8	17.2	ROCKHILL INS CO
4.5	3.6	63.1	47.4	-13.4	-19.3	65.6	29.9	95.5	94.9	-3.6	0.0	ROCKINGHAM CASUALTY CO
1.6	1.4	41.5	10.3	-3.5	-4.8	52.1	37.1	89.2	105.6	-0.1	40.3	ROCKINGHAM MUTUAL INS CO
2.3	1.3	51.6	134.4	-14.8	-25.5	41.6	32.7	74.3	109.4	-23.0	4.5	ROCKWOOD CASUALTY INS CO
4.0	3.2	89.9	43.0	-3.5	-10.4	62.3	26.7	89.0	98.4	-10.0	0.0	ROCKY MOUNTAIN FIRE & CAS CO
1.3	0.8	213.7	71.9	-4.4	-0.2	62.3	45.1	107.4	81.9	-19.7	0.0	ROYAL PALM INS CO
2.5	1.4	61.0	109.5	-8.2	-9.5	54.4	26.9	81.3	157.3	-9.2	7.5 •	RSUI INDEMNITY CO
6.4	4.6	98.8	35.1	-126.7	-121.9	97.7	1.1	98.8	47.8	-55.3	0.0 •	RURAL COMMUNITY INS CO
5.1	3.6	108.0	68.6	-4.3	-4.8	68.4	26.8	95.2	106.9	2.7	0.0	RURAL MUTUAL INS CO
1.1	0.7	85.0	178.6	3.8	2.4	67.7	82.2	149.9	82.8	-43.9	8.8	RUTGERS CASUALTY INS CO
N/A	N/A	-1.0	N/A	N/A	N/A	N/A	526.3	N/A	-0.3	-106.0	0.0	RUTGERS ENHANCED INS CO
7.5	6.5	14.5	7.4	-23.8	-20.2	48.9	68.3	117.2	2.8	-25.2	0.0	RVI AMERICA INS CO
7.5	7.0	0.6	1.4	N/A	N/A	999 +	734.5	999 +	7.3	N/A	0.0	RVI NATIONAL INS CO
1.3	1.1	106.5	12.0	-0.8	-1.0	91.3	43.6	134.9	77.8	-7.9	23.6	RVOS FARM MUTUAL INS CO
1.6	1.4	209.5	97.2	-6.9	-23.6	66.2	32.0	98.2	92.8	3.1	0.0	SAFE AUTO INS CO
2.2	1.5	82.0	7.6	-5.9	-1.8	36.5	43.2	79.7	135.0	-8.8	0.0	SAFE HARBOR INS CO
4.0	2.9	69.0	23.8	-4.7	-9.2	41.5	41.1	82.6	126.2	0.2	0.0	SAFE INS CO
20.9	19.7	8.3	0.5	-0.3	-1.0	N/A	14.4	14.4	695.7	0.0	0.0	SAFECARD SERVICE INS CO
2.1	1.4	228.9	205.0	-6.1	-6.4	67.0	31.2	98.2	105.3	-5.6	3.2 •	SAFECO INS CO OF AMERICA
1.7	1.0	167.3	149.8	-4.2	-5.9	67.0	31.2	98.2	102.7	-5.6	7.1 •	SAFECO INS CO OF ILLINOIS
1.4	0.7	N/A	N/A	N/A	N/A	N/A	N/A	N/A	14.5	0.0	0.0	SAFECO INS CO OF INDIANA
0.5	0.2	N/A	N/A	N/A	N/A	N/A	N/A	N/A	18.0	0.0	0.0	SAFECO INS CO OF OREGON
1.2	0.8	N/A	N/A	N/A	N/A	N/A	N/A	N/A	999 +	0.0	0.0	SAFECO LLOYDS INS CO
4.3	2.9	186.9	167.3	-3.2	-4.8	67.0	31.2	98.2	102.8	-5.6	0.0	SAFECO NATIONAL INS CO
10.1	9.1	N/A	N/A	N/A	N/A	N/A	N/A	N/A	999 +	0.0	0.0	SAFECO SURPLUS LINES INS CO
10.8	5.5	7.5	10.4	-0.1	-0.5	26.8	64.6	91.4	81.7	-2.4	0.0	SAFETY FIRST INS CO
3.8	3.0	98.5	69.7	-6.7	-13.0	64.1	27.8	91.9	100.2	-19.4	0.0	SAFETY INDEMNITY INS CO
4.5	3.7	88.8	62.8	-5.8	-10.6	64.1	27.3	91.4	106.1	-5.3	5.1 •	SAFETY INS CO
1.1	0.7	56.9	228.9	5.4	21.8	75.0	27.2	102.2	185.4	-0.6	3.1 •	SAFETY NATIONAL CASUALTY CORP
2.4	1.9	131.0	92.6	-9.0	-17.8	64.1	30.6	94.7	90.4	-38.6	0.0	SAFETY PROPERTY & CASUALTY INS CO
1.3	1.1	88.5	36.0	-1.1	-1.9	73.6	23.7	97.3	100.5	4.4	0.0	SAFEWAY DIRECT INS CO
1.6	1.5	57.8	23.5	-0.6	-1.0	73.5	22.8	96.3	97.5	4.6	45.9 •	SAFEWAY INS CO
1.9	1.6	110.6	44.9	-1.3	-2.1	73.6	26.5	100.1	97.0	4.4	0.0	SAFEWAY INS CO OF AL
2.0	1.6	106.0	43.1	-1.2	-2.0	73.6	25.7	99.3	98.2	4.4	0.0	SAFEWAY INS CO OF GEORGIA
2.6	2.1	95.9	39.0	-1.1	-1.9	73.6	21.8	95.4	97.4	4.4	0.0	SAFEWAY INS CO OF LA
1.6	1.1	78.7	7.4	-1.7	-1.1	25.4	38.9	64.3	141.9	44.3	0.0	SAFEWAY PROPERTY INS CO
16.7	12.1	22.9	16.6	-1.4	-1.7	64.9	38.9	103.8	82.2	-27.3	0.0	SAGAMORE INS CO
N/A	N/A	64.5	435.2	-12.7	-21.6	148.2	21.0	169.2	108.5	-0.9	0.0	SAIF CORP
4.0	2.5	43.3	52.5	-27.0	-10.7	9.9	21.5	31.4	125.0	-9.3	0.0	SAINT LUKES HEALTH SYSTEM RRG
N/A	N/A	N/A	N/A	N/A	N/A	N/A	999 +	999 +	1.5	0.0	0.0	SALEM COUNTY MUTUAL FIRE INS CO
1.5	1.0	77.3	68.9	-24.7	-2.6	62.0	11.5	73.5	273.6	6.2	0.0	SAMARITAN RRG INC
2.6	1.6	37.3	53.1	-7.5	-16.1	54.0	21.8	75.8	122.6	-14.6	0.0 •	SAMSUNG FIRE & MARINE INS CO LTD US
2.7	2.3	41.8	6.5	0.3	4.8	104.5	51.4	155.9	62.1	-24.4	0.0	SAN ANTONIO INDEMNITY CO
N/A	N/A	N/A	N/A	N/A	N/A	N/A	N/A	N/A	N/A	0.0	0.0	SAN DIEGO INS CO
N/A	N/A	N/A	9.7	-19.8	-19.4	N/A	N/A	N/A	N/A	0.0	0.0	SAN FRANCISCO REINSURANCE CO
1.2	1.1	55.8	9.0	-6.9	-11.1	81.2	48.7	129.9	73.6	3.6	0.0	SANILAC MUTUAL INS CO
0.5	0.4	250.9	25.4	4.3	N/A	62.9	50.3	113.2	97.9	18.0	0.0	SANTA FE AUTO INS CO
N/A	N/A	-0.7	0.1	-0.2	-0.1	-50.0	-605.1	-655.1	-13.2	-6.8	0.0	SAUCON MUTUAL INS CO
2.8	1.7	23.2	7.4	-1.6	-3.4	81.9	26.8	108.7	95.9	-5.2	0.0	SAUQUOIT VALLEY INS CO
1.9	1.1	156.6	194.1	-5.4	-8.4	62.0	30.3	92.3	128.1	8.5	0.0	SAVERS PROPERTY & CASUALTY INS CO
0.3	0.2	33.2	360.7	-13.3	-2.1	23.7	354.0	377.7	47.1	-69.6	0.0	SCAFFOLD INDUSTRY INS CO RRG INC
1.5	0.9	47.8	23.8	-0.2	N/A	153.9	-28.5	125.4	266.5	N/A	0.0	SCF PREMIER INS CO

999 + Denotes number greater than 999.9%
999 - Denotes number less than -999.99%
• Bullets denote a more detailed analysis is available in Section II.

INSURANCE COMPANY NAME	DOM. STATE	RATING	TOTAL ASSETS ($MIL)	CAPITAL & SURPLUS ($MIL)	ANNUAL NET PREMIUM ($MIL)	NET INCOME ($MIL)	CAPITAL-IZATION INDEX (PTS)	RESERVE ADQ INDEX (PTS)	PROFIT-ABILITY INDEX (PTS)	LIQUIDITY INDEX (PTS)	STAB. INDEX (PTS)	STABILITY FACTORS
▲SCHOOL BOARDS INS CO OF PA INC	PA	**E+**	200.9	56.1	79.2	0.3	3.8	3.6	5.9	5.8	0.5	T
SCHUYLKILL CROSSING RECIPROCAL RRG	VT	**E+**	25.1	3.2	4.4	0.1	0.3	6.0	1.1	9.1	0.1	CDFG
SCOR REINSURANCE CO	NY	**D**	1,450.6	514.5	388.5	8.6	4.1	3.5	3.9	7.8	1.4	FGRT
SCOTTSDALE INDEMNITY CO	OH	**B**	25.9	18.4	0.0	0.4	10.0	N/A	8.0	6.4	5.5	DG
SCOTTSDALE INS CO	OH	**B-**	1,727.0	537.3	610.9	12.1	8.2	6.2	7.4	5.9	4.9	T
SCOTTSDALE SURPLUS LINES INS CO	AZ	**B**	19.2	15.7	0.0	0.0	10.0	N/A	7.7	7.0	5.0	DGT
SCPIE INDEMNITY COMPANY	CA	**C**	478.4	204.3	58.9	3.9	7.6	7.0	6.8	7.4	3.0	FT
SCRUBS MUTUAL ASR CO RRG	NV	**D**	5.1	3.7	1.4	0.0	9.0	3.6	3.8	7.3	1.2	DGT
SEABRIGHT INS CO	IL	**D+**	767.4	276.4	256.6	1.2	4.3	4.9	6.8	6.4	2.0	T
SEATON INS CO	RI	**U** (1)	77.1	3.3	0.0	-21.3	N/A	0.3	0.5	0.6	0.0	CFLR
SEAWORTHY INS CO	MD	**C**	48.3	30.0	23.4	1.4	8.1	6.9	8.6	7.6	4.3	FT
SECURA INS A MUTUAL CO	WI	**B-**	600.5	203.2	268.9	-1.3	8.3	6.9	5.4	6.3	4.7	T
▲SECURA SUPREME INS CO	WI	**C+**	82.8	32.9	29.9	0.0	8.6	6.9	8.3	6.6	4.3	T
SECURIAN CASUALTY CO	MN	**B**	66.3	47.2	21.1	-0.4	9.1	6.2	4.1	6.9	4.2	DGT
SECURITY AMERICA RRG INC	VT	**D-**	5.0	2.2	1.6	0.0	4.7	7.0	4.6	8.0	0.0	DGT
SECURITY FIRST INS CO	FL	**C-**	43.2	20.9	12.9	0.4	7.1	4.8	2.9	6.4	2.7	DFGR
SECURITY MUTUAL INS CO	NY	**C**	73.5	29.3	31.0	0.7	7.9	4.5	6.7	6.8	3.9	T
SECURITY NATIONAL INS CO	TX	**B-**	43.7	15.4	2.7	0.0	10.0	N/A	4.0	10.0	5.1	DFGT
SECURITY NATIONAL INS CO	FL	**D+**	135.0	28.2	19.0	1.0	7.2	1.7	4.1	6.7	2.5	GT
SECURITY PLAN FIRE INS CO	LA	**D**	7.1	3.8	4.5	-0.3	1.7	3.0	1.3	1.7	1.8	CDFG
SELECT INS CO	TX	**U** (1)	67.9	66.9	0.0	2.3	N/A	0.5	8.0	7.0	0.8	T
SELECT MARKETS INS CO	IL	**D+**	14.0	11.4	0.0	0.1	10.0	4.6	6.9	7.1	2.0	DGT
SELECT RISK INS CO	PA	**B-**	35.3	8.5	13.9	-0.8	7.5	6.8	3.2	6.5	4.3	DGT
▲SELECTIVE AUTO INS CO OF NJ	NJ	**C+**	275.8	58.3	90.3	1.4	7.4	4.9	7.1	6.7	4.1	T
SELECTIVE INS CO OF AMERICA	NJ	**B**	2,215.7	421.1	745.3	-13.7	7.2	6.0	3.7	6.5	5.6	AT
▲SELECTIVE INS CO OF NEW ENGLAND	ME	**D**	29.8	12.6	7.5	-0.3	8.3	5.3	5.5	7.6	1.4	DGT
▲SELECTIVE INS CO OF NEW YORK	NY	**B**	306.1	63.7	105.4	1.0	7.3	6.0	6.6	6.6	5.4	AT
SELECTIVE INS CO OF SC	IN	**B-**	427.7	79.8	135.5	2.8	7.2	6.1	5.0	6.6	5.2	AT
SELECTIVE INS CO OF THE SOUTHEAST	IN	**B-**	321.5	59.7	105.4	-0.2	7.3	5.9	5.6	6.7	5.3	AT
SELECTIVE WAY INS CO	NJ	**B**	932.9	172.6	316.2	-4.0	6.8	6.0	3.6	6.3	5.5	AT
SEMINOLE CASUALTY INS CO	FL	**D**	54.8	9.1	32.2	-0.8	2.9	3.1	2.4	5.3	1.4	DFGR
SENECA INS CO INC	NY	**C**	329.3	146.7	98.1	1.8	8.9	9.5	8.9	8.5	3.5	T
SENECA SPECIALTY INS CO	AZ	**D**	27.3	24.8	2.1	-0.2	10.0	5.2	4.6	9.8	2.2	DGT
SENTINEL ASR RRG INC	HI	**D-**	13.4	7.3	4.4	0.2	8.6	6.1	9.6	6.9	1.1	DGT
SENTINEL INS CO LTD	CT	**B**	201.4	128.1	30.6	0.1	10.0	4.9	1.9	7.8	5.3	T
SENTRUITY CASUALTY CO	TX	**C**	23.1	14.8	2.2	0.2	10.0	N/A	2.6	10.0	2.7	DGT
SENTRY CASUALTY CO	WI	**B**	168.6	59.4	44.7	0.3	9.8	5.9	6.7	6.7	4.7	FRT
SENTRY INS A MUTUAL CO	WI	**A**	5,330.6	2,720.0	982.4	-113.5	7.9	8.3	4.7	6.9	7.5	T
SENTRY LLOYDS OF TX	TX	**B**	5.6	5.5	0.0	0.1	10.0	N/A	8.3	10.0	4.9	DG
SENTRY SELECT INS CO	WI	**B**	676.3	225.2	178.6	0.5	9.4	9.3	6.7	6.8	6.2	T
▲SEQUOIA INDEMNITY CO	NV	**C**	15.0	7.6	1.7	0.0	9.1	3.7	6.6	7.0	2.6	DGT
SEQUOIA INS CO	CA	**C+**	178.9	72.3	81.6	2.3	7.3	4.8	7.0	6.4	4.1	T
SERVICE INS CO	FL	**C**	19.2	14.2	3.0	-0.1	7.5	4.3	2.9	8.0	3.5	DGRT
SERVICE INS CO INC	NJ	**D-**	9.1	4.1	1.4	0.2	8.6	3.7	8.7	10.0	1.1	DGT
▲SERVICE LLOYDS INS CO	TX	**B-**	259.5	86.2	87.0	2.9	8.1	9.5	7.7	6.8	4.6	T
SEVEN SEAS INS CO INC	FL	**C**	16.3	12.6	19.3	1.5	7.2	6.4	9.3	7.3	3.1	DGRT
SFM MUTUAL INS CO	MN	**C**	351.8	71.9	101.8	1.6	4.8	3.8	7.8	6.3	4.0	CT
SFM SELECT INS CO	SD	**D-**	5.4	3.2	0.0	0.0	10.0	3.6	6.8	10.0	1.3	DGT
SHAMOKIN TOWNSHIP MUTUAL FIRE INS CO	PA	**U** (1)	0.1	0.1	0.0	0.0	N/A	3.7	2.9	10.0	0.5	FT
SHARED SERVICE INS GROUP INC	PA	**D**	2.7	1.1	1.8	-0.3	2.9	3.6	1.3	2.1	1.1	DFGL
SHEBOYGAN FALLS INS CO	WI	**C**	20.5	11.4	7.9	0.3	9.0	6.3	5.6	7.3	4.0	DFGT
SHEFFIELD INS CO	TN	**C-**	13.1	4.4	6.1	0.1	2.0	4.9	6.0	7.5	2.0	CDGT

See Page 27 for explanation of footnotes and Page 28 for explanation of stability factors.

Arrows denote recent upgrades ▲ or downgrades ▼ (see Section VII for explanations)

RISK ADJ. RATIO #1	CAPITAL RATIO #2	PREMIUM TO SURPLUS (%)	RESV. TO SURPLUS (%)	RESV. DEVELOP. 1 YEAR (%)	RESV. DEVELOP. 2 YEAR (%)	LOSS RATIO (%)	EXP. RATIO (%)	COMB RATIO (%)	CASH FROM UNDER-WRITING (%)	NET PREMIUM GROWTH (%)	INVEST. IN AFFIL (%)	INSURANCE COMPANY NAME
1.0	0.6	140.0	193.4	6.2	5.7	73.8	27.6	101.4	108.0	-11.7	0.0	SCHOOL BOARDS INS CO OF PA INC
0.4	0.3	308.3	983.1	8.9	-21.8	125.9	22.4	148.3	77.4	5.6	0.0	SCHUYLKILL CROSSING RECIPROCAL
1.0	0.7	77.2	132.0	-0.4	3.5	70.4	30.5	100.9	78.9	97.4	2.8 •	SCOR REINSURANCE CO
9.3	8.4	N/A	N/A	N/A	N/A	N/A	N/A	N/A	999 +	0.0	0.0	SCOTTSDALE INDEMNITY CO
2.3	1.8	117.7	78.1	0.6	-0.1	74.7	30.9	105.6	102.3	-1.7	12.4 •	SCOTTSDALE INS CO
13.9	12.5	N/A	N/A	N/A	N/A	N/A	N/A	N/A	175.0	0.0	0.0	SCOTTSDALE SURPLUS LINES INS CO
2.2	1.8	29.4	120.0	-6.2	-20.2	62.7	21.8	84.5	62.4	-10.2	15.7 •	SCPIE INDEMNITY COMPANY
6.0	3.7	36.2	2.9	0.1	N/A	54.2	14.3	68.5	999 +	N/A	0.0	SCRUBS MUTUAL ASR CO RRG
0.9	0.5	93.1	99.3	-8.4	-16.5	57.1	27.1	84.2	137.2	-2.3	0.0 •	SEABRIGHT INS CO
N/A	N/A	-0.3	999 +	74.5	70.0	999 +	999 +	999 +	N/A	N/A	0.0	SEATON INS CO
2.7	2.6	80.2	13.7	-4.2	-3.2	61.9	37.2	99.1	75.8	-25.6	0.0	SEAWORTHY INS CO
2.5	1.8	130.4	108.2	-2.0	-6.7	74.4	32.3	106.7	99.8	-3.8	6.8 •	SECURA INS A MUTUAL CO
3.2	2.3	91.3	75.8	-1.5	-6.1	74.4	30.4	104.8	95.9	-3.8	0.0	SECURA SUPREME INS CO
3.7	2.1	44.6	6.5	-1.0	-1.6	46.3	44.5	90.8	123.5	145.6	0.0	SECURIAN CASUALTY CO
1.0	0.6	74.5	61.3	-29.4	-37.2	28.7	55.8	84.5	138.4	6.0	0.0	SECURITY AMERICA RRG INC
1.9	1.3	63.6	9.9	-1.0	-11.3	70.6	44.4	115.0	96.8	215.4	0.0	SECURITY FIRST INS CO
2.2	1.7	105.5	84.6	-1.7	-1.5	61.9	37.5	99.4	107.1	0.2	0.0	SECURITY MUTUAL INS CO
3.5	3.1	17.5	6.7	N/A	N/A	122.5	4.0	126.5	999 +	0.0	0.0	SECURITY NATIONAL INS CO
1.8	1.4	75.4	49.9	10.6	50.5	80.2	12.8	93.0	116.4	73.7	0.0	SECURITY NATIONAL INS CO
0.4	0.4	143.7	20.9	1.2	-10.5	55.8	83.5	139.3	70.1	-8.5	0.0	SECURITY PLAN FIRE INS CO
N/A	N/A	N/A	N/A	N/A	N/A	N/A	N/A	N/A	N/A	0.0	0.0	SELECT INS CO
13.2	11.8	N/A	N/A	N/A	N/A	N/A	N/A	N/A	999 +	100.0	0.0	SELECT MARKETS INS CO
1.9	1.2	150.3	111.3	-5.3	-11.5	63.1	34.7	97.8	107.6	3.9	0.0	SELECT RISK INS CO
1.8	1.2	152.1	243.9	-2.2	-6.3	67.5	31.4	98.9	109.7	-4.7	0.0	SELECTIVE AUTO INS CO OF NJ
1.6	1.0	165.0	264.6	-2.0	-6.4	67.5	31.4	98.9	107.4	-4.7	0.0 •	SELECTIVE INS CO OF AMERICA
3.1	2.0	59.8	95.9	-0.8	-2.9	67.5	31.4	98.9	112.8	-4.7	0.0	SELECTIVE INS CO OF NEW ENGLAND
1.7	1.1	158.4	254.0	-2.0	-6.8	67.5	31.4	98.9	110.4	-4.7	0.0	SELECTIVE INS CO OF NEW YORK
1.7	1.0	166.0	266.3	-2.1	-6.9	67.5	31.4	98.9	112.7	-4.7	0.0	SELECTIVE INS CO OF SC
1.6	1.0	156.2	250.6	-1.9	-6.5	67.5	31.4	98.9	105.4	-4.7	0.0	SELECTIVE INS CO OF THE SOUTHEAST
1.5	1.0	194.0	311.1	-2.3	-7.2	67.5	31.3	98.8	108.1	-4.7	0.0 •	SELECTIVE WAY INS CO
0.5	0.4	315.6	107.5	10.7	16.7	75.8	33.5	109.3	81.7	-1.1	0.0	SEMINOLE CASUALTY INS CO
3.3	2.5	67.3	83.3	-12.8	-27.4	35.8	40.1	75.9	124.9	-0.5	8.3	SENECA INS CO INC
11.0	7.5	8.4	5.4	-1.1	-0.8	37.8	50.4	88.2	99.6	2.0	0.0	SENECA SPECIALTY INS CO
3.4	2.3	62.7	75.3	-44.9	-40.0	13.2	27.4	40.6	167.4	0.3	0.0	SENTINEL ASR RRG INC
12.4	7.9	24.2	40.1	-0.4	-0.6	64.1	6.1	70.2	110.9	-2.2	0.0	SENTINEL INS CO LTD
6.9	6.2	15.2	0.4	N/A	N/A	9.8	-8.8	1.0	365.5	N/A	0.0	SENTRUITY CASUALTY CO
4.1	2.8	75.6	122.1	-6.8	-14.6	74.5	26.8	101.3	90.9	-35.1	0.0	SENTRY CASUALTY CO
1.7	1.5	35.0	56.5	-2.8	-5.9	74.5	26.8	101.3	98.2	-5.6	33.8 •	SENTRY INS A MUTUAL CO
129.9	116.9	N/A	N/A	N/A	N/A	N/A	N/A	N/A	-43.3	0.0	0.0	SENTRY LLOYDS OF TX
4.1	2.7	79.5	128.4	-6.9	-15.4	74.5	26.8	101.3	95.9	-5.6	0.0 •	SENTRY SELECT INS CO
3.9	2.2	22.3	33.9	-10.0	-2.7	-11.8	31.0	19.2	-32.1	344.3	0.0	SEQUOIA INDEMNITY CO
2.1	1.4	116.4	75.7	-3.9	-10.0	54.2	40.9	95.1	99.9	-8.6	11.6	SEQUOIA INS CO
3.9	2.6	21.1	20.0	-13.0	-12.4	3.4	113.9	117.3	88.1	-50.7	0.0	SERVICE INS CO
2.6	2.3	35.6	21.3	2.2	4.2	25.9	29.9	55.8	247.4	5.9	0.0	SERVICE INS CO INC
2.9	1.8	102.5	67.1	-7.9	-14.4	39.2	50.1	89.3	115.1	-9.6	3.1	SERVICE LLOYDS INS CO
1.3	1.3	179.6	17.1	0.6	-6.6	26.1	13.7	39.8	299.1	27.9	0.0	SEVEN SEAS INS CO INC
1.1	0.7	142.1	289.5	-2.3	-2.0	81.7	20.4	102.1	111.1	-3.3	1.7	SFM MUTUAL INS CO
4.2	3.8	N/A	1.6	0.2	0.2	N/A	N/A	N/A	17.0	0.0	0.0	SFM SELECT INS CO
N/A	N/A	4.9	N/A	-2.8	-2.7	N/A	171.4	171.4	58.3	16.7	0.0	SHAMOKIN TOWNSHIP MUTUAL FIRE INS
0.5	0.4	153.9	58.1	-1.8	N/A	123.1	16.5	139.6	88.4	32.3	0.0	SHARED SERVICE INS GROUP INC
4.4	2.9	70.3	23.0	-3.2	-4.1	80.9	40.6	121.5	79.9	4.5	0.0	SHEBOYGAN FALLS INS CO
0.7	0.4	142.6	92.0	-14.6	-18.8	50.4	31.5	81.9	142.5	25.7	0.0	SHEFFIELD INS CO

999 + Denotes number greater than 999.9%
999 - Denotes number less than -999.99%
• Bullets denote a more detailed analysis is available in Section II.

INSURANCE COMPANY NAME	DOM. STATE	RATING	TOTAL ASSETS ($MIL)	CAPITAL & SURPLUS ($MIL)	ANNUAL NET PREMIUM ($MIL)	NET INCOME ($MIL)	CAPITAL-IZATION INDEX (PTS)	RESERVE ADQ INDEX (PTS)	PROFIT-ABILITY INDEX (PTS)	LIQUIDITY INDEX (PTS)	STAB. INDEX (PTS)	STABILITY FACTORS
SHELBY CASUALTY INS CO	TX	**F** (5)	0.0	0.0	0.0	0.0	10.0	8.0	2.4	2.1	0.0	DFLT
SHELBY INS CO	TX	**F** (5)	0.0	0.0	0.0	0.0	10.0	N/A	2.6	7.0	0.0	
SHELTER GENERAL INS CO	MO	**B-**	189.8	97.4	96.2	1.3	9.2	5.7	5.9	6.1	5.3	FT
SHELTER MUTUAL INS CO	MO	**B**	2,130.8	1,218.9	906.9	-22.3	7.9	8.2	5.1	5.8	5.5	FT
SHELTER REINSURANCE CO	MO	**B-**	229.9	140.8	72.7	2.4	9.2	9.3	8.8	6.8	4.3	RT
SHIELD INS CO	GA	**C**	24.8	20.4	0.0	0.0	10.0	3.7	3.6	7.4	3.8	DFG
▲SILVER OAK CASUALTY INC	LA	**C**	144.6	44.1	42.6	1.5	5.9	3.5	5.7	6.8	3.5	T
▲SIMED	PR	**D**	139.0	37.0	29.1	3.9	0.0	4.1	9.5	7.2	1.4	CRT
SLAVONIC INS CO OF TX	TX	**U** (1)	2.5	2.5	0.0	0.1	N/A	7.2	6.8	10.0	3.9	R
SLAVONIC MUTUAL FIRE INS ASN	TX	**C**	22.8	22.1	1.2	0.4	10.0	7.2	5.1	7.4	3.9	DFGT
▲SOCIETY INS	WI	**C+**	272.4	83.2	116.7	-1.7	8.0	5.0	6.0	6.4	4.4	T
SOMERSET CASUALTY INS CO	PA	**D**	24.3	11.5	4.5	0.5	5.7	5.9	8.9	7.8	2.3	DGT
SOMPO JAPAN FIRE & MAR INS CO AMER	NY	**C**	67.9	66.6	0.0	0.4	10.0	7.6	6.9	10.0	3.6	DGRT
▲SOMPO JAPAN INS CO OF AMERICA	NY	**C+**	792.8	381.2	61.5	4.0	8.5	6.0	6.6	8.7	4.5	RT
SONNENBERG MUTUAL INS ASSOC	OH	**B**	17.0	9.6	7.0	-0.2	8.9	8.7	3.9	6.8	4.4	DGT
SOPHIA PALMER NURSES RRG INC	NV	**D-**	1.3	0.5	0.6	0.0	1.7	3.6	2.1	5.7	0.0	DGT
SOUTH CAROLINA FARM BU MUTUAL INS CO	SC	**B**	111.1	60.2	48.8	-0.2	9.7	8.2	4.1	6.4	4.7	FT
SOUTHEAST EMPLOYERS MUT CAP INS CO	GA	**U** (5)	0.0	0.0	0.0	0.0	N/A	2.4	0.0	6.3	0.0	CFT
SOUTHEASTERN US INS INC	GA	**E**	42.5	1.9	21.6	-0.9	0.1	3.2	1.0	0.0	0.3	CDFG
▲SOUTHERN COUNTY MUTUAL INS CO	TX	**C**	27.6	23.1	0.0	0.0	10.0	N/A	2.9	10.0	3.5	DFGT
SOUTHERN EAGLE INS CO	FL	**D+**	31.9	10.5	10.2	0.0	5.1	5.1	5.5	3.7	2.5	CDFG
▼SOUTHERN FARM BUREAU CAS INS CO	MS	**B+**	1,807.1	1,058.7	1,318.7	2.6	8.0	8.2	4.7	5.0	5.0	FT
SOUTHERN FARM BUREAU PROPERTY	MS	**U** (1)	50.7	50.5	0.0	0.9	N/A	5.1	2.7	7.0	4.8	R
SOUTHERN FIDELITY INS CO INC	FL	**C-**	171.8	64.2	88.2	0.5	5.5	4.6	3.7	6.9	2.8	GT
▼SOUTHERN FIRE & CASUALTY CO	WI	**C+**	7.6	7.4	0.0	0.0	10.0	N/A	3.1	7.0	3.9	DGT
▼SOUTHERN GENERAL INS CO	GA	**C-**	53.5	17.6	43.6	-2.0	7.3	6.7	1.4	0.8	2.9	DFLT
SOUTHERN GENERAL UNDERWRITERS INS	GA	**C**	33.4	15.1	15.6	-0.9	8.8	8.4	2.9	7.0	3.0	DFGT
SOUTHERN GUARANTY INS CO	WI	**C**	182.5	58.5	84.7	-0.7	7.6	7.0	3.8	7.3	3.9	FT
SOUTHERN GUARANTY INS CO OF GEORGIA	GA	**C-**	6.1	5.4	0.5	-0.7	8.4	3.6	1.3	7.7	2.1	FGT
SOUTHERN INS CO	TX	**C+**	25.8	27.0	3.8	0.6	10.0	4.6	6.8	10.0	3.6	FGT
SOUTHERN INS CO OF VIRGINIA	VA	**B-**	137.8	63.6	74.3	-0.7	10.0	8.2	6.1	6.3	4.7	T
SOUTHERN MICHIGAN INS CO	MI	**U** (1)	6.1	5.3	0.0	0.0	N/A	5.0	2.7	7.0	3.9	T
SOUTHERN MUTUAL CHURCH INS CO	SC	**C**	41.1	18.8	19.3	-1.1	8.2	5.6	4.9	6.9	4.2	DGRT
▼SOUTHERN MUTUAL INS CO	GA	**C-**	20.4	9.1	11.9	-1.4	7.1	5.9	1.6	5.6	3.0	DFGR
▼SOUTHERN OAK INS CO	FL	**D-**	51.0	12.9	37.7	-0.1	0.9	2.3	2.9	7.1	1.2	CDGR
SOUTHERN PILOT INS CO	WI	**C**	13.2	12.1	0.0	-0.1	10.0	N/A	1.9	7.0	3.4	DGT
SOUTHERN PIONEER PROP & CAS INS CO	AR	**C-**	22.1	12.3	13.2	0.1	8.1	8.2	7.6	6.6	2.9	DGT
SOUTHERN STATES INS EXCHANGE	VA	**C**	30.1	13.2	12.3	0.4	7.2	6.6	3.8	6.7	3.5	DGT
SOUTHERN TRUST INS CO	GA	**C+**	39.3	20.7	21.8	0.3	8.6	8.3	8.1	6.5	4.5	DGT
SOUTHERN UNDERWRITERS INS CO	OK	**C+**	5.2	5.1	0.0	0.0	10.0	N/A	5.5	10.0	3.5	DGT
SOUTHERN UNITED FIRE INS CO	AL	**D+**	26.7	14.1	14.3	-1.5	7.3	6.3	1.2	2.9	2.7	DFGL
SOUTHERN VANGUARD INS CO	TX	**B-**	7.8	6.5	0.0	0.4	10.0	N/A	8.9	10.0	3.8	DGT
▲SOUTHERN-OWNERS INS CO	MI	**B+**	377.7	139.7	119.6	-5.4	9.6	4.8	5.5	6.7	6.4	T
SOUTHLAND LLOYDS INS CO	TX	**D+**	3.1	2.3	1.1	0.1	9.3	5.0	7.2	7.0	1.8	DFGT
SOUTHWEST CASUALTY CO	NM	**C**	23.2	13.0	0.0	0.2	9.6	N/A	8.7	10.0	3.5	DG
SOUTHWEST GENERAL INS CO	NM	**D**	5.2	2.2	1.9	0.1	8.5	9.4	6.4	7.5	1.9	DGT
SOUTHWEST MARINE & GEN INS CO	AZ	**B-**	44.6	26.1	12.0	-0.4	8.9	3.6	3.7	6.7	3.6	DGT
▲SOUTHWEST PHYSICIANS RRG INC	SC	**D**	27.3	8.6	8.9	0.2	1.8	3.6	9.6	8.2	1.8	CDGT
SPARTA INS CO	MA	**B**	306.0	252.1	25.3	-2.7	10.0	N/A	4.5	9.4	4.8	GT
SPARTAN INS CO	TX	**D**	7.9	3.3	5.1	0.1	7.4	7.0	2.4	7.0	2.1	DGT
SPARTAN PROPERTY INS CO	SC	**C**	27.5	18.1	16.1	1.4	7.5	6.1	8.7	8.3	3.8	DGT
SPECIALTY SURPLUS INS CO	IL	**U** (1)	35.1	32.4	0.0	15.7	N/A	7.0	5.4	10.0	5.5	FT

See Page 27 for explanation of footnotes and Page 28 for explanation of stability factors.
Arrows denote recent upgrades ▲ or downgrades ▼ (see Section VII for explanations)

RISK ADJ. RATIO #1	CAPITAL RATIO #2	PREMIUM TO SURPLUS (%)	RESV. TO SURPLUS (%)	RESV. DEVELOP. 1 YEAR (%)	RESV. DEVELOP. 2 YEAR (%)	LOSS RATIO (%)	EXP. RATIO (%)	COMB RATIO (%)	CASH FROM UNDER-WRITING (%)	NET PREMIUM GROWTH (%)	INVEST. IN AFFIL (%)	INSURANCE COMPANY NAME
5.1	4.6	N/A	4.7	-10.1	-8.8	N/A	N/A	N/A	26.3	0.0	0.0	SHELBY CASUALTY INS CO
19.5	17.2	N/A	N/A	N/A	N/A	N/A	N/A	N/A	1.9	0.0	0.0	SHELBY INS CO
3.6	2.8	100.7	57.8	-6.0	-14.0	73.0	27.1	100.1	87.7	1.2	4.7	SHELTER GENERAL INS CO
2.0	1.5	73.2	29.4	-2.5	-4.2	89.1	26.2	115.3	88.1	2.3	27.0 •	SHELTER MUTUAL INS CO
3.7	2.4	52.5	46.8	-5.1	-2.0	59.3	30.5	89.8	117.6	9.5	0.0	SHELTER REINSURANCE CO
10.3	5.9	N/A	N/A	N/A	N/A	N/A	N/A	N/A	2.0	0.0	0.0	SHIELD INS CO
1.7	1.3	100.2	174.2	-8.8	-21.5	60.7	19.8	80.5	128.4	-6.3	0.0	SILVER OAK CASUALTY INC
1.8	1.3	86.9	262.1	-38.4	-56.0	59.8	15.7	75.5	101.5	0.9	0.0	SIMED
N/A	N/A	1.5	0.2	-0.2	-0.2	5.6	155.6	161.2	63.2	38.5	0.0	SLAVONIC INS CO OF TX
7.5	7.0	5.7	0.7	-0.1	-0.1	160.0	56.4	216.4	46.0	-7.3	11.3	SLAVONIC MUTUAL FIRE INS ASN
2.2	1.6	134.6	123.0	-9.0	-22.4	61.8	30.6	92.4	102.7	3.5	0.0	SOCIETY INS
2.3	1.3	40.7	76.4	-21.2	-23.9	22.8	26.0	48.8	108.1	-23.1	0.0	SOMERSET CASUALTY INS CO
125.9	113.3	0.1	0.4	-0.1	-0.1	141.7	448.6	590.3	60.9	-71.1	0.0	SOMPO JAPAN FIRE & MAR INS CO AMER
3.3	2.4	16.1	65.4	-9.8	-22.5	49.8	34.2	84.0	93.6	-3.0	10.1 •	SOMPO JAPAN INS CO OF AMERICA
3.4	2.1	69.9	26.7	-1.8	-2.7	73.3	31.8	105.1	93.2	-0.4	0.2	SONNENBERG MUTUAL INS ASSOC
0.4	0.2	102.5	45.5	-3.6	N/A	48.1	60.1	108.2	172.8	101.7	0.0	SOPHIA PALMER NURSES RRG INC
3.3	2.8	81.0	13.9	-2.8	-3.0	76.5	33.0	109.5	92.3	21.0	6.0	SOUTH CAROLINA FARM BU MUTUAL INS
N/A	N/A	-19.4	898.6	-0.7	27.8	14.3	-478.6	-464.3	10.3	-138.9	0.0	SOUTHEAST EMPLOYERS MUT CAP INS
0.1	0.0	406.5	510.0	-35.3	9.2	59.7	62.0	121.7	76.7	-30.2	0.0	SOUTHEASTERN US INS INC
16.4	14.8	N/A	N/A	N/A	N/A	N/A	N/A	N/A	-34.0	0.0	0.0	SOUTHERN COUNTY MUTUAL INS CO
1.3	0.6	105.3	109.1	-28.1	-37.2	48.4	50.6	99.0	78.3	-32.3	0.0	SOUTHERN EAGLE INS CO
1.2	1.2	83.2	32.3	-3.4	-4.0	91.2	18.5	109.7	90.3	2.0	43.9 •	SOUTHERN FARM BUREAU CAS INS CO
N/A	N/A	N/A	N/A	N/A	0.1	N/A	N/A	N/A	N/A	0.0	0.0	SOUTHERN FARM BUREAU PROPERTY
1.5	0.9	140.5	40.7	-15.9	0.1	50.5	42.7	93.2	129.9	17.4	0.0	SOUTHERN FIDELITY INS CO INC
91.5	55.3	N/A	N/A	N/A	N/A	N/A	N/A	N/A	N/A	0.0	0.0	SOUTHERN FIRE & CASUALTY CO
1.2	1.0	203.6	59.0	6.6	3.5	72.2	43.3	115.5	80.8	-22.0	0.0	SOUTHERN GENERAL INS CO
2.0	1.6	103.3	27.6	-2.4	-4.6	84.9	29.3	114.2	65.2	387.8	0.0	SOUTHERN GENERAL UNDERWRITERS
3.3	2.3	143.6	178.0	-26.2	-19.4	52.3	36.1	88.4	64.1	-40.5	0.0	SOUTHERN GUARANTY INS CO
3.0	2.7	8.8	5.0	-0.3	N/A	59.8	285.0	344.8	17.7	-92.4	0.0	SOUTHERN GUARANTY INS CO OF
11.1	8.5	14.5	3.4	N/A	N/A	116.4	-5.3	111.1	-9.8	0.0	0.0	SOUTHERN INS CO
5.3	3.8	115.6	39.0	2.0	-1.9	71.3	32.4	103.7	100.8	11.9	0.0	SOUTHERN INS CO OF VIRGINIA
N/A	N/A	N/A	10.4	-13.1	-11.5	N/A	N/A	N/A	N/A	0.0	0.0	SOUTHERN MICHIGAN INS CO
2.0	1.6	95.3	30.5	-1.3	-3.0	63.3	34.4	97.7	107.6	12.5	0.0	SOUTHERN MUTUAL CHURCH INS CO
1.4	0.9	114.5	34.4	2.4	3.9	95.2	39.7	134.9	76.0	-10.3	0.0	SOUTHERN MUTUAL INS CO
0.5	0.3	344.1	60.9	18.9	21.3	69.2	29.1	98.3	117.5	9.3	0.0	SOUTHERN OAK INS CO
26.8	24.1	N/A	N/A	N/A	N/A	N/A	N/A	N/A	N/A	0.0	0.0	SOUTHERN PILOT INS CO
2.5	1.9	108.6	24.7	-1.1	-3.1	66.2	35.9	102.1	99.7	6.9	0.0	SOUTHERN PIONEER PROP & CAS INS
2.1	1.1	91.6	103.0	-1.6	2.7	66.5	28.0	94.5	95.3	-11.7	0.0	SOUTHERN STATES INS EXCHANGE
3.7	2.7	104.0	22.4	-3.7	-6.4	53.7	48.5	102.2	94.7	-1.4	0.0	SOUTHERN TRUST INS CO
77.7	37.0	N/A	N/A	N/A	N/A	N/A	N/A	N/A	180.0	0.0	0.0	SOUTHERN UNDERWRITERS INS CO
1.4	1.1	90.6	32.2	1.3	-3.0	99.2	44.0	143.2	64.0	39.1	0.0	SOUTHERN UNITED FIRE INS CO
12.1	10.9	N/A	N/A	N/A	N/A	N/A	N/A	N/A	-290.3	0.0	0.0	SOUTHERN VANGUARD INS CO
3.9	2.9	80.2	88.8	-9.5	-6.7	71.9	23.1	95.0	131.2	9.4	0.0 •	SOUTHERN-OWNERS INS CO
4.7	3.5	50.0	6.9	-5.5	N/A	31.9	73.5	105.4	89.5	-20.8	0.0	SOUTHLAND LLOYDS INS CO
5.2	2.6	N/A	39.8	N/A	N/A	N/A	N/A	N/A	-11.6	0.0	0.0	SOUTHWEST CASUALTY CO
2.3	2.1	89.5	27.0	-6.9	-19.1	53.9	36.6	90.5	108.3	-2.7	0.0	SOUTHWEST GENERAL INS CO
3.6	1.9	45.5	32.8	-0.8	N/A	69.4	29.2	98.6	217.2	57.2	0.0	SOUTHWEST MARINE & GEN INS CO
0.8	0.5	107.3	118.5	-28.5	N/A	46.2	16.0	62.2	419.0	-12.0	0.0	SOUTHWEST PHYSICIANS RRG INC
11.9	7.3	10.0	2.6	N/A	N/A	82.7	65.0	147.7	98.5	N/A	0.0 •	SPARTA INS CO
1.4	1.1	161.3	56.4	19.8	9.1	61.6	44.3	105.9	101.1	3.3	0.0	SPARTAN INS CO
2.0	1.7	95.8	1.5	-1.0	-1.6	4.4	60.7	65.1	153.6	5.2	0.0	SPARTAN PROPERTY INS CO
N/A	N/A	N/A	1.4	-88.4	-49.3	999 +	N/A	N/A	8.0	-100.0	0.0	SPECIALTY SURPLUS INS CO

999 + Denotes number greater than 999.9%
999 - Denotes number less than -999.99%
• Bullets denote a more detailed analysis is available in Section II.

INSURANCE COMPANY NAME	DOM. STATE	RATING	TOTAL ASSETS ($MIL)	CAPITAL & SURPLUS ($MIL)	ANNUAL NET PREMIUM ($MIL)	NET INCOME ($MIL)	CAPITAL-IZATION INDEX (PTS)	RESERVE ADQ INDEX (PTS)	PROFIT-ABILITY INDEX (PTS)	LIQUIDITY INDEX (PTS)	STAB. INDEX (PTS)	STABILITY FACTORS
SPIRIT MOUNTAIN INS CO RRG INC	DC	**D-**	5.6	1.8	2.5	0.0	5.0	5.1	8.1	9.1	1.3	DGRT
SPRING VALLEY MUTUAL INS CO	MN	**E**	8.0	2.0	6.3	-0.2	0.0	6.1	1.2	0.0	0.2	CDFG
SPRINGFIELD FIRE & CASUALTY CO	IL	**C**	11.0	7.1	2.0	0.1	10.0	6.4	6.4	8.8	2.6	DFGT
SPRINGFIELD INS CO INC	CA	**D**	80.3	27.7	22.3	0.4	3.2	3.8	8.5	6.7	2.3	DT
ST CHARLES INS CO RRG	SC	**E**	10.0	3.3	1.2	0.0	5.3	0.5	6.5	9.4	0.3	DGT
ST JOHNS INS CO INC	FL	**D-**	128.5	43.7	34.5	-2.0	1.0	3.8	2.5	1.7	1.2	CLT
ST LUKES HEALTH NETWORK INS CO RRG	VT	**E**	41.4	9.7	8.9	0.1	2.9	7.1	7.7	9.2	0.0	DGT
ST PAUL FIRE & CAS INS CO	WI	**B**	16.6	16.1	0.0	0.2	10.0	N/A	8.1	7.0	4.0	DGT
ST PAUL FIRE & MARINE INS CO	MN	**B**	19,047.7	6,436.6	4,711.5	179.1	7.5	4.5	5.1	6.8	5.7	T
ST PAUL GUARDIAN INS CO	MN	**B-**	78.2	27.0	18.1	0.7	7.7	5.6	8.6	6.8	3.7	T
▲ST PAUL MEDICAL LIABILITY INS CO	MN	**C+**	198.6	61.5	52.6	2.1	7.4	4.5	6.9	6.7	4.5	T
ST PAUL MERCURY INS CO	MN	**B-**	262.2	66.4	72.6	2.8	7.3	4.8	8.6	6.4	4.1	FT
ST PAUL PROTECTIVE INS CO	IL	**B-**	514.6	239.3	105.2	5.4	9.7	5.0	6.3	6.9	4.9	T
ST PAUL SURPLUS LINES INS CO	DE	**C**	610.7	188.1	159.6	6.4	7.3	4.2	6.8	6.8	3.9	T
STANDARD CASUALTY CO	TX	**C**	20.3	14.7	8.2	0.1	9.6	7.3	3.7	6.9	3.8	DGRT
▲STANDARD FIRE INS CO	CT	**B**	3,656.8	1,338.1	878.0	39.1	7.7	4.9	7.4	6.8	5.4	T
▲STANDARD GUARANTY INS CO	DE	**B-**	182.8	88.2	128.0	6.7	8.8	6.8	7.6	7.1	4.9	T
STANDARD MUTUAL INS CO	IL	**C**	63.3	26.8	38.8	-0.8	7.5	7.0	3.3	5.7	3.9	FRT
STAR CASUALTY INS CO	FL	**D**	21.9	10.1	4.5	-1.4	7.6	7.0	2.9	7.0	2.3	DFGR
STAR INS CO	MI	**C**	680.3	198.9	172.1	5.6	7.6	6.2	8.5	7.0	3.6	T
STARNET INS CO	DE	**C**	167.1	110.5	14.7	0.9	10.0	6.2	8.4	8.9	4.3	T
STARR INDEMNITY & LIABILITY CO	TX	**C+**	298.5	215.0	19.8	-0.4	10.0	N/A	4.5	9.1	4.0	RT
STATE & COUNTY MUTUAL FIRE INS CO	TX	**C**	2.7	2.0	0.0	0.0	10.0	N/A	3.6	7.0	2.4	DFGT
STATE AUTO FLORIDA INS CO	IN	**C**	11.1	9.7	0.0	0.1	10.0	3.6	5.2	7.0	3.5	ADFG
STATE AUTO INS CO OF OHIO	OH	**B**	41.0	12.4	14.5	0.0	7.6	7.0	5.8	5.4	4.0	ADFG
STATE AUTO INS CO OF WISCONSIN	WI	**B**	19.0	10.8	-0.1	0.1	10.0	3.6	3.6	8.6	4.3	ADG
STATE AUTO NATIONAL INS CO	OH	**B-**	99.4	65.0	42.2	-0.4	10.0	5.8	4.9	6.7	4.3	T
STATE AUTO PROPERTY & CASUALTY INS	IA	**B**	1,705.4	465.4	858.2	-7.5	7.6	7.0	3.7	5.9	4.3	AT
STATE AUTOMOBILE MUTUAL INS CO	OH	**B**	1,781.8	925.4	229.6	-3.4	7.8	6.3	4.4	6.9	4.3	AFT
STATE FARM CTY MUTUAL INS CO OF TX	TX	**A-**	99.4	40.5	24.5	0.2	10.0	4.7	3.7	6.5	6.8	DT
STATE FARM FIRE & CAS CO	IL	**B**	25,307.9	7,889.9	12,421.7	0.0	6.9	4.8	4.0	2.8	6.2	FLT
STATE FARM FLORIDA INS CO	FL	**C**	2,108.2	552.0	547.9	-54.0	4.1	7.0	2.0	3.9	3.9	CFLT
STATE FARM GENERAL INS CO	IL	**B**	4,555.6	1,982.6	1,681.9	66.8	7.3	6.3	8.3	5.5	6.3	T
STATE FARM GUARANTY INS CO	IL	**D+**	13.9	8.9	0.0	0.1	10.0	N/A	4.9	6.9	2.7	DFGT
STATE FARM INDEMNITY CO	IL	**B**	1,905.4	998.3	526.7	-3.1	10.0	7.0	3.1	6.5	5.4	T
▼STATE FARM LLOYDS	TX	**C+**	2,667.7	944.1	1,373.5	-43.6	5.2	8.9	2.3	1.0	4.3	FLT
STATE FARM MUTUAL AUTOMOBILE INS CO	IL	**B+**	88,473.2	50,979.0	31,963.4	89.2	8.2	6.4	5.3	6.3	6.7	T
STATE MUTUAL INS CO	ME	**C**	1.7	1.6	0.0	0.0	9.8	N/A	7.6	7.0	2.2	DGT
STATE NATIONAL FIRE INS CO	LA	**C-**	2.1	2.1	0.4	0.0	10.0	6.1	2.4	6.5	2.2	DFGT
STATE NATIONAL INS CO INC	TX	**C+**	188.7	113.4	57.3	2.2	8.3	6.1	8.5	6.9	4.6	FT
▲STATE VOLUNTEER MUTUAL INS CO	TN	**A-**	996.2	251.2	244.4	1.5	7.5	6.6	7.9	7.2	6.9	T
STATE-WIDE INS CO	NY	**C**	120.3	55.9	47.0	0.6	10.0	6.4	8.4	6.9	4.3	RT
▼STATES SELF-INSURERS RISK RET GROUP	VT	**E+**	20.2	6.3	1.8	0.2	0.3	2.6	3.1	3.8	0.5	CDGL
STEADFAST INS CO	DE	**C**	552.0	512.3	0.0	2.9	10.0	N/A	5.4	7.0	4.3	FT
▲STERLING CAS INS CO	CA	**E+**	26.9	8.0	21.9	-0.5	1.6	4.0	3.9	4.1	0.4	CDGL
STERLING INS CO	NY	**C**	104.5	46.2	44.5	-1.7	9.2	7.0	5.6	7.1	3.5	T
STEWARD RRG	DC	**U** (5)	0.0	0.0	0.8	0.0	N/A	3.6	2.5	7.5	1.8	DGRT
STICO MUTUAL INS CO A RRG	VT	**C**	18.8	8.7	3.2	-0.8	5.6	6.3	2.6	7.9	2.7	DGT
STONE VALLEY MUTUAL FIRE INS CO	PA	**U** (1)	0.6	0.6	0.1	0.0	N/A	9.2	8.3	10.0	1.7	T
STONEBRIDGE CASUALTY INS CO	OH	**C+**	296.6	130.9	107.9	-0.4	7.9	5.6	5.5	6.9	4.5	RT
▲STONETRUST COMMERCIAL INS CO	LA	**D**	64.3	18.2	25.4	0.4	2.3	2.8	8.5	6.8	1.7	CDT
STONEWALL INS CO	RI	**U** (1)	88.5	58.5	0.0	-0.6	N/A	4.5	3.4	10.0	5.5	CFT

See Page 27 for explanation of footnotes and Page 28 for explanation of stability factors.

Arrows denote recent upgrades ▲ or downgrades ▼ (see Section VII for explanations)

RISK ADJ. RATIO #1	CAPITAL RATIO #2	PREMIUM TO SURPLUS (%)	RESV. TO SURPLUS (%)	RESV. DEVELOP. 1 YEAR (%)	RESV. DEVELOP. 2 YEAR (%)	LOSS RATIO (%)	EXP. RATIO (%)	COMB RATIO (%)	CASH FROM UNDER-WRITING (%)	NET PREMIUM GROWTH (%)	INVEST. IN AFFIL (%)	INSURANCE COMPANY NAME
1.4	0.7	140.1	105.7	-108.8	-111.5	-4.5	40.5	36.0	169.6	24.2	0.0	SPIRIT MOUNTAIN INS CO RRG INC
0.1	0.1	300.7	43.8	0.9	0.2	73.7	41.9	115.6	83.6	-4.4	0.0	SPRING VALLEY MUTUAL INS CO
4.5	3.8	28.8	24.5	2.7	-0.6	38.9	48.7	87.6	78.8	-14.1	0.0	SPRINGFIELD FIRE & CASUALTY CO
0.9	0.5	81.6	146.1	-8.4	-15.0	73.5	26.5	100.0	104.8	4.1	0.0	SPRINGFIELD INS CO INC
1.3	0.5	35.8	194.0	N/A	N/A	60.0	43.1	103.1	174.3	-13.8	0.0	ST CHARLES INS CO RRG
0.4	0.4	75.3	67.0	-5.5	1.0	176.0	-27.4	148.6	97.5	-40.8	0.0	ST JOHNS INS CO INC
0.7	0.5	80.5	218.2	-3.8	-30.8	84.8	12.2	97.0	211.6	-1.6	0.0	ST LUKES HEALTH NETWORK INS CO
74.1	47.3	N/A	N/A	N/A	N/A	N/A	N/A	N/A	N/A	0.0	0.0	ST PAUL FIRE & CAS INS CO
1.7	1.4	74.0	152.2	-5.2	-6.7	61.4	30.6	92.0	97.1	0.9	17.7 •	ST PAUL FIRE & MARINE INS CO
2.3	1.5	69.0	141.4	-5.3	-11.7	61.5	30.0	91.5	104.9	-29.4	0.0	ST PAUL GUARDIAN INS CO
2.3	1.5	88.6	181.4	-6.7	-9.3	61.5	30.3	91.8	103.9	0.5	0.0	ST PAUL MEDICAL LIABILITY INS CO
1.9	1.2	114.0	233.4	-9.3	-26.4	61.5	30.5	92.0	104.6	-29.4	0.0	ST PAUL MERCURY INS CO
4.5	2.9	45.0	92.1	-3.5	-4.3	61.5	30.3	91.8	103.9	0.5	0.0 •	ST PAUL PROTECTIVE INS CO
2.1	1.4	87.9	179.9	-6.8	-9.4	61.5	30.5	92.0	103.9	0.5	0.0 •	ST PAUL SURPLUS LINES INS CO
3.7	2.7	55.4	3.3	-0.1	-1.0	39.5	56.4	95.9	116.3	3.4	0.0	STANDARD CASUALTY CO
2.0	1.6	67.2	137.5	-4.7	-6.5	61.5	30.5	92.0	103.9	0.7	16.4 •	STANDARD FIRE INS CO
3.4	2.3	157.6	18.7	-4.4	-9.8	47.6	41.3	88.9	106.0	-11.3	0.0	STANDARD GUARANTY INS CO
1.8	1.3	139.0	61.5	-7.1	-4.9	74.1	32.9	107.0	90.9	-0.2	0.0	STANDARD MUTUAL INS CO
1.8	1.5	37.0	30.8	3.8	7.6	79.3	61.4	140.7	44.0	-64.4	0.0	STAR CASUALTY INS CO
2.0	1.5	86.1	106.7	-3.1	-4.7	62.0	29.8	91.8	123.9	8.5	19.4 •	STAR INS CO
15.7	12.6	13.4	13.7	-0.7	-1.0	55.3	28.1	83.4	136.2	10.8	0.0	STARNET INS CO
13.2	9.7	9.2	2.8	N/A	N/A	107.2	43.7	150.9	94.2	0.0	0.0 •	STARR INDEMNITY & LIABILITY CO
6.7	6.0	N/A	N/A	N/A	N/A	N/A	N/A	N/A	304.5	-100.0	0.0	STATE & COUNTY MUTUAL FIRE INS CO
17.3	11.7	-0.4	N/A	N/A	N/A	N/A	N/A	N/A	999 +	51.1	0.0	STATE AUTO FLORIDA INS CO
2.1	1.3	114.7	74.3	-1.4	-5.1	75.2	33.4	108.6	89.9	19.6	0.0	STATE AUTO INS CO OF OHIO
5.2	4.7	-0.7	N/A	N/A	N/A	-119.2	-230.1	-349.3	112.6	54.7	0.0	STATE AUTO INS CO OF WISCONSIN
4.4	4.0	64.4	29.9	-1.6	-4.0	74.6	28.5	103.1	99.3	-1.3	0.0	STATE AUTO NATIONAL INS CO
2.1	1.3	177.2	114.2	-1.7	-6.0	74.8	33.2	108.0	109.1	18.9	0.0 •	STATE AUTO PROPERTY & CASUALTY
1.3	1.3	18.8	15.5	-0.7	-1.5	73.4	35.8	109.2	69.4	-27.7	61.3 •	STATE AUTOMOBILE MUTUAL INS CO
4.7	3.8	60.9	22.2	-0.2	N/A	95.0	23.0	118.0	94.1	20.2	0.0 •	STATE FARM CTY MUTUAL INS CO OF TX
1.5	0.9	151.8	87.7	4.0	7.5	95.5	27.9	123.4	88.8	5.4	0.0 •	STATE FARM FIRE & CAS CO
1.0	0.7	90.2	76.9	4.6	3.3	91.3	83.4	174.7	65.9	-17.8	0.0 •	STATE FARM FLORIDA INS CO
2.1	1.2	87.8	58.6	3.4	3.7	77.4	29.2	106.6	100.7	4.5	0.0 •	STATE FARM GENERAL INS CO
5.8	5.2	N/A	N/A	N/A	N/A	N/A	N/A	N/A	28.5	0.0	0.0	STATE FARM GUARANTY INS CO
5.0	3.8	52.6	62.9	8.2	6.9	117.6	24.2	141.8	83.6	3.1	0.5 •	STATE FARM INDEMNITY CO
1.0	0.7	139.8	33.8	N/A	-3.1	107.6	32.0	139.6	68.9	4.4	0.0 •	STATE FARM LLOYDS
2.1	1.7	60.0	38.4	-0.3	0.1	83.4	22.6	106.0	99.2	-0.2	22.7 •	STATE FARM MUTUAL AUTOMOBILE INS
5.2	3.1	N/A	N/A	N/A	N/A	N/A	N/A	N/A	N/A	0.0	0.0	STATE MUTUAL INS CO
3.1	2.9	17.6	1.5	1.0	2.4	109.4	106.7	216.1	49.1	-19.5	0.0	STATE NATIONAL FIRE INS CO
2.5	2.2	51.9	8.5	-0.3	-0.3	49.0	45.4	94.4	91.6	-14.6	26.8	STATE NATIONAL INS CO INC
1.9	1.4	95.5	205.8	-6.7	-11.5	75.5	7.8	83.3	153.2	35.8	0.0 •	STATE VOLUNTEER MUTUAL INS CO
4.8	4.0	82.0	40.4	-2.9	-4.1	68.0	25.2	93.2	100.6	-10.3	0.0	STATE-WIDE INS CO
0.2	0.1	28.9	183.1	24.2	37.8	199.7	-5.2	194.5	136.7	-2.0	0.0	STATES SELF-INSURERS RISK RET
3.3	3.2	N/A	N/A	N/A	N/A	N/A	N/A	N/A	234.8	0.0	32.5 •	STEADFAST INS CO
0.5	0.4	280.7	115.9	-6.6	-23.5	65.9	44.0	109.9	99.1	-45.1	0.0	STERLING CAS INS CO
3.4	2.6	91.2	54.6	-8.2	-13.2	51.3	34.3	85.6	121.4	0.1	0.1	STERLING INS CO
N/A	N/A	58.7	36.3	22.3	N/A	50.9	56.3	107.2	158.3	-0.8	0.0	STEWARD RRG
1.0	0.8	36.9	43.3	-5.5	-4.7	39.5	60.3	99.8	112.2	-5.6	0.0	STICO MUTUAL INS CO A RRG
N/A	N/A	10.6	0.2	N/A	-2.6	40.6	47.6	88.2	110.5	-7.4	0.0	STONE VALLEY MUTUAL FIRE INS CO
4.2	2.7	84.3	41.6	-3.3	-3.7	56.6	43.6	100.2	95.2	-18.4	0.0	STONEBRIDGE CASUALTY INS CO
0.8	0.4	140.7	147.7	-5.5	8.5	61.3	33.0	94.3	129.1	-12.0	0.0	STONETRUST COMMERCIAL INS CO
N/A	N/A	N/A	181.4	6.3	19.1	N/A	N/A	N/A	N/A	0.0	0.0	STONEWALL INS CO

999 + Denotes number greater than 999.9%
999 - Denotes number less than -999.99%
• Bullets denote a more detailed analysis is available in Section II.

INSURANCE COMPANY NAME	DOM. STATE	RATING	TOTAL ASSETS ($MIL)	CAPITAL & SURPLUS ($MIL)	ANNUAL NET PREMIUM ($MIL)	NET INCOME ($MIL)	CAPITAL-IZATION INDEX (PTS)	RESERVE ADQ INDEX (PTS)	PROFIT-ABILITY INDEX (PTS)	LIQUIDITY INDEX (PTS)	STAB. INDEX (PTS)	STABILITY FACTORS
STONEWOOD INS CO	NC	**C**	103.0	49.5	0.6	-1.0	7.3	6.5	5.4	7.0	3.7	T
STONINGTON INS CO	TX	**D+**	335.0	131.3	185.6	2.1	3.5	3.7	5.0	2.6	1.6	FLT
STONINGTON LLOYDS INS CO	TX	**C-**	7.0	3.4	0.2	0.0	10.0	N/A	5.2	6.5	3.2	DFGT
STRATFORD INS CO	NH	**B-**	175.3	58.4	19.6	0.9	7.5	8.4	8.6	8.0	4.7	DT
STRATHMORE INS CO	NY	**B**	46.3	20.0	10.8	0.4	7.6	4.8	8.7	7.0	4.0	DGT
SU INS CO	WI	**C-**	14.8	9.5	9.4	0.3	4.9	3.6	4.5	7.2	1.7	DFGT
SUA INS CO	IL	**C**	331.1	96.5	137.3	3.4	6.0	4.8	3.5	6.8	3.5	T
SUBLIMITY INS CO	OR	**C**	17.4	8.5	11.5	0.2	8.4	9.3	8.1	5.9	3.6	DGT
SUECIA INS CO	NY	**U** (1)	58.8	26.0	0.0	1.5	N/A	7.3	5.4	10.0	5.1	T
SUN SURETY INS CO	SD	**D**	12.2	5.5	2.4	0.3	9.0	N/A	7.2	7.4	1.4	DGT
SUNAPEE MUTUAL FIRE INS CO	NH	**B**	2.4	2.3	0.0	0.0	8.8	N/A	3.7	10.0	4.0	DGT
SUNBELT INS CO	TX	**U** (1)	4.7	2.6	0.0	1.0	N/A	4.6	2.9	10.0	3.0	GRT
SUNDERLAND MARINE MUTUAL CO LTD	AK	**E+**	8.3	5.6	2.3	-0.1	7.9	5.9	1.5	6.9	0.0	DGRT
SUNSHINE STATE INS CO	FL	**D+**	38.2	12.0	9.8	0.7	4.0	4.1	1.5	7.8	2.4	DG
▼SUNZ INS CO	FL	**D**	21.0	5.9	2.6	1.4	0.9	5.0	1.5	9.0	1.4	CDFG
SUPERIOR GUARANTY INS CO	FL	**U** (1)	6.9	5.9	0.0	-0.2	N/A	3.5	3.0	10.0	4.2	RT
SUPERIOR INS CO	FL	**U** (1)	5.7	-3.3	0.0	-6.8	N/A	0.7	0.7	7.0	-1.0	CFT
▲SUPERIOR INS CO RRG	SC	**D-**	14.1	4.8	5.0	0.2	2.4	2.2	4.7	7.2	0.9	DGT
▲SURETEC INS CO	TX	**C**	98.1	61.0	41.5	2.8	8.1	9.3	9.1	7.4	3.5	T
SURETY BONDING CO OF AMERICA	SD	**C+**	9.7	7.8	0.2	0.3	10.0	4.9	8.0	9.6	4.1	DGT
SUTTER INS CO	CA	**B-**	44.4	22.7	15.5	0.1	9.4	9.5	3.9	6.8	4.7	DFGT
SWISS REINSURANCE AMERICA CORP	NY	**C**	14,479.3	4,340.0	1,989.5	208.8	5.1	1.5	5.1	7.2	3.4	RT
▼SYNCORA GUARANTEE INC	NY	**E-**	3,409.9	-3,838.4	108.8	-1,445.2	0.0	0.3	0.0	9.2	0.0	CFGR
SYNERGY COMP INS CO	PA	**D-**	12.3	4.6	6.5	0.0	2.2	3.6	6.4	6.3	1.0	DGT
SYNERGY INS CO	NC	**C-**	9.6	3.6	2.6	-0.2	7.1	3.6	4.6	8.7	2.0	DGT
SYSTEM & AFFILIATE MEMBERS RECIP	VT	**E**	2.7	1.3	1.0	0.0	3.6	3.6	3.1	9.2	0.0	DGT
SYSTEMS PROTECTION ASR RRG INC	MT	**D-** (5)	0.0	0.0	0.9	0.0	9.4	3.6	9.4	9.1	1.0	DGT
T H E INS CO	LA	**C**	172.9	56.2	41.1	0.7	7.5	9.2	6.7	6.7	4.2	FT
TANK OWNER MEMBERS INS CO	TX	**D+**	21.7	10.7	4.6	0.4	8.1	9.5	3.1	8.6	2.5	DGT
TAXISURE EXCHANGE	NJ	**D-** (1)	7.4	2.7	3.3	0.4	2.8	2.7	2.8	1.2	1.2	DFGL
TEACHERS AUTO INS CO	NJ	**C**	14.7	8.4	0.0	0.1	10.0	4.8	6.4	7.7	2.8	DFGT
TEACHERS INS CO	IL	**B-**	280.2	97.9	197.2	3.8	7.2	5.0	5.0	3.1	5.1	ALT
TECHNOLOGY INS CO INC	NH	**C**	577.1	143.5	141.2	2.1	7.6	7.0	8.8	7.1	3.6	T
TENNESSEE FARMERS ASR CO	TN	**A**	879.3	557.2	431.7	-7.5	10.0	8.5	6.7	6.1	6.1	T
▲TENNESSEE FARMERS MUTUAL INS CO	TN	**A**	1,948.5	1,565.7	442.4	-1.6	8.6	7.5	8.0	6.7	6.1	T
TENNESSEE INS CO	TN	**U** (1)	10.7	2.5	0.0	-0.6	N/A	0.5	1.3	9.7	0.5	CFT
TERRA INS CO RRG	VT	**C+**	36.3	17.3	7.1	0.3	8.0	5.1	4.3	8.6	4.2	DFGT
▲TEXAS BUILDERS INS CO	TX	**D+**	14.6	4.1	6.0	-0.1	2.5	7.0	4.9	6.7	2.2	CDGT
TEXAS CONSTRUCTION INS CO RRG INC	NV	**U** (1)	0.5	0.5	-0.1	-0.1	N/A	3.6	2.8	7.0	0.0	FT
TEXAS FARM BUREAU MUTUAL INS CO	TX	**B-**	304.1	139.1	116.0	0.2	10.0	7.9	8.4	6.0	4.7	T
TEXAS FARM BUREAU UNDERWRITERS	TX	**C**	16.7	0.7	0.0	0.0	0.7	N/A	3.5	7.0	2.3	CDFG
TEXAS FARMERS INS CO	TX	**C**	242.3	77.9	117.9	0.7	8.1	4.1	6.9	1.9	3.9	FGLT
TEXAS GENERAL INDEMNITY CO	CO	**U** (1)	30.7	14.8	0.0	0.7	N/A	5.5	6.8	10.0	6.4	T
▲TEXAS HERITAGE INS CO	TX	**D**	35.3	22.8	9.9	0.1	10.0	3.6	3.4	6.8	1.5	DFGT
TEXAS HOSPITAL INS EXCHANGE	TX	**D**	28.4	9.8	6.4	0.0	5.7	7.1	7.7	6.7	2.1	DFGT
TEXAS LAWYERS INS EXCHANGE	TX	**D+**	71.4	37.4	14.5	0.9	9.9	9.4	8.3	7.6	2.6	T
▲TEXAS MEDICAL INS CO	TX	**D-**	21.1	12.0	3.6	0.1	4.3	3.6	4.2	7.9	0.9	DGRT
TEXAS MUTUAL INS CO	TX	**U** (5)	3,385.7	1,270.5	376.8	0.0	N/A	6.4	8.6	6.7	3.6	
TEXAS PACIFIC INDEMNITY CO	TX	**B**	5.9	4.8	0.0	0.0	10.0	N/A	8.0	7.0	4.5	DGT
TEXAS SELECT LLOYDS INS CO	TX	**F** (5)	0.0	0.0	8.6	0.0	4.6	N/A	3.1	0.0	0.0	DFL
THAMES INS CO INC	CT	**C**	34.6	14.1	13.9	0.1	7.6	4.1	3.6	6.8	4.1	DGT
THIRD COAST INS CO	IL	**U** (1)	13.9	13.5	0.0	0.5	N/A	6.9	5.6	10.0	5.5	T

See Page 27 for explanation of footnotes and Page 28 for explanation of stability factors.

Arrows denote recent upgrades ▲ or downgrades ▼ (see Section VII for explanations)

RISK ADJ. RATIO #1	CAPITAL RATIO #2	PREMIUM TO SURPLUS (%)	RESV. TO SURPLUS (%)	RESV. DEVELOP. 1 YEAR (%)	RESV. DEVELOP. 2 YEAR (%)	LOSS RATIO (%)	EXP. RATIO (%)	COMB RATIO (%)	CASH FROM UNDER-WRITING (%)	NET PREMIUM GROWTH (%)	INVEST. IN AFFIL (%)	INSURANCE COMPANY NAME
4.4	1.7	1.2	76.5	-3.6	-4.7	67.5	-244.6	-177.1	-26.8	-98.8	0.0	STONEWOOD INS CO
1.1	0.8	144.3	104.9	-19.1	-19.5	71.5	25.7	97.2	85.3	26.3	2.9	STONINGTON INS CO
2.9	2.6	4.5	N/A	N/A	N/A	N/A	217.3	217.3	40.6	113.7	0.0	STONINGTON LLOYDS INS CO
2.4	1.6	33.9	104.8	-3.2	-5.7	65.0	36.0	101.0	93.5	-17.7	0.0	STRATFORD INS CO
2.2	1.7	55.1	98.9	-2.6	-3.3	62.5	32.7	95.2	100.8	-6.0	0.0	STRATHMORE INS CO
1.0	0.8	101.3	13.0	-0.9	-0.9	72.1	24.5	96.6	99.1	18.6	0.0	SU INS CO
1.6	0.7	146.2	144.2	-2.0	-9.2	62.3	40.9	103.2	118.8	-8.1	0.0	SUA INS CO
2.5	1.9	136.3	40.1	-3.8	-7.2	64.5	32.8	97.3	108.4	9.4	0.1	SUBLIMITY INS CO
N/A	N/A	N/A	80.5	N/A	-0.4	999 +	999 +	999 +	0.1	-80.0	0.0	SUECIA INS CO
2.9	2.3	44.4	N/A	N/A	N/A	6.7	60.0	66.7	148.6	5.2	22.9	SUN SURETY INS CO
4.0	2.4	N/A	N/A	N/A	N/A	N/A	N/A	N/A	N/A	0.0	0.0	SUNAPEE MUTUAL FIRE INS CO
N/A	N/A	1.1	45.3	-59.5	-38.1	999 +	999 +	999 +	-16.4	350.0	0.0	SUNBELT INS CO
2.3	2.0	47.6	44.5	-2.9	17.0	72.4	29.7	102.1	90.9	-1.8	0.0	SUNDERLAND MARINE MUTUAL CO LTD
0.6	0.4	84.0	44.9	3.4	3.7	999 +	-46.7	999 +	999 +	158.5	0.0	SUNSHINE STATE INS CO
0.5	0.3	56.2	317.5	-3.4	-47.8	128.7	92.9	221.6	35.6	0.0	0.0	SUNZ INS CO
N/A	N/A	N/A	2.5	-0.6	-0.7	N/A	N/A	N/A	N/A	0.0	0.0	SUPERIOR GUARANTY INS CO
N/A	N/A	N/A	-5.5	-4.3	53.9	N/A	N/A	N/A	N/A	0.0	115.4	SUPERIOR INS CO
0.6	0.5	120.6	187.7	-19.2	35.2	44.5	36.0	80.5	105.3	14.8	0.0	SUPERIOR INS CO RRG
4.1	3.2	70.9	19.2	-9.6	-18.8	13.0	50.9	63.9	161.6	-10.1	0.0	SURETEC INS CO
5.4	3.5	3.2	15.1	6.1	8.0	246.7	-60.8	185.9	182.4	-7.0	0.0	SURETY BONDING CO OF AMERICA
4.3	3.2	67.6	38.1	-7.3	-16.4	60.0	38.4	98.4	73.8	-28.6	0.0	SUTTER INS CO
1.2	0.7	47.9	172.2	8.2	19.3	76.3	33.5	109.8	120.0	-3.1	2.9 •	SWISS REINSURANCE AMERICA CORP
-1.2	-0.9	-4.5	-202.1	999 +	999 +	999 +	150.7	999 +	8.7	N/A	1.1	SYNCORA GUARANTEE INC
0.6	0.4	143.5	80.4	-1.7	-0.5	67.4	23.8	91.2	190.9	73.3	0.0	SYNERGY COMP INS CO
1.8	1.0	69.9	48.5	4.0	N/A	76.0	15.5	91.5	141.4	44.6	0.0	SYNERGY INS CO
0.7	0.4	74.5	66.4	-0.3	N/A	67.7	32.0	99.7	189.3	11.9	0.0	SYSTEM & AFFILIATE MEMBERS RECIP
3.9	2.5	36.0	20.0	-7.2	N/A	25.3	14.9	40.2	439.5	298.3	0.0	SYSTEMS PROTECTION ASR RRG INC
1.8	1.4	76.0	174.6	-4.1	-14.5	72.0	39.9	111.9	80.8	-16.4	0.0	T H E INS CO
3.2	2.1	44.3	72.1	-5.5	-23.8	34.3	13.4	47.7	244.5	5.7	1.0	TANK OWNER MEMBERS INS CO
0.6	0.5	123.5	111.4	21.8	12.3	59.8	44.2	104.0	110.7	71.7	0.0	TAXISURE EXCHANGE
4.8	4.3	N/A	30.2	1.3	-3.1	N/A	N/A	N/A	0.5	0.0	0.0	TEACHERS AUTO INS CO
1.9	1.2	211.9	103.7	-4.0	-14.0	76.7	24.6	101.3	97.0	-1.9	0.0	TEACHERS INS CO
2.3	1.3	96.2	59.6	-6.5	-9.4	58.3	23.1	81.4	147.4	47.6	12.2	TECHNOLOGY INS CO INC
7.2	4.9	76.5	24.6	-3.8	-6.2	87.4	13.8	101.2	101.3	0.4	0.4 •	TENNESSEE FARMERS ASR CO
2.1	2.0	27.8	9.9	-1.4	-2.1	87.6	13.8	101.4	101.6	0.5	42.2 •	TENNESSEE FARMERS MUTUAL INS CO
N/A	N/A	N/A	277.6	30.6	55.9	N/A	N/A	N/A	N/A	0.0	0.0	TENNESSEE INS CO
1.4	1.0	37.4	27.2	-5.0	-6.6	35.7	47.5	83.2	90.6	9.7	0.0	TERRA INS CO RRG
0.8	0.4	140.6	217.1	-15.4	-28.4	51.6	49.2	100.8	97.6	-10.9	0.0	TEXAS BUILDERS INS CO
N/A	N/A	-15.3	N/A	-2.8	N/A	75.0	-83.1	-8.1	-426.1	-177.8	0.0	TEXAS CONSTRUCTION INS CO RRG INC
4.3	3.7	82.9	23.4	-1.4	-1.2	85.2	13.1	98.3	104.8	11.8	2.7	TEXAS FARM BUREAU MUTUAL INS CO
0.2	0.2	N/A	N/A	N/A	N/A	N/A	N/A	N/A	N/A	0.0	0.0	TEXAS FARM BUREAU UNDERWRITERS
2.9	1.9	152.4	104.4	-3.9	-1.1	75.8	29.7	105.5	51.1	-8.0	0.0	TEXAS FARMERS INS CO
N/A	N/A	N/A	38.0	1.7	4.0	N/A	N/A	N/A	N/A	0.0	0.0	TEXAS GENERAL INDEMNITY CO
4.7	3.7	43.6	5.1	-0.8	-0.1	71.1	42.3	113.4	83.3	-5.7	0.0	TEXAS HERITAGE INS CO
1.6	1.0	65.9	133.7	-62.1	-77.0	10.2	39.5	49.7	100.1	46.9	0.0	TEXAS HOSPITAL INS EXCHANGE
4.4	3.0	39.5	64.4	-5.4	-10.6	75.9	9.0	84.9	129.9	0.1	0.0	TEXAS LAWYERS INS EXCHANGE
0.8	0.6	30.4	47.0	-4.1	4.6	63.3	20.5	83.8	212.4	-0.4	0.0	TEXAS MEDICAL INS CO
N/A	N/A	58.7	84.5	-10.9	-11.6	61.1	44.4	105.5	99.1	-26.7	0.0	TEXAS MUTUAL INS CO
9.6	8.7	N/A	N/A	N/A	N/A	N/A	N/A	N/A	N/A	0.0	0.0	TEXAS PACIFIC INDEMNITY CO
1.0	0.6	87.9	N/A	N/A	N/A	N/A	84.5	84.5	88.8	-7.9	0.0	TEXAS SELECT LLOYDS INS CO
2.1	1.5	96.4	69.4	-4.1	-5.4	53.3	45.4	98.7	89.7	-4.9	0.0	THAMES INS CO INC
N/A	N/A	N/A	7.4	N/A	-5.5	N/A	N/A	N/A	N/A	0.0	0.0	THIRD COAST INS CO

999 + Denotes number greater than 999.9%
999 - Denotes number less than -999.99%
• Bullets denote a more detailed analysis is available in Section II.

INSURANCE COMPANY NAME	DOM. STATE	RATING	TOTAL ASSETS ($MIL)	CAPITAL & SURPLUS ($MIL)	ANNUAL NET PREMIUM ($MIL)	NET INCOME ($MIL)	CAPITAL-IZATION INDEX (PTS)	RESERVE ADQ INDEX (PTS)	PROFIT-ABILITY INDEX (PTS)	LIQUIDITY INDEX (PTS)	STAB. INDEX (PTS)	STABILITY FACTORS
THOMSON SECURITY INS CO	DE	**U** (5)	0.0	1.5	0.0	0.0	N/A	N/A	4.9	7.0	0.5	FT
TIFT AREA CAPTIVE INS CO	GA	**D**	5.8	1.5	1.2	0.2	5.0	5.6	3.1	8.6	1.1	DGRT
TIG INDEMNITY CO	CA	**U** (1)	27.2	23.9	0.0	0.9	N/A	N/A	3.8	7.0	5.0	T
▼TIG INS CO	CA	**D-**	1,722.5	479.0	12.6	-70.5	1.1	0.5	2.9	10.0	1.3	CFT
▲TITAN INDEMNITY CO	TX	**B-**	293.4	158.7	0.0	0.4	7.9	3.7	7.6	9.0	5.0	FGT
TITAN INS CO	MI	**C+**	116.2	106.2	0.0	0.7	10.0	3.6	4.5	8.9	4.6	FGT
TITAN INS CO INC RRG	SC	**D**	22.8	17.7	2.3	0.5	10.0	N/A	8.9	10.0	1.4	DGT
TITLE INDUSTRY ASR CO RRG	VT	**D**	8.9	2.5	1.2	0.0	6.2	9.3	1.9	8.4	2.0	DFGT
TITLE REINSURANCE CO	VT	**D+**	15.7	5.1	2.8	0.0	6.8	7.0	2.6	8.9	2.3	DFGT
TM CASUALTY INS CO	NY	**B**	2.7	2.5	0.0	0.0	10.0	4.9	4.0	10.0	4.9	DGT
TM SPECIALTY INS CO	AZ	**B**	21.3	21.1	0.0	0.1	10.0	N/A	6.8	10.0	4.5	DGT
TNUS INS CO	NY	**C+**	58.6	48.8	5.9	-0.2	8.7	3.1	5.1	7.6	3.4	DGRT
▲TOA-RE INS CO OF AMERICA	DE	**B-**	1,323.0	396.6	210.8	8.7	6.7	4.1	6.3	7.0	5.3	T
▲TOKIO MARINE & NICHIDO FIRE INS LTD	NY	**A**	1,706.6	607.9	312.1	6.1	7.3	7.0	8.5	7.0	7.4	T
TOPA INS CO	CA	**C+**	188.4	56.5	90.7	-0.1	7.1	7.0	3.7	6.1	4.4	T
▲TORUS SPECIALTY INS CO	DE	**C-**	61.1	49.2	9.8	-3.0	10.0	6.0	2.9	9.2	2.9	GT
TOWER BONDING & SURETY CO	PR	**D** (2)	3.2	1.6	4.0	0.4	1.2	2.7	4.9	3.5	1.3	CDGL
▲TOWER HILL PREFERRED INS CO	FL	**D**	42.9	22.9	7.4	0.0	3.6	5.1	2.9	6.3	1.5	DFGR
▲TOWER HILL PRIME INS CO	FL	**D-**	72.3	41.1	17.9	0.0	1.4	4.9	2.9	7.1	1.0	CFRT
TOWER HILL SELECT INS CO	FL	**D**	47.5	21.0	15.7	-0.3	5.5	5.6	3.3	7.3	1.4	DFGR
▲TOWER INS CO OF NEW YORK	NY	**C**	872.6	217.6	256.0	4.2	4.8	6.1	6.9	6.7	3.5	GRT
TOWER NATIONAL INS CO	MA	**F** (1)	63.7	12.2	29.5	1.3	1.5	4.6	6.4	6.8	0.0	CDGR
TOWN & COUNTRY MUTUAL INS CO	AR	**D+**	2.9	1.3	1.9	-0.2	2.9	6.2	1.0	1.4	1.3	CDFG
TOYOTA MOTOR INS CO	IA	**C**	341.5	94.9	52.6	-6.7	10.0	7.7	4.9	7.7	4.0	RT
TPA CAPTIVE INSURANCE CO INC	GA	**C-**	9.5	5.6	1.2	0.3	7.5	7.0	6.5	9.0	2.1	DGRT
TRADERS & GENERAL INS CO	TX	**U** (1)	46.9	46.6	0.0	0.6	N/A	N/A	7.2	7.0	4.9	GRT
TRADERS INS CO	MO	**C-**	13.3	4.0	10.4	0.1	4.9	6.8	1.9	5.4	2.2	DFGR
TRADEWIND INS CO LTD	HI	**C**	14.2	6.2	0.0	0.1	8.9	N/A	6.3	7.7	3.8	DG
TRANS CITY CASUALTY INS CO	AZ	**C**	19.7	10.3	4.8	0.1	6.7	7.0	8.4	6.8	2.5	DGRT
TRANS PACIFIC INS CO	NY	**B**	64.5	46.6	0.8	0.5	10.0	5.9	6.8	10.0	4.5	DT
TRANSATLANTIC REINSURANCE CO	NY	**C+**	11,688.1	3,508.7	3,488.9	74.4	5.1	2.2	7.0	6.5	4.4	CRT
TRANSGUARD INS CO OF AMERICA INC	IL	**C**	193.1	65.1	57.5	0.6	5.7	3.7	3.6	6.8	4.0	T
TRANSIT MUTUAL INS CORP OF WI	WI	**D**	11.8	5.9	2.8	-0.1	10.0	6.7	4.4	7.1	0.0	DGT
TRANSPORT INS CO	OH	**U** (1)	40.3	14.7	0.0	-7.4	N/A	3.3	1.2	10.0	0.2	CFRT
TRANSPORTATION INS CO	IL	**C**	35.5	35.1	0.0	0.4	10.0	N/A	1.9	7.3	3.4	AGT
TRANSPORTATION LIABILITY INS CO RRG	SC	**E-**	0.8	-1.3	-0.3	-0.6	0.0	1.3	0.0	7.0	0.0	CDFG
TRANSURANCE RRG INC	AZ	**E+** (4)	0.0	2.7	8.0	0.1	1.9	0.4	6.8	7.4	0.0	DGT
TRAVCO INS CO	CT	**B**	203.7	69.3	49.0	2.0	8.1	5.0	7.7	6.9	5.8	T
TRAVEL AIR INS CO KANSAS	KS	**U** (1)	6.1	5.1	0.0	0.9	N/A	6.3	4.8	10.0	4.3	T
TRAVELERS AUTO INS CO OF NJ	NJ	**B**	90.0	43.2	0.0	0.3	10.0	N/A	6.9	7.0	4.4	GT
TRAVELERS CASUALTY & SURETY CO	CT	**B**	15,135.9	5,432.5	3,694.0	120.7	7.3	4.6	7.9	6.8	5.9	T
▲TRAVELERS CASUALTY & SURETY CO OF	CT	**B-**	4,307.8	1,999.3	1,337.7	101.0	9.6	7.0	9.5	7.2	4.5	T
▲TRAVELERS CASUALTY CO OF	CT	**B**	312.5	87.7	85.3	3.7	7.3	4.6	8.6	6.9	5.5	T
▲TRAVELERS CASUALTY INS CO OF AMERICA	CT	**B**	1,830.4	519.3	495.2	21.2	7.3	4.6	8.1	6.6	5.4	T
▲TRAVELERS COMMERCIAL CASUALTY CO	CT	**B**	330.5	94.7	85.3	3.5	7.4	4.6	8.8	6.7	5.5	T
TRAVELERS COMMERCIAL INS CO	CT	**B**	322.3	91.9	85.3	3.5	7.4	5.0	8.5	6.9	5.8	T
TRAVELERS EXCESS & SURPLUS LINES CO	CT	**B**	197.7	62.9	49.0	2.0	7.8	5.0	8.3	6.8	5.8	T
TRAVELERS HOME & MARINE INS CO	CT	**B**	261.7	69.3	49.0	1.9	8.1	5.0	7.8	6.8	4.1	T
▲TRAVELERS INDEMNITY CO	CT	**A-**	20,531.8	7,713.4	4,226.9	183.1	7.9	4.9	7.4	6.9	6.9	T
TRAVELERS INDEMNITY CO OF AMERICA	CT	**B**	582.7	149.4	139.7	5.9	7.3	5.0	8.3	6.6	5.9	T
TRAVELERS INDEMNITY CO OF CT	CT	**B**	1,055.2	344.7	248.5	8.1	8.0	5.0	8.4	6.8	5.9	T
TRAVELERS LLOYDS INS CO	TX	**B-**	25.0	19.0	0.0	0.7	10.0	N/A	7.9	9.7	4.9	DG

See Page 27 for explanation of footnotes and Page 28 for explanation of stability factors.

Arrows denote recent upgrades ▲ or downgrades ▼ (see Section VII for explanations)

RISK ADJ. RATIO #1	CAPITAL RATIO #2	PREMIUM TO SURPLUS (%)	RESV. TO SURPLUS (%)	RESV. DEVELOP. 1 YEAR (%)	RESV. DEVELOP. 2 YEAR (%)	LOSS RATIO (%)	EXP. RATIO (%)	COMB RATIO (%)	CASH FROM UNDER-WRITING (%)	NET PREMIUM GROWTH (%)	INVEST. IN AFFIL (%)	INSURANCE COMPANY NAME
N/A	N/A	N/A	N/A	N/A	N/A	N/A	N/A	N/A	N/A	0.0	0.0	THOMSON SECURITY INS CO
1.1	0.8	96.3	230.7	-8.2	7.2	71.1	22.5	93.6	95.5	0.0	0.0	TIFT AREA CAPTIVE INS CO
N/A	N/A	N/A	N/A	N/A	N/A	N/A	N/A	N/A	N/A	0.0	0.0	TIG INDEMNITY CO
0.2	0.1	1.9	171.4	13.2	48.2	452.7	483.0	935.7	9.1	214.5	36.5 •	TIG INS CO
1.6	1.6	N/A	N/A	N/A	N/A	N/A	N/A	N/A	-159.3	0.0	64.5	TITAN INDEMNITY CO
43.7	33.3	N/A	N/A	N/A	N/A	N/A	N/A	N/A	-63.1	0.0	0.0	TITAN INS CO
10.0	8.0	13.4	N/A	N/A	N/A	N/A	-14.0	-14.0	265.2	-1.0	0.0	TITAN INS CO INC RRG
1.1	0.8	48.0	174.4	-17.2	-13.2	237.0	-4.0	233.0	57.1	-9.8	0.0	TITLE INDUSTRY ASR CO RRG
1.2	0.9	54.2	144.6	-27.5	-19.2	88.9	24.2	113.1	75.0	-9.8	0.0	TITLE REINSURANCE CO
9.8	6.9	0.8	4.2	N/A	0.8	N/A	-90.0	N/A	500.0	N/A	0.0	TM CASUALTY INS CO
218.7	133.7	N/A	0.3	N/A	N/A	N/A	N/A	N/A	4.6	0.0	0.0	TM SPECIALTY INS CO
2.9	1.8	12.0	10.8	0.5	-0.2	98.0	45.8	143.8	163.3	164.1	0.0	TNUS INS CO
1.6	1.0	52.4	186.3	-3.5	-2.7	64.2	27.1	91.3	94.0	-17.1	0.0 •	TOA-RE INS CO OF AMERICA
2.9	1.6	51.7	144.2	-24.6	-30.4	40.7	31.2	71.9	97.8	-9.5	5.2 •	TOKIO MARINE & NICHIDO FIRE INS LTD
1.5	0.9	148.2	140.1	-12.5	-22.7	66.5	36.7	103.2	94.1	4.3	5.0	TOPA INS CO
18.7	12.3	20.5	22.2	-1.8	1.9	50.2	36.6	86.8	605.0	-56.5	0.0	TORUS SPECIALTY INS CO
0.4	0.4	279.2	129.0	92.4	32.1	15.8	75.2	91.0	138.2	21.6	0.0	TOWER BONDING & SURETY CO
1.7	1.2	30.7	28.4	-3.3	-14.9	52.9	98.9	151.8	45.0	-72.2	0.0	TOWER HILL PREFERRED INS CO
0.6	0.5	43.6	21.1	-6.4	-12.5	41.5	66.4	107.9	54.9	-58.3	0.0	TOWER HILL PRIME INS CO
1.6	1.0	69.4	28.9	1.5	-3.7	51.8	69.7	121.5	64.8	-60.1	0.0	TOWER HILL SELECT INS CO
1.0	0.7	114.7	110.8	-3.8	-1.5	51.7	34.2	85.9	146.0	14.6	5.4 •	TOWER INS CO OF NEW YORK
0.3	0.3	243.0	103.0	-4.2	-1.8	51.7	14.9	66.6	329.1	556.8	0.0	TOWER NATIONAL INS CO
0.6	0.4	126.1	18.0	-6.6	-4.6	108.9	54.2	163.1	60.8	-16.7	0.0	TOWN & COUNTRY MUTUAL INS CO
5.6	4.6	51.3	8.0	1.0	-0.6	52.5	30.8	83.3	132.9	-21.8	0.0	TOYOTA MOTOR INS CO
2.6	1.6	21.4	44.7	-21.0	-14.7	-26.1	31.6	5.5	260.4	0.0	0.0	TPA CAPTIVE INSURANCE CO INC
N/A	N/A	N/A	N/A	N/A	N/A	N/A	N/A	N/A	N/A	0.0	0.0	TRADERS & GENERAL INS CO
0.8	0.7	259.7	108.1	-8.3	-4.8	61.7	40.4	102.1	80.7	-10.1	0.0	TRADERS INS CO
3.0	2.7	N/A	N/A	N/A	N/A	N/A	N/A	N/A	N/A	0.0	0.0	TRADEWIND INS CO LTD
3.1	1.3	47.0	70.1	-21.5	-18.0	58.4	25.1	83.5	103.7	-22.9	2.9	TRANS CITY CASUALTY INS CO
13.7	6.9	1.8	22.0	-1.0	0.1	137.0	-118.4	18.6	3.7	N/A	0.0	TRANS PACIFIC INS CO
1.1	0.7	98.7	187.5	N/A	5.8	71.1	28.7	99.8	111.0	1.7	5.0 •	TRANSATLANTIC REINSURANCE CO
1.3	0.7	82.7	137.4	-1.6	-0.7	62.7	34.2	96.9	110.0	22.7	0.0	TRANSGUARD INS CO OF AMERICA INC
3.5	2.9	47.2	62.6	-9.4	-13.7	58.6	27.1	85.7	126.6	10.4	0.0	TRANSIT MUTUAL INS CORP OF WI
N/A	N/A	N/A	571.5	7.1	2.7	N/A	N/A	N/A	-2.9	0.0	0.0	TRANSPORT INS CO
141.4	70.6	N/A	N/A	N/A	N/A	N/A	N/A	N/A	N/A	0.0	0.0	TRANSPORTATION INS CO
-0.3	-0.2	49.7	-425.1	149.6	52.6	217.1	-270.3	-53.2	11.0	-111.3	0.0	TRANSPORTATION LIABILITY INS CO RRG
0.7	0.4	296.2	372.0	-35.3	47.0	92.0	7.3	99.3	132.0	9.3	0.0	TRANSURANCE RRG INC
3.0	1.9	72.7	148.9	-5.5	-7.3	61.5	30.8	92.3	103.9	0.6	0.0	TRAVCO INS CO
N/A	N/A	N/A	3.1	0.1	-8.7	N/A	N/A	N/A	N/A	0.0	0.0	TRAVEL AIR INS CO KANSAS
6.7	6.0	N/A	N/A	N/A	N/A	N/A	N/A	N/A	N/A	0.0	0.0	TRAVELERS AUTO INS CO OF NJ
1.5	1.3	70.7	144.8	-5.2	-7.9	61.5	31.7	93.2	103.0	0.7	24.9 •	TRAVELERS CASUALTY & SURETY CO
6.0	3.8	77.1	63.4	-17.1	-32.5	19.2	34.4	53.6	185.3	-1.0	0.0 •	TRAVELERS CASUALTY & SURETY CO OF
2.1	1.4	99.4	203.6	-8.1	-9.9	61.5	30.4	91.9	103.9	0.9	0.0	TRAVELERS CASUALTY CO OF
2.2	1.4	99.1	203.0	-8.8	-10.5	61.5	30.3	91.8	104.0	0.6	0.0 •	TRAVELERS CASUALTY INS CO OF
2.3	1.5	93.5	191.4	-7.4	-10.0	61.5	30.4	91.9	104.0	0.9	0.0	TRAVELERS COMMERCIAL CASUALTY CO
2.2	1.4	96.4	197.4	-7.9	-10.0	61.5	30.5	92.0	103.9	0.9	0.0	TRAVELERS COMMERCIAL INS CO
2.7	1.7	80.4	164.7	-6.5	-8.2	61.5	30.6	92.1	103.9	0.6	0.0	TRAVELERS EXCESS & SURPLUS LINES
2.9	1.8	72.6	148.8	-5.5	-7.3	61.5	31.4	92.9	103.9	0.6	0.0	TRAVELERS HOME & MARINE INS CO
2.0	1.6	53.1	108.9	-3.8	-5.0	61.3	33.3	94.6	108.1	-0.1	19.8 •	TRAVELERS INDEMNITY CO
2.2	1.4	96.9	198.5	-7.9	-10.1	61.5	31.0	92.5	104.3	0.7	0.0	TRAVELERS INDEMNITY CO OF AMERICA
2.9	1.8	73.5	150.5	-5.8	-7.7	61.5	30.8	92.3	104.4	0.6	0.0 •	TRAVELERS INDEMNITY CO OF CT
11.1	10.0	N/A	N/A	N/A	N/A	N/A	N/A	N/A	N/A	0.0	0.0	TRAVELERS LLOYDS INS CO

999 + Denotes number greater than 999.9%
999 - Denotes number less than -999.99%
• Bullets denote a more detailed analysis is available in Section II.

INSURANCE COMPANY NAME	DOM. STATE	RATING	TOTAL ASSETS ($MIL)	CAPITAL & SURPLUS ($MIL)	ANNUAL NET PREMIUM ($MIL)	NET INCOME ($MIL)	CAPITAL-IZATION INDEX (PTS)	RESERVE ADQ INDEX (PTS)	PROFIT-ABILITY INDEX (PTS)	LIQUIDITY INDEX (PTS)	STAB. INDEX (PTS)	STABILITY FACTORS
TRAVELERS LLOYDS OF TEXAS INS CO	TX	**B**	22.0	14.4	0.0	0.4	10.0	N/A	6.8	10.0	4.9	DG
TRAVELERS PERSONAL INS CO	CT	**B**	194.4	62.8	49.0	2.0	7.7	5.0	7.6	6.9	5.8	T
TRAVELERS PERSONAL SECURITY INS CO	CT	**B**	197.5	65.2	49.0	2.1	7.8	5.0	7.7	6.9	5.8	T
TRAVELERS PROPERTY CAS OF AMERICA	CT	**B**	335.8	94.3	65.3	2.6	8.1	5.0	7.2	6.8	5.9	T
TRAVELERS PROPERTY CASUALTY INS CO	CT	**B**	218.3	69.4	54.4	2.2	7.7	5.0	8.2	6.6	5.8	T
TRENWICK AMERICA REINSURANCE CORP	CT	**F** (1)	158.3	30.5	-0.1	-10.9	3.9	1.5	1.2	10.0	0.0	FT
TRI CENTURY INS CO	PA	**D+**	28.4	8.0	1.8	0.2	4.2	3.5	5.0	7.5	2.7	DGRT
TRI STATE INS CO OF MINNESOTA	MN	**C**	33.0	32.8	0.0	0.3	10.0	N/A	6.8	10.0	4.2	DG
TRI-STATE CONSUMER INS CO	NY	**C**	95.1	32.8	26.8	0.1	8.6	9.9	4.3	6.8	4.1	T
TRIAD GUARANTY ASR CORP	IL	**B**	26.8	10.4	5.5	-0.6	3.8	5.8	1.7	6.8	4.4	CDGT
TRIAD GUARANTY INS CORP	IL	**D+**	1,036.4	393.3	236.6	-170.7	0.3	2.3	0.4	5.1	2.4	CT
TRIANGLE INS CO INC	OK	**C**	36.9	12.1	19.5	0.2	7.2	6.2	3.8	6.6	3.3	DGRT
▲TRINITY LLOYDS INS CO	TX	**B**	3.1	2.1	0.0	0.0	8.6	N/A	4.3	10.0	4.0	DFGT
TRINITY UNIVERSAL INS CO	TX	**B-**	2,583.6	697.1	1,720.0	7.7	7.4	7.0	3.0	3.0	4.9	AFLT
TRINITY UNIVERSAL INS CO OF KS	KS	**B**	32.6	9.9	2.6	-0.2	9.5	N/A	3.6	10.0	4.4	DFGT
TRIPLE S PROPIEDAD INC	PR	**C**	270.0	97.7	95.9	2.3	6.9	7.0	8.5	5.3	3.6	FRT
TRISTATE MEDICAL INS CO RRG	NV	**U** (1)	3.4	2.4	1.0	0.5	N/A	4.3	2.3	6.8	2.3	FRT
TRITON INS CO	TX	**B-**	768.2	348.6	309.5	15.6	10.0	7.8	3.6	7.3	5.3	GT
TRIUMPHE CASUALTY CO	PA	**C**	22.2	15.0	6.5	0.2	10.0	4.6	5.6	8.9	3.1	DGT
TRUCK INS EXCHANGE	CA	**C**	1,954.4	422.7	913.6	-8.4	5.6	3.7	4.1	5.7	3.4	T
TRUMBULL INS CO	CT	**B**	200.1	85.6	51.0	2.1	10.0	4.6	1.9	7.0	5.4	T
TRUSTGARD INS CO	OH	**B+**	66.4	32.4	37.5	0.4	7.9	8.3	7.4	6.5	5.0	T
TRUSTSTAR INS CO	MD	**D-**	2.2	1.7	0.7	0.0	9.0	7.4	5.5	7.4	1.3	DGT
TRYGG-HANSA INS CO LTD US BR	NY	**U** (1)	4.0	3.8	0.0	0.0	N/A	8.3	2.7	10.0	3.3	FRT
▲TUDOR INS CO	NH	**B-**	440.5	97.9	28.2	3.3	7.4	8.7	8.6	9.2	4.7	T
TUSCARORA WAYNE INS CO	PA	**C**	20.5	12.3	9.3	0.5	8.2	6.7	8.7	7.0	3.8	DGT
TUSCARORA WAYNE MUTUAL INS CO	PA	**B+**	54.2	31.2	13.9	0.0	8.0	8.2	7.2	7.0	5.0	T
TWIN CITY FIRE INS CO	IN	**B**	659.2	311.2	153.1	11.1	10.0	4.7	8.7	6.9	6.2	T
TWIN LIGHTS INS CO	NJ	**D**	11.8	5.7	0.0	0.0	10.0	N/A	4.9	10.0	1.4	DG
U S LLOYDS INS CO	TX	**D**	16.9	5.6	13.5	0.0	3.9	4.9	8.0	6.5	2.0	DGT
UFB CASUALTY INS CO	IN	**B**	7.8	7.8	0.0	0.0	10.0	N/A	6.0	10.0	4.8	DG
▲ULICO CASUALTY CO	DE	**C**	221.4	89.4	59.6	-1.4	5.4	4.9	5.0	8.2	3.5	GT
ULICO STANDARD OF AMER CAS CO	CA	**U** (1)	20.6	7.2	0.0	1.1	N/A	5.0	2.4	7.1	3.6	FT
UMIALIK INS CO	AK	**C**	42.6	15.4	23.4	0.4	3.3	7.0	5.8	5.0	3.7	CDGT
▲UNDERWRITER FOR THE PROFESSIONS INC	CO	**B-**	239.6	90.3	15.4	2.3	7.6	6.8	5.0	9.4	4.7	T
▼UNDERWRITERS AT LLOYDS	KY	**D+**	206.9	33.4	86.8	5.8	2.0	6.1	8.5	3.5	2.4	CFLT
UNDERWRITERS AT LLOYDS LONDON	IL	**E+**	687.7	230.8	80.7	16.3	1.1	3.0	2.9	7.0	0.0	CDFR
UNIGARD INDEMNITY CO	WA	**C**	77.8	22.9	27.2	-0.6	8.2	5.6	3.3	7.6	3.6	DFT
UNIGARD INS CO	WA	**C+**	646.6	208.6	169.4	-5.5	8.5	5.6	5.3	7.5	4.5	FT
UNION AMERICAN INS CO	FL	**F** (1)	2.1	0.4	0.0	1.1	0.4	0.2	0.1	9.3	0.0	CDFT
UNION INS CO	IA	**C**	92.4	27.8	0.0	0.3	10.0	N/A	7.2	6.9	4.2	T
UNION INS CO OF PROVIDENCE	IA	**B**	93.5	43.0	26.1	1.1	9.7	5.8	7.3	7.3	4.8	T
UNION MUTUAL FIRE INS CO	VT	**B-**	152.9	62.4	89.6	0.2	7.7	8.1	3.9	6.5	4.7	GT
UNION MUTUAL INS CO	OK	**E+**	4.0	1.0	3.3	-0.4	6.6	4.4	1.4	2.7	0.7	DFGL
UNION NATIONAL FIRE INS CO	LA	**B**	15.5	10.2	0.0	0.0	10.0	N/A	1.9	10.0	4.2	DGRT
UNION STANDARD INS CO	OK	**U** (1)	24.6	24.6	0.0	0.2	N/A	N/A	7.7	7.0	5.4	T
UNION STANDARD LLOYDS	TX	**C**	3.2	0.8	0.0	0.0	5.3	N/A	4.9	9.5	2.8	DFGT
UNIONE ITALIANA REINS CO OF AMERICA	NY	**U** (1)	77.6	30.8	0.0	-2.8	N/A	4.3	2.4	10.0	3.9	FRT
UNIQUE INS CO	IL	**D**	33.6	8.4	26.0	0.5	2.4	6.0	8.5	6.6	2.2	DGT
UNITED AMERICAS INS CO	NY	**U** (1)	8.3	5.8	0.0	-0.7	N/A	0.3	1.9	7.0	0.6	CFRT
▼UNITED AUTOMOBILE INS CO	FL	**E**	517.2	75.1	338.5	9.6	0.0	0.1	1.1	0.0	0.1	CFLT
UNITED BUSINESS INS CO	GA	**D-**	3.7	0.7	2.3	0.0	0.9	4.0	2.9	1.0	1.1	CDFG

See Page 27 for explanation of footnotes and Page 28 for explanation of stability factors.

Arrows denote recent upgrades ▲ or downgrades ▼ (see Section VII for explanations)

RISK ADJ. CAPITAL RATIO #1	RATIO #2	PREMIUM TO SURPLUS (%)	RESV. TO SURPLUS (%)	RESV. DEVELOP. 1 YEAR (%)	2 YEAR (%)	LOSS RATIO (%)	EXP. RATIO (%)	COMB RATIO (%)	CASH FROM UNDER-WRITING (%)	NET PREMIUM GROWTH (%)	INVEST. IN AFFIL (%)	INSURANCE COMPANY NAME
7.1	6.4	N/A	N/A	N/A	N/A	N/A	N/A	N/A	N/A	0.0	0.0	TRAVELERS LLOYDS OF TEXAS INS CO
2.7	1.7	82.9	169.8	-6.3	-8.3	61.5	30.6	92.1	103.9	0.6	0.0	TRAVELERS PERSONAL INS CO
2.8	1.8	79.5	162.9	-6.0	-8.0	61.5	30.5	92.0	103.9	0.6	0.0	TRAVELERS PERSONAL SECURITY INS
2.9	1.8	70.2	143.7	-5.4	-6.9	61.5	35.8	97.3	107.1	0.2	0.0	TRAVELERS PROPERTY CAS OF
2.7	1.7	81.0	165.8	-6.2	-8.5	61.5	31.0	92.5	103.9	0.5	0.0	TRAVELERS PROPERTY CASUALTY INS
1.0	0.5	-0.4	333.6	19.7	30.8	999 +	999 +	999 +	15.5	-112.2	0.4	TRENWICK AMERICA REINSURANCE
0.9	0.6	22.1	66.6	0.3	4.4	89.9	19.1	109.0	130.2	21.0	0.0	TRI CENTURY INS CO
94.5	44.9	N/A	N/A	N/A	N/A	N/A	N/A	N/A	-235.0	0.0	0.0	TRI STATE INS CO OF MINNESOTA
2.7	2.0	80.9	130.2	-11.1	-36.6	62.1	35.4	97.5	107.6	7.0	0.0	TRI-STATE CONSUMER INS CO
0.7	0.5	50.2	126.2	-13.0	1.9	214.6	35.4	250.0	123.9	3.0	0.0	TRIAD GUARANTY ASR CORP
1.1	0.8	268.7	988.0	-41.3	19.8	325.9	22.8	348.7	93.5	-14.9	1.3	TRIAD GUARANTY INS CORP
1.5	1.0	160.2	80.4	-1.7	1.0	80.4	23.3	103.7	122.5	19.7	0.0	TRIANGLE INS CO INC
4.4	3.9	-0.4	N/A	N/A	N/A	N/A	312.5	N/A	352.1	0.0	0.0	TRINITY LLOYDS INS CO
1.4	1.1	207.5	134.3	-6.3	-14.4	75.8	27.7	103.5	88.1	-4.0	11.6 •	TRINITY UNIVERSAL INS CO
2.6	2.3	25.7	4.4	N/A	N/A	71.4	17.3	88.7	999 +	0.0	0.0	TRINITY UNIVERSAL INS CO OF KS
1.5	1.0	98.1	72.7	-6.4	-13.7	50.0	47.9	97.9	87.8	-5.8	0.0	TRIPLE S PROPIEDAD INC
N/A	N/A	43.4	39.1	22.0	25.9	40.9	6.1	47.0	16.9	192.7	0.0	TRISTATE MEDICAL INS CO RRG
7.2	4.1	92.2	15.3	-2.0	-1.4	41.6	24.9	66.5	245.3	78.3	0.0 •	TRITON INS CO
6.3	4.4	44.2	25.3	0.6	-0.3	60.3	19.3	79.6	999 +	0.0	0.0	TRIUMPHE CASUALTY CO
1.0	0.8	213.3	147.9	-4.0	0.7	76.1	30.4	106.5	103.9	-8.0	21.4 •	TRUCK INS EXCHANGE
5.0	3.2	60.2	99.5	-0.6	-1.0	64.1	23.6	87.7	110.9	-2.2	0.0	TRUMBULL INS CO
3.1	1.9	115.4	55.3	-3.3	-8.0	67.8	22.1	89.9	95.4	2.6	0.0 •	TRUSTGARD INS CO
2.4	2.2	42.4	0.7	-0.4	-0.3	20.8	88.9	109.7	91.0	-0.4	0.0	TRUSTSTAR INS CO
N/A	N/A	N/A	169.6	-5.9	-7.4	N/A	N/A	N/A	-4.9	100.0	0.0	TRYGG-HANSA INS CO LTD US BR
2.7	1.7	29.8	99.0	-3.2	-6.4	65.0	35.7	100.7	64.9	-20.9	0.0	TUDOR INS CO
5.0	2.9	75.8	31.3	-4.3	-6.5	54.6	37.0	91.6	114.1	1.5	0.0	TUSCARORA WAYNE INS CO
1.9	1.7	44.1	19.8	-2.5	-3.7	55.2	38.1	93.3	103.8	1.4	38.5 •	TUSCARORA WAYNE MUTUAL INS CO
6.1	3.9	50.8	84.1	-2.0	-3.2	64.1	22.6	86.7	110.9	-2.2	0.0 •	TWIN CITY FIRE INS CO
3.2	2.9	N/A	N/A	N/A	N/A	N/A	N/A	N/A	999 +	0.0	0.0	TWIN LIGHTS INS CO
0.8	0.5	240.6	59.8	-20.6	-25.8	44.6	48.7	93.3	102.7	19.5	0.0	U S LLOYDS INS CO
211.7	105.9	N/A	N/A	N/A	N/A	N/A	N/A	N/A	N/A	0.0	0.0	UFB CASUALTY INS CO
1.3	0.9	66.7	88.4	-17.9	-20.0	54.4	40.8	95.2	149.0	62.7	0.0	ULICO CASUALTY CO
N/A	N/A	N/A	167.2	-8.9	-5.3	N/A	N/A	N/A	N/A	0.0	0.0	ULICO STANDARD OF AMER CAS CO
0.7	0.4	150.6	85.9	-6.6	-8.5	56.6	43.5	100.1	111.8	-3.6	0.0	UMIALIK INS CO
1.7	1.3	17.4	20.6	-3.0	-6.0	17.2	7.6	24.8	209.3	6.1	17.2	UNDERWRITER FOR THE PROFESSIONS
0.5	0.3	260.2	363.9	-142.5	-185.9	71.6	34.0	105.6	85.2	15.1	0.0	UNDERWRITERS AT LLOYDS
0.4	0.3	34.3	158.5	0.3	22.8	71.0	33.2	104.2	61.3	-6.3	0.0 •	UNDERWRITERS AT LLOYDS LONDON
2.5	1.8	116.7	135.3	-14.7	-10.5	52.3	33.8	86.1	73.1	-30.1	0.0	UNIGARD INDEMNITY CO
3.5	2.3	79.6	98.7	-13.3	-9.4	52.3	35.8	88.1	64.1	-40.5	5.0 •	UNIGARD INS CO
0.2	0.1	N/A	252.5	98.9	110.8	N/A	N/A	N/A	N/A	0.0	0.0	UNION AMERICAN INS CO
3.7	3.3	N/A	N/A	N/A	N/A	N/A	N/A	N/A	90.7	0.0	0.0	UNION INS CO
4.9	3.2	62.0	78.2	-3.6	-7.7	73.9	33.1	107.0	97.9	-3.5	0.0	UNION INS CO OF PROVIDENCE
1.6	1.4	138.9	56.6	-2.3	-4.9	68.8	36.3	105.1	149.8	113.5	23.6	UNION MUTUAL FIRE INS CO
0.9	0.8	236.8	21.9	9.8	-2.5	69.6	43.7	113.3	69.0	-11.8	0.0	UNION MUTUAL INS CO
6.3	5.7	N/A	N/A	N/A	N/A	N/A	N/A	N/A	-169.1	0.0	0.0	UNION NATIONAL FIRE INS CO
N/A	N/A	N/A	N/A	N/A	N/A	N/A	N/A	N/A	N/A	0.0	0.0	UNION STANDARD INS CO
0.9	0.8	N/A	N/A	N/A	N/A	N/A	N/A	N/A	244.9	0.0	0.0	UNION STANDARD LLOYDS
N/A	N/A	N/A	141.8	16.8	12.9	999 +	620.0	999 +	-0.8	N/A	0.0	UNIONE ITALIANA REINS CO OF AMERICA
0.6	0.5	312.1	173.6	-9.6	-27.1	49.9	42.3	92.2	113.0	4.4	0.0	UNIQUE INS CO
N/A	N/A	N/A	277.0	-6.7	109.6	N/A	N/A	N/A	1.0	0.0	0.0	UNITED AMERICAS INS CO
0.1	0.1	609.3	496.9	38.2	100.1	78.6	34.6	113.2	79.8	12.8	1.9	UNITED AUTOMOBILE INS CO
0.4	0.2	302.5	120.8	-18.2	55.3	60.4	40.3	100.7	91.6	-3.1	0.0	UNITED BUSINESS INS CO

999 + Denotes number greater than 999.9%
999 - Denotes number less than -999.99%
• Bullets denote a more detailed analysis is available in Section II.

INSURANCE COMPANY NAME	DOM. STATE	RATING	TOTAL ASSETS ($MIL)	CAPITAL & SURPLUS ($MIL)	ANNUAL NET PREMIUM ($MIL)	NET INCOME ($MIL)	CAPITAL-IZATION INDEX (PTS)	RESERVE ADQ INDEX (PTS)	PROFIT-ABILITY INDEX (PTS)	LIQUIDITY INDEX (PTS)	STAB. INDEX (PTS)	STABILITY FACTORS
UNITED CASUALTY & SURETY CO INC	MA	**D**	11.4	4.1	3.0	0.2	7.4	7.8	8.6	9.4	2.1	DGT
UNITED CASUALTY INS CO OF AMERICA	IL	**B**	16.1	9.3	2.9	0.1	10.0	4.9	2.7	6.9	4.3	DGT
▲UNITED CENTRAL PA RRG	VT	**D**	24.1	16.0	3.8	0.2	10.0	7.1	9.4	8.0	1.5	DGT
▲UNITED CONTRACTORS INS CO INC RRG	DC	**D**	26.1	14.2	9.5	0.0	3.3	4.8	9.1	6.4	1.5	CDFG
UNITED EDUCATORS INS A RECIP RRG	VT	**C**	500.6	169.5	92.7	3.1	7.3	6.1	7.8	8.0	3.5	T
UNITED EQUITABLE INS CO	IL	**D**	14.9	3.2	12.9	-0.3	1.0	1.3	1.5	2.7	1.4	CDFG
UNITED FARM FAMILY INS CO	NY	**B**	24.6	8.0	7.5	0.0	7.9	7.0	7.4	7.3	4.7	DFGT
▼UNITED FARM FAMILY MUTUAL INS CO	IN	**B+**	787.9	243.0	472.3	-23.6	8.2	5.7	2.5	3.4	6.4	FLT
UNITED FINANCIAL CASUALTY CO	OH	**C+**	1,839.0	408.8	1,185.8	40.8	4.7	5.8	7.0	5.3	4.3	T
UNITED FIRE & CAS CO	IA	**B-**	1,194.1	523.7	381.4	0.5	7.7	8.5	5.8	6.3	5.2	T
UNITED FIRE & INDEMNITY CO	TX	**C+**	39.0	14.7	13.8	0.0	7.5	9.1	6.3	7.4	4.5	GT
UNITED FIRE LLOYDS	TX	**C**	16.3	5.3	4.6	0.0	7.6	8.8	6.1	7.3	3.6	DFGT
UNITED FRONTIER MUTUAL INS CO	NY	**C-**	11.6	6.9	2.8	-0.5	8.7	8.2	4.1	6.7	2.7	DFGT
UNITED GROUP CAPTIVE INS CO	GA	**D**	2.3	1.6	0.7	0.0	8.9	5.6	5.4	9.3	1.4	DGT
UNITED GUAR RESIDENTIAL INS CO OF NC	NC	**D-**	1,106.8	240.9	236.7	45.8	1.2	10.0	1.1	0.0	0.9	CFGL
▲UNITED GUARANTY COML INS CO OF NC	NC	**D+**	266.3	34.8	23.4	2.1	7.3	7.1	5.3	6.9	2.5	FGT
UNITED GUARANTY CREDIT INS CO	NC	**B-**	22.3	16.9	1.4	4.8	6.8	7.3	1.6	7.6	4.6	DGT
UNITED GUARANTY INS CO	NC	**C**	242.1	73.0	47.4	-0.5	2.8	10.0	2.9	6.7	4.3	CGT
UNITED GUARANTY MORTGAGE INDEM CO	NC	**C**	378.2	127.5	46.4	0.1	6.4	4.0	2.9	7.0	4.3	CGT
UNITED GUARANTY MORTGAGE INS CO	NC	**C**	242.0	72.8	47.4	-0.6	2.8	10.0	2.9	6.9	4.3	CGT
UNITED GUARANTY MTG INS CO OF NC	NC	**C**	242.3	73.2	47.4	-0.5	2.8	10.0	2.9	6.7	4.3	CGT
UNITED GUARANTY RESIDENTIAL INS CO	NC	**D+**	2,518.8	1,079.0	472.9	4.8	7.2	4.7	2.9	6.5	2.4	GT
UNITED HERITAGE PROP & CAS CO	ID	**D+**	18.6	7.9	11.5	-0.1	7.3	4.7	4.3	5.1	1.4	DFGT
UNITED HOME INS CO	AR	**D**	12.6	5.7	9.7	-0.4	6.7	9.1	2.6	5.3	1.4	DFGR
UNITED HOME INS CO A RRG	VT	**U** (1)	9.2	2.9	0.0	0.4	N/A	N/A	5.2	10.0	0.0	FT
▲UNITED INS CO	UT	**C-** (1)	5.5	2.9	3.3	0.5	6.4	4.6	8.9	6.6	2.4	DGOT
UNITED INTERNATIONAL INS CO	NY	**U** (1)	4.4	4.1	0.0	-0.1	N/A	7.0	5.8	10.0	3.1	FT
UNITED MEDICAL LIABILITY INS CO RRG	HI	**D**	2.9	1.1	1.2	-0.1	2.8	4.7	1.5	8.8	1.2	DFGR
UNITED NATIONAL CASUALTY INS CO	IN	**C+**	52.9	24.3	3.8	-0.3	8.3	5.2	5.0	9.6	4.5	DGT
UNITED NATIONAL INS CO	PA	**C+**	643.6	316.3	60.3	17.0	7.3	5.7	3.4	7.4	4.3	FT
UNITED NATIONAL SPECIALTY INS CO	WI	**B-**	90.0	59.3	3.8	-0.1	9.7	6.2	6.7	7.4	4.4	DFT
UNITED OHIO INS CO	OH	**B**	203.1	94.9	104.6	-0.4	10.0	7.0	6.5	6.6	4.7	T
▲UNITED PROPERTY & CASUALTY INS CO	FL	**C-**	157.5	54.6	82.4	-0.9	6.8	3.2	2.9	6.8	2.9	T
UNITED SECURITY INS CO	CO	**C**	11.7	11.0	1.2	-0.4	10.0	4.6	3.5	9.3	2.4	DFGT
UNITED SERVICES AUTOMOBILE ASN	TX	**A+**	19,904.8	13,360.9	4,890.9	79.3	7.7	6.2	8.3	6.7	7.9	T
▲UNITED STATES FIDELITY & GUARANTY CO	MD	**B-**	4,250.9	2,099.7	800.0	33.7	9.3	4.5	4.5	6.9	5.0	T
UNITED STATES FIRE INS CO	DE	**C**	2,603.1	763.1	579.5	1.8	6.1	5.8	5.5	6.4	3.7	AFT
▼UNITED STATES LIABILITY INS CO	PA	**C**	406.1	203.8	84.9	70.9	7.1	9.4	3.0	6.6	4.3	T
UNITED STATES SURETY CO	MD	**C**	61.9	38.6	23.5	1.3	9.2	9.4	8.6	7.1	3.6	DT
UNITED SURETY & INDEMNITY CO	PR	**B-**	101.8	49.3	24.0	2.0	5.9	4.5	8.4	6.2	4.9	T
UNITED WISCONSIN INS CO	WI	**C+**	306.2	77.0	86.1	1.0	7.1	5.9	8.9	6.3	4.5	T
UNITRIN ADVANTAGE INS CO	NY	**D**	3.7	2.1	0.2	0.0	8.8	6.0	2.9	9.8	2.2	DFGT
UNITRIN AUTO & HOME INS CO	NY	**C-**	171.1	28.7	40.0	0.7	7.6	6.9	5.4	5.5	2.9	T
UNITRIN COUNTY MUTUAL INS CO	TX	**C+**	37.4	3.7	0.0	0.0	4.3	N/A	4.7	9.7	3.2	CDG
▲UNITRIN DIRECT INS CO	IL	**C+**	33.9	14.1	7.5	0.0	7.6	4.6	2.3	6.6	4.4	DGT
UNITRIN DIRECT PROPERTY & CAS CO	IL	**B-**	50.6	13.0	16.7	0.2	2.0	5.8	2.2	1.5	4.8	CDFL
UNITRIN PREFERRED INS CO	NY	**C-**	47.1	15.7	8.9	0.2	8.7	7.0	8.4	6.8	2.9	DGT
UNITRIN SAFEGUARD INS CO	WI	**B**	15.4	10.5	0.0	0.1	10.0	N/A	4.6	9.4	4.1	DGT
UNIVERSAL CASUALTY CO	IL	**C**	98.4	25.0	53.0	-0.7	6.6	9.2	2.1	5.8	3.4	RT
UNIVERSAL FIRE & CASUALTY INS CO	IN	**C-**	8.9	6.1	2.2	0.0	9.0	4.0	8.1	8.2	1.7	DGRT
UNIVERSAL INS CO	PR	**B**	517.7	214.0	123.0	4.5	8.0	7.9	8.7	7.0	4.7	FT
UNIVERSAL INS CO	NC	**D**	25.6	8.9	16.5	-0.6	3.2	6.7	4.2	0.8	1.7	DFGL

RISK ADJ. RATIO #1	CAPITAL RATIO #2	PREMIUM TO SURPLUS (%)	RESV. TO SURPLUS (%)	RESV. DEVELOP. 1 YEAR (%)	RESV. DEVELOP. 2 YEAR (%)	LOSS RATIO (%)	EXP. RATIO (%)	COMB RATIO (%)	CASH FROM UNDER-WRITING (%)	NET PREMIUM GROWTH (%)	INVEST. IN AFFIL (%)	INSURANCE COMPANY NAME
1.6	1.4	75.6	2.8	-2.9	-3.4	N/A	81.7	81.7	125.1	-1.5	0.0	UNITED CASUALTY & SURETY CO INC
4.9	4.4	31.2	2.4	0.9	1.1	38.1	46.9	85.0	102.4	-7.4	0.0	UNITED CASUALTY INS CO OF AMERICA
5.7	3.5	23.6	30.8	-22.6	-45.3	-17.0	8.0	-9.0	186.2	-1.4	0.0	UNITED CENTRAL PA RRG
1.1	0.6	67.9	79.0	-1.2	-0.9	27.0	57.1	84.1	99.6	-35.7	0.0	UNITED CONTRACTORS INS CO INC RRG
1.4	1.2	54.3	151.8	0.1	-1.6	73.8	18.4	92.2	127.9	5.9	0.0 •	UNITED EDUCATORS INS A RECIP RRG
0.2	0.2	370.7	193.2	29.8	30.8	67.6	42.8	110.4	95.7	1.6	0.0	UNITED EQUITABLE INS CO
2.6	2.1	93.2	116.1	-5.9	-16.3	76.4	26.2	102.6	80.9	-2.8	0.0	UNITED FARM FAMILY INS CO
2.2	1.5	169.1	84.6	1.9	4.5	89.3	23.2	112.5	90.0	-2.1	6.3 •	UNITED FARM FAMILY MUTUAL INS CO
1.1	0.8	337.7	222.5	2.0	14.2	72.5	20.6	93.1	118.8	-5.9	0.6 •	UNITED FINANCIAL CASUALTY CO
1.7	1.4	69.0	79.2	1.3	-0.6	84.6	28.1	112.7	99.6	-2.3	28.1 •	UNITED FIRE & CAS CO
2.1	1.4	94.4	108.5	2.0	-1.1	84.6	28.5	113.1	103.4	-2.3	0.0	UNITED FIRE & INDEMNITY CO
2.1	1.5	87.0	99.9	1.9	-1.0	84.6	28.5	113.1	64.9	-2.3	0.0	UNITED FIRE LLOYDS
3.2	2.0	36.8	30.8	-7.4	-5.9	41.2	37.2	78.4	93.9	1.6	0.0	UNITED FRONTIER MUTUAL INS CO
2.9	2.3	44.3	44.3	1.8	-1.1	66.4	33.9	100.3	111.4	-3.2	0.0	UNITED GROUP CAPTIVE INS CO
0.3	0.3	118.6	351.0	1.8	-65.7	386.4	99.3	485.7	32.9	15.6	29.0 •	UNITED GUAR RESIDENTIAL INS CO OF
1.8	1.3	71.5	133.7	-36.5	-71.4	103.2	29.0	132.2	49.0	-64.0	0.0	UNITED GUARANTY COML INS CO OF NC
1.5	1.5	11.8	7.0	0.4	-0.1	83.9	562.0	645.9	113.5	12.1	0.0	UNITED GUARANTY CREDIT INS CO
0.8	0.6	91.1	307.5	30.9	-17.8	236.9	19.4	256.3	154.9	71.2	0.0	UNITED GUARANTY INS CO
1.3	0.9	36.3	181.6	2.5	31.1	383.1	3.7	386.8	77.9	0.8	0.0	UNITED GUARANTY MORTGAGE INDEM
0.8	0.6	91.2	307.8	30.7	-17.7	236.9	19.4	256.3	154.9	71.2	0.0	UNITED GUARANTY MORTGAGE INS CO
0.8	0.6	90.8	306.4	30.7	-17.7	236.9	19.4	256.3	154.9	71.2	0.0	UNITED GUARANTY MTG INS CO OF NC
1.5	1.2	42.8	119.2	25.4	42.9	259.9	11.0	270.9	97.0	10.8	8.1 •	UNITED GUARANTY RESIDENTIAL INS CO
1.4	1.2	138.1	33.3	1.0	3.9	81.6	33.4	115.0	90.1	-4.8	0.0	UNITED HERITAGE PROP & CAS CO
1.7	1.2	154.8	17.6	-15.3	-1.8	82.9	30.5	113.4	80.2	9.6	0.5	UNITED HOME INS CO
N/A	N/A	0.4	N/A	N/A	N/A	N/A	999 +	999 +	10.3	-86.7	0.0	UNITED HOME INS CO A RRG
1.2	0.9	111.8	23.6	0.1	-0.6	59.5	16.6	76.1	153.7	75.6	0.0	UNITED INS CO
N/A	N/A	N/A	6.3	3.2	5.4	N/A	N/A	N/A	N/A	0.0	0.0	UNITED INTERNATIONAL INS CO
0.7	0.5	98.2	82.9	12.1	-3.1	61.9	46.7	108.6	89.1	125.5	0.0	UNITED MEDICAL LIABILITY INS CO RRG
1.9	1.1	15.5	57.2	5.5	0.5	104.4	36.9	141.3	341.5	-45.7	0.0	UNITED NATIONAL CASUALTY INS CO
1.5	1.2	19.2	71.1	5.0	0.5	100.9	27.3	128.2	72.9	-45.7	32.8 •	UNITED NATIONAL INS CO
5.1	3.0	6.4	23.5	2.4	0.2	97.5	36.9	134.4	42.6	-45.7	0.0	UNITED NATIONAL SPECIALTY INS CO
5.2	3.9	109.0	52.3	-14.4	-20.3	60.2	31.4	91.6	106.2	6.4	0.0	UNITED OHIO INS CO
2.1	1.7	150.7	35.1	-7.9	-11.4	35.6	52.3	87.9	105.0	15.3	0.0	UNITED PROPERTY & CASUALTY INS CO
7.5	7.1	10.5	16.6	-2.9	1.7	150.0	68.3	218.3	62.7	-29.4	0.0	UNITED SECURITY INS CO
1.5	1.4	36.3	22.0	-1.3	-2.0	85.0	14.2	99.2	109.2	2.0	50.3 •	UNITED SERVICES AUTOMOBILE ASN
4.6	3.1	38.7	79.3	-3.2	-3.4	61.5	30.4	91.9	105.2	0.7	1.8 •	UNITED STATES FIDELITY & GUARANTY
1.1	0.7	61.4	176.1	-4.2	-8.1	78.2	50.4	128.6	81.2	-22.0	13.0 •	UNITED STATES FIRE INS CO
1.0	0.9	30.2	42.4	-7.7	-29.0	32.0	41.1	73.1	118.1	215.0	51.0 •	UNITED STATES LIABILITY INS CO
3.4	2.6	62.7	15.6	-14.9	-9.1	3.6	52.1	55.7	171.8	-0.5	0.0	UNITED STATES SURETY CO
1.2	0.8	47.2	46.3	-6.1	-5.4	21.9	51.5	73.4	138.8	-0.1	0.0	UNITED SURETY & INDEMNITY CO
1.4	1.0	113.2	137.3	0.9	2.1	69.8	17.7	87.5	106.8	22.5	0.0	UNITED WISCONSIN INS CO
3.6	3.3	10.0	26.5	-10.2	-29.5	24.1	31.4	55.5	57.7	-44.8	0.0	UNITRIN ADVANTAGE INS CO
3.1	2.3	142.4	68.1	-6.7	-12.5	80.2	29.5	109.7	108.9	-3.3	0.0	UNITRIN AUTO & HOME INS CO
0.7	0.6	N/A	N/A	N/A	N/A	N/A	N/A	N/A	-601.6	0.0	0.0	UNITRIN COUNTY MUTUAL INS CO
1.9	1.5	60.0	36.1	2.6	2.0	97.9	30.3	128.2	94.8	4.0	0.0	UNITRIN DIRECT INS CO
0.7	0.6	131.0	71.1	1.1	4.0	81.5	35.4	116.9	90.0	10.1	0.0	UNITRIN DIRECT PROPERTY & CAS CO
3.4	3.0	57.6	36.0	-5.8	-11.9	62.7	29.0	91.7	127.1	-2.9	0.0	UNITRIN PREFERRED INS CO
7.0	6.3	N/A	N/A	N/A	N/A	N/A	N/A	N/A	310.2	0.0	0.0	UNITRIN SAFEGUARD INS CO
1.1	0.9	210.6	157.3	-11.6	-16.7	64.7	39.1	103.8	93.4	3.1	0.0	UNIVERSAL CASUALTY CO
2.5	2.3	36.8	N/A	N/A	N/A	N/A	96.0	96.0	103.5	8.1	0.0	UNIVERSAL FIRE & CASUALTY INS CO
1.9	1.6	57.6	30.8	-4.4	-5.6	63.6	36.9	100.5	85.2	-9.4	22.9 •	UNIVERSAL INS CO
0.5	0.4	168.9	43.8	1.3	-7.4	61.2	43.9	105.1	91.7	5.6	0.0	UNIVERSAL INS CO

999 + Denotes number greater than 999.9%
999 - Denotes number less than -999.99%
• Bullets denote a more detailed analysis is available in Section II.

INSURANCE COMPANY NAME	DOM. STATE	RATING	TOTAL ASSETS ($MIL)	CAPITAL & SURPLUS ($MIL)	ANNUAL NET PREMIUM ($MIL)	NET INCOME ($MIL)	CAPITAL-IZATION INDEX (PTS)	RESERVE ADQ INDEX (PTS)	PROFIT-ABILITY INDEX (PTS)	LIQUIDITY INDEX (PTS)	STAB. INDEX (PTS)	STABILITY FACTORS
▲UNIVERSAL INS CO OF NORTH AMERICA	FL	**C+**	105.5	46.4	34.6	0.2	5.3	5.6	3.7	6.8	4.3	ORT
UNIVERSAL INS EXCHANGE	TX	**U** (5)	0.0	0.0	6.1	0.0	N/A	4.6	5.5	7.7	3.1	DRT
▲UNIVERSAL NORTH AMERICA INS CO	TX	**C-**	44.5	23.2	24.6	0.4	8.2	3.7	3.2	6.8	2.9	GT
UNIVERSAL PROPERTY & CASUALTY INS	FL	**E+**	374.8	98.5	150.8	2.3	0.5	0.5	3.3	1.7	0.6	CLT
UNIVERSAL SURETY CO	NE	**C**	82.8	65.5	3.0	-0.7	8.1	7.8	3.8	9.8	2.1	DT
UNIVERSAL SURETY OF AMERICA	SD	**C**	25.5	13.6	3.7	0.1	8.8	9.6	8.0	9.1	3.8	DGT
UNIVERSAL UNDERWRITERS INS CO	KS	**C**	429.9	354.7	0.0	2.1	10.0	N/A	3.2	9.5	4.3	FT
UNIVERSAL UNDERWRITERS OF TX	TX	**C+**	14.8	9.5	0.0	0.1	9.4	N/A	3.1	7.3	4.3	DG
UPLAND MUTUAL INS INC	KS	**C**	17.6	9.0	10.1	0.0	8.4	8.4	3.2	6.3	2.9	DFGR
UPPER HUDSON NATIONAL INS CO	NY	**D+**	6.1	5.9	0.3	-0.1	10.0	3.6	1.9	9.5	2.1	DFGT
URGENT CARE ASR CO RRG INC	NV	**D**	1.4	0.7	0.3	-0.1	6.1	3.6	1.6	7.4	0.0	DGT
US AGENCIES CASUALTY INS CO INC	LA	**C**	89.1	49.6	0.2	0.7	10.0	8.0	7.8	10.0	3.4	FG
▼US FIDELIS INS CO RRG INC	MT	**D+**	0.7	0.5	-0.2	0.0	10.0	N/A	1.5	7.0	1.0	DGT
US INS CO OF AMERICA	IL	**D**	3.0	2.5	0.3	-0.1	7.8	N/A	2.1	7.0	1.9	DFGT
US RAIL INS CO A RRG	VT	**D**	2.3	1.5	0.9	-0.1	7.3	N/A	2.8	7.2	1.4	DGT
US SECURITY INS CO	FL	**C**	72.3	27.0	39.0	-2.6	7.2	5.0	3.3	4.9	3.4	FLRT
US SPECIALTY INS CO	TX	**B-**	1,212.9	326.4	429.1	13.1	7.9	6.4	8.8	6.9	4.7	RT
▼US UNDERWRITERS INS CO	ND	**B-**	140.1	52.6	24.3	1.4	7.5	9.7	1.9	9.2	4.0	T
▲USA INS CO	MS	**E**	8.2	2.1	13.9	0.3	0.4	3.6	0.2	0.0	0.1	CDGL
USAA CASUALTY INS CO	TX	**A+**	6,714.4	3,249.1	3,373.4	111.8	10.0	6.3	8.9	6.4	7.9	T
USAA COUNTY MUTUAL INS CO	TX	**B**	132.8	7.9	0.0	0.0	5.1	N/A	5.7	9.3	4.9	CDFT
▼USAA GENERAL INDEMNITY CO	TX	**B+**	452.4	141.0	311.2	0.6	7.9	8.3	2.6	5.3	6.4	GLT
USAA TEXAS LLOYDS CO	TX	**B**	349.1	176.5	148.1	0.3	9.1	6.6	8.9	6.8	5.2	T
USAGENCIES DIRECT INS CO	NY	**U** (1)	7.7	7.2	0.0	0.0	N/A	7.0	2.4	7.0	3.6	FT
USF INS CO	MI	**C**	151.5	61.1	27.4	1.4	0.8	4.7	8.6	6.4	3.8	CT
USIC OF FLORIDA INC	FL	**C-**	6.0	5.7	0.3	0.0	10.0	4.6	5.1	7.8	2.9	DFGO
USPLATE GLASS INS CO	IL	**C**	17.1	11.5	10.1	0.8	7.6	3.8	8.4	6.9	3.1	DGRT
▲UTAH BUILDERS INS CO INC	UT	**E+**	10.7	4.1	9.1	0.0	1.2	3.9	2.9	2.7	0.5	CDGL
▲UTAH MEDICAL INS ASN	UT	**C+**	271.0	57.6	62.0	1.1	7.1	7.0	7.3	7.4	3.6	DRT
▲UTICA FIRST INS CO	NY	**C+**	179.8	73.5	57.9	2.3	8.2	5.9	8.9	6.8	4.3	T
UTICA LLOYDS OF TX	TX	**B**	7.4	5.0	0.0	0.2	10.0	N/A	8.8	10.0	4.0	DG
UTICA MUTUAL INS CO	NY	**B-**	2,101.3	716.7	540.3	7.8	8.6	6.3	7.4	6.9	4.9	T
UTICA NATIONAL ASR CO	NY	**C**	56.8	25.9	12.1	0.0	9.3	6.2	8.6	7.3	4.1	T
UTICA NATIONAL INS CO OF TX	TX	**B-**	29.5	13.8	6.1	0.1	9.6	6.2	8.6	7.6	4.9	DGT
UTICA SPECIALTY RISK INS CO	TX	**C+**	26.0	25.9	0.0	0.3	10.0	N/A	7.8	10.0	4.8	DGT
VA FARM BUREAU TOWN & COUNTRY INS	VA	**C**	48.2	15.4	25.2	0.3	7.5	9.3	6.8	5.7	3.9	DT
VALIANT INS CO	DE	**C+**	67.7	50.4	6.0	-3.3	8.8	N/A	3.2	9.0	3.4	DFGT
VALLEY FORGE INS CO	PA	**C**	55.7	55.4	0.0	0.5	10.0	N/A	6.4	6.9	3.8	A
VALLEY INS CO	CA	**B**	27.7	21.4	0.9	0.3	8.6	8.9	8.5	9.5	5.6	DGT
VALLEY PROPERTY & CASUALTY INS CO	OR	**B-**	16.8	9.8	0.0	0.1	10.0	N/A	8.2	7.0	4.4	DG
VANLINER INS CO	MO	**C+**	475.9	105.5	149.2	2.5	7.7	6.0	3.9	6.5	4.5	T
VANTAGE CASUALTY INS CO	IN	**U** (1)	128.7	52.3	0.0	2.8	N/A	4.7	7.1	10.0	6.1	CT
VANTAPRO SPECIALTY INS CO	AR	**U** (1)	3.2	3.1	0.0	0.1	N/A	N/A	2.7	7.0	3.9	RT
VASA SPRING GARDEN MUTUAL INS CO	MN	**D-**	2.7	1.5	1.6	0.1	9.2	6.2	4.7	6.1	1.3	DFGT
VEHICULAR SERVICE INS CO RRG	OK	**U** (1)	1.8	1.6	0.1	0.0	N/A	2.0	4.8	9.5	2.1	GT
VEREX ASR INC	WI	**B-**	28.8	20.7	0.2	0.1	10.0	8.4	8.0	10.0	5.2	DG
VERLAN FIRE INS CO	NH	**C**	23.2	21.5	15.1	0.7	9.8	6.1	8.6	7.5	4.2	DGT
VERMONT ACCIDENT INS CO INC	VT	**B**	5.6	5.5	0.0	0.0	10.0	N/A	5.3	7.0	4.6	DGT
VERMONT MUTUAL INS CO	VT	**C+**	413.9	161.1	213.0	-1.3	8.4	8.5	6.1	6.7	4.4	RT
VERSANT CASUALTY INS CO	MS	**C-**	15.1	5.9	3.5	0.2	6.7	6.9	4.6	7.4	3.1	DGT
VESTA FIRE INS CO	TX	**F** (5)	0.0	0.0	207.5	0.0	1.6	1.2	0.8	1.3	0.0	CFLT
VESTA INS CORP	TX	**F** (5)	0.0	0.0	0.0	0.0	10.0	N/A	3.9	8.1	0.0	DGT

RISK ADJ. RATIO #1	CAPITAL RATIO #2	PREMIUM TO SURPLUS (%)	RESV. TO SURPLUS (%)	RESV. DEVELOP. 1 YEAR (%)	RESV. DEVELOP. 2 YEAR (%)	LOSS RATIO (%)	EXP. RATIO (%)	COMB RATIO (%)	CASH FROM UNDER-WRITING (%)	NET PREMIUM GROWTH (%)	INVEST. IN AFFIL (%)	INSURANCE COMPANY NAME
2.0	1.3	75.0	23.4	-4.5	-5.9	43.3	39.7	83.0	112.4	-31.5	0.0	UNIVERSAL INS CO OF NORTH AMERICA
N/A	N/A	177.4	116.2	-13.0	26.8	55.0	37.7	92.7	111.4	9.9	0.3	UNIVERSAL INS EXCHANGE
2.8	1.7	108.4	26.2	-15.1	-2.6	88.5	28.2	116.7	127.3	492.6	0.0	UNIVERSAL NORTH AMERICA INS CO
0.2	0.1	160.4	47.4	5.6	21.1	56.0	27.4	83.4	124.6	7.4	0.0	UNIVERSAL PROPERTY & CASUALTY INS
3.1	1.9	3.7	7.3	-2.3	-2.4	16.2	56.1	72.3	151.1	7.0	0.0	UNIVERSAL SURETY CO
2.9	2.3	27.2	30.6	-4.3	-15.5	16.5	80.2	96.7	109.1	-2.3	0.0	UNIVERSAL SURETY OF AMERICA
5.4	5.1	N/A	N/A	N/A	N/A	N/A	N/A	N/A	-72.1	0.0	19.8 •	UNIVERSAL UNDERWRITERS INS CO
5.9	5.3	N/A	N/A	N/A	N/A	N/A	N/A	N/A	406.8	0.0	0.0	UNIVERSAL UNDERWRITERS OF TX
2.3	2.0	112.3	5.9	-2.9	-4.4	80.0	32.9	112.9	78.2	-6.9	0.0	UPLAND MUTUAL INS INC
5.9	5.4	5.9	0.6	-0.5	-0.1	5.7	194.6	200.3	73.9	42.1	0.0	UPPER HUDSON NATIONAL INS CO
1.0	0.9	47.3	40.3	13.4	N/A	94.4	87.2	181.6	117.3	-38.7	0.0	URGENT CARE ASR CO RRG INC
8.8	7.9	0.3	5.6	-1.2	-2.4	-702.5	-304.3	999 +	-211.1	101.4	0.0	US AGENCIES CASUALTY INS CO INC
4.8	4.3	-15.8	N/A	N/A	N/A	N/A	17.8	N/A	-1.3	-200.0	0.0	US FIDELIS INS CO RRG INC
1.1	1.0	11.0	4.9	N/A	N/A	N/A	164.6	164.6	55.9	N/A	0.0	US INS CO OF AMERICA
1.8	1.2	57.9	19.2	N/A	N/A	50.6	50.7	101.3	162.6	529.8	0.0	US RAIL INS CO A RRG
1.4	1.0	123.5	91.4	-4.4	-19.5	83.9	20.0	103.9	90.2	-13.7	0.0	US SECURITY INS CO
2.4	1.6	137.0	164.0	-1.6	-8.2	62.9	24.4	87.3	169.5	24.4	1.2 •	US SPECIALTY INS CO
2.0	1.3	44.1	130.4	-5.1	-64.4	26.4	36.7	63.1	125.0	143.2	0.0	US UNDERWRITERS INS CO
0.4	0.3	785.3	173.5	39.1	377.4	55.3	36.6	91.9	95.3	-18.0	0.0	USA INS CO
5.0	3.9	107.7	57.0	-3.4	-3.3	79.1	13.7	92.8	108.3	4.1	1.3 •	USAA CASUALTY INS CO
0.8	0.7	N/A	N/A	N/A	N/A	N/A	N/A	N/A	-37.0	0.0	0.0	USAA COUNTY MUTUAL INS CO
1.9	1.4	224.6	103.8	-7.4	-6.6	92.5	14.0	106.5	109.4	58.3	0.0 •	USAA GENERAL INDEMNITY CO
3.2	2.4	84.2	29.2	-1.7	-3.9	86.6	12.5	99.1	104.2	4.1	0.0 •	USAA TEXAS LLOYDS CO
N/A	N/A	N/A	N/A	N/A	-18.4	N/A	N/A	N/A	862.5	-100.0	0.0	USAGENCIES DIRECT INS CO
0.3	0.2	45.6	102.5	-18.0	-11.3	65.7	7.5	73.2	136.4	-0.5	12.9	USF INS CO
10.0	7.3	6.1	5.2	2.8	0.5	123.2	54.0	177.2	72.1	-32.1	0.0	USIC OF FLORIDA INC
2.1	1.7	93.5	4.6	-0.1	4.7	9.4	55.9	65.3	148.1	-5.4	0.0	USPLATE GLASS INS CO
0.5	0.3	220.3	96.6	-34.0	-9.0	61.4	40.0	101.4	116.1	62.6	0.0	UTAH BUILDERS INS CO INC
1.6	1.3	107.7	245.2	-10.8	-4.2	79.6	9.2	88.8	123.5	5.6	0.0	UTAH MEDICAL INS ASN
2.6	2.3	80.7	97.7	-3.8	-4.6	56.2	25.8	82.0	130.5	-2.7	0.0	UTICA FIRST INS CO
6.1	5.4	N/A	N/A	N/A	N/A	N/A	N/A	N/A	N/A	0.0	0.0	UTICA LLOYDS OF TX
3.3	2.2	74.6	139.8	-1.4	-3.6	61.7	37.2	98.9	99.0	0.2	5.6 •	UTICA MUTUAL INS CO
4.3	2.8	46.9	87.9	-0.9	-2.4	61.7	36.2	97.9	99.0	0.2	0.0	UTICA NATIONAL ASR CO
4.5	3.0	44.1	82.6	-0.9	-2.2	61.7	36.8	98.5	99.3	0.2	0.0	UTICA NATIONAL INS CO OF TX
110.8	53.5	N/A	N/A	N/A	N/A	N/A	N/A	N/A	N/A	0.0	0.0	UTICA SPECIALTY RISK INS CO
1.7	1.4	161.5	75.2	-8.3	-11.2	62.7	31.4	94.1	99.2	1.3	0.0	VA FARM BUREAU TOWN & COUNTRY
2.2	1.7	11.8	3.4	N/A	N/A	80.0	200.1	280.1	52.0	N/A	27.2	VALIANT INS CO
152.5	74.7	N/A	N/A	N/A	N/A	N/A	N/A	N/A	N/A	0.0	0.0	VALLEY FORGE INS CO
5.0	3.3	4.2	12.9	-6.7	-11.5	-46.6	51.8	5.2	355.1	-27.2	0.0	VALLEY INS CO
5.1	4.6	N/A	N/A	N/A	N/A	N/A	N/A	N/A	0.9	0.0	0.0	VALLEY PROPERTY & CASUALTY INS CO
2.4	1.4	139.6	257.4	-41.5	-47.6	66.3	20.5	86.8	117.2	-2.0	0.0	VANLINER INS CO
N/A	N/A	N/A	99.3	7.8	N/A	184.8	N/A	N/A	N/A	0.0	0.0	VANTAGE CASUALTY INS CO
N/A	N/A	N/A	N/A	N/A	N/A	N/A	N/A	N/A	N/A	0.0	0.0	VANTAPRO SPECIALTY INS CO
3.1	2.8	116.4	0.1	-1.3	0.5	65.6	34.5	100.1	86.4	19.2	0.0	VASA SPRING GARDEN MUTUAL INS CO
N/A	N/A	5.5	N/A	N/A	N/A	N/A	114.4	114.4	87.4	-9.1	0.0	VEHICULAR SERVICE INS CO RRG
10.0	9.0	1.1	0.4	-0.6	-2.0	0.4	57.7	58.1	100.5	-11.6	0.0	VEREX ASR INC
16.0	8.1	74.2	11.8	-3.7	-3.2	18.0	27.6	45.6	207.4	66.6	0.0	VERLAN FIRE INS CO
13.0	7.6	N/A	N/A	N/A	N/A	N/A	N/A	N/A	N/A	0.0	0.0	VERMONT ACCIDENT INS CO INC
3.0	2.1	123.7	61.0	-5.5	-8.3	55.4	36.8	92.2	110.0	0.8	2.0 •	VERMONT MUTUAL INS CO
1.5	1.3	60.8	8.7	0.1	-0.2	55.7	29.1	84.8	119.5	-26.4	20.7	VERSANT CASUALTY INS CO
0.4	0.3	250.7	165.3	31.2	54.6	83.5	45.4	128.9	66.0	13.5	25.6	VESTA FIRE INS CO
4.8	4.3	N/A	N/A	N/A	N/A	N/A	N/A	N/A	159.8	0.0	0.0	VESTA INS CORP

999 + Denotes number greater than 999.9%
999 - Denotes number less than -999.99%
• Bullets denote a more detailed analysis is available in Section II.

INSURANCE COMPANY NAME	DOM. STATE	RATING	TOTAL ASSETS ($MIL)	CAPITAL & SURPLUS ($MIL)	ANNUAL NET PREMIUM ($MIL)	NET INCOME ($MIL)	CAPITAL-IZATION INDEX (PTS)	RESERVE ADQ INDEX (PTS)	PROFIT-ABILITY INDEX (PTS)	LIQUIDITY INDEX (PTS)	STAB. INDEX (PTS)	STABILITY FACTORS
▲VETERINARY PET INS CO	CA	**C**	152.7	48.9	147.1	1.8	7.8	6.6	4.2	5.2	3.4	T
VFH CAPTIVE INS CO	GA	**E+**	5.7	1.6	3.3	0.1	4.4	4.6	3.2	7.0	0.5	DGT
VICTORE INS CO	OK	**D+**	4.7	3.5	2.2	0.0	7.7	9.8	8.7	8.8	2.1	DGT
VICTORIA AUTOMOBILE INS CO	IN	**B**	17.0	8.2	0.0	0.0	10.0	N/A	6.6	7.0	4.2	DFG
▲VICTORIA FIRE & CASUALTY CO	OH	**B-**	512.6	32.1	79.0	-1.3	7.7	8.1	3.3	5.4	4.8	FGT
VICTORIA NATIONAL INS CO	OH	**U** (1)	3.3	3.3	0.0	0.1	N/A	N/A	6.9	7.0	3.5	DT
VICTORIA SELECT INS CO	OH	**B-**	45.6	7.6	0.0	0.2	7.3	N/A	7.0	7.0	4.1	DFGT
VICTORIA SPECIALTY INSURANCE CO	OH	**D**	23.5	3.4	0.0	0.1	5.8	N/A	7.0	6.7	1.9	DFGT
▼VICTORY INS CO INC	MT	**D**	4.0	1.9	1.5	0.1	1.7	N/A	0.3	0.9	1.3	CDFG
VIGILANT INS CO	NY	**B**	375.6	157.2	44.2	4.9	10.0	6.3	8.8	6.8	6.0	T
VIKING COUNTY MUTUAL INS CO	TX	**C**	2.6	2.3	0.0	0.0	10.0	N/A	4.1	7.0	2.0	DFGT
VIKING INS CO OF WI	WI	**C**	406.7	146.4	89.3	1.5	9.1	9.3	2.9	6.8	3.4	T
VININGS INS CO	SC	**C**	44.0	15.2	10.4	-0.2	5.6	4.9	6.0	6.7	4.0	CDGT
VINTAGE INS CO	CA	**U** (1)	20.5	20.0	0.0	0.8	N/A	5.1	7.9	7.0	5.4	RT
VIRGINIA FARM BUREAU FIRE & CAS INS	VA	**C**	40.7	15.0	23.7	0.3	7.4	9.3	6.8	5.6	3.9	DGT
VIRGINIA FARM BUREAU MUTUAL INS CO	VA	**C**	261.7	120.2	134.0	0.4	8.3	8.9	8.6	6.0	4.3	T
VIRGINIA HEALTH SYSTEMS ALLIANCE RRG	VT	**D-**	91.0	24.4	20.3	-1.7	3.4	7.0	3.7	7.1	0.9	DRT
▲VIRGINIA SURETY CO INC	IL	**C+**	1,015.5	275.6	341.9	10.2	6.2	3.1	3.5	6.9	4.4	T
VISION INS CO	TX	**D+**	13.3	6.4	16.2	-0.4	4.3	3.8	4.0	2.7	2.4	DFGL
VOYAGER INDEMNITY INS CO	GA	**C+**	88.9	26.6	33.2	0.8	7.9	8.5	3.6	7.1	4.8	T
WACO FIRE & CAS INS CO	GA	**D**	39.8	15.1	2.1	0.5	3.3	6.1	4.7	6.3	1.4	DFGT
WADENA INS CO	IA	**C**	36.4	8.0	5.5	0.2	8.4	3.8	4.5	6.6	2.9	DGT
WALLROSE MUTUAL INS CO	PA	**D**	1.0	0.5	0.2	0.0	8.6	6.0	3.9	7.6	1.0	DFGO
WARNER INS CO	CT	**C-**	25.4	14.6	9.1	-0.5	7.3	7.4	2.4	6.8	2.9	DFGT
▼WARRANTY UNDERWRITERS INS CO	TX	**D**	43.9	4.6	9.7	-0.2	1.0	9.6	1.0	9.2	2.3	CDGT
WARREN RRG INC	VT	**E+**	8.3	2.6	1.5	0.0	6.7	6.1	7.2	9.3	0.0	DGT
WASHINGTON CASUALTY CO	WA	**F** (1)	38.1	15.5	7.5	-2.5	3.2	3.5	0.3	6.8	0.0	DR
WASHINGTON COUNTY CO-OPERATIVE INS	NY	**E+**	6.0	4.1	1.3	0.0	10.0	7.6	4.3	7.5	0.8	DGT
WASHINGTON INTERNATIONAL INS CO	NH	**C+**	116.2	63.7	7.7	3.9	10.0	8.4	8.7	9.6	4.3	T
WASHINGTON MUT F I C OF LAWRENCE CTY	PA	**D** (1)	1.6	1.5	0.0	0.0	10.0	7.3	5.7	10.0	1.3	DOT
WASHINGTON MUTUAL FIRE & STORM INS	PA	**D+**	3.3	1.8	0.9	0.0	7.1	6.9	5.6	7.3	2.4	DGRT
WAUSAU BUSINESS INS CO	WI	**B-**	255.2	54.0	42.8	0.9	7.6	3.7	6.4	6.9	4.9	AT
WAUSAU GENERAL INS CO	WI	**B-**	36.1	29.2	0.0	0.2	10.0	3.4	3.6	9.9	3.7	ADGT
WAUSAU UNDERWRITERS INS CO	WI	**C+**	385.2	92.6	42.8	1.2	9.5	5.4	5.6	6.9	4.4	AFT
WAWANESA GENERAL INS CO	CA	**C**	334.8	115.7	242.3	-2.9	7.8	5.0	3.9	2.6	4.2	LRT
WAWANESA MUTUAL INS CO US BR	CA	**B**	250.3	197.2	56.3	3.1	10.0	6.2	8.6	6.9	5.4	RT
WAYNE COOPERATIVE INS CO	NY	**C-**	19.3	7.9	10.6	0.0	7.9	8.6	5.9	5.8	2.7	DGT
WAYNE MUTUAL INS CO	OH	**C**	28.3	12.5	17.1	-0.6	8.2	9.4	2.6	6.0	3.5	DFGT
WEA PROPERTY & CASUALTY INS CO	WI	**C**	14.0	5.0	9.2	0.1	7.1	7.0	5.7	5.2	3.4	DGT
▲WELLINGTON INS CO	TX	**C-**	31.7	13.4	22.3	-0.2	3.7	5.8	5.7	6.2	2.5	DGT
▲WELLSPAN RRG	VT	**D**	27.9	8.7	5.0	0.0	5.3	4.1	2.9	7.0	1.6	DGT
▲WESCO INS CO	DE	**C+**	205.3	36.6	22.6	1.1	10.0	7.5	4.0	7.5	3.7	GT
WESCO-FINANCIAL INS CO	NE	**B+**	2,526.8	2,086.2	298.6	9.9	9.9	5.0	5.9	7.2	5.1	GT
WEST AMERICAN INSURANCE CO	IN	**C**	404.3	209.5	0.0	2.2	10.0	3.5	3.6	7.0	3.8	AT
▼WEST BEND MUTUAL INS CO	WI	**B+**	1,438.7	390.2	690.7	-18.8	7.8	5.9	3.7	5.5	5.0	T
WEST BRANCH MUTUAL INS CO	PA	**U** (1)	0.5	0.4	0.1	0.0	N/A	6.2	2.2	7.0	1.1	T
WEST VIRGINIA FARMERS MUT INS ASSOC	WV	**C-**	4.4	3.6	0.8	0.0	10.0	6.0	8.8	7.4	2.9	DGT
WEST VIRGINIA MUTUAL INS CO	WV	**D-**	156.9	61.1	40.3	1.0	9.5	6.1	7.7	7.7	1.2	T
WEST VIRGINIA NATIONAL AUTO INS CO	WV	**D**	9.2	4.6	7.5	0.0	7.2	6.9	4.4	6.3	2.2	DGT
WESTCHESTER FIRE INS CO	NY	**C-**	2,561.4	785.0	502.2	30.2	2.4	2.6	7.1	6.9	2.9	CT
WESTCHESTER SURPLUS LINES INS CO	GA	**C**	421.4	169.6	26.6	3.7	7.1	5.2	7.5	7.1	4.1	FT
WESTERN AGRICULTURAL INS CO	IA	**B+**	309.2	50.6	79.0	0.8	8.1	7.0	5.4	3.8	5.0	FGLT

See Page 27 for explanation of footnotes and Page 28 for explanation of stability factors.

Arrows denote recent upgrades ▲ or downgrades ▼ (see Section VII for explanations)

RISK ADJ. CAPITAL RATIO #1	RATIO #2	PREMIUM TO SURPLUS (%)	RESV. TO SURPLUS (%)	RESV. DEVELOP. 1 YEAR (%)	2 YEAR (%)	LOSS RATIO (%)	EXP. RATIO (%)	COMB RATIO (%)	CASH FROM UNDER-WRITING (%)	NET PREMIUM GROWTH (%)	INVEST. IN AFFIL (%)	INSURANCE COMPANY NAME
3.7	2.0	324.2	28.4	-5.8	2.2	61.2	29.3	90.5	106.5	16.8	0.0	VETERINARY PET INS CO
0.9	0.7	225.9	178.4	-2.1	24.5	58.1	31.7	89.8	99.8	0.1	22.9	VFH CAPTIVE INS CO
2.1	1.8	63.8	25.3	-21.2	-42.5	-0.9	64.2	63.3	156.2	3.2	0.0	VICTORE INS CO
3.7	3.3	N/A	N/A	N/A	N/A	N/A	N/A	N/A	79.7	0.0	0.0	VICTORIA AUTOMOBILE INS CO
0.8	0.7	142.7	63.4	-1.6	-1.6	75.8	42.2	118.0	82.4	9.2	25.6	VICTORIA FIRE & CASUALTY CO
N/A	N/A	N/A	N/A	N/A	N/A	N/A	N/A	N/A	7.0	0.0	0.0	VICTORIA NATIONAL INS CO
1.4	1.2	N/A	N/A	N/A	N/A	N/A	N/A	N/A	419.9	0.0	0.0	VICTORIA SELECT INS CO
0.9	0.8	N/A	N/A	N/A	N/A	N/A	N/A	N/A	126.7	0.0	0.0	VICTORIA SPECIALTY INSURANCE CO
0.7	0.5	99.1	30.4	N/A	N/A	47.0	119.5	166.5	63.9	980.0	0.0	VICTORY INS CO INC
4.1	3.2	29.0	52.2	-1.8	-3.6	61.3	28.7	90.0	123.5	-2.6	12.2	VIGILANT INS CO
16.7	15.0	N/A	N/A	N/A	N/A	N/A	N/A	N/A	311.1	0.0	0.0	VIKING COUNTY MUTUAL INS CO
3.2	2.3	62.0	100.1	-5.3	-11.4	74.5	26.8	101.3	92.2	-5.6	5.4	VIKING INS CO OF WI
2.0	0.7	68.9	116.1	-10.8	-10.7	60.1	40.7	100.8	106.5	-41.3	0.0	VININGS INS CO
N/A	N/A	N/A	0.1	N/A	-0.4	300.0	N/A	300.0	N/A	0.0	0.0	VINTAGE INS CO
1.8	1.4	156.8	77.8	-8.6	-11.4	62.7	34.0	96.7	96.2	-1.1	0.0	VIRGINIA FARM BUREAU FIRE & CAS INS
2.3	1.8	110.5	50.7	-3.7	-6.8	63.9	33.3	97.2	100.7	-1.0	15.1	VIRGINIA FARM BUREAU MUTUAL INS CO
0.5	0.4	67.2	135.1	-10.6	-15.9	68.1	5.9	74.0	183.6	-7.9	0.0	VIRGINIA HEALTH SYSTEMS ALLIANCE
1.6	0.9	130.6	122.8	46.9	51.0	104.0	-8.5	95.5	120.2	14.5	0.7 •	VIRGINIA SURETY CO INC
0.8	0.6	238.3	81.7	-10.5	-6.3	65.8	37.9	103.7	95.0	-9.9	0.0	VISION INS CO
1.8	1.4	123.7	6.5	-0.3	-0.9	29.9	55.0	84.9	147.7	15.4	0.0	VOYAGER INDEMNITY INS CO
1.2	0.7	13.3	160.0	-55.6	-56.2	-158.1	241.2	83.1	12.9	-54.2	0.0	WACO FIRE & CAS INS CO
1.8	1.6	70.6	26.6	-2.9	-4.8	62.2	30.1	92.3	122.1	4.6	0.0	WADENA INS CO
2.2	1.9	43.5	10.5	-0.2	4.4	75.2	22.6	97.8	55.4	-8.5	0.0	WALLROSE MUTUAL INS CO
1.1	1.1	54.4	32.9	1.4	-0.6	83.9	29.2	113.1	81.8	5.8	57.8	WARNER INS CO
0.2	0.2	184.2	302.8	-27.6	-13.2	130.5	38.7	169.2	116.4	222.3	1.9	WARRANTY UNDERWRITERS INS CO
1.2	0.9	57.9	175.3	-65.9	-84.5	10.6	53.8	64.4	276.5	-13.6	0.0	WARREN RRG INC
0.9	0.8	48.2	116.9	18.3	-5.5	150.7	23.6	174.3	86.7	25.7	0.0	WASHINGTON CASUALTY CO
6.0	3.9	30.3	13.1	-1.0	-2.1	72.4	29.6	102.0	106.0	14.3	0.0	WASHINGTON COUNTY CO-OPERATIVE
9.3	8.4	12.7	17.9	-0.4	-1.8	28.6	32.1	60.7	167.3	-9.4	0.0	WASHINGTON INTERNATIONAL INS CO
28.4	25.3	1.7	0.5	-0.5	-0.3	65.4	92.3	157.7	50.0	-10.3	0.0	WASHINGTON MUT F I C OF LAWRENCE
1.6	1.0	46.2	20.3	-3.7	-10.7	40.4	50.4	90.8	94.7	-2.9	0.0	WASHINGTON MUTUAL FIRE & STORM
2.5	1.5	79.8	148.1	-2.7	2.0	83.6	24.1	107.7	96.6	-11.9	0.0	WAUSAU BUSINESS INS CO
14.9	13.4	N/A	N/A	N/A	N/A	N/A	N/A	N/A	881.3	100.0	0.0	WAUSAU GENERAL INS CO
4.2	2.6	46.7	86.7	-1.5	1.1	83.6	24.1	107.7	85.1	-11.9	0.0	WAUSAU UNDERWRITERS INS CO
2.0	1.5	204.5	61.1	6.5	8.1	98.3	7.8	106.1	97.2	6.6	0.0	WAWANESA GENERAL INS CO
15.4	10.1	29.0	8.7	0.7	0.6	84.7	8.6	93.3	104.8	-3.1	0.0 •	WAWANESA MUTUAL INS CO US BR
2.0	1.5	133.0	58.8	-4.8	-6.9	74.4	28.0	102.4	96.9	6.3	0.0	WAYNE COOPERATIVE INS CO
2.5	1.7	126.6	50.8	-9.0	-9.8	78.1	32.1	110.2	92.5	2.3	0.3	WAYNE MUTUAL INS CO
1.5	1.1	188.9	77.5	-5.5	-12.9	72.6	33.8	106.4	99.1	1.8	0.0	WEA PROPERTY & CASUALTY INS CO
0.9	0.6	165.3	28.9	-3.6	-6.2	62.2	34.6	96.8	116.2	-1.3	0.0	WELLINGTON INS CO
1.3	1.0	56.0	155.7	-65.2	-65.1	61.5	9.6	71.1	131.4	1.7	0.0	WELLSPAN RRG
3.8	3.4	60.7	17.0	-0.3	-3.0	58.7	-10.4	48.3	324.6	181.9	0.0	WESCO INS CO
3.3	2.6	12.8	7.9	-0.1	-0.2	69.9	30.9	100.8	177.6	744.9	5.2 •	WESCO-FINANCIAL INS CO
22.3	20.1	N/A	N/A	N/A	N/A	N/A	N/A	N/A	86.9	0.0	0.0 •	WEST AMERICAN INSURANCE CO
2.2	1.4	173.9	160.5	0.9	1.2	74.1	29.7	103.8	103.8	2.8	1.9 •	WEST BEND MUTUAL INS CO
N/A	N/A	29.8	2.2	N/A	-0.9	23.7	98.2	121.9	114.6	-5.2	0.0	WEST BRANCH MUTUAL INS CO
9.8	7.3	23.7	3.7	-0.3	0.6	56.1	17.8	73.9	128.1	-7.0	0.0	WEST VIRGINIA FARMERS MUT INS
3.2	2.2	57.9	97.1	-16.9	-16.7	52.0	25.0	77.0	167.0	-8.3	0.0	WEST VIRGINIA MUTUAL INS CO
1.2	1.1	165.0	76.6	-3.6	-5.6	73.2	29.2	102.4	100.3	16.2	0.0	WEST VIRGINIA NATIONAL AUTO INS CO
0.6	0.4	66.1	173.6	-6.5	1.6	68.0	31.6	99.6	115.9	-2.5	0.0 •	WESTCHESTER FIRE INS CO
1.8	1.2	16.1	42.5	-0.8	7.0	91.4	24.7	116.1	34.1	-0.8	0.0 •	WESTCHESTER SURPLUS LINES INS CO
2.8	1.8	152.8	82.7	-2.2	-8.5	85.2	24.6	109.8	94.7	18.9	3.0 •	WESTERN AGRICULTURAL INS CO

999 + Denotes number greater than 999.9%
999 - Denotes number less than -999.99%
• Bullets denote a more detailed analysis is available in Section II.

INSURANCE COMPANY NAME	DOM. STATE	RATING	TOTAL ASSETS ($MIL)	CAPITAL & SURPLUS ($MIL)	ANNUAL NET PREMIUM ($MIL)	NET INCOME ($MIL)	CAPITAL-IZATION INDEX (PTS)	RESERVE ADQ INDEX (PTS)	PROFIT-ABILITY INDEX (PTS)	LIQUIDITY INDEX (PTS)	STAB. INDEX (PTS)	STABILITY FACTORS
WESTERN COMMUNITY INS CO	ID	**B+**	30.0	21.3	0.1	0.3	10.0	6.0	8.6	8.9	5.0	DG
WESTERN GENERAL INS CO	CA	**C**	76.8	31.1	39.5	0.0	7.1	5.8	6.7	5.5	4.0	RT
WESTERN HERITAGE INS CO	AZ	**B**	117.6	93.1	0.0	1.7	10.0	N/A	8.1	10.0	5.4	FT
WESTERN HOME INS CO	MN	**C-**	33.1	16.4	10.3	0.5	5.7	6.7	5.9	6.7	3.2	GT
WESTERN INS RRG INC	AZ	**D** (1)	1.1	0.8	0.2	0.0	8.0	6.0	6.7	9.8	1.2	DT
▲WESTERN MUTUAL INS CO	CA	**C-**	45.6	27.6	18.0	0.9	7.4	9.0	8.7	6.8	2.7	GRT
WESTERN NATIONAL ASR CO	MN	**C**	41.5	16.6	14.5	0.5	5.4	8.5	5.8	6.6	3.2	DFGT
▲WESTERN NATIONAL MUTUAL INS CO	MN	**B-**	488.1	214.5	171.8	5.6	7.2	5.7	8.8	6.3	4.5	T
WESTERN PACIFIC MUT INS CO RISK RET	CO	**C**	122.1	63.5	6.2	1.2	9.9	8.8	6.0	9.5	3.9	DT
WESTERN PROFESSIONAL INS CO	WA	**U** (1)	12.4	12.1	0.0	0.3	N/A	N/A	6.8	7.0	5.0	T
WESTERN PROTECTORS INS CO	OR	**C**	13.5	8.1	-1.5	0.1	10.0	8.0	5.0	7.0	3.5	DFGT
WESTERN RESERVE MUTUAL CAS CO	OH	**B-**	139.4	83.0	56.1	-1.4	10.0	8.6	3.7	6.7	4.7	T
WESTERN SELECT INS CO	CA	**U** (1)	13.9	13.5	0.0	0.4	N/A	6.2	7.7	7.0	5.0	T
WESTERN SURETY CO	SD	**C**	1,232.9	574.7	427.8	20.3	7.9	5.9	9.1	7.1	4.1	T
WESTERN UNDERWRITERS INS CO	CA	**C**	16.8	16.8	0.2	0.0	10.0	4.6	8.1	10.0	3.6	DFGR
WESTERN UNITED INS CO	IN	**C+**	148.6	86.4	26.9	2.0	10.0	7.5	8.9	7.1	4.4	T
▲WESTERN WORLD INS CO	NH	**C+**	1,019.6	317.6	157.4	5.3	5.4	9.1	8.6	7.1	4.3	T
WESTFIELD INS CO	OH	**B-**	2,029.3	533.6	1,050.4	-8.0	8.0	5.0	4.0	6.0	4.6	T
WESTFIELD NATIONAL INS CO	OH	**B+**	437.0	142.2	213.4	0.5	8.3	5.0	5.0	6.5	5.0	T
▲WESTGUARD INS CO	PA	**D+**	29.7	8.7	10.0	0.1	4.8	6.0	6.7	6.9	2.4	CDGT
WESTMINSTER AMERICAN INS CO	MD	**C-**	11.1	7.2	3.9	0.5	8.4	6.0	7.0	7.0	2.2	DGT
WESTPORT INS CORP	MO	**C**	7,822.1	1,669.3	140.0	-62.3	2.5	2.7	1.3	7.0	4.0	CFGT
WESTWARD INS CO	CA	**U** (1)	2.4	2.4	0.0	0.1	N/A	4.6	2.5	7.0	3.7	T
WHITE MOUNTAINS REINS CO OF AMER	NY	**C-**	2,449.0	692.0	554.9	0.5	7.1	2.5	2.0	7.0	3.1	FRT
WHITECAP SURETY CO	MN	**D-**	1.3	1.1	3.7	0.0	0.5	N/A	6.7	0.6	0.9	CDGL
WI LAWYERS MUTUAL INS CO	WI	**C**	25.6	15.9	3.8	-0.2	10.0	9.3	5.0	8.0	3.9	DGRT
WILLIAMSBURG NATIONAL INS CO	MI	**C-**	99.5	23.0	34.7	1.0	5.2	5.7	7.2	6.8	3.2	DT
WILMINGTON INS CO	DE	**D**	4.5	3.2	0.4	0.0	7.1	6.0	4.3	7.7	2.1	DFGR
WILSHIRE INS CO	NC	**C**	129.8	61.3	69.7	1.1	7.8	5.0	4.1	5.8	2.7	RT
WILSON MUTUAL INS CO	WI	**B**	76.3	15.4	19.1	-0.5	7.0	5.5	3.4	6.4	5.6	T
▲WINDHAVEN INS CO	FL	**E+**	8.7	4.4	2.6	-0.1	7.9	3.1	3.3	9.2	0.5	DFGT
WINDSOR MOUNT JOY MUTUAL INS CO	PA	**C**	43.2	26.5	15.6	0.3	10.0	8.9	8.8	7.9	4.2	DGT
WISCONSIN AMERICAN MUTUAL INS CO	WI	**C**	4.8	2.6	3.6	-0.1	7.0	2.5	1.6	1.5	2.0	DFGL
WISCONSIN COUNTY MUTUAL INS CORP	WI	**C**	56.6	17.8	13.5	0.5	7.1	9.3	4.1	7.3	4.2	DRT
WISCONSIN MUNICIPAL MUTUAL INS CO	WI	**D+**	49.7	33.7	3.0	0.0	7.1	5.7	4.1	8.3	2.7	DGT
WISCONSIN MUTUAL INS CO	WI	**C**	86.7	43.4	51.6	0.6	8.8	8.6	8.4	5.5	4.1	T
WISCONSIN REINSURANCE CORP	WI	**C**	71.7	34.2	34.3	0.0	5.7	6.8	3.7	5.3	4.1	FRT
WMAC CREDIT INS CORP	WI	**U** (1)	6.2	6.1	0.0	0.2	N/A	3.6	6.9	7.0	4.5	T
WOLVERINE MUTUAL INS CO	MI	**C**	41.6	12.0	28.5	-0.3	7.1	6.9	2.5	5.0	3.3	DFGT
▼WORK FIRST CASUALTY CO	DE	**D**	33.8	10.0	24.8	0.2	0.7	3.6	4.3	6.3	1.9	CDGT
WORKCOMP HAWAII INS CO INC	HI	**U** (1)	19.8	17.1	0.0	0.1	N/A	9.7	7.4	10.0	5.0	FT
WORKCOMP HAWAII SELECT INS CO INC	HI	**U** (1)	13.3	11.0	0.0	-0.1	N/A	9.7	6.7	10.0	4.7	FT
WORKERS COMPENSATION EXCHANGE	ID	**E**	8.5	0.1	3.1	0.2	0.0	0.1	1.9	0.0	0.1	CDFG
WORKERS COMPENSATION FUND OF UTAH	UT	**U** (5)	1,379.4	462.7	131.2	0.0	N/A	3.9	7.8	7.1	3.5	T
WORKMENS AUTO INS CO	CA	**D**	60.5	19.3	52.0	0.0	4.0	4.4	2.6	0.8	1.9	DFLT
WORTH CASUALTY CO	TX	**C**	4.7	2.7	2.1	0.0	7.9	6.0	2.2	5.9	3.0	DFGO
WRM AMERICA INDEMNITY CO INC	NY	**U** (1)	61.9	60.8	0.0	-0.4	N/A	N/A	5.9	7.0	5.0	FGT
WVA INS CO	WV	**D**	36.3	27.8	11.4	0.2	10.0	6.4	8.8	7.0	2.1	DGT
X L INS CO OF NY	NY	**D**	210.5	68.2	53.8	0.8	1.8	3.7	8.0	8.3	2.3	AGT
▲XL INS AMERICA INC	DE	**C-**	629.4	221.1	179.4	-1.9	2.7	3.7	6.0	6.9	3.3	CGT
XL LLOYDS INS CO	TX	**U** (1)	3.3	3.1	0.0	0.0	N/A	N/A	7.7	7.0	4.2	T
▲XL REINS AMERICA INC	NY	**C**	5,090.1	2,072.3	1,166.4	42.3	5.2	4.2	7.1	6.9	3.5	AGT

See Page 27 for explanation of footnotes and Page 28 for explanation of stability factors.

Arrows denote recent upgrades ▲ or downgrades ▼ (see Section VII for explanations)

RISK ADJ. RATIO #1	CAPITAL RATIO #2	PREMIUM TO SURPLUS (%)	RESV. TO SURPLUS (%)	RESV. DEVELOP. 1 YEAR (%)	RESV. DEVELOP. 2 YEAR (%)	LOSS RATIO (%)	EXP. RATIO (%)	COMB RATIO (%)	CASH FROM UNDER-WRITING (%)	NET PREMIUM GROWTH (%)	INVEST. IN AFFIL (%)	INSURANCE COMPANY NAME
9.6	8.7	0.6	1.3	N/A	-0.1	61.8	-459.4	-397.6	-143.4	-2.9	0.0 •	WESTERN COMMUNITY INS CO
1.8	1.3	126.5	40.7	-7.8	-2.5	60.3	48.1	108.4	105.4	-41.5	0.0	WESTERN GENERAL INS CO
23.3	20.9	N/A	N/A	N/A	N/A	N/A	N/A	N/A	-132.5	0.0	0.0	WESTERN HERITAGE INS CO
1.7	1.1	65.2	65.8	-3.1	-6.1	69.3	27.5	96.8	116.0	-3.0	0.0	WESTERN HOME INS CO
3.9	2.3	19.5	28.3	-31.3	-34.5	N/A	31.6	31.6	999 +	0.6	0.0	WESTERN INS RRG INC
2.4	1.8	66.7	22.8	-5.8	-13.5	50.5	34.1	84.6	116.2	0.2	12.0	WESTERN MUTUAL INS CO
1.2	0.8	89.9	90.6	-4.2	-8.1	69.3	27.2	96.5	90.2	-3.0	0.0	WESTERN NATIONAL ASR CO
1.8	1.2	81.6	82.2	-3.6	-6.4	69.3	26.7	96.0	110.3	-3.0	12.1 •	WESTERN NATIONAL MUTUAL INS CO
5.2	3.3	9.4	40.2	-7.0	-4.9	64.2	55.9	120.1	93.6	-40.3	0.0	WESTERN PACIFIC MUT INS CO RISK
N/A	N/A	N/A	N/A	N/A	N/A	N/A	N/A	N/A	N/A	-100.0	0.0	WESTERN PROFESSIONAL INS CO
5.0	4.5	-18.3	6.5	-0.6	-7.6	N/A	92.5	N/A	312.1	-189.1	0.0	WESTERN PROTECTORS INS CO
5.4	3.2	64.5	24.6	-1.7	-2.5	73.3	31.8	105.1	93.2	-0.4	0.2	WESTERN RESERVE MUTUAL CAS CO
N/A	N/A	N/A	N/A	N/A	-1.4	N/A	N/A	N/A	N/A	0.0	0.0	WESTERN SELECT INS CO
2.5	1.9	77.1	59.3	-9.8	-17.0	18.2	53.6	71.8	157.7	0.8	1.9 •	WESTERN SURETY CO
22.3	14.7	1.0	0.3	0.3	N/A	N/A	164.0	164.0	20.0	-53.0	0.0	WESTERN UNDERWRITERS INS CO
11.8	10.7	32.8	13.3	-2.2	-1.7	65.6	1.7	67.3	247.7	-2.7	0.1	WESTERN UNITED INS CO
1.3	0.9	50.7	156.3	-4.6	-8.4	65.0	35.5	100.5	111.9	-17.7	20.7 •	WESTERN WORLD INS CO
2.1	1.5	179.2	147.9	-8.8	-4.0	66.7	31.9	98.6	107.2	3.0	0.0 •	WESTFIELD INS CO
2.6	1.8	138.0	113.9	-7.2	-3.4	66.7	32.3	99.0	107.2	3.0	0.0 •	WESTFIELD NATIONAL INS CO
1.0	0.4	117.0	171.9	-17.0	-17.0	56.7	29.6	86.3	142.0	1.5	0.0	WESTGUARD INS CO
3.1	2.0	59.0	17.3	-8.2	-9.9	42.1	48.0	90.1	107.4	-3.5	0.0	WESTMINSTER AMERICAN INS CO
0.6	0.4	7.7	170.6	-6.7	0.2	75.1	75.1	150.2	12.9	125.1	1.2 •	WESTPORT INS CORP
N/A	N/A	N/A	N/A	-0.1	N/A	-40.0	N/A	N/A	N/A	0.0	0.0	WESTWARD INS CO
1.5	1.0	78.3	205.5	16.8	23.8	101.0	24.0	125.0	79.1	-34.0	0.6 •	WHITE MOUNTAINS REINS CO OF AMER
0.2	0.2	354.4	N/A	N/A	N/A	N/A	94.8	94.8	103.8	-0.3	0.0	WHITECAP SURETY CO
5.8	3.6	22.7	36.5	-6.6	-5.4	49.8	24.2	74.0	101.5	-1.1	0.0	WI LAWYERS MUTUAL INS CO
1.5	0.9	157.9	195.8	-5.3	-8.2	62.0	30.2	92.2	116.2	8.5	0.0	WILLIAMSBURG NATIONAL INS CO
2.5	1.9	13.1	12.6	-1.2	-4.7	44.8	82.5	127.3	26.4	-9.7	0.0	WILMINGTON INS CO
3.1	1.8	97.9	67.7	-3.9	-9.0	64.5	34.2	98.7	102.8	21.6	0.0	WILSHIRE INS CO
1.5	0.9	120.6	100.3	-2.9	-5.5	73.5	32.4	105.9	106.7	3.5	0.0	WILSON MUTUAL INS CO
3.2	2.5	50.0	25.8	-3.9	11.9	70.7	28.9	99.6	71.5	-62.6	0.0	WINDHAVEN INS CO
5.0	4.1	59.5	17.8	-9.4	-9.8	35.2	44.3	79.5	119.1	-4.4	0.0	WINDSOR MOUNT JOY MUTUAL INS CO
1.6	1.1	132.6	41.8	20.2	26.2	96.7	34.8	131.5	66.7	-24.5	0.0	WISCONSIN AMERICAN MUTUAL INS CO
1.7	1.0	75.7	116.7	-14.4	-13.1	45.3	28.3	73.6	152.5	9.3	13.2	WISCONSIN COUNTY MUTUAL INS CORP
1.2	0.9	9.0	20.3	2.2	-8.5	75.2	27.1	102.3	196.2	24.1	0.0	WISCONSIN MUNICIPAL MUTUAL INS CO
3.9	2.7	121.1	65.3	0.1	-1.7	81.1	21.6	102.7	98.8	0.1	0.0	WISCONSIN MUTUAL INS CO
1.0	0.8	98.7	89.7	-10.2	-12.5	99.3	17.7	117.0	90.6	14.3	18.8	WISCONSIN REINSURANCE CORP
N/A	N/A	N/A	N/A	N/A	N/A	N/A	N/A	N/A	N/A	0.0	0.0	WMAC CREDIT INS CORP
1.5	1.1	237.7	96.5	-3.9	-5.0	79.2	31.7	110.9	87.1	-4.2	0.0	WOLVERINE MUTUAL INS CO
0.3	0.2	231.0	168.5	6.7	3.3	72.0	18.9	90.9	179.1	49.8	0.0	WORK FIRST CASUALTY CO
N/A	N/A	N/A	11.8	-5.7	-10.4	999 +	-300.0	999 +	0.3	150.0	0.0	WORKCOMP HAWAII INS CO INC
N/A	N/A	N/A	16.4	-5.3	-13.4	N/A	N/A	N/A	N/A	0.0	0.0	WORKCOMP HAWAII SELECT INS CO INC
0.0	0.0	999 +	999 +	155.2	675.1	98.8	9.7	108.5	46.1	-35.8	0.0	WORKERS COMPENSATION EXCHANGE
N/A	N/A	73.2	244.7	-0.9	N/A	82.7	13.9	96.6	157.3	-9.5	0.8	WORKERS COMPENSATION FUND OF
0.7	0.6	272.0	96.7	10.2	2.6	72.1	38.1	110.2	91.6	-6.6	1.2	WORKMENS AUTO INS CO
2.0	1.5	76.8	33.9	2.9	2.3	114.9	17.9	132.8	84.3	5.8	0.0	WORTH CASUALTY CO
N/A	N/A	N/A	N/A	N/A	N/A	N/A	N/A	N/A	N/A	0.0	0.0	WRM AMERICA INDEMNITY CO INC
7.4	6.5	41.2	7.3	-1.4	-2.7	64.5	17.6	82.1	123.1	-1.0	0.0	WVA INS CO
0.7	0.5	80.1	115.8	-11.4	-8.4	60.4	20.9	81.3	185.7	128.2	0.0	X L INS CO OF NY
0.7	0.4	72.3	104.4	-10.2	-7.7	60.4	20.0	80.4	185.7	128.2	21.6 •	XL INS AMERICA INC
N/A	N/A	N/A	N/A	N/A	N/A	N/A	N/A	N/A	32.2	0.0	0.0	XL LLOYDS INS CO
1.1	0.7	50.3	72.7	-6.9	-4.8	60.4	23.1	83.5	187.2	128.2	15.8 •	XL REINS AMERICA INC

999 + Denotes number greater than 999.9%
999 - Denotes number less than -999.99%
• Bullets denote a more detailed analysis is available in Section II.

INSURANCE COMPANY NAME	DOM. STATE	RATING	TOTAL ASSETS ($MIL)	CAPITAL & SURPLUS ($MIL)	ANNUAL NET PREMIUM ($MIL)	NET INCOME ($MIL)	CAPITAL-IZATION INDEX (PTS)	RESERVE ADQ INDEX (PTS)	PROFIT-ABILITY INDEX (PTS)	LIQUIDITY INDEX (PTS)	STAB. INDEX (PTS)	STABILITY FACTORS
XL SELECT INS CO	DE	**D+**	128.7	52.0	35.9	-0.4	2.5	3.9	6.2	6.8	2.7	CGT
XL SPECIALTY INS CO	DE	**C+**	510.3	161.9	107.7	-0.6	4.1	4.0	5.9	7.8	3.8	ACGT
YEL CO INS	FL	**C-**	13.7	9.3	1.2	0.2	10.0	9.3	7.3	10.0	2.9	DGT
YELLOWSTONE INS EXCH RRG	VT	**D-**	22.2	7.1	4.5	0.1	6.3	7.0	5.2	7.4	1.3	DGRT
YORK INS CO	RI	**U** (1)	23.4	9.6	-0.1	4.1	N/A	4.0	3.9	10.0	4.6	CFT
YORK INS CO OF MAINE	ME	**C+**	15.9	15.7	0.0	0.5	10.0	N/A	2.7	7.0	4.3	DG
YOSEMITE INS CO	IN	**C+**	335.2	242.2	60.8	7.6	10.0	7.3	3.4	9.2	4.5	T
YOUNG AMERICA INS CO	TX	**C**	39.8	14.1	36.1	-0.2	5.9	8.3	5.2	8.0	3.4	DGT
ZALE INDEMNITY CO	TX	**C**	13.9	8.6	5.5	0.6	9.5	8.7	7.5	7.0	3.8	DGT
ZC SPECIALTY INS CO	TX	**C**	99.0	85.7	0.0	0.2	10.0	6.9	2.9	10.0	2.6	DFGR
▲ZENITH INS CO	CA	**C+**	2,089.6	989.1	578.6	-7.6	7.3	5.0	6.4	6.8	4.4	AFT
ZEPHYR INS CO INC	HI	**E+**	57.2	28.9	-1.0	2.6	10.0	3.6	9.9	9.3	0.4	DR
▲ZNAT INS CO	CA	**C+**	60.5	26.1	11.8	0.3	7.1	6.0	8.8	8.7	4.1	AFT
ZURICH AMERICAN INS CO	NY	**C-**	29,566.7	6,123.9	4,934.3	56.7	5.4	2.0	4.5	6.7	3.3	T
ZURICH AMERICAN INS CO OF IL	IL	**C+**	54.3	41.3	0.0	-0.3	10.0	N/A	3.4	9.5	4.6	T
ZURICH INS (GUAM) INC	GU	**U** (5)	--	--	--	--	N/A	--	--	--	--	Z

RISK ADJ. CAPITAL RATIO #1	RATIO #2	PREMIUM TO SURPLUS (%)	RESV. TO SURPLUS (%)	RESV. DEVELOP. 1 YEAR (%)	2 YEAR (%)	LOSS RATIO (%)	EXP. RATIO (%)	COMB RATIO (%)	CASH FROM UNDER-WRITING (%)	NET PREMIUM GROWTH (%)	INVEST. IN AFFIL (%)	INSURANCE COMPANY NAME
0.6	0.4	68.0	98.2	-9.2	-6.8	60.4	23.6	84.0	185.7	128.2	0.0	XL SELECT INS CO
0.8	0.5	59.2	85.6	-8.6	-5.8	60.4	25.4	85.8	185.7	128.2	10.5 •	XL SPECIALTY INS CO
6.8	6.2	13.2	38.0	-5.6	-9.5	9.0	7.8	16.8	584.4	0.0	0.0	YEL CO INS
2.3	1.7	63.2	68.9	-9.6	-22.0	46.3	47.0	93.3	104.3	15.6	0.0	YELLOWSTONE INS EXCH RRG
N/A	N/A	-0.6	121.0	-66.3	-135.0	999 +	-938.3	999 +	-1.6	-100.0	0.0	YORK INS CO
149.9	74.9	N/A	N/A	N/A	N/A	N/A	N/A	N/A	N/A	0.0	0.0	YORK INS CO OF MAINE
4.7	4.1	19.4	10.3	-1.2	-0.7	33.1	19.1	52.2	192.4	3.7	13.0 •	YOSEMITE INS CO
0.9	0.8	253.2	100.8	-8.2	-7.6	66.4	35.6	102.0	107.1	64.3	0.0	YOUNG AMERICA INS CO
3.5	1.9	47.9	13.6	-11.3	-10.9	14.5	25.9	40.4	215.0	57.3	0.0	ZALE INDEMNITY CO
31.1	28.0	N/A	6.1	0.6	-0.8	632.1	N/A	N/A	N/A	100.0	0.0	ZC SPECIALTY INS CO
3.2	2.2	57.0	97.1	-17.0	-38.4	46.1	38.5	84.6	96.1	-17.7	1.4 •	ZENITH INS CO
6.5	5.9	-3.5	N/A	N/A	N/A	N/A	999 +	999 +	-48.9	59.9	0.0	ZEPHYR INS CO INC
2.7	1.9	45.7	77.8	-12.8	-36.7	46.1	38.5	84.6	95.4	-17.7	0.0	ZNAT INS CO
1.3	0.7	79.1	234.7	-2.6	1.8	83.4	20.5	103.9	101.8	-15.9	7.5 •	ZURICH AMERICAN INS CO
15.0	13.5	N/A	N/A	N/A	N/A	N/A	N/A	N/A	-114.8	0.0	0.0	ZURICH AMERICAN INS CO OF IL
N/A	N/A	--	--	--	--	--	--	--	--	--	--	ZURICH INS (GUAM) INC

999 + Denotes number greater than 999.9%
999 - Denotes number less than -999.99%
• Bullets denote a more detailed analysis is available in Section II.

Section II

Analysis of Largest Companies

A summary analysis of TheStreet.com Recommended

U.S. Property and Casualty Insurers,

along with the largest companies based on capital and surplus.

Companies are listed in alphabetical order.

Section II Contents

This section contains rating factors, historical data and general information on each of the 450 largest property and casualty insurers in the U.S. that have the most recent quarterly financial information available.

1. **Financial Strength Rating** The current rating appears to the right of the company name. Our ratings are designed to distinguish levels of insolvency risk and are measured on a scale from A (Excellent) to F (Failed). Highly-rated companies are, in our opinion, less likely to experience financial difficulties than lower-rated firms. See *About TheStreet.com Financial Strength Ratings* on page 9 for more information.

2. **Major Rating Factors** A synopsis of the key indexes and sub-factors that have most influenced the rating of a particular insurer. Items are presented in the approximate order of their importance to the rating. There may be additional factors which have influenced the rating but do not appear due to space limitations or confidentiality agreements with insurers.

3. **Other Rating Factors** A summary of those TheStreet.com Ratings indexes that were not included as Major Rating Factors, but nevertheless, may have had some impact on the final grade.

4. **Principal Business** The major types of policies written by an insurer along with the percentages for each line in relation to the entire book of business. Lines of business written by property and casualty insurers include personal and commercial insurance lines such as homeowners', auto, workers' compensation, commercial multiple peril, medical malpractice and product liability, among others.

5. **Principal Investments** The major investments in an insurer's portfolio. These include cash, investment grade bonds, non investment grade bonds, common and preferred stock, and real estate.

6. **Investments in Affiliates** The percentage of bonds, common and preferred stocks and other financial instruments an insurer has invested with affiliated companies.

7. **Group Affiliation** The name of the group of companies to which a particular insurer belongs.

8. **Licensed in** List of the states in which an insurer is licensed to conduct business.

9. **Commenced Business** The month and year the company started its operations.

10. **Address** The address of an insurer's corporate headquarters. This location may differ from the company's state of domicile.

11. Phone The telephone number of an insurer's corporate headquarters.

12. Domicile State The state that has primary regulatory responsibility for this company. You do not have to live in the domicile state to do business with this firm, provided it is registered to do business in your state.

13. NAIC Code The identification number assigned to an insurer by the National Association of Insurance Commissioners (NAIC).

14. Historical Data Five years of background data for TheStreet.com Financial Strength Rating, risk-adjusted capital ratios (moderate and severe loss scenarios), total assets, capital, net premium, and net income. See the following page for more details on how to read the historical data table.

15. Customized Graph (or Table) A graph or table depicting one of the company's major strengths or weaknesses.

How to Read the Historical Data Table

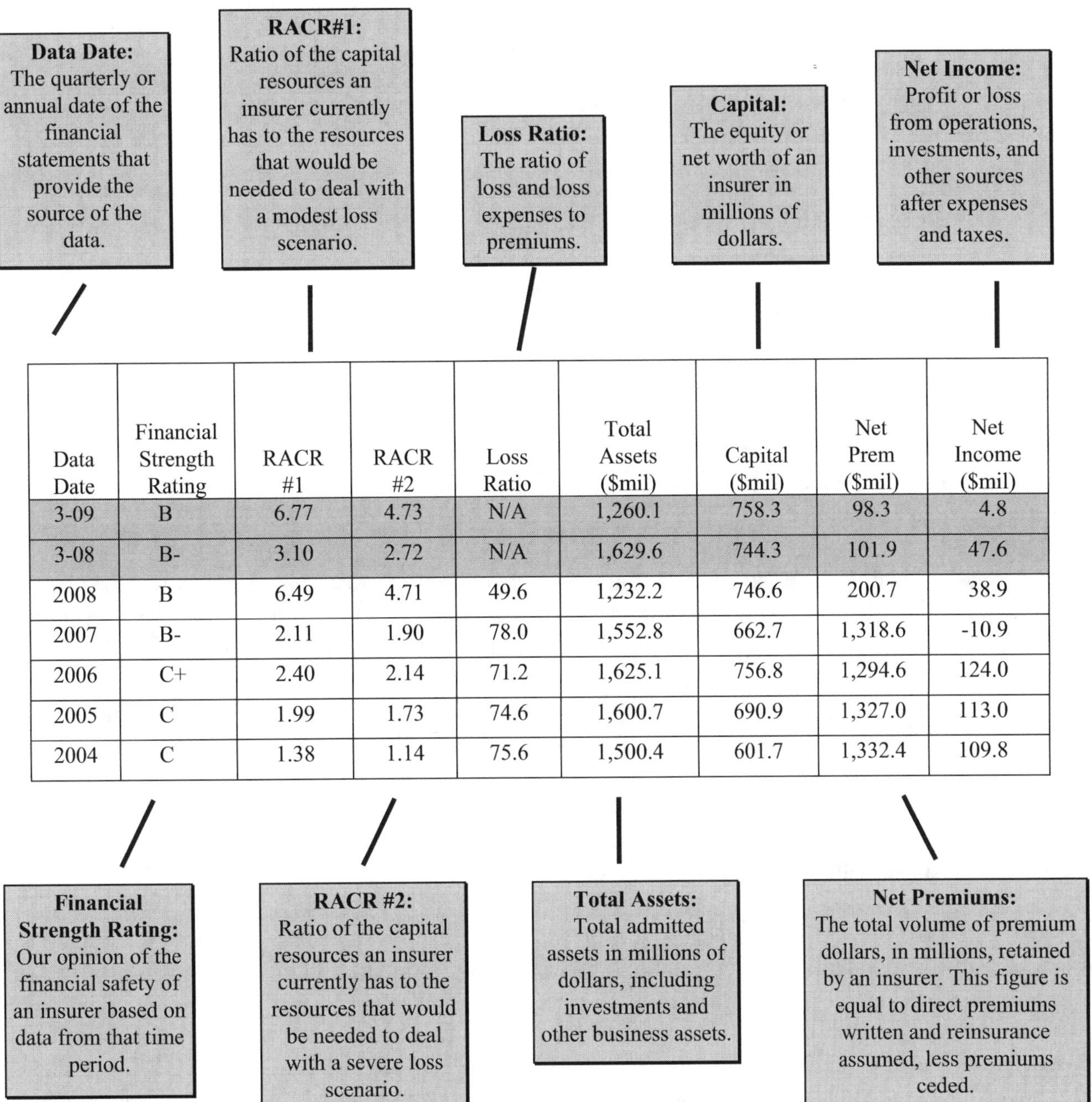

Data Date	Financial Strength Rating	RACR #1	RACR #2	Loss Ratio	Total Assets ($mil)	Capital ($mil)	Net Prem ($mil)	Net Income ($mil)
3-09	B	6.77	4.73	N/A	1,260.1	758.3	98.3	4.8
3-08	B-	3.10	2.72	N/A	1,629.6	744.3	101.9	47.6
2008	B	6.49	4.71	49.6	1,232.2	746.6	200.7	38.9
2007	B-	2.11	1.90	78.0	1,552.8	662.7	1,318.6	-10.9
2006	C+	2.40	2.14	71.2	1,625.1	756.8	1,294.6	124.0
2005	C	1.99	1.73	74.6	1,600.7	690.9	1,327.0	113.0
2004	C	1.38	1.14	75.6	1,500.4	601.7	1,332.4	109.8

Row Descriptions:

Row 1 contains the most recent quarterly data as filed with state regulators and is presented on a year-to-date basis. For example, the figure for year-end premiums includes premiums received through the year-end. **Row 2** consists of data from the same quarter of the prior year so that you can compare current quarterly results to those of a year ago.

Row 3 contains data from the most recent annual statutory filing. **Rows 4-7** include data from year-end statements going back four years from the most recent annual filing so that you can compare current year-end results to those of the previous four years. With the exception of Total Assets and Capital, quarterly data are not comparable with annual data.

Customized Graphs

In the lower right-hand corner of each company section, a customized graph or text block highlights a key factor affecting that company's financial strength. One of eleven types of information is found, identified by one of the following headings:

Capital plots the company's reported capital in millions of dollars over the last five years. Volatile changes in capital levels may indicate unstable operations.

Group Affiliation shows the group name, a composite TheStreet.com Financial Strength Rating for the group, and a list of the largest members with their ratings. The composite Financial Strength Rating is made up of the weighted average, by assets, of the individual ratings of each company in the group (including life/health companies, property/casualty companies or HMOs) plus a factor for the financial strength of the holding company, where applicable.

Income Trends shows underwriting and net income results over the last five years.

Liquidity Index evaluates a company's ability to raise the cash necessary to pay claims. Various cash flow scenarios are modeled to determine how the company might fare in the event of an unexpected spike in claims costs.

Rating Indexes illustrate the score and range -- strong, good, fair or weak -- on the five TheStreet.com indexes: Risk-Adjusted Capital Index #2 (Cap2), Stability Index (Stab.), Reserve Adequacy Index (Res.), Profitability Index (Prof.), and Liquidity Index (Liq.).

Reserve Deficiency shows whether the company has set aside sufficient funds to pay claims. A positive number indicates insufficient reserving and a negative number adequate reserving.

Reserves to Capital analyzes the relationship between loss and loss expense reserves to capital. Operating results and capital levels for companies with a high ratio are more susceptible to fluctuations than those with lower ratios.

Risk-Adjusted Capital Ratio #1 answers the question: In each of the past five years, does the insurer have sufficient capital to cover potential losses in its investments and business operations in a *moderate* loss scenario?

Risk-Adjusted Capital Ratio #2 answers the question: In each of the past five years, does the insurer have sufficient capital to cover potential losses in its investments and business operations in a *severe* loss scenario?

21ST CENTURY INS CO — B — Good

Major Rating Factors: History of adequate reserve strength (5.6 on a scale of 0 to 10) as reserves have been consistently at an acceptable level. Good overall profitability index (5.5) despite operating losses during 2007. Return on equity has been good over the last five years, averaging 10.5%.

Other Rating Factors: Good liquidity (6.7) with sufficient resources (cash flows and marketable investments) to handle a spike in claims. Good overall results on stability tests (5.5) despite negative cash flow from operations for 2008. Stability strengths include good operational trends and excellent risk diversification. Strong long-term capitalization index (10.0) based on excellent current risk adjusted capital (severe and moderate loss scenarios), despite some fluctuation in capital levels.

Principal Business: Auto liability (57%) and auto physical damage (43%).

Principal Investments: Investment grade bonds (98%), non investment grade bonds (1%), and real estate (1%).

Investments in Affiliates: None

Group Affiliation: American International Group

Licensed in: AL, AK, AR, CA, CO, CT, DC, DE, FL, GA, ID, IL, IN, IA, KS, KY, ME, MD, MI, MN, MO, NE, NV, NJ, NY, ND, OH, OK, OR, PA, SC, SD, TN, TX, UT, VT, WA, WV, WI

Commenced Business: December 1968

Address: 6301 Owensmouth Ave, Woodland Hills, CA 91367

Phone: (818) 704-3700 **Domicile State:** CA **NAIC Code:** 12963

Data Date	Rating	RACR #1	RACR #2	Loss Ratio %	Total Assets ($mil)	Capital ($mil)	Net Premium ($mil)	Net Income ($mil)
3-09	B	6.77	4.73	N/A	1,260.1	758.3	98.3	4.8
3-08	B-	3.10	2.72	N/A	1,629.6	744.3	101.9	47.6
2008	B	6.49	4.71	79.6	1,232.2	746.6	200.7	38.9
2007	B-	2.11	1.90	78.0	1,552.8	662.7	1,318.6	-10.9
2006	C+	2.40	2.14	71.2	1,625.1	756.8	1,294.6	124.0
2005	C	1.99	1.73	74.6	1,600.7	690.9	1,327.0	113.0
2004	C	1.38	1.14	75.6	1,500.4	601.7	1,332.4	109.8

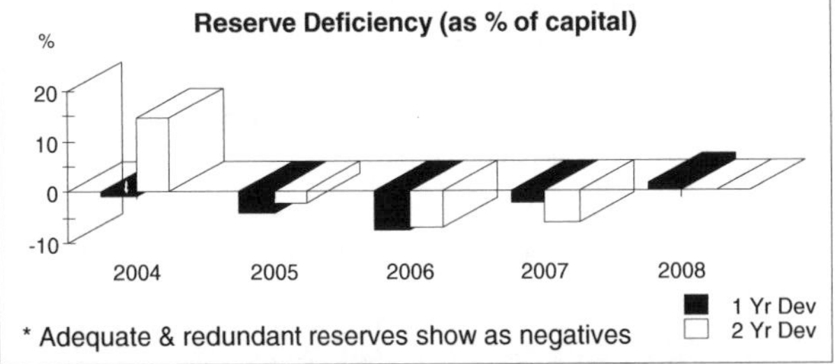

* Adequate & redundant reserves show as negatives

ACCIDENT FUND INS CO OF AMERICA — C+ — Fair

Major Rating Factors: Fair overall results on stability tests (4.4 on a scale of 0 to 10) including potential drain of affiliation with Blue Cross Blue Shield of Michigan. Good overall long-term capitalization (5.3) based on good current risk adjusted capital (severe and moderate loss scenarios). However, capital levels have fluctuated somewhat during past years.

Other Rating Factors: History of adequate reserve strength (6.2) as reserves have been consistently at an acceptable level. Good profitability index (5.0) despite operating losses during 2008. Return on equity has been fair, averaging 5.4% over the past five years. Good liquidity (5.6) with sufficient resources (cash flows and marketable investments) to handle a spike in claims.

Principal Business: Workers compensation (99%) and other liability (1%).

Principal Investments: Investment grade bonds (61%), misc. investments (36%), non investment grade bonds (3%), and real estate (1%).

Investments in Affiliates: 21%

Group Affiliation: Blue Cross Blue Shield of Michigan

Licensed in: All states except CA, FL, NY, OH, WA, WV, WY, PR

Commenced Business: December 1994

Address: 232 S Capitol Ave, Lansing, MI 48933

Phone: (517) 342-4200 **Domicile State:** MI **NAIC Code:** 10166

Data Date	Rating	RACR #1	RACR #2	Loss Ratio %	Total Assets ($mil)	Capital ($mil)	Net Premium ($mil)	Net Income ($mil)
3-09	C+	0.99	0.79	N/A	2,092.9	578.4	158.3	14.1
3-08	C+	1.18	0.93	N/A	2,102.0	665.4	164.4	20.4
2008	C+	0.99	0.79	69.6	1,988.9	577.3	689.6	-58.8
2007	C+	1.19	0.94	66.5	2,108.2	656.8	573.6	55.7
2006	C	1.17	0.87	73.8	1,870.9	502.8	503.7	22.5
2005	C	1.29	0.99	69.7	1,885.6	493.9	499.3	36.2
2004	C	1.29	0.94	60.8	1,636.7	483.1	490.7	76.5

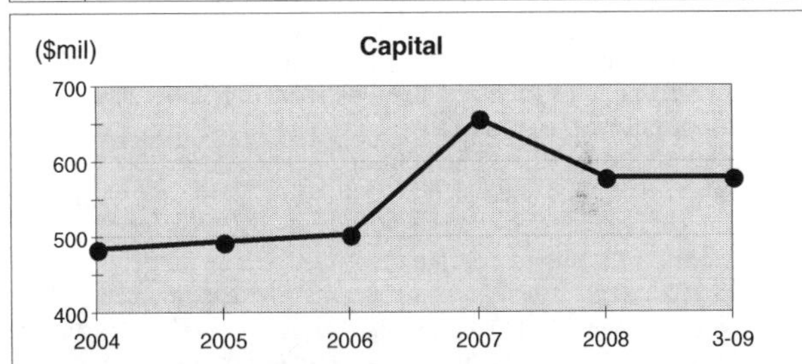

ACE AMERICAN INS CO — C+ — Fair

Major Rating Factors: Fair overall results on stability tests (4.4 on a scale of 0 to 10) including potential drain of affiliation with ACE Ltd. Good long-term capitalization index (6.0) based on good current risk adjusted capital (moderate loss scenario), despite some fluctuation in capital levels.

Other Rating Factors: History of adequate reserve strength (5.0) as reserves have been consistently at an acceptable level. Excellent profitability (7.5) with operating gains in each of the last five years. Return on equity has been good over the last five years, averaging 11.6%. Excellent liquidity (7.1) with ample operational cash flow and liquid investments.

Principal Business: Other liability (43%), workers compensation (14%), commercial multiple peril (12%), group accident & health (11%), auto liability (6%), aircraft (3%), and other lines (10%).

Principal Investments: Investment grade bonds (62%), misc. investments (33%), cash (2%), non investment grade bonds (2%), and real estate (1%).

Investments in Affiliates: 15%

Group Affiliation: ACE Ltd

Licensed in: All states, the District of Columbia and Puerto Rico

Commenced Business: January 1946

Address: 1601 Chestnut St, Philadelphia, PA 19192

Phone: (215) 761-1000 **Domicile State:** PA **NAIC Code:** 22667

Data Date	Rating	RACR #1	RACR #2	Loss Ratio %	Total Assets ($mil)	Capital ($mil)	Net Premium ($mil)	Net Income ($mil)
3-09	C+	1.38	1.04	N/A	8,025.1	1,784.2	272.8	39.4
3-08	C	1.41	1.00	N/A	8,041.1	2,042.8	264.3	33.5
2008	C+	1.41	1.07	62.5	8,051.1	1,789.6	1,029.2	204.6
2007	C	1.42	1.02	63.5	7,799.1	1,976.2	1,281.2	252.7
2006	C	1.31	0.91	60.3	7,313.3	1,688.1	1,416.8	264.1
2005	C	1.14	0.78	125.0	6,506.5	1,291.1	1,434.6	136.2
2004	C	0.94	0.67	72.7	5,374.0	881.6	1,372.7	74.0

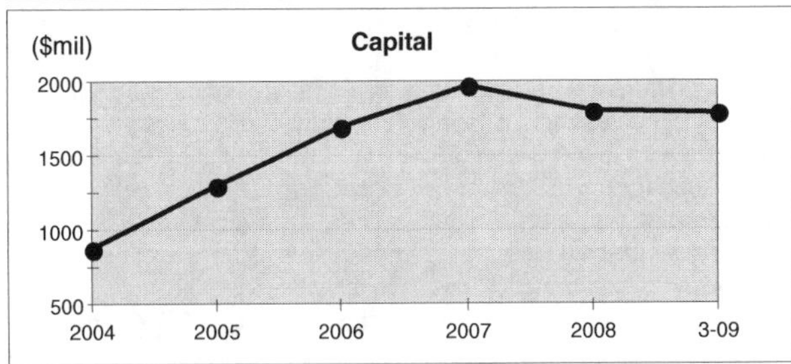

ACE PROPERTY & CASUALTY INS CO — C — Fair

Major Rating Factors: Fair overall results on stability tests (3.4 on a scale of 0 to 10) including fair financial strength of affiliated ACE Ltd. History of adequate reserve strength (5.0) as reserves have been consistently at an acceptable level.
Other Rating Factors: Good overall profitability index (5.8) despite operating losses during the first three months of 2008. Return on equity has been good over the last five years, averaging 11.4%. Good liquidity (6.7) with sufficient resources (cash flows and marketable investments) to handle a spike in claims. Strong long-term capitalization index (7.1) based on excellent current risk adjusted capital (severe and moderate loss scenarios), despite some fluctuation in capital levels.
Principal Business: Allied lines (85%), workers compensation (6%), other liability (6%), aircraft (1%), and auto liability (1%).
Principal Investments: Investment grade bonds (77%), misc. investments (21%), and non investment grade bonds (2%).
Investments in Affiliates: 4%
Group Affiliation: ACE Ltd
Licensed in: All states, the District of Columbia and Puerto Rico
Commenced Business: August 1819
Address: 1601 Chestnut St, Philadelphia, PA 19192
Phone: (215) 761-2324 **Domicile State:** PA **NAIC Code:** 20699

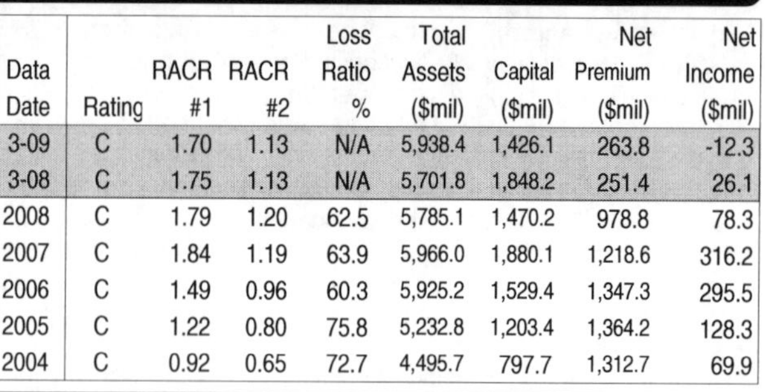

Data Date	Rating	RACR #1	RACR #2	Loss Ratio %	Total Assets ($mil)	Capital ($mil)	Net Premium ($mil)	Net Income ($mil)
3-09	C	1.70	1.13	N/A	5,938.4	1,426.1	263.8	-12.3
3-08	C	1.75	1.13	N/A	5,701.8	1,848.2	251.4	26.1
2008	C	1.79	1.20	62.5	5,785.1	1,470.2	978.8	78.3
2007	C	1.84	1.19	63.9	5,966.0	1,880.1	1,218.6	316.2
2006	C	1.49	0.96	60.3	5,925.2	1,529.4	1,347.3	295.5
2005	C	1.22	0.80	75.8	5,232.8	1,203.4	1,364.2	128.3
2004	C	0.92	0.65	72.7	4,495.7	797.7	1,312.7	69.9

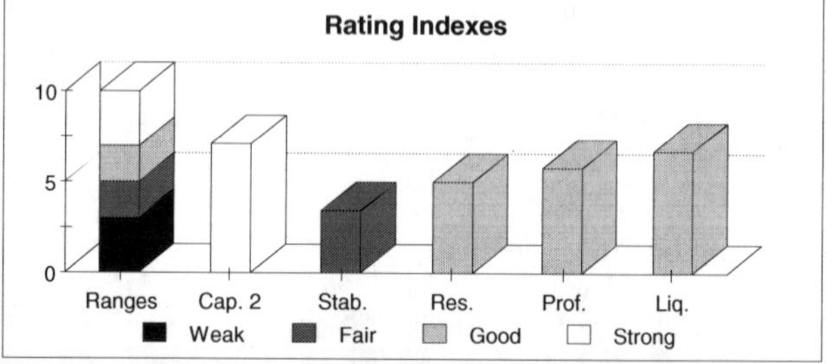

ACUITY A MUTUAL INS CO — B — Good

Major Rating Factors: Good liquidity (6.5 on a scale of 0 to 10) with sufficient resources (cash flows and marketable investments) to handle a spike in claims. Fair overall results on stability tests (4.7) including potential drain of affiliation with ACUITY Ins Group.
Other Rating Factors: Strong long-term capitalization index (9.3) based on excellent current risk adjusted capital (severe and moderate loss scenarios), despite some fluctuation in capital levels. Ample reserve history (7.0) that can protect against increases in claims costs. Excellent profitability (7.2) with operating gains in each of the last five years. Return on equity has been good over the last five years, averaging 13.6%.
Principal Business: Workers compensation (26%), auto liability (24%), auto physical damage (13%), other liability (10%), commercial multiple peril (10%), homeowners multiple peril (6%), and other lines (10%).
Principal Investments: Investment grade bonds (79%), misc. investments (17%), real estate (3%), and non investment grade bonds (2%).
Investments in Affiliates: 0%
Group Affiliation: ACUITY Ins Group
Licensed in: AL, AZ, AR, CO, DE, FL, GA, ID, IL, IN, IA, KS, KY, MI, MN, MS, MO, NE, NV, ND, OH, OR, PA, SD, TN, TX, VA, WA, WV, WI, WY
Commenced Business: September 1925
Address: 2800 S Taylor Dr, Sheboygan, WI 53081-8470
Phone: (920) 458-9131 **Domicile State:** WI **NAIC Code:** 14184

Data Date	Rating	RACR #1	RACR #2	Loss Ratio %	Total Assets ($mil)	Capital ($mil)	Net Premium ($mil)	Net Income ($mil)
3-09	B	3.76	2.52	N/A	1,817.0	617.6	175.7	18.0
3-08	B	4.06	2.65	N/A	1,859.4	698.1	186.4	16.5
2008	B	3.78	2.55	69.8	1,823.9	617.4	742.4	37.9
2007	B	4.08	2.67	66.8	1,865.0	705.4	765.9	78.9
2006	B	3.67	2.44	58.8	1,706.4	633.4	760.8	98.6
2005	B	2.94	1.98	55.7	1,488.6	517.8	720.6	98.4
2004	B	2.19	1.47	60.6	1,280.8	414.3	654.8	67.8

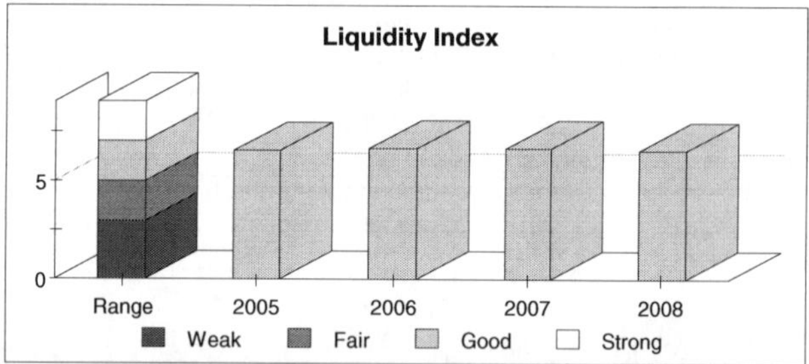

ADMIRAL INS CO — C — Fair

Major Rating Factors: Fair overall long-term capitalization (4.5 on a scale of 0 to 10) based on good current risk adjusted capital (severe loss scenario). However, capital levels have fluctuated somewhat during past years. Fair reserve development (4.5) as the level of reserves has at times been insufficient to cover claims. In 2005 and 2004 the two year reserve development was 17% and 29% deficient respectively.
Other Rating Factors: Fair overall results on stability tests (4.1). The largest net exposure for one risk is conservative at 1.5% of capital. Good overall profitability index (6.5) despite operating losses during the first three months of 2008. Return on equity has been good over the last five years, averaging 12.9%. Excellent liquidity (7.0) with ample operational cash flow and liquid investments.
Principal Business: Other liability (55%), medical malpractice (19%), products liability (16%), fire (6%), allied lines (1%), commercial multiple peril (1%), and auto liability (1%).
Principal Investments: Investment grade bonds (53%), misc. investments (44%), non investment grade bonds (2%), and cash (1%).
Investments in Affiliates: 28%
Group Affiliation: W R Berkley Corp
Licensed in: DE, NJ
Commenced Business: November 1952
Address: 1255 Orange Street, Wilmington, DE 19801
Phone: (609) 429-9200 **Domicile State:** DE **NAIC Code:** 24856

Data Date	Rating	RACR #1	RACR #2	Loss Ratio %	Total Assets ($mil)	Capital ($mil)	Net Premium ($mil)	Net Income ($mil)
3-09	C	1.10	0.77	N/A	2,494.8	1,031.7	106.6	-6.7
3-08	C+	1.00	0.70	N/A	2,792.3	1,071.9	131.7	31.8
2008	C+	1.13	0.80	62.4	2,514.5	1,057.4	431.0	104.6
2007	C+	1.14	0.80	56.6	2,756.2	1,215.4	571.6	190.0
2006	C+	1.10	0.78	59.3	2,585.0	1,109.4	604.5	140.5
2005	C	0.98	0.67	59.9	2,313.4	941.6	603.4	130.5
2004	C	0.98	0.66	61.2	1,902.4	728.8	597.6	119.7

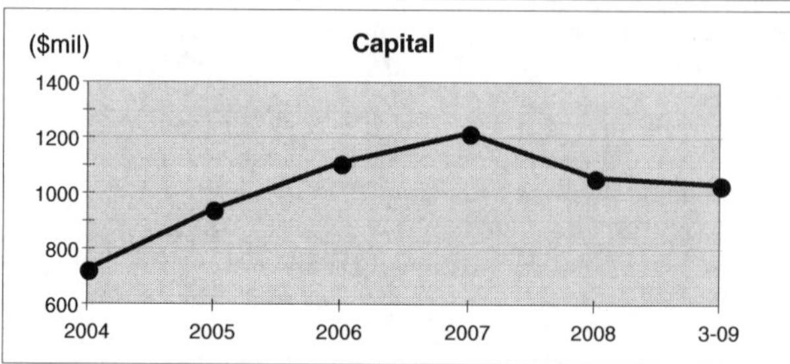

AFFILIATED FM INS CO — C — Fair

Major Rating Factors: Fair reserve development (3.9 on a scale of 0 to 10) as the level of reserves has at times been insufficient to cover claims. In 2005 and 2004 the two year reserve development was 20% and 64% deficient respectively. Fair overall results on stability tests (3.3). The largest net exposure for one risk is excessive at 9.3% of capital.

Other Rating Factors: Strong long-term capitalization index (9.9) based on excellent current risk adjusted capital (severe and moderate loss scenarios). Moreover, capital levels have been consistent in recent years. Excellent profitability (8.9) with operating gains in each of the last five years. Return on equity has been good over the last five years, averaging 11.7%. Excellent liquidity (7.0) with ample operational cash flow and liquid investments.

Principal Business: Fire (34%), inland marine (25%), allied lines (20%), commercial multiple peril (11%), boiler & machinery (6%), and ocean marine (4%).

Principal Investments: Investment grade bonds (94%) and misc. investments (6%).

Investments in Affiliates: None

Group Affiliation: FM Global

Licensed in: All states, the District of Columbia and Puerto Rico

Commenced Business: June 1950

Address: 1301 Atwood Avenue, Johnston, RI 02919-4908

Phone: (401) 275-3000 **Domicile State:** RI **NAIC Code:** 10014

Data Date	Rating	RACR #1	RACR #2	Loss Ratio %	Total Assets ($mil)	Capital ($mil)	Net Premium ($mil)	Net Income ($mil)
3-09	C	6.23	3.32	N/A	1,486.6	717.9	87.8	28.0
3-08	C	6.45	3.27	N/A	1,388.1	679.0	79.7	5.8
2008	C	5.88	3.13	77.6	1,470.5	695.5	336.2	32.9
2007	C	6.41	3.25	44.6	1,361.2	675.5	333.7	101.0
2006	C	5.24	2.68	51.3	1,275.1	572.0	347.3	79.2
2005	C	2.63	1.81	53.4	1,112.3	489.3	332.1	68.5
2004	C	2.08	1.42	49.6	949.6	420.0	154.6	41.0

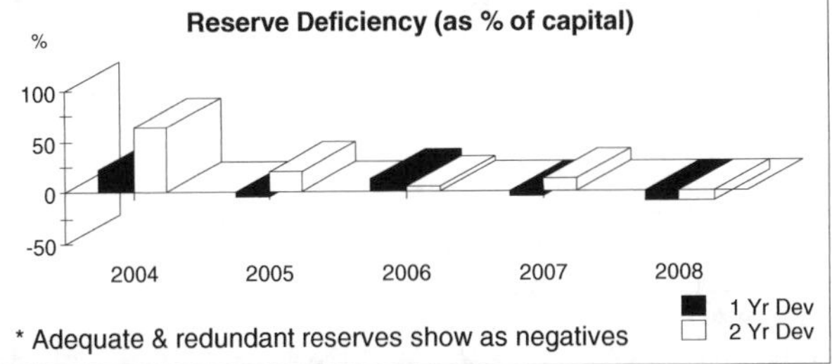

AGRI GENERAL INS CO — B- — Good

Major Rating Factors: Fair overall results on stability tests (4.3 on a scale of 0 to 10) including excessive premium growth and weak results on operational trends. Good long-term capitalization (6.7) based on good current risk adjusted capital (moderate loss scenario) reflecting improvement over results in 2008.

Other Rating Factors: Ample reserve history (7.6) that can protect against increases in claims costs. Excellent profitability (9.2) with operating gains in each of the last five years. Excellent expense controls. Return on equity has been excellent over the last five years averaging 23.7%. Vulnerable liquidity (2.5) as a spike in claims may stretch capacity.

Principal Business: Allied lines (100%).

Principal Investments: Investment grade bonds (58%) and misc. investments (42%).

Investments in Affiliates: None

Group Affiliation: Rain & Hail Ins Service Inc

Licensed in: All states except AK, DC, HI, NH, PR

Commenced Business: September 1983

Address: 1501 50th Regency W.1#200, West Des Moines, IA 50266-5962

Phone: (515) 224-3075 **Domicile State:** IA **NAIC Code:** 42757

Data Date	Rating	RACR #1	RACR #2	Loss Ratio %	Total Assets ($mil)	Capital ($mil)	Net Premium ($mil)	Net Income ($mil)
3-09	B-	2.12	1.33	N/A	753.7	487.8	51.2	8.9
3-08	B-	7.97	4.64	N/A	543.3	441.5	13.9	5.8
2008	B-	1.29	0.84	82.8	1,007.5	518.2	981.9	83.0
2007	B-	7.35	4.35	58.4	601.4	457.0	498.0	136.5
2006	C+	7.64	4.86	73.9	431.3	333.9	327.2	64.5
2005	C+	5.94	3.98	61.5	376.6	274.4	289.9	81.3
2004	C+	1.81	1.27	74.7	315.4	202.6	336.2	56.5

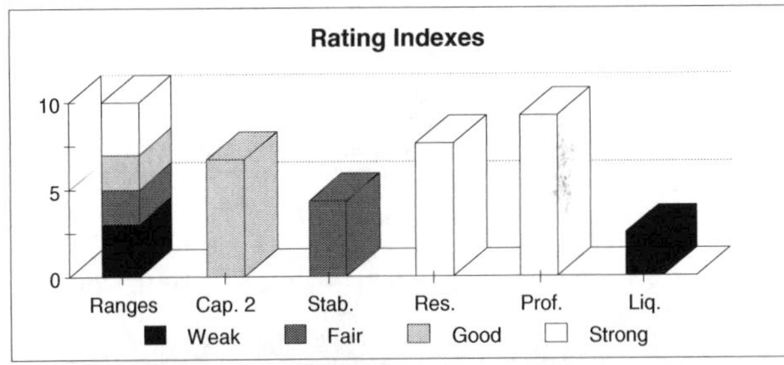

AGRINATIONAL INS CO — E — Very Weak

Major Rating Factors: Weak overall results on stability tests (0.0 on a scale of 0 to 10) including weak results on operational trends. The largest net exposure for one risk is excessive at 31.1% of capital. Fair long-term capitalization index (3.4) based on fair current risk adjusted capital (severe and moderate loss scenarios), although results have slipped from the excellent range over the last two years.

Other Rating Factors: Fair reserve development (3.6) as the level of reserves has at times been insufficient to cover claims. In 2004 and 2005 the two year reserve development was 354% and 411% deficient respectively. Fair profitability index (3.5) with operating losses during the first three months of 2008. Return on equity has been low, averaging 3.7% over the past five years. Good liquidity (5.3) with sufficient resources (cash flows and marketable investments) to handle a spike in claims.

Principal Business: Commercial multiple peril (70%), ocean marine (16%), credit (7%), auto liability (5%), and other liability (2%).

Principal Investments: Misc. investments (50%), investment grade bonds (31%), and cash (19%).

Investments in Affiliates: 56%

Group Affiliation: None

Licensed in: VT

Commenced Business: September 1987

Address: (No address available)

Phone: (802) 264-4715 **Domicile State:** VT **NAIC Code:** 10541

Data Date	Rating	RACR #1	RACR #2	Loss Ratio %	Total Assets ($mil)	Capital ($mil)	Net Premium ($mil)	Net Income ($mil)
3-09	E	0.71	0.59	N/A	513.6	156.7	20.6	-7.9
3-08	E	1.51	1.06	N/A	404.8	156.0	18.9	0.4
2008	E	0.67	0.54	162.4	520.6	165.8	95.0	-36.0
2007	E	1.57	1.10	80.6	402.0	155.9	79.2	10.8
2006	N/A	N/A	N/A	71.6	412.3	144.8	74.4	15.5
2005	N/A	N/A	N/A	53.2	344.7	128.9	73.0	12.3
2004	N/A	N/A	N/A	42.0	159.9	59.4	45.9	11.2

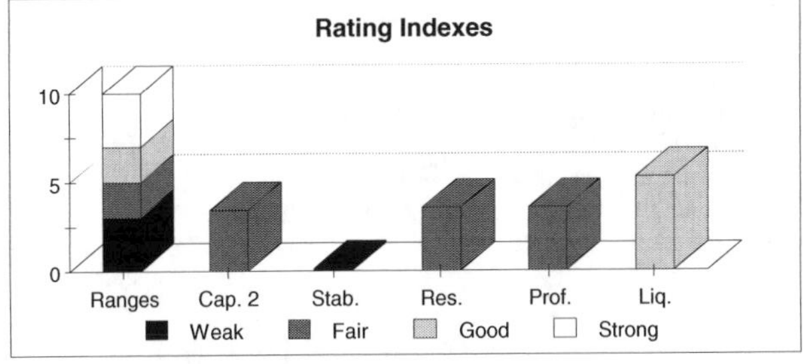

AIG CASUALTY CO C+ Fair

Major Rating Factors: Fair overall results on stability tests (4.3 on a scale of 0 to 10). Strengths include potentially strong support from affiliation with American International Group. Fair profitability index (4.9) with operating losses during 2004 and 2005. Return on equity has been fair, averaging 5.8% over the past five years.

Other Rating Factors: Good liquidity (6.4) with sufficient resources (cash flows and marketable investments) to handle a spike in claims. A history of deficient reserves (2.3). Underreserving can have an adverse impact on capital and profits. Deficiencies in the two year reserve development occurred in three of the previous five years and ranged between 39% and 62%. Strong long-term capitalization index (7.2) based on excellent current risk adjusted capital (severe and moderate loss scenarios), despite some fluctuation in capital levels.

Principal Business: Workers compensation (29%), fire (23%), auto liability (17%), other liability (13%), auto physical damage (11%), boiler & machinery (4%), and other lines (3%).

Principal Investments: Investment grade bonds (64%) and misc. investments (36%).

Investments in Affiliates: 16%

Group Affiliation: American International Group

Licensed in: All states except HI, PR

Commenced Business: August 1871

Address: 70 Pine St 3rd Floor, New York, NY 10270

Phone: (212) 770-7000 **Domicile State:** PA **NAIC Code:** 19402

Data Date	Rating	RACR #1	RACR #2	Loss Ratio %	Total Assets ($mil)	Capital ($mil)	Net Premium ($mil)	Net Income ($mil)
3-09	C+	1.73	1.26	N/A	4,051.5	1,460.7	209.4	28.2
3-08	C+	1.70	1.26	N/A	4,535.6	1,740.5	232.8	48.1
2008	C+	1.70	1.24	78.1	4,125.7	1,456.7	865.7	170.9
2007	C+	1.74	1.29	69.6	4,835.8	1,884.0	1,023.2	180.7
2006	C+	1.46	1.07	71.1	4,146.0	1,334.0	1,028.1	122.2
2005	C+	1.23	0.90	90.2	3,486.8	949.3	932.5	-2.6
2004	B-	1.17	0.82	86.4	2,893.2	673.6	924.9	-11.7

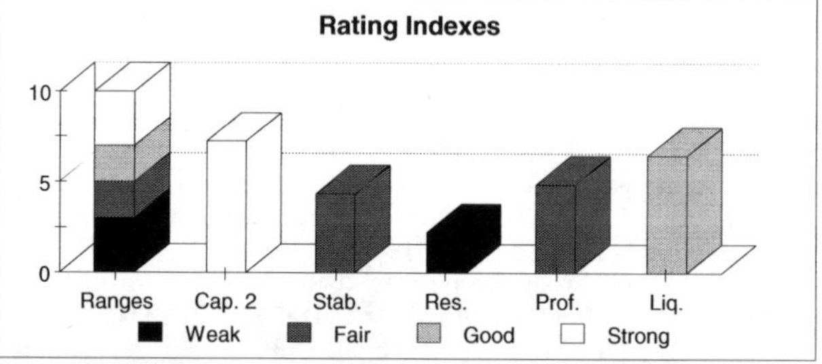

AIG CENTENNIAL INS CO B Good

Major Rating Factors: History of adequate reserve strength (6.6 on a scale of 0 to 10) as reserves have been consistently at an acceptable level. Good liquidity (6.2) with sufficient resources (cash flows and marketable investments) to handle a spike in claims.

Other Rating Factors: Good overall results on stability tests (5.4). Stability strengths include good operational trends and excellent risk diversification. Fair profitability index (4.3) with operating losses during 2007 and 2008. Return on equity has been low, averaging 1.9% over the past five years. Strong long-term capitalization index (7.3) based on excellent current risk adjusted capital (severe and moderate loss scenarios), despite some fluctuation in capital levels.

Principal Business: Auto liability (54%), auto physical damage (29%), ocean marine (13%), inland marine (2%), other liability (1%), and homeowners multiple peril (1%).

Principal Investments: Investment grade bonds (61%) and misc. investments (39%).

Investments in Affiliates: 37%

Group Affiliation: American International Group

Licensed in: All states except PR

Commenced Business: November 1977

Address: 500 Virginia Drive, Ft. Washington, PA 19034

Phone: (610) 650-2000 **Domicile State:** PA **NAIC Code:** 34789

Data Date	Rating	RACR #1	RACR #2	Loss Ratio %	Total Assets ($mil)	Capital ($mil)	Net Premium ($mil)	Net Income ($mil)
3-09	B	1.39	1.21	N/A	802.9	298.6	98.3	6.4
3-08	B	1.43	1.24	N/A	791.2	316.9	107.9	-9.9
2008	B	1.40	1.24	79.6	815.5	304.9	437.6	-15.2
2007	B	1.57	1.42	77.2	630.7	335.0	302.3	-3.1
2006	B	1.61	1.47	70.1	614.1	320.9	289.5	23.5
2005	B-	1.50	1.35	75.6	587.3	266.0	286.5	13.1
2004	C+	1.35	1.19	83.0	582.2	239.8	222.2	3.2

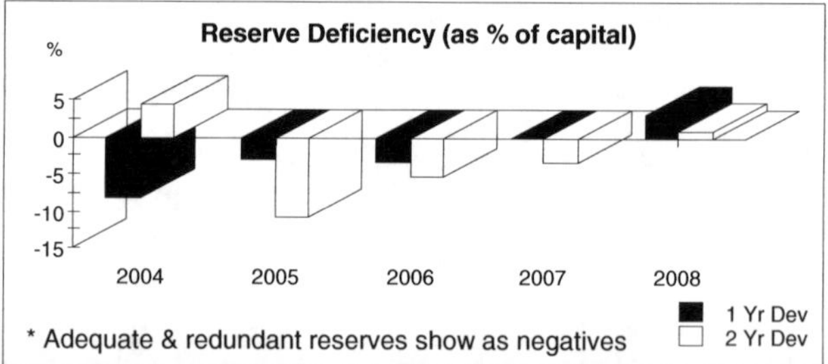

AIG EXCESS LIABILITY INS CO LTD C+ Fair

Major Rating Factors: Fair overall results on stability tests (3.0 on a scale of 0 to 10). The largest net exposure for one risk is excessive at 10.5% of capital. Strengths include potentially strong support from affiliation with American International Group. Good long-term capitalization index (6.5) based on good current risk adjusted capital (moderate loss scenario). Moreover, capital levels have been consistent in recent years.

Other Rating Factors: History of adequate reserve strength (5.7) as reserves have been consistently at an acceptable level. Excellent profitability (8.8) with operating gains in each of the last five years. Return on equity has been good over the last five years, averaging 13.3%. Excellent liquidity (7.0) with ample operational cash flow and liquid investments.

Principal Business: Other liability (88%) and products liability (12%).

Principal Investments: Investment grade bonds (86%) and misc. investments (14%).

Investments in Affiliates: 10%

Group Affiliation: American International Group

Licensed in: DE

Commenced Business: June 1998

Address: 70 Pine Street, New York, NY 10270

Phone: (212) 770-7000 **Domicile State:** DE **NAIC Code:** 10932

Data Date	Rating	RACR #1	RACR #2	Loss Ratio %	Total Assets ($mil)	Capital ($mil)	Net Premium ($mil)	Net Income ($mil)
3-09	C+	1.86	1.21	N/A	4,028.7	1,505.3	200.3	61.7
3-08	B-	1.11	0.77	N/A	3,799.7	1,390.0	236.7	65.8
2008	C+	1.80	1.18	80.5	4,042.7	1,437.9	899.8	133.7
2007	B	1.03	0.71	59.1	3,514.8	1,248.1	965.0	257.9
2006	B	0.85	0.59	62.9	2,967.9	949.5	932.1	206.0
2005	B	0.80	0.56	82.7	2,520.3	714.2	782.4	80.7
2004	B	0.80	0.55	86.7	2,185.7	577.8	722.6	14.6

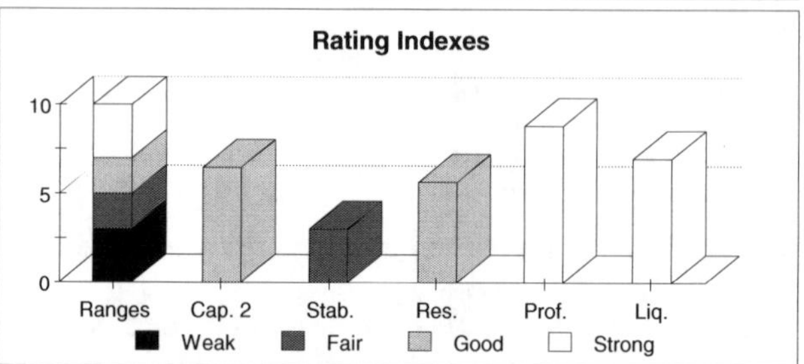

AIG GLOBAL TRADE & POL RISK INS CO — C+ — Fair

Major Rating Factors: Fair overall results on stability tests (4.5 on a scale of 0 to 10). The largest net exposure for one risk is excessive at 5.5% of capital. Good overall profitability index (6.7). Good expense controls. Return on equity has been excellent over the last five years averaging 17.1%.

Other Rating Factors: Strong long-term capitalization index (9.6) based on excellent current risk adjusted capital (severe and moderate loss scenarios), despite some fluctuation in capital levels. Ample reserve history (7.0) that can protect against increases in claims costs. Excellent liquidity (7.7) with ample operational cash flow and liquid investments.

Principal Business: (This company is a reinsurer.)

Principal Investments: Investment grade bonds (80%), cash (13%), and misc. investments (7%).

Investments in Affiliates: 8%

Group Affiliation: American International Group

Licensed in: NJ, NY

Commenced Business: April 1996

Address: 70 Pine Street, New York, NY 10270

Phone: (212) 770-7000 **Domicile State:** NJ **NAIC Code:** 10651

Data Date	Rating	RACR #1	RACR #2	Loss Ratio %	Total Assets ($mil)	Capital ($mil)	Net Premium ($mil)	Net Income ($mil)
3-09	C+	3.06	2.72	N/A	369.2	175.1	19.1	0.7
3-08	B	2.71	2.40	N/A	370.4	149.9	17.8	6.0
2008	C+	3.04	2.71	60.0	374.3	171.2	82.7	19.4
2007	B	3.01	2.66	40.4	378.4	164.3	74.2	35.6
2006	B	4.71	4.18	N/A	413.9	215.4	55.4	46.7
2005	B	3.38	2.94	13.2	418.8	162.7	47.2	37.5
2004	B	4.07	3.45	77.8	404.6	127.2	40.0	14.8

American International Group
Composite Group Rating: C-

Largest Group Members	Assets ($mil)	Rating
AMERICAN LIFE INS CO	86338	C-
VARIABLE ANNUITY LIFE INS CO	53699	B
WESTERN NATIONAL LIFE INS CO	45803	B-
AMERICAN GENERAL LIFE INS CO	38638	C+
NATIONAL UNION FIRE INS CO OF PITTSB	33707	B

AIU INS CO — C+ — Fair

Major Rating Factors: Fair overall results on stability tests (3.7 on a scale of 0 to 10) including negative cash flow from operations for 2008. The largest net exposure for one risk is excessive at 8.3% of capital. Strengths include potentially strong support from affiliation with American International Group. Fair reserve development (4.6) as reserves have generally been sufficient to cover claims.

Other Rating Factors: Good liquidity (5.6) with sufficient resources (cash flows and marketable investments) to handle a spike in claims. Weak profitability index (2.5) with operating losses during 2008. Return on equity has been low, averaging 4.4% over the past five years. Strong long-term capitalization index (7.3) based on excellent current risk adjusted capital (severe and moderate loss scenarios), despite some fluctuation in capital levels.

Principal Business: Other accident & health (36%), auto liability (18%), other liability (14%), homeowners multiple peril (12%), auto physical damage (8%), fire (7%), and other lines (5%).

Principal Investments: Investment grade bonds (57%), misc. investments (27%), and cash (16%).

Investments in Affiliates: 12%

Group Affiliation: American International Group

Licensed in: All states except HI, WY, PR

Commenced Business: April 1851

Address: 70 Pine St, New York, NY 10270

Phone: (212) 770-7000 **Domicile State:** NY **NAIC Code:** 19399

Data Date	Rating	RACR #1	RACR #2	Loss Ratio %	Total Assets ($mil)	Capital ($mil)	Net Premium ($mil)	Net Income ($mil)
3-09	C+	1.47	1.06	N/A	2,824.7	665.9	245.4	7.9
3-08	B	2.13	1.66	N/A	2,934.7	1,022.3	201.7	-18.7
2008	B-	1.64	1.21	68.4	3,156.8	725.7	1,175.2	-104.7
2007	B	2.89	2.25	64.0	3,104.2	1,398.5	699.0	47.9
2006	B	3.75	2.57	64.8	3,268.2	1,222.4	808.1	113.9
2005	B	3.38	2.17	70.0	3,256.2	1,038.1	697.1	112.7
2004	B	2.55	1.75	68.6	3,014.8	590.5	746.9	76.3

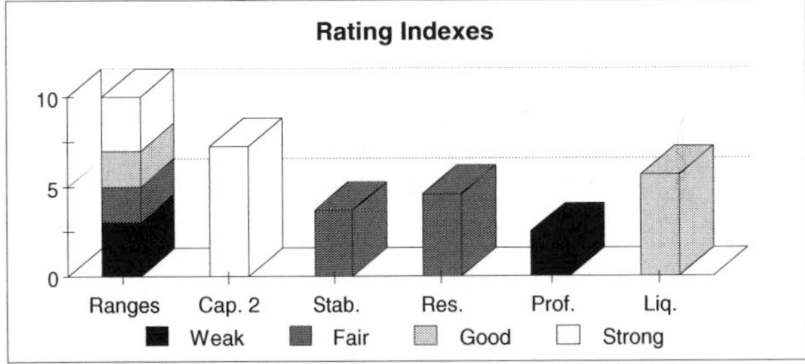

ALAMANCE INS CO — C- — Fair

Major Rating Factors: Weak overall results on stability tests (2.6 on a scale of 0 to 10) including potential drain of affiliation with IFG Companies. Good long-term capitalization index (6.2) based on good current risk adjusted capital (moderate loss scenario). Moreover, capital levels have been consistent in recent years.

Other Rating Factors: History of adequate reserve strength (6.0) as reserves have been consistently at an acceptable level. Excellent profitability (8.7) with operating gains in each of the last five years. Excellent liquidity (7.0) with ample operational cash flow and liquid investments.

Principal Business: (This company is a reinsurer.)

Principal Investments: Misc. investments (53%) and investment grade bonds (47%).

Investments in Affiliates: 50%

Group Affiliation: IFG Companies

Licensed in: AK, AR, DE, FL, GA, HI, IL, IN, IA, KS, LA, MD, MI, MT, NE, NV, NM, NC, ND, OH, OK, PA, SC, SD, TN, TX, UT, VA, WA, WV, WI, WY

Commenced Business: December 1998

Address: 238 International Road, Burlington, NC 27215

Phone: (336) 586-2830 **Domicile State:** IL **NAIC Code:** 10957

Data Date	Rating	RACR #1	RACR #2	Loss Ratio %	Total Assets ($mil)	Capital ($mil)	Net Premium ($mil)	Net Income ($mil)
3-09	C-	1.41	1.28	N/A	421.7	273.6	10.2	2.7
3-08	C-	1.38	1.22	N/A	412.1	251.9	14.0	3.9
2008	C-	1.40	1.26	56.3	421.0	269.7	45.1	16.8
2007	C-	1.36	1.20	62.9	407.0	245.0	62.3	17.2
2006	D+	1.33	1.15	58.0	374.9	216.5	73.9	18.3
2005	D+	1.18	1.00	58.6	328.0	179.9	75.4	12.9
2004	D	1.17	1.02	58.4	260.1	155.7	54.0	6.3

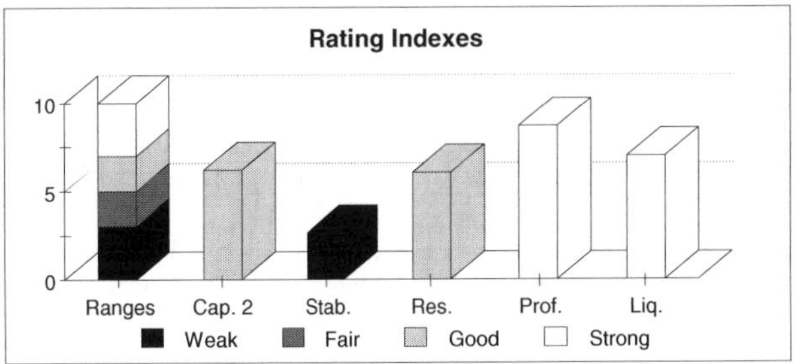

ALASKA NATIONAL INS CO — B — Good

Major Rating Factors: History of adequate reserve strength (6.0 on a scale of 0 to 10) as reserves have been consistently at an acceptable level. Good liquidity (6.9) with sufficient resources (cash flows and marketable investments) to handle a spike in claims.

Other Rating Factors: Good overall results on stability tests (5.5). Stability strengths include good operational trends and excellent risk diversification. Strong long-term capitalization index (7.9) based on excellent current risk adjusted capital (severe and moderate loss scenarios). Moreover, capital levels have been consistent in recent years. Excellent profitability (9.2) with operating gains in each of the last five years. Return on equity has been excellent over the last five years averaging 18.1%.

Principal Business: Workers compensation (66%), other liability (12%), auto liability (8%), commercial multiple peril (8%), inland marine (2%), auto physical damage (2%), and other lines (3%).

Principal Investments: Investment grade bonds (92%), misc. investments (7%), and cash (1%).

Investments in Affiliates: None

Group Affiliation: Alaska National Corp

Licensed in: AL, AK, AZ, CA, CO, FL, HI, ID, IL, IA, KS, LA, MN, MS, MO, MT, NV, NM, ND, OK, OR, SD, TX, UT, WA, WY

Commenced Business: October 1980

Address: 7001 Jewell Lake Rd, Anchorage, AK 99502-2800

Phone: (907) 248-2642 **Domicile State:** AK **NAIC Code:** 38733

Data Date	Rating	RACR #1	RACR #2	Loss Ratio %	Total Assets ($mil)	Capital ($mil)	Net Premium ($mil)	Net Income ($mil)
3-09	B	3.54	1.87	N/A	696.6	267.0	36.1	17.8
3-08	B-	2.94	1.56	N/A	716.1	250.6	41.5	16.0
2008	B	3.55	1.85	43.4	705.3	265.8	168.7	45.5
2007	B-	2.91	1.53	60.2	708.2	245.0	177.4	47.8
2006	B-	2.66	1.36	51.7	645.2	225.0	181.5	55.6
2005	B-	2.07	1.07	62.0	594.4	187.1	191.6	30.0
2004	B-	1.60	0.85	73.0	526.8	164.4	175.0	18.0

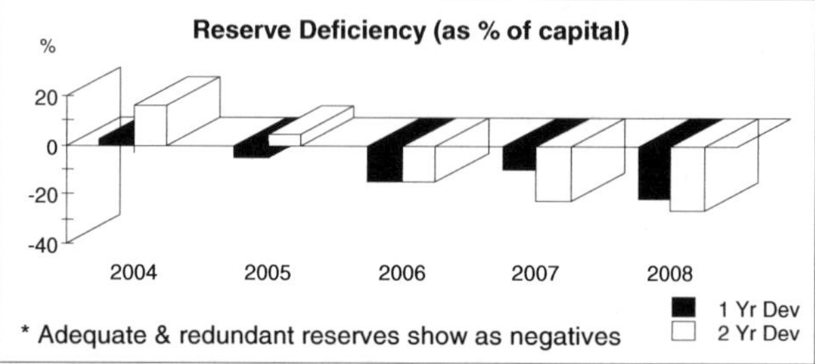

ALFA MUTUAL FIRE INS CO — B — Good

Major Rating Factors: Good overall long-term capitalization (6.1 on a scale of 0 to 10) based on good current risk adjusted capital (moderate loss scenario). However, capital levels have fluctuated during prior years. History of adequate reserve strength (6.0) as reserves have been consistently at an acceptable level.

Other Rating Factors: Fair overall results on stability tests (4.9) including weak results on operational trends. Strengths include potentially strong support from affiliation with Alfa Ins Group. Weak profitability index (2.0) with operating losses during 2004, 2005 and the first three months of 2008. Vulnerable liquidity (2.5) as a spike in claims may stretch capacity.

Principal Business: Fire (70%), allied lines (24%), and inland marine (6%).

Principal Investments: Investment grade bonds (60%), misc. investments (32%), cash (4%), non investment grade bonds (2%), and real estate (2%).

Investments in Affiliates: 57%

Group Affiliation: Alfa Ins Group

Licensed in: AL, IL, NC, VA

Commenced Business: August 1946

Address: 2108 East South Blvd, Montgomery, AL 36116

Phone: (334) 288-3900 **Domicile State:** AL **NAIC Code:** 19143

Data Date	Rating	RACR #1	RACR #2	Loss Ratio %	Total Assets ($mil)	Capital ($mil)	Net Premium ($mil)	Net Income ($mil)
3-09	B	1.24	0.86	N/A	571.5	331.1	80.5	-1.9
3-08	A-	4.02	2.95	N/A	901.9	642.7	81.8	-11.1
2008	B	1.27	0.89	70.9	572.0	337.1	383.6	-35.7
2007	A-	4.55	3.36	65.1	800.4	657.9	169.1	43.1
2006	A-	4.47	3.24	77.3	773.9	618.6	154.0	39.9
2005	A-	4.07	3.05	143.8	764.0	590.1	126.7	-38.9
2004	A-	4.78	3.42	133.0	785.1	608.8	154.4	-22.2

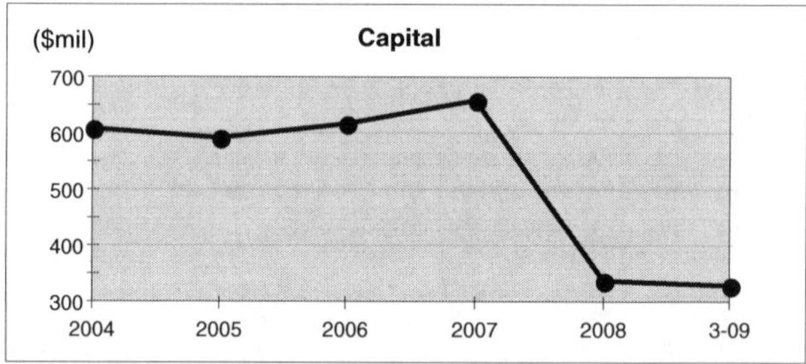

ALFA MUTUAL INS CO — B — Good

Major Rating Factors: Good overall results on stability tests (5.5 on a scale of 0 to 10). Strengths include potentially strong support from affiliation with Alfa Ins Group, good operational trends and excellent risk diversification. Strong long-term capitalization index (7.3) based on excellent current risk adjusted capital (severe and moderate loss scenarios), despite some fluctuation in capital levels.

Other Rating Factors: Ample reserve history (7.4) that can protect against increases in claims costs. Weak profitability index (2.4) with operating losses during 2005 and the first three months of 2008. Vulnerable liquidity (2.2) as a spike in claims may stretch capacity.

Principal Business: Homeowners multiple peril (31%), auto liability (29%), auto physical damage (28%), farmowners multiple peril (7%), commercial multiple peril (3%), and inland marine (1%).

Principal Investments: Misc. investments (58%), investment grade bonds (33%), real estate (7%), and cash (2%).

Investments in Affiliates: 46%

Group Affiliation: Alfa Ins Group

Licensed in: AL, CT, FL, GA, IL, IN, KY, MA, MI, NY, NC, OH, PA, SC, TN, VA, WI

Commenced Business: October 1947

Address: 2108 East South Blvd, Montgomery, AL 36116

Phone: (334) 288-3900 **Domicile State:** AL **NAIC Code:** 19135

Data Date	Rating	RACR #1	RACR #2	Loss Ratio %	Total Assets ($mil)	Capital ($mil)	Net Premium ($mil)	Net Income ($mil)
3-09	B	1.62	1.18	N/A	1,089.8	659.4	118.6	-7.0
3-08	A-	2.11	1.86	N/A	1,383.3	890.7	119.0	7.1
2008	B	1.69	1.25	74.7	1,088.8	663.6	593.5	-42.9
2007	A-	2.35	2.10	82.2	1,339.8	974.1	151.7	50.8
2006	A-	2.28	1.97	99.8	1,338.6	928.4	152.2	41.8
2005	A-	2.28	1.92	136.6	1,274.4	879.4	134.8	-9.5
2004	A	2.49	2.08	91.1	1,273.8	871.7	113.8	36.3

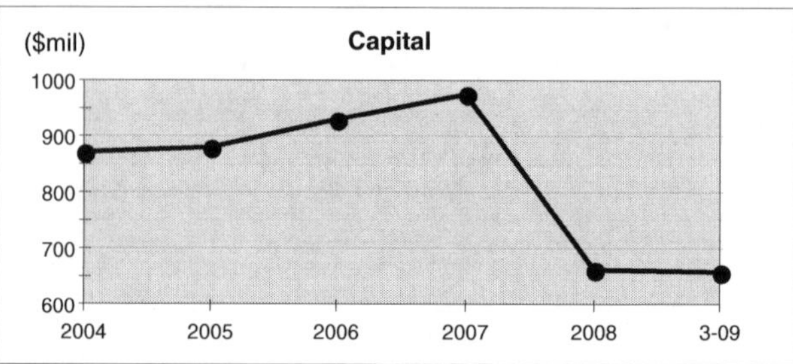

ALLIANZ GLOBAL RISKS US INS CO — C+ Fair

Major Rating Factors: Fair overall results on stability tests (4.5 on a scale of 0 to 10) including potential drain of affiliation with Allianz Ins Group and excessive premium growth. History of adequate reserve strength (6.0) as reserves have been consistently at an acceptable level.

Other Rating Factors: Good overall profitability index (5.1) despite operating losses during the first three months of 2008. Return on equity has been low, averaging 1.7% over the past five years. Good liquidity (6.9) with sufficient resources (cash flows and marketable investments) to handle a spike in claims. Strong long-term capitalization index (7.4) based on excellent current risk adjusted capital (severe and moderate loss scenarios), despite some fluctuation in capital levels.

Principal Business: Aircraft (29%), fire (25%), inland marine (10%), allied lines (10%), products liability (6%), other liability (5%), and other lines (14%).

Principal Investments: Misc. investments (70%), investment grade bonds (29%), and cash (1%).

Investments in Affiliates: 67%

Group Affiliation: Allianz Ins Group

Licensed in: All states, the District of Columbia and Puerto Rico

Commenced Business: December 1977

Address: 3400 Riverside Dr Ste 300, Burbank, CA 91505-4670

Phone: (818) 972-8000 **Domicile State:** CA **NAIC Code:** 35300

Data Date	Rating	RACR #1	RACR #2	Loss Ratio %	Total Assets ($mil)	Capital ($mil)	Net Premium ($mil)	Net Income ($mil)
3-09	C+	1.32	1.23	N/A	5,045.2	3,791.5	98.6	-32.4
3-08	C+	1.33	1.26	N/A	4,951.7	3,822.5	58.5	15.6
2008	C+	1.32	1.26	53.2	4,846.4	3,721.4	412.5	142.6
2007	C+	1.28	1.23	59.3	4,707.8	3,599.5	274.9	92.6
2006	C+	1.23	1.21	44.1	4,713.8	3,631.5	116.8	86.1
2005	C+	1.22	1.19	225.4	4,498.0	3,407.3	37.7	9.2
2004	C+	1.21	1.17	105.7	4,598.8	3,475.6	41.7	30.4

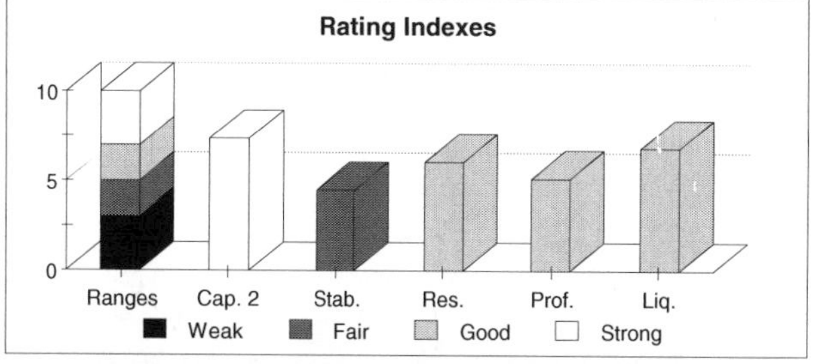

ALLIED WORLD REINS CO — C Fair

Major Rating Factors: Fair overall results on stability tests (3.4 on a scale of 0 to 10) including potential drain of affiliation with Allied World Asr Holding Group and weak results on operational trends. Fair profitability index (3.0) with operating losses during 2004, 2007 and 2008. Average return on equity over the last five years has been poor at -5.8%.

Other Rating Factors: History of adequate reserve strength (6.1) as reserves have been consistently at an acceptable level. Strong long-term capitalization index (7.9) based on excellent current risk adjusted capital (severe and moderate loss scenarios), despite some fluctuation in capital levels. Superior liquidity (9.2) with ample operational cash flow and liquid investments.

Principal Business: Auto liability (-43%).

Principal Investments: Misc. investments (56%) and investment grade bonds (44%).

Investments in Affiliates: 91%

Group Affiliation: Allied World Asr Holding Group

Licensed in: All states except NH, PR

Commenced Business: October 1986

Address: 2337 Lemoine Ave Suite 14, Fort Lee, NJ 07024

Phone: (203) 965-8800 **Domicile State:** NJ **NAIC Code:** 22730

Data Date	Rating	RACR #1	RACR #2	Loss Ratio %	Total Assets ($mil)	Capital ($mil)	Net Premium ($mil)	Net Income ($mil)
3-09	C	1.22	1.21	N/A	795.0	620.7	6.7	4.2
3-08	C	198.34	99.11	N/A	507.5	506.9	0.0	1.0
2008	C	1.47	1.75	33.9	684.8	592.0	32.3	-21.6
2007	C	17.61	12.34	N/A	57.7	46.0	-20.0	-11.5
2006	C	28.26	21.03	N/A	73.2	64.1	0.0	1.2
2005	C	21.25	19.13	0.0	76.6	62.0	0.0	0.6
2004	C	14.36	12.92	0.0	85.1	59.3	0.0	-3.2

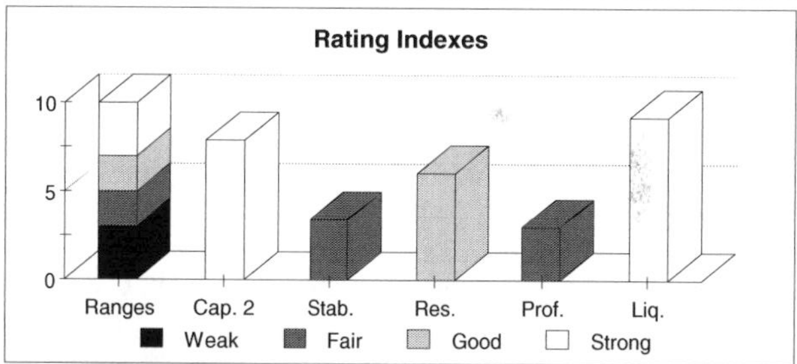

ALLSTATE FLORIDIAN INS CO — B- Good

Major Rating Factors: Good overall results on stability tests (5.2 on a scale of 0 to 10) despite excessive premium growth, negative cash flow from operations for 2008 and fair results on operational trends. The largest net exposure for one risk is high at 3.5% of capital. Strengths include potentially strong support from affiliation with Allstate Group. Good long-term capitalization index (5.5) based on good current risk adjusted capital (moderate loss scenario), despite some fluctuation in capital levels.

Other Rating Factors: History of adequate reserve strength (5.8) as reserves have been consistently at an acceptable level. Good liquidity (5.9) with sufficient resources (cash flows and marketable investments) to handle a spike in claims. Weak profitability index (0.8) with operating losses during 2004, 2005, 2007 and 2008. Average return on equity over the last five years has been poor at -73.2%.

Principal Business: Homeowners multiple peril (90%), inland marine (9%), and other liability (1%).

Principal Investments: Investment grade bonds (83%) and misc. investments (20%).

Investments in Affiliates: 11%

Group Affiliation: Allstate Group

Licensed in: FL, IL

Commenced Business: November 1988

Address: 780 Carillon Parkway, St. Petersburg, FL 33716

Phone: (847) 402-2242 **Domicile State:** IL **NAIC Code:** 30511

Data Date	Rating	RACR #1	RACR #2	Loss Ratio %	Total Assets ($mil)	Capital ($mil)	Net Premium ($mil)	Net Income ($mil)
3-09	B-	1.16	0.93	N/A	363.6	164.1	33.4	4.3
3-08	B-	3.15	2.54	N/A	398.8	178.0	5.4	-29.0
2008	B-	1.51	1.11	158.3	360.5	162.5	56.4	-50.4
2007	B-	2.79	2.21	136.3	431.7	206.7	34.0	-42.3
2006	B-	0.56	0.49	52.0	580.0	247.9	204.3	27.6
2005	B-	0.28	0.24	152.4	788.4	232.7	394.1	-185.8
2004	B-	0.21	0.17	364.3	1,013.6	272.1	485.1	-725.0

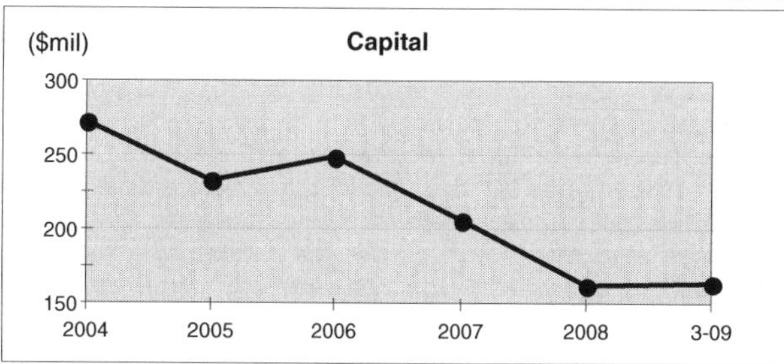

ALLSTATE INS CO * B+ Good

Major Rating Factors: Good overall results on stability tests (6.4 on a scale of 0 to 10). Strengths include potentially strong support from affiliation with Allstate Group, good operational trends and excellent risk diversification. History of adequate reserve strength (6.5) as reserves have been consistently at an acceptable level.

Other Rating Factors: Good liquidity (5.1) with sufficient resources (cash flows and marketable investments) to handle a spike in claims. Strong long-term capitalization index (7.7) based on excellent current risk adjusted capital (severe and moderate loss scenarios), despite some fluctuation in capital levels. Fair profitability index (3.2). Good expense controls. Return on equity has been fair, averaging 18.0% over the past five years.

Principal Business: Auto liability (35%), auto physical damage (28%), homeowners multiple peril (28%), commercial multiple peril (4%), allied lines (3%), other liability (2%), and inland marine (1%).

Principal Investments: Investment grade bonds (66%), misc. investments (28%), non investment grade bonds (5%), and real estate (1%).

Investments in Affiliates: 14%

Group Affiliation: Allstate Group

Licensed in: All states except NJ

Commenced Business: April 1931

Address: 3075 Sanders Rd, Ste G2H, Northbrook, IL 60062-7127

Phone: (847) 402-5000 **Domicile State:** IL **NAIC Code:** 19232

Data Date	Rating	RACR #1	RACR #2	Loss Ratio %	Total Assets ($mil)	Capital ($mil)	Net Premium ($mil)	Net Income ($mil)
3-09	B+	1.84	1.45	N/A	39,333.3	13,090.0	6,029.7	144.6
3-08	A-	2.43	1.85	N/A	44,022.5	16,724.8	6,234.2	603.2
2008	B+	1.82	1.44	74.3	39,944.6	13,021.1	24,431.4	686.9
2007	A-	2.54	1.94	64.8	46,162.4	18,034.5	25,055.8	4,958.2
2006	A-	2.43	1.86	58.9	47,679.7	19,129.2	25,167.5	4,921.5
2005	A-	1.83	1.37	78.3	45,243.5	14,833.7	25,081.4	1,750.0
2004	A-	2.14	1.66	63.6	44,711.7	16,766.7	24,133.3	3,863.5

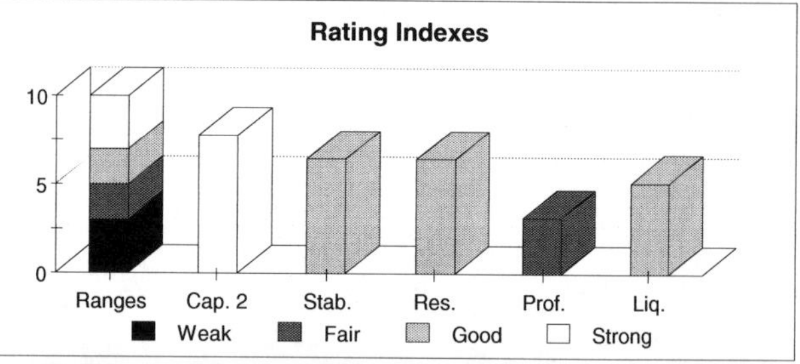

ALLSTATE NJ INS CO B- Good

Major Rating Factors: Fair reserve development (4.8 on a scale of 0 to 10) as reserves have generally been sufficient to cover claims. Fair profitability index (3.5) with operating losses during the first three months of 2008. Return on equity has been fair, averaging 15.2% over the past five years.

Other Rating Factors: Good liquidity (5.9) with sufficient resources (cash flows and marketable investments) to handle a spike in claims. Good overall results on stability tests (5.3). Stability strengths include good operational trends and excellent risk diversification. Strong long-term capitalization index (7.8) based on excellent current risk adjusted capital (severe and moderate loss scenarios), despite some fluctuation in capital levels.

Principal Business: Auto liability (43%), auto physical damage (31%), homeowners multiple peril (22%), other liability (2%), allied lines (1%), inland marine (1%), and commercial multiple peril (1%).

Principal Investments: Investment grade bonds (94%) and misc. investments (8%).

Investments in Affiliates: 3%

Group Affiliation: Allstate Group

Licensed in: IL, NJ

Commenced Business: November 1997

Address: 721 U.S. Hwy 202/206,Ste 300, Bridgewater, NJ 08807-1759

Phone: (847) 402-5000 **Domicile State:** IL **NAIC Code:** 10852

Data Date	Rating	RACR #1	RACR #2	Loss Ratio %	Total Assets ($mil)	Capital ($mil)	Net Premium ($mil)	Net Income ($mil)
3-09	B-	1.96	1.53	N/A	2,258.5	608.3	283.3	-0.8
3-08	B-	2.22	1.71	N/A	2,286.5	673.1	283.8	19.9
2008	B-	1.91	1.57	81.0	2,331.6	629.4	1,132.4	-12.4
2007	B-	2.11	1.70	74.4	2,271.3	679.8	1,141.6	113.6
2006	B-	2.27	1.58	69.5	2,398.4	779.4	1,169.4	159.7
2005	B-	2.18	1.53	67.0	2,372.9	747.1	1,213.3	181.0
2004	B-	2.03	1.48	67.3	2,316.9	728.0	1,271.2	149.6

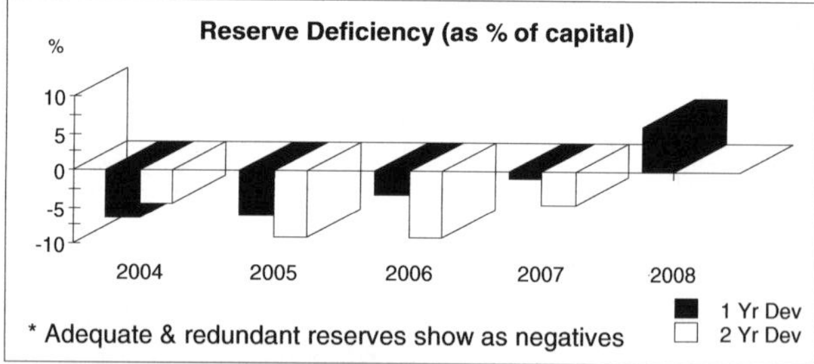

AMBAC ASSURANCE CORP D Weak

Major Rating Factors: Weak overall results on stability tests (1.4 on a scale of 0 to 10) including negative cash flow from operations for 2008. The largest net exposure for one risk is excessive at 372.2% of capital. Strengths include potentially strong support from affiliation with AMBAC Assurance Corp. Fair long-term capitalization index (3.6) based on weak current risk adjusted capital (severe and moderate loss scenarios), although results have slipped from the fair range during the last year.

Other Rating Factors: A history of deficient reserves (2.6). Underreserving can have an adverse impact on capital and profits. Weak profitability index (0.6) with operating losses during the first three months of 2008. Average return on equity over the last five years has been poor at -48.8%. Excellent liquidity (8.4) with ample operational cash flow and liquid investments.

Principal Business: Financial guaranty (100%).

Principal Investments: Investment grade bonds (98%) and non investment grade bonds (2%).

Investments in Affiliates: 2%

Group Affiliation: AMBAC Assurance Corp

Licensed in: All states, the District of Columbia and Puerto Rico

Commenced Business: March 1970

Address: 2 E Mifflin St Suite 600, Madison, WI 53703

Phone: (212) 668-0340 **Domicile State:** WI **NAIC Code:** 18708

Data Date	Rating	RACR #1	RACR #2	Loss Ratio %	Total Assets ($mil)	Capital ($mil)	Net Premium ($mil)	Net Income ($mil)
3-09	D	0.62	0.28	N/A	9,392.4	372.8	191.1	-232.2
3-08	C	4.81	1.76	N/A	12,282.0	3,629.3	182.2	-845.0
2008	D	1.53	0.68	150.6	10,781.1	1,554.4	502.3	-4,034.7
2007	C+	4.84	1.67	8.1	10,791.6	3,316.1	778.3	54.0
2006	B+	5.60	1.87	5.3	10,014.6	3,696.9	913.0	789.0
2005	U	N/A	N/A	5.8	8,994.4	3,327.5	1,009.4	707.4
2004	U	4.00	1.36	5.9	8,329.1	3,198.7	986.5	693.2

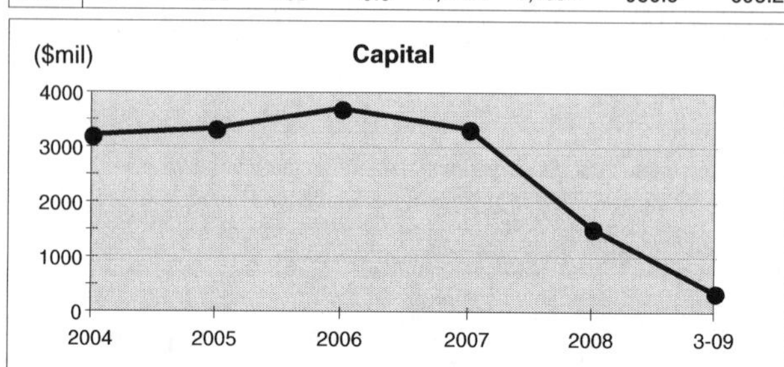

AMCO INS CO B Good

Major Rating Factors: Good overall results on stability tests (5.4 on a scale of 0 to 10). Stability strengths include good operational trends and excellent risk diversification. Fair profitability index (4.3). Good expense controls. Return on equity has been low, averaging 4.7% over the past five years.
Other Rating Factors: Strong long-term capitalization index (10.0) based on excellent current risk adjusted capital (severe and moderate loss scenarios), despite some fluctuation in capital levels. Superior liquidity (9.5) with ample operational cash flow and liquid investments.
Principal Business: Commercial multiple peril (33%), homeowners multiple peril (24%), auto liability (17%), auto physical damage (11%), other liability (6%), workers compensation (3%), and other lines (8%).
Principal Investments: Investment grade bonds (83%), misc. investments (29%), and non investment grade bonds (1%).
Investments in Affiliates: 6%
Group Affiliation: Nationwide Corp
Licensed in: AZ, CA, CO, DE, GA, ID, IL, IN, IA, KS, KY, MD, MI, MN, MO, MT, NE, NV, NM, NC, ND, OH, OR, PA, SC, SD, TN, TX, UT, VA, WA, WI, WY
Commenced Business: April 1959
Address: 1100 Locust St Dept 2007, Des Moines, IA 50391-2007
Phone: (515) 280-4211 **Domicile State:** IA **NAIC Code:** 19100

Data Date	Rating	RACR #1	RACR #2	Loss Ratio %	Total Assets ($mil)	Capital ($mil)	Net Premium ($mil)	Net Income ($mil)
3-09	B	7.97	5.70	N/A	2,453.5	416.1	0.0	3.9
3-08	B	39.65	27.42	N/A	969.6	491.7	0.0	4.0
2008	B	9.19	7.13	0.0	2,061.9	416.5	0.0	16.6
2007	B	39.25	30.76	0.0	966.6	487.2	0.0	24.1
2006	B	37.58	26.27	0.0	997.5	479.6	0.0	22.6
2005	B	29.71	21.67	0.0	988.8	398.5	0.0	19.7
2004	B	29.37	17.73	0.0	969.7	390.9	0.0	19.4

Nationwide Corp Composite Group Rating: B+ Largest Group Members	Assets ($mil)	Rating
NATIONWIDE LIFE INS CO	77310	B+
NATIONWIDE MUTUAL INS CO	28843	B
NATIONWIDE LIFE INS CO OF AMERICA	4994	B+
NATIONWIDE LIFE ANNUITY INS CO	4349	B
NATIONWIDE MUTUAL FIRE INS CO	4319	B+

AMERICAN AGRICULTURAL INS CO B Good

Major Rating Factors: History of adequate reserve strength (6.9 on a scale of 0 to 10) as reserves have been consistently at an acceptable level. Good overall profitability index (5.4) despite operating losses during the first three months of 2008. Return on equity has been fair, averaging 5.0% over the past five years.
Other Rating Factors: Good liquidity (6.7) with sufficient resources (cash flows and marketable investments) to handle a spike in claims. Good overall results on stability tests (5.6). Stability strengths include good operational trends and excellent risk diversification. Strong long-term capitalization index (8.0) based on excellent current risk adjusted capital (severe and moderate loss scenarios), despite some fluctuation in capital levels.
Principal Business: Allied lines (100%).
Principal Investments: Investment grade bonds (91%), misc. investments (6%), and cash (3%).
Investments in Affiliates: 0%
Group Affiliation: None
Licensed in: AL, AZ, AR, CO, DE, FL, GA, IL, IN, IA, KS, KY, LA, MI, MS, MO, MT, NE, NM, NC, OH, OK, OR, PA, SC, TN, TX, UT, VT, VA, WA, WI, WY, PR
Commenced Business: May 1948
Address: 225 South East sT, Indianapolis, IN 46202
Phone: (847) 969-2900 **Domicile State:** IN **NAIC Code:** 10103

Data Date	Rating	RACR #1	RACR #2	Loss Ratio %	Total Assets ($mil)	Capital ($mil)	Net Premium ($mil)	Net Income ($mil)
3-09	B	2.61	1.81	N/A	1,597.7	490.1	93.7	-4.0
3-08	B	2.27	1.56	N/A	1,496.7	557.3	94.2	10.9
2008	B	2.75	1.89	87.3	1,188.2	505.1	367.8	2.2
2007	B	2.31	1.58	67.3	1,290.4	553.3	460.2	68.2
2006	C+	2.32	1.62	85.2	1,134.9	484.5	428.8	24.4
2005	C+	2.43	1.66	70.4	1,161.5	459.0	441.6	27.3
2004	C+	1.52	1.05	77.0	985.8	331.9	484.6	11.5

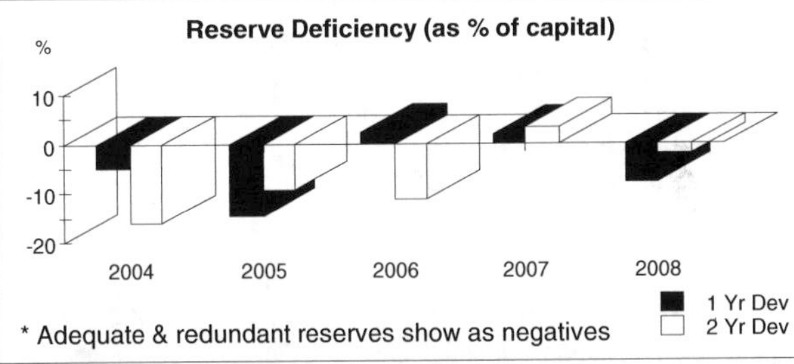

AMERICAN AUTOMOBILE INS CO C Fair

Major Rating Factors: Fair overall results on stability tests (4.3 on a scale of 0 to 10). History of adequate reserve strength (5.7) as reserves have been consistently at an acceptable level.
Other Rating Factors: Good liquidity (6.6) with sufficient resources (cash flows and marketable investments) to handle a spike in claims. Strong long-term capitalization index (7.7) based on excellent current risk adjusted capital (severe and moderate loss scenarios). Moreover, capital levels have been consistent in recent years. Excellent profitability (8.7) with operating gains in each of the last five years. Return on equity has been good over the last five years, averaging 10.7%.
Principal Business: Commercial multiple peril (29%), homeowners multiple peril (23%), other liability (23%), auto liability (9%), workers compensation (6%), inland marine (5%), and other lines (6%).
Principal Investments: Investment grade bonds (78%) and misc. investments (22%).
Investments in Affiliates: 20%
Group Affiliation: Allianz Ins Group
Licensed in: All states except PR
Commenced Business: January 1912
Address: 777 San Marin Dr, Novato, CA 94998
Phone: (415) 899-2000 **Domicile State:** MO **NAIC Code:** 21849

Data Date	Rating	RACR #1	RACR #2	Loss Ratio %	Total Assets ($mil)	Capital ($mil)	Net Premium ($mil)	Net Income ($mil)
3-09	C	2.12	1.68	N/A	457.0	213.6	27.1	5.8
3-08	C	2.05	1.54	N/A	443.1	205.9	25.8	6.8
2008	C	2.10	1.66	75.0	468.3	212.6	119.7	13.6
2007	C	1.96	1.46	62.0	447.5	196.7	116.2	22.6
2006	C	1.66	1.21	58.0	402.8	161.9	114.6	23.6
2005	C	1.62	1.13	66.7	370.2	145.6	107.4	15.7
2004	C	1.49	1.02	66.0	347.3	124.4	105.3	12.8

Allianz Ins Group Composite Group Rating: C+ Largest Group Members	Assets ($mil)	Rating
ALLIANZ LIFE INS CO OF NORTH AMERICA	66375	B-
FIREMANS FUND INS CO	10673	C
ALLIANZ GLOBAL RISKS US INS CO	4846	C+
AMERICAN INS CO	1449	B-
ALLIANZ LIFE INS CO OF NY	881	C

AMERICAN BANKERS INS CO OF FL B- Good

Major Rating Factors: Fair overall results on stability tests (4.9 on a scale of 0 to 10) including fair financial strength of affiliated Assurant Inc. Good liquidity (6.3) with sufficient resources (cash flows and marketable investments) to handle a spike in claims.

Other Rating Factors: Strong long-term capitalization index (7.8) based on excellent current risk adjusted capital (severe and moderate loss scenarios). Moreover, capital levels have been consistent in recent years. Ample reserve history (8.8) that helps to protect the company against sharp claims increases. Excellent profitability (7.0) with operating gains in each of the last five years.

Principal Business: Credit accident & health (29%), inland marine (24%), allied lines (13%), homeowners multiple peril (10%), auto physical damage (6%), auto liability (1%), and other lines (17%).

Principal Investments: Investment grade bonds (86%), misc. investments (9%), non investment grade bonds (4%), and cash (1%).

Investments in Affiliates: 1%

Group Affiliation: Assurant Inc

Licensed in: All states, the District of Columbia and Puerto Rico

Commenced Business: October 1947

Address: 11222 Quail Roost Dr, Miami, FL 33157

Phone: (305) 253-2244 **Domicile State:** FL **NAIC Code:** 10111

Data Date	Rating	RACR #1	RACR #2	Loss Ratio %	Total Assets ($mil)	Capital ($mil)	Net Premium ($mil)	Net Income ($mil)
3-09	B-	2.60	1.83	N/A	1,253.6	479.3	199.9	28.6
3-08	C+	1.74	1.29	N/A	1,317.1	389.6	203.9	32.2
2008	B-	2.43	1.72	43.9	1,270.2	449.9	778.4	59.2
2007	C+	1.76	1.31	37.1	1,428.1	404.1	799.2	36.8
2006	C	1.94	1.41	40.3	1,319.4	364.5	753.6	36.3
2005	C	1.38	1.02	43.3	1,369.0	289.9	689.6	4.4
2004	C	1.75	1.22	49.6	1,196.0	271.8	563.2	26.9

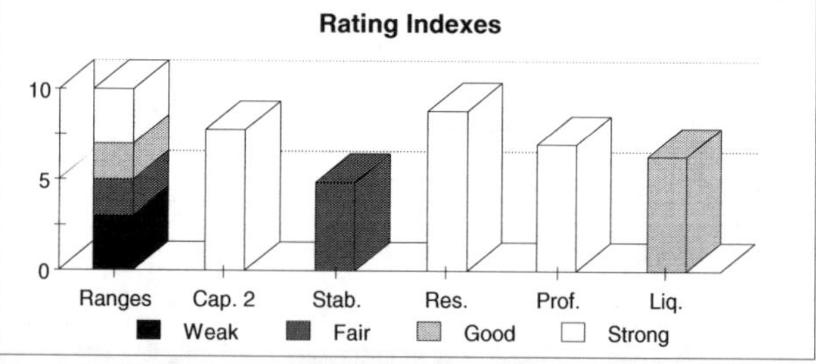

AMERICAN ECONOMY INS CO B- Good

Major Rating Factors: Fair overall results on stability tests (4.9 on a scale of 0 to 10). Strengths include potentially strong support from affiliation with Liberty Mutual Group. The largest net exposure for one risk is conservative at 1.1% of capital. History of adequate reserve strength (6.9) as reserves have been consistently at an acceptable level.

Other Rating Factors: Good liquidity (5.9) with sufficient resources (cash flows and marketable investments) to handle a spike in claims. Strong long-term capitalization index (7.6) based on excellent current risk adjusted capital (severe and moderate loss scenarios), despite some fluctuation in capital levels. Weak profitability index (2.6). Fair expense controls. Return on equity has been fair, averaging 21.5% over the past five years.

Principal Business: Commercial multiple peril (71%), auto liability (11%), workers compensation (8%), auto physical damage (2%), farmowners multiple peril (2%), other liability (2%), and other lines (4%).

Principal Investments: Investment grade bonds (83%), misc. investments (15%), and non investment grade bonds (2%).

Investments in Affiliates: 2%

Group Affiliation: Liberty Mutual Group

Licensed in: All states except NJ, PR

Commenced Business: October 1959

Address: 500 N Meridian St, Indianapolis, IN 46204

Phone: (206) 545-5000 **Domicile State:** IN **NAIC Code:** 19690

Data Date	Rating	RACR #1	RACR #2	Loss Ratio %	Total Assets ($mil)	Capital ($mil)	Net Premium ($mil)	Net Income ($mil)
3-09	B-	2.63	1.80	N/A	1,774.2	430.7	149.7	11.3
3-08	B-	2.08	1.39	N/A	1,511.1	408.7	194.1	21.4
2008	B-	1.86	1.30	67.0	1,438.5	309.1	747.7	62.2
2007	B-	2.05	1.38	62.9	1,525.3	400.3	791.9	97.9
2006	B-	2.61	1.72	58.5	1,634.8	528.8	785.9	121.1
2005	B-	2.24	1.51	62.3	1,643.3	502.5	814.0	105.2
2004	C+	2.24	1.52	63.2	1,567.9	491.3	794.6	108.3

Liberty Mutual Group
Composite Group Rating: C+

Largest Group Members	Assets ($mil)	Rating
LIBERTY MUTUAL INS CO	32550	B-
LIBERTY LIFE ASR CO OF BOSTON	11605	B-
PEERLESS INS CO	7069	C+
OHIO CASUALTY INS CO	4869	C+
SAFECO INS CO OF AMERICA	3952	B-

AMERICAN FAMILY HOME INS CO * B+ Good

Major Rating Factors: Good overall results on stability tests (5.0 on a scale of 0 to 10) despite potential drain of affiliation with Munich Re America Corp. Stability strengths include good operational trends and excellent risk diversification. History of adequate reserve strength (6.9) as reserves have been consistently at an acceptable level.

Other Rating Factors: Good overall profitability index (6.7). Weak expense controls. Return on equity has been good over the last five years, averaging 13.0%. Good liquidity (6.3) with sufficient resources (cash flows and marketable investments) to handle a spike in claims. Strong long-term capitalization index (8.2) based on excellent current risk adjusted capital (severe and moderate loss scenarios), despite some fluctuation in capital levels.

Principal Business: Homeowners multiple peril (78%), inland marine (11%), fire (4%), auto liability (3%), auto physical damage (2%), and allied lines (2%).

Principal Investments: Investment grade bonds (88%) and misc. investments (15%).

Investments in Affiliates: 8%

Group Affiliation: Munich Re America Corp

Licensed in: All states except ME, NH, TX, PR

Commenced Business: May 1965

Address: 1301 River Place Blvd Ste 1300, Jacksonville, FL 32207

Phone: (800) 543-2644 **Domicile State:** FL **NAIC Code:** 23450

Data Date	Rating	RACR #1	RACR #2	Loss Ratio %	Total Assets ($mil)	Capital ($mil)	Net Premium ($mil)	Net Income ($mil)
3-09	B+	2.58	1.81	N/A	443.6	129.0	55.6	4.8
3-08	B+	2.10	1.47	N/A	450.9	139.4	55.4	4.4
2008	B+	2.55	1.80	53.0	451.9	130.2	222.2	1.1
2007	B+	2.13	1.50	43.4	447.2	139.0	211.2	19.0
2006	B+	2.54	1.77	45.5	429.4	137.3	173.3	20.2
2005	B+	2.18	1.55	45.3	420.8	115.9	185.8	19.2
2004	B+	2.53	1.64	51.7	374.4	105.6	201.6	19.8

Munich Re America Corp
Composite Group Rating: C

Largest Group Members	Assets ($mil)	Rating
MUNICH REINSURANCE AMERICA INC	16355	C
MUNICH AMERICAN REASSURANCE CO	5506	C+
HARTFORD SM BOIL INSPECTION INS	1112	B-
AMERICAN MODERN HOME INS CO	909	B+
AMERICAN ALTERNATIVE INS CORP	462	C

AMERICAN FAMILY MUT INS CO — B- Good

Major Rating Factors: Fair overall results on stability tests (4.9 on a scale of 0 to 10) including negative cash flow from operations for 2008. Strengths include potentially strong support from affiliation with American Family Ins Group. History of adequate reserve strength (5.8) as reserves have been consistently at an acceptable level.

Other Rating Factors: Strong long-term capitalization index (7.6) based on excellent current risk adjusted capital (severe and moderate loss scenarios), despite some fluctuation in capital levels. Weak profitability index (2.3) with operating losses during 2006, 2007 and 2008. Vulnerable liquidity (2.9) as a spike in claims may stretch capacity.

Principal Business: Auto liability (32%), homeowners multiple peril (26%), auto physical damage (25%), commercial multiple peril (8%), other accident & health (3%), other liability (2%), and other lines (4%).

Principal Investments: Investment grade bonds (74%), misc. investments (23%), and real estate (3%).

Investments in Affiliates: 8%

Group Affiliation: American Family Ins Group

Licensed in: AZ, CO, ID, IL, IN, IA, KS, MN, MO, MT, NE, NV, NM, NC, ND, OH, OR, SC, SD, UT, WA, WI, WY

Commenced Business: October 1927

Address: 6000 American Pkwy, Madison, WI 53783-0001

Phone: (608) 249-2111 **Domicile State:** WI **NAIC Code:** 19275

Data Date	Rating	RACR #1	RACR #2	Loss Ratio %	Total Assets ($mil)	Capital ($mil)	Net Premium ($mil)	Net Income ($mil)
3-09	B-	2.06	1.44	N/A	10,575.6	3,193.6	1,366.0	159.0
3-08	B	2.30	1.60	N/A	11,283.6	4,066.5	1,460.7	71.4
2008	B-	2.01	1.41	88.5	10,609.1	3,199.2	5,786.2	-550.9
2007	B	2.34	1.64	86.1	11,342.7	4,144.7	5,952.8	-46.4
2006	B	2.41	1.69	86.1	11,009.9	4,191.6	5,905.0	-103.6
2005	B	2.47	1.71	68.5	10,467.2	4,022.0	5,975.6	573.1
2004	B	2.04	1.41	71.7	9,560.7	3,286.5	5,955.8	479.9

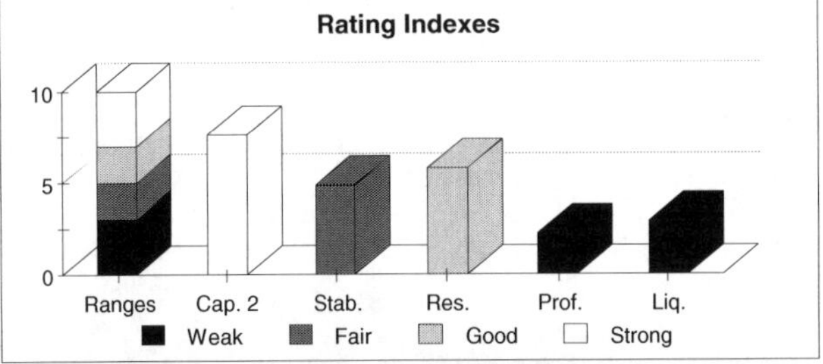

AMERICAN GUARANTEE & LIABILITY INS — C Fair

Major Rating Factors: Fair overall results on stability tests (3.9 on a scale of 0 to 10).

Other Rating Factors: Strong long-term capitalization index (10.0) based on excellent current risk adjusted capital (severe and moderate loss scenarios), despite some fluctuation in capital levels. Excellent profitability (7.7) despite modest operating losses during 2008. Excellent liquidity (7.0) with ample operational cash flow and liquid investments.

Principal Business: Other liability (48%), allied lines (14%), fire (12%), workers compensation (7%), products liability (6%), auto liability (6%), and other lines (7%).

Principal Investments: Investment grade bonds (100%) and cash (1%).

Investments in Affiliates: None

Group Affiliation: Zurich Financial Services Group

Licensed in: All states except PR

Commenced Business: September 1939

Address: 1400 American Lane, Schaumburg, IL 60196

Phone: (847) 605-6429 **Domicile State:** NY **NAIC Code:** 26247

Data Date	Rating	RACR #1	RACR #2	Loss Ratio %	Total Assets ($mil)	Capital ($mil)	Net Premium ($mil)	Net Income ($mil)
3-09	C	22.16	19.95	N/A	212.0	155.8	0.0	0.1
3-08	C	29.67	26.70	N/A	193.0	156.6	0.0	3.0
2008	C	21.82	19.64	0.0	215.5	156.3	0.0	-1.1
2007	C	15.71	14.14	0.0	339.9	153.6	0.0	9.1
2006	C	16.00	14.40	0.0	259.7	146.0	0.0	7.0
2005	C	21.45	19.30	0.0	187.9	140.0	0.0	7.0
2004	C	15.34	13.81	0.0	213.8	128.1	0.0	4.6

Zurich Financial Services Group
Composite Group Rating: C-

Largest Group Members	Assets ($mil)	Rating
ZURICH AMERICAN INS CO	29634	C-
KEMPER INVESTORS LIFE INS CO	13886	C
FARMERS INS EXCHANGE	13368	C
FARMERS NEW WORLD LIFE INS CO	6444	B-
MID-CENTURY INS CO	3273	C-

AMERICAN HOME ASR CO — C+ Fair

Major Rating Factors: Fair overall results on stability tests (4.3 on a scale of 0 to 10) including negative cash flow from operations for 2008. Strengths include potentially strong support from affiliation with American International Group. The largest net exposure for one risk is conservative at 1.4% of capital. Fair profitability index (4.6) with operating losses during 2004 and 2005. Return on equity has been fair, averaging 5.6% over the past five years.

Other Rating Factors: Good long-term capitalization index (5.5) based on good current risk adjusted capital (moderate loss scenario). Good liquidity (5.5) with sufficient resources (cash flows and marketable investments) to handle a spike in claims. A history of deficient reserves (1.8). Underreserving can have an adverse impact on capital and profits. Deficiencies in the two year reserve development occurred in three of the previous five years and ranged between 57% and 86%.

Principal Business: Other accident & health (22%), inland marine (16%), workers compensation (12%), ocean marine (11%), other liability (10%), auto liability (8%), and other lines (20%).

Principal Investments: Investment grade bonds (76%), misc. investments (23%), and non investment grade bonds (1%).

Investments in Affiliates: 7%

Group Affiliation: American International Group

Licensed in: All states except PR

Commenced Business: February 1899

Address: 70 Pine Street, 3rd Floor, New York, NY 10270

Phone: (212) 770-7000 **Domicile State:** NY **NAIC Code:** 19380

Data Date	Rating	RACR #1	RACR #2	Loss Ratio %	Total Assets ($mil)	Capital ($mil)	Net Premium ($mil)	Net Income ($mil)
3-09	C+	1.16	0.77	N/A	24,768.6	5,171.0	1,661.5	2.7
3-08	B-	1.36	0.91	N/A	28,265.3	6,806.0	1,800.3	10.6
2008	C+	1.26	0.83	75.7	26,862.8	5,701.9	6,846.0	21.1
2007	B-	1.45	0.98	68.6	28,856.3	7,297.0	7,660.0	1,347.7
2006	B	1.17	0.82	70.3	28,409.6	6,211.9	7,884.0	979.2
2005	B	1.02	0.72	92.3	24,004.5	5,049.7	7,151.3	-185.7
2004	B	0.97	0.67	84.3	19,983.5	3,339.3	6,989.8	-46.2

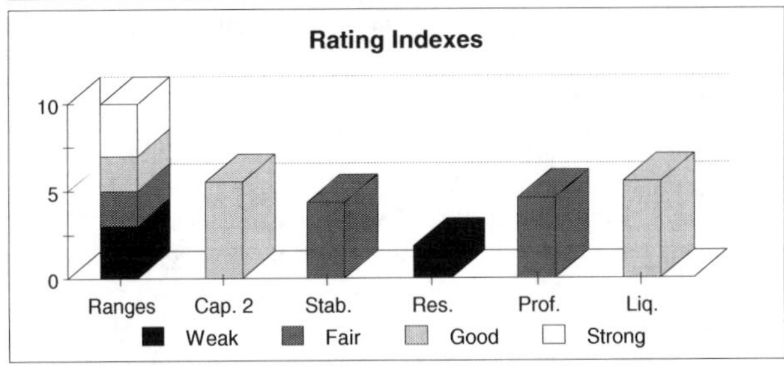

AMERICAN INS CO B- Good

Major Rating Factors: Fair profitability index (3.4 on a scale of 0 to 10). Fair expense controls. Return on equity has been fair, averaging 15.6% over the past five years. Fair overall results on stability tests (4.9).

Other Rating Factors: Good overall long-term capitalization (5.5) based on good current risk adjusted capital (moderate loss scenario). However, capital levels have fluctuated during prior years. History of adequate reserve strength (5.5) as reserves have been consistently at an acceptable level. Good liquidity (5.5) with sufficient resources (cash flows and marketable investments) to handle a spike in claims.

Principal Business: Commercial multiple peril (39%), homeowners multiple peril (22%), other liability (12%), workers compensation (9%), inland marine (6%), farmowners multiple peril (3%), and other lines (8%).

Principal Investments: Investment grade bonds (94%), misc. investments (5%), and non investment grade bonds (1%).

Investments in Affiliates: 4%

Group Affiliation: Allianz Ins Group

Licensed in: All states, the District of Columbia and Puerto Rico

Commenced Business: April 1846

Address: 777 San Marin Dr, Novato, CA 94998

Phone: (415) 889-2000 **Domicile State:** OH **NAIC Code:** 21857

Data Date	Rating	RACR #1	RACR #2	Loss Ratio %	Total Assets ($mil)	Capital ($mil)	Net Premium ($mil)	Net Income ($mil)
3-09	B-	1.16	0.80	N/A	1,425.7	382.8	124.5	17.1
3-08	B-	1.97	1.29	N/A	1,657.4	664.3	118.5	17.4
2008	B-	1.19	0.82	75.0	1,449.2	394.5	550.8	34.5
2007	B-	1.91	1.25	62.0	1,655.1	656.4	534.7	110.8
2006	B-	1.61	1.04	58.0	1,566.0	564.6	527.4	113.1
2005	C	1.54	0.96	66.7	1,499.0	507.6	493.9	90.8
2004	C	1.36	0.82	66.0	1,324.1	418.6	484.2	58.0

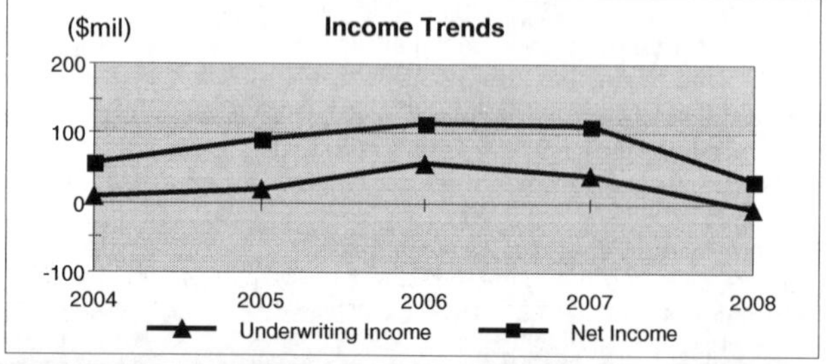

AMERICAN INTERNATIONAL INS CO B Good

Major Rating Factors: History of adequate reserve strength (5.3 on a scale of 0 to 10) as reserves have been consistently at an acceptable level. Good overall profitability index (6.6). Fair expense controls. Return on equity has been fair, averaging 8.2% over the past five years.

Other Rating Factors: Good overall results on stability tests (5.6) despite negative cash flow from operations for 2008. Stability strengths include good operational trends and excellent risk diversification. Strong long-term capitalization index (8.0) based on excellent current risk adjusted capital (severe and moderate loss scenarios), despite some fluctuation in capital levels. Vulnerable liquidity (0.7) as a spike in claims may stretch capacity.

Principal Business: Homeowners multiple peril (47%), other liability (15%), auto liability (14%), inland marine (12%), auto physical damage (9%), allied lines (2%), and earthquake (1%).

Principal Investments: Investment grade bonds (87%), misc. investments (7%), and cash (6%).

Investments in Affiliates: 10%

Group Affiliation: American International Group

Licensed in: All states except CA, KS, ME, NJ, NC, OH, OR, TN, VT, VA, WY, PR

Commenced Business: May 1975

Address: 505 Carr Rd, Wilmington, DE 19809

Phone: (302) 761-3000 **Domicile State:** NY **NAIC Code:** 32220

Data Date	Rating	RACR #1	RACR #2	Loss Ratio %	Total Assets ($mil)	Capital ($mil)	Net Premium ($mil)	Net Income ($mil)
3-09	B	2.34	1.77	N/A	1,612.1	364.3	113.1	6.0
3-08	B	2.02	1.47	N/A	1,312.5	363.3	137.9	0.2
2008	B	2.26	1.77	79.6	1,726.2	373.7	508.3	3.8
2007	B	2.08	1.57	77.2	1,221.9	367.2	520.6	6.3
2006	B	2.18	1.71	70.1	1,175.3	358.1	498.6	38.3
2005	B	1.89	1.52	75.6	1,140.4	303.6	493.5	18.7
2004	B	1.23	0.98	72.5	1,120.3	271.0	653.4	59.8

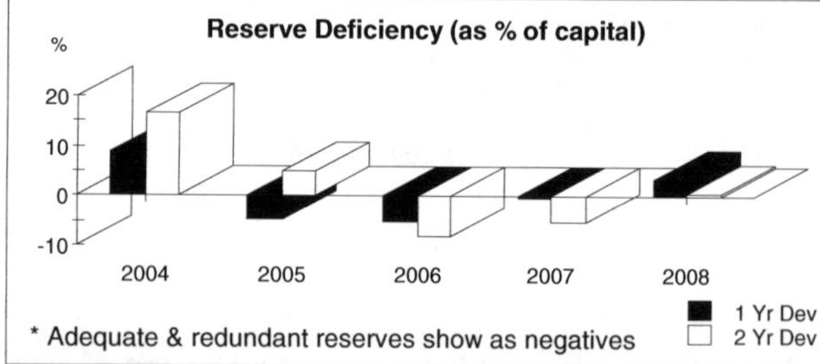

AMERICAN INTERSTATE INS CO C+ Fair

Major Rating Factors: Fair overall results on stability tests (4.5 on a scale of 0 to 10) including potential drain of affiliation with Amerisafe Inc. Fair reserve development (4.6) as the level of reserves has at times been insufficient to cover claims. In 2004 and 2005 the two year reserve development was 16% and 28% deficient respectively.

Other Rating Factors: Good liquidity (6.9) with sufficient resources (cash flows and marketable investments) to handle a spike in claims. Strong long-term capitalization index (7.3) based on excellent current risk adjusted capital (severe and moderate loss scenarios). Moreover, capital levels have been consistent in recent years. Excellent profitability (7.4). Return on equity has been good over the last five years, averaging 10.1%.

Principal Business: Workers compensation (100%).

Principal Investments: Investment grade bonds (88%) and misc. investments (13%).

Investments in Affiliates: 8%

Group Affiliation: Amerisafe Inc

Licensed in: All states except AZ, CT, NJ, OH, WV, PR

Commenced Business: April 1974

Address: 2301 Highway 190 West, Deridder, LA 70634

Phone: (318) 463-9052 **Domicile State:** LA **NAIC Code:** 31895

Data Date	Rating	RACR #1	RACR #2	Loss Ratio %	Total Assets ($mil)	Capital ($mil)	Net Premium ($mil)	Net Income ($mil)
3-09	C+	1.92	1.50	N/A	934.9	282.9	56.2	8.5
3-08	C	1.65	1.29	N/A	879.3	247.9	59.6	8.8
2008	C+	1.92	1.50	60.9	903.4	276.3	231.3	25.9
2007	C	1.64	1.29	64.8	851.6	241.0	246.9	45.6
2006	C	1.30	0.94	66.8	766.0	196.0	250.8	32.6
2005	C	1.12	0.80	79.5	670.8	157.7	216.7	-1.7
2004	C	1.13	0.89	74.4	499.1	112.3	195.3	7.1

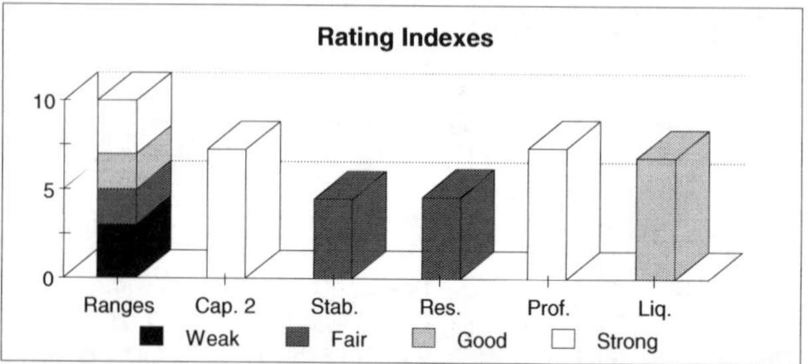

AMERICAN INTL SPECIALTY LINES INS CO — C — Fair

Major Rating Factors: Fair overall results on stability tests (4.2 on a scale of 0 to 10) including fair risk adjusted capital in prior years. The largest net exposure for one risk is excessive at 5.4% of capital. Strengths include potentially strong support from affiliation with American International Group. Fair profitability index (4.9) with operating losses during 2005 and 2008. Return on equity has been fair, averaging 6.0% over the past five years.

Other Rating Factors: Poor long-term capitalization index (1.9) based on fair current risk adjusted capital (moderate loss scenario). A history of deficient reserves (2.8). Underreserving can have an adverse impact on capital and profits. Deficiencies in the two year reserve development occurred in three of the previous five years and ranged between 23% and 50%. Good liquidity (6.3) with sufficient resources (cash flows and marketable investments) to handle a spike in claims.

Principal Business: Other liability (93%), auto liability (5%), and workers compensation (2%).

Principal Investments: Investment grade bonds (86%) and misc. investments (14%).

Investments in Affiliates: None

Group Affiliation: American International Group

Licensed in: AK

Commenced Business: July 1973

Address: Harborside Financial Ctr 401, Jersey City, NJ 07311

Phone: (201) 309-1100 **Domicile State:** IL **NAIC Code:** 26883

Data Date	Rating	RACR #1	RACR #2	Loss Ratio %	Total Assets ($mil)	Capital ($mil)	Net Premium ($mil)	Net Income ($mil)
3-09	C	0.75	0.54	N/A	2,497.8	754.5	78.3	21.9
3-08	C	0.70	0.51	N/A	2,551.9	721.1	66.4	19.8
2008	C	0.69	0.50	98.5	2,653.9	726.2	198.2	-96.4
2007	C	0.62	0.45	65.1	2,817.8	637.6	258.6	118.8
2006	C	0.40	0.29	79.8	2,727.8	492.5	298.9	46.0
2005	C	0.50	0.34	121.5	2,544.3	358.7	317.5	-36.4
2004	C+	1.11	0.69	57.1	2,389.9	351.1	372.2	84.8

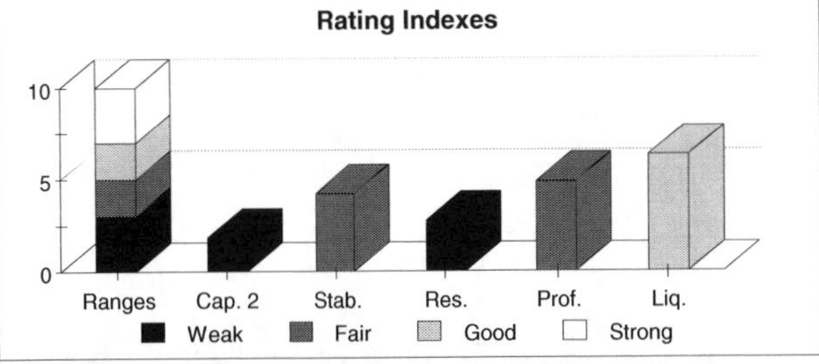

AMERICAN MERCURY INS CO * — B+ — Good

Major Rating Factors: History of adequate reserve strength (6.3 on a scale of 0 to 10) as reserves have been consistently at an acceptable level. Good liquidity (5.2) with sufficient resources (cash flows and marketable investments) to handle a spike in claims.

Other Rating Factors: Good overall results on stability tests (6.4) despite negative cash flow from operations for 2008. Stability strengths include good operational trends and excellent risk diversification. Strong long-term capitalization index (8.1) based on excellent current risk adjusted capital (severe and moderate loss scenarios), despite some fluctuation in capital levels. Fair profitability index (4.0) with operating losses during 2004 and 2008. Return on equity has been low, averaging 0.4% over the past five years.

Principal Business: Auto liability (29%), auto physical damage (23%), homeowners multiple peril (16%), and other liability (7%).

Principal Investments: Investment grade bonds (96%), misc. investments (3%), and cash (1%).

Investments in Affiliates: 3%

Group Affiliation: Mercury General Group

Licensed in: AL, AK, AZ, AR, CA, CO, FL, GA, ID, IL, IN, IA, KS, KY, LA, MN, MS, MO, MT, NE, NV, NJ, NM, ND, OK, OR, PA, SD, TN, TX, UT, VA, WA, WI, WY

Commenced Business: December 1962

Address: 2000 N Classen Center, Oklahoma City, OK 73106-6092

Phone: (405) 523-2000 **Domicile State:** OK **NAIC Code:** 16810

Data Date	Rating	RACR #1	RACR #2	Loss Ratio %	Total Assets ($mil)	Capital ($mil)	Net Premium ($mil)	Net Income ($mil)
3-09	B+	2.84	1.90	N/A	334.3	108.7	49.4	1.6
3-08	B+	3.06	2.10	N/A	356.8	119.9	52.7	4.0
2008	B+	2.75	1.87	83.0	335.3	107.3	196.3	-14.5
2007	B+	3.05	2.13	71.2	363.6	123.5	221.8	11.8
2006	B	2.26	1.54	66.8	345.3	113.2	235.2	12.2
2005	B	1.36	0.96	70.3	291.1	70.5	248.1	2.0
2004	B	1.86	1.23	77.0	230.3	72.6	142.3	-6.4

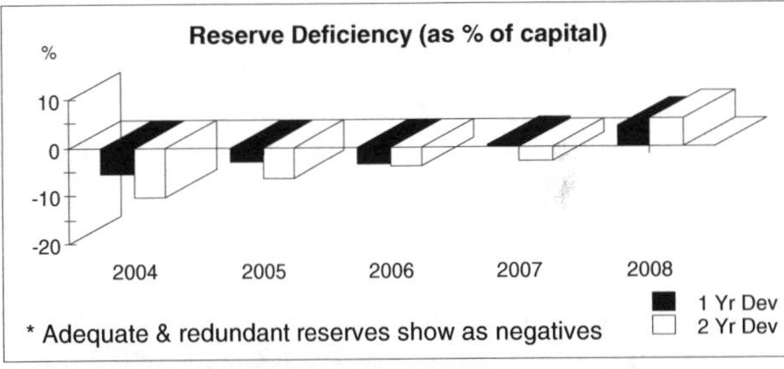

AMERICAN MODERN HOME INS CO * — B+ — Good

Major Rating Factors: Good overall results on stability tests (5.0 on a scale of 0 to 10) despite potential drain of affiliation with Munich Re America Corp and negative cash flow from operations for 2008. Stability strengths include good operational trends and excellent risk diversification. History of adequate reserve strength (6.9) as reserves have been consistently at an acceptable level.

Other Rating Factors: Good liquidity (6.0) with sufficient resources (cash flows and marketable investments) to handle a spike in claims. Strong long-term capitalization index (8.2) based on excellent current risk adjusted capital (severe and moderate loss scenarios), despite some fluctuation in capital levels. Excellent profitability (7.5) with operating gains in each of the last five years. Return on equity has been good over the last five years, averaging 12.3%.

Principal Business: Homeowners multiple peril (31%), fire (24%), allied lines (15%), inland marine (10%), auto physical damage (9%), auto liability (5%), and other lines (6%).

Principal Investments: Investment grade bonds (73%) and misc. investments (29%).

Investments in Affiliates: 22%

Group Affiliation: Munich Re America Corp

Licensed in: All states except PR

Commenced Business: September 1965

Address: 7000 Midland Blvd, Amelia, OH 45102-2607

Phone: (800) 543-2644 **Domicile State:** OH **NAIC Code:** 23469

Data Date	Rating	RACR #1	RACR #2	Loss Ratio %	Total Assets ($mil)	Capital ($mil)	Net Premium ($mil)	Net Income ($mil)
3-09	B+	2.24	1.77	N/A	888.8	270.7	97.8	6.3
3-08	B+	1.91	1.44	N/A	895.7	282.1	97.4	7.7
2008	B+	2.23	1.77	53.0	908.8	272.7	388.9	7.4
2007	B+	1.96	1.49	43.4	877.7	282.6	375.5	37.6
2006	B+	2.25	1.71	45.5	824.3	273.2	279.6	43.2
2005	B+	1.93	1.46	45.3	816.1	237.4	383.9	40.9
2004	B+	1.82	1.34	51.7	753.7	218.9	416.6	28.2

Munich Re America Corp
Composite Group Rating: C

Largest Group Members	Assets ($mil)	Rating
MUNICH REINSURANCE AMERICA INC	16355	C
MUNICH AMERICAN REASSURANCE CO	5506	C+
HARTFORD SM BOIL INSPECTION INS	1112	B-
AMERICAN MODERN HOME INS CO	909	B+
AMERICAN ALTERNATIVE INS CORP	462	C

AMERICAN MUTUAL SHARE INS CORP C- Fair

Major Rating Factors: Weak overall results on stability tests (1.5 on a scale of 0 to 10). The largest net exposure for one risk is excessive at 449.5% of capital. Strengths include potentially strong support from affiliation with American Mutual Share Group. Fair profitability index (3.6). Weak expense controls.

Other Rating Factors: Strong long-term capitalization index (10.0) based on excellent current risk adjusted capital (severe and moderate loss scenarios), despite some fluctuation in capital levels. Ample reserve history (7.8) that can protect against increases in claims costs. Superior liquidity (10.0) with ample operational cash flow and liquid investments.

Principal Business: Aggregate write-ins for other lines of business (100%).

Principal Investments: Investment grade bonds (80%), misc. investments (12%), and cash (8%).

Investments in Affiliates: 11%

Group Affiliation: American Mutual Share Group

Licensed in: CA, ID, IL, IN, ME, NV, NH, NJ, OH, PA

Commenced Business: June 1974

Address: 5656 Frantz Rd, Dublin, OH 43017

Phone: (614) 764-1900 **Domicile State:** OH **NAIC Code:** 12700

Data Date	Rating	RACR #1	RACR #2	Loss Ratio %	Total Assets ($mil)	Capital ($mil)	Net Premium ($mil)	Net Income ($mil)
3-09	C-	8.62	8.24	N/A	184.2	167.1	0.1	0.0
3-08	C-	9.69	9.08	N/A	226.8	176.2	0.4	0.5
2008	C-	8.57	8.21	98.6	185.6	170.4	1.2	0.5
2007	C-	11.89	11.37	78.8	219.8	210.5	1.5	3.2
2006	C-	12.97	12.36	59.4	214.3	204.1	1.6	2.6
2005	C-	13.92	13.19	52.5	200.0	192.6	1.7	2.3
2004	C-	14.48	13.63	83.2	191.3	184.7	1.6	0.8

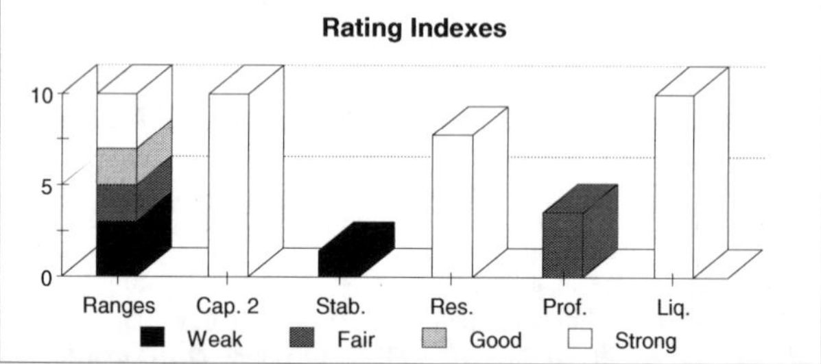

AMERICAN NATIONAL GENERAL INS CO * B+ Good

Major Rating Factors: Good overall results on stability tests (6.4 on a scale of 0 to 10). Stability strengths include good operational trends and excellent risk diversification. The largest net exposure for one risk is conservative at 1.4% of capital. History of adequate reserve strength (6.9) as reserves have been consistently at an acceptable level.

Other Rating Factors: Good liquidity (6.8) with sufficient resources (cash flows and marketable investments) to handle a spike in claims. Strong long-term capitalization index (10.0) based on excellent current risk adjusted capital (severe and moderate loss scenarios), despite some fluctuation in capital levels. Excellent profitability (8.2) with operating gains in each of the last five years.

Principal Business: Auto liability (47%), auto physical damage (28%), homeowners multiple peril (24%), and credit (1%).

Principal Investments: Investment grade bonds (88%), misc. investments (11%), and non investment grade bonds (2%).

Investments in Affiliates: 4%

Group Affiliation: American National Group Inc

Licensed in: AL, AZ, AR, CA, CO, CT, DE, FL, GA, ID, IL, IN, IA, KS, KY, LA, MD, MN, MS, MO, MT, NE, NV, NM, ND, OH, OK, OR, PA, SC, SD, TN, TX, UT, VA, WA, WV, WI, WY

Commenced Business: April 1981

Address: 1949 E Sunshine, Springfield, MO 65899

Phone: (417) 887-0220 **Domicile State:** MO **NAIC Code:** 39942

Data Date	Rating	RACR #1	RACR #2	Loss Ratio %	Total Assets ($mil)	Capital ($mil)	Net Premium ($mil)	Net Income ($mil)
3-09	B+	6.61	4.46	N/A	99.8	69.8	6.4	0.7
3-08	B+	5.15	4.20	N/A	98.8	71.7	5.5	1.3
2008	B+	7.03	4.88	69.6	99.3	69.0	22.1	0.3
2007	B+	4.92	4.05	61.4	99.2	70.4	22.9	7.3
2006	B+	4.31	3.41	76.4	100.6	64.0	28.6	5.0
2005	B+	4.23	3.21	79.3	103.0	59.2	36.2	4.9
2004	B+	3.03	2.38	75.9	103.2	54.4	43.9	6.5

American National Group Inc
Composite Group Rating: B+

Largest Group Members	Assets ($mil)	Rating
AMERICAN NATIONAL INS CO	13586	B+
AMERICAN NATIONAL PROPERTY CAS CO	1107	B+
FARM FAMILY LIFE INS CO	991	B+
FARM FAMILY CASUALTY INS CO	944	B
STANDARD LIFE ACCIDENT INS CO	490	A-

AMERICAN NATIONAL PROPERTY & CAS CO * B+ Good

Major Rating Factors: History of adequate reserve strength (6.9 on a scale of 0 to 10) as reserves have been consistently at an acceptable level. Good overall results on stability tests (6.4) despite negative cash flow from operations for 2008. Other stability subfactors include potential support from affiliation with American National Group Inc, good operational trends and excellent risk diversification.

Other Rating Factors: Strong long-term capitalization index (7.3) based on excellent current risk adjusted capital (severe and moderate loss scenarios), despite some fluctuation in capital levels. Fair liquidity (3.3) as cash resources may not be adequate to cover a spike in claims. Weak profitability index (2.9) with operating losses during the first three months of 2008. Return on equity has been fair, averaging 6.5% over the past five years.

Principal Business: Auto liability (30%), homeowners multiple peril (22%), auto physical damage (17%), credit (16%), allied lines (5%), inland marine (2%), and other lines (7%).

Principal Investments: Investment grade bonds (70%), misc. investments (29%), real estate (2%), and non investment grade bonds (1%).

Investments in Affiliates: 14%

Group Affiliation: American National Group Inc

Licensed in: All states except AK, CT, HI, MA, NY

Commenced Business: January 1974

Address: 1949 E Sunshine, Springfield, MO 65899-0001

Phone: (417) 887-0220 **Domicile State:** MO **NAIC Code:** 28401

Data Date	Rating	RACR #1	RACR #2	Loss Ratio %	Total Assets ($mil)	Capital ($mil)	Net Premium ($mil)	Net Income ($mil)
3-09	B+	1.67	1.17	N/A	1,068.4	357.0	143.1	-7.0
3-08	A-	2.24	1.64	N/A	1,186.1	504.0	147.1	9.3
2008	B+	1.77	1.25	90.8	1,107.2	386.2	563.1	-55.5
2007	A-	2.21	1.62	73.9	1,181.7	494.0	573.2	63.7
2006	B+	2.23	1.71	79.3	1,128.7	442.7	601.8	26.1
2005	B+	1.85	1.39	73.5	1,134.8	380.9	671.4	56.9
2004	B	1.67	1.28	71.3	1,005.3	380.2	636.9	63.5

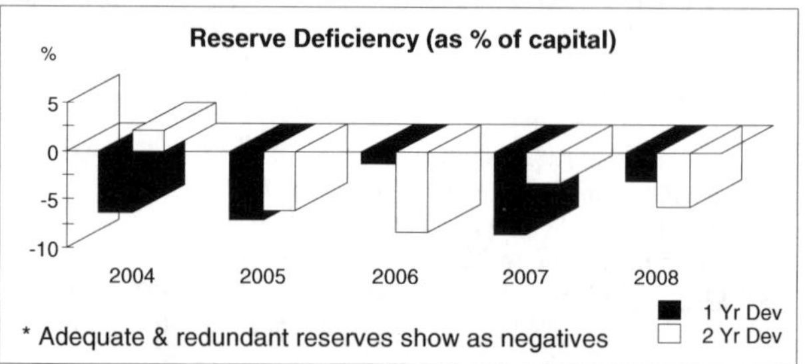

* Adequate & redundant reserves show as negatives

AMERICAN PHYSICIANS ASR CORP D+ Weak

Major Rating Factors: Weak overall results on stability tests (2.3 on a scale of 0 to 10) including potential drain of affiliation with American Physicians Capital Inc. Fair profitability index (3.7). Good expense controls. Return on equity has been fair, averaging 21.9% over the past five years.

Other Rating Factors: Good long-term capitalization index (6.7) based on good current risk adjusted capital (moderate loss scenario), despite some fluctuation in capital levels. History of adequate reserve strength (5.0) as reserves have been consistently at an acceptable level. Excellent liquidity (8.4) with ample operational cash flow and liquid investments.

Principal Business: Medical malpractice (100%).

Principal Investments: Investment grade bonds (91%), misc. investments (8%), and real estate (1%).

Investments in Affiliates: 3%

Group Affiliation: American Physicians Capital Inc

Licensed in: FL, IL, IN, IA, KS, KY, MI, MN, NE, NV, NM, NC, ND, OH, SD, TN, VA, WI

Commenced Business: May 1976

Address: 1301 N Hagadorn Rd, E Lansing, MI 48823

Phone: (517) 351-1150 **Domicile State:** MI **NAIC Code:** 33006

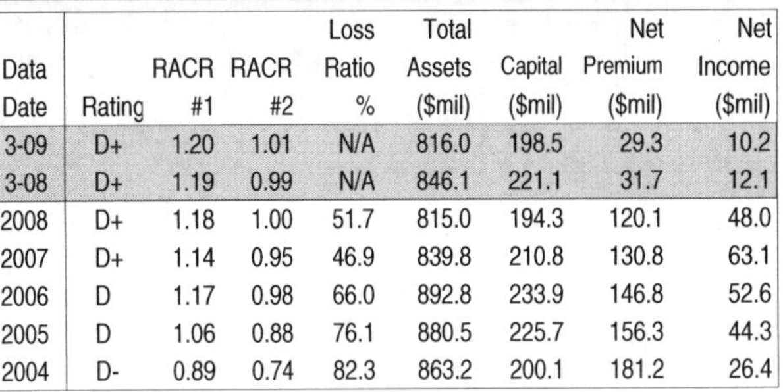

Data Date	Rating	RACR #1	RACR #2	Loss Ratio %	Total Assets ($mil)	Capital ($mil)	Net Premium ($mil)	Net Income ($mil)
3-09	D+	1.20	1.01	N/A	816.0	198.5	29.3	10.2
3-08	D+	1.19	0.99	N/A	846.1	221.1	31.7	12.1
2008	D+	1.18	1.00	51.7	815.0	194.3	120.1	48.0
2007	D+	1.14	0.95	46.9	839.8	210.8	130.8	63.1
2006	D	1.17	0.98	66.0	892.8	233.9	146.8	52.6
2005	D	1.06	0.88	76.1	880.5	225.7	156.3	44.3
2004	D-	0.89	0.74	82.3	863.2	200.1	181.2	26.4

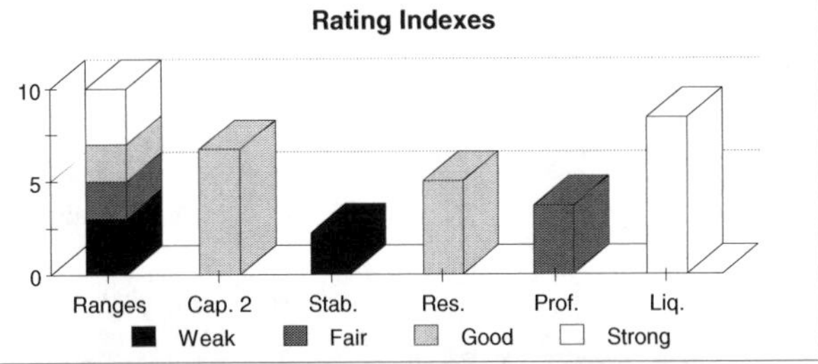

AMERICAN ROAD INS CO C Fair

Major Rating Factors: Fair overall results on stability tests (4.3 on a scale of 0 to 10) including fair results on operational trends. The largest net exposure for one risk is excessive at 6.8% of capital. Weak profitability index (2.7) with operating losses during the first three months of 2008. Return on equity has been fair, averaging 14.6% over the past five years.

Other Rating Factors: Strong long-term capitalization index (10.0) based on excellent current risk adjusted capital (severe and moderate loss scenarios), despite some fluctuation in capital levels. Ample reserve history (7.6) that can protect against increases in claims costs. Excellent liquidity (7.0) with ample operational cash flow and liquid investments.

Principal Business: Aggregate write-ins for other lines of business (44%), inland marine (2%), and surety (1%).

Principal Investments: Investment grade bonds (84%), misc. investments (15%), and cash (1%).

Investments in Affiliates: 7%

Group Affiliation: American Road Group

Licensed in: All states except PR

Commenced Business: December 1959

Address: The American Rd, Dearborn, MI 48121-6027

Phone: (313) 322-7287 **Domicile State:** MI **NAIC Code:** 19631

Data Date	Rating	RACR #1	RACR #2	Loss Ratio %	Total Assets ($mil)	Capital ($mil)	Net Premium ($mil)	Net Income ($mil)
3-09	C	4.82	3.71	N/A	564.2	277.9	29.0	-26.1
3-08	C	5.18	3.68	N/A	686.5	380.5	39.5	13.8
2008	C	4.65	3.56	71.3	590.4	271.1	112.7	42.0
2007	C	5.31	3.82	42.3	675.2	366.4	154.9	99.7
2006	C	7.04	4.78	71.1	719.0	399.5	177.8	60.9
2005	C	6.91	4.86	73.7	763.6	459.2	179.8	55.2
2004	C	6.67	4.66	62.4	706.3	396.1	210.9	63.9

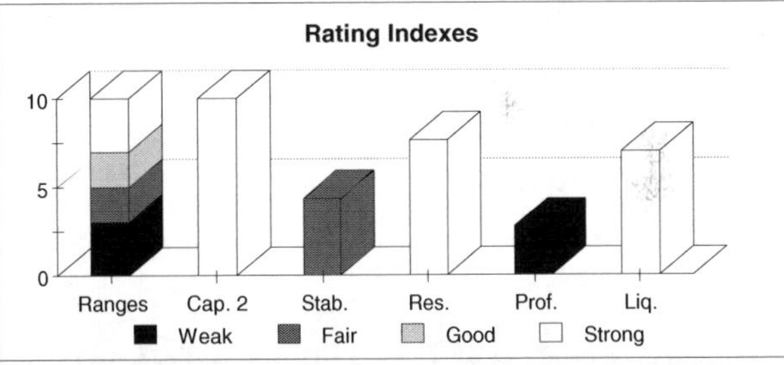

AMERICAN SECURITY INS CO B Good

Major Rating Factors: Good overall results on stability tests (5.2 on a scale of 0 to 10) despite potential drain of affiliation with Assurant Inc and weak results on operational trends. History of adequate reserve strength (6.3) as reserves have been consistently at an acceptable level.

Other Rating Factors: Good liquidity (6.8) with sufficient resources (cash flows and marketable investments) to handle a spike in claims. Strong long-term capitalization index (9.3) based on excellent current risk adjusted capital (severe and moderate loss scenarios). Moreover, capital levels have been consistent in recent years. Excellent profitability (9.4) with operating gains in each of the last five years. Return on equity has been excellent over the last five years averaging 32.4%.

Principal Business: Fire (64%), allied lines (24%), credit accident & health (4%), homeowners multiple peril (3%), other liability (2%), auto physical damage (2%), and inland marine (1%).

Principal Investments: Investment grade bonds (86%), misc. investments (13%), non investment grade bonds (3%), and real estate (2%).

Investments in Affiliates: 5%

Group Affiliation: Assurant Inc

Licensed in: All states except NH

Commenced Business: September 1938

Address: 260 Interstate N Circle NW, Atlanta, GA 30339-2111

Phone: (770) 763-1000 **Domicile State:** DE **NAIC Code:** 42978

Data Date	Rating	RACR #1	RACR #2	Loss Ratio %	Total Assets ($mil)	Capital ($mil)	Net Premium ($mil)	Net Income ($mil)
3-09	B	4.18	2.67	N/A	1,854.3	850.1	337.1	64.9
3-08	B	3.57	2.38	N/A	1,835.8	808.1	317.9	80.5
2008	B	3.95	2.53	29.5	1,881.1	785.3	1,542.7	297.7
2007	B	3.39	2.27	28.6	1,660.4	715.8	1,307.9	213.4
2006	B	3.07	2.07	30.6	1,085.1	431.5	857.2	178.4
2005	B	1.75	1.33	29.6	833.8	267.0	486.5	87.8
2004	B	1.56	1.25	35.4	656.3	225.1	389.3	46.4

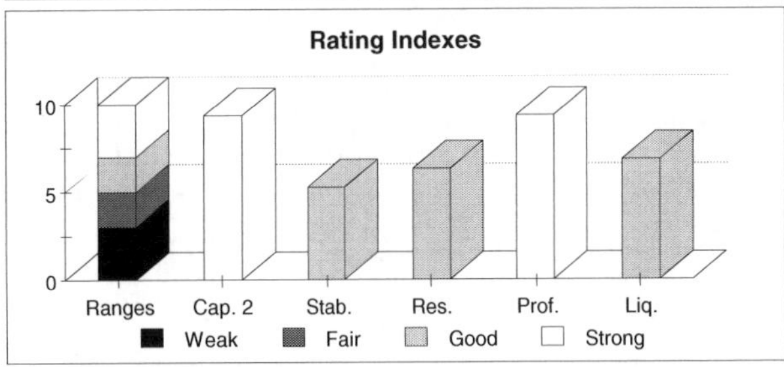

AMERICAN STANDARD INS CO OF WI * B+ Good

Major Rating Factors: Good overall results on stability tests (6.4 on a scale of 0 to 10). Strengths include potential support from affiliation with American Family Ins Group, good operational trends and excellent risk diversification. Strong long-term capitalization index (10.0) based on excellent current risk adjusted capital (severe and moderate loss scenarios). Moreover, capital levels have been consistent in recent years.

Other Rating Factors: Excellent profitability (8.2) with operating gains in each of the last five years. Excellent expense controls. Superior liquidity (10.0) with ample operational cash flow and liquid investments.

Principal Business: Auto liability (64%) and auto physical damage (36%).

Principal Investments: Investment grade bonds (89%) and misc. investments (11%).

Investments in Affiliates: None

Group Affiliation: American Family Ins Group

Licensed in: AZ, CO, ID, IL, IN, IA, KS, MN, MO, MT, NE, NV, NM, NC, ND, OH, OR, SC, SD, UT, WA, WI, WY

Commenced Business: September 1961

Address: 6000 American Parkway, Madison, WI 53783-0001

Phone: (608) 249-2111 **Domicile State:** WI **NAIC Code:** 19283

Data Date	Rating	RACR #1	RACR #2	Loss Ratio %	Total Assets ($mil)	Capital ($mil)	Net Premium ($mil)	Net Income ($mil)
3-09	B+	28.58	25.72	N/A	394.2	264.8	0.0	2.0
3-08	B+	28.02	25.22	N/A	363.3	254.4	0.0	3.2
2008	B+	30.12	27.10	0.0	356.8	262.9	0.0	11.3
2007	B+	27.44	24.69	0.0	368.4	251.2	0.0	12.5
2006	B+	26.08	23.47	0.0	355.2	238.6	0.0	11.8
2005	B+	24.54	22.08	0.0	354.0	226.8	0.0	11.7
2004	B+	23.03	20.73	0.0	353.2	215.1	0.0	11.5

American Family Ins Group
Composite Group Rating: C+

Largest Group Members	Assets ($mil)	Rating
AMERICAN FAMILY MUT INS CO	10609	B-
AMERICAN FAMILY LIFE INS CO	3861	A+
AMERICAN STANDARD INS CO OF WI	357	B+
AMERICAN FAMILY INS CO	53	B
AMERICAN STANDARD INS CO OF OH	11	B

AMERICAN STATES INS CO B- Good

Major Rating Factors: Fair profitability index (3.2 on a scale of 0 to 10). Fair expense controls. Return on equity has been fair, averaging 21.8% over the past five years. Fair overall results on stability tests (4.9).

Other Rating Factors: History of adequate reserve strength (6.9) as reserves have been consistently at an acceptable level. Good liquidity (6.4) with sufficient resources (cash flows and marketable investments) to handle a spike in claims. Strong long-term capitalization index (8.0) based on excellent current risk adjusted capital (severe and moderate loss scenarios), despite some fluctuation in capital levels.

Principal Business: Commercial multiple peril (26%), auto liability (26%), other liability (21%), workers compensation (9%), auto physical damage (6%), inland marine (4%), and other lines (8%).

Principal Investments: Investment grade bonds (95%), misc. investments (4%), and non investment grade bonds (1%).

Investments in Affiliates: None

Group Affiliation: Liberty Mutual Group

Licensed in: All states except PR

Commenced Business: July 1929

Address: 500 N Meridian St, Indianapolis, IN 46204

Phone: (206) 545-5000 **Domicile State:** IN **NAIC Code:** 19704

Data Date	Rating	RACR #1	RACR #2	Loss Ratio %	Total Assets ($mil)	Capital ($mil)	Net Premium ($mil)	Net Income ($mil)
3-09	B-	2.53	1.71	N/A	3,359.1	563.6	203.2	9.9
3-08	B-	2.02	1.34	N/A	2,067.8	520.4	263.5	33.1
2008	B-	2.43	1.69	67.0	2,077.1	541.2	1,014.8	95.9
2007	B-	1.99	1.33	62.9	2,070.0	512.1	1,074.7	144.9
2006	B-	2.90	1.90	58.5	2,337.8	770.7	1,066.6	164.9
2005	B-	2.63	1.76	62.3	2,340.0	772.8	1,104.7	163.7
2004	C+	2.76	1.86	63.2	2,267.8	801.5	1,078.4	192.1

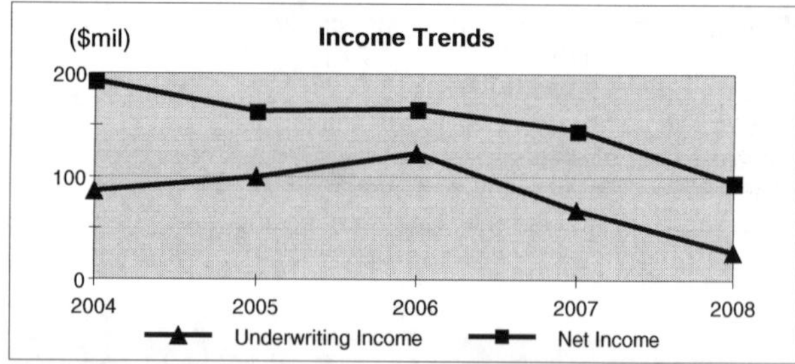

AMERICAN ZURICH INS CO B- Good

Major Rating Factors: Fair profitability index (3.6 on a scale of 0 to 10). Good expense controls. Return on equity has been fair, averaging 5.2% over the past five years. Fair overall results on stability tests (4.9).

Other Rating Factors: Strong long-term capitalization index (10.0) based on excellent current risk adjusted capital (severe and moderate loss scenarios), despite some fluctuation in capital levels. Excellent liquidity (7.0) with ample operational cash flow and liquid investments.

Principal Business: Workers compensation (79%), commercial multiple peril (9%), other liability (4%), auto liability (4%), aggregate write-ins for other lines of business (2%), products liability (1%), and auto physical damage (1%).

Principal Investments: Investment grade bonds (76%), misc. investments (23%), and cash (1%).

Investments in Affiliates: 24%

Group Affiliation: Zurich Financial Services Group

Licensed in: All states except PR

Commenced Business: September 1981

Address: 1400 American Ln Zurich Towers, Schaumburg, IL 60196-1056

Phone: (847) 605-6429 **Domicile State:** IL **NAIC Code:** 40142

Data Date	Rating	RACR #1	RACR #2	Loss Ratio %	Total Assets ($mil)	Capital ($mil)	Net Premium ($mil)	Net Income ($mil)
3-09	B-	4.35	4.24	N/A	195.0	166.6	0.0	0.2
3-08	B-	4.43	4.29	N/A	273.4	180.7	0.0	1.9
2008	B-	4.36	4.25	0.0	188.0	166.5	0.0	8.0
2007	B-	4.42	4.31	0.0	263.7	178.2	0.0	24.7
2006	B-	3.87	3.82	0.0	221.2	208.9	0.0	6.5
2005	B-	3.89	3.83	0.0	209.4	199.6	0.0	5.7
2004	B-	4.24	4.19	0.0	188.8	172.0	0.0	4.7

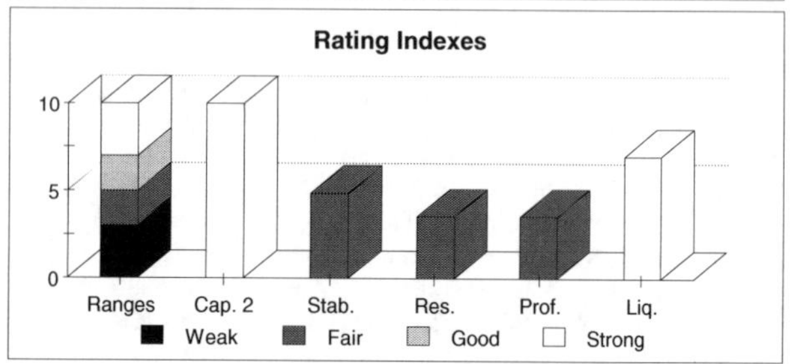

AMERISURE INS CO — B- Good

Major Rating Factors: Fair overall results on stability tests (4.7 on a scale of 0 to 10) including potential drain of affiliation with Amerisure Companies. The largest net exposure for one risk is conservative at 1.1% of capital. History of adequate reserve strength (5.8) as reserves have been consistently at an acceptable level.

Other Rating Factors: Strong long-term capitalization index (7.8) based on excellent current risk adjusted capital (severe and moderate loss scenarios). Moreover, capital levels have been consistent in recent years. Excellent profitability (8.6) with operating gains in each of the last five years. Excellent liquidity (7.0) with ample operational cash flow and liquid investments.

Principal Business: Workers compensation (45%), commercial multiple peril (19%), auto liability (15%), other liability (13%), products liability (4%), and auto physical damage (4%).

Principal Investments: Investment grade bonds (99%), cash (3%), and non investment grade bonds (1%).

Investments in Affiliates: None

Group Affiliation: Amerisure Companies

Licensed in: AL, AZ, AR, CT, FL, GA, IL, IN, KS, KY, ME, MD, MA, MI, MS, MO, NH, NJ, NY, NC, OH, RI, SC, TN, TX, VA, WI

Commenced Business: September 1968

Address: 26777 Halsted Road, Farmington Hills, MI 48331-3586

Phone: (248) 615-9000 **Domicile State:** MI **NAIC Code:** 19488

Data Date	Rating	RACR #1	RACR #2	Loss Ratio %	Total Assets ($mil)	Capital ($mil)	Net Premium ($mil)	Net Income ($mil)
3-09	B-	2.68	1.76	N/A	647.9	179.1	39.0	2.9
3-08	C+	2.56	1.71	N/A	623.2	169.8	43.5	3.9
2008	B-	2.70	1.79	64.5	622.4	177.3	167.7	11.7
2007	C+	2.58	1.74	61.7	607.0	166.8	181.0	17.5
2006	C	2.31	1.56	61.1	567.0	149.2	184.7	5.2
2005	C	2.34	1.59	60.9	553.8	143.9	179.3	19.2
2004	C	1.76	1.21	70.5	498.8	124.4	175.6	8.8

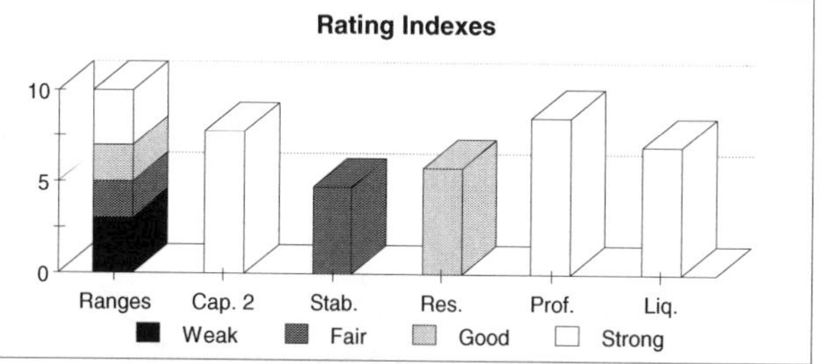

AMERISURE MUTUAL INS CO — C+ Fair

Major Rating Factors: Fair overall results on stability tests (4.5 on a scale of 0 to 10) including potential drain of affiliation with Amerisure Companies. History of adequate reserve strength (5.7) as reserves have been consistently at an acceptable level.

Other Rating Factors: Good overall profitability index (6.7) despite modest operating losses during the first three months of 2008. Good liquidity (6.9) with sufficient resources (cash flows and marketable investments) to handle a spike in claims. Strong long-term capitalization index (7.5) based on excellent current risk adjusted capital (severe and moderate loss scenarios), despite some fluctuation in capital levels.

Principal Business: Workers compensation (47%), commercial multiple peril (19%), other liability (16%), auto liability (10%), auto physical damage (3%), products liability (2%), and other lines (3%).

Principal Investments: Investment grade bonds (70%), misc. investments (24%), cash (4%), non investment grade bonds (1%), and real estate (1%).

Investments in Affiliates: 14%

Group Affiliation: Amerisure Companies

Licensed in: All states except PR

Commenced Business: September 1912

Address: 26777 Halsted Rd, Farmington Hills, MI 48331-3586

Phone: (248) 615-9000 **Domicile State:** MI **NAIC Code:** 23396

Data Date	Rating	RACR #1	RACR #2	Loss Ratio %	Total Assets ($mil)	Capital ($mil)	Net Premium ($mil)	Net Income ($mil)
3-09	C+	1.77	1.35	N/A	1,645.4	501.1	91.0	-0.2
3-08	C+	2.04	1.56	N/A	1,719.4	580.7	100.4	6.6
2008	C+	1.82	1.39	64.5	1,659.0	512.1	391.3	4.8
2007	C+	2.12	1.62	61.7	1,719.4	594.8	422.2	48.1
2006	C	2.04	1.54	61.1	1,632.6	545.9	431.0	55.4
2005	C	1.76	1.36	60.9	1,491.5	454.4	418.3	42.4
2004	C	1.48	1.11	70.5	1,391.4	405.1	409.8	26.7

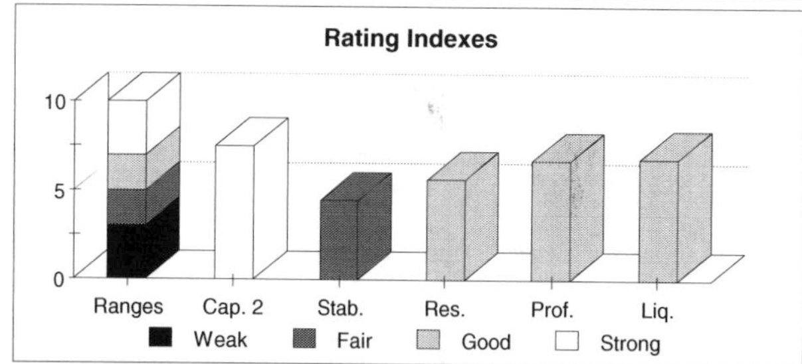

AMEX ASSURANCE CO — B- Good

Major Rating Factors: Fair overall results on stability tests (3.8 on a scale of 0 to 10) including weak results on operational trends. The largest net exposure for one risk is acceptable at 2.5% of capital. Good liquidity (6.6) with sufficient resources (cash flows and marketable investments) to handle a spike in claims.

Other Rating Factors: Strong long-term capitalization index (10.0) based on excellent current risk adjusted capital (severe and moderate loss scenarios), despite some fluctuation in capital levels. Ample reserve history (7.0) that can protect against increases in claims costs. Excellent profitability (8.1) with operating gains in each of the last five years. Return on equity has been excellent over the last five years averaging 28.0%.

Principal Business: Group accident & health (50%) and inland marine (50%).

Principal Investments: Investment grade bonds (89%) and misc. investments (11%).

Investments in Affiliates: None

Group Affiliation: American Express Company

Licensed in: All states, the District of Columbia and Puerto Rico

Commenced Business: February 1973

Address: 227 W Monroe St Ste 3600, Chicago, IL 60606

Phone: (920) 330-5100 **Domicile State:** IL **NAIC Code:** 27928

Data Date	Rating	RACR #1	RACR #2	Loss Ratio %	Total Assets ($mil)	Capital ($mil)	Net Premium ($mil)	Net Income ($mil)
3-09	B-	9.38	5.36	N/A	312.6	242.1	61.0	21.9
3-08	B-	9.34	5.60	N/A	266.5	175.8	74.7	30.4
2008	B-	8.53	4.86	30.7	283.4	220.2	267.2	102.8
2007	B-	8.92	5.49	24.8	232.4	145.7	81.8	27.0
2006	B-	30.56	27.51	0.0	142.6	117.8	0.0	7.1
2005	B-	3.87	3.00	N/A	141.4	115.2	118.9	24.9
2004	B-	5.31	3.18	18.0	283.6	216.8	246.1	98.0

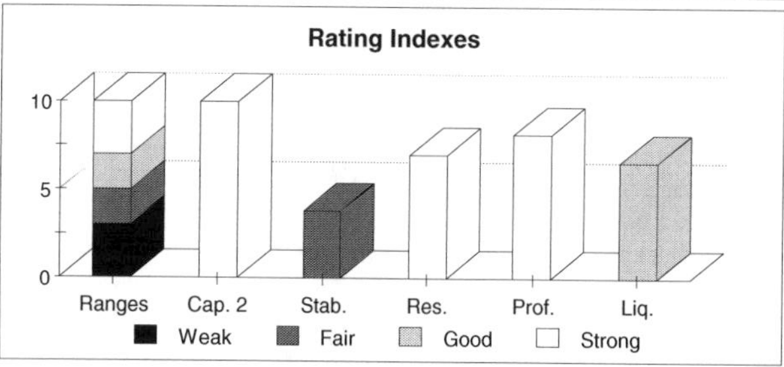

AMICA LLOYDS OF TEXAS * B+ Good

Major Rating Factors: Good liquidity (6.9 on a scale of 0 to 10) with sufficient resources (cash flows and marketable investments) to handle a spike in claims. Good overall results on stability tests (6.7) despite negative cash flow from operations for 2008. Stability strengths include good operational trends and excellent risk diversification. The largest net exposure for one risk is conservative at 1.1% of capital.

Other Rating Factors: Strong long-term capitalization index (10.0) based on excellent current risk adjusted capital (severe and moderate loss scenarios), despite some fluctuation in capital levels. Ample reserve history (8.7) that helps to protect the company against sharp claims increases. Excellent profitability (7.3). Excellent expense controls. Return on equity has been good over the last five years, averaging 14.8%.

Principal Business: Homeowners multiple peril (95%), allied lines (3%), inland marine (2%), and fire (1%).

Principal Investments: Investment grade bonds (98%) and misc. investments (2%).

Investments in Affiliates: None

Group Affiliation: Amica Mutual Group

Licensed in: TX

Commenced Business: December 1998

Address: (No address available)

Phone: (800) 992-6422 **Domicile State:** TX **NAIC Code:** 10896

Data Date	Rating	RACR #1	RACR #2	Loss Ratio %	Total Assets ($mil)	Capital ($mil)	Net Premium ($mil)	Net Income ($mil)
3-09	B+	10.67	7.56	N/A	70.2	57.4	2.2	0.7
3-08	B+	20.87	15.92	N/A	71.1	59.1	2.2	1.2
2008	B+	10.40	7.37	148.3	70.8	56.8	8.8	-0.7
2007	B+	14.45	11.22	7.0	70.1	58.2	8.8	10.7
2006	B	5.76	4.40	21.9	66.6	49.5	18.1	9.3
2005	B	4.16	2.81	38.3	58.6	40.3	18.5	6.1
2004	B	3.45	2.55	29.0	52.3	34.2	18.9	8.6

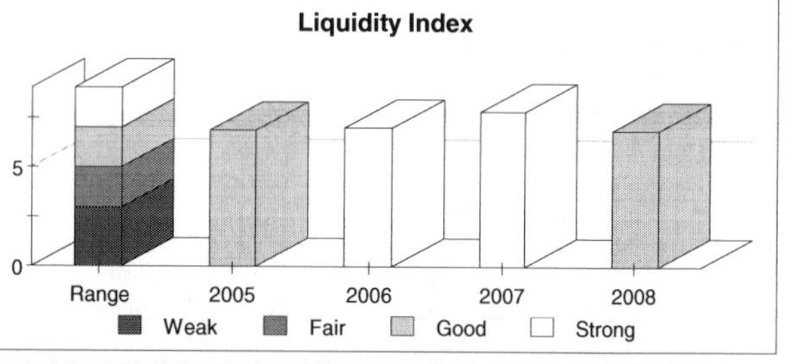

AMICA MUTUAL INS CO B Good

Major Rating Factors: Good overall profitability index (5.9 on a scale of 0 to 10). Good expense controls. Good liquidity (6.1) with sufficient resources (cash flows and marketable investments) to handle a spike in claims.

Other Rating Factors: Good overall results on stability tests (6.0). Stability strengths include good operational trends and excellent risk diversification. Strong long-term capitalization index (8.4) based on excellent current risk adjusted capital (severe and moderate loss scenarios), despite some fluctuation in capital levels. Ample reserve history (8.9) that helps to protect the company against sharp claims increases.

Principal Business: Auto liability (40%), homeowners multiple peril (29%), auto physical damage (25%), other liability (3%), earthquake (1%), and inland marine (1%).

Principal Investments: Investment grade bonds (56%), misc. investments (43%), and real estate (2%).

Investments in Affiliates: 6%

Group Affiliation: Amica Mutual Group

Licensed in: All states except HI, PR

Commenced Business: April 1907

Address: 100 Amica Way, Lincoln, RI 02865

Phone: (401) 334-6000 **Domicile State:** RI **NAIC Code:** 19976

Data Date	Rating	RACR #1	RACR #2	Loss Ratio %	Total Assets ($mil)	Capital ($mil)	Net Premium ($mil)	Net Income ($mil)
3-09	B	2.86	1.88	N/A	3,433.2	1,803.0	323.4	9.5
3-08	B	3.30	2.15	N/A	3,915.0	2,232.8	325.1	39.5
2008	B	2.93	1.94	67.4	3,582.2	1,909.6	1,321.7	112.7
2007	B	3.32	2.19	60.3	4,077.4	2,289.9	1,303.6	246.7
2006	B	3.17	2.08	57.9	3,890.1	2,090.5	1,312.6	247.2
2005	A-	2.94	1.93	65.8	3,585.0	1,796.2	1,357.2	145.4
2004	A-	2.78	1.82	71.6	3,384.4	1,602.3	1,357.6	84.6

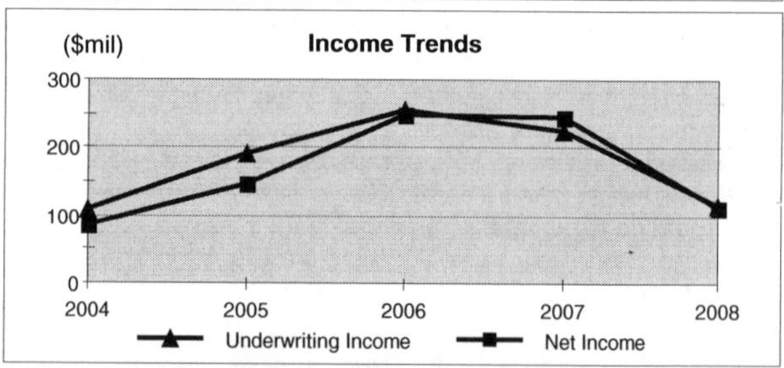

ARBELLA MUTUAL INS CO C+ Fair

Major Rating Factors: Fair overall results on stability tests (4.3 on a scale of 0 to 10) including potential drain of affiliation with Arbella Ins Group. Good liquidity (6.6) with sufficient resources (cash flows and marketable investments) to handle a spike in claims.

Other Rating Factors: Strong long-term capitalization index (8.9) based on excellent current risk adjusted capital (severe and moderate loss scenarios), despite some fluctuation in capital levels. Ample reserve history (9.3) that helps to protect the company against sharp claims increases. Excellent profitability (8.0) despite modest operating losses during the first three months of 2008.

Principal Business: Auto liability (48%), auto physical damage (29%), homeowners multiple peril (20%), fire (1%), inland marine (1%), and other liability (1%).

Principal Investments: Investment grade bonds (77%), misc. investments (23%), and non investment grade bonds (2%).

Investments in Affiliates: 15%

Group Affiliation: Arbella Ins Group

Licensed in: MA

Commenced Business: October 1988

Address: 1100 Crown Colony Dr, Quincy, MA 02269

Phone: (617) 328-2936 **Domicile State:** MA **NAIC Code:** 17000

Data Date	Rating	RACR #1	RACR #2	Loss Ratio %	Total Assets ($mil)	Capital ($mil)	Net Premium ($mil)	Net Income ($mil)
3-09	C+	3.03	2.47	N/A	920.8	429.5	103.7	-0.4
3-08	C+	2.97	2.38	N/A	946.4	440.8	111.9	3.6
2008	C+	3.05	2.48	63.6	948.8	437.8	430.8	21.9
2007	C+	2.95	2.37	55.4	961.8	441.3	414.5	26.1
2006	C+	2.85	2.23	56.4	954.3	391.1	481.1	37.6
2005	C+	2.42	2.02	67.2	898.1	345.1	465.1	25.1
2004	C+	2.34	1.93	66.3	831.1	310.8	445.6	23.4

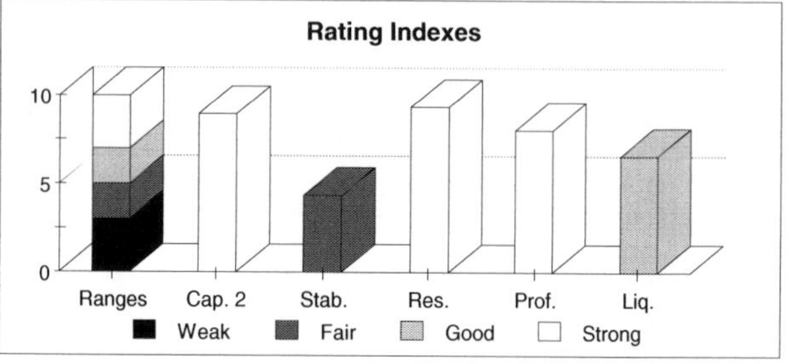

ARCH INS CO C+ Fair

Major Rating Factors: Fair overall results on stability tests (3.4 on a scale of 0 to 10) including potential drain of affiliation with Arch Capital Group Ltd. Good long-term capitalization index (5.3) based on good current risk adjusted capital (severe and moderate loss scenarios). Moreover, capital levels have been consistent over the last several years.

Other Rating Factors: History of adequate reserve strength (6.2) as reserves have been consistently at an acceptable level. Good liquidity (6.8) with sufficient resources (cash flows and marketable investments) to handle a spike in claims. Excellent profitability (7.7) with operating gains in each of the last five years.

Principal Business: Other liability (36%), workers compensation (15%), auto liability (9%), surety (8%), commercial multiple peril (7%), inland marine (6%), and other lines (20%).

Principal Investments: Investment grade bonds (63%), misc. investments (35%), and cash (2%).

Investments in Affiliates: 30%

Group Affiliation: Arch Capital Group Ltd

Licensed in: All states, the District of Columbia and Puerto Rico

Commenced Business: June 1980

Address: 3100 Broadway Suite 1000, Kansas City, MO 64111

Phone: (201) 743-4000 **Domicile State:** MO **NAIC Code:** 11150

Data Date	Rating	RACR #1	RACR #2	Loss Ratio %	Total Assets ($mil)	Capital ($mil)	Net Premium ($mil)	Net Income ($mil)
3-09	C+	0.97	0.79	N/A	1,680.7	598.1	73.0	14.9
3-08	C	1.02	0.83	N/A	1,524.8	549.4	70.5	15.0
2008	C+	0.96	0.78	75.0	1,563.2	577.0	298.8	22.3
2007	C	1.04	0.85	69.2	1,465.0	540.5	311.8	5.7
2006	C	1.59	1.34	76.1	1,187.7	518.9	170.3	6.0
2005	C	1.30	1.06	78.6	1,076.7	476.1	140.1	12.4
2004	C	1.11	0.82	69.2	807.2	337.0	152.8	9.4

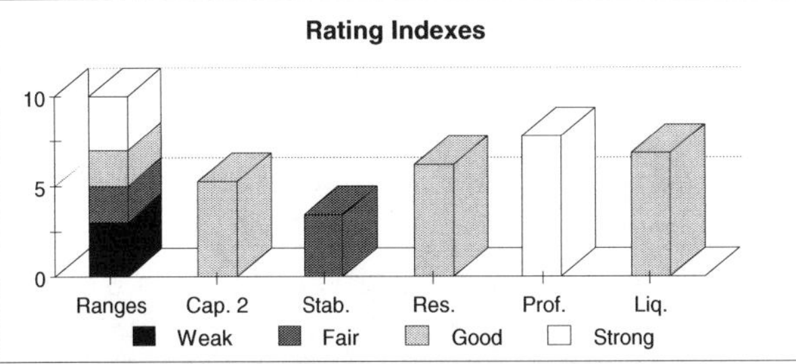

ARCH REINSURANCE CO C Fair

Major Rating Factors: Weak overall results on stability tests (2.7 on a scale of 0 to 10) including potential drain of affiliation with Arch Capital Group Ltd. History of adequate reserve strength (6.2) as reserves have been consistently at an acceptable level.

Other Rating Factors: Strong long-term capitalization index (7.9) based on excellent current risk adjusted capital (severe and moderate loss scenarios). Moreover, capital levels have been consistent in recent years. Excellent profitability (7.6) with operating gains in each of the last five years. Excellent liquidity (8.0) with ample operational cash flow and liquid investments.

Principal Business: Surety (100%).

Principal Investments: Misc. investments (58%), investment grade bonds (40%), and cash (2%).

Investments in Affiliates: 54%

Group Affiliation: Arch Capital Group Ltd

Licensed in: All states except ME, NC, WI, WY, PR

Commenced Business: July 1995

Address: 10306 Regency Parkway Dr, Omaha, NE 68113

Phone: (973) 898-9575 **Domicile State:** NE **NAIC Code:** 10348

Data Date	Rating	RACR #1	RACR #2	Loss Ratio %	Total Assets ($mil)	Capital ($mil)	Net Premium ($mil)	Net Income ($mil)
3-09	C	1.64	1.60	N/A	1,212.8	791.7	21.7	6.3
3-08	C-	1.62	1.59	N/A	1,167.8	729.9	22.3	1.4
2008	C	1.61	1.59	74.6	1,142.5	766.0	83.5	10.0
2007	C-	1.61	1.59	65.1	1,114.5	719.0	94.1	14.3
2006	C-	1.61	1.59	65.8	1,076.2	691.7	93.8	20.6
2005	C-	1.48	1.40	60.2	1,072.8	636.4	65.3	21.4
2004	C-	1.56	1.44	85.5	887.0	479.4	76.8	31.4

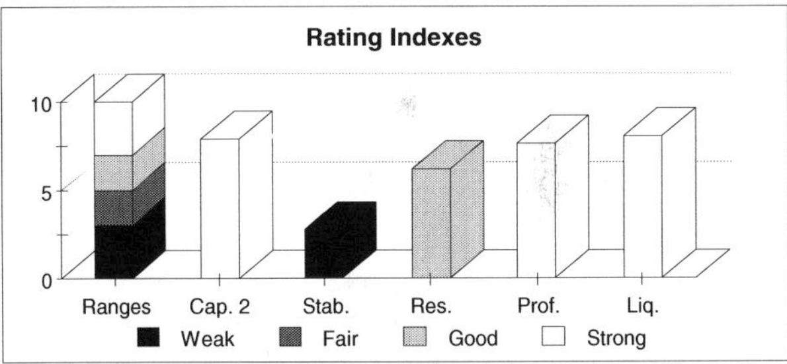

ARCH SPECIALTY INS CO * B+ Good

Major Rating Factors: Good overall results on stability tests (5.1 on a scale of 0 to 10) despite weak results on operational trends and negative cash flow from operations for 2008. Strong long-term capitalization index (10.0) based on excellent current risk adjusted capital (severe and moderate loss scenarios). Moreover, capital levels have been consistent in recent years.

Other Rating Factors: Ample reserve history (7.5) that can protect against increases in claims costs. Excellent profitability (8.6) despite modest operating losses during 2004. Excellent expense controls. Superior liquidity (9.7) with ample operational cash flow and liquid investments.

Principal Business: Other liability (42%), allied lines (17%), medical malpractice (14%), fire (11%), earthquake (6%), auto liability (5%), and other lines (5%).

Principal Investments: Investment grade bonds (95%) and cash (6%).

Investments in Affiliates: None

Group Affiliation: Arch Capital Group Ltd

Licensed in: IL, NE, WI

Commenced Business: January 1965

Address: 10909 Mill Valley Rd, Omaha, NE 68113

Phone: (201) 743-4000 **Domicile State:** NE **NAIC Code:** 21199

Data Date	Rating	RACR #1	RACR #2	Loss Ratio %	Total Assets ($mil)	Capital ($mil)	Net Premium ($mil)	Net Income ($mil)
3-09	B+	10.03	6.51	N/A	437.3	306.9	0.0	3.4
3-08	B+	6.99	4.57	N/A	465.1	289.3	0.2	2.7
2008	B+	9.84	6.42	776.4	406.7	303.1	0.3	12.5
2007	B+	7.26	4.78	N/A	441.5	288.6	-23.6	20.4
2006	B	2.19	1.44	84.4	592.9	272.1	49.2	27.7
2005	B	1.52	1.01	102.0	526.7	243.9	54.7	20.4
2004	B	0.45	0.34	89.1	393.4	120.4	61.0	-0.6

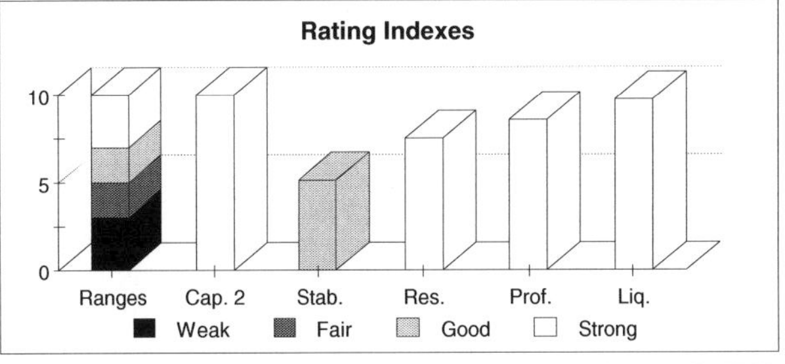

* Denotes a TheStreet.com Recommended Company

ARGONAUT INS CO — C Fair

Major Rating Factors: Fair overall results on stability tests (3.3 on a scale of 0 to 10) including potential drain of affiliation with Argo Group Intl Holdings Ltd and fair results on operational trends. Fair profitability index (3.1) with operating losses during 2005 and the first three months of 2008. Return on equity has been fair, averaging 5.3% over the past five years.

Other Rating Factors: Good overall long-term capitalization (5.1) based on good current risk adjusted capital (moderate loss scenario). However, capital levels have fluctuated during prior years. History of adequate reserve strength (5.5) as reserves have been consistently at an acceptable level. Good liquidity (6.9) with sufficient resources (cash flows and marketable investments) to handle a spike in claims.

Principal Business: Workers compensation (36%), commercial multiple peril (16%), other liability (15%), auto liability (11%), inland marine (9%), international (7%), and other lines (6%).

Principal Investments: Investment grade bonds (68%), misc. investments (31%), and cash (1%).

Investments in Affiliates: 18%

Group Affiliation: Argo Group Intl Holdings Ltd

Licensed in: All states except PR

Commenced Business: May 1957

Address: 225 W Washington St 6th Floor, Chicago, IL 60606

Phone: (800) 470-7958 **Domicile State:** IL **NAIC Code:** 19801

Data Date	Rating	RACR #1	RACR #2	Loss Ratio %	Total Assets ($mil)	Capital ($mil)	Net Premium ($mil)	Net Income ($mil)
3-09	C	1.05	0.76	N/A	1,390.6	286.8	63.4	-5.8
3-08	C	1.09	0.82	N/A	1,565.9	466.6	59.4	12.9
2008	C	1.06	0.77	72.2	1,385.3	288.7	264.8	20.3
2007	C	1.09	0.82	74.4	1,567.9	469.9	299.0	69.8
2006	C-	0.74	0.52	66.0	1,280.3	465.8	118.0	46.3
2005	D	0.51	0.34	60.7	1,275.5	351.4	216.5	-26.4
2004	D	0.46	0.33	61.4	1,195.9	372.4	220.8	20.4

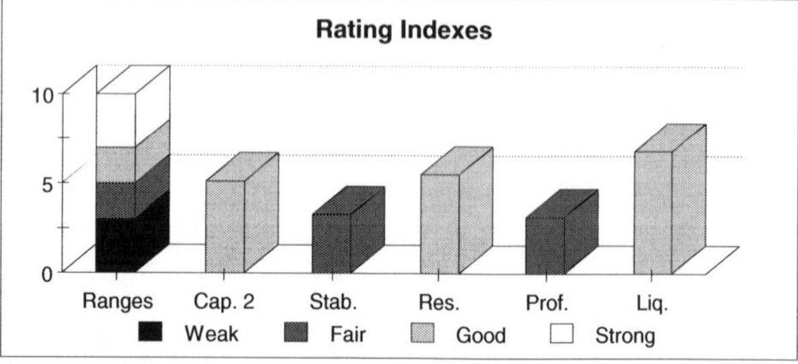

ARROWOOD INDEMNITY CO — D Weak

Major Rating Factors: Poor long-term capitalization (1.7 on a scale of 0 to 10) based on weak current risk adjusted capital (moderate loss scenario), although results have slipped from the good range over the last two years. A history of deficient reserves (1.0) that places pressure on both capital and profits. In four of the last five years reserves (two year development) were between 25% and 59% deficient.

Other Rating Factors: Weak profitability index (0.6) with operating losses during each of the last five years. However, profits have turned positive in the first three months of 2008. Average return on equity over the last five years has been poor at -43.3%. Weak overall results on stability tests (1.8) including weak risk adjusted capital in prior years and negative cash flow from operations for 2008. The largest net exposure for one risk is conservative at 1.9% of capital. Excellent liquidity (7.3) with ample operational cash flow and liquid investments.

Principal Business: (Not applicable due to unusual reinsurance transactions.)

Principal Investments: Investment grade bonds (90%), misc. investments (8%), cash (1%), and non investment grade bonds (1%).

Investments in Affiliates: 7%

Group Affiliation: Arrowpoint Capital Group

Licensed in: All states except PR

Commenced Business: February 1911

Address: 2711 Centerville Rd Suite 400, Wilmington, DE 19808

Phone: (704) 522-2000 **Domicile State:** DE **NAIC Code:** 24678

Data Date	Rating	RACR #1	RACR #2	Loss Ratio %	Total Assets ($mil)	Capital ($mil)	Net Premium ($mil)	Net Income ($mil)
3-09	D	0.56	0.33	N/A	2,370.5	320.8	0.9	0.6
3-08	D	0.99	0.56	N/A	2,943.0	425.4	1.5	-35.2
2008	D	0.58	0.34	N/A	2,510.7	331.5	-5.7	-101.3
2007	D	1.01	0.56	N/A	2,998.2	445.6	-1.8	-362.1
2006	D	1.05	0.79	785.6	3,922.7	576.4	-7.2	-202.5
2005	D	1.23	0.83	444.8	3,899.8	717.6	-22.5	-185.7
2004	D	0.93	0.65	134.8	5,258.6	893.5	147.3	-490.5

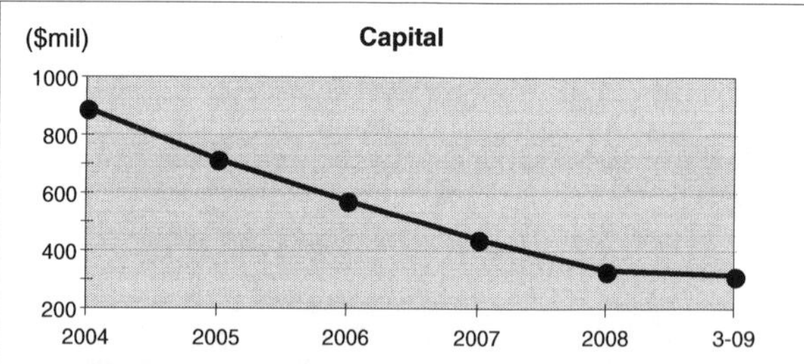

ASSURED GUARANTY CORP — C Fair

Major Rating Factors: Weak overall results on stability tests (2.0 on a scale of 0 to 10) including excessive premium growth and weak results on operational trends. The largest net exposure for one risk is excessive at 25.7% of capital. Strengths include potentially strong support from affiliation with ACE Ltd. History of adequate reserve strength (5.8) as reserves have been consistently at an acceptable level.

Other Rating Factors: Strong long-term capitalization index (9.9) based on excellent current risk adjusted capital (severe and moderate loss scenarios), despite some fluctuation in capital levels. Excellent profitability (7.2) with operating gains in each of the last five years. Return on equity has been excellent over the last five years averaging 24.9%. Superior liquidity (9.0) with ample operational cash flow and liquid investments.

Principal Business: Financial guaranty (100%).

Principal Investments: Investment grade bonds (85%), misc. investments (13%), and cash (2%).

Investments in Affiliates: 4%

Group Affiliation: ACE Ltd

Licensed in: All states except WI

Commenced Business: January 1988

Address: 1325 Ave Of The Americas 18 Fl, New York, NY 10019

Phone: (212) 974-3703 **Domicile State:** MD **NAIC Code:** 30180

Data Date	Rating	RACR #1	RACR #2	Loss Ratio %	Total Assets ($mil)	Capital ($mil)	Net Premium ($mil)	Net Income ($mil)
3-09	C	3.57	2.44	N/A	1,926.3	355.7	79.0	18.4
3-08	C	5.54	4.09	N/A	1,518.4	380.1	34.0	17.7
2008	C	4.30	3.09	90.3	1,803.1	378.1	429.4	27.7
2007	C	6.07	4.54	N/A	1,361.5	399.6	170.6	71.6
2006	C+	4.50	3.46	4.5	1,248.3	286.0	114.1	64.3
2005	U	8.34	6.11	18.2	1,140.7	295.7	-83.0	100.9
2004	U	3.12	2.60	N/A	1,278.2	236.7	59.8	103.2

ACE Ltd
Composite Group Rating: C+

Largest Group Members	Assets ($mil)	Rating
ACE AMERICAN INS CO	8051	C+
ACE PROPERTY CASUALTY INS CO	5785	C
WESTCHESTER FIRE INS CO	2561	C-
PACIFIC EMPLOYERS INS CO	2446	C+
COMBINED INS CO OF AMERICA	2382	B-

ATLANTIC STATES INS CO — B — Good

Major Rating Factors: Good liquidity (6.6 on a scale of 0 to 10) with sufficient resources (cash flows and marketable investments) to handle a spike in claims. Fair overall results on stability tests (4.7) including potential drain of affiliation with Donegal Group.

Other Rating Factors: Strong long-term capitalization index (10.0) based on excellent current risk adjusted capital (severe and moderate loss scenarios). Moreover, capital levels have been consistent in recent years. Ample reserve history (9.0) that helps to protect the company against sharp claims increases. Excellent profitability (8.6) with operating gains in each of the last five years. Return on equity has been good over the last five years, averaging 12.9%.

Principal Business: Auto liability (32%), auto physical damage (26%), commercial multiple peril (14%), workers compensation (13%), homeowners multiple peril (13%), farmowners multiple peril (1%), and fire (1%).

Principal Investments: Investment grade bonds (93%) and misc. investments (7%).

Investments in Affiliates: None

Group Affiliation: Donegal Group

Licensed in: CT, DE, GA, IN, MD, NY, OH, PA, TN, VA

Commenced Business: October 1986

Address: 1195 River Rd, Marietta, PA 17547-0302

Phone: (717) 426-1931 **Domicile State:** PA **NAIC Code:** 22586

Data Date	Rating	RACR #1	RACR #2	Loss Ratio %	Total Assets ($mil)	Capital ($mil)	Net Premium ($mil)	Net Income ($mil)
3-09	B	4.70	3.40	N/A	451.2	184.1	53.8	1.7
3-08	B	5.40	3.84	N/A	446.5	182.8	50.4	3.0
2008	B	4.71	3.37	63.1	445.4	182.4	229.8	18.4
2007	B	5.46	3.89	57.9	417.2	180.7	189.5	24.1
2006	B	5.10	3.64	55.2	419.1	169.9	188.1	26.7
2005	B	4.45	3.21	57.4	394.9	148.5	184.0	21.9
2004	B	3.99	2.87	61.4	365.9	127.2	170.5	16.3

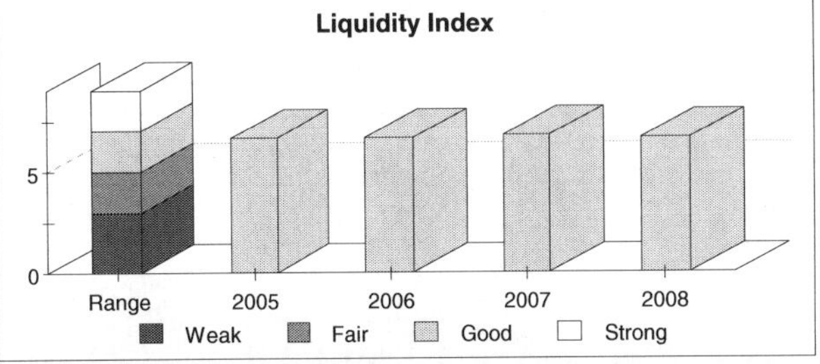

AUTO CLUB CASUALTY CO * — B+ — Good

Major Rating Factors: Good overall results on stability tests (5.0 on a scale of 0 to 10) despite weak results on operational trends. Strengths include potential support from affiliation with Auto Club Enterprises Ins Group. Strong long-term capitalization index (10.0) based on excellent current risk adjusted capital (severe and moderate loss scenarios), despite some fluctuation in capital levels.

Other Rating Factors: Excellent profitability (7.5) with operating gains in each of the last five years. Excellent expense controls. Excellent liquidity (7.0) with ample operational cash flow and liquid investments.

Principal Business: Auto physical damage (51%) and auto liability (49%).

Principal Investments: Investment grade bonds (96%), misc. investments (2%), and cash (2%).

Investments in Affiliates: None

Group Affiliation: Auto Club Enterprises Ins Group

Licensed in: TX

Commenced Business: December 1999

Address: 3333 Fairview Road, Costa Mesa, CA 92626-1698

Phone: (714) 885-2170 **Domicile State:** TX **NAIC Code:** 11009

Data Date	Rating	RACR #1	RACR #2	Loss Ratio %	Total Assets ($mil)	Capital ($mil)	Net Premium ($mil)	Net Income ($mil)
3-09	B+	57.20	51.48	N/A	2.8	2.7	0.0	0.0
3-08	B+	36.16	32.54	N/A	2.7	2.6	0.0	0.0
2008	B+	39.59	35.64	0.0	2.8	2.6	0.0	0.1
2007	B+	23.40	21.06	0.0	2.8	2.6	0.0	0.1
2006	B+	20.52	18.47	0.0	2.8	2.5	0.0	0.1
2005	B+	10.32	9.29	0.0	3.0	2.4	0.0	0.1
2004	B+	5.27	4.74	0.0	3.4	2.4	0.0	0.1

Auto Club Enterprises Ins Group Composite Group Rating: A+ Largest Group Members	Assets ($mil)	Rating
INTERINS EXCH OF THE AUTOMOBILE CLUB	5392	A+
AUTOMOBILE CLUB OF SOUTHERN CA INS	411	B
AUTOMOBILE CLUB INTERINSURANCE EXCH	279	C+
AUTO CLUB FAMILY INS CO	70	C
AAA TEXAS COUNTY MUTUAL INS CO	58	C-

AUTO CLUB INDEMNITY CO * — B+ — Good

Major Rating Factors: Good overall results on stability tests (5.0 on a scale of 0 to 10) despite weak results on operational trends and negative cash flow from operations for 2008. Strengths include potential support from affiliation with Auto Club Enterprises Ins Group. Strong long-term capitalization index (7.5) based on excellent current risk adjusted capital (severe and moderate loss scenarios), despite some fluctuation in capital levels.

Other Rating Factors: Excellent profitability (7.6) with operating gains in each of the last five years. Excellent expense controls. Fair liquidity (3.6) as cash resources may not be adequate to cover a spike in claims.

Principal Business: Homeowners multiple peril (97%), auto liability (1%), other liability (1%), and auto physical damage (1%).

Principal Investments: Investment grade bonds (92%) and cash (9%).

Investments in Affiliates: None

Group Affiliation: Auto Club Enterprises Ins Group

Licensed in: TX

Commenced Business: December 1999

Address: 3333 Fairview Road, Costa Mesa, CA 92626-1698

Phone: (714) 885-2170 **Domicile State:** TX **NAIC Code:** 11008

Data Date	Rating	RACR #1	RACR #2	Loss Ratio %	Total Assets ($mil)	Capital ($mil)	Net Premium ($mil)	Net Income ($mil)
3-09	B+	1.55	1.39	N/A	8.7	2.7	0.0	0.0
3-08	B+	2.10	1.89	N/A	6.5	2.6	0.0	0.0
2008	B+	1.48	1.33	0.0	9.0	2.6	0.0	0.1
2007	B+	2.37	2.14	0.0	5.9	2.6	0.0	0.1
2006	B+	2.46	2.21	0.0	5.6	2.5	0.0	0.1
2005	B+	2.93	2.64	0.0	4.9	2.4	0.0	0.1
2004	B+	2.76	2.49	0.0	4.9	2.4	0.0	0.1

Auto Club Enterprises Ins Group Composite Group Rating: A+ Largest Group Members	Assets ($mil)	Rating
INTERINS EXCH OF THE AUTOMOBILE CLUB	5392	A+
AUTOMOBILE CLUB OF SOUTHERN CA INS	411	B
AUTOMOBILE CLUB INTERINSURANCE EXCH	279	C+
AUTO CLUB FAMILY INS CO	70	C
AAA TEXAS COUNTY MUTUAL INS CO	58	C-

AUTO CLUB INS ASSN — B — Good

Major Rating Factors: Good liquidity (6.3 on a scale of 0 to 10) with sufficient resources (cash flows and marketable investments) to handle a spike in claims. Fair reserve development (3.9) as reserves have generally been sufficient to cover claims.

Other Rating Factors: Fair overall results on stability tests (4.9). Strong long-term capitalization index (8.7) based on excellent current risk adjusted capital (severe and moderate loss scenarios), despite some fluctuation in capital levels. Weak profitability index (2.9) with operating losses during the first three months of 2008.

Principal Business: Auto liability (46%), auto physical damage (42%), homeowners multiple peril (12%), and other liability (1%).

Principal Investments: Investment grade bonds (67%), misc. investments (26%), non investment grade bonds (6%), and real estate (3%).

Investments in Affiliates: 11%

Group Affiliation: Automobile Club of Michigan Group

Licensed in: ME, MI, MN, NH, NY, PA, WI

Commenced Business: March 1922

Address: One Auto Club Dr, Dearborn, MI 48126

Phone: (313) 336-1234 **Domicile State:** MI **NAIC Code:** 21202

Data Date	Rating	RACR #1	RACR #2	Loss Ratio %	Total Assets ($mil)	Capital ($mil)	Net Premium ($mil)	Net Income ($mil)
3-09	B	2.79	2.10	N/A	2,905.4	1,314.2	297.3	-15.2
3-08	B	3.08	2.25	N/A	3,250.2	1,646.4	293.5	-3.1
2008	B	2.74	2.10	78.4	2,990.8	1,375.5	1,193.3	-83.3
2007	B	3.09	2.29	70.8	3,355.3	1,726.9	1,190.2	90.5
2006	B	3.05	2.20	72.0	3,334.7	1,642.0	1,225.9	104.7
2005	B	2.90	2.12	70.1	3,180.3	1,483.2	1,268.0	62.3
2004	B	2.79	2.12	69.9	3,089.6	1,373.3	1,336.4	88.4

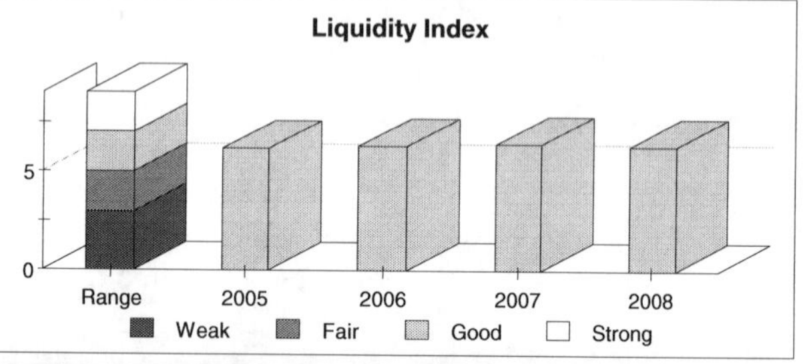

AUTO-OWNERS INS CO * — A — Excellent

Major Rating Factors: Strong long-term capitalization index (8.5 on a scale of 0 to 10) based on excellent current risk adjusted capital (severe and moderate loss scenarios). Furthermore, this high level of risk adjusted capital has been consistently maintained in previous years. Excellent profitability (7.2) with operating gains in each of the last five years.

Other Rating Factors: Excellent overall results on stability tests (7.4). Stability strengths include good operational trends and excellent risk diversification. History of adequate reserve strength (6.1) as reserves have been consistently at an acceptable level. Good liquidity (6.6) with sufficient resources (cash flows and marketable investments) to handle a spike in claims.

Principal Business: Auto liability (23%), auto physical damage (15%), commercial multiple peril (14%), homeowners multiple peril (13%), fire (10%), workers compensation (10%), and other lines (15%).

Principal Investments: Investment grade bonds (67%), misc. investments (33%), and real estate (1%).

Investments in Affiliates: 21%

Group Affiliation: Auto-Owners Group

Licensed in: AL, AZ, AR, CO, FL, GA, ID, IL, IN, IA, KS, KY, MI, MN, MS, MO, NE, NV, NM, NC, ND, OH, OR, PA, SC, SD, TN, UT, VA, WA, WI

Commenced Business: July 1916

Address: 6101 Anacapri Blvd, Lansing, MI 48917

Phone: (517) 323-1200 **Domicile State:** MI **NAIC Code:** 18988

Data Date	Rating	RACR #1	RACR #2	Loss Ratio %	Total Assets ($mil)	Capital ($mil)	Net Premium ($mil)	Net Income ($mil)
3-09	A	2.64	2.28	N/A	8,899.8	5,028.0	537.4	18.7
3-08	A	2.60	2.22	N/A	9,446.0	5,337.1	577.9	113.5
2008	A	2.68	2.31	73.4	9,052.0	5,180.7	2,207.8	209.1
2007	A	2.57	2.19	66.4	9,507.2	5,335.7	2,412.7	349.9
2006	A	2.51	2.14	62.5	9,038.0	4,845.7	2,510.6	422.0
2005	A	2.22	1.80	61.1	8,373.0	4,129.3	2,708.5	388.6
2004	A	1.92	1.51	79.7	7,715.7	3,519.9	2,841.0	44.5

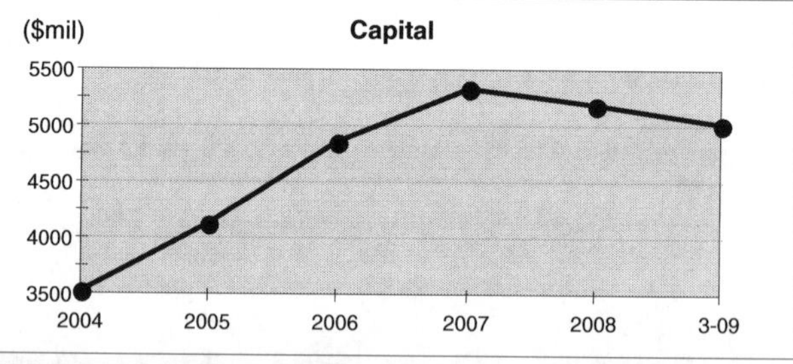

AUTOMOBILE INS CO OF HARTFORD CT — B — Good

Major Rating Factors: History of adequate reserve strength (5.0 on a scale of 0 to 10) as reserves have been consistently at an acceptable level. Good liquidity (6.7) with sufficient resources (cash flows and marketable investments) to handle a spike in claims.

Other Rating Factors: Good overall results on stability tests (6.0). Affiliation with Travelers Companies Inc is a strength. Strong long-term capitalization index (7.9) based on excellent current risk adjusted capital (severe and moderate loss scenarios), despite some fluctuation in capital levels. Excellent profitability (7.0) with operating gains in each of the last five years. Return on equity has been excellent over the last five years averaging 18.5%.

Principal Business: Homeowners multiple peril (61%), other liability (10%), fire (9%), auto liability (8%), allied lines (7%), auto physical damage (4%), and inland marine (1%).

Principal Investments: Investment grade bonds (92%) and misc. investments (8%).

Investments in Affiliates: None

Group Affiliation: Travelers Companies Inc

Licensed in: All states except CA, PR

Commenced Business: August 1968

Address: One Tower Square, Hartford, CT 06183

Phone: (860) 277-0111 **Domicile State:** CT **NAIC Code:** 19062

Data Date	Rating	RACR #1	RACR #2	Loss Ratio %	Total Assets ($mil)	Capital ($mil)	Net Premium ($mil)	Net Income ($mil)
3-09	B	2.52	1.61	N/A	954.1	293.7	61.8	14.3
3-08	B	2.87	1.65	N/A	982.0	331.3	61.3	14.5
2008	B	2.47	1.58	61.5	955.0	284.2	248.5	62.0
2007	B	2.70	1.55	59.0	964.5	308.1	247.0	55.3
2006	B	2.27	1.41	58.4	928.7	283.9	237.1	62.0
2005	B	1.88	1.22	75.1	914.7	258.7	223.8	30.7
2004	B	1.92	1.28	63.7	900.7	254.4	253.5	47.5

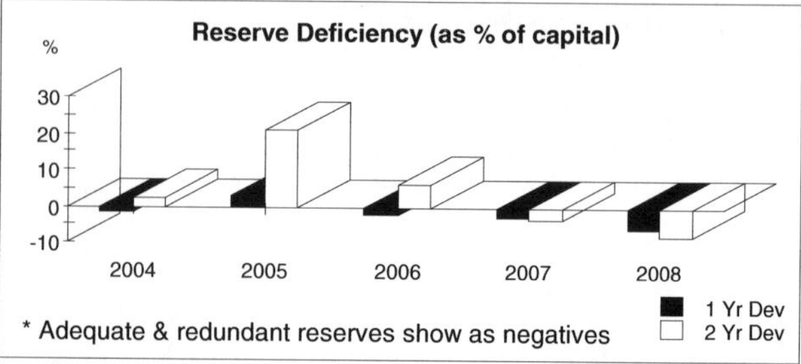

AXIS INS CO — C — Fair

Major Rating Factors: Fair profitability index (4.6) with operating losses during 2007. Return on equity has been low, averaging 2.0% over the past five years.
Other Rating Factors: Fair overall results on stability tests (3.1) including excessive premium growth and weak results on operational trends. The largest net exposure for one risk is acceptable at 2.2% of capital. Strong long-term capitalization index (7.9) based on excellent current risk adjusted capital (severe and moderate loss scenarios). Moreover, capital levels have been consistent in recent years. Excellent liquidity (8.7) with ample operational cash flow and liquid investments.
Principal Business: Other liability (76%), fire (10%), ocean marine (6%), allied lines (3%), earthquake (2%), inland marine (1%), and fidelity (1%).
Principal Investments: Investment grade bonds (55%) and misc. investments (45%).
Investments in Affiliates: 46%
Group Affiliation: AXIS Specialty Ltd
Licensed in: All states except CA, NH, PR
Commenced Business: November 1979
Address: 3333 North Mayfair Rd, Wauwatosa, WI 53222
Phone: (414) 778-3333 **Domicile State:** IL **NAIC Code:** 37273

Data Date	Rating	RACR #1	RACR #2	Loss Ratio %	Total Assets ($mil)	Capital ($mil)	Net Premium ($mil)	Net Income ($mil)
3-09	C	1.73	1.67	N/A	621.6	420.2	28.0	1.6
3-08	C	1.79	1.74	N/A	560.7	413.7	9.4	12.1
2008	C	1.69	1.63	80.0	674.9	414.2	115.7	13.8
2007	B-	1.71	1.69	62.1	479.9	385.1	34.4	-5.2
2006	U	159.57	79.78	0.0	107.2	106.9	0.0	1.9
2005	U	588.27	294.70	0.0	19.0	19.0	0.0	0.6
2004	U	76.27	68.64	0.0	18.9	18.4	0.0	0.6

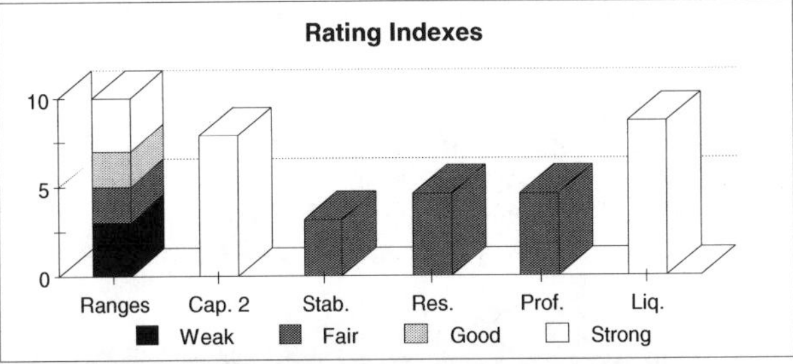

AXIS REINS CO — C+ — Fair

Major Rating Factors: Fair overall results on stability tests (4.2 on a scale of 0 to 10) including potential drain of affiliation with AXIS Specialty Ltd. The largest net exposure for one risk is conservative at 1.8% of capital. Good overall long-term capitalization (5.9) based on good current risk adjusted capital (moderate loss scenario). However, capital levels have fluctuated during prior years.
Other Rating Factors: History of adequate reserve strength (6.5) as reserves have been consistently at an acceptable level. Weak profitability index (2.9) with operating losses during 2004, 2005 and the first three months of 2008. Average return on equity over the last five years has been poor at -1.5%. Excellent liquidity (8.7) with ample operational cash flow and liquid investments.
Principal Business: Other liability (30%), earthquake (29%), ocean marine (23%), fire (10%), inland marine (3%), allied lines (3%), and fidelity (1%).
Principal Investments: Investment grade bonds (86%) and misc. investments (14%).
Investments in Affiliates: None
Group Affiliation: AXIS Specialty Ltd
Licensed in: All states, the District of Columbia and Puerto Rico
Commenced Business: January 1992
Address: 9300 Arrowpoint Blvd, Chalotte, NC 28201
Phone: (704) 522-2000 **Domicile State:** NY **NAIC Code:** 20370

Data Date	Rating	RACR #1	RACR #2	Loss Ratio %	Total Assets ($mil)	Capital ($mil)	Net Premium ($mil)	Net Income ($mil)
3-09	C+	1.57	0.84	N/A	2,116.6	517.5	87.3	-19.5
3-08	C+	1.86	1.11	N/A	2,043.6	585.4	101.6	-2.1
2008	C+	1.61	0.87	75.6	1,862.5	519.7	387.6	-62.6
2007	C+	2.01	1.20	71.9	2,007.4	607.1	196.8	79.1
2006	C	1.34	0.88	68.9	1,832.0	550.9	508.2	38.6
2005	C	1.04	0.70	80.8	1,462.3	524.1	573.6	-50.5
2004	C	1.95	1.40	79.4	973.1	517.0	218.6	-14.0

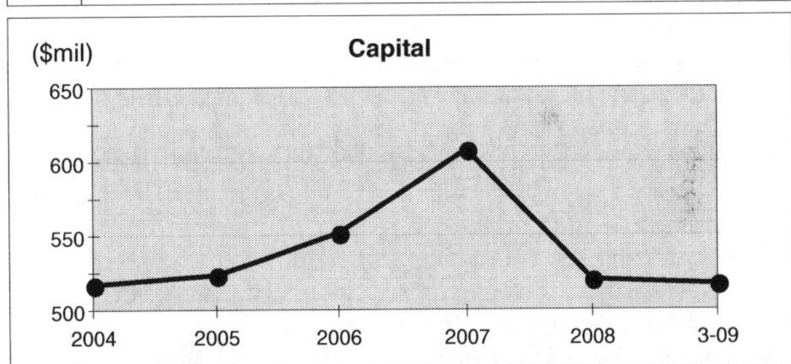

BALBOA INS CO — B — Good

Major Rating Factors: Good overall results on stability tests (5.2 on a scale of 0 to 10) despite potential drain of affiliation with Bank of America Corp. Stability strengths include good operational trends and excellent risk diversification. History of adequate reserve strength (6.2) as reserves have been consistently at an acceptable level.
Other Rating Factors: Good liquidity (6.8) with sufficient resources (cash flows and marketable investments) to handle a spike in claims. Strong long-term capitalization index (9.0) based on excellent current risk adjusted capital (severe and moderate loss scenarios). Moreover, capital levels have been consistent in recent years. Excellent profitability (9.3) with operating gains in each of the last five years. Return on equity has been excellent over the last five years averaging 17.2%.
Principal Business: Fire (29%), allied lines (23%), auto physical damage (22%), homeowners multiple peril (17%), auto liability (4%), other liability (1%), and other lines (3%).
Principal Investments: Investment grade bonds (88%), misc. investments (11%), and non investment grade bonds (1%).
Investments in Affiliates: 8%
Group Affiliation: Bank of America Corp
Licensed in: All states except LA, PR
Commenced Business: April 1948
Address: 18581 Teller Ave, Irvine, CA 92612-1627
Phone: (949) 553-0700 **Domicile State:** CA **NAIC Code:** 24813

Data Date	Rating	RACR #1	RACR #2	Loss Ratio %	Total Assets ($mil)	Capital ($mil)	Net Premium ($mil)	Net Income ($mil)
3-09	B	4.20	2.96	N/A	2,605.2	1,348.2	388.2	115.8
3-08	B	2.94	2.01	N/A	2,397.3	1,013.7	368.6	131.2
2008	B	3.85	2.70	41.1	2,581.5	1,255.1	1,517.6	392.5
2007	B	2.03	1.39	44.8	2,175.4	875.9	1,359.4	187.1
2006	B	2.56	1.79	47.7	1,533.2	656.0	885.5	115.5
2005	B	2.06	1.38	59.2	1,297.2	474.7	813.7	4.5
2004	B	1.86	1.24	55.9	896.5	336.4	609.5	35.8

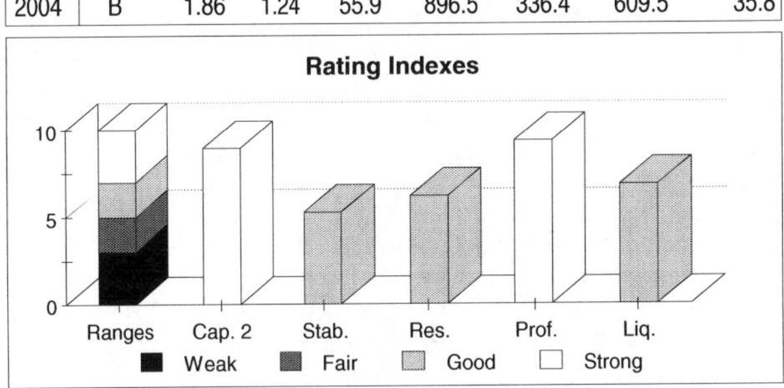

BAY STATE INS CO * B+ Good

Major Rating Factors: Good overall results on stability tests (5.0 on a scale of 0 to 10) despite potential drain of affiliation with Andover Group. Stability strengths include good operational trends and excellent risk diversification. History of adequate reserve strength (6.0) as reserves have been consistently at an acceptable level.

Other Rating Factors: Strong long-term capitalization index (10.0) based on excellent current risk adjusted capital (severe and moderate loss scenarios), despite some fluctuation in capital levels. Excellent profitability (8.1) with operating gains in each of the last five years. Excellent liquidity (7.7) with ample operational cash flow and liquid investments.

Principal Business: Homeowners multiple peril (88%), commercial multiple peril (4%), other liability (4%), and inland marine (3%).

Principal Investments: Investment grade bonds (77%), misc. investments (21%), and cash (2%).

Investments in Affiliates: None

Group Affiliation: Andover Group

Licensed in: CT, IL, ME, MA, NH, NJ, NY, RI

Commenced Business: July 1955

Address: 95 Old River Rd, Andover, MA 01810

Phone: (978) 475-3300 **Domicile State:** MA **NAIC Code:** 19763

Data Date	Rating	RACR #1	RACR #2	Loss Ratio %	Total Assets ($mil)	Capital ($mil)	Net Premium ($mil)	Net Income ($mil)
3-09	B+	6.93	4.72	N/A	285.6	179.6	15.1	3.3
3-08	B+	7.10	5.01	N/A	289.1	184.6	15.8	2.7
2008	B+	7.21	4.89	59.7	293.9	180.2	65.4	10.7
2007	B+	7.25	5.04	52.6	288.6	182.9	68.3	12.4
2006	B+	6.01	4.40	45.4	269.4	166.5	70.0	15.8
2005	B+	4.09	3.12	66.1	252.3	146.6	68.8	4.7
2004	B+	5.40	3.92	58.2	231.2	140.6	63.6	7.9

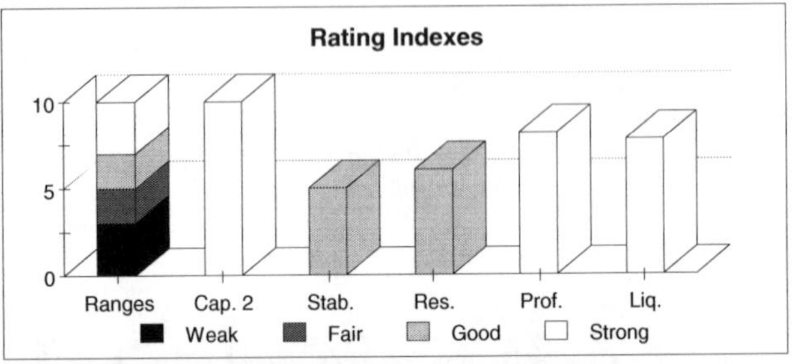

BERKLEY INS CO C Fair

Major Rating Factors: Fair overall results on stability tests (3.5 on a scale of 0 to 10) including weak risk adjusted capital in prior years. Strengths include potentially strong support from affiliation with W R Berkley Corp. Fair reserve development (3.2) as the level of reserves has at times been insufficient to cover claims. In 2005 and 2004 the two year reserve development was 33% and 44% deficient respectively.

Other Rating Factors: Poor long-term capitalization (1.9) based on weak current risk adjusted capital (moderate loss scenario), although results have slipped from the fair range over the last two years. Good overall profitability index (5.9) despite operating losses during the first three months of 2008. Return on equity has been good over the last five years, averaging 14.0%. Good liquidity (6.9) with sufficient resources (cash flows and marketable investments) to handle a spike in claims.

Principal Business: International (39%), commercial multiple peril (25%), aircraft (15%), other liability (11%), auto liability (8%), auto physical damage (2%), and surety (1%).

Principal Investments: Investment grade bonds (69%), misc. investments (28%), cash (1%), non investment grade bonds (1%), and real estate (1%).

Investments in Affiliates: 17%

Group Affiliation: W R Berkley Corp

Licensed in: All states except AZ, ME, MO, NH, VA, WY

Commenced Business: December 1975

Address: 100 Campus Drive, Florham Park, NJ 07932

Data Date	Rating	RACR #1	RACR #2	Loss Ratio %	Total Assets ($mil)	Capital ($mil)	Net Premium ($mil)	Net Income ($mil)
3-09	C	0.67	0.42	N/A	6,918.5	2,000.1	312.0	-9.9
3-08	C+	0.88	0.53	N/A	7,236.4	2,280.4	367.6	134.4
2008	C	0.68	0.43	65.8	6,846.5	2,036.6	1,232.3	264.6
2007	C+	0.86	0.52	62.4	7,014.5	2,210.1	1,525.3	452.9
2006	C+	0.90	0.55	68.3	6,796.3	2,178.7	1,800.7	442.6
2005	D+	0.75	0.46	72.6	5,870.2	1,785.2	1,739.2	180.7
2004	C-	0.78	0.49	71.5	4,777.9	1,511.6	1,599.7	154.8

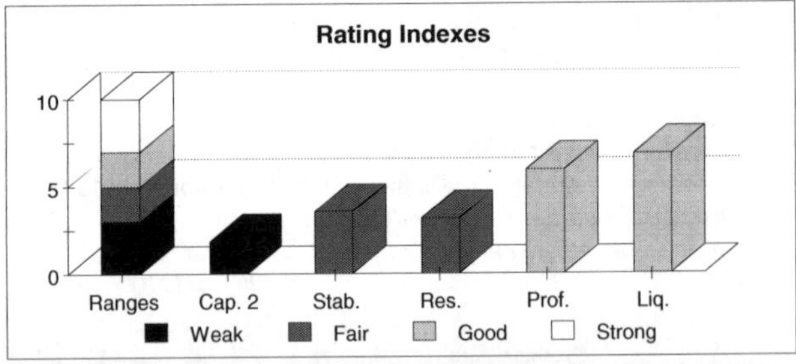

BERKLEY REGIONAL INS CO B- Good

Major Rating Factors: Fair reserve development (4.5 on a scale of 0 to 10) as reserves have generally been sufficient to cover claims. In 2004, the two year reserve development was 16% deficient. Fair profitability index (3.8). Fair expense controls. Return on equity has been fair, averaging 15.9% over the past five years.

Other Rating Factors: Good overall results on stability tests (5.1) despite potential drain of affiliation with W R Berkley Corp. Stability strengths include good operational trends, good risk adjusted capital for prior years and excellent risk diversification. Good overall long-term capitalization (6.5) based on good current risk adjusted capital (moderate loss scenario). However, capital levels have fluctuated during prior years. Good liquidity (6.4) with sufficient resources (cash flows and marketable investments) to handle a spike in claims.

Principal Business: Surety (58%), workers compensation (42%), and burglary & theft (1%).

Principal Investments: Investment grade bonds (62%), misc. investments (35%), non investment grade bonds (2%), and cash (1%).

Investments in Affiliates: 18%

Group Affiliation: W R Berkley Corp

Licensed in: All states except PR

Commenced Business: January 1987

Address: 165 Mason Street, Greenwich, CT 06836-2518

Phone: (314) 928-9960 **Domicile State:** DE **NAIC Code:** 29580

Data Date	Rating	RACR #1	RACR #2	Loss Ratio %	Total Assets ($mil)	Capital ($mil)	Net Premium ($mil)	Net Income ($mil)
3-09	B-	1.06	0.87	N/A	2,639.6	566.8	302.6	5.2
3-08	B-	1.18	0.98	N/A	2,707.0	656.3	328.4	16.4
2008	B-	1.15	0.96	64.8	2,665.5	610.3	1,276.9	19.6
2007	B-	1.21	1.02	58.8	2,565.9	654.2	1,309.1	132.1
2006	B-	1.28	1.09	59.2	2,402.3	665.0	1,274.5	140.8
2005	C+	1.23	1.02	55.5	2,248.4	715.1	1,205.2	139.9
2004	C+	1.06	0.85	55.4	1,946.8	632.0	1,141.4	114.5

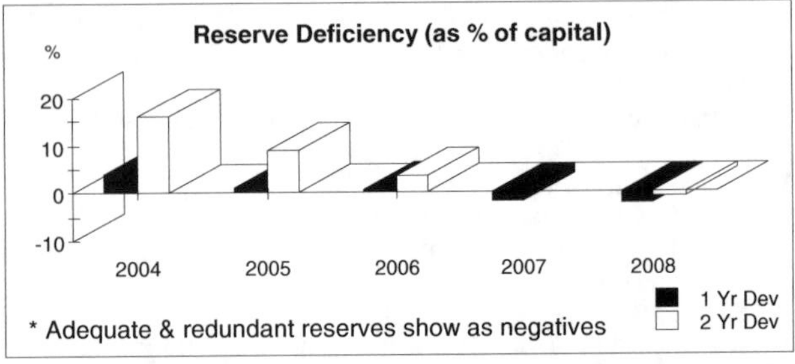

BITUMINOUS CASUALTY CORP * A- Excellent

Major Rating Factors: Strong long-term capitalization index (8.4 on a scale of 0 to 10) based on excellent current risk adjusted capital (severe and moderate loss scenarios), despite some fluctuation in capital levels. Good liquidity (6.8) with sufficient resources (cash flows and marketable investments) to handle a spike in claims.

Other Rating Factors: Good overall results on stability tests (6.9). Strengths that enhance stability include potential support from affiliation with Old Republic Group, good operational trends and excellent risk diversification. Fair reserve development (4.4) as reserves have generally been sufficient to cover claims. Fair profitability index (4.7) with operating losses during 2008. Return on equity has been fair, averaging 6.6% over the past five years.

Principal Business: Workers compensation (29%), commercial multiple peril (23%), auto liability (20%), other liability (14%), inland marine (8%), and auto physical damage (6%).

Principal Investments: Investment grade bonds (87%), misc. investments (13%), and non investment grade bonds (1%).

Investments in Affiliates: None

Group Affiliation: Old Republic Group

Licensed in: All states except HI, NH, PR

Commenced Business: August 1928

Address: 320 18th St, Rock Island, IL 61201

Phone: (309) 786-5401 **Domicile State:** IL **NAIC Code:** 20095

Data Date	Rating	RACR #1	RACR #2	Loss Ratio %	Total Assets ($mil)	Capital ($mil)	Net Premium ($mil)	Net Income ($mil)
3-09	A-	3.19	1.93	N/A	725.4	227.5	49.0	2.4
3-08	A-	3.03	1.84	N/A	762.0	252.9	57.7	7.3
2008	A-	3.33	2.02	66.8	741.8	237.4	211.7	-20.5
2007	A-	3.20	1.94	69.3	791.5	272.2	239.7	25.7
2006	A-	3.29	2.03	69.1	759.3	261.4	247.5	25.2
2005	A-	2.97	1.89	71.1	706.1	232.4	243.8	23.7
2004	A-	2.90	1.90	68.3	659.7	214.0	238.1	28.1

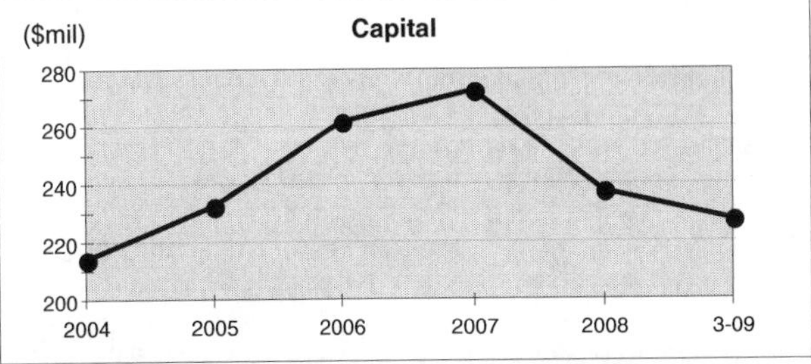

BITUMINOUS FIRE & MARINE INS CO * A- Excellent

Major Rating Factors: Strong long-term capitalization index (7.3 on a scale of 0 to 10) based on excellent current risk adjusted capital (severe and moderate loss scenarios), despite some fluctuation in capital levels. History of adequate reserve strength (5.0) as reserves have been consistently at an acceptable level.

Other Rating Factors: Good overall profitability index (6.7). Fair expense controls. Return on equity has been fair, averaging 8.9% over the past five years. Good liquidity (6.4) with sufficient resources (cash flows and marketable investments) to handle a spike in claims. Good overall results on stability tests (6.9).

Principal Business: Workers compensation (63%), commercial multiple peril (18%), auto liability (10%), inland marine (5%), auto physical damage (2%), and other liability (2%).

Principal Investments: Investment grade bonds (95%), misc. investments (4%), and non investment grade bonds (1%).

Investments in Affiliates: None

Group Affiliation: Old Republic Group

Licensed in: All states except AK, CT, HI, ME, NH, RI, VT, PR

Commenced Business: October 1942

Address: 320 18th St, Rock Island, IL 61201

Phone: (309) 786-5401 **Domicile State:** IL **NAIC Code:** 20109

Data Date	Rating	RACR #1	RACR #2	Loss Ratio %	Total Assets ($mil)	Capital ($mil)	Net Premium ($mil)	Net Income ($mil)
3-09	A-	2.09	1.33	N/A	463.7	106.8	30.9	3.2
3-08	A-	1.96	1.29	N/A	492.5	119.4	37.4	3.7
2008	A-	2.06	1.31	64.2	464.0	104.6	133.7	1.0
2007	A-	2.05	1.35	69.2	527.3	125.7	167.3	15.9
2006	A-	1.89	1.25	65.5	492.4	113.5	183.2	4.9
2005	A-	1.86	1.27	63.2	327.9	83.4	150.9	10.9
2004	A-	1.88	1.29	65.8	302.8	80.0	145.3	10.1

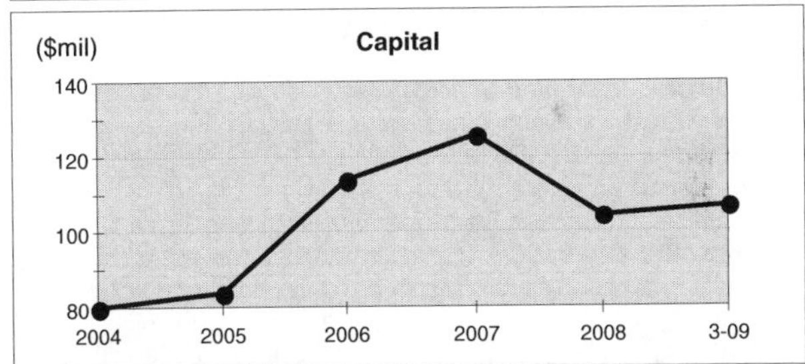

BRICKSTREET MUTUAL INS CO D- Weak

Major Rating Factors: Weak overall results on stability tests (1.0 on a scale of 0 to 10) including weak results on operational trends. Good long-term capitalization index (5.8) based on good current risk adjusted capital (severe loss scenario). Moreover, capital levels have been consistent over the last several years.

Other Rating Factors: Fair reserve development (4.1) as reserves have generally been sufficient to cover claims. Excellent profitability (9.4). Excellent liquidity (7.0) with ample operational cash flow and liquid investments.

Principal Business: Workers compensation (100%).

Principal Investments: Investment grade bonds (88%), misc. investments (7%), cash (3%), and real estate (2%).

Investments in Affiliates: None

Group Affiliation: None

Licensed in: WV

Commenced Business: January 2006

Address: (No address available)

Phone: (304) 926-3470 **Domicile State:** WV **NAIC Code:** 12372

Data Date	Rating	RACR #1	RACR #2	Loss Ratio %	Total Assets ($mil)	Capital ($mil)	Net Premium ($mil)	Net Income ($mil)
3-09	D-	2.12	0.84	N/A	1,529.6	484.3	90.5	8.6
3-08	E+	1.54	0.77	N/A	1,479.2	455.3	129.7	13.1
2008	D-	2.11	0.86	65.8	1,514.9	485.0	420.8	113.6
2007	E+	1.61	0.82	62.5	1,359.0	447.0	702.6	185.5
2006	E	0.43	0.26	92.3	985.6	268.1	762.0	70.7
2005	N/A	N/A	N/A	0.0	0.0	0.0	0.0	0.0
2004	N/A	N/A	N/A	0.0	0.0	0.0	0.0	0.0

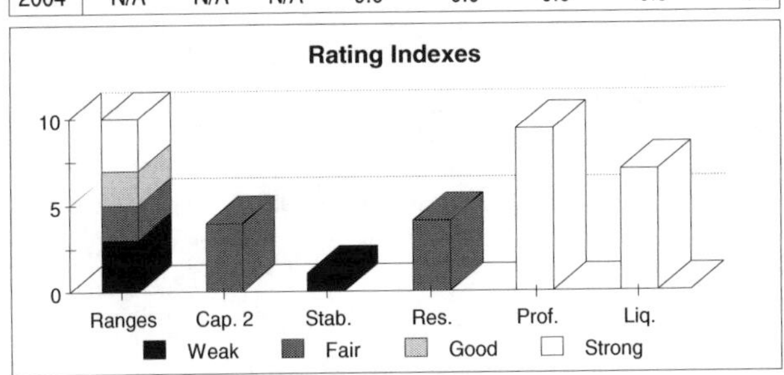

BUILDERS MUTUAL INS CO — B Good

Major Rating Factors: Good long-term capitalization index (5.9 on a scale of 0 to 10) based on good current risk adjusted capital (moderate loss scenario), despite some fluctuation in capital levels. Good liquidity (6.9) with sufficient resources (cash flows and marketable investments) to handle a spike in claims.

Other Rating Factors: Good overall results on stability tests (5.4). Stability strengths include good operational trends and excellent risk diversification. Ample reserve history (7.0) that can protect against increases in claims costs. Excellent profitability (8.3) with operating gains in each of the last five years. Return on equity has been good over the last five years, averaging 11.0%.

Principal Business: Workers compensation (63%), commercial multiple peril (20%), products liability (5%), inland marine (4%), auto liability (3%), other liability (3%), and auto physical damage (1%).

Principal Investments: Investment grade bonds (93%) and misc. investments (7%).

Investments in Affiliates: 2%

Group Affiliation: Builders Group

Licensed in: NC, SC, TN, VA, WI

Commenced Business: September 1997

Address: 6716 Six Forks Road, Raleigh, NC 27615

Phone: (919) 845-1976 **Domicile State:** NC **NAIC Code:** 10844

Data Date	Rating	RACR #1	RACR #2	Loss Ratio %	Total Assets ($mil)	Capital ($mil)	Net Premium ($mil)	Net Income ($mil)
3-09	B	1.68	1.05	N/A	481.6	184.2	22.9	2.2
3-08	B	1.88	1.18	N/A	508.2	189.9	34.9	5.1
2008	B	1.73	1.09	45.9	487.7	195.4	120.1	21.8
2007	B	1.92	1.21	43.3	505.9	190.7	142.4	35.4
2006	B	1.64	1.02	53.6	468.4	154.9	149.7	25.3
2005	B	1.53	0.96	66.7	424.0	128.1	148.7	7.6
2004	B	0.99	0.65	68.4	386.2	111.6	148.2	5.2

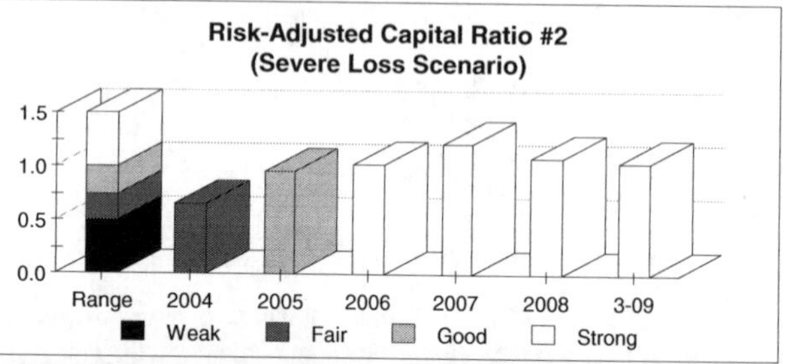

CALIFORNIA CAPITAL INS CO — B- Good

Major Rating Factors: Fair overall results on stability tests (4.7 on a scale of 0 to 10) including potential drain of affiliation with Capital Ins Group. Good liquidity (6.2) with sufficient resources (cash flows and marketable investments) to handle a spike in claims.

Other Rating Factors: Strong long-term capitalization index (7.9) based on excellent current risk adjusted capital (severe and moderate loss scenarios). Moreover, capital levels have been consistent in recent years. Ample reserve history (8.1) that helps to protect the company against sharp claims increases. Excellent profitability (8.7) with operating gains in each of the last five years.

Principal Business: Commercial multiple peril (40%), homeowners multiple peril (20%), auto liability (12%), auto physical damage (9%), farmowners multiple peril (6%), other liability (4%), and other lines (9%).

Principal Investments: Investment grade bonds (74%) and misc. investments (26%).

Investments in Affiliates: 24%

Group Affiliation: Capital Ins Group

Licensed in: AZ, CA, ID, MT, NV, TX

Commenced Business: August 1898

Address: 2300 Garden Rd, Monterey, CA 93942-3110

Phone: (408) 649-1155 **Domicile State:** CA **NAIC Code:** 13544

Data Date	Rating	RACR #1	RACR #2	Loss Ratio %	Total Assets ($mil)	Capital ($mil)	Net Premium ($mil)	Net Income ($mil)
3-09	B-	2.34	1.84	N/A	425.3	242.4	40.4	3.0
3-08	B-	2.28	1.76	N/A	412.8	222.3	40.7	2.6
2008	B-	2.31	1.83	57.7	426.2	237.8	166.4	13.7
2007	B-	2.25	1.73	56.8	433.1	217.6	164.6	16.1
2006	B-	2.14	1.61	52.7	406.9	190.8	153.2	20.6
2005	C+	1.68	1.16	54.8	379.1	156.1	177.3	17.1
2004	C+	1.27	0.86	53.5	329.4	127.8	160.5	16.2

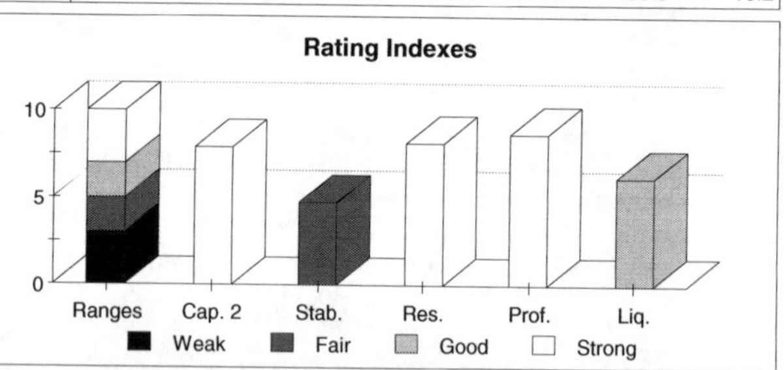

CALIFORNIA CASUALTY INDEMNITY EXCH — C Fair

Major Rating Factors: Fair overall results on stability tests (4.3 on a scale of 0 to 10) including fair financial strength of affiliated California Casualty Ins Group. Good overall profitability index (5.6). Fair expense controls.

Other Rating Factors: Good liquidity (6.8) with sufficient resources (cash flows and marketable investments) to handle a spike in claims. Strong long-term capitalization index (8.2) based on excellent current risk adjusted capital (severe and moderate loss scenarios), despite some fluctuation in capital levels. Ample reserve history (7.6) that can protect against increases in claims costs.

Principal Business: Auto liability (39%), auto physical damage (35%), homeowners multiple peril (25%), and earthquake (1%).

Principal Investments: Misc. investments (54%) and investment grade bonds (48%).

Investments in Affiliates: 42%

Group Affiliation: California Casualty Ins Group

Licensed in: All states except AK, MI, NJ, PR

Commenced Business: January 1914

Address: 1900 Alameda De Las Pulgas, San Mateo, CA 94403

Phone: (650) 572-4000 **Domicile State:** CA **NAIC Code:** 20117

Data Date	Rating	RACR #1	RACR #2	Loss Ratio %	Total Assets ($mil)	Capital ($mil)	Net Premium ($mil)	Net Income ($mil)
3-09	C	1.98	1.83	N/A	539.9	303.8	38.1	1.0
3-08	C	2.00	1.83	N/A	529.7	319.7	39.4	4.2
2008	C	1.98	1.83	76.3	533.5	304.7	154.7	3.0
2007	C	1.96	1.79	74.6	611.4	318.1	159.5	10.2
2006	C	1.91	1.74	71.9	534.5	305.7	168.4	9.3
2005	C	1.90	1.76	72.7	507.2	289.9	117.9	33.2
2004	C	1.64	1.42	80.5	398.8	260.0	141.4	0.7

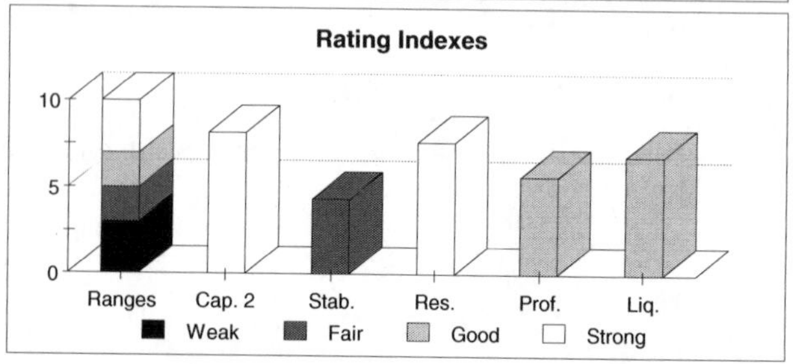

CALIFORNIA STATE AUTO ASN INTER-INS * A- Excellent

Major Rating Factors: Strong long-term capitalization index (10.0 on a scale of 0 to 10) based on excellent current risk adjusted capital (severe and moderate loss scenarios), despite some fluctuation in capital levels. Ample reserve history (7.7) that can protect against increases in claims costs.

Other Rating Factors: Good overall results on stability tests (5.5) despite potential drain of affiliation with California State Auto Group. Stability strengths include good operational trends and excellent risk diversification. Good overall profitability index (5.2) despite operating losses during the first three months of 2008. Good liquidity (6.3) with sufficient resources (cash flows and marketable investments) to handle a spike in claims.

Principal Business: Auto liability (40%), auto physical damage (35%), homeowners multiple peril (23%), other liability (1%), allied lines (1%), and inland marine (1%).

Principal Investments: Investment grade bonds (58%), misc. investments (34%), real estate (5%), and non investment grade bonds (4%).

Investments in Affiliates: 4%

Group Affiliation: California State Auto Group

Licensed in: CA, NV, UT, WY

Commenced Business: August 1914

Address: 100 Van Ness Ave, San Francisco, CA 94102

Phone: (415) 565-2012 **Domicile State:** CA **NAIC Code:** 15539

Data Date	Rating	RACR #1	RACR #2	Loss Ratio %	Total Assets ($mil)	Capital ($mil)	Net Premium ($mil)	Net Income ($mil)
3-09	A-	4.51	3.13	N/A	5,291.7	2,639.8	580.8	-37.2
3-08	A-	4.47	3.03	N/A	5,632.4	3,061.3	607.1	101.2
2008	A-	4.44	3.10	65.6	5,100.4	2,737.5	2,357.1	81.8
2007	A-	4.42	3.05	67.2	5,550.9	3,097.0	2,422.0	296.6
2006	A-	4.12	2.79	65.5	5,468.5	2,929.2	2,304.1	246.3
2005	A-	4.32	2.97	64.3	5,037.6	2,649.9	2,214.0	267.8
2004	A-	4.05	2.80	67.2	4,727.8	2,404.2	2,093.1	249.2

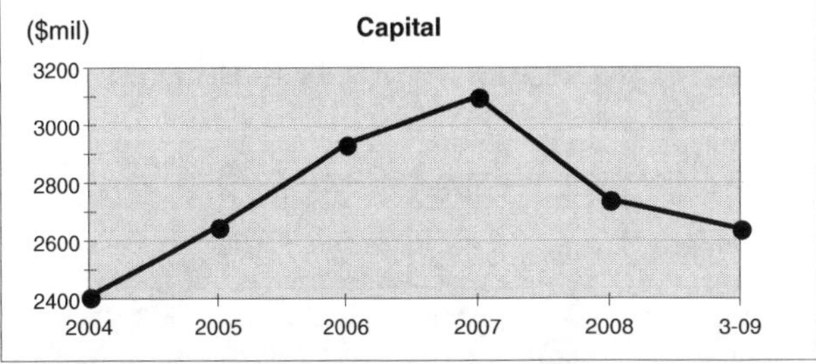

CAMBRIDGE MUTUAL FIRE INS CO B Good

Major Rating Factors: History of adequate reserve strength (5.9 on a scale of 0 to 10) as reserves have been consistently at an acceptable level. Fair overall results on stability tests (4.8) including potential drain of affiliation with Andover Group.

Other Rating Factors: Strong long-term capitalization index (10.0) based on excellent current risk adjusted capital (severe and moderate loss scenarios). Moreover, capital levels have been consistent in recent years. Excellent profitability (8.5) with operating gains in each of the last five years. Excellent liquidity (7.7) with ample operational cash flow and liquid investments.

Principal Business: Homeowners multiple peril (51%), commercial multiple peril (25%), fire (9%), allied lines (7%), other liability (6%), and inland marine (2%).

Principal Investments: Investment grade bonds (80%), misc. investments (17%), and cash (3%).

Investments in Affiliates: None

Group Affiliation: Andover Group

Licensed in: CT, IL, ME, MA, NH, NJ, NY, RI, VT

Commenced Business: January 1834

Address: 95 Old River Rd, Andover, MA 01810

Phone: (978) 475-3300 **Domicile State:** MA **NAIC Code:** 19771

Data Date	Rating	RACR #1	RACR #2	Loss Ratio %	Total Assets ($mil)	Capital ($mil)	Net Premium ($mil)	Net Income ($mil)
3-09	B	5.08	3.55	N/A	537.4	284.9	35.2	6.7
3-08	B	5.27	3.92	N/A	519.5	284.3	37.0	5.2
2008	B	5.09	3.49	59.7	559.9	285.4	152.7	17.0
2007	B	5.35	3.90	52.6	521.0	281.0	159.4	24.6
2006	B	4.25	3.20	45.4	502.7	260.4	163.4	33.7
2005	B	2.73	2.11	66.1	472.8	222.4	160.6	7.0
2004	B+	3.68	2.72	58.2	429.2	214.8	148.3	14.7

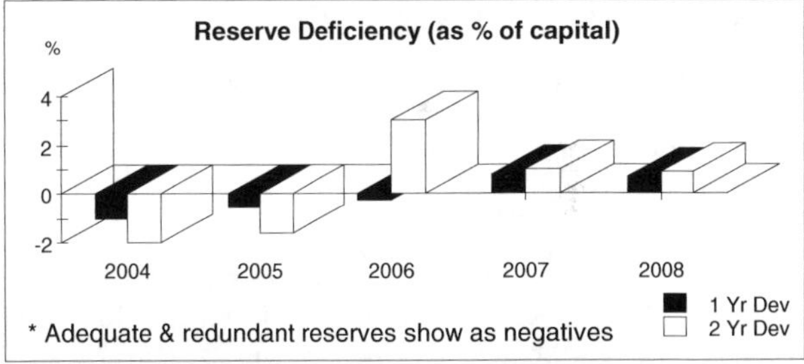

CANAL INS CO * B+ Good

Major Rating Factors: Good liquidity (6.7 on a scale of 0 to 10) with sufficient resources (cash flows and marketable investments) to handle a spike in claims. Good overall results on stability tests (5.8) despite negative cash flow from operations for 2008. Stability strengths include good operational trends and excellent risk diversification.

Other Rating Factors: Strong long-term capitalization index (7.5) based on excellent current risk adjusted capital (severe and moderate loss scenarios), despite some fluctuation in capital levels. Fair reserve development (4.3) as reserves have generally been sufficient to cover claims. Fair profitability index (3.6). Fair expense controls. Return on equity has been fair, averaging 7.7% over the past five years.

Principal Business: Auto liability (64%), auto physical damage (20%), inland marine (10%), workers compensation (6%), and other liability (1%).

Principal Investments: Investment grade bonds (74%) and misc. investments (26%).

Investments in Affiliates: 4%

Group Affiliation: Canal Group

Licensed in: All states except AK, HI, NJ, PR

Commenced Business: March 1939

Address: 400 E Stone Ave, Greenville, SC 29601

Phone: (864) 242-5365 **Domicile State:** SC **NAIC Code:** 10464

Data Date	Rating	RACR #1	RACR #2	Loss Ratio %	Total Assets ($mil)	Capital ($mil)	Net Premium ($mil)	Net Income ($mil)
3-09	B+	2.59	1.83	N/A	1,010.6	455.9	56.8	10.0
3-08	B+	2.46	1.66	N/A	1,245.2	519.7	89.9	12.4
2008	B+	2.52	1.78	76.7	1,044.0	465.1	238.2	41.5
2007	B+	2.40	1.61	75.4	1,377.4	530.5	433.5	44.3
2006	A-	2.60	1.74	73.2	1,324.3	585.8	472.3	45.7
2005	A-	2.68	1.72	70.9	1,227.3	527.7	487.7	34.6
2004	A-	2.28	1.46	69.0	1,123.0	487.6	475.5	31.1

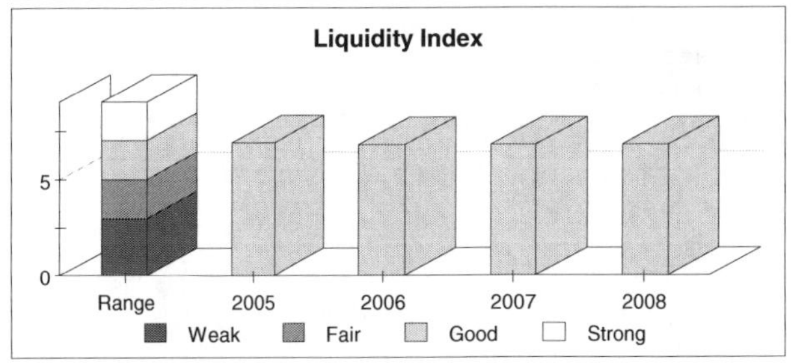

CAPITOL INDEMNITY CORP — C Fair

Major Rating Factors: Fair reserve development (4.8 on a scale of 0 to 10) as reserves have generally been sufficient to cover claims. In 2004, the two year reserve development was 27% deficient. Fair profitability index (4.6) with operating losses during 2008. Return on equity has been fair, averaging 9.9% over the past five years.

Other Rating Factors: Fair overall results on stability tests (4.0) including fair financial strength of affiliated Alleghany Corp Group. Good liquidity (6.9) with sufficient resources (cash flows and marketable investments) to handle a spike in claims. Strong long-term capitalization index (8.1) based on excellent current risk adjusted capital (severe and moderate loss scenarios), despite some fluctuation in capital levels.

Principal Business: Commercial multiple peril (62%), other liability (19%), workers compensation (7%), surety (5%), fire (1%), group accident & health (1%), and other lines (4%).

Principal Investments: Investment grade bonds (80%) and misc. investments (20%).

Investments in Affiliates: 8%

Group Affiliation: Alleghany Corp Group

Licensed in: All states except CA, ME, NH, NJ, NC, VT, PR

Commenced Business: June 1960

Address: 4610 University Ave, Madison, WI 53705-0900

Phone: (608) 231-4450 **Domicile State:** WI **NAIC Code:** 10472

Data Date	Rating	RACR #1	RACR #2	Loss Ratio %	Total Assets ($mil)	Capital ($mil)	Net Premium ($mil)	Net Income ($mil)
3-09	C	2.37	1.56	N/A	379.0	149.6	29.4	0.5
3-08	C	2.65	1.75	N/A	444.5	207.3	32.8	6.6
2008	C	2.73	1.81	48.2	405.5	169.8	124.2	-13.2
2007	C	2.58	1.71	48.8	446.8	210.1	122.7	33.5
2006	C	1.85	1.23	45.4	445.5	181.3	160.0	22.7
2005	C-	1.17	0.79	52.5	418.0	171.9	163.5	32.8
2004	C-	0.87	0.57	60.2	430.3	138.9	196.3	16.1

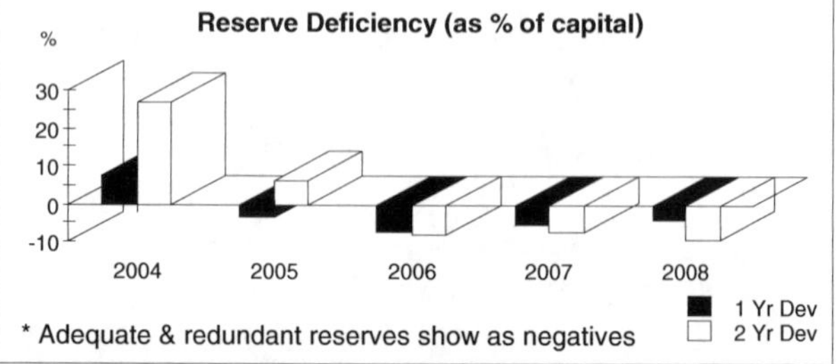

CAROLINA CASUALTY INS CO — C Fair

Major Rating Factors: Good long-term capitalization index (5.0 on a scale of 0 to 10) based on fair current risk adjusted capital (severe loss scenario), although results have slipped from the good range over the last two years. Fair profitability index (3.8) with operating losses during 2005 and 2008. Return on equity has been fair, averaging 7.4% over the past five years.

Other Rating Factors: Fair overall results on stability tests (3.8) including fair risk adjusted capital in prior years. The largest net exposure for one risk is acceptable at 2.4% of capital. A history of deficient reserves (2.8). Underreserving can have an adverse impact on capital and profits. Deficiencies in the two year reserve development occurred in three of the previous five years and ranged between 35% and 38%. Good liquidity (6.2) with sufficient resources (cash flows and marketable investments) to handle a spike in claims.

Principal Business: Auto liability (49%), other liability (28%), auto physical damage (9%), workers compensation (8%), inland marine (4%), and surety (1%).

Principal Investments: Investment grade bonds (96%), misc. investments (4%), and non investment grade bonds (1%).

Investments in Affiliates: None

Group Affiliation: W R Berkley Corp

Licensed in: All states except PR

Commenced Business: December 1952

Address: 11201 Douglas Ave, Urbandale, IA 50322-3707

Phone: (904) 363-0900 **Domicile State:** IA **NAIC Code:** 10510

Data Date	Rating	RACR #1	RACR #2	Loss Ratio %	Total Assets ($mil)	Capital ($mil)	Net Premium ($mil)	Net Income ($mil)
3-09	C	1.04	0.72	N/A	786.5	212.9	68.8	2.7
3-08	C+	1.22	0.85	N/A	893.3	267.4	84.8	11.2
2008	C	1.02	0.71	73.6	797.4	210.6	308.6	-3.3
2007	C+	1.17	0.82	69.1	873.0	257.4	351.0	39.2
2006	C+	1.12	0.78	68.4	881.7	260.7	354.8	39.9
2005	C-	0.98	0.66	85.5	824.3	221.9	351.0	-1.1
2004	C-	1.05	0.68	72.0	689.9	189.6	351.4	17.2

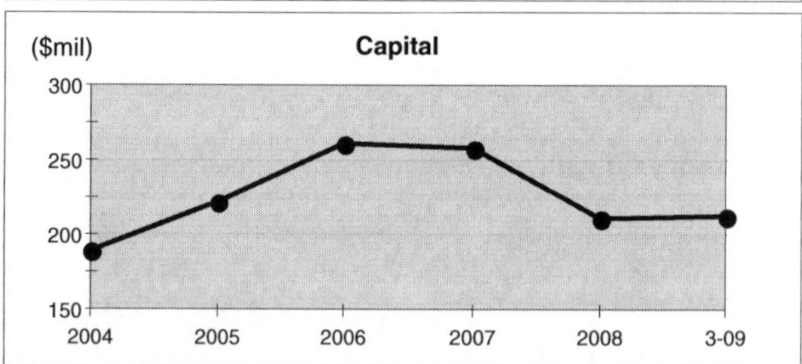

CATASTROPHE REINS CO — E+ Very Weak

Major Rating Factors: Weak overall results on stability tests (0.0 on a scale of 0 to 10) including weak results on operational trends. The largest net exposure for one risk is excessive at 94.0% of capital.

Other Rating Factors: Strong long-term capitalization index (10.0) based on excellent current risk adjusted capital (severe and moderate loss scenarios), despite some fluctuation in capital levels. Excellent profitability (8.0). Excellent expense controls. Excellent liquidity (7.8) with ample operational cash flow and liquid investments.

Principal Business: (This company is a reinsurer.)

Principal Investments: Investment grade bonds (94%) and misc. investments (6%).

Investments in Affiliates: None

Group Affiliation: USAA Group

Licensed in: TX

Commenced Business: June 2006

Address: (No address available)

Phone: (210) 498-2211 **Domicile State:** TX **NAIC Code:** 12578

Data Date	Rating	RACR #1	RACR #2	Loss Ratio %	Total Assets ($mil)	Capital ($mil)	Net Premium ($mil)	Net Income ($mil)
3-09	E+	5.55	3.91	N/A	1,417.9	1,273.0	54.9	-16.8
3-08	E+	3.28	2.45	N/A	1,262.3	1,172.5	63.1	51.3
2008	E+	5.71	4.16	15.7	1,419.5	1,290.0	219.5	168.9
2007	E+	4.25	3.15	0.0	1,236.8	1,121.4	252.5	123.9
2006	E+	29.89	24.76	0.0	334.6	316.3	26.2	15.6
2005	N/A	N/A	N/A	0.0	0.0	0.0	0.0	0.0
2004	N/A	N/A	N/A	0.0	0.0	0.0	0.0	0.0

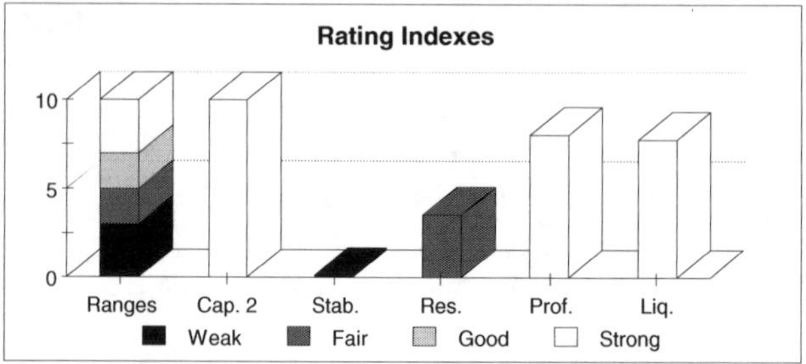

CENTRAL MUTUAL INS CO * B+ Good

Major Rating Factors: History of adequate reserve strength (5.4 on a scale of 0 to 10) as reserves have been consistently at an acceptable level. Good overall profitability index (5.2) despite operating losses during the first three months of 2008.

Other Rating Factors: Good liquidity (6.6) with sufficient resources (cash flows and marketable investments) to handle a spike in claims. Good overall results on stability tests (6.7). Strong long-term capitalization index (8.4) based on excellent current risk adjusted capital (severe and moderate loss scenarios), despite some fluctuation in capital levels.

Principal Business: Auto liability (24%), homeowners multiple peril (20%), commercial multiple peril (18%), auto physical damage (14%), workers compensation (6%), other liability (6%), and other lines (11%).

Principal Investments: Investment grade bonds (77%), misc. investments (19%), and real estate (6%).

Investments in Affiliates: 10%

Group Affiliation: Central Mutual Ins Group

Licensed in: AZ, CA, CO, CT, DE, GA, IL, IN, IA, KY, MA, MI, NV, NH, NJ, NM, NY, NC, OH, OK, PA, SC, TN, TX, VA, WI

Commenced Business: October 1876

Address: 800 S Washington St, Van Wert, OH 45891

Phone: (419) 238-5551 **Domicile State:** OH **NAIC Code:** 20230

Data Date	Rating	RACR #1	RACR #2	Loss Ratio %	Total Assets ($mil)	Capital ($mil)	Net Premium ($mil)	Net Income ($mil)
3-09	B+	2.65	1.95	N/A	1,238.6	471.6	111.2	-7.4
3-08	B+	3.02	2.24	N/A	1,229.3	534.7	115.5	4.2
2008	B+	2.72	2.02	79.4	1,244.6	483.1	460.2	-21.2
2007	B+	3.00	2.23	58.6	1,239.5	533.6	469.3	63.5
2006	B+	2.81	2.05	55.1	1,138.0	468.2	466.3	62.6
2005	B+	2.57	1.85	62.3	1,021.8	385.3	440.3	44.9
2004	B+	2.34	1.72	67.9	902.8	329.4	429.2	22.6

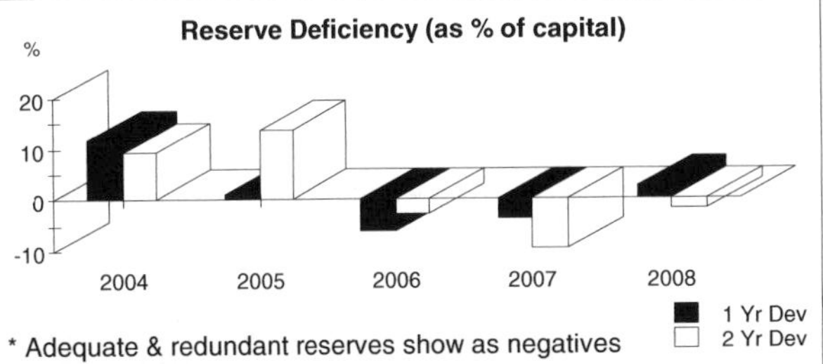

* Adequate & redundant reserves show as negatives

CENTRAL STATES INDEMNITY CO OF OMAHA * B+ Good

Major Rating Factors: Good overall results on stability tests (5.3 on a scale of 0 to 10). Stability strengths include good operational trends and excellent risk diversification. Strong long-term capitalization index (8.8) based on excellent current risk adjusted capital (severe and moderate loss scenarios), despite some fluctuation in capital levels.

Other Rating Factors: Ample reserve history (8.1) that helps to protect the company against sharp claims increases. Excellent liquidity (7.4) with ample operational cash flow and liquid investments. Fair profitability index (4.8). Weak expense controls. Return on equity has been low, averaging 3.3% over the past five years.

Principal Business: Aggregate write-ins for other lines of business (41%), inland marine (24%), credit accident & health (17%), aircraft (9%), other accident & health (5%), and group accident & health (3%).

Principal Investments: Non investment grade bonds (44%), misc. investments (34%), and investment grade bonds (22%).

Investments in Affiliates: 7%

Group Affiliation: Berkshire-Hathaway

Licensed in: All states, the District of Columbia and Puerto Rico

Commenced Business: June 1977

Address: 1212 N 96th St, Omaha, NE 68114

Phone: (402) 397-1111 **Domicile State:** NE **NAIC Code:** 34274

Data Date	Rating	RACR #1	RACR #2	Loss Ratio %	Total Assets ($mil)	Capital ($mil)	Net Premium ($mil)	Net Income ($mil)
3-09	B+	4.02	2.59	N/A	209.1	183.4	11.5	0.9
3-08	A-	4.04	3.00	N/A	250.3	207.4	12.6	6.5
2008	B+	3.82	2.43	15.8	222.7	192.5	48.5	13.4
2007	A-	3.78	2.75	14.3	259.4	210.6	51.6	7.2
2006	A-	3.20	2.41	0.1	260.9	207.5	54.9	5.3
2005	A-	4.02	2.93	41.9	269.3	192.0	100.6	3.8
2004	A-	3.43	2.77	12.5	246.8	183.1	66.7	3.5

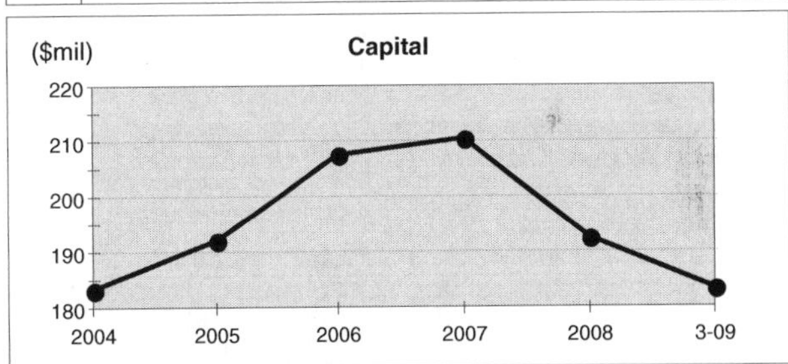

CENTURION CASUALTY CO B Good

Major Rating Factors: History of adequate reserve strength (6.1 on a scale of 0 to 10) as reserves have been consistently at an acceptable level. Fair overall results on stability tests (4.5) including weak results on operational trends.

Other Rating Factors: Strong long-term capitalization index (10.0) based on excellent current risk adjusted capital (severe and moderate loss scenarios). Moreover, capital levels have been consistent in recent years. Excellent profitability (9.0) with operating gains in each of the last five years. Excellent expense controls. Superior liquidity (9.3) with ample operational cash flow and liquid investments.

Principal Business: Aggregate write-ins for other lines of business (80%) and inland marine (20%).

Principal Investments: Investment grade bonds (95%), misc. investments (3%), cash (1%), and non investment grade bonds (1%).

Investments in Affiliates: None

Group Affiliation: Wells Fargo Group

Licensed in: All states except AK, AR, DC, GA, MI, NH, NY, PA, VT, PR

Commenced Business: March 1983

Address: 206 Eighth Street, Des Moines, IA 50309

Phone: (515) 243-2131 **Domicile State:** IA **NAIC Code:** 42765

Data Date	Rating	RACR #1	RACR #2	Loss Ratio %	Total Assets ($mil)	Capital ($mil)	Net Premium ($mil)	Net Income ($mil)
3-09	B	74.13	42.12	N/A	394.7	370.8	9.2	7.2
3-08	B	80.11	49.43	N/A	367.7	340.8	9.1	9.5
2008	B	50.85	30.25	11.5	383.5	363.8	36.5	33.0
2007	B	93.99	51.35	6.8	348.8	331.3	28.8	28.5
2006	B	88.49	53.14	9.9	322.0	302.8	12.1	24.0
2005	B	53.82	39.32	12.7	315.2	279.6	16.1	21.6
2004	B	48.38	31.95	19.6	295.2	258.3	16.9	19.7

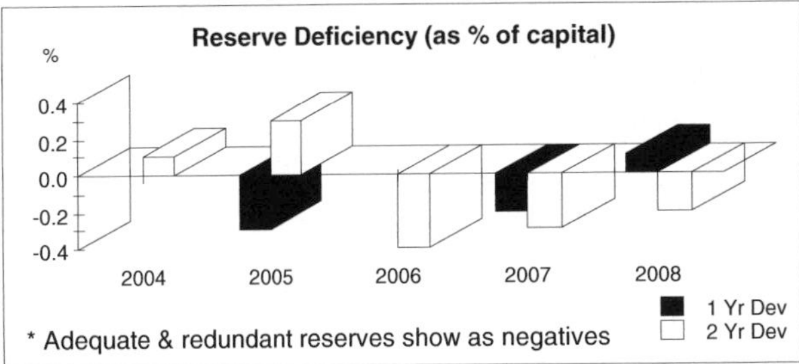

* Adequate & redundant reserves show as negatives

CENTURY-NATIONAL INS CO C+ Fair

Major Rating Factors: Fair overall results on stability tests (4.4 on a scale of 0 to 10) including negative cash flow from operations for 2008. Good liquidity (6.4) with sufficient resources (cash flows and marketable investments) to handle a spike in claims.

Other Rating Factors: Strong long-term capitalization index (7.5) based on excellent current risk adjusted capital (severe and moderate loss scenarios), despite some fluctuation in capital levels. Ample reserve history (9.7) that helps to protect the company against sharp claims increases. Excellent profitability (7.1) with operating gains in each of the last five years. Return on equity has been excellent over the last five years averaging 16.3%.

Principal Business: Homeowners multiple peril (52%), auto liability (23%), auto physical damage (8%), fire (7%), allied lines (6%), and earthquake (4%).

Principal Investments: Investment grade bonds (82%), misc. investments (11%), non investment grade bonds (6%), and cash (1%).

Investments in Affiliates: None

Group Affiliation: Kramer-Wilson Co Inc

Licensed in: AK, AZ, AR, CA, CO, DE, FL, GA, ID, IL, IN, IA, KY, LA, MD, MN, MS, MO, MT, NE, NV, NJ, NM, NC, ND, OH, OK, OR, PA, SC, SD, TN, TX, UT, VA, WA, WI, WY

Commenced Business: December 1956

Address: 12200 Sylvan St, N Hollywood, CA 91606-3216

Phone: (818) 760-0880 **Domicile State:** CA **NAIC Code:** 26905

Data Date	Rating	RACR #1	RACR #2	Loss Ratio %	Total Assets ($mil)	Capital ($mil)	Net Premium ($mil)	Net Income ($mil)
3-09	C+	2.25	1.59	N/A	484.5	226.7	35.6	5.3
3-08	C+	2.19	1.51	N/A	558.8	253.1	40.4	8.3
2008	C+	2.17	1.53	42.0	503.5	223.5	142.3	23.5
2007	C+	2.16	1.49	50.8	586.8	255.9	161.8	45.4
2006	C	1.62	1.13	53.0	572.0	215.9	185.1	37.2
2005	C	1.25	0.89	54.1	529.4	173.5	202.1	42.5
2004	C	0.87	0.60	68.7	495.1	133.0	213.9	17.7

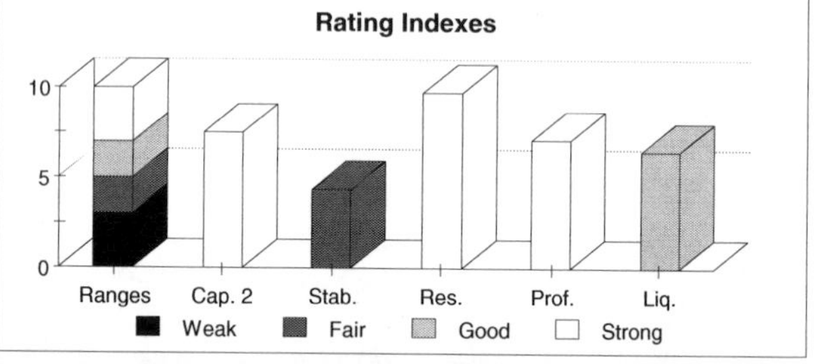

CHARTER OAK FIRE INS CO B Good

Major Rating Factors: Good liquidity (6.6 on a scale of 0 to 10) with sufficient resources (cash flows and marketable investments) to handle a spike in claims. Good overall results on stability tests (5.4).

Other Rating Factors: Fair reserve development (4.6) as reserves have generally been sufficient to cover claims. In 2005, the two year reserve development was 27% deficient. Strong long-term capitalization index (7.4) based on excellent current risk adjusted capital (severe and moderate loss scenarios), despite some fluctuation in capital levels. Excellent profitability (8.1) with operating gains in each of the last five years. Return on equity has been excellent over the last five years averaging 20.0%.

Principal Business: Commercial multiple peril (29%), auto liability (21%), workers compensation (18%), homeowners multiple peril (13%), auto physical damage (8%), other liability (6%), and other lines (4%).

Principal Investments: Investment grade bonds (92%) and misc. investments (8%).

Investments in Affiliates: None

Group Affiliation: Travelers Companies Inc

Licensed in: All states except CA

Commenced Business: October 1935

Address: One Tower Square, Hartford, CT 06183

Phone: (860) 277-0111 **Domicile State:** CT **NAIC Code:** 25615

Data Date	Rating	RACR #1	RACR #2	Loss Ratio %	Total Assets ($mil)	Capital ($mil)	Net Premium ($mil)	Net Income ($mil)
3-09	B	2.11	1.35	N/A	894.8	229.1	57.3	6.3
3-08	B-	2.25	1.30	N/A	842.6	240.8	56.9	13.9
2008	B	2.08	1.33	61.5	865.5	222.0	230.4	39.6
2007	B-	2.17	1.24	59.0	836.1	228.4	228.7	44.7
2006	C+	1.71	1.06	58.4	805.7	199.0	220.4	48.3
2005	C+	1.40	0.92	75.1	789.5	180.6	207.9	27.9
2004	C+	1.57	1.05	63.7	796.6	194.4	235.8	48.5

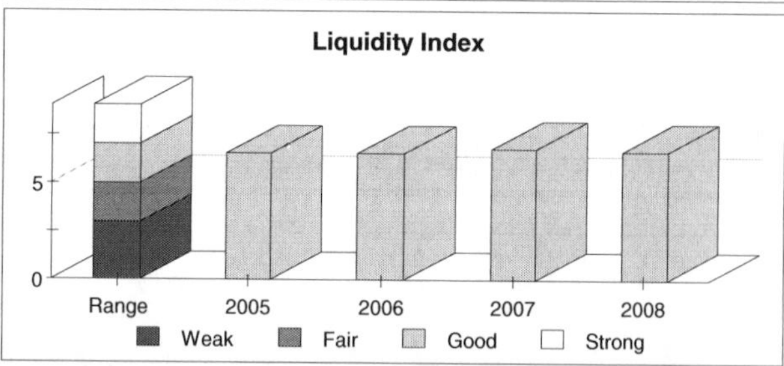

CHURCH MUTUAL INS CO * A Excellent

Major Rating Factors: Strong long-term capitalization index (8.4 on a scale of 0 to 10) based on excellent current risk adjusted capital (severe and moderate loss scenarios). Furthermore, this high level of risk adjusted capital has been consistently maintained in previous years. Ample reserve history (9.3) that helps to protect the company against sharp claims increases.

Other Rating Factors: Excellent overall results on stability tests (7.5). Stability strengths include excellent operational trends and excellent risk diversification. Good overall profitability index (6.8) despite modest operating losses during the first three months of 2008. Good liquidity (6.0) with sufficient resources (cash flows and marketable investments) to handle a spike in claims.

Principal Business: Commercial multiple peril (72%), workers compensation (13%), auto liability (7%), other liability (4%), auto physical damage (2%), homeowners multiple peril (1%), and medical malpractice (1%).

Principal Investments: Investment grade bonds (93%), misc. investments (6%), and real estate (2%).

Investments in Affiliates: None

Group Affiliation: None

Licensed in: All states except PR

Commenced Business: June 1897

Address: 3000 Schuster Lane, Merrill, WI 54452

Phone: (715) 536-5577 **Domicile State:** WI **NAIC Code:** 18767

Data Date	Rating	RACR #1	RACR #2	Loss Ratio %	Total Assets ($mil)	Capital ($mil)	Net Premium ($mil)	Net Income ($mil)
3-09	A	2.23	1.87	N/A	1,150.7	345.0	113.8	-0.1
3-08	A	2.35	1.98	N/A	1,194.8	385.0	116.6	2.4
2008	A	2.28	1.92	83.2	1,142.2	349.4	467.5	-3.0
2007	A	2.47	2.09	67.2	1,178.6	389.4	473.7	56.6
2006	A-	2.22	1.88	67.1	1,066.3	328.6	444.7	50.6
2005	A-	1.76	1.43	68.8	963.9	272.5	415.9	36.1
2004	A-	1.57	1.24	74.3	836.2	231.4	372.5	21.5

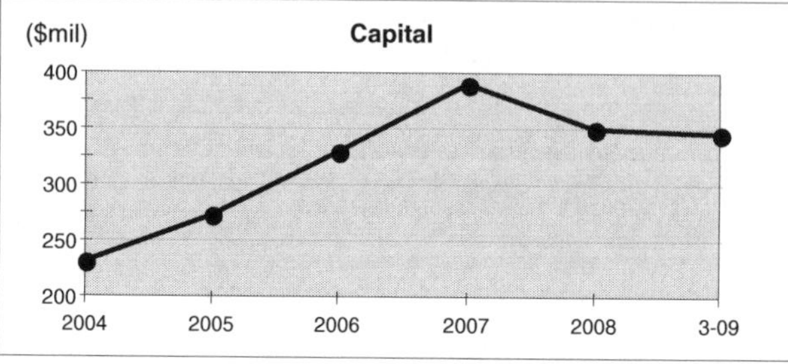

CINCINNATI CASUALTY CO — B — Good

Major Rating Factors: Good overall results on stability tests (5.8 on a scale of 0 to 10). Stability strengths include good operational trends and excellent risk diversification. Fair profitability index (4.8). Weak expense controls. Return on equity has been fair, averaging 5.5% over the past five years.

Other Rating Factors: Strong long-term capitalization index (10.0) based on excellent current risk adjusted capital (severe and moderate loss scenarios), despite some fluctuation in capital levels. Superior liquidity (10.0) with ample operational cash flow and liquid investments.

Principal Business: Workers compensation (100%).

Principal Investments: Investment grade bonds (69%), misc. investments (15%), cash (15%), and non investment grade bonds (1%).

Investments in Affiliates: None

Group Affiliation: Cincinnati Financial Corp

Licensed in: All states except AK, CA, CT, DC, HI, LA, ME, MA, NV, NJ, RI, PR

Commenced Business: March 1973

Address: 6200 S Gilmore Rd, Fairfield, OH 45014-5141

Phone: (513) 870-2000 **Domicile State:** OH **NAIC Code:** 28665

Data Date	Rating	RACR #1	RACR #2	Loss Ratio %	Total Assets ($mil)	Capital ($mil)	Net Premium ($mil)	Net Income ($mil)
3-09	B	19.18	10.72	N/A	297.7	240.0	0.0	11.5
3-08	B	7.41	4.33	N/A	324.7	273.2	0.0	3.7
2008	B	12.28	7.07	0.0	297.5	262.7	0.0	15.7
2007	B	6.67	3.92	0.0	331.9	278.5	0.0	12.2
2006	B	5.54	3.27	0.0	349.6	281.5	0.0	14.9
2005	B	5.63	3.32	0.0	335.4	262.9	0.0	12.7
2004	B	5.17	3.07	0.0	323.5	259.3	0.0	9.1

Cincinnati Financial Corp
Composite Group Rating: B+

Largest Group Members	Assets ($mil)	Rating
CINCINNATI INS CO	8636	A-
CINCINNATI LIFE INS CO	2478	B
CINCINNATI CASUALTY CO	298	B
CINCINNATI SPECIALTY UNDERWRITER	193	C+
CINCINNATI INDEMNITY CO	76	A-

CINCINNATI INDEMNITY CO * — A- — Excellent

Major Rating Factors: Strong long-term capitalization index (10.0 on a scale of 0 to 10) based on excellent current risk adjusted capital (severe and moderate loss scenarios), despite some fluctuation in capital levels. Excellent profitability (7.0) with operating gains in each of the last five years.

Other Rating Factors: Excellent liquidity (7.0) with ample operational cash flow and liquid investments. Good overall results on stability tests (6.2). Strengths that enhance stability include potential support from affiliation with Cincinnati Financial Corp, good operational trends and excellent risk diversification.

Principal Business: Workers compensation (98%) and other liability (1%).

Principal Investments: Investment grade bonds (72%), misc. investments (17%), cash (9%), and non investment grade bonds (2%).

Investments in Affiliates: None

Group Affiliation: Cincinnati Financial Corp

Licensed in: AL, AZ, AR, DE, FL, GA, ID, IL, IN, IA, KS, KY, MD, MI, MN, MO, MT, NE, NY, NC, ND, OH, OR, PA, SC, SD, TN, VA, WA, WV, WI

Commenced Business: January 1989

Address: 6200 S Gilmore Rd, Fairfield, OH 45014-5141

Phone: (513) 870-2000 **Domicile State:** OH **NAIC Code:** 23280

Data Date	Rating	RACR #1	RACR #2	Loss Ratio %	Total Assets ($mil)	Capital ($mil)	Net Premium ($mil)	Net Income ($mil)
3-09	A-	16.43	10.86	N/A	87.6	64.0	0.0	3.5
3-08	A-	7.78	4.53	N/A	77.2	65.6	0.0	0.6
2008	A-	9.05	5.25	0.0	75.6	65.5	0.0	2.5
2007	A-	7.44	4.35	0.0	77.5	63.3	0.0	1.1
2006	A-	7.72	4.49	0.0	74.5	61.9	0.0	2.2
2005	A-	8.99	5.08	0.0	82.9	62.7	0.0	2.1
2004	A-	8.25	4.63	0.0	71.6	60.2	0.0	2.3

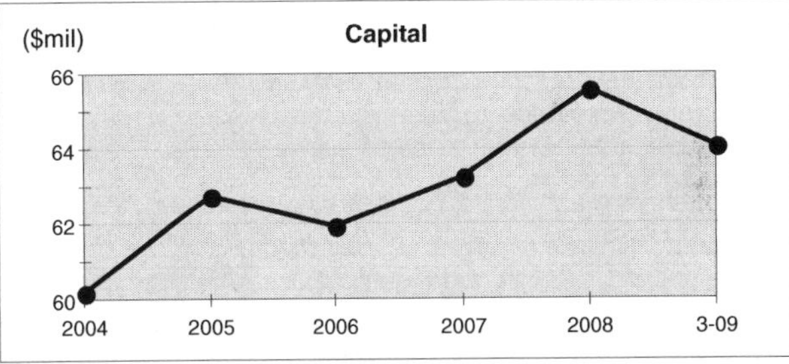

CINCINNATI INS CO * — A- — Excellent

Major Rating Factors: Strong long-term capitalization index (8.2 on a scale of 0 to 10) based on excellent current risk adjusted capital (severe and moderate loss scenarios), despite some fluctuation in capital levels. Ample reserve history (8.8) that helps to protect the company against sharp claims increases.

Other Rating Factors: Good overall results on stability tests (6.9). Strengths include potentially strong support from affiliation with Cincinnati Financial Corp, good operational trends and excellent risk diversification. Good liquidity (6.3) with sufficient resources (cash flows and marketable investments) to handle a spike in claims. Fair profitability index (3.1). Fair expense controls. Return on equity has been fair, averaging 11.4% over the past five years.

Principal Business: Commercial multiple peril (30%), other liability (17%), auto liability (17%), homeowners multiple peril (10%), auto physical damage (8%), workers compensation (5%), and other lines (12%).

Principal Investments: Investment grade bonds (55%), misc. investments (38%), non investment grade bonds (4%), and cash (3%).

Investments in Affiliates: 11%

Group Affiliation: Cincinnati Financial Corp

Licensed in: All states, the District of Columbia and Puerto Rico

Commenced Business: January 1951

Address: 6200 S Gilmore Rd, Fairfield, OH 45014-5141

Phone: (513) 870-2000 **Domicile State:** OH **NAIC Code:** 10677

Data Date	Rating	RACR #1	RACR #2	Loss Ratio %	Total Assets ($mil)	Capital ($mil)	Net Premium ($mil)	Net Income ($mil)
3-09	A-	2.34	1.76	N/A	8,454.0	3,105.4	730.0	11.0
3-08	A-	2.09	1.54	N/A	9,997.8	4,027.3	753.5	-53.0
2008	A-	2.41	1.81	68.2	8,636.1	3,360.3	2,998.5	194.3
2007	A-	2.14	1.57	58.6	10,019.7	4,307.2	3,119.2	658.3
2006	A-	2.27	1.59	63.4	10,917.9	4,750.2	3,180.4	572.2
2005	A-	2.20	1.55	59.2	9,993.0	4,219.8	3,078.5	517.1
2004	A-	2.13	1.49	60.0	9,820.1	4,191.2	2,999.4	587.7

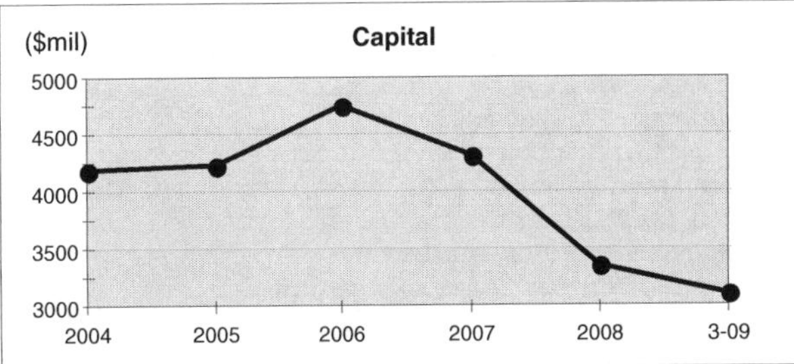

CINCINNATI SPECIALTY UNDERWRITER C+ Fair

Major Rating Factors: Fair overall results on stability tests (4.3 on a scale of 0 to 10) including excessive premium growth and weak results on operational trends.
Other Rating Factors: Weak profitability index (2.1) with operating losses during the first three months of 2008. Strong long-term capitalization index (10.0) based on excellent current risk adjusted capital (severe and moderate loss scenarios), despite some fluctuation in capital levels. Superior liquidity (9.1) with ample operational cash flow and liquid investments.
Principal Business: Other liability (47%), products liability (44%), fire (7%), and allied lines (2%).
Principal Investments: Investment grade bonds (71%), misc. investments (20%), and cash (9%).
Investments in Affiliates: None
Group Affiliation: Cincinnati Financial Corp
Licensed in: DE
Commenced Business: November 2007
Address: 1807 N Market St, Wilmington, DE 19802-4810
Phone: (513) 870-2000 **Domicile State:** DE **NAIC Code:** 13037

Data Date	Rating	RACR #1	RACR #2	Loss Ratio %	Total Assets ($mil)	Capital ($mil)	Net Premium ($mil)	Net Income ($mil)
3-09	C+	9.87	5.52	N/A	198.2	170.7	4.2	-4.1
3-08	N/A	N/A	N/A	N/A	215.8	192.9	0.0	0.8
2008	C+	12.12	6.99	109.5	193.3	174.3	13.7	-38.1
2007	N/A	N/A	N/A	0.0	210.2	195.9	0.0	0.2
2006	N/A	N/A	N/A	0.0	0.0	0.0	0.0	0.0
2005	N/A	N/A	N/A	0.0	0.0	0.0	0.0	0.0
2004	N/A	N/A	N/A	0.0	0.0	0.0	0.0	0.0

Cincinnati Financial Corp
Composite Group Rating: B+

Largest Group Members	Assets ($mil)	Rating
CINCINNATI INS CO	8636	A-
CINCINNATI LIFE INS CO	2478	B
CINCINNATI CASUALTY CO	298	B
CINCINNATI SPECIALTY UNDERWRITER	193	C+
CINCINNATI INDEMNITY CO	76	A-

CITATION INS CO * B+ Good

Major Rating Factors: Good liquidity (6.6 on a scale of 0 to 10) with sufficient resources (cash flows and marketable investments) to handle a spike in claims. Good overall results on stability tests (5.0). Stability strengths include good operational trends and excellent risk diversification. The largest net exposure for one risk is conservative at 1.8% of capital.
Other Rating Factors: Strong long-term capitalization index (9.9) based on excellent current risk adjusted capital (severe and moderate loss scenarios), despite some fluctuation in capital levels. Ample reserve history (8.1) that helps to protect the company against sharp claims increases. Fair profitability index (3.5) with operating losses during 2008. Return on equity has been fair, averaging 10.9% over the past five years.
Principal Business: Homeowners multiple peril (84%), auto liability (7%), auto physical damage (4%), inland marine (3%), and other liability (2%).
Principal Investments: Investment grade bonds (93%), misc. investments (4%), non investment grade bonds (2%), and cash (1%).
Investments in Affiliates: None
Group Affiliation: MAPFRE Ins Group
Licensed in: MA
Commenced Business: November 1981
Address: 211 Main St, Webster, MA 01570-0758
Phone: (508) 943-9000 **Domicile State:** MA **NAIC Code:** 40274

Data Date	Rating	RACR #1	RACR #2	Loss Ratio %	Total Assets ($mil)	Capital ($mil)	Net Premium ($mil)	Net Income ($mil)
3-09	B+	3.44	2.88	N/A	304.8	108.4	36.4	1.4
3-08	B+	3.93	3.31	N/A	358.8	135.4	39.1	0.5
2008	B+	3.44	2.99	68.0	321.3	114.8	149.5	-2.2
2007	B+	3.58	3.12	64.0	402.1	132.5	155.6	19.1
2006	B+	2.87	2.42	59.9	409.0	139.4	182.5	21.2
2005	B+	2.57	2.17	60.8	379.0	140.6	173.6	28.0
2004	B+	1.61	1.34	62.8	348.2	121.0	224.2	10.2

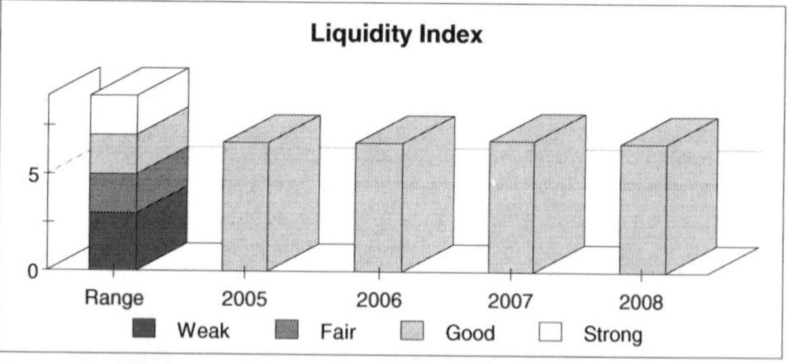

CITIZENS INS CO OF AMERICA B Good

Major Rating Factors: Good overall results on stability tests (5.2 on a scale of 0 to 10) despite potential drain of affiliation with Hanover Ins Group Inc. Good liquidity (6.5) with sufficient resources (cash flows and marketable investments) to handle a spike in claims.
Other Rating Factors: Fair profitability index (3.8). Fair expense controls. Return on equity has been fair, averaging 13.8% over the past five years. Strong long-term capitalization index (10.0) based on excellent current risk adjusted capital (severe and moderate loss scenarios), despite some fluctuation in capital levels. Ample reserve history (9.3) that helps to protect the company against sharp claims increases.
Principal Business: Homeowners multiple peril (31%), auto liability (28%), auto physical damage (20%), commercial multiple peril (14%), workers compensation (3%), other liability (2%), and inland marine (1%).
Principal Investments: Investment grade bonds (95%), misc. investments (6%), and real estate (1%).
Investments in Affiliates: 0%
Group Affiliation: Hanover Ins Group Inc
Licensed in: AL, CT, GA, IL, IN, KS, ME, MA, MI, MO, NH, NJ, NY, NC, OH, PA, RI, SC, VT, VA, WI
Commenced Business: August 1974
Address: 645 W Grand River, Howell, MI 48843
Phone: (517) 546-2160 **Domicile State:** MI **NAIC Code:** 31534

Data Date	Rating	RACR #1	RACR #2	Loss Ratio %	Total Assets ($mil)	Capital ($mil)	Net Premium ($mil)	Net Income ($mil)
3-09	B	5.04	3.52	N/A	1,489.6	643.1	167.6	0.9
3-08	B	5.77	3.76	N/A	1,665.2	755.3	175.0	11.0
2008	B	4.91	3.44	64.5	1,528.0	638.3	692.3	72.3
2007	B	5.43	3.68	59.4	1,666.7	737.1	700.1	116.7
2006	B	5.07	3.41	61.9	1,763.3	736.8	757.1	101.0
2005	B	4.86	3.25	61.9	1,831.3	733.0	780.2	123.3
2004	B	3.65	2.45	63.9	1,765.0	609.7	875.0	89.8

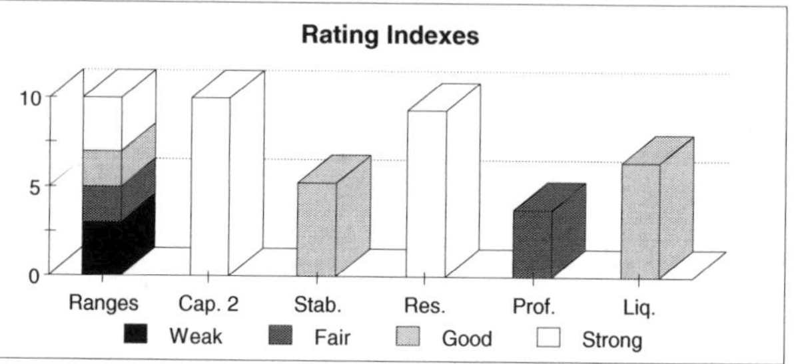

CLARENDON NATIONAL INS CO — C- Fair

Major Rating Factors: Weak profitability index (1.3 on a scale of 0 to 10) with operating losses during 2004, 2006, 2007 and the first three months of 2008. Average return on equity over the last five years has been poor at -13.1%. Weak overall results on stability tests (2.9) including weak results on operational trends and negative cash flow from operations for 2008.

Other Rating Factors: Good long-term capitalization index (5.2) based on good current risk adjusted capital (severe loss scenario), although results have slipped from the excellent range over the last two years. History of adequate reserve strength (5.5) as reserves have been consistently at an acceptable level. Excellent liquidity (7.0) with ample operational cash flow and liquid investments.

Principal Business: (Not applicable due to unusual reinsurance transactions.)

Principal Investments: Investment grade bonds (78%), misc. investments (19%), and cash (3%).

Investments in Affiliates: 27%

Group Affiliation: Hannover Group

Licensed in: All states, the District of Columbia and Puerto Rico

Commenced Business: November 1941

Address: 1177 Avenue Of The Americas, New York, NY 10036

Phone: (212) 805-9700 **Domicile State:** NJ **NAIC Code:** 20532

Data Date	Rating	RACR #1	RACR #2	Loss Ratio %	Total Assets ($mil)	Capital ($mil)	Net Premium ($mil)	Net Income ($mil)
3-09	C-	1.21	0.77	N/A	748.2	318.8	0.0	-23.1
3-08	C	1.38	0.86	N/A	903.1	396.9	-1.4	-67.4
2008	C-	1.27	0.80	N/A	791.8	341.3	-8.3	-122.4
2007	C	1.69	1.07	N/A	950.5	439.8	-32.9	-60.1
2006	C	1.75	1.17	N/A	1,430.9	496.0	-0.7	-62.7
2005	C	2.04	1.34	50.7	1,896.2	664.9	-47.6	147.1
2004	C-	0.81	0.56	86.1	2,022.9	564.6	318.9	-120.8

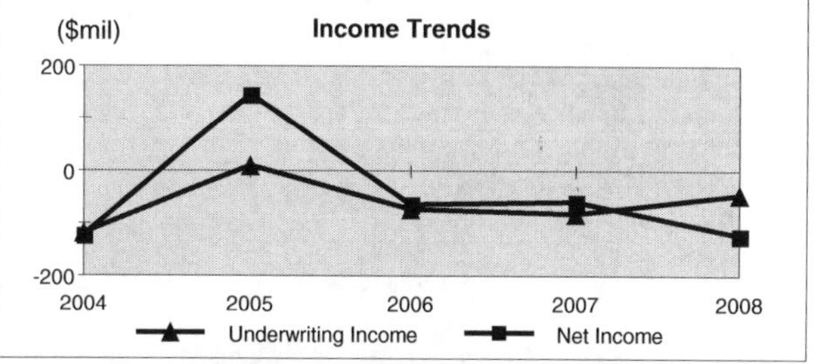

CLEARWATER INS CO — D Weak

Major Rating Factors: A history of deficient reserves (1.5 on a scale of 0 to 10) that places pressure on both capital and profits. In the last five years, reserves (two year development) fluctuated between 43% and 40% deficeint. Weak overall results on stability tests (2.1) including weak results on operational trends and negative cash flow from operations for 2008.

Other Rating Factors: Fair long-term capitalization index (3.7) based on fair current risk adjusted capital (severe loss scenario). Fair profitability index (3.7) with operating losses during 2004 and 2005. Average return on equity over the last five years has been poor at -0.2%. Good liquidity (6.7) with sufficient resources (cash flows and marketable investments) to handle a spike in claims.

Principal Business: Allied lines (59%), ocean marine (28%), auto physical damage (12%), auto liability (1%), and inland marine (1%).

Principal Investments: Misc. investments (49%), investment grade bonds (46%), and non investment grade bonds (5%).

Investments in Affiliates: 37%

Group Affiliation: Fairfax Financial

Licensed in: All states except CO, FL, ME, MA, MN

Commenced Business: July 1974

Address: 300 First Stamford Place, Stamford, CT 06902

Phone: (212) 978-4700 **Domicile State:** DE **NAIC Code:** 25070

Data Date	Rating	RACR #1	RACR #2	Loss Ratio %	Total Assets ($mil)	Capital ($mil)	Net Premium ($mil)	Net Income ($mil)
3-09	D	0.86	0.58	N/A	1,242.4	637.1	1.1	5.0
3-08	D	0.82	0.54	N/A	1,298.3	672.8	3.7	19.8
2008	D	0.83	0.55	276.1	1,283.5	635.5	40.5	3.0
2007	D	0.78	0.51	298.2	1,326.0	670.2	45.7	82.4
2006	D	0.69	0.47	519.1	1,308.3	660.4	18.4	29.0
2005	D	0.53	0.37	667.3	1,127.5	602.9	22.6	-61.8
2004	C-	0.66	0.46	844.1	1,102.5	583.4	15.4	-52.1

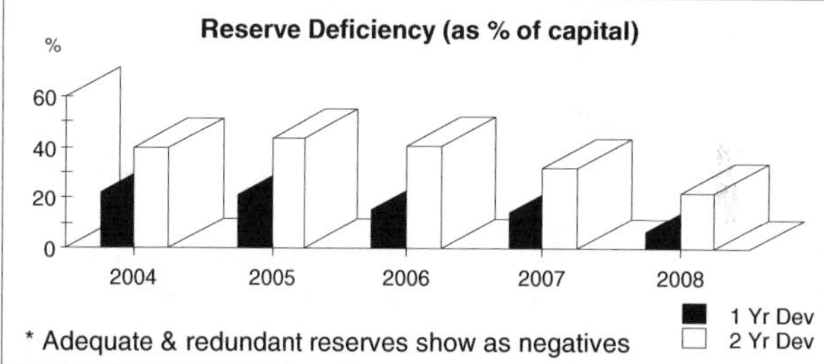

* Adequate & redundant reserves show as negatives

COAST NATIONAL INS CO — D+ Weak

Major Rating Factors: Weak overall results on stability tests (2.6 on a scale of 0 to 10) including potential drain of affiliation with Zurich Financial Services Group and negative cash flow from operations for 2008. Fair reserve development (4.5) as reserves have generally been sufficient to cover claims. In 2004, the two year reserve development was 33% deficient.

Other Rating Factors: Strong long-term capitalization index (10.0) based on excellent current risk adjusted capital (severe and moderate loss scenarios). Moreover, capital levels have been consistent in recent years. Excellent profitability (8.9) with operating gains in each of the last five years. Excellent expense controls. Excellent liquidity (7.6) with ample operational cash flow and liquid investments.

Principal Business: Auto liability (67%) and auto physical damage (33%).

Principal Investments: Investment grade bonds (92%) and misc. investments (11%).

Investments in Affiliates: 11%

Group Affiliation: Zurich Financial Services Group

Licensed in: AZ, CA, FL, GA, MS, NV, OR, PA, TN

Commenced Business: March 1987

Address: 5701 Stirling Road, Davie, FL 33314

Phone: (954) 316-5200 **Domicile State:** CA **NAIC Code:** 25089

Data Date	Rating	RACR #1	RACR #2	Loss Ratio %	Total Assets ($mil)	Capital ($mil)	Net Premium ($mil)	Net Income ($mil)
3-09	D+	8.16	7.35	N/A	559.1	360.8	0.0	2.7
3-08	D+	8.21	7.40	N/A	545.4	345.0	7.0	4.6
2008	D+	8.32	7.66	75.6	542.9	354.1	2.6	15.8
2007	D+	8.41	7.68	66.9	540.8	349.0	-177.5	69.2
2006	D+	1.75	1.56	65.7	774.7	328.1	549.8	23.5
2005	D	1.38	1.21	63.8	730.8	288.2	588.5	30.6
2004	D	1.34	1.08	68.0	566.0	249.4	372.2	16.4

Zurich Financial Services Group
Composite Group Rating: C-

Largest Group Members	Assets ($mil)	Rating
ZURICH AMERICAN INS CO	29634	C-
KEMPER INVESTORS LIFE INS CO	13886	C
FARMERS INS EXCHANGE	13368	C
FARMERS NEW WORLD LIFE INS CO	6444	B-
MID-CENTURY INS CO	3273	C-

COLISEUM REINS CO — C — Fair

Major Rating Factors: Fair reserve development (4.9 on a scale of 0 to 10) as reserves have generally been sufficient to cover claims. In 2004, the two year reserve development was 16% deficient. Fair overall results on stability tests (3.4) including weak results on operational trends and negative cash flow from operations for 2008. The largest net exposure for one risk is high at 4.0% of capital.

Other Rating Factors: Weak profitability index (2.7) with operating losses during 2008. Return on equity has been low, averaging 1.5% over the past five years. Strong long-term capitalization index (8.2) based on excellent current risk adjusted capital (severe and moderate loss scenarios), despite some fluctuation in capital levels. Superior liquidity (9.0) with ample operational cash flow and liquid investments.

Principal Business: (Not applicable due to unusual reinsurance transactions.)

Principal Investments: Misc. investments (53%), investment grade bonds (45%), and cash (2%).

Investments in Affiliates: -5%

Group Affiliation: AXA Ins Group

Licensed in: All states except FL, ME, MO, NH, PA, VT, VA, WV, WY, PR

Commenced Business: December 1978

Address: 1209 Orange St, Wilmington, DE 19801

Phone: (212) 493-9300 **Domicile State:** DE **NAIC Code:** 36552

Data Date	Rating	RACR #1	RACR #2	Loss Ratio %	Total Assets ($mil)	Capital ($mil)	Net Premium ($mil)	Net Income ($mil)
3-09	C	1.73	1.19	N/A	430.9	248.5	0.0	0.3
3-08	C	1.30	1.11	N/A	907.4	676.4	-0.1	-1.5
2008	C	2.94	2.01	N/A	618.9	430.5	-1.2	-4.6
2007	C	1.26	1.07	52.8	918.8	677.8	22.3	9.6
2006	C	1.33	1.15	101.4	932.2	653.8	15.9	0.7
2005	C	1.38	1.26	123.9	872.2	547.1	2.1	6.4
2004	C	1.40	1.27	79.4	994.6	571.6	9.0	36.2

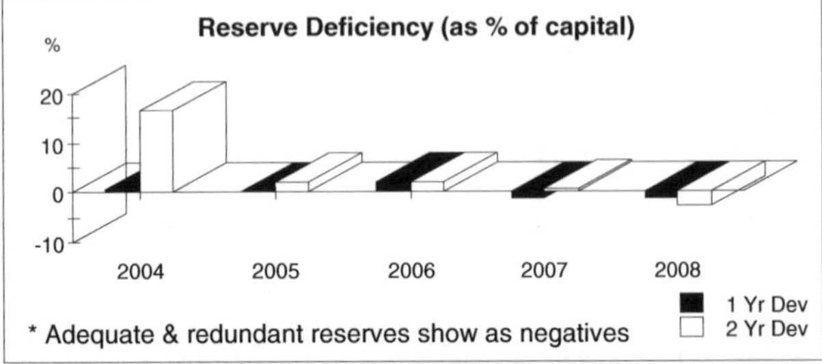

COLONY INS CO — C — Fair

Major Rating Factors: Fair overall results on stability tests (3.3 on a scale of 0 to 10) including potential drain of affiliation with Argo Group Intl Holdings Ltd and excessive premium growth. History of adequate reserve strength (5.9) as reserves have been consistently at an acceptable level.

Other Rating Factors: Good overall profitability index (6.4) despite operating losses during the first three months of 2008. Return on equity has been fair, averaging 7.4% over the past five years. Strong long-term capitalization index (7.0) based on excellent current risk adjusted capital (severe and moderate loss scenarios). Moreover, capital levels have been consistent in recent years. Excellent liquidity (7.1) with ample operational cash flow and liquid investments.

Principal Business: Other liability (54%), commercial multiple peril (15%), products liability (10%), allied lines (9%), auto liability (6%), auto physical damage (3%), and inland marine (1%).

Principal Investments: Investment grade bonds (81%), misc. investments (20%), and non investment grade bonds (1%).

Investments in Affiliates: 19%

Group Affiliation: Argo Group Intl Holdings Ltd

Licensed in: VA

Commenced Business: July 1981

Address: 9201 Forest Hill Ave, Ste 200, Richmond, VA 23235-6865

Phone: (804) 327-1700 **Domicile State:** VA **NAIC Code:** 39993

Data Date	Rating	RACR #1	RACR #2	Loss Ratio %	Total Assets ($mil)	Capital ($mil)	Net Premium ($mil)	Net Income ($mil)
3-09	C	1.65	1.09	N/A	1,390.5	394.1	57.9	-6.8
3-08	C	1.94	1.29	N/A	903.7	324.4	44.5	7.5
2008	C	1.99	1.52	51.9	1,040.3	382.9	150.0	24.6
2007	C	1.90	1.27	55.8	878.9	315.1	242.6	37.8
2006	C	1.84	1.22	54.4	789.3	282.3	274.7	26.2
2005	C	1.64	1.10	62.0	618.1	196.6	175.5	12.2
2004	C-	1.31	0.93	65.3	464.2	155.9	149.7	10.6

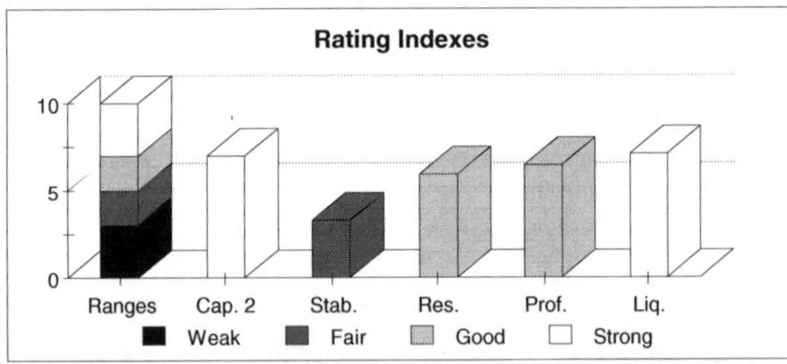

COLUMBIA CASUALTY CO — C — Fair

Major Rating Factors: Fair overall results on stability tests (3.5 on a scale of 0 to 10) including fair financial strength of affiliated CNA Financial Corp and fair results on operational trends.

Other Rating Factors: Strong long-term capitalization index (10.0) based on excellent current risk adjusted capital (severe and moderate loss scenarios). Moreover, capital levels have been consistent in recent years. Excellent profitability (7.8) with operating gains in each of the last five years. Superior liquidity (9.2) with ample operational cash flow and liquid investments.

Principal Business: Other liability (61%), medical malpractice (19%), products liability (15%), allied lines (2%), and inland marine (1%).

Principal Investments: Investment grade bonds (100%).

Investments in Affiliates: None

Group Affiliation: CNA Financial Corp

Licensed in: IL

Commenced Business: March 1974

Address: CNA Center, Chicago, IL 60685

Phone: (312) 822-5000 **Domicile State:** IL **NAIC Code:** 31127

Data Date	Rating	RACR #1	RACR #2	Loss Ratio %	Total Assets ($mil)	Capital ($mil)	Net Premium ($mil)	Net Income ($mil)
3-09	C	232.40	116.20	N/A	274.7	274.4	0.0	0.6
3-08	C	187.87	93.94	N/A	268.9	268.2	0.0	1.5
2008	C	753.19	376.60	0.0	274.1	273.9	0.0	8.8
2007	C	378.80	189.40	0.0	267.5	266.9	0.0	9.8
2006	C	359.39	179.70	0.0	256.3	256.3	0.0	5.1
2005	C-	97.83	48.91	0.0	132.0	132.0	0.0	6.0
2004	C-	127.10	63.57	0.0	124.9	124.9	0.0	3.8

CNA Financial Corp
Composite Group Rating: C

Largest Group Members	Assets ($mil)	Rating
CONTINENTAL CASUALTY CO	38650	C
CONTINENTAL INS CO	3748	C+
CONTINENTAL ASSURANCE CO	3334	C
WESTERN SURETY CO	1210	C
FIRST INS CO OF HI LTD	593	C+

COLUMBIA INS CO — C+ Fair

Data Date	Rating	RACR #1	RACR #2	Loss Ratio %	Total Assets ($mil)	Capital ($mil)	Net Premium ($mil)	Net Income ($mil)
3-09	C+	1.34	0.93	N/A	8,967.5	6,038.8	121.4	114.7
3-08	B-	1.86	1.25	N/A	13,433.4	8,784.9	115.5	149.7
2008	B-	1.63	1.13	48.9	11,050.0	7,370.6	486.5	661.0
2007	B-	1.85	1.25	30.3	13,419.4	8,736.6	558.5	1,265.3
2006	B-	1.38	0.97	47.8	13,360.5	7,986.4	679.4	706.6
2005	B-	1.02	0.77	120.0	13,710.3	8,846.0	2,161.8	4,339.4
2004	B-	2.45	1.70	37.0	10,281.8	7,451.3	383.9	500.0

Major Rating Factors: Fair reserve development (4.3 on a scale of 0 to 10) as the level of reserves has at times been insufficient to cover claims. In 2005 and 2006 the two year reserve development was 17% and 20% deficient respectively. Fair profitability index (3.8). Good expense controls. Return on equity has been fair, averaging 17.1% over the past five years.

Other Rating Factors: Fair overall results on stability tests (4.5) including fair financial strength of affiliated Berkshire-Hathaway and weak results on operational trends. The largest net exposure for one risk is acceptable at 2.1% of capital. Good long-term capitalization index (6.7) based on good current risk adjusted capital (moderate loss scenario), despite some fluctuation in capital levels. Excellent liquidity (7.7) with ample operational cash flow and liquid investments.

Principal Business: Auto liability (75%), auto physical damage (23%), inland marine (1%), and other liability (1%).

Principal Investments: Misc. investments (93%), investment grade bonds (5%), cash (1%), and non investment grade bonds (1%).

Investments in Affiliates: 12%

Group Affiliation: Berkshire-Hathaway

Licensed in: AK, AZ, CA, CO, DE, FL, ID, IL, IN, IA, LA, MN, MO, MT, NE, NV, NM, ND, OR, SC, SD, TN, TX, UT, VA, WA, WY

Commenced Business: January 1970

Address: 3024 Harney St, Omaha, NE 68131-3580

Phone: (402) 536-3000 **Domicile State:** NE **NAIC Code:** 27812

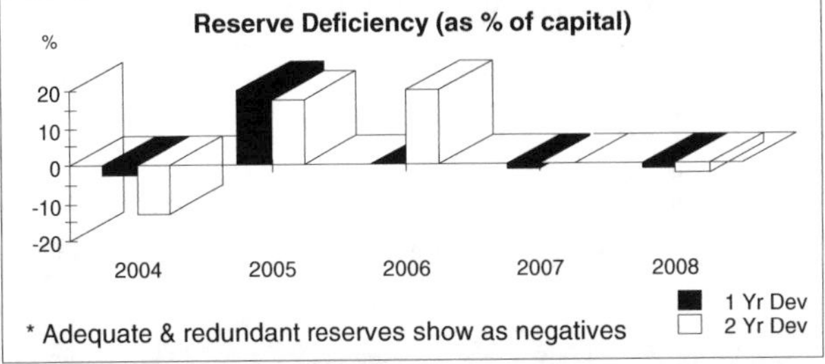

COMMERCE & INDUSTRY INS CO — C+ Fair

Data Date	Rating	RACR #1	RACR #2	Loss Ratio %	Total Assets ($mil)	Capital ($mil)	Net Premium ($mil)	Net Income ($mil)
3-09	C+	1.78	1.20	N/A	8,533.0	2,610.1	460.8	31.9
3-08	C+	1.85	1.23	N/A	9,078.0	2,779.1	512.3	-20.3
2008	C+	1.81	1.22	78.6	8,665.9	2,678.0	2,023.3	68.0
2007	C+	1.89	1.26	70.4	8,622.5	2,687.9	2,046.5	1,012.4
2006	C+	1.19	0.83	72.0	7,355.8	1,808.7	2,056.3	257.9
2005	C+	1.06	0.74	95.5	6,595.6	1,407.5	1,865.0	26.8
2004	B-	1.25	0.85	86.4	5,693.4	1,202.7	1,849.8	-50.4

Major Rating Factors: Fair overall results on stability tests (4.4 on a scale of 0 to 10). Strengths include potentially strong support from affiliation with American International Group. Good overall profitability index (6.7) despite operating losses during 2004. Return on equity has been good over the last five years, averaging 10.2%.

Other Rating Factors: Good liquidity (6.2) with sufficient resources (cash flows and marketable investments) to handle a spike in claims. A history of deficient reserves (2.0). Underreserving can have an adverse impact on capital and profits. Deficiencies in the two year reserve development occurred in three of the previous five years and ranged between 44% and 70%. Strong long-term capitalization index (7.0) based on excellent current risk adjusted capital (severe and moderate loss scenarios), despite some fluctuation in capital levels.

Principal Business: Workers compensation (64%), other liability (16%), auto liability (14%), auto physical damage (5%), and inland marine (1%).

Principal Investments: Investment grade bonds (76%) and misc. investments (24%).

Investments in Affiliates: 8%

Group Affiliation: American International Group

Licensed in: All states except PR

Commenced Business: December 1957

Address: 70 Pine St 3rd Floor, New York, NY 10270

Phone: (212) 770-7000 **Domicile State:** NY **NAIC Code:** 19410

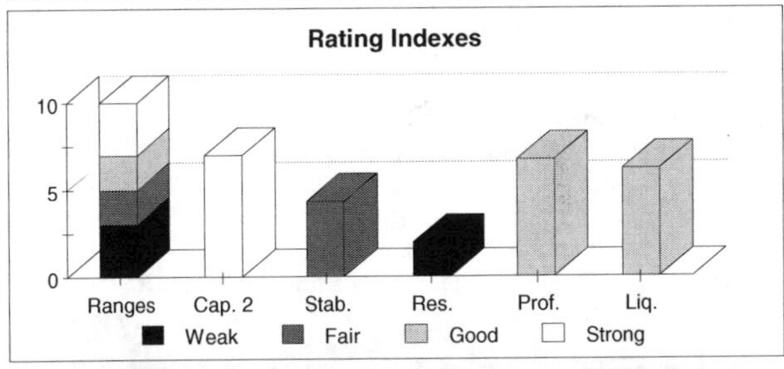

COMMERCE INS CO * — B+ Good

Data Date	Rating	RACR #1	RACR #2	Loss Ratio %	Total Assets ($mil)	Capital ($mil)	Net Premium ($mil)	Net Income ($mil)
3-09	B+	3.35	2.78	N/A	2,513.5	931.3	311.7	27.4
3-08	B+	3.42	2.86	N/A	2,951.0	1,137.0	334.8	17.8
2008	B+	3.35	2.85	68.0	2,579.4	977.8	1,279.8	86.0
2007	B+	3.25	2.80	63.9	2,878.1	1,127.8	1,357.2	178.3
2006	B+	2.95	2.40	59.9	3,113.0	1,205.9	1,452.9	186.9
2005	B+	2.74	2.22	60.8	2,924.8	1,173.0	1,382.0	181.9
2004	B+	2.33	1.86	62.8	2,654.0	1,031.8	1,296.6	206.3

Major Rating Factors: Good liquidity (5.9 on a scale of 0 to 10) with sufficient resources (cash flows and marketable investments) to handle a spike in claims. Good overall results on stability tests (5.0). Stability strengths include good operational trends and excellent risk diversification.

Other Rating Factors: Strong long-term capitalization index (9.7) based on excellent current risk adjusted capital (severe and moderate loss scenarios), despite some fluctuation in capital levels. Ample reserve history (8.2) that helps to protect the company against sharp claims increases. Fair profitability index (3.5). Fair expense controls. Return on equity has been fair, averaging 15.0% over the past five years.

Principal Business: Auto liability (57%), auto physical damage (35%), homeowners multiple peril (6%), commercial multiple peril (1%), and fire (1%).

Principal Investments: Investment grade bonds (73%), misc. investments (15%), cash (6%), non investment grade bonds (3%), and real estate (3%).

Investments in Affiliates: 6%

Group Affiliation: MAPFRE Ins Group

Licensed in: CT, ME, MA, NH, RI, VT

Commenced Business: May 1972

Address: 211 W Main St, Webster, MA 01570-0758

Phone: (508) 949-9000 **Domicile State:** MA **NAIC Code:** 34754

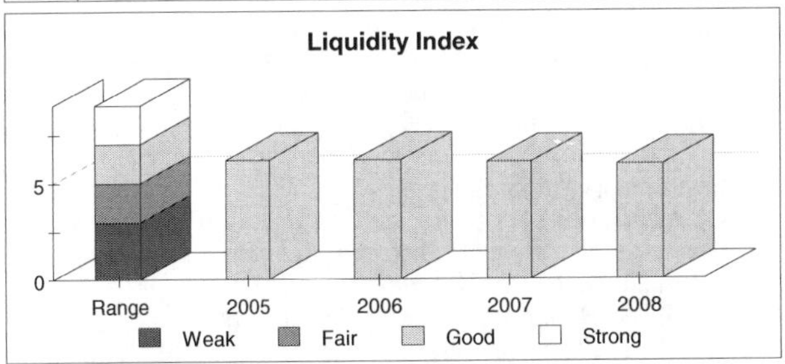

COMMONWEALTH MORTGAGE ASR CO OF TX — C — Fair

Major Rating Factors: Fair reserve development (4.5 on a scale of 0 to 10) as reserves have generally been sufficient to cover claims. In 2004, the one year reserve development was 23% deficient. Fair overall results on stability tests (4.2) including excessive premium growth and weak results on operational trends.

Other Rating Factors: Weak profitability index (2.1) with operating losses during 2004, 2005, 2007 and the first three months of 2008. Average return on equity over the last five years has been poor at -35.9%. Good long-term capitalization index (6.1) based on good current risk adjusted capital (moderate loss scenario). Good liquidity (6.5) with sufficient resources (cash flows and marketable investments) to handle a spike in claims.

Principal Business: (This company is a reinsurer.)

Principal Investments: Misc. investments (61%) and investment grade bonds (39%).

Investments in Affiliates: None

Group Affiliation: Radian Group Inc

Licensed in: TX

Commenced Business: January 1994

Address: 1601 Market Street, 12th Floor, Philadelphia, PA 19910

Phone: (800) 523-1988 **Domicile State:** TX **NAIC Code:** 15909

Data Date	Rating	RACR #1	RACR #2	Loss Ratio %	Total Assets ($mil)	Capital ($mil)	Net Premium ($mil)	Net Income ($mil)
3-09	C	1.03	0.80	N/A	573.8	183.2	21.9	-11.0
3-08	C	3.48	2.66	N/A	331.3	188.1	9.4	-27.4
2008	C	1.18	0.91	291.7	587.1	194.2	86.7	-160.9
2007	C	4.78	3.75	181.7	330.9	200.2	46.5	-87.8
2006	C	5.73	4.28	131.7	333.3	242.0	39.9	15.0
2005	C	3.84	2.90	199.9	204.0	127.9	30.8	-31.2
2004	B-	3.16	2.40	231.4	145.5	82.6	23.3	-30.9

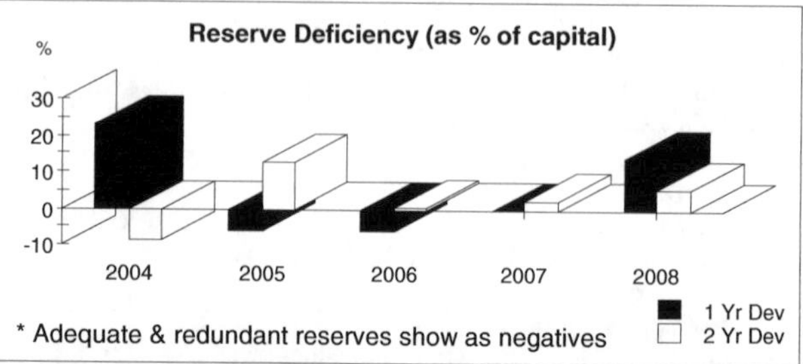

COMPANION PROPERTY & CASUALTY INS CO — B — Good

Major Rating Factors: History of adequate reserve strength (5.7 on a scale of 0 to 10) as reserves have been consistently at an acceptable level. Good overall results on stability tests (5.9). Stability strengths include good operational trends and excellent risk diversification.

Other Rating Factors: Strong long-term capitalization index (8.3) based on excellent current risk adjusted capital (severe and moderate loss scenarios). Moreover, capital levels have been consistent in recent years. Excellent profitability (7.4) with operating gains in each of the last five years. Excellent liquidity (7.5) with ample operational cash flow and liquid investments.

Principal Business: Workers compensation (66%), commercial multiple peril (9%), homeowners multiple peril (7%), other liability (6%), surety (4%), inland marine (4%), and auto liability (3%).

Principal Investments: Investment grade bonds (60%) and misc. investments (40%).

Investments in Affiliates: 11%

Group Affiliation: Blue Cross Blue Shield of SC Group

Licensed in: AL, AZ, AR, CO, DC, DE, FL, GA, IL, IN, IA, KS, KY, LA, MD, MI, MS, MO, NE, NV, NJ, NC, OH, OK, OR, PA, SC, TN, TX, VT, VA, WV, WI

Commenced Business: July 1984

Address: 51 Clemson Road, Columbia, SC 29223

Phone: (803) 735-0672 **Domicile State:** SC **NAIC Code:** 12157

Data Date	Rating	RACR #1	RACR #2	Loss Ratio %	Total Assets ($mil)	Capital ($mil)	Net Premium ($mil)	Net Income ($mil)
3-09	B	3.01	2.26	N/A	536.7	196.1	33.1	2.9
3-08	B	3.09	2.13	N/A	464.4	153.8	31.1	3.1
2008	B	2.84	2.15	60.7	506.6	179.5	152.3	9.9
2007	B	3.25	2.26	66.9	456.7	151.1	126.4	13.3
2006	B-	2.28	1.56	69.2	384.6	112.4	127.2	11.2
2005	B-	1.22	0.87	76.8	356.8	88.5	153.3	4.7
2004	B-	1.10	0.78	79.8	302.8	86.1	140.5	2.0

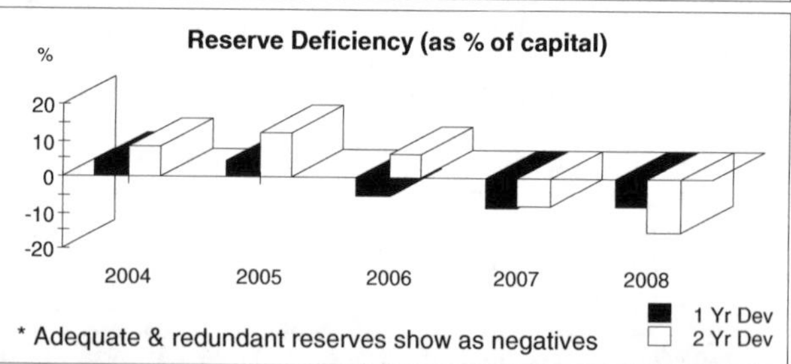

CONTINENTAL CASUALTY CO — C — Fair

Major Rating Factors: Fair reserve development (3.1 on a scale of 0 to 10) as the level of reserves has at times been insufficient to cover claims. Deficiencies in the two year reserve development occurred in three of the previous five years and ranged between 19% and 56%. Fair overall results on stability tests (3.9) including fair financial strength of affiliated CNA Financial Corp.

Other Rating Factors: Good overall profitability index (5.2) despite operating losses during the first three months of 2008. Return on equity has been fair, averaging 5.1% over the past five years. Good liquidity (6.9) with sufficient resources (cash flows and marketable investments) to handle a spike in claims. Strong long-term capitalization index (7.1) based on excellent current risk adjusted capital (severe and moderate loss scenarios), despite some fluctuation in capital levels.

Principal Business: Other liability (31%), inland marine (27%), other accident & health (10%), allied lines (5%), commercial multiple peril (5%), medical malpractice (5%), and other lines (17%).

Principal Investments: Investment grade bonds (72%), misc. investments (21%), and non investment grade bonds (7%).

Investments in Affiliates: 10%

Group Affiliation: CNA Financial Corp

Licensed in: All states, the District of Columbia and Puerto Rico

Commenced Business: December 1897

Address: 333 S Wabash Ave, Chicago, IL 60604

Phone: (312) 822-5000 **Domicile State:** IL **NAIC Code:** 20443

Data Date	Rating	RACR #1	RACR #2	Loss Ratio %	Total Assets ($mil)	Capital ($mil)	Net Premium ($mil)	Net Income ($mil)
3-09	C	1.62	1.11	N/A	38,541.1	7,750.5	1,442.4	-269.7
3-08	C	1.37	0.97	N/A	38,395.2	7,933.3	1,391.9	190.9
2008	C	1.63	1.13	87.0	38,649.5	7,819.0	6,135.3	459.5
2007	C	1.45	1.04	82.6	38,899.6	8,348.0	6,453.6	350.1
2006	C	1.34	0.94	80.9	38,198.4	7,939.4	6,808.0	513.6
2005	C	1.09	0.78	94.3	35,903.4	6,733.5	6,752.7	394.2
2004	C	1.10	0.86	78.1	34,211.8	6,815.3	7,028.4	521.4

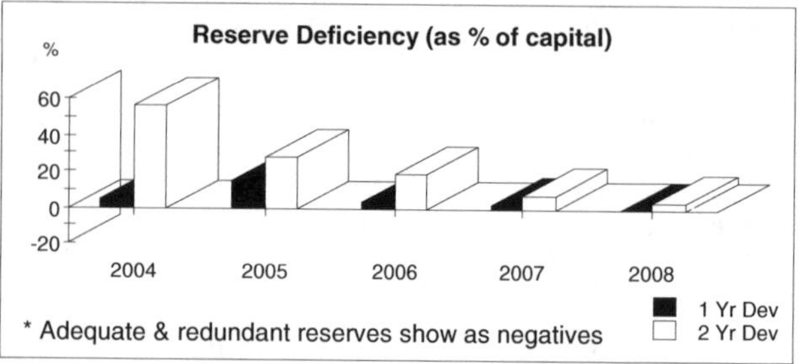

CONTINENTAL INS CO — C+ Fair

Major Rating Factors: Fair overall results on stability tests (4.5 on a scale of 0 to 10) including potential drain of affiliation with CNA Financial Corp and fair results on operational trends. The largest net exposure for one risk is conservative at 1.8% of capital. Fair profitability index (3.5). Weak expense controls. Return on equity has been low, averaging 4.7% over the past five years.

Other Rating Factors: Strong long-term capitalization index (10.0) based on excellent current risk adjusted capital (severe and moderate loss scenarios), despite some fluctuation in capital levels. Ample reserve history (7.3) that can protect against increases in claims costs. Superior liquidity (10.0) with ample operational cash flow and liquid investments.

Principal Business: Other liability (28%), workers compensation (20%), ocean marine (19%), commercial multiple peril (10%), auto liability (8%), fidelity (2%), and other lines (12%).

Principal Investments: Investment grade bonds (87%), misc. investments (7%), and non investment grade bonds (6%).

Investments in Affiliates: 7%

Group Affiliation: CNA Financial Corp

Licensed in: All states, the District of Columbia and Puerto Rico

Commenced Business: December 1977

Address: 1320 Main St Suite 1700, Columbia, SC 29201

Phone: (312) 822-5000 **Domicile State:** PA **NAIC Code:** 35289

Data Date	Rating	RACR #1	RACR #2	Loss Ratio %	Total Assets ($mil)	Capital ($mil)	Net Premium ($mil)	Net Income ($mil)
3-09	C+	5.57	4.31	N/A	3,668.1	1,426.5	0.0	9.8
3-08	C+	7.97	6.45	N/A	4,292.3	2,098.7	0.0	28.5
2008	C+	6.05	4.76	0.0	3,747.6	1,509.3	0.0	95.5
2007	C+	8.18	6.82	0.0	4,258.8	2,069.8	0.0	106.9
2006	C	8.82	7.76	N/A	4,057.4	1,925.4	3.6	102.3
2005	C	1.73	1.68	0.0	4,023.2	1,766.9	0.0	68.8
2004	C	1.68	1.62	0.0	3,896.6	1,685.8	0.0	51.4

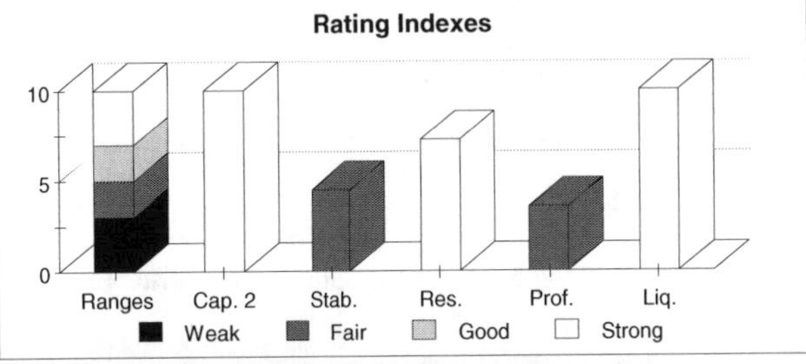

COOPERATIVA D SEGUROS MULTIPLES D PR * — A- Excellent

Major Rating Factors: Strong long-term capitalization index (8.1 on a scale of 0 to 10) based on excellent current risk adjusted capital (severe and moderate loss scenarios), despite some fluctuation in capital levels. History of adequate reserve strength (6.2) as reserves have been consistently at an acceptable level.

Other Rating Factors: Good liquidity (6.7) with sufficient resources (cash flows and marketable investments) to handle a spike in claims. Good overall results on stability tests (6.8) despite negative cash flow from operations for 2008. Stability strengths include good operational trends and excellent risk diversification. Fair profitability index (3.5) with operating losses during the first three months of 2008. Return on equity has been low, averaging 2.1% over the past five years.

Principal Business: Auto physical damage (47%), auto liability (19%), commercial multiple peril (10%), allied lines (5%), homeowners multiple peril (4%), earthquake (4%), and other lines (11%).

Principal Investments: Investment grade bonds (49%), misc. investments (40%), cash (8%), and real estate (3%).

Investments in Affiliates: 16%

Group Affiliation: Cooperativa de Seguros Multiples

Licensed in: FL, PR

Commenced Business: February 1965

Address: 38 Nevarez St/Americo Miranda, Rio Piedras, PR 00927

Phone: (787) 758-8585 **Domicile State:** PR **NAIC Code:** 18163

Data Date	Rating	RACR #1	RACR #2	Loss Ratio %	Total Assets ($mil)	Capital ($mil)	Net Premium ($mil)	Net Income ($mil)
3-09	A-	2.26	1.80	N/A	455.9	205.3	37.2	-4.1
3-08	A-	2.65	2.03	N/A	515.8	246.1	41.1	2.7
2008	A-	2.33	1.85	63.1	469.4	214.1	151.2	0.3
2007	A-	2.66	2.04	67.9	513.2	244.1	165.8	13.0
2006	A-	2.50	1.89	69.8	528.6	222.2	180.0	9.5
2005	A-	2.38	1.81	72.3	537.1	208.5	188.4	5.4
2004	A-	2.69	2.06	78.5	545.9	207.5	186.0	1.4

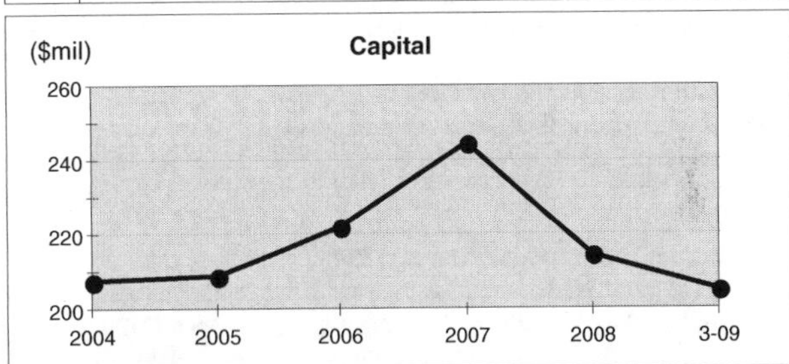

COPIC INS CO * — B+ Good

Major Rating Factors: Good overall results on stability tests (6.4 on a scale of 0 to 10). Stability strengths include good operational trends and excellent risk diversification. The largest net exposure for one risk is acceptable at 2.3% of capital. Strong long-term capitalization index (7.3) based on excellent current risk adjusted capital (severe and moderate loss scenarios), despite some fluctuation in capital levels.

Other Rating Factors: Ample reserve history (7.0) that can protect against increases in claims costs. Excellent liquidity (7.1) with ample operational cash flow and liquid investments. Fair profitability index (3.0) with operating losses during the first three months of 2008. Return on equity has been low, averaging 2.7% over the past five years.

Principal Business: Medical malpractice (94%), group accident & health (3%), and other liability (3%).

Principal Investments: Investment grade bonds (76%), misc. investments (22%), and cash (2%).

Investments in Affiliates: None

Group Affiliation: COPIC Trust

Licensed in: AZ, CO, ID, IA, KS, MT, NE, UT, WY

Commenced Business: September 1984

Address: 7800 E Dorado Pl Suite 200, Englewood, CO 80111

Phone: (303) 779-0044 **Domicile State:** CO **NAIC Code:** 11860

Data Date	Rating	RACR #1	RACR #2	Loss Ratio %	Total Assets ($mil)	Capital ($mil)	Net Premium ($mil)	Net Income ($mil)
3-09	B+	1.55	1.15	N/A	435.6	121.5	24.3	-11.1
3-08	B+	1.60	1.17	N/A	456.1	142.0	24.5	3.5
2008	B+	1.71	1.26	51.4	439.5	132.7	100.9	-16.1
2007	B+	1.71	1.24	70.9	460.5	150.5	100.7	20.5
2006	B	1.55	1.22	70.9	434.2	143.8	104.1	12.6
2005	B	1.46	1.10	73.6	390.0	123.3	104.0	7.7
2004	B	1.74	1.26	81.0	333.7	110.0	86.0	7.5

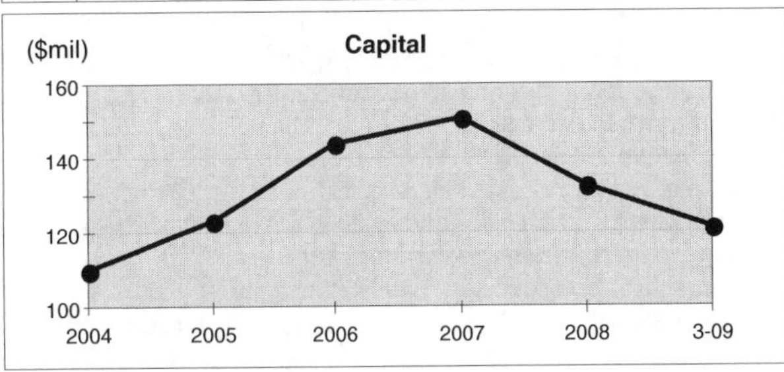

CORNHUSKER CASUALTY CO * B+ Good

Major Rating Factors: Strong long-term capitalization index (8.7 on a scale of 0 to 10) based on excellent current risk adjusted capital (severe and moderate loss scenarios), despite some fluctuation in capital levels. Ample reserve history (7.5) that can protect against increases in claims costs.

Other Rating Factors: Excellent liquidity (8.6) with ample operational cash flow and liquid investments. Fair profitability index (4.6). Fair expense controls. Return on equity has been fair, averaging 11.0% over the past five years. Good overall results on stability tests (5.3). Stability strengths include good operational trends and excellent risk diversification.

Principal Business: Auto liability (40%), workers compensation (26%), auto physical damage (13%), other liability (6%), products liability (5%), commercial multiple peril (4%), and other lines (5%).

Principal Investments: Misc. investments (57%), investment grade bonds (26%), non investment grade bonds (12%), and cash (5%).

Investments in Affiliates: None

Group Affiliation: Berkshire-Hathaway

Licensed in: AK, AR, CA, CO, ID, IA, KS, MS, NE, NC, OR, SC, SD, VA, WA, WI, WY

Commenced Business: February 1970

Address: 9290 W Dodge Rd, Omaha, NE 68114-3363

Phone: (402) 393-7255 **Domicile State:** NE **NAIC Code:** 20044

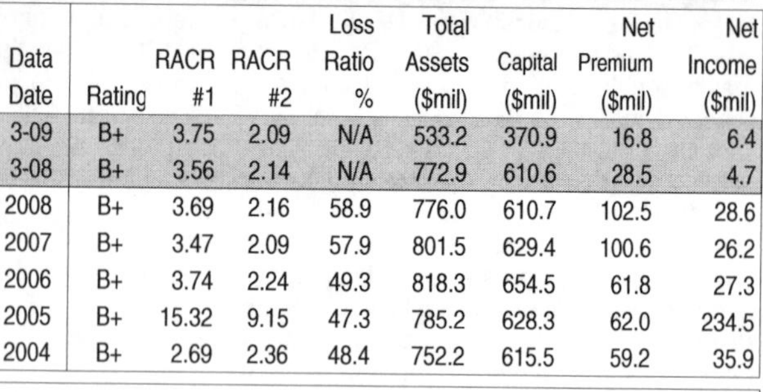

Data Date	Rating	RACR #1	RACR #2	Loss Ratio %	Total Assets ($mil)	Capital ($mil)	Net Premium ($mil)	Net Income ($mil)
3-09	B+	3.75	2.09	N/A	533.2	370.9	16.8	6.4
3-08	B+	3.56	2.14	N/A	772.9	610.6	28.5	4.7
2008	B+	3.69	2.16	58.9	776.0	610.7	102.5	28.6
2007	B+	3.47	2.09	57.9	801.5	629.4	100.6	26.2
2006	B+	3.74	2.24	49.3	818.3	654.5	61.8	27.3
2005	B+	15.32	9.15	47.3	785.2	628.3	62.0	234.5
2004	B+	2.69	2.36	48.4	752.2	615.5	59.2	35.9

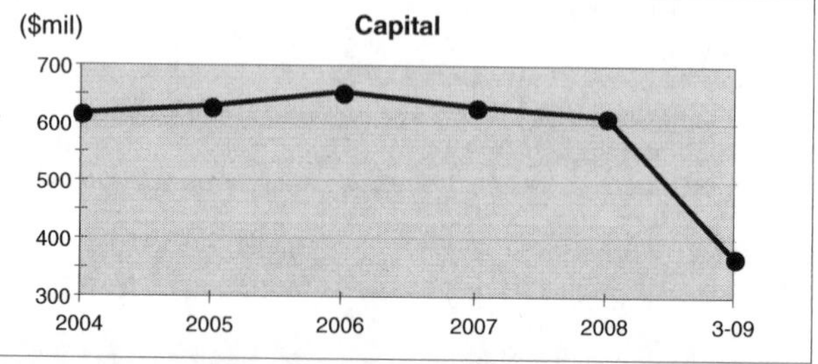

COUNTRY CASUALTY INS CO * B+ Good

Major Rating Factors: Good overall results on stability tests (6.3 on a scale of 0 to 10). Strengths include potential support from affiliation with COUNTRY Financial, good operational trends and excellent risk diversification. Strong long-term capitalization index (10.0) based on excellent current risk adjusted capital (severe and moderate loss scenarios), despite some fluctuation in capital levels.

Other Rating Factors: Excellent profitability (7.4) with operating gains in each of the last five years. Excellent expense controls. Excellent liquidity (7.0) with ample operational cash flow and liquid investments.

Principal Business: Auto liability (38%), homeowners multiple peril (26%), auto physical damage (18%), commercial multiple peril (12%), other liability (4%), workers compensation (1%), and inland marine (1%).

Principal Investments: Investment grade bonds (99%) and misc. investments (1%).

Investments in Affiliates: None

Group Affiliation: COUNTRY Financial

Licensed in: AL, AK, AZ, AR, CO, CT, DE, FL, GA, ID, IL, IN, IA, KS, KY, ME, MD, MA, MI, MN, MO, MT, NE, NV, NM, ND, OH, OK, OR, PA, RI, SD, TN, TX, WA, WI, WY

Commenced Business: March 1964

Address: 1701 N. Towanda Ave, Bloomington, IL 61701

Phone: (309) 821-3000 **Domicile State:** IL **NAIC Code:** 20982

Data Date	Rating	RACR #1	RACR #2	Loss Ratio %	Total Assets ($mil)	Capital ($mil)	Net Premium ($mil)	Net Income ($mil)
3-09	B+	20.93	18.84	N/A	75.7	61.1	0.0	0.3
3-08	B+	17.73	15.96	N/A	78.5	59.8	0.0	0.3
2008	B+	20.26	18.23	0.0	76.0	60.8	0.0	1.4
2007	B+	18.56	16.70	0.0	76.5	59.4	0.0	1.7
2006	B+	18.60	16.74	0.0	73.8	57.6	0.0	1.4
2005	B+	17.35	15.62	0.0	74.1	56.5	0.0	1.6
2004	B+	17.61	15.85	0.0	71.5	55.0	0.0	1.8

COUNTRY Financial Composite Group Rating: A+ Largest Group Members	Assets ($mil)	Rating
COUNTRY LIFE INS CO	7271	A+
COUNTRY MUTUAL INS CO	3378	A
COTTON STATES LIFE INS CO	281	B+
MIDDLESEX MUTUAL ASR CO	252	B-
COTTON STATES MUTUAL INS CO	245	C

COUNTRY MUTUAL INS CO * A Excellent

Major Rating Factors: Strong long-term capitalization index (9.5 on a scale of 0 to 10) based on excellent current risk adjusted capital (severe and moderate loss scenarios). Furthermore, this high level of risk adjusted capital has been consistently maintained in previous years. Ample reserve history (7.5) that can protect against increases in claims costs.

Other Rating Factors: Excellent overall results on stability tests (7.6). Stability strengths include excellent operational trends and excellent risk diversification. Good overall profitability index (5.9). Fair expense controls. Good liquidity (5.7) with sufficient resources (cash flows and marketable investments) to handle a spike in claims.

Principal Business: Homeowners multiple peril (31%), auto liability (22%), auto physical damage (15%), allied lines (12%), farmowners multiple peril (8%), workers compensation (5%), and other lines (8%).

Principal Investments: Investment grade bonds (78%), misc. investments (20%), cash (1%), and non investment grade bonds (1%).

Investments in Affiliates: 4%

Group Affiliation: COUNTRY Financial

Licensed in: AL, AK, AZ, AR, CO, CT, DE, FL, GA, ID, IL, IN, IA, KS, KY, ME, MA, MI, MN, MO, MT, NE, NV, ND, OK, OR, PA, RI, SD, TN, TX, WA, WI, WY

Commenced Business: November 1925

Address: 1701 N. Towanda Ave, Bloomington, IL 61701

Phone: (309) 821-3000 **Domicile State:** IL **NAIC Code:** 20990

Data Date	Rating	RACR #1	RACR #2	Loss Ratio %	Total Assets ($mil)	Capital ($mil)	Net Premium ($mil)	Net Income ($mil)
3-09	A	3.64	2.68	N/A	3,364.1	1,375.3	411.3	5.2
3-08	A	4.00	2.91	N/A	3,450.7	1,552.6	416.6	6.5
2008	A	3.65	2.66	75.4	3,378.4	1,416.2	1,802.4	8.6
2007	A	4.04	2.92	66.9	3,464.3	1,577.0	1,763.0	133.5
2006	A	3.59	2.62	68.1	3,321.1	1,445.3	1,795.2	114.5
2005	A	3.20	2.34	64.0	3,068.8	1,308.3	1,783.3	124.2
2004	A	3.56	2.65	62.7	2,756.3	1,199.2	1,496.8	122.7

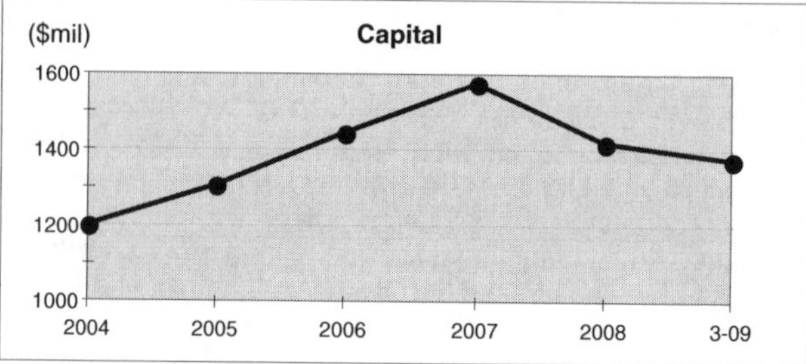

CUMBERLAND MUTUAL FIRE INS CO * B+ Good

Major Rating Factors: Good overall results on stability tests (5.2 on a scale of 0 to 10) despite potential drain of affiliation with Cumberland Group and negative cash flow from operations for 2008. History of adequate reserve strength (6.1) as reserves have been consistently at an acceptable level.

Other Rating Factors: Good liquidity (6.8) with sufficient resources (cash flows and marketable investments) to handle a spike in claims. Strong long-term capitalization index (9.4) based on excellent current risk adjusted capital (severe and moderate loss scenarios), despite some fluctuation in capital levels. Fair profitability index (4.3) with operating losses during 2005 and the first three months of 2008.

Principal Business: Homeowners multiple peril (60%), commercial multiple peril (20%), fire (7%), allied lines (5%), other liability (3%), boiler & machinery (2%), and other lines (3%).

Principal Investments: Investment grade bonds (74%), misc. investments (16%), real estate (6%), and cash (4%).

Investments in Affiliates: 9%

Group Affiliation: Cumberland Group

Licensed in: DE, MD, NJ, OH, PA

Commenced Business: May 1844

Address: 633 Shiloh Pike, Bridgeton, NJ 08302

Phone: (609) 451-4050 **Domicile State:** NJ **NAIC Code:** 13684

Data Date	Rating	RACR #1	RACR #2	Loss Ratio %	Total Assets ($mil)	Capital ($mil)	Net Premium ($mil)	Net Income ($mil)
3-09	B+	3.46	2.54	N/A	245.0	132.9	20.3	-5.2
3-08	B+	3.42	2.39	N/A	259.5	141.5	21.4	0.1
2008	B+	3.70	2.68	64.4	249.4	140.2	84.3	2.8
2007	B+	3.46	2.43	66.5	261.6	140.4	85.5	4.2
2006	B+	3.20	2.32	58.5	261.7	139.8	88.3	11.5
2005	B+	2.84	1.95	76.0	249.8	128.5	89.2	-1.6
2004	B+	3.04	2.17	72.7	233.5	130.8	79.4	1.8

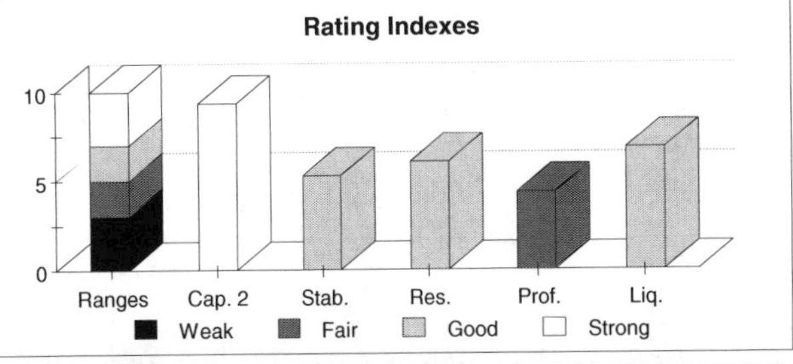

CUMIS INS SOCIETY INC * B+ Good

Major Rating Factors: Good overall results on stability tests (6.2 on a scale of 0 to 10). Stability strengths include good operational trends and excellent risk diversification. The largest net exposure for one risk is acceptable at 2.3% of capital. Strong long-term capitalization index (7.4) based on excellent current risk adjusted capital (severe and moderate loss scenarios), despite some fluctuation in capital levels.

Other Rating Factors: Ample reserve history (9.3) that helps to protect the company against sharp claims increases. Fair profitability index (4.6) with operating losses during the first three months of 2008. Return on equity has been fair, averaging 7.3% over the past five years. Fair liquidity (3.3) as cash resources may not be adequate to cover a spike in claims.

Principal Business: Other liability (22%), fidelity (18%), auto physical damage (18%), allied lines (14%), commercial multiple peril (12%), inland marine (9%), and other lines (7%).

Principal Investments: Investment grade bonds (70%), misc. investments (26%), non investment grade bonds (3%), and cash (1%).

Investments in Affiliates: 5%

Group Affiliation: CUNA Mutual Ins Group

Licensed in: All states, the District of Columbia and Puerto Rico

Commenced Business: June 1960

Address: 5910 Mineral Point Rd, Madison, WI 53705

Phone: (608) 238-5851 **Domicile State:** IA **NAIC Code:** 10847

Data Date	Rating	RACR #1	RACR #2	Loss Ratio %	Total Assets ($mil)	Capital ($mil)	Net Premium ($mil)	Net Income ($mil)
3-09	B+	1.93	1.25	N/A	1,228.8	413.8	156.5	-28.6
3-08	B+	2.52	1.62	N/A	1,346.9	497.3	157.9	1.7
2008	B+	1.95	1.26	65.1	1,323.5	448.8	850.5	30.5
2007	B+	2.63	1.69	59.1	1,301.7	508.4	710.4	80.7
2006	B+	2.49	1.71	64.1	1,173.0	460.9	569.9	44.8
2005	B+	2.22	1.59	68.7	1,057.2	414.7	506.7	11.7
2004	B+	2.56	1.88	60.0	973.2	402.8	437.9	41.0

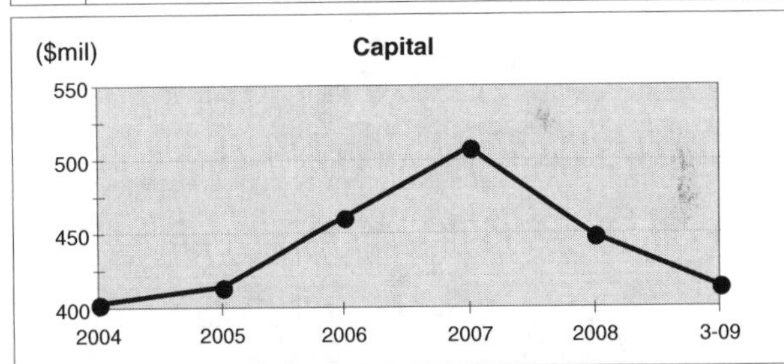

CYPRESS INS CO B- Good

Major Rating Factors: Good overall results on stability tests (5.3 on a scale of 0 to 10) despite potential drain of affiliation with Berkshire-Hathaway, excessive premium growth and fair results on operational trends. Good overall profitability index (5.5) despite operating losses during the first three months of 2008. Return on equity has been good over the last five years, averaging 17.5%.

Other Rating Factors: Strong long-term capitalization index (7.4) based on excellent current risk adjusted capital (severe and moderate loss scenarios), despite some fluctuation in capital levels. Ample reserve history (8.7) that helps to protect the company against sharp claims increases. Superior liquidity (9.0) with ample operational cash flow and liquid investments.

Principal Business: Workers compensation (88%), auto liability (6%), auto physical damage (2%), other liability (2%), fire (1%), and allied lines (1%).

Principal Investments: Investment grade bonds (69%), misc. investments (25%), cash (3%), and non investment grade bonds (3%).

Investments in Affiliates: None

Group Affiliation: Berkshire-Hathaway

Licensed in: AR, CA, GA, ID, MS, NM, SC, TN

Commenced Business: March 1963

Address: 395 Oyster Point Blvd.,Ste 401, S.san Francisco, CA 94080

Phone: (402) 393-7255 **Domicile State:** CA **NAIC Code:** 10855

Data Date	Rating	RACR #1	RACR #2	Loss Ratio %	Total Assets ($mil)	Capital ($mil)	Net Premium ($mil)	Net Income ($mil)
3-09	B-	1.59	1.06	N/A	582.9	208.6	57.6	-3.9
3-08	B	2.84	1.62	N/A	536.9	260.2	26.8	0.2
2008	B	2.06	1.35	80.6	594.4	239.1	196.7	-5.6
2007	B	2.95	1.69	63.5	529.1	263.2	94.2	16.1
2006	B	2.86	1.69	53.8	520.3	228.5	109.3	110.7
2005	B	1.74	1.31	62.8	432.4	238.5	92.3	96.2
2004	B	1.82	1.41	75.8	347.6	203.0	43.9	1.9

Berkshire-Hathaway Composite Group Rating: C Largest Group Members	Assets ($mil)	Rating
NATIONAL INDEMNITY CO	61720	C+
GENERAL REINSURANCE CORP	14446	B-
GOVERNMENT EMPLOYEES INS CO	12496	B+
COLUMBIA INS CO	11050	C+
GEICO INDEMNITY CO	4873	B+

DAIRYLAND INS CO * A+ Excellent

Major Rating Factors: Strong long-term capitalization index (9.9 on a scale of 0 to 10) based on excellent current risk adjusted capital (severe and moderate loss scenarios). Furthermore, this high level of risk adjusted capital has been consistently maintained in previous years. Ample reserve history (9.3) that helps to protect the company against sharp claims increases.

Other Rating Factors: Excellent overall results on stability tests (7.4). Stability strengths include good operational trends and excellent risk diversification. Good overall profitability index (6.8). Fair expense controls. Return on equity has been good over the last five years, averaging 10.0%. Good liquidity (6.7) with sufficient resources (cash flows and marketable investments) to handle a spike in claims.

Principal Business: Auto liability (74%) and auto physical damage (26%).

Principal Investments: Investment grade bonds (98%) and misc. investments (2%).

Investments in Affiliates: None

Group Affiliation: Sentry Ins Group

Licensed in: All states except CA, DC, HI, LA, NJ, OK, PR

Commenced Business: February 1953

Address: 1800 North Point Dr, Stevens Point, WI 54481

Phone: (715) 346-6000 **Domicile State:** WI **NAIC Code:** 21164

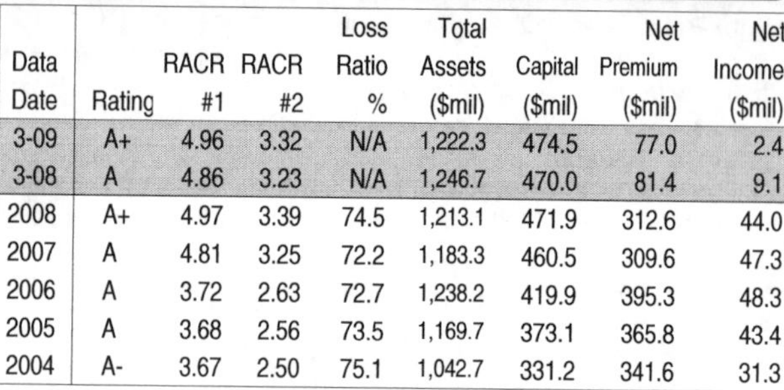

Data Date	Rating	RACR #1	RACR #2	Loss Ratio %	Total Assets ($mil)	Capital ($mil)	Net Premium ($mil)	Net Income ($mil)
3-09	A+	4.96	3.32	N/A	1,222.3	474.5	77.0	2.4
3-08	A	4.86	3.23	N/A	1,246.7	470.0	81.4	9.1
2008	A+	4.97	3.39	74.5	1,213.1	471.9	312.6	44.0
2007	A	4.81	3.25	72.2	1,183.3	460.5	309.6	47.3
2006	A	3.72	2.63	72.7	1,238.2	419.9	395.3	48.3
2005	A	3.68	2.56	73.5	1,169.7	373.1	365.8	43.4
2004	A-	3.67	2.50	75.1	1,042.7	331.2	341.6	31.3

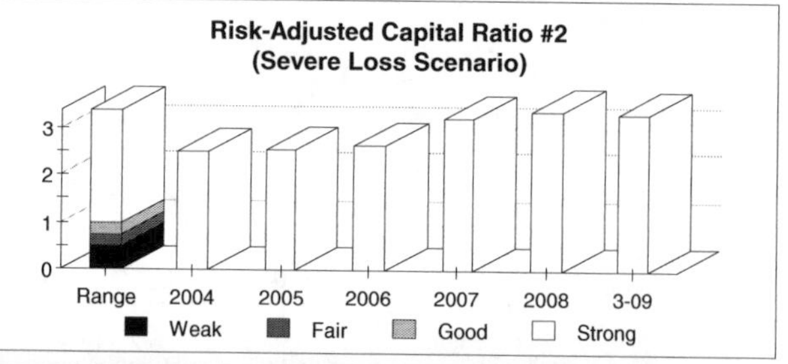

DARWIN NATIONAL ASR CO C Fair

Major Rating Factors: Fair overall results on stability tests (4.2 on a scale of 0 to 10). The largest net exposure for one risk is conservative at 1.8% of capital. History of adequate reserve strength (6.9) as reserves have been consistently at an acceptable level.

Other Rating Factors: Good overall profitability index (5.5) despite operating losses during 2004 and 2005. Return on equity has been low, averaging 4.9% over the past five years. Strong long-term capitalization (7.1) based on excellent current risk adjusted capital (severe and moderate loss scenarios) reflecting improvement over results in 2008. Excellent liquidity (7.1) with ample operational cash flow and liquid investments.

Principal Business: Other liability (75%) and medical malpractice (25%).

Principal Investments: Investment grade bonds (87%), misc. investments (12%), and cash (1%).

Investments in Affiliates: 9%

Group Affiliation: Allied World Asr Holding Group

Licensed in: All states except CA, WY, PR

Commenced Business: January 1972

Address: 10 Exchange Place, Jersey City, NJ 07302-3905

Phone: (201) 521-1200 **Domicile State:** DE **NAIC Code:** 16624

Data Date	Rating	RACR #1	RACR #2	Loss Ratio %	Total Assets ($mil)	Capital ($mil)	Net Premium ($mil)	Net Income ($mil)
3-09	C	2.11	1.27	N/A	687.3	266.4	43.6	16.1
3-08	C	3.19	1.79	N/A	626.9	231.8	49.2	12.4
2008	C	1.55	0.96	40.0	690.5	255.5	190.1	36.5
2007	C	3.17	1.80	55.7	585.9	218.8	188.5	35.8
2006	C	3.18	1.76	67.1	442.0	183.9	148.7	8.6
2005	C	2.43	1.57	71.7	334.2	173.6	80.4	-20.8
2004	C	3.58	2.75	65.2	47.3	31.0	6.8	-1.1

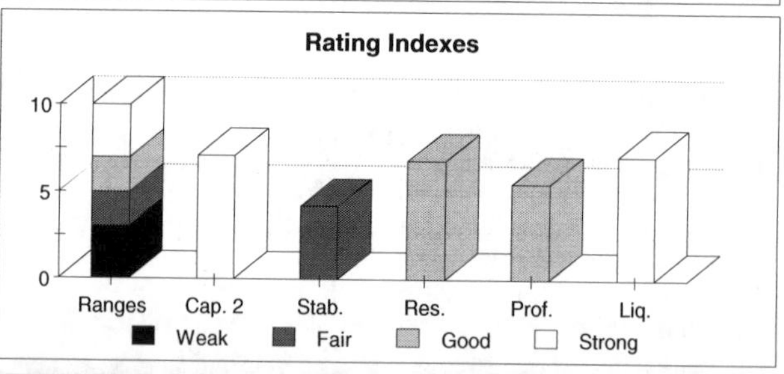

DELOS INS CO D+ Weak

Major Rating Factors: Poor long-term capitalization index (1.2 on a scale of 0 to 10) based on weak current risk adjusted capital (severe and moderate loss scenarios), although results have slipped from the good range over the last two years. Vulnerable liquidity (2.6) as a spike in claims may stretch capacity.

Other Rating Factors: Weak overall results on stability tests (2.4) including weak risk adjusted capital in prior years. History of adequate reserve strength (6.1) as reserves have been consistently at an acceptable level. Good overall profitability index (6.9) despite modest operating losses during 2008. Return on equity has been low, averaging 3.3% over the past five years.

Principal Business: Workers compensation (47%), group accident & health (16%), auto liability (14%), commercial multiple peril (10%), auto physical damage (7%), other liability (4%), and other lines (2%).

Principal Investments: Investment grade bonds (81%), misc. investments (14%), and cash (5%).

Investments in Affiliates: 5%

Group Affiliation: Lightyear Delos Acquisition Corp

Licensed in: All states except PR

Commenced Business: January 1978

Address: 32 Loockerman Sq Ste L100, Dover, DE 19901

Phone: (212) 702-3700 **Domicile State:** DE **NAIC Code:** 35408

Data Date	Rating	RACR #1	RACR #2	Loss Ratio %	Total Assets ($mil)	Capital ($mil)	Net Premium ($mil)	Net Income ($mil)
3-09	D+	0.32	0.27	N/A	568.2	197.5	57.5	1.9
3-08	B	1.08	0.85	N/A	490.9	206.6	49.1	1.5
2008	D+	0.33	0.28	65.1	539.7	200.5	262.8	-0.7
2007	B	1.21	0.96	63.2	463.0	207.8	186.2	3.0
2006	B-	1.41	1.10	62.8	370.4	203.8	63.2	9.6
2005	B	0.79	0.61	66.6	309.6	107.4	86.9	7.8
2004	B+	1.02	0.67	68.1	287.9	82.2	106.0	2.5

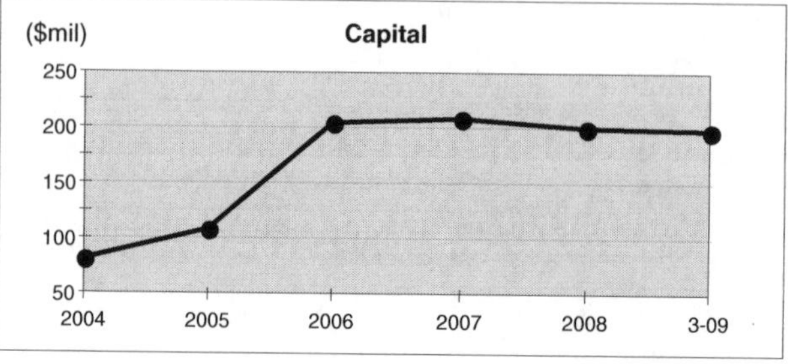

DOCTORS CO AN INTERINSURANCE EXCH — B- Good

Major Rating Factors: Fair overall results on stability tests (4.7 on a scale of 0 to 10) including potential drain of affiliation with Doctors Co Group. Fair reserve development (4.9) as reserves have generally been sufficient to cover claims. In 2004, the one year reserve development was 17% deficient.

Other Rating Factors: Good liquidity (6.9) with sufficient resources (cash flows and marketable investments) to handle a spike in claims. Strong long-term capitalization index (7.0) based on excellent current risk adjusted capital (severe and moderate loss scenarios), despite some fluctuation in capital levels. Excellent profitability (8.4) with operating gains in each of the last five years. Return on equity has been good over the last five years, averaging 14.1%.

Principal Business: Medical malpractice (100%).

Principal Investments: Misc. investments (58%), investment grade bonds (39%), cash (1%), non investment grade bonds (1%), and real estate (1%).

Investments in Affiliates: 30%

Group Affiliation: Doctors Co Group

Licensed in: All states except NY, PR

Commenced Business: April 1976

Address: 185 Greenwood Dr, Napa, CA 94558

Phone: (707) 226-0100 **Domicile State:** CA **NAIC Code:** 34495

Data Date	Rating	RACR #1	RACR #2	Loss Ratio %	Total Assets ($mil)	Capital ($mil)	Net Premium ($mil)	Net Income ($mil)
3-09	B-	1.30	1.12	N/A	2,076.4	791.6	138.6	8.9
3-08	B-	1.42	1.19	N/A	2,157.5	809.2	128.7	26.4
2008	B-	1.30	1.13	47.8	2,011.9	785.7	500.5	72.7
2007	B-	1.43	1.19	49.0	2,099.9	804.1	516.7	156.6
2006	C+	1.04	0.88	51.9	1,939.5	656.0	493.1	137.6
2005	C+	0.76	0.64	63.0	1,725.2	503.2	455.2	77.6
2004	C+	0.58	0.47	82.5	1,559.6	405.6	459.7	32.4

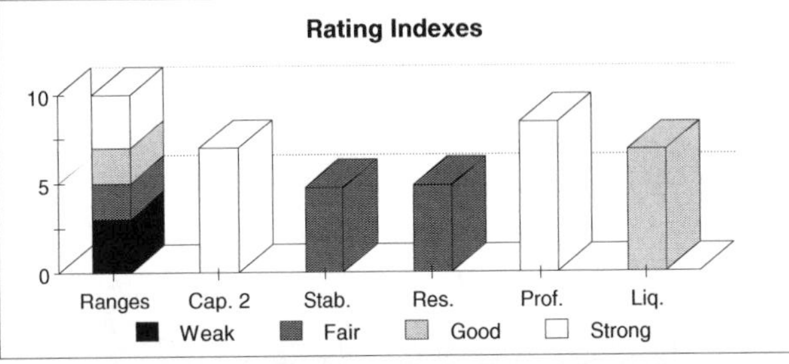

DONEGAL MUTUAL INS CO — C+ Fair

Major Rating Factors: Fair long-term capitalization index (3.7 on a scale of 0 to 10) based on good current risk adjusted capital (severe and moderate loss scenarios). Moreover, capital levels have been consistent over the last several years. Fair overall results on stability tests (4.3) including negative cash flow from operations for 2008.

Other Rating Factors: Good liquidity (5.7) with sufficient resources (cash flows and marketable investments) to handle a spike in claims. Ample reserve history (8.2) that helps to protect the company against sharp claims increases. Excellent profitability (8.4) despite modest operating losses during the first three months of 2008.

Principal Business: Homeowners multiple peril (24%), auto liability (23%), auto physical damage (20%), commercial multiple peril (14%), workers compensation (9%), other liability (4%), and other lines (5%).

Principal Investments: Misc. investments (82%), real estate (14%), and investment grade bonds (6%).

Investments in Affiliates: 75%

Group Affiliation: Donegal Group

Licensed in: DE, IL, IN, MD, NY, NC, OH, PA, SD, TN, VA

Commenced Business: May 1889

Address: 1195 River Rd, Marietta, PA 17547-0302

Phone: (717) 426-1931 **Domicile State:** PA **NAIC Code:** 13692

Data Date	Rating	RACR #1	RACR #2	Loss Ratio %	Total Assets ($mil)	Capital ($mil)	Net Premium ($mil)	Net Income ($mil)
3-09	C+	0.93	0.85	N/A	302.1	158.4	15.3	-0.3
3-08	B-	1.01	0.92	N/A	293.2	155.6	19.4	3.6
2008	B-	0.92	0.84	72.1	304.5	158.0	51.5	4.1
2007	B-	1.00	0.93	55.8	309.5	153.3	86.8	13.0
2006	C+	0.99	0.91	54.1	296.5	136.1	85.9	13.7
2005	C+	0.95	0.86	58.5	268.9	114.7	83.9	10.3
2004	C+	0.92	0.81	66.1	235.4	92.8	76.9	4.9

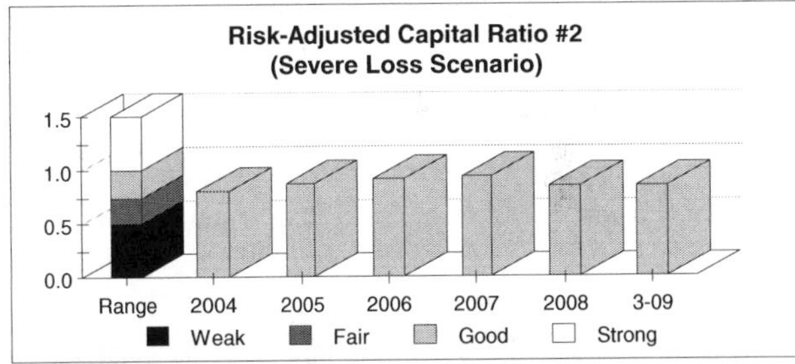

DORINCO REINSURANCE CO — D Weak

Major Rating Factors: Poor long-term capitalization index (1.4 on a scale of 0 to 10) based on weak current risk adjusted capital (severe and moderate loss scenarios). Weak overall results on stability tests (1.8) including weak risk adjusted capital in prior years, weak results on operational trends and negative cash flow from operations for 2008. The largest net exposure for one risk is high at 4.5% of capital.

Other Rating Factors: Good overall profitability index (6.1). Good expense controls. Return on equity has been good over the last five years, averaging 10.1%. Good liquidity (6.6) with sufficient resources (cash flows and marketable investments) to handle a spike in claims. Ample reserve history (9.4) that helps to protect the company against sharp claims increases.

Principal Business: Other liability (65%) and fire (35%).

Principal Investments: Investment grade bonds (70%), misc. investments (28%), and non investment grade bonds (2%).

Investments in Affiliates: None

Group Affiliation: Dow Chemical Co

Licensed in: AZ, CA, GA, ID, IL, IN, IA, LA, MI, MS, MO, OH, OK, OR, PA, TX, UT, WV, WI

Commenced Business: March 1977

Address: 1320 Waldo Rd #200, Midland, MI 48642

Phone: (989) 636-0047 **Domicile State:** MI **NAIC Code:** 33499

Data Date	Rating	RACR #1	RACR #2	Loss Ratio %	Total Assets ($mil)	Capital ($mil)	Net Premium ($mil)	Net Income ($mil)
3-09	D	0.53	0.38	N/A	1,545.7	535.0	52.0	11.2
3-08	D	0.72	0.49	N/A	1,751.0	574.8	40.1	26.6
2008	D	0.53	0.38	59.4	1,610.5	531.7	174.2	76.4
2007	D	0.71	0.49	54.5	1,938.1	589.3	109.3	114.8
2006	D	0.65	0.44	83.9	1,910.7	565.5	297.6	33.7
2005	D	0.54	0.42	89.1	1,726.4	495.0	276.8	44.8
2004	D-	0.50	0.33	106.6	1,671.3	415.8	217.1	8.5

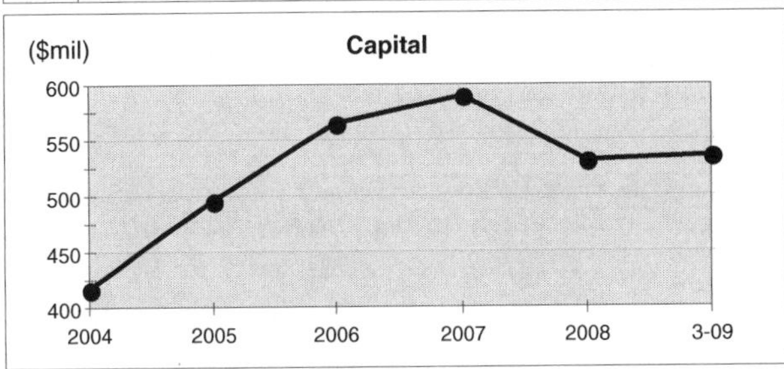

ECONOMY FIRE & CAS CO — B- Good

Major Rating Factors: Good overall results on stability tests (5.1 on a scale of 0 to 10). Stability strengths include good operational trends and excellent risk diversification. Strong long-term capitalization index (10.0) based on excellent current risk adjusted capital (severe and moderate loss scenarios), despite some fluctuation in capital levels.
Other Rating Factors: Excellent profitability (8.0) with operating gains in each of the last five years. Excellent liquidity (7.0) with ample operational cash flow and liquid investments.
Principal Business: Homeowners multiple peril (51%), auto liability (26%), auto physical damage (22%), inland marine (1%), and earthquake (1%).
Principal Investments: Investment grade bonds (83%), misc. investments (16%), and real estate (1%).
Investments in Affiliates: 12%
Group Affiliation: MetLife Inc
Licensed in: All states except DC, DE, HI, ME, MA, NH, NJ, RI, SC, VT, VA, PR
Commenced Business: January 1935
Address: 500 Economy Court, Freeport, IL 61032
Phone: (401) 827-2400 **Domicile State:** IL **NAIC Code:** 22926

Data Date	Rating	RACR #1	RACR #2	Loss Ratio %	Total Assets ($mil)	Capital ($mil)	Net Premium ($mil)	Net Income ($mil)
3-09	B-	8.37	7.40	N/A	388.6	367.1	0.0	4.5
3-08	B-	8.31	7.44	N/A	370.3	349.8	0.0	4.5
2008	B-	8.29	7.34	0.0	378.7	362.8	0.0	16.5
2007	B-	8.25	7.41	0.0	360.1	345.4	0.0	14.4
2006	B-	8.11	7.24	0.0	344.9	331.1	0.0	17.6
2005	B-	8.04	7.15	0.0	326.1	314.3	0.0	24.8
2004	B-	8.11	7.05	0.0	372.8	362.3	0.0	19.3

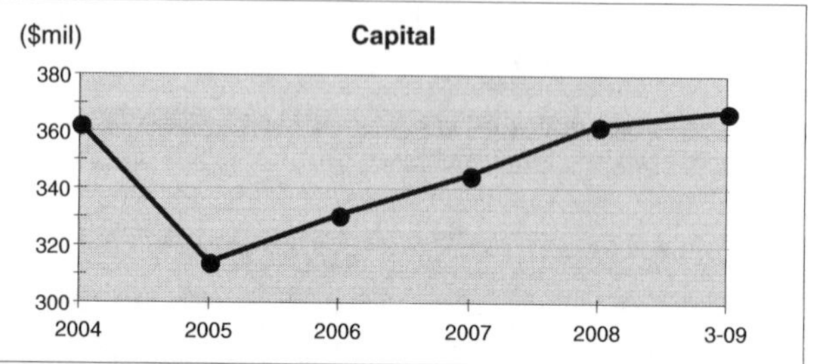

ELECTRIC INS CO — C+ Fair

Major Rating Factors: Good long-term capitalization index (5.4 on a scale of 0 to 10) based on fair current risk adjusted capital (severe loss scenario), although results have slipped from the good range over the last two years. Fair overall results on stability tests (3.4) including fair risk adjusted capital in prior years. The largest net exposure for one risk is excessive at 7.5% of capital.
Other Rating Factors: Good overall profitability index (6.6). Good expense controls. Return on equity has been fair, averaging 7.2% over the past five years. Good liquidity (6.3) with sufficient resources (cash flows and marketable investments) to handle a spike in claims. A history of deficient reserves (2.9) that places pressure on both capital and profits. Deficiencies in the two year reserve development occurred in three of the previous five years and ranged between 23% and 33%.
Principal Business: Workers compensation (25%), products liability (25%), auto liability (23%), auto physical damage (12%), homeowners multiple peril (12%), and other liability (2%).
Principal Investments: Investment grade bonds (83%), misc. investments (19%), and real estate (1%).
Investments in Affiliates: 4%
Group Affiliation: Electric Mutual
Licensed in: All states, the District of Columbia and Puerto Rico
Commenced Business: September 1966
Address: 75 Sam Fonzo Dr., Beverly, MA 01915
Phone: (978) 921-0660 **Domicile State:** MA **NAIC Code:** 21261

Data Date	Rating	RACR #1	RACR #2	Loss Ratio %	Total Assets ($mil)	Capital ($mil)	Net Premium ($mil)	Net Income ($mil)
3-09	C+	1.27	0.69	N/A	1,423.1	344.4	96.4	3.1
3-08	C+	1.61	0.88	N/A	1,392.0	371.3	96.4	5.6
2008	C+	1.30	0.71	87.1	1,250.6	350.0	370.1	14.3
2007	C+	1.61	0.88	84.5	1,246.0	372.0	367.7	46.4
2006	C+	1.17	0.71	87.4	1,200.1	331.8	371.0	30.6
2005	D+	1.49	0.86	88.5	1,142.5	298.6	399.3	20.6
2004	D+	1.15	0.65	91.6	1,144.3	275.0	425.8	11.2

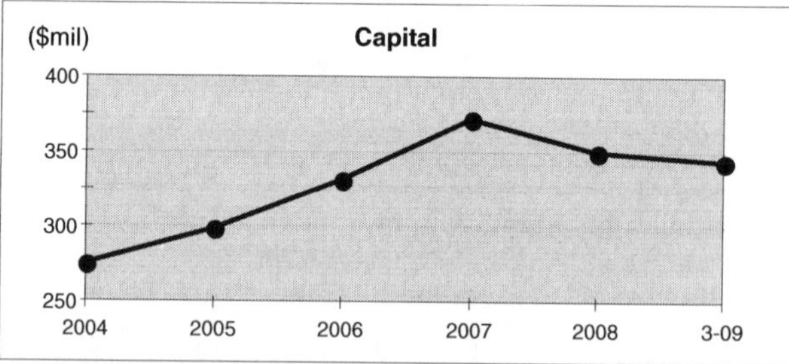

EMPLOYERS COMPENSATION INS CO — B- Good

Major Rating Factors: Good liquidity (6.7 on a scale of 0 to 10) with sufficient resources (cash flows and marketable investments) to handle a spike in claims. Good overall results on stability tests (5.0). Stability strengths include good operational trends and excellent risk diversification.
Other Rating Factors: Strong long-term capitalization index (8.6) based on excellent current risk adjusted capital (severe and moderate loss scenarios). Moreover, capital levels have been consistent in recent years. Ample reserve history (9.5) that helps to protect the company against sharp claims increases. Excellent profitability (8.8) with operating gains in each of the last five years. Return on equity has been excellent over the last five years averaging 15.6%.
Principal Business: Workers compensation (100%).
Principal Investments: Investment grade bonds (95%), misc. investments (3%), and cash (2%).
Investments in Affiliates: None
Group Affiliation: Employers Group Inc
Licensed in: AZ, CA, CO, ID, IL, MD, MT, NM, NY, OR, PA, TX, UT
Commenced Business: September 2002
Address: 500 North Brand Blvd, Glendale, CA 91203-3392
Phone: (818) 549-4654 **Domicile State:** CA **NAIC Code:** 11512

Data Date	Rating	RACR #1	RACR #2	Loss Ratio %	Total Assets ($mil)	Capital ($mil)	Net Premium ($mil)	Net Income ($mil)
3-09	B-	3.35	2.40	N/A	1,296.7	343.7	30.1	6.5
3-08	C+	2.63	1.77	N/A	1,475.8	348.3	35.7	13.0
2008	B-	3.37	2.44	46.2	1,275.5	337.4	146.6	52.5
2007	C+	2.59	1.75	46.5	1,469.1	335.3	159.1	49.2
2006	C	1.84	1.27	37.9	1,479.5	314.1	182.0	61.0
2005	C	0.88	0.61	58.4	1,443.6	277.2	206.7	44.6
2004	C-	0.71	0.49	61.3	1,141.4	205.2	198.5	29.4

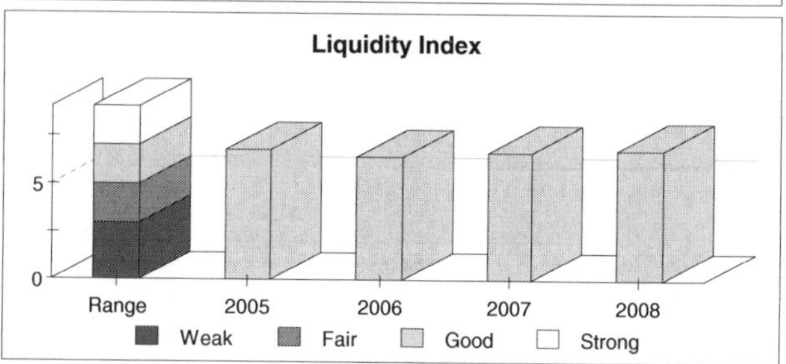

EMPLOYERS INS CO OF NEVADA INC — C — Fair

Major Rating Factors: Fair profitability index (3.2 on a scale of 0 to 10). Fair expense controls. Return on equity has been fair, averaging 14.5% over the past five years. Fair overall results on stability tests (4.1) including excessive premium growth.

Other Rating Factors: Good overall long-term capitalization (6.7) based on good current risk adjusted capital (moderate loss scenario). However, capital levels have fluctuated during prior years. Ample reserve history (9.4) that helps to protect the company against sharp claims increases. Superior liquidity (10.0) with ample operational cash flow and liquid investments.

Principal Business: Workers compensation (100%).

Principal Investments: Investment grade bonds (63%) and misc. investments (37%).

Investments in Affiliates: 31%

Group Affiliation: Employers Group Inc

Licensed in: NV

Commenced Business: January 2000

Address: 9790 Gateway Dr Suite 100, Reno, NV 89521

Phone: (775) 327-2468 **Domicile State:** NV **NAIC Code:** 10640

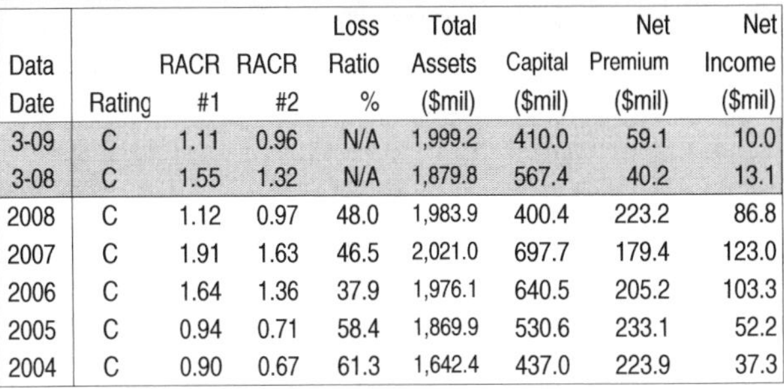

Data Date	Rating	RACR #1	RACR #2	Loss Ratio %	Total Assets ($mil)	Capital ($mil)	Net Premium ($mil)	Net Income ($mil)
3-09	C	1.11	0.96	N/A	1,999.2	410.0	59.1	10.0
3-08	C	1.55	1.32	N/A	1,879.8	567.4	40.2	13.1
2008	C	1.12	0.97	48.0	1,983.9	400.4	223.2	86.8
2007	C	1.91	1.63	46.5	2,021.0	697.7	179.4	123.0
2006	C	1.64	1.36	37.9	1,976.1	640.5	205.2	103.3
2005	C	0.94	0.71	58.4	1,869.9	530.6	233.1	52.2
2004	C	0.90	0.67	61.3	1,642.4	437.0	223.9	37.3

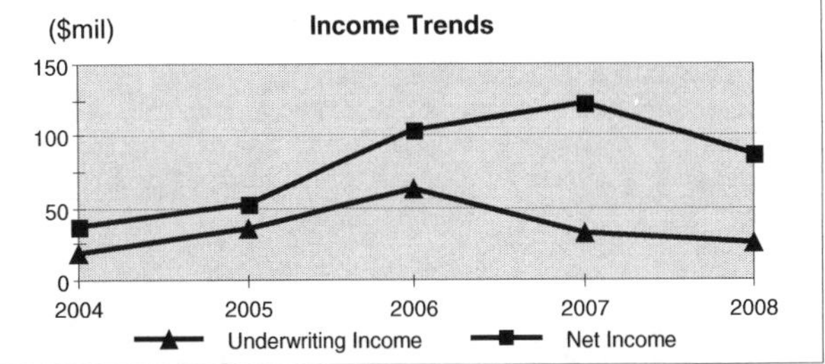

EMPLOYERS INS OF WAUSAU — B- — Good

Major Rating Factors: Fair reserve development (3.1 on a scale of 0 to 10) as the level of reserves has at times been insufficient to cover claims. Deficiencies in the two year reserve development occurred in three of the previous five years and ranged between 22% and 38%. Fair profitability index (3.6). Fair expense controls. Return on equity has been fair, averaging 8.6% over the past five years.

Other Rating Factors: Fair overall results on stability tests (4.9). Good liquidity (5.8) with sufficient resources (cash flows and marketable investments) to handle a spike in claims. Strong long-term capitalization index (7.1) based on excellent current risk adjusted capital (severe and moderate loss scenarios), despite some fluctuation in capital levels.

Principal Business: Workers compensation (73%), other liability (11%), commercial multiple peril (9%), auto liability (5%), and auto physical damage (1%).

Principal Investments: Investment grade bonds (71%), misc. investments (24%), non investment grade bonds (4%), and real estate (1%).

Investments in Affiliates: 13%

Group Affiliation: Liberty Mutual Group

Licensed in: All states, the District of Columbia and Puerto Rico

Commenced Business: September 1911

Address: 2000 Westwood Dr, Wausau, WI 54401

Phone: (715) 845-5211 **Domicile State:** WI **NAIC Code:** 21458

Data Date	Rating	RACR #1	RACR #2	Loss Ratio %	Total Assets ($mil)	Capital ($mil)	Net Premium ($mil)	Net Income ($mil)
3-09	B-	1.57	1.12	N/A	4,009.7	912.5	205.9	8.5
3-08	B-	2.30	1.37	N/A	4,733.2	1,296.8	275.6	10.0
2008	B-	1.53	1.07	83.5	3,719.9	949.5	1,070.7	96.1
2007	B-	2.29	1.36	77.8	4,077.2	1,298.4	980.3	142.1
2006	B-	1.52	0.89	76.4	5,295.6	1,208.4	1,898.3	90.1
2005	B-	1.42	0.86	82.6	4,687.2	1,070.7	1,695.4	59.2
2004	B-	1.21	0.78	82.8	4,423.2	995.1	1,588.6	100.5

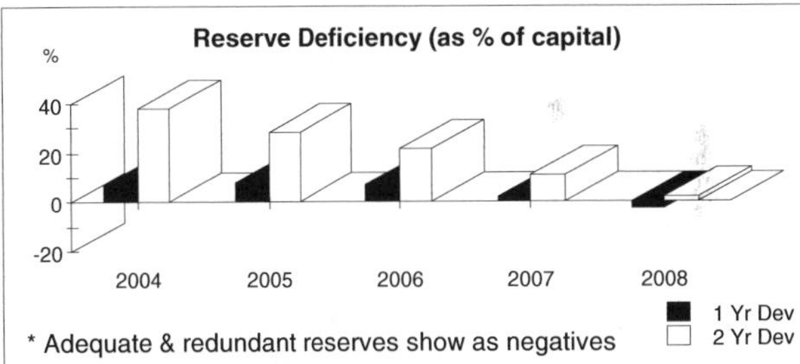

EMPLOYERS MUTUAL CAS CO — B- — Good

Major Rating Factors: Fair overall results on stability tests (4.8 on a scale of 0 to 10) including potential drain of affiliation with Employers Mutual Group and negative cash flow from operations for 2008. The largest net exposure for one risk is high at 3.4% of capital. Fair profitability index (4.2) with operating losses during 2004 and 2008.

Other Rating Factors: History of adequate reserve strength (5.8) as reserves have been consistently at an acceptable level. Good liquidity (6.6) with sufficient resources (cash flows and marketable investments) to handle a spike in claims. Strong long-term capitalization index (7.6) based on excellent current risk adjusted capital (severe and moderate loss scenarios), despite some fluctuation in capital levels.

Principal Business: Other liability (25%), auto liability (19%), workers compensation (18%), allied lines (7%), auto physical damage (7%), inland marine (6%), and other lines (18%).

Principal Investments: Investment grade bonds (54%), misc. investments (41%), real estate (6%), and non investment grade bonds (1%).

Investments in Affiliates: 18%

Group Affiliation: Employers Mutual Group

Licensed in: All states except PR

Commenced Business: July 1913

Address: 717 Mulberry St, Des Moines, IA 50309-3872

Phone: (515) 280-2511 **Domicile State:** IA **NAIC Code:** 21415

Data Date	Rating	RACR #1	RACR #2	Loss Ratio %	Total Assets ($mil)	Capital ($mil)	Net Premium ($mil)	Net Income ($mil)
3-09	B-	1.81	1.37	N/A	2,009.8	711.5	158.2	0.2
3-08	B-	1.95	1.47	N/A	2,154.0	875.3	164.4	17.1
2008	B-	1.83	1.38	74.9	1,994.7	723.8	651.7	-45.9
2007	B-	1.96	1.48	61.7	2,151.8	896.2	688.4	63.3
2006	B-	1.86	1.37	57.1	1,976.8	791.1	633.2	93.7
2005	B-	1.69	1.24	65.3	1,832.2	663.2	597.2	61.6
2004	B-	1.49	1.07	81.5	1,837.5	577.0	710.2	-22.8

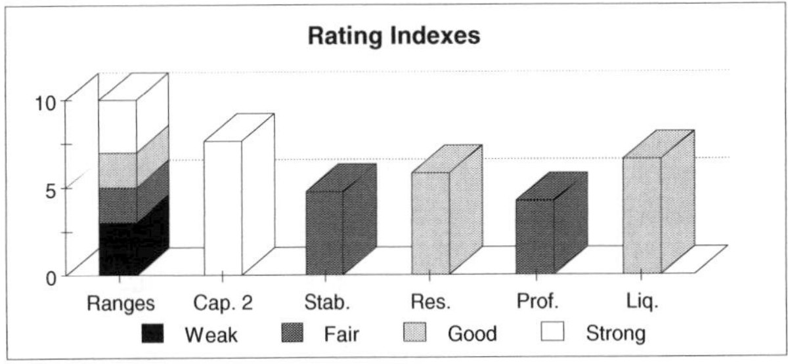

EMPLOYERS PREFERRED INS CO — C — Fair

Major Rating Factors: Fair overall results on stability tests (3.3 on a scale of 0 to 10) including potential drain of affiliation with Employers Group Inc and negative cash flow from operations for 2008. Fair liquidity (4.0) as cash resources may not be adequate to cover a spike in claims.
Other Rating Factors: Good overall profitability index (6.0) despite operating losses during 2004. Return on equity has been low, averaging 3.7% over the past five years. Strong long-term capitalization index (7.2) based on excellent current risk adjusted capital (severe and moderate loss scenarios). Moreover, capital levels have been consistent in recent years. Ample reserve history (9.4) that helps to protect the company against sharp claims increases.
Principal Business: Workers compensation (100%).
Principal Investments: Investment grade bonds (63%) and misc. investments (37%).
Investments in Affiliates: 36%
Group Affiliation: Employers Group Inc
Licensed in: DC, FL, GA, IL, IN, KY, MN, SC, TN, TX, VA
Commenced Business: January 1982
Address: 701 U.S. Hwy 1, Suite 200, North Palm Beach, FL 33408
Phone: (800) 226-1898 **Domicile State:** FL **NAIC Code:** 10346

Data Date	Rating	RACR #1	RACR #2	Loss Ratio %	Total Assets ($mil)	Capital ($mil)	Net Premium ($mil)	Net Income ($mil)
3-09	C	1.91	1.69	N/A	442.9	178.4	11.2	1.5
3-08	C	1.57	1.39	N/A	417.3	178.4	32.9	3.1
2008	C	1.87	1.64	59.1	448.9	177.4	56.7	12.1
2007	C	1.52	1.34	54.5	423.7	176.5	139.3	12.7
2006	C	1.40	1.20	61.2	410.2	155.5	166.8	8.6
2005	D+	1.05	0.86	56.3	325.6	96.2	168.6	5.9
2004	D+	0.95	0.75	66.5	268.3	80.5	137.0	-5.6

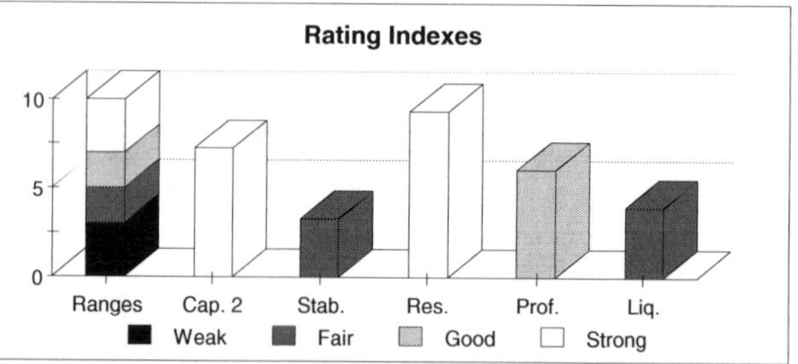

ENDURANCE REINS CORP OF AMERICA — C+ — Fair

Major Rating Factors: Fair overall results on stability tests (4.4 on a scale of 0 to 10). The largest net exposure for one risk is acceptable at 2.8% of capital. Good long-term capitalization (6.1) based on good current risk adjusted capital (moderate loss scenario) reflecting improvement over results in 2008.
Other Rating Factors: History of adequate reserve strength (6.6) as reserves have been consistently at an acceptable level. Good overall profitability index (5.1) despite operating losses during 2004 and 2005. Return on equity has been low, averaging 0.2% over the past five years. Good liquidity (6.8) with sufficient resources (cash flows and marketable investments) to handle a spike in claims.
Principal Business: Workers compensation (100%).
Principal Investments: Investment grade bonds (71%), misc. investments (27%), and cash (2%).
Investments in Affiliates: 20%
Group Affiliation: Endurance Specialty Holdings
Licensed in: AZ, CA, DC, DE, GA, ID, IN, KS, MD, MA, MI, MT, NE, NV, NM, NY, ND, OH, OK, OR, PA, SC, TX, UT, WV
Commenced Business: December 2002
Address: 333 Westchester Ave, White Plains, NY 10604
Phone: (914) 468-8000 **Domicile State:** DE **NAIC Code:** 11551

Data Date	Rating	RACR #1	RACR #2	Loss Ratio %	Total Assets ($mil)	Capital ($mil)	Net Premium ($mil)	Net Income ($mil)
3-09	C+	1.69	1.06	N/A	1,884.9	605.1	82.6	13.1
3-08	C+	2.04	1.32	N/A	1,872.8	603.6	89.3	8.3
2008	C+	1.32	0.83	74.2	1,920.4	592.8	445.5	25.0
2007	C+	2.08	1.37	63.7	1,613.4	592.9	366.2	26.3
2006	C	2.57	1.58	51.0	1,572.8	571.4	322.4	63.4
2005	C-	1.40	0.89	89.7	1,449.2	514.8	271.6	-66.7
2004	C-	3.81	2.09	76.8	1,288.3	504.5	339.1	-41.1

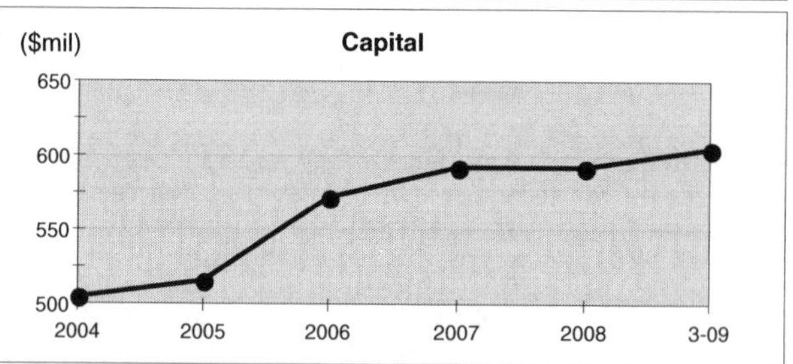

ERIE INS CO — B — Good

Major Rating Factors: Good overall results on stability tests (5.1 on a scale of 0 to 10) despite potential drain of affiliation with Erie Ins Group. Stability strengths include good operational trends and excellent risk diversification. Good overall profitability index (5.9) despite operating losses during the first three months of 2008. Return on equity has been fair, averaging 8.1% over the past five years.
Other Rating Factors: Good liquidity (6.7) with sufficient resources (cash flows and marketable investments) to handle a spike in claims. Strong long-term capitalization index (9.6) based on excellent current risk adjusted capital (severe and moderate loss scenarios), despite some fluctuation in capital levels. Ample reserve history (7.0) that can protect against increases in claims costs.
Principal Business: Auto liability (46%), auto physical damage (29%), commercial multiple peril (9%), workers compensation (7%), homeowners multiple peril (5%), surety (2%), and other liability (1%).
Principal Investments: Investment grade bonds (89%), misc. investments (8%), and non investment grade bonds (3%).
Investments in Affiliates: 5%
Group Affiliation: Erie Ins Group
Licensed in: DC, IL, IN, KY, MD, MN, NY, NC, OH, PA, TN, VA, WV, WI
Commenced Business: January 1973
Address: 100 Erie Ins Place, Erie, PA 16530
Phone: (814) 870-2000 **Domicile State:** PA **NAIC Code:** 26263

Data Date	Rating	RACR #1	RACR #2	Loss Ratio %	Total Assets ($mil)	Capital ($mil)	Net Premium ($mil)	Net Income ($mil)
3-09	B	4.27	2.77	N/A	601.5	200.6	46.8	-2.7
3-08	B	4.52	2.93	N/A	622.5	218.5	47.0	1.0
2008	B	4.49	2.95	66.0	610.3	209.5	189.4	-10.0
2007	B	4.54	2.97	60.6	622.7	215.4	188.8	28.1
2006	B	4.03	2.79	65.3	602.9	186.3	190.3	21.7
2005	B	3.56	2.46	65.1	600.9	161.7	194.7	22.9
2004	B	2.77	1.94	73.3	564.6	140.4	196.7	13.4

Erie Ins Group
Composite Group Rating: B

Largest Group Members	Assets ($mil)	Rating
ERIE INS EXCHANGE	9149	B
ERIE FAMILY LIFE INS CO	1534	B
ERIE INS CO	610	B
ERIE INS PROPERTY CASUALTY CO	62	B
ERIE INS CO OF NY	57	B+

ERIE INS CO OF NY * B+ Good

Major Rating Factors: Good liquidity (6.8 on a scale of 0 to 10) with sufficient resources (cash flows and marketable investments) to handle a spike in claims. Good overall results on stability tests (5.1).

Other Rating Factors: Strong long-term capitalization index (8.3) based on excellent current risk adjusted capital (severe and moderate loss scenarios), despite some fluctuation in capital levels. Ample reserve history (7.0) that can protect against increases in claims costs. Excellent profitability (8.3) with operating gains in each of the last five years. Return on equity has been good over the last five years, averaging 10.9%.

Principal Business: Workers compensation (90%), auto liability (7%), and auto physical damage (4%).

Principal Investments: Investment grade bonds (96%), non investment grade bonds (3%), and cash (1%).

Investments in Affiliates: None

Group Affiliation: Erie Ins Group

Licensed in: IL, MN, NY, PA, TN

Commenced Business: September 1885

Address: 120 Corporate Woods Suite 150, Rochester, NY 14623

Phone: (814) 870-2000 **Domicile State:** NY **NAIC Code:** 16233

Data Date	Rating	RACR #1	RACR #2	Loss Ratio %	Total Assets ($mil)	Capital ($mil)	Net Premium ($mil)	Net Income ($mil)
3-09	B+	3.32	2.05	N/A	58.4	19.8	4.7	0.0
3-08	B	3.23	2.01	N/A	55.6	19.3	4.7	0.4
2008	B+	3.37	2.11	66.0	57.2	19.9	18.9	1.2
2007	B	3.14	1.98	60.8	51.9	18.8	18.9	2.8
2006	B	2.60	1.79	65.5	48.2	16.0	19.0	2.0
2005	B	2.18	1.51	65.4	47.8	13.8	19.5	2.1
2004	B	1.63	1.15	73.7	45.8	11.8	19.7	1.0

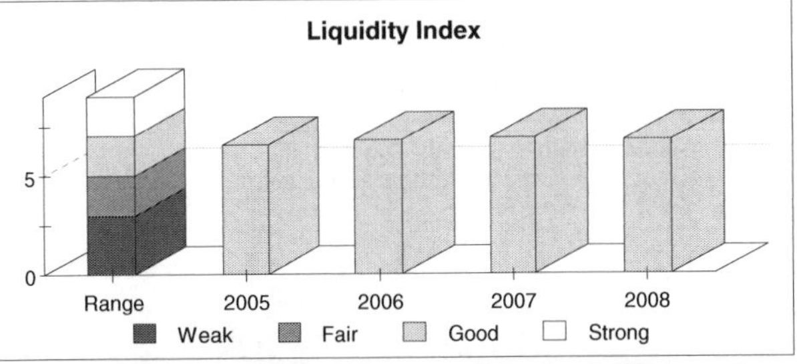

ERIE INS EXCHANGE B Good

Major Rating Factors: Good overall results on stability tests (5.1 on a scale of 0 to 10) despite potential drain of affiliation with Erie Ins Group. Stability strengths include good operational trends and excellent risk diversification. Good liquidity (6.6) with sufficient resources (cash flows and marketable investments) to handle a spike in claims.

Other Rating Factors: Fair profitability index (3.9) with operating losses during the first three months of 2008. Strong long-term capitalization index (9.7) based on excellent current risk adjusted capital (severe and moderate loss scenarios), despite some fluctuation in capital levels. Ample reserve history (7.0) that can protect against increases in claims costs.

Principal Business: Auto liability (34%), homeowners multiple peril (22%), auto physical damage (20%), commercial multiple peril (14%), workers compensation (6%), other liability (3%), and inland marine (1%).

Principal Investments: Investment grade bonds (58%), misc. investments (42%), and non investment grade bonds (1%).

Investments in Affiliates: 1%

Group Affiliation: Erie Ins Group

Licensed in: CT, DC, IL, IN, KY, ME, MD, MN, NC, OH, PA, RI, TN, VA, WV, WI

Commenced Business: April 1925

Address: 100 Erie Ins Place, Erie, PA 16530

Phone: (814) 870-2000 **Domicile State:** PA **NAIC Code:** 26271

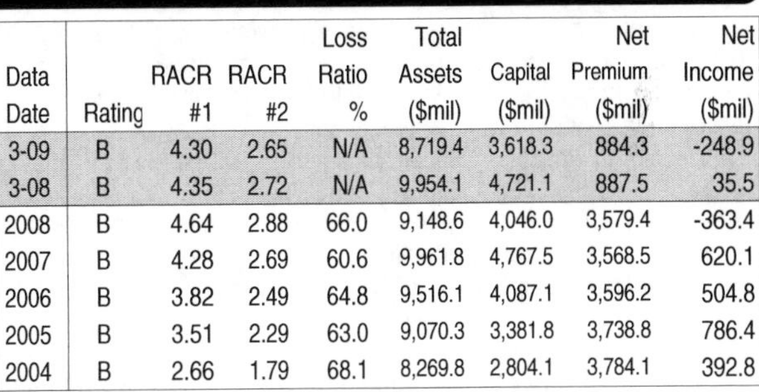

Data Date	Rating	RACR #1	RACR #2	Loss Ratio %	Total Assets ($mil)	Capital ($mil)	Net Premium ($mil)	Net Income ($mil)
3-09	B	4.30	2.65	N/A	8,719.4	3,618.3	884.3	-248.9
3-08	B	4.35	2.72	N/A	9,954.1	4,721.1	887.5	35.5
2008	B	4.64	2.88	66.0	9,148.6	4,046.0	3,579.4	-363.4
2007	B	4.28	2.69	60.6	9,961.8	4,767.5	3,568.5	620.1
2006	B	3.82	2.49	64.8	9,516.1	4,087.1	3,596.2	504.8
2005	B	3.51	2.29	63.0	9,070.3	3,381.8	3,738.8	786.4
2004	B	2.66	1.79	68.1	8,269.8	2,804.1	3,784.1	392.8

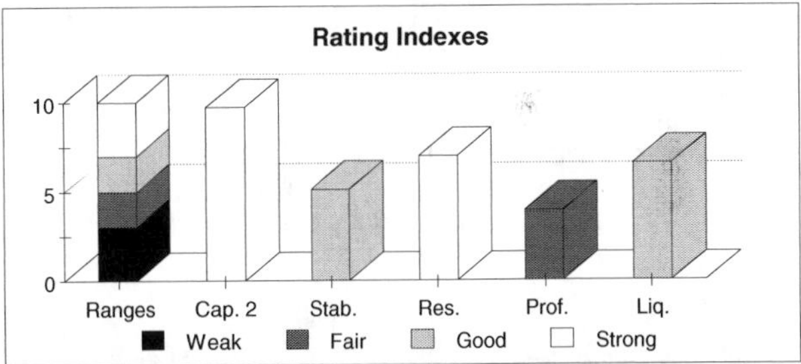

ESSEX INS CO C Fair

Major Rating Factors: Fair overall results on stability tests (3.4 on a scale of 0 to 10) including potential drain of affiliation with Markel Corp. The largest net exposure for one risk is conservative at 1.7% of capital. Good long-term capitalization index (5.1) based on good current risk adjusted capital (severe loss scenario).

Other Rating Factors: Fair reserve development (4.8) as reserves have generally been sufficient to cover claims. In 2004, the two year reserve development was 46% deficient. Good overall profitability index (6.2). Weak expense controls. Return on equity has been excellent over the last five years averaging 16.7%. Good liquidity (6.8) with sufficient resources (cash flows and marketable investments) to handle a spike in claims.

Principal Business: Other liability (37%), inland marine (22%), commercial multiple peril (10%), allied lines (8%), fire (6%), auto physical damage (6%), and other lines (11%).

Principal Investments: Investment grade bonds (86%), misc. investments (11%), cash (2%), and non investment grade bonds (1%).

Investments in Affiliates: None

Group Affiliation: Markel Corp

Licensed in: DE

Commenced Business: October 1980

Address: 1209 Orange St, Wilmington, DE 19801

Phone: (804) 273-1400 **Domicile State:** DE **NAIC Code:** 39020

Data Date	Rating	RACR #1	RACR #2	Loss Ratio %	Total Assets ($mil)	Capital ($mil)	Net Premium ($mil)	Net Income ($mil)
3-09	C	1.13	0.75	N/A	1,033.7	277.7	67.6	2.2
3-08	C-	0.92	0.60	N/A	1,056.3	248.2	90.8	6.6
2008	C	1.17	0.78	53.4	1,074.5	296.1	304.3	20.8
2007	C-	1.26	0.82	40.3	1,144.0	343.0	349.9	108.4
2006	D+	1.09	0.70	45.2	1,201.2	334.2	434.6	91.6
2005	D+	0.75	0.48	72.2	1,045.1	225.4	391.8	2.4
2004	C-	0.81	0.53	51.5	939.5	276.5	391.4	54.3

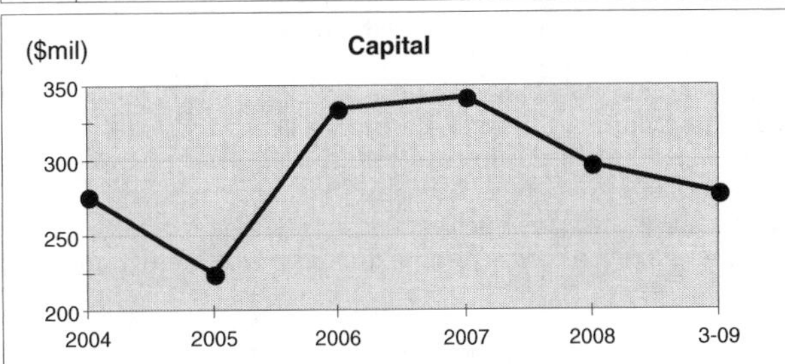

EULER HERMES AMERICAN CREDIT IND CO B- Good

Major Rating Factors: Fair overall results on stability tests (4.2 on a scale of 0 to 10). The largest net exposure for one risk is excessive at 6.9% of capital. Good overall profitability index (6.3) despite operating losses during the first three months of 2008. Return on equity has been good over the last five years, averaging 13.2%.

Other Rating Factors: Strong long-term capitalization index (10.0) based on excellent current risk adjusted capital (severe and moderate loss scenarios), despite some fluctuation in capital levels. Ample reserve history (8.0) that helps to protect the company against sharp claims increases. Excellent liquidity (7.0) with ample operational cash flow and liquid investments.

Principal Business: Credit (100%).

Principal Investments: Investment grade bonds (75%), cash (19%), and misc. investments (6%).

Investments in Affiliates: None

Group Affiliation: Allianz Ins Group

Licensed in: All states except PR

Commenced Business: May 1893

Address: 100 East Pratt St.,5th Floor, Baltimore, MD 21202-1008

Phone: (410) 554-0865 **Domicile State:** MD **NAIC Code:** 20516

Data Date	Rating	RACR #1	RACR #2	Loss Ratio %	Total Assets ($mil)	Capital ($mil)	Net Premium ($mil)	Net Income ($mil)
3-09	B-	5.04	3.28	N/A	444.7	159.6	29.1	-2.4
3-08	B-	4.76	2.89	N/A	379.2	169.8	29.3	-2.7
2008	B-	6.00	3.90	82.0	426.4	168.4	123.9	-1.8
2007	B-	5.98	3.62	52.8	362.1	172.1	112.4	32.2
2006	B-	4.87	2.93	45.4	325.4	160.1	117.1	31.6
2005	C+	8.45	5.16	34.4	306.2	161.8	108.1	32.9
2004	C	7.35	4.61	47.7	273.5	134.1	85.5	17.5

Allianz Ins Group Composite Group Rating: C+ Largest Group Members	Assets ($mil)	Rating
ALLIANZ LIFE INS CO OF NORTH AMERICA	66375	B-
FIREMANS FUND INS CO	10673	C
ALLIANZ GLOBAL RISKS US INS CO	4846	C+
AMERICAN INS CO	1449	B-
ALLIANZ LIFE INS CO OF NY	881	C

EVANSTON INS CO C Fair

Major Rating Factors: Fair long-term capitalization index (3.6 on a scale of 0 to 10) based on fair current risk adjusted capital (severe loss scenario). Fair overall results on stability tests (3.6) including fair risk adjusted capital in prior years. The largest net exposure for one risk is conservative at 1.0% of capital.

Other Rating Factors: Weak profitability index (2.7). Weak expense controls. Return on equity has been fair, averaging 19.9% over the past five years. Ample reserve history (7.1) that can protect against increases in claims costs. Excellent liquidity (7.1) with ample operational cash flow and liquid investments.

Principal Business: Other liability (47%), medical malpractice (20%), products liability (15%), inland marine (6%), commercial multiple peril (5%), fire (5%), and allied lines (2%).

Principal Investments: Investment grade bonds (80%), misc. investments (16%), cash (3%), and non investment grade bonds (1%).

Investments in Affiliates: None

Group Affiliation: Markel Corp

Licensed in: IL

Commenced Business: December 1977

Address: Ten Parkway North, Deerfield, IL 60015

Phone: (847) 572-6000 **Domicile State:** IL **NAIC Code:** 35378

Data Date	Rating	RACR #1	RACR #2	Loss Ratio %	Total Assets ($mil)	Capital ($mil)	Net Premium ($mil)	Net Income ($mil)
3-09	C	0.82	0.56	N/A	2,108.9	370.5	149.4	7.4
3-08	C	1.07	0.66	N/A	2,306.2	582.7	169.3	18.8
2008	C	0.83	0.57	58.1	2,112.6	369.8	597.6	38.0
2007	C	1.08	0.67	46.5	2,284.6	581.8	689.6	134.7
2006	C	1.20	0.75	40.5	2,304.8	647.7	683.3	187.5
2005	C	1.06	0.63	55.0	2,185.2	527.8	691.0	119.2
2004	C-	0.99	0.59	59.9	2,012.4	512.5	718.3	89.3

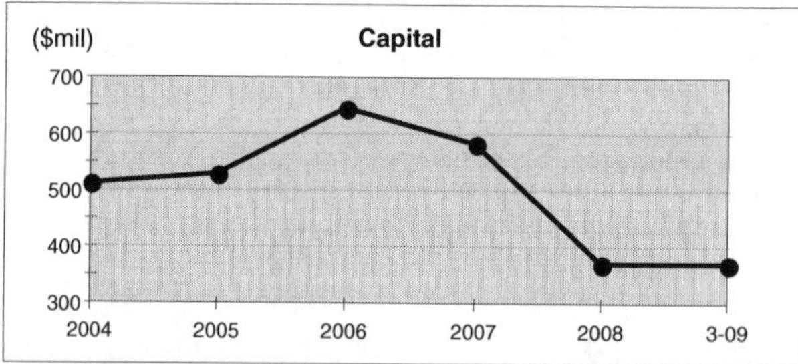

EVEREST NATIONAL INS CO C Fair

Major Rating Factors: Fair overall results on stability tests (4.3 on a scale of 0 to 10) including fair financial strength of affiliated Everest Reinsurance Group. History of adequate reserve strength (5.1) as reserves have been consistently at an acceptable level.

Other Rating Factors: Strong long-term capitalization index (7.0) based on excellent current risk adjusted capital (severe and moderate loss scenarios). Moreover, capital levels have been consistent in recent years. Excellent profitability (8.7) with operating gains in each of the last five years. Excellent liquidity (7.7) with ample operational cash flow and liquid investments.

Principal Business: Workers compensation (33%), auto liability (25%), other liability (22%), commercial multiple peril (19%), products liability (2%), and auto physical damage (1%).

Principal Investments: Investment grade bonds (96%), cash (6%), and non investment grade bonds (1%).

Investments in Affiliates: None

Group Affiliation: Everest Reinsurance Group

Licensed in: All states except HI, NC, VT, PR

Commenced Business: November 1985

Address: 477 Martinsville Road, Liberty Corner, NJ 07938-0830

Phone: (201) 802-8780 **Domicile State:** DE **NAIC Code:** 10120

Data Date	Rating	RACR #1	RACR #2	Loss Ratio %	Total Assets ($mil)	Capital ($mil)	Net Premium ($mil)	Net Income ($mil)
3-09	C	2.17	1.19	N/A	467.9	186.4	20.1	0.8
3-08	C	2.22	1.18	N/A	461.8	179.3	20.0	3.6
2008	C	2.19	1.20	72.9	466.4	184.7	78.1	6.3
2007	C	2.23	1.19	63.6	448.4	178.6	79.1	9.3
2006	C	3.02	1.57	55.7	574.7	165.0	88.0	21.0
2005	C	2.51	1.37	58.7	608.6	136.8	105.5	19.8
2004	C-	1.23	0.75	67.9	764.4	115.8	137.2	13.7

Everest Reinsurance Group Composite Group Rating: D+ Largest Group Members	Assets ($mil)	Rating
EVEREST REINSURANCE CO	8345	C-
EVEREST NATIONAL INS CO	466	C
EVEREST INDEMNITY INS CO	158	C
MT MCKINLEY INS CO	50	U
EVEREST SECURITY INS CO	33	C

EVEREST REINSURANCE CO — C- Fair

Major Rating Factors: Poor long-term capitalization index (2.4 on a scale of 0 to 10) based on good current risk adjusted capital (moderate loss scenario). Weak overall results on stability tests (2.9) including negative cash flow from operations for 2008.

Other Rating Factors: Fair reserve development (3.7) as reserves have generally been sufficient to cover claims. In 2004, the two year reserve development was 29% deficient. Fair profitability index (4.1) with operating losses during 2005. Return on equity has been fair, averaging 9.1% over the past five years. Good liquidity (6.5) with sufficient resources (cash flows and marketable investments) to handle a spike in claims.

Principal Business: Other liability (34%), auto liability (32%), workers compensation (18%), commercial multiple peril (13%), products liability (1%), and auto physical damage (1%).

Principal Investments: Investment grade bonds (81%), misc. investments (17%), cash (1%), and non investment grade bonds (1%).

Investments in Affiliates: 9%

Group Affiliation: Everest Reinsurance Group

Licensed in: All states except NV, NH, WY, PR

Commenced Business: June 1973

Address: 477 Martinsville Road, Liberty Corner, NJ 07938-0830

Phone: (908) 604-3000 **Domicile State:** DE **NAIC Code:** 26921

Data Date	Rating	RACR #1	RACR #2	Loss Ratio %	Total Assets ($mil)	Capital ($mil)	Net Premium ($mil)	Net Income ($mil)
3-09	C-	1.01	0.65	N/A	8,311.4	2,422.4	416.2	65.8
3-08	C-	0.83	0.55	N/A	9,743.8	2,869.6	474.0	68.6
2008	C-	0.96	0.62	61.7	8,344.6	2,342.4	838.8	74.4
2007	C	0.83	0.55	68.1	9,661.8	2,886.6	1,978.9	673.1
2006	C	0.94	0.60	70.2	9,731.9	2,704.1	2,187.1	298.7
2005	C	1.09	0.67	92.0	9,315.6	2,327.6	2,289.2	-26.9
2004	C-	0.81	0.52	77.4	8,572.7	2,093.2	2,800.5	175.8

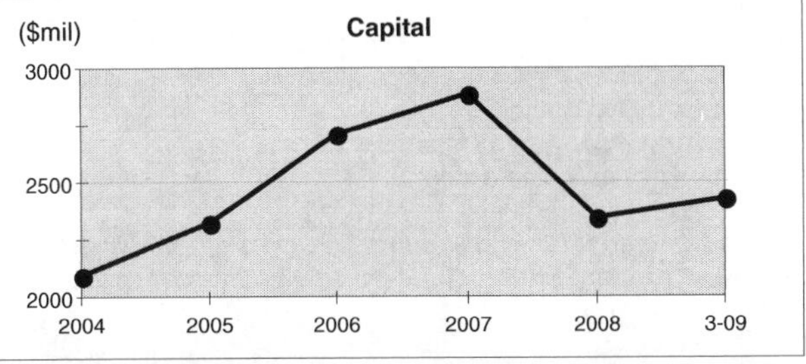

EXECUTIVE RISK INDEMNITY INC — B Good

Major Rating Factors: History of adequate reserve strength (5.6 on a scale of 0 to 10) as reserves have been consistently at an acceptable level. Good liquidity (6.7) with sufficient resources (cash flows and marketable investments) to handle a spike in claims.

Other Rating Factors: Good overall results on stability tests (6.0). The largest net exposure for one risk is high at 3.3% of capital. Stability strengths include good operational trends and excellent risk diversification. Strong long-term capitalization index (7.8) based on excellent current risk adjusted capital (severe and moderate loss scenarios). Moreover, capital levels have been consistent in recent years. Excellent profitability (9.1) with operating gains in each of the last five years. Return on equity has been excellent over the last five years averaging 19.5%.

Principal Business: Other liability (98%) and fidelity (1%).

Principal Investments: Investment grade bonds (92%), misc. investments (7%), and real estate (1%).

Investments in Affiliates: 3%

Group Affiliation: Chubb Corp

Licensed in: All states except CT

Commenced Business: January 1978

Address: 1209 Orange St, Wilmington, DE 19801-1120

Phone: (860) 408-2488 **Domicile State:** DE **NAIC Code:** 35181

Data Date	Rating	RACR #1	RACR #2	Loss Ratio %	Total Assets ($mil)	Capital ($mil)	Net Premium ($mil)	Net Income ($mil)
3-09	B	2.77	1.82	N/A	2,691.1	936.7	176.5	45.9
3-08	B	2.55	1.61	N/A	2,621.2	867.5	180.0	48.6
2008	B	2.74	1.79	61.3	2,710.1	921.7	707.5	136.1
2007	B	2.44	1.53	54.0	2,604.0	820.6	726.0	190.2
2006	B-	2.42	1.49	55.3	2,633.7	810.1	754.8	199.9
2005	B-	1.96	1.40	65.7	2,435.8	656.4	785.9	107.0
2004	B-	1.58	1.12	63.7	2,225.4	585.2	781.7	107.0

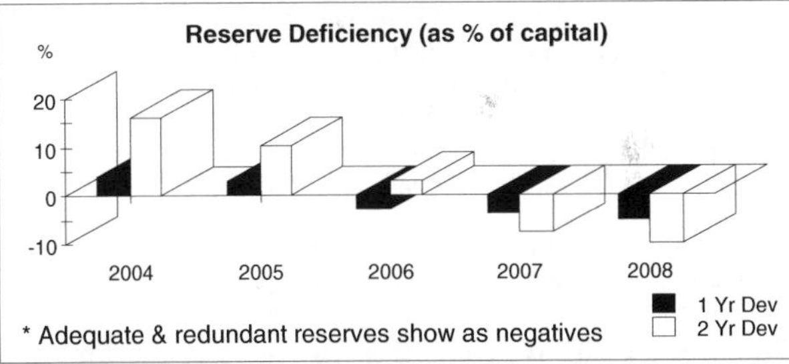

FACTORY MUTUAL INS CO — C Fair

Major Rating Factors: Fair overall results on stability tests (4.1 on a scale of 0 to 10) including fair financial strength of affiliated FM Global. The largest net exposure for one risk is high at 4.8% of capital. History of adequate reserve strength (5.5) as reserves have been consistently at an acceptable level.

Other Rating Factors: Good overall profitability index (5.6) despite operating losses during 2008. Good liquidity (6.6) with sufficient resources (cash flows and marketable investments) to handle a spike in claims. Strong long-term capitalization index (7.9) based on excellent current risk adjusted capital (severe and moderate loss scenarios), despite some fluctuation in capital levels.

Principal Business: Allied lines (40%), inland marine (25%), fire (22%), and boiler & machinery (12%).

Principal Investments: Misc. investments (60%), investment grade bonds (38%), cash (1%), and non investment grade bonds (1%).

Investments in Affiliates: 23%

Group Affiliation: FM Global

Licensed in: All states, the District of Columbia and Puerto Rico

Commenced Business: December 1835

Address: 1301 Atwood Avenue, Johnston, RI 02919-4908

Phone: (401) 275-3000 **Domicile State:** RI **NAIC Code:** 21482

Data Date	Rating	RACR #1	RACR #2	Loss Ratio %	Total Assets ($mil)	Capital ($mil)	Net Premium ($mil)	Net Income ($mil)
3-09	C	2.02	1.63	N/A	8,433.0	4,667.6	629.0	189.2
3-08	C	1.97	1.50	N/A	9,564.1	5,466.6	571.2	9.7
2008	C	1.99	1.59	77.6	8,602.6	4,734.2	2,262.5	-596.2
2007	C	2.02	1.52	44.6	9,961.9	5,770.5	2,384.0	835.8
2006	C	2.16	1.57	51.3	9,152.6	5,016.7	2,449.6	591.7
2005	C	1.91	1.41	53.4	7,979.3	4,204.2	2,265.2	525.8
2004	C	1.62	1.18	48.5	6,974.5	3,532.8	2,081.2	501.5

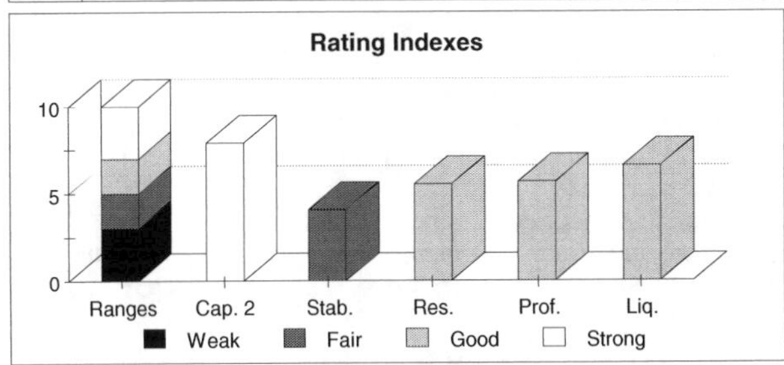

FAIRMONT PREMIER INS CO C- Fair

Major Rating Factors: Fair reserve development (4.0 on a scale of 0 to 10) as the level of reserves has at times been insufficient to cover claims. In 2004 and 2005 the two year reserve development was 22% and 47% deficient respectively. Fair overall results on stability tests (3.1) including weak financial strength of affiliated Fairfax Financial, weak results on operational trends and negative cash flow from operations for 2008.

Other Rating Factors: Strong long-term capitalization index (7.1) based on excellent current risk adjusted capital (severe and moderate loss scenarios), despite some fluctuation in capital levels. Excellent profitability (7.2) despite modest operating losses during the first three months of 2008. Excellent expense controls. Superior liquidity (10.0) with ample operational cash flow and liquid investments.

Principal Business: (Not applicable due to unusual reinsurance transactions.)

Principal Investments: Misc. investments (83%) and investment grade bonds (17%).

Investments in Affiliates: 78%

Group Affiliation: Fairfax Financial

Licensed in: All states except NH, NY, PR

Commenced Business: August 1941

Address: 5205 N.O'Conner Blvd, 2nd Fl, Irving, TX 75015

Phone: (714) 937-2700 **Domicile State:** CA **NAIC Code:** 25518

Data Date	Rating	RACR #1	RACR #2	Loss Ratio %	Total Assets ($mil)	Capital ($mil)	Net Premium ($mil)	Net Income ($mil)
3-09	C-	1.28	1.27	N/A	209.7	186.7	-0.1	-0.1
3-08	C-	1.33	1.30	N/A	209.5	184.2	0.0	0.0
2008	C-	1.30	1.29	N/A	212.3	189.6	-0.2	0.2
2007	C-	1.31	1.30	N/A	206.9	177.2	0.1	4.3
2006	C-	1.28	1.28	72.6	185.6	139.4	2.3	1.2
2005	C-	1.28	1.27	63.3	188.0	137.2	31.8	3.3
2004	C+	1.15	1.14	64.4	168.5	119.9	33.3	-0.7

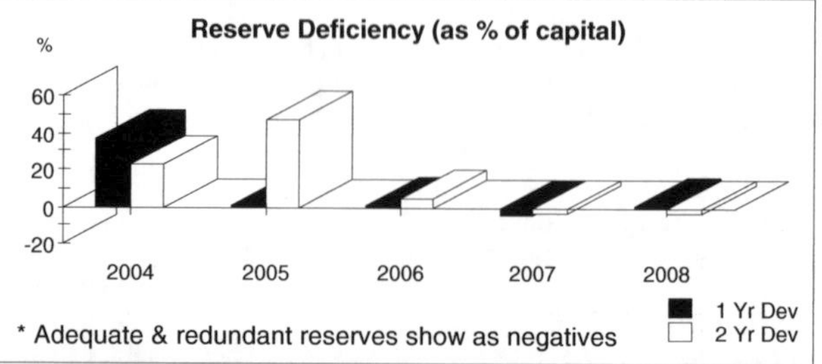

FARM BUREAU MUTUAL INS CO * A- Excellent

Major Rating Factors: Strong long-term capitalization index (8.4 on a scale of 0 to 10) based on excellent current risk adjusted capital (severe and moderate loss scenarios). Furthermore, this high level of risk adjusted capital has been consistently maintained in previous years. Ample reserve history (7.0) that can protect against increases in claims costs.

Other Rating Factors: Excellent overall results on stability tests (7.0). Stability strengths include excellent operational trends and excellent risk diversification. Good overall profitability index (5.2) despite operating losses during 2008. Good liquidity (5.6) with sufficient resources (cash flows and marketable investments) to handle a spike in claims.

Principal Business: Auto liability (26%), auto physical damage (23%), farmowners multiple peril (20%), homeowners multiple peril (20%), commercial multiple peril (5%), workers compensation (4%), and other liability (2%).

Principal Investments: Investment grade bonds (78%), misc. investments (19%), real estate (3%), and non investment grade bonds (1%).

Investments in Affiliates: 6%

Group Affiliation: Iowa Farm Bureau

Licensed in: AZ, IA, KS, MN, MO, NE, NM, SD, UT

Commenced Business: May 1939

Address: 5400 University Ave, West Des Moines, IA 50265-0540

Phone: (515) 225-5400 **Domicile State:** IA **NAIC Code:** 13773

Data Date	Rating	RACR #1	RACR #2	Loss Ratio %	Total Assets ($mil)	Capital ($mil)	Net Premium ($mil)	Net Income ($mil)
3-09	A-	2.79	1.93	N/A	1,586.9	560.9	183.6	13.2
3-08	A-	3.67	2.61	N/A	1,484.3	650.9	175.9	17.8
2008	A-	2.75	1.91	85.1	1,601.1	574.6	908.8	-47.8
2007	A-	3.65	2.63	67.2	1,460.0	633.9	764.5	53.8
2006	B+	3.39	2.39	63.7	1,380.2	587.4	701.4	72.8
2005	B	3.22	2.23	63.8	1,299.0	521.9	704.2	91.2
2004	B	2.63	1.82	67.0	1,272.1	440.3	701.7	60.1

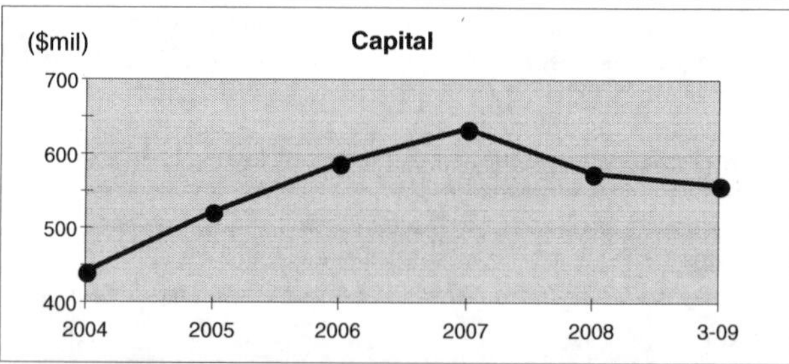

FARM BUREAU MUTUAL INS CO OF ID * B+ Good

Major Rating Factors: Good overall results on stability tests (5.0 on a scale of 0 to 10) despite potential drain of affiliation with Farm Bureau Group of Idaho. Stability strengths include good operational trends and excellent risk diversification. Good liquidity (6.4) with sufficient resources (cash flows and marketable investments) to handle a spike in claims.

Other Rating Factors: Strong long-term capitalization index (9.5) based on excellent current risk adjusted capital (severe and moderate loss scenarios), despite some fluctuation in capital levels. Ample reserve history (8.0) that helps to protect the company against sharp claims increases. Excellent profitability (8.0) with operating gains in each of the last five years.

Principal Business: Auto liability (34%), auto physical damage (25%), farmowners multiple peril (18%), homeowners multiple peril (15%), inland marine (3%), other liability (2%), and allied lines (2%).

Principal Investments: Investment grade bonds (68%), misc. investments (26%), real estate (5%), and cash (1%).

Investments in Affiliates: 13%

Group Affiliation: Farm Bureau Group of Idaho

Licensed in: ID

Commenced Business: May 1947

Address: 1001 N 7th Centennial Plaza, Pocatello, ID 83201

Phone: (208) 232-7914 **Domicile State:** ID **NAIC Code:** 13765

Data Date	Rating	RACR #1	RACR #2	Loss Ratio %	Total Assets ($mil)	Capital ($mil)	Net Premium ($mil)	Net Income ($mil)
3-09	B+	3.74	2.89	N/A	346.7	190.9	32.1	1.7
3-08	B+	3.45	2.78	N/A	355.6	197.4	33.7	-0.4
2008	B+	3.71	2.87	72.6	354.0	193.5	132.7	7.7
2007	B+	3.47	2.78	64.5	365.5	200.9	141.3	18.8
2006	B+	3.12	2.49	68.4	348.4	180.9	142.9	15.8
2005	B+	2.82	2.20	64.1	325.2	159.5	134.1	16.5
2004	B+	2.51	1.93	69.3	295.1	138.3	132.2	10.2

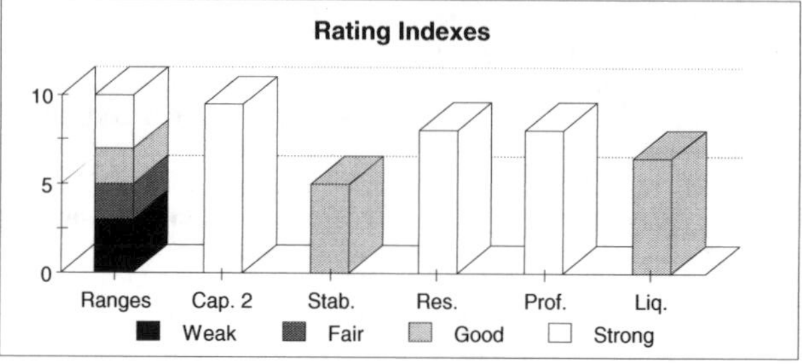

FARM BUREAU MUTUAL INS CO OF MI — B- Good

Major Rating Factors: Fair profitability index (3.6 on a scale of 0 to 10) with operating losses during the first three months of 2008. Fair overall results on stability tests (4.9).

Other Rating Factors: History of adequate reserve strength (6.5) as reserves have been consistently at an acceptable level. Good liquidity (5.3) with sufficient resources (cash flows and marketable investments) to handle a spike in claims. Strong long-term capitalization index (8.9) based on excellent current risk adjusted capital (severe and moderate loss scenarios), despite some fluctuation in capital levels.

Principal Business: Farmowners multiple peril (42%), auto liability (28%), auto physical damage (20%), workers compensation (6%), inland marine (2%), and other liability (1%).

Principal Investments: Investment grade bonds (86%), misc. investments (14%), and non investment grade bonds (1%).

Investments in Affiliates: None

Group Affiliation: Michigan Farm Bureau

Licensed in: MI

Commenced Business: March 1949

Address: 7373 W Saginaw Hwy, Lansing, MI 48917

Phone: (517) 323-7000 **Domicile State:** MI **NAIC Code:** 21555

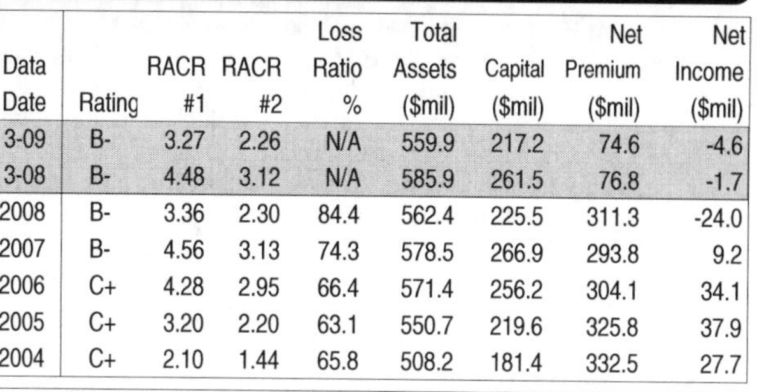

Data Date	Rating	RACR #1	RACR #2	Loss Ratio %	Total Assets ($mil)	Capital ($mil)	Net Premium ($mil)	Net Income ($mil)
3-09	B-	3.27	2.26	N/A	559.9	217.2	74.6	-4.6
3-08	B-	4.48	3.12	N/A	585.9	261.5	76.8	-1.7
2008	B-	3.36	2.30	84.4	562.4	225.5	311.3	-24.0
2007	B-	4.56	3.13	74.3	578.5	266.9	293.8	9.2
2006	C+	4.28	2.95	66.4	571.4	256.2	304.1	34.1
2005	C+	3.20	2.20	63.1	550.7	219.6	325.8	37.9
2004	C+	2.10	1.44	65.8	508.2	181.4	332.5	27.7

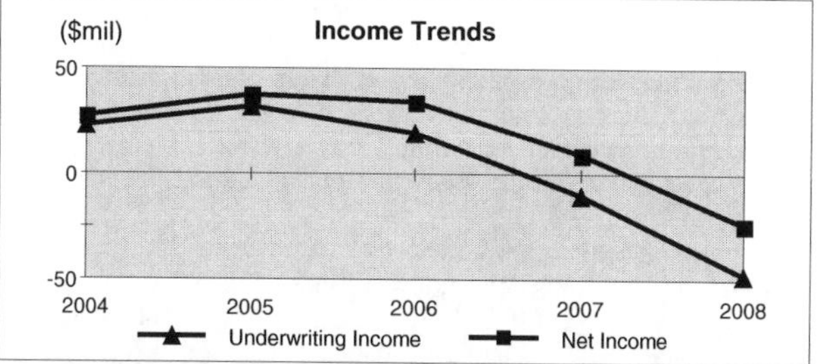

FARM FAMILY CASUALTY INS CO — B Good

Major Rating Factors: Good overall profitability index (6.9 on a scale of 0 to 10) despite operating losses during the first three months of 2008. Return on equity has been good over the last five years, averaging 12.0%. Good liquidity (6.3) with sufficient resources (cash flows and marketable investments) to handle a spike in claims.

Other Rating Factors: Good overall results on stability tests (5.5). Stability strengths include good operational trends and excellent risk diversification. Strong long-term capitalization index (8.6) based on excellent current risk adjusted capital (severe and moderate loss scenarios), despite some fluctuation in capital levels. Ample reserve history (7.0) that can protect against increases in claims costs.

Principal Business: Auto liability (28%), workers compensation (12%), auto physical damage (11%), other liability (11%), commercial multiple peril (10%), fire (9%), and other lines (19%).

Principal Investments: Investment grade bonds (91%), misc. investments (7%), cash (1%), and non investment grade bonds (1%).

Investments in Affiliates: None

Group Affiliation: American National Group Inc

Licensed in: CT, DE, ME, MA, MO, NH, NJ, NY, RI, VT, WV

Commenced Business: November 1956

Address: 344 Route 9W, Glenmont, NY 12077-2910

Phone: (518) 431-5000 **Domicile State:** NY **NAIC Code:** 13803

Data Date	Rating	RACR #1	RACR #2	Loss Ratio %	Total Assets ($mil)	Capital ($mil)	Net Premium ($mil)	Net Income ($mil)
3-09	B	3.32	2.25	N/A	954.1	273.4	89.4	-2.0
3-08	B	3.38	2.31	N/A	961.2	280.2	93.1	2.8
2008	B	3.33	2.29	76.4	944.2	272.2	367.2	11.9
2007	B	3.45	2.40	70.4	948.4	280.8	377.8	38.4
2006	B-	3.00	2.12	70.5	913.2	243.2	389.8	38.2
2005	B-	2.14	1.52	71.6	813.9	204.0	402.7	35.6
2004	B-	1.57	1.10	75.2	722.4	172.0	396.0	21.4

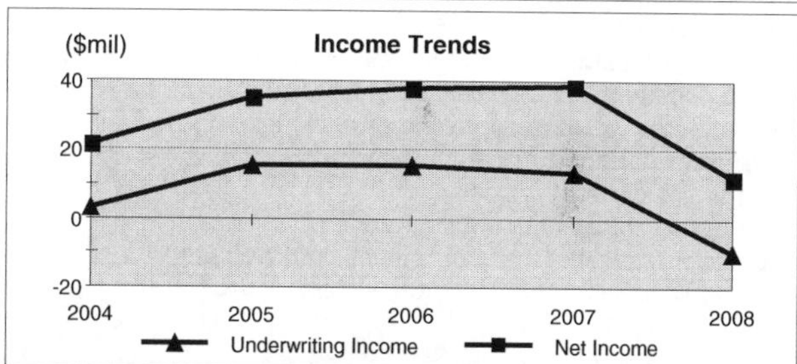

FARMERS AUTOMOBILE INS ASN * — B+ Good

Major Rating Factors: Good overall results on stability tests (6.0 on a scale of 0 to 10). Affiliation with Farmers Automobile Ins Assn is a strength. Good liquidity (6.2) with sufficient resources (cash flows and marketable investments) to handle a spike in claims.

Other Rating Factors: Strong long-term capitalization index (8.5) based on excellent current risk adjusted capital (severe and moderate loss scenarios), despite some fluctuation in capital levels. Ample reserve history (9.3) that helps to protect the company against sharp claims increases. Fair profitability index (4.5) with operating losses during the first three months of 2008.

Principal Business: Auto liability (33%), auto physical damage (31%), homeowners multiple peril (29%), allied lines (3%), fire (2%), and inland marine (1%).

Principal Investments: Investment grade bonds (74%), misc. investments (24%), cash (1%), and real estate (1%).

Investments in Affiliates: 21%

Group Affiliation: Farmers Automobile Ins Assn

Licensed in: IL, IN, IA, MI, OH, WI

Commenced Business: April 1921

Address: 2505 Court St, Pekin, IL 61558

Phone: (309) 346-1161 **Domicile State:** IL **NAIC Code:** 24201

Data Date	Rating	RACR #1	RACR #2	Loss Ratio %	Total Assets ($mil)	Capital ($mil)	Net Premium ($mil)	Net Income ($mil)
3-09	B+	2.26	1.95	N/A	852.7	369.7	77.2	-1.2
3-08	B+	2.49	2.18	N/A	860.5	408.7	78.6	-1.2
2008	B+	2.30	2.00	89.9	850.7	375.7	318.7	-15.9
2007	B+	2.54	2.24	72.4	859.1	416.4	319.6	24.7
2006	B+	2.61	2.31	71.4	811.1	393.2	317.3	24.0
2005	B+	2.58	2.25	63.3	744.2	354.3	316.2	38.7
2004	B+	2.35	2.00	61.8	665.0	304.4	302.4	36.8

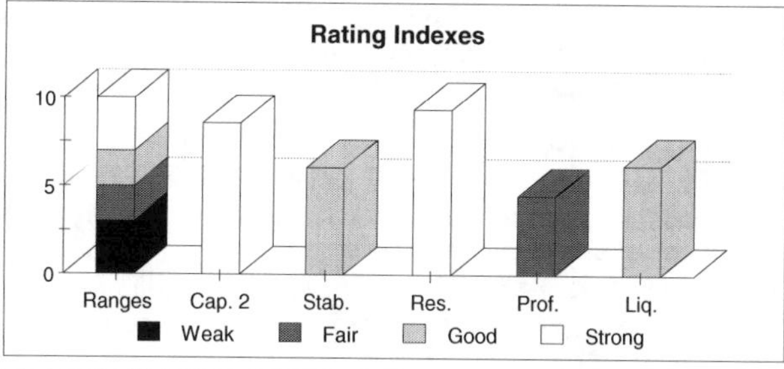

FARMERS INS CO OF OR B- Good

Major Rating Factors: Fair reserve development (4.4 on a scale of 0 to 10) as the level of reserves has at times been insufficient to cover claims. In 2005 and 2004 the two year reserve development was 16% and 24% deficient respectively. Fair overall results on stability tests (4.9) including fair financial strength of affiliated Zurich Financial Services Group.

Other Rating Factors: Good overall profitability index (6.8). Fair expense controls. Return on equity has been fair, averaging 6.8% over the past five years. Good liquidity (6.3) with sufficient resources (cash flows and marketable investments) to handle a spike in claims. Strong long-term capitalization index (8.2) based on excellent current risk adjusted capital (severe and moderate loss scenarios), despite some fluctuation in capital levels.

Principal Business: Auto liability (50%), auto physical damage (26%), homeowners multiple peril (18%), commercial multiple peril (3%), earthquake (1%), and allied lines (1%).

Principal Investments: Investment grade bonds (105%) and non investment grade bonds (1%).

Investments in Affiliates: None

Group Affiliation: Zurich Financial Services Group

Licensed in: CA, MI, OR

Commenced Business: October 1970

Address: 13333 SW 68th Parkway, Tigard, OR 97223

Phone: (503) 620-6200 **Domicile State:** OR **NAIC Code:** 21636

Data Date	Rating	RACR #1	RACR #2	Loss Ratio %	Total Assets ($mil)	Capital ($mil)	Net Premium ($mil)	Net Income ($mil)
3-09	B-	2.90	1.90	N/A	1,505.0	524.6	181.3	5.1
3-08	B-	2.54	1.66	N/A	1,611.6	529.9	218.4	7.7
2008	B-	2.75	1.84	75.5	1,523.6	520.4	825.2	3.5
2007	B-	2.53	1.68	69.6	1,579.2	522.9	896.9	39.5
2006	C+	2.79	1.80	67.0	1,501.8	519.9	811.7	49.6
2005	C+	2.65	1.73	68.2	1,429.9	466.6	757.3	48.9
2004	C+	2.61	1.71	70.3	1,218.8	422.5	674.2	26.9

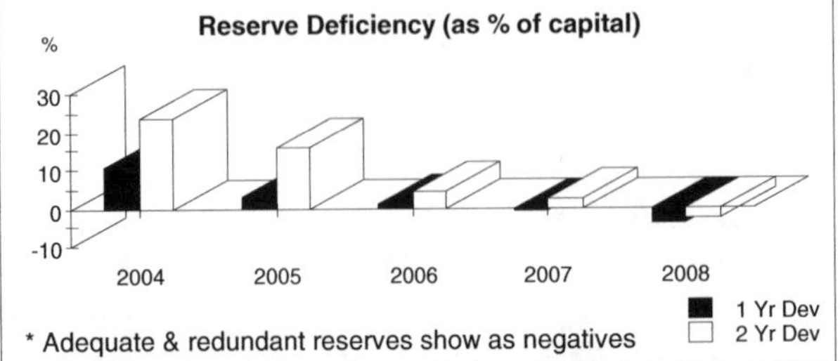

FARMERS INS CO OF WA C+ Fair

Major Rating Factors: Fair reserve development (4.7 on a scale of 0 to 10) as reserves have generally been sufficient to cover claims. In 2004, the two year reserve development was 23% deficient. Fair overall results on stability tests (4.7) including fair financial strength of affiliated Zurich Financial Services Group.

Other Rating Factors: Good liquidity (6.5) with sufficient resources (cash flows and marketable investments) to handle a spike in claims. Strong long-term capitalization index (8.4) based on excellent current risk adjusted capital (severe and moderate loss scenarios). Moreover, capital levels have been consistent in recent years. Excellent profitability (7.2) with operating gains in each of the last five years.

Principal Business: Auto liability (48%), homeowners multiple peril (26%), auto physical damage (21%), commercial multiple peril (4%), earthquake (1%), and allied lines (1%).

Principal Investments: Investment grade bonds (106%) and non investment grade bonds (1%).

Investments in Affiliates: None

Group Affiliation: Zurich Financial Services Group

Licensed in: WA

Commenced Business: October 1970

Address: 5306 NE Gher Rd, Vancouver, WA 98682

Phone: (206) 253-7200 **Domicile State:** WA **NAIC Code:** 21644

Data Date	Rating	RACR #1	RACR #2	Loss Ratio %	Total Assets ($mil)	Capital ($mil)	Net Premium ($mil)	Net Income ($mil)
3-09	C+	3.21	2.10	N/A	501.2	165.6	51.8	1.9
3-08	C+	2.75	1.80	N/A	530.6	164.2	62.4	2.6
2008	C+	3.06	2.04	74.9	488.0	164.3	235.8	4.3
2007	C+	2.74	1.82	68.3	520.2	161.6	256.3	13.3
2006	C+	2.75	1.77	66.8	477.2	147.0	231.9	15.0
2005	C+	2.60	1.70	67.9	438.9	131.2	216.4	15.0
2004	C+	2.56	1.67	69.8	342.9	118.0	192.6	9.2

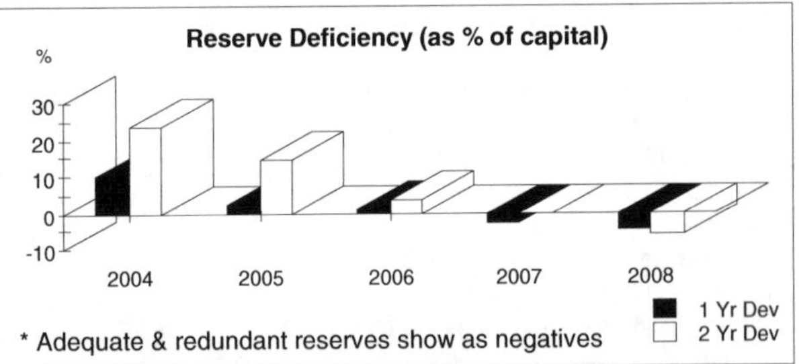

FARMERS INS EXCHANGE C Fair

Major Rating Factors: Fair reserve development (3.7 on a scale of 0 to 10) as the level of reserves has at times been insufficient to cover claims. In 2005 and 2004 the two year reserve development was 22% and 33% deficient respectively. Fair overall results on stability tests (3.4) including negative cash flow from operations for 2008.

Other Rating Factors: Good overall profitability index (5.3) despite operating losses during the first three months of 2008. Good liquidity (5.9) with sufficient resources (cash flows and marketable investments) to handle a spike in claims. Strong long-term capitalization index (7.2) based on excellent current risk adjusted capital (severe and moderate loss scenarios), despite some fluctuation in capital levels.

Principal Business: Auto liability (36%), homeowners multiple peril (23%), auto physical damage (23%), commercial multiple peril (13%), other liability (2%), workers compensation (2%), and fire (1%).

Principal Investments: Investment grade bonds (76%) and misc. investments (25%).

Investments in Affiliates: 21%

Group Affiliation: Zurich Financial Services Group

Licensed in: All states except AK, CT, DE, HI, NY, PA, VT, WV, PR

Commenced Business: April 1928

Address: 4680 Wilshire Blvd, Los Angeles, CA 90010

Phone: (213) 932-3441 **Domicile State:** CA **NAIC Code:** 21652

Data Date	Rating	RACR #1	RACR #2	Loss Ratio %	Total Assets ($mil)	Capital ($mil)	Net Premium ($mil)	Net Income ($mil)
3-09	C	1.40	1.15	N/A	13,763.9	3,253.9	1,340.1	-5.2
3-08	C	1.20	0.99	N/A	13,500.0	3,475.6	1,614.2	40.9
2008	C	1.39	1.15	76.2	13,368.0	3,253.9	6,100.5	-32.0
2007	C	1.20	1.00	71.2	13,053.2	3,446.7	6,630.9	154.5
2006	C	1.23	1.00	67.1	11,919.1	3,148.6	6,000.6	244.7
2005	C	1.19	0.97	68.5	11,402.7	2,721.0	5,598.8	220.7
2004	C	1.09	0.90	70.6	10,117.2	2,401.2	4,984.3	63.3

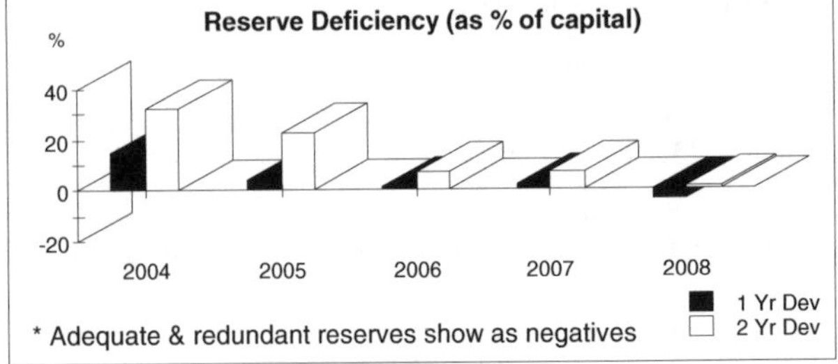

FARMERS MUTUAL HAIL INS CO OF IA — C+ Fair

Major Rating Factors: Fair overall results on stability tests (4.0 on a scale of 0 to 10) including potential drain of affiliation with Farmers Mutual Hail Ins Co, excessive premium growth and weak results on operational trends. The largest net exposure for one risk is high at 3.7% of capital. Fair profitability index (3.1) with operating losses during the first three months of 2008.

Other Rating Factors: Good long-term capitalization (6.8) based on good current risk adjusted capital (moderate loss scenario) reflecting improvement over results in 2008. History of adequate reserve strength (6.0) as reserves have been consistently at an acceptable level. Vulnerable liquidity (1.3) as a spike in claims may stretch capacity.

Principal Business: Allied lines (100%).

Principal Investments: Investment grade bonds (54%), cash (28%), misc. investments (14%), and real estate (4%).

Investments in Affiliates: 3%

Group Affiliation: Farmers Mutual Hail Ins Co

Licensed in: All states except AK, DC, HI, LA, ME, NV, NM, RI, VT, WV, PR

Commenced Business: March 1893

Address: 6785 Westown Parkway, West Des Moines, IA 50266

Phone: (515) 282-9104 **Domicile State:** IA **NAIC Code:** 13897

Data Date	Rating	RACR #1	RACR #2	Loss Ratio %	Total Assets ($mil)	Capital ($mil)	Net Premium ($mil)	Net Income ($mil)
3-09	C+	2.65	1.59	N/A	497.8	234.6	8.4	-27.8
3-08	C	2.06	1.33	N/A	410.8	253.6	4.3	-10.2
2008	C+	1.23	0.77	85.2	605.3	259.9	384.9	5.3
2007	C	1.91	1.23	56.9	388.1	265.3	229.9	42.4
2006	C	1.90	1.24	55.7	315.5	221.2	174.0	33.4
2005	C	1.46	0.97	62.4	292.9	189.3	169.1	23.5
2004	C+	1.22	0.80	62.7	272.7	168.5	160.4	29.4

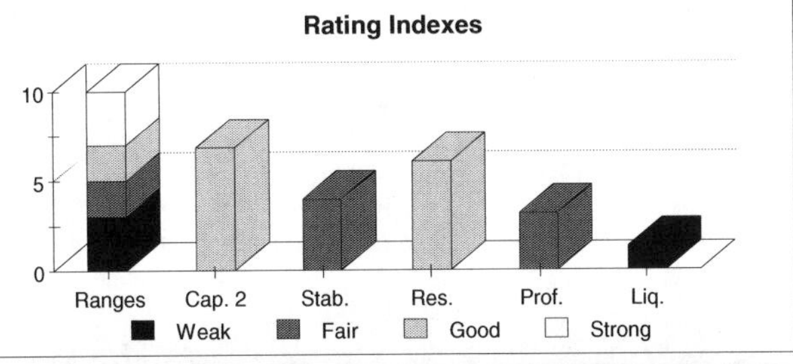

FARMERS MUTUAL INS CO OF NE — B- Good

Major Rating Factors: Good liquidity (6.8 on a scale of 0 to 10) with sufficient resources (cash flows and marketable investments) to handle a spike in claims. Good overall results on stability tests (5.3) despite negative cash flow from operations for 2008.

Other Rating Factors: Strong long-term capitalization index (10.0) based on excellent current risk adjusted capital (severe and moderate loss scenarios), despite some fluctuation in capital levels. Ample reserve history (8.2) that helps to protect the company against sharp claims increases. Excellent profitability (8.2) with operating gains in each of the last five years. Return on equity has been good over the last five years, averaging 10.3%.

Principal Business: Homeowners multiple peril (28%), farmowners multiple peril (25%), auto liability (21%), auto physical damage (20%), allied lines (2%), fire (2%), and other liability (1%).

Principal Investments: Investment grade bonds (86%), misc. investments (14%), and real estate (1%).

Investments in Affiliates: None

Group Affiliation: None

Licensed in: IL, IN, IA, KS, NE, ND, SD

Commenced Business: November 1891

Address: 1220 Lincoln Mall, Lincoln, NE 68501

Phone: (402) 434-8342 **Domicile State:** NE **NAIC Code:** 13889

Data Date	Rating	RACR #1	RACR #2	Loss Ratio %	Total Assets ($mil)	Capital ($mil)	Net Premium ($mil)	Net Income ($mil)
3-09	B-	6.08	4.67	N/A	431.3	249.5	47.4	6.9
3-08	B-	5.93	4.57	N/A	436.9	263.0	46.6	13.6
2008	B-	6.01	4.44	79.9	427.0	249.9	185.9	4.0
2007	B-	5.66	4.21	67.0	431.1	255.0	194.1	20.8
2006	B-	5.64	4.17	54.6	392.1	235.9	175.3	31.6
2005	B-	5.07	3.55	63.1	352.2	200.5	174.5	21.9
2004	B-	4.75	3.34	52.8	323.6	178.2	167.8	30.5

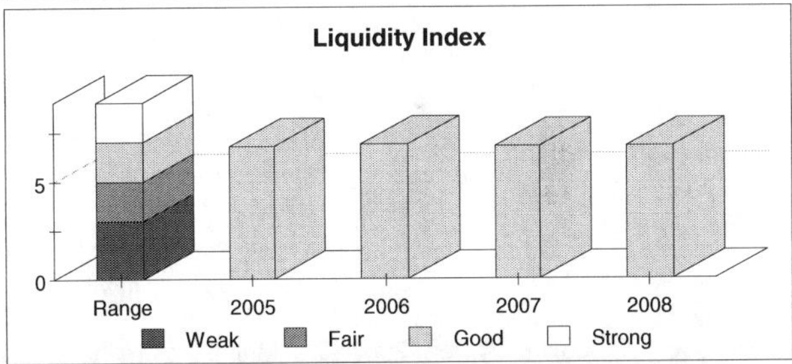

FARMERS REINS CO — C+ Fair

Major Rating Factors: Fair profitability index (4.4 on a scale of 0 to 10) with operating losses during the first three months of 2008. Return on equity has been low, averaging 3.9% over the past five years. Fair overall results on stability tests (4.5) including fair financial strength of affiliated Zurich Financial Services Group and excessive premium growth.

Other Rating Factors: History of adequate reserve strength (5.3) as reserves have been consistently at an acceptable level. Good liquidity (6.9) with sufficient resources (cash flows and marketable investments) to handle a spike in claims. Strong long-term capitalization index (10.0) based on excellent current risk adjusted capital (severe and moderate loss scenarios), despite some fluctuation in capital levels.

Principal Business: (This company is a reinsurer.)

Principal Investments: Investment grade bonds (51%) and misc. investments (49%).

Investments in Affiliates: None

Group Affiliation: Zurich Financial Services Group

Licensed in: CA

Commenced Business: August 1997

Address: 4680 Wilshire Blvd, Los Angeles, CA 90010

Phone: (213) 932-3441 **Domicile State:** CA **NAIC Code:** 10873

Data Date	Rating	RACR #1	RACR #2	Loss Ratio %	Total Assets ($mil)	Capital ($mil)	Net Premium ($mil)	Net Income ($mil)
3-09	C+	7.66	4.75	N/A	1,536.5	971.9	221.8	-12.6
3-08	C+	13.08	7.58	N/A	1,316.9	1,049.3	82.8	10.3
2008	C+	9.11	5.44	68.2	1,450.4	985.5	676.2	-29.3
2007	C+	12.25	7.13	66.6	1,267.1	1,054.7	346.2	55.8
2006	C	12.03	6.92	64.6	1,283.1	996.3	348.0	50.5
2005	C	13.03	7.43	60.4	1,326.3	939.8	430.6	67.8
2004	C	6.64	4.35	54.8	1,292.1	878.5	625.6	63.7

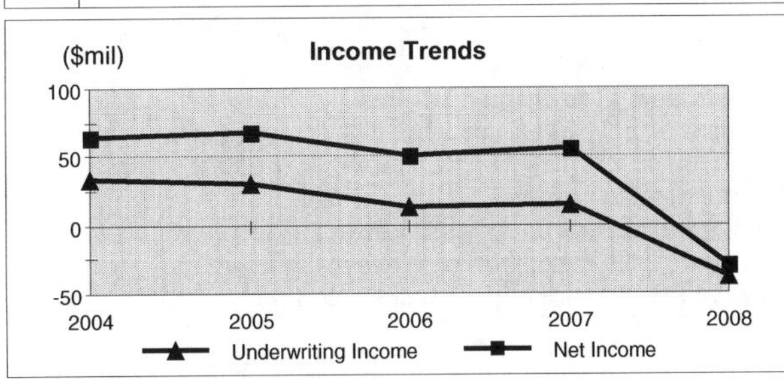

FARMINGTON CASUALTY CO — B — Good

Major Rating Factors: Good liquidity (6.6 on a scale of 0 to 10) with sufficient resources (cash flows and marketable investments) to handle a spike in claims. Good overall results on stability tests (5.4).

Other Rating Factors: Fair reserve development (4.6) as reserves have generally been sufficient to cover claims. In 2005, the two year reserve development was 29% deficient. Strong long-term capitalization index (7.5) based on excellent current risk adjusted capital (severe and moderate loss scenarios), despite some fluctuation in capital levels. Excellent profitability (8.4) with operating gains in each of the last five years. Return on equity has been excellent over the last five years averaging 19.0%.

Principal Business: Homeowners multiple peril (46%), workers compensation (45%), auto liability (7%), auto physical damage (1%), and surety (1%).

Principal Investments: Investment grade bonds (94%), misc. investments (5%), and non investment grade bonds (1%).

Investments in Affiliates: 2%

Group Affiliation: Travelers Companies Inc

Licensed in: All states except PR

Commenced Business: October 1982

Address: One Tower Square, Hartford, CT 06183

Phone: (860) 277-0111 **Domicile State:** CT **NAIC Code:** 41483

Data Date	Rating	RACR #1	RACR #2	Loss Ratio %	Total Assets ($mil)	Capital ($mil)	Net Premium ($mil)	Net Income ($mil)
3-09	B	2.18	1.40	N/A	976.9	277.4	66.7	11.0
3-08	B-	2.27	1.32	N/A	989.2	287.2	66.3	15.4
2008	B	2.14	1.38	61.5	983.2	268.4	268.5	44.1
2007	B-	2.19	1.27	59.0	981.9	272.8	266.4	54.5
2006	C+	1.75	1.09	58.4	941.9	240.7	257.2	53.4
2005	C+	1.44	0.94	75.1	931.5	218.0	242.4	28.1
2004	C+	1.56	1.04	63.7	944.5	228.0	275.5	55.9

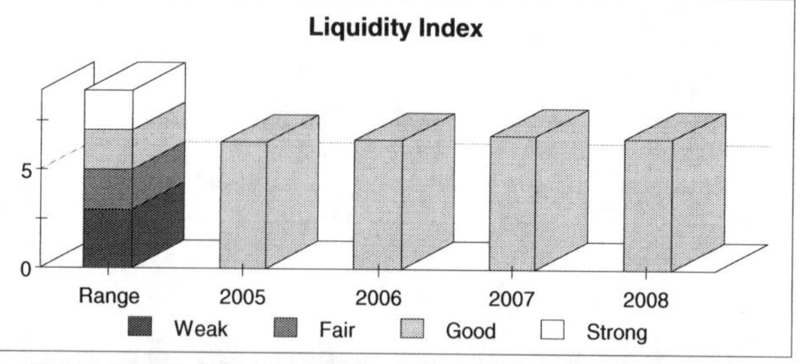

FARMLAND MUTUAL INS CO * — B+ — Good

Major Rating Factors: Good overall results on stability tests (6.4 on a scale of 0 to 10) despite negative cash flow from operations for 2008. Stability strengths include good operational trends and excellent risk diversification. History of adequate reserve strength (6.2) as reserves have been consistently at an acceptable level.

Other Rating Factors: Good liquidity (6.0) with sufficient resources (cash flows and marketable investments) to handle a spike in claims. Strong long-term capitalization index (9.9) based on excellent current risk adjusted capital (severe and moderate loss scenarios). Moreover, capital levels have been consistent in recent years. Excellent profitability (7.9) with operating gains in each of the last five years.

Principal Business: Commercial multiple peril (44%), workers compensation (22%), auto liability (16%), other liability (10%), auto physical damage (5%), products liability (2%), and surety (1%).

Principal Investments: Investment grade bonds (70%), misc. investments (23%), and cash (7%).

Investments in Affiliates: None

Group Affiliation: Nationwide Corp

Licensed in: AL, AZ, AR, CA, CO, DC, DE, FL, GA, ID, IL, IN, IA, KS, KY, MD, MI, MN, MS, MO, MT, NE, NV, NC, ND, OH, OK, OR, PA, SC, SD, TN, TX, UT, VA, WA, WV, WI, WY

Commenced Business: June 1909

Address: 1100 Locust St Dept 2007, Des Moines, IA 50391-2007

Data Date	Rating	RACR #1	RACR #2	Loss Ratio %	Total Assets ($mil)	Capital ($mil)	Net Premium ($mil)	Net Income ($mil)
3-09	B+	4.49	3.21	N/A	371.1	154.3	37.6	2.2
3-08	B+	4.65	3.37	N/A	322.7	154.1	38.2	2.9
2008	B+	4.42	3.17	74.7	367.1	152.1	152.7	2.0
2007	B+	4.54	3.30	64.5	331.3	151.1	155.4	10.9
2006	B+	4.40	3.21	60.7	332.3	140.9	155.9	18.0
2005	B+	3.84	2.80	65.8	338.2	118.5	148.0	9.8
2004	B+	3.39	2.49	64.5	317.1	108.7	140.1	13.6

Nationwide Corp Composite Group Rating: B+ Largest Group Members	Assets ($mil)	Rating
NATIONWIDE LIFE INS CO	77310	B+
NATIONWIDE MUTUAL INS CO	28843	B
NATIONWIDE LIFE INS CO OF AMERICA	4994	B+
NATIONWIDE LIFE ANNUITY INS CO	4349	B
NATIONWIDE MUTUAL FIRE INS CO	4319	B+

FCCI INS CO — C+ — Fair

Major Rating Factors: Fair overall results on stability tests (4.2 on a scale of 0 to 10) including potential drain of affiliation with FCCI Ins Group. Fair profitability index (4.8) with operating losses during the first three months of 2008. Return on equity has been low, averaging 4.6% over the past five years.

Other Rating Factors: Good long-term capitalization index (6.9) based on good current risk adjusted capital (moderate loss scenario), despite some fluctuation in capital levels. Good liquidity (6.2) with sufficient resources (cash flows and marketable investments) to handle a spike in claims. Ample reserve history (9.4) that helps to protect the company against sharp claims increases.

Principal Business: Workers compensation (69%), commercial multiple peril (8%), auto liability (7%), other liability (6%), allied lines (4%), fire (2%), and other lines (4%).

Principal Investments: Investment grade bonds (83%), misc. investments (14%), and real estate (3%).

Investments in Affiliates: 9%

Group Affiliation: FCCI Ins Group

Licensed in: AL, AZ, CT, FL, GA, IL, IN, IA, KS, KY, MD, MI, MS, MO, NE, NC, OH, OK, PA, SC, TN, VA

Commenced Business: April 1959

Address: 2601 Cattlemen Rd, Sarasota, FL 34232

Phone: (941) 951-3603 **Domicile State:** FL **NAIC Code:** 10178

Data Date	Rating	RACR #1	RACR #2	Loss Ratio %	Total Assets ($mil)	Capital ($mil)	Net Premium ($mil)	Net Income ($mil)
3-09	C+	1.26	0.98	N/A	1,450.2	360.9	112.5	-3.5
3-08	C	1.32	1.03	N/A	1,486.2	413.3	121.1	0.3
2008	C+	1.32	1.03	69.7	1,400.0	376.8	474.9	11.2
2007	C	1.34	1.06	67.2	1,407.3	420.6	508.5	28.1
2006	C	1.11	0.88	64.9	1,342.3	390.1	539.7	30.2
2005	C	0.93	0.74	67.2	1,242.4	347.5	583.0	19.4
2004	C	2.15	1.44	66.6	1,052.1	327.2	434.8	7.1

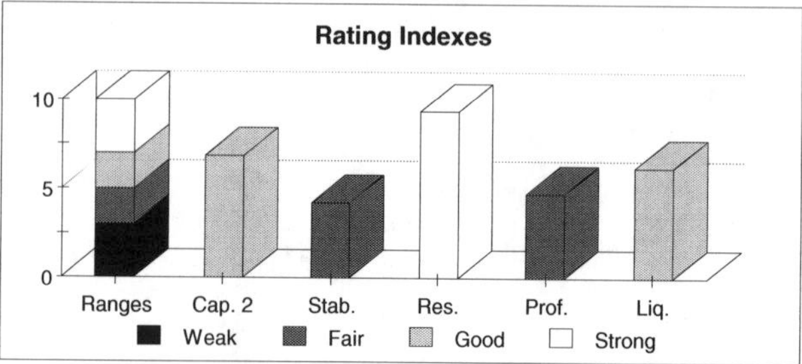

FEDERAL INS CO * B+ Good

Major Rating Factors: History of adequate reserve strength (5.6 on a scale of 0 to 10) as reserves have been consistently at an acceptable level. Good liquidity (6.8) with sufficient resources (cash flows and marketable investments) to handle a spike in claims.

Other Rating Factors: Good overall results on stability tests (6.8). Stability strengths include good operational trends and excellent risk diversification. The largest net exposure for one risk is acceptable at 2.2% of capital. Strong long-term capitalization index (7.3) based on excellent current risk adjusted capital (severe and moderate loss scenarios), despite some fluctuation in capital levels. Excellent profitability (7.7) with operating gains in each of the last five years. Return on equity has been good over the last five years, averaging 14.3%.

Principal Business: Other liability (34%), commercial multiple peril (18%), workers compensation (8%), homeowners multiple peril (8%), surety (5%), fidelity (4%), and other lines (23%).

Principal Investments: Investment grade bonds (57%), misc. investments (42%), and non investment grade bonds (1%).

Investments in Affiliates: 32%

Group Affiliation: Chubb Corp

Licensed in: All states, the District of Columbia and Puerto Rico

Commenced Business: March 1901

Address: 211 N Pennsylvania St #1350, Indianapolis, IN 46204-1927

Phone: (908) 903-2000 **Domicile State:** IN **NAIC Code:** 20281

Data Date	Rating	RACR #1	RACR #2	Loss Ratio %	Total Assets ($mil)	Capital ($mil)	Net Premium ($mil)	Net Income ($mil)
3-09	B+	1.49	1.34	N/A	28,842.9	12,301.0	1,655.7	397.5
3-08	B+	1.67	1.47	N/A	29,772.6	13,198.2	1,687.4	519.2
2008	B+	1.47	1.33	59.0	28,856.6	12,135.8	6,660.6	1,187.9
2007	B+	1.65	1.46	51.8	29,671.1	12,877.2	6,815.7	2,362.4
2006	B+	1.56	1.36	55.0	28,363.1	11,276.7	6,997.7	1,647.2
2005	B+	1.45	1.26	65.0	25,377.5	8,833.1	7,195.0	1,353.4
2004	B+	1.32	1.12	63.9	23,128.7	7,764.7	7,135.7	1,056.0

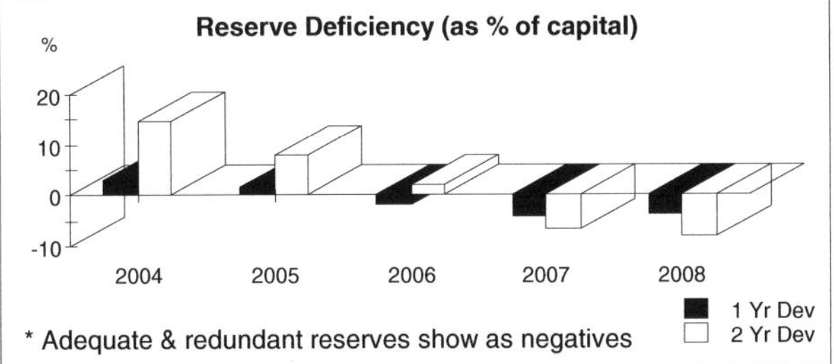

FEDERATED MUTUAL INS CO * A- Excellent

Major Rating Factors: Strong long-term capitalization index (9.0 on a scale of 0 to 10) based on excellent current risk adjusted capital (severe and moderate loss scenarios). Moreover, capital levels have been consistent in recent years. Ample reserve history (7.0) that can protect against increases in claims costs.

Other Rating Factors: Excellent profitability (8.6) with operating gains in each of the last five years. Good overall results on stability tests (5.5) despite potential drain of affiliation with Federated Mutual Ins Group. Stability strengths include good operational trends and excellent risk diversification. Good liquidity (6.8) with sufficient resources (cash flows and marketable investments) to handle a spike in claims.

Principal Business: Group accident & health (33%), workers compensation (15%), other liability (15%), auto liability (13%), commercial multiple peril (8%), auto physical damage (4%), and other lines (12%).

Principal Investments: Investment grade bonds (78%), misc. investments (19%), real estate (2%), and non investment grade bonds (1%).

Investments in Affiliates: 13%

Group Affiliation: Federated Mutual Ins Group

Licensed in: All states except AK, HI, PR

Commenced Business: August 1904

Address: 121 E Park Square, Owatonna, MN 55060

Phone: (507) 455-5200 **Domicile State:** MN **NAIC Code:** 13935

Data Date	Rating	RACR #1	RACR #2	Loss Ratio %	Total Assets ($mil)	Capital ($mil)	Net Premium ($mil)	Net Income ($mil)
3-09	A-	3.39	2.66	N/A	3,817.8	1,812.7	223.2	27.1
3-08	B+	3.25	2.52	N/A	3,909.0	1,787.5	252.0	35.5
2008	A-	3.39	2.67	66.7	3,829.0	1,809.3	929.8	129.0
2007	B+	3.26	2.54	67.7	3,905.2	1,784.4	1,024.5	158.3
2006	B+	3.00	2.31	63.5	3,722.4	1,590.9	1,041.1	224.2
2005	B+	2.76	2.07	72.7	3,581.0	1,413.4	1,044.6	128.5
2004	B+	2.76	2.06	77.4	3,359.8	1,293.9	1,034.4	109.4

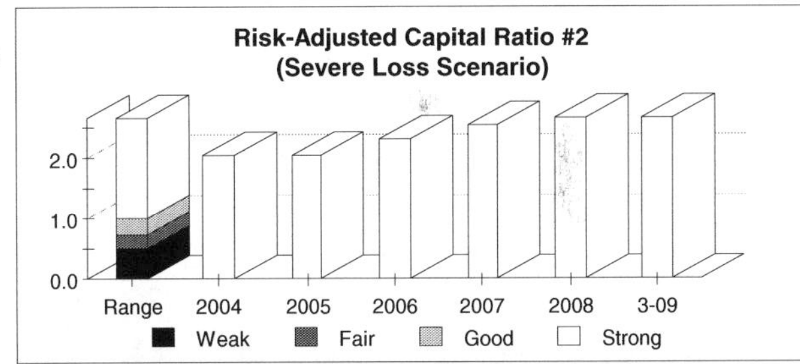

FEDERATED SERVICE INS CO * B+ Good

Major Rating Factors: Good overall results on stability tests (5.4 on a scale of 0 to 10) despite potential drain of affiliation with Federated Mutual Ins Group. The largest net exposure for one risk is acceptable at 2.1% of capital. Good liquidity (6.7) with sufficient resources (cash flows and marketable investments) to handle a spike in claims.

Other Rating Factors: Strong long-term capitalization index (9.0) based on excellent current risk adjusted capital (severe and moderate loss scenarios). Moreover, capital levels have been consistent in recent years. Ample reserve history (7.0) that can protect against increases in claims costs. Excellent profitability (8.5) with operating gains in each of the last five years. Return on equity has been good over the last five years, averaging 12.3%.

Principal Business: Other liability (32%), auto liability (18%), workers compensation (17%), auto physical damage (7%), products liability (6%), allied lines (5%), and other lines (16%).

Principal Investments: Investment grade bonds (99%) and misc. investments (1%).

Investments in Affiliates: None

Group Affiliation: Federated Mutual Ins Group

Licensed in: All states except AK, HI, NH, NJ, RI, VT, PR

Commenced Business: January 1975

Address: 121 E Park Square, Owatonna, MN 55060

Phone: (507) 455-5200 **Domicile State:** MN **NAIC Code:** 28304

Data Date	Rating	RACR #1	RACR #2	Loss Ratio %	Total Assets ($mil)	Capital ($mil)	Net Premium ($mil)	Net Income ($mil)
3-09	B+	4.51	2.86	N/A	358.9	137.2	24.8	3.3
3-08	B	3.92	2.52	N/A	356.2	124.1	28.0	3.2
2008	B+	4.45	2.84	66.7	358.1	134.3	103.3	13.4
2007	B	3.91	2.52	67.7	363.2	121.7	113.8	15.3
2006	B	3.10	2.04	63.5	339.5	106.6	115.7	19.4
2005	B	2.44	1.63	72.7	340.1	92.9	116.1	12.5
2004	B	2.26	1.52	77.4	320.4	84.6	114.9	7.0

Federated Mutual Ins Group
Composite Group Rating: B+

Largest Group Members	Assets ($mil)	Rating
FEDERATED MUTUAL INS CO	3829	A-
FEDERATED LIFE INS CO	955	A
FEDERATED SERVICE INS CO	358	B+

FIDELITY & DEPOSIT CO OF MARYLAND C+ Fair

Major Rating Factors: Fair profitability index (3.9 on a scale of 0 to 10). Excellent expense controls. Return on equity has been fair, averaging 5.8% over the past five years. Fair overall results on stability tests (4.6) including negative cash flow from operations for 2008.

Other Rating Factors: Strong long-term capitalization index (10.0) based on excellent current risk adjusted capital (severe and moderate loss scenarios), despite some fluctuation in capital levels. Excellent liquidity (7.0) with ample operational cash flow and liquid investments.

Principal Business: Surety (74%), fidelity (8%), commercial multiple peril (6%), other liability (4%), allied lines (2%), homeowners multiple peril (1%), and other lines (4%).

Principal Investments: Investment grade bonds (85%), misc. investments (14%), and cash (1%).

Investments in Affiliates: 13%

Group Affiliation: Zurich Financial Services Group

Licensed in: All states, the District of Columbia and Puerto Rico

Commenced Business: January 1982

Address: 210 North Charles St, Baltimore, MD 21203

Phone: (410) 539-0800 **Domicile State:** MD **NAIC Code:** 39306

Data Date	Rating	RACR #1	RACR #2	Loss Ratio %	Total Assets ($mil)	Capital ($mil)	Net Premium ($mil)	Net Income ($mil)
3-09	C+	8.09	7.57	N/A	229.1	180.5	0.0	2.0
3-08	C+	6.98	5.88	N/A	248.7	205.1	0.0	3.4
2008	C+	8.06	7.57	0.0	223.7	178.6	0.0	26.2
2007	C+	6.90	5.84	0.0	315.4	200.6	0.0	6.8
2006	C+	7.25	6.23	0.0	263.2	194.8	0.0	7.2
2005	C+	7.12	6.09	0.0	213.8	186.8	0.0	6.7
2004	C+	5.09	4.98	0.0	216.5	178.7	0.0	6.9

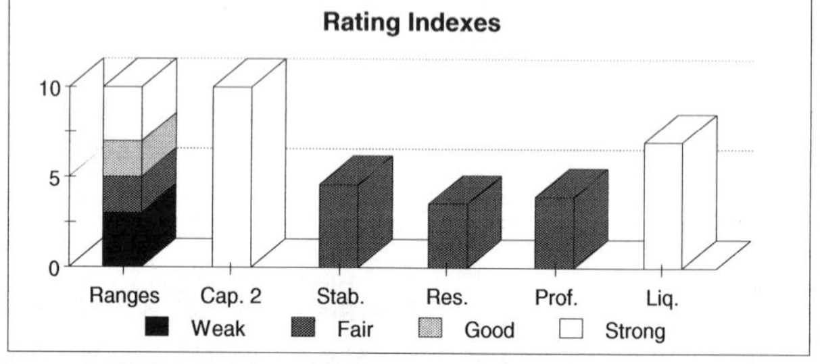

FINANCIAL GUARANTY INS CO D- Weak

Major Rating Factors: Weak overall results on stability tests (0.9 on a scale of 0 to 10) including excessive premium growth and weak risk adjusted capital in prior years. The largest net exposure for one risk is excessive at 258.8% of capital. Strengths include potentially strong support from affiliation with PMI Group Inc. Poor long-term capitalization index (0.1) based on weak current risk adjusted capital (severe and moderate loss scenarios), although results have slipped from the fair range over the last two years.

Other Rating Factors: A history of deficient reserves (2.6). Underreserving can have an adverse impact on capital and profits. Weak profitability index (0.3) with operating losses during the first nine months of 2007. Average return on equity over the last five years has been poor at -103.3%. Good liquidity (6.7) with sufficient resources (cash flows and marketable investments) to handle a spike in claims.

Principal Business: Financial guaranty (100%).

Principal Investments: Investment grade bonds (127%) and cash (5%).

Investments in Affiliates: 0%

Group Affiliation: PMI Group Inc

Licensed in: All states, the District of Columbia and Puerto Rico

Commenced Business: July 1972

Address: 125 Park Ave, New York, NY 10017

Phone: (212) 312-3000 **Domicile State:** NY **NAIC Code:** 12815

Data Date	Rating	RACR #1	RACR #2	Loss Ratio %	Total Assets ($mil)	Capital ($mil)	Net Premium ($mil)	Net Income ($mil)
9-08	D-	0.26	0.11	N/A	3,301.3	350.2	392.9	-287.6
9-07	C	1.37	0.46	N/A	4,133.4	1,094.8	190.3	187.6
2007	D	0.30	0.13	772.1	4,298.8	260.9	311.2	-1,502.5
2006	A-	1.65	0.55	N/A	3,894.1	1,130.8	352.3	220.5
2005	A-	1.68	0.56	12.1	3,504.1	1,162.9	374.9	192.0
2004	U	1.69	0.57	1.4	3,115.8	1,172.6	313.9	144.1
2003	U	1.61	0.55	N/A	2,740.7	1,153.5	266.0	178.4

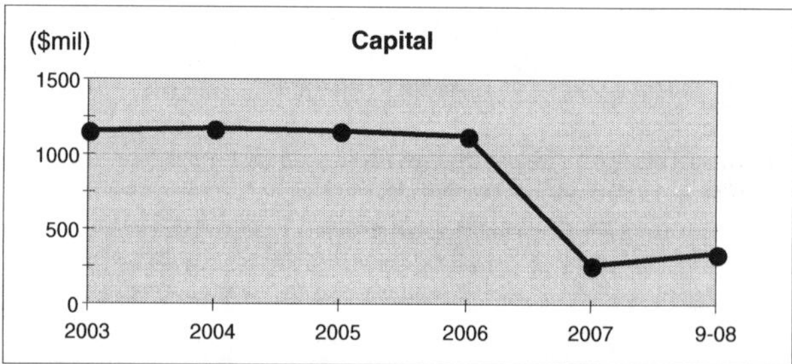

FINANCIAL SECURITY ASR INC D+ Weak

Major Rating Factors: Weak overall results on stability tests (2.4 on a scale of 0 to 10) including weak risk adjusted capital in prior years. The largest net exposure for one risk is excessive at 23.5% of capital. Strengths include potentially strong support from affiliation with Financial Security Asr Holdings Ltd. Poor long-term capitalization (2.4) based on fair current risk adjusted capital (severe and moderate loss scenarios) reflecting improvement over results in 2008.

Other Rating Factors: Weak profitability index (0.9) with operating losses during the first three months of 2008. Average return on equity over the last five years has been poor at -12.9%. Fair reserve development (3.0) as reserves have generally been sufficient to cover claims. In 2008, the one year reserve development was 45% deficient. Excellent liquidity (8.3) with ample operational cash flow and liquid investments.

Principal Business: Financial guaranty (100%).

Principal Investments: Investment grade bonds (91%) and misc. investments (9%).

Investments in Affiliates: 11%

Group Affiliation: Financial Security Asr Holdings Ltd

Licensed in: All states except WI

Commenced Business: September 1985

Address: 31 W 52nd St, New York, NY 10019

Phone: (212) 823-1146 **Domicile State:** NY **NAIC Code:** 18287

Data Date	Rating	RACR #1	RACR #2	Loss Ratio %	Total Assets ($mil)	Capital ($mil)	Net Premium ($mil)	Net Income ($mil)
3-09	D+	0.92	0.52	N/A	4,298.5	843.7	62.2	-11.3
3-08	B-	1.96	1.39	N/A	4,705.3	1,854.9	66.2	-70.3
2008	D+	0.69	0.40	477.0	4,434.2	620.4	528.2	-800.7
2007	B-	1.87	1.36	16.7	4,289.3	1,628.9	395.2	215.9
2006	B+	1.92	1.35	0.2	3,953.5	1,566.2	370.8	280.6
2005	B+	1.93	1.35	1.9	3,789.8	1,538.5	395.7	245.9
2004	U	1.94	1.14	5.0	3,480.0	1,144.7	403.7	175.8

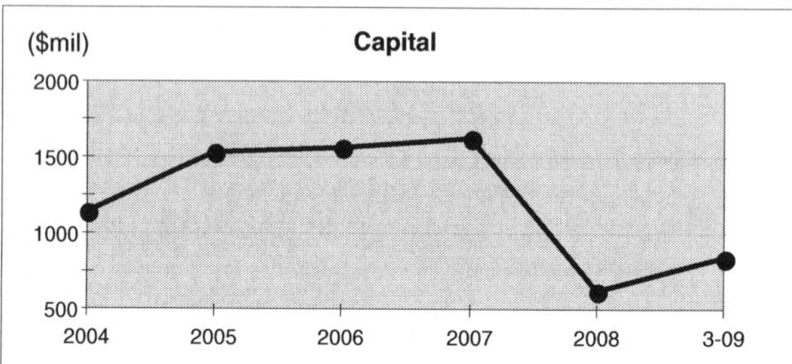

FINIAL REINS CO — D — Weak

Major Rating Factors: Weak profitability index (2.9 on a scale of 0 to 10) with operating losses during 2004, 2006 and 2008. Average return on equity over the last five years has been poor at -18.5%. Weak overall results on stability tests (2.3) including weak results on operational trends and negative cash flow from operations for 2008.

Other Rating Factors: Fair reserve development (3.9) as the level of reserves has at times been insufficient to cover claims. In 2005 and 2004 the two year reserve development was 47% and 61% deficient respectively. Strong long-term capitalization index (7.4) based on excellent current risk adjusted capital (severe and moderate loss scenarios), despite some fluctuation in capital levels. Superior liquidity (10.0) with ample operational cash flow and liquid investments.

Principal Business: (Not applicable due to unusual reinsurance transactions.)

Principal Investments: Investment grade bonds (58%), cash (34%), non investment grade bonds (5%), and misc. investments (3%).

Investments in Affiliates: None

Group Affiliation: Berkshire-Hathaway

Licensed in: AR, CA, CO, CT, GA, IL, IN, IA, KS, LA, MI, MT, NE, NV, NJ, NM, NY, OH, OK, PA, SD, TN, TX, UT, WA, WV, WI

Commenced Business: February 1993

Address: 100 First Stamford Pl, Stamford, CT 06902

Phone: (402) 536-3000 **Domicile State:** CT **NAIC Code:** 39136

Data Date	Rating	RACR #1	RACR #2	Loss Ratio %	Total Assets ($mil)	Capital ($mil)	Net Premium ($mil)	Net Income ($mil)
3-09	D	2.57	1.39	N/A	1,278.3	459.8	0.0	11.8
3-08	D	1.21	0.72	N/A	1,318.0	417.5	-2.4	-23.4
2008	D	2.46	1.34	143.0	1,310.5	447.7	-1.0	-8.5
2007	D	1.21	0.69	N/A	1,323.5	395.6	1.1	31.7
2006	D-	1.00	0.58	257.0	1,450.4	377.5	16.5	-47.2
2005	D-	0.76	0.46	59.0	1,695.9	394.8	32.4	34.1
2004	D-	0.37	0.23	143.8	2,545.4	349.3	348.3	-355.7

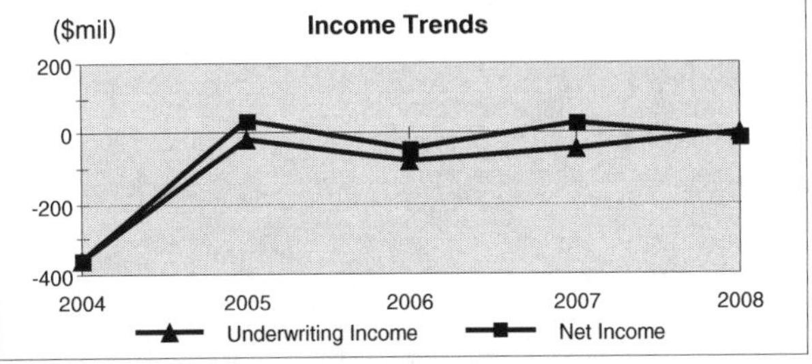

FIRE INS EXCHANGE — C — Fair

Major Rating Factors: Fair reserve development (3.9 on a scale of 0 to 10) as the level of reserves has at times been insufficient to cover claims. In 2005 and 2004 the two year reserve development was 21% and 31% deficient respectively. Fair overall results on stability tests (3.4).

Other Rating Factors: Good long-term capitalization index (5.6) based on good current risk adjusted capital (severe and moderate loss scenarios), although results have slipped from the excellent range over the last two years. Good overall profitability index (5.4) despite operating losses during the first three months of 2008. Good liquidity (5.5) with sufficient resources (cash flows and marketable investments) to handle a spike in claims.

Principal Business: Homeowners multiple peril (73%), commercial multiple peril (13%), allied lines (6%), fire (6%), and inland marine (1%).

Principal Investments: Investment grade bonds (57%), misc. investments (42%), and cash (1%).

Investments in Affiliates: 32%

Group Affiliation: Zurich Financial Services Group

Licensed in: AL, AZ, AR, CA, CO, FL, GA, ID, IL, IN, IA, KS, MI, MN, MO, MT, NE, NV, NH, NJ, NM, ND, OH, OK, OR, SD, TX, UT, WA, WI, WY

Commenced Business: November 1942

Address: 4680 Wilshire Blvd, Los Angeles, CA 90010

Phone: (213) 932-3441 **Domicile State:** CA **NAIC Code:** 21660

Data Date	Rating	RACR #1	RACR #2	Loss Ratio %	Total Assets ($mil)	Capital ($mil)	Net Premium ($mil)	Net Income ($mil)
3-09	C	0.96	0.83	N/A	2,315.5	530.2	194.2	-4.3
3-08	C	1.39	1.13	N/A	2,359.8	600.8	233.9	6.1
2008	C	0.98	0.84	76.1	2,344.6	545.9	884.1	8.1
2007	C	1.40	1.16	71.1	2,151.8	595.1	961.0	27.4
2006	C	1.42	1.15	67.1	2,063.0	543.8	869.7	45.1
2005	C	1.32	1.06	68.4	1,837.7	456.8	811.4	39.5
2004	C	1.22	1.00	70.5	1,623.5	404.5	722.4	27.3

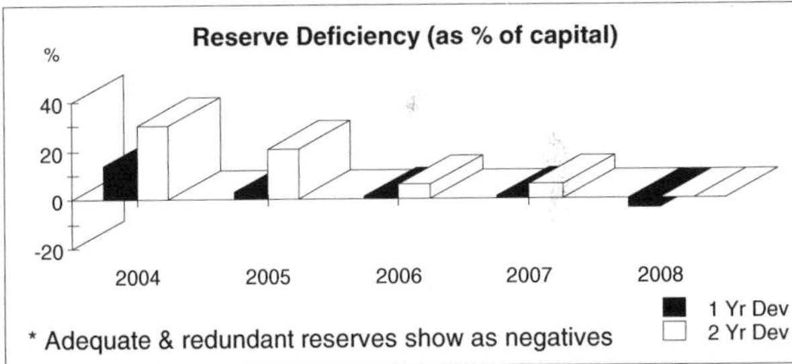

FIREMANS FUND INS CO — C — Fair

Major Rating Factors: Fair overall results on stability tests (3.4 on a scale of 0 to 10). Good long-term capitalization index (6.2) based on good current risk adjusted capital (moderate loss scenario).

Other Rating Factors: History of adequate reserve strength (5.6) as reserves have been consistently at an acceptable level. Good profitability index (5.0). Fair expense controls. Return on equity has been excellent over the last five years averaging 15.5%. Good liquidity (5.4) with sufficient resources (cash flows and marketable investments) to handle a spike in claims.

Principal Business: Allied lines (38%), inland marine (15%), commercial multiple peril (14%), homeowners multiple peril (12%), ocean marine (8%), other liability (7%), and other lines (7%).

Principal Investments: Investment grade bonds (75%), misc. investments (26%), and non investment grade bonds (1%).

Investments in Affiliates: 18%

Group Affiliation: Allianz Ins Group

Licensed in: All states, the District of Columbia and Puerto Rico

Commenced Business: September 1864

Address: 777 San Marin Dr, Novato, CA 94998

Phone: (415) 899-2000 **Domicile State:** CA **NAIC Code:** 21873

Data Date	Rating	RACR #1	RACR #2	Loss Ratio %	Total Assets ($mil)	Capital ($mil)	Net Premium ($mil)	Net Income ($mil)
3-09	C	1.26	0.94	N/A	9,398.7	2,958.3	820.6	75.8
3-08	C	1.21	0.88	N/A	9,372.4	3,118.3	772.9	70.9
2008	C	1.18	0.88	75.0	10,673.0	2,861.6	3,592.2	116.7
2007	C	1.11	0.80	62.0	9,982.5	2,894.2	3,487.0	415.5
2006	C	1.18	0.83	58.0	10,066.5	3,032.6	3,439.4	1,073.2
2005	C	1.11	0.78	66.7	9,695.6	2,850.2	3,221.0	487.6
2004	C-	1.26	0.85	66.0	9,913.2	2,930.1	3,157.7	231.0

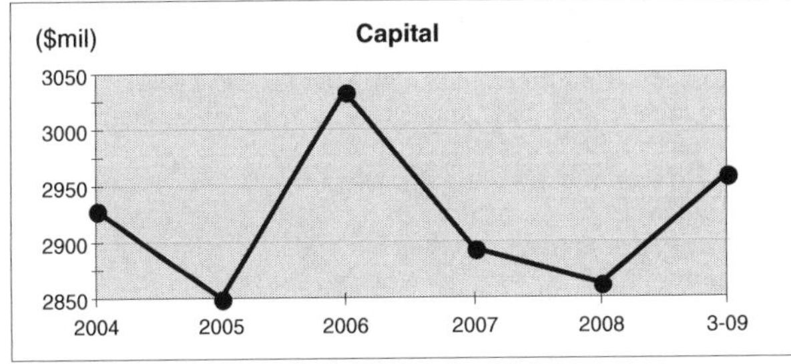

FIRST FINANCIAL INS CO C- Fair

Major Rating Factors: Weak overall results on stability tests (2.6 on a scale of 0 to 10) including potential drain of affiliation with IFG Companies. Fair reserve development (3.3) as the level of reserves has at times been insufficient to cover claims. In 2005 and 2004 the two year reserve development was 18% and 32% deficient respectively.

Other Rating Factors: Fair profitability index (4.8) with operating losses during 2004. Return on equity has been low, averaging 1.2% over the past five years. Good long-term capitalization index (6.0) based on excellent current risk adjusted capital (severe and moderate loss scenarios). Moreover, capital levels have been consistent in recent years. Excellent liquidity (7.3) with ample operational cash flow and liquid investments.

Principal Business: Other liability (88%), auto liability (5%), commercial multiple peril (5%), and auto physical damage (2%).

Principal Investments: Misc. investments (65%) and investment grade bonds (35%).

Investments in Affiliates: 62%

Group Affiliation: IFG Companies

Licensed in: All states except CT, LA, ME, MA, PA, SC, PR

Commenced Business: May 1970

Address: 238 International Road, Burlington, NC 27215

Phone: (910) 586-2830 **Domicile State:** IL **NAIC Code:** 11177

Data Date	Rating	RACR #1	RACR #2	Loss Ratio %	Total Assets ($mil)	Capital ($mil)	Net Premium ($mil)	Net Income ($mil)
3-09	C-	1.22	1.19	N/A	492.2	311.6	7.7	2.2
3-08	C-	1.21	1.18	N/A	492.0	290.4	10.5	0.5
2008	C-	1.21	1.19	83.7	498.6	307.0	33.8	6.4
2007	C-	1.20	1.17	74.4	503.7	284.8	46.8	13.8
2006	C-	1.16	1.05	92.2	510.4	251.9	55.4	2.2
2005	C-	1.03	0.87	85.3	487.4	220.6	56.6	4.6
2004	C-	1.04	0.86	116.6	410.9	197.6	40.5	-8.7

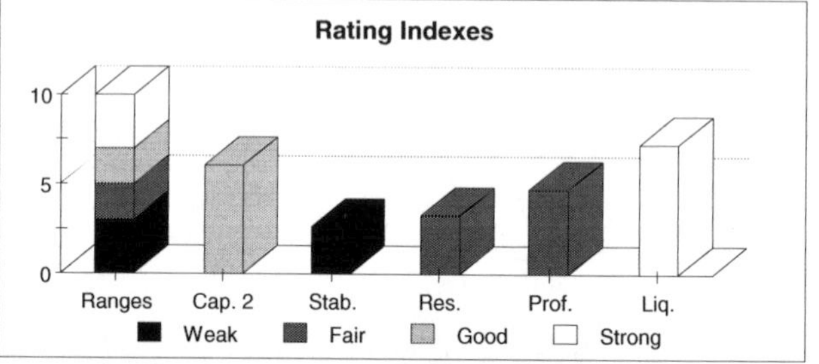

FIRST FLORIDIAN AUTO & HOME INS CO B Good

Major Rating Factors: Good overall profitability index (6.0 on a scale of 0 to 10) despite operating losses during 2004. Return on equity has been good over the last five years, averaging 13.9%. Good liquidity (6.8) with sufficient resources (cash flows and marketable investments) to handle a spike in claims.

Other Rating Factors: Good overall results on stability tests (5.4). Stability strengths include good operational trends and excellent risk diversification. The largest net exposure for one risk is acceptable at 2.7% of capital. Strong long-term capitalization index (10.0) based on excellent current risk adjusted capital (severe and moderate loss scenarios). Moreover, capital levels have been consistent in recent years. Ample reserve history (9.4) that helps to protect the company against sharp claims increases.

Principal Business: Auto liability (53%), homeowners multiple peril (26%), auto physical damage (20%), and other liability (1%).

Principal Investments: Investment grade bonds (98%) and misc. investments (3%).

Investments in Affiliates: None

Group Affiliation: Travelers Companies Inc

Licensed in: FL

Commenced Business: June 1996

Address: 7840 Woodland Ctr Blvd, Tampa, FL 33614

Phone: (813) 890-4369 **Domicile State:** FL **NAIC Code:** 10647

Data Date	Rating	RACR #1	RACR #2	Loss Ratio %	Total Assets ($mil)	Capital ($mil)	Net Premium ($mil)	Net Income ($mil)
3-09	B	7.39	5.65	N/A	410.3	253.4	34.7	17.9
3-08	B-	4.56	3.27	N/A	444.3	231.8	43.9	15.2
2008	B	6.12	4.88	39.5	402.3	235.4	144.3	57.4
2007	B-	3.95	2.94	67.4	450.7	217.4	194.9	29.7
2006	B-	2.88	2.11	51.3	496.1	210.9	233.9	70.5
2005	B-	1.53	1.07	73.5	492.2	164.0	276.3	6.6
2004	B-	1.89	1.23	96.3	426.7	155.0	231.1	-14.7

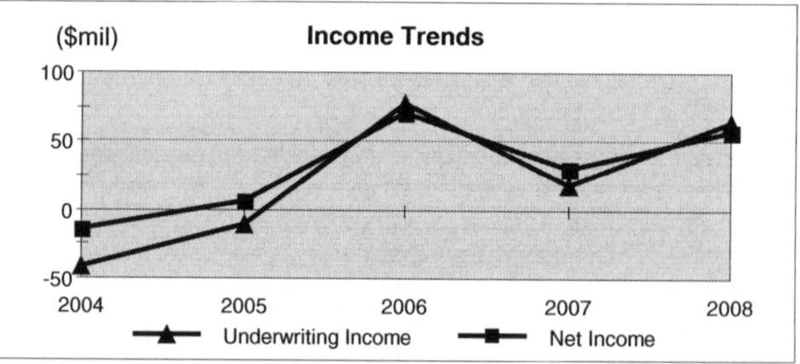

FIRST INS CO OF HI LTD C+ Fair

Major Rating Factors: Fair overall results on stability tests (4.3 on a scale of 0 to 10) including fair financial strength of affiliated CNA Financial Corp. The largest net exposure for one risk is conservative at 1.5% of capital. Strong long-term capitalization index (8.5) based on excellent current risk adjusted capital (severe and moderate loss scenarios), despite some fluctuation in capital levels.

Other Rating Factors: Ample reserve history (8.8) that helps to protect the company against sharp claims increases. Excellent profitability (8.2) with operating gains in each of the last five years. Return on equity has been good over the last five years, averaging 13.0%. Excellent liquidity (7.3) with ample operational cash flow and liquid investments.

Principal Business: Workers compensation (23%), auto liability (15%), homeowners multiple peril (15%), other liability (12%), commercial multiple peril (11%), allied lines (11%), and other lines (13%).

Principal Investments: Investment grade bonds (90%), misc. investments (9%), and non investment grade bonds (1%).

Investments in Affiliates: 3%

Group Affiliation: CNA Financial Corp

Licensed in: HI

Commenced Business: September 1982

Address: 1100 Ward Ave, Honolulu, HI 96814

Phone: (808) 527-7777 **Domicile State:** HI **NAIC Code:** 41742

Data Date	Rating	RACR #1	RACR #2	Loss Ratio %	Total Assets ($mil)	Capital ($mil)	Net Premium ($mil)	Net Income ($mil)
3-09	C+	3.43	2.24	N/A	602.2	198.4	34.5	3.7
3-08	C+	3.35	1.95	N/A	593.2	195.8	37.6	6.6
2008	C+	3.33	2.18	58.4	593.4	189.9	146.6	21.5
2007	C+	3.40	1.99	60.7	590.6	196.0	156.1	27.4
2006	C+	3.15	1.84	61.9	552.0	183.3	168.5	25.1
2005	C+	2.97	1.77	64.5	514.2	166.3	161.0	20.7
2004	C+	2.90	1.77	61.7	482.7	158.4	152.6	23.5

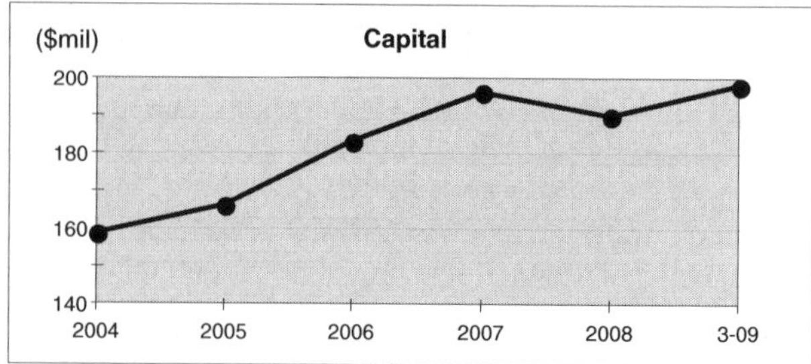

FIRST MERCURY INS CO D+ Weak

Major Rating Factors: A history of deficient reserves (2.0 on a scale of 0 to 10). Underreserving can have an adverse impact on capital and profits. In four of the last five years reserves (two year development) were between 16% and 69% deficient. Weak overall results on stability tests (2.5).

Other Rating Factors: Fair long-term capitalization index (3.6) based on fair current risk adjusted capital (severe loss scenario). Good liquidity (6.6) with sufficient resources (cash flows and marketable investments) to handle a spike in claims. Excellent profitability (8.8) with operating gains in each of the last five years. Return on equity has been good over the last five years, averaging 10.9%.

Principal Business: Other liability (80%), products liability (11%), fire (8%), and commercial multiple peril (1%).

Principal Investments: Investment grade bonds (86%), misc. investments (11%), non investment grade bonds (3%), and real estate (1%).

Investments in Affiliates: None

Group Affiliation: First Mercury Financial Corp

Licensed in: IL, MI

Commenced Business: June 1996

Address: 29621 Northwestern Hwy, Southfield, MI 48034

Phone: (248) 358-4010 **Domicile State:** IL **NAIC Code:** 10657

Data Date	Rating	RACR #1	RACR #2	Loss Ratio %	Total Assets ($mil)	Capital ($mil)	Net Premium ($mil)	Net Income ($mil)
3-09	D+	0.81	0.51	N/A	579.6	184.2	47.3	7.4
3-08	D	0.84	0.53	N/A	479.6	166.9	38.1	6.0
2008	D+	0.83	0.52	55.8	555.0	177.2	196.7	20.8
2007	D	0.74	0.47	52.0	441.3	161.3	139.3	30.1
2006	D	0.77	0.49	50.3	296.7	128.0	124.7	7.3
2005	D+	0.65	0.41	57.5	213.9	77.0	90.3	6.2
2004	C-	1.11	0.75	44.7	165.0	67.0	60.4	6.0

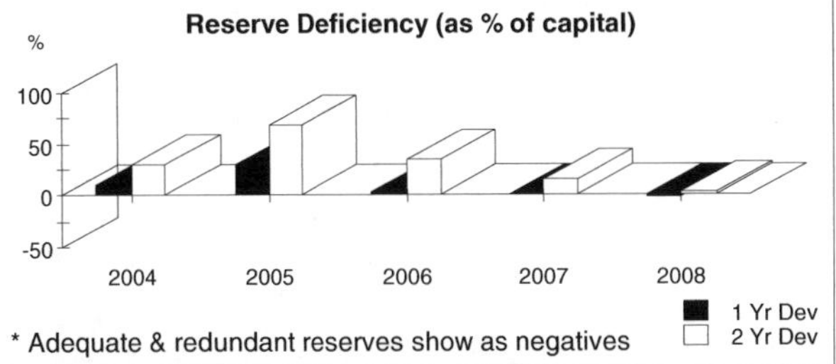

FIRST PROFESSIONALS INS CO INC C+ Fair

Major Rating Factors: Fair overall results on stability tests (4.2 on a scale of 0 to 10) including potential drain of affiliation with FPIC Ins Group Inc. Strong long-term capitalization index (7.9) based on excellent current risk adjusted capital (severe and moderate loss scenarios), despite some fluctuation in capital levels.

Other Rating Factors: Ample reserve history (7.0) that can protect against increases in claims costs. Excellent profitability (7.5) with operating gains in each of the last five years. Excellent liquidity (7.4) with ample operational cash flow and liquid investments.

Principal Business: Medical malpractice (100%).

Principal Investments: Investment grade bonds (84%), misc. investments (11%), cash (2%), non investment grade bonds (2%), and real estate (1%).

Investments in Affiliates: 11%

Group Affiliation: FPIC Ins Group Inc

Licensed in: AL, AZ, AR, DE, FL, GA, IL, IN, KS, KY, MD, MI, MN, MS, MO, MT, NV, NC, OH, OR, PA, SC, TN, TX, UT, VA, WA, WV

Commenced Business: December 1976

Address: 1000 Riverside Ave, Suite 800, Jacksonville, FL 32204

Phone: (904) 354-5910 **Domicile State:** FL **NAIC Code:** 33383

Data Date	Rating	RACR #1	RACR #2	Loss Ratio %	Total Assets ($mil)	Capital ($mil)	Net Premium ($mil)	Net Income ($mil)
3-09	C+	2.10	1.70	N/A	615.6	213.7	26.6	3.6
3-08	C	2.05	1.69	N/A	673.6	243.4	31.7	6.8
2008	C+	2.16	1.76	57.6	625.2	220.8	116.1	20.8
2007	C	1.95	1.62	45.1	761.6	235.1	92.4	41.9
2006	C	1.43	1.12	69.4	753.1	200.4	162.0	19.5
2005	C	1.46	1.15	59.8	741.1	172.9	183.8	9.9
2004	C	1.55	1.21	81.8	662.8	145.4	136.5	9.1

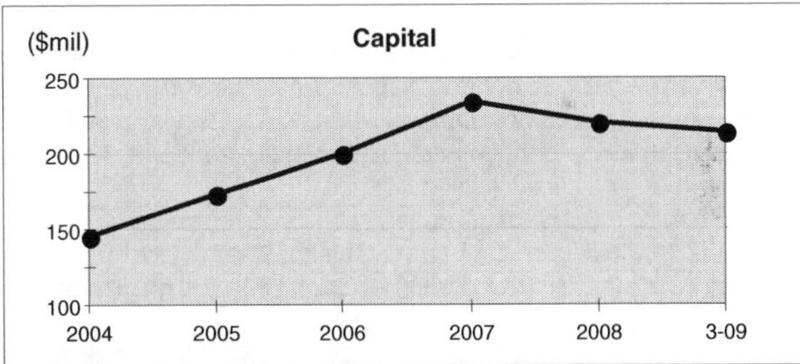

FIRST TRENTON INDEMNITY CO B- Good

Major Rating Factors: Fair profitability index (4.4 on a scale of 0 to 10) with operating losses during the first three months of 2008. Return on equity has been fair, averaging 9.0% over the past five years. Good liquidity (6.2) with sufficient resources (cash flows and marketable investments) to handle a spike in claims.

Other Rating Factors: Good overall results on stability tests (5.3) despite negative cash flow from operations for 2008. Stability strengths include good operational trends and excellent risk diversification. Strong long-term capitalization index (8.3) based on excellent current risk adjusted capital (severe and moderate loss scenarios), despite some fluctuation in capital levels. Ample reserve history (8.2) that helps to protect the company against sharp claims increases.

Principal Business: Auto liability (55%), auto physical damage (26%), homeowners multiple peril (15%), other liability (3%), and inland marine (2%).

Principal Investments: Investment grade bonds (95%) and misc. investments (6%).

Investments in Affiliates: 6%

Group Affiliation: Travelers Companies Inc

Licensed in: NJ

Commenced Business: March 1992

Address: 402 Lippincott Dr, Marlton, NJ 08053

Phone: (856) 983-2400 **Domicile State:** NJ **NAIC Code:** 29930

Data Date	Rating	RACR #1	RACR #2	Loss Ratio %	Total Assets ($mil)	Capital ($mil)	Net Premium ($mil)	Net Income ($mil)
3-09	B-	2.28	1.79	N/A	862.1	277.5	98.3	-9.8
3-08	B-	2.88	2.25	N/A	882.9	325.2	98.0	3.9
2008	B-	2.32	1.87	81.6	858.8	288.0	385.0	1.1
2007	B-	2.71	2.19	71.4	902.4	321.6	386.3	34.2
2006	B-	2.54	2.10	73.2	925.4	311.1	396.4	28.8
2005	B-	2.18	1.81	72.8	848.4	266.4	386.7	33.8
2004	B-	2.04	1.73	69.9	813.3	241.7	401.7	43.3

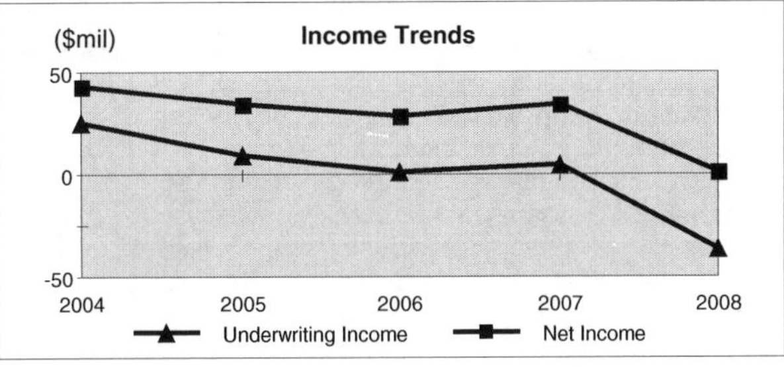

FLORIDA FARM BU CASUALTY INS CO B- Good

Major Rating Factors: Fair overall results on stability tests (4.8 on a scale of 0 to 10) including potential drain of affiliation with Southern Farm Bureau Casualty. Fair profitability index (4.9) with operating losses during 2004 and 2005. Return on equity has been low, averaging 1.2% over the past five years.

Other Rating Factors: Good liquidity (6.6) with sufficient resources (cash flows and marketable investments) to handle a spike in claims. Strong long-term capitalization index (8.5) based on excellent current risk adjusted capital (severe and moderate loss scenarios), despite some fluctuation in capital levels. Ample reserve history (9.3) that helps to protect the company against sharp claims increases.

Principal Business: Homeowners multiple peril (70%), auto liability (21%), and auto physical damage (9%).

Principal Investments: Investment grade bonds (89%), misc. investments (6%), real estate (3%), and cash (2%).

Investments in Affiliates: 2%

Group Affiliation: Southern Farm Bureau Casualty

Licensed in: FL

Commenced Business: July 1974

Address: 5700 SW 34th St, Gainesville, FL 32608

Phone: (352) 378-8100 **Domicile State:** FL **NAIC Code:** 31216

Data Date	Rating	RACR #1	RACR #2	Loss Ratio %	Total Assets ($mil)	Capital ($mil)	Net Premium ($mil)	Net Income ($mil)
3-09	B-	3.39	2.22	N/A	424.6	198.9	42.6	2.5
3-08	B-	3.19	2.11	N/A	397.5	182.5	43.6	2.2
2008	B-	3.36	2.22	74.5	417.2	197.8	172.1	16.1
2007	B-	3.23	2.16	78.6	397.7	181.4	169.4	16.2
2006	B-	2.77	1.86	70.0	397.0	168.2	163.2	19.5
2005	B-	1.98	1.35	99.4	379.5	150.5	178.6	-13.5
2004	B	2.18	1.46	114.8	409.2	161.0	184.5	-23.9

Southern Farm Bureau Casualty Composite Group Rating: B+ Largest Group Members	Assets ($mil)	Rating
SOUTHERN FARM BUREAU CAS INS CO	2649	B+
FLORIDA FARM BU CASUALTY INS CO	417	B-
MISSISSIPPI FARM BUREAU CAS INS CO	278	B
SOUTHERN FARM BUREAU PROPERTY	51	U
LOUISIANA FARM BUREAU CAS INS CO	10	B

FOREMOST INS CO * B+ Good

Major Rating Factors: History of adequate reserve strength (6.0 on a scale of 0 to 10) as reserves have been consistently at an acceptable level. Good overall profitability index (5.7) despite operating losses during 2008. Return on equity has been fair, averaging 9.4% over the past five years.

Other Rating Factors: Good overall results on stability tests (5.6) despite negative cash flow from operations for 2008. Stability strengths include good operational trends and excellent risk diversification. Strong long-term capitalization index (7.9) based on excellent current risk adjusted capital (severe and moderate loss scenarios), despite some fluctuation in capital levels. Fair liquidity (4.3) as cash resources may not be adequate to cover a spike in claims.

Principal Business: Homeowners multiple peril (52%), fire (13%), auto physical damage (12%), auto liability (9%), allied lines (5%), other liability (4%), and other lines (5%).

Principal Investments: Investment grade bonds (95%), misc. investments (7%), non investment grade bonds (1%), and real estate (1%).

Investments in Affiliates: 4%

Group Affiliation: Zurich Financial Services Group

Licensed in: All states except PR

Commenced Business: June 1952

Address: 5600 Beech Tree Lane, Caledonia, MI 49316-0050

Phone: (616) 956-8102 **Domicile State:** MI **NAIC Code:** 11185

Data Date	Rating	RACR #1	RACR #2	Loss Ratio %	Total Assets ($mil)	Capital ($mil)	Net Premium ($mil)	Net Income ($mil)
3-09	B+	1.96	1.67	N/A	2,024.3	584.2	340.3	3.4
3-08	A-	2.07	1.79	N/A	1,997.1	625.3	328.5	12.4
2008	B+	1.98	1.58	64.2	1,919.2	583.4	1,325.7	-27.7
2007	A-	2.07	1.67	53.9	1,902.8	615.6	1,333.7	83.7
2006	A-	1.99	1.61	51.2	1,813.0	587.0	1,309.2	90.1
2005	A-	1.75	1.41	51.6	1,613.7	473.5	1,206.2	74.9
2004	A-	1.60	1.30	54.1	1,441.6	410.9	1,107.9	36.5

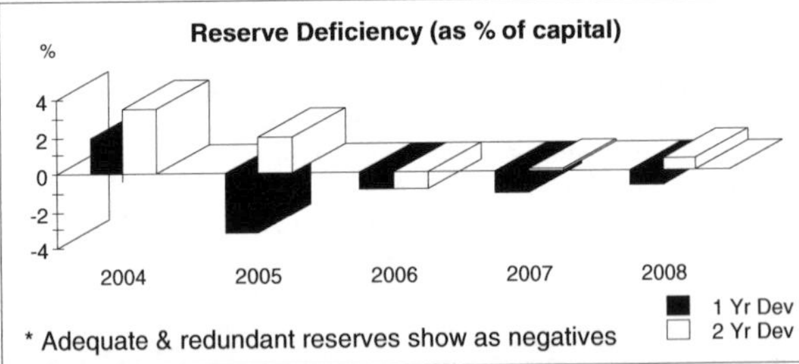

FRANKENMUTH MUTUAL INS CO * A Excellent

Major Rating Factors: Strong long-term capitalization index (8.6 on a scale of 0 to 10) based on excellent current risk adjusted capital (severe and moderate loss scenarios). Furthermore, this high level of risk adjusted capital has been consistently maintained in previous years. Ample reserve history (9.4) that helps to protect the company against sharp claims increases.

Other Rating Factors: Excellent overall results on stability tests (7.6). Stability strengths include excellent operational trends and excellent risk diversification. Good liquidity (6.6) with sufficient resources (cash flows and marketable investments) to handle a spike in claims. Fair profitability index (4.5) with operating losses during 2008.

Principal Business: Auto liability (21%), workers compensation (20%), homeowners multiple peril (17%), auto physical damage (17%), commercial multiple peril (16%), other liability (4%), and other lines (5%).

Principal Investments: Investment grade bonds (83%), misc. investments (14%), and real estate (4%).

Investments in Affiliates: 11%

Group Affiliation: Frankenmuth Mutual Group

Licensed in: All states except AK, CA, DC, HI, PR

Commenced Business: March 1922

Address: One Mutual Avenue, Frankenmuth, MI 48787-0001

Phone: (989) 652-6121 **Domicile State:** MI **NAIC Code:** 13986

Data Date	Rating	RACR #1	RACR #2	Loss Ratio %	Total Assets ($mil)	Capital ($mil)	Net Premium ($mil)	Net Income ($mil)
3-09	A	2.73	2.06	N/A	955.3	319.9	102.0	5.2
3-08	A	2.89	2.12	N/A	959.7	362.1	96.1	-10.3
2008	A	2.75	2.10	84.1	948.8	314.2	415.9	-28.0
2007	A	3.00	2.23	61.2	981.1	377.7	403.8	26.7
2006	A	3.49	2.35	57.1	868.0	321.7	333.3	35.2
2005	A	3.29	2.26	58.9	803.6	285.8	327.0	28.4
2004	A	2.97	2.08	62.9	738.1	253.5	313.1	24.1

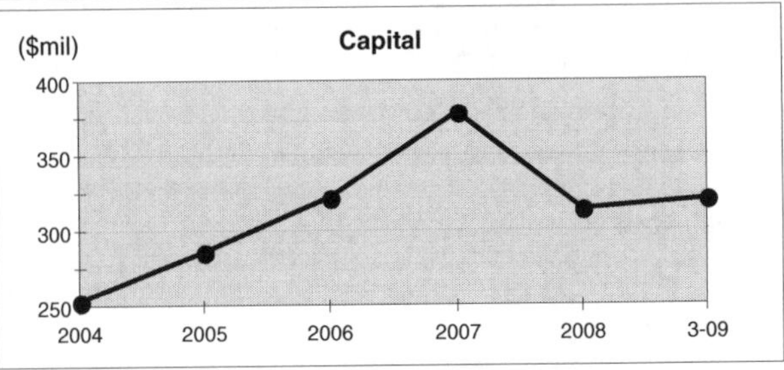

FRANKLIN MUTUAL INS CO — B — Good

Major Rating Factors: Good overall results on stability tests (5.6 on a scale of 0 to 10) despite potential drain of affiliation with Franklin Mutual Group. History of adequate reserve strength (6.5) as reserves have been consistently at an acceptable level.
Other Rating Factors: Good overall profitability index (6.2) with small operating losses during 2004. Strong long-term capitalization index (8.3) based on excellent current risk adjusted capital (severe and moderate loss scenarios), despite some fluctuation in capital levels. Excellent liquidity (8.8) with ample operational cash flow and liquid investments.
Principal Business: Homeowners multiple peril (38%), commercial multiple peril (22%), fire (13%), allied lines (11%), other liability (9%), workers compensation (5%), and inland marine (1%).
Principal Investments: Misc. investments (51%), investment grade bonds (49%), and real estate (1%).
Investments in Affiliates: 7%
Group Affiliation: Franklin Mutual Group
Licensed in: NJ
Commenced Business: June 1879
Address: 5 Broad St, Branchville, NJ 07826
Phone: (201) 948-3120 **Domicile State:** NJ **NAIC Code:** 16454

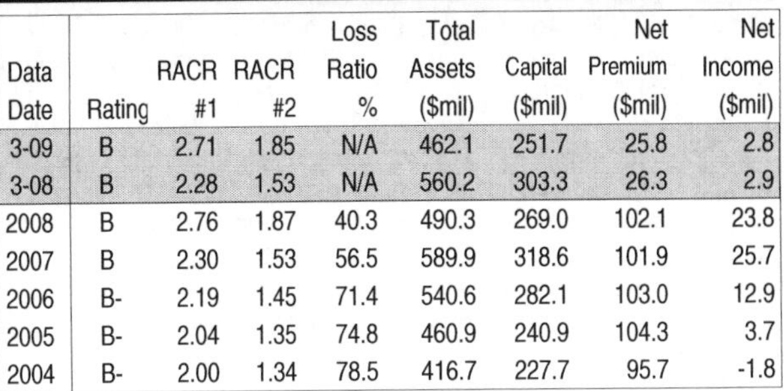

Data Date	Rating	RACR #1	RACR #2	Loss Ratio %	Total Assets ($mil)	Capital ($mil)	Net Premium ($mil)	Net Income ($mil)
3-09	B	2.71	1.85	N/A	462.1	251.7	25.8	2.8
3-08	B	2.28	1.53	N/A	560.2	303.3	26.3	2.9
2008	B	2.76	1.87	40.3	490.3	269.0	102.1	23.8
2007	B	2.30	1.53	56.5	589.9	318.6	101.9	25.7
2006	B-	2.19	1.45	71.4	540.6	282.1	103.0	12.9
2005	B-	2.04	1.35	74.8	460.9	240.9	104.3	3.7
2004	B-	2.00	1.34	78.5	416.7	227.7	95.7	-1.8

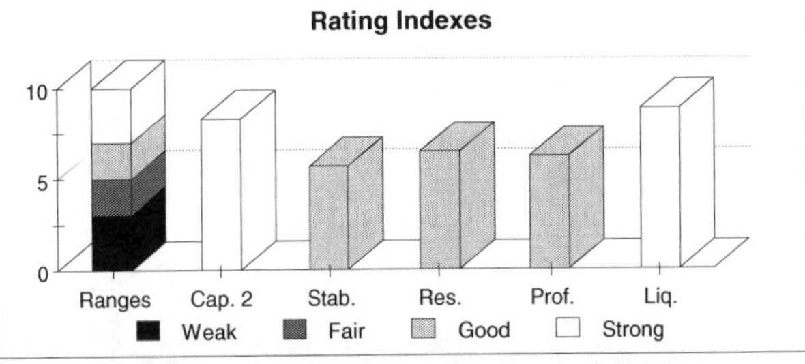

FSA INS CO — D — Weak

Major Rating Factors: Weak profitability index (1.3 on a scale of 0 to 10) with operating losses during the first three months of 2008. Average return on equity over the last five years has been poor at -10.1%. Weak overall results on stability tests (0.8). The largest net exposure for one risk is excessive at 22.2% of capital.
Other Rating Factors: Fair long-term capitalization (4.8) based on fair current risk adjusted capital (moderate loss scenario), although results have slipped from the good range over the last two years. History of adequate reserve strength (6.1) as reserves have been consistently at an acceptable level. Excellent liquidity (8.4) with ample operational cash flow and liquid investments.
Principal Business: (This company is a reinsurer.)
Principal Investments: Investment grade bonds (88%), misc. investments (11%), and cash (1%).
Investments in Affiliates: 14%
Group Affiliation: Financial Security Asr Holdings Ltd
Licensed in: NY, OK
Commenced Business: July 1997
Address: 201 Robert S Kerr Ave, Oklahoma City, OK 73102
Phone: (212) 826-0100 **Domicile State:** OK **NAIC Code:** 10843

Data Date	Rating	RACR #1	RACR #2	Loss Ratio %	Total Assets ($mil)	Capital ($mil)	Net Premium ($mil)	Net Income ($mil)
3-09	D	0.81	0.69	N/A	2,034.9	423.1	27.1	-3.6
3-08	C	3.79	3.49	N/A	2,163.7	1,047.1	28.9	-51.5
2008	D+	0.86	0.74	522.2	2,091.9	443.9	251.8	-472.3
2007	C	3.28	3.10	18.2	1,838.3	879.3	182.2	96.2
2006	C	4.03	3.78	0.4	1,650.9	818.8	166.2	104.7
2005	C	4.94	4.57	1.5	1,520.5	787.8	164.3	169.7
2004	U	3.28	3.02	4.1	1,225.5	519.2	161.9	46.6

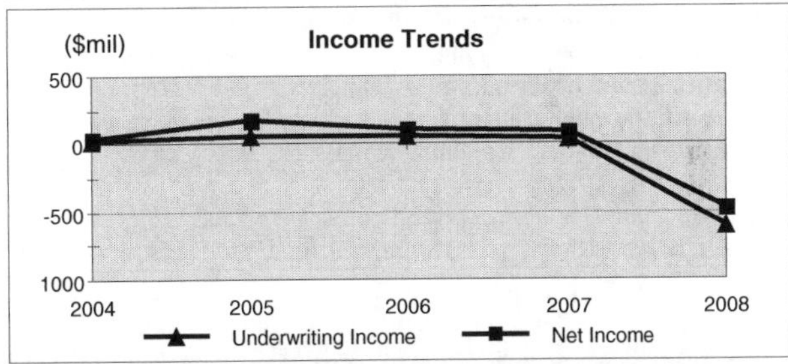

GEICO GENERAL INS CO * — B+ — Good

Major Rating Factors: Good overall results on stability tests (5.3 on a scale of 0 to 10). Stability strengths include good operational trends and excellent risk diversification. Strong long-term capitalization index (10.0) based on excellent current risk adjusted capital (severe and moderate loss scenarios). Moreover, capital levels have been consistent in recent years.
Other Rating Factors: Excellent profitability (8.8) with operating gains in each of the last five years. Excellent expense controls. Excellent liquidity (7.0) with ample operational cash flow and liquid investments.
Principal Business: Auto liability (61%) and auto physical damage (39%).
Principal Investments: Investment grade bonds (74%), misc. investments (18%), and non investment grade bonds (8%).
Investments in Affiliates: None
Group Affiliation: Berkshire-Hathaway
Licensed in: All states except PR
Commenced Business: May 1934
Address: 5260 Western Avenue, Chevy Chase, MD 20815-3799
Phone: (800) 841-3000 **Domicile State:** MD **NAIC Code:** 35882

Data Date	Rating	RACR #1	RACR #2	Loss Ratio %	Total Assets ($mil)	Capital ($mil)	Net Premium ($mil)	Net Income ($mil)
3-09	B+	10.82	9.74	N/A	175.2	90.1	0.0	1.0
3-08	B+	9.12	8.21	N/A	166.9	77.7	0.0	1.1
2008	B+	11.21	10.09	0.0	163.8	88.4	0.0	4.4
2007	B+	9.57	8.61	0.0	153.9	76.4	0.0	5.8
2006	B+	8.71	7.84	0.0	151.1	70.7	0.0	6.0
2005	B+	8.40	7.56	0.0	138.1	65.3	0.0	4.9
2004	B+	7.34	6.61	0.0	125.9	56.1	0.0	4.2

Berkshire-Hathaway
Composite Group Rating: C

Largest Group Members	Assets ($mil)	Rating
NATIONAL INDEMNITY CO	61720	C+
GENERAL REINSURANCE CORP	14446	B-
GOVERNMENT EMPLOYEES INS CO	12496	B+
COLUMBIA INS CO	11050	C+
GEICO INDEMNITY CO	4873	B+

GEICO INDEMNITY CO * B+ Good

Major Rating Factors: Good overall profitability index (6.0 on a scale of 0 to 10) despite operating losses during 2008. Return on equity has been good over the last five years, averaging 10.5%. Good overall results on stability tests (5.3).

Other Rating Factors: Strong long-term capitalization index (7.7) based on excellent current risk adjusted capital (severe and moderate loss scenarios), despite some fluctuation in capital levels. Ample reserve history (9.3) that helps to protect the company against sharp claims increases. Fair liquidity (4.9) as cash resources may not be adequate to cover a spike in claims.

Principal Business: Auto liability (65%) and auto physical damage (35%).

Principal Investments: Investment grade bonds (46%), misc. investments (43%), and non investment grade bonds (11%).

Investments in Affiliates: 3%

Group Affiliation: Berkshire-Hathaway

Licensed in: All states except MA, PR

Commenced Business: September 1961

Address: One Geico Plaza, Washington, DC 20076-0001

Phone: (800) 841-3000 **Domicile State:** MD **NAIC Code:** 22055

Data Date	Rating	RACR #1	RACR #2	Loss Ratio %	Total Assets ($mil)	Capital ($mil)	Net Premium ($mil)	Net Income ($mil)
3-09	B+	1.63	1.30	N/A	5,117.3	1,687.4	979.4	11.0
3-08	A-	1.96	1.68	N/A	4,578.5	1,743.7	855.4	10.9
2008	B+	1.77	1.52	78.4	4,872.9	1,774.2	3,736.7	-95.4
2007	A-	2.01	1.76	76.0	4,514.0	1,827.2	3,315.2	238.2
2006	A-	2.03	1.72	71.8	4,288.4	1,824.4	3,113.1	293.9
2005	A	2.07	1.86	69.3	3,987.7	1,714.0	2,850.1	277.5
2004	A	2.14	1.94	67.0	3,409.4	1,409.3	2,435.9	201.3

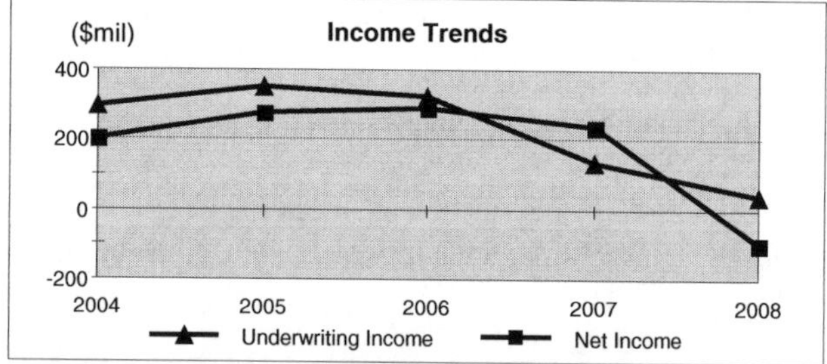

GENERAL CASUALTY CO OF WI B- Good

Major Rating Factors: Fair profitability index (3.4 on a scale of 0 to 10) with operating losses during the first three months of 2008. Return on equity has been fair, averaging 17.0% over the past five years. Fair overall results on stability tests (4.5).

Other Rating Factors: History of adequate reserve strength (5.2) as reserves have been consistently at an acceptable level. Strong long-term capitalization index (7.3) based on excellent current risk adjusted capital (severe and moderate loss scenarios), despite some fluctuation in capital levels. Excellent liquidity (7.4) with ample operational cash flow and liquid investments.

Principal Business: Commercial multiple peril (23%), auto liability (23%), workers compensation (16%), auto physical damage (12%), homeowners multiple peril (11%), other liability (8%), and other lines (5%).

Principal Investments: Misc. investments (50%), cash (30%), investment grade bonds (16%), and real estate (4%).

Investments in Affiliates: 44%

Group Affiliation: QBE Ins Group Ltd

Licensed in: All states except DC, NH, NJ, VT

Commenced Business: May 1925

Address: One General Dr, Sun Prairie, WI 53596

Phone: (608) 825-5528 **Domicile State:** WI **NAIC Code:** 24414

Data Date	Rating	RACR #1	RACR #2	Loss Ratio %	Total Assets ($mil)	Capital ($mil)	Net Premium ($mil)	Net Income ($mil)
3-09	B-	1.25	1.18	N/A	1,150.7	515.1	90.7	-6.4
3-08	B-	1.51	1.35	N/A	1,395.3	529.3	122.3	119.2
2008	B-	1.30	1.22	52.3	1,208.0	537.9	370.7	172.5
2007	B-	2.15	1.94	69.0	1,558.1	744.6	466.2	74.1
2006	B-	1.75	1.54	65.6	1,555.1	741.4	508.4	120.0
2005	B-	1.64	1.40	63.7	1,450.3	698.3	426.6	63.5
2004	B-	1.69	1.35	67.3	1,528.0	530.4	639.3	121.7

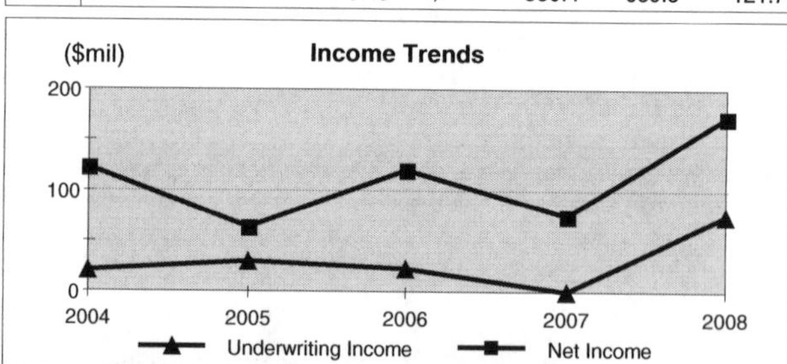

GENERAL FIDELITY INS CO B- Good

Major Rating Factors: Fair profitability index (4.6 on a scale of 0 to 10) with operating losses during 2006 and 2008. Return on equity has been low, averaging 2.1% over the past five years. Fair overall results on stability tests (4.0) including weak results on operational trends. The largest net exposure for one risk is conservative at 2.0% of capital.

Other Rating Factors: History of adequate reserve strength (5.9) as reserves have been consistently at an acceptable level. Good liquidity (6.9) with sufficient resources (cash flows and marketable investments) to handle a spike in claims. Strong long-term capitalization index (7.2) based on excellent current risk adjusted capital (severe and moderate loss scenarios), despite some fluctuation in capital levels.

Principal Business: Other liability (58%).

Principal Investments: Investment grade bonds (89%), misc. investments (9%), cash (1%), and non investment grade bonds (1%).

Investments in Affiliates: None

Group Affiliation: BankAmerica Corp

Licensed in: All states except PR

Commenced Business: July 1987

Address: 450 B St Ste 800, San Diego, CA 92101

Phone: (619) 231-7019 **Domicile State:** SC **NAIC Code:** 30007

Data Date	Rating	RACR #1	RACR #2	Loss Ratio %	Total Assets ($mil)	Capital ($mil)	Net Premium ($mil)	Net Income ($mil)
3-09	B-	1.82	1.20	N/A	699.3	357.7	37.7	0.1
3-08	B-	2.71	1.64	N/A	708.9	412.3	64.3	5.5
2008	B-	1.62	1.07	65.4	731.2	381.9	218.0	-0.4
2007	B-	2.41	1.49	58.0	718.1	415.7	258.7	27.3
2006	B-	3.77	2.35	67.2	598.6	403.0	170.3	-15.1
2005	B	6.56	4.21	59.0	195.7	159.7	29.4	4.7
2004	B	10.22	6.11	N/A	166.8	154.4	4.7	8.6

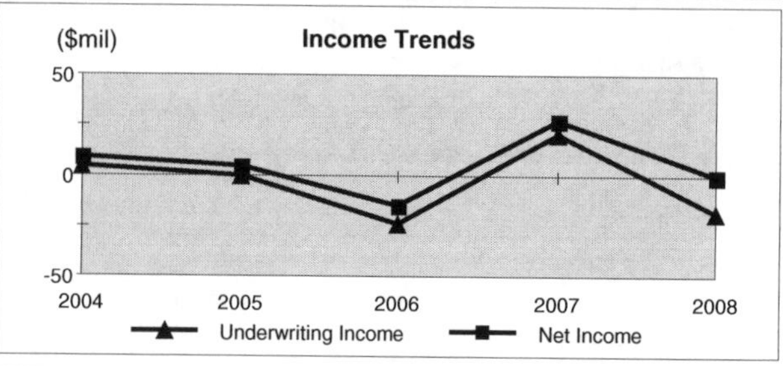

GENERAL INS CO OF AMERICA — B- Good

Major Rating Factors: Fair overall results on stability tests (4.9 on a scale of 0 to 10). Strengths include potentially strong support from affiliation with Liberty Mutual Group. The largest net exposure for one risk is conservative at 1.1% of capital. History of adequate reserve strength (6.9) as reserves have been consistently at an acceptable level.

Other Rating Factors: Good liquidity (5.7) with sufficient resources (cash flows and marketable investments) to handle a spike in claims. Strong long-term capitalization index (7.3) based on excellent current risk adjusted capital (severe and moderate loss scenarios), despite some fluctuation in capital levels. Weak profitability index (2.4). Fair expense controls. Return on equity has been fair, averaging 21.9% over the past five years.

Principal Business: Auto liability (33%), allied lines (18%), commercial multiple peril (15%), auto physical damage (15%), other liability (12%), workers compensation (2%), and other lines (5%).

Principal Investments: Investment grade bonds (93%), misc. investments (5%), and non investment grade bonds (2%).

Investments in Affiliates: 1%

Group Affiliation: Liberty Mutual Group

Licensed in: All states, the District of Columbia and Puerto Rico

Commenced Business: May 1923

Address: Safeco Plaza, Seattle, WA 98185

Phone: (206) 545-5000 **Domicile State:** WA **NAIC Code:** 24732

Data Date	Rating	RACR #1	RACR #2	Loss Ratio %	Total Assets ($mil)	Capital ($mil)	Net Premium ($mil)	Net Income ($mil)
3-09	B-	1.72	1.16	N/A	3,068.0	454.7	245.9	11.1
3-08	B-	1.68	1.12	N/A	2,342.2	522.7	318.9	29.1
2008	B-	1.68	1.17	67.0	2,302.0	447.6	1,228.4	74.0
2007	B-	1.90	1.27	62.9	2,432.4	594.3	1,300.9	168.8
2006	B-	2.72	1.78	58.5	2,702.7	876.6	1,291.2	225.9
2005	B-	2.28	1.53	62.3	2,725.4	814.3	1,337.2	170.4
2004	C+	2.03	1.37	63.2	2,455.7	721.0	1,305.4	148.9

Liberty Mutual Group
Composite Group Rating: C+

Largest Group Members	Assets ($mil)	Rating
LIBERTY MUTUAL INS CO	32550	B-
LIBERTY LIFE ASR CO OF BOSTON	11605	B-
PEERLESS INS CO	7069	C+
OHIO CASUALTY INS CO	4869	C+
SAFECO INS CO OF AMERICA	3952	B-

GENERAL REINSURANCE CORP — B- Good

Major Rating Factors: Good overall results on stability tests (5.0 on a scale of 0 to 10) despite potential drain of affiliation with Berkshire-Hathaway. Stability strengths include good operational trends and excellent risk diversification. History of adequate reserve strength (5.0) as reserves have been consistently at an acceptable level.

Other Rating Factors: Good overall profitability index (6.6). Weak expense controls. Return on equity has been fair, averaging 6.9% over the past five years. Strong long-term capitalization index (7.1) based on excellent current risk adjusted capital (severe and moderate loss scenarios), despite some fluctuation in capital levels. Excellent liquidity (7.4) with ample operational cash flow and liquid investments.

Principal Business: Aircraft (100%).

Principal Investments: Misc. investments (82%), investment grade bonds (13%), and non investment grade bonds (5%).

Investments in Affiliates: 45%

Group Affiliation: Berkshire-Hathaway

Licensed in: All states except HI

Commenced Business: January 1973

Address: 695 E Main St, Stamford, CT 06904-2350

Phone: (203) 328-5000 **Domicile State:** DE **NAIC Code:** 22039

Data Date	Rating	RACR #1	RACR #2	Loss Ratio %	Total Assets ($mil)	Capital ($mil)	Net Premium ($mil)	Net Income ($mil)
3-09	B-	1.27	1.12	N/A	13,285.1	7,921.8	158.6	143.2
3-08	B-	1.55	1.28	N/A	15,653.1	9,594.8	162.9	177.4
2008	B-	1.36	1.18	60.8	14,446.1	8,936.8	625.6	300.2
2007	B-	1.55	1.27	39.2	16,414.7	9,887.6	708.0	763.1
2006	B-	1.61	1.34	41.1	15,457.7	8,692.2	749.1	631.3
2005	B-	1.78	1.47	104.0	14,632.6	7,894.1	-4,482.4	721.1
2004	B-	1.07	0.79	76.1	19,614.1	7,159.0	2,262.4	485.8

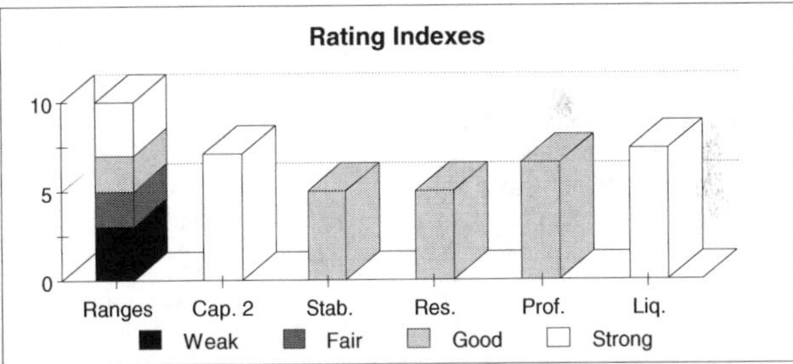

GENERAL STAR INDEMNITY CO — B Good

Major Rating Factors: Good overall results on stability tests (5.3 on a scale of 0 to 10). Stability strengths include good operational trends and excellent risk diversification. The largest net exposure for one risk is conservative at 1.1% of capital. Strong long-term capitalization index (10.0) based on excellent current risk adjusted capital (severe and moderate loss scenarios), despite some fluctuation in capital levels.

Other Rating Factors: Ample reserve history (7.1) that can protect against increases in claims costs. Excellent profitability (7.7) with operating gains in each of the last five years. Excellent liquidity (7.0) with ample operational cash flow and liquid investments.

Principal Business: (Not applicable due to unusual reinsurance transactions.)

Principal Investments: Investment grade bonds (74%), misc. investments (23%), and non investment grade bonds (3%).

Investments in Affiliates: 2%

Group Affiliation: Berkshire-Hathaway

Licensed in: CT

Commenced Business: May 1979

Address: 695 E Main St, Stamford, CT 06904-2354

Phone: (203) 328-5700 **Domicile State:** CT **NAIC Code:** 37362

Data Date	Rating	RACR #1	RACR #2	Loss Ratio %	Total Assets ($mil)	Capital ($mil)	Net Premium ($mil)	Net Income ($mil)
3-09	B	6.50	4.77	N/A	888.7	623.6	13.9	7.8
3-08	B	6.09	4.51	N/A	998.8	688.4	21.3	16.1
2008	B	6.77	4.92	8.1	985.4	710.5	57.9	55.6
2007	B	5.41	4.05	18.2	1,060.3	669.8	98.2	72.6
2006	B	4.01	3.15	36.0	1,051.0	610.6	125.5	53.4
2005	B	7.81	6.97	121.0	1,042.1	549.7	-279.1	68.0
2004	B	1.81	1.28	73.3	1,214.9	476.7	279.5	23.9

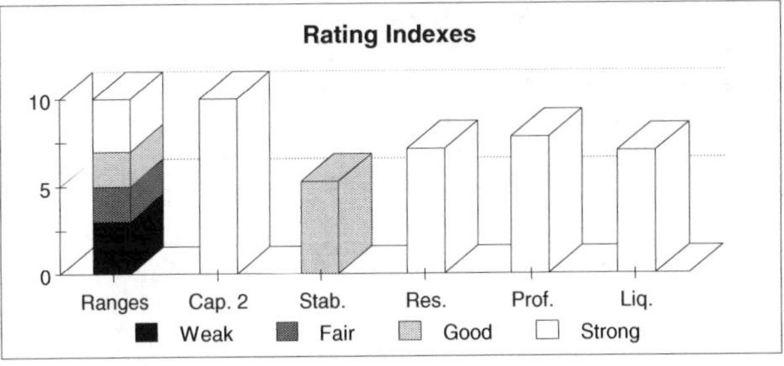

GENERAL STAR NATIONAL INS CO * A- Excellent

Major Rating Factors: Strong long-term capitalization index (10.0 on a scale of 0 to 10) based on excellent current risk adjusted capital (severe and moderate loss scenarios), despite some fluctuation in capital levels. Ample reserve history (7.0) that can protect against increases in claims costs.

Other Rating Factors: Superior liquidity (10.0) with ample operational cash flow and liquid investments. Good overall profitability index (6.0) despite operating losses during the first three months of 2008. Return on equity has been fair, averaging 5.7% over the past five years. Good overall results on stability tests (5.5) despite fair results on operational trends. The largest net exposure for one risk is high at 3.1% of capital.

Principal Business: (Not applicable due to unusual reinsurance transactions.)

Principal Investments: Investment grade bonds (92%) and misc. investments (8%).

Investments in Affiliates: None

Group Affiliation: Berkshire-Hathaway

Licensed in: All states except CT

Commenced Business: September 1864

Address: 695 E Main St, Stamford, CT 06904-2360

Phone: (203) 328-5700 **Domicile State:** OH **NAIC Code:** 11967

Data Date	Rating	RACR #1	RACR #2	Loss Ratio %	Total Assets ($mil)	Capital ($mil)	Net Premium ($mil)	Net Income ($mil)
3-09	A-	5.86	4.44	N/A	340.1	232.9	6.3	-1.6
3-08	A-	8.65	6.58	N/A	384.9	234.8	6.2	1.9
2008	A-	6.30	4.79	42.7	344.9	242.3	27.7	8.8
2007	A-	12.63	9.46	18.2	536.8	232.3	17.3	16.9
2006	A-	9.34	7.02	36.0	518.8	202.2	22.1	14.0
2005	A-	12.49	9.01	121.0	554.0	190.2	-49.3	15.9
2004	A-	4.23	2.98	73.3	530.0	173.2	49.3	7.7

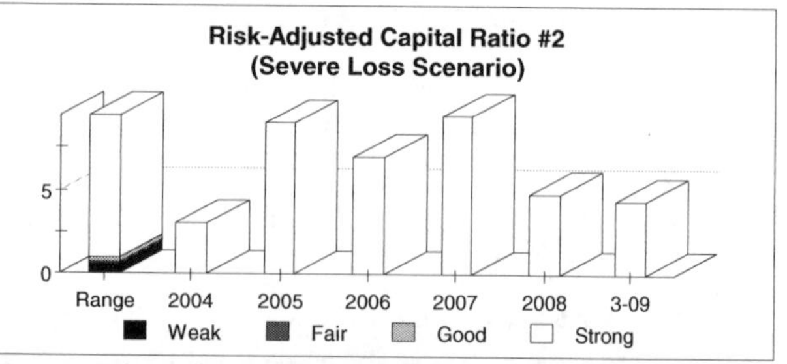

GENWORTH MORTGAGE INS CORP C Fair

Major Rating Factors: Fair overall results on stability tests (4.0 on a scale of 0 to 10) including weak risk adjusted capital in prior years. Strengths include potentially strong support from affiliation with Genworth Financial. Fair liquidity (3.5) as cash resources may not be adequate to cover a spike in claims.

Other Rating Factors: Poor long-term capitalization index (0.8) based on weak current risk adjusted capital (severe and moderate loss scenarios), although results have slipped from the good range over the last two years. Weak profitability index (2.8) with operating losses during the first three months of 2008. Return on equity has been fair, averaging 29.5% over the past five years. History of adequate reserve strength (6.0) as reserves have been consistently at an acceptable level.

Principal Business: Mortgage guaranty (100%).

Principal Investments: Investment grade bonds (84%), misc. investments (15%), and non investment grade bonds (1%).

Investments in Affiliates: None

Group Affiliation: Genworth Financial

Licensed in: All states except PR

Commenced Business: May 1980

Address: 6601 Six Forks Road, Raleigh, NC 27615

Phone: (919) 846-4125 **Domicile State:** NC **NAIC Code:** 38458

Data Date	Rating	RACR #1	RACR #2	Loss Ratio %	Total Assets ($mil)	Capital ($mil)	Net Premium ($mil)	Net Income ($mil)
3-09	C	0.21	0.17	N/A	3,060.0	212.7	146.5	-180.8
3-08	B-	1.02	0.67	N/A	2,936.9	250.2	153.8	-34.3
2008	C	0.30	0.24	144.6	3,023.1	276.8	657.0	-295.9
2007	B-	1.26	0.83	67.7	2,817.4	243.5	570.8	132.0
2006	B-	1.97	1.35	28.5	2,790.4	244.8	432.4	212.9
2005	C+	1.49	1.06	26.8	2,847.8	188.3	397.9	188.8
2004	C	1.54	1.09	27.1	2,724.0	186.2	415.3	195.9

Genworth Financial
Composite Group Rating: C+

Largest Group Members	Assets ($mil)	Rating
GENWORTH LIFE INS CO	34734	C+
GENWORTH LIFE ANNUITY INS CO	25964	B
GENWORTH LIFE INS CO OF NEW YORK	6999	C
GENWORTH MORTGAGE INS CORP	3023	C
GENWORTH MTG INS CORP OF NC	490	C+

GENWORTH MTG INS CORP OF NC C+ Fair

Major Rating Factors: Fair long-term capitalization (4.4 on a scale of 0 to 10) based on good current risk adjusted capital (moderate loss scenario) reflecting improvement over results in 2008. Fair overall results on stability tests (4.3) including weak results on operational trends.

Other Rating Factors: Weak profitability index (2.9) with operating losses during the first three months of 2008. Return on equity has been fair, averaging 32.1% over the past five years. Ample reserve history (9.4) that helps to protect the company against sharp claims increases. Excellent liquidity (7.2) with ample operational cash flow and liquid investments.

Principal Business: Mortgage guaranty (100%).

Principal Investments: Investment grade bonds (79%) and misc. investments (21%).

Investments in Affiliates: None

Group Affiliation: Genworth Financial

Licensed in: All states except HI, ME, NH, PR

Commenced Business: April 1961

Address: 6601 Six Forks Rd, Raleigh, NC 27615

Phone: (919) 846-4100 **Domicile State:** NC **NAIC Code:** 16675

Data Date	Rating	RACR #1	RACR #2	Loss Ratio %	Total Assets ($mil)	Capital ($mil)	Net Premium ($mil)	Net Income ($mil)
3-09	C+	1.60	1.19	N/A	601.6	269.4	20.4	-40.4
3-08	C+	2.41	1.61	N/A	344.4	104.6	26.0	-7.7
2008	C+	1.24	0.93	257.0	489.9	196.3	99.5	-106.7
2007	C+	1.65	1.09	67.6	275.2	51.1	87.7	23.4
2006	C	2.50	1.64	37.7	189.6	30.6	47.7	22.9
2005	C	2.97	1.95	21.9	170.0	28.9	38.1	27.2
2004	C	6.96	4.63	36.4	213.3	89.8	36.5	21.1

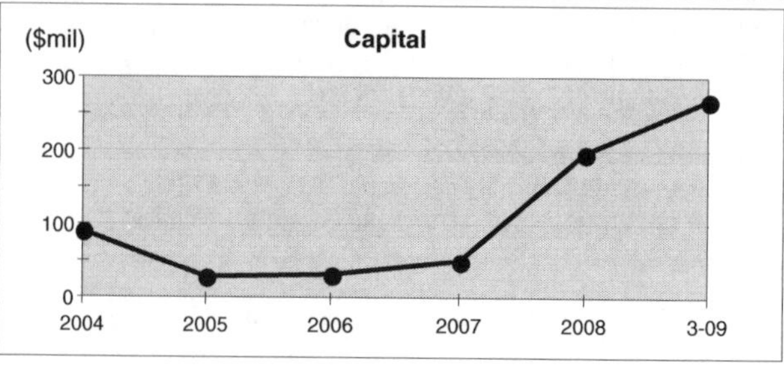

GEORGIA FARM BUREAU MUTUAL INS CO — B Good

Major Rating Factors: Fair reserve development (4.7 on a scale of 0 to 10) as reserves have generally been sufficient to cover claims. Fair liquidity (4.8) as cash resources may not be adequate to cover a spike in claims.
Other Rating Factors: Fair overall results on stability tests (4.8) including negative cash flow from operations for 2008. Strong long-term capitalization index (8.0) based on excellent current risk adjusted capital (severe and moderate loss scenarios), despite some fluctuation in capital levels. Weak profitability index (2.2) with operating losses during 2005, 2007 and the first three months of 2008.
Principal Business: Auto physical damage (29%), homeowners multiple peril (27%), auto liability (26%), farmowners multiple peril (12%), commercial multiple peril (2%), fire (2%), and allied lines (1%).
Principal Investments: Investment grade bonds (81%), misc. investments (15%), and cash (4%).
Investments in Affiliates: 1%
Group Affiliation: Georgia Farm Bureau Ins
Licensed in: GA
Commenced Business: January 1959
Address: 1620 Bass Rd, Macon, GA 31210
Phone: (912) 474-8411 **Domicile State:** GA **NAIC Code:** 14001

Data Date	Rating	RACR #1	RACR #2	Loss Ratio %	Total Assets ($mil)	Capital ($mil)	Net Premium ($mil)	Net Income ($mil)
3-09	B	2.31	1.53	N/A	743.0	282.0	127.6	-24.3
3-08	A-	3.46	2.31	N/A	828.9	354.4	136.4	-16.2
2008	B+	2.47	1.67	89.3	759.9	307.0	521.3	-45.9
2007	A-	3.71	2.54	87.2	830.3	377.4	552.8	-8.1
2006	A-	3.37	2.30	83.6	779.9	338.3	550.6	14.1
2005	A	3.43	2.39	88.4	734.6	324.1	513.0	-7.6
2004	A	3.79	2.68	81.6	712.3	337.9	481.3	13.1

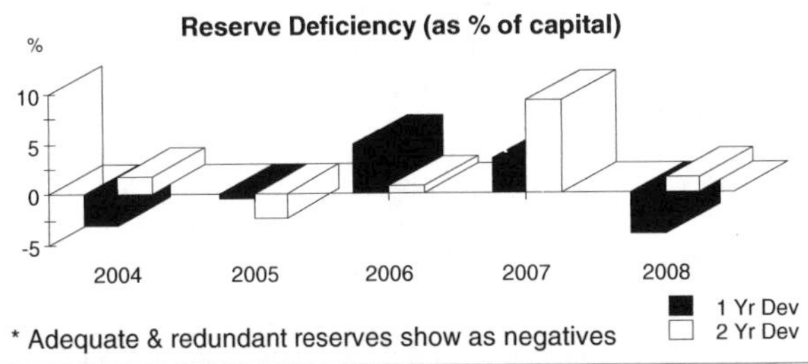

* Adequate & redundant reserves show as negatives

GERMANIA FARM MUTUAL INS ASN — B Good

Major Rating Factors: Good liquidity (6.0 on a scale of 0 to 10) with sufficient resources (cash flows and marketable investments) to handle a spike in claims. Fair overall results on stability tests (4.9) including potential drain of affiliation with Germania Ins Group.
Other Rating Factors: Fair profitability index (4.4) with operating losses during the first three months of 2008. Strong long-term capitalization index (7.9) based on excellent current risk adjusted capital (severe and moderate loss scenarios), despite some fluctuation in capital levels. Ample reserve history (7.5) that can protect against increases in claims costs.
Principal Business: Fire (99%) and inland marine (1%).
Principal Investments: Misc. investments (51%), investment grade bonds (49%), and real estate (2%).
Investments in Affiliates: 44%
Group Affiliation: Germania Ins Group
Licensed in: TX
Commenced Business: November 1897
Address: 507 Highway 290 East, Brenham, TX 77833
Phone: (979) 836-5224 **Domicile State:** TX **NAIC Code:** 29610

Data Date	Rating	RACR #1	RACR #2	Loss Ratio %	Total Assets ($mil)	Capital ($mil)	Net Premium ($mil)	Net Income ($mil)
3-09	B	1.68	1.57	N/A	312.7	193.3	35.9	-3.3
3-08	B+	2.21	2.08	N/A	326.5	224.9	36.8	5.9
2008	B	1.74	1.64	95.2	310.4	196.9	152.0	18.2
2007	B+	2.17	2.05	55.2	325.3	219.0	143.1	20.1
2006	B+	2.05	1.89	62.0	318.9	211.3	140.8	13.4
2005	B+	2.13	1.92	56.4	307.4	191.8	147.8	19.0
2004	B+	2.07	1.83	50.4	277.8	170.4	146.4	27.2

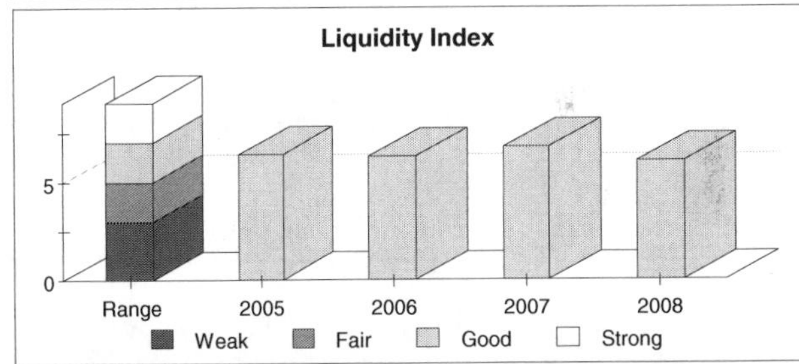

GOLDEN EAGLE INS CORP — C+ Fair

Major Rating Factors: Good liquidity (5.8 on a scale of 0 to 10) with sufficient resources (cash flows and marketable investments) to handle a spike in claims. Weak overall results on stability tests (2.9). The largest net exposure for one risk is excessive at 13.8% of capital. Strengths include potentially strong support from affiliation with Liberty Mutual Group.
Other Rating Factors: Weak profitability index (2.8). Fair expense controls. Return on equity has been fair, averaging 11.4% over the past five years. Strong long-term capitalization index (7.4) based on excellent current risk adjusted capital (severe and moderate loss scenarios), despite some fluctuation in capital levels. Ample reserve history (7.0) that can protect against increases in claims costs.
Principal Business: Commercial multiple peril (62%), other liability (18%), auto liability (14%), auto physical damage (4%), and earthquake (1%).
Principal Investments: Investment grade bonds (93%), misc. investments (6%), and non investment grade bonds (1%).
Investments in Affiliates: None
Group Affiliation: Liberty Mutual Group
Licensed in: AZ, CA
Commenced Business: August 1997
Address: 175 Berkley St, Mailstop 3E, Boston, MA 02117
Phone: (619) 744-6000 **Domicile State:** CA **NAIC Code:** 10836

Data Date	Rating	RACR #1	RACR #2	Loss Ratio %	Total Assets ($mil)	Capital ($mil)	Net Premium ($mil)	Net Income ($mil)
3-09	C+	2.17	1.47	N/A	975.7	187.9	80.2	7.0
3-08	B-	1.99	1.35	N/A	1,188.5	312.3	104.8	2.5
2008	C+	1.81	1.23	63.2	957.2	180.9	372.8	45.0
2007	B-	2.00	1.36	62.7	1,168.7	312.4	492.2	32.5
2006	B-	1.90	1.33	66.2	1,095.1	279.5	476.3	17.6
2005	B-	2.17	1.60	62.5	894.1	287.3	389.0	15.1
2004	B-	2.10	1.57	66.5	752.3	263.9	450.3	24.0

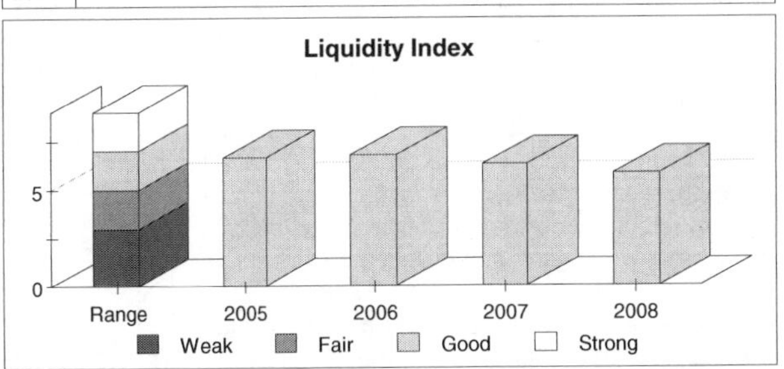

GOVERNMENT EMPLOYEES INS CO * B+ Good

Major Rating Factors: Good overall results on stability tests (5.3 on a scale of 0 to 10). Stability strengths include good operational trends and excellent risk diversification. Strong long-term capitalization index (7.4) based on excellent current risk adjusted capital (severe and moderate loss scenarios), despite some fluctuation in capital levels.

Other Rating Factors: Ample reserve history (9.3) that helps to protect the company against sharp claims increases. Fair profitability index (3.5) with operating losses during the first three months of 2008. Return on equity has been fair, averaging 15.6% over the past five years. Vulnerable liquidity (2.6) as a spike in claims may stretch capacity.

Principal Business: Auto liability (58%), auto physical damage (39%), and other liability (2%).

Principal Investments: Misc. investments (56%), investment grade bonds (30%), non investment grade bonds (14%), and real estate (2%).

Investments in Affiliates: 4%

Group Affiliation: Berkshire-Hathaway

Licensed in: All states except PR

Commenced Business: December 1937

Address: One Geico Plaza, Washington, DC 20076-0001

Phone: (800) 841-3000 **Domicile State:** MD **NAIC Code:** 22063

Data Date	Rating	RACR #1	RACR #2	Loss Ratio %	Total Assets ($mil)	Capital ($mil)	Net Premium ($mil)	Net Income ($mil)
3-09	B+	1.66	1.25	N/A	12,473.2	3,968.3	2,218.4	-172.8
3-08	B+	2.06	1.49	N/A	12,630.1	4,831.6	2,117.4	152.6
2008	B+	1.65	1.27	75.5	12,495.5	4,131.1	8,763.3	287.9
2007	B+	2.05	1.49	72.9	12,908.3	5,104.4	8,383.8	1,174.6
2006	B+	2.01	1.50	70.9	12,268.6	4,706.7	7,964.2	1,073.4
2005	A	2.35	1.71	73.4	12,462.3	5,686.8	7,224.4	941.9
2004	A	2.50	1.90	74.8	11,160.6	4,796.8	6,574.5	814.5

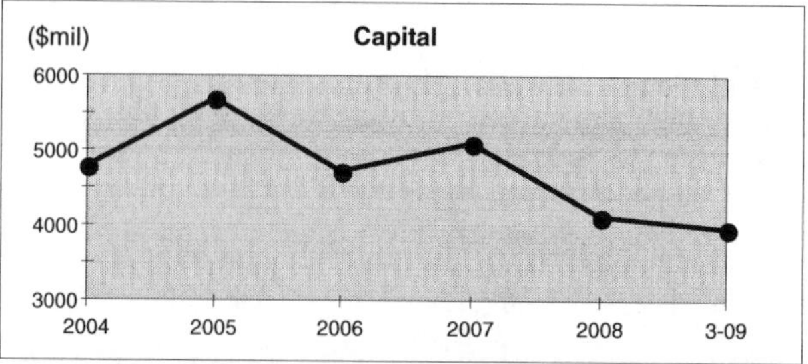

GRANGE MUTUAL CAS CO * A- Excellent

Major Rating Factors: Strong long-term capitalization index (8.3 on a scale of 0 to 10) based on excellent current risk adjusted capital (severe and moderate loss scenarios), despite some fluctuation in capital levels. Ample reserve history (8.1) that helps to protect the company against sharp claims increases.

Other Rating Factors: Good overall profitability index (5.5) despite operating losses during the first three months of 2008. Good liquidity (5.5) with sufficient resources (cash flows and marketable investments) to handle a spike in claims. Good overall results on stability tests (5.5) despite negative cash flow from operations for 2008.

Principal Business: Auto liability (34%), auto physical damage (24%), homeowners multiple peril (19%), commercial multiple peril (13%), farmowners multiple peril (3%), other liability (2%), and other lines (6%).

Principal Investments: Investment grade bonds (66%), misc. investments (22%), real estate (10%), and non investment grade bonds (4%).

Investments in Affiliates: 10%

Group Affiliation: Grange Mutual Casualty Group

Licensed in: AL, GA, IL, IN, IA, KS, KY, MN, MO, OH, PA, TN, WI

Commenced Business: April 1935

Address: 650 S Front St, Columbus, OH 43206-1014

Phone: (614) 445-2900 **Domicile State:** OH **NAIC Code:** 14060

Data Date	Rating	RACR #1	RACR #2	Loss Ratio %	Total Assets ($mil)	Capital ($mil)	Net Premium ($mil)	Net Income ($mil)
3-09	A-	2.71	1.82	N/A	1,525.7	682.0	219.4	-14.0
3-08	A-	2.89	1.91	N/A	1,617.2	759.4	224.7	7.3
2008	A-	2.79	1.88	67.8	1,561.8	713.1	899.0	15.5
2007	A-	2.88	1.93	64.2	1,721.9	772.2	908.0	42.1
2006	A-	2.70	1.89	64.4	1,652.4	715.3	941.6	34.2
2005	A-	2.63	1.87	62.0	1,492.6	636.1	898.4	69.0
2004	A-	2.26	1.61	62.4	1,346.9	551.8	887.6	66.9

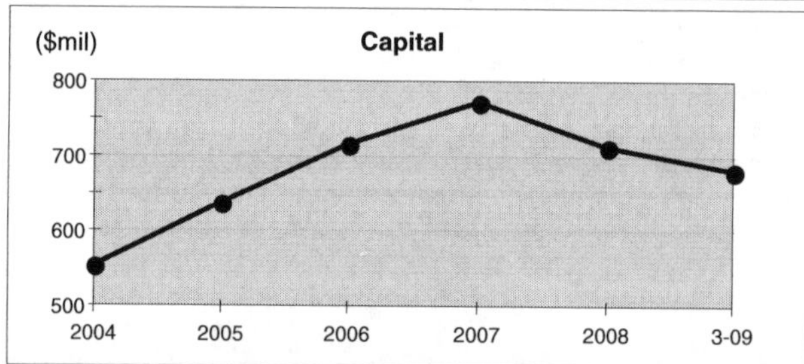

GREAT AMERICAN INS CO C Fair

Major Rating Factors: Fair reserve development (3.3 on a scale of 0 to 10) as the level of reserves has at times been insufficient to cover claims. Deficiencies in the two year reserve development occurred in three of the previous five years and ranged between 24% and 29%. Fair profitability index (3.6). Fair expense controls. Return on equity has been fair, averaging 13.7% over the past five years.

Other Rating Factors: Fair overall results on stability tests (3.5). The largest net exposure for one risk is high at 4.3% of capital. Good overall long-term capitalization (5.5) based on good current risk adjusted capital (severe loss scenario). However, capital levels have fluctuated during prior years. Good liquidity (6.5) with sufficient resources (cash flows and marketable investments) to handle a spike in claims.

Principal Business: Other liability (40%), surety (11%), aggregate write-ins for other lines of business (10%), fidelity (8%), inland marine (5%), allied lines (5%), and other lines (21%).

Principal Investments: Investment grade bonds (72%), misc. investments (21%), non investment grade bonds (5%), cash (1%), and real estate (1%).

Investments in Affiliates: 9%

Group Affiliation: American Financial Corp

Licensed in: All states, the District of Columbia and Puerto Rico

Commenced Business: March 1872

Address: 580 Walnut St, Cincinnati, OH 45202

Phone: (513) 369-5000 **Domicile State:** OH **NAIC Code:** 16691

Data Date	Rating	RACR #1	RACR #2	Loss Ratio %	Total Assets ($mil)	Capital ($mil)	Net Premium ($mil)	Net Income ($mil)
3-09	C	1.34	0.82	N/A	5,206.4	1,289.6	383.6	60.8
3-08	C-	1.09	0.69	N/A	5,126.9	1,244.8	398.6	30.0
2008	C	1.30	0.79	62.6	5,641.6	1,286.5	1,952.7	34.5
2007	C-	1.17	0.74	60.3	5,358.8	1,359.8	1,805.7	149.3
2006	C-	1.16	0.81	64.1	5,461.8	1,602.6	1,669.6	301.3
2005	C-	1.06	0.75	88.2	5,163.1	1,455.3	1,441.9	10.5
2004	C	1.37	0.99	73.2	5,084.6	1,445.3	1,262.1	488.9

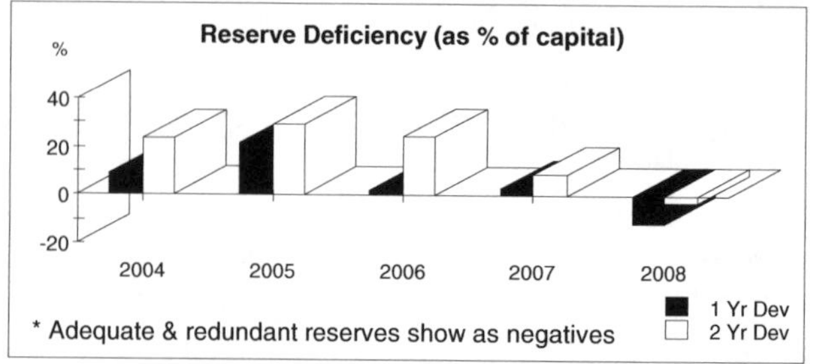

* Adequate & redundant reserves show as negatives

GREAT NORTHERN INS CO * B+ Good

Major Rating Factors: History of adequate reserve strength (5.6 on a scale of 0 to 10) as reserves have been consistently at an acceptable level. Good liquidity (6.7) with sufficient resources (cash flows and marketable investments) to handle a spike in claims.

Other Rating Factors: Good overall results on stability tests (5.8). The largest net exposure for one risk is high at 3.8% of capital. Strong long-term capitalization index (7.5) based on excellent current risk adjusted capital (severe and moderate loss scenarios). Moreover, capital levels have been consistent in recent years. Excellent profitability (9.3) with operating gains in each of the last five years. Return on equity has been excellent over the last five years averaging 21.9%.

Principal Business: Homeowners multiple peril (42%), commercial multiple peril (22%), inland marine (9%), auto liability (7%), auto physical damage (5%), other liability (5%), and other lines (10%).

Principal Investments: Investment grade bonds (98%), misc. investments (1%), and non investment grade bonds (1%).

Investments in Affiliates: None

Group Affiliation: Chubb Corp

Licensed in: All states except PR

Commenced Business: August 1952

Address: 100 S 5th St #1800, Minneapolis, MN 55402-1225

Phone: (908) 903-2000 **Domicile State:** IN **NAIC Code:** 20303

Data Date	Rating	RACR #1	RACR #2	Loss Ratio %	Total Assets ($mil)	Capital ($mil)	Net Premium ($mil)	Net Income ($mil)
3-09	B+	2.38	1.57	N/A	1,518.9	400.5	88.2	23.2
3-08	B+	2.25	1.50	N/A	1,491.9	384.1	90.0	24.9
2008	B+	2.33	1.54	61.3	1,554.2	385.9	353.8	68.8
2007	B+	2.22	1.49	54.0	1,519.6	374.3	363.0	90.7
2006	B+	2.10	1.40	55.3	1,508.9	351.3	377.4	85.1
2005	B+	1.67	1.12	65.7	1,411.9	284.0	393.0	59.3
2004	B+	1.36	0.93	63.7	1,297.3	255.0	390.9	56.1

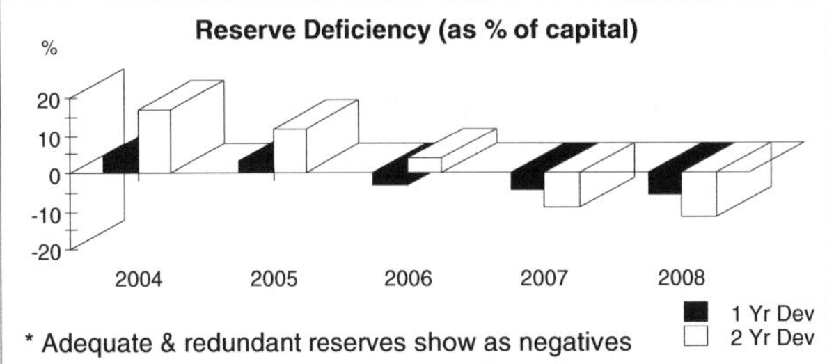

GREAT WEST CASUALTY CO * A- Excellent

Major Rating Factors: Strong long-term capitalization index (9.1 on a scale of 0 to 10) based on excellent current risk adjusted capital (severe and moderate loss scenarios), despite some fluctuation in capital levels. Ample reserve history (9.4) that helps to protect the company against sharp claims increases.

Other Rating Factors: Good liquidity (6.4) with sufficient resources (cash flows and marketable investments) to handle a spike in claims. Good overall results on stability tests (6.9). Strengths that enhance stability include potential support from affiliation with Old Republic Group, good operational trends and excellent risk diversification. Fair profitability index (3.8) with operating losses during 2008. Return on equity has been fair, averaging 8.2% over the past five years.

Principal Business: Auto liability (55%), auto physical damage (24%), inland marine (9%), workers compensation (8%), and other liability (4%).

Principal Investments: Investment grade bonds (92%), misc. investments (5%), cash (1%), non investment grade bonds (1%), and real estate (1%).

Investments in Affiliates: None

Group Affiliation: Old Republic Group

Licensed in: All states except HI, PR

Commenced Business: April 1956

Address: 1100 W 29th St, South Sioux City, NE 68776

Phone: (402) 494-2411 **Domicile State:** NE **NAIC Code:** 11371

Data Date	Rating	RACR #1	RACR #2	Loss Ratio %	Total Assets ($mil)	Capital ($mil)	Net Premium ($mil)	Net Income ($mil)
3-09	A-	3.75	2.38	N/A	1,460.5	375.0	131.6	15.0
3-08	A-	3.76	2.35	N/A	1,545.7	425.7	145.2	15.8
2008	A-	3.72	2.37	73.2	1,472.5	372.1	572.5	-53.5
2007	A-	4.00	2.49	71.2	1,595.0	473.0	595.5	71.4
2006	A-	3.77	2.37	75.5	1,564.4	439.3	668.8	43.5
2005	A-	3.69	2.30	68.9	1,410.9	400.7	676.1	67.7
2004	B+	3.37	2.22	69.9	1,230.0	355.6	543.4	40.7

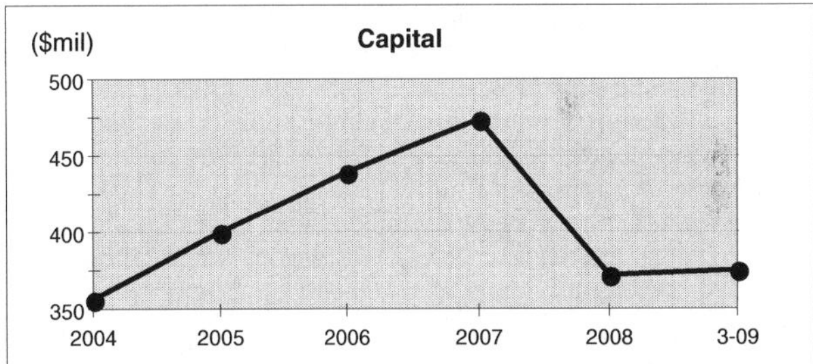

GREATER NEW YORK MUTUAL INS CO B Good

Major Rating Factors: Fair reserve development (4.8 on a scale of 0 to 10) as reserves have generally been sufficient to cover claims. Fair overall results on stability tests (4.9).

Other Rating Factors: Strong long-term capitalization index (8.2) based on excellent current risk adjusted capital (severe and moderate loss scenarios). Moreover, capital levels have been consistent in recent years. Excellent profitability (8.7) with operating gains in each of the last five years. Excellent liquidity (7.0) with ample operational cash flow and liquid investments.

Principal Business: Commercial multiple peril (91%), workers compensation (4%), other liability (2%), auto liability (1%), and auto physical damage (1%).

Principal Investments: Investment grade bonds (82%), misc. investments (17%), and cash (1%).

Investments in Affiliates: 15%

Group Affiliation: Greater New York Group

Licensed in: All states except AK, CA, FL, HI, ME, TX, PR

Commenced Business: November 1927

Address: 200 Madison Avenue, New York, NY 10016

Phone: (212) 683-9700 **Domicile State:** NY **NAIC Code:** 22187

Data Date	Rating	RACR #1	RACR #2	Loss Ratio %	Total Assets ($mil)	Capital ($mil)	Net Premium ($mil)	Net Income ($mil)
3-09	B	2.55	2.16	N/A	810.8	364.7	45.7	6.6
3-08	B	2.40	1.97	N/A	792.7	334.5	47.7	8.6
2008	B	2.52	2.15	62.5	809.8	357.1	181.1	26.4
2007	B	2.32	1.90	62.9	812.2	324.5	195.0	27.4
2006	B	2.06	1.61	64.3	769.4	292.1	216.8	22.4
2005	B	2.25	1.61	67.6	708.5	262.6	203.7	11.7
2004	B+	2.03	1.46	66.9	652.7	249.4	200.4	14.8

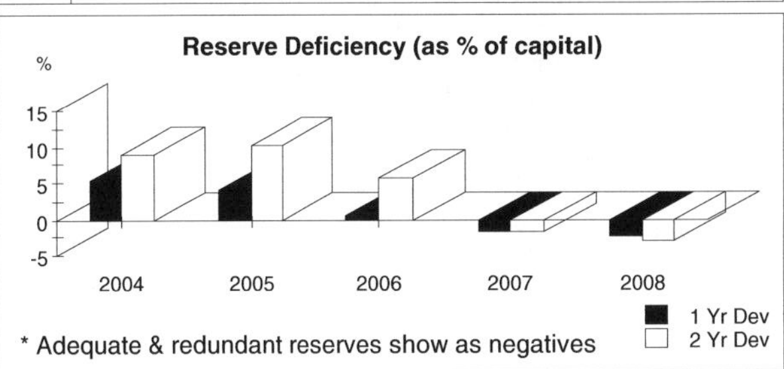

GREENWICH INS CO D+ Weak

Major Rating Factors: Weak overall results on stability tests (2.8 on a scale of 0 to 10) including weak financial strength of affiliated XL Capital Ltd. The largest net exposure for one risk is acceptable at 2.3% of capital. Fair reserve development (4.0) as reserves have generally been sufficient to cover claims. In 2004, the two year reserve development was 110% deficient.

Other Rating Factors: Good long-term capitalization index (5.1) based on fair current risk adjusted capital (severe loss scenario), although results have slipped from the good range during the last year. Good liquidity (6.8) with sufficient resources (cash flows and marketable investments) to handle a spike in claims. Excellent profitability (7.8) with operating gains in each of the last five years.

Principal Business: Allied lines (39%), other liability (32%), auto liability (4%), fire (3%), commercial multiple peril (2%), inland marine (1%), and other lines (19%).

Principal Investments: Investment grade bonds (64%), misc. investments (29%), and cash (7%).

Investments in Affiliates: 32%

Group Affiliation: XL Capital Ltd

Licensed in: All states, the District of Columbia and Puerto Rico

Commenced Business: May 1946

Address: 1201 N Market St Suite 501, Wilmington, DE 19801

Phone: (203) 964-5200 **Domicile State:** DE **NAIC Code:** 22322

Data Date	Rating	RACR #1	RACR #2	Loss Ratio %	Total Assets ($mil)	Capital ($mil)	Net Premium ($mil)	Net Income ($mil)
3-09	D+	1.01	0.70	N/A	919.6	419.8	39.7	19.4
3-08	D	0.93	0.64	N/A	863.1	390.6	45.4	1.9
2008	D+	1.10	0.77	60.4	901.9	444.5	215.3	22.6
2007	D	0.91	0.64	70.8	816.6	367.2	94.4	20.4
2006	D	0.90	0.63	69.3	785.9	355.6	101.4	26.4
2005	D	0.83	0.58	88.4	728.3	303.2	95.2	0.7
2004	D+	0.57	0.40	71.8	674.6	292.7	100.8	12.4

XL Capital Ltd
Composite Group Rating: C

Largest Group Members	Assets ($mil)	Rating
XL REINS AMERICA INC	5278	C
GREENWICH INS CO	902	D+
XL INS AMERICA INC	648	C-
XL SPECIALTY INS CO	577	C+
X L INS CO OF NY	210	D

GRINNELL MUTUAL REINSURANCE CO B- Good

Major Rating Factors: Fair overall results on stability tests (4.7 on a scale of 0 to 10) including potential drain of affiliation with Grinnell Mutual Group and negative cash flow from operations for 2008. History of adequate reserve strength (6.9) as reserves have been consistently at an acceptable level.

Other Rating Factors: Good overall profitability index (6.0) despite operating losses during 2008. Good liquidity (6.3) with sufficient resources (cash flows and marketable investments) to handle a spike in claims. Strong long-term capitalization index (8.2) based on excellent current risk adjusted capital (severe and moderate loss scenarios), despite some fluctuation in capital levels.

Principal Business: Auto liability (21%), workers compensation (16%), auto physical damage (16%), commercial multiple peril (15%), other liability (15%), allied lines (9%), and other lines (7%).

Principal Investments: Investment grade bonds (81%), misc. investments (13%), cash (4%), non investment grade bonds (1%), and real estate (1%).

Investments in Affiliates: 5%

Group Affiliation: Grinnell Mutual Group

Licensed in: IL, IN, IA, MN, MO, NE, ND, OH, SD, WI

Commenced Business: April 1909

Address: 4211 Highway 146, Grinnell, IA 50112-0790

Phone: (515) 236-6121 **Domicile State:** IA **NAIC Code:** 14117

Data Date	Rating	RACR #1	RACR #2	Loss Ratio %	Total Assets ($mil)	Capital ($mil)	Net Premium ($mil)	Net Income ($mil)
3-09	B-	2.42	1.70	N/A	725.2	289.6	86.6	6.6
3-08	B-	2.90	2.06	N/A	667.0	317.1	75.2	2.3
2008	B-	2.55	1.81	78.3	652.6	285.3	303.3	-2.0
2007	B-	2.94	2.10	63.1	675.3	320.2	309.5	31.5
2006	B-	2.71	1.96	66.1	640.6	287.2	316.5	23.2
2005	B-	2.57	1.90	63.2	603.6	258.3	312.6	36.6
2004	B-	2.43	1.81	67.4	555.3	225.0	310.2	18.4

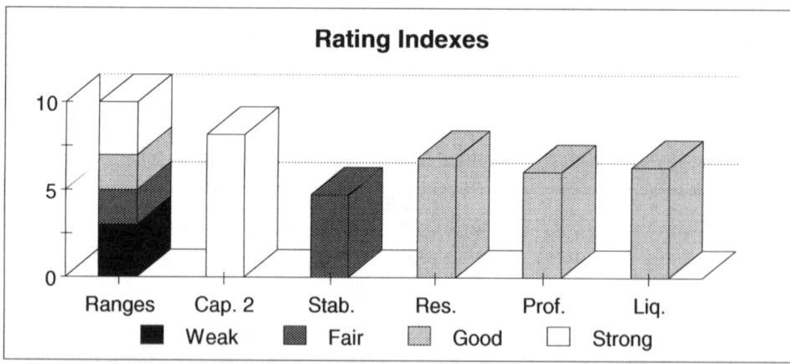

GUIDEONE MUTUAL INS CO C+ Fair

Major Rating Factors: Fair overall results on stability tests (4.5 on a scale of 0 to 10) including potential drain of affiliation with GuideOne Group and negative cash flow from operations for 2008. History of adequate reserve strength (5.8) as reserves have been consistently at an acceptable level.

Other Rating Factors: Good liquidity (6.6) with sufficient resources (cash flows and marketable investments) to handle a spike in claims. Strong long-term capitalization index (7.5) based on excellent current risk adjusted capital (severe and moderate loss scenarios). Moreover, capital levels have been consistent in recent years. Excellent profitability (8.5) with operating gains in each of the last five years.

Principal Business: Commercial multiple peril (38%), workers compensation (16%), homeowners multiple peril (14%), auto liability (11%), allied lines (9%), other liability (8%), and other lines (5%).

Principal Investments: Investment grade bonds (73%), misc. investments (27%), non investment grade bonds (1%), and real estate (1%).

Investments in Affiliates: 21%

Group Affiliation: GuideOne Group

Licensed in: All states except PR

Commenced Business: April 1947

Address: 1111 Ashworth Rd, West Des Moines, IA 50265-3538

Phone: (515) 267-5000 **Domicile State:** IA **NAIC Code:** 15032

Data Date	Rating	RACR #1	RACR #2	Loss Ratio %	Total Assets ($mil)	Capital ($mil)	Net Premium ($mil)	Net Income ($mil)
3-09	C+	1.87	1.56	N/A	1,000.8	362.0	77.8	4.1
3-08	C	1.85	1.56	N/A	1,011.1	357.1	78.5	4.5
2008	C+	1.87	1.57	70.7	1,010.9	360.1	298.1	8.6
2007	C	1.83	1.55	59.2	1,020.1	349.2	312.8	47.8
2006	C	1.59	1.37	61.1	950.7	298.4	324.8	21.0
2005	C	1.51	1.24	68.2	847.5	264.0	322.6	4.7
2004	C	1.59	1.38	69.8	686.7	248.1	326.8	4.1

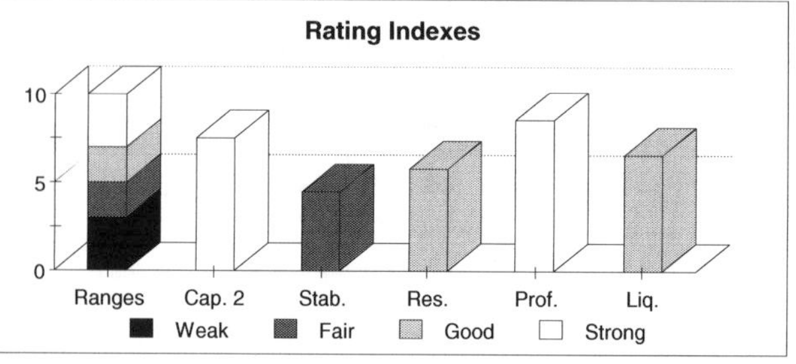

GUIDEONE PROPERTY & CASUALTY INS CO B Good

Major Rating Factors: Good overall results on stability tests (5.5 on a scale of 0 to 10) despite potential drain of affiliation with GuideOne Group, negative cash flow from operations for 2008 and fair results on operational trends. History of adequate reserve strength (6.7) as reserves have been consistently at an acceptable level.
Other Rating Factors: Good liquidity (6.9) with sufficient resources (cash flows and marketable investments) to handle a spike in claims. Strong long-term capitalization index (10.0) based on excellent current risk adjusted capital (severe and moderate loss scenarios). Moreover, capital levels have been consistent in recent years. Excellent profitability (8.5) with operating gains in each of the last five years.
Principal Business: (This company is a reinsurer.)
Principal Investments: Investment grade bonds (86%) and misc. investments (14%).
Investments in Affiliates: 9%
Group Affiliation: GuideOne Group
Licensed in: IA
Commenced Business: December 1993
Address: 1111 Ashworth Road, West Des Moines, IA 50265-3538
Phone: (515) 267-5092 **Domicile State:** IA **NAIC Code:** 13984

Data Date	Rating	RACR #1	RACR #2	Loss Ratio %	Total Assets ($mil)	Capital ($mil)	Net Premium ($mil)	Net Income ($mil)
3-09	B	4.62	3.47	N/A	376.0	195.1	24.3	2.1
3-08	B-	4.41	3.17	N/A	379.6	189.7	24.5	2.1
2008	B	4.63	3.49	70.7	375.0	194.1	93.2	8.0
2007	B-	4.42	3.19	59.2	378.3	187.4	97.8	15.7
2006	C+	4.19	2.89	61.1	399.3	180.3	101.5	16.9
2005	C+	3.60	2.56	68.2	365.4	152.1	100.8	11.8
2004	C+	3.88	2.96	69.8	328.8	143.5	102.1	4.7

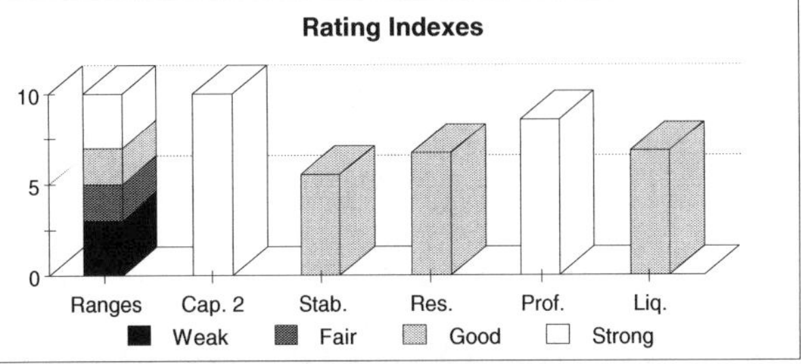

GUILFORD INS CO C- Fair

Major Rating Factors: Weak overall results on stability tests (2.6 on a scale of 0 to 10) including potential drain of affiliation with IFG Companies. Good long-term capitalization index (6.1) based on good current risk adjusted capital (moderate loss scenario). Moreover, capital levels have been consistent in recent years.
Other Rating Factors: History of adequate reserve strength (5.9) as reserves have been consistently at an acceptable level. Excellent profitability (8.8) with operating gains in each of the last five years. Excellent liquidity (7.0) with ample operational cash flow and liquid investments.
Principal Business: Other liability (90%), commercial multiple peril (7%), auto liability (2%), and auto physical damage (1%).
Principal Investments: Investment grade bonds (56%) and misc. investments (44%).
Investments in Affiliates: 41%
Group Affiliation: IFG Companies
Licensed in: IL
Commenced Business: December 1998
Address: 238 International Road, Burlington, NC 27215
Phone: (336) 586-2830 **Domicile State:** IL **NAIC Code:** 10956

Data Date	Rating	RACR #1	RACR #2	Loss Ratio %	Total Assets ($mil)	Capital ($mil)	Net Premium ($mil)	Net Income ($mil)
3-09	C-	1.50	1.26	N/A	356.4	208.0	10.2	2.4
3-08	D+	1.44	1.17	N/A	353.7	193.3	14.0	3.5
2008	C-	1.49	1.24	56.3	357.2	205.6	45.1	14.5
2007	D+	1.41	1.15	62.9	351.5	188.6	62.3	14.7
2006	D	1.36	1.09	58.0	335.7	168.3	73.9	16.1
2005	D	1.17	0.92	58.6	294.6	142.6	75.4	11.2
2004	D	1.16	0.97	58.4	233.2	125.6	54.0	6.3

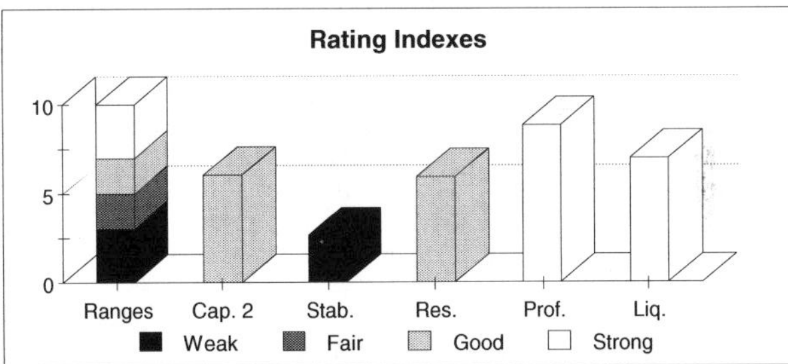

HANOVER INS CO B- Good

Major Rating Factors: Good overall results on stability tests (5.1 on a scale of 0 to 10) despite potential drain of affiliation with Hanover Ins Group Inc. Good overall profitability index (5.9) despite operating losses during 2005. Return on equity has been fair, averaging 7.9% over the past five years.
Other Rating Factors: Good liquidity (6.5) with sufficient resources (cash flows and marketable investments) to handle a spike in claims. Strong long-term capitalization index (7.8) based on excellent current risk adjusted capital (severe and moderate loss scenarios), despite some fluctuation in capital levels. Ample reserve history (7.0) that can protect against increases in claims costs.
Principal Business: Auto liability (18%), commercial multiple peril (17%), inland marine (15%), surety (12%), other liability (8%), auto physical damage (8%), and other lines (21%).
Principal Investments: Investment grade bonds (64%), misc. investments (36%), and non investment grade bonds (1%).
Investments in Affiliates: 23%
Group Affiliation: Hanover Ins Group Inc
Licensed in: All states except PR
Commenced Business: April 1852
Address: 100 North Parkway, Worcester, MA 01605
Phone: (508) 853-7200 **Domicile State:** NH **NAIC Code:** 22292

Data Date	Rating	RACR #1	RACR #2	Loss Ratio %	Total Assets ($mil)	Capital ($mil)	Net Premium ($mil)	Net Income ($mil)
3-09	B-	1.68	1.47	N/A	4,742.8	1,519.8	465.6	18.8
3-08	B-	1.80	1.58	N/A	4,551.5	1,742.4	437.6	49.8
2008	B-	1.74	1.55	65.6	4,451.2	1,537.6	1,782.4	178.1
2007	B-	1.75	1.56	62.2	4,330.8	1,666.4	1,712.3	227.2
2006	B-	1.62	1.43	62.8	4,027.1	1,463.6	1,548.9	230.9
2005	B-	1.33	1.19	80.7	3,730.8	1,204.6	1,370.6	-34.2
2004	B-	1.38	1.23	72.7	3,448.6	1,098.8	1,361.7	20.5

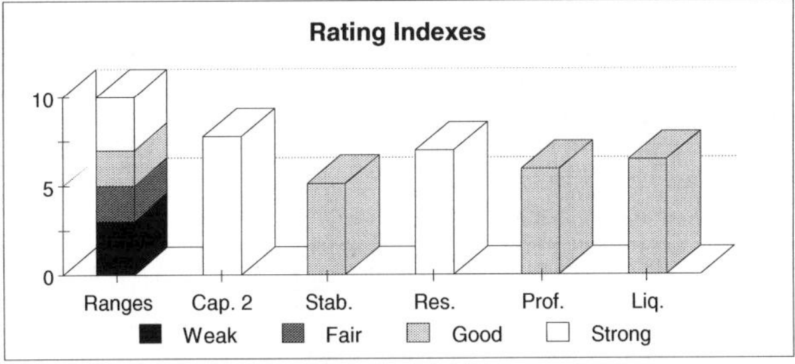

HARBOR POINT REINS US INC — B — Good

Major Rating Factors: Good overall profitability index (6.1 on a scale of 0 to 10) with small operating losses during 2007. Return on equity has been excellent over the last five years averaging 22.0%.

Other Rating Factors: Fair overall results on stability tests (4.1) including excessive premium growth and weak results on operational trends. Strong long-term capitalization index (10.0) based on excellent current risk adjusted capital (severe and moderate loss scenarios), despite some fluctuation in capital levels. Superior liquidity (9.2) with ample operational cash flow and liquid investments.

Principal Business: N/A

Principal Investments: Investment grade bonds (89%), misc. investments (6%), and cash (5%).

Investments in Affiliates: None

Group Affiliation: Harbor Point US Holdings Inc

Licensed in: All states except AL, AZ, CO, ID, KY, MN, UT, PR

Commenced Business: September 1997

Address: 82 Hopmeadow Street, Simsbury, CT 06070

Phone: (908) 903-2000 **Domicile State:** CT **NAIC Code:** 10829

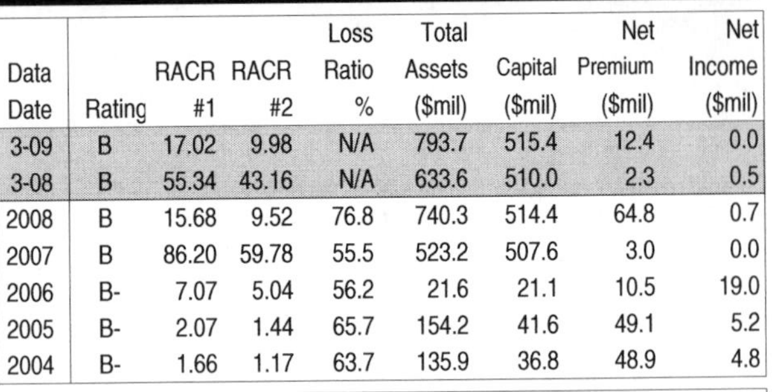

Data Date	Rating	RACR #1	RACR #2	Loss Ratio %	Total Assets ($mil)	Capital ($mil)	Net Premium ($mil)	Net Income ($mil)
3-09	B	17.02	9.98	N/A	793.7	515.4	12.4	0.0
3-08	B	55.34	43.16	N/A	633.6	510.0	2.3	0.5
2008	B	15.68	9.52	76.8	740.3	514.4	64.8	0.7
2007	B	86.20	59.78	55.5	523.2	507.6	3.0	0.0
2006	B-	7.07	5.04	56.2	21.6	21.1	10.5	19.0
2005	B-	2.07	1.44	65.7	154.2	41.6	49.1	5.2
2004	B-	1.66	1.17	63.7	135.9	36.8	48.9	4.8

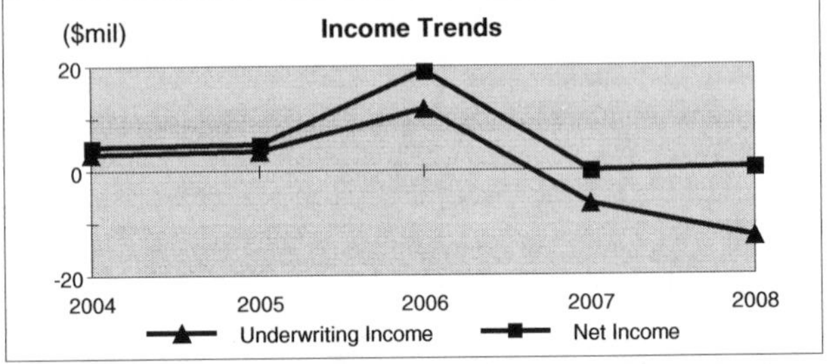

HARLEYSVILLE MUTUAL INS CO — B- — Good

Major Rating Factors: Fair overall results on stability tests (4.8 on a scale of 0 to 10) including potential drain of affiliation with Harleysville Group and negative cash flow from operations for 2008. Fair reserve development (4.9) as reserves have generally been sufficient to cover claims.

Other Rating Factors: Good overall profitability index (6.8). Weak expense controls. Good liquidity (6.9) with sufficient resources (cash flows and marketable investments) to handle a spike in claims. Strong long-term capitalization index (7.3) based on excellent current risk adjusted capital (severe and moderate loss scenarios). Moreover, capital levels have been consistent in recent years.

Principal Business: Commercial multiple peril (32%), auto liability (20%), allied lines (14%), workers compensation (9%), homeowners multiple peril (7%), other liability (6%), and other lines (11%).

Principal Investments: Investment grade bonds (57%) and misc. investments (44%).

Investments in Affiliates: 35%

Group Affiliation: Harleysville Group

Licensed in: All states except AK, AZ, WY, PR

Commenced Business: October 1917

Address: 355 Maple Ave, Harleysville, PA 19438-2297

Phone: (215) 256-5000 **Domicile State:** PA **NAIC Code:** 14168

Data Date	Rating	RACR #1	RACR #2	Loss Ratio %	Total Assets ($mil)	Capital ($mil)	Net Premium ($mil)	Net Income ($mil)
3-09	B-	1.98	1.84	N/A	1,296.4	741.0	43.6	0.4
3-08	B-	1.68	1.54	N/A	1,364.5	730.8	45.9	26.1
2008	B-	1.97	1.82	69.3	1,310.5	742.6	140.9	44.5
2007	B-	1.60	1.43	63.9	1,559.6	726.5	267.7	65.7
2006	C+	1.50	1.35	65.7	1,506.3	666.5	268.0	55.8
2005	C+	1.49	1.33	65.6	1,391.6	579.2	279.6	37.1
2004	C+	1.46	1.29	73.1	1,261.8	521.7	280.0	53.6

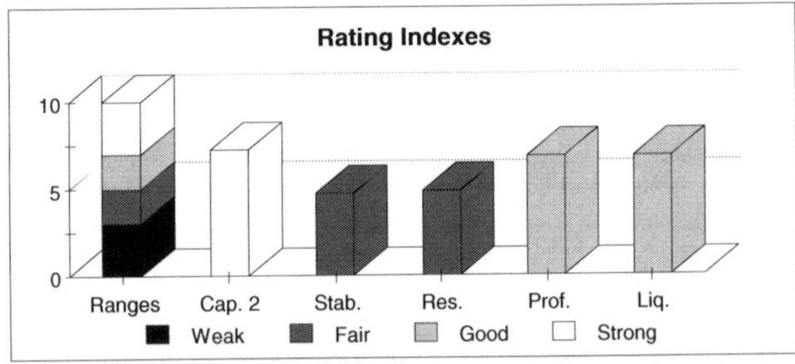

HARTFORD ACCIDENT & INDEMNITY CO — C+ — Fair

Major Rating Factors: Fair reserve development (4.3 on a scale of 0 to 10) as reserves have generally been sufficient to cover claims. In 2004, the two year reserve development was 60% deficient. Fair profitability index (3.5) with operating losses during the first three months of 2008. Return on equity has been fair, averaging 10.9% over the past five years.

Other Rating Factors: Fair overall results on stability tests (4.3). Good liquidity (6.8) with sufficient resources (cash flows and marketable investments) to handle a spike in claims. Strong long-term capitalization index (7.7) based on excellent current risk adjusted capital (severe and moderate loss scenarios), despite some fluctuation in capital levels.

Principal Business: Workers compensation (40%), auto liability (18%), commercial multiple peril (13%), auto physical damage (11%), homeowners multiple peril (10%), surety (7%), and other liability (2%).

Principal Investments: Investment grade bonds (75%), misc. investments (23%), and non investment grade bonds (2%).

Investments in Affiliates: 8%

Group Affiliation: Hartford Financial Services Inc

Licensed in: All states, the District of Columbia and Puerto Rico

Commenced Business: August 1913

Address: Hartford Plaza, Hartford, CT 06115

Phone: (860) 547-5000 **Domicile State:** CT **NAIC Code:** 22357

Data Date	Rating	RACR #1	RACR #2	Loss Ratio %	Total Assets ($mil)	Capital ($mil)	Net Premium ($mil)	Net Income ($mil)
3-09	C+	2.02	1.46	N/A	10,829.4	2,765.0	825.7	-44.7
3-08	C+	2.30	1.60	N/A	12,227.4	3,937.3	848.6	53.0
2008	C+	2.06	1.50	64.1	10,935.3	2,835.8	3,337.5	63.7
2007	C+	2.33	1.63	64.6	12,046.6	3,942.0	3,411.9	708.5
2006	C+	2.27	1.66	67.5	11,193.6	3,778.0	3,454.5	446.0
2005	C+	2.15	1.58	66.0	10,195.9	3,260.7	3,405.1	462.0
2004	C+	1.87	1.41	70.5	9,280.3	2,838.9	3,068.5	358.9

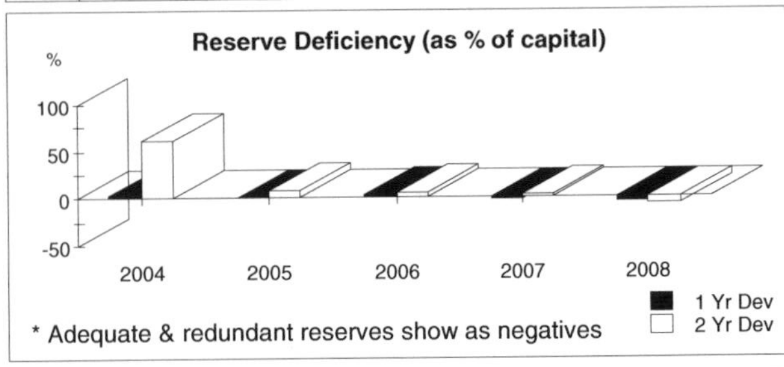

HARTFORD CASUALTY INS CO B Good

Major Rating Factors: Good liquidity (6.9 on a scale of 0 to 10) with sufficient resources (cash flows and marketable investments) to handle a spike in claims. Good overall results on stability tests (5.9).

Other Rating Factors: Fair reserve development (4.7) as reserves have generally been sufficient to cover claims. In 2004, the two year reserve development was 23% deficient. Fair profitability index (4.6) with operating losses during 2006 and the first three months of 2008. Return on equity has been fair, averaging 7.6% over the past five years. Strong long-term capitalization index (10.0) based on excellent current risk adjusted capital (severe and moderate loss scenarios), despite some fluctuation in capital levels.

Principal Business: Commercial multiple peril (55%), workers compensation (15%), other liability (13%), auto liability (6%), homeowners multiple peril (4%), auto physical damage (3%), and other lines (3%).

Principal Investments: Investment grade bonds (90%), misc. investments (8%), and non investment grade bonds (2%).

Investments in Affiliates: None

Group Affiliation: Hartford Financial Services Inc

Licensed in: All states except PR

Commenced Business: July 1987

Address: 4040 Vincennes Cir Suite 100, Indianapolis, IN 46268

Phone: (860) 547-5000 **Domicile State:** IN **NAIC Code:** 29424

Data Date	Rating	RACR #1	RACR #2	Loss Ratio %	Total Assets ($mil)	Capital ($mil)	Net Premium ($mil)	Net Income ($mil)
3-09	B	4.70	3.04	N/A	2,124.5	847.0	138.9	-60.5
3-08	B	4.74	2.83	N/A	2,202.9	962.5	142.8	42.6
2008	B	4.71	3.06	64.1	2,105.7	837.3	561.5	107.0
2007	B	4.58	2.75	64.6	2,164.6	920.2	574.0	116.2
2006	B	4.61	2.93	67.5	2,115.4	905.2	581.2	-2.3
2005	B	3.34	2.39	66.0	1,943.4	823.5	572.9	99.6
2004	B	2.85	2.15	70.5	1,760.2	754.2	516.3	75.0

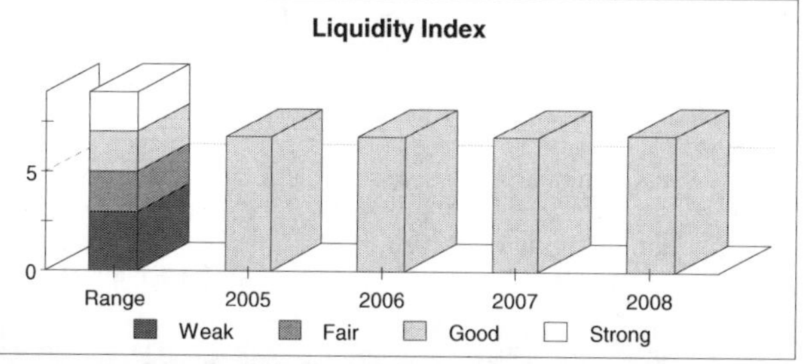

HARTFORD FIRE INS CO * B+ Good

Major Rating Factors: Good overall profitability index (6.9 on a scale of 0 to 10). Fair expense controls. Return on equity has been fair, averaging 6.0% over the past five years. Good liquidity (6.9) with sufficient resources (cash flows and marketable investments) to handle a spike in claims.

Other Rating Factors: Good overall results on stability tests (6.4). Stability strengths include good operational trends and excellent risk diversification. Strong long-term capitalization index (8.9) based on excellent current risk adjusted capital (severe and moderate loss scenarios), despite some fluctuation in capital levels. Fair reserve development (4.8) as reserves have generally been sufficient to cover claims. In 2004, the two year reserve development was 18% deficient.

Principal Business: Commercial multiple peril (29%), workers compensation (18%), inland marine (13%), auto liability (11%), surety (9%), other liability (7%), and other lines (14%).

Principal Investments: Investment grade bonds (66%), misc. investments (31%), cash (1%), non investment grade bonds (1%), and real estate (1%).

Investments in Affiliates: 26%

Group Affiliation: Hartford Financial Services Inc

Licensed in: All states, the District of Columbia and Puerto Rico

Commenced Business: August 1810

Address: Hartford Plaza, Hartford, CT 06115

Phone: (860) 547-5000 **Domicile State:** CT **NAIC Code:** 19682

Data Date	Rating	RACR #1	RACR #2	Loss Ratio %	Total Assets ($mil)	Capital ($mil)	Net Premium ($mil)	Net Income ($mil)
3-09	B+	2.49	2.28	N/A	23,864.9	12,364.8	1,048.3	95.1
3-08	B+	2.23	2.04	N/A	25,588.1	13,865.0	1,077.3	162.9
2008	B+	2.50	2.30	64.1	24,453.6	12,491.5	4,237.0	955.6
2007	B+	2.34	2.14	64.6	26,570.5	14,442.3	4,331.4	1,082.8
2006	B+	2.17	2.01	67.5	24,589.9	13,020.9	4,385.6	498.3
2005	B+	1.98	1.83	66.0	21,569.8	10,480.1	4,322.8	808.4
2004	B+	1.92	1.76	70.5	20,101.6	9,754.4	3,895.5	390.8

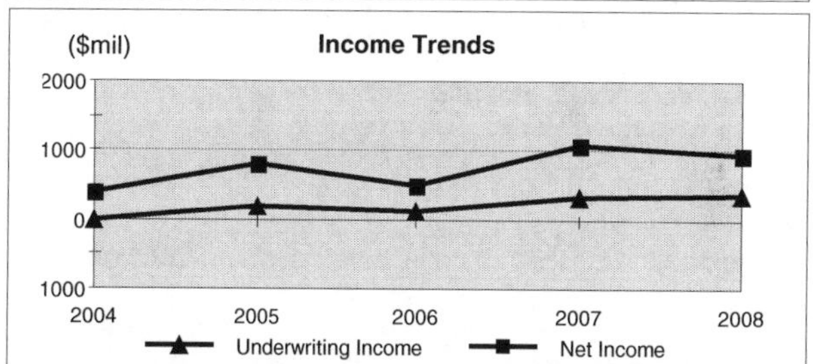

HARTFORD INS CO OF IL B Good

Major Rating Factors: Good profitability index (5.0 on a scale of 0 to 10). Fair expense controls. Return on equity has been good over the last five years, averaging 10.3%. Good liquidity (6.9) with sufficient resources (cash flows and marketable investments) to handle a spike in claims.

Other Rating Factors: Good overall results on stability tests (5.4). Stability strengths include good operational trends and excellent risk diversification. Fair reserve development (4.5) as reserves have generally been sufficient to cover claims. In 2004, the two year reserve development was 43% deficient. Strong long-term capitalization index (9.5) based on excellent current risk adjusted capital (severe and moderate loss scenarios), despite some fluctuation in capital levels.

Principal Business: Auto liability (49%), auto physical damage (25%), homeowners multiple peril (10%), workers compensation (10%), other liability (2%), inland marine (2%), and other lines (3%).

Principal Investments: Investment grade bonds (92%), misc. investments (7%), and non investment grade bonds (1%).

Investments in Affiliates: None

Group Affiliation: Hartford Financial Services Inc

Licensed in: IL, NY, PA

Commenced Business: January 1980

Address: 4245 Meridian Parkway, Aurora, IL 60504

Phone: (860) 547-5000 **Domicile State:** IL **NAIC Code:** 38288

Data Date	Rating	RACR #1	RACR #2	Loss Ratio %	Total Assets ($mil)	Capital ($mil)	Net Premium ($mil)	Net Income ($mil)
3-09	B	4.16	2.69	N/A	3,683.3	1,324.3	255.1	8.4
3-08	B-	4.10	2.46	N/A	3,813.3	1,492.9	262.2	55.3
2008	B	4.16	2.70	64.1	3,682.7	1,313.5	1,031.2	90.0
2007	B-	4.04	2.44	64.6	3,709.2	1,453.0	1,054.1	206.4
2006	B-	4.07	2.61	67.5	3,613.8	1,432.1	1,067.3	148.3
2005	B-	3.93	2.54	66.0	3,314.3	1,306.8	1,052.1	151.7
2004	B-	3.35	2.30	70.5	3,034.3	1,187.8	948.1	125.0

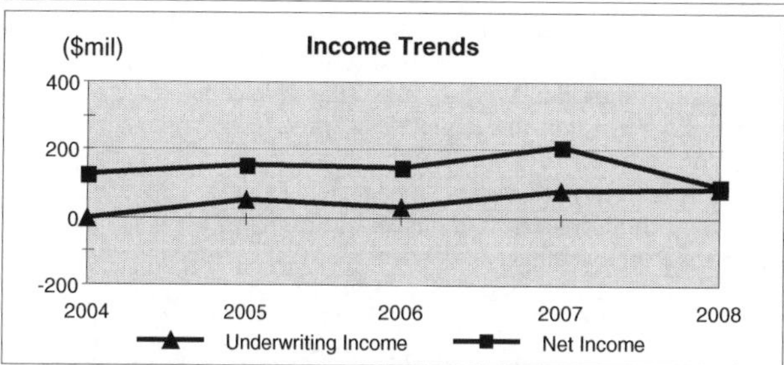

HARTFORD INS CO OF THE MIDWEST * B+ Good

Major Rating Factors: Good overall results on stability tests (6.4 on a scale of 0 to 10). Strong long-term capitalization index (10.0) based on excellent current risk adjusted capital (severe and moderate loss scenarios). Moreover, capital levels have been consistent in recent years.

Other Rating Factors: Excellent profitability (8.9) with operating gains in each of the last five years. Excellent expense controls. Return on equity has been good over the last five years, averaging 10.5%. Excellent liquidity (7.0) with ample operational cash flow and liquid investments. Fair reserve development (4.9) as reserves have generally been sufficient to cover claims.

Principal Business: Workers compensation (26%), auto liability (21%), homeowners multiple peril (16%), allied lines (14%), auto physical damage (12%), commercial multiple peril (8%), and other liability (2%).

Principal Investments: Investment grade bonds (95%), non investment grade bonds (3%), and misc. investments (2%).

Investments in Affiliates: None

Group Affiliation: Hartford Financial Services Inc

Licensed in: All states except PR

Commenced Business: January 1980

Address: 4040 Vincennes Cir Suite 100, Indianapolis, IN 46268

Phone: (860) 547-5000 **Domicile State:** IN **NAIC Code:** 37478

Data Date	Rating	RACR #1	RACR #2	Loss Ratio %	Total Assets ($mil)	Capital ($mil)	Net Premium ($mil)	Net Income ($mil)
3-09	B+	14.12	8.90	N/A	359.6	244.2	12.6	4.6
3-08	B+	12.27	7.11	N/A	331.1	219.4	13.0	5.7
2008	B+	14.05	8.91	64.1	356.0	240.2	51.0	22.7
2007	B+	12.09	7.06	64.6	325.9	213.5	52.2	22.8
2006	B+	11.24	6.96	67.5	297.4	189.9	52.8	19.3
2005	B+	10.45	6.56	66.0	267.2	168.1	52.1	18.9
2004	B+	8.67	5.81	70.5	241.9	147.2	46.9	17.2

Hartford Financial Services Inc
Composite Group Rating: D+

Largest Group Members	Assets ($mil)	Rating
HARTFORD LIFE INS CO	133562	C-
HARTFORD LIFE ANNUITY INS CO	65461	B-
HARTFORD FIRE INS CO	24454	B+
HARTFORD LIFE ACCIDENT INS CO	14414	B-
HARTFORD ACCIDENT INDEMNITY CO	10935	C+

HARTFORD SM BOIL INSPECTION & INS B- Good

Major Rating Factors: Fair profitability index (3.1 on a scale of 0 to 10) with operating losses during 2008. Return on equity has been fair, averaging 16.7% over the past five years. Fair overall results on stability tests (4.9). The largest net exposure for one risk is conservative at 1.9% of capital.

Other Rating Factors: Good liquidity (6.7) with sufficient resources (cash flows and marketable investments) to handle a spike in claims. Strong long-term capitalization index (8.0) based on excellent current risk adjusted capital (severe and moderate loss scenarios), despite some fluctuation in capital levels. Ample reserve history (9.3) that helps to protect the company against sharp claims increases.

Principal Business: Boiler & machinery (93%), inland marine (4%), commercial multiple peril (2%), and other liability (1%).

Principal Investments: Misc. investments (51%), investment grade bonds (48%), and cash (1%).

Investments in Affiliates: 13%

Group Affiliation: Munich Re Group

Licensed in: All states, the District of Columbia and Puerto Rico

Commenced Business: October 1866

Address: One State St, Hartford, CT 06102-5024

Phone: (860) 722-1866 **Domicile State:** CT **NAIC Code:** 11452

Data Date	Rating	RACR #1	RACR #2	Loss Ratio %	Total Assets ($mil)	Capital ($mil)	Net Premium ($mil)	Net Income ($mil)
3-09	B-	1.92	1.75	N/A	1,164.7	466.6	159.2	10.6
3-08	B	2.05	1.84	N/A	1,181.2	559.7	154.6	19.0
2008	B-	1.80	1.64	27.4	1,111.7	442.6	643.4	-4.0
2007	B	2.39	2.20	28.9	1,321.2	719.8	618.7	157.6
2006	B	2.62	2.37	23.9	1,203.3	617.6	571.0	146.0
2005	B	2.85	2.51	26.6	1,162.8	602.6	520.7	138.6
2004	B	2.40	1.99	26.5	1,180.4	604.5	545.0	107.7

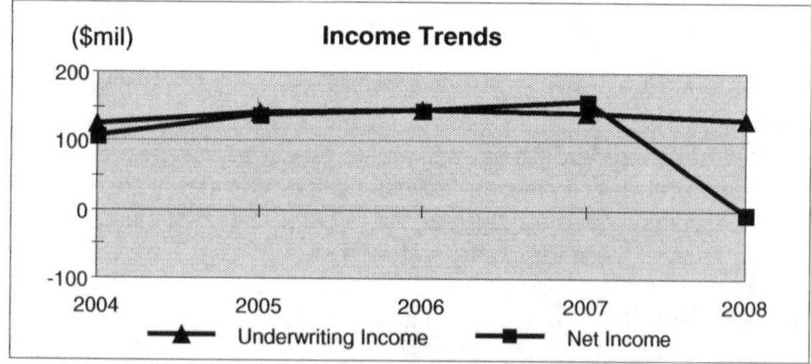

HARTFORD UNDERWRITERS INS CO * B+ Good

Major Rating Factors: Good overall profitability index (5.8 on a scale of 0 to 10) despite operating losses during the first three months of 2008. Return on equity has been good over the last five years, averaging 13.0%. Good liquidity (6.8) with sufficient resources (cash flows and marketable investments) to handle a spike in claims.

Other Rating Factors: Good overall results on stability tests (6.4). Stability strengths include good operational trends and excellent risk diversification. Strong long-term capitalization index (10.0) based on excellent current risk adjusted capital (severe and moderate loss scenarios), despite some fluctuation in capital levels. Fair reserve development (4.7) as reserves have generally been sufficient to cover claims. In 2004, the two year reserve development was 25% deficient.

Principal Business: Workers compensation (32%), auto liability (30%), auto physical damage (18%), homeowners multiple peril (11%), commercial multiple peril (4%), other liability (2%), and other lines (3%).

Principal Investments: Investment grade bonds (97%), misc. investments (2%), and non investment grade bonds (1%).

Investments in Affiliates: None

Group Affiliation: Hartford Financial Services Inc

Licensed in: All states except PR

Commenced Business: December 1987

Address: Hartford Plaza, Hartford, CT 06115

Phone: (860) 547-5000 **Domicile State:** CT **NAIC Code:** 30104

Data Date	Rating	RACR #1	RACR #2	Loss Ratio %	Total Assets ($mil)	Capital ($mil)	Net Premium ($mil)	Net Income ($mil)
3-09	B+	4.84	3.14	N/A	1,564.1	645.7	101.0	-18.9
3-08	B+	4.47	2.67	N/A	1,579.5	674.2	103.8	25.6
2008	B+	4.80	3.13	64.1	1,561.2	634.3	408.4	67.1
2007	B+	4.37	2.63	64.6	1,551.8	652.9	417.5	87.0
2006	B+	4.44	2.83	67.5	1,506.2	646.6	422.7	70.4
2005	B+	4.21	2.71	66.0	1,386.4	577.9	416.7	81.1
2004	B+	3.42	2.35	70.5	1,236.6	504.9	375.5	111.8

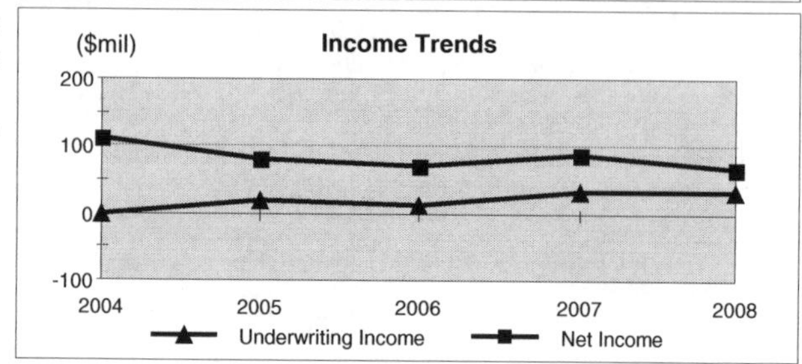

HASTINGS MUTUAL INS CO * A+ Excellent

Major Rating Factors: Strong long-term capitalization index (10.0 on a scale of 0 to 10) based on excellent current risk adjusted capital (severe and moderate loss scenarios). Furthermore, this high level of risk adjusted capital has been consistently maintained in previous years. Ample reserve history (9.3) that helps to protect the company against sharp claims increases.

Other Rating Factors: Excellent profitability (8.4) despite modest operating losses during the first three months of 2008. Return on equity has been good over the last five years, averaging 11.3%. Excellent overall results on stability tests (7.4). Stability strengths include excellent operational trends and excellent risk diversification. Good liquidity (6.6) with sufficient resources (cash flows and marketable investments) to handle a spike in claims.

Principal Business: Auto liability (21%), homeowners multiple peril (17%), commercial multiple peril (15%), workers compensation (14%), auto physical damage (13%), farmowners multiple peril (13%), and other lines (8%).

Principal Investments: Investment grade bonds (96%), misc. investments (4%), non investment grade bonds (1%), and real estate (1%).

Investments in Affiliates: None

Group Affiliation: None

Licensed in: IL, IN, KY, MI, OH, WI

Commenced Business: April 1885

Address: 404 E Woodlawn Ave, Hastings, MI 49058-1091

Phone: (800) 442-8277 **Domicile State:** MI **NAIC Code:** 14176

Data Date	Rating	RACR #1	RACR #2	Loss Ratio %	Total Assets ($mil)	Capital ($mil)	Net Premium ($mil)	Net Income ($mil)
3-09	A+	6.03	4.21	N/A	591.7	289.3	66.8	-0.4
3-08	A+	5.59	3.89	N/A	611.2	286.9	66.0	3.5
2008	A+	6.18	4.24	64.3	595.0	292.4	266.8	20.3
2007	A+	5.65	3.88	68.0	617.9	286.9	265.5	17.6
2006	A	5.57	3.89	58.5	584.2	269.4	256.7	31.1
2005	A-	4.53	3.31	54.9	552.7	235.3	266.0	38.3
2004	A-	3.81	2.75	55.2	510.8	196.7	266.9	36.3

Risk-Adjusted Capital Ratio #2 (Severe Loss Scenario)

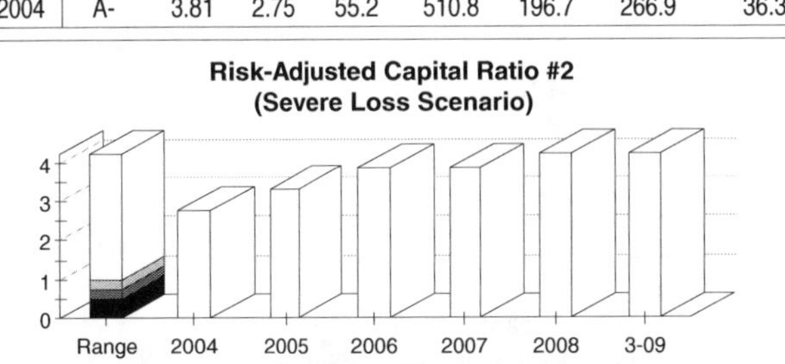

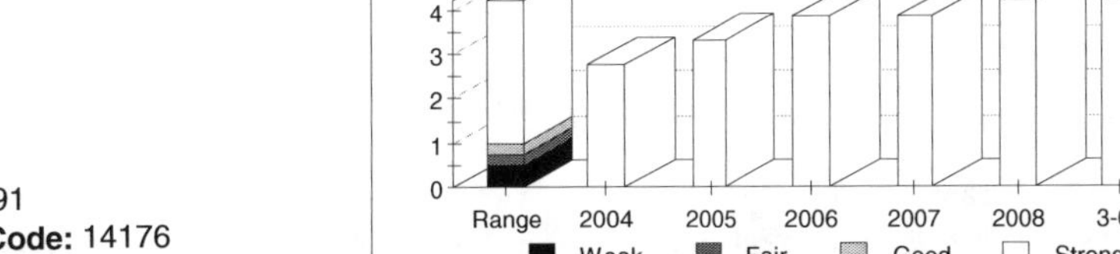

HEALTH CARE INDEMNITY INC C Fair

Major Rating Factors: Fair overall results on stability tests (4.3 on a scale of 0 to 10) including weak results on operational trends, negative cash flow from operations for 2008 and excessive premium growth. The largest net exposure for one risk is acceptable at 2.0% of capital. Strong long-term capitalization index (8.4) based on excellent current risk adjusted capital (severe and moderate loss scenarios), despite some fluctuation in capital levels.

Other Rating Factors: Ample reserve history (9.9) that helps to protect the company against sharp claims increases. Excellent profitability (7.0) with operating gains in each of the last five years. Excellent expense controls. Return on equity has been excellent over the last five years averaging 26.1%. Superior liquidity (9.1) with ample operational cash flow and liquid investments.

Principal Business: Medical malpractice (100%).

Principal Investments: Investment grade bonds (108%).

Investments in Affiliates: None

Group Affiliation: None

Licensed in: CO, FL, IL, IN, KS, KY, LA, MO, NV, OH, OK, SC, TN, TX, UT, WV

Commenced Business: August 1976

Address: One Park Plaza, Nashville, TN 37202-0555

Phone: (615) 344-5808 **Domicile State:** CO **NAIC Code:** 35904

Data Date	Rating	RACR #1	RACR #2	Loss Ratio %	Total Assets ($mil)	Capital ($mil)	Net Premium ($mil)	Net Income ($mil)
3-09	C	2.89	2.51	N/A	1,637.6	775.9	8.5	19.5
3-08	C	2.31	2.00	N/A	1,896.5	793.4	6.2	41.8
2008	C	3.07	2.68	16.9	1,742.6	872.8	32.9	113.9
2007	C	2.09	1.82	N/A	2,001.1	754.4	46.3	232.5
2006	C	0.90	0.79	52.6	2,174.9	521.9	313.0	318.9
2005	C	1.10	0.90	86.3	2,426.6	800.3	344.5	129.0
2004	C	1.02	0.85	95.1	2,337.2	767.8	370.1	103.7

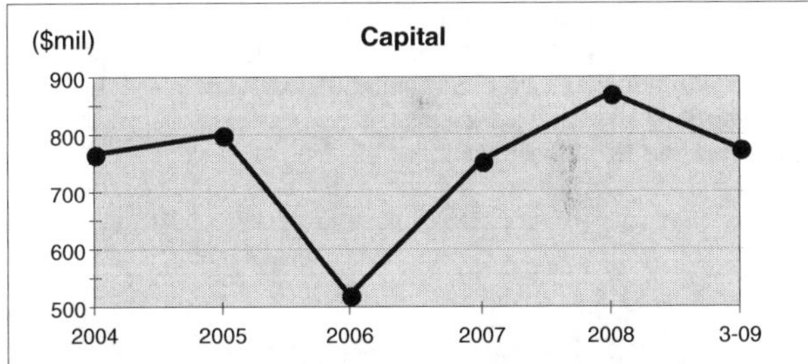

HIGH POINT PREFERRED INS CO C+ Fair

Major Rating Factors: Fair overall results on stability tests (4.4 on a scale of 0 to 10). The largest net exposure for one risk is conservative at 1.5% of capital. Good long-term capitalization index (6.1) based on good current risk adjusted capital (moderate loss scenario).

Other Rating Factors: Good overall profitability index (5.6). Fair expense controls. Return on equity has been fair, averaging 7.2% over the past five years. Good liquidity (6.1) with sufficient resources (cash flows and marketable investments) to handle a spike in claims. Ample reserve history (9.5) that helps to protect the company against sharp claims increases.

Principal Business: Homeowners multiple peril (59%), auto liability (24%), auto physical damage (11%), allied lines (3%), other liability (2%), inland marine (1%), and fire (1%).

Principal Investments: Investment grade bonds (69%), misc. investments (28%), and cash (3%).

Investments in Affiliates: 11%

Group Affiliation: Palisades Group

Licensed in: NJ

Commenced Business: October 1987

Address: 331 Newman Sprgs Rd, Ste 310, Red Bank, NJ 07701-5692

Phone: (732) 946-5000 **Domicile State:** NJ **NAIC Code:** 28959

Data Date	Rating	RACR #1	RACR #2	Loss Ratio %	Total Assets ($mil)	Capital ($mil)	Net Premium ($mil)	Net Income ($mil)
3-09	C+	1.20	0.88	N/A	866.7	221.2	108.2	3.1
3-08	C+	1.52	1.22	N/A	837.0	226.0	103.2	-5.7
2008	C+	1.20	0.89	72.1	854.0	225.0	497.3	14.9
2007	C+	1.60	1.33	75.1	822.4	248.0	370.4	10.7
2006	C	1.60	1.34	71.8	837.5	243.3	389.7	17.6
2005	C	1.43	1.23	77.2	829.8	210.8	371.3	20.2
2004	C	1.48	1.25	74.5	836.5	202.9	438.3	17.3

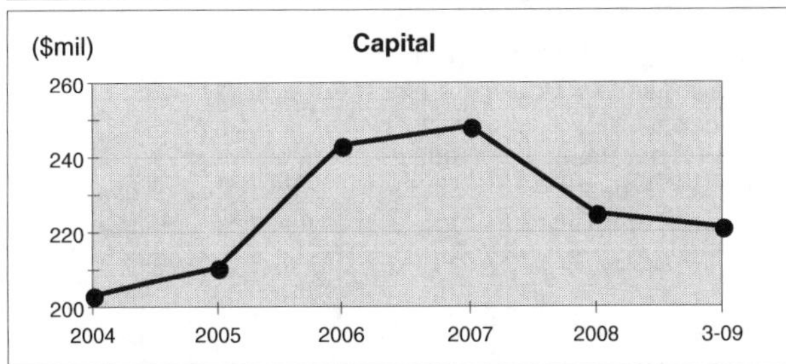

HOME-OWNERS INS CO * — A — Excellent

Major Rating Factors: Strong long-term capitalization index (8.4 on a scale of 0 to 10) based on excellent current risk adjusted capital (severe and moderate loss scenarios). Furthermore, this high level of risk adjusted capital has been consistently maintained in previous years. Ample reserve history (8.3) that helps to protect the company against sharp claims increases.

Other Rating Factors: Excellent overall results on stability tests (7.4). Strengths that enhance stability include potential support from affiliation with Auto-Owners Group, excellent operational trends and excellent risk diversification. Good overall profitability index (5.5) despite operating losses during 2007 and 2008. Return on equity has been fair, averaging 8.8% over the past five years. Fair liquidity (4.7) as cash resources may not be adequate to cover a spike in claims.

Principal Business: Homeowners multiple peril (34%), auto liability (28%), auto physical damage (25%), commercial multiple peril (7%), workers compensation (2%), inland marine (2%), and other liability (1%).

Principal Investments: Investment grade bonds (94%) and misc. investments (6%).

Investments in Affiliates: None

Group Affiliation: Auto-Owners Group

Licensed in: AL, AR, CO, IL, IN, IA, KY, MI, MO, NE, NV, ND, OH, PA, SC, SD, UT, VA, WI

Commenced Business: May 1863

Address: 6101 Anacapri Blvd, Lansing, MI 48917-3999

Phone: (517) 323-1200 **Domicile State:** MI **NAIC Code:** 26638

Data Date	Rating	RACR #1	RACR #2	Loss Ratio %	Total Assets ($mil)	Capital ($mil)	Net Premium ($mil)	Net Income ($mil)
3-09	A	2.95	1.93	N/A	1,353.2	451.9	192.4	11.1
3-08	A	3.20	2.06	N/A	1,276.3	426.8	179.4	-22.3
2008	A	2.86	1.91	90.8	1,335.9	449.4	770.2	-44.2
2007	A	3.46	2.29	87.5	1,258.7	461.0	690.3	-9.3
2006	A	4.30	2.92	71.8	1,146.5	465.6	646.7	62.6
2005	A	3.91	2.70	64.7	1,024.6	394.0	532.1	91.6
2004	A	3.00	1.90	67.1	884.1	316.7	442.5	59.3

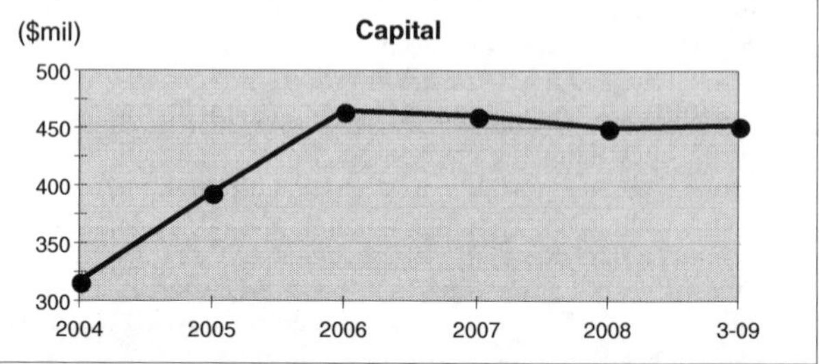

HOMELAND INS CO OF NEW YORK — C — Fair

Major Rating Factors: Fair profitability index (4.3 on a scale of 0 to 10) with operating losses during 2008. Return on equity has been fair, averaging 8.5% over the past five years. Fair overall results on stability tests (4.3) including fair financial strength of affiliated White Mountains Group.

Other Rating Factors: History of adequate reserve strength (5.6) as reserves have been consistently at an acceptable level. Strong long-term capitalization index (9.2) based on excellent current risk adjusted capital (severe and moderate loss scenarios), despite some fluctuation in capital levels. Excellent liquidity (7.1) with ample operational cash flow and liquid investments.

Principal Business: Medical malpractice (50%), other liability (19%), fire (17%), allied lines (7%), group accident & health (4%), and earthquake (2%).

Principal Investments: Investment grade bonds (75%), misc. investments (21%), and non investment grade bonds (4%).

Investments in Affiliates: None

Group Affiliation: White Mountains Group

Licensed in: NY

Commenced Business: October 1988

Address: 201 North Service Road, Melville, NY 11747-9088

Phone: (516) 423-4400 **Domicile State:** NY **NAIC Code:** 34452

Data Date	Rating	RACR #1	RACR #2	Loss Ratio %	Total Assets ($mil)	Capital ($mil)	Net Premium ($mil)	Net Income ($mil)
3-09	C	3.90	2.52	N/A	464.7	205.2	42.8	6.3
3-08	C	3.67	2.28	N/A	514.1	229.8	39.9	6.4
2008	C	3.80	2.44	60.2	467.6	200.7	172.8	-11.6
2007	C	3.93	2.45	58.3	530.8	248.2	161.9	22.3
2006	C	3.17	2.00	62.5	536.6	226.6	188.1	44.1
2005	C	2.33	1.55	70.7	531.8	189.8	200.3	30.1
2004	C	2.14	1.39	68.8	592.3	180.7	229.3	5.8

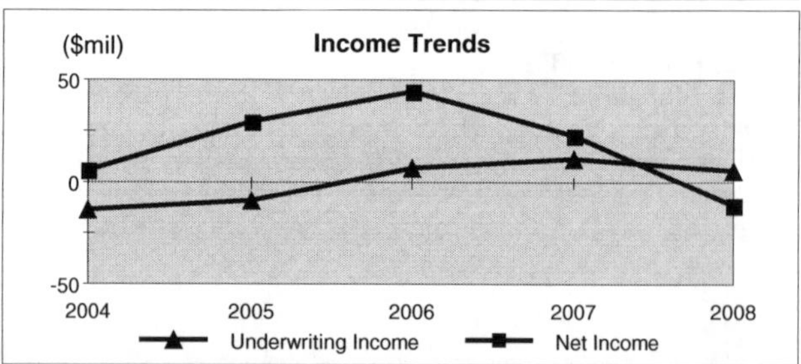

HOUSING ENTERPRISE INS CO * — B+ — Good

Major Rating Factors: Good overall profitability index (5.2 on a scale of 0 to 10) with small operating losses during 2004. Return on equity has been low, averaging 4.8% over the past five years. Good overall results on stability tests (5.0) despite weak results on operational trends. The largest net exposure for one risk is conservative at 1.9% of capital.

Other Rating Factors: Strong long-term capitalization index (7.8) based on excellent current risk adjusted capital (severe and moderate loss scenarios). Moreover, capital levels have been consistent in recent years. Ample reserve history (9.4) that helps to protect the company against sharp claims increases. Excellent liquidity (7.3) with ample operational cash flow and liquid investments.

Principal Business: (This company is a reinsurer.)

Principal Investments: Investment grade bonds (97%), cash (2%), and misc. investments (1%).

Investments in Affiliates: None

Group Affiliation: Housing Authority Property Group

Licensed in: VT

Commenced Business: August 2001

Address: (No address available)

Phone: (203) 272-8220 **Domicile State:** VT **NAIC Code:** 11206

Data Date	Rating	RACR #1	RACR #2	Loss Ratio %	Total Assets ($mil)	Capital ($mil)	Net Premium ($mil)	Net Income ($mil)
3-09	B+	3.51	2.03	N/A	36.4	26.6	1.1	0.2
3-08	A-	3.11	1.70	N/A	31.8	22.6	1.1	0.4
2008	B+	3.52	2.05	36.0	36.1	26.4	4.5	1.1
2007	A-	3.10	1.70	23.3	32.6	22.4	4.4	1.5
2006	N/A	N/A	N/A	47.9	22.4	10.9	5.8	1.1
2005	N/A	N/A	N/A	51.7	18.6	7.8	7.7	0.3
2004	N/A	N/A	N/A	51.9	15.8	7.5	7.4	0.0

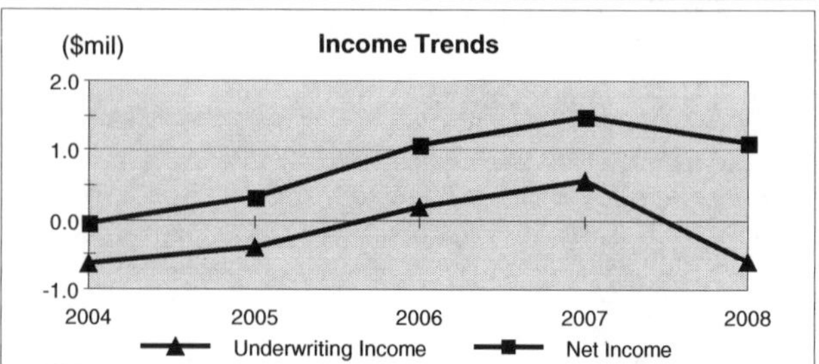

HOUSTON CASUALTY CO B- Good

Major Rating Factors: Fair overall results on stability tests (4.9 on a scale of 0 to 10). The largest net exposure for one risk is conservative at 1.4% of capital. History of adequate reserve strength (5.0) as reserves have been consistently at an acceptable level.

Other Rating Factors: Strong long-term capitalization index (7.4) based on excellent current risk adjusted capital (severe and moderate loss scenarios). Moreover, capital levels have been consistent in recent years. Excellent profitability (8.5) with operating gains in each of the last five years. Excellent liquidity (7.5) with ample operational cash flow and liquid investments.

Principal Business: Other liability (56%), ocean marine (22%), aircraft (6%), inland marine (4%), credit (4%), group accident & health (3%), and other lines (5%).

Principal Investments: Investment grade bonds (67%), misc. investments (32%), and cash (1%).

Investments in Affiliates: 27%

Group Affiliation: HCC Ins Holdings Inc

Licensed in: TX

Commenced Business: June 1981

Address: 13403 Northwest Freeway, Houston, TX 77040-6094

Phone: (713) 462-1000 **Domicile State:** TX **NAIC Code:** 42374

Data Date	Rating	RACR #1	RACR #2	Loss Ratio %	Total Assets ($mil)	Capital ($mil)	Net Premium ($mil)	Net Income ($mil)
3-09	B-	1.98	1.71	N/A	2,917.5	1,411.9	86.0	22.0
3-08	B-	1.87	1.47	N/A	2,844.8	1,317.2	91.4	15.9
2008	B-	1.91	1.67	48.0	2,845.7	1,345.3	372.0	179.9
2007	B-	1.82	1.44	52.0	2,782.0	1,260.2	424.9	136.6
2006	B-	1.63	1.21	56.2	2,520.4	952.1	485.6	160.8
2005	B-	1.48	1.06	75.9	2,235.1	812.5	499.5	4.7
2004	B-	1.46	1.09	69.4	1,663.7	604.4	471.0	18.5

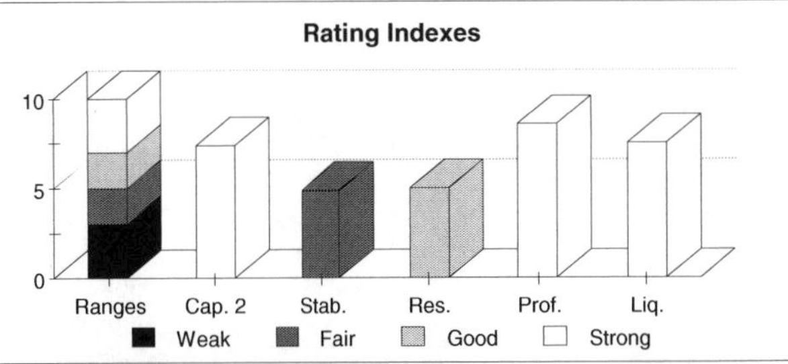

HSBC INS CO OF DELAWARE C Fair

Major Rating Factors: Fair profitability index (4.9 on a scale of 0 to 10) with operating losses during 2005 and the first three months of 2008. Return on equity has been fair, averaging 8.0% over the past five years. Fair overall results on stability tests (4.2) including fair financial strength of affiliated HSBC Holdings.

Other Rating Factors: Strong long-term capitalization index (10.0) based on excellent current risk adjusted capital (severe and moderate loss scenarios), despite some fluctuation in capital levels. Ample reserve history (9.2) that helps to protect the company against sharp claims increases. Excellent liquidity (7.4) with ample operational cash flow and liquid investments.

Principal Business: Credit (95%) and credit accident & health (5%).

Principal Investments: Investment grade bonds (83%) and misc. investments (17%).

Investments in Affiliates: None

Group Affiliation: HSBC Holdings

Licensed in: All states except CT, FL, NV, NH, NC, PR

Commenced Business: September 1965

Address: 200 Somerset Corp Blvd,Ste 100, Bridgewater, NJ 08807

Phone: (908) 203-2116 **Domicile State:** DE **NAIC Code:** 28657

Data Date	Rating	RACR #1	RACR #2	Loss Ratio %	Total Assets ($mil)	Capital ($mil)	Net Premium ($mil)	Net Income ($mil)
3-09	C	13.72	8.45	N/A	370.0	276.2	21.2	-11.3
3-08	C	16.39	9.73	N/A	458.0	354.1	26.5	11.9
2008	C	14.30	8.79	29.8	385.1	280.6	92.1	23.7
2007	C	18.48	10.95	27.1	507.8	398.5	106.9	55.5
2006	C	14.01	8.89	22.1	480.4	351.5	126.0	67.8
2005	C	1.82	1.15	26.1	264.5	110.1	126.8	-7.9
2004	U	0.20	0.60	0.2	20.5	15.7	-0.3	1.8

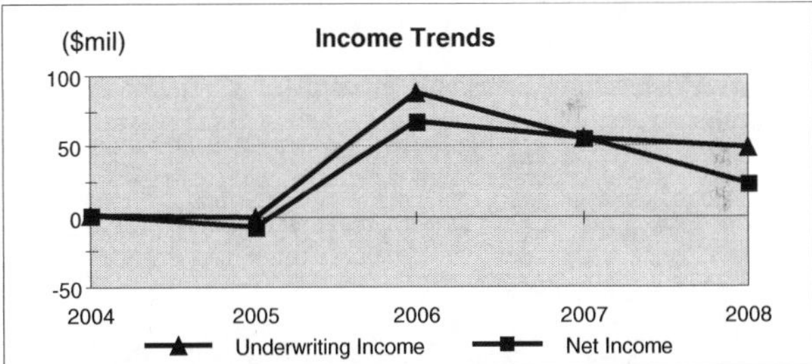

IDS PROPERTY CASUALTY INS CO B- Good

Major Rating Factors: Good overall profitability index (5.8 on a scale of 0 to 10). Good expense controls. Return on equity has been excellent over the last five years averaging 26.4%. Good liquidity (5.1) with sufficient resources (cash flows and marketable investments) to handle a spike in claims.

Other Rating Factors: Good overall results on stability tests (5.2). Strong long-term capitalization index (9.4) based on excellent current risk adjusted capital (severe and moderate loss scenarios), despite some fluctuation in capital levels. Ample reserve history (7.0) that can protect against increases in claims costs.

Principal Business: Auto liability (48%), auto physical damage (34%), and homeowners multiple peril (17%).

Principal Investments: Investment grade bonds (94%), misc. investments (7%), and non investment grade bonds (1%).

Investments in Affiliates: 5%

Group Affiliation: Ameriprise Financial Group

Licensed in: All states except LA, PR

Commenced Business: January 1973

Address: 3500 Packerland Dr, De Pere, WI 54115

Phone: (920) 330-5100 **Domicile State:** WI **NAIC Code:** 29068

Data Date	Rating	RACR #1	RACR #2	Loss Ratio %	Total Assets ($mil)	Capital ($mil)	Net Premium ($mil)	Net Income ($mil)
3-09	B-	3.21	2.67	N/A	972.4	450.2	155.9	13.8
3-08	B-	3.19	2.56	N/A	995.8	439.7	148.4	14.4
2008	B-	3.02	2.60	77.2	956.2	436.2	619.0	64.0
2007	B-	2.99	2.50	74.3	991.2	424.3	586.2	81.7
2006	C+	2.49	2.17	78.6	1,091.7	522.9	575.3	59.5
2005	C+	2.26	1.87	84.0	958.3	464.3	520.1	276.2
2004	C+	1.26	1.11	82.8	728.4	346.0	445.3	106.3

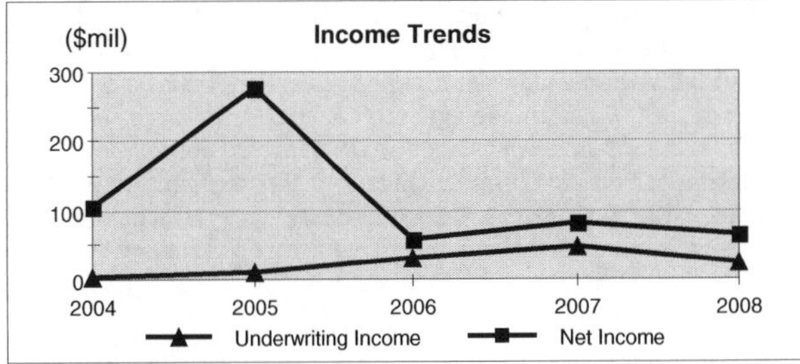

INDIANA INS CO C+ Fair

Major Rating Factors: Fair profitability index (4.0 on a scale of 0 to 10). Weak expense controls. Return on equity has been fair, averaging 14.2% over the past five years. Good liquidity (6.7) with sufficient resources (cash flows and marketable investments) to handle a spike in claims.

Other Rating Factors: Weak overall results on stability tests (2.9). The largest net exposure for one risk is excessive at 10.6% of capital. Strong long-term capitalization index (7.8) based on excellent current risk adjusted capital (severe and moderate loss scenarios), despite some fluctuation in capital levels. Ample reserve history (7.0) that can protect against increases in claims costs.

Principal Business: Auto liability (25%), homeowners multiple peril (21%), auto physical damage (16%), commercial multiple peril (13%), other liability (12%), workers compensation (9%), and other lines (5%).

Principal Investments: Investment grade bonds (89%), misc. investments (10%), and cash (1%).

Investments in Affiliates: 2%

Group Affiliation: Liberty Mutual Group

Licensed in: FL, IL, IN, IA, KY, MI, MN, NJ, OH, TN, WA, WI

Commenced Business: February 1851

Address: 350 E 96th St, Indianapolis, IN 46240

Phone: (603) 358-3810 **Domicile State:** IN **NAIC Code:** 22659

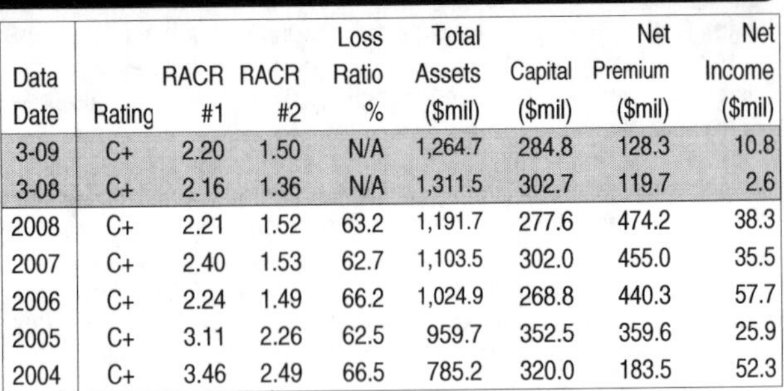

Data Date	Rating	RACR #1	RACR #2	Loss Ratio %	Total Assets ($mil)	Capital ($mil)	Net Premium ($mil)	Net Income ($mil)
3-09	C+	2.20	1.50	N/A	1,264.7	284.8	128.3	10.8
3-08	C+	2.16	1.36	N/A	1,311.5	302.7	119.7	2.6
2008	C+	2.21	1.52	63.2	1,191.7	277.6	474.2	38.3
2007	C+	2.40	1.53	62.7	1,103.5	302.0	455.0	35.5
2006	C+	2.24	1.49	66.2	1,024.9	268.8	440.3	57.7
2005	C+	3.11	2.26	62.5	959.7	352.5	359.6	25.9
2004	C+	3.46	2.49	66.5	785.2	320.0	183.5	52.3

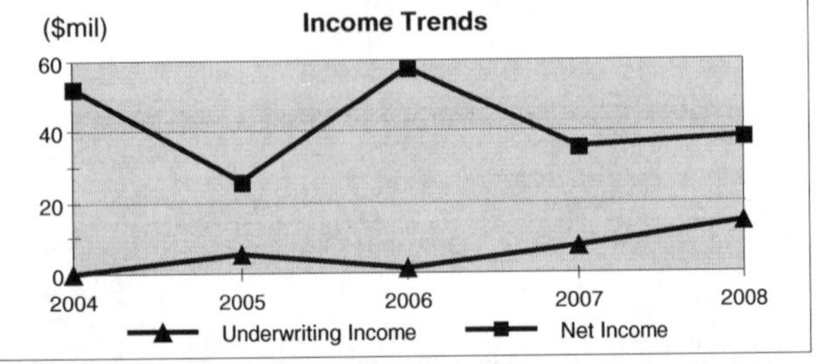

INDIANA OLD NATIONAL INS CO D Weak

Major Rating Factors: Weak overall results on stability tests (2.0 on a scale of 0 to 10) including negative cash flow from operations for 2008. Fair reserve development (4.6) as reserves have generally been sufficient to cover claims.

Other Rating Factors: Fair profitability index (3.4). Fair expense controls. Return on equity has been low, averaging 3.0% over the past five years. Strong long-term capitalization index (10.0) based on excellent current risk adjusted capital (severe and moderate loss scenarios), despite some fluctuation in capital levels. Superior liquidity (10.0) with ample operational cash flow and liquid investments.

Principal Business: Other liability (51%), fidelity (43%), earthquake (5%), and surety (1%).

Principal Investments: Investment grade bonds (57%), misc. investments (27%), and cash (16%).

Investments in Affiliates: None

Group Affiliation: Old National Bancorp

Licensed in: IN, VT

Commenced Business: March 1999

Address: 7 Burlington Square,6th Floor, Burlington, VT 05401

Phone: (802) 864-5599 **Domicile State:** VT **NAIC Code:** 11021

Data Date	Rating	RACR #1	RACR #2	Loss Ratio %	Total Assets ($mil)	Capital ($mil)	Net Premium ($mil)	Net Income ($mil)
3-09	D	57.38	23.72	N/A	1,597.5	1,571.1	0.5	15.9
3-08	D	108.75	44.89	N/A	1,999.4	1,987.5	0.4	8.7
2008	D	53.12	22.00	12.4	1,573.1	1,554.7	1.2	33.9
2007	D	98.07	39.98	25.9	1,989.0	1,972.1	1.5	40.9
2006	D	71.90	28.52	23.3	1,955.0	1,934.1	1.6	57.9
2005	D	49.21	19.16	30.4	1,899.1	1,875.4	1.6	65.2
2004	D	36.20	13.95	37.3	1,837.8	1,809.0	1.8	71.2

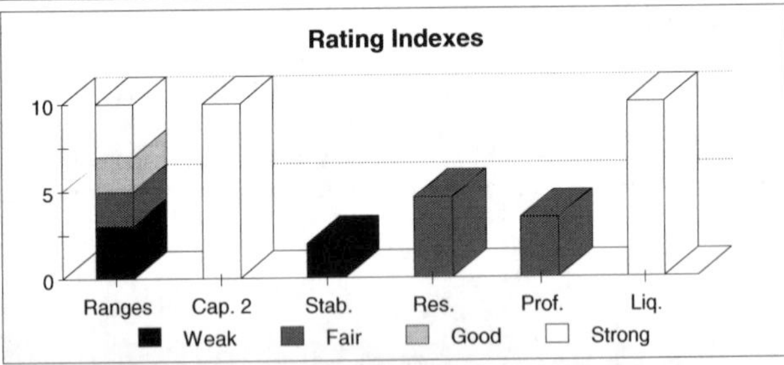

INFINITY INS CO B- Good

Major Rating Factors: Fair overall results on stability tests (4.9 on a scale of 0 to 10) including potential drain of affiliation with Infinity Property & Casualty Group. Fair profitability index (4.8). Good expense controls. Return on equity has been fair, averaging 18.7% over the past five years.

Other Rating Factors: Good liquidity (5.0) with sufficient resources (cash flows and marketable investments) to handle a spike in claims. Strong long-term capitalization index (7.8) based on excellent current risk adjusted capital (severe and moderate loss scenarios), despite some fluctuation in capital levels. Ample reserve history (9.1) that helps to protect the company against sharp claims increases.

Principal Business: Auto liability (61%) and auto physical damage (39%).

Principal Investments: Investment grade bonds (84%), misc. investments (15%), non investment grade bonds (4%), and real estate (1%).

Investments in Affiliates: 9%

Group Affiliation: Infinity Property & Casualty Group

Licensed in: All states except KS, LA, NH, NJ, VT, WY, PR

Commenced Business: October 1978

Address: 2204 Lakeshore Dr,Suite 125, Birmingham, AL 35209-6787

Phone: (205) 870-4000 **Domicile State:** IN **NAIC Code:** 22268

Data Date	Rating	RACR #1	RACR #2	Loss Ratio %	Total Assets ($mil)	Capital ($mil)	Net Premium ($mil)	Net Income ($mil)
3-09	B-	1.78	1.53	N/A	1,411.6	433.4	211.7	8.6
3-08	B-	1.66	1.43	N/A	1,587.3	462.2	231.8	9.1
2008	B-	1.66	1.49	70.3	1,386.0	425.2	879.6	34.1
2007	B-	1.61	1.44	70.6	1,541.1	473.4	1,000.1	78.5
2006	C+	1.74	1.56	67.0	1,596.4	492.9	968.4	113.9
2005	C+	1.64	1.45	68.7	1,679.1	552.2	1,116.0	160.4
2004	C+	1.90	1.72	62.1	901.9	322.5	528.1	62.7

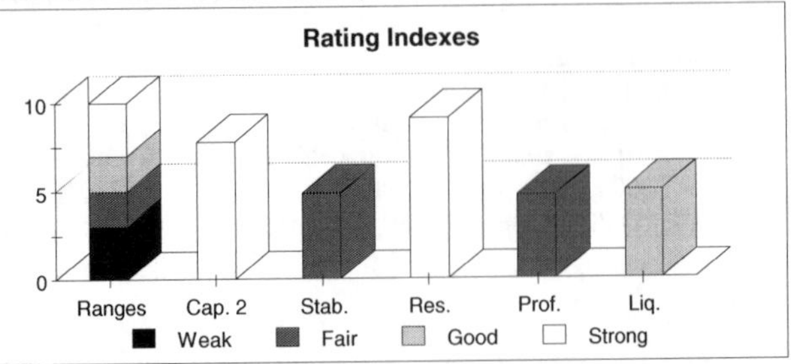

INS CO OF GREATER NY * B+ Good

Major Rating Factors: Good overall results on stability tests (5.0 on a scale of 0 to 10) despite potential drain of affiliation with Greater New York Group. Stability strengths include good operational trends and excellent risk diversification. The largest net exposure for one risk is conservative at 1.0% of capital. History of adequate reserve strength (5.4) as reserves have been consistently at an acceptable level.

Other Rating Factors: Strong long-term capitalization index (9.2) based on excellent current risk adjusted capital (severe and moderate loss scenarios). Moreover, capital levels have been consistent in recent years. Excellent profitability (8.7) with operating gains in each of the last five years. Excellent liquidity (7.1) with ample operational cash flow and liquid investments.

Principal Business: Commercial multiple peril (100%).

Principal Investments: Investment grade bonds (100%).

Investments in Affiliates: None

Group Affiliation: Greater New York Group

Licensed in: CT, DE, MD, MA, NJ, NY, PA

Commenced Business: November 1967

Address: 200 Madison Avenue, New York, NY 10016

Phone: (212) 683-9700 **Domicile State:** NY **NAIC Code:** 22195

Data Date	Rating	RACR #1	RACR #2	Loss Ratio %	Total Assets ($mil)	Capital ($mil)	Net Premium ($mil)	Net Income ($mil)
3-09	B+	3.83	2.89	N/A	101.2	48.5	5.4	0.9
3-08	B+	3.54	2.58	N/A	101.5	45.0	5.7	1.2
2008	B+	3.78	2.88	62.5	101.7	47.7	21.6	3.7
2007	B+	3.34	2.44	62.9	100.3	43.9	22.9	3.8
2006	B+	2.72	1.90	64.3	95.9	40.2	25.5	3.1
2005	B+	2.43	1.66	67.6	88.7	37.0	24.0	1.7
2004	B+	2.08	1.43	66.9	82.4	35.1	23.6	2.1

Greater New York Group
Composite Group Rating: B

Largest Group Members	Assets ($mil)	Rating
GREATER NEW YORK MUTUAL INS CO	810	B
INS CO OF GREATER NY	102	B+
GNY CUSTOM INS CO	48	B
STRATHMORE INS CO	47	B

INS CO OF NORTH AMERICA C Fair

Major Rating Factors: Fair overall results on stability tests (4.3 on a scale of 0 to 10) including fair financial strength of affiliated ACE Ltd. Good long-term capitalization index (6.9) based on good current risk adjusted capital (moderate loss scenario). Moreover, capital levels have been consistent in recent years.

Other Rating Factors: History of adequate reserve strength (5.0) as reserves have been consistently at an acceptable level. Good liquidity (6.7) with sufficient resources (cash flows and marketable investments) to handle a spike in claims. Excellent profitability (9.0) with operating gains in each of the last five years. Return on equity has been excellent over the last five years averaging 20.8%.

Principal Business: Ocean marine (31%), international (17%), other liability (14%), fire (13%), group accident & health (9%), products liability (8%), and other lines (8%).

Principal Investments: Investment grade bonds (69%), misc. investments (25%), and real estate (6%).

Investments in Affiliates: None

Group Affiliation: ACE Ltd

Licensed in: All states, the District of Columbia and Puerto Rico

Commenced Business: January 1792

Address: 1601 Chestnut St, Philadelphia, PA 19192

Phone: (215) 761-1000 **Domicile State:** PA **NAIC Code:** 22713

Data Date	Rating	RACR #1	RACR #2	Loss Ratio %	Total Assets ($mil)	Capital ($mil)	Net Premium ($mil)	Net Income ($mil)
3-09	C	1.97	1.30	N/A	764.4	249.3	37.7	5.4
3-08	C	1.51	0.97	N/A	701.7	239.9	35.9	8.0
2008	C	2.02	1.33	62.5	718.8	247.7	139.8	27.6
2007	C	1.54	0.98	63.9	712.6	233.1	174.1	48.5
2006	C-	1.17	0.74	60.3	628.6	175.0	192.5	53.3
2005	C-	0.62	0.39	75.8	511.0	87.2	194.9	17.2
2004	C-	0.61	0.41	72.7	508.4	68.3	187.5	16.9

ACE Ltd
Composite Group Rating: C+

Largest Group Members	Assets ($mil)	Rating
ACE AMERICAN INS CO	8051	C+
ACE PROPERTY CASUALTY INS CO	5785	C
WESTCHESTER FIRE INS CO	2561	C-
PACIFIC EMPLOYERS INS CO	2446	C+
COMBINED INS CO OF AMERICA	2382	B-

INS CO OF THE STATE OF PA C+ Fair

Major Rating Factors: Fair overall results on stability tests (4.4 on a scale of 0 to 10). Good long-term capitalization index (6.5) based on good current risk adjusted capital (moderate loss scenario), despite some fluctuation in capital levels.

Other Rating Factors: Good liquidity (6.7) with sufficient resources (cash flows and marketable investments) to handle a spike in claims. A history of deficient reserves (2.8). Underreserving can have an adverse impact on capital and profits. Deficiencies in the two year reserve development occurred in three of the previous five years and ranged between 30% and 53%. Excellent profitability (7.0) with operating gains in each of the last five years.

Principal Business: Workers compensation (52%), other liability (17%), auto liability (16%), fire (6%), auto physical damage (6%), and group accident & health (4%).

Principal Investments: Investment grade bonds (58%) and misc. investments (42%).

Investments in Affiliates: 36%

Group Affiliation: American International Group

Licensed in: All states except PR

Commenced Business: April 1794

Address: 70 Pine Street 3rd Floor, New York, NY 10270

Phone: (212) 770-7000 **Domicile State:** PA **NAIC Code:** 19429

Data Date	Rating	RACR #1	RACR #2	Loss Ratio %	Total Assets ($mil)	Capital ($mil)	Net Premium ($mil)	Net Income ($mil)
3-09	C+	1.41	1.24	N/A	4,578.1	1,986.1	209.4	52.6
3-08	C+	1.44	1.20	N/A	4,724.3	1,932.8	232.8	49.1
2008	C+	1.38	1.20	78.1	4,694.1	2,011.9	865.7	139.5
2007	C+	1.41	1.18	69.6	4,806.9	1,900.4	1,023.2	207.8
2006	C+	1.30	1.05	71.1	4,343.8	1,521.8	1,028.1	159.3
2005	C+	1.18	0.94	90.2	3,792.0	1,147.2	932.5	31.1
2004	B-	1.18	0.92	86.4	3,134.5	889.2	924.9	6.9

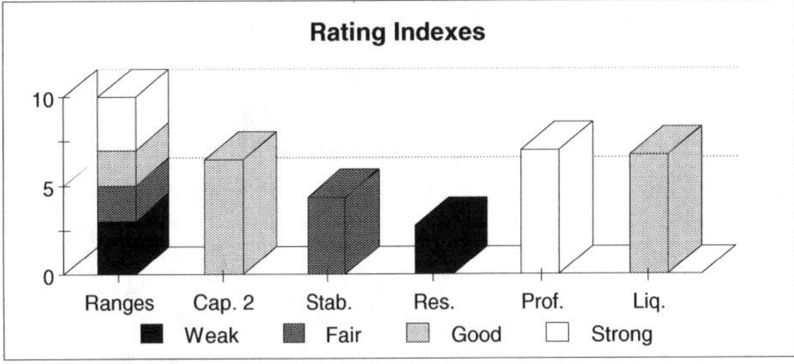

INS CO OF THE WEST — C — Fair

Major Rating Factors: Fair overall results on stability tests (3.7 on a scale of 0 to 10) including potential drain of affiliation with Western Insurance Holdings Inc and negative cash flow from operations for 2008. The largest net exposure for one risk is excessive at 7.1% of capital. Fair profitability index (4.7) with operating losses during 2008. Return on equity has been fair, averaging 9.8% over the past five years.

Other Rating Factors: Good long-term capitalization index (5.9) based on good current risk adjusted capital (moderate loss scenario). History of adequate reserve strength (5.6) as reserves have been consistently at an acceptable level. Good liquidity (6.1) with sufficient resources (cash flows and marketable investments) to handle a spike in claims.

Principal Business: Workers compensation (52%), earthquake (25%), surety (13%), inland marine (3%), fire (2%), auto liability (2%), and auto physical damage (2%).

Principal Investments: Investment grade bonds (71%), misc. investments (24%), cash (4%), and non investment grade bonds (1%).

Investments in Affiliates: 12%

Group Affiliation: Western Insurance Holdings Inc

Licensed in: All states except CT, DC, DE, NH, NY, PR

Commenced Business: May 1972

Address: 11455 El Camino Real, San Diego, CA 92130-2045

Phone: (858) 546-2400 **Domicile State:** CA **NAIC Code:** 27847

Data Date	Rating	RACR #1	RACR #2	Loss Ratio %	Total Assets ($mil)	Capital ($mil)	Net Premium ($mil)	Net Income ($mil)
3-09	C	1.35	0.79	N/A	801.8	347.0	74.3	6.1
3-08	C	1.29	0.79	N/A	854.0	433.2	69.0	9.1
2008	C	1.48	0.88	50.0	825.6	374.5	277.6	-11.9
2007	C	1.33	0.82	53.3	874.0	455.8	289.1	41.2
2006	C	1.40	0.88	53.9	845.9	453.3	253.1	160.5
2005	C	0.91	0.71	60.3	745.1	364.6	208.3	22.8
2004	C-	0.88	0.66	68.6	630.0	293.5	174.7	7.1

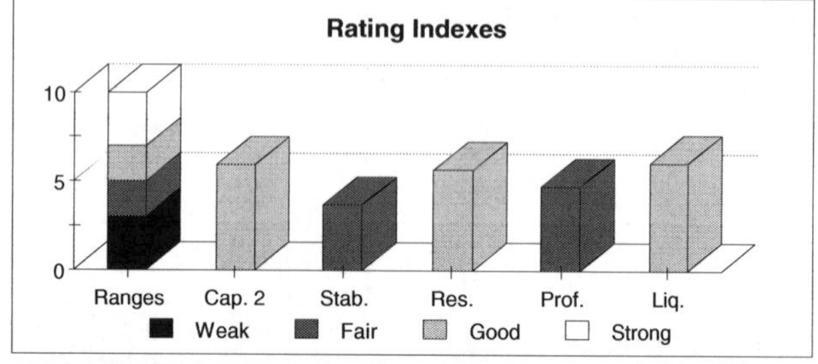

INTERINS EXCH OF THE AUTOMOBILE CLUB * — A+ — Excellent

Major Rating Factors: Strong long-term capitalization index (10.0 on a scale of 0 to 10) based on excellent current risk adjusted capital (severe and moderate loss scenarios). Furthermore, this high level of risk adjusted capital has been consistently maintained in previous years. Excellent profitability (7.9) with operating gains in each of the last five years.

Other Rating Factors: History of adequate reserve strength (6.5) as reserves have been consistently at an acceptable level. Good liquidity (6.5) with sufficient resources (cash flows and marketable investments) to handle a spike in claims. Good overall results on stability tests (6.5).

Principal Business: Auto liability (44%), auto physical damage (40%), homeowners multiple peril (15%), and other liability (1%).

Principal Investments: Investment grade bonds (74%), misc. investments (22%), non investment grade bonds (4%), and real estate (2%).

Investments in Affiliates: 1%

Group Affiliation: Auto Club Enterprises Ins Group

Licensed in: CA, HI, ME, NH, NM, OH, PA, TX, VT

Commenced Business: October 1912

Address: 3333 Fairview Road, Costa Mesa, CA 92626

Phone: (800) 924-6141 **Domicile State:** CA **NAIC Code:** 15598

Data Date	Rating	RACR #1	RACR #2	Loss Ratio %	Total Assets ($mil)	Capital ($mil)	Net Premium ($mil)	Net Income ($mil)
3-09	A+	6.03	4.24	N/A	5,434.9	3,146.8	588.3	78.2
3-08	A+	5.58	3.72	N/A	5,581.5	3,303.2	590.0	56.8
2008	A+	5.79	4.09	70.0	5,391.8	3,162.0	2,393.7	116.3
2007	A+	5.35	3.58	72.9	5,615.5	3,323.7	2,379.8	196.6
2006	A+	5.38	3.65	65.2	5,332.9	3,110.4	2,339.7	260.4
2005	A+	5.10	3.49	62.0	4,772.5	2,703.2	2,195.7	252.5
2004	A+	4.72	3.22	58.4	4,400.1	2,429.1	2,036.0	246.4

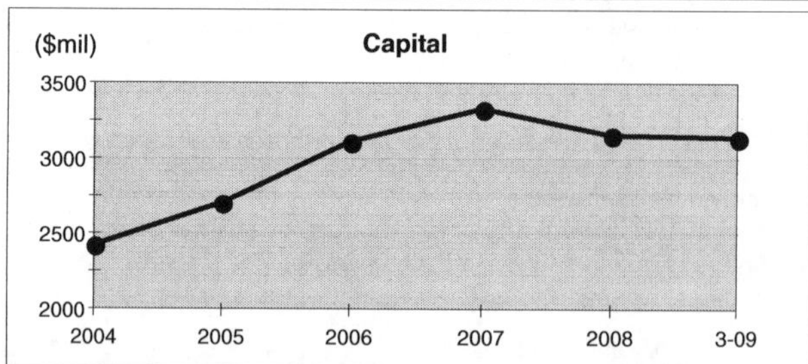

INTERSTATE FIRE & CAS CO — C — Fair

Major Rating Factors: Fair overall results on stability tests (4.3 on a scale of 0 to 10). History of adequate reserve strength (5.8) as reserves have been consistently at an acceptable level.

Other Rating Factors: Good liquidity (6.7) with sufficient resources (cash flows and marketable investments) to handle a spike in claims. Strong long-term capitalization index (7.4) based on excellent current risk adjusted capital (severe and moderate loss scenarios), despite some fluctuation in capital levels. Excellent profitability (7.3) with operating gains in each of the last five years.

Principal Business: Other liability (93%) and medical malpractice (7%).

Principal Investments: Investment grade bonds (71%) and misc. investments (29%).

Investments in Affiliates: 36%

Group Affiliation: Allianz Ins Group

Licensed in: IL, MI

Commenced Business: January 1951

Address: 55 E Monroe St, Chicago, IL 60603

Phone: (312) 346-6400 **Domicile State:** IL **NAIC Code:** 22829

Data Date	Rating	RACR #1	RACR #2	Loss Ratio %	Total Assets ($mil)	Capital ($mil)	Net Premium ($mil)	Net Income ($mil)
3-09	C	1.21	1.07	N/A	612.2	279.0	37.9	5.8
3-08	C	1.53	1.31	N/A	666.3	335.5	36.1	6.0
2008	C	1.54	1.36	75.0	688.4	354.3	167.6	8.3
2007	C	1.49	1.28	62.0	652.7	325.6	162.7	20.1
2006	C	1.40	1.17	58.0	612.1	285.6	160.5	22.3
2005	C	1.46	1.17	66.7	578.6	260.5	150.3	13.9
2004	C	1.19	0.96	66.0	514.9	214.5	147.4	17.4

Allianz Ins Group
Composite Group Rating: C+

Largest Group Members	Assets ($mil)	Rating
ALLIANZ LIFE INS CO OF NORTH AMERICA	66375	B-
FIREMANS FUND INS CO	10673	C
ALLIANZ GLOBAL RISKS US INS CO	4846	C+
AMERICAN INS CO	1449	B-
ALLIANZ LIFE INS CO OF NY	881	C

ISMIE MUTUAL INS CO C+ Fair

Major Rating Factors: Fair overall results on stability tests (4.5 on a scale of 0 to 10) including potential drain of affiliation with ISMIE Group. Fair reserve development (4.8) as the level of reserves has at times been insufficient to cover claims. In 2005 and 2004 the two year reserve development was 23% and 33% deficient respectively.

Other Rating Factors: Good overall profitability index (6.9). Good expense controls. Return on equity has been good over the last five years, averaging 12.2%. Strong long-term capitalization index (7.2) based on excellent current risk adjusted capital (severe and moderate loss scenarios). Moreover, capital levels have been consistent in recent years. Excellent liquidity (7.7) with ample operational cash flow and liquid investments.

Principal Business: Medical malpractice (100%).

Principal Investments: Investment grade bonds (97%) and misc. investments (4%).

Investments in Affiliates: 2%

Group Affiliation: ISMIE Group

Licensed in: IL, IN, IA, MO, WI

Commenced Business: June 1976

Address: 20 N Michigan Ave, Chicago, IL 60602-4811

Phone: (312) 782-1654 **Domicile State:** IL **NAIC Code:** 32921

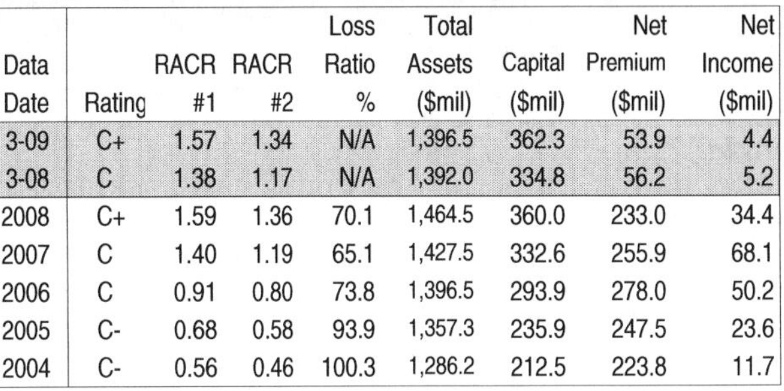

Data Date	Rating	RACR #1	RACR #2	Loss Ratio %	Total Assets ($mil)	Capital ($mil)	Net Premium ($mil)	Net Income ($mil)
3-09	C+	1.57	1.34	N/A	1,396.5	362.3	53.9	4.4
3-08	C	1.38	1.17	N/A	1,392.0	334.8	56.2	5.2
2008	C+	1.59	1.36	70.1	1,464.5	360.0	233.0	34.4
2007	C	1.40	1.19	65.1	1,427.5	332.6	255.9	68.1
2006	C	0.91	0.80	73.8	1,396.5	293.9	278.0	50.2
2005	C-	0.68	0.58	93.9	1,357.3	235.9	247.5	23.6
2004	C-	0.56	0.46	100.3	1,286.2	212.5	223.8	11.7

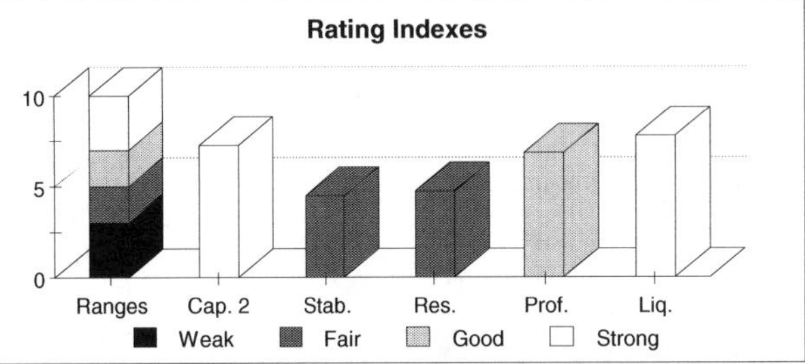

JAMES RIVER INS CO C Fair

Major Rating Factors: Fair overall results on stability tests (4.0 on a scale of 0 to 10) including weak results on operational trends. The largest net exposure for one risk is conservative at 1.1% of capital. History of adequate reserve strength (6.7) as reserves have been consistently at an acceptable level.

Other Rating Factors: Strong long-term capitalization index (7.5) based on excellent current risk adjusted capital (severe and moderate loss scenarios), despite some fluctuation in capital levels. Excellent profitability (7.0). Excellent liquidity (7.0) with ample operational cash flow and liquid investments.

Principal Business: Other liability (68%), products liability (17%), medical malpractice (6%), allied lines (5%), fire (2%), and earthquake (1%).

Principal Investments: Investment grade bonds (90%), non investment grade bonds (6%), and misc. investments (5%).

Investments in Affiliates: None

Group Affiliation: D.E. Shaw & Co.

Licensed in: OH

Commenced Business: September 1987

Address: 515 Main Street, Cincinnati, OH 45202

Phone: (513) 369-3000 **Domicile State:** OH **NAIC Code:** 12203

Data Date	Rating	RACR #1	RACR #2	Loss Ratio %	Total Assets ($mil)	Capital ($mil)	Net Premium ($mil)	Net Income ($mil)
3-09	C	3.82	2.06	N/A	471.3	181.3	12.1	-1.7
3-08	C	2.06	1.43	N/A	489.4	205.6	13.8	18.3
2008	C	3.66	1.98	65.3	446.2	179.3	-5.1	16.3
2007	C	1.82	1.27	57.7	585.2	189.4	204.1	35.8
2006	C	1.39	0.96	58.5	508.5	184.2	182.2	28.3
2005	C	4.22	2.86	67.4	359.5	122.6	119.1	5.5
2004	C	3.35	2.41	62.8	171.4	57.5	77.4	0.3

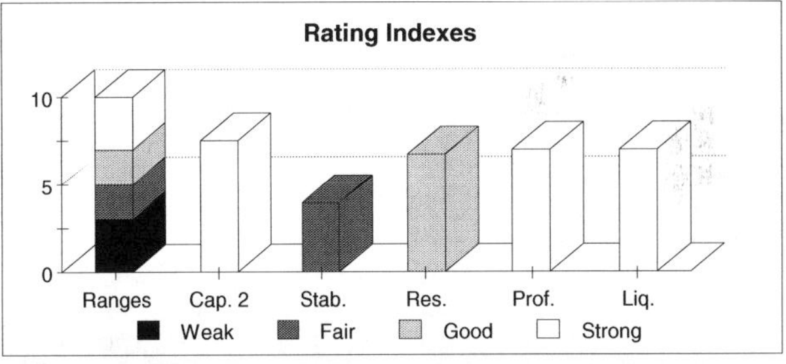

JEWELERS MUTUAL INS CO * A- Excellent

Major Rating Factors: Strong long-term capitalization index (10.0 on a scale of 0 to 10) based on excellent current risk adjusted capital (severe and moderate loss scenarios), despite some fluctuation in capital levels. Ample reserve history (7.5) that can protect against increases in claims costs.

Other Rating Factors: Good overall profitability index (6.1) despite operating losses during the first three months of 2008. Good liquidity (6.6) with sufficient resources (cash flows and marketable investments) to handle a spike in claims. Good overall results on stability tests (5.9). The largest net exposure for one risk is high at 3.6% of capital.

Principal Business: Inland marine (81%) and commercial multiple peril (19%).

Principal Investments: Investment grade bonds (69%), misc. investments (21%), real estate (9%), and non investment grade bonds (1%).

Investments in Affiliates: 0%

Group Affiliation: None

Licensed in: All states except DC, PR

Commenced Business: June 1914

Address: 24 Jewelers Park Dr, Neenah, WI 54957-3703

Phone: (414) 725-4326 **Domicile State:** WI **NAIC Code:** 14354

Data Date	Rating	RACR #1	RACR #2	Loss Ratio %	Total Assets ($mil)	Capital ($mil)	Net Premium ($mil)	Net Income ($mil)
3-09	A-	5.53	3.43	N/A	186.8	108.9	26.4	-1.3
3-08	A-	5.12	3.23	N/A	194.0	114.7	25.3	1.3
2008	A-	5.68	3.52	51.1	195.1	112.1	108.9	4.2
2007	A-	5.20	3.26	47.2	197.8	119.3	100.0	12.1
2006	B+	5.22	3.19	54.8	184.4	107.4	91.5	8.0
2005	B+	5.49	3.27	61.2	172.9	98.0	84.4	7.3
2004	B+	4.83	2.90	54.8	166.4	93.3	85.3	5.6

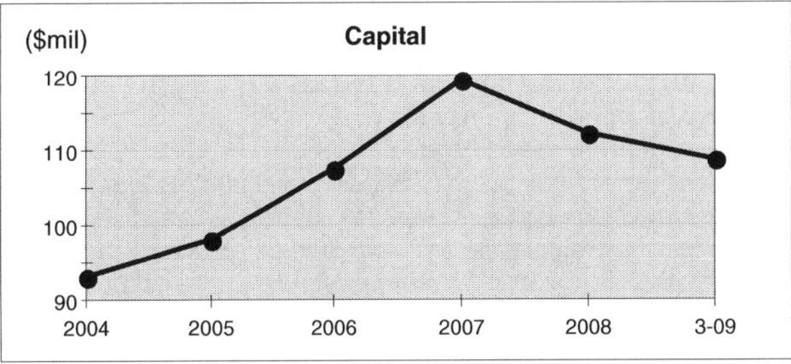

KENTUCKY FARM BUREAU MUTUAL INS CO * A Excellent

Major Rating Factors: Strong long-term capitalization index (10.0 on a scale of 0 to 10) based on excellent current risk adjusted capital (severe and moderate loss scenarios). Furthermore, this high level of risk adjusted capital has been consistently maintained in previous years. Ample reserve history (7.8) that can protect against increases in claims costs.

Other Rating Factors: Good liquidity (5.7) with sufficient resources (cash flows and marketable investments) to handle a spike in claims. Good overall results on stability tests (6.0) despite negative cash flow from operations for 2008. Fair profitability index (4.2) with operating losses during the first three months of 2008.

Principal Business: Auto liability (36%), auto physical damage (23%), homeowners multiple peril (22%), farmowners multiple peril (11%), commercial multiple peril (6%), and other liability (1%).

Principal Investments: Investment grade bonds (89%) and misc. investments (14%).

Investments in Affiliates: 3%

Group Affiliation: Kentucky Farm Bureau Group

Licensed in: KY

Commenced Business: December 1943

Address: 9201 Bunsen Parkway, Louisville, KY 40220-3793

Phone: (502) 495-5000 **Domicile State:** KY **NAIC Code:** 22993

Data Date	Rating	RACR #1	RACR #2	Loss Ratio %	Total Assets ($mil)	Capital ($mil)	Net Premium ($mil)	Net Income ($mil)
3-09	A	4.53	3.06	N/A	1,580.7	814.5	172.3	-51.3
3-08	A	5.58	3.98	N/A	1,660.1	958.7	177.4	-29.6
2008	A	5.02	3.45	91.2	1,617.8	890.5	719.4	-34.8
2007	A	5.80	4.13	72.7	1,696.7	1,016.3	709.9	74.0
2006	A	5.16	3.63	73.7	1,589.6	933.3	705.4	76.3
2005	A	4.86	3.48	64.9	1,484.1	825.2	651.5	94.6
2004	A	4.06	2.83	68.7	1,356.7	720.6	650.1	90.9

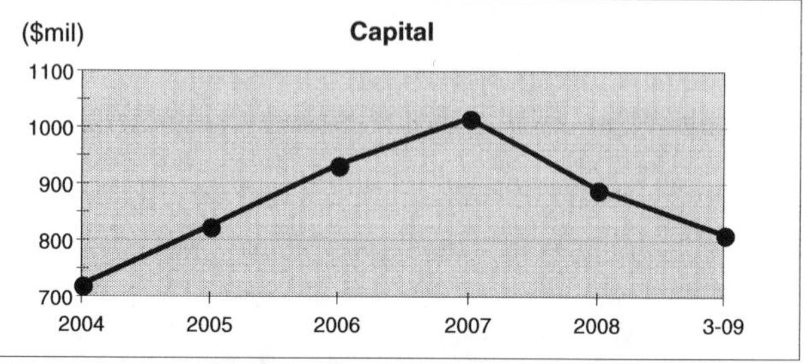

LEXINGTON INS CO C+ Fair

Major Rating Factors: Good overall long-term capitalization (5.3 on a scale of 0 to 10) based on good current risk adjusted capital (severe loss scenario). However, capital levels have fluctuated somewhat during past years. History of adequate reserve strength (5.8) as reserves have been consistently at an acceptable level.

Other Rating Factors: Good liquidity (6.8) with sufficient resources (cash flows and marketable investments) to handle a spike in claims. Weak overall results on stability tests (2.9). The largest net exposure for one risk is excessive at 15.9% of capital. Strengths include potentially strong support from affiliation with American International Group. Excellent profitability (7.4) with operating gains in each of the last five years. Return on equity has been good over the last five years, averaging 14.6%.

Principal Business: Other liability (33%), fire (26%), allied lines (16%), medical malpractice (8%), inland marine (4%), products liability (3%), and other lines (10%).

Principal Investments: Investment grade bonds (85%) and misc. investments (15%).

Investments in Affiliates: 3%

Group Affiliation: American International Group

Licensed in: DE

Commenced Business: April 1965

Address: 200 State Street 4th FLoor, Boston, MA 02109

Phone: (617) 330-1100 **Domicile State:** DE **NAIC Code:** 19437

Data Date	Rating	RACR #1	RACR #2	Loss Ratio %	Total Assets ($mil)	Capital ($mil)	Net Premium ($mil)	Net Income ($mil)
3-09	C+	1.39	0.87	N/A	15,208.1	4,379.3	890.3	174.9
3-08	B-	1.29	0.82	N/A	15,094.2	4,705.1	1,052.2	232.4
2008	C+	1.37	0.85	80.5	15,293.5	4,262.8	3,999.3	208.5
2007	B-	1.29	0.82	59.1	14,832.2	4,551.0	4,288.8	1,206.4
2006	B-	1.10	0.71	62.9	12,583.9	3,511.6	4,142.8	896.0
2005	B-	0.93	0.61	82.7	10,605.7	2,564.9	3,477.3	315.8
2004	B-	0.99	0.66	86.7	8,941.2	2,226.2	3,211.5	71.6

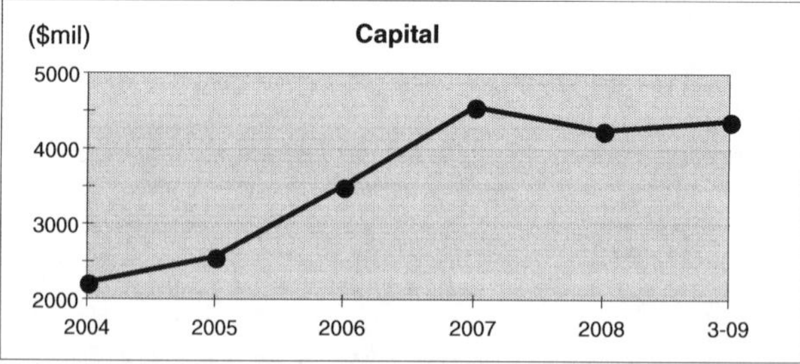

LIBERTY INS CORP C Fair

Major Rating Factors: Fair profitability index (3.5 on a scale of 0 to 10). Fair expense controls. Return on equity has been fair, averaging 7.9% over the past five years. Fair overall results on stability tests (3.8).

Other Rating Factors: A history of deficient reserves (2.7). Underreserving can have an adverse impact on capital and profits. Deficiencies in the two year reserve development occurred in three of the previous five years and ranged between 30% and 39%. Good liquidity (6.2) with sufficient resources (cash flows and marketable investments) to handle a spike in claims. Strong long-term capitalization index (7.0) based on good current risk adjusted capital (severe and moderate loss scenarios), although results have slipped from the excellent range during the last year.

Principal Business: Workers compensation (84%), auto liability (6%), other liability (5%), auto physical damage (3%), and commercial multiple peril (1%).

Principal Investments: Investment grade bonds (85%), misc. investments (14%), and non investment grade bonds (1%).

Investments in Affiliates: None

Group Affiliation: Liberty Mutual Group

Licensed in: All states, the District of Columbia and Puerto Rico

Commenced Business: November 1988

Address: 175 Berkeley St, Mailstop 3E, Boston, MA 02117

Phone: (617) 357-9500 **Domicile State:** IL **NAIC Code:** 42404

Data Date	Rating	RACR #1	RACR #2	Loss Ratio %	Total Assets ($mil)	Capital ($mil)	Net Premium ($mil)	Net Income ($mil)
3-09	C	1.59	0.99	N/A	1,101.9	256.1	77.2	4.9
3-08	C+	2.25	1.23	N/A	1,303.2	365.8	82.7	3.9
2008	C	1.60	1.01	83.5	1,044.3	255.4	321.2	27.4
2007	C+	2.21	1.21	77.8	1,198.8	364.0	247.1	54.7
2006	C+	0.98	0.57	76.4	1,850.5	329.7	711.8	23.8
2005	C+	0.91	0.55	82.6	1,632.8	290.8	635.8	7.7
2004	C+	0.81	0.52	82.8	1,639.8	270.2	595.7	10.3

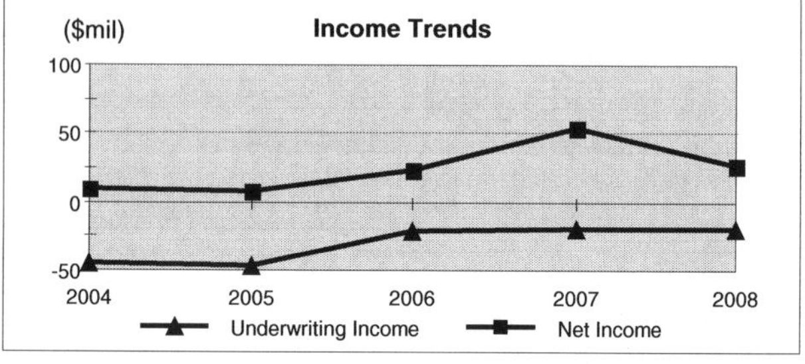

LIBERTY MUTUAL FIRE INS CO B- Good

Major Rating Factors: Fair reserve development (3.2 on a scale of 0 to 10) as the level of reserves has at times been insufficient to cover claims. Deficiencies in the two year reserve development occurred in three of the previous five years and ranged between 20% and 24%. Fair overall results on stability tests (4.9).

Other Rating Factors: Good long-term capitalization index (6.9) based on good current risk adjusted capital (moderate loss scenario), despite some fluctuation in capital levels. Good overall profitability index (6.2). Fair expense controls. Return on equity has been fair, averaging 5.8% over the past five years. Good liquidity (5.9) with sufficient resources (cash flows and marketable investments) to handle a spike in claims.

Principal Business: Auto liability (30%), homeowners multiple peril (24%), auto physical damage (19%), workers compensation (11%), fire (5%), other liability (5%), and other lines (6%).

Principal Investments: Investment grade bonds (68%), misc. investments (26%), and non investment grade bonds (6%).

Investments in Affiliates: 11%

Group Affiliation: Liberty Mutual Group

Licensed in: All states, the District of Columbia and Puerto Rico

Commenced Business: November 1908

Address: 175 Berkeley St,Mailstop 3E, Boston, MA 02117

Phone: (617) 357-9500 **Domicile State:** WI **NAIC Code:** 23035

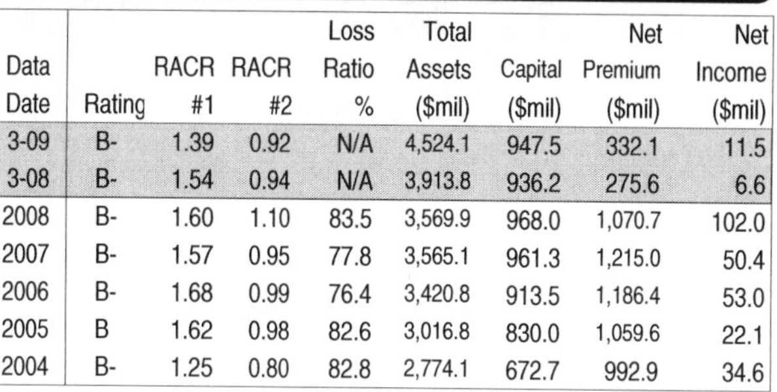

Data Date	Rating	RACR #1	RACR #2	Loss Ratio %	Total Assets ($mil)	Capital ($mil)	Net Premium ($mil)	Net Income ($mil)
3-09	B-	1.39	0.92	N/A	4,524.1	947.5	332.1	11.5
3-08	B-	1.54	0.94	N/A	3,913.8	936.2	275.6	6.6
2008	B-	1.60	1.10	83.5	3,569.9	968.0	1,070.7	102.0
2007	B-	1.57	0.95	77.8	3,565.1	961.3	1,215.0	50.4
2006	B-	1.68	0.99	76.4	3,420.8	913.5	1,186.4	53.0
2005	B	1.62	0.98	82.6	3,016.8	830.0	1,059.6	22.1
2004	B-	1.25	0.80	82.8	2,774.1	672.7	992.9	34.6

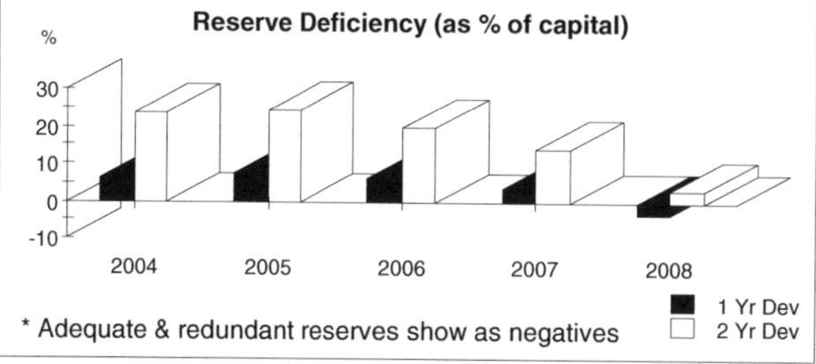

* Adequate & redundant reserves show as negatives

LIBERTY MUTUAL INS CO B- Good

Major Rating Factors: Fair reserve development (3.6 on a scale of 0 to 10) as reserves have generally been sufficient to cover claims. In 2004, the two year reserve development was 27% deficient. Fair overall results on stability tests (4.9).

Other Rating Factors: Good overall profitability index (6.2). Fair expense controls. Return on equity has been fair, averaging 7.4% over the past five years. Good liquidity (6.3) with sufficient resources (cash flows and marketable investments) to handle a spike in claims. Strong long-term capitalization index (7.0) based on excellent current risk adjusted capital (severe and moderate loss scenarios), despite some fluctuation in capital levels.

Principal Business: Inland marine (43%), other liability (15%), auto liability (11%), surety (8%), workers compensation (6%), auto physical damage (6%), and other lines (10%).

Principal Investments: Misc. investments (50%), investment grade bonds (43%), non investment grade bonds (4%), real estate (2%), and cash (1%).

Investments in Affiliates: 28%

Group Affiliation: Liberty Mutual Group

Licensed in: All states, the District of Columbia and Puerto Rico

Commenced Business: July 1912

Address: 175 Berkeley St,Mailstop 3E, Boston, MA 02117

Phone: (617) 357-9500 **Domicile State:** MA **NAIC Code:** 23043

Data Date	Rating	RACR #1	RACR #2	Loss Ratio %	Total Assets ($mil)	Capital ($mil)	Net Premium ($mil)	Net Income ($mil)
3-09	B-	1.25	1.04	N/A	33,672.9	10,223.6	1,930.6	26.6
3-08	B	1.60	1.22	N/A	36,821.0	11,794.2	2,091.9	47.0
2008	B-	1.26	1.06	83.5	32,549.8	10,334.7	8,126.3	1,500.7
2007	B	1.60	1.22	77.8	34,829.2	11,823.3	9,589.2	440.5
2006	B	1.93	1.39	76.4	29,920.0	9,952.1	7,889.6	1,007.0
2005	B	1.49	1.13	82.6	26,011.6	7,924.7	7,046.4	584.1
2004	B	1.36	1.07	82.8	23,957.0	7,255.4	6,698.5	216.9

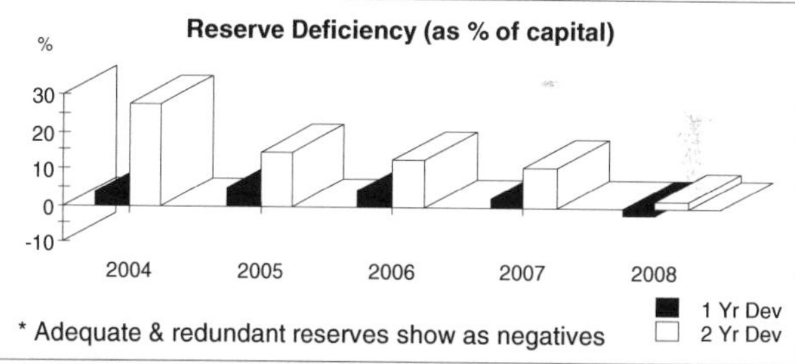

* Adequate & redundant reserves show as negatives

MAG MUTUAL INS CO B- Good

Major Rating Factors: Fair overall results on stability tests (4.7 on a scale of 0 to 10) including potential drain of affiliation with MAG Mutual Group. Strong long-term capitalization index (7.7) based on excellent current risk adjusted capital (severe and moderate loss scenarios). Moreover, capital levels have been consistent in recent years.

Other Rating Factors: Ample reserve history (9.7) that helps to protect the company against sharp claims increases. Excellent profitability (8.5) with operating gains in each of the last five years. Return on equity has been good over the last five years, averaging 11.1%. Excellent liquidity (7.8) with ample operational cash flow and liquid investments.

Principal Business: Medical malpractice (97%), workers compensation (2%), and commercial multiple peril (1%).

Principal Investments: Investment grade bonds (87%), misc. investments (12%), and cash (1%).

Investments in Affiliates: 2%

Group Affiliation: MAG Mutual Group

Licensed in: AL, AR, FL, GA, KY, MS, NC, SC, TN, VA, WV

Commenced Business: June 1982

Address: 8 Piedmont Ctr Ste 600, Atlanta, GA 30305-1533

Phone: (404) 842-5600 **Domicile State:** GA **NAIC Code:** 42617

Data Date	Rating	RACR #1	RACR #2	Loss Ratio %	Total Assets ($mil)	Capital ($mil)	Net Premium ($mil)	Net Income ($mil)
3-09	B-	2.26	1.81	N/A	1,367.0	356.2	53.4	7.2
3-08	B-	1.83	1.49	N/A	1,307.1	338.8	57.2	9.8
2008	B-	2.33	1.91	53.2	1,322.3	357.3	225.7	53.3
2007	B-	1.80	1.48	58.1	1,303.0	333.2	253.0	56.6
2006	C+	1.38	1.15	77.1	1,082.9	251.1	284.6	32.3
2005	C+	1.15	0.93	82.8	915.1	215.5	287.6	16.0
2004	C+	0.83	0.63	89.8	777.1	194.9	258.8	7.9

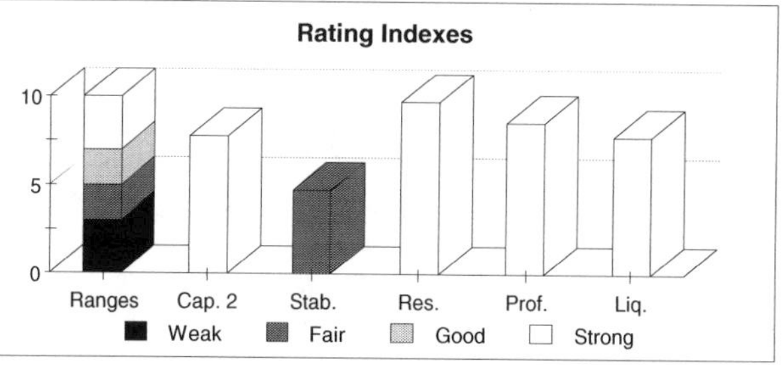

MAPFRE PRAICO INS CO — B — Good

Major Rating Factors: Good long-term capitalization index (6.7 on a scale of 0 to 10) based on good current risk adjusted capital (moderate loss scenario). Moreover, capital levels have been consistent in recent years. Good liquidity (5.9) with sufficient resources (cash flows and marketable investments) to handle a spike in claims.
Other Rating Factors: Fair overall results on stability tests (4.8) including potential drain of affiliation with MAPFRE Ins Group. Ample reserve history (8.2) that helps to protect the company against sharp claims increases. Excellent profitability (8.6) with operating gains in each of the last five years. Return on equity has been good over the last five years, averaging 12.3%.
Principal Business: Commercial multiple peril (26%), allied lines (15%), auto physical damage (14%), auto liability (12%), earthquake (12%), homeowners multiple peril (5%), and other lines (15%).
Principal Investments: Investment grade bonds (78%), misc. investments (9%), real estate (9%), and cash (4%).
Investments in Affiliates: 8%
Group Affiliation: MAPFRE Ins Group
Licensed in: PR
Commenced Business: December 1990
Address: #7 Chardon Ave, Hato Rey, PR 00936
Phone: (809) 250-6500 **Domicile State:** PR **NAIC Code:** 43052

Data Date	Rating	RACR #1	RACR #2	Loss Ratio %	Total Assets ($mil)	Capital ($mil)	Net Premium ($mil)	Net Income ($mil)
3-09	B	1.67	1.10	N/A	444.6	183.4	40.4	4.9
3-08	B	2.12	1.38	N/A	446.6	175.6	41.1	3.9
2008	B	1.62	1.07	60.9	449.4	177.9	169.4	28.6
2007	B	2.10	1.38	63.8	439.1	172.1	167.3	16.4
2006	B	1.99	1.28	60.9	420.4	149.8	173.8	18.9
2005	B	1.70	1.09	63.9	403.2	127.9	179.7	19.2
2004	B	1.84	1.17	62.7	368.4	111.0	162.5	9.5

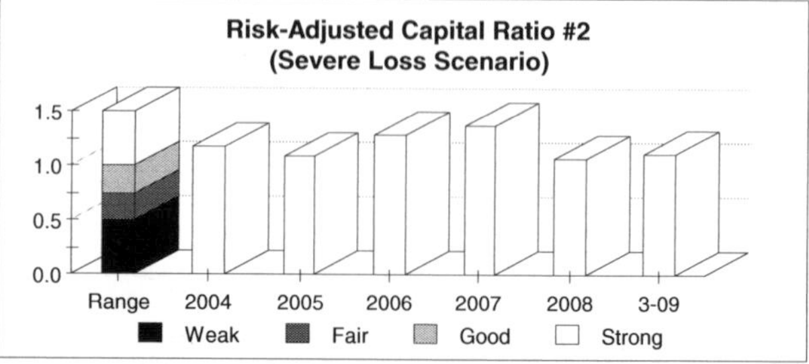

MARYLAND CASUALTY CO — C+ — Fair

Major Rating Factors: Fair overall results on stability tests (4.4 on a scale of 0 to 10) including negative cash flow from operations for 2008.
Other Rating Factors: Strong long-term capitalization index (10.0) based on excellent current risk adjusted capital (severe and moderate loss scenarios), despite some fluctuation in capital levels. Excellent profitability (8.5) with operating gains in each of the last five years. Excellent liquidity (7.0) with ample operational cash flow and liquid investments.
Principal Business: Commercial multiple peril (73%), workers compensation (12%), auto liability (10%), auto physical damage (3%), and inland marine (1%).
Principal Investments: Investment grade bonds (75%), misc. investments (19%), real estate (5%), and cash (1%).
Investments in Affiliates: 18%
Group Affiliation: Zurich Financial Services Group
Licensed in: All states, the District of Columbia and Puerto Rico
Commenced Business: March 1898
Address: 3910 Keswick Rd, Baltimore, MD 21211
Phone: (410) 366-1000 **Domicile State:** MD **NAIC Code:** 19356

Data Date	Rating	RACR #1	RACR #2	Loss Ratio %	Total Assets ($mil)	Capital ($mil)	Net Premium ($mil)	Net Income ($mil)
3-09	C+	5.64	5.10	N/A	384.6	434.7	0.0	1.5
3-08	C+	4.59	3.90	N/A	477.9	410.7	0.0	4.7
2008	C+	5.63	5.09	0.0	399.5	433.0	0.0	49.5
2007	C+	4.55	3.89	0.0	584.7	403.0	0.0	66.1
2006	C+	3.08	2.79	0.0	514.1	404.9	0.0	11.4
2005	C+	3.05	2.75	0.0	454.2	388.6	0.0	8.1
2004	C+	2.66	2.51	0.0	417.1	371.8	0.0	12.6

Zurich Financial Services Group
Composite Group Rating: C-

Largest Group Members	Assets ($mil)	Rating
ZURICH AMERICAN INS CO	29634	C-
KEMPER INVESTORS LIFE INS CO	13886	C
FARMERS INS EXCHANGE	13368	C
FARMERS NEW WORLD LIFE INS CO	6444	B-
MID-CENTURY INS CO	3273	C-

MBIA INS CORP — D+ — Weak

Major Rating Factors: Weak overall results on stability tests (2.6 on a scale of 0 to 10) including negative cash flow from operations for 2008. The largest net exposure for one risk is excessive at 26.5% of capital. Strengths include potentially strong support from affiliation with MBIA Inc. Fair long-term capitalization index (4.4) based on fair current risk adjusted capital (severe and moderate loss scenarios), although results have slipped from the good range over the last two years.
Other Rating Factors: Weak profitability index (2.2) with operating losses during the first three months of 2008. Return on equity has been low, averaging 3.9% over the past five years. Fair reserve development (3.2) as reserves have generally been sufficient to cover claims. In 2008, the one year reserve development was 23% deficient. Excellent liquidity (8.5) with ample operational cash flow and liquid investments.
Principal Business: Financial guaranty (100%).
Principal Investments: Investment grade bonds (187%), cash (5%), and real estate (2%).
Investments in Affiliates: 6%
Group Affiliation: MBIA Inc
Licensed in: All states, the District of Columbia and Puerto Rico
Commenced Business: May 1968
Address: 113 King St, Armonk, NY 10504-1610
Phone: (914) 273-4545 **Domicile State:** NY **NAIC Code:** 12041

Data Date	Rating	RACR #1	RACR #2	Loss Ratio %	Total Assets ($mil)	Capital ($mil)	Net Premium ($mil)	Net Income ($mil)
3-09	D+	1.29	0.56	N/A	6,123.8	2,515.5	101.5	-17.9
3-08	C	2.07	0.87	N/A	13,245.0	3,957.1	158.1	-1,091.1
2008	D+	1.64	0.71	339.0	13,532.6	3,502.4	1,429.4	-1,412.8
2007	C	2.24	0.88	114.3	11,410.2	3,663.1	764.7	182.1
2006	U	N/A	N/A	12.7	10,952.3	4,080.6	723.5	673.0
2005	U	N/A	N/A	25.7	11,037.0	3,800.4	812.5	634.1
2004	U	2.50	0.90	17.0	10,342.3	3,280.3	938.7	773.2

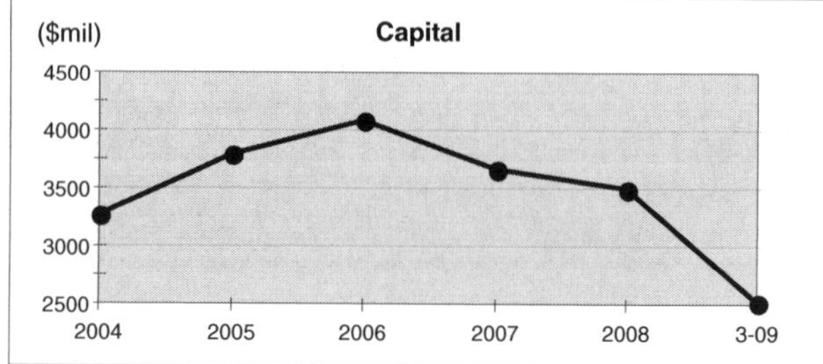

MEDICAL LIABILITY MUTUAL INS CO D+ Weak

Major Rating Factors: Weak overall results on stability tests (2.4 on a scale of 0 to 10) including weak risk adjusted capital in prior years. The largest net exposure for one risk is high at 4.5% of capital. Strengths include potentially strong support from affiliation with HUM Group of Companies. Poor long-term capitalization index (0.3) based on weak current risk adjusted capital (severe and moderate loss scenarios).

Other Rating Factors: Weak profitability index (2.6) with operating losses during 2004, 2005, 2006 and the first three months of 2008. History of adequate reserve strength (5.1) as reserves have been consistently at an acceptable level. Good liquidity (5.6) with sufficient resources (cash flows and marketable investments) to handle a spike in claims.

Principal Business: Medical malpractice (99%) and other liability (1%).

Principal Investments: Investment grade bonds (92%), misc. investments (7%), and non investment grade bonds (1%).

Investments in Affiliates: 5%

Group Affiliation: HUM Group of Companies

Licensed in: CT, DC, DE, GA, IA, KS, KY, ME, MD, MA, MT, NE, NH, NJ, NY, ND, OH, OR, PA, RI, SC, SD, TN, TX, VT, WY

Commenced Business: May 1977

Address: 8 British American Blvd, Latham, NY 12110

Phone: (800) 635-0666 **Domicile State:** NY **NAIC Code:** 34231

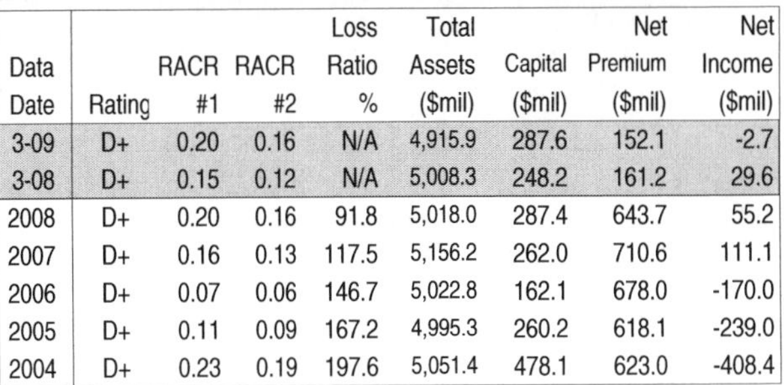

Data Date	Rating	RACR #1	RACR #2	Loss Ratio %	Total Assets ($mil)	Capital ($mil)	Net Premium ($mil)	Net Income ($mil)
3-09	D+	0.20	0.16	N/A	4,915.9	287.6	152.1	-2.7
3-08	D+	0.15	0.12	N/A	5,008.3	248.2	161.2	29.6
2008	D+	0.20	0.16	91.8	5,018.0	287.4	643.7	55.2
2007	D+	0.16	0.13	117.5	5,156.2	262.0	710.6	111.1
2006	D+	0.07	0.06	146.7	5,022.8	162.1	678.0	-170.0
2005	D+	0.11	0.09	167.2	4,995.3	260.2	618.1	-239.0
2004	D+	0.23	0.19	197.6	5,051.4	478.1	623.0	-408.4

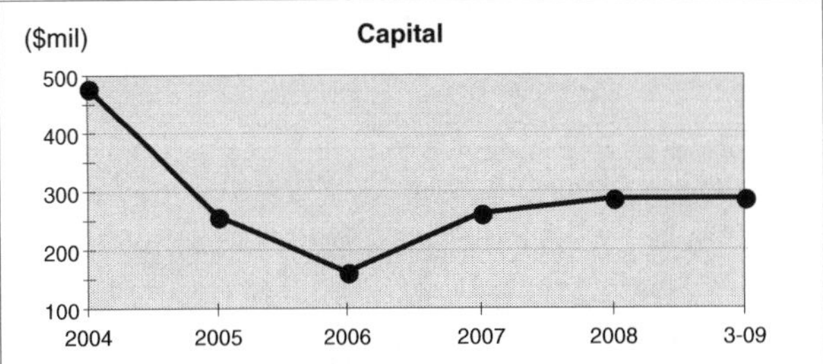

MEDICAL MUTUAL INS CO OF NC B- Good

Major Rating Factors: Fair overall results on stability tests (4.5 on a scale of 0 to 10) including potential drain of affiliation with Medical Ins Group. Strong long-term capitalization index (8.6) based on excellent current risk adjusted capital (severe and moderate loss scenarios). Moreover, capital levels have been consistent in recent years.

Other Rating Factors: Ample reserve history (7.0) that can protect against increases in claims costs. Excellent profitability (8.9) with operating gains in each of the last five years. Excellent expense controls. Return on equity has been good over the last five years, averaging 14.7%. Excellent liquidity (7.5) with ample operational cash flow and liquid investments.

Principal Business: Medical malpractice (100%).

Principal Investments: Investment grade bonds (77%), misc. investments (14%), and cash (9%).

Investments in Affiliates: 4%

Group Affiliation: Medical Ins Group

Licensed in: AL, AR, FL, GA, KY, MS, NC, SC, TN, VA

Commenced Business: October 1975

Address: 700 Spring Forest Rd, Raleigh, NC 27609

Phone: (919) 872-7117 **Domicile State:** NC **NAIC Code:** 32522

Data Date	Rating	RACR #1	RACR #2	Loss Ratio %	Total Assets ($mil)	Capital ($mil)	Net Premium ($mil)	Net Income ($mil)
3-09	B-	3.11	2.40	N/A	445.8	160.3	22.4	2.9
3-08	B-	2.58	1.94	N/A	435.4	152.4	22.4	3.1
2008	B-	3.20	2.48	53.9	422.5	157.0	85.7	24.8
2007	B-	2.68	2.01	59.4	416.2	153.1	94.6	26.1
2006	B-	2.11	1.58	68.3	371.3	127.7	91.9	24.3
2005	B-	1.77	1.29	82.5	321.5	91.2	90.6	13.0
2004	B-	1.40	1.02	86.5	272.3	76.1	78.9	6.8

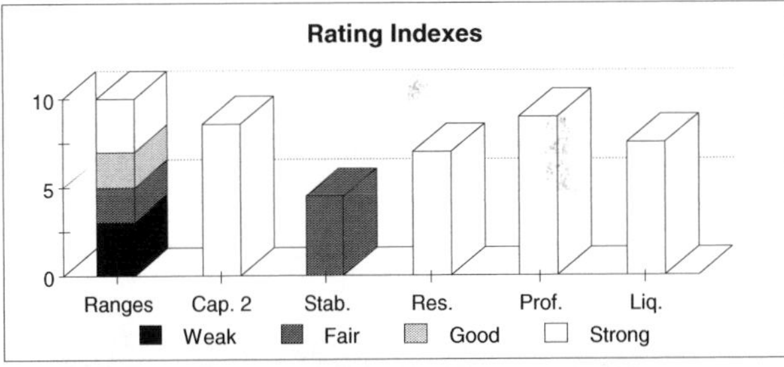

MEDICAL MUTUAL LIAB INS SOC OF MD B- Good

Major Rating Factors: Fair overall results on stability tests (4.6 on a scale of 0 to 10) including potential drain of affiliation with Medical Ins Group Of MD. Good overall profitability index (6.5) despite operating losses during the first three months of 2008.

Other Rating Factors: Strong long-term capitalization index (7.8) based on excellent current risk adjusted capital (severe and moderate loss scenarios). Moreover, capital levels have been consistent in recent years. Ample reserve history (9.9) that helps to protect the company against sharp claims increases. Excellent liquidity (7.4) with ample operational cash flow and liquid investments.

Principal Business: Medical malpractice (100%).

Principal Investments: Investment grade bonds (93%), misc. investments (6%), and real estate (1%).

Investments in Affiliates: 7%

Group Affiliation: Medical Ins Group Of MD

Licensed in: MD

Commenced Business: June 1975

Address: 225 International Cir, Hunt Valley, MD 21030

Phone: (410) 785-0050 **Domicile State:** MD **NAIC Code:** 32328

Data Date	Rating	RACR #1	RACR #2	Loss Ratio %	Total Assets ($mil)	Capital ($mil)	Net Premium ($mil)	Net Income ($mil)
3-09	B-	2.07	1.81	N/A	787.8	252.8	32.2	-1.1
3-08	B-	1.79	1.56	N/A	751.4	223.1	34.7	-0.9
2008	B-	2.11	1.86	45.4	742.5	253.1	138.9	20.1
2007	B-	1.84	1.61	36.9	661.5	223.1	150.6	7.3
2006	C+	1.51	1.30	52.2	688.4	210.6	160.9	51.1
2005	C+	1.20	1.01	73.1	641.1	172.3	155.9	25.8
2004	C+	1.18	1.00	121.1	576.7	139.1	119.2	0.5

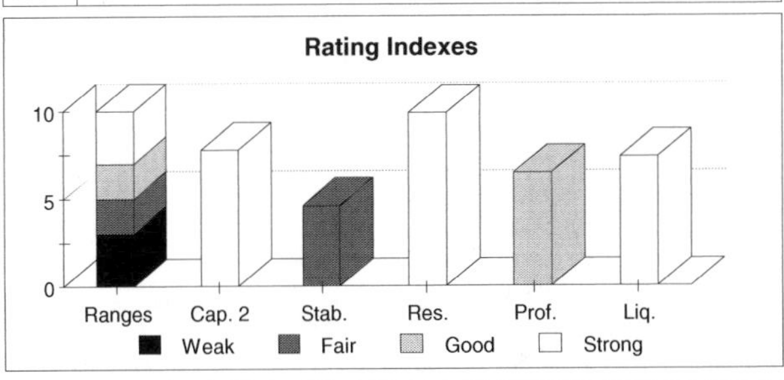

MEDICAL PROFESSIONAL MUTUAL INS CO — C+ Fair

Major Rating Factors: Fair overall results on stability tests (4.5 on a scale of 0 to 10) including potential drain of affiliation with ProMutual Companies. The largest net exposure for one risk is high at 3.5% of capital. Good long-term capitalization index (6.3) based on good current risk adjusted capital (moderate loss scenario), despite some fluctuation in capital levels.

Other Rating Factors: Good overall profitability index (6.7) despite operating losses during the first three months of 2008. Return on equity has been good over the last five years, averaging 10.3%. Good liquidity (6.9) with sufficient resources (cash flows and marketable investments) to handle a spike in claims. Ample reserve history (9.6) that helps to protect the company against sharp claims increases.

Principal Business: Medical malpractice (99%) and other liability (1%).

Principal Investments: Investment grade bonds (90%), misc. investments (8%), and non investment grade bonds (2%).

Investments in Affiliates: 2%

Group Affiliation: ProMutual Companies

Licensed in: MA

Commenced Business: July 1975

Address: 101 Arch St, Boston, MA 02110

Phone: (617) 330-1755 **Domicile State:** MA **NAIC Code:** 10206

Data Date	Rating	RACR #1	RACR #2	Loss Ratio %	Total Assets ($mil)	Capital ($mil)	Net Premium ($mil)	Net Income ($mil)
3-09	C+	1.20	1.00	N/A	2,198.8	585.0	73.9	-2.3
3-08	C	1.11	0.91	N/A	2,225.3	595.2	72.5	10.8
2008	C+	1.29	1.08	55.4	2,246.1	612.1	297.5	46.0
2007	C	1.14	0.94	67.4	2,228.4	602.8	316.3	108.9
2006	C	0.80	0.62	80.0	2,097.6	504.7	341.5	64.0
2005	C-	0.62	0.49	88.5	1,940.2	418.0	351.1	39.7
2004	C-	0.63	0.49	95.0	1,663.3	378.5	263.4	25.3

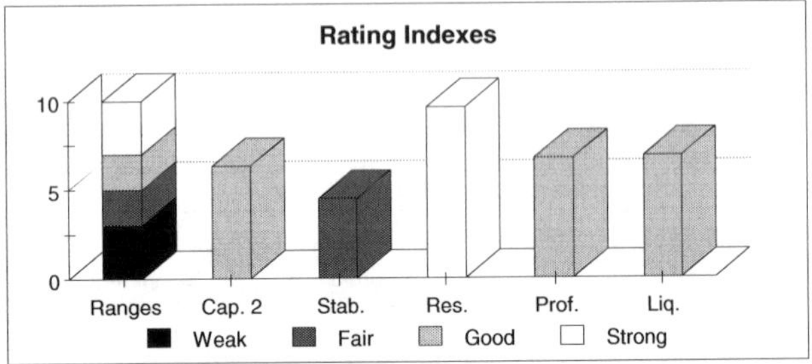

MEDICAL PROTECTIVE CO — B Good

Major Rating Factors: Good overall results on stability tests (5.6 on a scale of 0 to 10). Affiliation with Berkshire-Hathaway is a strength. History of adequate reserve strength (6.0) as reserves have been consistently at an acceptable level.

Other Rating Factors: Strong long-term capitalization index (7.4) based on excellent current risk adjusted capital (severe and moderate loss scenarios), despite some fluctuation in capital levels. Excellent profitability (7.0) with operating gains in each of the last five years. Return on equity has been good over the last five years, averaging 12.0%. Excellent liquidity (7.7) with ample operational cash flow and liquid investments.

Principal Business: Medical malpractice (100%).

Principal Investments: Investment grade bonds (68%), non investment grade bonds (21%), misc. investments (8%), cash (2%), and real estate (1%).

Investments in Affiliates: None

Group Affiliation: Berkshire-Hathaway

Licensed in: All states except PR

Commenced Business: January 1910

Address: 5814 Reed Rd, Fort Wayne, IN 46835

Phone: (219) 485-9622 **Domicile State:** IN **NAIC Code:** 11843

Data Date	Rating	RACR #1	RACR #2	Loss Ratio %	Total Assets ($mil)	Capital ($mil)	Net Premium ($mil)	Net Income ($mil)
3-09	B	1.49	1.17	N/A	1,922.5	554.5	83.0	10.1
3-08	B	1.87	1.47	N/A	1,880.6	632.5	84.3	9.4
2008	B	1.72	1.32	74.0	1,938.2	631.7	343.2	70.6
2007	B	1.96	1.53	80.4	1,805.2	639.7	343.1	61.3
2006	B	2.26	1.84	74.5	1,703.8	645.9	337.4	60.7
2005	B	2.94	2.50	103.1	2,254.9	571.3	-342.6	77.5
2004	B-	1.00	0.82	83.1	2,172.6	510.8	526.3	89.2

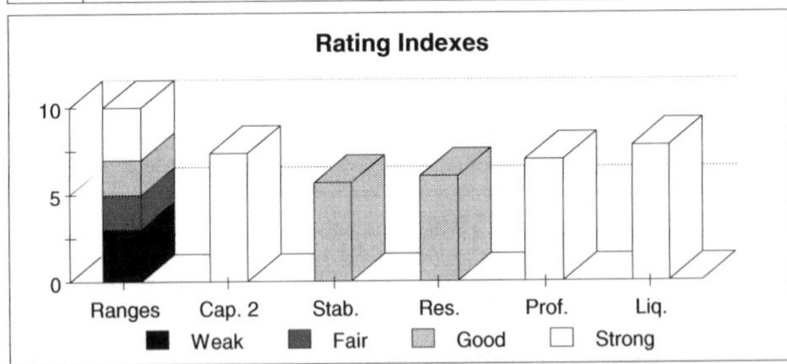

MERCURY CASUALTY CO * — A- Excellent

Major Rating Factors: Strong long-term capitalization index (7.7 on a scale of 0 to 10) based on excellent current risk adjusted capital (severe and moderate loss scenarios), despite some fluctuation in capital levels. Good overall results on stability tests (6.9). Strengths include potentially strong support from affiliation with Mercury General Group, good operational trends and excellent risk diversification.

Other Rating Factors: History of adequate reserve strength (5.9) as reserves have been consistently at an acceptable level. Good liquidity (6.2) with sufficient resources (cash flows and marketable investments) to handle a spike in claims. Fair profitability index (3.5) with modest operating losses during the first three months of 2008. Return on equity has been fair, averaging 13.1% over the past five years.

Principal Business: Auto liability (43%), homeowners multiple peril (27%), auto physical damage (24%), commercial multiple peril (5%), fire (1%), and other liability (1%).

Principal Investments: Investment grade bonds (50%), misc. investments (42%), real estate (6%), and non investment grade bonds (2%).

Investments in Affiliates: 31%

Group Affiliation: Mercury General Group

Licensed in: AZ, CA, FL, NV, NY, TX, VA, WA

Commenced Business: April 1962

Address: 4484 Wilshire Blvd, Los Angeles, CA 90010

Phone: (714) 671-6600 **Domicile State:** CA **NAIC Code:** 11908

Data Date	Rating	RACR #1	RACR #2	Loss Ratio %	Total Assets ($mil)	Capital ($mil)	Net Premium ($mil)	Net Income ($mil)
3-09	A-	1.67	1.46	N/A	2,212.7	1,056.6	252.3	-0.9
3-08	A-	1.75	1.55	N/A	2,382.1	1,368.4	270.2	29.5
2008	A-	1.67	1.48	74.7	2,073.8	1,049.6	1,042.5	18.8
2007	A-	1.78	1.59	68.4	2,401.4	1,391.6	1,135.4	210.4
2006	A-	1.66	1.50	68.8	2,336.3	1,284.3	1,257.4	216.9
2005	A	1.60	1.45	66.3	2,274.3	1,242.4	1,256.5	218.7
2004	A	1.50	1.36	60.6	1,992.8	1,152.1	1,105.1	200.4

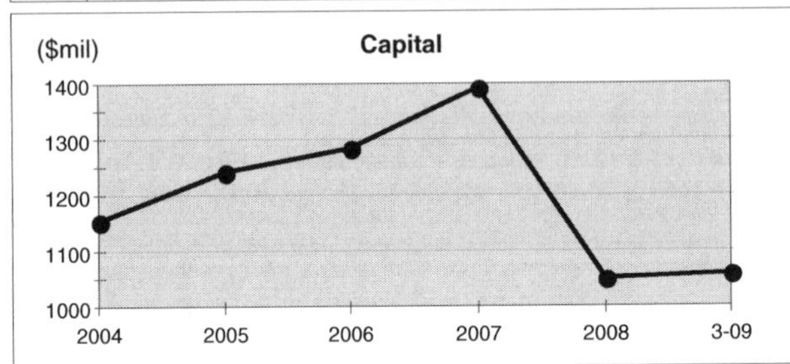

MERCURY INS CO * A- Excellent

Major Rating Factors: Strong long-term capitalization index (8.0 on a scale of 0 to 10) based on excellent current risk adjusted capital (severe and moderate loss scenarios), despite some fluctuation in capital levels. Good overall results on stability tests (6.9). Strengths include potentially strong support from affiliation with Mercury General Group, good operational trends and excellent risk diversification.

Other Rating Factors: History of adequate reserve strength (6.0) as reserves have been consistently at an acceptable level. Fair profitability index (3.3). Fair expense controls. Return on equity has been fair, averaging 14.3% over the past five years. Fair liquidity (3.0) as cash resources may not be adequate to cover a spike in claims.

Principal Business: Auto liability (58%) and auto physical damage (42%).

Principal Investments: Investment grade bonds (91%), misc. investments (8%), and non investment grade bonds (3%).

Investments in Affiliates: None

Group Affiliation: Mercury General Group

Licensed in: CA

Commenced Business: July 1978

Address: 4484 Wilshire Blvd, Los Angeles, CA 90010

Phone: (714) 671-6600 **Domicile State:** CA **NAIC Code:** 27553

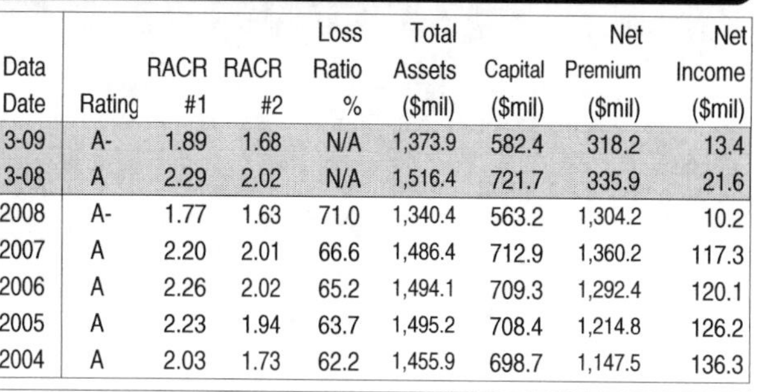

Data Date	Rating	RACR #1	RACR #2	Loss Ratio %	Total Assets ($mil)	Capital ($mil)	Net Premium ($mil)	Net Income ($mil)
3-09	A-	1.89	1.68	N/A	1,373.9	582.4	318.2	13.4
3-08	A	2.29	2.02	N/A	1,516.4	721.7	335.9	21.6
2008	A-	1.77	1.63	71.0	1,340.4	563.2	1,304.2	10.2
2007	A	2.20	2.01	66.6	1,486.4	712.9	1,360.2	117.3
2006	A	2.26	2.02	65.2	1,494.1	709.3	1,292.4	120.1
2005	A	2.23	1.94	63.7	1,495.2	708.4	1,214.8	126.2
2004	A	2.03	1.73	62.2	1,455.9	698.7	1,147.5	136.3

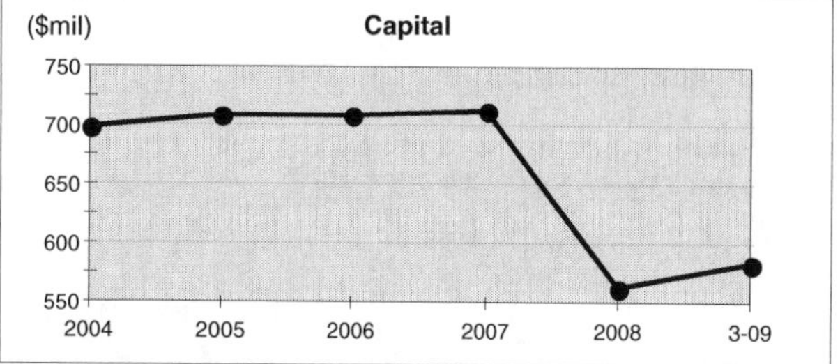

MERRIMACK MUTUAL FIRE INS CO * A Excellent

Major Rating Factors: Strong long-term capitalization index (8.9 on a scale of 0 to 10) based on excellent current risk adjusted capital (severe and moderate loss scenarios). Furthermore, this high level of risk adjusted capital has been consistently maintained in previous years. Excellent profitability (8.3) with operating gains in each of the last five years.

Other Rating Factors: Excellent liquidity (7.6) with ample operational cash flow and liquid investments. Good overall results on stability tests (6.0) despite potential drain of affiliation with Andover Group. Stability strengths include good operational trends and excellent risk diversification. History of adequate reserve strength (6.0) as reserves have been consistently at an acceptable level.

Principal Business: Homeowners multiple peril (54%), commercial multiple peril (20%), fire (11%), allied lines (7%), other liability (6%), and inland marine (2%).

Principal Investments: Investment grade bonds (63%), misc. investments (31%), cash (4%), and real estate (2%).

Investments in Affiliates: 21%

Group Affiliation: Andover Group

Licensed in: CT, IL, ME, MA, NH, NJ, NY, RI, VT

Commenced Business: April 1828

Address: 95 Old River Rd, Andover, MA 01810

Phone: (978) 475-3300 **Domicile State:** MA **NAIC Code:** 19798

Data Date	Rating	RACR #1	RACR #2	Loss Ratio %	Total Assets ($mil)	Capital ($mil)	Net Premium ($mil)	Net Income ($mil)
3-09	A	2.79	2.42	N/A	883.0	520.3	50.3	11.7
3-08	A-	2.83	2.52	N/A	861.0	524.1	52.8	7.1
2008	A	2.89	2.51	59.7	921.0	526.5	218.2	23.3
2007	A-	2.86	2.56	52.6	864.7	518.7	227.7	33.3
2006	A-	2.70	2.39	45.4	813.4	465.1	233.4	45.5
2005	A-	2.23	1.90	66.1	759.2	399.1	229.4	10.0
2004	A-	2.44	2.11	58.2	701.4	386.4	211.9	18.8

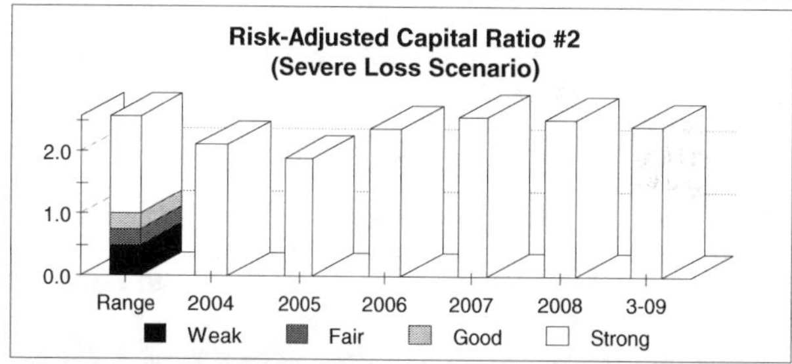

METROPOLITAN GROUP PROP & CAS INS CO B Good

Major Rating Factors: History of adequate reserve strength (5.3 on a scale of 0 to 10) as reserves have been consistently at an acceptable level. Good overall profitability index (6.8). Good expense controls. Return on equity has been good over the last five years, averaging 11.2%.

Other Rating Factors: Good overall results on stability tests (5.5) despite negative cash flow from operations for 2008. Stability strengths include good operational trends and excellent risk diversification. Strong long-term capitalization index (10.0) based on excellent current risk adjusted capital (severe and moderate loss scenarios), despite some fluctuation in capital levels. Superior liquidity (9.2) with ample operational cash flow and liquid investments.

Principal Business: (Not applicable due to unusual reinsurance transactions.)

Principal Investments: Investment grade bonds (92%), misc. investments (5%), and non investment grade bonds (3%).

Investments in Affiliates: 2%

Group Affiliation: MetLife Inc

Licensed in: All states except CO, HI, KY, ME, MN, NM, NC, OR, VA, WY, PR

Commenced Business: December 1977

Address: 700 Quaker Lane, Warwick, RI 02886

Phone: (401) 827-2400 **Domicile State:** RI **NAIC Code:** 34339

Data Date	Rating	RACR #1	RACR #2	Loss Ratio %	Total Assets ($mil)	Capital ($mil)	Net Premium ($mil)	Net Income ($mil)
3-09	B	11.14	8.22	N/A	414.3	305.1	0.0	3.7
3-08	B-	9.48	6.81	N/A	396.0	284.9	0.0	3.4
2008	B	11.49	8.68	0.0	402.6	300.0	0.0	12.1
2007	B-	9.44	6.89	0.0	390.2	277.2	0.0	12.7
2006	B-	9.18	5.05	0.0	381.5	259.6	0.0	13.0
2005	B-	9.61	5.89	0.0	374.7	260.6	0.0	98.8
2004	B-	7.01	4.03	0.0	364.5	198.6	0.0	12.2

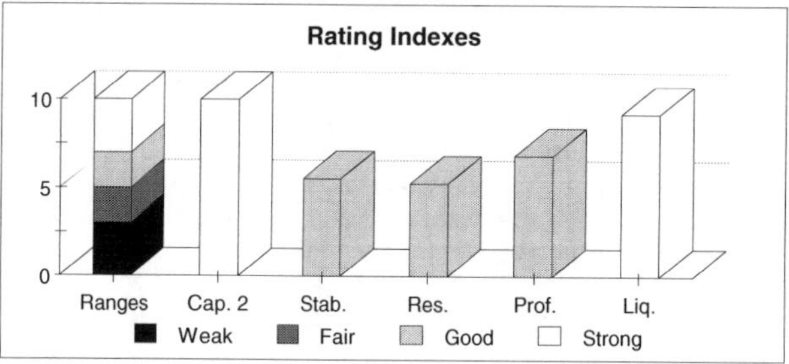

METROPOLITAN PROPERTY & CAS INS CO * B+ Good

Major Rating Factors: Good overall results on stability tests (6.4 on a scale of 0 to 10). Strengths include potentially strong support from affiliation with MetLife Inc. Strong long-term capitalization index (7.6) based on excellent current risk adjusted capital (severe and moderate loss scenarios), despite some fluctuation in capital levels.

Other Rating Factors: Ample reserve history (7.0) that can protect against increases in claims costs. Fair profitability index (4.6). Fair expense controls. Return on equity has been fair, averaging 18.5% over the past five years. Fair liquidity (3.5) as cash resources may not be adequate to cover a spike in claims.

Principal Business: Homeowners multiple peril (41%), auto liability (30%), auto physical damage (21%), other liability (2%), allied lines (2%), inland marine (2%), and other lines (2%).

Principal Investments: Investment grade bonds (70%), misc. investments (29%), and non investment grade bonds (4%).

Investments in Affiliates: 21%

Group Affiliation: MetLife Inc

Licensed in: All states except AK, CA, PR

Commenced Business: December 1972

Address: 700 Quaker Lane, Warwick, RI 02886

Phone: (401) 827-2400 **Domicile State:** RI **NAIC Code:** 26298

Data Date	Rating	RACR #1	RACR #2	Loss Ratio %	Total Assets ($mil)	Capital ($mil)	Net Premium ($mil)	Net Income ($mil)
3-09	B+	1.82	1.44	N/A	4,771.4	1,769.8	726.2	65.5
3-08	B+	1.95	1.52	N/A	5,183.1	1,917.3	747.8	88.3
2008	B+	1.78	1.42	64.3	4,855.6	1,762.3	2,962.5	272.8
2007	B+	1.84	1.45	60.8	5,333.5	1,825.8	2,990.1	400.5
2006	B	1.88	1.49	59.1	5,305.1	1,850.6	2,955.0	385.3
2005	B	1.81	1.44	68.8	5,348.2	1,782.7	2,929.2	289.0
2004	B+	1.96	1.57	70.3	5,192.2	1,875.0	2,963.3	355.7

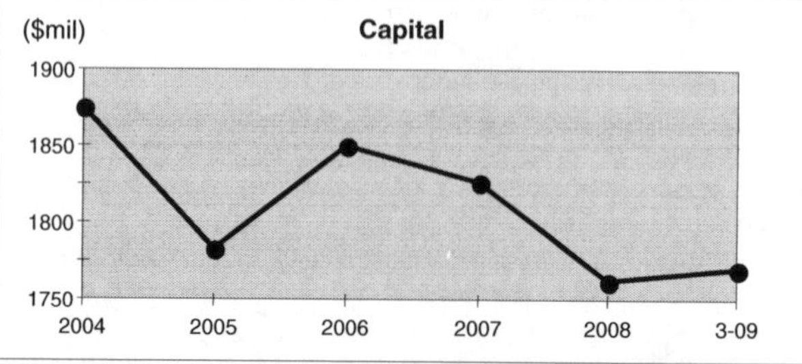

MGIC REINSURANCE CORP OF WI D Weak

Major Rating Factors: Poor long-term capitalization (2.2 on a scale of 0 to 10) based on weak current risk adjusted capital (moderate loss scenario), although results have slipped from the good range over the last two years. Weak profitability index (0.5) with operating losses during 2007 and the first three months of 2008. Average return on equity over the last five years has been poor at -45.2%.

Other Rating Factors: Fair reserve development (4.1) as reserves have generally been sufficient to cover claims. In 2008, the one year reserve development was 18% deficient. Weak overall results on stability tests (1.4) including excessive premium growth and weak risk adjusted capital in prior years. Excellent liquidity (7.7) with ample operational cash flow and liquid investments.

Principal Business: (This company is a reinsurer.)

Principal Investments: Investment grade bonds (95%) and misc. investments (5%).

Investments in Affiliates: None

Group Affiliation: Mortgage Guaranty Corp

Licensed in: WI

Commenced Business: April 1996

Address: 250 East Kilbourn Avenue, Milwaukee, WI 53202

Phone: (800) 558-9900 **Domicile State:** WI **NAIC Code:** 10247

Data Date	Rating	RACR #1	RACR #2	Loss Ratio %	Total Assets ($mil)	Capital ($mil)	Net Premium ($mil)	Net Income ($mil)
3-09	D	0.47	0.36	N/A	982.7	178.0	40.3	-90.5
3-08	B	2.81	1.94	N/A	714.7	316.9	23.5	-23.3
2008	C	0.55	0.41	331.1	951.2	183.0	144.0	-346.1
2007	B	3.24	2.24	273.0	709.8	341.3	96.3	-34.9
2006	B	4.98	3.46	89.7	714.7	420.9	92.2	21.1
2005	B	4.78	3.41	80.4	735.2	440.3	90.3	19.5
2004	U	3.90	3.37	88.5	780.2	497.4	84.8	18.8

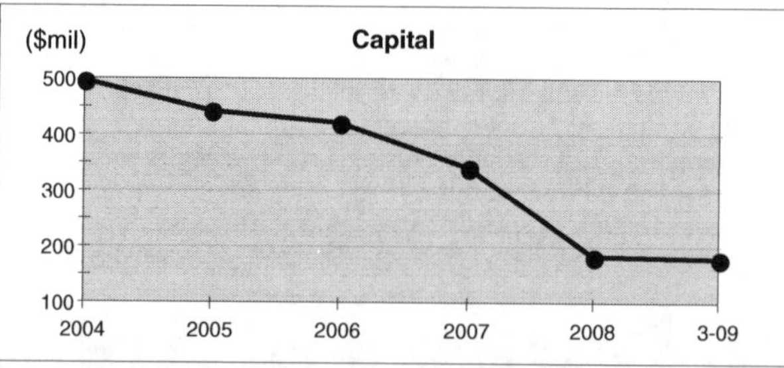

MID-CENTURY INS CO C- Fair

Major Rating Factors: A history of deficient reserves (1.6 on a scale of 0 to 10). Underreserving can have an adverse impact on capital and profits. Deficiencies in the two year reserve development occurred in three of the previous five years and ranged between 64% and 124%. Fair overall results on stability tests (3.2). Strengths include potentially strong support from affiliation with Zurich Financial Services Group.

Other Rating Factors: Fair profitability index (3.9) with operating losses during 2004, 2005 and 2008. Average return on equity over the last five years has been poor at -0.2%. Fair liquidity (4.2) as cash resources may not be adequate to cover a spike in claims. Good long-term capitalization index (5.1) based on good current risk adjusted capital (severe loss scenario).

Principal Business: Auto liability (47%), auto physical damage (27%), homeowners multiple peril (16%), commercial multiple peril (6%), and workers compensation (3%).

Principal Investments: Investment grade bonds (104%), misc. investments (6%), real estate (2%), and non investment grade bonds (1%).

Investments in Affiliates: 10%

Group Affiliation: Zurich Financial Services Group

Licensed in: All states except AK, CT, DC, ME, MA, NY, RI, WV, PR

Commenced Business: February 1953

Address: 4680 Wilshire Blvd, Los Angeles, CA 90010

Phone: (213) 932-3200 **Domicile State:** CA **NAIC Code:** 21687

Data Date	Rating	RACR #1	RACR #2	Loss Ratio %	Total Assets ($mil)	Capital ($mil)	Net Premium ($mil)	Net Income ($mil)
3-09	C-	1.10	0.77	N/A	3,285.3	616.9	414.3	23.7
3-08	C-	0.64	0.42	N/A	3,473.3	744.1	499.1	26.0
2008	C-	1.06	0.75	78.4	3,272.7	603.6	1,886.1	-32.8
2007	C-	0.62	0.42	69.0	3,388.4	724.4	2,050.1	102.5
2006	C-	0.32	0.26	70.1	3,198.1	610.6	1,855.3	81.7
2005	C-	0.21	0.17	84.2	3,238.2	483.0	1,731.0	-58.7
2004	C-	0.31	0.25	85.9	2,900.6	558.4	1,541.0	-83.9

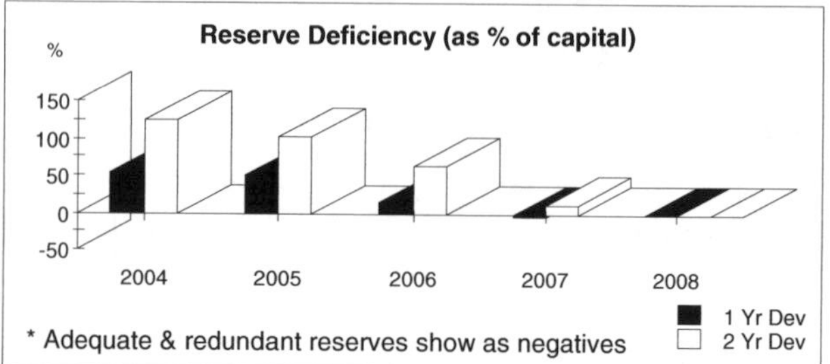

* Adequate & redundant reserves show as negatives

MID-CONTINENT CAS CO — C- Fair

Major Rating Factors: Fair long-term capitalization index (3.6 on a scale of 0 to 10) based on fair current risk adjusted capital (severe loss scenario), although results have slipped from the good range over the last two years. Fair profitability index (3.7). Fair expense controls. Return on equity has been fair, averaging 21.9% over the past five years.

Other Rating Factors: Fair overall results on stability tests (3.2) including fair risk adjusted capital in prior years. History of adequate reserve strength (5.0) as reserves have been consistently at an acceptable level. Excellent liquidity (7.1) with ample operational cash flow and liquid investments.

Principal Business: Other liability (57%), products liability (19%), auto liability (9%), inland marine (6%), surety (4%), auto physical damage (4%), and commercial multiple peril (1%).

Principal Investments: Investment grade bonds (88%), misc. investments (6%), non investment grade bonds (4%), and cash (2%).

Investments in Affiliates: 5%

Group Affiliation: American Financial Corp

Licensed in: AL, AZ, AR, CO, FL, GA, ID, IL, IN, IA, KS, LA, MD, MI, MN, MS, MO, MT, NE, NM, NC, ND, OH, OK, OR, SC, SD, TN, TX, UT, VA, WA, WY

Commenced Business: February 1948

Address: 1646 S Boulder Dr, Tulsa, OK 74119

Phone: (918) 587-7221 **Domicile State:** OH **NAIC Code:** 23418

Data Date	Rating	RACR #1	RACR #2	Loss Ratio %	Total Assets ($mil)	Capital ($mil)	Net Premium ($mil)	Net Income ($mil)
3-09	C-	0.88	0.60	N/A	696.5	217.8	47.8	16.8
3-08	C+	1.16	0.79	N/A	874.0	306.5	62.7	15.0
2008	C-	0.82	0.56	28.0	703.2	209.6	206.0	61.4
2007	C+	1.26	0.86	28.0	882.3	331.6	266.5	105.5
2006	C	1.24	0.84	46.9	876.2	292.8	301.5	62.0
2005	C	1.22	0.87	62.2	763.1	234.0	289.1	28.5
2004	C	1.20	0.88	64.2	621.5	178.3	272.0	22.3

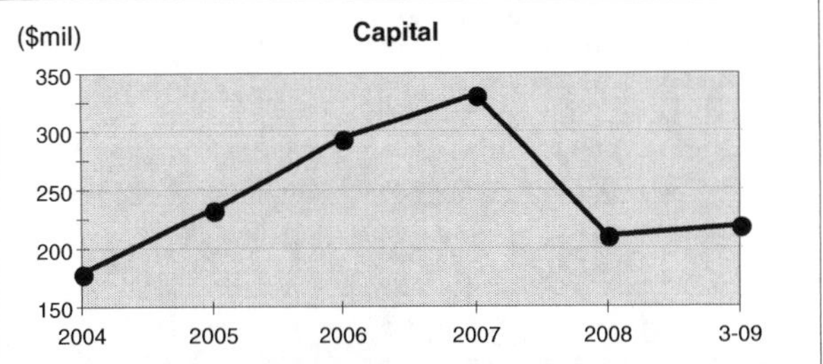

MIDDLESEX INS CO — B Good

Major Rating Factors: Good overall profitability index (6.7 on a scale of 0 to 10). Fair expense controls. Return on equity has been fair, averaging 9.8% over the past five years. Good liquidity (6.7) with sufficient resources (cash flows and marketable investments) to handle a spike in claims.

Other Rating Factors: Good overall results on stability tests (6.3). Stability strengths include good operational trends and excellent risk diversification. Strong long-term capitalization index (9.3) based on excellent current risk adjusted capital (severe and moderate loss scenarios). Moreover, capital levels have been consistent in recent years. Ample reserve history (9.3) that helps to protect the company against sharp claims increases.

Principal Business: Workers compensation (39%), auto liability (20%), homeowners multiple peril (17%), auto physical damage (14%), allied lines (4%), fire (3%), and other lines (5%).

Principal Investments: Investment grade bonds (95%), misc. investments (4%), and non investment grade bonds (1%).

Investments in Affiliates: 4%

Group Affiliation: Sentry Ins Group

Licensed in: All states except AK, HI, ID, NE, NM, ND, SD, WA, WV, WY, PR

Commenced Business: March 1826

Address: 1800 N Point Dr, Stevens Point, WI 54481

Phone: (715) 346-6000 **Domicile State:** WI **NAIC Code:** 23434

Data Date	Rating	RACR #1	RACR #2	Loss Ratio %	Total Assets ($mil)	Capital ($mil)	Net Premium ($mil)	Net Income ($mil)
3-09	B	4.06	2.81	N/A	660.8	241.1	44.0	2.5
3-08	B	3.91	2.69	N/A	672.7	236.7	46.5	4.6
2008	B	4.04	2.84	74.5	657.3	237.9	178.6	20.1
2007	B	3.87	2.70	72.2	644.5	231.8	189.2	23.9
2006	B	3.48	2.51	72.7	623.6	210.0	197.7	23.0
2005	B+	3.43	2.44	73.5	592.2	186.9	182.9	21.6
2004	B+	3.38	2.37	75.1	529.7	165.7	170.8	15.2

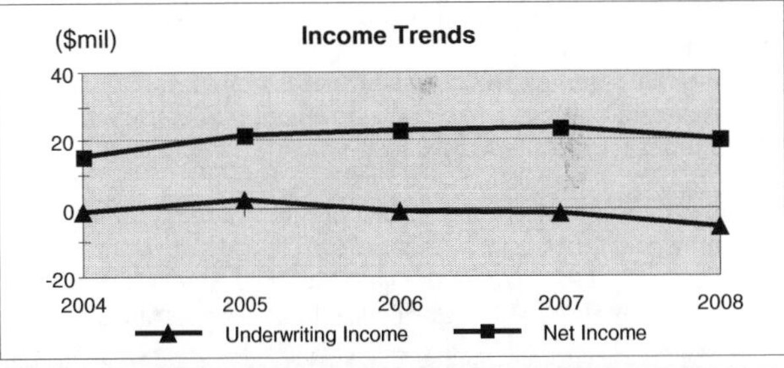

MIDWEST MEDICAL INS CO * — B+ Good

Major Rating Factors: History of adequate reserve strength (5.8 on a scale of 0 to 10) as reserves have been consistently at an acceptable level. Good overall profitability index (6.9). Good expense controls. Return on equity has been fair, averaging 8.2% over the past five years.

Other Rating Factors: Good liquidity (6.9) with sufficient resources (cash flows and marketable investments) to handle a spike in claims. Good overall results on stability tests (6.4). The largest net exposure for one risk is conservative at 1.3% of capital. Strong long-term capitalization index (8.2) based on excellent current risk adjusted capital (severe and moderate loss scenarios), despite some fluctuation in capital levels.

Principal Business: Medical malpractice (98%) and other liability (2%).

Principal Investments: Investment grade bonds (79%) and misc. investments (22%).

Investments in Affiliates: None

Group Affiliation: Midwest Medical Ins Holding Co

Licensed in: IL, IA, KS, MN, MO, MT, NE, ND, SD, WI

Commenced Business: October 1980

Address: 7650 Edinborough Way Ste 400, Minneapolis, MN 55435-5978

Phone: (952) 838-6700 **Domicile State:** MN **NAIC Code:** 16942

Data Date	Rating	RACR #1	RACR #2	Loss Ratio %	Total Assets ($mil)	Capital ($mil)	Net Premium ($mil)	Net Income ($mil)
3-09	B+	2.35	1.78	N/A	490.6	154.1	28.0	1.0
3-08	B	2.43	1.76	N/A	520.6	174.3	32.9	4.2
2008	B+	2.46	1.86	69.5	448.9	157.4	116.1	14.8
2007	B	2.49	1.81	74.1	488.7	177.3	123.1	22.2
2006	B	2.02	1.54	83.9	442.9	157.2	126.2	15.8
2005	B	1.61	1.31	89.7	401.5	137.8	118.3	8.0
2004	B-	1.54	1.23	93.9	342.3	128.1	98.7	6.2

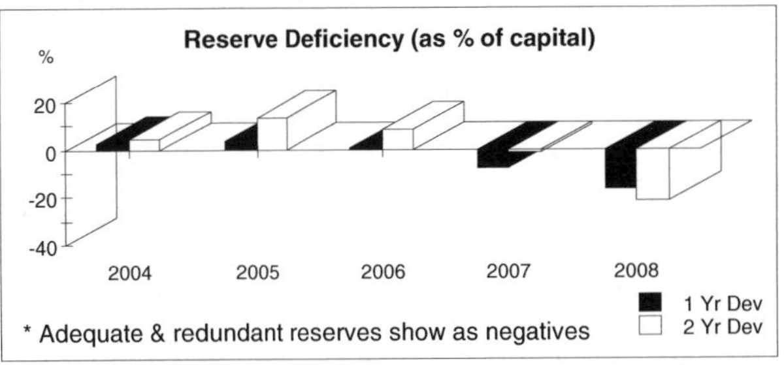

MISSISSIPPI FARM BUREAU CAS INS CO — B Good

Major Rating Factors: Good overall profitability index (6.4 on a scale of 0 to 10) despite operating losses during 2005. Return on equity has been fair, averaging 5.6% over the past five years. Good liquidity (6.7) with sufficient resources (cash flows and marketable investments) to handle a spike in claims.

Other Rating Factors: Fair reserve development (4.6) as reserves have generally been sufficient to cover claims. Fair overall results on stability tests (4.8). Strong long-term capitalization index (10.0) based on excellent current risk adjusted capital (severe and moderate loss scenarios). Moreover, capital levels have been consistent in recent years.

Principal Business: (Not applicable due to unusual reinsurance transactions.)

Principal Investments: Investment grade bonds (96%) and misc. investments (4%).

Investments in Affiliates: None

Group Affiliation: Southern Farm Bureau Casualty

Licensed in: MS

Commenced Business: September 1986

Address: 6310 I-55 North, Jackson, MS 39211

Phone: (601) 957-3200 **Domicile State:** MS **NAIC Code:** 27669

Data Date	Rating	RACR #1	RACR #2	Loss Ratio %	Total Assets ($mil)	Capital ($mil)	Net Premium ($mil)	Net Income ($mil)
3-09	B	5.43	4.42	N/A	293.8	178.1	30.7	3.6
3-08	B	3.72	2.39	N/A	304.1	164.6	32.8	4.3
2008	B	5.31	4.06	72.4	278.4	174.6	124.9	14.3
2007	B	3.81	2.37	54.6	268.9	160.5	124.3	25.8
2006	B	2.95	1.82	62.9	228.8	129.9	120.8	2.8
2005	B	4.47	2.71	100.0	103.3	74.0	20.7	-2.2
2004	B	68.53	40.93	0.0	33.1	32.1	0.0	1.3

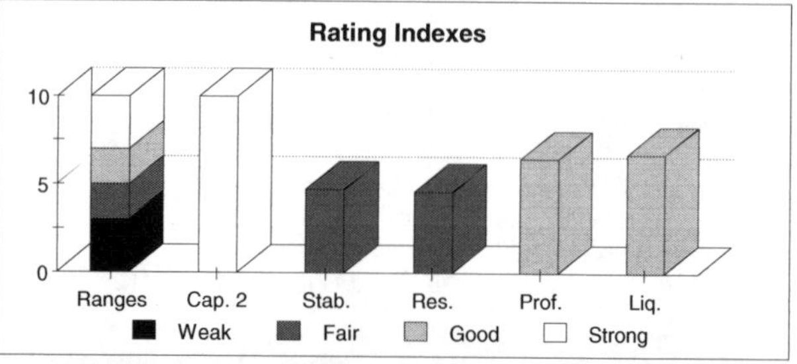

MITSUI SUMITOMO INS CO OF AMER — B Good

Major Rating Factors: History of adequate reserve strength (5.0 on a scale of 0 to 10) as reserves have been consistently at an acceptable level. Good overall profitability index (6.5) with small operating losses during 2004. Return on equity has been low, averaging 4.0% over the past five years.

Other Rating Factors: Good liquidity (6.9) with sufficient resources (cash flows and marketable investments) to handle a spike in claims. Good overall results on stability tests (5.5). Stability strengths include good operational trends and excellent risk diversification. The largest net exposure for one risk is conservative at 1.5% of capital. Strong long-term capitalization index (7.5) based on excellent current risk adjusted capital (severe and moderate loss scenarios). Moreover, capital levels have been consistent in recent years.

Principal Business: Commercial multiple peril (30%), workers compensation (22%), other liability (14%), ocean marine (13%), aircraft (11%), auto liability (5%), and other lines (5%).

Principal Investments: Investment grade bonds (90%), misc. investments (9%), and real estate (4%).

Investments in Affiliates: None

Group Affiliation: Mitsui Sumitomo Ins Group

Licensed in: All states, the District of Columbia and Puerto Rico

Commenced Business: January 1971

Address: 560 Lexington Ave 20th Floor, New York, NY 10022-6828

Phone: (908) 604-2900 **Domicile State:** NY **NAIC Code:** 20362

Data Date	Rating	RACR #1	RACR #2	Loss Ratio %	Total Assets ($mil)	Capital ($mil)	Net Premium ($mil)	Net Income ($mil)
3-09	B	2.82	1.53	N/A	712.3	231.6	33.1	1.5
3-08	B-	2.66	1.44	N/A	675.7	217.0	34.8	5.8
2008	B	2.84	1.54	61.4	700.1	229.5	141.4	14.9
2007	B-	2.64	1.43	66.0	674.6	214.1	135.2	20.2
2006	C+	2.16	1.19	82.3	670.2	190.1	141.0	4.7
2005	B-	1.60	1.02	78.6	635.1	136.7	168.0	4.0
2004	B-	1.32	0.87	78.8	621.5	131.9	191.3	-1.2

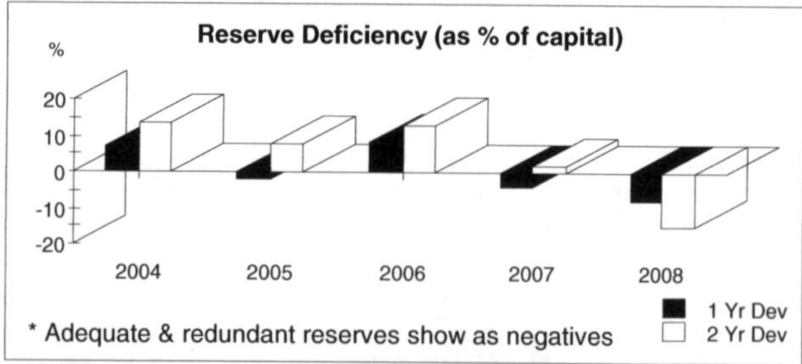

* Adequate & redundant reserves show as negatives

MORTGAGE GUARANTY INS CORP — D Weak

Major Rating Factors: Weak overall results on stability tests (1.4 on a scale of 0 to 10). Fair long-term capitalization index (3.2) based on weak current risk adjusted capital (moderate loss scenario), although results have slipped from the fair range during the last year.

Other Rating Factors: Fair reserve development (4.4) as the level of reserves has at times been insufficient to cover claims. In 2008 and 2007 the one year reserve development was 20% and 26% deficient respectively. Fair profitability index (4.7) with operating losses during the first three months of 2008. Return on equity has been fair, averaging 21.3% over the past five years. Excellent liquidity (7.5) with ample operational cash flow and liquid investments.

Principal Business: Mortgage guaranty (100%).

Principal Investments: Investment grade bonds (95%) and misc. investments (5%).

Investments in Affiliates: 5%

Group Affiliation: Mortgage Guaranty Corp

Licensed in: All states, the District of Columbia and Puerto Rico

Commenced Business: March 1979

Address: 250 East Kilbourn Avenue, Milwaukee, WI 53202

Phone: (800) 558-9900 **Domicile State:** WI **NAIC Code:** 29858

Data Date	Rating	RACR #1	RACR #2	Loss Ratio %	Total Assets ($mil)	Capital ($mil)	Net Premium ($mil)	Net Income ($mil)
3-09	D	0.66	0.47	N/A	7,527.3	1,350.0	304.6	-88.0
3-08	C-	0.88	0.63	N/A	7,776.7	1,721.0	303.1	-76.0
2008	D+	0.78	0.55	195.7	7,624.5	1,529.0	1,237.7	348.9
2007	C-	0.65	0.46	174.2	7,110.4	1,258.5	1,172.4	537.1
2006	U	N/A	N/A	48.0	7,364.3	1,549.7	1,056.2	400.4
2005	U	N/A	N/A	41.2	7,276.0	1,637.1	1,100.2	287.2
2004	U	0.75	0.56	49.4	7,022.5	1,776.8	1,148.9	164.0

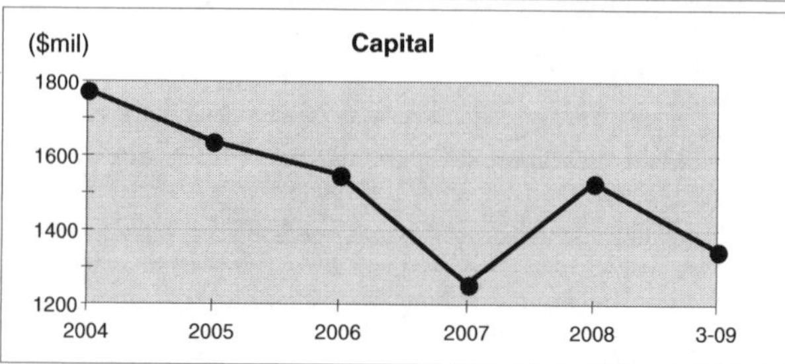

MOTORISTS MUTUAL INS CO * B+ Good

Major Rating Factors: History of adequate reserve strength (5.7 on a scale of 0 to 10) as reserves have been consistently at an acceptable level. Good liquidity (6.3) with sufficient resources (cash flows and marketable investments) to handle a spike in claims.

Other Rating Factors: Good overall results on stability tests (6.4). Strengths include potential support from affiliation with The Motorists Group. Strong long-term capitalization index (7.9) based on excellent current risk adjusted capital (severe and moderate loss scenarios), despite some fluctuation in capital levels. Fair profitability index (3.2) with operating losses during the first three months of 2008.

Principal Business: Auto liability (31%), homeowners multiple peril (21%), auto physical damage (20%), other liability (10%), commercial multiple peril (8%), workers compensation (5%), and other lines (6%).

Principal Investments: Investment grade bonds (76%), misc. investments (25%), and real estate (1%).

Investments in Affiliates: 5%

Group Affiliation: The Motorists Group

Licensed in: IN, KY, MI, OH, PA, WV

Commenced Business: November 1928

Address: 471 E Broad St, Columbus, OH 43215

Phone: (614) 225-8211 **Domicile State:** OH **NAIC Code:** 14621

Data Date	Rating	RACR #1	RACR #2	Loss Ratio %	Total Assets ($mil)	Capital ($mil)	Net Premium ($mil)	Net Income ($mil)
3-09	B+	2.29	1.52	N/A	1,212.1	388.4	114.9	-8.9
3-08	B+	2.90	1.97	N/A	1,213.3	525.0	112.3	-0.7
2008	B+	2.44	1.63	73.5	1,175.5	409.3	474.2	-18.3
2007	B+	3.08	2.09	66.0	1,213.9	535.1	458.2	34.4
2006	B+	3.18	2.21	65.1	1,183.0	499.9	460.0	44.0
2005	B+	2.85	1.99	61.4	1,119.2	454.1	465.2	55.6
2004	B+	2.30	1.61	67.4	1,035.8	404.5	458.4	40.1

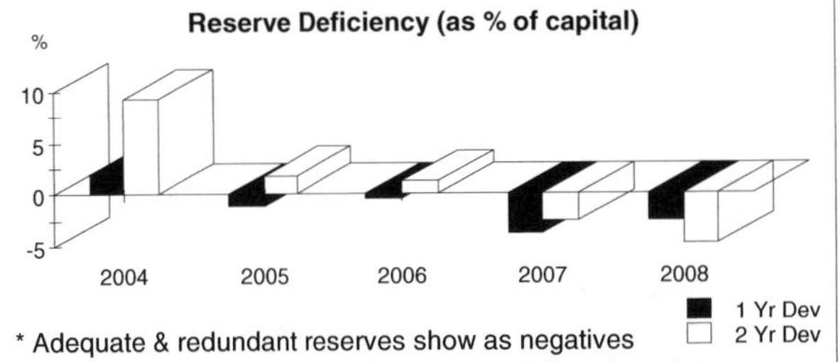

MOTORS INS CORP C+ Fair

Major Rating Factors: Fair profitability index (3.0 on a scale of 0 to 10) with operating losses during the first three months of 2008. Return on equity has been fair, averaging 21.9% over the past five years. Fair overall results on stability tests (4.3) including negative cash flow from operations for 2008. The largest net exposure for one risk is conservative at 1.2% of capital.

Other Rating Factors: History of adequate reserve strength (5.2) as reserves have been consistently at an acceptable level. Good liquidity (6.1) with sufficient resources (cash flows and marketable investments) to handle a spike in claims. Strong long-term capitalization index (8.2) based on excellent current risk adjusted capital (severe and moderate loss scenarios), despite some fluctuation in capital levels.

Principal Business: Auto physical damage (38%) and auto liability (12%).

Principal Investments: Investment grade bonds (80%), misc. investments (17%), and non investment grade bonds (3%).

Investments in Affiliates: 7%

Group Affiliation: General Motors Corp

Licensed in: All states except PR

Commenced Business: November 1939

Address: 300 Galleria Officentre, Southfield, MI 48034

Phone: (313) 556-5000 **Domicile State:** MI **NAIC Code:** 22012

Data Date	Rating	RACR #1	RACR #2	Loss Ratio %	Total Assets ($mil)	Capital ($mil)	Net Premium ($mil)	Net Income ($mil)
3-09	C+	2.58	1.85	N/A	5,444.4	1,681.2	507.6	-14.4
3-08	C+	2.08	1.43	N/A	6,960.8	1,919.7	703.9	74.9
2008	C+	2.50	1.79	63.5	5,407.5	1,692.4	2,186.0	325.4
2007	C+	2.03	1.41	67.8	6,601.5	1,883.4	2,607.6	429.0
2006	C+	2.15	1.62	67.7	7,770.6	2,812.2	2,855.3	1,102.2
2005	C+	2.10	1.36	72.1	8,368.7	2,501.1	2,863.3	417.7
2004	C+	1.83	1.19	76.4	7,780.7	2,073.8	2,864.0	366.3

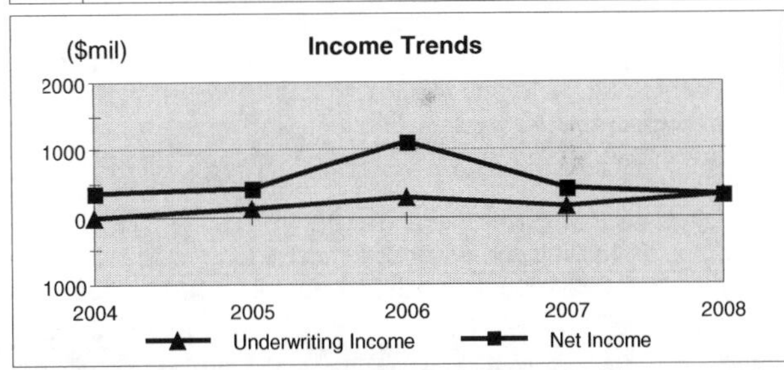

MOUNT VERNON FIRE INS CO B- Good

Major Rating Factors: Fair profitability index (3.2 on a scale of 0 to 10). Weak expense controls. Return on equity has been fair, averaging 18.9% over the past five years. Fair overall results on stability tests (4.6) including weak results on operational trends.

Other Rating Factors: Strong long-term capitalization index (7.8) based on excellent current risk adjusted capital (severe and moderate loss scenarios), despite some fluctuation in capital levels. Ample reserve history (9.5) that helps to protect the company against sharp claims increases. Superior liquidity (9.1) with ample operational cash flow and liquid investments.

Principal Business: Other liability (62%), fire (34%), products liability (1%), auto physical damage (1%), and inland marine (1%).

Principal Investments: Investment grade bonds (67%), non investment grade bonds (22%), and misc. investments (13%).

Investments in Affiliates: 16%

Group Affiliation: Berkshire-Hathaway

Licensed in: AL, DE, IN, KY, ME, MA, NH, NY, PA, TN

Commenced Business: December 1958

Address: 190 S. Warner Road, Wayne, PA 19087

Phone: (610) 688-2535 **Domicile State:** PA **NAIC Code:** 26522

Data Date	Rating	RACR #1	RACR #2	Loss Ratio %	Total Assets ($mil)	Capital ($mil)	Net Premium ($mil)	Net Income ($mil)
3-09	B-	1.44	1.12	N/A	283.4	116.3	16.8	2.7
3-08	B-	1.41	1.24	N/A	369.5	200.9	16.8	2.7
2008	B-	2.27	1.73	31.4	390.8	216.0	68.6	116.2
2007	B-	1.40	1.23	187.6	368.7	198.8	-77.7	36.6
2006	B	2.01	1.75	50.8	671.9	337.0	128.2	26.8
2005	B	2.03	1.74	45.6	595.3	317.7	122.0	24.5
2004	B	1.98	1.71	50.5	531.6	275.3	121.3	24.6

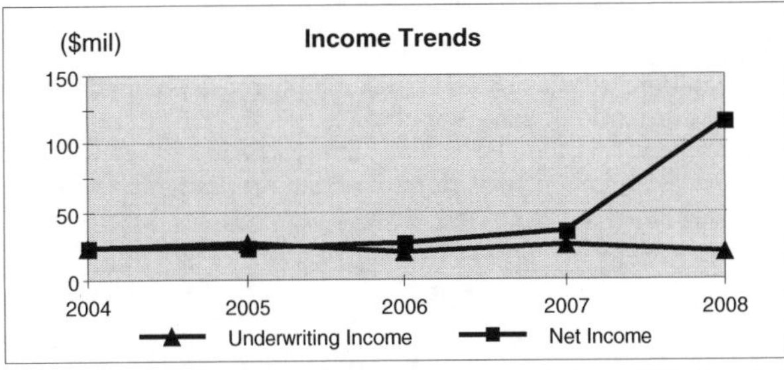

MOUNTAIN WEST FARM BU MUTUAL INS CO * A Excellent

Major Rating Factors: Strong long-term capitalization index (10.0 on a scale of 0 to 10) based on excellent current risk adjusted capital (severe and moderate loss scenarios). Furthermore, this high level of risk adjusted capital has been consistently maintained in previous years. Ample reserve history (9.2) that helps to protect the company against sharp claims increases.

Other Rating Factors: Excellent profitability (7.5) with operating gains in each of the last five years. Excellent overall results on stability tests (7.2). Stability strengths include excellent operational trends and excellent risk diversification. Good liquidity (6.7) with sufficient resources (cash flows and marketable investments) to handle a spike in claims.

Principal Business: Auto liability (24%), auto physical damage (23%), homeowners multiple peril (19%), farmowners multiple peril (18%), commercial multiple peril (12%), other liability (2%), and fire (2%).

Principal Investments: Investment grade bonds (84%), misc. investments (8%), cash (6%), and real estate (2%).

Investments in Affiliates: None

Group Affiliation: None

Licensed in: AZ, MT, WY

Commenced Business: August 1948

Address: 931 Boulder Dr, Laramie, WY 82070

Phone: (307) 745-4835 **Domicile State:** WY **NAIC Code:** 29440

Data Date	Rating	RACR #1	RACR #2	Loss Ratio %	Total Assets ($mil)	Capital ($mil)	Net Premium ($mil)	Net Income ($mil)
3-09	A	5.43	3.75	N/A	339.7	173.3	28.9	2.3
3-08	A-	6.12	4.08	N/A	344.8	182.1	26.6	2.1
2008	A	5.41	3.68	80.3	337.0	176.1	118.8	1.6
2007	A-	6.04	3.99	81.7	335.9	181.8	111.8	9.9
2006	B+	5.80	3.74	62.8	326.6	176.7	112.0	21.6
2005	B+	5.44	3.50	67.3	297.5	153.1	101.7	16.2
2004	B+	4.52	2.94	67.5	266.3	134.8	99.7	14.0

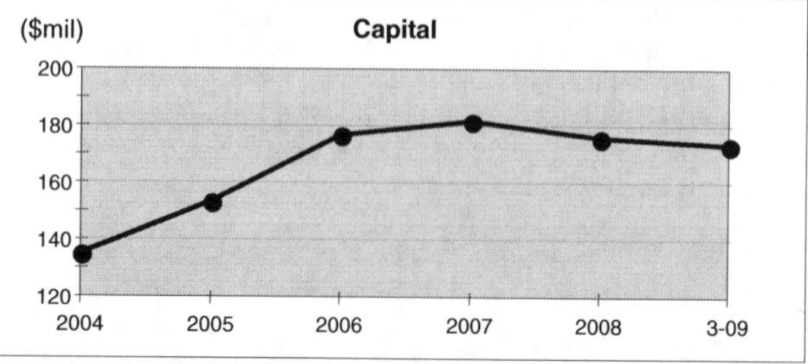

MT HAWLEY INS CO C+ Fair

Major Rating Factors: Fair overall results on stability tests (4.3 on a scale of 0 to 10). Strengths include potential support from affiliation with RLI Corp. The largest net exposure for one risk is conservative at 1.5% of capital. Good liquidity (6.9) with sufficient resources (cash flows and marketable investments) to handle a spike in claims.

Other Rating Factors: Strong long-term capitalization index (7.3) based on excellent current risk adjusted capital (severe and moderate loss scenarios). Moreover, capital levels have been consistent in recent years. Ample reserve history (9.5) that helps to protect the company against sharp claims increases. Excellent profitability (8.7) with operating gains in each of the last five years. Return on equity has been good over the last five years, averaging 14.0%.

Principal Business: Other liability (56%), allied lines (14%), fire (10%), inland marine (9%), earthquake (8%), and products liability (3%).

Principal Investments: Investment grade bonds (80%) and misc. investments (20%).

Investments in Affiliates: 7%

Group Affiliation: RLI Corp

Licensed in: IL

Commenced Business: December 1979

Address: 9025 N Lindbergh Dr, Peoria, IL 61615

Phone: (309) 692-1000 **Domicile State:** IL **NAIC Code:** 37974

Data Date	Rating	RACR #1	RACR #2	Loss Ratio %	Total Assets ($mil)	Capital ($mil)	Net Premium ($mil)	Net Income ($mil)
3-09	C+	2.25	1.55	N/A	1,050.6	471.7	57.6	15.3
3-08	C+	1.72	0.99	N/A	1,047.2	454.6	71.7	19.0
2008	C+	2.16	1.49	49.2	1,052.3	470.1	238.6	46.2
2007	C+	1.73	1.00	33.6	1,040.4	454.2	284.9	104.6
2006	C+	1.57	0.92	50.2	1,024.7	416.4	321.5	59.1
2005	C+	1.78	1.22	50.1	940.3	367.1	277.8	55.8
2004	C+	1.53	1.18	64.7	787.8	309.1	266.9	25.2

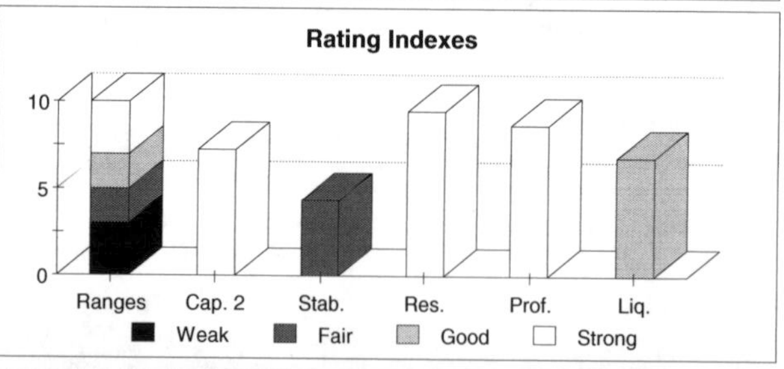

MUNICH REINSURANCE AMERICA INC C Fair

Major Rating Factors: Fair overall results on stability tests (3.7 on a scale of 0 to 10) including potential drain of affiliation with Munich Re America Corp. The largest net exposure for one risk is high at 3.2% of capital. Weak profitability index (2.9) with operating losses during 2005 and the first three months of 2008. Average return on equity over the last five years has been poor at -3.2%.

Other Rating Factors: History of adequate reserve strength (5.0) as reserves have been consistently at an acceptable level. Strong long-term capitalization index (7.4) based on excellent current risk adjusted capital (severe and moderate loss scenarios), despite some fluctuation in capital levels. Excellent liquidity (7.3) with ample operational cash flow and liquid investments.

Principal Business: Surety (85%), other liability (15%), and auto liability (1%).

Principal Investments: Investment grade bonds (99%) and real estate (1%).

Investments in Affiliates: 0%

Group Affiliation: Munich Re America Corp

Licensed in: All states, the District of Columbia and Puerto Rico

Commenced Business: April 1917

Address: 555 College Rd E, Princeton, NJ 08543

Phone: (609) 243-4200 **Domicile State:** DE **NAIC Code:** 10227

Data Date	Rating	RACR #1	RACR #2	Loss Ratio %	Total Assets ($mil)	Capital ($mil)	Net Premium ($mil)	Net Income ($mil)
3-09	C	1.87	1.19	N/A	15,783.4	3,299.2	582.6	-176.5
3-08	C	2.91	1.84	N/A	17,125.9	4,470.2	525.2	287.4
2008	C	2.07	1.33	78.6	16,355.2	3,546.6	2,290.0	-2.8
2007	C	2.84	1.81	68.1	17,948.0	4,321.6	2,298.0	456.5
2006	C	2.48	1.61	68.7	17,207.2	3,773.9	2,523.0	615.8
2005	D+	4.70	2.66	77.0	17,160.8	3,041.4	-4,747.2	-1,401.0
2004	C-	1.00	0.60	95.5	15,486.1	3,304.7	1,819.3	259.0

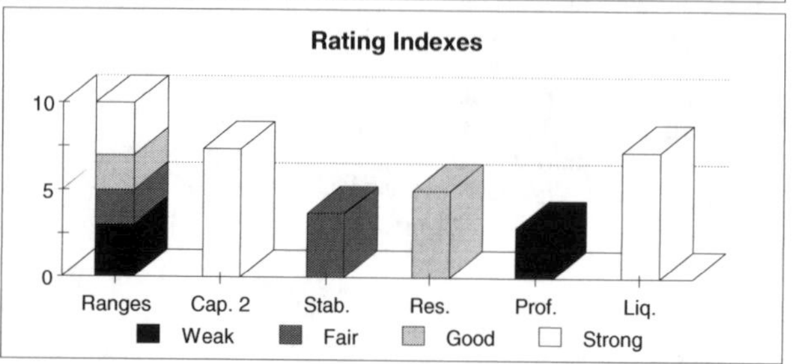

MUTUAL INS CO OF AZ * A- Excellent

Major Rating Factors: Strong long-term capitalization index (9.1 on a scale of 0 to 10) based on excellent current risk adjusted capital (severe and moderate loss scenarios). Furthermore, this high level of risk adjusted capital has been consistently maintained in previous years. Ample reserve history (7.1) that can protect against increases in claims costs.

Other Rating Factors: Excellent profitability (8.0) with operating gains in each of the last five years. Excellent liquidity (7.5) with ample operational cash flow and liquid investments. Excellent overall results on stability tests (7.0). Stability strengths include good operational trends and excellent risk diversification.

Principal Business: Medical malpractice (100%).

Principal Investments: Investment grade bonds (97%) and misc. investments (3%).

Investments in Affiliates: None

Group Affiliation: None

Licensed in: AZ, CO, NM, UT

Commenced Business: March 1976

Address: 2602 East Thomas Rd, Phoenix, AZ 85016

Phone: (602) 808-2173 **Domicile State:** AZ **NAIC Code:** 32832

Data Date	Rating	RACR #1	RACR #2	Loss Ratio %	Total Assets ($mil)	Capital ($mil)	Net Premium ($mil)	Net Income ($mil)
3-09	A-	3.41	2.84	N/A	891.6	356.2	35.4	8.1
3-08	B+	2.53	2.11	N/A	885.4	309.0	37.8	6.3
2008	A-	3.49	2.92	29.6	914.2	351.5	149.2	64.9
2007	B+	2.63	2.21	56.8	909.5	306.9	162.5	35.2
2006	B+	2.01	1.56	72.8	847.2	268.7	159.7	31.0
2005	B+	1.72	1.33	98.2	758.2	235.0	173.4	3.8
2004	B+	2.04	1.64	105.2	670.6	235.0	136.1	4.6

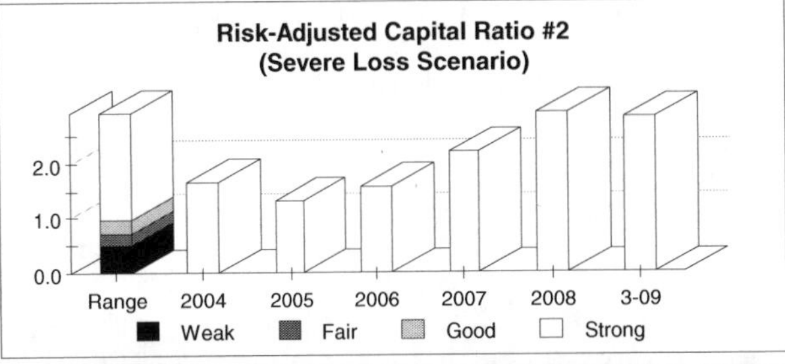

MUTUAL OF ENUMCLAW INS CO B Good

Major Rating Factors: Good liquidity (6.2 on a scale of 0 to 10) with sufficient resources (cash flows and marketable investments) to handle a spike in claims. Good overall results on stability tests (5.4).

Other Rating Factors: Fair reserve development (4.5) as reserves have generally been sufficient to cover claims. In 2004, the two year reserve development was 20% deficient. Strong long-term capitalization index (8.2) based on excellent current risk adjusted capital (severe and moderate loss scenarios), despite some fluctuation in capital levels. Excellent profitability (8.0) with operating gains in each of the last five years.

Principal Business: Auto liability (32%), homeowners multiple peril (22%), auto physical damage (18%), commercial multiple peril (12%), farmowners multiple peril (7%), other liability (3%), and other lines (5%).

Principal Investments: Investment grade bonds (92%), misc. investments (4%), cash (3%), and real estate (1%).

Investments in Affiliates: 2%

Group Affiliation: Enumclaw Ins Group

Licensed in: AZ, ID, NV, OR, UT, WA

Commenced Business: March 1898

Address: 1460 Wells St, Enumclaw, WA 98022

Phone: (360) 825-2591 **Domicile State:** WA **NAIC Code:** 14761

Data Date	Rating	RACR #1	RACR #2	Loss Ratio %	Total Assets ($mil)	Capital ($mil)	Net Premium ($mil)	Net Income ($mil)
3-09	B	2.85	1.90	N/A	533.6	207.5	77.7	4.6
3-08	B-	2.52	1.69	N/A	548.2	212.1	75.1	3.9
2008	B	2.77	1.81	64.9	539.7	204.7	311.3	9.7
2007	B-	2.50	1.66	65.3	554.3	210.9	303.8	19.9
2006	B-	2.20	1.43	68.9	528.5	192.2	287.1	16.2
2005	B-	2.13	1.40	59.9	515.1	185.4	281.0	22.7
2004	B-	1.88	1.23	67.1	481.8	161.5	276.2	10.4

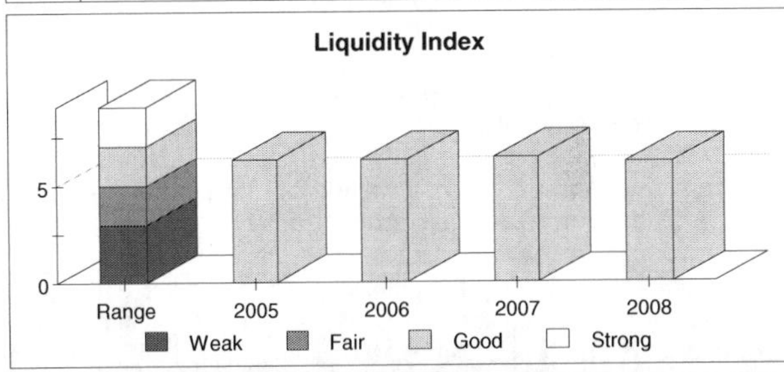

NATIONAL CASUALTY CO * B+ Good

Major Rating Factors: History of adequate reserve strength (5.0 on a scale of 0 to 10) as reserves have been consistently at an acceptable level. Good overall profitability index (6.9). Fair expense controls. Return on equity has been low, averaging 3.5% over the past five years.

Other Rating Factors: Good overall results on stability tests (6.4) despite negative cash flow from operations for 2008. Stability strengths include good operational trends and excellent risk diversification. Strong long-term capitalization index (10.0) based on excellent current risk adjusted capital (severe and moderate loss scenarios), despite some fluctuation in capital levels. Superior liquidity (10.0) with ample operational cash flow and liquid investments.

Principal Business: Other liability (43%), auto liability (30%), auto physical damage (7%), ocean marine (4%), commercial multiple peril (3%), fire (2%), and other lines (11%).

Principal Investments: Investment grade bonds (85%), misc. investments (14%), and cash (1%).

Investments in Affiliates: None

Group Affiliation: Nationwide Corp

Licensed in: All states except PR

Commenced Business: December 1904

Address: 8877 N Gainey Center Dr, Scottsdale, AZ 85258-2108

Phone: (602) 948-0505 **Domicile State:** WI **NAIC Code:** 11991

Data Date	Rating	RACR #1	RACR #2	Loss Ratio %	Total Assets ($mil)	Capital ($mil)	Net Premium ($mil)	Net Income ($mil)
3-09	B+	20.19	18.17	N/A	144.3	107.5	0.0	1.4
3-08	B+	14.02	12.62	N/A	169.3	104.2	0.0	0.7
2008	B+	19.61	17.65	0.0	144.4	106.6	0.0	3.1
2007	B+	12.64	11.38	0.0	185.5	103.6	0.0	3.3
2006	B+	14.24	12.82	0.0	156.7	100.3	0.0	3.6
2005	B+	53.96	48.56	0.0	103.0	96.6	0.0	3.5
2004	B+	55.21	38.43	0.0	98.9	93.1	0.0	3.4

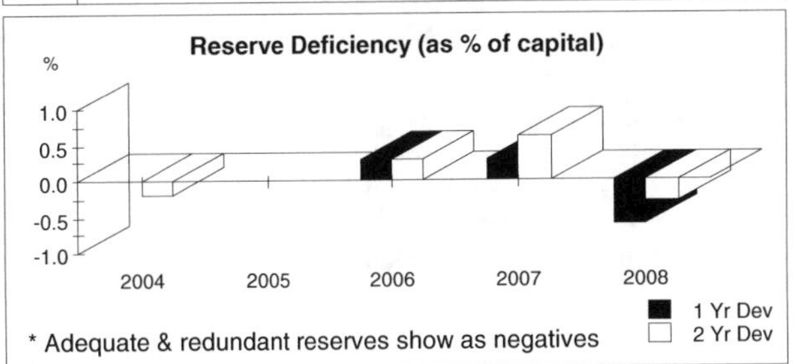

NATIONAL FIRE & MARINE INS CO — C — Fair

Major Rating Factors: Fair profitability index (4.0 on a scale of 0 to 10) with operating losses during the first three months of 2008. Return on equity has been fair, averaging 16.1% over the past five years. Fair overall results on stability tests (4.1). The largest net exposure for one risk is high at 4.0% of capital.

Other Rating Factors: Strong long-term capitalization index (8.5) based on excellent current risk adjusted capital (severe and moderate loss scenarios), despite some fluctuation in capital levels. Ample reserve history (7.5) that can protect against increases in claims costs. Excellent liquidity (7.6) with ample operational cash flow and liquid investments.

Principal Business: Commercial multiple peril (36%), other liability (20%), aircraft (19%), medical malpractice (13%), auto liability (4%), allied lines (3%), and other lines (5%).

Principal Investments: Misc. investments (85%), non investment grade bonds (9%), investment grade bonds (4%), and cash (2%).

Investments in Affiliates: 8%

Group Affiliation: Berkshire-Hathaway

Licensed in: NE

Commenced Business: January 1950

Address: 3024 Harney St, Omaha, NE 68131

Phone: (402) 536-3000 **Domicile State:** NE **NAIC Code:** 20079

Data Date	Rating	RACR #1	RACR #2	Loss Ratio %	Total Assets ($mil)	Capital ($mil)	Net Premium ($mil)	Net Income ($mil)
3-09	C	2.46	1.63	N/A	3,829.2	2,488.0	58.3	-48.4
3-08	C	3.20	2.12	N/A	5,387.5	3,550.5	125.2	72.5
2008	C	3.17	2.09	70.1	4,680.6	3,102.4	282.8	208.9
2007	C	3.24	2.14	28.1	5,665.9	3,699.2	503.4	478.0
2006	C	2.89	1.86	39.2	5,054.8	3,095.5	606.2	245.1
2005	B	4.49	2.90	27.7	5,226.2	3,592.5	356.1	1,979.9
2004	B	1.81	1.52	66.9	5,078.7	3,506.2	378.2	129.8

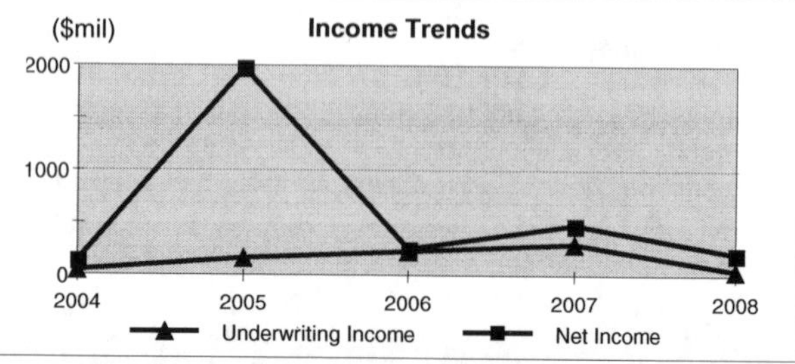

NATIONAL INDEMNITY CO — C+ — Fair

Major Rating Factors: Fair overall results on stability tests (4.3 on a scale of 0 to 10) including excessive premium growth and fair risk adjusted capital in prior years. The largest net exposure for one risk is excessive at 6.3% of capital. Strengths include potentially strong support from affiliation with Berkshire-Hathaway. Fair long-term capitalization index (3.0) based on weak current risk adjusted capital (severe and moderate loss scenarios), although results have slipped from the fair range during the last year.

Other Rating Factors: Fair reserve development (3.9) as the level of reserves has at times been insufficient to cover claims. In 2005 and 2006 the two year reserve development was 21% and 22% deficient respectively. Fair profitability index (3.7) with operating losses during the first three months of 2008. Return on equity has been fair, averaging 8.2% over the past five years. Good liquidity (6.8) with sufficient resources (cash flows and marketable investments) to handle a spike in claims.

Principal Business: Aircraft (43%), auto liability (27%), auto physical damage (10%), other liability (7%), surety (6%), commercial multiple peril (4%), and other lines (4%).

Principal Investments: Misc. investments (88%), investment grade bonds (9%), cash (2%), and non investment grade bonds (1%).

Investments in Affiliates: 31%

Group Affiliation: Berkshire-Hathaway

Licensed in: All states except HI, MA, NJ, NY, PR

Commenced Business: May 1940

Data Date	Rating	RACR #1	RACR #2	Loss Ratio %	Total Assets ($mil)	Capital ($mil)	Net Premium ($mil)	Net Income ($mil)
3-09	C+	0.62	0.49	N/A	59,159.5	24,111.0	1,294.0	-2,172.9
3-08	B	1.17	0.88	N/A	73,327.8	34,791.4	970.6	356.8
2008	B-	0.72	0.56	64.1	61,719.5	27,613.1	5,171.8	1,089.1
2007	B	1.17	0.88	46.3	74,163.5	35,582.0	4,237.0	3,999.2
2006	B	1.10	0.83	46.4	67,168.0	35,562.6	4,832.4	6,770.3
2005	B	0.72	0.56	112.5	62,010.6	28,720.4	8,822.5	2,809.8
2004	B+	1.43	1.09	49.9	50,959.6	27,224.8	2,808.6	2,186.0

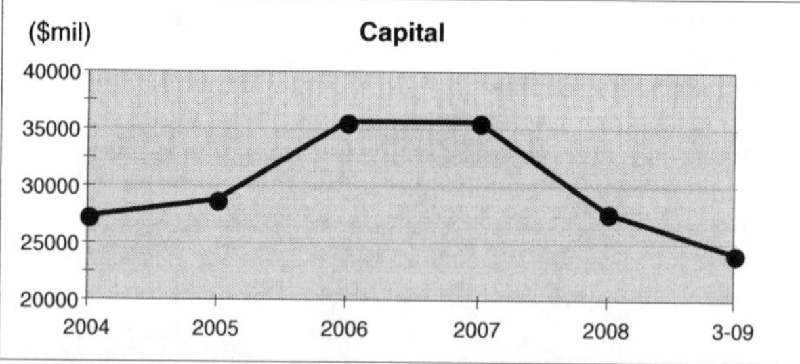

NATIONAL INTERSTATE INS CO — C+ — Fair

Major Rating Factors: Fair overall results on stability tests (4.7 on a scale of 0 to 10) including potential drain of affiliation with American Financial Corp. Strong long-term capitalization index (9.2) based on excellent current risk adjusted capital (severe and moderate loss scenarios), despite some fluctuation in capital levels.

Other Rating Factors: Ample reserve history (8.2) that helps to protect the company against sharp claims increases. Excellent profitability (8.8) with operating gains in each of the last five years. Return on equity has been excellent over the last five years averaging 17.6%. Excellent liquidity (7.3) with ample operational cash flow and liquid investments.

Principal Business: Auto liability (56%), auto physical damage (19%), workers compensation (13%), other liability (7%), and inland marine (4%).

Principal Investments: Investment grade bonds (75%), misc. investments (23%), and real estate (3%).

Investments in Affiliates: 4%

Group Affiliation: American Financial Corp

Licensed in: All states except PR

Commenced Business: March 1989

Address: 3250 Interstate Drive, Richfield, OH 44286

Phone: (800) 929-1500 **Domicile State:** OH **NAIC Code:** 32620

Data Date	Rating	RACR #1	RACR #2	Loss Ratio %	Total Assets ($mil)	Capital ($mil)	Net Premium ($mil)	Net Income ($mil)
3-09	C+	3.87	2.54	N/A	740.4	186.6	51.7	7.2
3-08	C+	3.70	2.39	N/A	757.7	184.6	50.8	4.9
2008	C+	3.93	2.60	59.3	730.1	190.1	217.9	7.6
2007	C+	3.81	2.48	50.7	694.7	182.3	203.6	37.7
2006	C+	3.26	2.06	56.1	631.5	148.3	185.6	26.6
2005	C+	2.37	1.79	55.5	384.9	122.8	172.2	29.3
2004	C+	4.11	2.51	55.3	297.9	92.1	141.0	20.5

American Financial Corp Composite Group Rating: B- Largest Group Members	Assets ($mil)	Rating
GREAT AMERICAN LIFE INS CO	9628	B-
GREAT AMERICAN INS CO	5642	C
ANNUITY INVESTORS LIFE INS CO	1742	B-
REPUBLIC INDEMNITY CO OF AMERICA	858	B-
NATIONAL INTERSTATE INS CO	730	C+

NATIONAL LIABILITY & FIRE INS CO * A- Excellent

Major Rating Factors: Strong long-term capitalization index (8.2 on a scale of 0 to 10) based on excellent current risk adjusted capital (severe and moderate loss scenarios), despite some fluctuation in capital levels. Ample reserve history (9.3) that helps to protect the company against sharp claims increases.

Other Rating Factors: Superior liquidity (9.0) with ample operational cash flow and liquid investments. Good overall profitability index (6.9). Good expense controls. Return on equity has been excellent over the last five years averaging 19.1%. Good overall results on stability tests (5.5). The largest net exposure for one risk is high at 3.9% of capital. Stability strengths include good operational trends and excellent risk diversification.

Principal Business: Ocean marine (48%), aircraft (18%), auto liability (15%), workers compensation (12%), and auto physical damage (5%).

Principal Investments: Cash (35%), investment grade bonds (30%), non investment grade bonds (20%), and misc. investments (15%).

Investments in Affiliates: None

Group Affiliation: Berkshire-Hathaway

Licensed in: All states except MA, NH, PR

Commenced Business: December 1958

Address: 100 First Stamford Place, Stamford, CT 68131-3580

Phone: (402) 536-3000 **Domicile State:** CT **NAIC Code:** 20052

Data Date	Rating	RACR #1	RACR #2	Loss Ratio %	Total Assets ($mil)	Capital ($mil)	Net Premium ($mil)	Net Income ($mil)
3-09	A-	5.03	2.26	N/A	1,040.7	499.0	69.9	2.4
3-08	A-	5.21	2.49	N/A	1,199.2	630.8	57.6	10.2
2008	A-	5.06	2.40	43.3	1,055.7	546.7	190.4	79.5
2007	A-	4.97	2.43	47.3	1,203.1	629.2	286.3	103.8
2006	B+	3.52	2.41	47.2	1,155.4	496.7	439.8	115.2
2005	B+	2.72	1.80	57.9	883.0	306.7	294.1	101.5
2004	B+	2.54	1.73	39.9	654.8	278.8	158.9	35.0

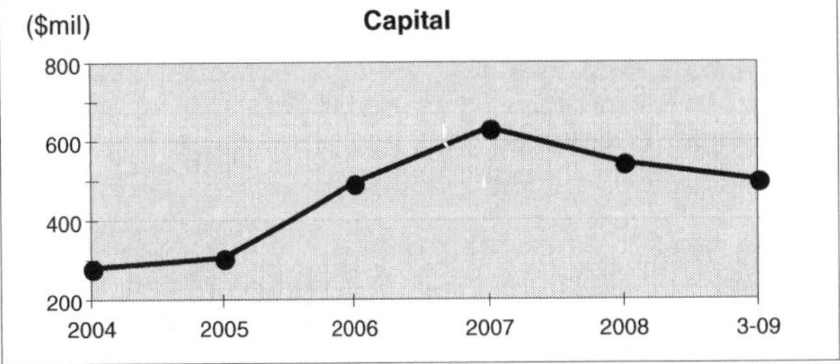

NATIONAL SURETY CORP C Fair

Major Rating Factors: Fair overall results on stability tests (4.3 on a scale of 0 to 10). History of adequate reserve strength (5.5) as reserves have been consistently at an acceptable level.

Other Rating Factors: Good liquidity (6.4) with sufficient resources (cash flows and marketable investments) to handle a spike in claims. Strong long-term capitalization index (7.4) based on excellent current risk adjusted capital (severe and moderate loss scenarios), despite some fluctuation in capital levels. Excellent profitability (8.6) with operating gains in each of the last five years. Return on equity has been good over the last five years, averaging 14.5%.

Principal Business: Commercial multiple peril (54%), other liability (19%), homeowners multiple peril (11%), workers compensation (4%), auto liability (3%), products liability (2%), and other lines (7%).

Principal Investments: Investment grade bonds (96%) and misc. investments (4%).

Investments in Affiliates: None

Group Affiliation: Allianz Ins Group

Licensed in: All states, the District of Columbia and Puerto Rico

Commenced Business: October 1970

Address: 777 San Marin Drive, Novato, CA 94998

Phone: (312) 441-5400 **Domicile State:** IL **NAIC Code:** 21881

Data Date	Rating	RACR #1	RACR #2	Loss Ratio %	Total Assets ($mil)	Capital ($mil)	Net Premium ($mil)	Net Income ($mil)
3-09	C	2.04	1.41	N/A	624.0	231.1	43.3	6.9
3-08	C	1.91	1.24	N/A	584.7	223.4	41.2	8.0
2008	C	2.02	1.39	75.0	622.3	232.3	191.6	15.7
2007	C	1.84	1.19	62.0	585.4	219.0	186.0	36.8
2006	C	1.56	1.01	58.0	553.5	189.7	183.4	39.7
2005	C	1.50	0.92	66.7	515.0	170.0	171.8	24.9
2004	C	1.36	0.82	66.0	465.1	143.1	168.4	19.9

Allianz Ins Group
Composite Group Rating: C+

Largest Group Members	Assets ($mil)	Rating
ALLIANZ LIFE INS CO OF NORTH AMERICA	66375	B-
FIREMANS FUND INS CO	10673	C
ALLIANZ GLOBAL RISKS US INS CO	4846	C+
AMERICAN INS CO	1449	B-
ALLIANZ LIFE INS CO OF NY	881	C

NATIONAL UNION FIRE INS CO OF PITTSB B Good

Major Rating Factors: Good overall results on stability tests (5.4 on a scale of 0 to 10). Strengths include potentially strong support from affiliation with American International Group, good operational trends and excellent risk diversification. Good long-term capitalization index (6.2) based on good current risk adjusted capital (moderate loss scenario), despite some fluctuation in capital levels.

Other Rating Factors: Good liquidity (6.6) with sufficient resources (cash flows and marketable investments) to handle a spike in claims. Excellent profitability (7.1) with operating gains in each of the last five years. A history of deficient reserves (2.9). Underreserving can have an adverse impact on capital and profits. Deficiencies in the two year reserve development occurred in three of the previous five years and ranged between 27% and 48%.

Principal Business: Other liability (45%), group accident & health (15%), workers compensation (13%), auto liability (6%), inland marine (5%), aircraft (4%), and other lines (13%).

Principal Investments: Investment grade bonds (51%) and misc. investments (49%).

Investments in Affiliates: 32%

Group Affiliation: American International Group

Licensed in: All states, the District of Columbia and Puerto Rico

Commenced Business: March 1901

Address: 70 Pine St 22 Fl, New York, NY 10270

Phone: (212) 770-8596 **Domicile State:** PA **NAIC Code:** 19445

Data Date	Rating	RACR #1	RACR #2	Loss Ratio %	Total Assets ($mil)	Capital ($mil)	Net Premium ($mil)	Net Income ($mil)
3-09	B	1.27	1.08	N/A	33,210.5	11,993.7	1,591.7	164.6
3-08	B	1.29	1.08	N/A	34,236.3	12,311.5	1,769.6	324.9
2008	B	1.25	1.07	78.1	33,706.8	11,825.4	6,579.2	1,369.7
2007	B	1.28	1.08	69.6	34,575.4	12,157.0	7,776.6	1,284.9
2006	B	1.22	1.00	71.1	31,667.5	10,420.2	7,813.8	1,120.9
2005	B	1.08	0.88	90.2	28,761.7	8,120.2	7,087.0	131.9
2004	B+	1.22	0.99	86.4	25,702.2	7,376.8	7,029.3	326.4

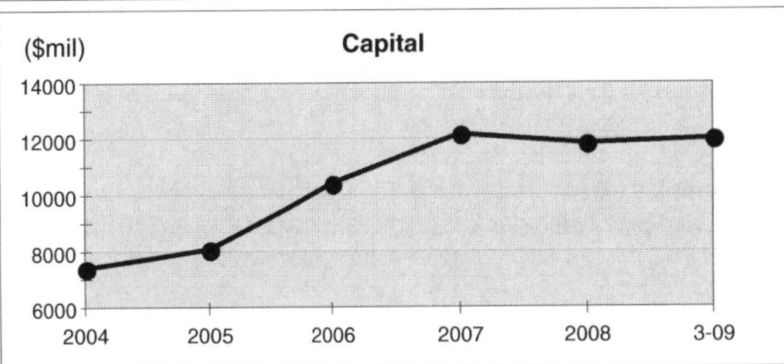

NATIONWIDE INDEMNITY CO — C+ Fair

Major Rating Factors: Fair overall results on stability tests (4.5 on a scale of 0 to 10) including excessive premium growth, weak risk adjusted capital in prior years, weak results on operational trends and negative cash flow from operations for 2008. Strengths include potentially strong support from affiliation with Nationwide Corp. Fair profitability index (3.9) with operating losses during 2004 and 2005. Average return on equity over the last five years has been poor at -14.1%.

Other Rating Factors: Poor long-term capitalization index (0.4) based on weak current risk adjusted capital (severe and moderate loss scenarios). A history of deficient reserves (0.5). Underreserving can have an adverse impact on capital and profits. In the last five years, reserves (two year development) fluctuated between 190% and 108% deficeint. Superior liquidity (9.5) with ample operational cash flow and liquid investments.

Principal Business: (This company is a reinsurer.)

Principal Investments: Investment grade bonds (88%), misc. investments (10%), and non investment grade bonds (2%).

Investments in Affiliates: None

Group Affiliation: Nationwide Corp

Licensed in: IL, IA, NY, OH

Commenced Business: April 1994

Address: One Nationwide Plaza, Columbus, OH 43216

Phone: (614) 249-3004 **Domicile State:** OH **NAIC Code:** 10070

Data Date	Rating	RACR #1	RACR #2	Loss Ratio %	Total Assets ($mil)	Capital ($mil)	Net Premium ($mil)	Net Income ($mil)
3-09	C+	0.20	0.16	N/A	3,670.8	850.1	0.9	50.9
3-08	C+	0.16	0.13	N/A	3,743.7	808.0	0.1	12.0
2008	C+	0.19	0.16	N/A	3,679.8	834.1	1.4	28.9
2007	C+	0.15	0.13	N/A	3,729.6	780.4	2.4	13.0
2006	C+	0.15	0.12	N/A	3,718.6	785.4	-0.2	2.8
2005	C	0.13	0.10	N/A	3,849.1	765.4	3.5	-351.9
2004	C	0.16	0.12	N/A	3,347.5	722.3	5.0	-285.1

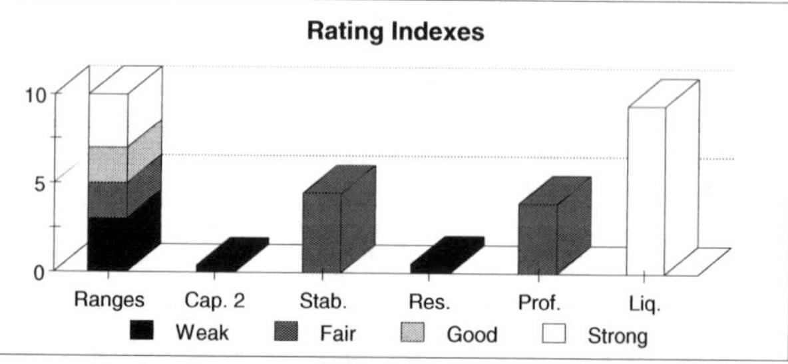

NATIONWIDE INS CO OF FLORIDA — C+ Fair

Major Rating Factors: Fair overall results on stability tests (4.5 on a scale of 0 to 10) including negative cash flow from operations for 2008. Strengths include potentially strong support from affiliation with Nationwide Corp. The largest net exposure for one risk is conservative at 2.0% of capital. Fair reserve development (4.2) as reserves have generally been sufficient to cover claims. In 2005, the one year reserve development was 41% deficient.

Other Rating Factors: Good long-term capitalization index (5.4) based on good current risk adjusted capital (moderate loss scenario), despite some fluctuation in capital levels. Good liquidity (6.7) with sufficient resources (cash flows and marketable investments) to handle a spike in claims. Weak profitability index (2.8) with operating losses during 2004, 2005 and 2007. Average return on equity over the last five years has been poor at -48.1%.

Principal Business: Homeowners multiple peril (95%) and inland marine (4%).

Principal Investments: Investment grade bonds (91%), misc. investments (8%), and non investment grade bonds (1%).

Investments in Affiliates: None

Group Affiliation: Nationwide Corp

Licensed in: FL, OH

Commenced Business: August 1998

Address: One Nationwide Plaza, Columbus, OH 43216

Phone: (614) 249-9585 **Domicile State:** OH **NAIC Code:** 10948

Data Date	Rating	RACR #1	RACR #2	Loss Ratio %	Total Assets ($mil)	Capital ($mil)	Net Premium ($mil)	Net Income ($mil)
3-09	C+	1.61	1.16	N/A	436.1	263.0	31.4	10.1
3-08	C+	0.97	0.68	N/A	454.0	251.2	34.8	19.2
2008	C+	1.48	1.07	92.9	429.8	249.3	104.7	27.6
2007	C+	0.98	0.68	66.1	601.0	238.6	131.8	-12.2
2006	C+	0.47	0.41	35.2	584.4	246.1	192.3	54.8
2005	C+	0.26	0.22	128.3	612.2	188.4	259.0	-94.6
2004	C	0.25	0.21	327.9	449.7	133.5	209.5	-313.2

Nationwide Corp
Composite Group Rating: B+

Largest Group Members	Assets ($mil)	Rating
NATIONWIDE LIFE INS CO	77310	B+
NATIONWIDE MUTUAL INS CO	28843	B
NATIONWIDE LIFE INS CO OF AMERICA	4994	B+
NATIONWIDE LIFE ANNUITY INS CO	4349	B
NATIONWIDE MUTUAL FIRE INS CO	4319	B+

NATIONWIDE MUTUAL FIRE INS CO * — B+ Good

Major Rating Factors: Good overall results on stability tests (6.4 on a scale of 0 to 10). Stability strengths include good operational trends and excellent risk diversification. History of adequate reserve strength (6.2) as reserves have been consistently at an acceptable level.

Other Rating Factors: Good liquidity (6.3) with sufficient resources (cash flows and marketable investments) to handle a spike in claims. Strong long-term capitalization index (10.0) based on excellent current risk adjusted capital (severe and moderate loss scenarios), despite some fluctuation in capital levels. Excellent profitability (7.8) with operating gains in each of the last five years.

Principal Business: Homeowners multiple peril (44%), auto liability (24%), auto physical damage (14%), allied lines (6%), commercial multiple peril (5%), fire (2%), and other lines (5%).

Principal Investments: Investment grade bonds (78%), misc. investments (20%), and non investment grade bonds (2%).

Investments in Affiliates: 5%

Group Affiliation: Nationwide Corp

Licensed in: All states except PR

Commenced Business: April 1934

Address: One Nationwide Plaza, Columbus, OH 43216

Phone: (614) 249-3004 **Domicile State:** OH **NAIC Code:** 23779

Data Date	Rating	RACR #1	RACR #2	Loss Ratio %	Total Assets ($mil)	Capital ($mil)	Net Premium ($mil)	Net Income ($mil)
3-09	B+	4.84	3.55	N/A	4,143.4	1,986.0	424.4	30.3
3-08	B+	5.20	3.81	N/A	4,310.3	2,127.2	431.9	66.9
2008	B+	5.11	3.76	74.7	4,318.7	2,109.4	1,725.8	124.9
2007	B+	5.01	3.68	64.5	4,330.9	2,060.6	1,756.4	197.4
2006	B+	3.77	2.72	60.7	4,219.1	1,912.5	1,762.0	243.6
2005	B+	3.55	2.55	65.8	4,591.4	1,673.4	1,672.8	148.9
2004	B+	3.19	2.29	64.5	4,279.3	1,490.7	1,582.8	188.6

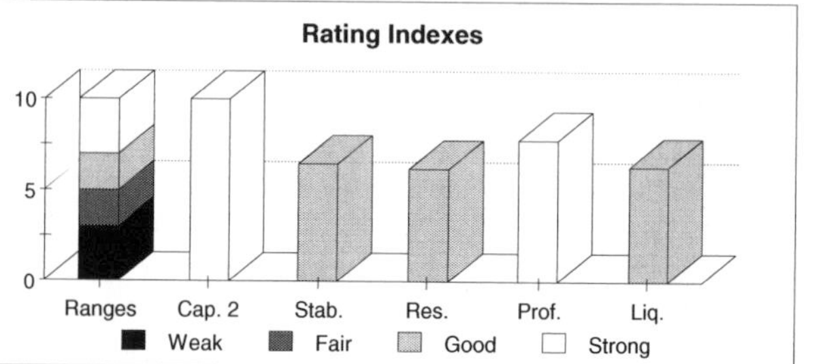

NATIONWIDE MUTUAL INS CO — B — Good

Major Rating Factors: History of adequate reserve strength (6.3 on a scale of 0 to 10) as reserves have been consistently at an acceptable level. Good overall profitability index (6.2). Fair expense controls.

Other Rating Factors: Good liquidity (5.8) with sufficient resources (cash flows and marketable investments) to handle a spike in claims. Good overall results on stability tests (5.4). Stability strengths include good operational trends and excellent risk diversification. Strong long-term capitalization index (7.5) based on excellent current risk adjusted capital (severe and moderate loss scenarios), despite some fluctuation in capital levels.

Principal Business: Auto liability (46%), auto physical damage (29%), commercial multiple peril (7%), homeowners multiple peril (4%), farmowners multiple peril (4%), other liability (4%), and other lines (5%).

Principal Investments: Misc. investments (52%), investment grade bonds (42%), non investment grade bonds (4%), and real estate (3%).

Investments in Affiliates: 27%

Group Affiliation: Nationwide Corp

Licensed in: All states except NJ, PR

Commenced Business: April 1926

Address: One Nationwide Plaza, Columbus, OH 43216

Phone: (614) 249-7111 **Domicile State:** OH **NAIC Code:** 23787

Data Date	Rating	RACR #1	RACR #2	Loss Ratio %	Total Assets ($mil)	Capital ($mil)	Net Premium ($mil)	Net Income ($mil)
3-09	B	1.17	1.02	N/A	25,410.2	7,633.1	3,143.4	85.9
3-08	B	1.75	1.50	N/A	28,893.0	11,512.5	3,198.8	277.2
2008	B	1.66	1.45	74.7	28,842.8	10,886.5	12,783.2	562.9
2007	B	1.72	1.48	64.3	29,520.7	11,361.5	13,052.8	813.4
2006	B-	1.39	1.22	60.8	28,374.8	10,806.0	13,057.7	1,080.5
2005	B-	1.21	1.05	65.8	26,282.4	8,265.8	12,391.0	652.2
2004	B-	1.15	0.98	64.5	24,183.4	7,581.2	11,723.6	1,028.2

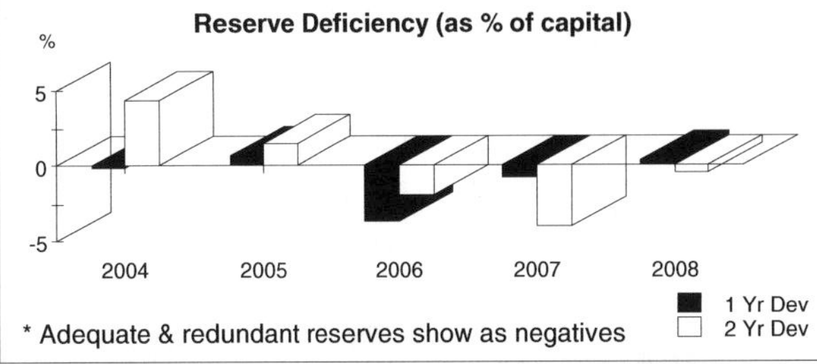

NAU COUNTRY INS CO — C- — Fair

Major Rating Factors: Vulnerable liquidity (0.9 on a scale of 0 to 10) as a spike in claims may stretch capacity. Weak overall results on stability tests (2.9) including excessive premium growth and weak results on operational trends.

Other Rating Factors: Fair long-term capitalization index (3.6) based on fair current risk adjusted capital (severe loss scenario), although results have slipped from the good range over the last two years. Fair reserve development (3.6) as reserves have generally been sufficient to cover claims. In 2005, the one year reserve development was 34% deficient. Good overall profitability index (5.3) despite operating losses during the first three months of 2008. Return on equity has been good over the last five years, averaging 29.6%.

Principal Business: Allied lines (100%).

Principal Investments: Misc. investments (56%), investment grade bonds (43%), and cash (1%).

Investments in Affiliates: None

Group Affiliation: The Lightyear Fund LP

Licensed in: AL, AZ, AR, CA, ID, IL, IN, IA, KS, KY, MI, MN, MS, MO, MT, NE, NM, ND, OH, OK, OR, PA, SC, SD, TX, WA, WI

Commenced Business: May 1919

Address: 7333 Sunwood Dr, Ramsey, MN 55303-5119

Phone: (763) 427-3770 **Domicile State:** MN **NAIC Code:** 25240

Data Date	Rating	RACR #1	RACR #2	Loss Ratio %	Total Assets ($mil)	Capital ($mil)	Net Premium ($mil)	Net Income ($mil)
3-09	C-	1.00	0.64	N/A	447.1	188.1	8.0	-8.4
3-08	C	2.49	1.55	N/A	295.9	191.9	4.3	-5.6
2008	C-	0.77	0.50	94.2	773.7	231.5	555.3	44.8
2007	C	1.34	0.85	60.9	379.9	198.3	330.1	96.7
2006	C-	0.64	0.49	66.4	269.6	121.4	192.4	51.6
2005	D+	0.52	0.46	69.4	124.7	64.3	111.1	8.6
2004	D+	0.72	0.58	85.2	35.6	17.9	36.1	6.4

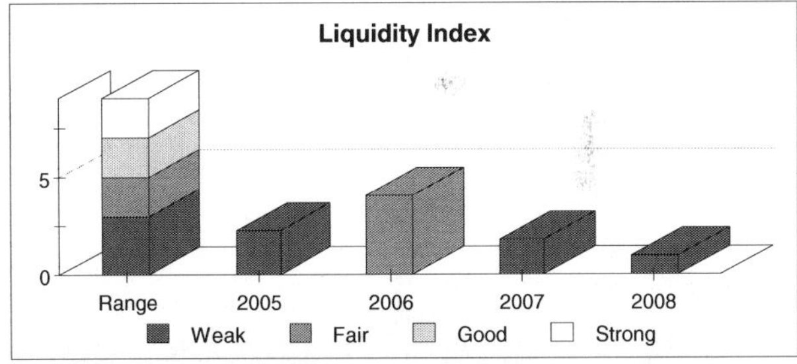

NAUTILUS INS CO — C+ — Fair

Major Rating Factors: Fair overall results on stability tests (4.3 on a scale of 0 to 10). The largest net exposure for one risk is conservative at 1.0% of capital. History of adequate reserve strength (5.9) as reserves have been consistently at an acceptable level.

Other Rating Factors: Strong long-term capitalization index (7.4) based on excellent current risk adjusted capital (severe and moderate loss scenarios), despite some fluctuation in capital levels. Excellent profitability (8.6) with operating gains in each of the last five years. Return on equity has been excellent over the last five years averaging 17.8%. Excellent liquidity (7.1) with ample operational cash flow and liquid investments.

Principal Business: Other liability (60%), products liability (19%), fire (11%), allied lines (5%), medical malpractice (4%), and inland marine (1%).

Principal Investments: Investment grade bonds (85%), misc. investments (13%), non investment grade bonds (1%), and real estate (1%).

Investments in Affiliates: 7%

Group Affiliation: W R Berkley Corp

Licensed in: AZ, NC, VA

Commenced Business: October 1985

Address: 7273 East Butherus Drive, Scottsdale, AZ 85260

Phone: (480) 951-0905 **Domicile State:** AZ **NAIC Code:** 17370

Data Date	Rating	RACR #1	RACR #2	Loss Ratio %	Total Assets ($mil)	Capital ($mil)	Net Premium ($mil)	Net Income ($mil)
3-09	C+	1.95	1.49	N/A	1,408.7	471.0	104.7	23.5
3-08	C+	1.77	1.39	N/A	1,391.1	480.8	116.2	26.3
2008	C+	1.88	1.45	44.8	1,395.4	453.4	423.8	45.9
2007	C+	1.74	1.37	45.8	1,371.0	462.3	473.4	102.5
2006	C+	1.49	1.12	52.0	1,222.5	408.8	488.8	85.4
2005	C	1.20	0.93	47.5	947.5	307.0	420.2	68.7
2004	C	0.89	0.70	51.1	664.6	201.3	325.3	26.4

W R Berkley Corp
Composite Group Rating: C

Largest Group Members	Assets ($mil)	Rating
BERKLEY INS CO	6846	C
BERKLEY REGIONAL INS CO	2665	B-
ADMIRAL INS CO	2514	C
NAUTILUS INS CO	1395	C+
CAROLINA CASUALTY INS CO	797	C

NAVIGATORS INS CO B Good

Major Rating Factors: Good overall results on stability tests (5.6 on a scale of 0 to 10) despite potential drain of affiliation with Navigators Group Inc. The largest net exposure for one risk is conservative at 1.1% of capital. Fair reserve development (4.9) as reserves have generally been sufficient to cover claims.

Other Rating Factors: Strong long-term capitalization index (8.2) based on excellent current risk adjusted capital (severe and moderate loss scenarios), despite some fluctuation in capital levels. Excellent profitability (8.6) despite modest operating losses during the first three months of 2008. Excellent liquidity (7.1) with ample operational cash flow and liquid investments.

Principal Business: Other liability (49%), ocean marine (39%), inland marine (4%), commercial multiple peril (4%), auto liability (2%), surety (2%), and auto physical damage (1%).

Principal Investments: Investment grade bonds (85%), misc. investments (12%), and cash (3%).

Investments in Affiliates: 7%

Group Affiliation: Navigators Group Inc

Licensed in: All states, the District of Columbia and Puerto Rico

Commenced Business: March 1983

Address: One Penn Plaza, 55th Floor, New York, NY 10119

Phone: (212) 349-1600 **Domicile State:** NY **NAIC Code:** 42307

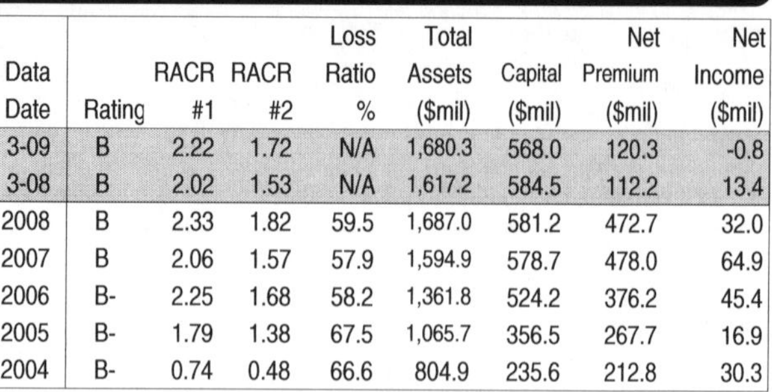

Data Date	Rating	RACR #1	RACR #2	Loss Ratio %	Total Assets ($mil)	Capital ($mil)	Net Premium ($mil)	Net Income ($mil)
3-09	B	2.22	1.72	N/A	1,680.3	568.0	120.3	-0.8
3-08	B	2.02	1.53	N/A	1,617.2	584.5	112.2	13.4
2008	B	2.33	1.82	59.5	1,687.0	581.2	472.7	32.0
2007	B	2.06	1.57	57.9	1,594.9	578.7	478.0	64.9
2006	B-	2.25	1.68	58.2	1,361.8	524.2	376.2	45.4
2005	B-	1.79	1.38	67.5	1,065.7	356.5	267.7	16.9
2004	B-	0.74	0.48	66.6	804.9	235.6	212.8	30.3

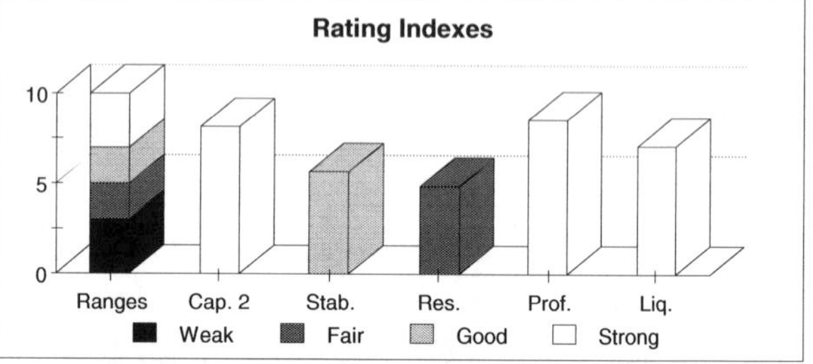

NEW HAMPSHIRE INS CO C+ Fair

Major Rating Factors: Fair overall results on stability tests (4.4 on a scale of 0 to 10) including negative cash flow from operations for 2008. Strengths include potentially strong support from affiliation with American International Group. Good long-term capitalization index (5.4) based on excellent current risk adjusted capital (severe and moderate loss scenarios), despite some fluctuation in capital levels.

Other Rating Factors: Good liquidity (6.7) with sufficient resources (cash flows and marketable investments) to handle a spike in claims. A history of deficient reserves (2.5). Underreserving can have an adverse impact on capital and profits. Deficiencies in the two year reserve development occurred in three of the previous five years and ranged between 33% and 62%. Excellent profitability (7.1) with operating gains in each of the last five years.

Principal Business: Workers compensation (62%), auto liability (12%), commercial multiple peril (7%), other liability (3%), allied lines (3%), auto physical damage (2%), and other lines (12%).

Principal Investments: Investment grade bonds (64%), misc. investments (35%), and non investment grade bonds (1%).

Investments in Affiliates: 31%

Group Affiliation: American International Group

Licensed in: All states, the District of Columbia and Puerto Rico

Commenced Business: April 1870

Address: 70 Pine Street 3rd Floor, New York, NY 10270

Phone: (212) 770-7000 **Domicile State:** PA **NAIC Code:** 23841

Data Date	Rating	RACR #1	RACR #2	Loss Ratio %	Total Assets ($mil)	Capital ($mil)	Net Premium ($mil)	Net Income ($mil)
3-09	C+	1.19	1.01	N/A	4,181.7	1,511.2	209.4	9.1
3-08	C+	1.48	1.10	N/A	4,444.2	1,390.9	232.8	22.6
2008	C+	1.28	1.09	78.1	4,585.6	1,652.1	865.7	76.5
2007	C+	1.47	1.10	69.6	4,452.3	1,369.3	1,023.2	189.8
2006	B-	1.13	0.82	71.1	4,001.2	1,029.3	1,028.1	156.5
2005	B-	1.01	0.75	90.2	3,465.5	867.1	932.5	44.0
2004	B	1.27	0.94	86.4	3,111.6	810.4	924.9	50.8

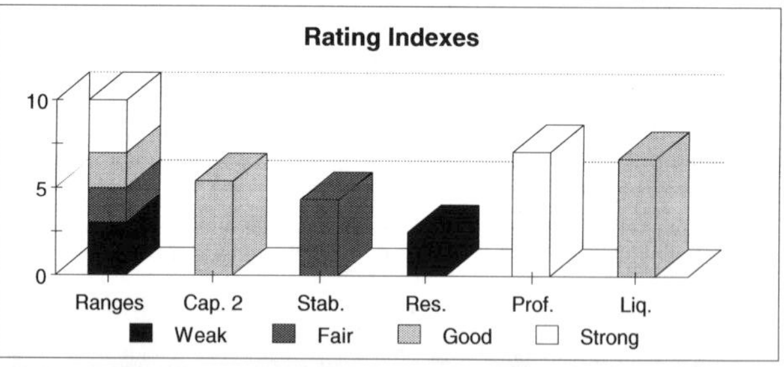

NEW JERSEY MANUFACTURERS INS CO B Good

Major Rating Factors: Good overall results on stability tests (5.7 on a scale of 0 to 10) despite potential drain of affiliation with NJ Manufacturers. Good liquidity (6.9) with sufficient resources (cash flows and marketable investments) to handle a spike in claims.

Other Rating Factors: Fair profitability index (4.8) with operating losses during the first three months of 2008. Return on equity has been low, averaging 3.0% over the past five years. Strong long-term capitalization index (8.3) based on excellent current risk adjusted capital (severe and moderate loss scenarios), despite some fluctuation in capital levels. Ample reserve history (8.6) that helps to protect the company against sharp claims increases.

Principal Business: Auto liability (39%), workers compensation (29%), auto physical damage (20%), and homeowners multiple peril (11%).

Principal Investments: Investment grade bonds (71%), misc. investments (28%), and real estate (1%).

Investments in Affiliates: 20%

Group Affiliation: NJ Manufacturers

Licensed in: CT, DE, ME, NJ, NY, PA, RI

Commenced Business: July 1913

Address: 301 Sullivan Way, West Trenton, NJ 08628

Phone: (609) 883-1300 **Domicile State:** NJ **NAIC Code:** 12122

Data Date	Rating	RACR #1	RACR #2	Loss Ratio %	Total Assets ($mil)	Capital ($mil)	Net Premium ($mil)	Net Income ($mil)
3-09	B	2.10	1.79	N/A	4,941.6	2,108.6	303.5	-16.9
3-08	B	2.28	1.95	N/A	4,956.5	2,241.2	317.1	34.0
2008	B	2.15	1.85	80.1	4,947.9	2,140.3	1,266.3	22.9
2007	B	2.28	1.96	76.4	4,911.8	2,241.0	1,283.0	53.1
2006	B	2.33	2.00	73.6	4,645.4	2,114.8	1,223.7	127.4
2005	B	2.24	1.93	83.2	4,337.2	1,920.0	1,164.3	30.3
2004	B	2.20	1.90	74.8	4,099.3	1,887.4	1,087.0	98.7

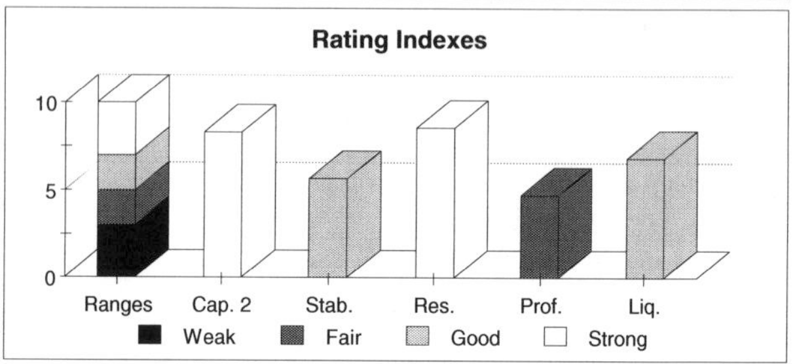

NEW JERSEY RE-INS CO — B — Good

Major Rating Factors: Good overall results on stability tests (5.5 on a scale of 0 to 10) despite potential drain of affiliation with NJ Manufacturers. Stability strengths include good operational trends and excellent risk diversification. History of adequate reserve strength (5.6) as reserves have been consistently at an acceptable level.

Other Rating Factors: Good overall profitability index (5.7) despite operating losses during 2005. Return on equity has been low, averaging 3.4% over the past five years. Strong long-term capitalization index (7.5) based on excellent current risk adjusted capital (severe and moderate loss scenarios), despite some fluctuation in capital levels. Excellent liquidity (8.2) with ample operational cash flow and liquid investments.

Principal Business: Auto liability (44%), auto physical damage (17%), workers compensation (17%), allied lines (10%), other liability (8%), homeowners multiple peril (2%), and fire (1%).

Principal Investments: Investment grade bonds (98%) and misc. investments (2%).

Investments in Affiliates: None

Group Affiliation: NJ Manufacturers

Licensed in: DE, NJ, OH, PA, WA

Commenced Business: January 1978

Address: 301 Sullivan Way, West Trenton, NJ 08628

Phone: (609) 883-1300 **Domicile State:** NJ **NAIC Code:** 35432

Data Date	Rating	RACR #1	RACR #2	Loss Ratio %	Total Assets ($mil)	Capital ($mil)	Net Premium ($mil)	Net Income ($mil)
3-09	B	2.74	1.84	N/A	1,506.3	710.5	24.3	7.2
3-08	B	2.68	1.80	N/A	1,518.8	697.5	28.7	8.8
2008	B	2.71	1.82	98.5	1,506.2	706.5	102.4	31.5
2007	B	2.65	1.79	90.8	1,523.7	693.7	121.0	53.1
2006	B-	2.20	1.51	104.6	1,509.7	642.6	187.4	26.3
2005	B-	2.25	1.55	122.9	1,448.6	615.3	192.5	-6.6
2004	B	2.65	1.80	106.5	1,366.8	621.7	201.4	11.5

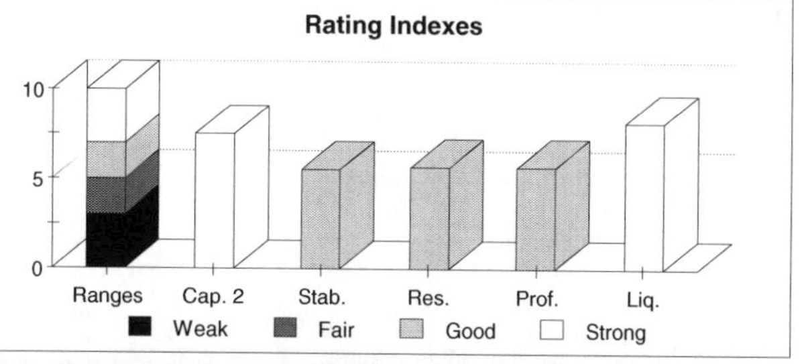

NEW YORK CENTRAL MUTUAL FIRE INS CO — B- — Good

Major Rating Factors: Fair overall results on stability tests (4.7 on a scale of 0 to 10) including potential drain of affiliation with Central Services Group. History of adequate reserve strength (5.8) as reserves have been consistently at an acceptable level.

Other Rating Factors: Good liquidity (6.3) with sufficient resources (cash flows and marketable investments) to handle a spike in claims. Strong long-term capitalization index (8.9) based on excellent current risk adjusted capital (severe and moderate loss scenarios). Moreover, capital levels have been consistent in recent years. Excellent profitability (8.7) with operating gains in each of the last five years.

Principal Business: Homeowners multiple peril (38%), auto liability (35%), auto physical damage (20%), commercial multiple peril (3%), fire (1%), other liability (1%), and allied lines (1%).

Principal Investments: Investment grade bonds (91%), misc. investments (9%), and real estate (1%).

Investments in Affiliates: 2%

Group Affiliation: Central Services Group

Licensed in: NY

Commenced Business: April 1899

Address: 1899 Central Plaza E, Edmeston, NY 13335

Phone: (607) 965-8321 **Domicile State:** NY **NAIC Code:** 14834

Data Date	Rating	RACR #1	RACR #2	Loss Ratio %	Total Assets ($mil)	Capital ($mil)	Net Premium ($mil)	Net Income ($mil)
3-09	B-	3.50	2.63	N/A	915.1	365.1	103.6	2.3
3-08	C+	3.27	2.46	N/A	926.0	359.7	103.6	10.4
2008	B-	3.32	2.55	68.1	944.4	365.7	410.8	21.8
2007	C+	3.05	2.35	68.0	945.5	355.6	420.4	25.6
2006	C+	2.69	2.11	68.1	916.9	325.1	421.3	31.0
2005	C+	2.24	1.78	67.2	900.7	290.2	451.2	31.3
2004	C+	1.88	1.55	70.2	835.4	253.7	462.0	28.2

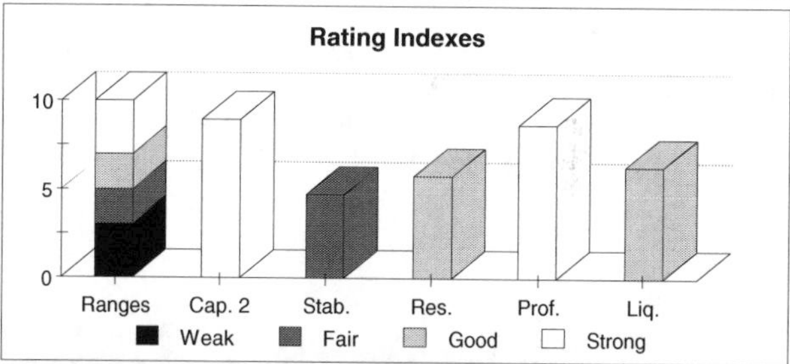

NEW YORK MARINE & GENERAL INS CO — B — Good

Major Rating Factors: Fair profitability index (4.0 on a scale of 0 to 10) with operating losses during the first three months of 2008. Return on equity has been low, averaging 2.6% over the past five years. Fair overall results on stability tests (4.9). The largest net exposure for one risk is acceptable at 2.6% of capital.

Other Rating Factors: Strong long-term capitalization index (7.3) based on excellent current risk adjusted capital (severe and moderate loss scenarios), despite some fluctuation in capital levels. Ample reserve history (9.4) that helps to protect the company against sharp claims increases. Excellent liquidity (7.0) with ample operational cash flow and liquid investments.

Principal Business: Other liability (50%), ocean marine (39%), fire (5%), auto liability (3%), inland marine (1%), and surety (1%).

Principal Investments: Investment grade bonds (54%), misc. investments (42%), and cash (4%).

Investments in Affiliates: 14%

Group Affiliation: NYMAGIC INC

Licensed in: All states except DC

Commenced Business: July 1972

Address: 919 Third Ave, New York, NY 10022

Phone: (212) 551-0600 **Domicile State:** NY **NAIC Code:** 16608

Data Date	Rating	RACR #1	RACR #2	Loss Ratio %	Total Assets ($mil)	Capital ($mil)	Net Premium ($mil)	Net Income ($mil)
3-09	B	1.63	1.21	N/A	598.4	176.4	31.0	-2.5
3-08	A-	1.72	1.30	N/A	601.6	187.3	35.7	3.2
2008	B	1.62	1.20	55.0	580.3	175.5	129.3	-32.4
2007	A-	1.79	1.36	53.0	593.6	191.1	135.2	24.8
2006	A-	1.67	1.28	58.8	590.8	181.1	131.7	26.8
2005	A-	2.18	1.58	65.2	560.1	171.4	113.8	4.3
2004	A-	2.04	1.49	55.3	530.2	167.0	116.6	5.6

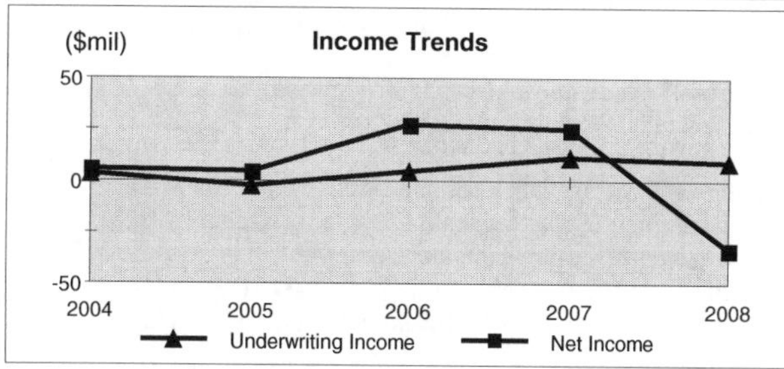

NGM INS CO B- Good

Major Rating Factors: Fair overall results on stability tests (4.6 on a scale of 0 to 10) including potential drain of affiliation with Main Street America Group Inc. History of adequate reserve strength (5.6) as reserves have been consistently at an acceptable level.

Other Rating Factors: Good liquidity (6.3) with sufficient resources (cash flows and marketable investments) to handle a spike in claims. Strong long-term capitalization index (7.8) based on excellent current risk adjusted capital (severe and moderate loss scenarios), despite some fluctuation in capital levels. Excellent profitability (7.9) with operating gains in each of the last five years.

Principal Business: Commercial multiple peril (29%), auto liability (25%), homeowners multiple peril (18%), auto physical damage (12%), workers compensation (9%), surety (3%), and other lines (4%).

Principal Investments: Investment grade bonds (80%), misc. investments (19%), and non investment grade bonds (1%).

Investments in Affiliates: 13%

Group Affiliation: Main Street America Group Inc

Licensed in: All states except AK, CA, HI, LA, MN, MS, PR

Commenced Business: July 1923

Address: 4601 Touchton Rd E Suite 3400, Jacksonville, FL 32245

Phone: (904) 380-7282 **Domicile State:** FL **NAIC Code:** 14788

Data Date	Rating	RACR #1	RACR #2	Loss Ratio %	Total Assets ($mil)	Capital ($mil)	Net Premium ($mil)	Net Income ($mil)
3-09	B-	2.12	1.54	N/A	1,790.2	617.8	194.5	11.0
3-08	B-	1.69	1.26	N/A	1,801.9	606.0	200.3	11.4
2008	B-	2.11	1.54	62.8	1,787.8	607.5	806.4	9.3
2007	B-	1.74	1.30	63.2	1,817.1	619.6	1,085.5	165.6
2006	B-	1.67	1.45	65.1	1,008.6	560.3	331.9	34.7
2005	B-	1.84	1.55	71.7	801.9	378.0	321.1	7.4
2004	B-	1.80	1.51	68.7	723.1	358.3	303.0	14.8

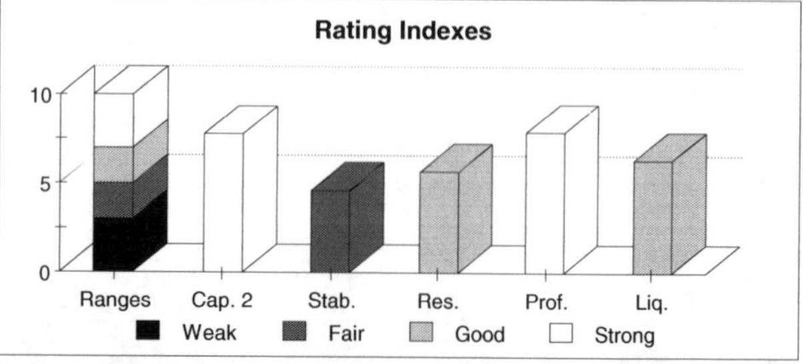

NORCAL MUTUAL INS CO B- Good

Major Rating Factors: Fair overall results on stability tests (4.6 on a scale of 0 to 10) including potential drain of affiliation with Medical Group Holdings Inc. Fair profitability index (4.6) with operating losses during the first three months of 2008.

Other Rating Factors: Strong long-term capitalization index (7.4) based on excellent current risk adjusted capital (severe and moderate loss scenarios), despite some fluctuation in capital levels. Ample reserve history (9.5) that helps to protect the company against sharp claims increases. Excellent liquidity (7.1) with ample operational cash flow and liquid investments.

Principal Business: Medical malpractice (100%).

Principal Investments: Investment grade bonds (62%), misc. investments (35%), and non investment grade bonds (3%).

Investments in Affiliates: 17%

Group Affiliation: Medical Group Holdings Inc

Licensed in: AK, AZ, CA, CT, DC, MA, NV, NJ, NM, OR, PA, RI

Commenced Business: November 1975

Address: 560 Davis Street, 2nd Floor, San Francisco, CA 94111-1902

Phone: (415) 397-9700 **Domicile State:** CA **NAIC Code:** 33200

Data Date	Rating	RACR #1	RACR #2	Loss Ratio %	Total Assets ($mil)	Capital ($mil)	Net Premium ($mil)	Net Income ($mil)
3-09	B-	1.50	1.25	N/A	1,142.9	366.2	44.6	-11.0
3-08	B-	1.55	1.25	N/A	1,218.2	416.3	43.5	-1.5
2008	B-	1.60	1.33	54.9	1,060.3	388.9	182.2	-13.9
2007	B-	1.65	1.34	73.9	1,135.6	441.5	186.8	28.2
2006	B-	1.20	1.01	68.8	1,027.5	398.9	200.8	35.4
2005	B	1.05	0.89	87.1	963.8	338.4	199.6	12.1
2004	B	1.04	0.88	94.0	886.6	311.6	200.8	17.0

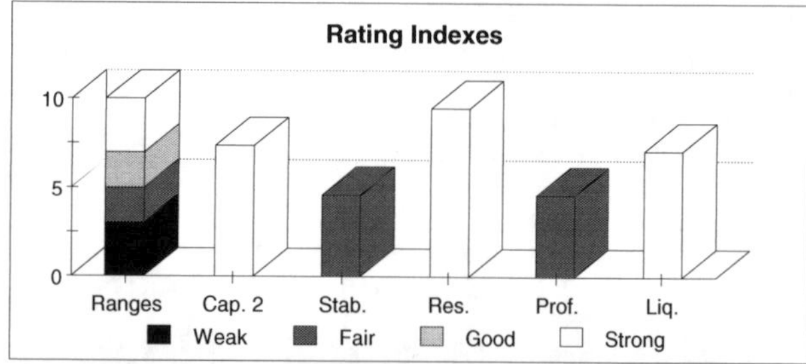

NORTH AMERICAN SPECIALTY INS CO C Fair

Major Rating Factors: Fair overall results on stability tests (3.6 on a scale of 0 to 10) including potential drain of affiliation with Swiss Reinsurance and weak results on operational trends. The largest net exposure for one risk is conservative at 1.5% of capital. Good overall profitability index (6.4). Excellent expense controls. Return on equity has been good over the last five years, averaging 10.5%.

Other Rating Factors: Strong long-term capitalization index (10.0) based on excellent current risk adjusted capital (severe and moderate loss scenarios), despite some fluctuation in capital levels. Ample reserve history (7.0) that can protect against increases in claims costs. Superior liquidity (9.6) with ample operational cash flow and liquid investments.

Principal Business: Inland marine (28%), surety (25%), workers compensation (19%), other liability (10%), ocean marine (7%), aircraft (6%), and other lines (6%).

Principal Investments: Investment grade bonds (71%), misc. investments (21%), and cash (8%).

Investments in Affiliates: 16%

Group Affiliation: Swiss Reinsurance

Licensed in: All states except PR

Commenced Business: October 1974

Address: 650 Elm St, Manchester, NH 03101-2524

Phone: (603) 644-6600 **Domicile State:** NH **NAIC Code:** 29874

Data Date	Rating	RACR #1	RACR #2	Loss Ratio %	Total Assets ($mil)	Capital ($mil)	Net Premium ($mil)	Net Income ($mil)
3-09	C	4.38	3.90	N/A	541.9	282.9	2.4	9.9
3-08	C	3.97	3.41	N/A	503.7	250.1	3.6	7.9
2008	C	4.32	3.90	N/A	505.8	273.4	10.9	34.9
2007	C	3.95	3.43	20.5	459.9	243.5	3.4	28.5
2006	C	3.11	2.58	229.6	447.5	212.7	27.5	12.4
2005	C	3.80	3.55	N/A	645.2	394.1	10.9	50.0
2004	C	3.68	3.43	N/A	606.3	343.1	11.1	30.1

Swiss Reinsurance
Composite Group Rating: C+

Largest Group Members	Assets ($mil)	Rating
REASSURE AMERICA LIFE INS CO	16470	C+
SWISS REINSURANCE AMERICA CORP	14402	C
SWISS RE LIFE HEALTH AMER INC	12775	B-
WESTPORT INS CORP	8047	C
NORTH AMERICAN SPECIALTY INS CO	506	C

NORTH CAROLINA FARM BU MUTUAL INS CO * A Excellent

Major Rating Factors: Strong long-term capitalization index (10.0 on a scale of 0 to 10) based on excellent current risk adjusted capital (severe and moderate loss scenarios). Furthermore, this high level of risk adjusted capital has been consistently maintained in previous years. Excellent profitability (8.3) with operating gains in each of the last five years.

Other Rating Factors: Good overall results on stability tests (6.0) despite potential drain of affiliation with NC Farm Bureau Ins. History of adequate reserve strength (6.1) as reserves have been consistently at an acceptable level. Good liquidity (6.4) with sufficient resources (cash flows and marketable investments) to handle a spike in claims.

Principal Business: Auto liability (33%), homeowners multiple peril (27%), auto physical damage (19%), allied lines (5%), fire (3%), workers compensation (3%), and other lines (9%).

Principal Investments: Investment grade bonds (87%) and misc. investments (14%).

Investments in Affiliates: 1%

Group Affiliation: NC Farm Bureau Ins

Licensed in: NC

Commenced Business: October 1953

Address: 5301 Glenwood Ave, Raleigh, NC 27612

Phone: (919) 782-1705 **Domicile State:** NC **NAIC Code:** 14842

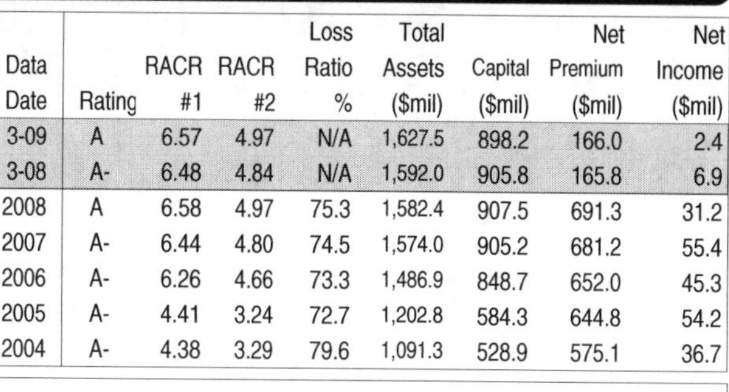

Data Date	Rating	RACR #1	RACR #2	Loss Ratio %	Total Assets ($mil)	Capital ($mil)	Net Premium ($mil)	Net Income ($mil)
3-09	A	6.57	4.97	N/A	1,627.5	898.2	166.0	2.4
3-08	A-	6.48	4.84	N/A	1,592.0	905.8	165.8	6.9
2008	A	6.58	4.97	75.3	1,582.4	907.5	691.3	31.2
2007	A-	6.44	4.80	74.5	1,574.0	905.2	681.2	55.4
2006	A-	6.26	4.66	73.3	1,486.9	848.7	652.0	45.3
2005	A-	4.41	3.24	72.7	1,202.8	584.3	644.8	54.2
2004	A-	4.38	3.29	79.6	1,091.3	528.9	575.1	36.7

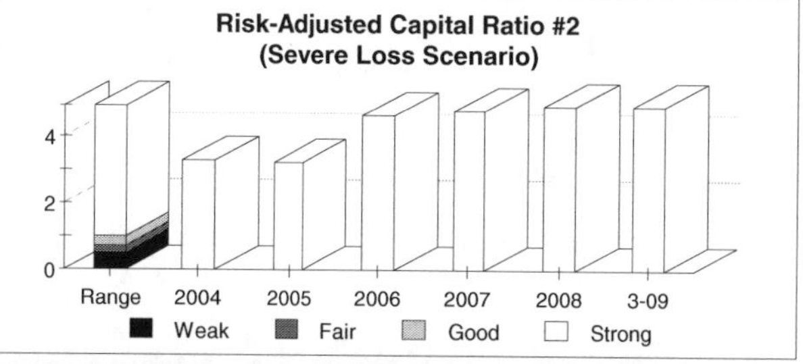

NORTH RIVER INS CO C Fair

Major Rating Factors: Fair overall results on stability tests (3.5 on a scale of 0 to 10) including potential drain of affiliation with Fairfax Financial and negative cash flow from operations for 2008. History of adequate reserve strength (5.8) as reserves have been consistently at an acceptable level.

Other Rating Factors: Good overall profitability index (6.6). Weak expense controls. Return on equity has been good over the last five years, averaging 10.3%. Strong long-term capitalization index (7.1) based on excellent current risk adjusted capital (severe and moderate loss scenarios), despite some fluctuation in capital levels. Excellent liquidity (7.8) with ample operational cash flow and liquid investments.

Principal Business: Other liability (41%), workers compensation (28%), auto liability (10%), inland marine (8%), products liability (5%), commercial multiple peril (3%), and other lines (5%).

Principal Investments: Investment grade bonds (61%), misc. investments (20%), non investment grade bonds (11%), and cash (8%).

Investments in Affiliates: 16%

Group Affiliation: Fairfax Financial

Licensed in: All states, the District of Columbia and Puerto Rico

Commenced Business: October 1972

Address: 305 Madison Avenue, Morristown, NJ 07960

Phone: (973) 490-6600 **Domicile State:** NJ **NAIC Code:** 21105

Data Date	Rating	RACR #1	RACR #2	Loss Ratio %	Total Assets ($mil)	Capital ($mil)	Net Premium ($mil)	Net Income ($mil)
3-09	C	1.59	1.08	N/A	1,011.9	393.8	39.7	36.8
3-08	C	2.29	1.54	N/A	1,018.3	495.1	52.9	-1.2
2008	C	1.88	1.29	78.2	1,095.5	441.3	167.7	1.0
2007	C	2.18	1.47	66.9	971.1	453.8	215.0	34.7
2006	D+	1.96	1.25	63.0	956.4	409.9	226.6	75.0
2005	D	1.48	0.96	74.1	891.4	348.1	163.9	33.6
2004	D	1.34	0.87	89.5	844.9	304.4	175.3	27.7

Fairfax Financial
Composite Group Rating: C

Largest Group Members	Assets ($mil)	Rating
ODYSSEY AMERICA REINSURANCE CO	7312	C
UNITED STATES FIRE INS CO	3051	C
TIG INS CO	1956	D-
CLEARWATER INS CO	1283	D
NORTH RIVER INS CO	1095	C

NORTH STAR MUTUAL INS CO * B+ Good

Major Rating Factors: Good overall results on stability tests (5.0 on a scale of 0 to 10) despite potential drain of affiliation with North Star Companies. Good liquidity (6.7) with sufficient resources (cash flows and marketable investments) to handle a spike in claims.

Other Rating Factors: Strong long-term capitalization index (10.0) based on excellent current risk adjusted capital (severe and moderate loss scenarios), despite some fluctuation in capital levels. Ample reserve history (7.5) that can protect against increases in claims costs. Excellent profitability (8.3) with operating gains in each of the last five years. Return on equity has been excellent over the last five years averaging 15.4%.

Principal Business: Allied lines (25%), homeowners multiple peril (25%), auto liability (11%), auto physical damage (10%), other liability (9%), farmowners multiple peril (7%), and other lines (13%).

Principal Investments: Investment grade bonds (85%), misc. investments (12%), cash (2%), and real estate (1%).

Investments in Affiliates: 1%

Group Affiliation: North Star Companies

Licensed in: MN, NE, ND, OK, SD

Commenced Business: February 1920

Address: 269 Barstad Rd S, Cottonwood, MN 56229

Phone: (507) 423-6262 **Domicile State:** MN **NAIC Code:** 14850

Data Date	Rating	RACR #1	RACR #2	Loss Ratio %	Total Assets ($mil)	Capital ($mil)	Net Premium ($mil)	Net Income ($mil)
3-09	B+	6.92	4.77	N/A	340.1	197.6	37.9	8.5
3-08	B+	6.88	4.56	N/A	328.8	204.5	37.5	11.8
2008	B+	6.72	4.55	69.1	331.3	191.9	151.6	16.1
2007	B+	6.46	4.21	61.8	325.0	197.1	141.8	17.8
2006	B+	6.11	4.03	45.6	300.4	175.9	148.6	32.2
2005	B+	5.04	3.41	47.3	264.1	142.9	143.7	27.7
2004	B+	3.96	2.65	45.0	228.1	113.8	133.6	24.4

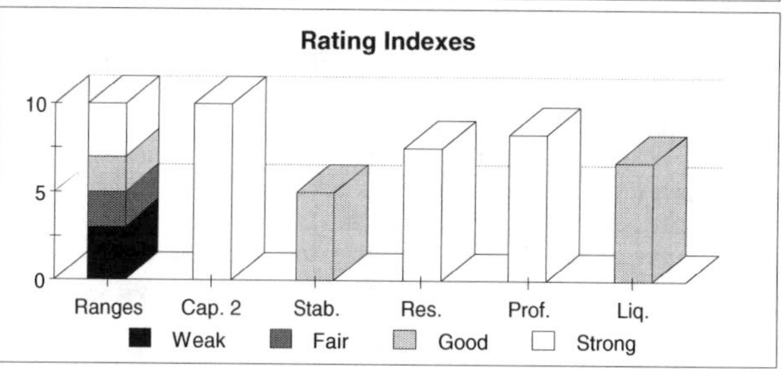

NORTHLAND INS CO — B Good

Major Rating Factors: History of adequate reserve strength (5.5 on a scale of 0 to 10) as reserves have been consistently at an acceptable level. Good liquidity (6.9) with sufficient resources (cash flows and marketable investments) to handle a spike in claims.

Other Rating Factors: Good overall results on stability tests (5.9) despite fair results on operational trends. Affiliation with Travelers Companies Inc is a strength. Strong long-term capitalization index (8.9) based on excellent current risk adjusted capital (severe and moderate loss scenarios), despite some fluctuation in capital levels. Excellent profitability (7.4) with operating gains in each of the last five years. Return on equity has been good over the last five years, averaging 11.6%.

Principal Business: Auto liability (59%), auto physical damage (28%), inland marine (9%), other liability (2%), and commercial multiple peril (1%).

Principal Investments: Investment grade bonds (82%), misc. investments (17%), and non investment grade bonds (2%).

Investments in Affiliates: 14%

Group Affiliation: Travelers Companies Inc

Licensed in: All states except AK, MA, PR

Commenced Business: March 1948

Address: 385 Washington St, St. Paul, MN 55102-1309

Phone: (651) 310-4100 **Domicile State:** MN **NAIC Code:** 24015

Data Date	Rating	RACR #1	RACR #2	Loss Ratio %	Total Assets ($mil)	Capital ($mil)	Net Premium ($mil)	Net Income ($mil)
3-09	B	3.20	2.53	N/A	1,176.4	578.3	55.0	10.9
3-08	B	3.35	2.51	N/A	1,236.4	620.1	54.6	11.3
2008	B	3.16	2.50	61.5	1,166.9	560.8	221.3	71.1
2007	B	3.21	2.37	47.5	1,216.6	602.9	175.4	105.7
2006	B-	2.37	1.68	60.6	1,227.4	567.3	402.3	74.0
2005	B-	1.96	1.35	70.0	1,139.9	479.2	348.4	33.8
2004	B-	1.82	1.23	69.6	1,100.3	434.7	330.5	38.1

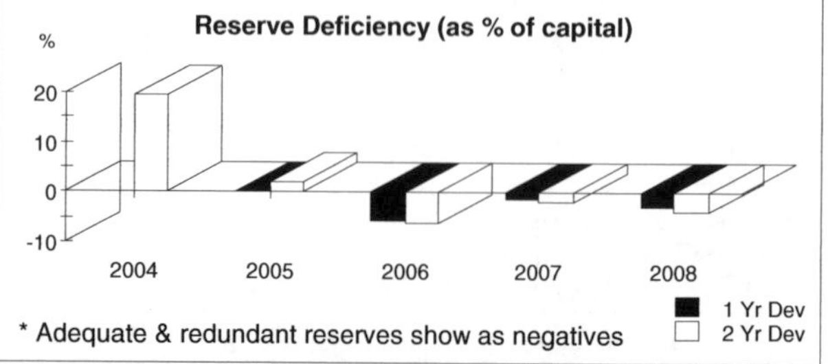

NUCLEAR ELECTRIC INS LTD — E+ Very Weak

Major Rating Factors: Weak profitability index (2.6 on a scale of 0 to 10) with operating losses during 2008. Weak overall results on stability tests (0.0) including weak results on operational trends and negative cash flow from operations for 2008. The largest net exposure for one risk is excessive at 75.1% of capital.

Other Rating Factors: History of adequate reserve strength (6.0) as reserves have been consistently at an acceptable level. Strong long-term capitalization index (9.9) based on excellent current risk adjusted capital (severe and moderate loss scenarios), despite some fluctuation in capital levels. Excellent liquidity (7.0) with ample operational cash flow and liquid investments.

Principal Business: Commercial multiple peril (100%).

Principal Investments: Misc. investments (48%), investment grade bonds (47%), cash (4%), and non investment grade bonds (1%).

Investments in Affiliates: 0%

Group Affiliation: None

Licensed in: DE

Commenced Business: September 1980

Address: 1201 Market St Ste 1200, Wilmington, DE 19801

Phone: (302) 888-3000 **Domicile State:** DE **NAIC Code:** 34215

Data Date	Rating	RACR #1	RACR #2	Loss Ratio %	Total Assets ($mil)	Capital ($mil)	Net Premium ($mil)	Net Income ($mil)
2008	E+	5.11	3.20	207.5	3,950.3	2,988.6	211.4	-635.7
2007	E+	4.83	2.92	42.3	5,116.3	3,951.5	206.3	98.3
2006	E+	4.11	2.49	N/A	5,066.5	3,875.4	217.4	345.2
2005	D	N/A	N/A	73.4	4,984.5	3,538.2	220.2	46.2
2004	D	4.96	2.96	68.3	4,911.7	3,464.0	219.6	73.6

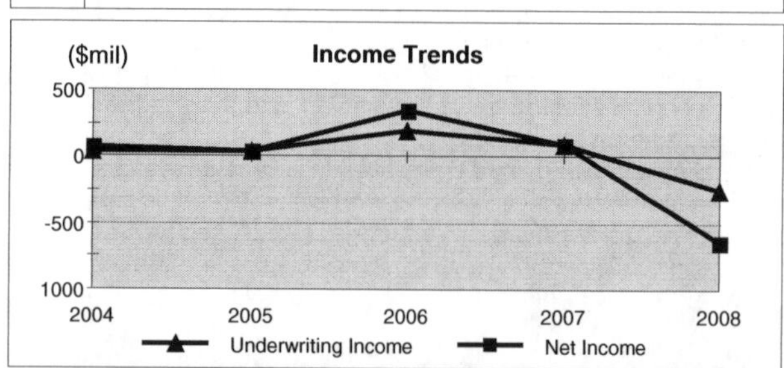

ODYSSEY AMERICA REINSURANCE CO — C Fair

Major Rating Factors: Fair overall results on stability tests (3.7 on a scale of 0 to 10) including potential drain of affiliation with Fairfax Financial. The largest net exposure for one risk is high at 3.9% of capital. Fair reserve development (4.0) as the level of reserves has at times been insufficient to cover claims. In 2005 and 2004 the two year reserve development was 15% and 19% deficient respectively.

Other Rating Factors: Good long-term capitalization index (6.0) based on good current risk adjusted capital (moderate loss scenario). Over the last several years, capital levels have remained relatively consistent. Good overall profitability index (6.0) despite operating losses during 2005 and the first three months of 2008. Return on equity has been fair, averaging 9.7% over the past five years. Excellent liquidity (7.1) with ample operational cash flow and liquid investments.

Principal Business: (This company is a reinsurer.)

Principal Investments: Investment grade bonds (54%), misc. investments (38%), non investment grade bonds (5%), and cash (3%).

Investments in Affiliates: 14%

Group Affiliation: Fairfax Financial

Licensed in: All states except MO

Commenced Business: September 1986

Address: 300 First Stamford Pl, Stamford, CT 06902

Phone: (203) 977-8000 **Domicile State:** CT **NAIC Code:** 23680

Data Date	Rating	RACR #1	RACR #2	Loss Ratio %	Total Assets ($mil)	Capital ($mil)	Net Premium ($mil)	Net Income ($mil)
3-09	C	1.27	0.88	N/A	6,880.8	2,671.1	416.4	-21.6
3-08	C	1.40	0.99	N/A	7,184.4	3,059.6	417.4	196.6
2008	C	1.42	0.99	68.8	7,312.4	2,951.3	1,702.4	544.8
2007	C	1.36	0.96	62.0	6,855.7	2,922.8	1,692.6	235.0
2006	C	1.16	0.83	64.3	6,392.4	2,501.6	1,741.2	561.7
2005	C	0.93	0.68	89.1	5,886.9	2,071.3	1,875.2	-135.3
2004	C	0.96	0.69	67.0	4,855.1	1,675.9	1,986.3	159.4

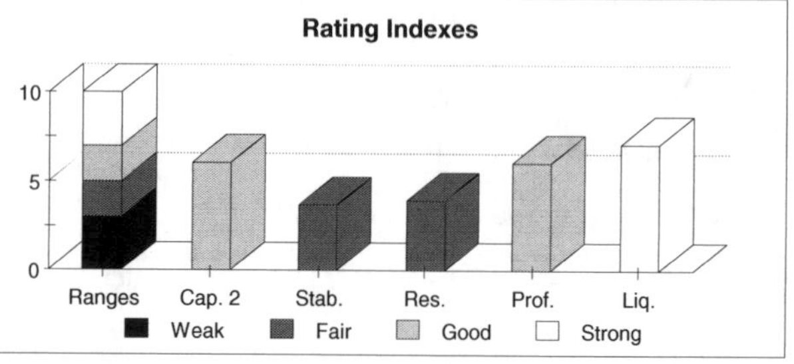

OHIO CASUALTY INS CO — C+ — Fair

Major Rating Factors: Good overall profitability index (6.0 on a scale of 0 to 10). Fair expense controls. Return on equity has been excellent over the last five years averaging 17.8%. Good liquidity (6.6) with sufficient resources (cash flows and marketable investments) to handle a spike in claims.
Other Rating Factors: Weak overall results on stability tests (2.9). The largest net exposure for one risk is excessive at 11.8% of capital. Strong long-term capitalization index (7.3) based on excellent current risk adjusted capital (severe and moderate loss scenarios), despite some fluctuation in capital levels. Ample reserve history (7.0) that can protect against increases in claims costs.
Principal Business: Other liability (33%), commercial multiple peril (19%), auto liability (13%), surety (11%), workers compensation (8%), auto physical damage (5%), and other lines (11%).
Principal Investments: Investment grade bonds (85%), misc. investments (14%), and non investment grade bonds (1%).
Investments in Affiliates: 8%
Group Affiliation: Liberty Mutual Group
Licensed in: All states except CA, PR
Commenced Business: March 1920
Address: 9450 Seward Rd, Fairfield, OH 45014
Phone: (513) 603-2400 **Domicile State:** OH **NAIC Code:** 24074

Data Date	Rating	RACR #1	RACR #2	Loss Ratio %	Total Assets ($mil)	Capital ($mil)	Net Premium ($mil)	Net Income ($mil)
3-09	C+	1.70	1.22	N/A	5,328.1	1,072.8	545.3	34.4
3-08	C+	2.09	1.54	N/A	6,800.0	1,362.9	508.9	12.2
2008	C+	1.68	1.22	63.2	4,869.3	1,035.4	2,272.1	53.2
2007	C+	2.31	1.76	58.0	4,581.1	1,356.4	1,335.3	141.8
2006	C+	1.75	1.30	61.8	4,349.8	1,082.7	1,412.4	206.0
2005	C+	1.62	1.21	61.5	4,271.3	1,004.5	1,795.5	415.0
2004	C+	1.34	1.21	63.6	2,595.5	972.0	680.0	138.3

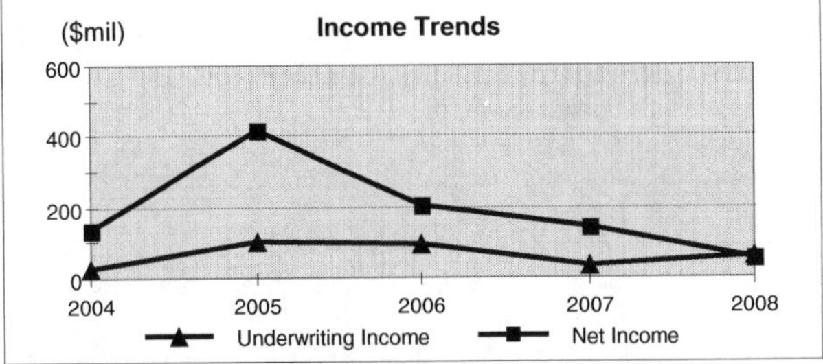

OHIO FARMERS INS CO — B — Good

Major Rating Factors: History of adequate reserve strength (5.0 on a scale of 0 to 10) as reserves have been consistently at an acceptable level. Good overall profitability index (5.7). Weak expense controls.
Other Rating Factors: Fair overall results on stability tests (4.6) including potential drain of affiliation with Westfield Companies and negative cash flow from operations for 2008. Strong long-term capitalization index (7.3) based on excellent current risk adjusted capital (severe and moderate loss scenarios), despite some fluctuation in capital levels. Excellent liquidity (7.0) with ample operational cash flow and liquid investments.
Principal Business: Surety (99%) and fidelity (1%).
Principal Investments: Misc. investments (76%), investment grade bonds (17%), real estate (5%), and cash (2%).
Investments in Affiliates: 73%
Group Affiliation: Westfield Companies
Licensed in: All states except AK, CA, CT, HI, ID, ME, NH, OR, PR
Commenced Business: July 1848
Address: 9040 Greenwich Rd, Westfield Center, OH 44251-5001
Phone: (330) 887-0101 **Domicile State:** OH **NAIC Code:** 24104

Data Date	Rating	RACR #1	RACR #2	Loss Ratio %	Total Assets ($mil)	Capital ($mil)	Net Premium ($mil)	Net Income ($mil)
3-09	B	1.21	1.19	N/A	1,314.5	1,029.7	32.4	21.2
3-08	B	1.22	1.19	N/A	1,567.4	1,248.2	31.6	-1.4
2008	B	1.25	1.22	66.7	1,422.6	1,075.6	147.7	6.8
2007	B	1.23	1.20	64.4	1,588.9	1,265.4	143.4	12.8
2006	B+	1.21	1.18	60.9	1,483.0	1,167.7	136.0	5.7
2005	B+	1.21	1.17	60.8	1,314.3	1,007.5	131.9	11.1
2004	B+	1.21	1.17	58.7	1,202.1	919.7	126.5	24.2

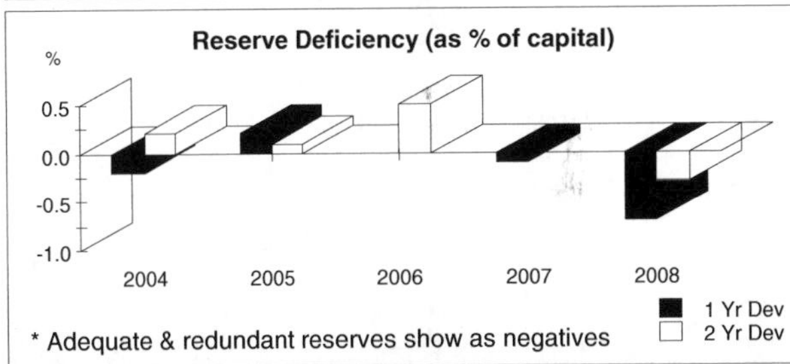

OLD REPUBLIC GENERAL INS CORP * — A- — Excellent

Major Rating Factors: Ample reserve history (9.3 on a scale of 0 to 10) that helps to protect the company against sharp claims increases. Good long-term capitalization index (6.8) based on good current risk adjusted capital (moderate loss scenario). Furthermore, this high level of risk adjusted capital has been consistently maintained in previous years.
Other Rating Factors: Good overall profitability index (6.9) despite operating losses during 2008. Return on equity has been good over the last five years, averaging 14.1%. Good liquidity (6.7) with sufficient resources (cash flows and marketable investments) to handle a spike in claims. Good overall results on stability tests (6.6). Stability strengths include good operational trends and excellent risk diversification. The largest net exposure for one risk is conservative at 1.0% of capital.
Principal Business: Workers compensation (57%), other liability (32%), auto liability (9%), and auto physical damage (1%).
Principal Investments: Investment grade bonds (94%), misc. investments (4%), cash (1%), and non investment grade bonds (1%).
Investments in Affiliates: None
Group Affiliation: Old Republic Group
Licensed in: All states except HI, PR
Commenced Business: January 1961
Address: 307 North Michigan Avenue, Chicago, IL 60601
Phone: (312) 346-8100 **Domicile State:** IL **NAIC Code:** 24139

Data Date	Rating	RACR #1	RACR #2	Loss Ratio %	Total Assets ($mil)	Capital ($mil)	Net Premium ($mil)	Net Income ($mil)
3-09	A-	2.03	1.06	N/A	985.4	254.9	40.2	4.9
3-08	A-	2.41	1.26	N/A	987.3	242.2	70.3	4.8
2008	A-	2.01	1.06	92.3	999.2	255.2	220.0	-8.1
2007	A-	2.82	1.48	91.5	991.3	275.0	267.2	29.1
2006	A-	3.29	1.78	70.3	853.8	270.0	223.6	51.5
2005	A-	2.15	1.15	79.2	622.4	167.2	220.6	33.7
2004	B+	2.49	1.37	72.9	546.3	150.7	177.3	38.5

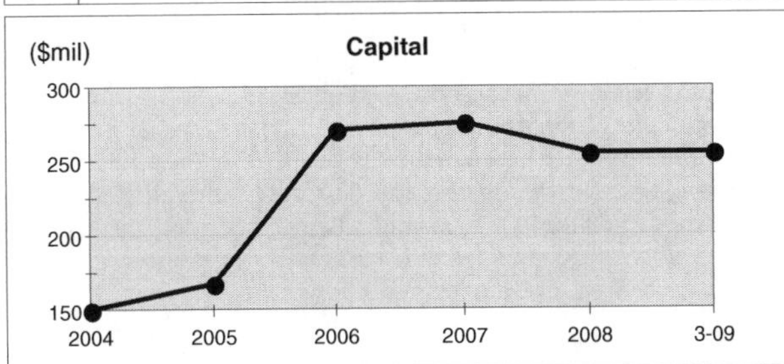

OLD REPUBLIC INS CO * A- Excellent

Major Rating Factors: Strong long-term capitalization index (8.6 on a scale of 0 to 10) based on excellent current risk adjusted capital (severe and moderate loss scenarios). Furthermore, this high level of risk adjusted capital has been consistently maintained in previous years. Ample reserve history (8.5) that helps to protect the company against sharp claims increases.

Other Rating Factors: Excellent liquidity (7.5) with ample operational cash flow and liquid investments. Excellent overall results on stability tests (7.3). Stability strengths include good operational trends and excellent risk diversification. Good overall profitability index (6.3). Fair expense controls. Return on equity has been good over the last five years, averaging 12.4%.

Principal Business: Credit (24%), inland marine (23%), workers compensation (16%), other liability (15%), aircraft (9%), other accident & health (5%), and other lines (8%).

Principal Investments: Investment grade bonds (90%), misc. investments (8%), cash (1%), and non investment grade bonds (1%).

Investments in Affiliates: 1%

Group Affiliation: Old Republic Group

Licensed in: All states, the District of Columbia and Puerto Rico

Commenced Business: April 1935

Address: 414 W Pittsburgh St, Greensburg, PA 15601-0789

Phone: (412) 834-5000 **Domicile State:** PA **NAIC Code:** 24147

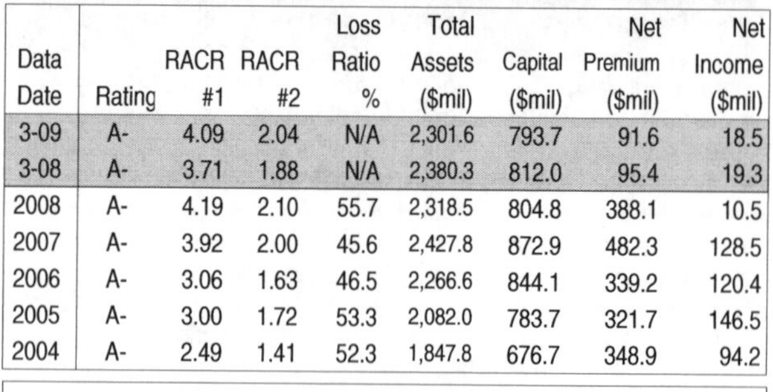

Data Date	Rating	RACR #1	RACR #2	Loss Ratio %	Total Assets ($mil)	Capital ($mil)	Net Premium ($mil)	Net Income ($mil)
3-09	A-	4.09	2.04	N/A	2,301.6	793.7	91.6	18.5
3-08	A-	3.71	1.88	N/A	2,380.3	812.0	95.4	19.3
2008	A-	4.19	2.10	55.7	2,318.5	804.8	388.1	10.5
2007	A-	3.92	2.00	45.6	2,427.8	872.9	482.3	128.5
2006	A-	3.06	1.63	46.5	2,266.6	844.1	339.2	120.4
2005	A-	3.00	1.72	53.3	2,082.0	783.7	321.7	146.5
2004	A-	2.49	1.41	52.3	1,847.8	676.7	348.9	94.2

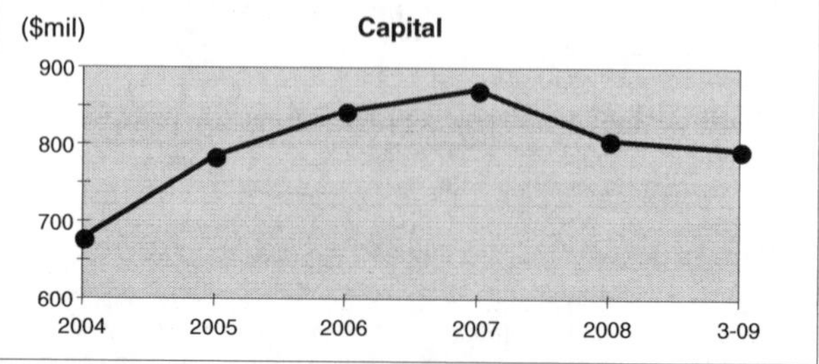

OLD REPUBLIC SURETY CO * A- Excellent

Major Rating Factors: Strong long-term capitalization index (7.6 on a scale of 0 to 10) based on excellent current risk adjusted capital (severe and moderate loss scenarios), despite some fluctuation in capital levels. Ample reserve history (9.3) that helps to protect the company against sharp claims increases.

Other Rating Factors: Good overall profitability index (6.4). Weak expense controls. Return on equity has been good over the last five years, averaging 11.7%. Good liquidity (6.9) with sufficient resources (cash flows and marketable investments) to handle a spike in claims. Good overall results on stability tests (6.0). The largest net exposure for one risk is high at 3.6% of capital.

Principal Business: Surety (85%) and fidelity (15%).

Principal Investments: Investment grade bonds (89%), misc. investments (6%), cash (3%), and non investment grade bonds (2%).

Investments in Affiliates: 0%

Group Affiliation: Old Republic Group

Licensed in: AL, AZ, AR, CA, CO, DC, FL, GA, ID, IL, IN, IA, KS, MD, MN, MS, MO, MT, NE, NV, NM, NC, ND, OH, OK, OR, PA, SC, SD, TN, TX, UT, VA, WA, WV, WI, WY

Commenced Business: December 1981

Address: 445 S Moorland Rd Suite 301, Brookfield, WI 53005

Phone: (414) 797-2645 **Domicile State:** WI **NAIC Code:** 40444

Data Date	Rating	RACR #1	RACR #2	Loss Ratio %	Total Assets ($mil)	Capital ($mil)	Net Premium ($mil)	Net Income ($mil)
3-09	A-	1.58	1.32	N/A	94.2	42.1	10.3	0.2
3-08	A-	1.78	1.47	N/A	96.6	44.5	10.3	1.6
2008	A-	1.65	1.39	14.3	94.1	42.8	40.0	3.1
2007	A-	1.88	1.55	15.4	99.1	45.7	40.7	6.9
2006	A-	1.79	1.49	14.8	96.7	42.8	39.8	5.5
2005	A-	1.60	1.34	17.8	91.4	39.6	38.1	4.3
2004	B+	1.57	1.30	15.8	88.2	38.2	37.3	5.5

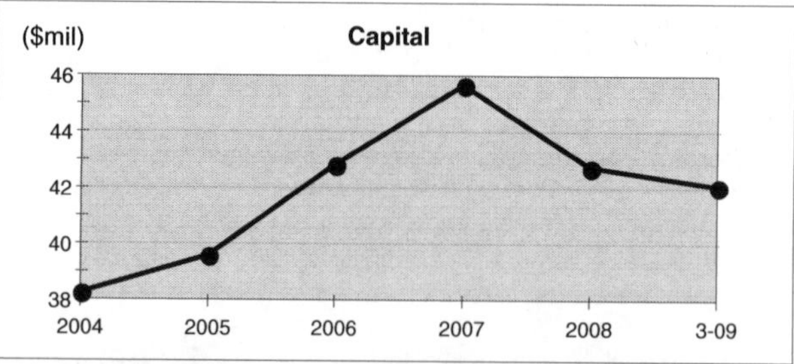

OLD UNITED CAS CO B- Good

Major Rating Factors: Fair overall results on stability tests (4.7 on a scale of 0 to 10) including potential drain of affiliation with Van Enterprises Group. History of adequate reserve strength (5.3) as reserves have been consistently at an acceptable level.

Other Rating Factors: Strong long-term capitalization index (10.0) based on excellent current risk adjusted capital (severe and moderate loss scenarios). Moreover, capital levels have been consistent in recent years. Excellent profitability (9.3) with operating gains in each of the last five years. Return on equity has been excellent over the last five years averaging 20.8%. Excellent liquidity (7.6) with ample operational cash flow and liquid investments.

Principal Business: (Not applicable due to unusual reinsurance transactions.)

Principal Investments: Investment grade bonds (77%), misc. investments (22%), and non investment grade bonds (1%).

Investments in Affiliates: None

Group Affiliation: Van Enterprises Group

Licensed in: All states except PR

Commenced Business: April 1989

Address: 8500 Shawnee Mission Pkwy 200, Merriam, KS 66202

Phone: (913) 432-6400 **Domicile State:** KS **NAIC Code:** 37060

Data Date	Rating	RACR #1	RACR #2	Loss Ratio %	Total Assets ($mil)	Capital ($mil)	Net Premium ($mil)	Net Income ($mil)
3-09	B-	11.30	5.61	N/A	376.9	166.5	19.5	8.8
3-08	B-	9.88	5.47	N/A	369.0	149.7	19.3	7.4
2008	B-	11.05	5.50	51.2	372.0	158.0	71.9	22.1
2007	B-	9.21	5.15	47.4	365.9	145.9	85.2	30.8
2006	C+	7.58	4.24	48.4	353.4	116.8	81.4	24.7
2005	C+	6.46	3.59	50.9	312.5	91.2	88.3	20.8
2004	C+	7.18	4.05	49.8	253.0	69.8	72.5	17.5

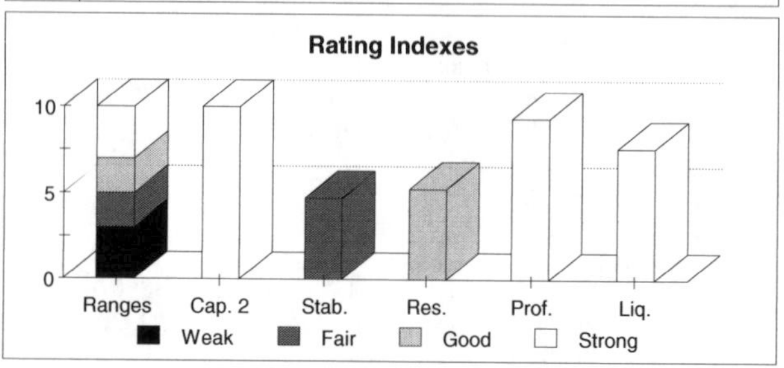

ONEBEACON AMERICA INS CO — C — Fair

Major Rating Factors: Fair overall results on stability tests (3.5 on a scale of 0 to 10). Weak profitability index (2.4) with operating losses during 2008. Return on equity has been fair, averaging 6.8% over the past five years.

Other Rating Factors: History of adequate reserve strength (6.3) as reserves have been consistently at an acceptable level. Strong long-term capitalization index (8.7) based on excellent current risk adjusted capital (severe and moderate loss scenarios), despite some fluctuation in capital levels. Excellent liquidity (7.0) with ample operational cash flow and liquid investments.

Principal Business: Commercial multiple peril (37%), workers compensation (13%), other liability (13%), auto liability (11%), inland marine (7%), group accident & health (6%), and other lines (13%).

Principal Investments: Investment grade bonds (63%), misc. investments (33%), and non investment grade bonds (4%).

Investments in Affiliates: 3%

Group Affiliation: White Mountains Group

Licensed in: All states, the District of Columbia and Puerto Rico

Commenced Business: December 1971

Address: One Beacon St, Boston, MA 02108-3100

Phone: (617) 725-6522 **Domicile State:** MA **NAIC Code:** 20621

Data Date	Rating	RACR #1	RACR #2	Loss Ratio %	Total Assets ($mil)	Capital ($mil)	Net Premium ($mil)	Net Income ($mil)
3-09	C	3.32	2.18	N/A	722.9	296.7	70.2	12.0
3-08	C	3.49	2.17	N/A	891.2	430.4	65.4	10.9
2008	C	3.20	2.09	60.2	731.1	296.3	283.4	-59.3
2007	C	3.58	2.24	58.3	904.3	433.1	265.5	62.3
2006	C	3.68	2.38	62.5	1,057.0	520.9	308.4	114.9
2005	C-	3.09	2.08	70.7	1,052.0	462.2	328.5	34.7
2004	C-	4.55	3.08	68.8	1,299.6	596.6	346.5	45.8

White Mountains Group
Composite Group Rating: B

Largest Group Members	Assets ($mil)	Rating
SYMETRA LIFE INS CO	18646	B
ONEBEACON INS CO	2965	B-
WHITE MOUNTAINS REINS CO OF AMER	2505	C-
ONEBEACON AMERICA INS CO	731	C
HOMELAND INS CO OF NEW YORK	468	C

ONEBEACON INS CO — B- — Good

Major Rating Factors: Fair profitability index (3.2 on a scale of 0 to 10) with operating losses during 2008. Return on equity has been fair, averaging 12.4% over the past five years. Fair overall results on stability tests (4.9) including negative cash flow from operations for 2008.

Other Rating Factors: History of adequate reserve strength (6.4) as reserves have been consistently at an acceptable level. Good liquidity (6.9) with sufficient resources (cash flows and marketable investments) to handle a spike in claims. Strong long-term capitalization index (7.3) based on excellent current risk adjusted capital (severe and moderate loss scenarios), despite some fluctuation in capital levels.

Principal Business: Other liability (35%), farmowners multiple peril (29%), ocean marine (17%), allied lines (6%), medical malpractice (4%), homeowners multiple peril (3%), and other lines (6%).

Principal Investments: Misc. investments (48%), investment grade bonds (47%), non investment grade bonds (3%), and cash (2%).

Investments in Affiliates: 36%

Group Affiliation: White Mountains Group

Licensed in: All states, the District of Columbia and Puerto Rico

Commenced Business: July 1956

Address: 436 Walnut St, Philadelphia, PA 19106-3786

Phone: (617) 725-6000 **Domicile State:** PA **NAIC Code:** 21970

Data Date	Rating	RACR #1	RACR #2	Loss Ratio %	Total Assets ($mil)	Capital ($mil)	Net Premium ($mil)	Net Income ($mil)
3-09	B-	1.34	1.21	N/A	2,859.8	1,173.5	231.0	40.7
3-08	B-	1.43	1.26	N/A	3,345.4	1,629.4	215.2	25.5
2008	B-	1.31	1.17	60.2	2,965.3	1,164.2	933.2	-25.2
2007	B-	1.44	1.27	58.3	3,494.1	1,639.9	874.2	288.1
2006	C+	1.39	1.24	62.5	3,758.3	1,694.1	1,015.6	197.8
2005	C+	1.15	1.04	70.7	3,602.5	1,399.4	1,081.8	207.9
2004	C+	0.99	0.90	68.8	3,849.9	1,361.5	1,084.5	266.7

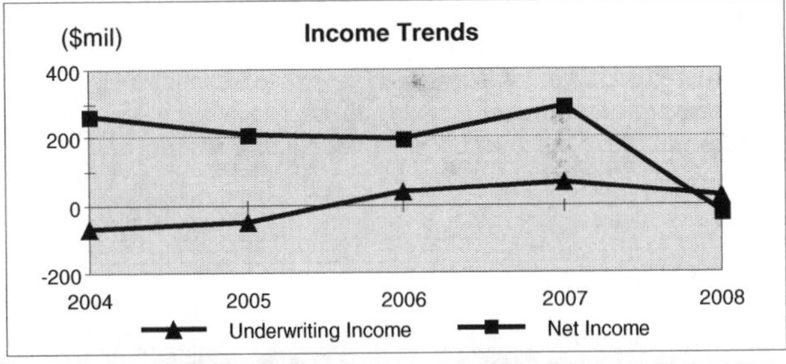

OTSEGO MUTUAL FIRE INS CO * — A- — Excellent

Major Rating Factors: Strong long-term capitalization index (10.0 on a scale of 0 to 10) based on excellent current risk adjusted capital (severe and moderate loss scenarios), despite some fluctuation in capital levels. Ample reserve history (7.5) that can protect against increases in claims costs.

Other Rating Factors: Excellent profitability (7.4) with operating gains in each of the last five years. Excellent expense controls. Excellent liquidity (7.1) with ample operational cash flow and liquid investments. Good overall results on stability tests (6.2). Stability strengths include excellent operational trends and good risk diversification.

Principal Business: Homeowners multiple peril (81%), fire (10%), allied lines (7%), and other liability (2%).

Principal Investments: Misc. investments (54%), investment grade bonds (45%), and real estate (1%).

Investments in Affiliates: None

Group Affiliation: None

Licensed in: NY

Commenced Business: April 1897

Address: 143 Arnold Road, Burlington Flats, NY 13315-0040

Phone: (607) 965-8211 **Domicile State:** NY **NAIC Code:** 14915

Data Date	Rating	RACR #1	RACR #2	Loss Ratio %	Total Assets ($mil)	Capital ($mil)	Net Premium ($mil)	Net Income ($mil)
3-09	A-	6.14	3.67	N/A	70.8	62.1	0.7	0.2
3-08	B+	5.23	3.15	N/A	77.5	65.8	0.8	0.6
2008	A-	5.76	3.44	48.7	72.3	63.9	4.3	3.8
2007	B+	5.05	3.03	50.3	78.3	66.5	4.3	4.3
2006	B+	4.70	2.83	50.7	75.4	62.7	4.3	3.3
2005	B+	4.63	2.79	76.6	69.3	57.9	4.0	2.5
2004	B+	4.14	2.49	73.1	65.6	56.0	3.7	2.3

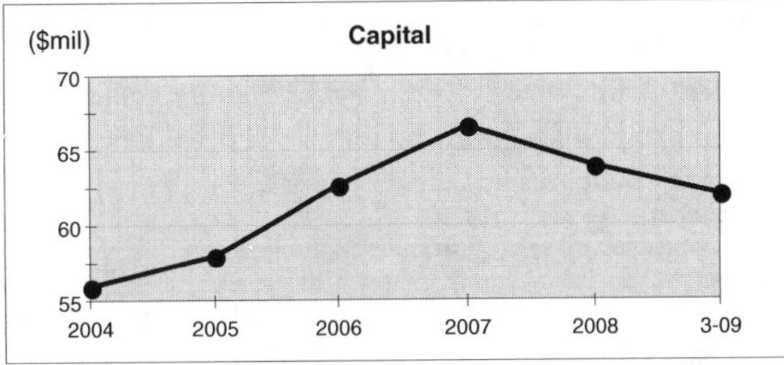

OWNERS INS CO * A- Excellent

Major Rating Factors: Strong long-term capitalization index (8.3 on a scale of 0 to 10) based on excellent current risk adjusted capital (severe and moderate loss scenarios). Furthermore, this high level of risk adjusted capital has been consistently maintained in previous years. Excellent overall results on stability tests (7.0). Stability strengths include excellent operational trends and excellent risk diversification.

Other Rating Factors: History of adequate reserve strength (5.8) as reserves have been consistently at an acceptable level. Good overall profitability index (6.6). Good expense controls. Return on equity has been fair, averaging 9.8% over the past five years. Good liquidity (5.5) with sufficient resources (cash flows and marketable investments) to handle a spike in claims.

Principal Business: Auto liability (24%), commercial multiple peril (22%), auto physical damage (19%), homeowners multiple peril (19%), workers compensation (10%), inland marine (3%), and other lines (4%).

Principal Investments: Investment grade bonds (91%) and misc. investments (9%).

Investments in Affiliates: None

Group Affiliation: Auto-Owners Group

Licensed in: AL, AZ, AR, CO, FL, GA, ID, IL, IN, IA, KS, KY, MI, MN, MS, MO, NE, NV, NM, NC, ND, OH, OR, PA, SC, SD, TN, UT, VA, WA, WI

Commenced Business: December 1975

Address: 2325 N Cole St, Lima, OH 45801

Phone: (517) 323-1200 **Domicile State:** OH **NAIC Code:** 32700

Data Date	Rating	RACR #1	RACR #2	Loss Ratio %	Total Assets ($mil)	Capital ($mil)	Net Premium ($mil)	Net Income ($mil)
3-09	A-	2.86	1.78	N/A	2,535.6	781.0	271.0	1.4
3-08	A-	3.53	2.31	N/A	2,447.7	860.4	260.7	20.7
2008	A-	3.04	1.90	82.8	2,440.9	793.8	1,086.7	4.1
2007	A-	3.58	2.35	71.9	2,371.2	851.0	1,043.7	87.1
2006	B+	3.31	2.25	67.5	2,166.0	760.3	1,027.8	100.8
2005	B+	2.76	1.92	63.6	1,876.8	644.5	959.6	106.4
2004	A-	1.91	1.29	67.6	1,642.4	538.2	828.8	59.2

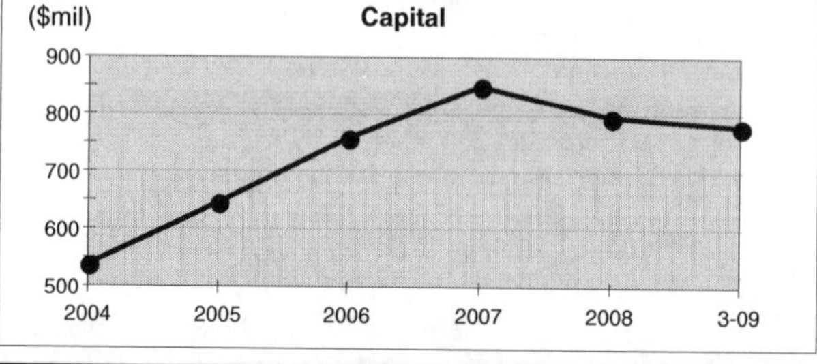

PACIFIC EMPLOYERS INS CO C+ Fair

Major Rating Factors: Fair overall results on stability tests (4.4 on a scale of 0 to 10) including potential drain of affiliation with ACE Ltd. Good long-term capitalization index (6.1) based on good current risk adjusted capital (moderate loss scenario). Moreover, capital levels have been consistent in recent years.

Other Rating Factors: History of adequate reserve strength (5.0) as reserves have been consistently at an acceptable level. Good liquidity (6.8) with sufficient resources (cash flows and marketable investments) to handle a spike in claims. Excellent profitability (8.8) with operating gains in each of the last five years. Return on equity has been good over the last five years, averaging 13.6%.

Principal Business: Workers compensation (100%).

Principal Investments: Investment grade bonds (78%) and misc. investments (22%).

Investments in Affiliates: 7%

Group Affiliation: ACE Ltd

Licensed in: All states except PR

Commenced Business: October 1923

Address: 1601 Chestnut St, Philadelphia, PA 19192

Phone: (215) 761-2324 **Domicile State:** PA **NAIC Code:** 22748

Data Date	Rating	RACR #1	RACR #2	Loss Ratio %	Total Assets ($mil)	Capital ($mil)	Net Premium ($mil)	Net Income ($mil)
3-09	C+	1.79	1.21	N/A	2,554.7	809.4	134.2	22.5
3-08	C	1.27	0.83	N/A	2,358.1	714.7	127.8	19.0
2008	C+	1.80	1.22	62.5	2,446.3	801.6	497.8	107.5
2007	C	1.29	0.84	63.9	2,385.9	694.5	619.7	112.5
2006	C	1.06	0.68	60.3	2,247.2	573.0	685.2	122.1
2005	C	0.91	0.58	75.8	1,959.7	459.3	693.8	29.3
2004	C	0.72	0.51	72.7	1,561.6	315.3	667.6	34.9

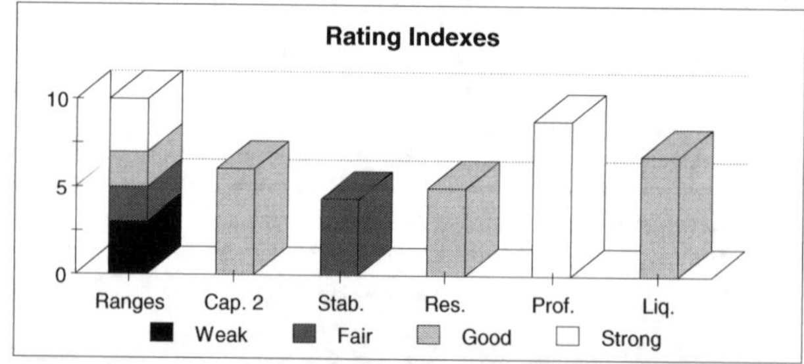

PACIFIC INDEMNITY CO * B+ Good

Major Rating Factors: History of adequate reserve strength (5.6 on a scale of 0 to 10) as reserves have been consistently at an acceptable level. Good liquidity (6.7) with sufficient resources (cash flows and marketable investments) to handle a spike in claims.

Other Rating Factors: Good overall results on stability tests (6.0). The largest net exposure for one risk is high at 3.5% of capital. Stability strengths include good operational trends and excellent risk diversification. Strong long-term capitalization index (7.9) based on excellent current risk adjusted capital (severe and moderate loss scenarios), despite some fluctuation in capital levels. Excellent profitability (9.0) with operating gains in each of the last five years. Return on equity has been excellent over the last five years averaging 20.2%.

Principal Business: Homeowners multiple peril (44%), workers compensation (19%), inland marine (11%), commercial multiple peril (6%), auto liability (5%), other liability (5%), and other lines (10%).

Principal Investments: Investment grade bonds (91%) and misc. investments (9%).

Investments in Affiliates: 0%

Group Affiliation: Chubb Corp

Licensed in: All states except PR

Commenced Business: February 1926

Address: Two Plaza East Suite 1450, Milwaukee, WI 53202-3146

Phone: (908) 903-2000 **Domicile State:** WI **NAIC Code:** 20346

Data Date	Rating	RACR #1	RACR #2	Loss Ratio %	Total Assets ($mil)	Capital ($mil)	Net Premium ($mil)	Net Income ($mil)
3-09	B+	2.80	1.83	N/A	5,651.8	1,862.6	377.8	84.6
3-08	B	2.77	1.85	N/A	5,673.6	1,874.5	386.4	112.4
2008	B+	2.78	1.82	62.4	5,687.7	1,831.7	1,523.2	244.2
2007	B	2.78	1.85	54.0	5,636.2	1,842.9	1,544.1	364.9
2006	B	2.47	1.66	55.1	5,465.1	1,608.1	1,604.8	374.6
2005	B	1.95	1.31	65.8	5,049.2	1,279.2	1,671.0	295.5
2004	B	1.57	1.07	63.7	4,612.5	1,151.9	1,662.3	254.8

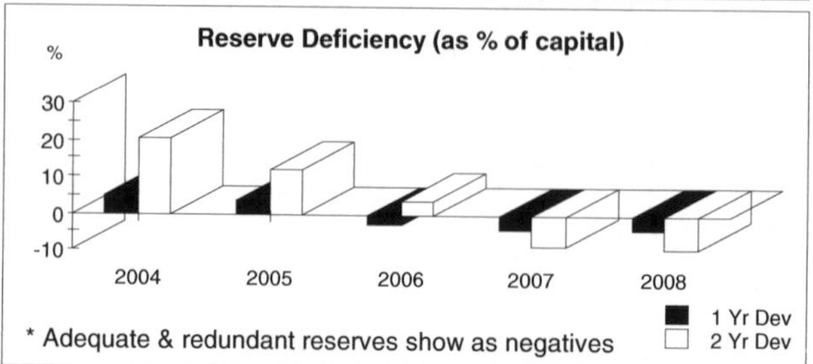

* Adequate & redundant reserves show as negatives

PACIFIC INS CO LTD — B Good

Major Rating Factors: Good overall results on stability tests (5.4 on a scale of 0 to 10). Stability strengths include good operational trends and excellent risk diversification. Fair reserve development (4.8) as reserves have generally been sufficient to cover claims.

Other Rating Factors: Fair profitability index (3.3). Fair expense controls. Return on equity has been fair, averaging 9.0% over the past five years. Strong long-term capitalization index (9.3) based on excellent current risk adjusted capital (severe and moderate loss scenarios), despite some fluctuation in capital levels. Excellent liquidity (7.0) with ample operational cash flow and liquid investments.

Principal Business: Inland marine (41%), workers compensation (21%), other liability (16%), fire (10%), allied lines (10%), and homeowners multiple peril (1%).

Principal Investments: Investment grade bonds (89%), misc. investments (9%), and non investment grade bonds (2%).

Investments in Affiliates: None

Group Affiliation: Hartford Financial Services Inc

Licensed in: CT, HI

Commenced Business: January 1995

Address: Hartford Plaza, Hartford, CT 06115

Phone: (617) 526-7600 **Domicile State:** CT **NAIC Code:** 10046

Data Date	Rating	RACR #1	RACR #2	Loss Ratio %	Total Assets ($mil)	Capital ($mil)	Net Premium ($mil)	Net Income ($mil)
3-09	B	3.96	2.55	N/A	622.5	227.7	42.9	5.5
3-08	B	4.63	2.77	N/A	686.1	305.8	44.1	7.1
2008	B	3.89	2.52	64.1	615.4	222.2	173.6	7.9
2007	B	4.56	2.75	64.6	677.4	297.8	177.4	36.1
2006	B	4.71	3.01	67.5	665.6	298.7	179.6	25.5
2005	B	4.52	2.92	66.0	607.5	270.4	177.1	27.4
2004	B-	3.89	2.67	70.5	560.1	246.8	159.6	26.2

Hartford Financial Services Inc
Composite Group Rating: D+

Largest Group Members	Assets ($mil)	Rating
HARTFORD LIFE INS CO	133562	C-
HARTFORD LIFE ANNUITY INS CO	65461	B-
HARTFORD FIRE INS CO	24454	B+
HARTFORD LIFE ACCIDENT INS CO	14414	B-
HARTFORD ACCIDENT INDEMNITY CO	10935	C+

PALISADES SAFETY & INS ASSOC — C Fair

Major Rating Factors: Fair overall results on stability tests (3.5 on a scale of 0 to 10) including potential drain of affiliation with Palisades Group, weak results on operational trends and excessive premium growth. The largest net exposure for one risk is conservative at 1.0% of capital. Fair reserve development (4.5) as reserves have generally been sufficient to cover claims. In 2008, the one year reserve development was 44% deficient.

Other Rating Factors: Fair profitability index (4.8) with operating losses during 2008. Good long-term capitalization index (5.0) based on good current risk adjusted capital (severe and moderate loss scenarios), although results have slipped from the excellent range over the last two years. Good liquidity (6.8) with sufficient resources (cash flows and marketable investments) to handle a spike in claims.

Principal Business: Auto liability (62%) and auto physical damage (38%).

Principal Investments: Investment grade bonds (54%) and misc. investments (46%).

Investments in Affiliates: 39%

Group Affiliation: Palisades Group

Licensed in: NJ

Commenced Business: May 1992

Address: 5 Marineview Plaza, Ste 102, Hoboken, NJ 07030

Phone: (201) 420-8700 **Domicile State:** NJ **NAIC Code:** 22050

Data Date	Rating	RACR #1	RACR #2	Loss Ratio %	Total Assets ($mil)	Capital ($mil)	Net Premium ($mil)	Net Income ($mil)
3-09	C	0.82	0.75	N/A	754.6	287.3	56.0	3.8
3-08	C	1.12	1.09	N/A	493.6	274.9	40.7	0.2
2008	C	0.82	0.75	89.2	764.3	287.9	382.2	-6.4
2007	C	1.15	1.10	70.3	514.7	291.6	163.6	5.8
2006	C-	0.98	0.93	61.9	463.5	242.6	153.9	9.9
2005	D+	0.73	0.70	62.5	375.6	157.5	152.2	8.5
2004	D	0.52	0.50	68.2	266.6	101.5	60.2	7.7

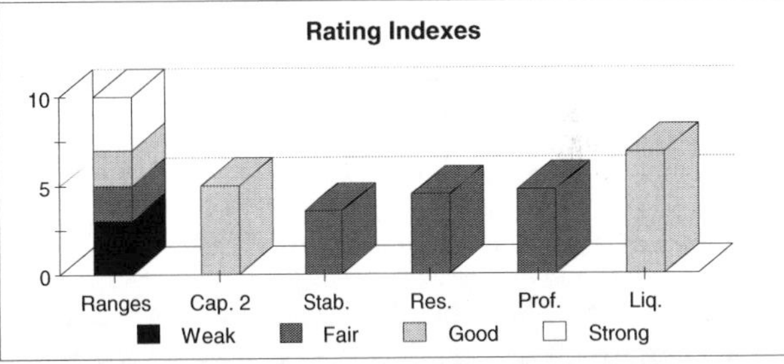

PARTNER REINSURANCE CO OF THE US — D Weak

Major Rating Factors: Poor long-term capitalization index (1.0 on a scale of 0 to 10) based on weak current risk adjusted capital (severe and moderate loss scenarios). Weak overall results on stability tests (1.4) including weak risk adjusted capital in prior years. The largest net exposure for one risk is high at 3.9% of capital.

Other Rating Factors: Fair profitability index (3.5) with operating losses during the first three months of 2008. Return on equity has been low, averaging 2.2% over the past five years. History of adequate reserve strength (5.8) as reserves have been consistently at an acceptable level. Good liquidity (6.3) with sufficient resources (cash flows and marketable investments) to handle a spike in claims.

Principal Business: (This company is a reinsurer.)

Principal Investments: Investment grade bonds (78%), misc. investments (21%), and non investment grade bonds (1%).

Investments in Affiliates: 4%

Group Affiliation: PartnerRe Ltd

Licensed in: AL, AK, AZ, CA, CO, DC, GA, IL, IA, KS, LA, MI, MS, NE, NV, NY, OH, SD, TX, UT, WA

Commenced Business: May 1980

Address: 245 Park Ave 24th Floor, New York, NY 10167

Phone: (203) 485-4200 **Domicile State:** NY **NAIC Code:** 38636

Data Date	Rating	RACR #1	RACR #2	Loss Ratio %	Total Assets ($mil)	Capital ($mil)	Net Premium ($mil)	Net Income ($mil)
3-09	D	0.33	0.24	N/A	3,410.2	596.9	171.8	-13.7
3-08	D+	0.32	0.22	N/A	3,326.9	646.2	188.9	8.9
2008	D	0.34	0.25	75.0	3,281.1	608.3	757.9	-30.1
2007	C-	0.35	0.24	67.0	3,213.6	677.1	711.2	35.9
2006	C-	0.33	0.22	72.4	3,177.3	652.5	716.8	66.6
2005	C-	0.33	0.22	87.8	3,010.9	565.6	678.3	10.4
2004	C	0.38	0.25	77.9	2,717.6	586.5	877.4	7.3

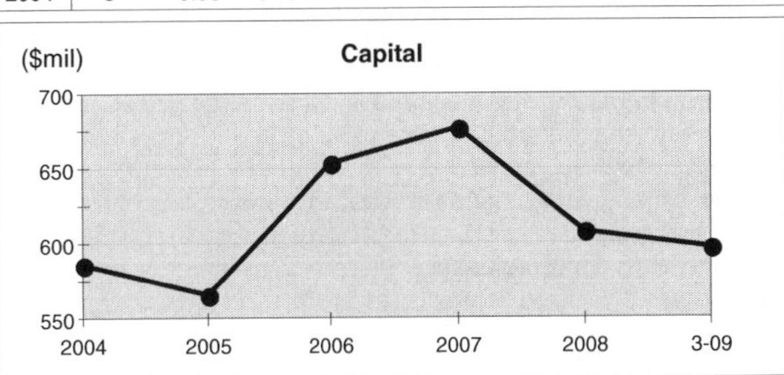

PEERLESS INDEMNITY INS CO C Fair

Major Rating Factors: Weak profitability index (2.9 on a scale of 0 to 10) with operating losses during 2006, 2007 and 2008. Average return on equity over the last five years has been poor at -7.5%. Weak overall results on stability tests (2.7) including weak results on operational trends. The largest net exposure for one risk is excessive at 10.3% of capital.

Other Rating Factors: History of adequate reserve strength (5.0) as reserves have been consistently at an acceptable level. Strong long-term capitalization index (7.5) based on excellent current risk adjusted capital (severe and moderate loss scenarios), despite some fluctuation in capital levels. Excellent liquidity (8.7) with ample operational cash flow and liquid investments.

Principal Business: Commercial multiple peril (44%), auto liability (28%), auto physical damage (12%), homeowners multiple peril (10%), other liability (3%), workers compensation (1%), and other lines (2%).

Principal Investments: Investment grade bonds (99%) and misc. investments (1%).

Investments in Affiliates: None

Group Affiliation: Liberty Mutual Group

Licensed in: All states except PR

Commenced Business: January 1978

Address: 62 Maple Avenue, Keene, NH 03431

Phone: (609) 275-2727 **Domicile State:** IL **NAIC Code:** 18333

Data Date	Rating	RACR #1	RACR #2	Loss Ratio %	Total Assets ($mil)	Capital ($mil)	Net Premium ($mil)	Net Income ($mil)
3-09	C	1.90	1.31	N/A	789.6	186.5	80.2	7.2
3-08	C	3.81	2.08	N/A	764.2	170.1	74.8	1.8
2008	C	1.88	1.30	63.2	747.9	179.9	418.7	-0.2
2007	C+	36.86	29.14	62.7	196.3	166.9	11.1	-0.9
2006	C+	20.83	18.75	66.2	246.2	168.1	10.8	-99.0
2005	B-	3.40	3.22	62.5	633.8	576.4	-351.2	59.8
2004	B-	2.32	1.79	66.5	1,579.9	544.6	786.1	33.8

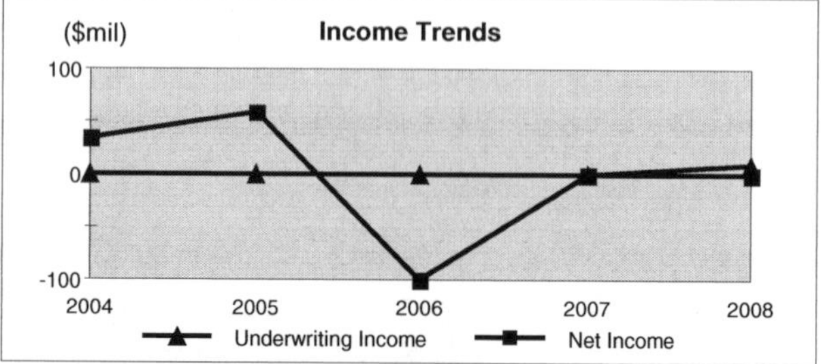

PEERLESS INS CO C+ Fair

Major Rating Factors: Fair overall results on stability tests (3.3 on a scale of 0 to 10) including fair results on operational trends. The largest net exposure for one risk is excessive at 7.9% of capital. History of adequate reserve strength (5.0) as reserves have been consistently at an acceptable level.

Other Rating Factors: Good liquidity (6.5) with sufficient resources (cash flows and marketable investments) to handle a spike in claims. Strong long-term capitalization index (7.2) based on excellent current risk adjusted capital (severe and moderate loss scenarios). Moreover, capital levels have been consistent in recent years. Excellent profitability (8.5) with operating gains in each of the last five years. Return on equity has been excellent over the last five years averaging 15.9%.

Principal Business: Commercial multiple peril (25%), auto liability (22%), homeowners multiple peril (15%), auto physical damage (12%), workers compensation (8%), other liability (8%), and other lines (10%).

Principal Investments: Investment grade bonds (77%), misc. investments (24%), and non investment grade bonds (1%).

Investments in Affiliates: 17%

Group Affiliation: Liberty Mutual Group

Licensed in: All states except HI, NJ, PR

Commenced Business: November 1903

Address: 62 Maple Ave, Keene, NH 03431

Phone: (603) 352-3221 **Domicile State:** NH **NAIC Code:** 24198

Data Date	Rating	RACR #1	RACR #2	Loss Ratio %	Total Assets ($mil)	Capital ($mil)	Net Premium ($mil)	Net Income ($mil)
3-09	C+	1.76	1.42	N/A	12,656.5	2,012.8	673.7	58.4
3-08	C+	1.61	1.12	N/A	9,392.5	1,472.4	628.7	11.7
2008	C+	1.85	1.54	63.2	7,069.0	2,019.1	2,379.5	186.7
2007	C+	1.71	1.23	62.7	6,025.0	1,470.3	2,634.6	188.0
2006	C+	1.84	1.25	66.2	5,707.9	1,219.2	2,549.7	579.5
2005	C+	1.30	1.03	62.5	4,551.5	1,016.7	2,472.8	39.0
2004	C	1.53	1.35	66.5	2,542.0	862.1	1,194.9	63.0

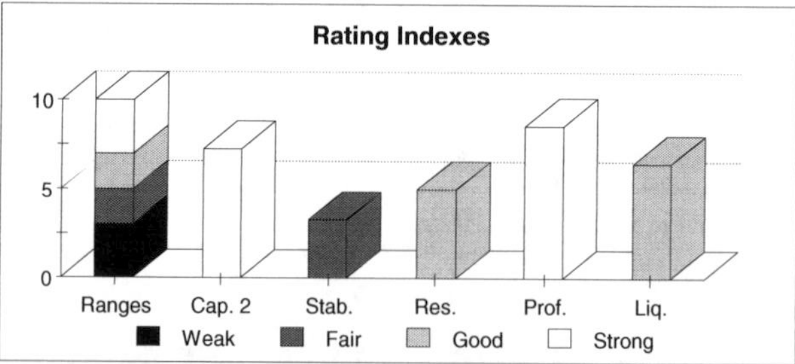

PEKIN INS CO * B+ Good

Major Rating Factors: Good overall results on stability tests (6.0 on a scale of 0 to 10). Stability strengths include good operational trends and excellent risk diversification. Good overall profitability index (5.3) despite operating losses during 2008. Return on equity has been fair, averaging 7.6% over the past five years.

Other Rating Factors: Good liquidity (6.2) with sufficient resources (cash flows and marketable investments) to handle a spike in claims. Strong long-term capitalization index (10.0) based on excellent current risk adjusted capital (severe and moderate loss scenarios), despite some fluctuation in capital levels. Ample reserve history (9.3) that helps to protect the company against sharp claims increases.

Principal Business: Commercial multiple peril (29%), workers compensation (25%), auto liability (15%), homeowners multiple peril (13%), auto physical damage (10%), other liability (5%), and other lines (3%).

Principal Investments: Investment grade bonds (91%), misc. investments (8%), and non investment grade bonds (1%).

Investments in Affiliates: 5%

Group Affiliation: Farmers Automobile Ins Assn

Licensed in: IL, IN, IA, MI, OH, WI

Commenced Business: July 1961

Address: 2505 Court St, Pekin, IL 61558

Phone: (309) 346-1161 **Domicile State:** IL **NAIC Code:** 24228

Data Date	Rating	RACR #1	RACR #2	Loss Ratio %	Total Assets ($mil)	Capital ($mil)	Net Premium ($mil)	Net Income ($mil)
3-09	B+	4.19	2.94	N/A	195.5	84.7	19.3	0.3
3-08	B+	4.83	3.48	N/A	194.6	91.2	19.6	-0.2
2008	B+	4.22	3.01	89.9	194.5	85.0	79.7	-4.1
2007	B+	4.94	3.61	72.4	193.9	92.5	79.9	6.7
2006	B+	4.89	3.61	71.4	181.3	86.0	79.3	6.5
2005	B+	4.47	3.32	63.3	165.9	77.3	79.1	10.0
2004	B	3.68	2.71	61.8	150.1	67.3	75.6	11.1

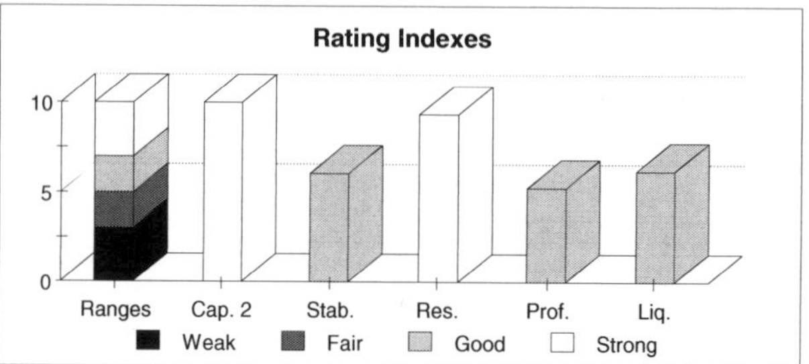

PEMCO MUTUAL INS CO — B — Good

Major Rating Factors: History of adequate reserve strength (6.9 on a scale of 0 to 10) as reserves have been consistently at an acceptable level. Good liquidity (6.5) with sufficient resources (cash flows and marketable investments) to handle a spike in claims.

Other Rating Factors: Fair overall results on stability tests (4.7) including potential drain of affiliation with PEMCO Corp. Fair profitability index (4.7) with operating losses during the first three months of 2008. Strong long-term capitalization index (8.5) based on excellent current risk adjusted capital (severe and moderate loss scenarios), despite some fluctuation in capital levels.

Principal Business: Auto liability (41%), homeowners multiple peril (33%), auto physical damage (19%), earthquake (2%), other liability (2%), fire (1%), and inland marine (1%).

Principal Investments: Investment grade bonds (71%), misc. investments (25%), real estate (3%), and cash (1%).

Investments in Affiliates: 20%

Group Affiliation: PEMCO Corp

Licensed in: OR, WA

Commenced Business: February 1949

Address: 325 Eastlake Ave E, Seattle, WA 98109-5466

Phone: (206) 628-4290 **Domicile State:** WA **NAIC Code:** 24341

Data Date	Rating	RACR #1	RACR #2	Loss Ratio %	Total Assets ($mil)	Capital ($mil)	Net Premium ($mil)	Net Income ($mil)
3-09	B	2.32	2.00	N/A	492.9	212.6	58.0	-0.8
3-08	B	2.27	1.97	N/A	515.4	234.0	57.2	2.2
2008	B	2.29	1.98	69.9	502.9	212.5	234.0	-0.5
2007	B	2.27	1.97	65.3	525.3	238.7	229.1	22.1
2006	B	2.06	1.77	80.1	537.2	216.2	231.1	12.4
2005	B-	1.92	1.61	67.9	498.4	197.9	233.2	24.6
2004	B-	1.47	1.04	72.3	475.9	181.1	241.3	21.3

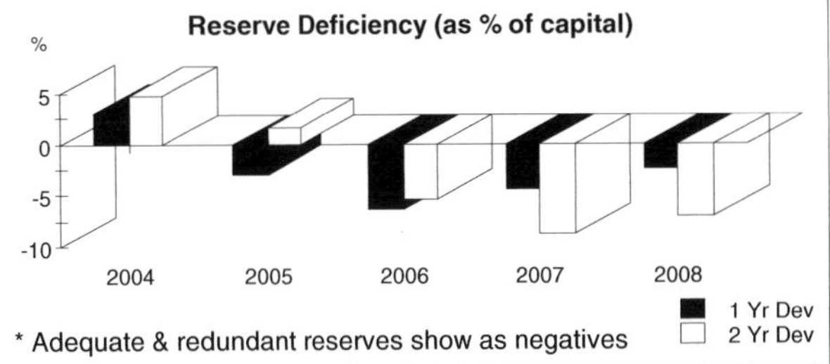

* Adequate & redundant reserves show as negatives

PENN NATIONAL SECURITY INS CO — C+ — Fair

Major Rating Factors: Fair overall results on stability tests (4.5 on a scale of 0 to 10) including potential drain of affiliation with Pennsylvania National Ins Group. History of adequate reserve strength (5.8) as reserves have been consistently at an acceptable level.

Other Rating Factors: Good liquidity (6.6) with sufficient resources (cash flows and marketable investments) to handle a spike in claims. Strong long-term capitalization index (8.5) based on excellent current risk adjusted capital (severe and moderate loss scenarios). Moreover, capital levels have been consistent in recent years. Excellent profitability (8.4) with operating gains in each of the last five years. Return on equity has been good over the last five years, averaging 11.9%.

Principal Business: Workers compensation (44%), auto liability (18%), fire (13%), other liability (10%), products liability (6%), auto physical damage (5%), and inland marine (4%).

Principal Investments: Investment grade bonds (94%) and cash (6%).

Investments in Affiliates: None

Group Affiliation: Pennsylvania National Ins Group

Licensed in: AL, DE, MD, NC, PA, SC, TN, VA

Commenced Business: January 1989

Address: Two North Second Street, Harrisburg, PA 17101

Phone: (717) 234-4941 **Domicile State:** PA **NAIC Code:** 32441

Data Date	Rating	RACR #1	RACR #2	Loss Ratio %	Total Assets ($mil)	Capital ($mil)	Net Premium ($mil)	Net Income ($mil)
3-09	C+	3.59	2.29	N/A	659.6	213.9	54.2	1.9
3-08	C	3.36	2.14	N/A	665.5	207.1	57.7	1.5
2008	C+	3.62	2.32	64.3	657.9	213.4	222.4	18.0
2007	C	3.46	2.21	61.9	654.6	207.8	237.2	24.5
2006	C	3.10	1.95	59.9	617.5	183.5	243.9	25.5
2005	C	2.51	1.62	63.1	575.3	151.7	252.3	21.3
2004	C	2.33	1.55	65.4	535.8	132.0	244.9	17.5

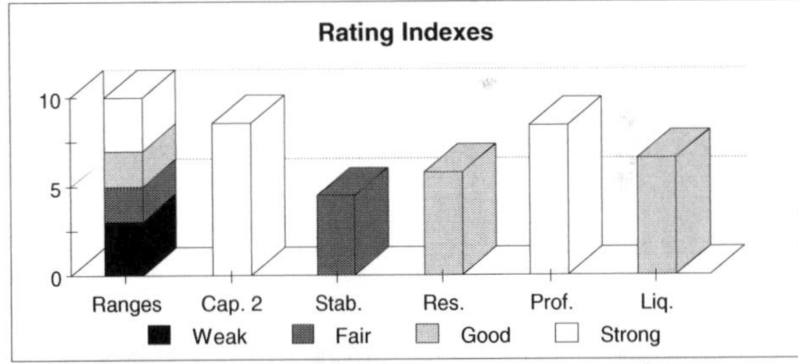

PENN-AMERICA INS CO — B- — Good

Major Rating Factors: Fair overall results on stability tests (4.7 on a scale of 0 to 10) including negative cash flow from operations for 2008. History of adequate reserve strength (5.0) as reserves have been consistently at an acceptable level.

Other Rating Factors: Strong long-term capitalization index (7.6) based on excellent current risk adjusted capital (severe and moderate loss scenarios), despite some fluctuation in capital levels. Excellent profitability (7.8) with operating gains in each of the last five years. Excellent liquidity (7.3) with ample operational cash flow and liquid investments.

Principal Business: Commercial multiple peril (54%), other liability (37%), products liability (4%), fire (3%), inland marine (2%), and allied lines (1%).

Principal Investments: Investment grade bonds (65%), misc. investments (34%), and cash (1%).

Investments in Affiliates: 32%

Group Affiliation: United America Indemnity Ltd

Licensed in: AL, AK, AZ, AR, CA, CO, DE, HI, ID, IL, IN, IA, KS, KY, MI, MN, MS, MO, MT, NE, NV, NM, NY, ND, OH, OR, PA, SD, TN, UT, WA, WI

Commenced Business: April 1976

Address: 420 S York Rd, Hatboro, PA 19040

Phone: (215) 443-3600 **Domicile State:** PA **NAIC Code:** 32859

Data Date	Rating	RACR #1	RACR #2	Loss Ratio %	Total Assets ($mil)	Capital ($mil)	Net Premium ($mil)	Net Income ($mil)
3-09	B-	1.93	1.81	N/A	350.9	191.8	8.4	1.4
3-08	B-	2.07	1.92	N/A	366.1	202.3	13.4	2.2
2008	B-	1.93	1.82	60.8	340.5	188.5	38.7	9.1
2007	B-	2.05	1.92	61.0	367.6	198.2	47.3	23.5
2006	B-	1.92	1.65	60.1	358.4	181.0	80.6	19.6
2005	B-	1.97	1.77	59.8	335.6	163.5	61.2	22.0
2004	B-	1.10	0.82	61.2	337.0	140.3	146.2	10.8

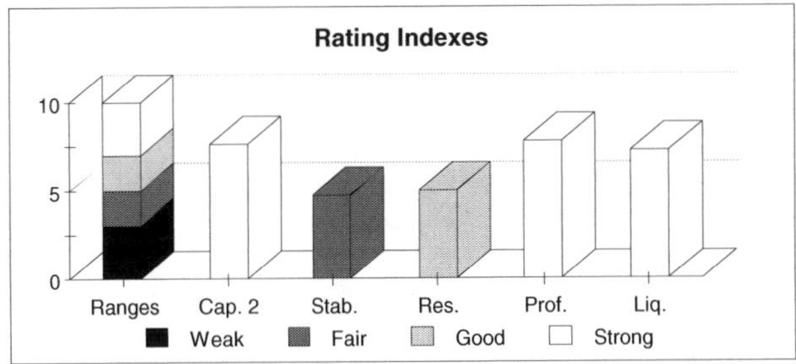

PENNSYLVANIA MANUFACTURERS ASN INS — C Fair

Major Rating Factors: Fair overall results on stability tests (3.5 on a scale of 0 to 10) including fair financial strength of affiliated PMA Capital Corp. History of adequate reserve strength (5.1) as reserves have been consistently at an acceptable level.

Other Rating Factors: Good overall profitability index (6.2). Fair expense controls. Return on equity has been low, averaging 3.5% over the past five years. Good liquidity (6.4) with sufficient resources (cash flows and marketable investments) to handle a spike in claims. Strong long-term capitalization index (7.8) based on excellent current risk adjusted capital (severe and moderate loss scenarios), despite some fluctuation in capital levels.

Principal Business: Workers compensation (87%), auto liability (5%), other liability (4%), commercial multiple peril (2%), auto physical damage (1%), and inland marine (1%).

Principal Investments: Investment grade bonds (90%), misc. investments (4%), non investment grade bonds (3%), real estate (2%), and cash (1%).

Investments in Affiliates: None

Group Affiliation: PMA Capital Corp

Licensed in: All states, the District of Columbia and Puerto Rico

Commenced Business: July 1964

Address: 380 Sentry Parkway, Blue Bell, PA 19422-0754

Phone: (610) 397-5000 **Domicile State:** PA **NAIC Code:** 12262

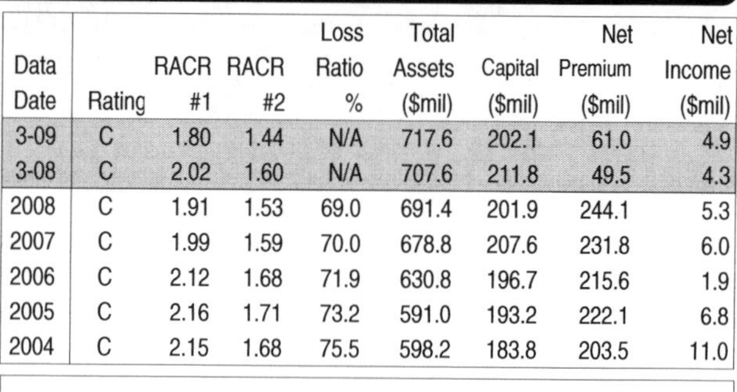

Data Date	Rating	RACR #1	RACR #2	Loss Ratio %	Total Assets ($mil)	Capital ($mil)	Net Premium ($mil)	Net Income ($mil)
3-09	C	1.80	1.44	N/A	717.6	202.1	61.0	4.9
3-08	C	2.02	1.60	N/A	707.6	211.8	49.5	4.3
2008	C	1.91	1.53	69.0	691.4	201.9	244.1	5.3
2007	C	1.99	1.59	70.0	678.8	207.6	231.8	6.0
2006	C	2.12	1.68	71.9	630.8	196.7	215.6	1.9
2005	C	2.16	1.71	73.2	591.0	193.2	222.1	6.8
2004	C	2.15	1.68	75.5	598.2	183.8	203.5	11.0

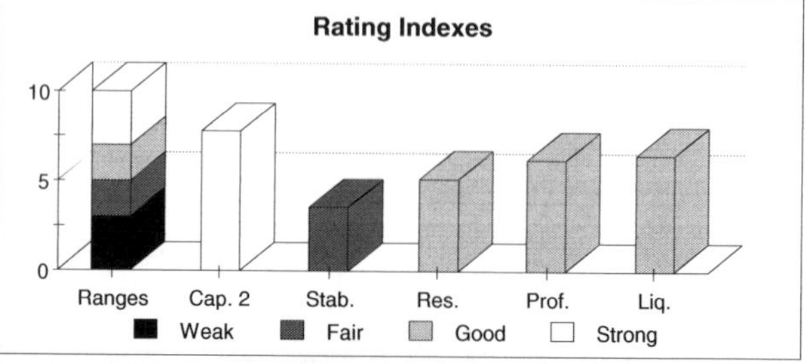

PENNSYLVANIA NTL MUTUAL CAS INS CO — B- Good

Major Rating Factors: Fair overall results on stability tests (4.7 on a scale of 0 to 10) including potential drain of affiliation with Pennsylvania National Ins Group. Fair reserve development (4.2) as reserves have generally been sufficient to cover claims.

Other Rating Factors: Good overall profitability index (6.9). Fair expense controls. Good liquidity (6.6) with sufficient resources (cash flows and marketable investments) to handle a spike in claims. Strong long-term capitalization index (7.5) based on excellent current risk adjusted capital (severe and moderate loss scenarios), despite some fluctuation in capital levels.

Principal Business: Auto liability (25%), other liability (17%), workers compensation (14%), auto physical damage (12%), homeowners multiple peril (10%), commercial multiple peril (7%), and other lines (15%).

Principal Investments: Investment grade bonds (59%), misc. investments (40%), and cash (1%).

Investments in Affiliates: 30%

Group Affiliation: Pennsylvania National Ins Group

Licensed in: All states except CA, CT, HI, NV, NH, ND, WY, PR

Commenced Business: April 1920

Address: Two North Second Street, Harrisburg, PA 17101

Phone: (717) 234-4941 **Domicile State:** PA **NAIC Code:** 14990

Data Date	Rating	RACR #1	RACR #2	Loss Ratio %	Total Assets ($mil)	Capital ($mil)	Net Premium ($mil)	Net Income ($mil)
3-09	B-	1.68	1.50	N/A	1,025.3	425.1	68.6	2.0
3-08	C+	1.68	1.47	N/A	1,058.0	432.5	73.2	-0.5
2008	B-	1.68	1.50	65.6	1,038.9	427.2	284.3	17.1
2007	C+	1.71	1.50	67.3	1,059.4	439.9	299.7	14.6
2006	C+	1.71	1.48	66.7	993.2	398.9	309.2	13.3
2005	C+	1.67	1.43	68.0	903.6	336.8	320.6	15.1
2004	C+	1.69	1.43	67.6	833.9	304.6	309.8	10.7

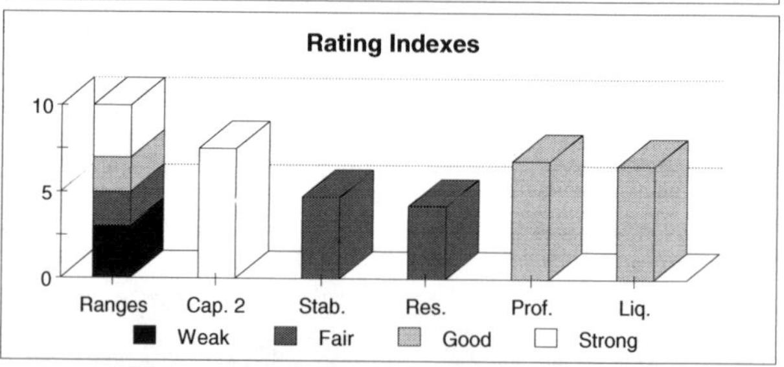

PHILADELPHIA CBSP FOR INS OF HOUSES — B Good

Major Rating Factors: History of adequate reserve strength (5.1 on a scale of 0 to 10) as reserves have been consistently at an acceptable level. Good liquidity (6.7) with sufficient resources (cash flows and marketable investments) to handle a spike in claims.

Other Rating Factors: Fair overall results on stability tests (4.1) including potential drain of affiliation with Philadelphia Contrib Group and weak results on operational trends. Fair profitability index (4.5) with operating losses during 2004. Strong long-term capitalization index (7.0) based on good current risk adjusted capital (severe and moderate loss scenarios), although results have slipped from the excellent range during the last year.

Principal Business: (This company is a reinsurer.)

Principal Investments: Misc. investments (90%), investment grade bonds (9%), and real estate (1%).

Investments in Affiliates: 58%

Group Affiliation: Philadelphia Contrib Group

Licensed in: NJ, PA

Commenced Business: March 1753

Address: 212 S Fourth St, Philadelphia, PA 19106

Phone: (215) 627-1752 **Domicile State:** PA **NAIC Code:** 17930

Data Date	Rating	RACR #1	RACR #2	Loss Ratio %	Total Assets ($mil)	Capital ($mil)	Net Premium ($mil)	Net Income ($mil)
3-09	B	1.05	0.95	N/A	235.6	169.9	8.3	0.5
3-08	B	1.17	1.00	N/A	293.9	206.2	8.3	0.8
2008	B	1.16	1.03	51.2	259.0	189.4	33.3	4.2
2007	B	1.18	1.01	62.4	297.6	208.2	36.0	1.0
2006	B	1.30	1.13	N/A	239.4	189.6	0.1	4.7
2005	B	1.23	1.05	N/A	222.6	159.9	0.1	9.9
2004	B	1.22	1.04	N/A	216.1	154.0	0.4	-10.2

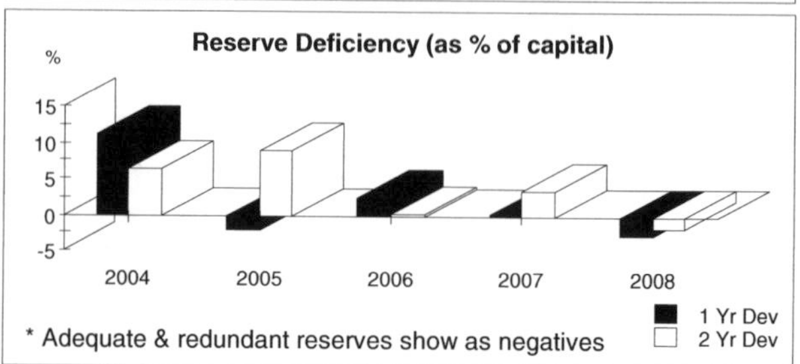

PHILADELPHIA INDEMNITY INS CO — B — Good

Major Rating Factors: History of adequate reserve strength (5.9 on a scale of 0 to 10) as reserves have been consistently at an acceptable level. Good liquidity (6.6) with sufficient resources (cash flows and marketable investments) to handle a spike in claims.

Other Rating Factors: Fair overall results on stability tests (4.6) including potential drain of affiliation with Tokio Marine Holdings Inc. Strong long-term capitalization index (8.4) based on excellent current risk adjusted capital (severe and moderate loss scenarios). Moreover, capital levels have been consistent in recent years. Excellent profitability (9.0) with operating gains in each of the last five years. Return on equity has been excellent over the last five years averaging 18.5%.

Principal Business: Commercial multiple peril (53%), other liability (24%), auto liability (14%), auto physical damage (5%), inland marine (3%), and allied lines (1%).

Principal Investments: Investment grade bonds (88%) and misc. investments (13%).

Investments in Affiliates: None

Group Affiliation: Tokio Marine Holdings Inc

Licensed in: All states except PR

Commenced Business: March 1927

Address: 1 Bala Plz #100, Bala Cynwyd, PA 19004-1401

Phone: (610) 617-7900 **Domicile State:** PA **NAIC Code:** 18058

Data Date	Rating	RACR #1	RACR #2	Loss Ratio %	Total Assets ($mil)	Capital ($mil)	Net Premium ($mil)	Net Income ($mil)
3-09	B	2.47	1.92	N/A	3,975.6	1,229.8	409.3	3.5
3-08	B-	2.86	2.24	N/A	3,414.6	1,159.1	358.0	54.5
2008	B	2.53	1.98	55.0	3,853.2	1,205.0	1,604.5	133.3
2007	B-	3.03	2.38	44.7	3,328.3	1,169.0	1,394.1	280.6
2006	B-	2.05	1.63	39.6	2,674.0	890.2	1,198.8	251.3
2005	B-	1.41	1.14	50.6	2,165.3	595.8	1,007.4	149.2
2004	B-	1.14	0.86	59.7	1,706.9	417.8	760.3	35.6

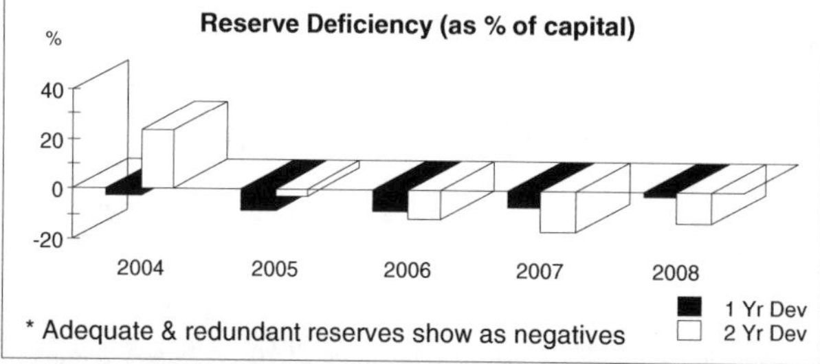

PHOENIX INS CO — B — Good

Major Rating Factors: Good liquidity (6.7 on a scale of 0 to 10) with sufficient resources (cash flows and marketable investments) to handle a spike in claims. Good overall results on stability tests (5.5).

Other Rating Factors: Fair reserve development (4.9) as reserves have generally been sufficient to cover claims. In 2005, the two year reserve development was 20% deficient. Strong long-term capitalization index (7.6) based on excellent current risk adjusted capital (severe and moderate loss scenarios), despite some fluctuation in capital levels. Excellent profitability (8.2) with operating gains in each of the last five years. Return on equity has been excellent over the last five years averaging 20.2%.

Principal Business: Commercial multiple peril (22%), workers compensation (20%), auto liability (20%), homeowners multiple peril (16%), auto physical damage (10%), inland marine (6%), and other lines (7%).

Principal Investments: Investment grade bonds (76%), misc. investments (23%), and non investment grade bonds (1%).

Investments in Affiliates: 18%

Group Affiliation: Travelers Companies Inc

Licensed in: All states except CA, PR

Commenced Business: July 1850

Address: One Tower Square, Hartford, CT 06183

Phone: (860) 277-0111 **Domicile State:** CT **NAIC Code:** 25623

Data Date	Rating	RACR #1	RACR #2	Loss Ratio %	Total Assets ($mil)	Capital ($mil)	Net Premium ($mil)	Net Income ($mil)
3-09	B	1.78	1.42	N/A	3,614.1	1,206.6	225.4	31.0
3-08	B-	1.86	1.39	N/A	3,609.0	1,239.9	223.8	52.4
2008	B	1.75	1.40	61.5	3,573.1	1,170.2	907.0	219.5
2007	B-	1.79	1.34	59.0	3,569.5	1,173.7	900.9	240.8
2006	C+	1.72	1.31	58.4	3,510.1	1,150.5	866.6	254.4
2005	C+	1.51	1.15	75.1	3,425.4	1,019.8	816.8	184.1
2004	B-	1.45	1.14	63.7	3,371.3	995.7	929.0	237.8

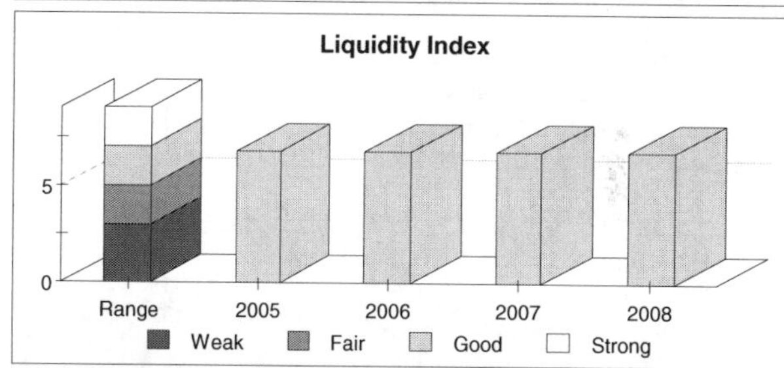

PIONEER STATE MUTUAL INS CO * — A — Excellent

Major Rating Factors: Strong long-term capitalization index (10.0 on a scale of 0 to 10) based on excellent current risk adjusted capital (severe and moderate loss scenarios). Furthermore, this high level of risk adjusted capital has been consistently maintained in previous years. Ample reserve history (8.9) that helps to protect the company against sharp claims increases.

Other Rating Factors: Excellent overall results on stability tests (7.0). Stability strengths include good operational trends and excellent risk diversification. Good overall profitability index (6.6). Fair expense controls. Good liquidity (6.6) with sufficient resources (cash flows and marketable investments) to handle a spike in claims.

Principal Business: Auto liability (33%), homeowners multiple peril (31%), auto physical damage (23%), farmowners multiple peril (7%), inland marine (2%), fire (2%), and other lines (2%).

Principal Investments: Investment grade bonds (79%), misc. investments (20%), real estate (2%), and non investment grade bonds (1%).

Investments in Affiliates: None

Group Affiliation: None

Licensed in: IN, MI

Commenced Business: June 1908

Address: 1510 N Elms Rd, Flint, MI 48532

Phone: (800) 837-7674 **Domicile State:** MI **NAIC Code:** 18309

Data Date	Rating	RACR #1	RACR #2	Loss Ratio %	Total Assets ($mil)	Capital ($mil)	Net Premium ($mil)	Net Income ($mil)
3-09	A	5.39	3.64	N/A	294.4	169.9	31.9	0.3
3-08	A	5.19	3.37	N/A	317.6	191.0	31.0	2.4
2008	A	5.45	3.63	77.7	302.3	176.4	127.7	5.7
2007	A	5.07	3.25	70.4	328.2	195.2	125.8	12.1
2006	A-	4.92	3.19	60.7	313.4	180.5	125.3	18.1
2005	A-	4.02	2.64	60.0	286.0	158.3	131.9	19.0
2004	A-	2.80	1.89	64.3	258.1	137.9	131.9	12.9

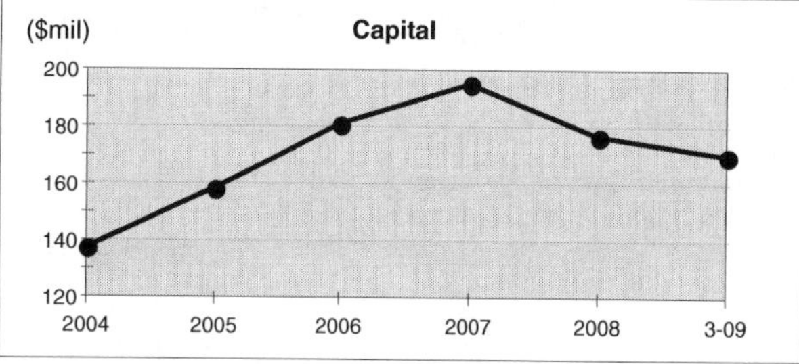

PLATINUM UNDERWRITERS REINS CO C Fair

Major Rating Factors: Good long-term capitalization index (5.6 on a scale of 0 to 10) based on fair current risk adjusted capital (severe loss scenario), although results have slipped from the good range over the last two years. Fair overall results on stability tests (3.5) including fair risk adjusted capital in prior years. The largest net exposure for one risk is excessive at 6.8% of capital.
Other Rating Factors: Good overall profitability index (6.4) despite operating losses during 2005. Return on equity has been fair, averaging 6.7% over the past five years. Ample reserve history (8.8) that helps to protect the company against sharp claims increases. Excellent liquidity (7.5) with ample operational cash flow and liquid investments.
Principal Business: (This company is a reinsurer.)
Principal Investments: Investment grade bonds (90%) and misc. investments (10%).
Investments in Affiliates: None
Group Affiliation: Platinum Underwriters Holdings Ltd
Licensed in: AR, CO, DC, FL, GA, IL, IA, KS, KY, LA, MD, MA, MI, MS, NE, NY, OH, OK, OR, PA, SC, TN, TX, VA, WA, WV, WY
Commenced Business: December 1995
Address: 5801 Centennial Way, LA303, Baltimore, MD 21209-3653
Phone: (651) 310-7911 **Domicile State:** MD **NAIC Code:** 10357

Data Date	Rating	RACR #1	RACR #2	Loss Ratio %	Total Assets ($mil)	Capital ($mil)	Net Premium ($mil)	Net Income ($mil)
3-09	C	1.35	0.68	N/A	1,770.8	575.2	156.3	5.8
3-08	C	1.57	0.81	N/A	1,528.1	555.7	134.7	10.3
2008	C	1.45	0.74	72.2	1,656.8	574.1	566.0	15.0
2007	C	1.75	0.89	61.0	1,466.4	548.0	365.7	51.1
2006	C	1.66	0.85	35.8	1,519.7	530.8	307.3	118.0
2005	C	0.71	0.43	57.9	1,623.2	447.2	601.8	-21.9
2004	C	0.60	0.37	45.4	1,421.3	403.1	715.4	20.6

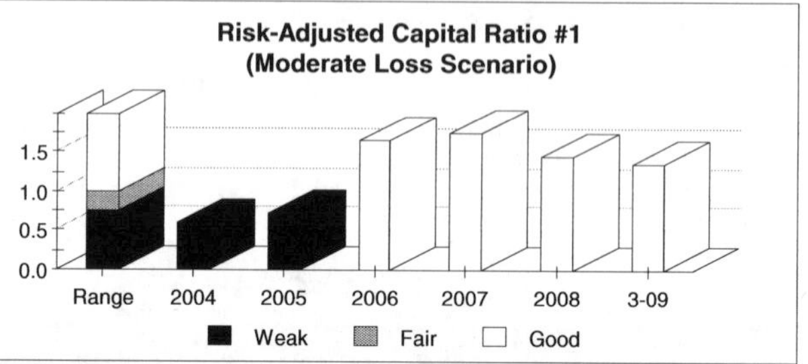

PMI MORTGAGE INS CO D- Weak

Major Rating Factors: Poor long-term capitalization index (1.3 on a scale of 0 to 10) based on weak current risk adjusted capital (severe and moderate loss scenarios). Weak profitability index (1.3) with operating losses during 2007 and the first three months of 2008. Average return on equity over the last five years has been poor at -20.6%.
Other Rating Factors: Weak overall results on stability tests (1.1) including weak risk adjusted capital in prior years and negative cash flow from operations for 2008. Fair reserve development (3.3) as the level of reserves has at times been insufficient to cover claims. In 2008 and 2007 the one year reserve development was 24% and 31% deficient respectively. Excellent liquidity (7.1) with ample operational cash flow and liquid investments.
Principal Business: Mortgage guaranty (100%).
Principal Investments: Investment grade bonds (80%), misc. investments (19%), and cash (1%).
Investments in Affiliates: 6%
Group Affiliation: PMI Group Inc
Licensed in: All states, the District of Columbia and Puerto Rico
Commenced Business: April 1973
Address: 2999 N 44th St Suite 250, Phoenix, AZ 85018
Phone: (800) 288-1970 **Domicile State:** AZ **NAIC Code:** 27251

Data Date	Rating	RACR #1	RACR #2	Loss Ratio %	Total Assets ($mil)	Capital ($mil)	Net Premium ($mil)	Net Income ($mil)
3-09	D-	0.29	0.23	N/A	3,434.9	379.3	162.1	-181.1
3-08	D	0.44	0.39	N/A	3,765.7	624.0	187.3	-255.6
2008	D-	0.38	0.30	239.6	3,503.8	462.1	653.8	-601.4
2007	D	0.36	0.33	136.0	3,682.6	495.5	670.9	-258.8
2006	B-	0.57	0.54	36.8	3,487.3	518.3	550.6	253.0
2005	B	0.68	0.63	38.7	3,506.6	510.8	594.0	157.8
2004	B+	0.92	0.84	36.3	3,421.7	645.5	527.4	273.8

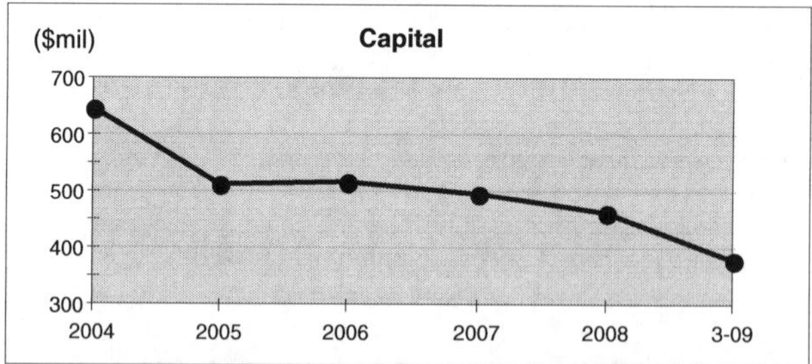

PMSLIC INS CO C+ Fair

Major Rating Factors: Fair reserve development (4.9 on a scale of 0 to 10) as the level of reserves has at times been insufficient to cover claims. In 2004, the one year reserve development was 16% deficient. Fair overall results on stability tests (4.3) including fair financial strength of affiliated Medical Group Holdings Inc. The largest net exposure for one risk is conservative at 1.8% of capital.
Other Rating Factors: Good overall profitability index (6.8) despite operating losses during the first three months of 2008. Return on equity has been fair, averaging 9.7% over the past five years. Strong long-term capitalization index (8.8) based on excellent current risk adjusted capital (severe and moderate loss scenarios), despite some fluctuation in capital levels. Excellent liquidity (7.8) with ample operational cash flow and liquid investments.
Principal Business: Medical malpractice (100%).
Principal Investments: Investment grade bonds (92%) and misc. investments (8%).
Investments in Affiliates: None
Group Affiliation: Medical Group Holdings Inc
Licensed in: DE, NJ, OH, PA
Commenced Business: January 1978
Address: 777 E Park Dr, Harrisburg, PA 17111
Phone: (717) 558-7500 **Domicile State:** PA **NAIC Code:** 35114

Data Date	Rating	RACR #1	RACR #2	Loss Ratio %	Total Assets ($mil)	Capital ($mil)	Net Premium ($mil)	Net Income ($mil)
3-09	C+	3.10	2.53	N/A	482.4	162.7	16.5	-1.4
3-08	C	2.06	1.72	N/A	493.2	154.3	16.1	-0.3
2008	C+	3.28	2.71	54.9	418.3	165.3	67.4	15.0
2007	C	2.08	1.76	73.9	405.2	154.8	77.2	13.7
2006	C-	1.18	1.05	55.9	457.3	146.0	83.1	21.9
2005	C-	0.90	0.79	80.1	444.8	127.5	89.7	14.0
2004	C	0.78	0.69	91.0	435.8	114.9	84.9	9.1

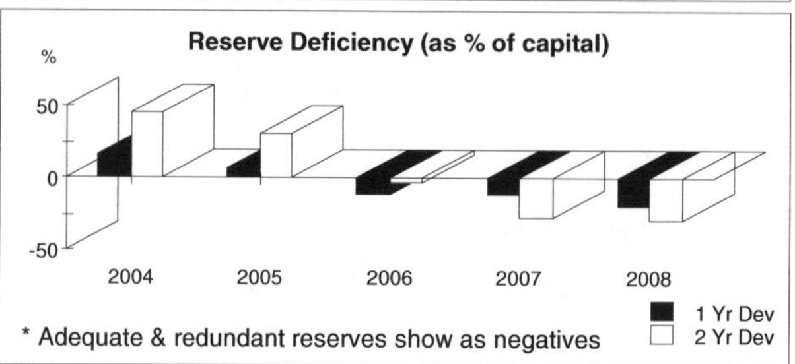

PRAETORIAN INS CO — C+ Fair

Major Rating Factors: Fair overall results on stability tests (4.5 on a scale of 0 to 10) including potential drain of affiliation with QBE Ins Group Ltd, negative cash flow from operations for 2008 and fair results on operational trends. The largest net exposure for one risk is acceptable at 2.6% of capital. Good long-term capitalization index (5.2) based on good current risk adjusted capital (severe loss scenario).

Other Rating Factors: Fair profitability index (4.6) with operating losses during 2005 and the first three months of 2008. Return on equity has been fair, averaging 5.4% over the past five years. History of adequate reserve strength (6.9) as reserves have been consistently at an acceptable level. Excellent liquidity (8.0) with ample operational cash flow and liquid investments.

Principal Business: Workers compensation (26%), auto liability (22%), commercial multiple peril (21%), inland marine (15%), auto physical damage (7%), other liability (4%), and other lines (6%).

Principal Investments: Cash (48%), investment grade bonds (46%), and misc. investments (6%).

Investments in Affiliates: 6%

Group Affiliation: QBE Ins Group Ltd

Licensed in: All states, the District of Columbia and Puerto Rico

Commenced Business: August 1979

Address: 3435 Wilshire Blvd, Ste 700, Los Angeles, CA 90010

Phone: (213) 613-0108 **Domicile State:** IL **NAIC Code:** 37257

Data Date	Rating	RACR #1	RACR #2	Loss Ratio %	Total Assets ($mil)	Capital ($mil)	Net Premium ($mil)	Net Income ($mil)
3-09	C+	1.25	0.82	N/A	934.9	334.3	78.4	-5.7
3-08	C+	1.18	0.84	N/A	1,351.0	470.1	96.6	8.8
2008	C+	1.31	0.86	59.5	1,063.1	349.8	248.0	19.4
2007	C+	1.13	0.81	63.5	1,290.3	461.0	401.2	32.6
2006	C+	1.21	0.83	61.0	1,739.2	398.7	511.5	51.6
2005	B-	1.63	1.09	68.2	1,054.0	324.8	399.6	-19.8
2004	C+	1.40	1.05	54.0	732.5	179.9	67.9	19.4

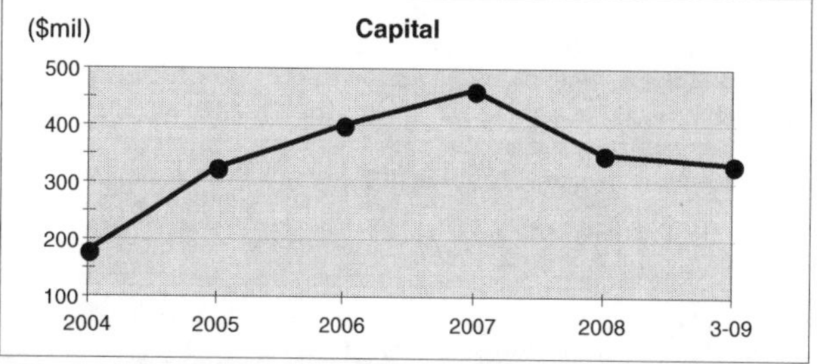

PREMIER INS CO OF MASSACHUSETTS — B- Good

Major Rating Factors: Fair profitability index (3.7 on a scale of 0 to 10). Good expense controls. Return on equity has been fair, averaging 24.1% over the past five years. Good liquidity (6.4) with sufficient resources (cash flows and marketable investments) to handle a spike in claims.

Other Rating Factors: Good overall results on stability tests (5.3). Stability strengths include good operational trends and excellent risk diversification. Strong long-term capitalization index (9.7) based on excellent current risk adjusted capital (severe and moderate loss scenarios), despite some fluctuation in capital levels. Ample reserve history (9.4) that helps to protect the company against sharp claims increases.

Principal Business: Auto liability (63%) and auto physical damage (37%).

Principal Investments: Investment grade bonds (103%).

Investments in Affiliates: None

Group Affiliation: Travelers Companies Inc

Licensed in: MA

Commenced Business: July 1993

Address: Ten Chestnut St., Suite 410, Worcester, MA 01608-2898

Phone: (508) 751-4339 **Domicile State:** MA **NAIC Code:** 12850

Data Date	Rating	RACR #1	RACR #2	Loss Ratio %	Total Assets ($mil)	Capital ($mil)	Net Premium ($mil)	Net Income ($mil)
3-09	B-	3.61	3.23	N/A	447.7	208.6	55.1	1.6
3-08	B-	3.34	2.98	N/A	484.1	216.1	63.9	4.8
2008	B-	3.33	3.09	70.3	457.7	208.1	231.1	22.4
2007	B-	3.04	2.83	65.6	493.4	211.9	262.5	42.4
2006	B-	2.96	2.75	56.5	566.8	231.9	302.0	66.7
2005	B-	2.97	2.72	43.3	629.0	272.2	327.4	105.0
2004	B-	2.26	2.05	67.3	693.6	228.2	348.1	62.6

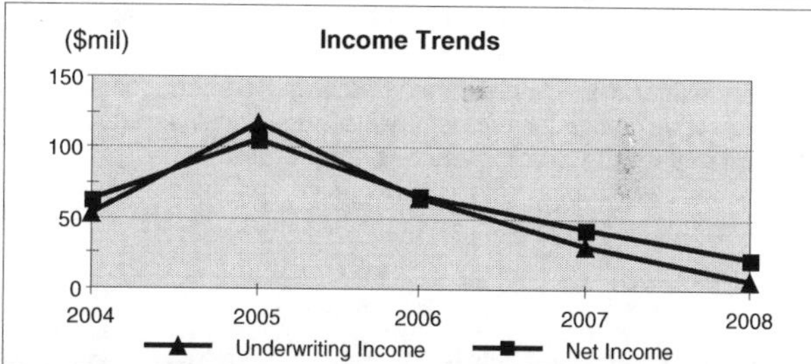

PRINCETON INS CO — D+ Weak

Major Rating Factors: Weak overall results on stability tests (2.6 on a scale of 0 to 10). Strengths include potentially strong support from affiliation with HUM Group of Companies. The largest net exposure for one risk is conservative at 1.7% of capital. A history of deficient reserves (0.6) that places pressure on both capital and profits. In the last five years, reserves (two year development) fluctuated between 98% and 63% deficeint.

Other Rating Factors: Fair long-term capitalization index (4.8) based on good current risk adjusted capital (moderate loss scenario). Over the last several years, capital levels have remained relatively consistent. Good liquidity (6.7) with sufficient resources (cash flows and marketable investments) to handle a spike in claims. Excellent profitability (7.5) with operating gains in each of the last five years. Return on equity has been good over the last five years, averaging 11.0%.

Principal Business: (Not applicable due to unusual reinsurance transactions.)

Principal Investments: Investment grade bonds (88%), misc. investments (8%), cash (2%), non investment grade bonds (1%), and real estate (1%).

Investments in Affiliates: None

Group Affiliation: HUM Group of Companies

Licensed in: AZ, CT, DC, DE, GA, IL, IN, MD, MI, NJ, NY, NC, PA, SC, VA, WA, WV

Commenced Business: February 1982

Address: 746 Alexander Rd, CN-5322, Princeton, NJ 08543-5322

Phone: (609) 951-5808 **Domicile State:** NJ **NAIC Code:** 42226

Data Date	Rating	RACR #1	RACR #2	Loss Ratio %	Total Assets ($mil)	Capital ($mil)	Net Premium ($mil)	Net Income ($mil)
3-09	D+	1.14	0.86	N/A	976.8	266.3	39.6	14.1
3-08	D+	0.97	0.69	N/A	1,034.7	274.9	44.5	15.1
2008	D+	1.10	0.84	77.8	962.9	259.5	164.6	5.6
2007	D+	0.96	0.68	61.8	1,012.9	269.8	188.4	56.6
2006	D+	0.72	0.52	86.9	1,007.7	222.3	173.6	18.3
2005	D	0.49	0.35	88.2	1,002.8	190.5	200.8	18.9
2004	D	0.42	0.30	92.9	976.4	166.6	186.2	18.2

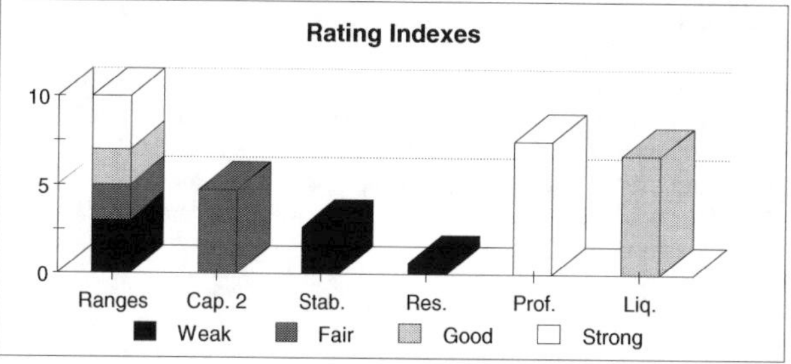

PROASSURANCE CASUALTY CO C+ Fair

Major Rating Factors: Fair overall results on stability tests (4.5 on a scale of 0 to 10) including potential drain of affiliation with ProAssurance Group and negative cash flow from operations for 2008. Good long-term capitalization index (5.8) based on good current risk adjusted capital (moderate loss scenario), despite some fluctuation in capital levels.

Other Rating Factors: History of adequate reserve strength (5.6) as reserves have been consistently at an acceptable level. Good overall profitability index (6.8). Good expense controls. Return on equity has been excellent over the last five years averaging 34.4%. Excellent liquidity (7.0) with ample operational cash flow and liquid investments.

Principal Business: Medical malpractice (94%) and other liability (6%).

Principal Investments: Investment grade bonds (95%), non investment grade bonds (3%), cash (1%), and misc. investments (1%).

Investments in Affiliates: None

Group Affiliation: ProAssurance Group

Licensed in: DE, FL, GA, IL, IN, IA, KS, KY, MD, MI, MO, NJ, OH, PA, SC, TN, VA, WV, WI

Commenced Business: June 1980

Address: 2600 Professionals Dr, Okemos, MI 48805-0150

Phone: (517) 349-6500 **Domicile State:** MI **NAIC Code:** 38954

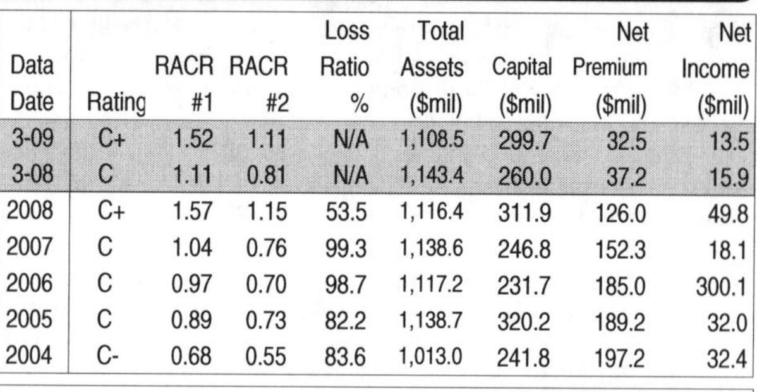

Data Date	Rating	RACR #1	RACR #2	Loss Ratio %	Total Assets ($mil)	Capital ($mil)	Net Premium ($mil)	Net Income ($mil)
3-09	C+	1.52	1.11	N/A	1,108.5	299.7	32.5	13.5
3-08	C	1.11	0.81	N/A	1,143.4	260.0	37.2	15.9
2008	C+	1.57	1.15	53.5	1,116.4	311.9	126.0	49.8
2007	C	1.04	0.76	99.3	1,138.6	246.8	152.3	18.1
2006	C	0.97	0.70	98.7	1,117.2	231.7	185.0	300.1
2005	C	0.89	0.73	82.2	1,138.7	320.2	189.2	32.0
2004	C-	0.68	0.55	83.6	1,013.0	241.8	197.2	32.4

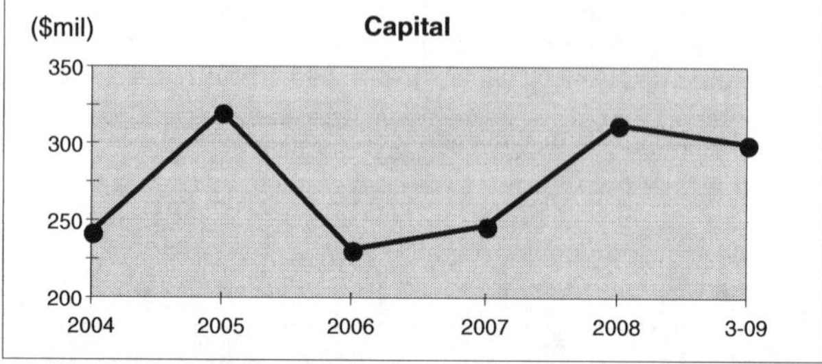

PROASSURANCE INDEMNTIY CO INC B Good

Major Rating Factors: Fair overall results on stability tests (4.6 on a scale of 0 to 10) including potential drain of affiliation with ProAssurance Group. Strong long-term capitalization index (7.9) based on excellent current risk adjusted capital (severe and moderate loss scenarios), despite some fluctuation in capital levels.

Other Rating Factors: Ample reserve history (7.1) that can protect against increases in claims costs. Excellent profitability (9.0) with operating gains in each of the last five years. Return on equity has been excellent over the last five years averaging 18.2%. Excellent liquidity (7.8) with ample operational cash flow and liquid investments.

Principal Business: (Not applicable due to unusual reinsurance transactions.)

Principal Investments: Investment grade bonds (95%), non investment grade bonds (3%), misc. investments (1%), and real estate (1%).

Investments in Affiliates: 0%

Group Affiliation: ProAssurance Group

Licensed in: All states except CT, ME, MS, NH, NJ, NY, VT, PR

Commenced Business: April 1977

Address: 100 Brookwood Pl, Birmingham, AL 35209

Phone: (205) 877-4400 **Domicile State:** AL **NAIC Code:** 33391

Data Date	Rating	RACR #1	RACR #2	Loss Ratio %	Total Assets ($mil)	Capital ($mil)	Net Premium ($mil)	Net Income ($mil)
3-09	B	2.47	2.07	N/A	1,822.2	584.9	53.8	21.8
3-08	B-	2.27	1.90	N/A	1,879.2	579.4	63.0	28.9
2008	B	2.41	2.03	30.8	1,818.2	566.3	228.8	129.4
2007	B-	2.21	1.86	37.5	1,881.4	569.4	263.3	132.4
2006	B-	1.41	1.21	57.9	1,720.5	429.1	288.9	99.2
2005	B-	1.11	0.94	78.6	1,570.7	328.7	298.5	54.0
2004	B-	0.95	0.75	92.9	1,391.5	276.9	322.9	17.6

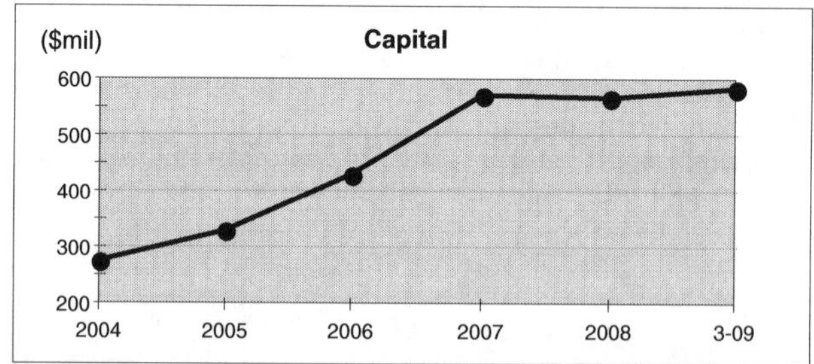

PROGRESSIVE CASUALTY INS CO C Fair

Major Rating Factors: Fair profitability index (3.2 on a scale of 0 to 10). Good expense controls. Return on equity has been fair, averaging 29.4% over the past five years. Fair overall results on stability tests (4.1).

Other Rating Factors: Vulnerable liquidity (1.1) as a spike in claims may stretch capacity. Good overall long-term capitalization (5.1) based on good current risk adjusted capital (severe and moderate loss scenarios). However, capital levels have fluctuated during prior years. History of adequate reserve strength (6.5) as reserves have been consistently at an acceptable level.

Principal Business: Auto liability (53%), auto physical damage (31%), other liability (7%), inland marine (5%), homeowners multiple peril (2%), and fidelity (2%).

Principal Investments: Investment grade bonds (46%), misc. investments (39%), real estate (12%), and cash (3%).

Investments in Affiliates: 29%

Group Affiliation: Progressive Group

Licensed in: All states, the District of Columbia and Puerto Rico

Commenced Business: December 1956

Address: 6300 Wilson Mills Rd,W33, Mayfield Village, OH 44143-2182

Phone: (440) 461-5000 **Domicile State:** OH **NAIC Code:** 24260

Data Date	Rating	RACR #1	RACR #2	Loss Ratio %	Total Assets ($mil)	Capital ($mil)	Net Premium ($mil)	Net Income ($mil)
3-09	C	0.91	0.80	N/A	5,072.6	1,271.5	980.4	80.2
3-08	C	0.79	0.68	N/A	5,061.6	1,268.7	1,000.3	47.3
2008	C	0.84	0.75	73.5	4,835.1	1,214.5	3,952.4	52.9
2007	C	0.77	0.66	71.4	4,772.6	1,253.9	3,998.1	357.3
2006	C+	0.95	0.81	66.1	5,588.1	1,592.7	4,713.9	661.0
2005	C+	0.96	0.80	67.0	5,917.4	1,654.0	5,064.0	537.3
2004	C+	0.99	0.80	64.4	6,508.1	1,773.9	5,203.3	727.6

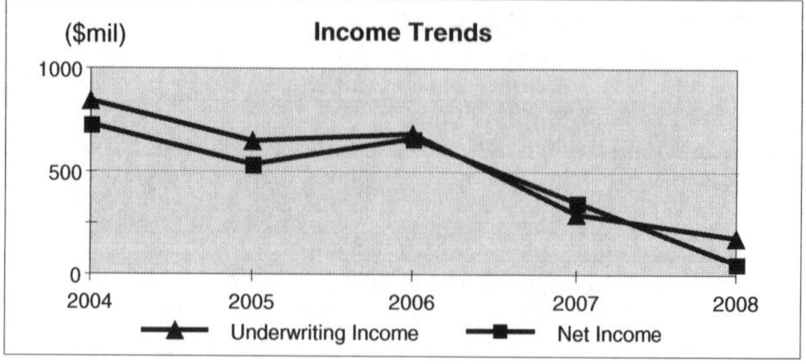

PROGRESSIVE DIRECT INS CO — C- Fair

Major Rating Factors: Vulnerable liquidity (2.0 on a scale of 0 to 10) as a spike in claims may stretch capacity. Weak overall results on stability tests (2.9). The largest net exposure for one risk is conservative at 1.6% of capital.

Other Rating Factors: Strong long-term capitalization index (7.2) based on excellent current risk adjusted capital (severe and moderate loss scenarios), despite some fluctuation in capital levels. Ample reserve history (8.3) that helps to protect the company against sharp claims increases. Excellent profitability (7.7). Return on equity has been good over the last five years, averaging 16.3%.

Principal Business: Auto liability (62%), auto physical damage (37%), and inland marine (1%).

Principal Investments: Investment grade bonds (73%), misc. investments (18%), and real estate (9%).

Investments in Affiliates: None

Group Affiliation: Progressive Group

Licensed in: All states except AZ, FL, MA, MI, NJ, TX, PR

Commenced Business: January 1987

Address: 6300 Wilson Mills Rd, Mayfield Village, OH 44143-2182

Phone: (440) 461-5000 **Domicile State:** OH **NAIC Code:** 16322

Data Date	Rating	RACR #1	RACR #2	Loss Ratio %	Total Assets ($mil)	Capital ($mil)	Net Premium ($mil)	Net Income ($mil)
3-09	C-	1.32	1.17	N/A	3,169.5	948.4	756.5	47.8
3-08	C-	1.25	1.05	N/A	2,887.3	866.8	696.0	4.6
2008	C-	1.21	1.10	73.7	3,011.6	884.0	2,926.7	-26.5
2007	C-	1.21	1.04	71.9	2,836.0	862.4	2,758.6	194.0
2006	C-	1.33	1.18	68.1	2,708.1	900.2	2,626.6	251.0
2005	C-	1.17	1.05	70.1	2,376.2	731.6	2,402.8	155.0
2004	C-	1.12	0.96	67.5	1,841.3	683.6	2,075.3	80.2

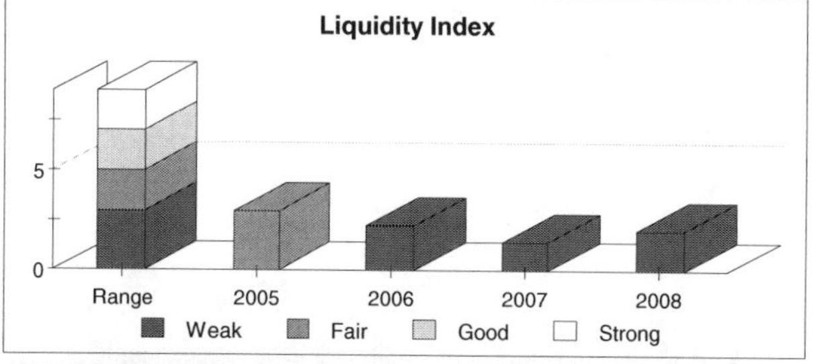

PROGRESSIVE GULF INS CO — B Good

Major Rating Factors: History of adequate reserve strength (6.4 on a scale of 0 to 10) as reserves have been consistently at an acceptable level. Good liquidity (6.5) with sufficient resources (cash flows and marketable investments) to handle a spike in claims.

Other Rating Factors: Fair overall results on stability tests (4.5) including potential drain of affiliation with Progressive Group. Strong long-term capitalization index (10.0) based on excellent current risk adjusted capital (severe and moderate loss scenarios). Moreover, capital levels have been consistent in recent years. Excellent profitability (8.9) with operating gains in each of the last five years. Return on equity has been excellent over the last five years averaging 15.3%.

Principal Business: Auto liability (61%), auto physical damage (36%), inland marine (2%), and other liability (1%).

Principal Investments: Investment grade bonds (99%) and non investment grade bonds (2%).

Investments in Affiliates: None

Group Affiliation: Progressive Group

Licensed in: GA, MS, OH, VA

Commenced Business: January 1983

Address: 6300 Wilson Mills Rd W33, Mayfield Village, OH 44143-2182

Phone: (440) 461-5000 **Domicile State:** OH **NAIC Code:** 42412

Data Date	Rating	RACR #1	RACR #2	Loss Ratio %	Total Assets ($mil)	Capital ($mil)	Net Premium ($mil)	Net Income ($mil)
3-09	B	5.36	4.67	N/A	340.1	196.3	40.0	5.9
3-08	B	4.93	4.25	N/A	331.1	184.8	40.8	5.1
2008	B	4.99	4.51	73.5	332.2	190.0	161.3	11.1
2007	B	4.69	4.17	71.4	329.8	183.4	167.4	18.9
2006	B	4.03	3.64	66.1	315.0	164.6	177.9	26.4
2005	B	3.10	2.74	67.0	313.7	138.6	192.7	25.4
2004	B	2.18	1.82	64.4	278.7	114.2	196.4	30.7

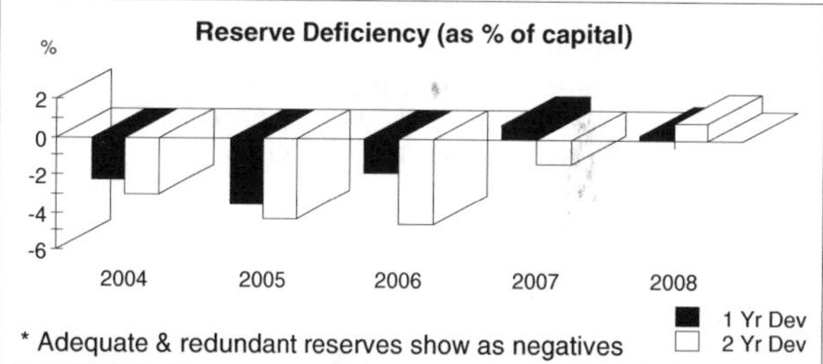

PROGRESSIVE NORTHERN INS CO — C+ Fair

Major Rating Factors: Fair overall results on stability tests (4.4 on a scale of 0 to 10) including potential drain of affiliation with Progressive Group. Fair profitability index (3.3). Good expense controls. Return on equity has been fair, averaging 32.3% over the past five years.

Other Rating Factors: Fair liquidity (3.2) as cash resources may not be adequate to cover a spike in claims. History of adequate reserve strength (6.5) as reserves have been consistently at an acceptable level. Strong long-term capitalization index (7.3) based on excellent current risk adjusted capital (severe and moderate loss scenarios), despite some fluctuation in capital levels.

Principal Business: Auto liability (57%), auto physical damage (39%), inland marine (2%), other liability (1%), and homeowners multiple peril (1%).

Principal Investments: Investment grade bonds (82%), misc. investments (17%), and non investment grade bonds (1%).

Investments in Affiliates: None

Group Affiliation: Progressive Group

Licensed in: All states except AL, AR, CA, FL, MA, MI, MO, NJ, ND, TN, TX, PR

Commenced Business: March 1981

Address: 8025 Excelsior Dr Suite 200, Madison, WI 53717

Phone: (440) 461-5000 **Domicile State:** WI **NAIC Code:** 38628

Data Date	Rating	RACR #1	RACR #2	Loss Ratio %	Total Assets ($mil)	Capital ($mil)	Net Premium ($mil)	Net Income ($mil)
3-09	C+	1.48	1.29	N/A	1,147.5	322.1	240.1	25.1
3-08	C+	1.31	1.05	N/A	1,167.3	317.3	245.0	16.8
2008	C+	1.31	1.16	73.5	1,126.9	298.6	967.9	34.2
2007	C+	1.24	1.01	71.4	1,167.2	314.9	1,004.4	92.6
2006	B-	1.37	1.13	66.1	1,269.4	357.6	1,067.3	146.7
2005	B-	1.36	1.15	67.0	1,305.2	373.1	1,156.0	141.5
2004	B-	1.36	1.10	64.4	1,426.1	435.9	1,178.1	182.8

Progressive Group
Composite Group Rating: C

Largest Group Members	Assets ($mil)	Rating
PROGRESSIVE CASUALTY INS CO	4835	C
PROGRESSIVE DIRECT INS CO	3012	C-
UNITED FINANCIAL CASUALTY CO	1783	C+
PROGRESSIVE NORTHERN INS CO	1127	C+
PROGRESSIVE NORTHWESTERN INS CO	1093	C+

PROGRESSIVE NORTHWESTERN INS CO — C+ Fair

Major Rating Factors: Fair overall results on stability tests (4.5 on a scale of 0 to 10) including potential drain of affiliation with Progressive Group. Fair profitability index (3.3). Good expense controls. Return on equity has been fair, averaging 31.4% over the past five years.

Other Rating Factors: Fair liquidity (3.9) as cash resources may not be adequate to cover a spike in claims. History of adequate reserve strength (6.5) as reserves have been consistently at an acceptable level. Strong long-term capitalization index (7.3) based on excellent current risk adjusted capital (severe and moderate loss scenarios), despite some fluctuation in capital levels.

Principal Business: Auto liability (60%), auto physical damage (37%), inland marine (2%), and other liability (1%).

Principal Investments: Investment grade bonds (87%), misc. investments (12%), and non investment grade bonds (1%).

Investments in Affiliates: None

Group Affiliation: Progressive Group

Licensed in: All states except AL, FL, IL, MA, MI, NH, PA, VT, WY, PR

Commenced Business: September 1983

Address: 6300 Wilson Mills Rd W33, Mayfield Village, OH 44143-2182

Phone: (440) 461-5000 **Domicile State:** OH **NAIC Code:** 42919

Data Date	Rating	RACR #1	RACR #2	Loss Ratio %	Total Assets ($mil)	Capital ($mil)	Net Premium ($mil)	Net Income ($mil)
3-09	C+	1.52	1.33	N/A	1,118.3	332.7	240.1	29.5
3-08	C+	1.28	1.00	N/A	1,115.8	314.0	245.0	13.9
2008	C+	1.30	1.17	73.5	1,092.8	297.3	967.9	38.9
2007	C+	1.24	0.98	71.4	1,141.0	320.0	1,004.4	85.6
2006	B-	1.35	1.09	66.1	1,206.9	359.3	1,067.3	140.5
2005	B-	1.34	1.11	67.0	1,271.6	373.6	1,156.0	138.7
2004	B	1.35	1.08	64.4	1,393.4	438.5	1,178.1	174.2

Progressive Group
Composite Group Rating: C

Largest Group Members	Assets ($mil)	Rating
PROGRESSIVE CASUALTY INS CO	4835	C
PROGRESSIVE DIRECT INS CO	3012	C-
UNITED FINANCIAL CASUALTY CO	1783	C+
PROGRESSIVE NORTHERN INS CO	1127	C+
PROGRESSIVE NORTHWESTERN INS CO	1093	C+

PROGRESSIVE PREFERRED INS CO — C Fair

Major Rating Factors: Fair overall results on stability tests (4.0 on a scale of 0 to 10) including potential drain of affiliation with Progressive Group. Fair profitability index (3.9). Good expense controls. Return on equity has been fair, averaging 37.3% over the past five years.

Other Rating Factors: Fair liquidity (4.3) as cash resources may not be adequate to cover a spike in claims. History of adequate reserve strength (6.5) as reserves have been consistently at an acceptable level. Strong long-term capitalization index (7.4) based on excellent current risk adjusted capital (severe and moderate loss scenarios), despite some fluctuation in capital levels.

Principal Business: Auto liability (63%), auto physical damage (36%), and inland marine (1%).

Principal Investments: Investment grade bonds (95%) and misc. investments (5%).

Investments in Affiliates: None

Group Affiliation: Progressive Group

Licensed in: AK, AZ, CO, DC, DE, GA, HI, ID, IN, IA, KY, ME, MD, MI, MN, MS, MO, MT, NE, NV, NJ, NM, NY, NC, OH, OK, OR, RI, SC, SD, TN, TX, UT, VA, WA, WV

Commenced Business: April 1980

Address: 6300 Wilson Mills Rd,W33, Mayfield Village, OH 44143-2182

Phone: (440) 461-5000 **Domicile State:** OH **NAIC Code:** 37834

Data Date	Rating	RACR #1	RACR #2	Loss Ratio %	Total Assets ($mil)	Capital ($mil)	Net Premium ($mil)	Net Income ($mil)
3-09	C	1.67	1.47	N/A	604.6	182.3	120.0	17.1
3-08	C	1.72	1.51	N/A	629.8	191.1	122.5	29.2
2008	C	1.46	1.33	73.5	589.9	165.3	484.0	61.8
2007	C	1.39	1.26	71.4	587.0	160.1	502.2	44.9
2006	C	1.42	1.29	66.1	617.8	171.5	533.7	71.3
2005	C+	1.39	1.23	67.0	652.1	184.2	578.0	65.7
2004	C+	1.27	1.06	64.4	692.9	198.1	589.1	87.0

Progressive Group
Composite Group Rating: C

Largest Group Members	Assets ($mil)	Rating
PROGRESSIVE CASUALTY INS CO	4835	C
PROGRESSIVE DIRECT INS CO	3012	C-
UNITED FINANCIAL CASUALTY CO	1783	C+
PROGRESSIVE NORTHERN INS CO	1127	C+
PROGRESSIVE NORTHWESTERN INS CO	1093	C+

PROGRESSIVE SPECIALTY INS CO — B Good

Major Rating Factors: History of adequate reserve strength (6.4 on a scale of 0 to 10) as reserves have been consistently at an acceptable level. Good overall profitability index (5.9) despite operating losses during 2008. Return on equity has been good over the last five years, averaging 10.9%.

Other Rating Factors: Good liquidity (6.5) with sufficient resources (cash flows and marketable investments) to handle a spike in claims. Fair overall results on stability tests (4.5) including potential drain of affiliation with Progressive Group. Strong long-term capitalization index (10.0) based on excellent current risk adjusted capital (severe and moderate loss scenarios), despite some fluctuation in capital levels.

Principal Business: Auto liability (60%), auto physical damage (38%), and inland marine (1%).

Principal Investments: Investment grade bonds (80%) and misc. investments (20%).

Investments in Affiliates: None

Group Affiliation: Progressive Group

Licensed in: All states except LA, MA, NH, NC, WY, PR

Commenced Business: May 1976

Address: 6300 Wilson Mills Rd,W33, Mayfield Village, OH 44143-2182

Phone: (440) 461-5000 **Domicile State:** OH **NAIC Code:** 32786

Data Date	Rating	RACR #1	RACR #2	Loss Ratio %	Total Assets ($mil)	Capital ($mil)	Net Premium ($mil)	Net Income ($mil)
3-09	B	4.64	4.01	N/A	1,061.2	594.4	140.1	16.5
3-08	B	4.56	3.61	N/A	1,133.6	655.9	142.9	12.5
2008	B	4.40	3.87	73.5	1,061.1	589.4	564.6	-62.3
2007	B	4.39	3.52	71.4	1,152.6	668.5	585.9	61.4
2006	B	4.01	3.30	66.1	1,120.6	619.5	622.6	89.2
2005	B	3.17	2.69	67.0	1,048.1	509.7	674.3	83.8
2004	B	2.29	1.87	64.4	987.0	427.4	687.2	107.1

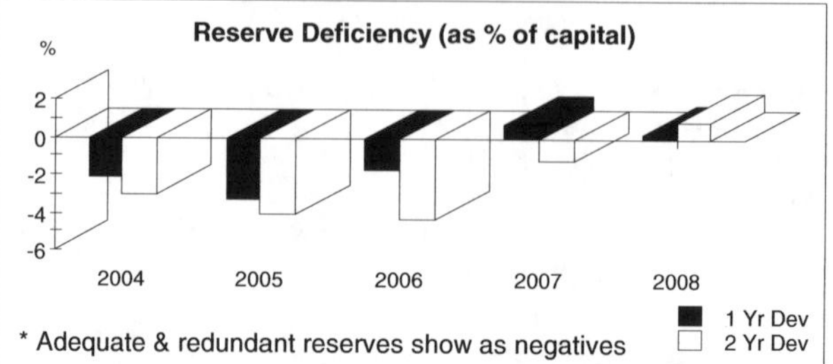

PROPERTY-OWNERS INS CO * A- Excellent

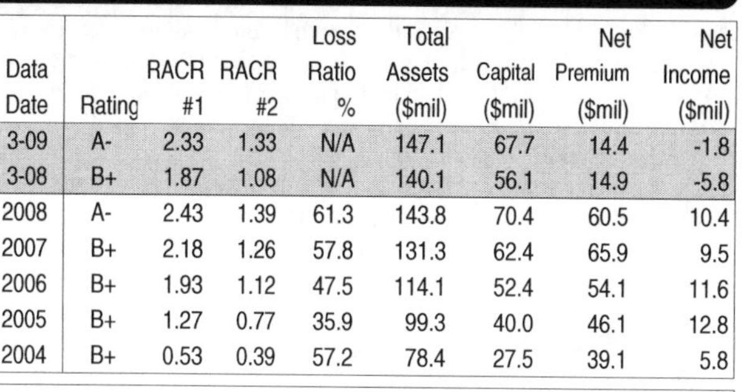

Data Date	Rating	RACR #1	RACR #2	Loss Ratio %	Total Assets ($mil)	Capital ($mil)	Net Premium ($mil)	Net Income ($mil)
3-09	A-	2.33	1.33	N/A	147.1	67.7	14.4	-1.8
3-08	B+	1.87	1.08	N/A	140.1	56.1	14.9	-5.8
2008	A-	2.43	1.39	61.3	143.8	70.4	60.5	10.4
2007	B+	2.18	1.26	57.8	131.3	62.4	65.9	9.5
2006	B+	1.93	1.12	47.5	114.1	52.4	54.1	11.6
2005	B+	1.27	0.77	35.9	99.3	40.0	46.1	12.8
2004	B+	0.53	0.39	57.2	78.4	27.5	39.1	5.8

Major Rating Factors: Strong long-term capitalization index (7.3 on a scale of 0 to 10) based on excellent current risk adjusted capital (severe and moderate loss scenarios), despite some fluctuation in capital levels. Ample reserve history (7.0) that can protect against increases in claims costs.

Other Rating Factors: Good overall profitability index (5.8) despite operating losses during the first three months of 2008. Return on equity has been good over the last five years, averaging 19.5%. Good liquidity (5.6) with sufficient resources (cash flows and marketable investments) to handle a spike in claims. Good overall results on stability tests (6.9).

Principal Business: Commercial multiple peril (35%), homeowners multiple peril (30%), workers compensation (10%), auto liability (8%), auto physical damage (7%), inland marine (5%), and other lines (7%).

Principal Investments: Investment grade bonds (91%) and misc. investments (9%).

Investments in Affiliates: None

Group Affiliation: Auto-Owners Group

Licensed in: AL, AR, IL, IN, IA, KY, MI, MO, NE, NV, ND, SC, SD, UT, VA, WI

Commenced Business: September 1976

Address: 3950 W Delphi Pike, Marion, IN 46952-9266

Phone: (517) 323-1200 **Domicile State:** IN **NAIC Code:** 32905

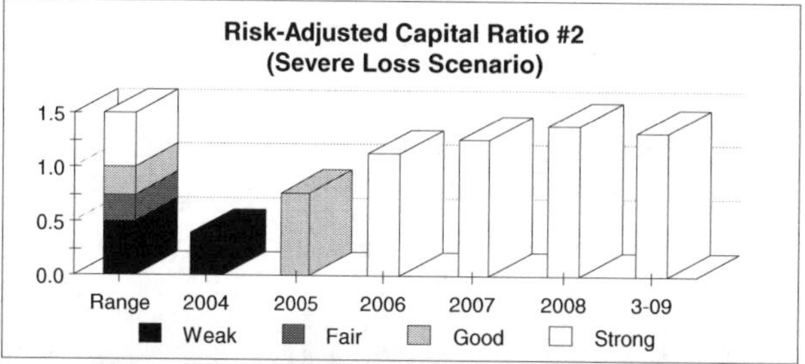

PROTECTIVE INS CO * A Excellent

Data Date	Rating	RACR #1	RACR #2	Loss Ratio %	Total Assets ($mil)	Capital ($mil)	Net Premium ($mil)	Net Income ($mil)
3-09	A	1.79	1.46	N/A	529.3	310.0	37.5	4.4
3-08	A+	2.09	1.63	N/A	604.0	347.8	35.0	-1.0
2008	A	1.78	1.45	63.2	541.7	314.2	148.6	12.7
2007	A+	2.26	1.78	59.3	619.8	359.6	130.8	27.9
2006	A+	2.23	1.71	67.7	596.0	342.7	117.4	20.9
2005	A+	2.12	1.60	81.7	579.7	330.5	131.8	11.4
2004	A+	1.96	1.47	77.7	525.5	318.2	110.6	14.4

Major Rating Factors: Strong long-term capitalization index (7.7 on a scale of 0 to 10) based on excellent current risk adjusted capital (severe and moderate loss scenarios). Furthermore, this high level of risk adjusted capital has been consistently maintained in previous years. Ample reserve history (9.1) that helps to protect the company against sharp claims increases.

Other Rating Factors: Excellent overall results on stability tests (7.3). Stability strengths include excellent operational trends and excellent risk diversification. Good liquidity (6.8) with sufficient resources (cash flows and marketable investments) to handle a spike in claims. Fair profitability index (3.9). Good expense controls. Return on equity has been fair, averaging 5.2% over the past five years.

Principal Business: Workers compensation (30%), other liability (28%), auto physical damage (20%), group accident & health (11%), auto liability (10%), and surety (1%).

Principal Investments: Misc. investments (58%) and investment grade bonds (44%).

Investments in Affiliates: 27%

Group Affiliation: Protective Ins Group

Licensed in: All states except PR

Commenced Business: December 1954

Address: 1099 N Meridian St, Indianapolis, IN 46204

Phone: (317) 636-9800 **Domicile State:** IN **NAIC Code:** 12416

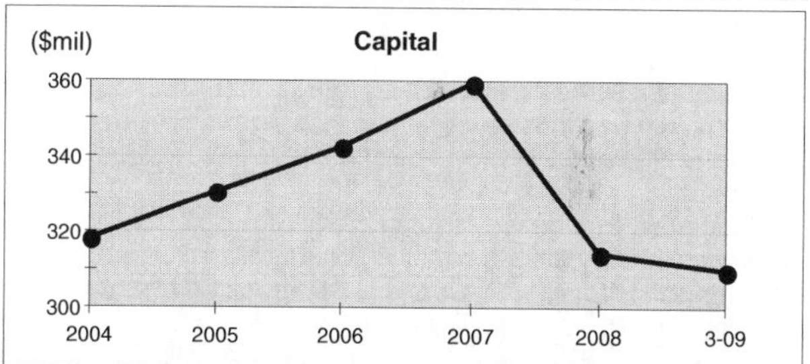

PUBLIC SERVICE MUTUAL INS CO C+ Fair

Data Date	Rating	RACR #1	RACR #2	Loss Ratio %	Total Assets ($mil)	Capital ($mil)	Net Premium ($mil)	Net Income ($mil)
3-09	C+	2.98	2.05	N/A	639.5	274.3	36.2	1.3
3-08	C	2.49	1.57	N/A	656.0	273.4	35.3	3.6
2008	C+	2.98	2.05	65.3	639.2	271.8	140.4	-1.6
2007	C	2.47	1.56	60.6	669.3	275.9	145.9	22.9
2006	C	N/A	N/A	61.3	680.1	250.8	164.1	22.5
2005	C	1.26	0.81	67.3	645.6	200.4	159.4	20.3
2004	C	0.76	0.50	65.8	629.5	172.7	168.4	21.2

Major Rating Factors: Fair overall results on stability tests (4.4 on a scale of 0 to 10) including potential drain of affiliation with Public Service Group and negative cash flow from operations for 2008. The largest net exposure for one risk is conservative at 1.3% of capital. Fair reserve development (4.6) as reserves have generally been sufficient to cover claims. In 2004, the two year reserve development was 41% deficient.

Other Rating Factors: Strong long-term capitalization index (8.2) based on excellent current risk adjusted capital (severe and moderate loss scenarios), despite some fluctuation in capital levels. Excellent profitability (7.7) despite modest operating losses during 2008. Excellent liquidity (7.0) with ample operational cash flow and liquid investments.

Principal Business: Commercial multiple peril (66%), workers compensation (26%), other liability (3%), fire (2%), homeowners multiple peril (1%), and allied lines (1%).

Principal Investments: Investment grade bonds (82%) and misc. investments (19%).

Investments in Affiliates: 10%

Group Affiliation: Public Service Group

Licensed in: All states except PR

Commenced Business: August 1925

Address: One Park Avenue, New York, NY 10016

Phone: (212) 591-9600 **Domicile State:** NY **NAIC Code:** 15059

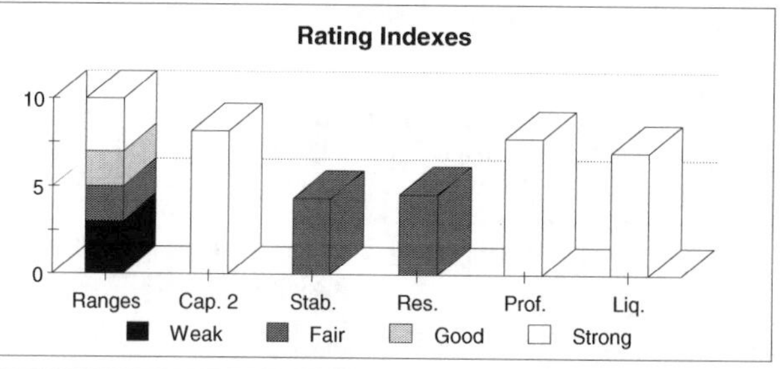

PUTNAM REINSURANCE CO — C Fair

Major Rating Factors: Fair long-term capitalization index (4.1 on a scale of 0 to 10) based on fair current risk adjusted capital (severe loss scenario). Fair overall results on stability tests (4.2) including fair risk adjusted capital in prior years.
Other Rating Factors: A history of deficient reserves (2.5). Underreserving can have an adverse impact on capital and profits. In four of the last five years reserves (two year development) were between 20% and 38% deficient. Good liquidity (6.2) with sufficient resources (cash flows and marketable investments) to handle a spike in claims. Excellent profitability (7.0) with operating gains in each of the last five years. Return on equity has been good over the last five years, averaging 11.1%.
Principal Business: (This company is a reinsurer.)
Principal Investments: Investment grade bonds (99%) and misc. investments (1%).
Investments in Affiliates: None
Group Affiliation: American International Group
Licensed in: AK, AZ, AR, CA, CO, DC, DE, FL, GA, HI, ID, IL, IN, IA, KY, LA, MD, MI, MN, MS, MO, MT, NE, NV, NM, NY, OH, OK, PA, SC, TX, UT, WA, WI
Commenced Business: September 1985
Address: 80 Pine St, 7th Floor, New York, NY 10005
Phone: (212) 770-2000 **Domicile State:** NY **NAIC Code:** 35157

Data Date	Rating	RACR #1	RACR #2	Loss Ratio %	Total Assets ($mil)	Capital ($mil)	Net Premium ($mil)	Net Income ($mil)
3-09	C	0.99	0.62	N/A	623.2	172.8	43.6	7.2
3-08	C	0.80	0.52	N/A	583.4	159.2	46.6	7.6
2008	C	0.95	0.60	71.1	606.8	165.9	183.6	24.7
2007	C	0.79	0.52	67.0	554.0	151.7	180.6	22.5
2006	C	0.86	0.56	67.9	505.3	138.1	165.5	23.9
2005	C	0.74	0.49	85.5	431.1	114.2	154.5	0.6
2004	C+	0.91	0.60	75.0	404.7	125.6	169.7	8.5

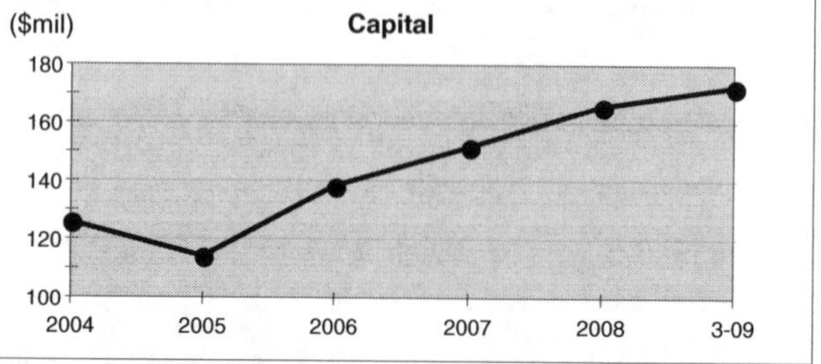

QBE INS CORP — B- Good

Major Rating Factors: Fair reserve development (4.3 on a scale of 0 to 10) as reserves have generally been sufficient to cover claims. Fair profitability index (3.5) with operating losses during the first three months of 2008. Return on equity has been low, averaging 2.3% over the past five years.
Other Rating Factors: Good overall results on stability tests (5.2) despite potential drain of affiliation with QBE Ins Group Ltd and excessive premium growth. Strong long-term capitalization index (7.2) based on good current risk adjusted capital (severe and moderate loss scenarios), although results have slipped from the excellent range during the last year. Excellent liquidity (8.8) with ample operational cash flow and liquid investments.
Principal Business: Commercial multiple peril (39%), group accident & health (24%), allied lines (11%), auto liability (10%), other liability (8%), auto physical damage (3%), and other lines (5%).
Principal Investments: Cash (55%), misc. investments (36%), and investment grade bonds (9%).
Investments in Affiliates: 41%
Group Affiliation: QBE Ins Group Ltd
Licensed in: All states except PR
Commenced Business: October 1980
Address: 1209 Orange St, Wilmington, DE 19801
Phone: (212) 422-9888 **Domicile State:** PA **NAIC Code:** 39217

Data Date	Rating	RACR #1	RACR #2	Loss Ratio %	Total Assets ($mil)	Capital ($mil)	Net Premium ($mil)	Net Income ($mil)
3-09	B-	1.26	0.90	N/A	844.5	256.2	61.2	-25.5
3-08	B-	1.71	1.29	N/A	493.0	169.4	31.4	5.2
2008	B-	1.69	1.47	72.5	610.5	272.3	131.6	-4.4
2007	B-	1.61	1.21	53.6	469.7	161.6	108.4	15.8
2006	B-	1.15	0.81	56.4	479.0	137.4	141.8	5.7
2005	B-	1.47	1.07	58.2	376.9	138.7	93.1	10.7
2004	B-	1.42	0.98	68.9	357.5	130.8	85.7	2.6

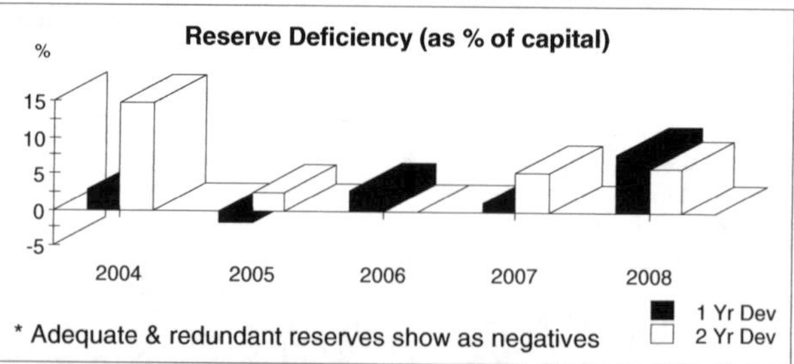

QBE REINSURANCE CORP — B- Good

Major Rating Factors: Fair reserve development (3.3 on a scale of 0 to 10) as the level of reserves has at times been insufficient to cover claims. In 2008 and 2004 the two year reserve development was 18% and 19% deficient respectively. Fair profitability index (4.7) with operating losses during 2008. Return on equity has been fair, averaging 5.2% over the past five years.
Other Rating Factors: Good overall results on stability tests (5.0). The largest net exposure for one risk is high at 3.0% of capital. Stability strengths include good operational trends and excellent risk diversification. Strong long-term capitalization index (7.3) based on excellent current risk adjusted capital (severe and moderate loss scenarios), despite some fluctuation in capital levels. Excellent liquidity (7.5) with ample operational cash flow and liquid investments.
Principal Business: (This company is a reinsurer.)
Principal Investments: Misc. investments (39%), cash (38%), and investment grade bonds (23%).
Investments in Affiliates: 26%
Group Affiliation: QBE Ins Group Ltd
Licensed in: AZ, AR, CA, DC, DE, FL, GA, HI, ID, IL, IN, IA, KS, LA, MI, MN, MS, NE, NV, NH, NJ, NY, OH, OK, OR, PA, TX, UT, VA, WA, WV, WI, PR
Commenced Business: October 1964
Address: 88 Pine Street, 16th Floorr, New York, NY 10005
Phone: (212) 422-1212 **Domicile State:** PA **NAIC Code:** 10219

Data Date	Rating	RACR #1	RACR #2	Loss Ratio %	Total Assets ($mil)	Capital ($mil)	Net Premium ($mil)	Net Income ($mil)
3-09	B-	1.65	1.37	N/A	1,129.0	547.7	83.9	37.7
3-08	B-	1.31	1.02	N/A	1,308.1	573.9	123.6	9.8
2008	B-	1.44	1.13	74.9	1,438.8	538.8	667.6	-11.9
2007	B-	1.33	1.04	68.4	1,258.5	569.2	482.2	12.0
2006	B-	1.38	1.08	59.5	1,171.7	545.6	468.8	44.7
2005	B-	1.37	1.06	60.9	1,122.9	539.5	427.5	27.2
2004	C+	1.12	0.76	60.1	1,010.8	435.6	449.4	32.3

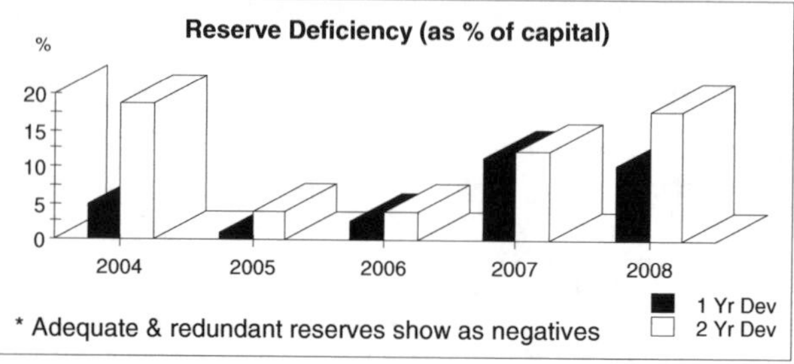

QUINCY MUTUAL FIRE INS CO B Good

Major Rating Factors: Good liquidity (6.9 on a scale of 0 to 10) with sufficient resources (cash flows and marketable investments) to handle a spike in claims. Fair overall results on stability tests (4.7) including potential drain of affiliation with Quincy Mutual Group.

Other Rating Factors: Fair profitability index (3.9) with operating losses during 2008. Strong long-term capitalization index (9.2) based on excellent current risk adjusted capital (severe and moderate loss scenarios), despite some fluctuation in capital levels. Ample reserve history (7.4) that can protect against increases in claims costs.

Principal Business: Homeowners multiple peril (48%), auto liability (19%), commercial multiple peril (15%), auto physical damage (11%), allied lines (3%), fire (3%), and workers compensation (1%).

Principal Investments: Investment grade bonds (52%), misc. investments (45%), non investment grade bonds (2%), and real estate (1%).

Investments in Affiliates: 3%

Group Affiliation: Quincy Mutual Group

Licensed in: CT, ME, MA, NH, NJ, NY, OH, PA, RI, VT

Commenced Business: May 1851

Address: 57 Washington St, Quincy, MA 02169

Phone: (617) 770-5100 **Domicile State:** MA **NAIC Code:** 15067

Data Date	Rating	RACR #1	RACR #2	Loss Ratio %	Total Assets ($mil)	Capital ($mil)	Net Premium ($mil)	Net Income ($mil)
3-09	B	3.81	2.43	N/A	997.9	584.9	62.3	3.6
3-08	B	3.66	2.28	N/A	1,214.9	727.5	64.0	5.5
2008	B	3.90	2.48	60.6	1,061.0	620.0	261.5	-40.4
2007	B	3.56	2.21	58.6	1,277.6	759.5	268.7	39.3
2006	B	3.25	2.02	56.2	1,259.2	721.9	323.3	48.9
2005	B	3.54	2.15	60.1	1,156.7	633.8	335.1	60.3
2004	B	2.99	1.83	63.0	1,029.3	533.1	323.2	27.7

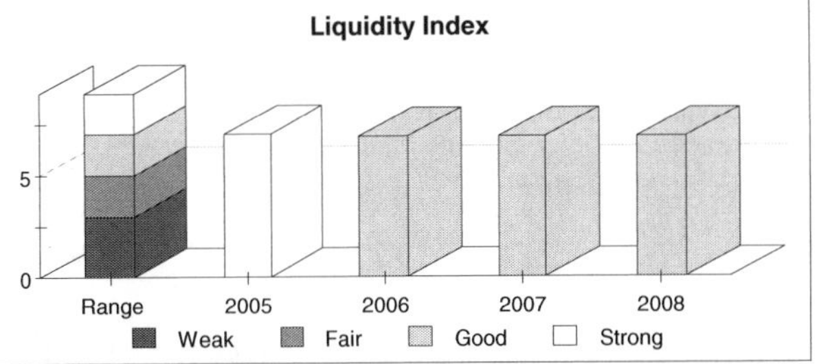

RADIAN ASSET ASR CO B Good

Major Rating Factors: History of adequate reserve strength (5.0 on a scale of 0 to 10) as reserves have been consistently at an acceptable level. Fair profitability index (4.5). Weak expense controls. Return on equity has been fair, averaging 6.4% over the past five years.

Other Rating Factors: Fair overall results on stability tests (4.5) including negative cash flow from operations for 2008. The largest net exposure for one risk is excessive at 6.3% of capital. Strong long-term capitalization index (10.0) based on excellent current risk adjusted capital (severe and moderate loss scenarios), despite some fluctuation in capital levels. Superior liquidity (9.1) with ample operational cash flow and liquid investments.

Principal Business: Financial guaranty (100%).

Principal Investments: Investment grade bonds (94%) and misc. investments (6%).

Investments in Affiliates: 4%

Group Affiliation: Radian Group Inc

Licensed in: All states except PR

Commenced Business: April 1986

Address: 360 Madison Ave, 25th Floor, New York, NY 10017-4605

Phone: (212) 983-5859 **Domicile State:** NY **NAIC Code:** 36250

Data Date	Rating	RACR #1	RACR #2	Loss Ratio %	Total Assets ($mil)	Capital ($mil)	Net Premium ($mil)	Net Income ($mil)
3-09	B	5.51	4.71	N/A	2,309.6	997.3	45.3	11.0
3-08	B+	8.43	6.68	N/A	2,504.2	1,075.4	48.6	-36.8
2008	B	5.53	4.80	73.0	2,324.6	965.4	79.6	5.4
2007	A-	9.17	7.41	4.8	2,529.8	1,137.4	259.2	124.6
2006	A-	8.48	6.86	50.2	2,258.2	1,001.3	257.7	52.1
2005	A-	6.97	5.96	N/A	2,084.1	994.5	187.6	117.0
2004	U	6.79	5.69	74.1	2,070.0	1,003.7	153.6	42.4

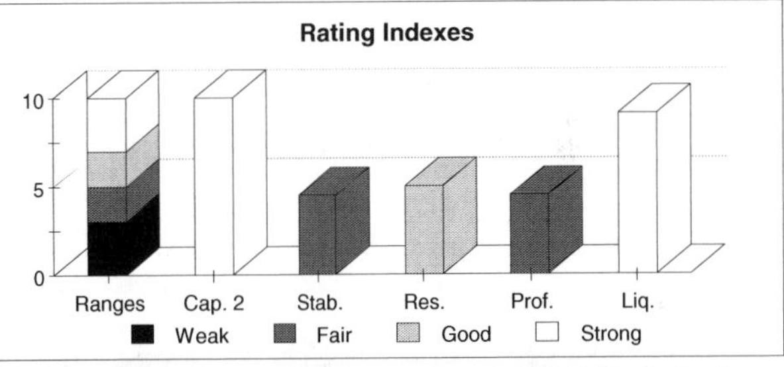

RADIAN GUARANTY INC D Weak

Major Rating Factors: Weak overall results on stability tests (1.9 on a scale of 0 to 10) including weak risk adjusted capital in prior years and negative cash flow from operations for 2008. Strengths include potentially strong support from affiliation with Radian Group Inc. Poor long-term capitalization index (0.7) based on weak current risk adjusted capital (severe and moderate loss scenarios).

Other Rating Factors: Weak profitability index (0.3) with operating losses during 2007 and the first three months of 2008. Average return on equity over the last five years has been poor at -29.1%. History of adequate reserve strength (5.8) as reserves have been consistently at an acceptable level. Good liquidity (5.5) with sufficient resources (cash flows and marketable investments) to handle a spike in claims.

Principal Business: Mortgage guaranty (100%).

Principal Investments: Investment grade bonds (63%) and misc. investments (37%).

Investments in Affiliates: 29%

Group Affiliation: Radian Group Inc

Licensed in: All states except PR

Commenced Business: April 1977

Address: 1601 Market Street, 12th Floor, Philadelphia, PA 19103

Phone: (215) 564-6600 **Domicile State:** PA **NAIC Code:** 33790

Data Date	Rating	RACR #1	RACR #2	Loss Ratio %	Total Assets ($mil)	Capital ($mil)	Net Premium ($mil)	Net Income ($mil)
3-09	D	0.23	0.20	N/A	4,318.0	399.2	158.2	-55.6
3-08	D	0.13	0.11	N/A	4,038.7	159.6	181.4	-351.3
2008	D	0.24	0.20	238.9	4,263.0	406.6	688.5	-1,622.9
2007	D	0.16	0.14	143.9	3,995.0	2,423.6	780.5	-157.1
2006	C	0.50	0.45	39.7	3,952.5	496.4	671.8	380.7
2005	C	0.88	0.70	41.9	3,567.9	413.4	702.9	460.2
2004	A-	0.97	0.76	43.8	3,248.7	421.8	710.4	331.4

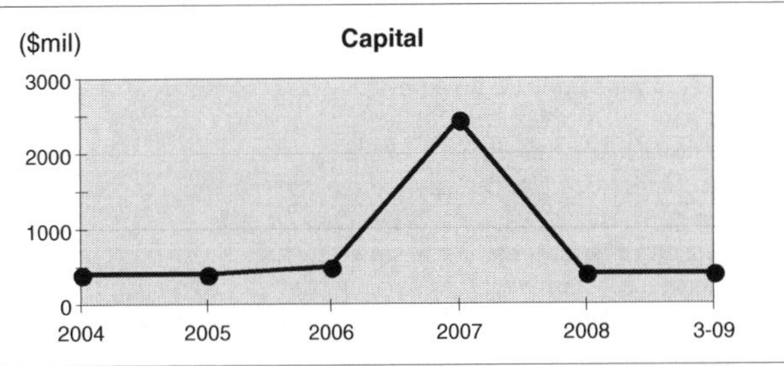

REDWOOD FIRE & CAS INS CO B Good

Major Rating Factors: Good overall results on stability tests (5.3 on a scale of 0 to 10) despite potential drain of affiliation with Berkshire-Hathaway and negative cash flow from operations for 2008. Stability strengths include good operational trends and excellent risk diversification. Good long-term capitalization index (6.1) based on good current risk adjusted capital (moderate loss scenario). Moreover, capital levels have been consistent in recent years.

Other Rating Factors: Ample reserve history (7.0) that can protect against increases in claims costs. Excellent profitability (7.8). Return on equity has been good over the last five years, averaging 22.8%. Excellent liquidity (8.4) with ample operational cash flow and liquid investments.

Principal Business: Workers compensation (90%), auto liability (7%), and auto physical damage (2%).

Principal Investments: Investment grade bonds (62%), non investment grade bonds (31%), misc. investments (6%), and cash (1%).

Investments in Affiliates: None

Group Affiliation: Berkshire-Hathaway

Licensed in: AZ, CA, CO, DE, HI, ID, NE, NV, NM, TX, UT

Commenced Business: January 1970

Address: 9290 W Dodge Road,Ste 300, Omaha, NE 68114-3363

Phone: (402) 393-7255 **Domicile State:** NE **NAIC Code:** 11673

Data Date	Rating	RACR #1	RACR #2	Loss Ratio %	Total Assets ($mil)	Capital ($mil)	Net Premium ($mil)	Net Income ($mil)
3-09	B	2.56	1.38	N/A	863.5	378.6	13.0	8.0
3-08	B	1.53	0.94	N/A	924.6	367.6	36.4	4.9
2008	B	2.27	1.24	60.6	877.8	372.5	121.0	37.4
2007	B	1.35	0.84	65.8	912.5	361.4	238.4	35.0
2006	B	0.72	0.47	61.6	800.8	305.2	424.7	56.8
2005	B+	0.87	0.57	74.0	547.6	236.2	250.9	193.0
2004	A-	1.14	1.03	89.5	329.7	216.2	60.0	-5.5

Berkshire-Hathaway
Composite Group Rating: C

Largest Group Members	Assets ($mil)	Rating
NATIONAL INDEMNITY CO	61720	C+
GENERAL REINSURANCE CORP	14446	B-
GOVERNMENT EMPLOYEES INS CO	12496	B+
COLUMBIA INS CO	11050	C+
GEICO INDEMNITY CO	4873	B+

REPUBLIC INDEMNITY CO OF AMERICA B- Good

Major Rating Factors: Fair overall results on stability tests (4.9 on a scale of 0 to 10) including potential drain of affiliation with American Financial Corp. History of adequate reserve strength (5.9) as reserves have been consistently at an acceptable level.

Other Rating Factors: Good overall profitability index (5.3). Fair expense controls. Return on equity has been excellent over the last five years averaging 18.8%. Good liquidity (6.9) with sufficient resources (cash flows and marketable investments) to handle a spike in claims. Strong long-term capitalization index (7.4) based on excellent current risk adjusted capital (severe and moderate loss scenarios), despite some fluctuation in capital levels.

Principal Business: Workers compensation (79%) and other liability (21%).

Principal Investments: Investment grade bonds (94%), misc. investments (3%), non investment grade bonds (2%), and cash (1%).

Investments in Affiliates: 3%

Group Affiliation: American Financial Corp

Licensed in: AL, AK, AZ, AR, CA, CO, DC, DE, GA, HI, ID, IL, IN, IA, KS, KY, LA, ME, MD, MI, MS, MO, MT, NE, NV, NM, NC, OH, OK, OR, RI, SC, SD, TN, TX, UT, WA, WV, WI

Commenced Business: March 1973

Address: 15821 Ventura Blvd, Suite 370, Encino, CA 91436

Phone: (818) 382-1051 **Domicile State:** CA **NAIC Code:** 22179

Data Date	Rating	RACR #1	RACR #2	Loss Ratio %	Total Assets ($mil)	Capital ($mil)	Net Premium ($mil)	Net Income ($mil)
3-09	B-	2.18	1.45	N/A	862.6	294.2	42.3	4.5
3-08	B-	2.03	1.35	N/A	890.1	308.9	49.9	9.9
2008	B-	2.20	1.46	47.0	858.0	292.9	206.7	41.8
2007	B-	2.14	1.41	51.2	891.2	323.0	226.0	56.6
2006	C+	1.88	1.25	51.4	893.4	320.8	276.9	69.7
2005	C+	1.64	0.94	49.9	875.4	310.2	334.1	83.8
2004	C+	1.30	0.78	67.2	797.8	242.6	328.6	40.0

American Financial Corp
Composite Group Rating: B-

Largest Group Members	Assets ($mil)	Rating
GREAT AMERICAN LIFE INS CO	9628	B-
GREAT AMERICAN INS CO	5642	C
ANNUITY INVESTORS LIFE INS CO	1742	B-
REPUBLIC INDEMNITY CO OF AMERICA	858	B-
NATIONAL INTERSTATE INS CO	730	C+

REPUBLIC UNDERWRITERS INS CO B- Good

Major Rating Factors: Fair overall results on stability tests (4.5 on a scale of 0 to 10) including potential drain of affiliation with Delek Group Ltd and negative cash flow from operations for 2008. Fair profitability index (4.7) with operating losses during 2008. Return on equity has been low, averaging 4.9% over the past five years.

Other Rating Factors: History of adequate reserve strength (5.9) as reserves have been consistently at an acceptable level. Good liquidity (6.1) with sufficient resources (cash flows and marketable investments) to handle a spike in claims. Strong long-term capitalization index (7.4) based on excellent current risk adjusted capital (severe and moderate loss scenarios). Moreover, capital levels have been consistent in recent years.

Principal Business: Commercial multiple peril (32%), workers compensation (18%), auto liability (16%), other liability (13%), homeowners multiple peril (8%), auto physical damage (6%), and other lines (7%).

Principal Investments: Investment grade bonds (87%) and misc. investments (15%).

Investments in Affiliates: 13%

Group Affiliation: Delek Group Ltd

Licensed in: AZ, CO, LA, NV, NM, OK, TX, UT

Commenced Business: October 1965

Address: 2727 Turtle Creek Blvd, Dallas, TX 75219

Phone: (214) 559-1222 **Domicile State:** TX **NAIC Code:** 24538

Data Date	Rating	RACR #1	RACR #2	Loss Ratio %	Total Assets ($mil)	Capital ($mil)	Net Premium ($mil)	Net Income ($mil)
3-09	B-	1.88	1.30	N/A	694.4	242.3	102.3	4.4
3-08	B-	2.02	1.39	N/A	646.3	226.8	99.3	9.9
2008	B-	1.86	1.29	70.0	710.0	235.6	409.8	-30.1
2007	B-	2.06	1.42	54.2	657.1	218.3	415.0	16.9
2006	C+	1.89	1.46	51.0	531.3	182.1	338.1	13.1
2005	C	1.33	0.99	54.3	463.1	169.4	269.5	15.9
2004	C	1.26	0.95	55.1	417.5	152.2	243.6	18.8

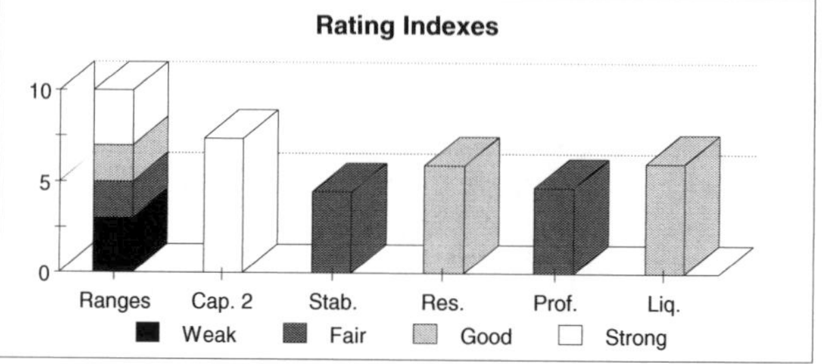

RLI INS CO — B — Good

Major Rating Factors: Good overall results on stability tests (5.4 on a scale of 0 to 10) despite potential drain of affiliation with RLI Corp. The largest net exposure for one risk is conservative at 1.1% of capital. Fair profitability index (4.7) with operating losses during the first three months of 2008. Return on equity has been fair, averaging 7.7% over the past five years.

Other Rating Factors: Strong long-term capitalization index (7.3) based on excellent current risk adjusted capital (severe and moderate loss scenarios), despite some fluctuation in capital levels. Ample reserve history (8.0) that helps to protect the company against sharp claims increases. Excellent liquidity (7.0) with ample operational cash flow and liquid investments.

Principal Business: Other liability (40%), surety (21%), ocean marine (14%), auto liability (14%), inland marine (3%), homeowners multiple peril (3%), and other lines (5%).

Principal Investments: Misc. investments (53%), investment grade bonds (46%), and real estate (1%).

Investments in Affiliates: 40%

Group Affiliation: RLI Corp

Licensed in: All states, the District of Columbia and Puerto Rico

Commenced Business: November 1960

Address: 9025 N Lindbergh Dr, Peoria, IL 61615

Phone: (309) 692-1000 **Domicile State:** IL **NAIC Code:** 13056

Data Date	Rating	RACR #1	RACR #2	Loss Ratio %	Total Assets ($mil)	Capital ($mil)	Net Premium ($mil)	Net Income ($mil)
3-09	B	1.34	1.19	N/A	1,266.2	663.1	68.0	-11.4
3-08	B	1.36	1.19	N/A	1,313.1	705.3	64.1	8.4
2008	B	1.35	1.20	44.4	1,279.1	678.0	274.4	26.7
2007	B	1.44	1.25	36.8	1,351.9	752.0	253.3	126.2
2006	B-	1.52	1.28	45.9	1,366.3	746.9	229.4	75.7
2005	B-	1.46	1.23	52.6	1,300.3	690.5	216.5	38.3
2004	B-	1.40	1.13	54.9	1,216.0	606.0	244.9	35.9

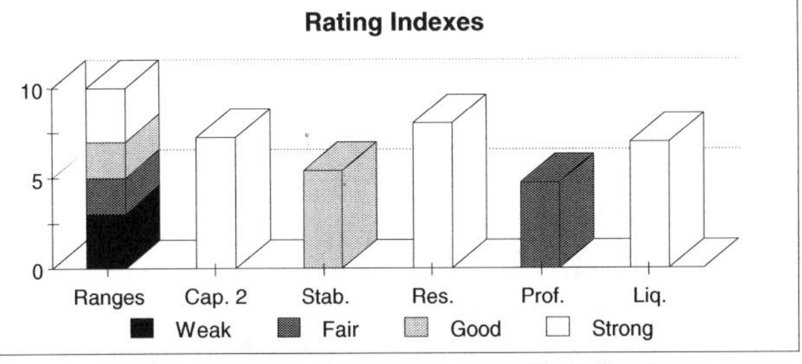

RSUI INDEMNITY CO — C — Fair

Major Rating Factors: Fair overall results on stability tests (3.5 on a scale of 0 to 10) including potential drain of affiliation with Alleghany Corp Group. The largest net exposure for one risk is conservative at 1.0% of capital. History of adequate reserve strength (6.3) as reserves have been consistently at an acceptable level.

Other Rating Factors: Good overall profitability index (6.1) despite operating losses during 2005. Return on equity has been fair, averaging 8.5% over the past five years. Strong long-term capitalization index (7.5) based on excellent current risk adjusted capital (severe and moderate loss scenarios), despite some fluctuation in capital levels. Excellent liquidity (7.0) with ample operational cash flow and liquid investments.

Principal Business: Other liability (67%), allied lines (16%), fire (12%), and inland marine (4%).

Principal Investments: Investment grade bonds (84%), misc. investments (15%), and cash (1%).

Investments in Affiliates: 8%

Group Affiliation: Alleghany Corp Group

Licensed in: All states except CT, ME, NC, PR

Commenced Business: December 1977

Address: 26050 Mureau Rd, Calabasas, CA 91302

Phone: (818) 878-9500 **Domicile State:** NH **NAIC Code:** 22314

Data Date	Rating	RACR #1	RACR #2	Loss Ratio %	Total Assets ($mil)	Capital ($mil)	Net Premium ($mil)	Net Income ($mil)
3-09	C	2.54	1.43	N/A	2,480.2	984.4	150.4	18.0
3-08	C	2.62	1.51	N/A	2,497.1	1,059.4	166.5	44.8
2008	C	2.62	1.48	54.4	2,490.9	1,001.9	610.7	7.0
2007	C	2.70	1.57	46.6	2,499.8	1,084.0	672.3	216.4
2006	C-	2.21	1.29	50.1	2,257.9	920.6	632.3	159.4
2005	C-	1.28	0.80	101.7	1,957.7	738.6	580.6	-60.2
2004	C-	1.14	0.79	67.0	1,471.9	647.3	589.1	83.3

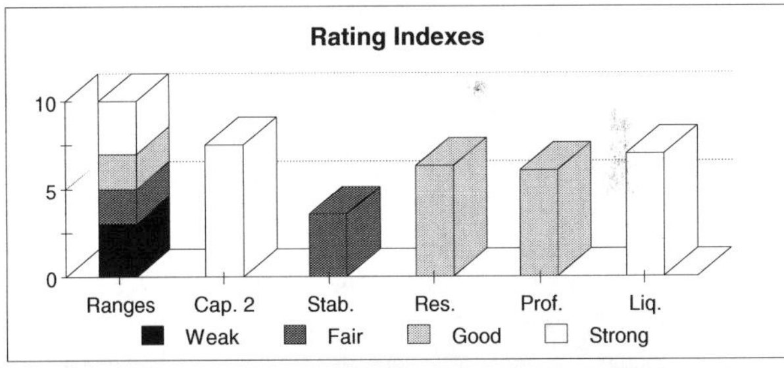

RURAL COMMUNITY INS CO — B- — Good

Major Rating Factors: Fair overall results on stability tests (4.9 on a scale of 0 to 10) including negative cash flow from operations for 2008 and fair results on operational trends. Strong long-term capitalization index (7.7) based on excellent current risk adjusted capital (severe and moderate loss scenarios). Moreover, capital levels have been consistent in recent years.

Other Rating Factors: Ample reserve history (10.0) that helps to protect the company against sharp claims increases. Excellent profitability (8.9) with operating gains in each of the last five years. Excellent expense controls. Return on equity has been good over the last five years, averaging 11.6%. Vulnerable liquidity (1.8) as a spike in claims may stretch capacity.

Principal Business: Allied lines (100%).

Principal Investments: Investment grade bonds (59%) and misc. investments (41%).

Investments in Affiliates: None

Group Affiliation: Wells Fargo Group

Licensed in: All states except CO, DC, NH, NY, NC, TN, WY, PR

Commenced Business: April 1980

Address: 3501 Thurston Avenue, Anoka, MN 55303

Phone: (605) 575-4947 **Domicile State:** MN **NAIC Code:** 39039

Data Date	Rating	RACR #1	RACR #2	Loss Ratio %	Total Assets ($mil)	Capital ($mil)	Net Premium ($mil)	Net Income ($mil)
3-09	B-	6.48	4.62	N/A	856.9	339.5	11.5	19.4
3-08	C+	0.85	0.74	N/A	763.9	319.5	42.3	9.4
2008	B-	2.97	2.02	97.7	4,387.5	322.3	318.6	18.8
2007	C+	0.73	0.61	53.3	3,085.4	315.1	712.1	35.8
2006	C+	0.99	0.79	98.5	2,658.7	273.8	507.0	22.3
2005	C+	0.67	0.57	50.3	2,189.3	252.8	408.6	43.1
2004	C+	0.40	0.29	114.2	2,167.0	122.3	467.7	15.8

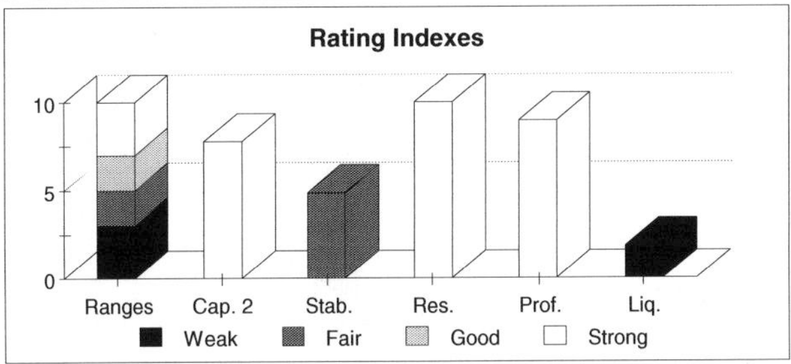

SAFECO INS CO OF AMERICA — B- Good

Major Rating Factors: Fair overall results on stability tests (4.9 on a scale of 0 to 10). Strengths include potentially strong support from affiliation with Liberty Mutual Group. Fair profitability index (3.0). Fair expense controls. Return on equity has been fair, averaging 23.2% over the past five years.
Other Rating Factors: History of adequate reserve strength (6.9) as reserves have been consistently at an acceptable level. Good liquidity (5.7) with sufficient resources (cash flows and marketable investments) to handle a spike in claims. Strong long-term capitalization index (7.5) based on excellent current risk adjusted capital (severe and moderate loss scenarios), despite some fluctuation in capital levels.
Principal Business: Homeowners multiple peril (27%), surety (21%), auto liability (21%), auto physical damage (16%), fire (5%), allied lines (3%), and other lines (7%).
Principal Investments: Investment grade bonds (87%), misc. investments (16%), and non investment grade bonds (2%).
Investments in Affiliates: 3%
Group Affiliation: Liberty Mutual Group
Licensed in: All states except PR
Commenced Business: October 1953
Address: Safeco Plaza, Seattle, WA 98185
Phone: (206) 545-5000 **Domicile State:** WA **NAIC Code:** 24740

Data Date	Rating	RACR #1	RACR #2	Loss Ratio %	Total Assets ($mil)	Capital ($mil)	Net Premium ($mil)	Net Income ($mil)
3-09	B-	2.14	1.41	N/A	7,272.4	955.7	406.3	20.1
3-08	B-	1.81	1.19	N/A	4,013.0	816.4	457.6	51.5
2008	B-	1.91	1.34	67.0	3,952.2	769.8	1,762.5	163.8
2007	B-	1.86	1.23	62.9	4,067.2	838.6	1,866.5	248.4
2006	B-	2.58	1.70	58.5	4,522.0	1,155.4	1,852.6	288.8
2005	B-	2.43	1.63	62.3	4,469.0	1,197.9	1,918.6	256.0
2004	C+	2.04	1.37	63.2	3,785.6	1,043.4	1,873.0	232.1

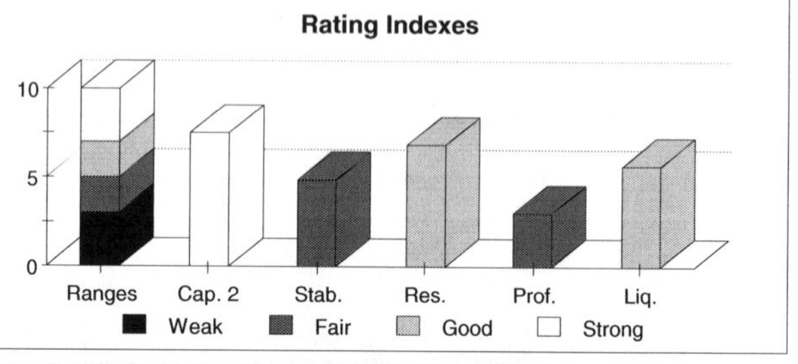

SAFECO INS CO OF ILLINOIS — B Good

Major Rating Factors: History of adequate reserve strength (6.9 on a scale of 0 to 10) as reserves have been consistently at an acceptable level. Good liquidity (6.7) with sufficient resources (cash flows and marketable investments) to handle a spike in claims.
Other Rating Factors: Good overall results on stability tests (5.6). Stability strengths include good operational trends and excellent risk diversification. Fair profitability index (3.7). Fair expense controls. Return on equity has been fair, averaging 18.1% over the past five years. Strong long-term capitalization index (7.8) based on excellent current risk adjusted capital (severe and moderate loss scenarios), despite some fluctuation in capital levels.
Principal Business: Auto liability (55%), auto physical damage (33%), homeowners multiple peril (8%), and earthquake (3%).
Principal Investments: Investment grade bonds (83%), misc. investments (14%), and non investment grade bonds (3%).
Investments in Affiliates: 7%
Group Affiliation: Liberty Mutual Group
Licensed in: AL, AK, AZ, AR, CA, CO, CT, FL, GA, ID, IL, IN, IA, KS, KY, LA, MD, MI, MN, MS, MO, MT, NE, NV, NM, OH, OK, OR, PA, TN, TX, UT, VA, WA, WI, WY
Commenced Business: January 1981
Address: 2800 W Higgins Rd, Hoffman Estates, IL 60195
Phone: (206) 545-5000 **Domicile State:** IL **NAIC Code:** 39012

Data Date	Rating	RACR #1	RACR #2	Loss Ratio %	Total Assets ($mil)	Capital ($mil)	Net Premium ($mil)	Net Income ($mil)
3-09	B	1.77	1.07	N/A	1,767.4	155.0	53.5	2.3
3-08	B	2.05	1.40	N/A	676.4	184.6	69.3	7.6
2008	B	2.32	1.68	67.0	640.8	159.6	267.0	18.8
2007	B	2.06	1.42	62.9	671.1	185.5	282.8	30.7
2006	B	2.11	1.45	58.5	664.1	188.7	280.7	41.1
2005	B	1.88	1.30	62.3	665.0	173.8	290.7	36.0
2004	B	1.84	1.28	63.2	542.5	166.4	283.8	37.7

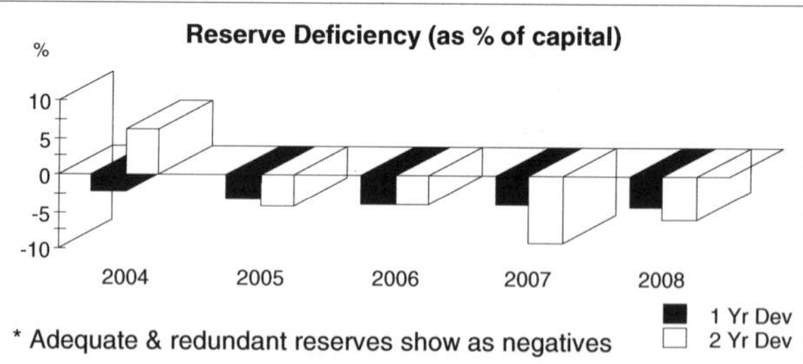

* Adequate & redundant reserves show as negatives

SAFETY INS CO * — B+ Good

Major Rating Factors: Good overall results on stability tests (5.0 on a scale of 0 to 10) despite potential drain of affiliation with Safety Group. Stability strengths include good operational trends and excellent risk diversification. Good liquidity (6.7) with sufficient resources (cash flows and marketable investments) to handle a spike in claims.
Other Rating Factors: Strong long-term capitalization index (10.0) based on excellent current risk adjusted capital (severe and moderate loss scenarios), despite some fluctuation in capital levels. Ample reserve history (7.0) that can protect against increases in claims costs. Excellent profitability (8.7) with operating gains in each of the last five years. Return on equity has been excellent over the last five years averaging 18.3%.
Principal Business: Auto liability (59%), auto physical damage (33%), homeowners multiple peril (4%), commercial multiple peril (2%), and other liability (1%).
Principal Investments: Investment grade bonds (99%) and misc. investments (3%).
Investments in Affiliates: 5%
Group Affiliation: Safety Group
Licensed in: MA
Commenced Business: January 1980
Address: 20 Custom House St, Boston, MA 02110
Phone: (617) 951-0600 **Domicile State:** MA **NAIC Code:** 39454

Data Date	Rating	RACR #1	RACR #2	Loss Ratio %	Total Assets ($mil)	Capital ($mil)	Net Premium ($mil)	Net Income ($mil)
3-09	B+	4.59	3.75	N/A	1,190.4	550.8	121.8	10.7
3-08	B+	4.13	3.40	N/A	1,223.1	525.3	135.7	15.4
2008	B+	4.44	3.76	64.1	1,226.1	560.5	497.6	68.5
2007	B+	3.91	3.35	61.5	1,212.4	515.0	525.5	83.4
2006	B+	3.22	2.74	56.6	1,155.5	457.5	589.9	110.1
2005	B+	2.43	2.08	61.9	1,048.7	350.8	601.2	92.4
2004	B+	1.95	1.68	71.7	982.5	278.2	588.0	42.3

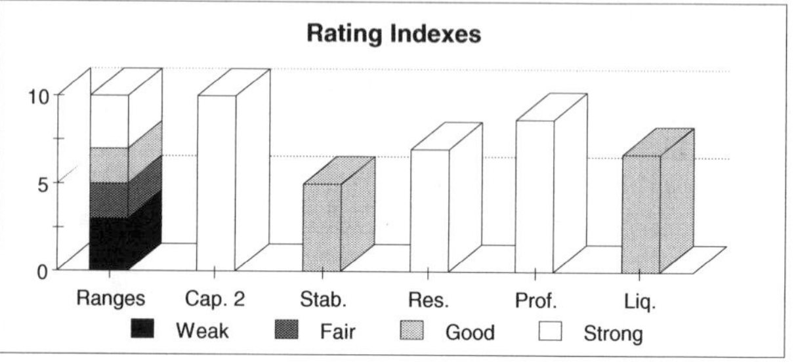

SAFETY NATIONAL CASUALTY CORP — C — Fair

Major Rating Factors: Fair overall results on stability tests (4.3 on a scale of 0 to 10) including fair results on operational trends. Strengths include potentially strong support from affiliation with Delphi Financial Group. The largest net exposure for one risk is conservative at 2.0% of capital. Fair long-term capitalization index (4.8) based on fair current risk adjusted capital (severe loss scenario), although results have slipped from the good range during the last year.

Other Rating Factors: A history of deficient reserves (1.5) that places pressure on both capital and profits. In the last five years, reserves (two year development) fluctuated between 54% and 31% deficeint. Good overall profitability index (6.7) despite operating losses during the first three months of 2008. Return on equity has been fair, averaging 8.9% over the past five years. Excellent liquidity (7.0) with ample operational cash flow and liquid investments.

Principal Business: Other liability (90%), workers compensation (6%), and surety (3%).

Principal Investments: Investment grade bonds (80%), misc. investments (15%), non investment grade bonds (3%), cash (1%), and real estate (1%).

Investments in Affiliates: 3%

Group Affiliation: Delphi Financial Group

Licensed in: All states except PR

Commenced Business: December 1942

Address: 2043 Woodland Pkwy. Ste 200, St Louis, MO 63146

Phone: (314) 995-5300 **Domicile State:** MO **NAIC Code:** 15105

Data Date	Rating	RACR #1	RACR #2	Loss Ratio %	Total Assets ($mil)	Capital ($mil)	Net Premium ($mil)	Net Income ($mil)
3-09	C	1.10	0.73	N/A	1,969.0	529.8	76.1	-1.9
3-08	C+	1.26	0.80	N/A	1,779.8	464.6	74.7	21.0
2008	C	1.12	0.75	75.0	1,903.8	530.9	302.0	46.1
2007	C+	1.31	0.83	74.7	1,778.5	463.0	303.9	53.9
2006	C+	1.20	0.82	76.5	1,522.9	416.0	311.0	42.3
2005	C+	1.04	0.76	87.0	1,319.1	359.1	271.7	16.7
2004	C+	0.97	0.73	73.3	1,095.5	286.2	233.2	34.1

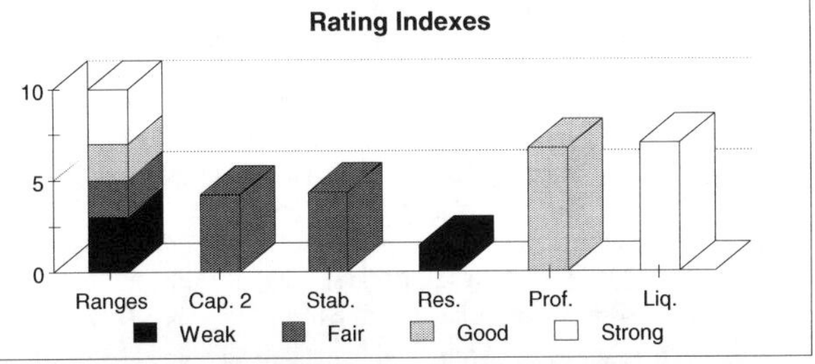

SAFEWAY INS CO — B- — Good

Major Rating Factors: Fair overall results on stability tests (4.5 on a scale of 0 to 10) including potential drain of affiliation with Safeway Ins Group. Fair reserve development (4.9) as reserves have generally been sufficient to cover claims.

Other Rating Factors: Good overall profitability index (5.7). Fair expense controls. Return on equity has been low, averaging 4.9% over the past five years. Good liquidity (6.6) with sufficient resources (cash flows and marketable investments) to handle a spike in claims. Strong long-term capitalization index (7.8) based on excellent current risk adjusted capital (severe and moderate loss scenarios), despite some fluctuation in capital levels.

Principal Business: Auto liability (60%) and auto physical damage (40%).

Principal Investments: Misc. investments (59%), investment grade bonds (35%), cash (4%), non investment grade bonds (1%), and real estate (1%).

Investments in Affiliates: 46%

Group Affiliation: Safeway Ins Group

Licensed in: AZ, CA, CO, DC, DE, FL, GA, IL, IN, IA, KS, MD, MS, MT, NE, NV, NJ, NM, ND, OK, OR, PA, SD, TX, UT, WV, WI

Commenced Business: December 1962

Address: 790 Pasquinelli, Westmont, IL 60559

Phone: (630) 887-8300 **Domicile State:** IL **NAIC Code:** 12521

Data Date	Rating	RACR #1	RACR #2	Loss Ratio %	Total Assets ($mil)	Capital ($mil)	Net Premium ($mil)	Net Income ($mil)
3-09	B-	1.67	1.52	N/A	334.5	243.3	30.0	1.5
3-08	B-	1.75	1.58	N/A	367.7	257.1	35.9	-1.1
2008	B-	1.66	1.52	73.5	339.9	244.0	141.1	16.2
2007	B-	1.78	1.60	73.7	370.3	263.3	135.0	6.8
2006	C+	1.79	1.60	70.6	370.9	257.0	125.6	11.7
2005	C+	1.81	1.63	67.7	375.4	239.0	159.0	9.6
2004	C+	1.78	1.60	67.3	360.5	220.2	186.2	16.2

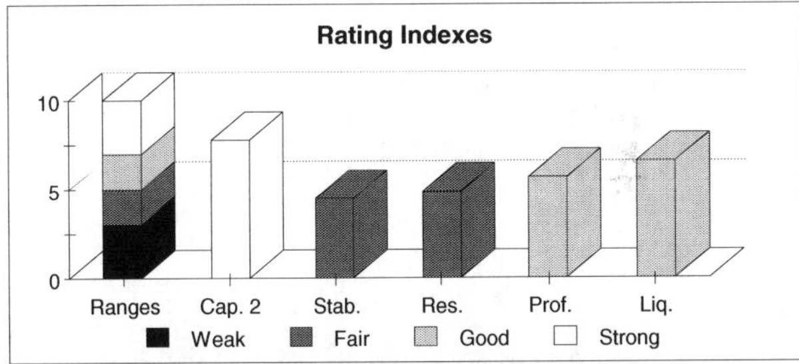

SAMSUNG FIRE & MARINE INS CO LTD US * — B+ — Good

Major Rating Factors: Good overall results on stability tests (5.7 on a scale of 0 to 10). The largest net exposure for one risk is high at 3.9% of capital. Strong long-term capitalization index (7.7) based on excellent current risk adjusted capital (severe and moderate loss scenarios), despite some fluctuation in capital levels.

Other Rating Factors: Ample reserve history (9.5) that helps to protect the company against sharp claims increases. Excellent profitability (8.1) with operating gains in each of the last five years. Return on equity has been good over the last five years, averaging 13.1%. Excellent liquidity (7.0) with ample operational cash flow and liquid investments.

Principal Business: Ocean marine (92%), commercial multiple peril (3%), auto liability (3%), auto physical damage (1%), and products liability (1%).

Principal Investments: Investment grade bonds (91%), misc. investments (8%), and cash (1%).

Investments in Affiliates: None

Group Affiliation: Chubb Corp

Licensed in: CA, NY

Commenced Business: April 1990

Address: 55 Water St, New York, NY 10041-2899

Phone: (908) 903-2000 **Domicile State:** NY **NAIC Code:** 38300

Data Date	Rating	RACR #1	RACR #2	Loss Ratio %	Total Assets ($mil)	Capital ($mil)	Net Premium ($mil)	Net Income ($mil)
3-09	B+	2.60	1.66	N/A	69.7	36.1	3.3	0.2
3-08	B	3.02	1.88	N/A	64.7	35.5	3.5	1.2
2008	B+	2.64	1.69	54.0	67.0	36.1	13.5	3.4
2007	B	2.99	1.87	47.7	63.3	34.1	15.8	4.7
2006	B-	2.27	1.41	44.5	67.5	23.6	11.0	3.9
2005	B-	3.15	1.96	40.3	55.1	25.8	12.9	3.3
2004	B-	2.02	1.26	40.8	50.6	22.5	10.8	3.4

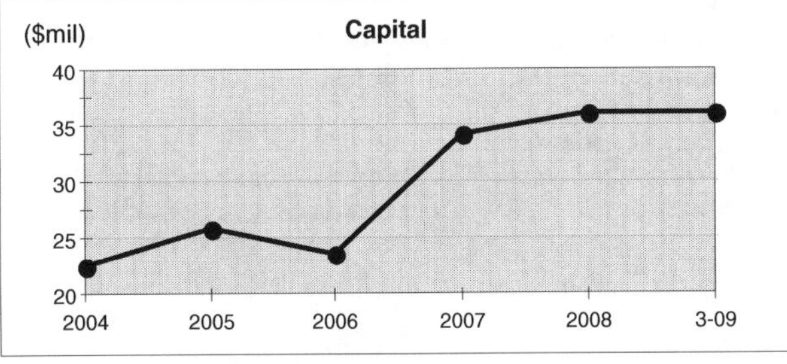

SCOR REINSURANCE CO D Weak

Major Rating Factors: Weak overall results on stability tests (1.4 on a scale of 0 to 10) including excessive premium growth, weak results on operational trends and negative cash flow from operations for 2008. The largest net exposure for one risk is conservative at 2.0% of capital. Fair long-term capitalization index (4.4) based on fair current risk adjusted capital (severe loss scenario), although results have slipped from the good range over the last two years.

Other Rating Factors: Fair reserve development (3.5) as the level of reserves has at times been insufficient to cover claims. In 2005 and 2004 the two year reserve development was 17% and 62% deficient respectively. Fair profitability index (3.9) with operating losses during 2004, 2005 and 2008. Average return on equity over the last five years has been poor at -1.2%. Excellent liquidity (7.8) with ample operational cash flow and liquid investments.

Principal Business: (This company is a reinsurer.)

Principal Investments: Investment grade bonds (96%) and misc. investments (4%).

Investments in Affiliates: 3%

Group Affiliation: Scor Reinsurance Group

Licensed in: AL, AK, AZ, CA, DC, DE, HI, ID, IL, IN, IA, KY, LA, MI, MN, MS, MT, NE, NM, NY, NC, ND, OH, OK, OR, PA, RI, TN, TX, UT, WA, WI, PR

Commenced Business: September 1985

Address: 199 Water St, New York, NY 10038-3526

Phone: (212) 390-5233 **Domicile State:** NY **NAIC Code:** 30058

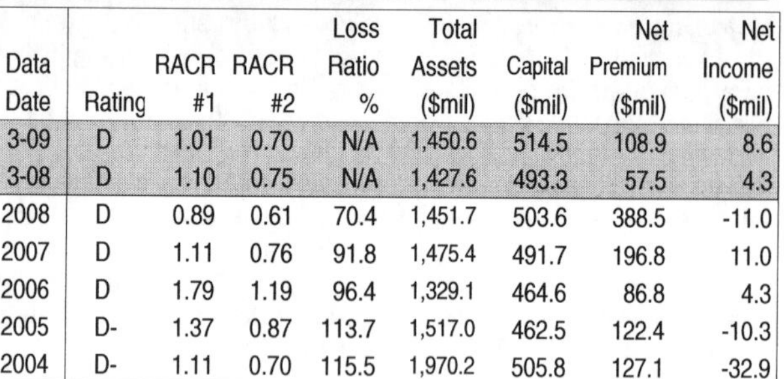

Data Date	Rating	RACR #1	RACR #2	Loss Ratio %	Total Assets ($mil)	Capital ($mil)	Net Premium ($mil)	Net Income ($mil)
3-09	D	1.01	0.70	N/A	1,450.6	514.5	108.9	8.6
3-08	D	1.10	0.75	N/A	1,427.6	493.3	57.5	4.3
2008	D	0.89	0.61	70.4	1,451.7	503.6	388.5	-11.0
2007	D	1.11	0.76	91.8	1,475.4	491.7	196.8	11.0
2006	D	1.79	1.19	96.4	1,329.1	464.6	86.8	4.3
2005	D-	1.37	0.87	113.7	1,517.0	462.5	122.4	-10.3
2004	D-	1.11	0.70	115.5	1,970.2	505.8	127.1	-32.9

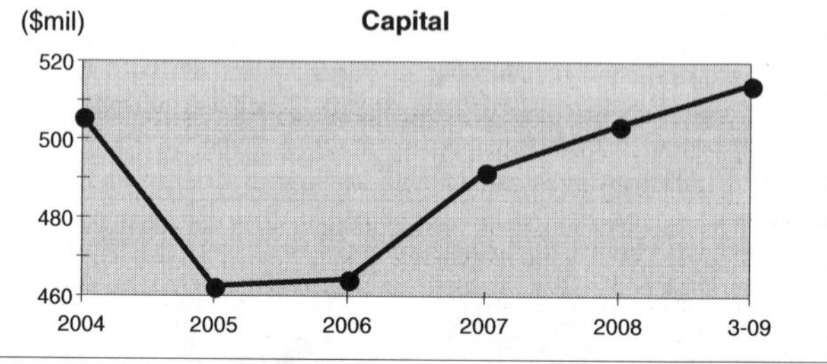

SCOTTSDALE INS CO B- Good

Major Rating Factors: Fair overall results on stability tests (4.9 on a scale of 0 to 10). History of adequate reserve strength (6.2) as reserves have been consistently at an acceptable level.

Other Rating Factors: Good liquidity (5.9) with sufficient resources (cash flows and marketable investments) to handle a spike in claims. Strong long-term capitalization index (8.1) based on excellent current risk adjusted capital (severe and moderate loss scenarios), despite some fluctuation in capital levels. Excellent profitability (7.4) with operating gains in each of the last five years.

Principal Business: Other liability (53%), commercial multiple peril (21%), allied lines (9%), auto liability (5%), fire (4%), products liability (3%), and other lines (6%).

Principal Investments: Investment grade bonds (84%) and misc. investments (20%).

Investments in Affiliates: 12%

Group Affiliation: Nationwide Corp

Licensed in: AZ, DE, OH

Commenced Business: July 1982

Address: 8877 N. Gainey Center Dr, Scottsdale, AZ 85258

Phone: (602) 948-0505 **Domicile State:** OH **NAIC Code:** 41297

Data Date	Rating	RACR #1	RACR #2	Loss Ratio %	Total Assets ($mil)	Capital ($mil)	Net Premium ($mil)	Net Income ($mil)
3-09	B-	2.37	1.84	N/A	1,727.0	537.3	150.2	12.1
3-08	B-	2.67	2.06	N/A	1,517.9	544.9	152.9	12.5
2008	B-	2.32	1.81	74.7	1,700.3	518.9	610.9	9.5
2007	B-	2.63	2.03	64.5	1,595.7	534.0	621.7	46.7
2006	B-	2.60	1.99	60.7	1,614.8	494.2	623.7	72.5
2005	B-	2.22	1.69	65.9	1,703.1	409.7	592.1	41.8
2004	B-	2.07	1.58	64.5	1,605.8	378.5	560.3	53.3

Nationwide Corp
Composite Group Rating: B+

Largest Group Members	Assets ($mil)	Rating
NATIONWIDE LIFE INS CO	77310	B+
NATIONWIDE MUTUAL INS CO	28843	B
NATIONWIDE LIFE INS CO OF AMERICA	4994	B+
NATIONWIDE LIFE ANNUITY INS CO	4349	B
NATIONWIDE MUTUAL FIRE INS CO	4319	B+

SCPIE INDEMNITY COMPANY C Fair

Major Rating Factors: Fair overall results on stability tests (3.0 on a scale of 0 to 10) including potential drain of affiliation with Doctors Co Group and negative cash flow from operations for 2008. Good overall profitability index (6.8) despite operating losses during 2004. Return on equity has been fair, averaging 8.7% over the past five years.

Other Rating Factors: Strong long-term capitalization index (7.7) based on excellent current risk adjusted capital (severe and moderate loss scenarios). Moreover, capital levels have been consistent in recent years. Ample reserve history (7.0) that can protect against increases in claims costs. Excellent liquidity (7.4) with ample operational cash flow and liquid investments.

Principal Business: Medical malpractice (98%) and other liability (2%).

Principal Investments: Investment grade bonds (83%) and misc. investments (17%).

Investments in Affiliates: 16%

Group Affiliation: Doctors Co Group

Licensed in: CA

Commenced Business: October 1995

Address: 1888 Century Park E Ste 800, Los Angeles, CA 90067-1708

Phone: (310) 551-5900 **Domicile State:** CA **NAIC Code:** 10352

Data Date	Rating	RACR #1	RACR #2	Loss Ratio %	Total Assets ($mil)	Capital ($mil)	Net Premium ($mil)	Net Income ($mil)
3-09	C	2.25	1.83	N/A	478.4	204.3	4.9	3.9
3-08	C	2.15	1.72	N/A	538.0	203.7	15.8	5.2
2008	C	2.16	1.76	62.7	481.8	200.5	58.9	24.4
2007	C	2.07	1.66	57.9	490.4	195.8	65.7	31.9
2006	C	1.51	1.13	71.6	520.0	164.4	60.2	22.4
2005	D+	0.92	0.70	76.2	536.8	145.6	115.4	8.9
2004	D+	0.55	0.38	108.8	640.9	136.5	110.7	-6.4

Doctors Co Group
Composite Group Rating: B-

Largest Group Members	Assets ($mil)	Rating
DOCTORS CO AN INTERINSURANCE EXCH	2012	B-
SCPIE INDEMNITY COMPANY	482	C
UNDERWRITER FOR THE PROFESSIONS INC	268	B-
OHIC INS CO	235	C-
NORTHWEST PHYSICIANS INS CO	139	C

SEABRIGHT INS CO — D+ Weak

Major Rating Factors: Weak overall results on stability tests (2.0 on a scale of 0 to 10) including potential drain of affiliation with SeaBright Insurance Holdings Inc. Fair long-term capitalization index (3.8) based on fair current risk adjusted capital (severe loss scenario).

Other Rating Factors: Fair reserve development (4.9) as reserves have generally been sufficient to cover claims. Good overall profitability index (6.8) despite operating losses during 2004. Return on equity has been fair, averaging 7.6% over the past five years. Good liquidity (6.4) with sufficient resources (cash flows and marketable investments) to handle a spike in claims.

Principal Business: Workers compensation (99%) and ocean marine (1%).

Principal Investments: Investment grade bonds (95%) and misc. investments (5%).

Investments in Affiliates: None

Group Affiliation: SeaBright Insurance Holdings Inc

Licensed in: All states except ME, NH, NC, ND, WV, PR

Commenced Business: January 1962

Address: 161 N Clark St Suite 3525, Chicago, IL 60601

Phone: (206) 269-8500 **Domicile State:** IL **NAIC Code:** 15563

Data Date	Rating	RACR #1	RACR #2	Loss Ratio %	Total Assets ($mil)	Capital ($mil)	Net Premium ($mil)	Net Income ($mil)
3-09	D+	0.92	0.58	N/A	767.4	276.4	58.0	1.2
3-08	D+	1.09	0.68	N/A	696.0	262.5	56.7	8.9
2008	D+	0.94	0.59	57.1	736.9	275.7	256.6	24.4
2007	D+	1.10	0.68	55.2	675.2	256.3	262.6	33.7
2006	D+	0.88	0.56	56.7	550.9	222.3	213.6	27.0
2005	D	0.71	0.45	65.4	378.0	144.7	182.6	12.5
2004	D-	0.49	0.32	65.9	183.5	54.5	119.6	-1.7

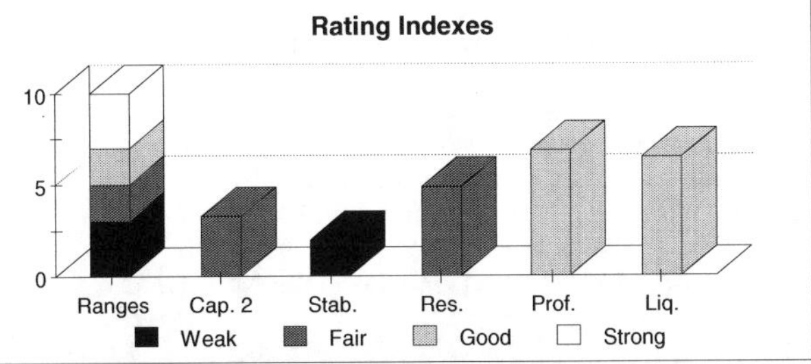

SECURA INS A MUTUAL CO — B- Good

Major Rating Factors: Fair overall results on stability tests (4.7 on a scale of 0 to 10) including potential drain of affiliation with SECURA Group. History of adequate reserve strength (6.9) as reserves have been consistently at an acceptable level.

Other Rating Factors: Good overall profitability index (5.4) despite operating losses during the first three months of 2008. Good liquidity (6.3) with sufficient resources (cash flows and marketable investments) to handle a spike in claims. Strong long-term capitalization index (8.3) based on excellent current risk adjusted capital (severe and moderate loss scenarios), despite some fluctuation in capital levels.

Principal Business: Workers compensation (32%), commercial multiple peril (25%), auto liability (15%), farmowners multiple peril (8%), auto physical damage (6%), other liability (6%), and other lines (8%).

Principal Investments: Investment grade bonds (85%), misc. investments (13%), and real estate (3%).

Investments in Affiliates: 7%

Group Affiliation: SECURA Group

Licensed in: AZ, CO, IL, IN, IA, KS, KY, MI, MN, MO, ND, OH, OK, OR, PA, SD, WI

Commenced Business: May 1900

Address: 2401 S Memorial Dr, Appleton, WI 54915

Phone: (920) 739-3161 **Domicile State:** WI **NAIC Code:** 22543

Data Date	Rating	RACR #1	RACR #2	Loss Ratio %	Total Assets ($mil)	Capital ($mil)	Net Premium ($mil)	Net Income ($mil)
3-09	B-	2.52	1.87	N/A	600.5	203.2	68.3	-1.3
3-08	B-	2.65	1.94	N/A	602.8	222.8	68.5	-1.4
2008	B-	2.56	1.90	74.4	597.8	206.2	268.9	-8.9
2007	B-	2.72	2.01	66.3	599.3	227.0	279.6	13.9
2006	B-	2.77	2.03	61.1	561.7	210.1	272.2	20.8
2005	B-	2.20	1.60	59.8	501.1	179.3	265.4	23.9
2004	B-	1.98	1.45	58.5	437.5	153.5	256.8	23.5

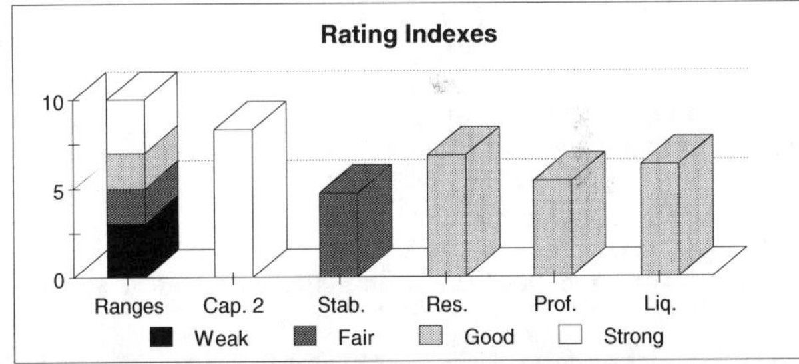

SELECTIVE INS CO OF AMERICA — B Good

Major Rating Factors: History of adequate reserve strength (6.0 on a scale of 0 to 10) as reserves have been consistently at an acceptable level. Good liquidity (6.5) with sufficient resources (cash flows and marketable investments) to handle a spike in claims.

Other Rating Factors: Good overall results on stability tests (5.6). Fair profitability index (3.7) with operating losses during the first three months of 2008. Return on equity has been fair, averaging 15.0% over the past five years. Strong long-term capitalization index (7.2) based on excellent current risk adjusted capital (severe and moderate loss scenarios), despite some fluctuation in capital levels.

Principal Business: Workers compensation (32%), other liability (16%), allied lines (14%), auto liability (12%), homeowners multiple peril (5%), products liability (4%), and other lines (16%).

Principal Investments: Investment grade bonds (87%), misc. investments (14%), and non investment grade bonds (1%).

Investments in Affiliates: None

Group Affiliation: Selective Ins

Licensed in: All states except AZ, CO, FL, ID, LA, ME, NH, NM, OK, UT, VT, PR

Commenced Business: April 1926

Address: 40 Wantage Ave, Branchville, NJ 07890

Phone: (973) 948-3000 **Domicile State:** NJ **NAIC Code:** 12572

Data Date	Rating	RACR #1	RACR #2	Loss Ratio %	Total Assets ($mil)	Capital ($mil)	Net Premium ($mil)	Net Income ($mil)
3-09	B	1.65	1.05	N/A	2,215.7	421.1	181.2	-13.7
3-08	B	1.97	1.25	N/A	2,277.8	518.0	191.4	17.7
2008	B	1.81	1.16	67.5	2,241.2	451.7	745.3	51.5
2007	B	2.09	1.33	65.7	2,281.1	535.4	781.8	101.4
2006	B	1.96	1.26	64.1	2,133.2	534.3	776.0	94.3
2005	B	1.69	1.09	63.9	2,139.5	519.7	821.8	82.6
2004	B	1.51	1.02	65.7	1,924.3	463.5	768.2	83.7

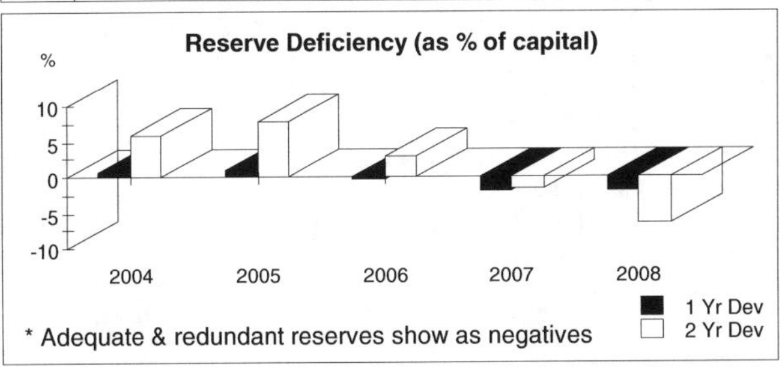

SELECTIVE WAY INS CO — B Good

Major Rating Factors: Good long-term capitalization (6.9 on a scale of 0 to 10) based on good current risk adjusted capital (moderate loss scenario) reflecting improvement over results in 2008. History of adequate reserve strength (6.0) as reserves have been consistently at an acceptable level.

Other Rating Factors: Good liquidity (6.3) with sufficient resources (cash flows and marketable investments) to handle a spike in claims. Good overall results on stability tests (5.5). Stability strengths include excellent operational trends, good risk adjusted capital for prior years and excellent risk diversification. Fair profitability index (3.6) with operating losses during the first three months of 2008. Return on equity has been fair, averaging 13.1% over the past five years.

Principal Business: Other liability (30%), auto liability (22%), workers compensation (7%), fire (7%), allied lines (7%), products liability (7%), and other lines (21%).

Principal Investments: Investment grade bonds (91%) and misc. investments (9%).

Investments in Affiliates: None

Group Affiliation: Selective Ins

Licensed in: DC, DE, GA, MD, MI, NJ, NY, PA, SC, VA

Commenced Business: November 1973

Address: 40 Wantage Ave, Branchville, NJ 07890

Phone: (973) 948-3000 **Domicile State:** NJ **NAIC Code:** 26301

Data Date	Rating	RACR #1	RACR #2	Loss Ratio %	Total Assets ($mil)	Capital ($mil)	Net Premium ($mil)	Net Income ($mil)
3-09	B	1.59	1.01	N/A	932.9	172.6	76.9	-4.0
3-08	B	1.79	1.13	N/A	933.2	200.3	81.2	6.0
2008	B	1.53	0.98	67.5	918.9	163.0	316.2	20.8
2007	B	1.83	1.16	65.7	922.6	200.1	331.7	25.7
2006	B-	1.81	1.15	64.1	879.4	201.7	327.4	28.5
2005	C+	1.61	1.03	63.9	791.8	182.7	311.0	28.8
2004	C+	1.44	0.98	65.7	721.7	161.7	287.7	25.2

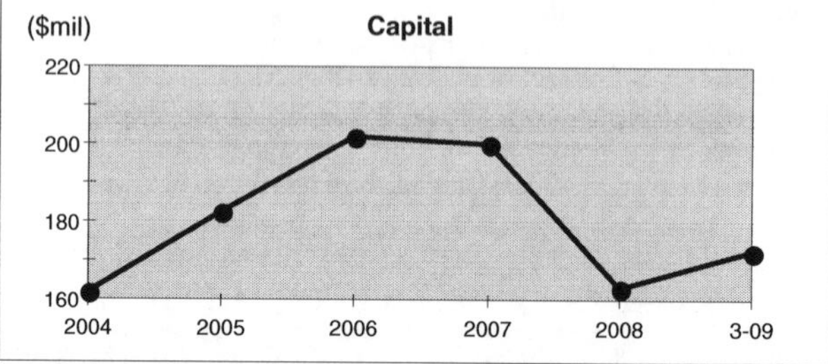

SENTRY INS A MUTUAL CO * — A Excellent

Major Rating Factors: Strong long-term capitalization index (7.8 on a scale of 0 to 10) based on excellent current risk adjusted capital (severe and moderate loss scenarios). Furthermore, this high level of risk adjusted capital has been consistently maintained in previous years. Ample reserve history (8.3) that helps to protect the company against sharp claims increases.

Other Rating Factors: Excellent overall results on stability tests (7.5). Stability strengths include good operational trends and excellent risk diversification. Good liquidity (6.9) with sufficient resources (cash flows and marketable investments) to handle a spike in claims. Fair profitability index (4.7) with operating losses during the first three months of 2008.

Principal Business: Workers compensation (48%), auto liability (15%), other liability (7%), homeowners multiple peril (7%), auto physical damage (5%), products liability (5%), and other lines (13%).

Principal Investments: Misc. investments (52%), investment grade bonds (48%), and real estate (1%).

Investments in Affiliates: 34%

Group Affiliation: Sentry Ins Group

Licensed in: All states, the District of Columbia and Puerto Rico

Commenced Business: August 1914

Address: 1800 N Point Dr, Stevens Point, WI 54481

Phone: (715) 346-6000 **Domicile State:** WI **NAIC Code:** 24988

Data Date	Rating	RACR #1	RACR #2	Loss Ratio %	Total Assets ($mil)	Capital ($mil)	Net Premium ($mil)	Net Income ($mil)
3-09	A	1.73	1.57	N/A	5,330.6	2,720.0	241.9	-113.5
3-08	A	1.83	1.63	N/A	5,609.6	2,974.0	255.9	9.3
2008	A	1.78	1.61	74.5	5,368.6	2,806.8	982.4	-24.7
2007	A	1.85	1.65	72.2	5,525.4	3,015.1	1,040.5	183.0
2006	A	1.81	1.61	72.7	5,280.7	2,793.8	1,042.3	154.0
2005	A	1.75	1.56	73.5	5,231.5	2,493.2	1,097.5	176.2
2004	A	2.21	1.92	75.1	4,667.6	2,366.7	1,024.9	125.9

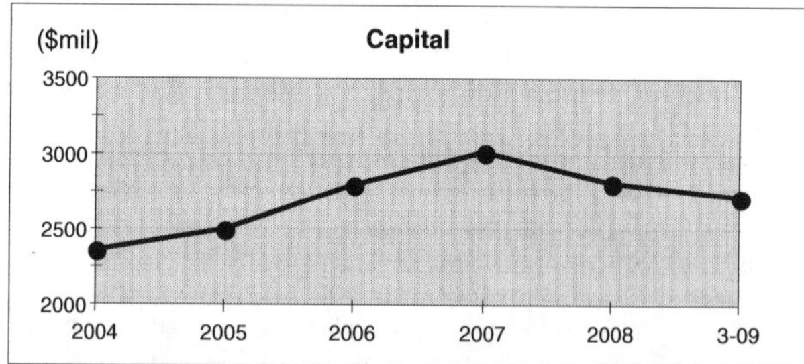

SENTRY SELECT INS CO — B Good

Major Rating Factors: Good overall profitability index (6.7 on a scale of 0 to 10). Fair expense controls. Return on equity has been good over the last five years, averaging 10.4%. Good liquidity (6.8) with sufficient resources (cash flows and marketable investments) to handle a spike in claims.

Other Rating Factors: Good overall results on stability tests (6.2). Stability strengths include good operational trends and excellent risk diversification. The largest net exposure for one risk is conservative at 1.1% of capital. Strong long-term capitalization index (9.2) based on excellent current risk adjusted capital (severe and moderate loss scenarios). Moreover, capital levels have been consistent in recent years. Ample reserve history (9.3) that helps to protect the company against sharp claims increases.

Principal Business: Auto liability (45%), auto physical damage (15%), inland marine (12%), other liability (10%), workers compensation (8%), fire (4%), and other lines (7%).

Principal Investments: Investment grade bonds (98%), misc. investments (1%), and non investment grade bonds (1%).

Investments in Affiliates: None

Group Affiliation: Sentry Ins Group

Licensed in: All states except PR

Commenced Business: August 1929

Address: 3400 80th St, Moline, IL 61265

Phone: (800) 447-0633 **Domicile State:** WI **NAIC Code:** 21180

Data Date	Rating	RACR #1	RACR #2	Loss Ratio %	Total Assets ($mil)	Capital ($mil)	Net Premium ($mil)	Net Income ($mil)
3-09	B	4.11	2.75	N/A	676.3	225.2	44.0	0.5
3-08	B	3.97	2.64	N/A	696.7	223.8	46.5	4.7
2008	B	4.13	2.81	74.5	680.6	224.6	178.6	19.9
2007	B	3.94	2.67	72.2	654.9	219.7	189.2	22.2
2006	B	3.45	2.43	72.7	631.3	194.6	197.7	23.3
2005	B	3.41	2.36	73.5	593.5	174.2	182.9	22.4
2004	B	3.29	2.27	75.1	556.7	152.5	170.8	16.1

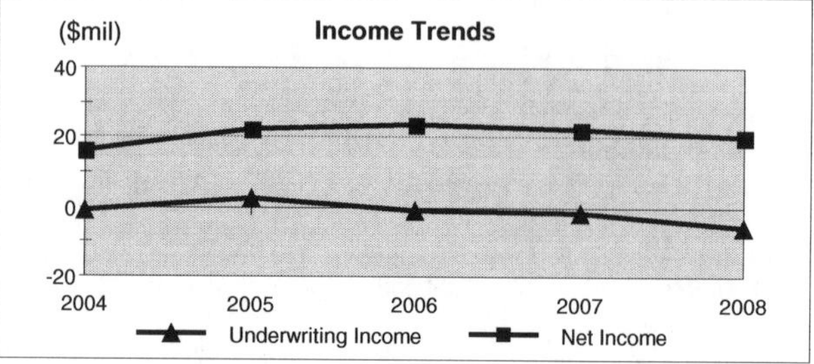

SHELTER MUTUAL INS CO — B — Good

Major Rating Factors: Good overall results on stability tests (5.5 on a scale of 0 to 10) despite potential drain of affiliation with Shelter Ins Companies and negative cash flow from operations for 2008. Good overall profitability index (5.1) despite operating losses during the first three months of 2008.

Other Rating Factors: Good liquidity (5.8) with sufficient resources (cash flows and marketable investments) to handle a spike in claims. Strong long-term capitalization index (7.9) based on excellent current risk adjusted capital (severe and moderate loss scenarios), despite some fluctuation in capital levels. Ample reserve history (8.2) that helps to protect the company against sharp claims increases.

Principal Business: Auto liability (32%), homeowners multiple peril (28%), auto physical damage (23%), fire (4%), allied lines (4%), farmowners multiple peril (3%), and other lines (6%).

Principal Investments: Investment grade bonds (54%), misc. investments (43%), real estate (2%), and cash (1%).

Investments in Affiliates: 27%

Group Affiliation: Shelter Ins Companies

Licensed in: AR, CO, IL, IN, IA, KS, KY, LA, MD, MS, MO, NE, NV, OH, OK, TN, TX, VT

Commenced Business: January 1946

Address: 1817 W Broadway, Columbia, MO 65218

Phone: (573) 445-8441 **Domicile State:** MO **NAIC Code:** 23388

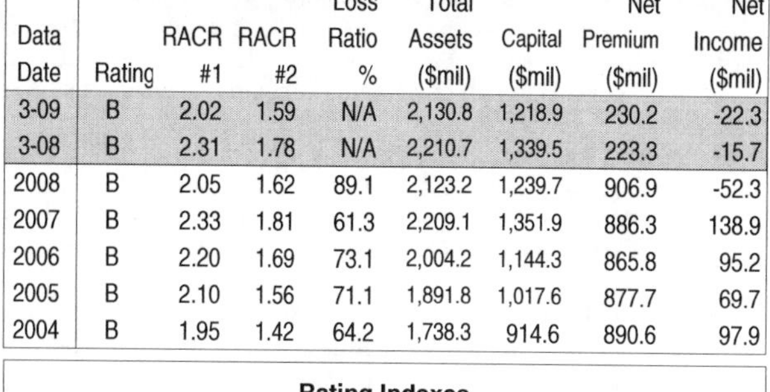

Data Date	Rating	RACR #1	RACR #2	Loss Ratio %	Total Assets ($mil)	Capital ($mil)	Net Premium ($mil)	Net Income ($mil)
3-09	B	2.02	1.59	N/A	2,130.8	1,218.9	230.2	-22.3
3-08	B	2.31	1.78	N/A	2,210.7	1,339.5	223.3	-15.7
2008	B	2.05	1.62	89.1	2,123.2	1,239.7	906.9	-52.3
2007	B	2.33	1.81	61.3	2,209.1	1,351.9	886.3	138.9
2006	B	2.20	1.69	73.1	2,004.2	1,144.3	865.8	95.2
2005	B	2.10	1.56	71.1	1,891.8	1,017.6	877.7	69.7
2004	B	1.95	1.42	64.2	1,738.3	914.6	890.6	97.9

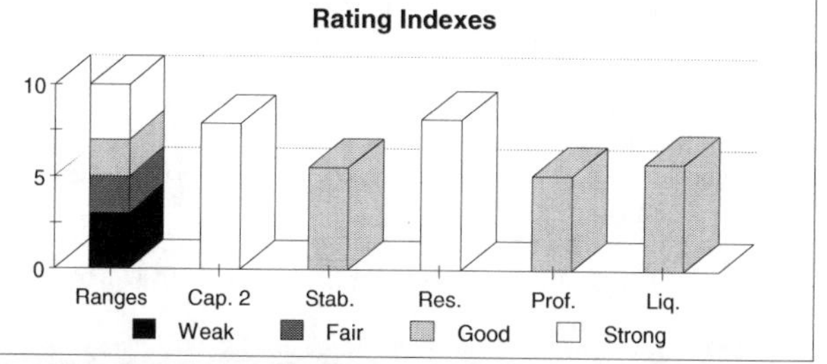

SOMPO JAPAN INS CO OF AMERICA — C+ — Fair

Major Rating Factors: Fair overall results on stability tests (4.5 on a scale of 0 to 10). History of adequate reserve strength (6.0) as reserves have been consistently at an acceptable level.

Other Rating Factors: Good overall profitability index (6.6) despite operating losses during 2004 and 2005. Return on equity has been low, averaging 3.2% over the past five years. Strong long-term capitalization index (8.3) based on excellent current risk adjusted capital (severe and moderate loss scenarios), despite some fluctuation in capital levels. Excellent liquidity (8.7) with ample operational cash flow and liquid investments.

Principal Business: Commercial multiple peril (41%), products liability (18%), workers compensation (15%), ocean marine (9%), auto liability (5%), fire (4%), and other lines (9%).

Principal Investments: Investment grade bonds (65%), misc. investments (32%), and cash (3%).

Investments in Affiliates: 10%

Group Affiliation: Sompo Japan Ins Group

Licensed in: All states except PR

Commenced Business: January 1963

Address: 225 Liberty Street,43rd Fl, New York, NY 10281

Phone: (212) 416-1200 **Domicile State:** NY **NAIC Code:** 11126

Data Date	Rating	RACR #1	RACR #2	Loss Ratio %	Total Assets ($mil)	Capital ($mil)	Net Premium ($mil)	Net Income ($mil)
3-09	C+	3.35	2.44	N/A	792.8	381.2	15.7	4.0
3-08	C	2.98	2.12	N/A	790.6	343.3	14.4	6.5
2008	C+	3.42	2.50	49.8	795.1	382.2	61.5	35.8
2007	C	3.07	2.19	67.4	770.8	349.8	63.3	29.7
2006	C	1.83	1.30	85.6	534.1	206.1	65.6	7.9
2005	C	2.23	1.34	85.1	518.9	196.2	63.4	-2.1
2004	C-	3.38	2.00	91.7	518.1	198.3	71.8	-10.2

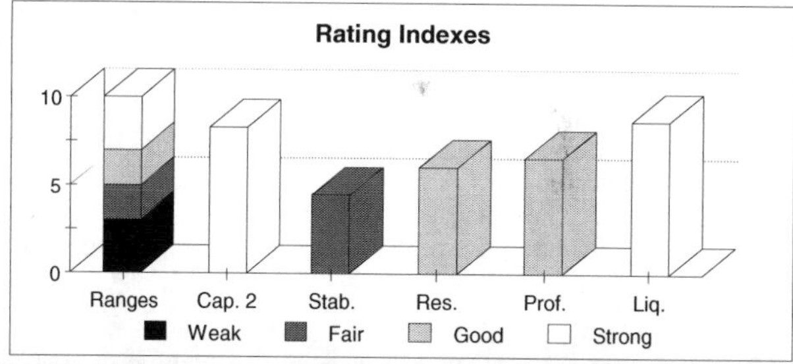

SOUTHERN FARM BUREAU CAS INS CO * — B+ — Good

Major Rating Factors: Good liquidity (5.0 on a scale of 0 to 10) with sufficient resources (cash flows and marketable investments) to handle a spike in claims. Strong long-term capitalization index (7.8) based on excellent current risk adjusted capital (severe and moderate loss scenarios), despite some fluctuation in capital levels.

Other Rating Factors: Ample reserve history (8.2) that helps to protect the company against sharp claims increases. Good overall results on stability tests (5.0) despite potential drain of affiliation with Southern Farm Bureau Casualty and negative cash flow from operations for 2008. Stability strengths include good operational trends and excellent risk diversification. Fair profitability index (4.7) with operating losses during 2005 and 2008. Return on equity has been low, averaging 3.4% over the past five years.

Principal Business: Auto liability (51%), auto physical damage (45%), other liability (3%), and allied lines (1%).

Principal Investments: Investment grade bonds (60%), misc. investments (40%), and real estate (1%).

Investments in Affiliates: 44%

Group Affiliation: Southern Farm Bureau Casualty

Licensed in: AR, CO, FL, LA, MS, SC, TX

Commenced Business: September 1947

Address: 1800 E County Line Rd, Ridgeland, MS 39157

Phone: (601) 957-7777 **Domicile State:** MS **NAIC Code:** 18325

Data Date	Rating	RACR #1	RACR #2	Loss Ratio %	Total Assets ($mil)	Capital ($mil)	Net Premium ($mil)	Net Income ($mil)
3-09	B+	1.26	1.21	N/A	1,807.1	1,058.7	202.2	2.6
3-08	A-	3.30	2.81	N/A	2,748.2	1,637.9	322.1	18.5
2008	B+	1.76	1.64	91.2	2,648.8	1,585.8	1,318.7	-29.8
2007	A-	3.27	2.81	78.0	2,654.9	1,628.7	1,293.0	135.0
2006	A-	3.23	2.76	80.8	2,490.3	1,459.6	1,301.9	125.5
2005	A-	2.92	2.40	83.8	2,507.5	1,333.9	1,269.6	-100.7
2004	A-	3.37	2.84	74.6	2,472.5	1,478.8	1,294.7	152.8

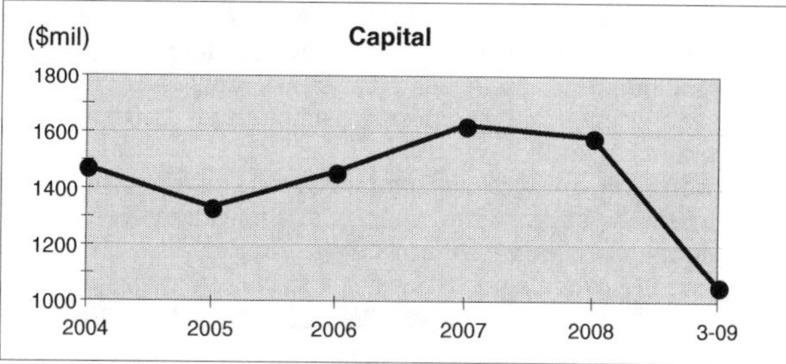

SOUTHERN-OWNERS INS CO * B+ Good

Major Rating Factors: Good overall profitability index (5.5 on a scale of 0 to 10) despite operating losses during the first three months of 2008. Return on equity has been fair, averaging 9.3% over the past five years. Good liquidity (6.7) with sufficient resources (cash flows and marketable investments) to handle a spike in claims.

Other Rating Factors: Good overall results on stability tests (6.4). Strong long-term capitalization index (10.0) based on excellent current risk adjusted capital (severe and moderate loss scenarios), despite some fluctuation in capital levels. Fair reserve development (4.8) as reserves have generally been sufficient to cover claims. In 2004, the two year reserve development was 30% deficient.

Principal Business: Auto liability (42%), auto physical damage (18%), other liability (17%), commercial multiple peril (15%), homeowners multiple peril (4%), inland marine (3%), and workers compensation (2%).

Principal Investments: Investment grade bonds (91%) and misc. investments (9%).

Investments in Affiliates: None

Group Affiliation: Auto-Owners Group

Licensed in: AR, FL, IL, IN, IA, KY, MI, MO, NE, NV, ND, SC, SD, UT, VA, WI

Commenced Business: June 1995

Address: 6101 Anacapri Blvd, Lansing, MI 48917-3968

Phone: (517) 323-1200 **Domicile State:** MI **NAIC Code:** 10190

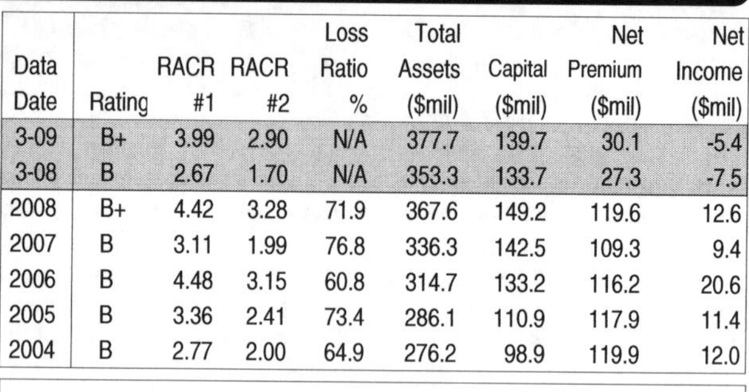

Data Date	Rating	RACR #1	RACR #2	Loss Ratio %	Total Assets ($mil)	Capital ($mil)	Net Premium ($mil)	Net Income ($mil)
3-09	B+	3.99	2.90	N/A	377.7	139.7	30.1	-5.4
3-08	B	2.67	1.70	N/A	353.3	133.7	27.3	-7.5
2008	B+	4.42	3.28	71.9	367.6	149.2	119.6	12.6
2007	B	3.11	1.99	76.8	336.3	142.5	109.3	9.4
2006	B	4.48	3.15	60.8	314.7	133.2	116.2	20.6
2005	B	3.36	2.41	73.4	286.1	110.9	117.9	11.4
2004	B	2.77	2.00	64.9	276.2	98.9	119.9	12.0

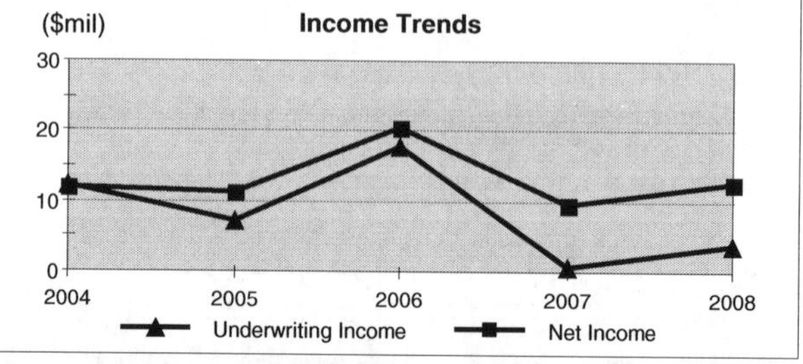

SPARTA INS CO B Good

Major Rating Factors: Fair profitability index (4.5 on a scale of 0 to 10) with operating losses during the first three months of 2008. Return on equity has been fair, averaging 9.7% over the past five years. Fair overall results on stability tests (4.8) including excessive premium growth and weak results on operational trends.

Other Rating Factors: Strong long-term capitalization index (10.0) based on excellent current risk adjusted capital (severe and moderate loss scenarios), despite some fluctuation in capital levels. Superior liquidity (9.4) with ample operational cash flow and liquid investments.

Principal Business: Workers compensation (68%), auto liability (23%), auto physical damage (6%), other liability (2%), products liability (1%), and commercial multiple peril (1%).

Principal Investments: Investment grade bonds (97%) and misc. investments (3%).

Investments in Affiliates: None

Group Affiliation: SPARTA Insurance Holdings Inc

Licensed in: All states except PR

Commenced Business: March 1923

Address: One Beacon St, Boston, MA 02108

Phone: (617) 725-6000 **Domicile State:** MA **NAIC Code:** 20613

Data Date	Rating	RACR #1	RACR #2	Loss Ratio %	Total Assets ($mil)	Capital ($mil)	Net Premium ($mil)	Net Income ($mil)
3-09	B	11.97	7.34	N/A	306.0	252.1	9.0	-2.7
3-08	B	41.39	34.62	N/A	262.6	257.0	0.4	1.1
2008	B	14.49	9.14	82.7	280.4	254.1	25.3	-2.1
2007	A-	61.53	51.28	74.0	257.7	255.6	1.4	0.5
2006	U	N/A	N/A	0.0	35.4	35.2	0.0	4.3
2005	U	185.62	92.81	0.0	37.5	37.4	0.0	11.5
2004	U	3.30	3.23	0.0	123.6	122.8	-34.2	11.9

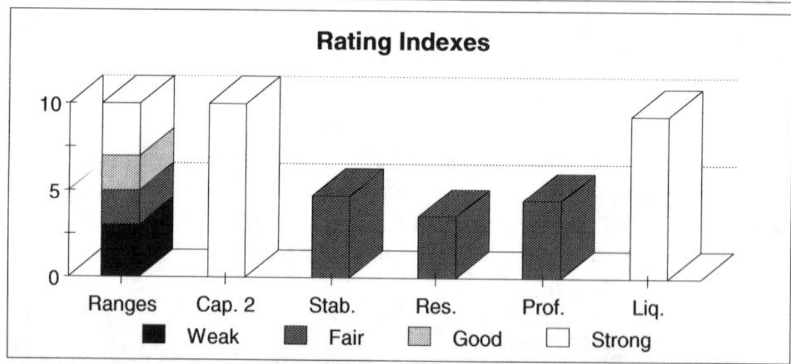

ST PAUL FIRE & MARINE INS CO B Good

Major Rating Factors: Good overall results on stability tests (5.7 on a scale of 0 to 10) despite potential drain of affiliation with Travelers Companies Inc. Stability strengths include good operational trends and excellent risk diversification. Good overall profitability index (5.1). Fair expense controls. Return on equity has been good over the last five years, averaging 12.1%.

Other Rating Factors: Good liquidity (6.8) with sufficient resources (cash flows and marketable investments) to handle a spike in claims. Fair reserve development (4.5) as the level of reserves has at times been insufficient to cover claims. In 2005 and 2004 the two year reserve development was 20% and 40% deficient respectively. Strong long-term capitalization index (7.6) based on excellent current risk adjusted capital (severe and moderate loss scenarios), despite some fluctuation in capital levels.

Principal Business: Other liability (50%), ocean marine (12%), auto liability (9%), fire (8%), products liability (7%), inland marine (4%), and other lines (9%).

Principal Investments: Investment grade bonds (71%), misc. investments (24%), real estate (4%), and non investment grade bonds (1%).

Investments in Affiliates: 18%

Group Affiliation: Travelers Companies Inc

Licensed in: All states, the District of Columbia and Puerto Rico

Commenced Business: April 1925

Address: 385 Washington St, St Paul, MN 55102

Phone: (651) 310-7911 **Domicile State:** MN **NAIC Code:** 24767

Data Date	Rating	RACR #1	RACR #2	Loss Ratio %	Total Assets ($mil)	Capital ($mil)	Net Premium ($mil)	Net Income ($mil)
3-09	B	1.79	1.41	N/A	19,047.7	6,436.6	1,174.2	179.1
3-08	B-	1.84	1.42	N/A	19,785.7	7,174.5	1,171.6	322.6
2008	B	1.77	1.40	61.4	19,163.0	6,366.5	4,711.5	849.4
2007	B-	1.78	1.38	58.6	19,842.7	6,881.1	4,670.8	1,147.8
2006	B-	1.83	1.45	58.6	20,172.0	7,019.9	4,654.6	858.4
2005	B-	1.65	1.26	74.2	19,900.5	6,575.9	4,550.0	983.3
2004	B-	1.37	1.02	92.2	19,049.3	5,508.7	4,481.1	190.5

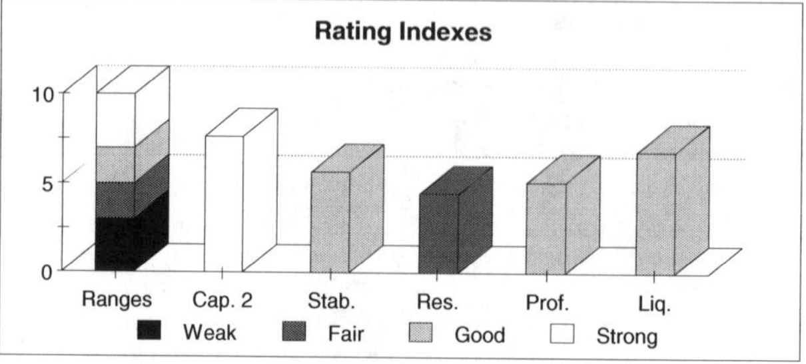

ST PAUL PROTECTIVE INS CO — B- Good

Major Rating Factors: Fair overall results on stability tests (4.9 on a scale of 0 to 10) including fair financial strength of affiliated Travelers Companies Inc. History of adequate reserve strength (5.0) as reserves have been consistently at an acceptable level.

Other Rating Factors: Good overall profitability index (6.3). Fair expense controls. Return on equity has been fair, averaging 8.0% over the past five years. Good liquidity (6.9) with sufficient resources (cash flows and marketable investments) to handle a spike in claims. Strong long-term capitalization index (9.9) based on excellent current risk adjusted capital (severe and moderate loss scenarios), despite some fluctuation in capital levels.

Principal Business: Other liability (29%), fire (22%), allied lines (22%), auto liability (12%), auto physical damage (6%), commercial multiple peril (4%), and other lines (5%).

Principal Investments: Investment grade bonds (99%) and misc. investments (1%).

Investments in Affiliates: None

Group Affiliation: Travelers Companies Inc

Licensed in: All states, the District of Columbia and Puerto Rico

Commenced Business: February 1932

Address: 200 N LaSalle St, Chicago, IL 60661

Phone: (651) 310-7911 **Domicile State:** IL **NAIC Code:** 19224

Data Date	Rating	RACR #1	RACR #2	Loss Ratio %	Total Assets ($mil)	Capital ($mil)	Net Premium ($mil)	Net Income ($mil)
3-09	B-	4.55	2.97	N/A	514.6	239.3	26.2	5.4
3-08	B-	4.57	2.70	N/A	515.1	239.0	26.0	7.2
2008	B-	4.51	2.94	61.5	509.4	233.9	105.2	22.6
2007	B-	4.51	2.65	59.0	510.2	232.3	104.7	25.6
2006	B-	4.56	2.80	58.4	504.8	231.4	100.2	25.7
2005	B-	3.38	2.19	75.1	494.3	216.5	119.6	8.9
2004	B-	7.18	4.29	92.2	369.4	225.8	48.7	8.9

Travelers Companies Inc
Composite Group Rating: B+

Largest Group Members	Assets ($mil)	Rating
TRAVELERS INDEMNITY CO	20788	A-
ST PAUL FIRE MARINE INS CO	19163	B
TRAVELERS CASUALTY SURETY CO	14960	B
UNITED STATES FIDELITY GUARANTY CO	4193	B-
TRAVELERS CASUALTY SURETY CO OF AM	4096	B-

ST PAUL SURPLUS LINES INS CO — C Fair

Major Rating Factors: Fair reserve development (4.2 on a scale of 0 to 10) as the level of reserves has at times been insufficient to cover claims. In 2005 and 2004 the two year reserve development was 39% and 93% deficient respectively. Fair overall results on stability tests (3.9).

Other Rating Factors: Good overall profitability index (6.8) with small operating losses during 2004. Return on equity has been good over the last five years, averaging 13.3%. Good liquidity (6.8) with sufficient resources (cash flows and marketable investments) to handle a spike in claims. Strong long-term capitalization index (7.5) based on excellent current risk adjusted capital (severe and moderate loss scenarios). Moreover, capital levels have been consistent in recent years.

Principal Business: Other liability (54%), inland marine (40%), fire (3%), allied lines (2%), and products liability (1%).

Principal Investments: Investment grade bonds (99%) and misc. investments (1%).

Investments in Affiliates: None

Group Affiliation: Travelers Companies Inc

Licensed in: DE

Commenced Business: December 1974

Address: 2711 Centerville Rd Suite 400, Wilmington, DE 19808

Phone: (651) 310-7911 **Domicile State:** DE **NAIC Code:** 30481

Data Date	Rating	RACR #1	RACR #2	Loss Ratio %	Total Assets ($mil)	Capital ($mil)	Net Premium ($mil)	Net Income ($mil)
3-09	C	2.15	1.41	N/A	610.7	188.1	39.7	6.4
3-08	C	2.17	1.29	N/A	607.7	187.0	39.4	9.4
2008	C	2.10	1.38	61.5	614.6	181.7	159.6	28.1
2007	C	2.10	1.25	59.0	600.1	178.5	158.8	31.7
2006	C	1.94	1.20	58.4	575.2	161.3	152.0	31.9
2005	C	1.48	0.95	75.1	570.3	149.6	149.4	20.1
2004	C	1.18	0.75	92.2	562.2	133.7	146.1	-0.4

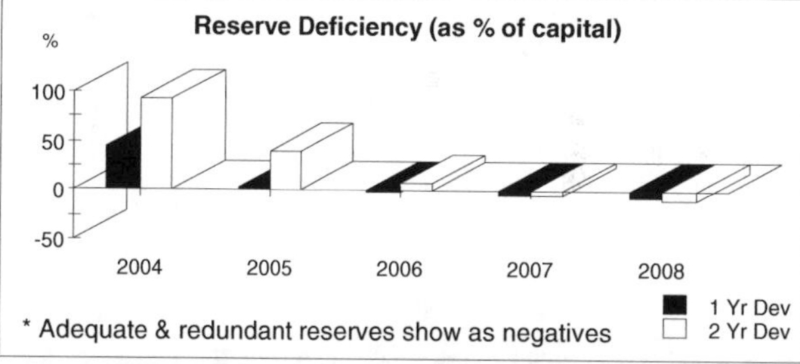

STANDARD FIRE INS CO — B Good

Major Rating Factors: Good liquidity (6.8 on a scale of 0 to 10) with sufficient resources (cash flows and marketable investments) to handle a spike in claims. Good overall results on stability tests (5.4).

Other Rating Factors: Fair reserve development (4.9) as reserves have generally been sufficient to cover claims. In 2005, the two year reserve development was 21% deficient. Strong long-term capitalization index (7.9) based on excellent current risk adjusted capital (severe and moderate loss scenarios), despite some fluctuation in capital levels. Excellent profitability (7.4) with operating gains in each of the last five years. Return on equity has been excellent over the last five years averaging 17.2%.

Principal Business: Homeowners multiple peril (51%), allied lines (14%), auto liability (13%), auto physical damage (8%), workers compensation (6%), ocean marine (4%), and other lines (4%).

Principal Investments: Investment grade bonds (77%), misc. investments (22%), and non investment grade bonds (1%).

Investments in Affiliates: 16%

Group Affiliation: Travelers Companies Inc

Licensed in: All states, the District of Columbia and Puerto Rico

Commenced Business: March 1910

Address: One Tower Square, Hartford, CT 06183

Phone: (860) 277-0111 **Domicile State:** CT **NAIC Code:** 19070

Data Date	Rating	RACR #1	RACR #2	Loss Ratio %	Total Assets ($mil)	Capital ($mil)	Net Premium ($mil)	Net Income ($mil)
3-09	B	2.08	1.63	N/A	3,656.8	1,338.1	218.2	39.1
3-08	B-	2.11	1.58	N/A	3,714.5	1,410.3	216.7	59.7
2008	B	2.06	1.62	61.5	3,653.3	1,307.3	878.0	217.8
2007	B-	2.16	1.63	59.0	3,750.2	1,422.1	871.7	277.7
2006	C+	1.95	1.49	58.4	3,599.6	1,276.2	840.0	206.3
2005	C+	1.51	1.16	75.1	3,347.7	1,003.8	791.6	152.8
2004	B-	1.39	1.08	63.7	3,244.0	924.7	900.4	184.8

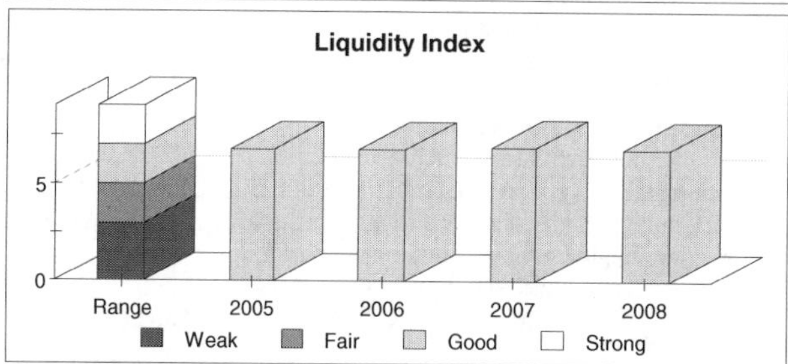

STAR INS CO — C — Fair

Major Rating Factors: Fair overall results on stability tests (3.6 on a scale of 0 to 10) including potential drain of affiliation with Meadowbrook Ins Group. The largest net exposure for one risk is conservative at 1.1% of capital. History of adequate reserve strength (6.2) as reserves have been consistently at an acceptable level.

Other Rating Factors: Strong long-term capitalization index (7.9) based on excellent current risk adjusted capital (severe and moderate loss scenarios), despite some fluctuation in capital levels. Excellent profitability (8.5) with operating gains in each of the last five years. Excellent liquidity (7.0) with ample operational cash flow and liquid investments.

Principal Business: Workers compensation (37%), other liability (23%), commercial multiple peril (15%), auto liability (13%), auto physical damage (4%), medical malpractice (4%), and other lines (5%).

Principal Investments: Investment grade bonds (76%), misc. investments (23%), and cash (1%).

Investments in Affiliates: 19%

Group Affiliation: Meadowbrook Ins Group

Licensed in: All states except PR

Commenced Business: November 1985

Address: 26255 American Drive, Southfield, MI 48034-6112

Phone: (810) 358-4020 **Domicile State:** MI **NAIC Code:** 18023

Data Date	Rating	RACR #1	RACR #2	Loss Ratio %	Total Assets ($mil)	Capital ($mil)	Net Premium ($mil)	Net Income ($mil)
3-09	C	2.02	1.59	N/A	680.3	198.9	46.2	5.6
3-08	C	1.86	1.47	N/A	539.5	195.4	37.4	3.2
2008	C	2.12	1.70	62.0	567.5	199.9	172.1	27.2
2007	C	1.83	1.45	61.1	524.6	188.4	158.6	13.9
2006	C	1.61	1.24	62.3	468.2	165.1	148.7	9.5
2005	C	1.18	0.88	65.0	407.6	141.1	134.5	13.4
2004	C	1.24	0.86	63.9	410.1	120.7	187.6	7.0

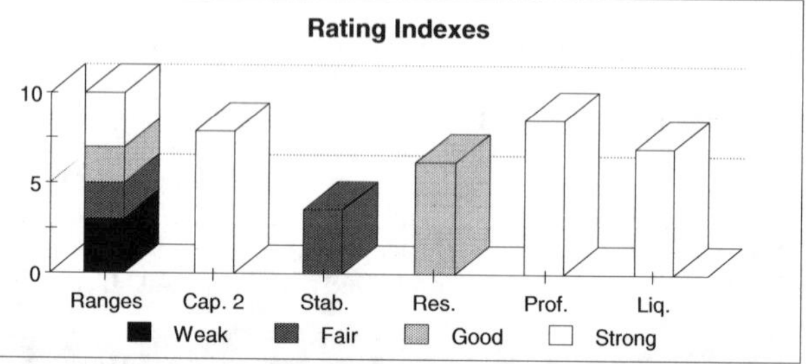

STARR INDEMNITY & LIABILITY CO — C+ — Fair

Major Rating Factors: Fair profitability index (4.5 on a scale of 0 to 10) with operating losses during 2006 and the first three months of 2008. Return on equity has been low, averaging 3.5% over the past five years. Fair overall results on stability tests (4.0) including excessive premium growth and weak results on operational trends. The largest net exposure for one risk is conservative at 1.4% of capital.

Other Rating Factors: Strong long-term capitalization index (10.0) based on excellent current risk adjusted capital (severe and moderate loss scenarios), despite some fluctuation in capital levels. Superior liquidity (9.1) with ample operational cash flow and liquid investments.

Principal Business: Group accident & health (100%).

Principal Investments: Investment grade bonds (75%), misc. investments (20%), and cash (5%).

Investments in Affiliates: None

Group Affiliation: Starr International Co Inc

Licensed in: All states except AL, CT, HI, MD, MA, MI, MT, SD, VT

Commenced Business: May 1919

Address: 2727 Turtle Creek Blvd, Dallas, TX 75219

Phone: (214) 559-1222 **Domicile State:** TX **NAIC Code:** 38318

Data Date	Rating	RACR #1	RACR #2	Loss Ratio %	Total Assets ($mil)	Capital ($mil)	Net Premium ($mil)	Net Income ($mil)
3-09	C+	13.21	9.72	N/A	298.5	215.0	13.2	-0.4
3-08	U	N/A	N/A	N/A	281.0	219.1	0.2	1.1
2008	C+	16.14	11.65	107.2	288.6	215.1	19.8	-2.2
2007	U	N/A	N/A	0.0	277.9	218.1	0.0	0.7
2006	U	N/A	N/A	0.0	81.9	16.5	0.0	-0.2
2005	U	N/A	N/A	0.0	80.1	11.5	0.0	1.4
2004	U	1.11	1.00	0.0	73.3	14.6	0.0	1.2

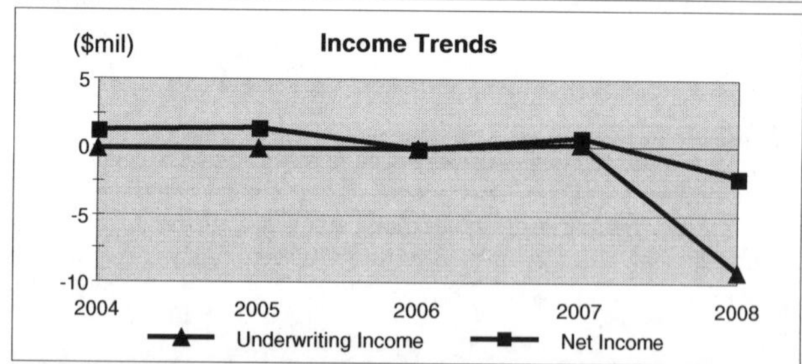

STATE AUTO PROPERTY & CASUALTY INS — B — Good

Major Rating Factors: Good liquidity (5.9 on a scale of 0 to 10) with sufficient resources (cash flows and marketable investments) to handle a spike in claims. Fair overall results on stability tests (4.3) including potential drain of affiliation with State Auto Mutual Group.

Other Rating Factors: Fair profitability index (3.7) with operating losses during the first three months of 2008. Return on equity has been fair, averaging 11.1% over the past five years. Strong long-term capitalization index (7.6) based on excellent current risk adjusted capital (severe and moderate loss scenarios), despite some fluctuation in capital levels. Ample reserve history (7.0) that can protect against increases in claims costs.

Principal Business: Auto liability (28%), homeowners multiple peril (20%), auto physical damage (16%), commercial multiple peril (13%), other liability (7%), fire (5%), and other lines (12%).

Principal Investments: Investment grade bonds (94%) and misc. investments (6%).

Investments in Affiliates: None

Group Affiliation: State Auto Mutual Group

Licensed in: AL, AZ, AR, DC, FL, GA, IL, IN, IA, KS, KY, MD, MI, MN, MS, MO, MT, NE, NC, ND, OH, OK, PA, SC, SD, TN, UT, VA, WV, WI, WY

Commenced Business: April 1950

Address: 112 S Main St, Greer, SC 29650

Phone: (614) 464-5000 **Domicile State:** IA **NAIC Code:** 25127

Data Date	Rating	RACR #1	RACR #2	Loss Ratio %	Total Assets ($mil)	Capital ($mil)	Net Premium ($mil)	Net Income ($mil)
3-09	B	2.11	1.32	N/A	1,705.4	465.4	203.5	-7.5
3-08	B+	2.91	1.81	N/A	1,741.6	595.6	198.3	-9.9
2008	B	2.25	1.42	74.8	1,728.4	484.4	858.2	-39.8
2007	B+	3.17	1.97	57.5	1,604.5	616.0	721.9	91.6
2006	B+	2.89	1.81	56.5	1,555.3	578.9	721.9	99.2
2005	B+	2.26	1.44	58.0	1,498.9	473.8	753.9	86.5
2004	B+	2.24	1.46	60.6	1,343.5	419.7	703.6	74.2

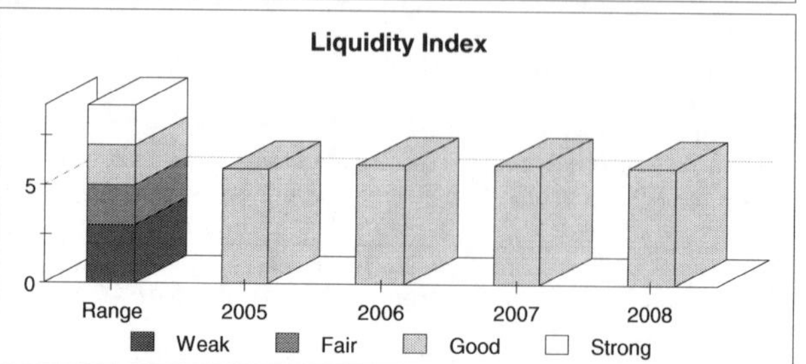

STATE AUTOMOBILE MUTUAL INS CO — B — Good

Major Rating Factors: History of adequate reserve strength (6.3 on a scale of 0 to 10) as reserves have been consistently at an acceptable level. Good liquidity (6.9) with sufficient resources (cash flows and marketable investments) to handle a spike in claims.

Other Rating Factors: Fair overall results on stability tests (4.3) including potential drain of affiliation with State Auto Mutual Group and negative cash flow from operations for 2008. Fair profitability index (4.4) with operating losses during the first three months of 2008. Strong long-term capitalization index (7.7) based on excellent current risk adjusted capital (severe and moderate loss scenarios), despite some fluctuation in capital levels.

Principal Business: Auto liability (26%), auto physical damage (16%), homeowners multiple peril (15%), other liability (11%), workers compensation (7%), fire (7%), and other lines (18%).

Principal Investments: Misc. investments (61%), investment grade bonds (33%), cash (3%), and real estate (3%).

Investments in Affiliates: 61%

Group Affiliation: State Auto Mutual Group

Licensed in: AL, AZ, AR, CO, DC, FL, GA, ID, IL, IN, IA, KS, KY, MD, MI, MN, MS, MO, MT, NE, NV, NM, NC, ND, OH, OK, OR, PA, SC, SD, TN, TX, UT, VA, WA, WV, WI, WY

Commenced Business: September 1921

Address: 518 E Broad St, Columbus, OH 43215-3976

Phone: (614) 464-5000 **Domicile State:** OH **NAIC Code:** 25135

Data Date	Rating	RACR #1	RACR #2	Loss Ratio %	Total Assets ($mil)	Capital ($mil)	Net Premium ($mil)	Net Income ($mil)
3-09	B	1.35	1.32	N/A	1,781.8	925.4	65.5	-3.4
3-08	B	1.74	1.63	N/A	1,883.6	1,243.1	63.1	20.2
2008	B	1.76	1.70	73.4	1,911.4	1,223.9	229.6	32.0
2007	B	1.69	1.58	55.8	1,845.2	1,193.8	317.4	57.9
2006	B+	1.52	1.43	56.6	1,941.5	1,328.9	277.1	49.4
2005	B+	1.47	1.39	67.4	1,966.3	1,320.4	288.3	20.7
2004	B+	1.57	1.47	60.5	1,654.2	1,089.3	238.1	31.5

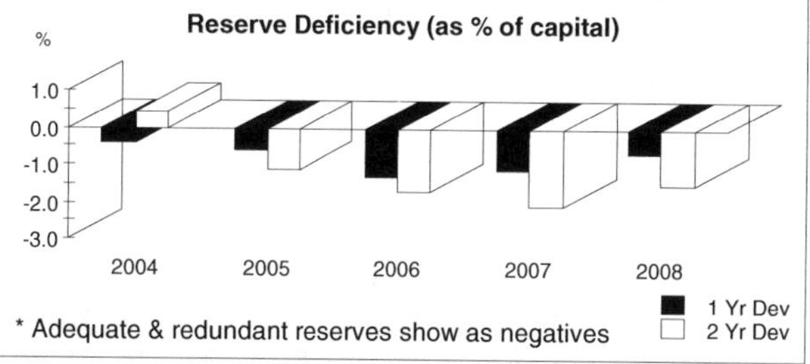

* Adequate & redundant reserves show as negatives

STATE FARM CTY MUTUAL INS CO OF TX * — A- — Excellent

Major Rating Factors: Strong long-term capitalization index (10.0 on a scale of 0 to 10) based on excellent current risk adjusted capital (severe and moderate loss scenarios), despite some fluctuation in capital levels. Good liquidity (6.5) with sufficient resources (cash flows and marketable investments) to handle a spike in claims.

Other Rating Factors: Good overall results on stability tests (6.8). Fair reserve development (4.7) as reserves have generally been sufficient to cover claims. Fair profitability index (3.7) with operating losses during 2007 and 2008.

Principal Business: Auto liability (52%), auto physical damage (36%), and inland marine (12%).

Principal Investments: Investment grade bonds (95%) and misc. investments (5%).

Investments in Affiliates: None

Group Affiliation: State Farm Group

Licensed in: TX

Commenced Business: November 1960

Address: 17301 Preston Road, Dallas, TX 75379

Phone: (214) 732-5000 **Domicile State:** TX **NAIC Code:** 26816

Data Date	Rating	RACR #1	RACR #2	Loss Ratio %	Total Assets ($mil)	Capital ($mil)	Net Premium ($mil)	Net Income ($mil)
3-09	A-	4.78	3.85	N/A	99.4	40.5	6.3	0.2
3-08	A-	6.08	4.87	N/A	93.4	42.0	5.3	-0.2
2008	A-	4.75	3.94	95.0	95.7	40.2	24.5	-1.9
2007	A-	6.02	4.99	89.6	86.9	42.3	20.4	-0.2
2006	A	6.64	5.51	82.8	83.4	42.0	19.1	1.8
2005	A	6.70	5.50	73.7	82.1	40.2	17.0	2.8
2004	A	6.13	5.05	73.2	75.2	37.3	16.4	2.9

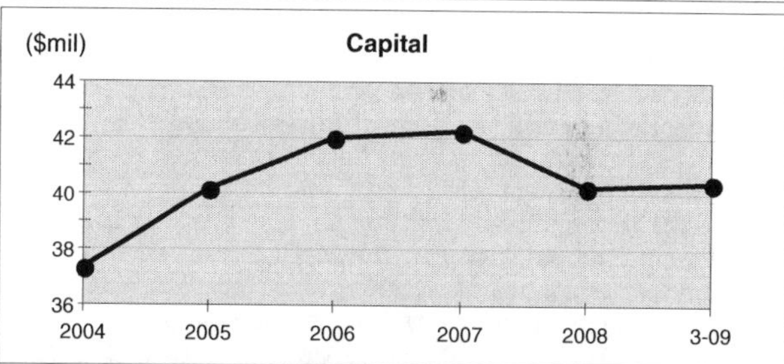

STATE FARM FIRE & CAS CO — B — Good

Major Rating Factors: Good long-term capitalization index (6.8 on a scale of 0 to 10) based on good current risk adjusted capital (moderate loss scenario). Good overall results on stability tests (6.2) despite negative cash flow from operations for 2008. Stability strengths include excellent operational trends, good risk adjusted capital for prior years and excellent risk diversification.

Other Rating Factors: Fair reserve development (4.8) as reserves have generally been sufficient to cover claims. Fair profitability index (4.0) with operating losses during 2008. Return on equity has been fair, averaging 10.1% over the past five years. Vulnerable liquidity (2.8) as a spike in claims may stretch capacity.

Principal Business: Homeowners multiple peril (66%), auto liability (8%), commercial multiple peril (7%), auto physical damage (5%), other liability (4%), inland marine (3%), and other lines (7%).

Principal Investments: Investment grade bonds (85%) and misc. investments (15%).

Investments in Affiliates: None

Group Affiliation: State Farm Group

Licensed in: All states except PR

Commenced Business: June 1935

Address: One State Farm Plaza, Bloomington, IL 61710

Phone: (309) 766-2311 **Domicile State:** IL **NAIC Code:** 25143

Data Date	Rating	RACR #1	RACR #2	Loss Ratio %	Total Assets ($mil)	Capital ($mil)	Net Premium ($mil)	Net Income ($mil)
3-09	B	1.59	0.94	N/A	25,307.9	7,889.9	3,092.6	0.0
3-08	B	2.24	1.40	N/A	26,338.4	10,235.3	3,010.9	212.2
2008	B	1.67	0.99	95.5	25,815.8	8,184.6	12,421.7	-1,192.6
2007	B	2.26	1.38	69.9	26,187.6	10,161.5	11,788.9	956.1
2006	B	2.11	1.29	69.8	24,413.6	8,948.1	11,635.7	939.5
2005	B	1.97	1.22	67.1	23,781.7	7,666.7	11,159.8	1,250.3
2004	B-	1.74	1.09	59.7	20,636.3	6,519.6	10,829.2	2,031.8

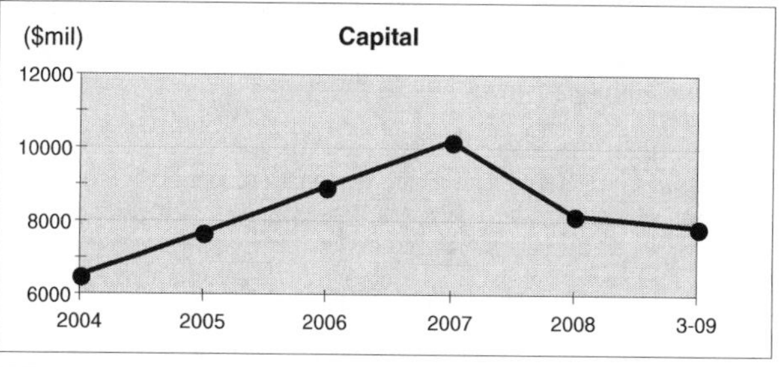

STATE FARM FLORIDA INS CO — C Fair

Major Rating Factors: Fair overall results on stability tests (3.9 on a scale of 0 to 10) including negative cash flow from operations for 2008 and fair risk adjusted capital in prior years. The largest net exposure for one risk is high at 4.5% of capital. Strengths include potentially strong support from affiliation with State Farm Group. Fair long-term capitalization index (4.1) based on fair current risk adjusted capital (severe loss scenario), although results have slipped from the good range over the last two years.

Other Rating Factors: Fair liquidity (3.9) as cash resources may not be adequate to cover a spike in claims. Weak profitability index (2.0) with operating losses during 2004 and the first three months of 2008. Average return on equity over the last five years has been poor at -27.7%. Ample reserve history (7.0) that can protect against increases in claims costs.

Principal Business: Homeowners multiple peril (84%), commercial multiple peril (7%), inland marine (4%), and other liability (4%).

Principal Investments: Investment grade bonds (99%) and misc. investments (1%).

Investments in Affiliates: None

Group Affiliation: State Farm Group

Licensed in: FL, IL

Commenced Business: December 1998

Address: One State Farm Plaza, Bloomington, IL 61710

Phone: (309) 766-1093 **Domicile State:** FL **NAIC Code:** 10739

Data Date	Rating	RACR #1	RACR #2	Loss Ratio %	Total Assets ($mil)	Capital ($mil)	Net Premium ($mil)	Net Income ($mil)
3-09	C	1.05	0.72	N/A	2,108.2	552.0	126.3	-54.0
3-08	C	1.32	0.87	N/A	2,327.1	839.3	229.2	20.3
2008	C	1.04	0.71	91.3	2,138.1	607.6	547.9	-184.5
2007	C	1.29	0.85	52.4	2,343.6	822.2	666.3	108.1
2006	C	0.54	0.37	41.6	2,391.7	718.9	1,140.5	134.0
2005	C	0.47	0.32	71.3	2,432.1	561.4	1,031.2	26.9
2004	C	0.43	0.29	216.0	2,466.0	544.0	891.9	-771.3

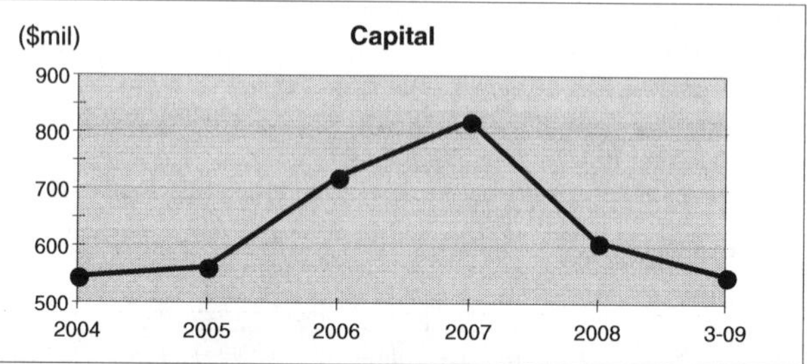

STATE FARM GENERAL INS CO — B Good

Major Rating Factors: Good overall results on stability tests (6.3 on a scale of 0 to 10). Stability strengths include good operational trends and excellent risk diversification. The largest net exposure for one risk is conservative at 1.3% of capital. History of adequate reserve strength (6.3) as reserves have been consistently at an acceptable level.

Other Rating Factors: Good liquidity (5.5) with sufficient resources (cash flows and marketable investments) to handle a spike in claims. Strong long-term capitalization index (7.2) based on excellent current risk adjusted capital (severe and moderate loss scenarios). Moreover, capital levels have been consistent in recent years. Excellent profitability (8.3) with operating gains in each of the last five years. Return on equity has been excellent over the last five years averaging 19.0%.

Principal Business: Homeowners multiple peril (67%), commercial multiple peril (18%), other liability (7%), earthquake (3%), inland marine (3%), and farmowners multiple peril (1%).

Principal Investments: Investment grade bonds (94%) and misc. investments (6%).

Investments in Affiliates: None

Group Affiliation: State Farm Group

Licensed in: All states except CT, MA, RI, PR

Commenced Business: May 1962

Address: One State Farm Plaza, Bloomington, IL 61710

Phone: (309) 766-2020 **Domicile State:** IL **NAIC Code:** 25151

Data Date	Rating	RACR #1	RACR #2	Loss Ratio %	Total Assets ($mil)	Capital ($mil)	Net Premium ($mil)	Net Income ($mil)
3-09	B	2.14	1.29	N/A	4,555.6	1,982.6	422.6	66.8
3-08	B	2.22	1.35	N/A	4,366.8	1,895.2	416.1	28.6
2008	B	2.07	1.23	77.4	4,497.2	1,914.8	1,681.9	48.0
2007	B	2.15	1.30	78.3	4,360.2	1,863.5	1,609.5	93.6
2006	B	2.01	1.22	44.1	4,192.5	1,850.7	1,832.5	463.5
2005	B-	1.56	0.95	44.6	3,899.7	1,466.8	1,831.5	488.3
2004	B-	1.11	0.66	49.6	3,492.5	1,080.1	1,726.2	326.9

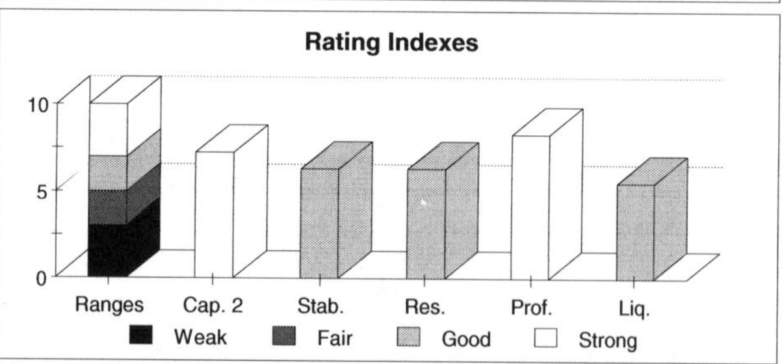

STATE FARM INDEMNITY CO — B Good

Major Rating Factors: Good liquidity (6.5 on a scale of 0 to 10) with sufficient resources (cash flows and marketable investments) to handle a spike in claims. Good overall results on stability tests (5.4). Stability strengths include good operational trends and excellent risk diversification.

Other Rating Factors: Fair profitability index (3.1) with operating losses during 2007 and the first three months of 2008. Return on equity has been fair, averaging 6.9% over the past five years. Strong long-term capitalization index (10.0) based on excellent current risk adjusted capital (severe and moderate loss scenarios), despite some fluctuation in capital levels. Ample reserve history (7.0) that can protect against increases in claims costs.

Principal Business: Auto liability (69%) and auto physical damage (31%).

Principal Investments: Investment grade bonds (97%) and misc. investments (3%).

Investments in Affiliates: 1%

Group Affiliation: State Farm Group

Licensed in: IL, NJ

Commenced Business: March 1991

Address: One State Farm Plaza, Bloomington, IL 61710

Phone: (309) 766-2020 **Domicile State:** IL **NAIC Code:** 43796

Data Date	Rating	RACR #1	RACR #2	Loss Ratio %	Total Assets ($mil)	Capital ($mil)	Net Premium ($mil)	Net Income ($mil)
3-09	B	5.02	3.87	N/A	1,905.4	998.3	134.1	-3.1
3-08	B	6.87	5.47	N/A	1,869.9	1,086.6	128.3	4.2
2008	B	4.78	3.91	117.6	1,902.6	1,002.2	526.7	-81.6
2007	B	6.42	5.42	90.2	1,873.3	1,083.4	510.9	-5.3
2006	B-	6.50	5.61	71.8	1,874.8	1,090.3	535.6	26.8
2005	B-	5.78	4.84	65.1	1,969.0	1,070.9	604.9	161.4
2004	B-	4.12	3.46	53.2	1,967.3	921.8	694.9	254.0

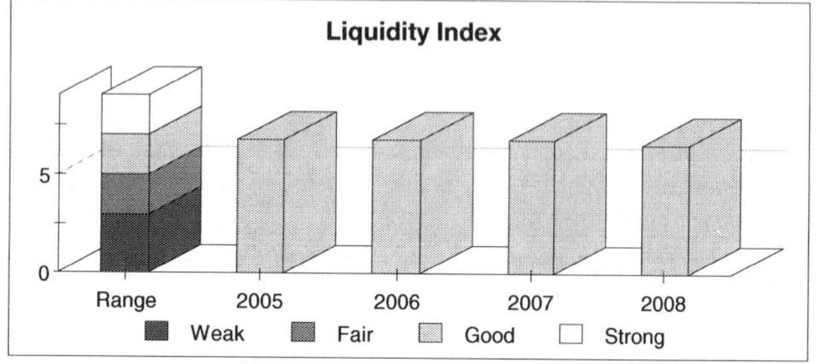

STATE FARM LLOYDS — C+ Fair

Major Rating Factors: Fair overall results on stability tests (4.3 on a scale of 0 to 10) including negative cash flow from operations for 2008. Strengths include potentially strong support from affiliation with State Farm Group. The largest net exposure for one risk is acceptable at 2.6% of capital. Good overall long-term capitalization (5.2) based on good current risk adjusted capital (moderate loss scenario). However, capital levels have fluctuated during prior years.

Other Rating Factors: Weak profitability index (2.3) with operating losses during the first three months of 2008. Vulnerable liquidity (1.0) as a spike in claims may stretch capacity. Ample reserve history (8.9) that helps to protect the company against sharp claims increases.

Principal Business: Homeowners multiple peril (94%), commercial multiple peril (4%), and farmowners multiple peril (2%).

Principal Investments: Investment grade bonds (97%) and misc. investments (3%).

Investments in Affiliates: None

Group Affiliation: State Farm Group

Licensed in: TX

Commenced Business: June 1983

Address: 17301 Preston Rd, Dallas, TX 75252

Phone: (214) 732-5000 **Domicile State:** TX **NAIC Code:** 43419

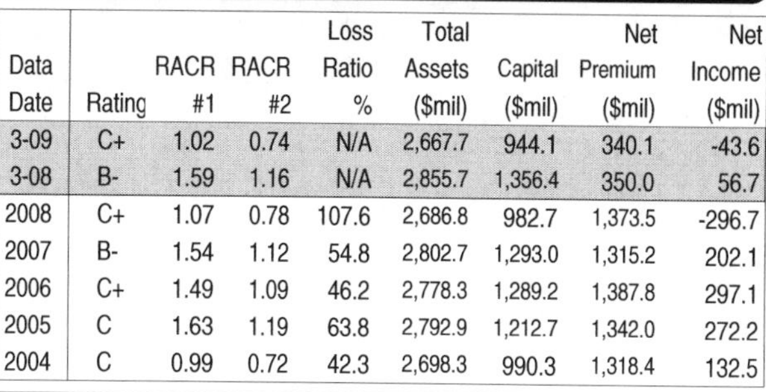

Data Date	Rating	RACR #1	RACR #2	Loss Ratio %	Total Assets ($mil)	Capital ($mil)	Net Premium ($mil)	Net Income ($mil)
3-09	C+	1.02	0.74	N/A	2,667.7	944.1	340.1	-43.6
3-08	B-	1.59	1.16	N/A	2,855.7	1,356.4	350.0	56.7
2008	C+	1.07	0.78	107.6	2,686.8	982.7	1,373.5	-296.7
2007	B-	1.54	1.12	54.8	2,802.7	1,293.0	1,315.2	202.1
2006	C+	1.49	1.09	46.2	2,778.3	1,289.2	1,387.8	297.1
2005	C	1.63	1.19	63.8	2,792.9	1,212.7	1,342.0	272.2
2004	C	0.99	0.72	42.3	2,698.3	990.3	1,318.4	132.5

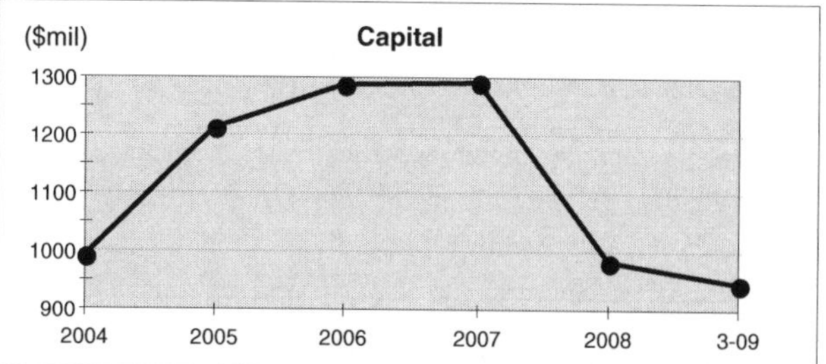

STATE FARM MUTUAL AUTOMOBILE INS CO * — B+ Good

Major Rating Factors: History of adequate reserve strength (6.4 on a scale of 0 to 10) as reserves have been consistently at an acceptable level. Good overall profitability index (5.3). Good expense controls.

Other Rating Factors: Good liquidity (6.3) with sufficient resources (cash flows and marketable investments) to handle a spike in claims. Good overall results on stability tests (6.7). Strong long-term capitalization index (8.2) based on excellent current risk adjusted capital (severe and moderate loss scenarios), despite some fluctuation in capital levels.

Principal Business: Auto liability (57%), auto physical damage (40%), other accident & health (3%), and group accident & health (1%).

Principal Investments: Misc. investments (56%), investment grade bonds (42%), and real estate (2%).

Investments in Affiliates: 23%

Group Affiliation: State Farm Group

Licensed in: All states except PR

Commenced Business: June 1922

Address: One State Farm Plaza, Bloomington, IL 61710

Phone: (309) 735-8480 **Domicile State:** IL **NAIC Code:** 25178

Data Date	Rating	RACR #1	RACR #2	Loss Ratio %	Total Assets ($mil)	Capital ($mil)	Net Premium ($mil)	Net Income ($mil)
3-09	B+	2.11	1.79	N/A	88,473.2	50,979.0	7,975.4	89.2
3-08	B+	2.17	1.79	N/A	103,031.2	62,513.3	7,785.2	399.9
2008	B+	2.15	1.81	83.4	92,017.5	53,274.0	31,963.4	1,036.0
2007	B+	2.17	1.79	78.7	104,842.4	63,577.3	32,019.1	3,664.3
2006	B+	2.30	1.86	73.6	98,348.1	58,034.3	32,100.3	2,977.1
2005	B+	2.23	1.79	87.4	89,982.0	50,187.3	31,938.1	847.4
2004	B+	2.24	1.79	76.2	84,405.2	46,144.2	32,285.4	3,075.9

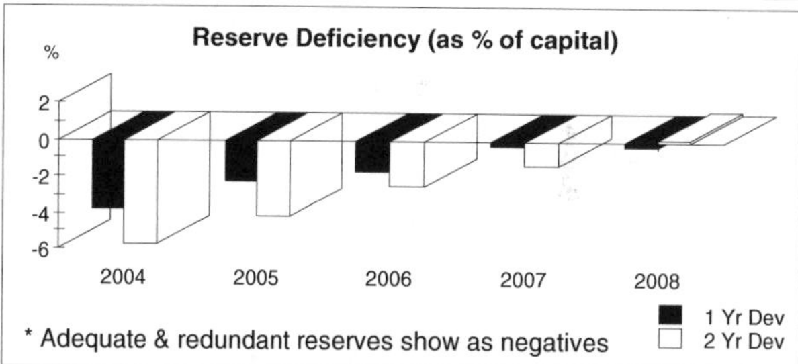

STATE VOLUNTEER MUTUAL INS CO * — A- Excellent

Major Rating Factors: Strong long-term capitalization index (7.8 on a scale of 0 to 10) based on excellent current risk adjusted capital (severe and moderate loss scenarios), despite some fluctuation in capital levels. Excellent profitability (7.9) with operating gains in each of the last five years. Excellent expense controls.

Other Rating Factors: Excellent liquidity (7.2) with ample operational cash flow and liquid investments. History of adequate reserve strength (6.6) as reserves have been consistently at an acceptable level. Good overall results on stability tests (6.9). Stability strengths include good operational trends and excellent risk diversification.

Principal Business: Medical malpractice (100%).

Principal Investments: Investment grade bonds (94%) and misc. investments (6%).

Investments in Affiliates: None

Group Affiliation: None

Licensed in: AL, AR, GA, IN, KY, MS, MO, NC, TN, VA

Commenced Business: May 1976

Address: 101 Westpark Dr Suite 300, Brentwood, TN 37024-1065

Phone: (615) 377-1999 **Domicile State:** TN **NAIC Code:** 33049

Data Date	Rating	RACR #1	RACR #2	Loss Ratio %	Total Assets ($mil)	Capital ($mil)	Net Premium ($mil)	Net Income ($mil)
3-09	A-	1.90	1.44	N/A	996.2	251.2	49.1	1.5
3-08	B+	1.82	1.43	N/A	949.8	240.8	54.0	2.5
2008	A-	1.99	1.52	75.5	983.5	255.9	244.4	26.0
2007	B+	1.95	1.55	86.7	941.0	245.2	180.0	30.5
2006	B+	1.39	1.12	90.3	870.2	217.4	190.9	23.0
2005	B+	1.10	0.87	94.1	805.9	184.3	161.0	14.7
2004	B+	0.95	0.74	97.4	765.6	167.9	150.0	10.8

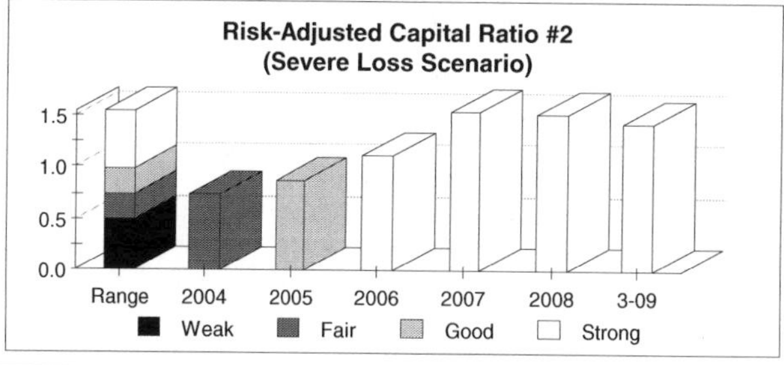

STEADFAST INS CO — C — Fair

Major Rating Factors: Fair overall results on stability tests (4.3 on a scale of 0 to 10) including negative cash flow from operations for 2008.
Other Rating Factors: Good overall profitability index (5.4). Good expense controls. Return on equity has been low, averaging 4.7% over the past five years. Strong long-term capitalization index (10.0) based on excellent current risk adjusted capital (severe and moderate loss scenarios), despite some fluctuation in capital levels. Excellent liquidity (7.0) with ample operational cash flow and liquid investments.
Principal Business: Other liability (71%), medical malpractice (12%), fire (4%), products liability (4%), allied lines (3%), credit (2%), and other lines (3%).
Principal Investments: Investment grade bonds (67%) and misc. investments (33%).
Investments in Affiliates: 33%
Group Affiliation: Zurich Financial Services Group
Licensed in: DE
Commenced Business: May 1988
Address: 1400 American Lane, Schaumburg, IL 60196-1056
Phone: (847) 605-6429 **Domicile State:** DE **NAIC Code:** 26387

Data Date	Rating	RACR #1	RACR #2	Loss Ratio %	Total Assets ($mil)	Capital ($mil)	Net Premium ($mil)	Net Income ($mil)
3-09	C	3.35	3.29	N/A	552.0	512.3	0.0	2.9
3-08	C	3.34	3.27	N/A	582.4	546.8	0.0	4.7
2008	C	3.34	3.28	0.0	537.3	510.2	0.0	35.1
2007	C	3.30	3.24	0.0	760.8	539.7	0.0	56.8
2006	C	3.05	3.00	0.0	772.9	581.6	0.0	16.5
2005	C	3.05	3.01	0.0	747.2	555.9	0.0	10.5
2004	C	2.54	2.52	0.0	557.1	397.8	0.0	7.9

Zurich Financial Services Group
Composite Group Rating: C-

Largest Group Members	Assets ($mil)	Rating
ZURICH AMERICAN INS CO	29634	C-
KEMPER INVESTORS LIFE INS CO	13886	C
FARMERS INS EXCHANGE	13368	C
FARMERS NEW WORLD LIFE INS CO	6444	B-
MID-CENTURY INS CO	3273	C-

SWISS REINSURANCE AMERICA CORP — C — Fair

Major Rating Factors: Fair overall results on stability tests (3.4 on a scale of 0 to 10) including excessive premium growth. The largest net exposure for one risk is excessive at 6.0% of capital. Strengths include potentially strong support from affiliation with Swiss Reinsurance. Good long-term capitalization index (5.2) based on good current risk adjusted capital (severe loss scenario). Moreover, capital levels have been consistent over the last several years.
Other Rating Factors: A history of deficient reserves (1.5) that places pressure on both capital and profits. In the last five years, reserves (two year development) fluctuated between 58% and 35% deficeint. Good overall profitability index (5.1) despite operating losses during 2004, 2005 and 2008. Return on equity has been low, averaging 1.2% over the past five years. Excellent liquidity (7.2) with ample operational cash flow and liquid investments.
Principal Business: (This company is a reinsurer.)
Principal Investments: Investment grade bonds (84%), misc. investments (10%), and non investment grade bonds (6%).
Investments in Affiliates: 3%
Group Affiliation: Swiss Reinsurance
Licensed in: All states except WY
Commenced Business: September 1940
Address: 175 King Street, Armonk, NY 10504
Phone: (914) 828-8000 **Domicile State:** NY **NAIC Code:** 25364

Data Date	Rating	RACR #1	RACR #2	Loss Ratio %	Total Assets ($mil)	Capital ($mil)	Net Premium ($mil)	Net Income ($mil)
3-09	C	1.22	0.79	N/A	14,479.3	4,340.0	611.5	208.8
3-08	C	1.07	0.70	N/A	14,538.9	4,091.3	464.4	92.7
2008	C	1.21	0.79	76.3	14,401.9	4,153.5	1,989.5	-4.8
2007	C	1.05	0.69	79.1	14,245.8	4,065.0	2,053.2	219.4
2006	C	1.03	0.66	86.3	14,544.8	3,861.8	2,043.1	625.4
2005	C	0.96	0.60	89.9	15,246.3	3,817.2	2,423.2	-420.0
2004	C	1.06	0.69	93.7	14,230.8	3,336.9	2,625.3	-302.5

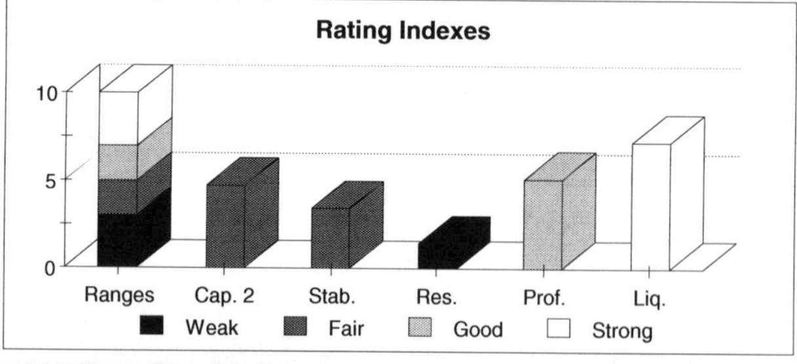

TENNESSEE FARMERS ASR CO * — A — Excellent

Major Rating Factors: Strong long-term capitalization index (10.0 on a scale of 0 to 10) based on excellent current risk adjusted capital (severe and moderate loss scenarios). Furthermore, this high level of risk adjusted capital has been consistently maintained in previous years. Ample reserve history (8.5) that helps to protect the company against sharp claims increases.
Other Rating Factors: Good overall results on stability tests (6.1). Affiliation with Tennessee Farmers Mutual is a strength. Good overall profitability index (6.7) despite operating losses during the first three months of 2008. Return on equity has been good over the last five years, averaging 11.4%. Good liquidity (6.1) with sufficient resources (cash flows and marketable investments) to handle a spike in claims.
Principal Business: Auto liability (56%) and auto physical damage (44%).
Principal Investments: Investment grade bonds (89%), cash (6%), and misc. investments (5%).
Investments in Affiliates: 0%
Group Affiliation: Tennessee Farmers Mutual
Licensed in: TN
Commenced Business: August 1991
Address: 147 Bear Creek Pike, Columbia, TN 38401-2266
Phone: (615) 388-7872 **Domicile State:** TN **NAIC Code:** 41220

Data Date	Rating	RACR #1	RACR #2	Loss Ratio %	Total Assets ($mil)	Capital ($mil)	Net Premium ($mil)	Net Income ($mil)
3-09	A	7.24	4.91	N/A	879.3	557.2	105.5	-7.5
3-08	A	6.87	5.12	N/A	883.8	513.6	99.7	-39.7
2008	A	7.33	5.08	87.4	883.3	564.5	431.7	16.3
2007	A	7.46	5.54	68.1	878.6	559.1	429.9	82.1
2006	A	6.51	4.69	81.1	786.9	479.0	405.5	42.5
2005	A	6.15	4.45	69.0	742.5	431.0	392.9	76.4
2004	A	5.44	3.97	70.7	654.0	352.8	367.2	59.7

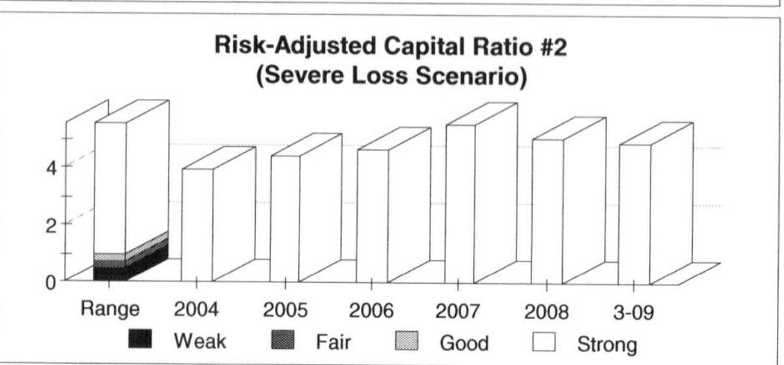

TENNESSEE FARMERS MUTUAL INS CO * A Excellent

Major Rating Factors: Strong long-term capitalization index (8.5 on a scale of 0 to 10) based on excellent current risk adjusted capital (severe and moderate loss scenarios). Furthermore, this high level of risk adjusted capital has been consistently maintained in previous years. Ample reserve history (7.5) that can protect against increases in claims costs.

Other Rating Factors: Excellent profitability (8.0) despite modest operating losses during the first three months of 2008. Good overall results on stability tests (6.1). Affiliation with Tennessee Farmers Mutual is a strength. Good liquidity (6.7) with sufficient resources (cash flows and marketable investments) to handle a spike in claims.

Principal Business: Auto liability (29%), auto physical damage (28%), homeowners multiple peril (25%), farmowners multiple peril (10%), fire (4%), other liability (2%), and commercial multiple peril (1%).

Principal Investments: Misc. investments (50%), investment grade bonds (48%), and cash (2%).

Investments in Affiliates: 42%

Group Affiliation: Tennessee Farmers Mutual

Licensed in: TN

Commenced Business: December 1952

Address: 147 Bear Creek Pike, Columbia, TN 38401-2266

Phone: (615) 388-7872 **Domicile State:** TN **NAIC Code:** 15245

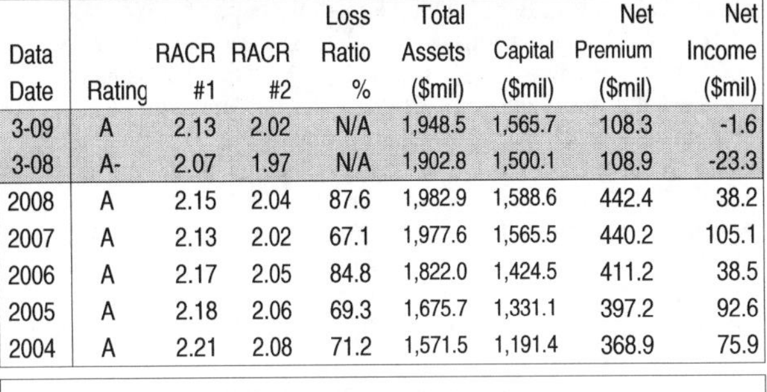

Data Date	Rating	RACR #1	RACR #2	Loss Ratio %	Total Assets ($mil)	Capital ($mil)	Net Premium ($mil)	Net Income ($mil)
3-09	A	2.13	2.02	N/A	1,948.5	1,565.7	108.3	-1.6
3-08	A-	2.07	1.97	N/A	1,902.8	1,500.1	108.9	-23.3
2008	A	2.15	2.04	87.6	1,982.9	1,588.6	442.4	38.2
2007	A	2.13	2.02	67.1	1,977.6	1,565.5	440.2	105.1
2006	A	2.17	2.05	84.8	1,822.0	1,424.5	411.2	38.5
2005	A	2.18	2.06	69.3	1,675.7	1,331.1	397.2	92.6
2004	A	2.21	2.08	71.2	1,571.5	1,191.4	368.9	75.9

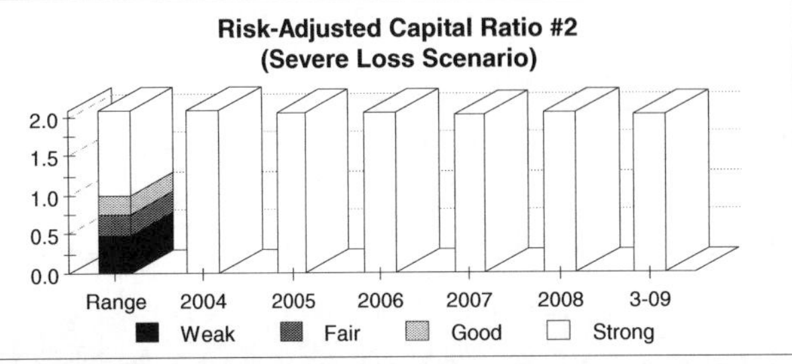

TIG INS CO D- Weak

Major Rating Factors: Weak overall results on stability tests (1.3 on a scale of 0 to 10) including weak risk adjusted capital in prior years, weak results on operational trends and negative cash flow from operations for 2008. Strengths include potentially strong support from affiliation with Fairfax Financial. The largest net exposure for one risk is acceptable at 2.1% of capital. Poor long-term capitalization index (0.9) based on weak current risk adjusted capital (severe and moderate loss scenarios).

Other Rating Factors: A history of deficient reserves (0.5) that places pressure on both capital and profits. In four of the last five years reserves (two year development) were between 48% and 64% deficient. Weak profitability index (2.9) with operating losses during 2004, 2005, 2007 and the first three months of 2008. Average return on equity over the last five years has been poor at -5.4%. Superior liquidity (10.0) with ample operational cash flow and liquid investments.

Principal Business: (Not applicable due to unusual reinsurance transactions.)

Principal Investments: Investment grade bonds (54%), misc. investments (45%), and non investment grade bonds (1%).

Investments in Affiliates: 37%

Group Affiliation: Fairfax Financial

Licensed in: All states except PR

Commenced Business: April 1915

Address: 5205 N OConnor Blvd,2nd Floor, Irving, TX 75015

Phone: (972) 831-5393 **Domicile State:** CA **NAIC Code:** 25534

Data Date	Rating	RACR #1	RACR #2	Loss Ratio %	Total Assets ($mil)	Capital ($mil)	Net Premium ($mil)	Net Income ($mil)
3-09	D-	0.22	0.18	N/A	1,722.5	479.0	0.5	-70.5
3-08	D	0.52	0.36	N/A	2,176.9	880.6	2.1	209.9
2008	D-	0.32	0.26	452.7	1,956.0	674.0	12.6	311.5
2007	D	0.42	0.29	N/A	2,061.6	738.4	-11.0	-91.8
2006	D	0.41	0.29	429.6	2,191.2	683.4	8.9	9.4
2005	D	0.98	0.75	N/A	2,375.0	597.3	-15.2	-179.3
2004	D	1.48	1.22	209.1	2,148.7	742.0	-21.2	-139.9

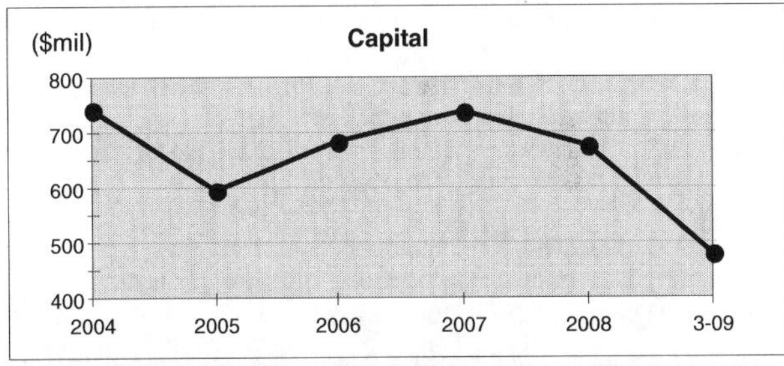

TOA-RE INS CO OF AMERICA B- Good

Major Rating Factors: Fair reserve development (4.1 on a scale of 0 to 10) as the level of reserves has at times been insufficient to cover claims. In 2004 and 2005 the two year reserve development was 19% and 21% deficient respectively. Good long-term capitalization index (6.6) based on good current risk adjusted capital (moderate loss scenario), despite some fluctuation in capital levels.

Other Rating Factors: Good overall profitability index (6.3). Fair expense controls. Return on equity has been fair, averaging 7.1% over the past five years. Good overall results on stability tests (5.3). Stability strengths include good operational trends and excellent risk diversification. The largest net exposure for one risk is conservative at 1.1% of capital. Excellent liquidity (7.0) with ample operational cash flow and liquid investments.

Principal Business: (This company is a reinsurer.)

Principal Investments: Investment grade bonds (84%) and misc. investments (16%).

Investments in Affiliates: None

Group Affiliation: Toa Reinsurance Co Ltd Japan

Licensed in: AZ, CA, CT, DC, DE, GA, IL, IA, KS, LA, MI, MS, NE, NV, NH, NJ, NY, OH, OK, PA, SD, TX, UT, WA, WI

Commenced Business: January 1972

Address: 2711 Centerville Rd Suite 400, Wilmington, DE 19808

Phone: (973) 898-9480 **Domicile State:** DE **NAIC Code:** 42439

Data Date	Rating	RACR #1	RACR #2	Loss Ratio %	Total Assets ($mil)	Capital ($mil)	Net Premium ($mil)	Net Income ($mil)
3-09	B-	1.62	1.07	N/A	1,323.0	396.6	59.2	8.7
3-08	C+	1.61	1.02	N/A	1,398.3	437.4	56.7	13.8
2008	B-	1.65	1.10	64.2	1,315.0	402.5	210.8	41.8
2007	C+	1.63	1.04	74.0	1,427.7	457.0	254.1	53.0
2006	C+	1.41	0.87	75.2	1,369.5	404.6	283.9	39.7
2005	C+	1.17	0.71	93.3	1,271.9	340.1	275.4	8.4
2004	C+	1.16	0.74	90.3	1,176.0	330.0	283.0	3.3

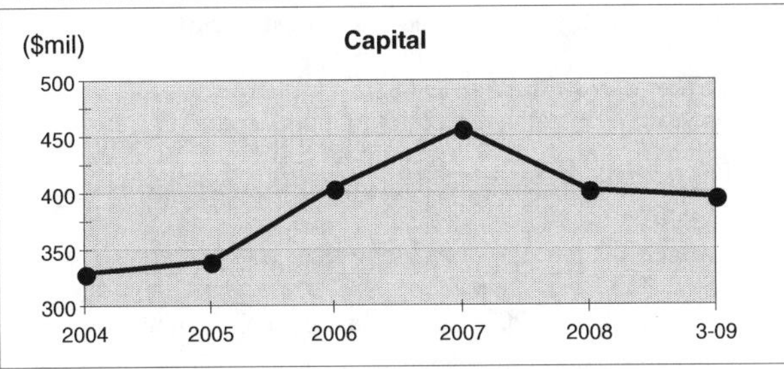

TOKIO MARINE & NICHIDO FIRE INS LTD * A Excellent

Major Rating Factors: Strong long-term capitalization index (7.6 on a scale of 0 to 10) based on excellent current risk adjusted capital (severe and moderate loss scenarios). Furthermore, this high level of risk adjusted capital has been consistently maintained in previous years. Ample reserve history (7.0) that can protect against increases in claims costs.

Other Rating Factors: Excellent profitability (8.5) with operating gains in each of the last five years. Excellent liquidity (7.0) with ample operational cash flow and liquid investments. Excellent overall results on stability tests (7.4). Stability strengths include excellent operational trends and excellent risk diversification.

Principal Business: Auto liability (13%), ocean marine (13%), other liability (12%), workers compensation (10%), commercial multiple peril (10%), fire (10%), and other lines (31%).

Principal Investments: Investment grade bonds (92%), misc. investments (6%), and cash (2%).

Investments in Affiliates: 5%

Group Affiliation: Millea Holdings Inc

Licensed in: All states, the District of Columbia and Puerto Rico

Commenced Business: December 1955

Address: 101 Park Ave, New York, NY 10178

Phone: (212) 297-6600 **Domicile State:** NY **NAIC Code:** 12904

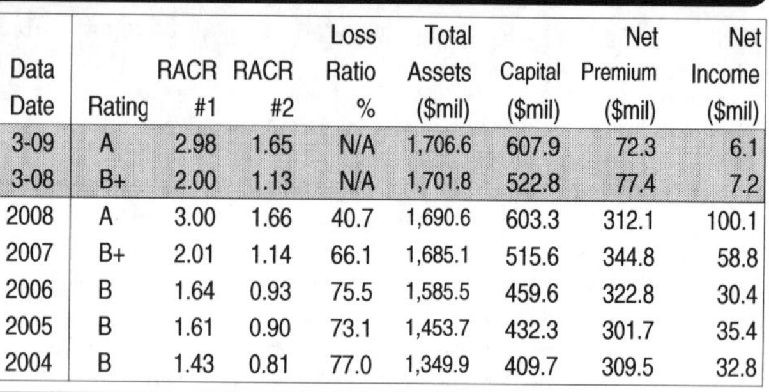

Data Date	Rating	RACR #1	RACR #2	Loss Ratio %	Total Assets ($mil)	Capital ($mil)	Net Premium ($mil)	Net Income ($mil)
3-09	A	2.98	1.65	N/A	1,706.6	607.9	72.3	6.1
3-08	B+	2.00	1.13	N/A	1,701.8	522.8	77.4	7.2
2008	A	3.00	1.66	40.7	1,690.6	603.3	312.1	100.1
2007	B+	2.01	1.14	66.1	1,685.1	515.6	344.8	58.8
2006	B	1.64	0.93	75.5	1,585.5	459.6	322.8	30.4
2005	B	1.61	0.90	73.1	1,453.7	432.3	301.7	35.4
2004	B	1.43	0.81	77.0	1,349.9	409.7	309.5	32.8

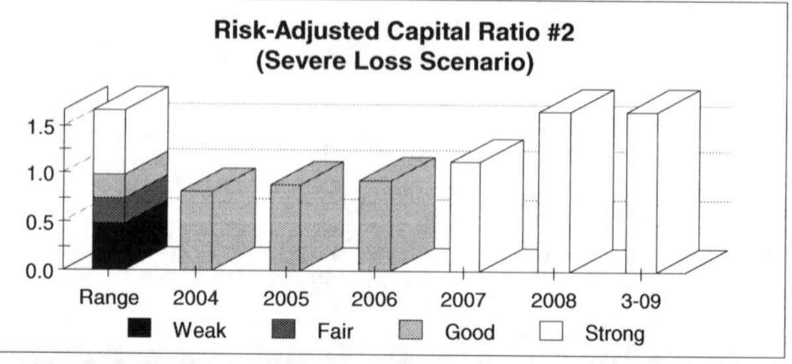

TOWER INS CO OF NEW YORK C Fair

Major Rating Factors: Fair overall results on stability tests (3.5 on a scale of 0 to 10). Good long-term capitalization index (5.1) based on good current risk adjusted capital (moderate loss scenario). Over the last several years, capital levels have remained relatively consistent.

Other Rating Factors: History of adequate reserve strength (6.1) as reserves have been consistently at an acceptable level. Good overall profitability index (6.9) despite operating losses during 2004. Return on equity has been fair, averaging 7.1% over the past five years. Good liquidity (6.7) with sufficient resources (cash flows and marketable investments) to handle a spike in claims.

Principal Business: Commercial multiple peril (36%), workers compensation (26%), homeowners multiple peril (16%), other liability (10%), auto liability (8%), fire (3%), and auto physical damage (2%).

Principal Investments: Investment grade bonds (81%), misc. investments (15%), and non investment grade bonds (4%).

Investments in Affiliates: 5%

Group Affiliation: Tower Group Inc

Licensed in: AK, AZ, AR, CO, DC, DE, FL, GA, IL, IN, KS, KY, ME, MD, MA, MI, MO, MT, NV, NJ, NY, NC, ND, OK, OR, PA, RI, SC, SD, TN, TX, UT, VT, VA, WA, WV

Commenced Business: December 1990

Address: 120 Broadway, 14th Floor, New York, NY 10271

Phone: (212) 655-2000 **Domicile State:** NY **NAIC Code:** 44300

Data Date	Rating	RACR #1	RACR #2	Loss Ratio %	Total Assets ($mil)	Capital ($mil)	Net Premium ($mil)	Net Income ($mil)
3-09	C	1.07	0.78	N/A	872.6	217.6	66.4	4.2
3-08	C-	0.86	0.56	N/A	697.1	214.2	54.1	10.4
2008	C	1.01	0.75	51.7	876.1	223.2	256.0	24.0
2007	C-	0.89	0.58	55.1	661.0	215.3	223.5	29.6
2006	C-	0.78	0.51	60.2	638.6	200.7	243.8	21.1
2005	C-	0.91	0.61	58.8	431.2	132.4	211.8	6.2
2004	D+	1.86	1.27	59.4	283.6	126.1	98.1	-5.7

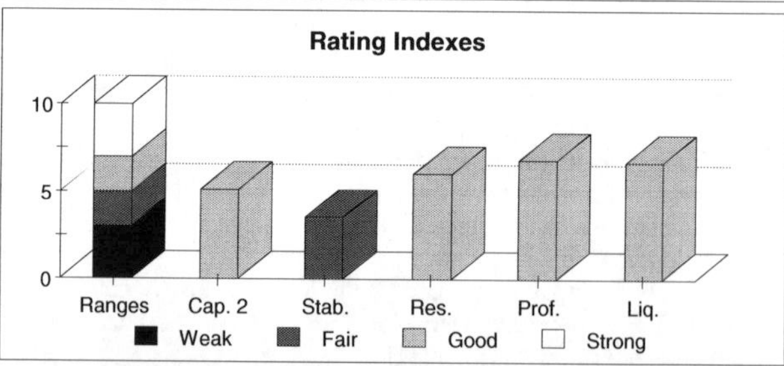

TRANSATLANTIC REINSURANCE CO C+ Fair

Major Rating Factors: Fair overall results on stability tests (4.4 on a scale of 0 to 10). Strengths include potentially strong support from affiliation with American International Group. Good long-term capitalization index (5.2) based on fair current risk adjusted capital (severe loss scenario), although results have slipped from the good range during the last year.

Other Rating Factors: Good liquidity (6.5) with sufficient resources (cash flows and marketable investments) to handle a spike in claims. A history of deficient reserves (2.2). Underreserving can have an adverse impact on capital and profits. In four of the last five years reserves (two year development) were between 16% and 52% deficient. Excellent profitability (7.0) with operating gains in each of the last five years.

Principal Business: (This company is a reinsurer.)

Principal Investments: Investment grade bonds (84%), misc. investments (14%), and cash (2%).

Investments in Affiliates: 5%

Group Affiliation: American International Group

Licensed in: AK, AZ, AR, CA, CO, CT, DC, DE, FL, GA, ID, IL, IN, IA, KS, KY, LA, MA, MI, MN, MS, NE, NV, NJ, NM, NY, OH, OK, PA, SC, SD, TX, UT, WA, WV, WI, PR

Commenced Business: January 1953

Address: 80 Pine St, New York, NY 10005

Phone: (212) 770-2000 **Domicile State:** NY **NAIC Code:** 19453

Data Date	Rating	RACR #1	RACR #2	Loss Ratio %	Total Assets ($mil)	Capital ($mil)	Net Premium ($mil)	Net Income ($mil)
3-09	C+	1.16	0.74	N/A	11,688.1	3,508.7	828.5	74.4
3-08	C+	0.99	0.65	N/A	12,897.2	3,347.9	886.2	79.8
2008	C+	1.17	0.75	71.1	11,451.4	3,534.1	3,488.9	103.4
2007	C+	1.03	0.68	67.0	12,633.2	3,368.8	3,430.7	391.7
2006	C+	1.11	0.73	67.9	10,161.5	3,059.5	3,145.4	384.7
2005	C+	0.99	0.66	85.5	9,031.4	2,618.0	2,935.2	17.2
2004	B-	0.78	0.52	75.0	7,483.0	1,944.5	3,223.6	141.8

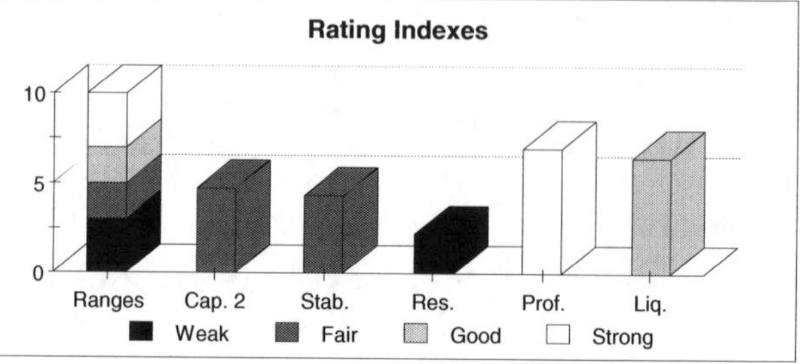

TRAVELERS CASUALTY & SURETY CO — B — Good

Major Rating Factors: Good liquidity (6.8 on a scale of 0 to 10) with sufficient resources (cash flows and marketable investments) to handle a spike in claims. Good overall results on stability tests (5.9). Affiliation with Travelers Companies Inc is a strength.

Other Rating Factors: Fair reserve development (4.6) as reserves have generally been sufficient to cover claims. In 2005, the two year reserve development was 26% deficient. Strong long-term capitalization index (7.3) based on excellent current risk adjusted capital (severe and moderate loss scenarios), despite some fluctuation in capital levels. Excellent profitability (7.9) with operating gains in each of the last five years. Return on equity has been excellent over the last five years averaging 18.5%.

Principal Business: Workers compensation (66%), surety (17%), homeowners multiple peril (14%), other liability (1%), and fire (1%).

Principal Investments: Investment grade bonds (67%), misc. investments (32%), and non investment grade bonds (1%).

Investments in Affiliates: 25%

Group Affiliation: Travelers Companies Inc

Licensed in: All states, the District of Columbia and Puerto Rico

Commenced Business: May 1907

Address: One Tower Square, Hartford, CT 06183

Phone: (860) 277-0111 **Domicile State:** CT **NAIC Code:** 19038

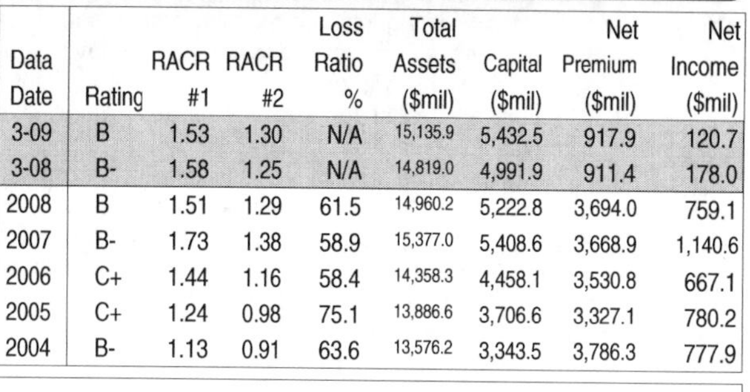

Data Date	Rating	RACR #1	RACR #2	Loss Ratio %	Total Assets ($mil)	Capital ($mil)	Net Premium ($mil)	Net Income ($mil)
3-09	B	1.53	1.30	N/A	15,135.9	5,432.5	917.9	120.7
3-08	B-	1.58	1.25	N/A	14,819.0	4,991.9	911.4	178.0
2008	B	1.51	1.29	61.5	14,960.2	5,222.8	3,694.0	759.1
2007	B-	1.73	1.38	58.9	15,377.0	5,408.6	3,668.9	1,140.6
2006	C+	1.44	1.16	58.4	14,358.3	4,458.1	3,530.8	667.1
2005	C+	1.24	0.98	75.1	13,886.6	3,706.6	3,327.1	780.2
2004	B-	1.13	0.91	63.6	13,576.2	3,343.5	3,786.3	777.9

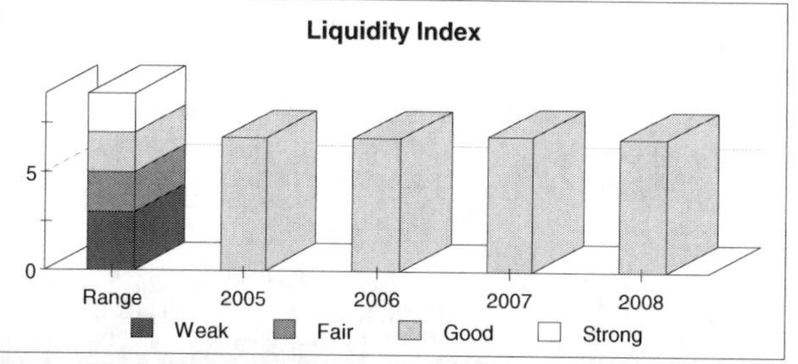

TRAVELERS CASUALTY & SURETY CO OF AM — B- — Good

Major Rating Factors: Fair overall results on stability tests (4.5 on a scale of 0 to 10). The largest net exposure for one risk is excessive at 6.3% of capital. Strong long-term capitalization index (9.9) based on excellent current risk adjusted capital (severe and moderate loss scenarios), despite some fluctuation in capital levels.

Other Rating Factors: Ample reserve history (7.0) that can protect against increases in claims costs. Excellent profitability (9.5) with operating gains in each of the last five years. Return on equity has been excellent over the last five years averaging 25.6%. Excellent liquidity (7.2) with ample operational cash flow and liquid investments.

Principal Business: Surety (65%), other liability (24%), fidelity (8%), and burglary & theft (2%).

Principal Investments: Investment grade bonds (94%), misc. investments (4%), and non investment grade bonds (3%).

Investments in Affiliates: None

Group Affiliation: Travelers Companies Inc

Licensed in: All states except PR

Commenced Business: July 1974

Address: One Tower Square, Hartford, CT 06183

Phone: (860) 277-0111 **Domicile State:** CT **NAIC Code:** 31194

Data Date	Rating	RACR #1	RACR #2	Loss Ratio %	Total Assets ($mil)	Capital ($mil)	Net Premium ($mil)	Net Income ($mil)
3-09	B-	6.08	3.83	N/A	4,307.8	1,999.3	312.8	101.0
3-08	C+	3.76	2.39	N/A	3,664.0	1,317.9	324.9	26.5
2008	B-	5.63	3.55	19.2	4,096.2	1,735.0	1,337.7	511.8
2007	C+	4.16	2.65	25.5	3,556.0	1,290.6	1,351.7	405.1
2006	C+	3.44	2.25	34.8	3,291.4	1,127.9	1,193.4	264.3
2005	C	2.95	1.94	35.9	2,680.4	856.9	990.9	189.0
2004	C	3.92	2.40	40.2	2,295.2	870.5	858.9	198.7

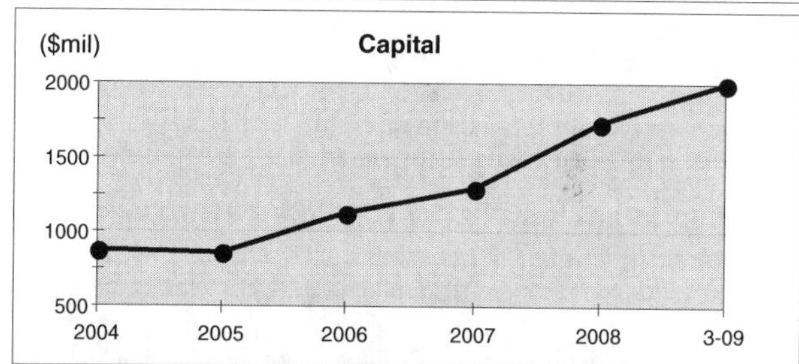

TRAVELERS CASUALTY INS CO OF AMERICA — B — Good

Major Rating Factors: Good liquidity (6.6 on a scale of 0 to 10) with sufficient resources (cash flows and marketable investments) to handle a spike in claims. Good overall results on stability tests (5.4).

Other Rating Factors: Fair reserve development (4.6) as reserves have generally been sufficient to cover claims. In 2005, the two year reserve development was 26% deficient. Strong long-term capitalization index (7.4) based on excellent current risk adjusted capital (severe and moderate loss scenarios), despite some fluctuation in capital levels. Excellent profitability (8.1) with operating gains in each of the last five years. Return on equity has been excellent over the last five years averaging 19.5%.

Principal Business: Commercial multiple peril (64%) and workers compensation (36%).

Principal Investments: Investment grade bonds (96%), misc. investments (3%), and non investment grade bonds (1%).

Investments in Affiliates: None

Group Affiliation: Travelers Companies Inc

Licensed in: All states except PR

Commenced Business: October 1971

Address: One Tower Square, Hartford, CT 06183

Phone: (860) 277-0111 **Domicile State:** CT **NAIC Code:** 19046

Data Date	Rating	RACR #1	RACR #2	Loss Ratio %	Total Assets ($mil)	Capital ($mil)	Net Premium ($mil)	Net Income ($mil)
3-09	B	2.25	1.44	N/A	1,830.4	519.3	123.1	21.2
3-08	B-	2.00	1.15	N/A	1,752.1	457.4	122.2	28.5
2008	B	2.20	1.40	61.5	1,810.3	499.6	495.2	86.5
2007	B-	1.92	1.10	59.0	1,740.1	432.4	492.2	93.0
2006	C+	1.80	1.12	58.4	1,750.8	447.8	472.6	111.0
2005	C+	1.43	0.93	75.1	1,705.4	393.3	445.7	53.7
2004	B-	1.60	1.06	63.7	1,716.7	424.0	505.8	89.9

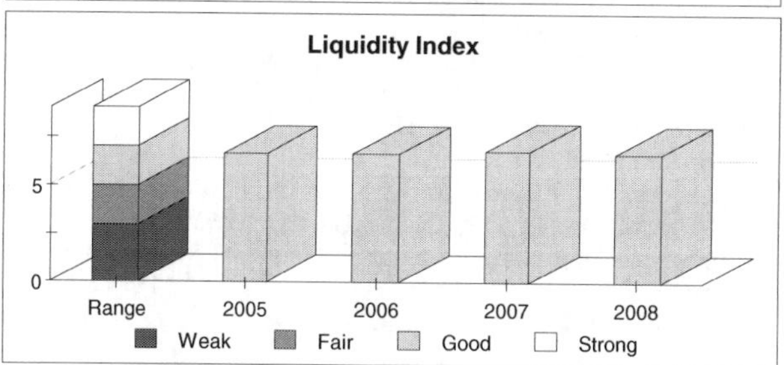

TRAVELERS INDEMNITY CO * A- Excellent

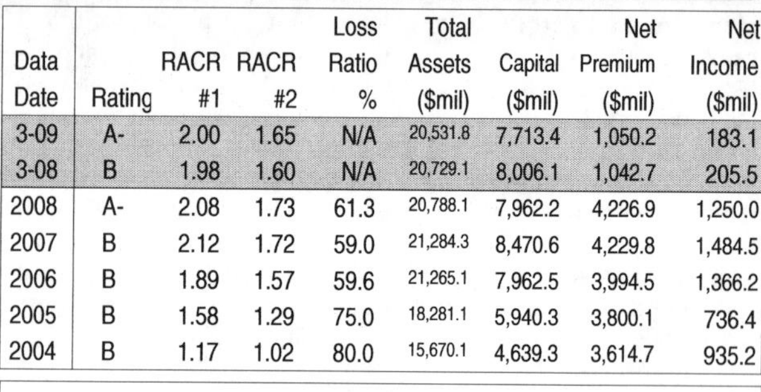

Data Date	Rating	RACR #1	RACR #2	Loss Ratio %	Total Assets ($mil)	Capital ($mil)	Net Premium ($mil)	Net Income ($mil)
3-09	A-	2.00	1.65	N/A	20,531.8	7,713.4	1,050.2	183.1
3-08	B	1.98	1.60	N/A	20,729.1	8,006.1	1,042.7	205.5
2008	A-	2.08	1.73	61.3	20,788.1	7,962.2	4,226.9	1,250.0
2007	B	2.12	1.72	59.0	21,284.3	8,470.6	4,229.8	1,484.5
2006	B	1.89	1.57	59.6	21,265.1	7,962.5	3,994.5	1,366.2
2005	B	1.58	1.29	75.0	18,281.1	5,940.3	3,800.1	736.4
2004	B	1.17	1.02	80.0	15,670.1	4,639.3	3,614.7	935.2

Major Rating Factors: Strong long-term capitalization index (8.1 on a scale of 0 to 10) based on excellent current risk adjusted capital (severe and moderate loss scenarios), despite some fluctuation in capital levels. Excellent profitability (7.4) with operating gains in each of the last five years. Return on equity has been excellent over the last five years averaging 16.3%.

Other Rating Factors: Good liquidity (6.9) with sufficient resources (cash flows and marketable investments) to handle a spike in claims. Good overall results on stability tests (6.9). Stability strengths include good operational trends and excellent risk diversification. Fair reserve development (4.9) as reserves have generally been sufficient to cover claims. In 2005, the two year reserve development was 19% deficient.

Principal Business: Workers compensation (26%), other liability (18%), commercial multiple peril (16%), auto liability (10%), fire (9%), allied lines (7%), and other lines (14%).

Principal Investments: Investment grade bonds (76%), misc. investments (23%), non investment grade bonds (3%), and real estate (1%).

Investments in Affiliates: 20%

Group Affiliation: Travelers Companies Inc

Licensed in: All states, the District of Columbia and Puerto Rico

Commenced Business: May 1906

Address: One Tower Square, Hartford, CT 06183

Phone: (860) 277-0111 **Domicile State:** CT **NAIC Code:** 25658

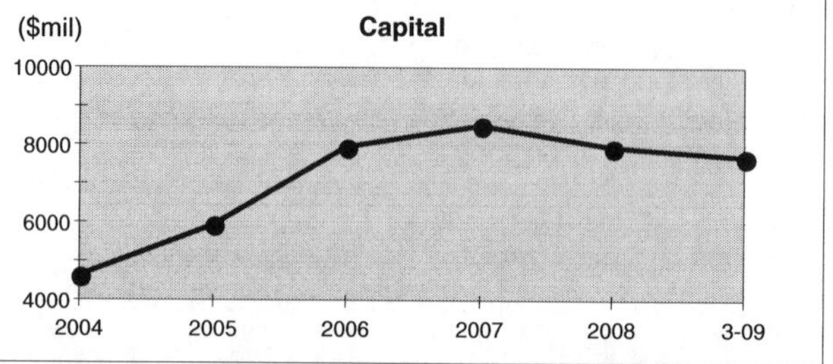

TRAVELERS INDEMNITY CO OF CT B Good

Data Date	Rating	RACR #1	RACR #2	Loss Ratio %	Total Assets ($mil)	Capital ($mil)	Net Premium ($mil)	Net Income ($mil)
3-09	B	2.94	1.88	N/A	1,055.2	344.7	61.8	8.1
3-08	B	2.97	1.71	N/A	994.1	343.2	61.3	15.5
2008	B	2.93	1.87	61.5	1,019.2	338.1	248.5	46.5
2007	B	2.89	1.66	59.0	988.0	329.0	247.0	54.4
2006	B-	2.43	1.51	58.4	949.2	304.5	237.1	59.2
2005	B-	2.01	1.31	75.1	931.6	276.4	223.8	34.3
2004	B-	2.23	1.48	63.7	944.9	293.7	253.5	54.3

Major Rating Factors: History of adequate reserve strength (5.0 on a scale of 0 to 10) as reserves have been consistently at an acceptable level. Good liquidity (6.8) with sufficient resources (cash flows and marketable investments) to handle a spike in claims.

Other Rating Factors: Good overall results on stability tests (5.9). Affiliation with Travelers Companies Inc is a strength. Strong long-term capitalization index (8.2) based on excellent current risk adjusted capital (severe and moderate loss scenarios), despite some fluctuation in capital levels. Excellent profitability (8.4) with operating gains in each of the last five years. Return on equity has been excellent over the last five years averaging 15.8%.

Principal Business: Workers compensation (37%), commercial multiple peril (36%), auto liability (13%), auto physical damage (5%), other liability (4%), farmowners multiple peril (2%), and other lines (2%).

Principal Investments: Investment grade bonds (92%) and misc. investments (8%).

Investments in Affiliates: None

Group Affiliation: Travelers Companies Inc

Licensed in: All states, the District of Columbia and Puerto Rico

Commenced Business: September 1860

Address: One Tower Square, Hartford, CT 06183

Phone: (860) 277-0111 **Domicile State:** CT **NAIC Code:** 25682

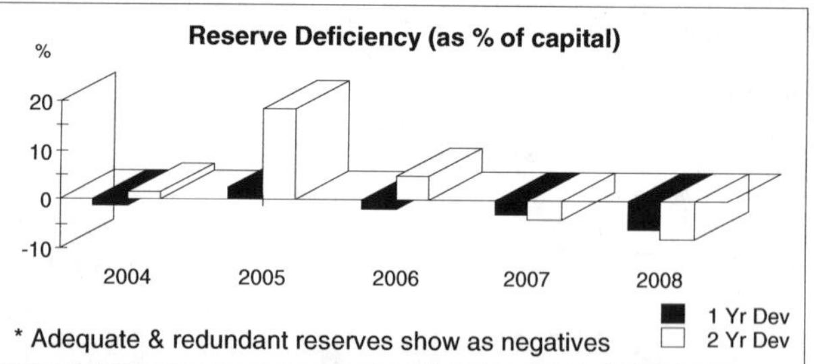

TRINITY UNIVERSAL INS CO B- Good

Data Date	Rating	RACR #1	RACR #2	Loss Ratio %	Total Assets ($mil)	Capital ($mil)	Net Premium ($mil)	Net Income ($mil)
3-09	B-	1.47	1.11	N/A	2,583.6	697.1	442.4	7.7
3-08	B-	1.68	1.22	N/A	3,195.1	1,127.3	456.6	-3.5
2008	B-	1.83	1.42	75.8	2,664.8	828.9	1,720.0	-59.8
2007	B-	1.70	1.24	67.7	3,239.8	1,145.4	1,791.2	109.8
2006	C+	1.71	1.21	65.4	3,334.8	1,184.3	1,775.8	161.9
2005	C+	1.64	1.16	68.0	3,400.6	1,153.0	1,807.4	100.0
2004	C+	1.33	0.94	68.0	3,272.0	1,061.2	1,829.3	100.5

Major Rating Factors: Fair overall results on stability tests (4.9 on a scale of 0 to 10) including negative cash flow from operations for 2008. Strengths include potentially strong support from affiliation with Unitrin Inc. Fair profitability index (3.0) with operating losses during 2008. Return on equity has been fair, averaging 6.7% over the past five years.

Other Rating Factors: Fair liquidity (3.0) as cash resources may not be adequate to cover a spike in claims. Strong long-term capitalization index (7.5) based on excellent current risk adjusted capital (severe and moderate loss scenarios), despite some fluctuation in capital levels. Ample reserve history (7.0) that can protect against increases in claims costs.

Principal Business: Auto liability (40%), auto physical damage (27%), homeowners multiple peril (25%), other liability (3%), inland marine (1%), allied lines (1%), and fire (1%).

Principal Investments: Investment grade bonds (55%), misc. investments (46%), and non investment grade bonds (1%).

Investments in Affiliates: 12%

Group Affiliation: Unitrin Inc

Licensed in: AL, AZ, AR, CA, CO, GA, ID, IL, IN, IA, KS, KY, LA, MI, MS, MO, MT, NE, NM, OH, OK, OR, TN, TX, UT, WA, WI, WY

Commenced Business: February 1926

Address: 10000 N Central Expressway, Dallas, TX 75231

Phone: (214) 360-8000 **Domicile State:** TX **NAIC Code:** 19887

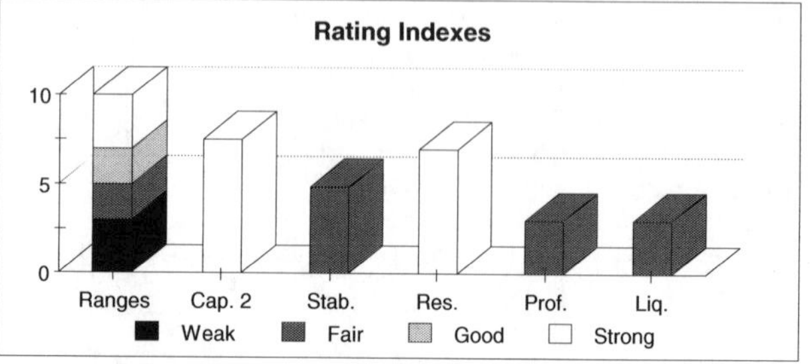

TRITON INS CO — B- Good

Major Rating Factors: Fair profitability index (3.6 on a scale of 0 to 10) with operating losses during 2008. Return on equity has been fair, averaging 15.2% over the past five years. Good overall results on stability tests (5.3) despite excessive premium growth. Stability strengths include good operational trends and excellent risk diversification.

Other Rating Factors: Strong long-term capitalization index (10.0) based on excellent current risk adjusted capital (severe and moderate loss scenarios), despite some fluctuation in capital levels. Ample reserve history (7.8) that can protect against increases in claims costs. Excellent liquidity (7.3) with ample operational cash flow and liquid investments.

Principal Business: Aggregate write-ins for other lines of business (49%), credit accident & health (47%), inland marine (4%), and other accident & health (1%).

Principal Investments: Investment grade bonds (90%), non investment grade bonds (5%), misc. investments (3%), and cash (2%).

Investments in Affiliates: None

Group Affiliation: Citigroup Inc

Licensed in: All states except PR

Commenced Business: July 1982

Address: 3001 Meacham Blvd Ste 200, Fort Worth, TX 76137-4615

Phone: (817) 348-7500 **Domicile State:** TX **NAIC Code:** 41211

Data Date	Rating	RACR #1	RACR #2	Loss Ratio %	Total Assets ($mil)	Capital ($mil)	Net Premium ($mil)	Net Income ($mil)
3-09	B-	7.20	4.11	N/A	768.2	348.6	53.3	15.6
3-08	B-	13.41	7.09	N/A	598.4	312.3	40.1	12.0
2008	B-	7.14	4.11	41.6	779.2	335.7	309.5	-5.5
2007	B-	13.40	7.09	33.7	587.2	301.3	173.6	63.3
2006	B-	6.72	4.06	30.4	715.7	446.7	172.1	93.5
2005	B-	9.81	5.76	26.3	775.3	498.6	223.3	141.3
2004	B-	2.70	2.17	25.2	684.0	374.8	277.8	24.0

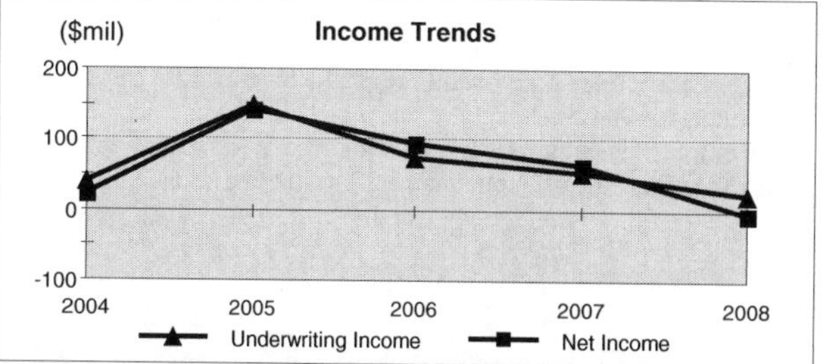

TRUCK INS EXCHANGE — C Fair

Major Rating Factors: Fair reserve development (3.7 on a scale of 0 to 10) as the level of reserves has at times been insufficient to cover claims. In 2005 and 2004 the two year reserve development was 24% and 36% deficient respectively. Fair profitability index (4.1) with operating losses during the first three months of 2008.

Other Rating Factors: Fair overall results on stability tests (3.4). Good long-term capitalization index (5.6) based on good current risk adjusted capital (moderate loss scenario). Good liquidity (5.7) with sufficient resources (cash flows and marketable investments) to handle a spike in claims.

Principal Business: Commercial multiple peril (42%), workers compensation (22%), auto liability (17%), other liability (8%), auto physical damage (7%), homeowners multiple peril (1%), and other lines (2%).

Principal Investments: Investment grade bonds (52%), misc. investments (31%), cash (16%), and non investment grade bonds (1%).

Investments in Affiliates: 21%

Group Affiliation: Zurich Financial Services Group

Licensed in: All states except DE, VT, PR

Commenced Business: February 1935

Address: 4680 Wilshire Blvd, Los Angeles, CA 90010

Phone: (323) 932-3200 **Domicile State:** CA **NAIC Code:** 21709

Data Date	Rating	RACR #1	RACR #2	Loss Ratio %	Total Assets ($mil)	Capital ($mil)	Net Premium ($mil)	Net Income ($mil)
3-09	C	1.02	0.83	N/A	1,954.4	422.7	200.7	-8.4
3-08	C	1.38	1.06	N/A	1,814.8	504.9	241.7	4.1
2008	C	1.02	0.82	76.1	1,917.0	428.3	913.6	-31.1
2007	C	1.38	1.06	71.1	1,773.1	504.1	993.0	47.7
2006	C	1.44	1.09	67.1	1,641.5	471.2	898.6	68.2
2005	C	1.36	1.03	68.4	1,632.7	399.3	838.5	37.7
2004	C	1.29	0.99	70.5	1,215.3	349.2	746.4	31.4

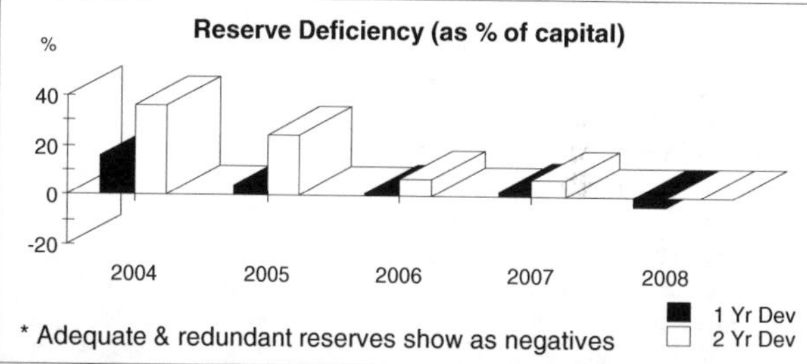

TRUSTGARD INS CO * — B+ Good

Major Rating Factors: Good liquidity (6.5 on a scale of 0 to 10) with sufficient resources (cash flows and marketable investments) to handle a spike in claims. Good overall results on stability tests (5.0) despite weak results on operational trends. The largest net exposure for one risk is high at 3.0% of capital.

Other Rating Factors: Strong long-term capitalization index (7.9) based on excellent current risk adjusted capital (severe and moderate loss scenarios). Moreover, capital levels have been consistent in recent years. Ample reserve history (8.3) that helps to protect the company against sharp claims increases. Excellent profitability (7.4) with operating gains in each of the last five years. Return on equity has been good over the last five years, averaging 14.2%.

Principal Business: Auto liability (45%), auto physical damage (28%), homeowners multiple peril (22%), workers compensation (1%), fire (1%), other liability (1%), and other lines (2%).

Principal Investments: Investment grade bonds (100%).

Investments in Affiliates: None

Group Affiliation: Grange Mutual Casualty Group

Licensed in: CO, GA, IL, IN, IA, KS, KY, MN, MO, NE, ND, OH, OR, PA, SC, SD, TN, TX, VA, WA, WI

Commenced Business: November 1981

Address: 650 S Front St, Columbus, OH 43206

Phone: (614) 445-2754 **Domicile State:** OH **NAIC Code:** 40118

Data Date	Rating	RACR #1	RACR #2	Loss Ratio %	Total Assets ($mil)	Capital ($mil)	Net Premium ($mil)	Net Income ($mil)
3-09	B+	3.10	1.94	N/A	66.4	32.4	9.1	0.4
3-08	B+	2.81	1.73	N/A	64.9	29.4	9.4	0.8
2008	B+	3.06	1.93	67.8	67.9	32.5	37.5	3.8
2007	B+	2.65	1.66	64.2	67.4	28.6	36.5	3.8
2006	B+	2.02	1.33	64.4	66.0	25.0	42.8	3.2
2005	B+	1.89	1.26	62.0	60.4	21.8	40.8	3.5
2004	B+	1.45	1.00	62.4	54.8	18.4	40.3	3.6

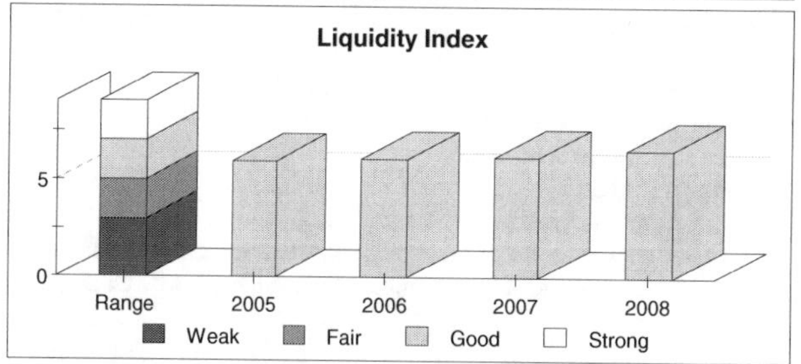

TUSCARORA WAYNE MUTUAL INS CO * B+ Good

Major Rating Factors: Good overall results on stability tests (5.0 on a scale of 0 to 10) despite excessive premium growth. Stability strengths include excellent operational trends and good risk diversification. Strong long-term capitalization index (8.1) based on excellent current risk adjusted capital (severe and moderate loss scenarios), despite some fluctuation in capital levels.

Other Rating Factors: Ample reserve history (8.2) that helps to protect the company against sharp claims increases. Excellent profitability (7.2). Excellent liquidity (7.0) with ample operational cash flow and liquid investments.

Principal Business: Homeowners multiple peril (34%), commercial multiple peril (32%), fire (13%), farmowners multiple peril (9%), allied lines (5%), other liability (4%), and inland marine (3%).

Principal Investments: Misc. investments (50%), investment grade bonds (49%), real estate (2%), and non investment grade bonds (1%).

Investments in Affiliates: 39%

Group Affiliation: Tuscarora Group

Licensed in: OH, PA

Commenced Business: September 1874

Address: 601 State St, Wyalusing, PA 18853

Phone: (570) 746-1515 **Domicile State:** PA **NAIC Code:** 17825

Data Date	Rating	RACR #1	RACR #2	Loss Ratio %	Total Assets ($mil)	Capital ($mil)	Net Premium ($mil)	Net Income ($mil)
3-09	B+	1.92	1.71	N/A	54.2	31.2	5.8	0.0
3-08	B+	1.99	1.74	N/A	53.7	33.7	3.5	0.6
2008	B+	1.95	1.73	55.2	52.2	31.5	13.9	0.7
2007	B+	1.98	1.72	47.6	55.7	33.5	13.7	2.2
2006	B+	2.00	1.74	44.8	49.3	29.7	13.1	2.3
2005	B+	1.82	1.53	44.3	46.5	25.7	13.1	2.2
2004	B+	1.62	1.34	51.6	43.1	22.6	12.8	1.3

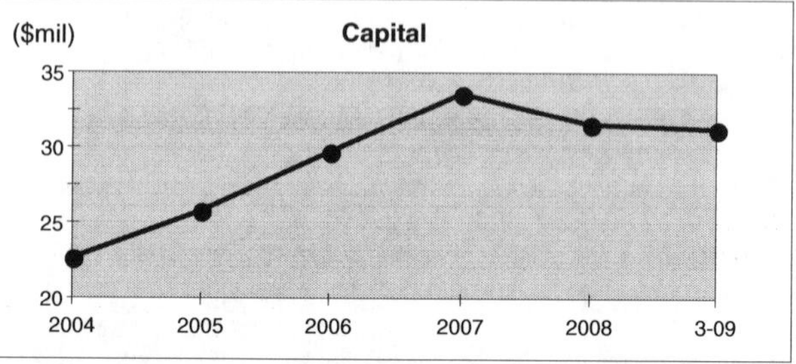

TWIN CITY FIRE INS CO B Good

Major Rating Factors: Good liquidity (6.9 on a scale of 0 to 10) with sufficient resources (cash flows and marketable investments) to handle a spike in claims. Good overall results on stability tests (6.2). Stability strengths include good operational trends and excellent risk diversification.

Other Rating Factors: Fair reserve development (4.7) as reserves have generally been sufficient to cover claims. In 2004, the two year reserve development was 23% deficient. Strong long-term capitalization index (10.0) based on excellent current risk adjusted capital (severe and moderate loss scenarios), despite some fluctuation in capital levels. Excellent profitability (8.7) with operating gains in each of the last five years. Return on equity has been good over the last five years, averaging 12.2%.

Principal Business: Workers compensation (45%), other liability (32%), auto liability (9%), commercial multiple peril (5%), auto physical damage (4%), products liability (3%), and homeowners multiple peril (2%).

Principal Investments: Investment grade bonds (97%), misc. investments (2%), and non investment grade bonds (1%).

Investments in Affiliates: None

Group Affiliation: Hartford Financial Services Inc

Licensed in: All states except PR

Commenced Business: July 1987

Address: 4040 Vincennes Cir Suite 100, Indianapolis, IN 46268

Phone: (860) 547-5000 **Domicile State:** IN **NAIC Code:** 29459

Data Date	Rating	RACR #1	RACR #2	Loss Ratio %	Total Assets ($mil)	Capital ($mil)	Net Premium ($mil)	Net Income ($mil)
3-09	B	6.12	3.95	N/A	659.2	311.2	37.9	11.1
3-08	B	5.56	3.31	N/A	650.4	315.0	38.9	11.1
2008	B	6.00	3.89	64.1	647.9	301.2	153.1	38.8
2007	B	5.41	3.25	64.6	637.6	303.2	156.6	40.0
2006	B	5.40	3.44	67.5	615.9	293.7	158.5	30.9
2005	B	5.02	3.24	66.0	564.2	258.5	156.2	32.0
2004	B	4.22	2.89	70.5	508.8	231.1	140.8	26.9

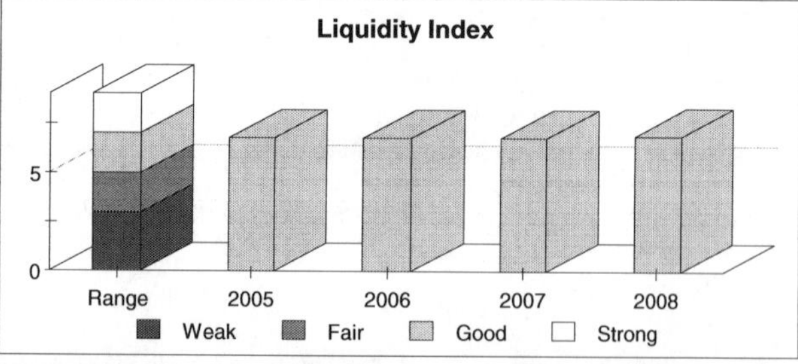

UNDERWRITERS AT LLOYDS LONDON E+ Very Weak

Major Rating Factors: Poor long-term capitalization index (1.2 on a scale of 0 to 10) based on weak current risk adjusted capital (severe and moderate loss scenarios). Weak profitability index (2.9) with operating losses during 2004 and 2007.

Other Rating Factors: Weak overall results on stability tests (0.0) including weak risk adjusted capital in prior years and negative cash flow from operations for 2008. The largest net exposure for one risk is excessive at 43.6% of capital. Fair reserve development (3.0) as the level of reserves has at times been insufficient to cover claims. Deficiencies in the two year reserve development occurred in three of the previous five years and ranged between 23% and 155%. Excellent liquidity (7.0) with ample operational cash flow and liquid investments.

Principal Business: Other liability (74%), group accident & health (7%), commercial multiple peril (7%), inland marine (4%), fidelity (3%), surety (1%), and other lines (3%).

Principal Investments: Investment grade bonds (103%).

Investments in Affiliates: None

Group Affiliation: None

Licensed in: IL

Commenced Business: February 1929

Address: 115 S La Salle Street, Chicago, IL 60603

Phone: (312) 443-0383 **Domicile State:** IL **NAIC Code:** 15792

Data Date	Rating	RACR #1	RACR #2	Loss Ratio %	Total Assets ($mil)	Capital ($mil)	Net Premium ($mil)	Net Income ($mil)
3-09	E+	0.40	0.30	N/A	687.7	230.8	22.2	16.3
3-08	E+	0.34	0.26	N/A	741.8	242.7	19.4	8.2
2008	E+	0.41	0.31	71.0	707.3	235.3	80.7	32.8
2007	E+	0.34	0.26	130.5	735.5	236.9	86.1	-20.3
2006	E+	0.33	0.25	16.3	730.6	218.2	86.2	68.5
2005	E+	0.27	0.22	50.7	751.7	201.2	108.6	36.4
2004	D-	0.20	0.16	290.4	695.1	165.9	75.1	-146.5

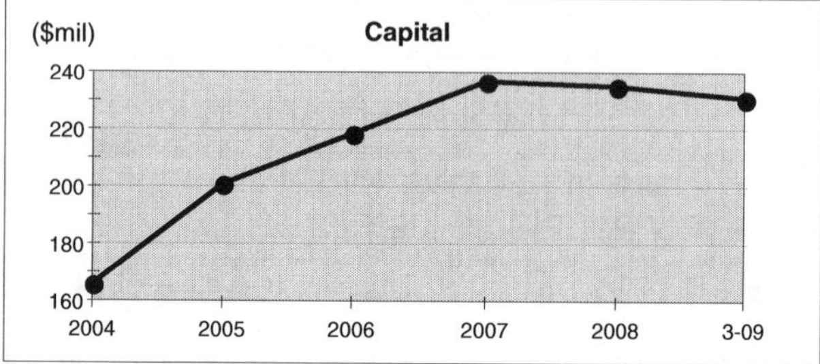

UNIGARD INS CO — C+ Fair

Major Rating Factors: Fair overall results on stability tests (4.5 on a scale of 0 to 10) including potential drain of affiliation with QBE Ins Group Ltd and negative cash flow from operations for 2008. History of adequate reserve strength (5.6) as reserves have been consistently at an acceptable level.

Other Rating Factors: Good overall profitability index (5.3) despite operating losses during the first three months of 2008. Return on equity has been good over the last five years, averaging 10.6%. Strong long-term capitalization index (8.4) based on excellent current risk adjusted capital (severe and moderate loss scenarios), despite some fluctuation in capital levels. Excellent liquidity (7.5) with ample operational cash flow and liquid investments.

Principal Business: Auto liability (31%), commercial multiple peril (26%), auto physical damage (14%), other liability (8%), homeowners multiple peril (7%), farmowners multiple peril (4%), and other lines (9%).

Principal Investments: Cash (48%), investment grade bonds (24%), misc. investments (18%), and real estate (10%).

Investments in Affiliates: 5%

Group Affiliation: QBE Ins Group Ltd

Licensed in: AK, AZ, CA, CO, ID, IL, MT, NV, NM, NY, NC, ND, OH, OR, PA, TN, TX, UT, WA, WV, WI, WY

Commenced Business: September 1960

Address: 15805 NE 24th St, Bellevue, WA 98008-2409

Phone: (425) 641-4321 **Domicile State:** WA **NAIC Code:** 25747

Data Date	Rating	RACR #1	RACR #2	Loss Ratio %	Total Assets ($mil)	Capital ($mil)	Net Premium ($mil)	Net Income ($mil)
3-09	C+	3.53	2.39	N/A	646.6	208.6	62.2	-5.5
3-08	C+	2.06	1.38	N/A	597.9	164.4	62.7	16.9
2008	C+	3.82	2.61	52.3	560.4	212.8	169.4	43.4
2007	C+	2.78	1.86	69.0	723.8	228.4	284.9	14.8
2006	C+	2.38	1.65	65.6	733.7	225.3	310.7	22.7
2005	C+	2.16	1.48	63.7	687.4	212.8	294.4	20.1
2004	C+	2.63	1.91	60.5	571.9	195.2	242.8	22.7

QBE Ins Group Ltd
Composite Group Rating: B-

Largest Group Members	Assets ($mil)	Rating
QBE REINSURANCE CORP	1439	B-
GENERAL CASUALTY CO OF WI	1208	B-
PRAETORIAN INS CO	1063	C+
QBE INS CORP	611	B-
UNIGARD INS CO	560	C+

UNITED EDUCATORS INS A RECIP RRG — C Fair

Major Rating Factors: Fair overall results on stability tests (3.5 on a scale of 0 to 10). The largest net exposure for one risk is high at 3.4% of capital. History of adequate reserve strength (6.1) as reserves have been consistently at an acceptable level.

Other Rating Factors: Strong long-term capitalization index (7.3) based on excellent current risk adjusted capital (severe and moderate loss scenarios), despite some fluctuation in capital levels. Excellent profitability (7.8) with operating gains in each of the last five years. Return on equity has been excellent over the last five years averaging 17.4%. Excellent liquidity (8.0) with ample operational cash flow and liquid investments.

Principal Business: Other liability (100%).

Principal Investments: Investment grade bonds (94%) and misc. investments (6%).

Investments in Affiliates: None

Group Affiliation: None

Licensed in: VT

Commenced Business: March 1987

Address: Two Wisconsin Circle,Ste 1040, Chevy Chase, MD 20815-9913

Phone: (802) 652-1553 **Domicile State:** VT **NAIC Code:** 10020

Data Date	Rating	RACR #1	RACR #2	Loss Ratio %	Total Assets ($mil)	Capital ($mil)	Net Premium ($mil)	Net Income ($mil)
3-09	C	1.48	1.22	N/A	500.6	169.5	23.0	3.1
3-08	C	1.67	1.36	N/A	486.5	178.3	21.6	4.1
2008	C	1.55	1.28	73.8	515.1	170.6	92.7	27.3
2007	C	1.70	1.39	70.6	503.9	176.9	87.5	25.2
2006	D+	1.61	1.18	66.5	461.7	157.4	86.9	34.2
2005	D+	1.36	1.01	67.3	409.4	133.2	106.0	25.3
2004	D+	1.20	0.90	66.9	338.3	113.1	111.7	20.9

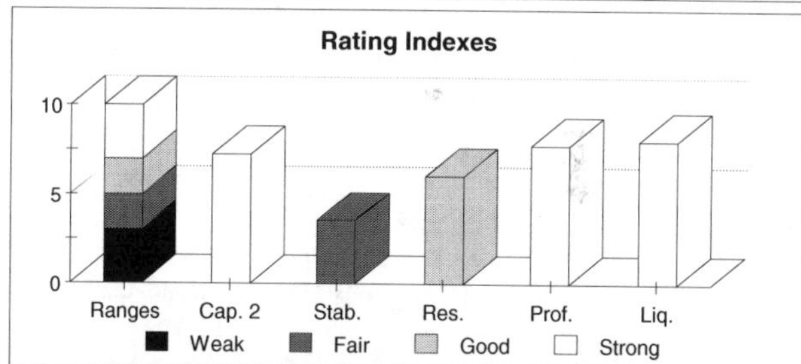

UNITED FARM FAMILY MUTUAL INS CO * — B+ Good

Major Rating Factors: History of adequate reserve strength (5.7 on a scale of 0 to 10) as reserves have been consistently at an acceptable level. Strong long-term capitalization index (8.1) based on excellent current risk adjusted capital (severe and moderate loss scenarios), despite some fluctuation in capital levels.

Other Rating Factors: Good overall results on stability tests (6.4) despite negative cash flow from operations for 2008. Other stability subfactors include potentially strong support from affiliation with Indiana Farm Bureau, good operational trends and excellent risk diversification. Fair liquidity (3.4) as cash resources may not be adequate to cover a spike in claims. Weak profitability index (2.5) with operating losses during the first three months of 2008.

Principal Business: Auto liability (28%), auto physical damage (23%), homeowners multiple peril (22%), farmowners multiple peril (12%), allied lines (7%), commercial multiple peril (5%), and workers compensation (2%).

Principal Investments: Investment grade bonds (75%) and misc. investments (25%).

Investments in Affiliates: 6%

Group Affiliation: Indiana Farm Bureau

Licensed in: IN, OH

Commenced Business: February 1935

Address: 225 South East St, Indianapolis, IN 46202-4056

Phone: (317) 692-7200 **Domicile State:** IN **NAIC Code:** 15288

Data Date	Rating	RACR #1	RACR #2	Loss Ratio %	Total Assets ($mil)	Capital ($mil)	Net Premium ($mil)	Net Income ($mil)
3-09	B+	2.21	1.55	N/A	787.9	243.0	109.6	-23.6
3-08	A-	3.09	2.33	N/A	840.3	339.9	110.5	-9.7
2008	B+	2.50	1.77	89.3	837.6	279.2	472.3	-26.2
2007	A-	3.21	2.41	74.4	869.9	360.0	482.3	21.5
2006	B+	3.06	2.32	73.6	828.5	331.9	478.7	24.1
2005	B+	2.90	2.22	68.4	793.6	301.6	477.2	38.9
2004	B+	2.57	1.95	70.4	746.8	261.7	478.1	34.0

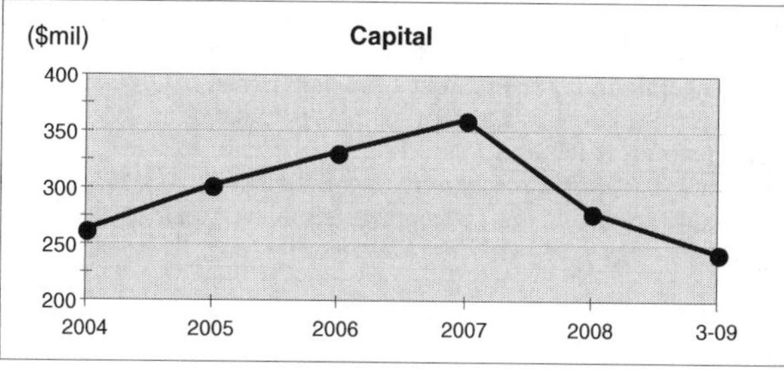

UNITED FINANCIAL CASUALTY CO C+ Fair

Major Rating Factors: Fair overall results on stability tests (4.3 on a scale of 0 to 10) including potential drain of affiliation with Progressive Group and fair risk adjusted capital in prior years. Good long-term capitalization (5.0) based on good current risk adjusted capital (severe loss scenario) reflecting some improvement over results in 2008.

Other Rating Factors: History of adequate reserve strength (5.8) as reserves have been consistently at an acceptable level. Good liquidity (5.3) with sufficient resources (cash flows and marketable investments) to handle a spike in claims. Excellent profitability (7.0) despite modest operating losses during 2008. Return on equity has been excellent over the last five years averaging 19.5%.

Principal Business: Auto liability (72%), auto physical damage (28%), and inland marine (1%).

Principal Investments: Investment grade bonds (88%) and misc. investments (12%).

Investments in Affiliates: 1%

Group Affiliation: Progressive Group

Licensed in: All states, the District of Columbia and Puerto Rico

Commenced Business: August 1984

Address: 6300 Wilson Mills Rd W33, Mayfield Village, OH 44143-2182

Phone: (440) 461-5000 **Domicile State:** OH **NAIC Code:** 11770

Data Date	Rating	RACR #1	RACR #2	Loss Ratio %	Total Assets ($mil)	Capital ($mil)	Net Premium ($mil)	Net Income ($mil)
3-09	C+	1.14	0.80	N/A	1,839.0	408.8	289.5	40.8
3-08	C+	0.89	0.66	N/A	1,802.4	417.4	305.7	23.2
2008	C+	0.96	0.68	72.5	1,783.1	351.1	1,185.8	-1.0
2007	C+	0.92	0.68	71.5	1,764.0	416.1	1,260.6	118.4
2006	B-	1.23	0.90	63.2	1,609.2	426.4	1,261.9	97.3
2005	B-	1.25	0.93	71.3	1,139.4	308.5	963.7	37.8
2004	B-	1.83	1.43	57.3	145.0	56.7	70.9	16.5

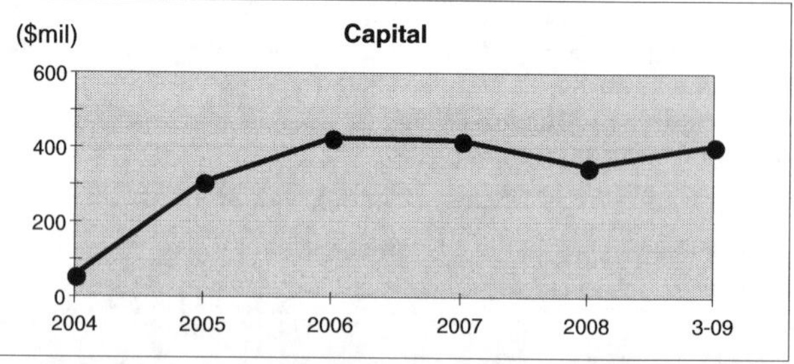

UNITED FIRE & CAS CO B- Good

Major Rating Factors: Good overall results on stability tests (5.2 on a scale of 0 to 10) despite potential drain of affiliation with United Fire & Casualty Group. Good overall profitability index (5.8) despite operating losses during 2008. Return on equity has been fair, averaging 8.2% over the past five years.

Other Rating Factors: Good liquidity (6.3) with sufficient resources (cash flows and marketable investments) to handle a spike in claims. Strong long-term capitalization index (7.7) based on excellent current risk adjusted capital (severe and moderate loss scenarios), despite some fluctuation in capital levels. Ample reserve history (8.5) that helps to protect the company against sharp claims increases.

Principal Business: Other liability (20%), auto liability (17%), workers compensation (14%), surety (8%), products liability (8%), auto physical damage (7%), and other lines (27%).

Principal Investments: Investment grade bonds (62%), misc. investments (38%), non investment grade bonds (1%), and real estate (1%).

Investments in Affiliates: 28%

Group Affiliation: United Fire & Casualty Group

Licensed in: All states except DC, DE, HI, ME, MA, NH, PA, RI, VT, VA, PR

Commenced Business: January 1947

Address: 118 Second Ave SE, Cedar Rapids, IA 52407

Phone: (319) 399-5700 **Domicile State:** IA **NAIC Code:** 13021

Data Date	Rating	RACR #1	RACR #2	Loss Ratio %	Total Assets ($mil)	Capital ($mil)	Net Premium ($mil)	Net Income ($mil)
3-09	B-	1.70	1.45	N/A	1,194.1	523.7	90.6	0.5
3-08	B-	1.95	1.66	N/A	1,262.2	655.2	94.1	14.0
2008	B-	1.76	1.50	84.6	1,221.0	553.1	381.4	-3.6
2007	B-	1.93	1.64	52.4	1,254.2	648.5	390.4	94.6
2006	C+	1.77	1.47	60.2	1,213.9	576.0	395.4	92.3
2005	C+	1.26	1.04	81.3	1,121.1	383.1	376.3	-0.8
2004	C+	1.36	1.14	56.6	991.6	384.0	383.5	50.0

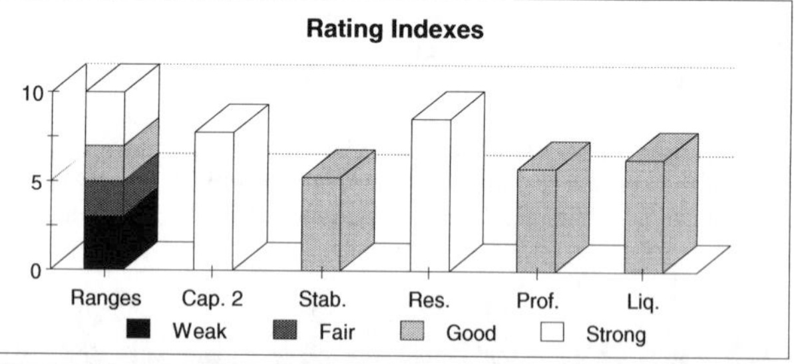

UNITED GUAR RESIDENTIAL INS CO OF NC D- Weak

Major Rating Factors: Poor long-term capitalization index (1.3 on a scale of 0 to 10) based on weak current risk adjusted capital (severe and moderate loss scenarios), although results have slipped from the fair range over the last two years. Weak profitability index (1.1) with operating losses during 2007 and 2008. Average return on equity over the last five years has been poor at -27.5%.

Other Rating Factors: Vulnerable liquidity (0.0) as a spike in claims may stretch capacity. Weak overall results on stability tests (0.9) including weak risk adjusted capital in prior years, weak results on operational trends and negative cash flow from operations for 2008. Ample reserve history (10.0) that helps to protect the company against sharp claims increases.

Principal Business: Credit (100%).

Principal Investments: Investment grade bonds (94%) and misc. investments (6%).

Investments in Affiliates: 29%

Group Affiliation: American International Group

Licensed in: All states except AZ, CA, NY, WY, PR

Commenced Business: May 1963

Address: 230 North Elm Street, Greensboro, NC 27401

Phone: (336) 373-0232 **Domicile State:** NC **NAIC Code:** 16667

Data Date	Rating	RACR #1	RACR #2	Loss Ratio %	Total Assets ($mil)	Capital ($mil)	Net Premium ($mil)	Net Income ($mil)
3-09	D-	0.38	0.32	N/A	1,106.8	240.9	56.1	45.8
3-08	C	0.77	0.62	N/A	783.8	229.2	55.6	-29.0
2008	D-	0.33	0.28	386.4	1,228.4	199.6	236.7	-645.1
2007	C	0.68	0.55	316.8	734.1	194.2	204.8	-239.9
2006	C+	1.21	0.85	90.9	371.2	65.8	192.7	67.8
2005	B	1.09	1.03	28.2	324.7	89.4	98.1	72.8
2004	B	1.07	1.02	58.1	288.8	122.2	68.4	121.3

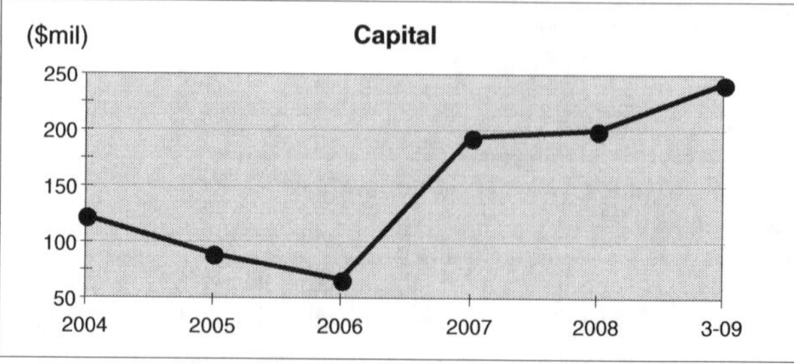

UNITED GUARANTY RESIDENTIAL INS CO — D+ Weak

Major Rating Factors: Weak profitability index (2.9 on a scale of 0 to 10) with operating losses during 2007 and 2008. Return on equity has been fair, averaging 32.6% over the past five years. Weak overall results on stability tests (2.4).

Other Rating Factors: Fair reserve development (4.7) as the level of reserves has at times been insufficient to cover claims. In 2008 and 2007 the one year reserve development was 25% and 36% deficient respectively. Good long-term capitalization index (5.3) based on good current risk adjusted capital (moderate loss scenario), despite some fluctuation in capital levels. Good liquidity (6.5) with sufficient resources (cash flows and marketable investments) to handle a spike in claims.

Principal Business: Mortgage guaranty (100%).

Principal Investments: Investment grade bonds (91%) and misc. investments (9%).

Investments in Affiliates: 8%

Group Affiliation: American International Group

Licensed in: All states, the District of Columbia and Puerto Rico

Commenced Business: December 1963

Address: 230 North Elm Street, Greensboro, NC 27401

Phone: (336) 373-0232 **Domicile State:** NC **NAIC Code:** 15873

Data Date	Rating	RACR #1	RACR #2	Loss Ratio %	Total Assets ($mil)	Capital ($mil)	Net Premium ($mil)	Net Income ($mil)
3-09	D+	1.54	1.20	N/A	2,518.8	1,079.0	114.5	4.8
3-08	C-	1.10	0.86	N/A	2,002.5	508.9	119.5	-94.3
2008	D+	1.48	1.15	259.9	2,535.3	1,105.8	472.9	-447.0
2007	C-	1.29	1.03	125.2	1,908.0	495.5	426.7	-52.9
2006	C	1.58	1.10	31.7	1,903.3	133.0	357.9	177.0
2005	B	3.79	2.67	24.3	1,940.4	375.6	310.0	169.8
2004	B	3.87	2.67	18.7	1,886.7	481.8	346.2	210.1

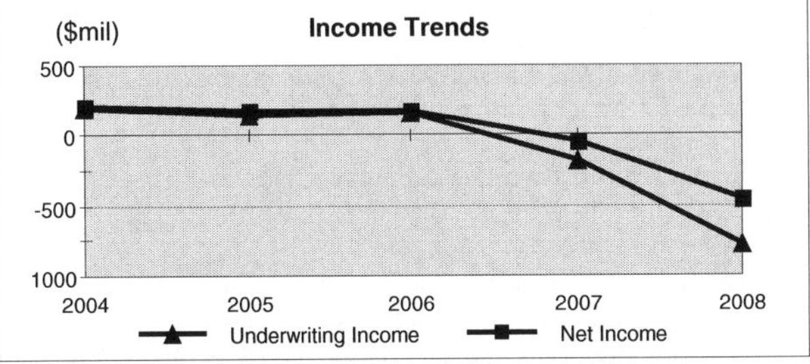

UNITED NATIONAL INS CO — C+ Fair

Major Rating Factors: Fair profitability index (3.4 on a scale of 0 to 10) with operating losses during 2008. Return on equity has been fair, averaging 6.9% over the past five years. Fair overall results on stability tests (4.3) including negative cash flow from operations for 2008.

Other Rating Factors: History of adequate reserve strength (5.7) as reserves have been consistently at an acceptable level. Strong long-term capitalization index (7.1) based on excellent current risk adjusted capital (severe and moderate loss scenarios), despite some fluctuation in capital levels. Excellent liquidity (7.4) with ample operational cash flow and liquid investments.

Principal Business: Other liability (50%), fire (18%), allied lines (12%), commercial multiple peril (11%), products liability (6%), auto physical damage (2%), and inland marine (1%).

Principal Investments: Misc. investments (58%), investment grade bonds (39%), cash (2%), and non investment grade bonds (1%).

Investments in Affiliates: 33%

Group Affiliation: Fox Paine & Co LLC

Licensed in: PA

Commenced Business: December 1960

Address: Three Bala Plaza E 300, Bala Cynwyd, PA 19004

Phone: (610) 664-1500 **Domicile State:** PA **NAIC Code:** 13064

Data Date	Rating	RACR #1	RACR #2	Loss Ratio %	Total Assets ($mil)	Capital ($mil)	Net Premium ($mil)	Net Income ($mil)
3-09	C+	1.55	1.29	N/A	643.6	316.3	13.5	17.0
3-08	C+	1.81	1.51	N/A	758.9	447.6	22.6	4.5
2008	C+	1.50	1.22	100.9	610.6	313.3	60.3	-13.7
2007	C+	1.82	1.52	53.2	774.0	452.5	111.0	46.9
2006	C+	1.75	1.46	51.0	788.3	412.0	105.6	65.3
2005	B-	1.46	1.16	61.6	732.4	359.5	96.6	12.8
2004	B-	2.25	1.61	61.5	733.7	373.7	61.0	20.8

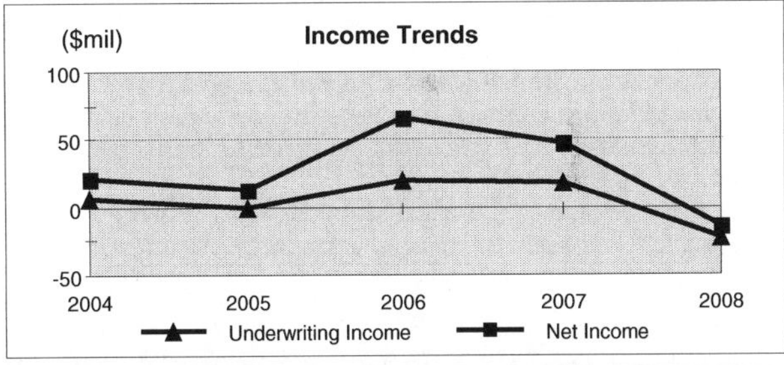

UNITED SERVICES AUTOMOBILE ASN * — A+ Excellent

Major Rating Factors: Strong long-term capitalization index (7.5 on a scale of 0 to 10) based on excellent current risk adjusted capital (severe and moderate loss scenarios). Furthermore, this high level of risk adjusted capital has been consistently maintained in previous years. Excellent profitability (8.3) with operating gains in each of the last five years.

Other Rating Factors: Excellent overall results on stability tests (7.9). Stability strengths include excellent operational trends and excellent risk diversification. History of adequate reserve strength (6.2) as reserves have been consistently at an acceptable level. Good liquidity (6.7) with sufficient resources (cash flows and marketable investments) to handle a spike in claims.

Principal Business: Auto liability (34%), homeowners multiple peril (30%), auto physical damage (29%), other liability (2%), allied lines (2%), inland marine (2%), and fire (1%).

Principal Investments: Misc. investments (63%), investment grade bonds (32%), and real estate (6%).

Investments in Affiliates: 50%

Group Affiliation: USAA Group

Licensed in: All states, the District of Columbia and Puerto Rico

Commenced Business: June 1922

Address: 9800 Fredericksburg Rd, San Antonio, TX 78288

Phone: (210) 498-2211 **Domicile State:** TX **NAIC Code:** 25941

Data Date	Rating	RACR #1	RACR #2	Loss Ratio %	Total Assets ($mil)	Capital ($mil)	Net Premium ($mil)	Net Income ($mil)
3-09	A+	1.56	1.46	N/A	19,904.8	13,360.9	1,260.9	79.3
3-08	A+	1.65	1.52	N/A	18,709.7	13,101.2	1,218.2	36.3
2008	A+	1.58	1.48	85.0	19,743.7	13,471.9	4,890.9	365.1
2007	A+	1.72	1.64	77.8	18,401.8	12,896.6	4,796.7	659.3
2006	A+	1.83	1.67	69.4	16,868.9	11,692.9	5,045.1	1,051.0
2005	A+	1.98	1.83	78.5	15,740.9	9,879.1	4,715.9	448.8
2004	A+	1.98	1.77	73.9	14,383.7	9,060.2	4,639.3	643.5

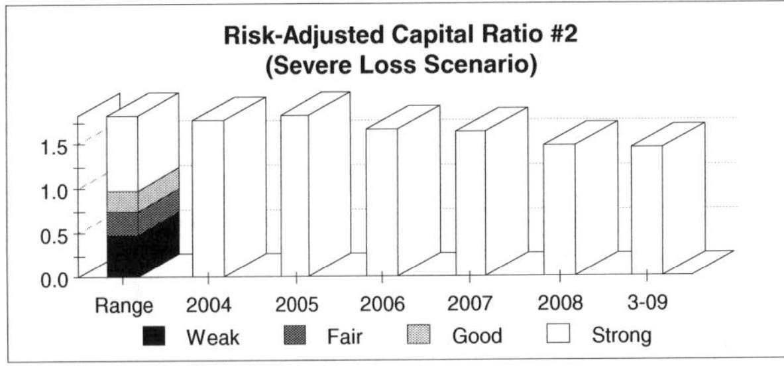

UNITED STATES FIDELITY & GUARANTY CO — B- Good

Major Rating Factors: Fair reserve development (4.5 on a scale of 0 to 10) as the level of reserves has at times been insufficient to cover claims. In 2004, the one year reserve development was 78% deficient. Fair profitability index (4.5) with operating losses during 2004. Return on equity has been low, averaging 1.4% over the past five years.

Other Rating Factors: Good liquidity (6.9) with sufficient resources (cash flows and marketable investments) to handle a spike in claims. Good overall results on stability tests (5.0) despite fair financial strength of affiliated Travelers Companies Inc. Stability strengths include good operational trends and excellent risk diversification. Strong long-term capitalization index (10.0) based on excellent current risk adjusted capital (severe and moderate loss scenarios), despite some fluctuation in capital levels.

Principal Business: Workers compensation (92%), other liability (6%), surety (2%), and inland marine (2%).

Principal Investments: Investment grade bonds (93%), misc. investments (6%), and non investment grade bonds (1%).

Investments in Affiliates: 2%

Group Affiliation: Travelers Companies Inc

Licensed in: All states, the District of Columbia and Puerto Rico

Commenced Business: August 1896

Address: 111 Schilling Rd, Hunt Valley, MD 21031

Phone: (651) 310-7911 **Domicile State:** MD **NAIC Code:** 25887

Data Date	Rating	RACR #1	RACR #2	Loss Ratio %	Total Assets ($mil)	Capital ($mil)	Net Premium ($mil)	Net Income ($mil)
3-09	B-	4.67	3.10	N/A	4,250.9	2,099.7	198.8	33.7
3-08	C+	4.41	2.69	N/A	4,139.4	1,984.6	197.4	57.9
2008	B-	4.65	3.09	61.5	4,192.7	2,065.9	800.0	173.5
2007	C+	4.33	2.64	59.0	4,079.6	1,928.5	794.4	145.4
2006	C	2.85	2.27	58.4	4,390.1	2,231.9	764.8	187.0
2005	C-	2.79	2.21	75.1	4,193.4	2,010.6	743.8	196.8
2004	C-	1.36	0.93	230.6	4,842.6	1,741.4	625.2	-495.8

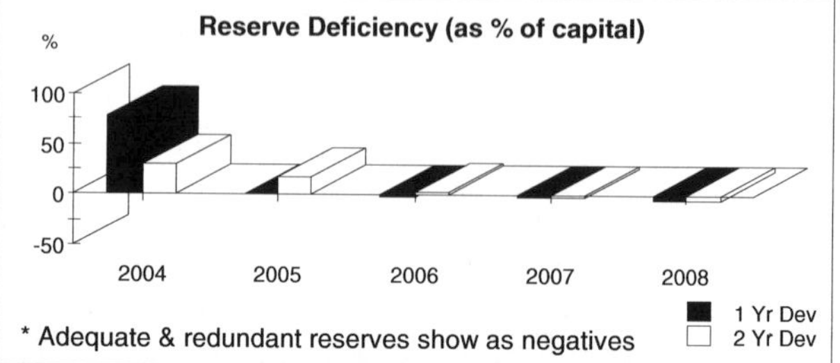

* Adequate & redundant reserves show as negatives

UNITED STATES FIRE INS CO — C Fair

Major Rating Factors: Fair overall results on stability tests (3.7 on a scale of 0 to 10) including potential drain of affiliation with Fairfax Financial and negative cash flow from operations for 2008. Good long-term capitalization index (5.7) based on good current risk adjusted capital (moderate loss scenario).

Other Rating Factors: History of adequate reserve strength (5.8) as reserves have been consistently at an acceptable level. Good overall profitability index (5.5). Weak expense controls. Return on equity has been excellent over the last five years averaging 17.6%. Good liquidity (6.4) with sufficient resources (cash flows and marketable investments) to handle a spike in claims.

Principal Business: Workers compensation (22%), auto liability (18%), group accident & health (15%), fire (9%), inland marine (9%), other liability (7%), and other lines (20%).

Principal Investments: Investment grade bonds (48%), misc. investments (41%), non investment grade bonds (9%), and cash (2%).

Investments in Affiliates: 13%

Group Affiliation: Fairfax Financial

Licensed in: All states, the District of Columbia and Puerto Rico

Commenced Business: April 1824

Address: 305 Madison Avenue, Morristown, NJ 07960

Phone: (201) 490-6600 **Domicile State:** DE **NAIC Code:** 21113

Data Date	Rating	RACR #1	RACR #2	Loss Ratio %	Total Assets ($mil)	Capital ($mil)	Net Premium ($mil)	Net Income ($mil)
3-09	C	1.13	0.77	N/A	2,603.1	763.1	137.0	1.8
3-08	C	1.77	1.11	N/A	3,585.4	1,114.8	182.7	120.5
2008	C	1.32	0.89	78.2	3,050.7	943.3	579.5	458.4
2007	C	1.84	1.17	66.9	3,694.7	1,160.9	742.8	137.1
2006	C-	1.51	0.93	63.0	3,328.7	973.9	782.9	162.2
2005	D+	1.31	0.83	74.1	3,089.7	945.2	566.4	94.0
2004	D+	1.24	0.77	89.5	2,934.2	885.3	605.6	43.6

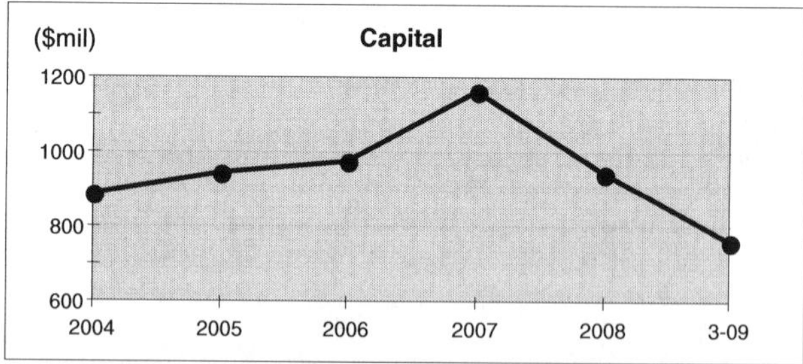

UNITED STATES LIABILITY INS CO — C Fair

Major Rating Factors: Fair profitability index (3.0 on a scale of 0 to 10). Weak expense controls. Return on equity has been fair, averaging 25.9% over the past five years. Fair overall results on stability tests (4.3) including fair results on operational trends.

Other Rating Factors: Good liquidity (6.6) with sufficient resources (cash flows and marketable investments) to handle a spike in claims. Strong long-term capitalization index (7.1) based on good current risk adjusted capital (severe and moderate loss scenarios), although results have slipped from the excellent range during the last year. Ample reserve history (9.4) that helps to protect the company against sharp claims increases.

Principal Business: Other liability (93%) and fire (7%).

Principal Investments: Misc. investments (70%), non investment grade bonds (16%), and investment grade bonds (15%).

Investments in Affiliates: 51%

Group Affiliation: Berkshire-Hathaway

Licensed in: All states except AL, IN, KY, ME, MA, NH, ND, TN, PR

Commenced Business: May 1951

Address: 190 S. Warner Road, Wayne, PA 19087

Phone: (610) 225-2212 **Domicile State:** PA **NAIC Code:** 25895

Data Date	Rating	RACR #1	RACR #2	Loss Ratio %	Total Assets ($mil)	Capital ($mil)	Net Premium ($mil)	Net Income ($mil)
3-09	C	1.03	0.95	N/A	406.1	203.8	18.7	70.9
3-08	B	1.42	1.25	N/A	474.7	291.9	18.7	2.7
2008	C+	1.24	1.08	32.0	476.9	281.5	84.9	19.6
2007	B	1.42	1.24	221.3	481.4	296.1	-73.8	218.3
2006	B	1.43	1.33	38.9	832.2	479.4	139.2	64.9
2005	B	1.37	1.31	51.8	722.8	419.6	131.7	17.9
2004	B	1.42	1.37	57.3	637.6	367.6	128.8	10.5

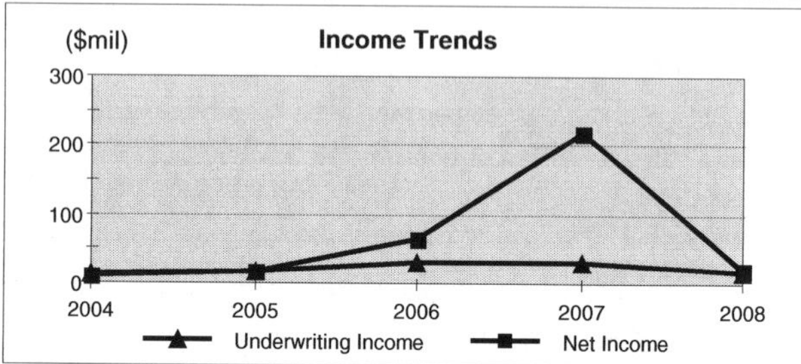

UNIVERSAL INS CO — B — Good

Major Rating Factors: Fair overall results on stability tests (4.7 on a scale of 0 to 10) including potential drain of affiliation with Universal Ins Co Group and negative cash flow from operations for 2008. Strong long-term capitalization index (7.5) based on excellent current risk adjusted capital (severe and moderate loss scenarios). Moreover, capital levels have been consistent in recent years.
Other Rating Factors: Ample reserve history (7.9) that can protect against increases in claims costs. Excellent profitability (8.7) with operating gains in each of the last five years. Excellent liquidity (7.0) with ample operational cash flow and liquid investments.
Principal Business: Auto physical damage (36%), commercial multiple peril (28%), auto liability (10%), homeowners multiple peril (7%), other liability (7%), allied lines (4%), and other lines (8%).
Principal Investments: Investment grade bonds (56%), misc. investments (33%), real estate (9%), cash (1%), and non investment grade bonds (1%).
Investments in Affiliates: 23%
Group Affiliation: Universal Ins Co Group
Licensed in: PR
Commenced Business: January 1972
Address: Metro Office Park St 1 Lot 10, Guaynabo, PR 00921
Phone: (787) 793-7202 **Domicile State:** PR **NAIC Code:** 31704

Data Date	Rating	RACR #1	RACR #2	Loss Ratio %	Total Assets ($mil)	Capital ($mil)	Net Premium ($mil)	Net Income ($mil)
3-09	B	1.97	1.65	N/A	517.7	214.0	32.9	4.5
3-08	B	2.22	1.80	N/A	511.2	211.9	35.8	5.2
2008	B	1.98	1.66	63.6	510.5	213.6	123.0	15.2
2007	B	2.25	1.84	65.2	510.5	207.8	135.8	16.7
2006	B	2.23	1.75	70.4	535.0	183.4	156.5	14.8
2005	B	2.29	1.65	66.6	547.7	167.1	170.6	15.2
2004	B	2.29	1.60	65.3	462.3	140.5	176.6	18.8

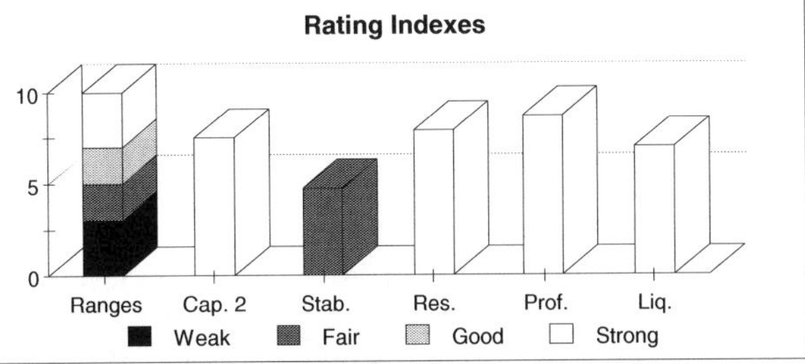

UNIVERSAL UNDERWRITERS INS CO — C — Fair

Major Rating Factors: Fair profitability index (3.2 on a scale of 0 to 10). Fair expense controls. Return on equity has been fair, averaging 8.5% over the past five years. Fair overall results on stability tests (4.3) including negative cash flow from operations for 2008.
Other Rating Factors: Strong long-term capitalization index (10.0) based on excellent current risk adjusted capital (severe and moderate loss scenarios), despite some fluctuation in capital levels. Superior liquidity (9.5) with ample operational cash flow and liquid investments.
Principal Business: Other liability (28%), auto liability (20%), auto physical damage (16%), allied lines (6%), fire (6%), products liability (4%), and other lines (20%).
Principal Investments: Investment grade bonds (77%), misc. investments (21%), and cash (2%).
Investments in Affiliates: 20%
Group Affiliation: Zurich Financial Services Group
Licensed in: All states except PR
Commenced Business: January 1982
Address: 7045 College Blvd, Overland Park, KS 66211
Phone: (913) 339-1000 **Domicile State:** KS **NAIC Code:** 41181

Data Date	Rating	RACR #1	RACR #2	Loss Ratio %	Total Assets ($mil)	Capital ($mil)	Net Premium ($mil)	Net Income ($mil)
3-09	C	5.44	5.19	N/A	429.9	354.7	0.0	2.1
3-08	C	6.47	6.01	N/A	429.2	352.5	0.0	3.4
2008	C	5.39	5.17	0.0	446.5	348.8	0.0	8.5
2007	C	6.54	6.22	0.0	418.3	342.9	0.0	51.9
2006	C	9.60	8.97	0.0	681.6	531.6	0.0	25.7
2005	C	8.82	7.87	0.0	586.0	505.8	0.0	87.0
2004	C	4.31	4.07	0.0	608.6	481.3	0.0	20.2

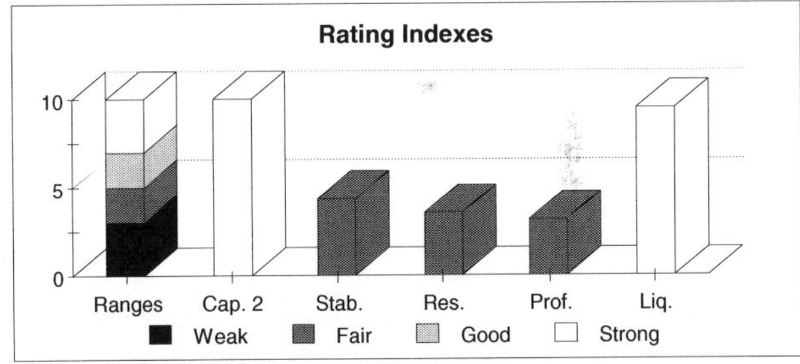

US SPECIALTY INS CO — B- — Good

Major Rating Factors: Fair overall results on stability tests (4.7 on a scale of 0 to 10) including excessive premium growth. The largest net exposure for one risk is excessive at 5.8% of capital. History of adequate reserve strength (6.4) as reserves have been consistently at an acceptable level.
Other Rating Factors: Good liquidity (6.9) with sufficient resources (cash flows and marketable investments) to handle a spike in claims. Strong long-term capitalization index (8.0) based on excellent current risk adjusted capital (severe and moderate loss scenarios). Moreover, capital levels have been consistent in recent years. Excellent profitability (8.8) with operating gains in each of the last five years. Return on equity has been excellent over the last five years averaging 16.1%.
Principal Business: Other liability (69%), aircraft (14%), group accident & health (6%), surety (6%), commercial multiple peril (2%), credit (1%), and other lines (2%).
Principal Investments: Investment grade bonds (90%) and misc. investments (10%).
Investments in Affiliates: 1%
Group Affiliation: HCC Ins Holdings Inc
Licensed in: All states except PR
Commenced Business: April 1987
Address: 13403 Northwest Freeway, Houston, TX 77040-6094
Phone: (713) 744-3700 **Domicile State:** TX **NAIC Code:** 29599

Data Date	Rating	RACR #1	RACR #2	Loss Ratio %	Total Assets ($mil)	Capital ($mil)	Net Premium ($mil)	Net Income ($mil)
3-09	B-	2.49	1.63	N/A	1,212.9	326.4	104.4	13.1
3-08	B-	2.83	1.79	N/A	971.6	295.1	82.3	16.7
2008	B-	2.57	1.69	62.9	1,161.3	313.1	429.1	31.6
2007	B-	2.83	1.80	55.9	945.5	277.1	345.0	68.1
2006	B-	2.43	1.62	59.2	762.5	198.5	335.6	45.0
2005	B-	1.35	0.92	62.4	599.7	167.4	253.6	22.0
2004	B	2.33	1.54	61.4	465.8	139.7	171.3	13.7

HCC Ins Holdings Inc
Composite Group Rating: C+

Largest Group Members	Assets ($mil)	Rating
HOUSTON CASUALTY CO	2846	B-
US SPECIALTY INS CO	1161	B-
HCC LIFE INS CO	585	B
AMERICAN CONTRACTORS INDEMNITY CO	245	C+
AVEMCO INS CO	119	B

USAA CASUALTY INS CO * A+ Excellent

Major Rating Factors: Strong long-term capitalization index (10.0 on a scale of 0 to 10) based on excellent current risk adjusted capital (severe and moderate loss scenarios). Furthermore, this high level of risk adjusted capital has been consistently maintained in previous years. Excellent profitability (8.9) with operating gains in each of the last five years. Return on equity has been good over the last five years, averaging 14.1%.

Other Rating Factors: Excellent overall results on stability tests (7.9). Stability strengths include excellent operational trends and excellent risk diversification. History of adequate reserve strength (6.3) as reserves have been consistently at an acceptable level. Good liquidity (6.4) with sufficient resources (cash flows and marketable investments) to handle a spike in claims.

Principal Business: Auto liability (37%), auto physical damage (31%), homeowners multiple peril (27%), inland marine (2%), other liability (1%), fire (1%), and allied lines (1%).

Principal Investments: Investment grade bonds (87%) and misc. investments (13%).

Investments in Affiliates: 1%

Group Affiliation: USAA Group

Licensed in: All states except PR

Commenced Business: December 1990

Address: 9800 Fredericksburg Rd, San Antonio, TX 78288

Phone: (210) 498-2211 **Domicile State:** TX **NAIC Code:** 25968

Data Date	Rating	RACR #1	RACR #2	Loss Ratio %	Total Assets ($mil)	Capital ($mil)	Net Premium ($mil)	Net Income ($mil)
3-09	A+	5.04	3.97	N/A	6,714.4	3,249.1	865.6	111.8
3-08	A+	4.84	3.84	N/A	6,182.5	2,953.4	822.6	95.9
2008	A+	4.75	3.86	79.1	6,371.2	3,133.2	3,373.4	278.1
2007	A+	4.47	3.64	75.1	6,040.6	2,849.4	3,239.0	316.6
2006	A+	3.98	3.15	67.9	5,724.2	2,495.7	3,342.4	448.4
2005	A+	3.35	2.67	71.7	5,007.5	1,993.0	3,163.5	289.6
2004	A+	2.94	2.36	68.2	4,721.1	1,702.5	3,058.3	308.2

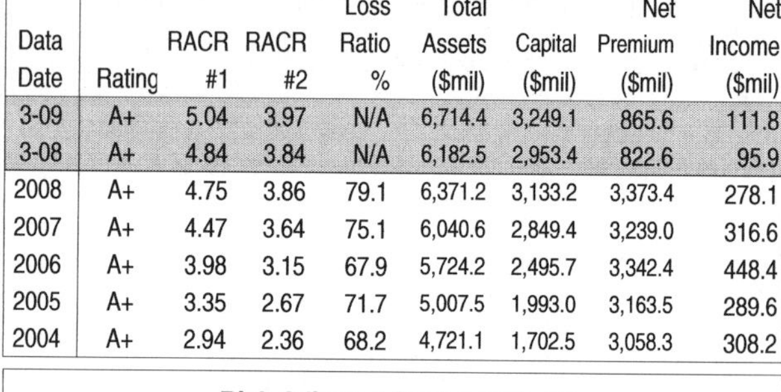

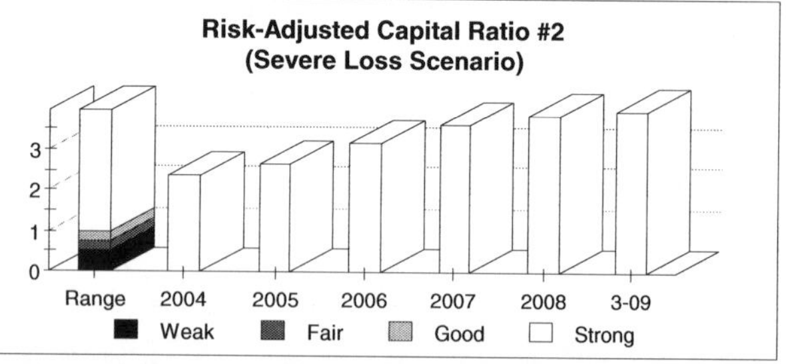

USAA GENERAL INDEMNITY CO * B+ Good

Major Rating Factors: Good overall results on stability tests (6.4 on a scale of 0 to 10) despite excessive premium growth. Other stability subfactors include potentially strong support from affiliation with USAA Group, good operational trends and excellent risk diversification. The largest net exposure for one risk is conservative at 1.6% of capital. Good liquidity (5.3) with sufficient resources (cash flows and marketable investments) to handle a spike in claims.

Other Rating Factors: Strong long-term capitalization index (7.8) based on excellent current risk adjusted capital (severe and moderate loss scenarios), despite some fluctuation in capital levels. Ample reserve history (8.3) that helps to protect the company against sharp claims increases. Weak profitability index (2.6) with operating losses during 2007 and 2008. Return on equity has been low, averaging 1.2% over the past five years.

Principal Business: Auto physical damage (35%), auto liability (34%), allied lines (25%), and homeowners multiple peril (6%).

Principal Investments: Investment grade bonds (94%), misc. investments (4%), and cash (2%).

Investments in Affiliates: None

Group Affiliation: USAA Group

Licensed in: All states except PR

Commenced Business: August 1972

Address: 9800 Fredericksburg Rd, San Antonio, TX 78288

Phone: (210) 498-2211 **Domicile State:** TX **NAIC Code:** 18600

Data Date	Rating	RACR #1	RACR #2	Loss Ratio %	Total Assets ($mil)	Capital ($mil)	Net Premium ($mil)	Net Income ($mil)
3-09	B+	1.92	1.42	N/A	452.4	141.0	89.4	0.6
3-08	A-	3.16	2.41	N/A	388.1	147.1	54.9	-6.0
2008	B+	2.05	1.57	92.5	443.9	138.6	311.2	-13.8
2007	A-	3.37	2.69	100.5	358.3	152.0	196.6	-13.3
2006	A-	4.43	3.81	82.9	343.5	163.1	156.3	5.5
2005	A-	3.60	3.11	74.5	432.1	155.3	170.6	10.2
2004	B+	2.65	2.14	64.7	394.6	146.4	211.5	21.2

USAA Group
Composite Group Rating: A+

Largest Group Members	Assets ($mil)	Rating
UNITED SERVICES AUTOMOBILE ASN	19744	A+
USAA LIFE INS CO	12584	A
USAA CASUALTY INS CO	6371	A+
CATASTROPHE REINS CO	1419	E+
USAA GENERAL INDEMNITY CO	444	B+

USAA TEXAS LLOYDS CO B Good

Major Rating Factors: History of adequate reserve strength (6.6 on a scale of 0 to 10) as reserves have been consistently at an acceptable level. Good liquidity (6.8) with sufficient resources (cash flows and marketable investments) to handle a spike in claims.

Other Rating Factors: Good overall results on stability tests (5.2). The largest net exposure for one risk is high at 4.7% of capital. Strong long-term capitalization index (8.9) based on excellent current risk adjusted capital (severe and moderate loss scenarios). Moreover, capital levels have been consistent in recent years. Excellent profitability (8.9) with operating gains in each of the last five years. Return on equity has been excellent over the last five years averaging 16.5%.

Principal Business: Homeowners multiple peril (95%), allied lines (4%), and fire (1%).

Principal Investments: Investment grade bonds (89%) and misc. investments (11%).

Investments in Affiliates: None

Group Affiliation: USAA Group

Licensed in: TX

Commenced Business: September 2001

Address: 9800 Fredericksburg Rd, San Antonio, TX 78288

Phone: (210) 498-2211 **Domicile State:** TX **NAIC Code:** 11120

Data Date	Rating	RACR #1	RACR #2	Loss Ratio %	Total Assets ($mil)	Capital ($mil)	Net Premium ($mil)	Net Income ($mil)
3-09	B	3.29	2.46	N/A	349.1	176.5	37.4	0.3
3-08	B	3.74	3.07	N/A	317.9	177.7	36.1	5.0
2008	B	3.41	2.45	86.6	350.1	175.9	148.1	6.4
2007	B	3.75	2.91	57.8	317.7	172.5	142.2	29.6
2006	B	2.87	2.25	56.1	277.4	143.3	135.9	27.5
2005	B	2.52	1.94	57.0	241.4	115.5	122.1	19.2
2004	B	2.23	1.76	43.5	205.6	95.4	116.8	28.4

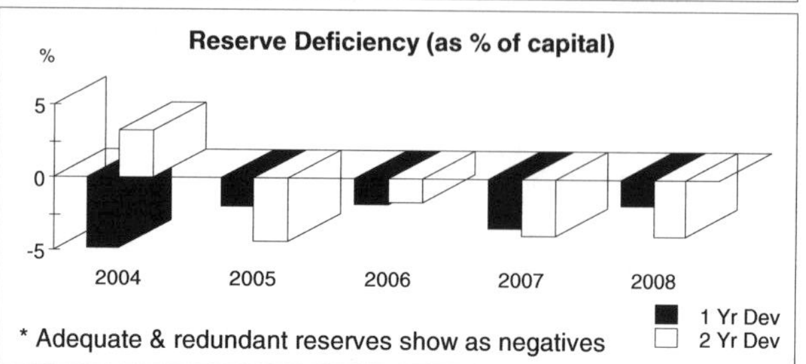

* Adequate & redundant reserves show as negatives

UTICA MUTUAL INS CO B- Good

Major Rating Factors: Fair overall results on stability tests (4.9 on a scale of 0 to 10) including potential drain of affiliation with Utica National Ins Group. The largest net exposure for one risk is conservative at 1.9% of capital. History of adequate reserve strength (6.3) as reserves have been consistently at an acceptable level.

Other Rating Factors: Good liquidity (6.9) with sufficient resources (cash flows and marketable investments) to handle a spike in claims. Strong long-term capitalization index (8.8) based on excellent current risk adjusted capital (severe and moderate loss scenarios), despite some fluctuation in capital levels. Excellent profitability (7.4) with operating gains in each of the last five years. Return on equity has been good over the last five years, averaging 10.3%.

Principal Business: Other liability (42%), workers compensation (18%), commercial multiple peril (14%), auto liability (12%), homeowners multiple peril (5%), auto physical damage (3%), and other lines (5%).

Principal Investments: Investment grade bonds (89%), misc. investments (10%), and real estate (1%).

Investments in Affiliates: 6%

Group Affiliation: Utica National Ins Group

Licensed in: All states, the District of Columbia and Puerto Rico

Commenced Business: July 1914

Address: 180 Genesee St, New Hartford, NY 13413

Phone: (315) 734-2000 **Domicile State:** NY **NAIC Code:** 25976

Data Date	Rating	RACR #1	RACR #2	Loss Ratio %	Total Assets ($mil)	Capital ($mil)	Net Premium ($mil)	Net Income ($mil)
3-09	B-	3.30	2.29	N/A	2,101.3	716.7	130.6	7.8
3-08	B-	3.36	2.26	N/A	2,153.0	765.1	136.8	13.9
2008	B-	3.34	2.33	61.7	2,145.9	723.8	540.3	53.2
2007	B-	3.38	2.28	58.4	2,187.6	764.5	539.2	66.4
2006	B-	3.04	2.04	57.4	2,141.9	692.0	552.4	79.0
2005	B-	2.29	1.58	61.4	2,051.4	588.0	563.5	64.5
2004	B-	2.01	1.38	62.4	1,994.7	510.3	588.4	74.2

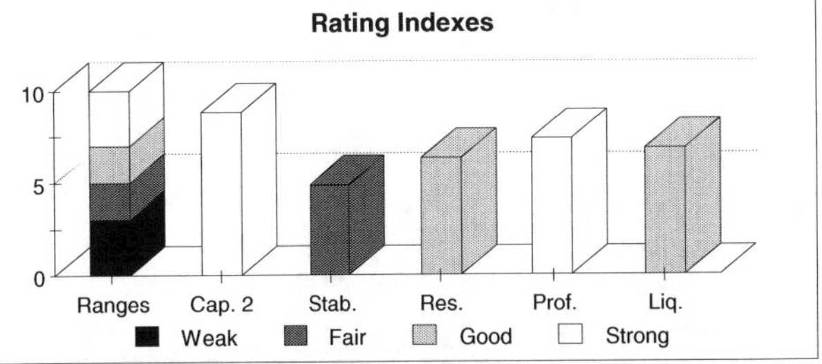

VERMONT MUTUAL INS CO C+ Fair

Major Rating Factors: Fair overall results on stability tests (4.4 on a scale of 0 to 10) including potential drain of affiliation with Vermont Mutual Group. Good overall profitability index (6.1) despite operating losses during the first three months of 2008. Return on equity has been good over the last five years, averaging 12.4%.

Other Rating Factors: Good liquidity (6.7) with sufficient resources (cash flows and marketable investments) to handle a spike in claims. Strong long-term capitalization index (8.6) based on excellent current risk adjusted capital (severe and moderate loss scenarios), despite some fluctuation in capital levels. Ample reserve history (8.5) that helps to protect the company against sharp claims increases.

Principal Business: Homeowners multiple peril (47%), commercial multiple peril (29%), auto liability (6%), auto physical damage (5%), fire (5%), allied lines (4%), and other lines (4%).

Principal Investments: Investment grade bonds (71%), misc. investments (20%), cash (6%), non investment grade bonds (2%), and real estate (1%).

Investments in Affiliates: 2%

Group Affiliation: Vermont Mutual Group

Licensed in: CT, ME, MA, NH, NY, RI, VT, VA

Commenced Business: March 1828

Address: 89 State St, Monteplier, VT 05602

Phone: (802) 223-2341 **Domicile State:** VT **NAIC Code:** 26018

Data Date	Rating	RACR #1	RACR #2	Loss Ratio %	Total Assets ($mil)	Capital ($mil)	Net Premium ($mil)	Net Income ($mil)
3-09	C+	3.00	2.15	N/A	413.9	161.1	53.4	-1.3
3-08	C+	2.90	2.01	N/A	427.6	177.0	52.2	0.0
2008	C+	3.04	2.08	55.4	437.6	172.2	213.0	1.8
2007	C+	2.99	2.02	56.6	435.1	182.4	211.3	18.6
2006	C	2.81	1.88	53.2	395.3	162.3	186.5	22.3
2005	C	2.40	1.62	54.9	359.1	133.0	200.0	17.9
2004	C	2.01	1.35	53.8	326.2	114.0	197.3	31.0

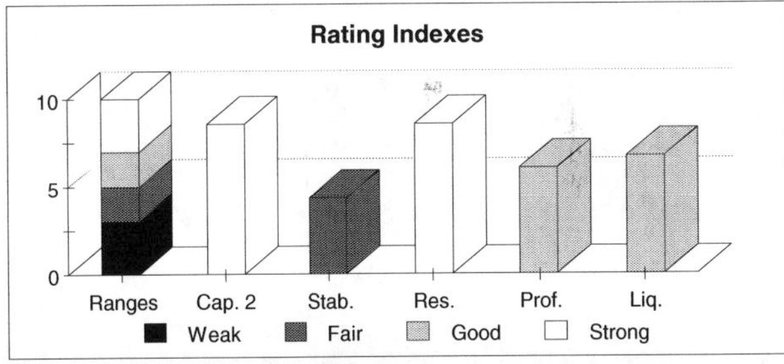

VIRGINIA SURETY CO INC C+ Fair

Major Rating Factors: Fair reserve development (3.1 on a scale of 0 to 10) as the level of reserves has at times been insufficient to cover claims. In 2008, the one year reserve development was 47% deficient. Fair profitability index (3.5). Excellent expense controls. Return on equity has been fair, averaging 22.7% over the past five years.

Other Rating Factors: Fair overall results on stability tests (4.4) including fair results on operational trends. Good overall long-term capitalization (5.8) based on good current risk adjusted capital (moderate loss scenario). However, capital levels have fluctuated during prior years. Good liquidity (6.9) with sufficient resources (cash flows and marketable investments) to handle a spike in claims.

Principal Business: Inland marine (10%), credit (10%), auto physical damage (3%), other accident & health (2%), and other liability (1%).

Principal Investments: Investment grade bonds (96%) and cash (5%).

Investments in Affiliates: 1%

Group Affiliation: Onex Corp

Licensed in: All states, the District of Columbia and Puerto Rico

Commenced Business: July 1982

Address: 175 W Jackson, Chicago, IL 60604

Phone: (312) 356-3000 **Domicile State:** IL **NAIC Code:** 40827

Data Date	Rating	RACR #1	RACR #2	Loss Ratio %	Total Assets ($mil)	Capital ($mil)	Net Premium ($mil)	Net Income ($mil)
3-09	C+	1.65	0.99	N/A	1,015.5	275.6	81.0	10.2
3-08	C	2.01	1.25	N/A	1,134.1	259.9	90.9	11.9
2008	C+	1.52	0.91	104.0	1,063.5	261.9	341.9	33.0
2007	C	1.83	1.15	73.2	1,135.1	250.4	298.6	43.1
2006	B-	N/A	N/A	84.2	1,163.0	255.7	662.3	145.4
2005	B-	1.57	1.03	74.0	1,915.4	526.9	593.7	41.1
2004	B-	1.57	0.96	76.2	1,927.4	461.6	723.5	98.0

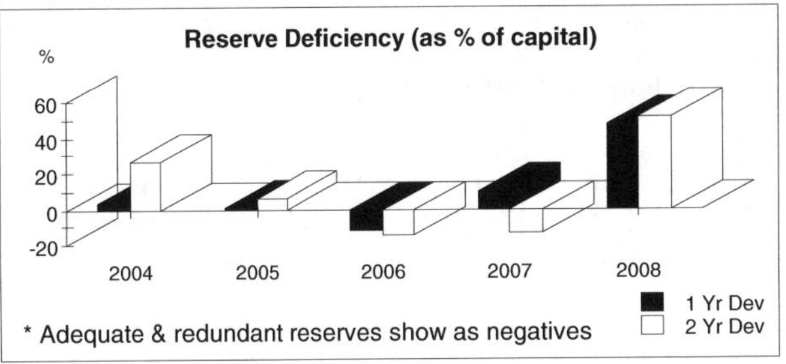

WAWANESA MUTUAL INS CO US BR — B Good

Major Rating Factors: Good overall results on stability tests (5.4 on a scale of 0 to 10) despite potential drain of affiliation with Wawanesa Ins Group. Stability strengths include good operational trends and excellent risk diversification. History of adequate reserve strength (6.2) as reserves have been consistently at an acceptable level.

Other Rating Factors: Good liquidity (6.9) with sufficient resources (cash flows and marketable investments) to handle a spike in claims. Strong long-term capitalization index (10.0) based on excellent current risk adjusted capital (severe and moderate loss scenarios). Moreover, capital levels have been consistent in recent years. Excellent profitability (8.6) with operating gains in each of the last five years. Excellent expense controls.

Principal Business: Auto physical damage (50%), auto liability (43%), homeowners multiple peril (6%), and earthquake (1%).

Principal Investments: Investment grade bonds (93%), real estate (6%), and misc. investments (1%).

Investments in Affiliates: None

Group Affiliation: Wawanesa Ins Group

Licensed in: CA

Commenced Business: May 1929

Address: 9050 Friars Rd, Suite 200, San Diego, CA 92108-5865

Phone: (858) 874-5000 **Domicile State:** CA **NAIC Code:** 31526

Data Date	Rating	RACR #1	RACR #2	Loss Ratio %	Total Assets ($mil)	Capital ($mil)	Net Premium ($mil)	Net Income ($mil)
3-09	B	15.42	10.11	N/A	250.3	197.2	13.8	3.1
3-08	B	15.17	9.88	N/A	239.3	186.5	14.4	4.5
2008	B	14.65	9.95	84.7	248.2	194.0	56.3	10.3
2007	B	13.90	9.35	87.0	240.1	182.5	58.1	8.8
2006	B-	11.13	8.36	77.1	235.6	175.0	64.5	12.6
2005	B-	9.02	6.79	80.2	228.1	162.6	66.7	12.4
2004	B-	7.35	5.49	79.1	216.0	150.0	69.0	13.8

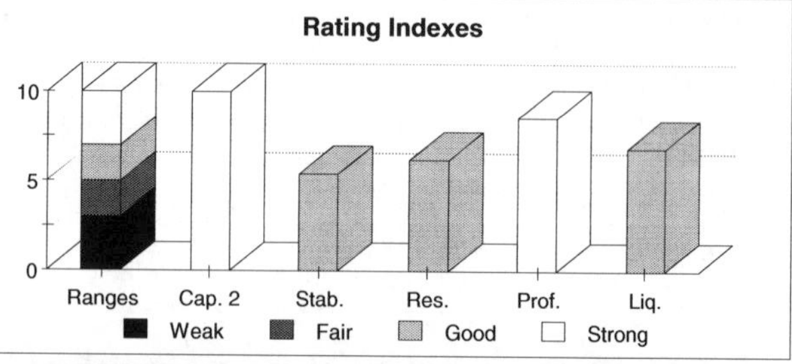

WESCO-FINANCIAL INS CO * — B+ Good

Major Rating Factors: History of adequate reserve strength (5.0 on a scale of 0 to 10) as reserves have been consistently at an acceptable level. Good overall profitability index (5.9). Fair expense controls. Return on equity has been fair, averaging 6.0% over the past five years.

Other Rating Factors: Good overall results on stability tests (5.1) despite excessive premium growth and weak results on operational trends. Strong long-term capitalization index (9.8) based on excellent current risk adjusted capital (severe and moderate loss scenarios), despite some fluctuation in capital levels. Excellent liquidity (7.2) with ample operational cash flow and liquid investments.

Principal Business: (This company is a reinsurer.)

Principal Investments: Misc. investments (92%), investment grade bonds (5%), and cash (3%).

Investments in Affiliates: 5%

Group Affiliation: Berkshire-Hathaway

Licensed in: IA, NE, UT

Commenced Business: September 1985

Address: 3024 Harney St, Omaha, NE 68131

Phone: (402) 536-3000 **Domicile State:** NE **NAIC Code:** 19500

Data Date	Rating	RACR #1	RACR #2	Loss Ratio %	Total Assets ($mil)	Capital ($mil)	Net Premium ($mil)	Net Income ($mil)
3-09	B+	3.39	2.60	N/A	2,526.8	2,086.2	75.6	9.9
3-08	B+	5.29	3.45	N/A	2,901.3	2,446.1	21.5	3.5
2008	B+	4.04	2.95	69.9	2,828.2	2,333.7	298.6	60.6
2007	B+	5.25	3.42	68.0	2,894.4	2,481.1	35.3	100.8
2006	B+	5.92	3.98	66.6	2,746.8	2,344.1	35.7	76.7
2005	B+	6.17	4.16	53.3	2,499.6	2,192.8	30.5	393.9
2004	B+	6.35	4.31	30.4	2,348.8	2,077.9	24.3	59.7

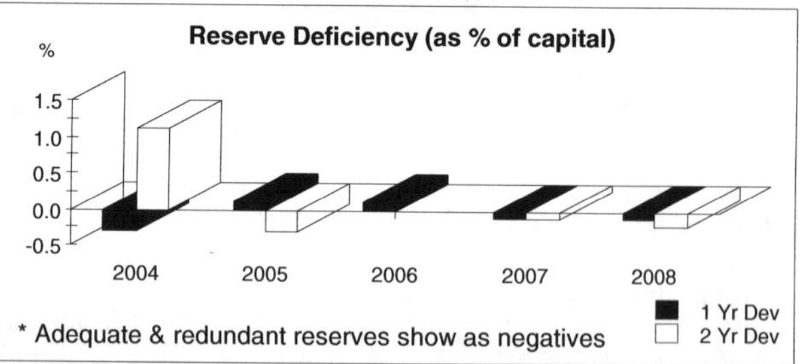

* Adequate & redundant reserves show as negatives

WEST AMERICAN INSURANCE CO — C Fair

Major Rating Factors: Fair overall results on stability tests (3.8 on a scale of 0 to 10) including potential drain of affiliation with Liberty Mutual Group.

Other Rating Factors: Fair profitability index (3.6). Fair expense controls. Return on equity has been fair, averaging 25.8% over the past five years. Strong long-term capitalization index (10.0) based on excellent current risk adjusted capital (severe and moderate loss scenarios), despite some fluctuation in capital levels. Excellent liquidity (7.0) with ample operational cash flow and liquid investments.

Principal Business: Auto liability (29%), commercial multiple peril (24%), homeowners multiple peril (19%), auto physical damage (16%), workers compensation (4%), other liability (2%), and other lines (5%).

Principal Investments: Investment grade bonds (85%), misc. investments (11%), cash (2%), and non investment grade bonds (2%).

Investments in Affiliates: None

Group Affiliation: Liberty Mutual Group

Licensed in: All states except CA, HI, ME, VT, PR

Commenced Business: May 1995

Address: 7999 Knue Rd Suite 450, Indianapolis, IN 46250-1901

Phone: (513) 603-2400 **Domicile State:** IN **NAIC Code:** 44393

Data Date	Rating	RACR #1	RACR #2	Loss Ratio %	Total Assets ($mil)	Capital ($mil)	Net Premium ($mil)	Net Income ($mil)
3-09	C	22.33	20.10	N/A	404.3	209.5	0.0	2.2
3-08	C	4.88	2.44	N/A	1,269.8	217.5	0.0	2.2
2008	C	25.23	22.70	0.0	298.7	207.0	0.0	10.2
2007	C	30.15	27.14	0.0	271.6	213.9	0.0	10.6
2006	C	32.39	29.15	0.0	264.6	216.0	0.0	1.4
2005	C	23.90	21.51	0.0	282.2	199.7	-303.8	218.4
2004	C+	2.12	1.50	63.6	1,884.1	484.6	680.0	71.3

Liberty Mutual Group
Composite Group Rating: C+

Largest Group Members	Assets ($mil)	Rating
LIBERTY MUTUAL INS CO	32550	B-
LIBERTY LIFE ASR CO OF BOSTON	11605	B-
PEERLESS INS CO	7069	C+
OHIO CASUALTY INS CO	4869	C+
SAFECO INS CO OF AMERICA	3952	B-

WEST BEND MUTUAL INS CO * B+ Good

Major Rating Factors: History of adequate reserve strength (5.9 on a scale of 0 to 10) as reserves have been consistently at an acceptable level. Good liquidity (5.5) with sufficient resources (cash flows and marketable investments) to handle a spike in claims.

Other Rating Factors: Good overall results on stability tests (5.0). Strong long-term capitalization index (7.7) based on excellent current risk adjusted capital (severe and moderate loss scenarios), despite some fluctuation in capital levels. Fair profitability index (3.7) with operating losses during the first three months of 2008.

Principal Business: Workers compensation (27%), other liability (18%), auto liability (18%), auto physical damage (11%), homeowners multiple peril (9%), fire (4%), and other lines (14%).

Principal Investments: Investment grade bonds (70%), misc. investments (17%), real estate (7%), and non investment grade bonds (6%).

Investments in Affiliates: 2%

Group Affiliation: West Bend Mutual Group

Licensed in: IL, IN, IA, MI, MN, OH, WI

Commenced Business: May 1894

Address: 1900 S 18th Ave, West Bend, WI 53095

Phone: (262) 334-5571 **Domicile State:** WI **NAIC Code:** 15350

Data Date	Rating	RACR #1	RACR #2	Loss Ratio %	Total Assets ($mil)	Capital ($mil)	Net Premium ($mil)	Net Income ($mil)
3-09	B+	2.24	1.46	N/A	1,438.7	390.2	168.2	-18.8
3-08	A-	2.72	1.77	N/A	1,483.6	490.4	166.9	6.6
2008	B+	2.30	1.50	74.1	1,446.5	397.2	690.7	-17.7
2007	A-	2.88	1.88	68.8	1,509.8	510.9	671.9	35.0
2006	A-	3.08	2.06	60.4	1,460.3	501.8	657.8	65.2
2005	A-	2.75	1.90	57.2	1,325.3	423.6	650.7	68.9
2004	A-	2.02	1.37	57.6	1,191.7	357.1	620.6	66.6

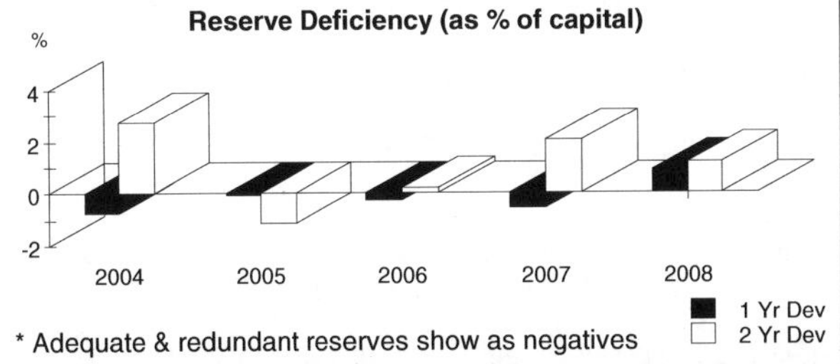

WESTCHESTER FIRE INS CO C- Fair

Major Rating Factors: Weak overall results on stability tests (2.9 on a scale of 0 to 10) including weak risk adjusted capital in prior years. Strengths include potentially strong support from affiliation with ACE Ltd. Poor long-term capitalization (2.0) based on weak current risk adjusted capital (moderate loss scenario), although results have slipped from the fair range over the last two years.

Other Rating Factors: A history of deficient reserves (2.6). Underreserving can have an adverse impact on capital and profits. Deficiencies in the two year reserve development occurred in three of the previous five years and ranged between 36% and 51%. Good liquidity (6.9) with sufficient resources (cash flows and marketable investments) to handle a spike in claims. Excellent profitability (7.1) with operating gains in each of the last five years. Return on equity has been good over the last five years, averaging 12.2%.

Principal Business: Other liability (52%), surety (26%), auto liability (7%), products liability (5%), fire (2%), inland marine (2%), and other lines (7%).

Principal Investments: Investment grade bonds (83%), misc. investments (12%), and cash (5%).

Investments in Affiliates: None

Group Affiliation: ACE Ltd

Licensed in: All states, the District of Columbia and Puerto Rico

Commenced Business: December 1837

Address: 6 Concourse Parkway, Ste 2500, Atlanta, GA 30328-5346

Phone: (770) 393-9955 **Domicile State:** NY **NAIC Code:** 21121

Data Date	Rating	RACR #1	RACR #2	Loss Ratio %	Total Assets ($mil)	Capital ($mil)	Net Premium ($mil)	Net Income ($mil)
3-09	C-	0.66	0.46	N/A	2,561.4	785.0	133.5	30.2
3-08	C-	0.94	0.63	N/A	2,389.7	833.4	140.8	53.0
2008	C-	0.62	0.43	68.0	2,561.3	759.5	502.2	53.0
2007	C-	0.89	0.60	66.0	2,542.9	802.9	515.2	147.9
2006	C-	0.64	0.41	76.8	2,297.7	657.8	607.2	91.9
2005	C-	0.33	0.21	78.8	2,242.6	540.0	646.3	98.7
2004	C-	0.29	0.19	93.4	1,892.2	500.2	655.1	13.1

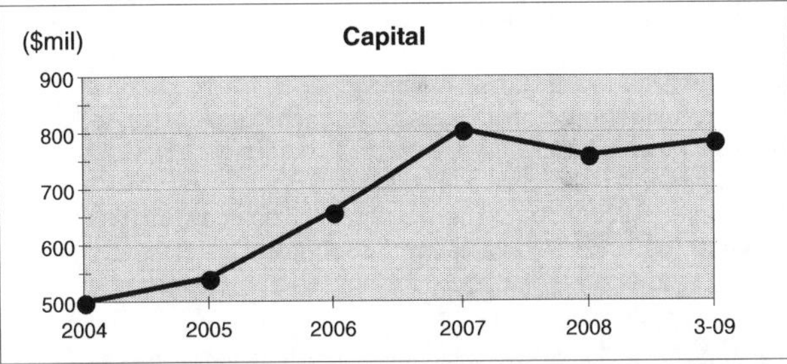

WESTCHESTER SURPLUS LINES INS CO C Fair

Major Rating Factors: Fair overall results on stability tests (4.1 on a scale of 0 to 10) including negative cash flow from operations for 2008. The largest net exposure for one risk is high at 3.3% of capital. Good long-term capitalization index (6.4) based on good current risk adjusted capital (moderate loss scenario). Moreover, capital levels have been consistent in recent years.

Other Rating Factors: History of adequate reserve strength (5.2) as reserves have been consistently at an acceptable level. Excellent profitability (7.5) with operating gains in each of the last five years. Excellent liquidity (7.1) with ample operational cash flow and liquid investments.

Principal Business: (Not applicable due to unusual reinsurance transactions.)

Principal Investments: Investment grade bonds (121%).

Investments in Affiliates: None

Group Affiliation: ACE Ltd

Licensed in: GA

Commenced Business: November 1971

Address: Six Concourse Parkway Ste 2500, Atlanta, GA 30328-5346

Phone: (770) 393-9955 **Domicile State:** GA **NAIC Code:** 10172

Data Date	Rating	RACR #1	RACR #2	Loss Ratio %	Total Assets ($mil)	Capital ($mil)	Net Premium ($mil)	Net Income ($mil)
3-09	C	1.86	1.29	N/A	421.4	169.6	7.0	3.7
3-08	C	1.86	1.31	N/A	338.8	168.2	7.4	6.4
2008	C	1.76	1.23	91.4	456.0	165.4	26.6	2.7
2007	C	1.66	1.17	76.2	367.9	157.6	26.8	10.3
2006	C	1.63	1.09	74.0	499.6	149.6	41.1	8.4
2005	C-	0.91	0.66	96.1	449.1	103.9	48.7	2.1
2004	D+	0.70	0.53	47.2	367.0	65.4	45.8	12.0

ACE Ltd Composite Group Rating: C+ Largest Group Members	Assets ($mil)	Rating
ACE AMERICAN INS CO	8051	C+
ACE PROPERTY CASUALTY INS CO	5785	C
WESTCHESTER FIRE INS CO	2561	C-
PACIFIC EMPLOYERS INS CO	2446	C+
COMBINED INS CO OF AMERICA	2382	B-

WESTERN AGRICULTURAL INS CO * B+ Good

Major Rating Factors: Good overall profitability index (5.4 on a scale of 0 to 10) despite operating losses during 2008. Return on equity has been fair, averaging 8.1% over the past five years. Good overall results on stability tests (5.0) despite negative cash flow from operations for 2008 and fair results on operational trends.

Other Rating Factors: Strong long-term capitalization index (8.1) based on excellent current risk adjusted capital (severe and moderate loss scenarios), despite some fluctuation in capital levels. Ample reserve history (7.0) that can protect against increases in claims costs. Fair liquidity (3.8) as cash resources may not be adequate to cover a spike in claims.

Principal Business: Allied lines (89%), auto liability (4%), farmowners multiple peril (4%), auto physical damage (2%), and workers compensation (1%).

Principal Investments: Investment grade bonds (93%) and misc. investments (7%).

Investments in Affiliates: 3%

Group Affiliation: Iowa Farm Bureau

Licensed in: AZ, CO, ID, IL, IN, IA, KS, MI, MN, MO, MT, NE, NV, NM, ND, OK, OR, SD, TN, UT, VA, WA, WI, WY

Commenced Business: January 1972

Address: 5400 University Ave, West Des Moines, IA 50266-5997

Phone: (515) 225-5400 **Domicile State:** IA **NAIC Code:** 27871

Data Date	Rating	RACR #1	RACR #2	Loss Ratio %	Total Assets ($mil)	Capital ($mil)	Net Premium ($mil)	Net Income ($mil)
3-09	B+	2.86	1.85	N/A	309.2	50.6	16.0	0.8
3-08	B+	3.50	2.43	N/A	130.8	57.1	15.3	1.6
2008	B+	2.74	1.73	85.2	326.6	51.7	79.0	-2.7
2007	B+	3.63	2.58	67.6	135.4	55.8	66.5	3.9
2006	B	3.41	2.43	62.9	143.1	52.2	57.0	7.3
2005	B	2.59	1.77	63.2	133.4	47.0	69.5	7.1
2004	B	1.95	1.25	68.6	112.8	39.2	69.2	3.9

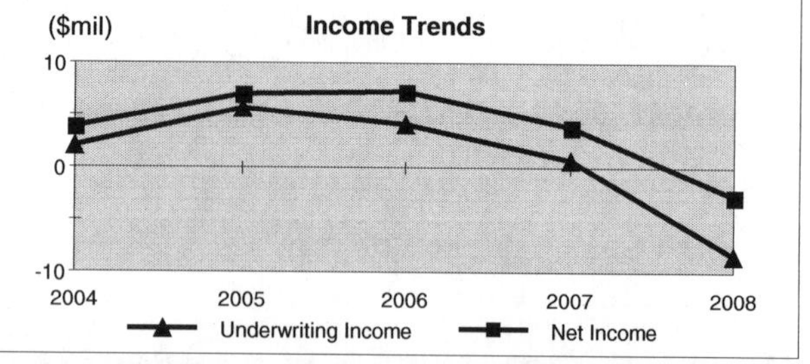

WESTERN COMMUNITY INS CO * B+ Good

Major Rating Factors: History of adequate reserve strength (6.0 on a scale of 0 to 10) as reserves have been consistently at an acceptable level. Good overall results on stability tests (5.0). Stability strengths include good operational trends and excellent risk diversification.

Other Rating Factors: Strong long-term capitalization index (10.0) based on excellent current risk adjusted capital (severe and moderate loss scenarios). Moreover, capital levels have been consistent in recent years. Excellent profitability (8.6) with operating gains in each of the last five years. Excellent expense controls. Excellent liquidity (8.9) with ample operational cash flow and liquid investments.

Principal Business: Commercial multiple peril (58%), auto liability (23%), auto physical damage (11%), inland marine (5%), and other liability (3%).

Principal Investments: Investment grade bonds (94%), misc. investments (5%), and cash (1%).

Investments in Affiliates: None

Group Affiliation: Farm Bureau Group of Idaho

Licensed in: ID, OR, WA

Commenced Business: July 1980

Address: 1001 N 7th Centennial Plaza, Pocatello, ID 83201

Phone: (208) 232-7914 **Domicile State:** ID **NAIC Code:** 39519

Data Date	Rating	RACR #1	RACR #2	Loss Ratio %	Total Assets ($mil)	Capital ($mil)	Net Premium ($mil)	Net Income ($mil)
3-09	B+	9.68	8.71	N/A	30.0	21.3	0.0	0.3
3-08	B+	8.03	7.22	N/A	31.4	20.4	0.0	0.3
2008	B+	8.71	7.84	61.9	31.1	21.1	0.1	1.2
2007	B+	7.60	6.84	43.0	32.1	20.1	0.1	1.3
2006	B+	6.92	6.23	75.7	31.5	18.8	0.2	1.3
2005	B+	6.93	6.24	111.7	28.4	17.5	0.2	1.0
2004	B+	7.11	6.40	60.7	25.9	16.5	0.2	0.9

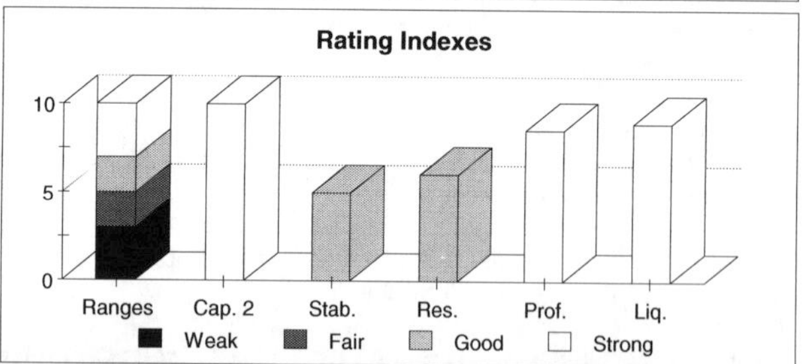

WESTERN NATIONAL MUTUAL INS CO B- Good

Major Rating Factors: Fair overall results on stability tests (4.5 on a scale of 0 to 10) including potential drain of affiliation with Western National Mutual. History of adequate reserve strength (5.7) as reserves have been consistently at an acceptable level.

Other Rating Factors: Good liquidity (6.3) with sufficient resources (cash flows and marketable investments) to handle a spike in claims. Strong long-term capitalization index (7.1) based on excellent current risk adjusted capital (severe and moderate loss scenarios). Moreover, capital levels have been consistent in recent years. Excellent profitability (8.8) with operating gains in each of the last five years. Return on equity has been good over the last five years, averaging 10.9%.

Principal Business: Auto liability (23%), workers compensation (22%), homeowners multiple peril (17%), auto physical damage (15%), other liability (9%), products liability (5%), and other lines (8%).

Principal Investments: Investment grade bonds (80%), misc. investments (18%), and real estate (2%).

Investments in Affiliates: 12%

Group Affiliation: Western National Mutual

Licensed in: IA, KS, MN, NE, ND, SD, WI

Commenced Business: June 1915

Address: 5350 W 78th St, Minneapolis, MN 55439

Phone: (612) 921-3807 **Domicile State:** MN **NAIC Code:** 15377

Data Date	Rating	RACR #1	RACR #2	Loss Ratio %	Total Assets ($mil)	Capital ($mil)	Net Premium ($mil)	Net Income ($mil)
3-09	B-	1.87	1.25	N/A	488.1	214.5	39.0	5.6
3-08	C+	1.75	1.16	N/A	475.6	211.6	41.7	5.5
2008	B-	1.83	1.23	69.3	479.0	210.5	171.8	9.0
2007	C+	1.74	1.16	67.6	463.1	206.3	177.0	18.6
2006	C	2.02	1.31	64.4	442.4	190.6	173.1	23.6
2005	C	1.31	0.83	65.6	387.9	133.5	186.6	18.5
2004	C	1.26	0.80	65.7	339.1	113.4	181.9	17.1

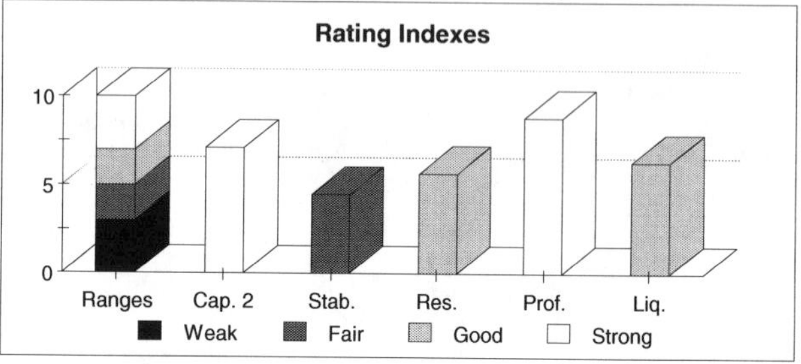

WESTERN SURETY CO C Fair

Major Rating Factors: Fair overall results on stability tests (4.1 on a scale of 0 to 10) including fair financial strength of affiliated CNA Financial Corp. History of adequate reserve strength (5.9) as reserves have been consistently at an acceptable level.

Other Rating Factors: Strong long-term capitalization index (7.8) based on excellent current risk adjusted capital (severe and moderate loss scenarios). Moreover, capital levels have been consistent in recent years. Excellent profitability (9.1) with operating gains in each of the last five years. Return on equity has been excellent over the last five years averaging 19.8%. Excellent liquidity (7.1) with ample operational cash flow and liquid investments.

Principal Business: Surety (91%), fidelity (7%), and other liability (1%).

Principal Investments: Investment grade bonds (94%), misc. investments (5%), and cash (1%).

Investments in Affiliates: 2%

Group Affiliation: CNA Financial Corp

Licensed in: All states, the District of Columbia and Puerto Rico

Commenced Business: July 1900

Address: 101 South Phillips Avenue, Sioux Falls, SD 57104-6703

Phone: (605) 336-0850 **Domicile State:** SD **NAIC Code:** 13188

Data Date	Rating	RACR #1	RACR #2	Loss Ratio %	Total Assets ($mil)	Capital ($mil)	Net Premium ($mil)	Net Income ($mil)
3-09	C	2.52	1.91	N/A	1,232.9	574.7	100.2	20.3
3-08	C	2.25	1.70	N/A	1,111.0	464.0	101.7	23.3
2008	C	2.50	1.91	18.2	1,209.6	554.6	427.8	108.5
2007	C	2.18	1.65	24.6	1,083.8	442.2	424.3	96.7
2006	C	1.86	1.41	24.4	959.6	349.0	405.3	87.7
2005	C	1.50	1.15	37.8	847.2	275.2	361.9	39.1
2004	C	1.45	1.12	30.8	786.7	252.4	313.0	49.2

CNA Financial Corp
Composite Group Rating: C

Largest Group Members	Assets ($mil)	Rating
CONTINENTAL CASUALTY CO	38650	C
CONTINENTAL INS CO	3748	C+
CONTINENTAL ASSURANCE CO	3334	C
WESTERN SURETY CO	1210	C
FIRST INS CO OF HI LTD	593	C+

WESTERN WORLD INS CO C+ Fair

Major Rating Factors: Fair overall results on stability tests (4.3 on a scale of 0 to 10). Good long-term capitalization index (5.2) based on good current risk adjusted capital (moderate loss scenario). Moreover, capital levels have been consistent over the last several years.

Other Rating Factors: Ample reserve history (9.1) that helps to protect the company against sharp claims increases. Excellent profitability (8.6) with operating gains in each of the last five years. Excellent liquidity (7.1) with ample operational cash flow and liquid investments.

Principal Business: Other liability (63%), commercial multiple peril (16%), products liability (10%), medical malpractice (6%), auto liability (4%), and auto physical damage (1%).

Principal Investments: Investment grade bonds (77%), misc. investments (23%), and non investment grade bonds (1%).

Investments in Affiliates: 21%

Group Affiliation: Western World Group

Licensed in: NH, NY

Commenced Business: April 1964

Address: 50 Washington St, Keene, NH 03431

Phone: (201) 847-8600 **Domicile State:** NH **NAIC Code:** 13196

Data Date	Rating	RACR #1	RACR #2	Loss Ratio %	Total Assets ($mil)	Capital ($mil)	Net Premium ($mil)	Net Income ($mil)
3-09	C+	1.33	0.98	N/A	1,019.6	317.6	37.2	5.3
3-08	C	1.13	0.81	N/A	1,026.2	302.5	46.4	6.5
2008	C+	1.31	0.97	65.0	1,015.0	310.2	157.4	21.5
2007	C	1.11	0.79	66.4	1,013.4	294.3	191.3	21.4
2006	C	0.97	0.73	66.7	952.8	271.7	205.7	19.1
2005	C	0.88	0.66	65.7	875.2	246.4	204.3	13.0
2004	C+	0.79	0.57	67.5	762.5	222.1	209.1	9.0

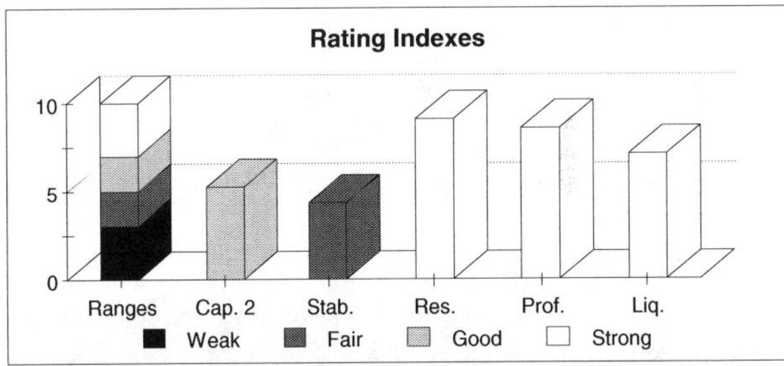

WESTFIELD INS CO B- Good

Major Rating Factors: Fair overall results on stability tests (4.6 on a scale of 0 to 10) including potential drain of affiliation with Westfield Companies. Fair profitability index (4.0) with operating losses during the first three months of 2008. Return on equity has been fair, averaging 7.1% over the past five years.

Other Rating Factors: History of adequate reserve strength (5.0) as reserves have been consistently at an acceptable level. Good liquidity (6.0) with sufficient resources (cash flows and marketable investments) to handle a spike in claims. Strong long-term capitalization index (7.9) based on excellent current risk adjusted capital (severe and moderate loss scenarios), despite some fluctuation in capital levels.

Principal Business: Allied lines (24%), commercial multiple peril (20%), auto liability (17%), auto physical damage (8%), workers compensation (8%), other liability (7%), and other lines (17%).

Principal Investments: Investment grade bonds (80%) and misc. investments (20%).

Investments in Affiliates: None

Group Affiliation: Westfield Companies

Licensed in: All states except AK, CA, CT, HI, ME, NH, PR

Commenced Business: July 1929

Address: 9040 Greenwich Rd, Westfield Center, OH 44251-5001

Phone: (330) 887-0101 **Domicile State:** OH **NAIC Code:** 24112

Data Date	Rating	RACR #1	RACR #2	Loss Ratio %	Total Assets ($mil)	Capital ($mil)	Net Premium ($mil)	Net Income ($mil)
3-09	B-	2.15	1.52	N/A	2,029.3	533.6	230.7	-8.0
3-08	B-	2.56	1.76	N/A	2,268.9	718.1	224.4	9.3
2008	B-	2.37	1.67	66.7	2,122.2	586.1	1,050.4	-3.9
2007	B-	2.57	1.77	64.4	2,235.5	727.3	1,020.0	56.5
2006	B-	2.50	1.71	60.9	2,074.9	683.1	967.1	69.8
2005	B-	2.25	1.54	60.8	1,919.7	586.1	938.2	51.7
2004	B-	1.99	1.35	58.7	1,825.6	517.6	899.5	64.1

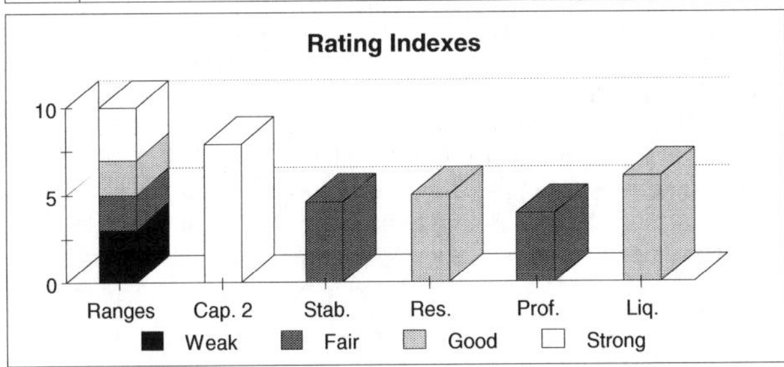

WESTFIELD NATIONAL INS CO * B+ Good

Major Rating Factors: History of adequate reserve strength (5.0 on a scale of 0 to 10) as reserves have been consistently at an acceptable level. Good profitability index (5.0) despite operating losses during 2008. Return on equity has been fair, averaging 6.2% over the past five years.

Other Rating Factors: Good liquidity (6.5) with sufficient resources (cash flows and marketable investments) to handle a spike in claims. Strong long-term capitalization index (8.3) based on excellent current risk adjusted capital (severe and moderate loss scenarios), despite some fluctuation in capital levels. Good overall results on stability tests (5.0). The largest net exposure for one risk is acceptable at 2.8% of capital.

Principal Business: Homeowners multiple peril (34%), auto liability (32%), auto physical damage (23%), other liability (4%), workers compensation (3%), inland marine (3%), and earthquake (1%).

Principal Investments: Investment grade bonds (76%) and misc. investments (24%).

Investments in Affiliates: None

Group Affiliation: Westfield Companies

Licensed in: AZ, CA, CO, FL, GA, IL, IN, IA, KY, MI, MN, NM, ND, OH, PA, SD, TN, TX, WV, WI

Commenced Business: April 1968

Address: 9040 Greenwich Rd, Westfield Center, OH 44251

Phone: (330) 887-0101 **Domicile State:** OH **NAIC Code:** 24120

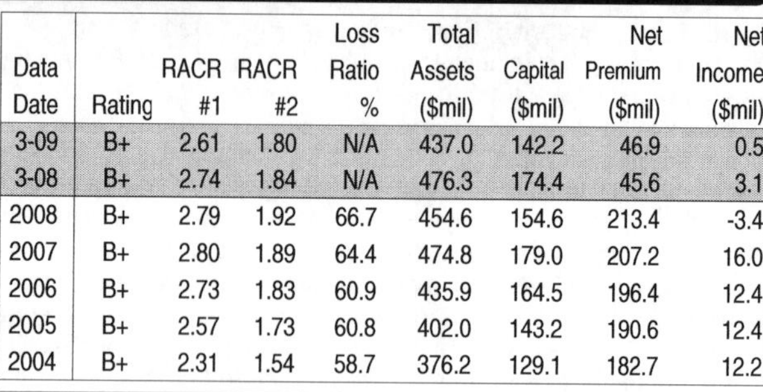

Data Date	Rating	RACR #1	RACR #2	Loss Ratio %	Total Assets ($mil)	Capital ($mil)	Net Premium ($mil)	Net Income ($mil)
3-09	B+	2.61	1.80	N/A	437.0	142.2	46.9	0.5
3-08	B+	2.74	1.84	N/A	476.3	174.4	45.6	3.1
2008	B+	2.79	1.92	66.7	454.6	154.6	213.4	-3.4
2007	B+	2.80	1.89	64.4	474.8	179.0	207.2	16.0
2006	B+	2.73	1.83	60.9	435.9	164.5	196.4	12.4
2005	B+	2.57	1.73	60.8	402.0	143.2	190.6	12.4
2004	B+	2.31	1.54	58.7	376.2	129.1	182.7	12.2

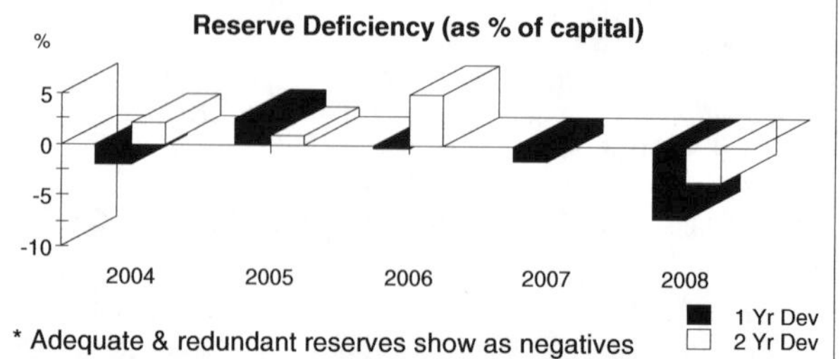

WESTPORT INS CORP C Fair

Major Rating Factors: Fair overall results on stability tests (4.0 on a scale of 0 to 10) including weak results on operational trends, weak risk adjusted capital in prior years and negative cash flow from operations for 2008. Strengths include potentially strong support from affiliation with Swiss Reinsurance. The largest net exposure for one risk is conservative at 2.0% of capital. Poor long-term capitalization index (1.6) based on weak current risk adjusted capital (moderate loss scenario).

Other Rating Factors: A history of deficient reserves (2.7). Underreserving can have an adverse impact on capital and profits. Deficiencies in the two year reserve development occurred in three of the previous five years and ranged between 30% and 58%. Weak profitability index (1.3) with operating losses during 2004, 2005, 2006 and the first three months of 2008. Average return on equity over the last five years has been poor at -6.3%. Excellent liquidity (7.0) with ample operational cash flow and liquid investments.

Principal Business: Other liability (40%), workers compensation (16%), fire (13%), allied lines (10%), commercial multiple peril (7%), group accident & health (4%), and other lines (10%).

Principal Investments: Investment grade bonds (97%), cash (2%), and misc. investments (1%).

Investments in Affiliates: 1%

Group Affiliation: Swiss Reinsurance

Licensed in: All states, the District of Columbia and Puerto Rico

Commenced Business: September 1981

Data Date	Rating	RACR #1	RACR #2	Loss Ratio %	Total Assets ($mil)	Capital ($mil)	Net Premium ($mil)	Net Income ($mil)
3-09	C	0.67	0.43	N/A	7,822.1	1,669.3	1.7	-62.3
3-08	C	0.72	0.44	N/A	11,258.1	3,167.0	82.0	126.4
2008	C	0.68	0.44	75.1	8,047.0	1,811.3	140.0	365.6
2007	C	0.74	0.45	539.2	11,411.2	3,062.0	-476.6	28.7
2006	C	0.58	0.36	97.7	15,488.0	3,606.3	1,050.8	-1,351.0
2005	C	0.76	0.50	168.9	18,203.6	5,388.9	2,034.0	-583.3
2004	C	0.92	0.63	106.3	16,759.2	5,513.1	3,099.5	-110.3

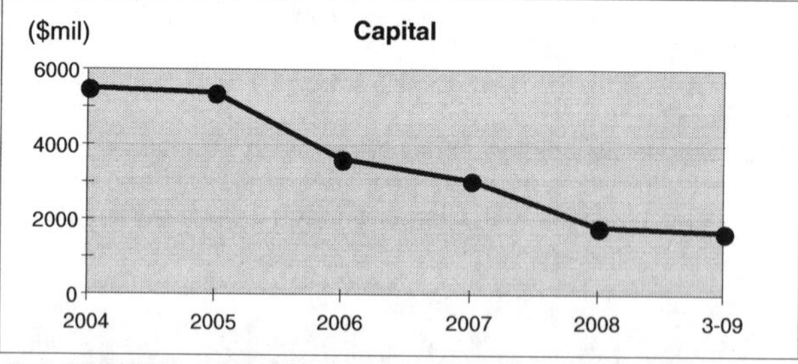

WHITE MOUNTAINS REINS CO OF AMER C- Fair

Major Rating Factors: A history of deficient reserves (2.5 on a scale of 0 to 10) that places pressure on both capital and profits. In 2007 and 2008 the two year reserve development was 22% and 24% deficient respectively. Weak profitability index (2.0) with operating losses during 2004, 2005 and 2008. Average return on equity over the last five years has been poor at -2.7%.

Other Rating Factors: Fair overall results on stability tests (3.1) including negative cash flow from operations for 2008. The largest net exposure for one risk is conservative at 1.8% of capital. Strong long-term capitalization index (7.1) based on excellent current risk adjusted capital (severe and moderate loss scenarios), despite some fluctuation in capital levels. Excellent liquidity (7.0) with ample operational cash flow and liquid investments.

Principal Business: N/A

Principal Investments: Investment grade bonds (88%), misc. investments (10%), cash (1%), and non investment grade bonds (1%).

Investments in Affiliates: 1%

Group Affiliation: White Mountains Group

Licensed in: All states except FL, HI, ME, MN, RI, SD, VT, WV, PR

Commenced Business: January 1980

Address: One Liberty Plaza, 19th Floor, New York, NY 10006

Phone: (212) 312-2500 **Domicile State:** NY **NAIC Code:** 38776

Data Date	Rating	RACR #1	RACR #2	Loss Ratio %	Total Assets ($mil)	Capital ($mil)	Net Premium ($mil)	Net Income ($mil)
3-09	C-	1.59	1.06	N/A	2,449.0	692.0	136.9	0.5
3-08	C-	1.64	1.14	N/A	2,863.3	874.2	172.4	0.0
2008	C-	1.60	1.08	101.0	2,505.0	708.8	554.9	-123.8
2007	C-	1.70	1.20	76.9	2,819.2	926.6	840.3	62.9
2006	C-	2.14	1.39	74.6	3,024.8	1,153.3	715.6	46.9
2005	C-	2.33	1.56	102.7	3,150.8	1,074.2	737.8	-81.7
2004	C-	2.08	1.40	76.3	2,746.1	917.4	993.1	-0.9

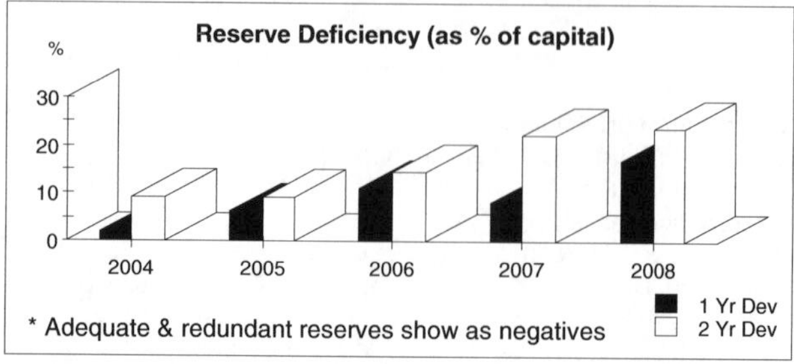

XL INS AMERICA INC — C- Fair

Major Rating Factors: Fair long-term capitalization index (3.4 on a scale of 0 to 10) based on weak current risk adjusted capital (severe loss scenario), although results have slipped from the fair range during the last year. Fair reserve development (3.7) as the level of reserves has at times been insufficient to cover claims. In 2006 and 2004 the two year reserve development was 16% and 48% deficient respectively.

Other Rating Factors: Fair overall results on stability tests (3.3) including weak financial strength of affiliated XL Capital Ltd and fair risk adjusted capital in prior years. The largest net exposure for one risk is high at 3.6% of capital. Good overall profitability index (6.0) despite operating losses during the first three months of 2008. Return on equity has been fair, averaging 6.5% over the past five years. Good liquidity (6.9) with sufficient resources (cash flows and marketable investments) to handle a spike in claims.

Principal Business: Other liability (40%), fire (26%), allied lines (15%), earthquake (5%), boiler & machinery (4%), auto liability (3%), and other lines (6%).

Principal Investments: Investment grade bonds (69%), cash (16%), misc. investments (14%), and non investment grade bonds (1%).

Investments in Affiliates: 22%

Group Affiliation: XL Capital Ltd

Licensed in: All states, the District of Columbia and Puerto Rico

Commenced Business: December 1945

Address: 1201 N Market St Suite 501, Wilmington, DE 19801

Data Date	Rating	RACR #1	RACR #2	Loss Ratio %	Total Assets ($mil)	Capital ($mil)	Net Premium ($mil)	Net Income ($mil)
3-09	C-	0.72	0.47	N/A	629.4	221.1	33.1	-1.9
3-08	D+	0.69	0.46	N/A	618.0	224.6	37.9	1.6
2008	C-	0.83	0.55	60.4	647.7	248.3	179.4	4.4
2007	D+	0.69	0.46	70.8	542.7	211.6	78.6	18.0
2006	D+	0.66	0.45	69.3	542.7	202.7	84.5	23.2
2005	D+	0.58	0.40	88.4	562.0	172.4	79.3	3.4
2004	C-	0.39	0.27	71.8	482.3	165.3	84.0	18.9

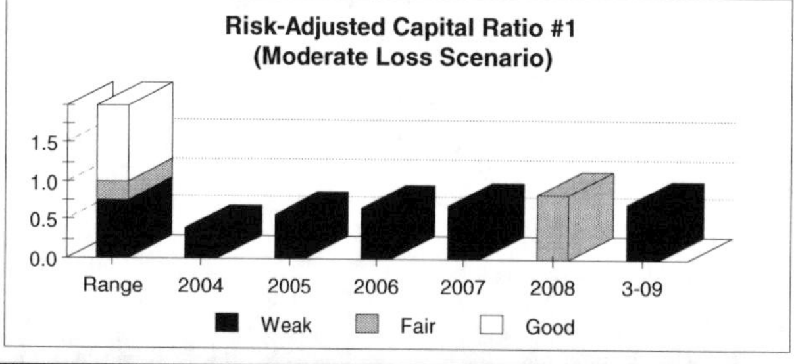

XL REINS AMERICA INC — C Fair

Major Rating Factors: Fair overall results on stability tests (3.5 on a scale of 0 to 10) including potential drain of affiliation with XL Capital Ltd. The largest net exposure for one risk is acceptable at 2.5% of capital. Fair reserve development (4.2) as reserves have generally been sufficient to cover claims. In 2004, the two year reserve development was 30% deficient.

Other Rating Factors: Good overall long-term capitalization (5.6) based on good current risk adjusted capital (moderate loss scenario). However, capital levels have fluctuated somewhat during past years. Good liquidity (6.9) with sufficient resources (cash flows and marketable investments) to handle a spike in claims. Excellent profitability (7.1) with operating gains in each of the last five years.

Principal Business: Other liability (100%).

Principal Investments: Investment grade bonds (80%), cash (11%), and misc. investments (9%).

Investments in Affiliates: 16%

Group Affiliation: XL Capital Ltd

Licensed in: All states, the District of Columbia and Puerto Rico

Commenced Business: October 1929

Address: 111 Broadway Suite 1802, New York, NY 10006

Phone: (203) 964-5200 **Domicile State:** NY **NAIC Code:** 20583

Data Date	Rating	RACR #1	RACR #2	Loss Ratio %	Total Assets ($mil)	Capital ($mil)	Net Premium ($mil)	Net Income ($mil)
3-09	C	1.13	0.73	N/A	5,090.1	2,072.3	214.8	42.3
3-08	C-	1.10	0.73	N/A	5,021.6	2,116.1	246.1	27.1
2008	C	1.30	0.85	60.4	5,277.6	2,319.1	1,166.4	130.1
2007	C-	1.12	0.74	70.8	5,027.6	2,044.5	511.2	190.8
2006	D+	1.18	0.79	69.3	4,939.8	2,133.6	549.2	172.5
2005	D+	1.04	0.72	88.4	4,695.5	1,856.2	515.4	46.9
2004	C	0.69	0.49	71.8	4,415.4	1,775.4	546.0	135.0

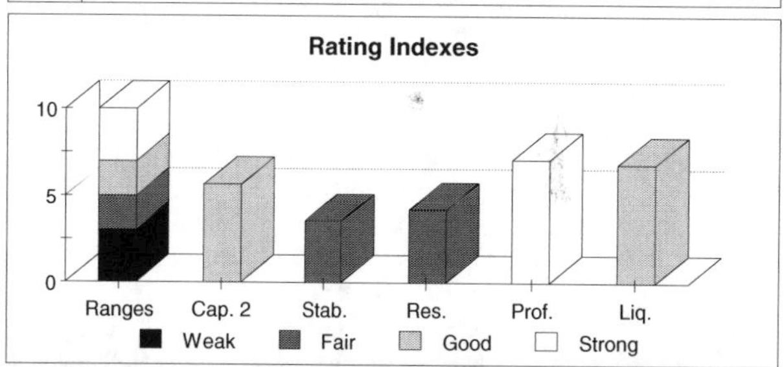

XL SPECIALTY INS CO — C+ Fair

Major Rating Factors: Fair overall results on stability tests (3.8 on a scale of 0 to 10) including potential drain of affiliation with XL Capital Ltd and fair risk adjusted capital in prior years. The largest net exposure for one risk is acceptable at 2.9% of capital. Good long-term capitalization index (5.0) based on fair current risk adjusted capital (severe loss scenario).

Other Rating Factors: Fair reserve development (4.0) as reserves have generally been sufficient to cover claims. In 2004, the two year reserve development was 43% deficient. Good overall profitability index (5.9) despite operating losses during the first three months of 2008. Return on equity has been fair, averaging 7.2% over the past five years. Excellent liquidity (7.8) with ample operational cash flow and liquid investments.

Principal Business: Other liability (60%), aircraft (16%), ocean marine (8%), inland marine (7%), workers compensation (6%), and auto liability (2%).

Principal Investments: Investment grade bonds (77%), cash (15%), and misc. investments (8%).

Investments in Affiliates: 11%

Group Affiliation: XL Capital Ltd

Licensed in: All states, the District of Columbia and Puerto Rico

Commenced Business: December 1979

Address: 1201 N Market St Suite 501, Wilmington, DE 19801

Phone: (203) 964-5200 **Domicile State:** DE **NAIC Code:** 37885

Data Date	Rating	RACR #1	RACR #2	Loss Ratio %	Total Assets ($mil)	Capital ($mil)	Net Premium ($mil)	Net Income ($mil)
3-09	C+	0.89	0.57	N/A	510.3	161.9	19.8	-0.6
3-08	C+	0.79	0.52	N/A	647.4	153.6	22.7	2.1
2008	C+	1.03	0.67	60.4	577.1	181.8	107.7	15.1
2007	C+	0.83	0.55	70.8	555.5	151.6	47.2	11.4
2006	C+	0.89	0.59	69.3	432.9	161.6	50.7	11.8
2005	D	0.82	0.55	88.4	523.8	142.2	47.6	4.1
2004	D+	0.56	0.39	71.8	633.6	140.2	50.4	17.2

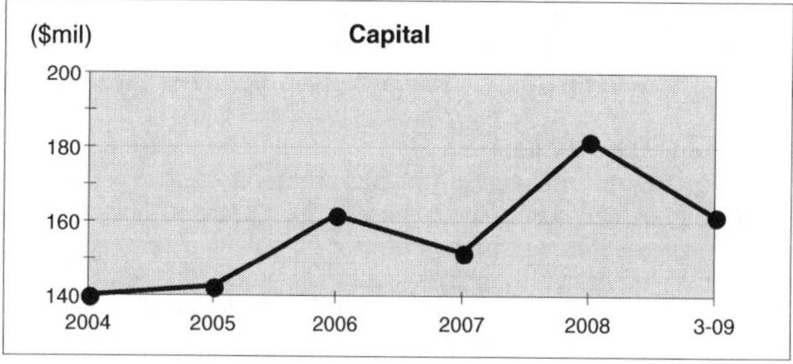

YOSEMITE INS CO C+ Fair

Major Rating Factors: Fair profitability index (3.4 on a scale of 0 to 10). Good expense controls. Return on equity has been fair, averaging 10.3% over the past five years. Fair overall results on stability tests (4.5).

Other Rating Factors: Strong long-term capitalization index (10.0) based on excellent current risk adjusted capital (severe and moderate loss scenarios), despite some fluctuation in capital levels. Ample reserve history (7.3) that can protect against increases in claims costs. Superior liquidity (9.2) with ample operational cash flow and liquid investments.

Principal Business: Auto physical damage (43%), aggregate write-ins for other lines of business (37%), fire (15%), and inland marine (5%).

Principal Investments: Investment grade bonds (104%).

Investments in Affiliates: 13%

Group Affiliation: American International Group

Licensed in: All states except AK, DC, NY, VT, PR

Commenced Business: August 1964

Address: 601 NW Second St, Evansville, IN 47708

Phone: (812) 424-8031 **Domicile State:** IN **NAIC Code:** 26220

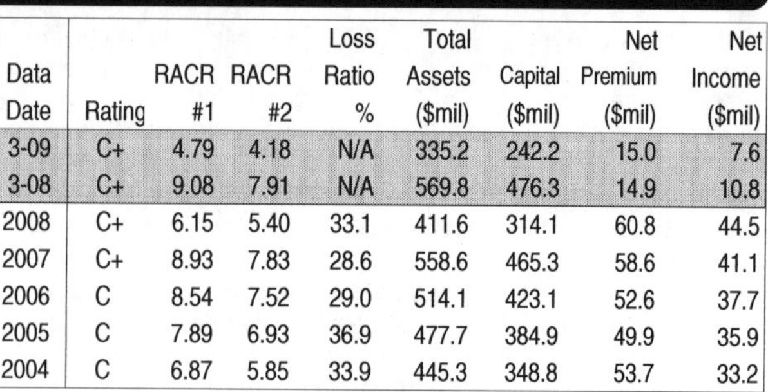

Data Date	Rating	RACR #1	RACR #2	Loss Ratio %	Total Assets ($mil)	Capital ($mil)	Net Premium ($mil)	Net Income ($mil)
3-09	C+	4.79	4.18	N/A	335.2	242.2	15.0	7.6
3-08	C+	9.08	7.91	N/A	569.8	476.3	14.9	10.8
2008	C+	6.15	5.40	33.1	411.6	314.1	60.8	44.5
2007	C+	8.93	7.83	28.6	558.6	465.3	58.6	41.1
2006	C	8.54	7.52	29.0	514.1	423.1	52.6	37.7
2005	C	7.89	6.93	36.9	477.7	384.9	49.9	35.9
2004	C	6.87	5.85	33.9	445.3	348.8	53.7	33.2

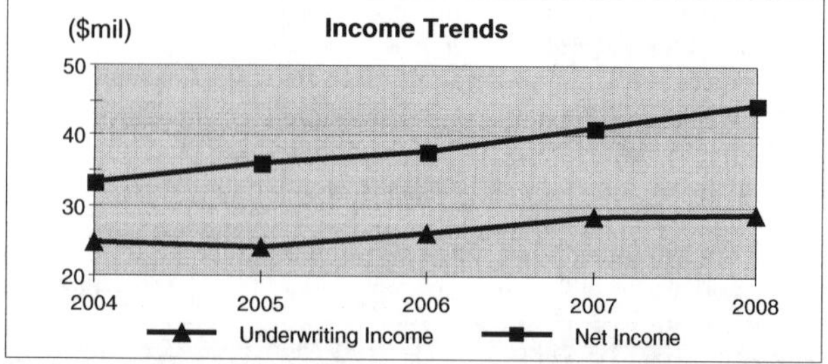

ZENITH INS CO C+ Fair

Major Rating Factors: Fair overall results on stability tests (4.4 on a scale of 0 to 10) including potential drain of affiliation with Zenith National Ins Group and negative cash flow from operations for 2008. History of adequate reserve strength (5.0) as reserves have been consistently at an acceptable level.

Other Rating Factors: Good overall profitability index (6.4) despite operating losses during the first three months of 2008. Return on equity has been good over the last five years, averaging 31.9%. Good liquidity (6.8) with sufficient resources (cash flows and marketable investments) to handle a spike in claims. Strong long-term capitalization index (7.6) based on excellent current risk adjusted capital (severe and moderate loss scenarios), despite some fluctuation in capital levels.

Principal Business: Workers compensation (100%).

Principal Investments: Investment grade bonds (85%), misc. investments (7%), non investment grade bonds (7%), and real estate (1%).

Investments in Affiliates: 1%

Group Affiliation: Zenith National Ins Group

Licensed in: All states except NH, ND, WV, WY, PR

Commenced Business: December 1950

Address: 21255 Califa St, Woodland Hills, CA 91367

Phone: (818) 713-1000 **Domicile State:** CA **NAIC Code:** 13269

Data Date	Rating	RACR #1	RACR #2	Loss Ratio %	Total Assets ($mil)	Capital ($mil)	Net Premium ($mil)	Net Income ($mil)
3-09	C+	3.22	2.26	N/A	2,089.6	989.1	115.6	-7.6
3-08	C	2.68	1.95	N/A	2,253.6	1,047.1	155.9	42.5
2008	C+	3.00	2.12	46.1	2,106.4	1,015.3	578.6	111.5
2007	C	1.18	0.87	34.2	2,252.9	451.1	703.1	238.9
2006	C	1.17	0.87	34.2	2,377.1	559.5	872.0	272.4
2005	C-	0.58	0.43	59.7	2,304.0	440.9	1,140.0	159.3
2004	C	0.80	0.59	66.6	1,981.8	576.7	969.8	111.7

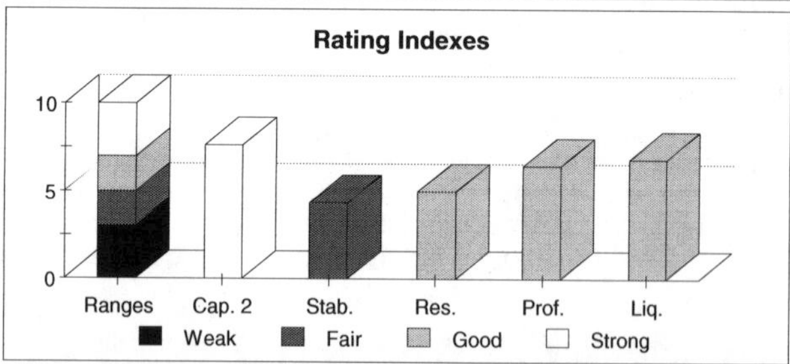

ZURICH AMERICAN INS CO C- Fair

Major Rating Factors: A history of deficient reserves (2.0 on a scale of 0 to 10). Underreserving can have an adverse impact on capital and profits. Deficiencies in the two year reserve development occurred in three of the previous five years and ranged between 29% and 111%. Good overall long-term capitalization (5.4) based on good current risk adjusted capital (severe loss scenario). However, capital levels have fluctuated somewhat during past years.

Other Rating Factors: Fair profitability index (4.5) with operating losses during 2004 and 2005. Return on equity has been low, averaging 0.2% over the past five years. Fair overall results on stability tests (3.3). The largest net exposure for one risk is high at 4.2% of capital. Good liquidity (6.7) with sufficient resources (cash flows and marketable investments) to handle a spike in claims.

Principal Business: Other liability (34%), workers compensation (28%), auto liability (9%), inland marine (7%), group accident & health (6%), commercial multiple peril (5%), and other lines (11%).

Principal Investments: Investment grade bonds (82%) and misc. investments (18%).

Investments in Affiliates: 8%

Group Affiliation: Zurich Financial Services Group

Licensed in: All states, the District of Columbia and Puerto Rico

Commenced Business: January 1913

Address: 165 Broadway, 28th Floor, New York, NY 10006

Phone: (847) 605-6429 **Domicile State:** NY **NAIC Code:** 16535

Data Date	Rating	RACR #1	RACR #2	Loss Ratio %	Total Assets ($mil)	Capital ($mil)	Net Premium ($mil)	Net Income ($mil)
3-09	C-	1.38	0.76	N/A	29,566.7	6,123.9	1,153.8	56.7
3-08	C-	1.31	0.73	N/A	32,377.6	6,917.7	1,327.7	245.7
2008	C-	1.40	0.77	83.4	29,634.5	6,239.8	4,934.3	249.1
2007	C-	1.29	0.72	78.0	31,808.0	6,744.7	5,864.8	1,276.0
2006	C-	1.11	0.65	82.3	31,513.4	6,036.8	5,434.0	321.6
2005	C-	1.08	0.63	99.5	28,479.7	5,527.9	5,201.6	-352.1
2004	C	1.08	0.69	102.4	25,058.8	4,924.6	7,248.7	-1,082.8

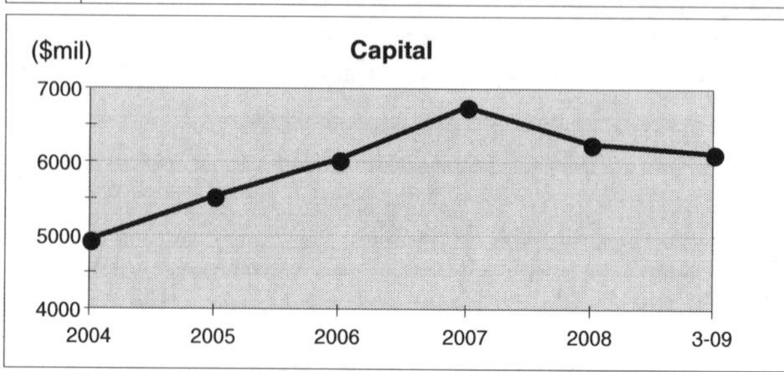

Section III

TheStreet.com Recommended Companies

A compilation of those

U.S. Property and Casualty Insurers

receiving a TheStreet.com Financial Strength Rating

of A+, A, A- or B+.

Companies are listed in alphabetical order.

Section III Contents

This section provides a list of recommended carriers (based strictly on financial safety) along with additional information you should have when shopping for insurance. It contains all insurers receiving a Financial Strength Rating of A+, A, A- or B+. If an insurer is not on this list, it should not be automatically assumed that the firm is weak. Indeed, there are many firms that have not achieved a B+ or better rating but are in relatively good condition with adequate resources to cover their risk during an average recession. Not being included in this list should not be construed as a recommendation to cancel a policy.

Left Pages

1. **Financial Strength Rating** Our rating is measured on a scale from A to F and considers a wide range of factors. Highly-rated companies are, in our opinion, less likely to experience financial difficulties than lower rated firms. See *About TheStreet.com Financial Strength Ratings* on page 9 for more information.

2. **Insurance Company Name** The legally-registered name, which can sometimes differ from the name that the company uses for advertising. An insurer's name can be very similar to the name of other companies which may not be on our Recommended List, so make sure you note the exact name before contacting your agent.

3. **Address** The address of the main office where you can contact the firm for additional financial data or for the location of local branches and/or registered agents.

4. **Telephone Number** The number to call for additional financial data or for the phone numbers of local branches and/or registered agents.

Right Pages

The right-side pages present the percentage of the company's business that is involved in each type of insurance. Specifically, the numbers shown are the amounts of direct premium (received directly from policyholders) for each line of business as a percent of total premiums.

1. **Domicile State** The state which has primary regulatory responsibility for the company. It may differ from the location of the company's corporate headquarters. You do not have to be living in the domicile state to purchase insurance from this firm, provided it is licensed to do business in your state.

2. **Auto** Coverage for damage to a policyholder's own automobile and for the financial loss from auto-related bodily injury or property damage.

3. Homeowners Multiple Peril	Package policies for homeowners providing a broad spectrum of property and liability coverages.
4. Farmowners Multiple Peril	Package policies for farm or ranch owners providing a broad spectrum of property and liability coverages.
5. Commercial Multiple Peril	Package policies for businesses and other commercial establishments providing a broad spectrum of property and liability coverages.
6. Commercial Auto Liability	Coverage against financial loss because of auto related injuries or damages to third parties.
7. Other Liability	Encompasses all third-party liability coverages not included in other business areas. It can include among others: professional liability, environmental liability, product liability, umbrella liability, general liability.
8. Medical Malpractice	Errors and omissions liability coverages for persons engaged in the practice of medicine, surgery, dentistry, nursing, pharmacy, or other health care services. Also covers health care institutions.
9. Workers' Compensation	Liability coverage issued to employers which provides for the payment of medical care, disability income or possible additional liability amounts to employees who are injured on the job.
10. Accident and Health	This includes three categories: (1) group accident and health, which consists of medical and hospitalization insurance plans under which a number of persons and their dependents are insured under a single policy issued to an employer or a common associated entity; (2) credit accident and health, which makes certain debt payments, usually for car or home loans, in the case of accident or illness; and (3) other accident and health, issued to individuals, to pay health care benefits or loss of income due to accidental injury or death.
11. Other	Fire, allied lines, mortgage guaranty, ocean marine, inland marine, financial guaranty, product liability, aircraft, fidelity, surety, glass, burglary and theft, boiler and machinery, credit, international, reinsurance, aggregate write-ins for other lines of business and other miscellaneous types of insurance.

TheStreet.com Financial Strength Ratings are not deemed to be a recommendation concerning the purchase or sale of the securities of any insurance company that is publicly owned.

RATING	INSURANCE COMPANY NAME	ADDRESS	CITY	STATE	ZIP	PHONE
B+	ALLSTATE INS CO	3075 SANDERS RD, STE G2H	NORTHBROOK	IL	60062	(847)-402-5000
B+	AMERICAN FAMILY HOME INS CO	1301 RIVER PLACE BLVD STE 1300	JACKSONVILLE	FL	32207	(800)-543-2644
B+	AMERICAN MERCURY INS CO	2000 N CLASSEN CENTER	OKLAHOMA CITY	OK	73106	(405)-523-2000
B+	AMERICAN MODERN HOME INS CO	7000 MIDLAND BLVD	AMELIA	OH	45102	(800)-543-2644
B+	AMERICAN NATIONAL GENERAL INS CO	1949 EAST SUNSHINE	SPRINGFIELD	MO	65899	(417)-887-0220
B+	AMERICAN NATIONAL PROPERTY & CAS CO	1949 E SUNSHINE	SPRINGFIELD	MO	65899	(417)-887-0220
B+	AMERICAN STANDARD INS CO OF WI	6000 AMERICAN PARKWAY	MADISON	WI	53783	(608)-249-2111
B+	AMICA LLOYDS OF TEXAS	P.O. BOX 6008	PROVIDENCE	RI	02940	(800)-992-6422
B+	ARCH SPECIALTY INS CO	10909 MILL VALLEY RD	OMAHA	NE	68113	201-743-4000
B+	AUTO CLUB CASUALTY CO	3333 FAIRVIEW ROAD	COSTA MESA	CA	92626	(714)-885-2170
B+	AUTO CLUB INDEMNITY CO	3333 FAIRVIEW ROAD	COSTA MESA	CA	92626	(714)-885-2170
A	AUTO-OWNERS INS CO	6101 ANACAPRI BLVD	LANSING	MI	48917	(517)-323-1200
B+	BAY STATE INS CO	95 OLD RIVER RD	ANDOVER	MA	01810	(978)-475-3300
A-	BITUMINOUS CASUALTY CORP	320 18TH ST	ROCK ISLAND	IL	61201	(309)-786-5401
A-	BITUMINOUS FIRE & MARINE INS CO	320 18TH ST	ROCK ISLAND	IL	61201	(309)-786-5401
A-	CALIFORNIA STATE AUTO ASN INTER-INS	100 VAN NESS AVE	SAN FRANCISCO	CA	94102	(415)-565-2012
B+	CANAL INS CO	400 E STONE AVE	GREENVILLE	SC	29601	(864)-242-5365
B+	CENTRAL MUTUAL INS CO	800 S WASHINGTON ST	VAN WERT	OH	45891	(419)-238-5551
B+	CENTRAL STATES INDEMNITY CO OF OMAHA	1212 N 96TH ST	OMAHA	NE	68114	(402)-397-1111
A	CHURCH MUTUAL INS CO	3000 SCHUSTER LANE	MERRILL	WI	54452	(715)-536-5577
A-	CINCINNATI INDEMNITY CO	6200 S GILMORE RD	FAIRFIELD	OH	45014	(513)-870-2000
A-	CINCINNATI INS CO	6200 S GILMORE RD	FAIRFIELD	OH	45014	(513)-870-2000
B+	CITATION INS CO	211 MAIN ST	WEBSTER	MA	01570	(508)-943-9000
B+	COMMERCE INS CO	211 W MAIN ST	WEBSTER	MA	01570	(508)-949-9000
A-	COOPERATIVA D SEGUROS MULTIPLES D PR	38 NEVAREZ ST/AMERICO MIRANDA	RIO PIEDRAS	PR	00927	(787)-758-8585
B+	COPIC INS CO	7800 E DORADO PL SUITE 200	ENGLEWOOD	CO	80111	(303)-779-0044
B+	CORNHUSKER CASUALTY CO	9290 W DODGE RD	OMAHA	NE	68114	(402)-393-7255
B+	COUNTRY CASUALTY INS CO	1701 N. TOWANDA AVE	BLOOMINGTON	IL	61701	(309)-821-3000
A	COUNTRY MUTUAL INS CO	1701 N. TOWANDA AVE	BLOOMINGTON	IL	61701	(309)-821-3000
B+	CUMBERLAND MUTUAL FIRE INS CO	633 SHILOH PIKE	BRIDGETON	NJ	08302	(609)-451-4050
B+	CUMIS INS SOCIETY INC	5910 MINERAL POINT RD	MADISON	WI	53705	(608)-238-5851
A+	DAIRYLAND INS CO	1800 NORTH POINT DR	STEVENS POINT	WI	54481	(715)-346-6000
B+	ERIE INS CO OF NY	120 CORPORATE WOODS SUITE 150	ROCHESTER	NY	14623	(814)-870-2000
A-	FARM BUREAU MUTUAL INS CO	5400 UNIVERSITY AVE	WEST DES MOINES	IA	50265	(515)-225-5400
B+	FARM BUREAU MUTUAL INS CO OF ID	1001 N 7TH CENTENNIAL PLAZA	POCATELLO	ID	83201	(208)-232-7914
B+	FARMERS AUTOMOBILE INS ASN	2505 COURT ST	PEKIN	IL	61558	(309)-346-1161
B+	FARMLAND MUTUAL INS CO	1100 LOCUST ST DEPT 2007	DES MOINES	IA	50391	(515)-245-8800
B+	FEDERAL INS CO	211 N PENNSYLVANIA ST #1350	INDIANAPOLIS	IN	46204	(908)-903-2000
A-	FEDERATED MUTUAL INS CO	121 E PARK SQUARE	OWATONNA	MN	55060	507-455-5200
B+	FEDERATED SERVICE INS CO	121 E PARK SQUARE	OWATONNA	MN	55060	(507)-455-5200
B+	FOREMOST INS CO	5600 BEECH TREE LANE	CALEDONIA	MI	49316	(616)-956-8102
A	FRANKENMUTH MUTUAL INS CO	ONE MUTUAL AVENUE	FRANKENMUTH	MI	48787	989-652-6121
B+	GEICO GENERAL INS CO	5260 WESTERN AVENUE	CHEVY CHASE	MD	20815	(800)-841-3000
B+	GEICO INDEMNITY CO	ONE GEICO PLAZA	WASHINGTON	DC	20076	(800)-841-3000
A-	GENERAL STAR NATIONAL INS CO	695 E MAIN ST	STAMFORD	CT	06904	(203)-328-5700
B+	GOVERNMENT EMPLOYEES INS CO	ONE GEICO PLAZA	WASHINGTON	DC	20076	(800)-841-3000
A-	GRANGE MUTUAL CAS CO	650 S FRONT ST	COLUMBUS	OH	43206	(614)-445-2900
B+	GREAT NORTHERN INS CO	100 S 5TH ST #1800	MINNEAPOLIS	MN	55402	(908)-903-2000
A-	GREAT WEST CASUALTY CO	1100 W 29TH ST	SOUTH SIOUX CITY	NE	68776	(402)-494-2411
B+	HARTFORD FIRE INS CO	HARTFORD PLAZA	HARTFORD	CT	06115	(860)-547-5000
B+	HARTFORD INS CO OF THE MIDWEST	4040 VINCENNES CIR SUITE 100	INDIANAPOLIS	IN	46268	(860)-547-5000
B+	HARTFORD UNDERWRITERS INS CO	HARTFORD PLAZA	HARTFORD	CT	06115	(860)-547-5000
A+	HASTINGS MUTUAL INS CO	404 E WOODLAWN AVE	HASTINGS	MI	49058	(800)-442-8277
A	HOME-OWNERS INS CO	6101 ANACAPRI BLVD	LANSING	MI	48917	(517)-323-1200
B+	HOUSING ENTERPRISE INS CO	PO BOX 189	CHESHIRE	CT	06410	203-272-8220-
B+	INS CO OF GREATER NY	200 MADISON AVENUE	NEW YORK	NY	10016	(212)-683-9700

DOM. STATE	AUTO	HOME MULT. PERIL	FARM MULT. PERIL	COMM. MULT. PERIL	COMM. AUTO LIAB.	OTHER LIABILITY	MED MALPRAC.	WORK. COMP.	ACCID. & HEALTH	OTHER	INSURANCE COMPANY NAME
IL	61	28	0	4	2	2	0	0	0	4	ALLSTATE INS CO
FL	5	78	0	0	0	0	0	0	0	16	AMERICAN FAMILY HOME INS CO
OK	46	16	0	0	5	7	0	0	0	0	AMERICAN MERCURY INS CO
OH	13	31	0	0	1	4	0	0	0	51	AMERICAN MODERN HOME INS CO
MO	75	24	0	0	0	0	0	0	0	1	AMERICAN NATIONAL GENERAL INS CO
MO	45	22	0	1	2	2	0	0	0	27	AMERICAN NATIONAL PROPERTY & CAS CO
WI	100	0	0	0	0	0	0	0	0	0	AMERICAN STANDARD INS CO OF WI
TX	0	95	0	0	0	0	0	0	0	5	AMICA LLOYDS OF TEXAS
NE	0	0	0	1	5	42	14	0	0	38	ARCH SPECIALTY INS CO
TX	100	0	0	0	0	0	0	0	0	0	AUTO CLUB CASUALTY CO
TX	2	97	0	0	0	1	0	0	0	0	AUTO CLUB INDEMNITY CO
MI	25	13	2	14	13	9	0	10	0	15	AUTO-OWNERS INS CO
MA	0	88	0	4	0	4	0	0	0	3	BAY STATE INS CO
IL	6	0	0	23	20	14	0	29	0	9	BITUMINOUS CASUALTY CORP
IL	2	0	0	18	10	2	0	63	0	5	BITUMINOUS FIRE & MARINE INS CO
CA	75	23	0	0	0	1	0	0	0	1	CALIFORNIA STATE AUTO ASN INTER-INS
SC	20	0	0	0	64	1	0	6	0	10	CANAL INS CO
OH	32	20	0	18	6	6	0	6	0	11	CENTRAL MUTUAL INS CO
NE	0	0	0	0	0	0	0	0	25	75	CENTRAL STATES INDEMNITY CO OF OMAHA
WI	2	1	0	72	7	4	1	13	0	0	CHURCH MUTUAL INS CO
OH	0	0	0	0	0	1	0	98	0	0	CINCINNATI INDEMNITY CO
OH	15	10	0	30	10	17	1	5	0	11	CINCINNATI INS CO
MA	4	84	0	0	7	2	0	0	0	3	CITATION INS CO
MA	88	6	0	1	4	0	0	0	0	1	COMMERCE INS CO
PR	63	4	0	10	3	3	0	0	0	16	COOPERATIVA D SEGUROS MULTIPLES D PR
CO	0	0	0	0	0	3	94	0	4	0	COPIC INS CO
NE	13	0	0	4	40	6	0	26	0	9	CORNHUSKER CASUALTY CO
IL	53	26	0	12	3	4	0	1	0	1	COUNTRY CASUALTY INS CO
IL	36	31	8	5	1	3	0	5	0	12	COUNTRY MUTUAL INS CO
NJ	0	60	0	20	0	3	0	0	0	17	CUMBERLAND MUTUAL FIRE INS CO
IA	18	4	0	12	1	22	0	1	1	41	CUMIS INS SOCIETY INC
WI	100	0	0	0	0	0	0	0	0	0	DAIRYLAND INS CO
NY	10	0	0	0	0	0	0	90	0	0	ERIE INS CO OF NY
IA	47	20	20	5	2	2	0	4	0	1	FARM BUREAU MUTUAL INS CO
ID	59	15	18	0	0	2	0	0	0	5	FARM BUREAU MUTUAL INS CO OF ID
IL	64	29	0	0	0	0	0	0	0	7	FARMERS AUTOMOBILE INS ASN
IA	5	0	0	44	16	10	0	22	0	3	FARMLAND MUTUAL INS CO
IN	2	8	0	18	2	34	0	8	4	24	FEDERAL INS CO
MN	4	0	0	8	13	15	0	15	33	12	FEDERATED MUTUAL INS CO
MN	7	0	0	4	18	32	0	17	0	23	FEDERATED SERVICE INS CO
MI	21	52	0	0	0	4	0	0	0	24	FOREMOST INS CO
MI	32	17	0	16	6	4	0	20	0	5	FRANKENMUTH MUTUAL INS CO
MD	100	0	0	0	0	0	0	0	0	0	GEICO GENERAL INS CO
MD	100	0	0	0	0	0	0	0	0	0	GEICO INDEMNITY CO
OH	0	0	0	0	0	89	9	0	0	2	GENERAL STAR NATIONAL INS CO
MD	98	0	0	0	0	2	0	0	0	0	GOVERNMENT EMPLOYEES INS CO
OH	52	19	3	13	6	2	0	2	0	4	GRANGE MUTUAL CAS CO
IN	10	42	0	22	3	5	0	4	0	15	GREAT NORTHERN INS CO
NE	24	0	0	0	55	4	0	8	0	9	GREAT WEST CASUALTY CO
CT	4	2	0	29	9	7	0	18	1	30	HARTFORD FIRE INS CO
IN	31	16	0	8	2	2	0	26	0	15	HARTFORD INS CO OF THE MIDWEST
CT	41	11	0	4	7	2	0	32	0	3	HARTFORD UNDERWRITERS INS CO
MI	28	17	13	15	6	4	0	14	0	4	HASTINGS MUTUAL INS CO
MI	51	34	0	7	2	1	0	2	0	2	HOME-OWNERS INS CO
VT (*)	0	0	0	0	0	0	0	0	0	0	HOUSING ENTERPRISE INS CO
NY	0	0	0	100	0	0	0	-1	0	0	INS CO OF GREATER NY

(*) Denotes reinsurers, companies that do not sell to consumers

RATING	INSURANCE COMPANY NAME	ADDRESS	CITY	STATE	ZIP	PHONE
A+	INTERINS EXCH OF THE AUTOMOBILE CLUB	3333 FAIRVIEW ROAD	COSTA MESA	CA	92626	(800)-924-6141
A-	JEWELERS MUTUAL INS CO	24 JEWELERS PARK DR	NEENAH	WI	54957	(414)-725-4326
A	KENTUCKY FARM BUREAU MUTUAL INS CO	9201 BUNSEN PARKWAY	LOUISVILLE	KY	40220	(502)-495-5000
A-	MERCURY CASUALTY CO	4484 WILSHIRE BLVD	LOS ANGELES	CA	90010	(714)-671-6600
A-	MERCURY INS CO	4484 WILSHIRE BLVD	LOS ANGELES	CA	90010	(714)-671-6600
A	MERRIMACK MUTUAL FIRE INS CO	95 OLD RIVER RD	ANDOVER	MA	01810	(978)-475-3300
B+	METROPOLITAN PROPERTY & CAS INS CO	700 QUAKER LANE	WARWICK	RI	02886	(401)-827-2400
B+	MIDWEST MEDICAL INS CO	7650 EDINBOROUGH WAY STE 400	MINNEAPOLIS	MN	55435	(952)-838-6700
B+	MOTORISTS MUTUAL INS CO	471 E BROAD ST	COLUMBUS	OH	43215	(614)-225-8211
A	MOUNTAIN WEST FARM BU MUTUAL INS CO	931 BOULDER DR	LARAMIE	WY	82070	(307)-745-4835
A-	MUTUAL INS CO OF AZ	2602 EAST THOMAS RD	PHOENIX	AZ	85016	(602)-808-2173
B+	NATIONAL CASUALTY CO	8877 N GAINEY CENTER DR	SCOTTSDALE	AZ	85258	(602)-948-0505
A-	NATIONAL LIABILITY & FIRE INS CO	100 FIRST STAMFORD PLACE	STAMFORD	CT	68131	(402)-536-3000
B+	NATIONWIDE MUTUAL FIRE INS CO	ONE NATIONWIDE PLAZA	COLUMBUS	OH	43216	(614)-249-3004
A	NORTH CAROLINA FARM BU MUTUAL INS CO	5301 GLENWOOD AVE	RALEIGH	NC	27612	(919)-782-1705
B+	NORTH STAR MUTUAL INS CO	269 BARSTAD RD S	COTTONWOOD	MN	56229	(507)-423-6262
A-	OLD REPUBLIC GENERAL INS CORP	307 NORTH MICHIGAN AVENUE	CHICAGO	IL	60601	(312)-346-8100
A-	OLD REPUBLIC INS CO	414 W PITTSBURGH ST	GREENSBURG	PA	15601	(412)-834-5000
A-	OLD REPUBLIC SURETY CO	445 S MOORLAND RD SUITE 301	BROOKFIELD	WI	53005	(414)-797-2645
A-	OTSEGO MUTUAL FIRE INS CO	143 ARNOLD ROAD RD	BURLINGTON FLATS	NY	13315	(607)-965-8211
A-	OWNERS INS CO	2325 N COLE ST	LIMA	OH	45801	(517)-323-1200
B+	PACIFIC INDEMNITY CO	TWO PLAZA EAST SUITE 1450	MILWAUKEE	WI	53202	(908)-903-2000
B+	PEKIN INS CO	2505 COURT ST	PEKIN	IL	61558	(309)-346-1161
A	PIONEER STATE MUTUAL INS CO	1510 N ELMS RD	FLINT	MI	48532	(800)-837-7674
A-	PROPERTY-OWNERS INS CO	3950 W DELPHI PIKE	MARION	IN	46952	(517)-323-1200
A	PROTECTIVE INS CO	1099 N MERIDIAN ST	INDIANAPOLIS	IN	46204	(317)-636-9800
B+	SAFETY INS CO	20 CUSTOM HOUSE ST	BOSTON	MA	02110	(617)-951-0600
B+	SAMSUNG FIRE & MARINE INS CO LTD US	55 WATER ST	NEW YORK	NY	10041	(908)-903-2000
A	SENTRY INS A MUTUAL CO	1800 N POINT DR	STEVENS POINT	WI	54481	(715)-346-6000
B+	SOUTHERN FARM BUREAU CAS INS CO	1800 E COUNTY LINE RD	RIDGELAND	MS	39157	(601)-957-7777
B+	SOUTHERN-OWNERS INS CO	6101 ANACAPRI BLVD	LANSING	MI	48917	(517)-323-1200
A-	STATE FARM CTY MUTUAL INS CO OF TX	17301 PRESTON ROAD	DALLAS	TX	75379	(214)-732-5000
B+	STATE FARM MUTUAL AUTOMOBILE INS CO	ONE STATE FARM PLAZA	BLOOMINGTON	IL	61710	(309)-735-8480
A-	STATE VOLUNTEER MUTUAL INS CO	101 WESTPARK DR SUITE 300	BRENTWOOD	TN	37024	(615)-377-1999
A	TENNESSEE FARMERS ASR CO	147 BEAR CREEK PIKE	COLUMBIA	TN	38401	(615)-388-7872
A	TENNESSEE FARMERS MUTUAL INS CO	147 BEAR CREEK PIKE	COLUMBIA	TN	38401	(615)-388-7872
A	TOKIO MARINE & NICHIDO FIRE INS LTD	101 PARK AVE	NEW YORK	NY	10178	(212)-297-6600
A-	TRAVELERS INDEMNITY CO	ONE TOWER SQUARE	HARTFORD	CT	06183	(860)-277-0111
B+	TRUSTGARD INS CO	650 S FRONT ST	COLUMBUS	OH	43206	(614)-445-2754
B+	TUSCARORA WAYNE MUTUAL INS CO	601 STATE ST	WYALUSING	PA	18853	(570)-746-1515
B+	UNITED FARM FAMILY MUTUAL INS CO	225 SOUTH EAST ST	INDIANAPOLIS	IN	46202	(317)-692-7200
A+	UNITED SERVICES AUTOMOBILE ASN	9800 FREDERICKSBURG RD	SAN ANTONIO	TX	78288	(210)-498-2211
A+	USAA CASUALTY INS CO	9800 FREDERICKSBURG RD	SAN ANTONIO	TX	78288	(210)-498-2211
B+	USAA GENERAL INDEMNITY CO	9800 FREDERICKSBURG RD	SAN ANTONIO	TX	78288	(210)-498-2211
B+	WESCO-FINANCIAL INS CO	3024 HARNEY ST	OMAHA	NE	68131	(402)-536-3000
B+	WEST BEND MUTUAL INS CO	1900 S 18TH AVE	WEST BEND	WI	53095	(262)-334-5571
B+	WESTERN AGRICULTURAL INS CO	5400 UNIVERSITY AVE	WEST DES MOINES	IA	50266	(515)-225-5400
B+	WESTERN COMMUNITY INS CO	1001 N 7TH CENTENNIAL PLAZA	POCATELLO	ID	83201	(208)-232-7914
B+	WESTFIELD NATIONAL INS CO	9040 GREENWICH RD	WESTFIELD CENTER	OH	44251	(330)-887-0101

DOM. STATE	AUTO	HOME MULT. PERIL	FARM MULT. PERIL	COMM. MULT. PERIL	COMM. AUTO LIAB.	OTHER LIABILITY	MED MALPRAC.	WORK. COMP.	ACCID. & HEALTH	OTHER	INSURANCE COMPANY NAME
CA	84	15	0	0	0	1	0	0	0	1	INTERINS EXCH OF THE AUTOMOBILE CLUB
WI	0	0	0	19	0	0	0	0	0	81	JEWELERS MUTUAL INS CO
KY	58	22	11	6	1	1	0	0	0	1	KENTUCKY FARM BUREAU MUTUAL INS CO
CA	59	27	0	5	7	1	0	0	0	1	MERCURY CASUALTY CO
CA	100	0	0	0	0	0	0	0	0	0	MERCURY INS CO
MA	0	54	0	20	0	6	0	0	0	20	MERRIMACK MUTUAL FIRE INS CO
RI	51	41	0	0	0	2	0	0	1	4	METROPOLITAN PROPERTY & CAS INS CO
MN	0	0	0	0	0	2	98	0	0	0	MIDWEST MEDICAL INS CO
OH	41	21	0	8	10	10	0	5	0	6	MOTORISTS MUTUAL INS CO
WY	47	19	18	12	1	2	0	0	0	2	MOUNTAIN WEST FARM BU MUTUAL INS CO
AZ	0	0	0	0	0	0	100	0	0	0	MUTUAL INS CO OF AZ
WI	7	1	0	3	30	43	1	0	0	7	NATIONAL CASUALTY CO
CT	5	0	0	0	15	0	0	12	0	68	NATIONAL LIABILITY & FIRE INS CO
OH	37	44	0	5	1	2	0	1	0	10	NATIONWIDE MUTUAL FIRE INS CO
NC	49	27	3	2	4	2	0	3	0	10	NORTH CAROLINA FARM BU MUTUAL INS CO
MN	20	25	7	4	0	9	0	0	0	34	NORTH STAR MUTUAL INS CO
IL	1	0	0	0	9	32	0	57	0	0	OLD REPUBLIC GENERAL INS CORP
PA	1	0	0	0	4	15	0	16	5	58	OLD REPUBLIC INS CO
WI	0	0	0	0	0	0	0	0	0	100	OLD REPUBLIC SURETY CO
NY	0	81	0	0	0	2	0	0	0	18	OTSEGO MUTUAL FIRE INS CO
OH	34	19	0	22	8	3	0	10	0	4	OWNERS INS CO
WI	9	44	0	6	0	5	0	19	0	17	PACIFIC INDEMNITY CO
IL	13	13	0	29	12	5	0	25	0	3	PEKIN INS CO
MI	55	31	7	0	0	0	0	1	0	4	PIONEER STATE MUTUAL INS CO
IN	7	30	1	35	8	3	0	10	0	7	PROPERTY-OWNERS INS CO
IN	20	0	0	0	10	28	0	30	11	1	PROTECTIVE INS CO
MA	85	4	0	2	7	1	0	0	0	1	SAFETY INS CO
NY	1	0	0	3	3	0	0	0	0	93	SAMSUNG FIRE & MARINE INS CO LTD US
WI	11	7	0	2	9	7	0	48	1	14	SENTRY INS A MUTUAL CO
MS	94	0	0	0	2	3	0	0	0	1	SOUTHERN FARM BUREAU CAS INS CO
MI	56	4	0	15	4	17	0	2	0	3	SOUTHERN-OWNERS INS CO
TX	86	0	0	0	1	0	0	0	0	12	STATE FARM CTY MUTUAL INS CO OF TX
IL	95	0	0	0	1	0	0	0	4	0	STATE FARM MUTUAL AUTOMOBILE INS CO
TN	0	0	0	0	0	0	100	0	0	0	STATE VOLUNTEER MUTUAL INS CO
TN	100	0	0	0	0	0	0	0	0	0	TENNESSEE FARMERS ASR CO
TN	57	25	10	1	1	2	0	0	0	5	TENNESSEE FARMERS MUTUAL INS CO
NY	7	2	0	10	11	12	0	10	0	47	TOKIO MARINE & NICHIDO FIRE INS LTD
CT	7	4	2	16	7	18	0	26	0	21	TRAVELERS INDEMNITY CO
OH	72	22	0	0	1	1	0	1	0	3	TRUSTGARD INS CO
PA	0	34	9	32	0	4	0	0	0	21	TUSCARORA WAYNE MUTUAL INS CO
IN	49	22	12	5	1	1	0	2	0	7	UNITED FARM FAMILY MUTUAL INS CO
TX	63	30	0	0	0	2	0	0	0	5	UNITED SERVICES AUTOMOBILE ASN
TX	69	27	0	0	0	1	0	0	0	4	USAA CASUALTY INS CO
TX	68	6	0	0	0	0	0	0	0	25	USAA GENERAL INDEMNITY CO
NE (*)	0	0	0	0	0	0	0	0	0	0	WESCO-FINANCIAL INS CO
WI	20	9	0	4	8	18	0	27	0	14	WEST BEND MUTUAL INS CO
IA	5	0	4	0	1	0	0	1	0	89	WESTERN AGRICULTURAL INS CO
ID	17	0	0	58	17	3	0	0	0	5	WESTERN COMMUNITY INS CO
OH	55	34	0	0	0	4	0	3	0	4	WESTFIELD NATIONAL INS CO

(*) Denotes reinsurers, companies that do not sell to consumers

Section IV

TheStreet.com Recommended Companies by Type of Business

A compilation of those

U.S. Property and Casualty Insurers

receiving a TheStreet.com Financial Strength Rating

of A+, A, A- or B+.

Companies are ranked by Financial Strength Rating in each line of business where they have received more than $1 million in direct premiums.

Section IV Contents

This section is broken into six subsections, each presenting a list of the recommended carriers receiving at least $1 million in direct premiums from a particular line of business: Auto, Commercial Multiple Peril, Fire and Allied, Homeowners Multiple Peril, Medical Malpractice, and Workers' Compensation. Recommended companies are those insurers receiving a Financial Strength Rating of A+, A, A- or B+. If an insurer is not on this list, it should not be automatically assumed that the firm is weak. Indeed, there are many firms that have not achieved a B+ or better rating but are in relatively good condition with adequate resources to cover their risk during an average recession. Not being included in this list should not be construed as a recommendation to cancel policies.

Companies are ranked within each line of business by their Financial Strength Rating. However, companies with the same rating should be viewed as having the same relative financial strength regardless of their ranking in these tables. While the specific order in which they appear on the page is based upon differences in our underlying indexes, you can assume that companies with the same rating have differences that are only minor and relatively inconsequential.

The six lines of business covered in this section are defined as follows:

Auto: Coverage for auto physical damage and auto liability. Auto physical covers damage to the policyholder's own automobile. Auto liability covers against financial loss from lawsuits (and legal settlements) for auto-related bodily injuries or property damage caused by the insured.

Commercial Multiple Peril: Package policies for business and other commercial establishments providing a broad spectrum of property and liability coverages.

Fire & Allied: Coverage for losses caused by fire, lightning, sprinkler damage, windstorm, and water damage.

Homeowners Multiple Peril: Package policies for homeowners providing a broad spectrum of property and liability coverages.

Medical Malpractice: Errors and omissions liability coverages for persons engaged in the practice of medicine, surgery, dentistry, nursing, pharmacy, or other health care services. Also covers health care institutions.

Workers' Compensation: Liability coverage issued to employers which provides for the payment of medical care, certain disability income benefits and possible additional liability amounts to employees who are injured on the job.

Column definitions are as follows:

1. **Insurance Company Name** The legally-registered name, which can sometimes differ from the name that the company uses for advertising. An insurer's name can be very similar to the name of other companies which may not be on our Recommended List, so make sure you note the exact name before contacting your agent.

2. **Domicile State** The state which has primary regulatory responsibility for the company. It may differ from the location of the company's corporate headquarters. You do not have to be living in the domicile state to purchase insurance from this firm, provided it is licensed to do business in your state.

3. **Total Premiums** Total direct premiums received by the company during the year for all types of policies.

4. **Policy-Type Premium** Direct premiums received by the company for a specific type of insurance coverage, such as Auto Premiums. Companies that have less than $1,000,000 in this type of premium are not listed.

5. **Maximum Benefit** Conservative consumers may want to limit the size of their policy with this company to the amount shown. This figure is based on the view that a policy's maximum benefits per risk should not exceed 1% of the company's capital and surplus.

TheStreet.com Financial Strength Ratings are not deemed to be a recommendation concerning the purchase or sale of the securities of any insurance company that is publicly owned.

Auto

INSURANCE COMPANY NAME	DOMICILE STATE	TOTAL PREMIUM ($)	AUTO PREMIUM ($)	MAXIMUM BENEFIT ($)
Rating: A+				
DAIRYLAND INS CO	WI	315,387,000	315,387,000	5,000,000
HASTINGS MUTUAL INS CO	MI	291,534,000	98,184,000	3,000,000
INTERINS EXCH OF THE AUTOMOBILE CLUB	CA	2,164,224,000	1,815,459,000	30,000,000
UNITED SERVICES AUTOMOBILE ASN	TX	5,268,487,000	3,297,494,000	100,000,000
USAA CASUALTY INS CO	TX	3,138,694,000	2,153,257,000	30,000,000
Rating: A				
AUTO-OWNERS INS CO	MI	2,119,833,000	800,947,000	50,000,000
CHURCH MUTUAL INS CO	WI	568,993,000	48,335,000	3,000,000
COUNTRY MUTUAL INS CO	IL	1,146,917,000	424,689,000	10,000,000
FRANKENMUTH MUTUAL INS CO	MI	399,711,000	151,898,000	3,000,000
HOME-OWNERS INS CO	MI	878,858,000	460,508,000	4,000,000
KENTUCKY FARM BUREAU MUTUAL INS CO	KY	725,745,000	426,392,000	9,000,000
MOUNTAIN WEST FARM BU MUTUAL INS CO	WY	115,768,000	55,077,000	2,000,000
NORTH CAROLINA FARM BU MUTUAL INS CO	NC	817,890,000	428,292,000	9,000,000
PIONEER STATE MUTUAL INS CO	MI	146,493,000	81,202,000	2,000,000
PROTECTIVE INS CO	IN	151,242,000	45,527,000	3,000,000
SENTRY INS A MUTUAL CO	WI	452,884,000	90,801,000	30,000,000
TENNESSEE FARMERS ASR CO	TN	6,658,000	6,657,000	6,000,000
TENNESSEE FARMERS MUTUAL INS CO	TN	889,514,000	510,557,000	10,000,000
TOKIO MARINE & NICHIDO FIRE INS LTD	NY	454,246,000	80,708,000	6,000,000
Rating: A-				
BITUMINOUS CASUALTY CORP	IL	345,575,000	87,366,000	2,000,000
BITUMINOUS FIRE & MARINE INS CO	IL	38,521,000	4,623,000	1,000,000
CALIFORNIA STATE AUTO ASN INTER-INS	CA	1,801,987,000	1,349,259,000	30,000,000
CINCINNATI INS CO	OH	2,904,103,000	728,036,000	30,000,000
COOPERATIVA D SEGUROS MULTIPLES D PR	PR	180,839,000	119,763,000	2,000,000
FARM BUREAU MUTUAL INS CO	IA	787,823,000	383,958,000	6,000,000
FEDERATED MUTUAL INS CO	MN	976,597,000	162,240,000	20,000,000
GRANGE MUTUAL CAS CO	OH	704,217,000	405,516,000	7,000,000
GREAT WEST CASUALTY CO	NE	707,568,000	557,648,000	4,000,000
MERCURY CASUALTY CO	CA	756,465,000	504,302,000	10,000,000
MERCURY INS CO	CA	1,304,229,000	1,304,229,000	6,000,000
NATIONAL LIABILITY & FIRE INS CO	CT	331,485,000	66,485,000	5,000,000
OLD REPUBLIC GENERAL INS CORP	IL	257,086,000	26,912,000	2,000,000
OLD REPUBLIC INS CO	PA	1,125,723,000	50,050,000	8,000,000
OWNERS INS CO	OH	1,198,095,000	509,316,000	8,000,000
PROPERTY-OWNERS INS CO	IN	69,517,000	10,278,000	700,000
STATE FARM CTY MUTUAL INS CO OF TX	TX	279,463,000	244,824,000	400,000
TRAVELERS INDEMNITY CO	CT	1,635,818,000	227,337,000	80,000,000
Rating: B+				
ALLSTATE INS CO	IL	10,871,407,000	6,790,637,000	100,000,000
AMERICAN FAMILY HOME INS CO	FL	191,855,000	9,352,000	1,000,000
AMERICAN MERCURY INS CO	OK	116,545,000	59,489,000	1,000,000
AMERICAN MODERN HOME INS CO	OH	425,522,000	57,031,000	3,000,000

Auto (Continued)

INSURANCE COMPANY NAME	DOMICILE STATE	TOTAL PREMIUM ($)	AUTO PREMIUM ($)	MAXIMUM BENEFIT ($)
Rating: B+ (Continued)				
AMERICAN NATIONAL GENERAL INS CO	MO	24,363,000	18,269,000	700,000
AMERICAN NATIONAL PROPERTY & CAS CO	MO	663,397,000	312,712,000	4,000,000
AMERICAN STANDARD INS CO OF WI	WI	376,525,000	376,525,000	3,000,000
ARCH SPECIALTY INS CO	NE	470,878,000	24,979,000	3,000,000
CANAL INS CO	SC	196,538,000	163,869,000	5,000,000
CENTRAL MUTUAL INS CO	OH	525,862,000	199,468,000	5,000,000
CITATION INS CO	MA	116,191,000	12,288,000	1,000,000
COMMERCE INS CO	MA	1,345,190,000	1,234,415,000	10,000,000
CORNHUSKER CASUALTY CO	NE	43,608,000	23,212,000	6,000,000
COUNTRY CASUALTY INS CO	IL	52,383,000	29,549,000	600,000
CUMIS INS SOCIETY INC	IA	521,552,000	96,561,000	4,000,000
ERIE INS CO OF NY	NY	27,198,000	2,831,000	200,000
FARM BUREAU MUTUAL INS CO OF ID	ID	106,674,000	63,387,000	2,000,000
FARMERS AUTOMOBILE INS ASN	IL	208,013,000	134,148,000	4,000,000
FARMLAND MUTUAL INS CO	IA	74,882,000	15,597,000	1,000,000
FEDERAL INS CO	IN	5,888,123,000	256,912,000	100,000,000
FEDERATED SERVICE INS CO	MN	90,926,000	22,455,000	1,000,000
FOREMOST INS CO	MI	985,797,000	203,278,000	6,000,000
GEICO GENERAL INS CO	MD	5,035,415,000	5,035,415,000	900,000
GEICO INDEMNITY CO	MD	3,334,950,000	3,334,950,000	20,000,000
GOVERNMENT EMPLOYEES INS CO	MD	3,734,600,000	3,655,281,000	40,000,000
GREAT NORTHERN INS CO	IN	1,328,556,000	169,239,000	4,000,000
HARTFORD FIRE INS CO	CT	1,854,925,000	254,216,000	100,000,000
HARTFORD INS CO OF THE MIDWEST	IN	1,543,379,000	502,947,000	2,000,000
HARTFORD UNDERWRITERS INS CO	CT	1,534,320,000	745,803,000	6,000,000
METROPOLITAN PROPERTY & CAS INS CO	RI	1,155,035,000	593,319,000	20,000,000
MOTORISTS MUTUAL INS CO	OH	413,035,000	209,166,000	4,000,000
NATIONAL CASUALTY CO	WI	546,193,000	202,952,000	1,000,000
NATIONWIDE MUTUAL FIRE INS CO	OH	2,576,627,000	995,380,000	20,000,000
NORTH STAR MUTUAL INS CO	MN	175,720,000	35,906,000	2,000,000
PACIFIC INDEMNITY CO	WI	607,808,000	55,356,000	20,000,000
PEKIN INS CO	IL	203,919,000	50,268,000	800,000
SAFETY INS CO	MA	499,074,000	459,304,000	6,000,000
SOUTHERN FARM BUREAU CAS INS CO	MS	565,300,000	543,218,000	10,000,000
SOUTHERN-OWNERS INS CO	MI	143,108,000	85,627,000	1,000,000
STATE FARM MUTUAL AUTOMOBILE INS CO	IL	28,952,522,000	27,887,832,000	500,000,000
TRUSTGARD INS CO	OH	151,559,000	110,686,000	300,000
UNITED FARM FAMILY MUTUAL INS CO	IN	493,726,000	250,946,000	3,000,000
USAA GENERAL INDEMNITY CO	TX	438,217,000	299,511,000	1,000,000
WEST BEND MUTUAL INS CO	WI	668,505,000	187,814,000	4,000,000
WESTERN AGRICULTURAL INS CO	IA	365,387,000	21,052,000	500,000
WESTERN COMMUNITY INS CO	ID	33,085,000	11,316,000	200,000
WESTFIELD NATIONAL INS CO	OH	257,473,000	141,052,000	1,000,000

Commercial Multiple Peril

INSURANCE COMPANY NAME	DOMICILE STATE	TOTAL PREMIUM ($)	COMM. MULT. PERIL PREMIUM ($)	MAXIMUM BENEFIT ($)
Rating: A+				
HASTINGS MUTUAL INS CO	MI	291,534,000	55,189,000	3,000,000
INTERINS EXCH OF THE AUTOMOBILE CLUB	CA	2,164,224,000	12,532,000	30,000,000
UNITED SERVICES AUTOMOBILE ASN	TX	5,268,487,000	94,091,000	100,000,000
USAA CASUALTY INS CO	TX	3,138,694,000	27,436,000	30,000,000
Rating: A				
AUTO-OWNERS INS CO	MI	2,119,833,000	476,731,000	50,000,000
CHURCH MUTUAL INS CO	WI	568,993,000	434,956,000	3,000,000
COUNTRY MUTUAL INS CO	IL	1,146,917,000	81,842,000	10,000,000
FRANKENMUTH MUTUAL INS CO	MI	399,711,000	80,193,000	3,000,000
HOME-OWNERS INS CO	MI	878,858,000	76,329,000	4,000,000
KENTUCKY FARM BUREAU MUTUAL INS CO	KY	725,745,000	51,888,000	9,000,000
MERRIMACK MUTUAL FIRE INS CO	MA	286,580,000	73,374,000	5,000,000
MOUNTAIN WEST FARM BU MUTUAL INS CO	WY	115,768,000	16,031,000	2,000,000
NORTH CAROLINA FARM BU MUTUAL INS CO	NC	817,890,000	36,847,000	9,000,000
PIONEER STATE MUTUAL INS CO	MI	146,493,000	1,226,000	2,000,000
PROTECTIVE INS CO	IN	151,242,000	42,250,000	3,000,000
SENTRY INS A MUTUAL CO	WI	452,884,000	44,687,000	30,000,000
TENNESSEE FARMERS MUTUAL INS CO	TN	889,514,000	24,759,000	10,000,000
TOKIO MARINE & NICHIDO FIRE INS LTD	NY	454,246,000	102,490,000	6,000,000
Rating: A-				
BITUMINOUS CASUALTY CORP	IL	345,575,000	127,977,000	2,000,000
BITUMINOUS FIRE & MARINE INS CO	IL	38,521,000	7,592,000	1,000,000
CALIFORNIA STATE AUTO ASN INTER-INS	CA	1,801,987,000	12,577,000	30,000,000
CINCINNATI INS CO	OH	2,904,103,000	1,379,419,000	30,000,000
COOPERATIVA D SEGUROS MULTIPLES D PR	PR	180,839,000	24,869,000	2,000,000
FARM BUREAU MUTUAL INS CO	IA	787,823,000	55,471,000	6,000,000
FEDERATED MUTUAL INS CO	MN	976,597,000	227,557,000	20,000,000
GENERAL STAR NATIONAL INS CO	OH	49,280,000	43,959,000	2,000,000
GRANGE MUTUAL CAS CO	OH	704,217,000	105,131,000	7,000,000
GREAT WEST CASUALTY CO	NE	707,568,000	28,226,000	4,000,000
JEWELERS MUTUAL INS CO	WI	117,289,000	22,218,000	1,000,000
MERCURY CASUALTY CO	CA	756,465,000	42,252,000	10,000,000
NATIONAL LIABILITY & FIRE INS CO	CT	331,485,000	2,122,000	5,000,000
OLD REPUBLIC GENERAL INS CORP	IL	257,086,000	82,626,000	2,000,000
OLD REPUBLIC INS CO	PA	1,125,723,000	171,936,000	8,000,000
OWNERS INS CO	OH	1,198,095,000	290,579,000	8,000,000
PROPERTY-OWNERS INS CO	IN	69,517,000	25,868,000	700,000
TRAVELERS INDEMNITY CO	CT	1,635,818,000	553,928,000	80,000,000
Rating: B+				
ALLSTATE INS CO	IL	10,871,407,000	636,017,000	100,000,000
AMERICAN MERCURY INS CO	OK	116,545,000	8,292,000	1,000,000
AMERICAN MODERN HOME INS CO	OH	425,522,000	17,383,000	3,000,000
AMERICAN NATIONAL PROPERTY & CAS CO	MO	663,397,000	22,542,000	4,000,000

Commercial Multiple Peril (Continued)

INSURANCE COMPANY NAME	DOMICILE STATE	TOTAL PREMIUM ($)	COMM. MULT. PERIL PREMIUM ($)	MAXIMUM BENEFIT ($)
Rating: B+ (Continued)				
ARCH SPECIALTY INS CO	NE	470,878,000	201,111,000	3,000,000
BAY STATE INS CO	MA	22,958,000	1,903,000	2,000,000
CANAL INS CO	SC	196,538,000	1,207,000	5,000,000
CENTRAL MUTUAL INS CO	OH	525,862,000	126,286,000	5,000,000
CITATION INS CO	MA	116,191,000	2,566,000	1,000,000
COMMERCE INS CO	MA	1,345,190,000	21,285,000	10,000,000
COPIC INS CO	CO	107,468,000	2,929,000	1,000,000
CORNHUSKER CASUALTY CO	NE	43,608,000	4,739,000	6,000,000
COUNTRY CASUALTY INS CO	IL	52,383,000	8,118,000	600,000
CUMBERLAND MUTUAL FIRE INS CO	NJ	99,651,000	22,960,000	1,000,000
CUMIS INS SOCIETY INC	IA	521,552,000	179,385,000	4,000,000
FARM BUREAU MUTUAL INS CO OF ID	ID	106,674,000	2,596,000	2,000,000
FARMLAND MUTUAL INS CO	IA	74,882,000	40,447,000	1,000,000
FEDERAL INS CO	IN	5,888,123,000	3,077,114,000	100,000,000
FEDERATED SERVICE INS CO	MN	90,926,000	32,284,000	1,000,000
FOREMOST INS CO	MI	985,797,000	35,704,000	6,000,000
GOVERNMENT EMPLOYEES INS CO	MD	3,734,600,000	79,144,000	40,000,000
GREAT NORTHERN INS CO	IN	1,328,556,000	351,400,000	4,000,000
HARTFORD FIRE INS CO	CT	1,854,925,000	678,008,000	100,000,000
HARTFORD INS CO OF THE MIDWEST	IN	1,543,379,000	149,792,000	2,000,000
HARTFORD UNDERWRITERS INS CO	CT	1,534,320,000	83,174,000	6,000,000
INS CO OF GREATER NY	NY	48,526,000	48,722,000	500,000
METROPOLITAN PROPERTY & CAS INS CO	RI	1,155,035,000	26,847,000	20,000,000
MIDWEST MEDICAL INS CO	MN	134,078,000	3,049,000	1,000,000
MOTORISTS MUTUAL INS CO	OH	413,035,000	74,603,000	4,000,000
NATIONAL CASUALTY CO	WI	546,193,000	248,604,000	1,000,000
NATIONWIDE MUTUAL FIRE INS CO	OH	2,576,627,000	175,171,000	20,000,000
NORTH STAR MUTUAL INS CO	MN	175,720,000	23,038,000	2,000,000
PACIFIC INDEMNITY CO	WI	607,808,000	65,969,000	20,000,000
PEKIN INS CO	IL	203,919,000	70,731,000	800,000
SAFETY INS CO	MA	499,074,000	15,228,000	6,000,000
SOUTHERN FARM BUREAU CAS INS CO	MS	565,300,000	15,602,000	10,000,000
SOUTHERN-OWNERS INS CO	MI	143,108,000	45,302,000	1,000,000
STATE FARM MUTUAL AUTOMOBILE INS CO	IL	28,952,522,000	9,934,000	500,000,000
TRUSTGARD INS CO	OH	151,559,000	1,310,000	300,000
TUSCARORA WAYNE MUTUAL INS CO	PA	25,661,000	9,152,000	300,000
UNITED FARM FAMILY MUTUAL INS CO	IN	493,726,000	31,652,000	3,000,000
WEST BEND MUTUAL INS CO	WI	668,505,000	149,575,000	4,000,000
WESTERN AGRICULTURAL INS CO	IA	365,387,000	1,291,000	500,000
WESTERN COMMUNITY INS CO	ID	33,085,000	20,013,000	200,000
WESTFIELD NATIONAL INS CO	OH	257,473,000	9,430,000	1,000,000

Fire & Allied

INSURANCE COMPANY NAME	DOMICILE STATE	TOTAL PREMIUM ($)	FIRE & ALLIED PREMIUM ($)	MAXIMUM BENEFIT ($)
Rating: A+				
HASTINGS MUTUAL INS CO	MI	291,534,000	8,330,000	3,000,000
INTERINS EXCH OF THE AUTOMOBILE CLUB	CA	2,164,224,000	7,285,000	30,000,000
UNITED SERVICES AUTOMOBILE ASN	TX	5,268,487,000	166,118,000	100,000,000
USAA CASUALTY INS CO	TX	3,138,694,000	53,159,000	30,000,000
Rating: A				
AUTO-OWNERS INS CO	MI	2,119,833,000	264,431,000	50,000,000
CHURCH MUTUAL INS CO	WI	568,993,000	1,799,000	3,000,000
COUNTRY MUTUAL INS CO	IL	1,146,917,000	136,704,000	10,000,000
FRANKENMUTH MUTUAL INS CO	MI	399,711,000	2,884,000	3,000,000
HOME-OWNERS INS CO	MI	878,858,000	1,496,000	4,000,000
KENTUCKY FARM BUREAU MUTUAL INS CO	KY	725,745,000	5,748,000	9,000,000
MERRIMACK MUTUAL FIRE INS CO	MA	286,580,000	50,979,000	5,000,000
MOUNTAIN WEST FARM BU MUTUAL INS CO	WY	115,768,000	2,369,000	2,000,000
NORTH CAROLINA FARM BU MUTUAL INS CO	NC	817,890,000	68,673,000	9,000,000
PIONEER STATE MUTUAL INS CO	MI	146,493,000	3,514,000	2,000,000
SENTRY INS A MUTUAL CO	WI	452,884,000	35,899,000	30,000,000
TENNESSEE FARMERS MUTUAL INS CO	TN	889,514,000	41,243,000	10,000,000
TOKIO MARINE & NICHIDO FIRE INS LTD	NY	454,246,000	70,049,000	6,000,000
Rating: A-				
CALIFORNIA STATE AUTO ASN INTER-INS	CA	1,801,987,000	11,039,000	30,000,000
CINCINNATI INS CO	OH	2,904,103,000	117,042,000	30,000,000
COOPERATIVA D SEGUROS MULTIPLES D PR	PR	180,839,000	9,421,000	2,000,000
FEDERATED MUTUAL INS CO	MN	976,597,000	51,627,000	20,000,000
GRANGE MUTUAL CAS CO	OH	704,217,000	17,411,000	7,000,000
MERCURY CASUALTY CO	CA	756,465,000	8,709,000	10,000,000
NATIONAL LIABILITY & FIRE INS CO	CT	331,485,000	1,529,000	5,000,000
OTSEGO MUTUAL FIRE INS CO	NY	16,690,000	2,901,000	600,000
OWNERS INS CO	OH	1,198,095,000	6,094,000	8,000,000
TRAVELERS INDEMNITY CO	CT	1,635,818,000	258,591,000	80,000,000
Rating: B+				
ALLSTATE INS CO	IL	10,871,407,000	326,758,000	100,000,000
AMERICAN FAMILY HOME INS CO	FL	191,855,000	10,328,000	1,000,000
AMERICAN MODERN HOME INS CO	OH	425,522,000	167,101,000	3,000,000
AMERICAN NATIONAL PROPERTY & CAS CO	MO	663,397,000	46,784,000	4,000,000
AMICA LLOYDS OF TEXAS	TX	46,284,000	1,483,000	600,000
ARCH SPECIALTY INS CO	NE	470,878,000	133,668,000	3,000,000
CENTRAL MUTUAL INS CO	OH	525,862,000	19,367,000	5,000,000
COMMERCE INS CO	MA	1,345,190,000	9,882,000	10,000,000
CORNHUSKER CASUALTY CO	NE	43,608,000	1,384,000	6,000,000
CUMBERLAND MUTUAL FIRE INS CO	NJ	99,651,000	11,881,000	1,000,000
CUMIS INS SOCIETY INC	IA	521,552,000	72,209,000	4,000,000
FARM BUREAU MUTUAL INS CO OF ID	ID	106,674,000	2,734,000	2,000,000

Fire & Allied (Continued)

INSURANCE COMPANY NAME	DOMICILE STATE	TOTAL PREMIUM ($)	FIRE & ALLIED PREMIUM ($)	MAXIMUM BENEFIT ($)
Rating: B+ (Continued)				
FARMERS AUTOMOBILE INS ASN	IL	208,013,000	11,129,000	4,000,000
FEDERAL INS CO	IN	5,888,123,000	31,619,000	100,000,000
FEDERATED SERVICE INS CO	MN	90,926,000	8,918,000	1,000,000
FOREMOST INS CO	MI	985,797,000	184,631,000	6,000,000
GREAT NORTHERN INS CO	IN	1,328,556,000	10,578,000	4,000,000
HARTFORD FIRE INS CO	CT	1,854,925,000	19,625,000	100,000,000
HARTFORD INS CO OF THE MIDWEST	IN	1,543,379,000	225,038,000	2,000,000
HARTFORD UNDERWRITERS INS CO	CT	1,534,320,000	21,478,000	6,000,000
METROPOLITAN PROPERTY & CAS INS CO	RI	1,155,035,000	24,750,000	20,000,000
MOTORISTS MUTUAL INS CO	OH	413,035,000	5,028,000	4,000,000
NATIONAL CASUALTY CO	WI	546,193,000	13,406,000	1,000,000
NATIONWIDE MUTUAL FIRE INS CO	OH	2,576,627,000	207,917,000	20,000,000
NORTH STAR MUTUAL INS CO	MN	175,720,000	54,403,000	2,000,000
PACIFIC INDEMNITY CO	WI	607,808,000	4,559,000	20,000,000
PEKIN INS CO	IL	203,919,000	1,283,000	800,000
SAFETY INS CO	MA	499,074,000	2,710,000	6,000,000
SOUTHERN FARM BUREAU CAS INS CO	MS	565,300,000	6,481,000	10,000,000
TRUSTGARD INS CO	OH	151,559,000	2,471,000	300,000
TUSCARORA WAYNE MUTUAL INS CO	PA	25,661,000	4,654,000	300,000
UNITED FARM FAMILY MUTUAL INS CO	IN	493,726,000	32,915,000	3,000,000
USAA GENERAL INDEMNITY CO	TX	438,217,000	109,994,000	1,000,000
WEST BEND MUTUAL INS CO	WI	668,505,000	51,198,000	4,000,000
WESTERN AGRICULTURAL INS CO	IA	365,387,000	324,427,000	500,000
WESTFIELD NATIONAL INS CO	OH	257,473,000	1,625,000	1,000,000

Homeowners Multiple Peril

INSURANCE COMPANY NAME	DOMICILE STATE	TOTAL PREMIUM ($)	HOME OWNERS PREMIUM ($)	MAXIMUM BENEFIT ($)
Rating: A+				
HASTINGS MUTUAL INS CO	MI	291,534,000	48,223,000	3,000,000
INTERINS EXCH OF THE AUTOMOBILE CLUB	CA	2,164,224,000	321,679,000	30,000,000
UNITED SERVICES AUTOMOBILE ASN	TX	5,268,487,000	1,590,704,000	100,000,000
USAA CASUALTY INS CO	TX	3,138,694,000	834,463,000	30,000,000
Rating: A				
AUTO-OWNERS INS CO	MI	2,119,833,000	280,002,000	50,000,000
CHURCH MUTUAL INS CO	WI	568,993,000	4,042,000	3,000,000
COUNTRY MUTUAL INS CO	IL	1,146,917,000	352,012,000	10,000,000
FRANKENMUTH MUTUAL INS CO	MI	399,711,000	68,796,000	3,000,000
HOME-OWNERS INS CO	MI	878,858,000	300,138,000	4,000,000
KENTUCKY FARM BUREAU MUTUAL INS CO	KY	725,745,000	160,922,000	9,000,000
MERRIMACK MUTUAL FIRE INS CO	MA	286,580,000	156,019,000	5,000,000
MOUNTAIN WEST FARM BU MUTUAL INS CO	WY	115,768,000	21,896,000	2,000,000
NORTH CAROLINA FARM BU MUTUAL INS CO	NC	817,890,000	222,191,000	9,000,000
PIONEER STATE MUTUAL INS CO	MI	146,493,000	45,960,000	2,000,000
SENTRY INS A MUTUAL CO	WI	452,884,000	32,935,000	30,000,000
TENNESSEE FARMERS MUTUAL INS CO	TN	889,514,000	225,544,000	10,000,000
TOKIO MARINE & NICHIDO FIRE INS LTD	NY	454,246,000	10,538,000	6,000,000
Rating: A-				
CALIFORNIA STATE AUTO ASN INTER-INS	CA	1,801,987,000	418,616,000	30,000,000
CINCINNATI INS CO	OH	2,904,103,000	302,802,000	30,000,000
COOPERATIVA D SEGUROS MULTIPLES D PR	PR	180,839,000	7,826,000	2,000,000
FARM BUREAU MUTUAL INS CO	IA	787,823,000	155,712,000	6,000,000
FEDERATED MUTUAL INS CO	MN	976,597,000	1,772,000	20,000,000
GRANGE MUTUAL CAS CO	OH	704,217,000	136,919,000	7,000,000
MERCURY CASUALTY CO	CA	756,465,000	200,812,000	10,000,000
OTSEGO MUTUAL FIRE INS CO	NY	16,690,000	13,463,000	600,000
OWNERS INS CO	OH	1,198,095,000	223,247,000	8,000,000
PROPERTY-OWNERS INS CO	IN	69,517,000	20,612,000	700,000
TRAVELERS INDEMNITY CO	CT	1,635,818,000	62,818,000	80,000,000
Rating: B+				
ALLSTATE INS CO	IL	10,871,407,000	2,995,673,000	100,000,000
AMERICAN FAMILY HOME INS CO	FL	191,855,000	150,457,000	1,000,000
AMERICAN MERCURY INS CO	OK	116,545,000	18,372,000	1,000,000
AMERICAN MODERN HOME INS CO	OH	425,522,000	133,866,000	3,000,000
AMERICAN NATIONAL GENERAL INS CO	MO	24,363,000	5,906,000	700,000
AMERICAN NATIONAL PROPERTY & CAS CO	MO	663,397,000	144,781,000	4,000,000
AMICA LLOYDS OF TEXAS	TX	46,284,000	43,858,000	600,000
AUTO CLUB INDEMNITY CO	TX	32,588,000	31,676,000	30,000
BAY STATE INS CO	MA	22,958,000	20,264,000	2,000,000
CENTRAL MUTUAL INS CO	OH	525,862,000	107,187,000	5,000,000
CITATION INS CO	MA	116,191,000	97,416,000	1,000,000
COMMERCE INS CO	MA	1,345,190,000	77,711,000	10,000,000

Homeowners Multiple Peril (Continued)

INSURANCE COMPANY NAME	DOMICILE STATE	TOTAL PREMIUM ($)	HOME OWNERS PREMIUM ($)	MAXIMUM BENEFIT ($)
Rating: B+ (Continued)				
COUNTRY CASUALTY INS CO	IL	52,383,000	13,584,000	600,000
CUMBERLAND MUTUAL FIRE INS CO	NJ	99,651,000	60,054,000	1,000,000
CUMIS INS SOCIETY INC	IA	521,552,000	18,513,000	4,000,000
FARM BUREAU MUTUAL INS CO OF ID	ID	106,674,000	16,203,000	2,000,000
FARMERS AUTOMOBILE INS ASN	IL	208,013,000	60,120,000	4,000,000
FEDERAL INS CO	IN	5,888,123,000	460,858,000	100,000,000
FOREMOST INS CO	MI	985,797,000	510,215,000	6,000,000
GREAT NORTHERN INS CO	IN	1,328,556,000	563,400,000	4,000,000
HARTFORD FIRE INS CO	CT	1,854,925,000	29,791,000	100,000,000
HARTFORD INS CO OF THE MIDWEST	IN	1,543,379,000	250,638,000	2,000,000
HARTFORD UNDERWRITERS INS CO	CT	1,534,320,000	174,380,000	6,000,000
METROPOLITAN PROPERTY & CAS INS CO	RI	1,155,035,000	475,944,000	20,000,000
MOTORISTS MUTUAL INS CO	OH	413,035,000	86,895,000	4,000,000
NATIONAL CASUALTY CO	WI	546,193,000	5,544,000	1,000,000
NATIONWIDE MUTUAL FIRE INS CO	OH	2,576,627,000	1,129,786,000	20,000,000
NORTH STAR MUTUAL INS CO	MN	175,720,000	43,239,000	2,000,000
PACIFIC INDEMNITY CO	WI	607,808,000	269,724,000	20,000,000
PEKIN INS CO	IL	203,919,000	25,819,000	800,000
SAFETY INS CO	MA	499,074,000	21,064,000	6,000,000
SOUTHERN-OWNERS INS CO	MI	143,108,000	5,189,000	1,000,000
TRUSTGARD INS CO	OH	151,559,000	32,891,000	300,000
TUSCARORA WAYNE MUTUAL INS CO	PA	25,661,000	8,679,000	300,000
UNITED FARM FAMILY MUTUAL INS CO	IN	493,726,000	107,825,000	3,000,000
USAA GENERAL INDEMNITY CO	TX	438,217,000	26,796,000	1,000,000
WEST BEND MUTUAL INS CO	WI	668,505,000	58,014,000	4,000,000
WESTFIELD NATIONAL INS CO	OH	257,473,000	87,667,000	1,000,000

Medical Malpractice

INSURANCE COMPANY NAME	DOMICILE STATE	TOTAL PREMIUM ($)	MEDICAL MALPRACTICE PREMIUM ($)	MAXIMUM BENEFIT ($)
Rating: A				
CHURCH MUTUAL INS CO	WI	568,993,000	3,919,000	3,000,000
Rating: A-				
CINCINNATI INS CO	OH	2,904,103,000	40,096,000	30,000,000
GENERAL STAR NATIONAL INS CO	OH	49,280,000	4,272,000	2,000,000
MUTUAL INS CO OF AZ	AZ	160,939,000	160,939,000	3,000,000
STATE VOLUNTEER MUTUAL INS CO	TN	245,921,000	245,779,000	2,000,000
Rating: B+				
ARCH SPECIALTY INS CO	NE	470,878,000	66,679,000	3,000,000
COPIC INS CO	CO	107,468,000	100,611,000	1,000,000
MIDWEST MEDICAL INS CO	MN	134,078,000	131,029,000	1,000,000
NATIONAL CASUALTY CO	WI	546,193,000	3,346,000	1,000,000

Workers' Compensation

INSURANCE COMPANY NAME	DOMICILE STATE	TOTAL PREMIUM ($)	WORKERS' COMPENSATION PREMIUM ($)	MAXIMUM BENEFIT ($)
Rating: A+				
HASTINGS MUTUAL INS CO	MI	291,534,000	41,856,000	3,000,000
Rating: A				
AUTO-OWNERS INS CO	MI	2,119,833,000	202,567,000	50,000,000
CHURCH MUTUAL INS CO	WI	568,993,000	75,817,000	3,000,000
COUNTRY MUTUAL INS CO	IL	1,146,917,000	52,758,000	10,000,000
FRANKENMUTH MUTUAL INS CO	MI	399,711,000	78,060,000	3,000,000
HOME-OWNERS INS CO	MI	878,858,000	20,247,000	4,000,000
NORTH CAROLINA FARM BU MUTUAL INS CO	NC	817,890,000	24,888,000	9,000,000
PIONEER STATE MUTUAL INS CO	MI	146,493,000	1,201,000	2,000,000
PROTECTIVE INS CO	IN	151,242,000	45,553,000	3,000,000
SENTRY INS A MUTUAL CO	WI	452,884,000	216,373,000	30,000,000
TOKIO MARINE & NICHIDO FIRE INS LTD	NY	454,246,000	47,338,000	6,000,000
Rating: A-				
BITUMINOUS CASUALTY CORP	IL	345,575,000	100,206,000	2,000,000
BITUMINOUS FIRE & MARINE INS CO	IL	38,521,000	24,209,000	1,000,000
CINCINNATI INDEMNITY CO	OH	77,334,000	76,149,000	600,000
CINCINNATI INS CO	OH	2,904,103,000	138,316,000	30,000,000
FARM BUREAU MUTUAL INS CO	IA	787,823,000	28,369,000	6,000,000
FEDERATED MUTUAL INS CO	MN	976,597,000	147,319,000	20,000,000
GRANGE MUTUAL CAS CO	OH	704,217,000	10,733,000	7,000,000
GREAT WEST CASUALTY CO	NE	707,568,000	59,409,000	4,000,000
NATIONAL LIABILITY & FIRE INS CO	CT	331,485,000	38,407,000	5,000,000
OLD REPUBLIC GENERAL INS CORP	IL	257,086,000	146,809,000	2,000,000
OLD REPUBLIC INS CO	PA	1,125,723,000	176,459,000	8,000,000
OWNERS INS CO	OH	1,198,095,000	125,188,000	8,000,000
PROPERTY-OWNERS INS CO	IN	69,517,000	6,922,000	700,000
TRAVELERS INDEMNITY CO	CT	1,635,818,000	425,018,000	80,000,000
Rating: B+				
AMERICAN NATIONAL PROPERTY & CAS CO	MO	663,397,000	2,851,000	4,000,000
CANAL INS CO	SC	196,538,000	11,358,000	5,000,000
CENTRAL MUTUAL INS CO	OH	525,862,000	33,328,000	5,000,000
CORNHUSKER CASUALTY CO	NE	43,608,000	11,540,000	6,000,000
CUMIS INS SOCIETY INC	IA	521,552,000	4,765,000	4,000,000
ERIE INS CO OF NY	NY	27,198,000	24,367,000	200,000
FARMLAND MUTUAL INS CO	IA	74,882,000	16,331,000	1,000,000
FEDERAL INS CO	IN	5,888,123,000	480,845,000	100,000,000
FEDERATED SERVICE INS CO	MN	90,926,000	15,341,000	1,000,000
GREAT NORTHERN INS CO	IN	1,328,556,000	49,513,000	4,000,000
HARTFORD FIRE INS CO	CT	1,854,925,000	326,135,000	100,000,000
HARTFORD INS CO OF THE MIDWEST	IN	1,543,379,000	402,718,000	2,000,000
HARTFORD UNDERWRITERS INS CO	CT	1,534,320,000	492,484,000	6,000,000
MOTORISTS MUTUAL INS CO	OH	413,035,000	18,847,000	4,000,000
NATIONWIDE MUTUAL FIRE INS CO	OH	2,576,627,000	15,135,000	20,000,000
PACIFIC INDEMNITY CO	WI	607,808,000	113,603,000	20,000,000

Workers' Compensation (Continued)

INSURANCE COMPANY NAME	DOMICILE STATE	TOTAL PREMIUM ($)	WORKERS' COMPENSATION PREMIUM ($)	MAXIMUM BENEFIT ($)
Rating: B+ (Continued)				
PEKIN INS CO	IL	203,919,000	51,986,000	800,000
SOUTHERN-OWNERS INS CO	MI	143,108,000	2,650,000	1,000,000
TRUSTGARD INS CO	OH	151,559,000	1,989,000	300,000
UNITED FARM FAMILY MUTUAL INS CO	IN	493,726,000	11,904,000	3,000,000
WEST BEND MUTUAL INS CO	WI	668,505,000	178,675,000	4,000,000
WESTERN AGRICULTURAL INS CO	IA	365,387,000	5,136,000	500,000
WESTFIELD NATIONAL INS CO	OH	257,473,000	8,622,000	1,000,000

Section V

TheStreet.com Recommended Companies by State

A compilation of those

U.S. Property and Casualty Insurers

receiving a TheStreet.com Financial Strength Rating

of A+, A, A- or B+.

Companies are ranked by Financial Strength Rating in each state where they are licensed to do business.

Section V Contents

This section provides a list of the recommended carriers licensed to do business in each state. It contains all insurers receiving a Financial Strength Rating of A+, A, A- or B+. If an insurer is not on this list, it should not be automatically assumed that the firm is weak. Indeed, there are many firms that have not achieved a B+ or better rating but are in relatively good condition with adequate resources to cover their risk during an average recession. Not being included in this list should not be construed as a recommendation to cancel policies.

Companies are ranked within each state by their Financial Strength Rating. However, companies with the same rating should be viewed as having the same relative safety regardless of their ranking in this table. While the specific order in which they appear on the page is based upon differences in our underlying indexes, you can assume that companies with the same rating have differences that are only minor and relatively inconsequential.

1. **Insurance Company Name** — The legally-registered name, which can sometimes differ from the name that the company uses for advertising. An insurer's name can be very similar to the name of other companies which may not be on our Recommended List, so make sure you note the exact name before contacting your agent.

2. **Domicile State** — The state which has primary regulatory responsibility for the company. It may differ from the location of the company's corporate headquarters. You do not have to be living in the domicile state to purchase insurance from this firm, provided it is licensed to do business in your state.

3. **Total Assets** — All assets admitted by state insurance regulators in millions of dollars. This includes investments and current business assets such as receivables from agents and reinsurers.

TheStreet.com Financial Strength Ratings are not deemed to be a recommendation concerning the purchase or sale of the securities of any insurance company that is publicly owned.

Alabama

INSURANCE COMPANY NAME	DOM. STATE	TOTAL ASSETS ($MIL)
Rating: A+		
DAIRYLAND INS CO	WI	1,222.3
UNITED SERVICES AUTOMOBILE ASN	TX	19,904.8
USAA CASUALTY INS CO	TX	6,714.4
Rating: A		
AUTO-OWNERS INS CO	MI	8,899.8
CHURCH MUTUAL INS CO	WI	1,150.7
COUNTRY MUTUAL INS CO	IL	3,364.1
FRANKENMUTH MUTUAL INS CO	MI	955.3
HOME-OWNERS INS CO	MI	1,353.2
PROTECTIVE INS CO	IN	529.3
SENTRY INS A MUTUAL CO	WI	5,330.6
TOKIO MARINE & NICHIDO FIRE INS LTD	NY	1,706.6
Rating: A-		
BITUMINOUS CASUALTY CORP	IL	725.4
BITUMINOUS FIRE & MARINE INS CO	IL	463.7
CINCINNATI INDEMNITY CO	OH	87.6
CINCINNATI INS CO	OH	8,454.0
FEDERATED MUTUAL INS CO	MN	3,817.8
GENERAL STAR NATIONAL INS CO	OH	340.1
GRANGE MUTUAL CAS CO	OH	1,525.7
GREAT WEST CASUALTY CO	NE	1,460.5
JEWELERS MUTUAL INS CO	WI	186.8
NATIONAL LIABILITY & FIRE INS CO	CT	1,040.7
OLD REPUBLIC GENERAL INS CORP	IL	985.4
OLD REPUBLIC INS CO	PA	2,301.6
OLD REPUBLIC SURETY CO	WI	94.2
OWNERS INS CO	OH	2,535.6
PROPERTY-OWNERS INS CO	IN	147.1
STATE VOLUNTEER MUTUAL INS CO	TN	996.2
TRAVELERS INDEMNITY CO	CT	20,531.8
Rating: B+		
ALLSTATE INS CO	IL	39,333.3
AMERICAN FAMILY HOME INS CO	FL	443.6
AMERICAN MERCURY INS CO	OK	334.3
AMERICAN MODERN HOME INS CO	OH	888.8
AMERICAN NATIONAL GENERAL INS CO	MO	99.8
AMERICAN NATIONAL PROPERTY & CAS CO	MO	1,068.4
CANAL INS CO	SC	1,010.6
CENTRAL STATES INDEMNITY CO OF OMAHA	NE	209.1
COUNTRY CASUALTY INS CO	IL	75.7
CUMIS INS SOCIETY INC	IA	1,228.8
FARMLAND MUTUAL INS CO	IA	371.1
FEDERAL INS CO	IN	28,842.9
FEDERATED SERVICE INS CO	MN	358.9
FOREMOST INS CO	MI	2,024.3
GEICO GENERAL INS CO	MD	175.2
GEICO INDEMNITY CO	MD	5,117.3
GOVERNMENT EMPLOYEES INS CO	MD	12,473.2
GREAT NORTHERN INS CO	IN	1,518.9
HARTFORD FIRE INS CO	CT	23,864.9
HARTFORD INS CO OF THE MIDWEST	IN	359.6
HARTFORD UNDERWRITERS INS CO	CT	1,564.1
METROPOLITAN PROPERTY & CAS INS CO	RI	4,771.4

INSURANCE COMPANY NAME	DOM. STATE	TOTAL ASSETS ($MIL)
NATIONAL CASUALTY CO	WI	144.3
NATIONWIDE MUTUAL FIRE INS CO	OH	4,143.4
PACIFIC INDEMNITY CO	WI	5,651.8
STATE FARM MUTUAL AUTOMOBILE INS CO	IL	88,473.2
USAA GENERAL INDEMNITY CO	TX	452.4

Alaska

INSURANCE COMPANY NAME	DOM. STATE	TOTAL ASSETS ($MIL)
Rating: A+		
DAIRYLAND INS CO	WI	1,222.3
UNITED SERVICES AUTOMOBILE ASN	TX	19,904.8
USAA CASUALTY INS CO	TX	6,714.4
Rating: A		
CHURCH MUTUAL INS CO	WI	1,150.7
COUNTRY MUTUAL INS CO	IL	3,364.1
PROTECTIVE INS CO	IN	529.3
SENTRY INS A MUTUAL CO	WI	5,330.6
TOKIO MARINE & NICHIDO FIRE INS LTD	NY	1,706.6
Rating: A-		
BITUMINOUS CASUALTY CORP	IL	725.4
CINCINNATI INS CO	OH	8,454.0
GENERAL STAR NATIONAL INS CO	OH	340.1
GREAT WEST CASUALTY CO	NE	1,460.5
JEWELERS MUTUAL INS CO	WI	186.8
NATIONAL LIABILITY & FIRE INS CO	CT	1,040.7
OLD REPUBLIC GENERAL INS CORP	IL	985.4
OLD REPUBLIC INS CO	PA	2,301.6
TRAVELERS INDEMNITY CO	CT	20,531.8
Rating: B+		
ALLSTATE INS CO	IL	39,333.3
AMERICAN FAMILY HOME INS CO	FL	443.6
AMERICAN MERCURY INS CO	OK	334.3
AMERICAN MODERN HOME INS CO	OH	888.8
CENTRAL STATES INDEMNITY CO OF OMAHA	NE	209.1
CORNHUSKER CASUALTY CO	NE	533.2
COUNTRY CASUALTY INS CO	IL	75.7
CUMIS INS SOCIETY INC	IA	1,228.8
FEDERAL INS CO	IN	28,842.9
FOREMOST INS CO	MI	2,024.3
GEICO GENERAL INS CO	MD	175.2
GEICO INDEMNITY CO	MD	5,117.3
GOVERNMENT EMPLOYEES INS CO	MD	12,473.2
GREAT NORTHERN INS CO	IN	1,518.9
HARTFORD FIRE INS CO	CT	23,864.9
HARTFORD INS CO OF THE MIDWEST	IN	359.6
HARTFORD UNDERWRITERS INS CO	CT	1,564.1
NATIONAL CASUALTY CO	WI	144.3
NATIONWIDE MUTUAL FIRE INS CO	OH	4,143.4
PACIFIC INDEMNITY CO	WI	5,651.8
STATE FARM MUTUAL AUTOMOBILE INS CO	IL	88,473.2
USAA GENERAL INDEMNITY CO	TX	452.4

Arizona

INSURANCE COMPANY NAME	DOM. STATE	TOTAL ASSETS ($MIL)
Rating: A+		
DAIRYLAND INS CO	WI	1,222.3
UNITED SERVICES AUTOMOBILE ASN	TX	19,904.8
USAA CASUALTY INS CO	TX	6,714.4
Rating: A		
AUTO-OWNERS INS CO	MI	8,899.8
CHURCH MUTUAL INS CO	WI	1,150.7
COUNTRY MUTUAL INS CO	IL	3,364.1
FRANKENMUTH MUTUAL INS CO	MI	955.3
MOUNTAIN WEST FARM BU MUTUAL INS CO	WY	339.7
PROTECTIVE INS CO	IN	529.3
SENTRY INS A MUTUAL CO	WI	5,330.6
TOKIO MARINE & NICHIDO FIRE INS LTD	NY	1,706.6
Rating: A-		
BITUMINOUS CASUALTY CORP	IL	725.4
BITUMINOUS FIRE & MARINE INS CO	IL	463.7
CINCINNATI INDEMNITY CO	OH	87.6
CINCINNATI INS CO	OH	8,454.0
FARM BUREAU MUTUAL INS CO	IA	1,586.9
FEDERATED MUTUAL INS CO	MN	3,817.8
GENERAL STAR NATIONAL INS CO	OH	340.1
GREAT WEST CASUALTY CO	NE	1,460.5
JEWELERS MUTUAL INS CO	WI	186.8
MERCURY CASUALTY CO	CA	2,212.7
MUTUAL INS CO OF AZ	AZ	891.6
NATIONAL LIABILITY & FIRE INS CO	CT	1,040.7
OLD REPUBLIC GENERAL INS CORP	IL	985.4
OLD REPUBLIC INS CO	PA	2,301.6
OLD REPUBLIC SURETY CO	WI	94.2
OWNERS INS CO	OH	2,535.6
TRAVELERS INDEMNITY CO	CT	20,531.8
Rating: B+		
ALLSTATE INS CO	IL	39,333.3
AMERICAN FAMILY HOME INS CO	FL	443.6
AMERICAN MERCURY INS CO	OK	334.3
AMERICAN MODERN HOME INS CO	OH	888.8
AMERICAN NATIONAL GENERAL INS CO	MO	99.8
AMERICAN NATIONAL PROPERTY & CAS CO	MO	1,068.4
AMERICAN STANDARD INS CO OF WI	WI	394.2
CANAL INS CO	SC	1,010.6
CENTRAL MUTUAL INS CO	OH	1,238.6
CENTRAL STATES INDEMNITY CO OF OMAHA	NE	209.1
COPIC INS CO	CO	435.6
COUNTRY CASUALTY INS CO	IL	75.7
CUMIS INS SOCIETY INC	IA	1,228.8
FARMLAND MUTUAL INS CO	IA	371.1
FEDERAL INS CO	IN	28,842.9
FEDERATED SERVICE INS CO	MN	358.9
FOREMOST INS CO	MI	2,024.3
GEICO GENERAL INS CO	MD	175.2
GEICO INDEMNITY CO	MD	5,117.3
GOVERNMENT EMPLOYEES INS CO	MD	12,473.2
GREAT NORTHERN INS CO	IN	1,518.9
HARTFORD FIRE INS CO	CT	23,864.9
HARTFORD INS CO OF THE MIDWEST	IN	359.6
HARTFORD UNDERWRITERS INS CO	CT	1,564.1
METROPOLITAN PROPERTY & CAS INS CO	RI	4,771.4
NATIONAL CASUALTY CO	WI	144.3
NATIONWIDE MUTUAL FIRE INS CO	OH	4,143.4
PACIFIC INDEMNITY CO	WI	5,651.8
STATE FARM MUTUAL AUTOMOBILE INS CO	IL	88,473.2
USAA GENERAL INDEMNITY CO	TX	452.4
WESTERN AGRICULTURAL INS CO	IA	309.2
WESTFIELD NATIONAL INS CO	OH	437.0

Arkansas

INSURANCE COMPANY NAME	DOM. STATE	TOTAL ASSETS ($MIL)
Rating: A+		
DAIRYLAND INS CO	WI	1,222.3
UNITED SERVICES AUTOMOBILE ASN	TX	19,904.8
USAA CASUALTY INS CO	TX	6,714.4
Rating: A		
AUTO-OWNERS INS CO	MI	8,899.8
CHURCH MUTUAL INS CO	WI	1,150.7
COUNTRY MUTUAL INS CO	IL	3,364.1
FRANKENMUTH MUTUAL INS CO	MI	955.3
HOME-OWNERS INS CO	MI	1,353.2
PROTECTIVE INS CO	IN	529.3
SENTRY INS A MUTUAL CO	WI	5,330.6
TOKIO MARINE & NICHIDO FIRE INS LTD	NY	1,706.6
Rating: A-		
BITUMINOUS CASUALTY CORP	IL	725.4
BITUMINOUS FIRE & MARINE INS CO	IL	463.7
CINCINNATI INDEMNITY CO	OH	87.6
CINCINNATI INS CO	OH	8,454.0
FEDERATED MUTUAL INS CO	MN	3,817.8
GENERAL STAR NATIONAL INS CO	OH	340.1
GREAT WEST CASUALTY CO	NE	1,460.5
JEWELERS MUTUAL INS CO	WI	186.8
NATIONAL LIABILITY & FIRE INS CO	CT	1,040.7
OLD REPUBLIC GENERAL INS CORP	IL	985.4
OLD REPUBLIC INS CO	PA	2,301.6
OLD REPUBLIC SURETY CO	WI	94.2
OWNERS INS CO	OH	2,535.6
PROPERTY-OWNERS INS CO	IN	147.1
STATE VOLUNTEER MUTUAL INS CO	TN	996.2
TRAVELERS INDEMNITY CO	CT	20,531.8
Rating: B+		
ALLSTATE INS CO	IL	39,333.3
AMERICAN FAMILY HOME INS CO	FL	443.6
AMERICAN MERCURY INS CO	OK	334.3
AMERICAN MODERN HOME INS CO	OH	888.8
AMERICAN NATIONAL GENERAL INS CO	MO	99.8
AMERICAN NATIONAL PROPERTY & CAS CO	MO	1,068.4
CANAL INS CO	SC	1,010.6
CENTRAL STATES INDEMNITY CO OF OMAHA	NE	209.1
CORNHUSKER CASUALTY CO	NE	533.2
COUNTRY CASUALTY INS CO	IL	75.7
CUMIS INS SOCIETY INC	IA	1,228.8
FARMLAND MUTUAL INS CO	IA	371.1
FEDERAL INS CO	IN	28,842.9
FEDERATED SERVICE INS CO	MN	358.9
FOREMOST INS CO	MI	2,024.3
GEICO GENERAL INS CO	MD	175.2
GEICO INDEMNITY CO	MD	5,117.3
GOVERNMENT EMPLOYEES INS CO	MD	12,473.2
GREAT NORTHERN INS CO	IN	1,518.9
HARTFORD FIRE INS CO	CT	23,864.9
HARTFORD INS CO OF THE MIDWEST	IN	359.6
HARTFORD UNDERWRITERS INS CO	CT	1,564.1
METROPOLITAN PROPERTY & CAS INS CO	RI	4,771.4
NATIONAL CASUALTY CO	WI	144.3
NATIONWIDE MUTUAL FIRE INS CO	OH	4,143.4
PACIFIC INDEMNITY CO	WI	5,651.8
SOUTHERN FARM BUREAU CAS INS CO	MS	1,807.1
SOUTHERN-OWNERS INS CO	MI	377.7
STATE FARM MUTUAL AUTOMOBILE INS CO	IL	88,473.2
USAA GENERAL INDEMNITY CO	TX	452.4

California

INSURANCE COMPANY NAME	DOM. STATE	TOTAL ASSETS ($MIL)
Rating: A+		
INTERINS EXCH OF THE AUTOMOBILE CLUB	CA	5,434.9
UNITED SERVICES AUTOMOBILE ASN	TX	19,904.8
USAA CASUALTY INS CO	TX	6,714.4
Rating: A		
CHURCH MUTUAL INS CO	WI	1,150.7
PROTECTIVE INS CO	IN	529.3
SENTRY INS A MUTUAL CO	WI	5,330.6
TOKIO MARINE & NICHIDO FIRE INS LTD	NY	1,706.6
Rating: A-		
BITUMINOUS CASUALTY CORP	IL	725.4
BITUMINOUS FIRE & MARINE INS CO	IL	463.7
CALIFORNIA STATE AUTO ASN INTER-INS	CA	5,291.7
CINCINNATI INS CO	OH	8,454.0
FEDERATED MUTUAL INS CO	MN	3,817.8
GENERAL STAR NATIONAL INS CO	OH	340.1
GREAT WEST CASUALTY CO	NE	1,460.5
JEWELERS MUTUAL INS CO	WI	186.8
MERCURY CASUALTY CO	CA	2,212.7
MERCURY INS CO	CA	1,373.9
NATIONAL LIABILITY & FIRE INS CO	CT	1,040.7
OLD REPUBLIC GENERAL INS CORP	IL	985.4
OLD REPUBLIC INS CO	PA	2,301.6
OLD REPUBLIC SURETY CO	WI	94.2
TRAVELERS INDEMNITY CO	CT	20,531.8
Rating: B+		
ALLSTATE INS CO	IL	39,333.3
AMERICAN FAMILY HOME INS CO	FL	443.6
AMERICAN MERCURY INS CO	OK	334.3
AMERICAN MODERN HOME INS CO	OH	888.8
AMERICAN NATIONAL GENERAL INS CO	MO	99.8
AMERICAN NATIONAL PROPERTY & CAS CO	MO	1,068.4
CANAL INS CO	SC	1,010.6
CENTRAL MUTUAL INS CO	OH	1,238.6
CENTRAL STATES INDEMNITY CO OF OMAHA	NE	209.1
CORNHUSKER CASUALTY CO	NE	533.2
CUMIS INS SOCIETY INC	IA	1,228.8
FARMLAND MUTUAL INS CO	IA	371.1
FEDERAL INS CO	IN	28,842.9
FEDERATED SERVICE INS CO	MN	358.9
FOREMOST INS CO	MI	2,024.3
GEICO GENERAL INS CO	MD	175.2
GEICO INDEMNITY CO	MD	5,117.3
GOVERNMENT EMPLOYEES INS CO	MD	12,473.2
GREAT NORTHERN INS CO	IN	1,518.9
HARTFORD FIRE INS CO	CT	23,864.9
HARTFORD INS CO OF THE MIDWEST	IN	359.6
HARTFORD UNDERWRITERS INS CO	CT	1,564.1
NATIONAL CASUALTY CO	WI	144.3
NATIONWIDE MUTUAL FIRE INS CO	OH	4,143.4
PACIFIC INDEMNITY CO	WI	5,651.8
SAMSUNG FIRE & MARINE INS CO LTD US	NY	69.7
STATE FARM MUTUAL AUTOMOBILE INS CO	IL	88,473.2
USAA GENERAL INDEMNITY CO	TX	452.4
WESTFIELD NATIONAL INS CO	OH	437.0

Colorado

INSURANCE COMPANY NAME	DOM. STATE	TOTAL ASSETS ($MIL)
Rating: A+		
DAIRYLAND INS CO	WI	1,222.3
UNITED SERVICES AUTOMOBILE ASN	TX	19,904.8
USAA CASUALTY INS CO	TX	6,714.4
Rating: A		
AUTO-OWNERS INS CO	MI	8,899.8
CHURCH MUTUAL INS CO	WI	1,150.7
COUNTRY MUTUAL INS CO	IL	3,364.1
FRANKENMUTH MUTUAL INS CO	MI	955.3
HOME-OWNERS INS CO	MI	1,353.2
PROTECTIVE INS CO	IN	529.3
SENTRY INS A MUTUAL CO	WI	5,330.6
TOKIO MARINE & NICHIDO FIRE INS LTD	NY	1,706.6
Rating: A-		
BITUMINOUS CASUALTY CORP	IL	725.4
BITUMINOUS FIRE & MARINE INS CO	IL	463.7
CINCINNATI INS CO	OH	8,454.0
FEDERATED MUTUAL INS CO	MN	3,817.8
GENERAL STAR NATIONAL INS CO	OH	340.1
GREAT WEST CASUALTY CO	NE	1,460.5
JEWELERS MUTUAL INS CO	WI	186.8
MUTUAL INS CO OF AZ	AZ	891.6
NATIONAL LIABILITY & FIRE INS CO	CT	1,040.7
OLD REPUBLIC GENERAL INS CORP	IL	985.4
OLD REPUBLIC INS CO	PA	2,301.6
OLD REPUBLIC SURETY CO	WI	94.2
OWNERS INS CO	OH	2,535.6
TRAVELERS INDEMNITY CO	CT	20,531.8
Rating: B+		
ALLSTATE INS CO	IL	39,333.3
AMERICAN FAMILY HOME INS CO	FL	443.6
AMERICAN MERCURY INS CO	OK	334.3
AMERICAN MODERN HOME INS CO	OH	888.8
AMERICAN NATIONAL GENERAL INS CO	MO	99.8
AMERICAN NATIONAL PROPERTY & CAS CO	MO	1,068.4
AMERICAN STANDARD INS CO OF WI	WI	394.2
CANAL INS CO	SC	1,010.6
CENTRAL MUTUAL INS CO	OH	1,238.6
CENTRAL STATES INDEMNITY CO OF OMAHA	NE	209.1
COPIC INS CO	CO	435.6
CORNHUSKER CASUALTY CO	NE	533.2
COUNTRY CASUALTY INS CO	IL	75.7
CUMIS INS SOCIETY INC	IA	1,228.8
FARMLAND MUTUAL INS CO	IA	371.1
FEDERAL INS CO	IN	28,842.9
FEDERATED SERVICE INS CO	MN	358.9
FOREMOST INS CO	MI	2,024.3
GEICO GENERAL INS CO	MD	175.2
GEICO INDEMNITY CO	MD	5,117.3
GOVERNMENT EMPLOYEES INS CO	MD	12,473.2
GREAT NORTHERN INS CO	IN	1,518.9
HARTFORD FIRE INS CO	CT	23,864.9
HARTFORD INS CO OF THE MIDWEST	IN	359.6
HARTFORD UNDERWRITERS INS CO	CT	1,564.1
METROPOLITAN PROPERTY & CAS INS CO	RI	4,771.4
NATIONAL CASUALTY CO	WI	144.3
NATIONWIDE MUTUAL FIRE INS CO	OH	4,143.4
PACIFIC INDEMNITY CO	WI	5,651.8
SOUTHERN FARM BUREAU CAS INS CO	MS	1,807.1
STATE FARM MUTUAL AUTOMOBILE INS CO	IL	88,473.2
TRUSTGARD INS CO	OH	66.4
USAA GENERAL INDEMNITY CO	TX	452.4
WESTERN AGRICULTURAL INS CO	IA	309.2
WESTFIELD NATIONAL INS CO	OH	437.0

Connecticut

INSURANCE COMPANY NAME	DOM. STATE	TOTAL ASSETS ($MIL)
Rating: A+		
DAIRYLAND INS CO	WI	1,222.3
UNITED SERVICES AUTOMOBILE ASN	TX	19,904.8
USAA CASUALTY INS CO	TX	6,714.4
Rating: A		
CHURCH MUTUAL INS CO	WI	1,150.7
COUNTRY MUTUAL INS CO	IL	3,364.1
FRANKENMUTH MUTUAL INS CO	MI	955.3
MERRIMACK MUTUAL FIRE INS CO	MA	883.0
PROTECTIVE INS CO	IN	529.3
SENTRY INS A MUTUAL CO	WI	5,330.6
TOKIO MARINE & NICHIDO FIRE INS LTD	NY	1,706.6
Rating: A-		
BITUMINOUS CASUALTY CORP	IL	725.4
CINCINNATI INS CO	OH	8,454.0
FEDERATED MUTUAL INS CO	MN	3,817.8
GREAT WEST CASUALTY CO	NE	1,460.5
JEWELERS MUTUAL INS CO	WI	186.8
NATIONAL LIABILITY & FIRE INS CO	CT	1,040.7
OLD REPUBLIC GENERAL INS CORP	IL	985.4
OLD REPUBLIC INS CO	PA	2,301.6
TRAVELERS INDEMNITY CO	CT	20,531.8
Rating: B+		
ALLSTATE INS CO	IL	39,333.3
AMERICAN FAMILY HOME INS CO	FL	443.6
AMERICAN MODERN HOME INS CO	OH	888.8
AMERICAN NATIONAL GENERAL INS CO	MO	99.8
BAY STATE INS CO	MA	285.6
CANAL INS CO	SC	1,010.6
CENTRAL MUTUAL INS CO	OH	1,238.6
CENTRAL STATES INDEMNITY CO OF OMAHA	NE	209.1
COMMERCE INS CO	MA	2,513.5
COUNTRY CASUALTY INS CO	IL	75.7
CUMIS INS SOCIETY INC	IA	1,228.8
FEDERAL INS CO	IN	28,842.9
FEDERATED SERVICE INS CO	MN	358.9
FOREMOST INS CO	MI	2,024.3
GEICO GENERAL INS CO	MD	175.2
GEICO INDEMNITY CO	MD	5,117.3
GOVERNMENT EMPLOYEES INS CO	MD	12,473.2
GREAT NORTHERN INS CO	IN	1,518.9
HARTFORD FIRE INS CO	CT	23,864.9
HARTFORD INS CO OF THE MIDWEST	IN	359.6
HARTFORD UNDERWRITERS INS CO	CT	1,564.1
INS CO OF GREATER NY	NY	101.2
METROPOLITAN PROPERTY & CAS INS CO	RI	4,771.4
NATIONAL CASUALTY CO	WI	144.3
NATIONWIDE MUTUAL FIRE INS CO	OH	4,143.4
PACIFIC INDEMNITY CO	WI	5,651.8
STATE FARM MUTUAL AUTOMOBILE INS CO	IL	88,473.2
USAA GENERAL INDEMNITY CO	TX	452.4

Delaware

INSURANCE COMPANY NAME	DOM. STATE	TOTAL ASSETS ($MIL)
Rating: A+		
DAIRYLAND INS CO	WI	1,222.3
UNITED SERVICES AUTOMOBILE ASN	TX	19,904.8
USAA CASUALTY INS CO	TX	6,714.4
Rating: A		
CHURCH MUTUAL INS CO	WI	1,150.7
COUNTRY MUTUAL INS CO	IL	3,364.1
FRANKENMUTH MUTUAL INS CO	MI	955.3
PROTECTIVE INS CO	IN	529.3
SENTRY INS A MUTUAL CO	WI	5,330.6
TOKIO MARINE & NICHIDO FIRE INS LTD	NY	1,706.6
Rating: A-		
BITUMINOUS CASUALTY CORP	IL	725.4
BITUMINOUS FIRE & MARINE INS CO	IL	463.7
CINCINNATI INDEMNITY CO	OH	87.6
CINCINNATI INS CO	OH	8,454.0
FEDERATED MUTUAL INS CO	MN	3,817.8
GENERAL STAR NATIONAL INS CO	OH	340.1
GREAT WEST CASUALTY CO	NE	1,460.5
JEWELERS MUTUAL INS CO	WI	186.8
NATIONAL LIABILITY & FIRE INS CO	CT	1,040.7
OLD REPUBLIC GENERAL INS CORP	IL	985.4
OLD REPUBLIC INS CO	PA	2,301.6
TRAVELERS INDEMNITY CO	CT	20,531.8
Rating: B+		
ALLSTATE INS CO	IL	39,333.3
AMERICAN FAMILY HOME INS CO	FL	443.6
AMERICAN MODERN HOME INS CO	OH	888.8
AMERICAN NATIONAL GENERAL INS CO	MO	99.8
AMERICAN NATIONAL PROPERTY & CAS CO	MO	1,068.4
CANAL INS CO	SC	1,010.6
CENTRAL MUTUAL INS CO	OH	1,238.6
CENTRAL STATES INDEMNITY CO OF OMAHA	NE	209.1
COUNTRY CASUALTY INS CO	IL	75.7
CUMBERLAND MUTUAL FIRE INS CO	NJ	245.0
CUMIS INS SOCIETY INC	IA	1,228.8
FARMLAND MUTUAL INS CO	IA	371.1
FEDERAL INS CO	IN	28,842.9
FEDERATED SERVICE INS CO	MN	358.9
FOREMOST INS CO	MI	2,024.3
GEICO GENERAL INS CO	MD	175.2
GEICO INDEMNITY CO	MD	5,117.3
GOVERNMENT EMPLOYEES INS CO	MD	12,473.2
GREAT NORTHERN INS CO	IN	1,518.9
HARTFORD FIRE INS CO	CT	23,864.9
HARTFORD INS CO OF THE MIDWEST	IN	359.6
HARTFORD UNDERWRITERS INS CO	CT	1,564.1
INS CO OF GREATER NY	NY	101.2
METROPOLITAN PROPERTY & CAS INS CO	RI	4,771.4
NATIONAL CASUALTY CO	WI	144.3
NATIONWIDE MUTUAL FIRE INS CO	OH	4,143.4
PACIFIC INDEMNITY CO	WI	5,651.8
STATE FARM MUTUAL AUTOMOBILE INS CO	IL	88,473.2
USAA GENERAL INDEMNITY CO	TX	452.4

District Of Columbia

INSURANCE COMPANY NAME	DOM. STATE	TOTAL ASSETS ($MIL)
Rating: A+		
UNITED SERVICES AUTOMOBILE ASN	TX	19,904.8
USAA CASUALTY INS CO	TX	6,714.4
Rating: A		
CHURCH MUTUAL INS CO	WI	1,150.7
PROTECTIVE INS CO	IN	529.3
SENTRY INS A MUTUAL CO	WI	5,330.6
TOKIO MARINE & NICHIDO FIRE INS LTD	NY	1,706.6
Rating: A-		
BITUMINOUS CASUALTY CORP	IL	725.4
BITUMINOUS FIRE & MARINE INS CO	IL	463.7
CINCINNATI INS CO	OH	8,454.0
FEDERATED MUTUAL INS CO	MN	3,817.8
GENERAL STAR NATIONAL INS CO	OH	340.1
GREAT WEST CASUALTY CO	NE	1,460.5
NATIONAL LIABILITY & FIRE INS CO	CT	1,040.7
OLD REPUBLIC GENERAL INS CORP	IL	985.4
OLD REPUBLIC INS CO	PA	2,301.6
OLD REPUBLIC SURETY CO	WI	94.2
TRAVELERS INDEMNITY CO	CT	20,531.8
Rating: B+		
ALLSTATE INS CO	IL	39,333.3
AMERICAN FAMILY HOME INS CO	FL	443.6
AMERICAN MODERN HOME INS CO	OH	888.8
AMERICAN NATIONAL PROPERTY & CAS CO	MO	1,068.4
CANAL INS CO	SC	1,010.6
CENTRAL STATES INDEMNITY CO OF OMAHA	NE	209.1
CUMIS INS SOCIETY INC	IA	1,228.8
FARMLAND MUTUAL INS CO	IA	371.1
FEDERAL INS CO	IN	28,842.9
FEDERATED SERVICE INS CO	MN	358.9
FOREMOST INS CO	MI	2,024.3
GEICO GENERAL INS CO	MD	175.2
GEICO INDEMNITY CO	MD	5,117.3
GOVERNMENT EMPLOYEES INS CO	MD	12,473.2
GREAT NORTHERN INS CO	IN	1,518.9
HARTFORD FIRE INS CO	CT	23,864.9
HARTFORD INS CO OF THE MIDWEST	IN	359.6
HARTFORD UNDERWRITERS INS CO	CT	1,564.1
METROPOLITAN PROPERTY & CAS INS CO	RI	4,771.4
NATIONAL CASUALTY CO	WI	144.3
NATIONWIDE MUTUAL FIRE INS CO	OH	4,143.4
PACIFIC INDEMNITY CO	WI	5,651.8
STATE FARM MUTUAL AUTOMOBILE INS CO	IL	88,473.2
USAA GENERAL INDEMNITY CO	TX	452.4

Florida

INSURANCE COMPANY NAME	DOM. STATE	TOTAL ASSETS ($MIL)
Rating: A+		
DAIRYLAND INS CO	WI	1,222.3
UNITED SERVICES AUTOMOBILE ASN	TX	19,904.8
USAA CASUALTY INS CO	TX	6,714.4
Rating: A		
AUTO-OWNERS INS CO	MI	8,899.8
CHURCH MUTUAL INS CO	WI	1,150.7
COUNTRY MUTUAL INS CO	IL	3,364.1
FRANKENMUTH MUTUAL INS CO	MI	955.3
PROTECTIVE INS CO	IN	529.3
SENTRY INS A MUTUAL CO	WI	5,330.6
TOKIO MARINE & NICHIDO FIRE INS LTD	NY	1,706.6
Rating: A-		
BITUMINOUS CASUALTY CORP	IL	725.4
BITUMINOUS FIRE & MARINE INS CO	IL	463.7
CINCINNATI INDEMNITY CO	OH	87.6
CINCINNATI INS CO	OH	8,454.0
COOPERATIVA D SEGUROS MULTIPLES D PR	PR	455.9
FEDERATED MUTUAL INS CO	MN	3,817.8
GENERAL STAR NATIONAL INS CO	OH	340.1
GREAT WEST CASUALTY CO	NE	1,460.5
JEWELERS MUTUAL INS CO	WI	186.8
MERCURY CASUALTY CO	CA	2,212.7
NATIONAL LIABILITY & FIRE INS CO	CT	1,040.7
OLD REPUBLIC GENERAL INS CORP	IL	985.4
OLD REPUBLIC INS CO	PA	2,301.6
OLD REPUBLIC SURETY CO	WI	94.2
OWNERS INS CO	OH	2,535.6
TRAVELERS INDEMNITY CO	CT	20,531.8
Rating: B+		
ALLSTATE INS CO	IL	39,333.3
AMERICAN FAMILY HOME INS CO	FL	443.6
AMERICAN MERCURY INS CO	OK	334.3
AMERICAN MODERN HOME INS CO	OH	888.8
AMERICAN NATIONAL GENERAL INS CO	MO	99.8
AMERICAN NATIONAL PROPERTY & CAS CO	MO	1,068.4
CANAL INS CO	SC	1,010.6
CENTRAL STATES INDEMNITY CO OF OMAHA	NE	209.1
COUNTRY CASUALTY INS CO	IL	75.7
CUMIS INS SOCIETY INC	IA	1,228.8
FARMLAND MUTUAL INS CO	IA	371.1
FEDERAL INS CO	IN	28,842.9
FEDERATED SERVICE INS CO	MN	358.9
FOREMOST INS CO	MI	2,024.3
GEICO GENERAL INS CO	MD	175.2
GEICO INDEMNITY CO	MD	5,117.3
GOVERNMENT EMPLOYEES INS CO	MD	12,473.2
GREAT NORTHERN INS CO	IN	1,518.9
HARTFORD FIRE INS CO	CT	23,864.9
HARTFORD INS CO OF THE MIDWEST	IN	359.6
HARTFORD UNDERWRITERS INS CO	CT	1,564.1
METROPOLITAN PROPERTY & CAS INS CO	RI	4,771.4
NATIONAL CASUALTY CO	WI	144.3
NATIONWIDE MUTUAL FIRE INS CO	OH	4,143.4
PACIFIC INDEMNITY CO	WI	5,651.8
SOUTHERN FARM BUREAU CAS INS CO	MS	1,807.1
SOUTHERN-OWNERS INS CO	MI	377.7
STATE FARM MUTUAL AUTOMOBILE INS CO	IL	88,473.2
USAA GENERAL INDEMNITY CO	TX	452.4
WESTFIELD NATIONAL INS CO	OH	437.0

Georgia

INSURANCE COMPANY NAME	DOM. STATE	TOTAL ASSETS ($MIL)
Rating: A+		
DAIRYLAND INS CO	WI	1,222.3
UNITED SERVICES AUTOMOBILE ASN	TX	19,904.8
USAA CASUALTY INS CO	TX	6,714.4
Rating: A		
AUTO-OWNERS INS CO	MI	8,899.8
CHURCH MUTUAL INS CO	WI	1,150.7
COUNTRY MUTUAL INS CO	IL	3,364.1
FRANKENMUTH MUTUAL INS CO	MI	955.3
PROTECTIVE INS CO	IN	529.3
SENTRY INS A MUTUAL CO	WI	5,330.6
TOKIO MARINE & NICHIDO FIRE INS LTD	NY	1,706.6
Rating: A-		
BITUMINOUS CASUALTY CORP	IL	725.4
BITUMINOUS FIRE & MARINE INS CO	IL	463.7
CINCINNATI INDEMNITY CO	OH	87.6
CINCINNATI INS CO	OH	8,454.0
FEDERATED MUTUAL INS CO	MN	3,817.8
GENERAL STAR NATIONAL INS CO	OH	340.1
GRANGE MUTUAL CAS CO	OH	1,525.7
GREAT WEST CASUALTY CO	NE	1,460.5
JEWELERS MUTUAL INS CO	WI	186.8
NATIONAL LIABILITY & FIRE INS CO	CT	1,040.7
OLD REPUBLIC GENERAL INS CORP	IL	985.4
OLD REPUBLIC INS CO	PA	2,301.6
OLD REPUBLIC SURETY CO	WI	94.2
OWNERS INS CO	OH	2,535.6
STATE VOLUNTEER MUTUAL INS CO	TN	996.2
TRAVELERS INDEMNITY CO	CT	20,531.8
Rating: B+		
ALLSTATE INS CO	IL	39,333.3
AMERICAN FAMILY HOME INS CO	FL	443.6
AMERICAN MERCURY INS CO	OK	334.3
AMERICAN MODERN HOME INS CO	OH	888.8
AMERICAN NATIONAL GENERAL INS CO	MO	99.8
AMERICAN NATIONAL PROPERTY & CAS CO	MO	1,068.4
CANAL INS CO	SC	1,010.6
CENTRAL MUTUAL INS CO	OH	1,238.6
CENTRAL STATES INDEMNITY CO OF OMAHA	NE	209.1
COUNTRY CASUALTY INS CO	IL	75.7
CUMIS INS SOCIETY INC	IA	1,228.8
FARMLAND MUTUAL INS CO	IA	371.1
FEDERAL INS CO	IN	28,842.9
FEDERATED SERVICE INS CO	MN	358.9
FOREMOST INS CO	MI	2,024.3
GEICO GENERAL INS CO	MD	175.2
GEICO INDEMNITY CO	MD	5,117.3
GOVERNMENT EMPLOYEES INS CO	MD	12,473.2
GREAT NORTHERN INS CO	IN	1,518.9
HARTFORD FIRE INS CO	CT	23,864.9
HARTFORD INS CO OF THE MIDWEST	IN	359.6
HARTFORD UNDERWRITERS INS CO	CT	1,564.1
METROPOLITAN PROPERTY & CAS INS CO	RI	4,771.4
NATIONAL CASUALTY CO	WI	144.3
NATIONWIDE MUTUAL FIRE INS CO	OH	4,143.4
PACIFIC INDEMNITY CO	WI	5,651.8
STATE FARM MUTUAL AUTOMOBILE INS CO	IL	88,473.2
TRUSTGARD INS CO	OH	66.4
USAA GENERAL INDEMNITY CO	TX	452.4
WESTFIELD NATIONAL INS CO	OH	437.0

Hawaii

INSURANCE COMPANY NAME	DOM. STATE	TOTAL ASSETS ($MIL)
Rating: A+		
INTERINS EXCH OF THE AUTOMOBILE CLUB	CA	5,434.9
UNITED SERVICES AUTOMOBILE ASN	TX	19,904.8
USAA CASUALTY INS CO	TX	6,714.4
Rating: A		
CHURCH MUTUAL INS CO	WI	1,150.7
PROTECTIVE INS CO	IN	529.3
SENTRY INS A MUTUAL CO	WI	5,330.6
TOKIO MARINE & NICHIDO FIRE INS LTD	NY	1,706.6
Rating: A-		
CINCINNATI INS CO	OH	8,454.0
GENERAL STAR NATIONAL INS CO	OH	340.1
JEWELERS MUTUAL INS CO	WI	186.8
NATIONAL LIABILITY & FIRE INS CO	CT	1,040.7
OLD REPUBLIC INS CO	PA	2,301.6
TRAVELERS INDEMNITY CO	CT	20,531.8
Rating: B+		
ALLSTATE INS CO	IL	39,333.3
AMERICAN FAMILY HOME INS CO	FL	443.6
AMERICAN MODERN HOME INS CO	OH	888.8
CENTRAL STATES INDEMNITY CO OF OMAHA	NE	209.1
CUMIS INS SOCIETY INC	IA	1,228.8
FEDERAL INS CO	IN	28,842.9
FOREMOST INS CO	MI	2,024.3
GEICO GENERAL INS CO	MD	175.2
GEICO INDEMNITY CO	MD	5,117.3
GOVERNMENT EMPLOYEES INS CO	MD	12,473.2
GREAT NORTHERN INS CO	IN	1,518.9
HARTFORD FIRE INS CO	CT	23,864.9
HARTFORD INS CO OF THE MIDWEST	IN	359.6
HARTFORD UNDERWRITERS INS CO	CT	1,564.1
METROPOLITAN PROPERTY & CAS INS CO	RI	4,771.4
NATIONAL CASUALTY CO	WI	144.3
NATIONWIDE MUTUAL FIRE INS CO	OH	4,143.4
PACIFIC INDEMNITY CO	WI	5,651.8
STATE FARM MUTUAL AUTOMOBILE INS CO	IL	88,473.2
USAA GENERAL INDEMNITY CO	TX	452.4

Idaho

INSURANCE COMPANY NAME	DOM. STATE	TOTAL ASSETS ($MIL)
Rating: A+		
DAIRYLAND INS CO	WI	1,222.3
UNITED SERVICES AUTOMOBILE ASN	TX	19,904.8
USAA CASUALTY INS CO	TX	6,714.4
Rating: A		
AUTO-OWNERS INS CO	MI	8,899.8
CHURCH MUTUAL INS CO	WI	1,150.7
COUNTRY MUTUAL INS CO	IL	3,364.1
FRANKENMUTH MUTUAL INS CO	MI	955.3
PROTECTIVE INS CO	IN	529.3
SENTRY INS A MUTUAL CO	WI	5,330.6
TOKIO MARINE & NICHIDO FIRE INS LTD	NY	1,706.6
Rating: A-		
BITUMINOUS CASUALTY CORP	IL	725.4
BITUMINOUS FIRE & MARINE INS CO	IL	463.7
CINCINNATI INDEMNITY CO	OH	87.6
CINCINNATI INS CO	OH	8,454.0
FEDERATED MUTUAL INS CO	MN	3,817.8
GENERAL STAR NATIONAL INS CO	OH	340.1
GREAT WEST CASUALTY CO	NE	1,460.5
JEWELERS MUTUAL INS CO	WI	186.8
NATIONAL LIABILITY & FIRE INS CO	CT	1,040.7
OLD REPUBLIC GENERAL INS CORP	IL	985.4
OLD REPUBLIC INS CO	PA	2,301.6
OLD REPUBLIC SURETY CO	WI	94.2
OWNERS INS CO	OH	2,535.6
TRAVELERS INDEMNITY CO	CT	20,531.8
Rating: B+		
ALLSTATE INS CO	IL	39,333.3
AMERICAN FAMILY HOME INS CO	FL	443.6
AMERICAN MERCURY INS CO	OK	334.3
AMERICAN MODERN HOME INS CO	OH	888.8
AMERICAN NATIONAL GENERAL INS CO	MO	99.8
AMERICAN NATIONAL PROPERTY & CAS CO	MO	1,068.4
AMERICAN STANDARD INS CO OF WI	WI	394.2
CANAL INS CO	SC	1,010.6
CENTRAL STATES INDEMNITY CO OF OMAHA	NE	209.1
COPIC INS CO	CO	435.6
CORNHUSKER CASUALTY CO	NE	533.2
COUNTRY CASUALTY INS CO	IL	75.7
CUMIS INS SOCIETY INC	IA	1,228.8
FARM BUREAU MUTUAL INS CO OF ID	ID	346.7
FARMLAND MUTUAL INS CO	IA	371.1
FEDERAL INS CO	IN	28,842.9
FEDERATED SERVICE INS CO	MN	358.9
FOREMOST INS CO	MI	2,024.3
GEICO GENERAL INS CO	MD	175.2
GEICO INDEMNITY CO	MD	5,117.3
GOVERNMENT EMPLOYEES INS CO	MD	12,473.2
GREAT NORTHERN INS CO	IN	1,518.9
HARTFORD FIRE INS CO	CT	23,864.9
HARTFORD INS CO OF THE MIDWEST	IN	359.6
HARTFORD UNDERWRITERS INS CO	CT	1,564.1
METROPOLITAN PROPERTY & CAS INS CO	RI	4,771.4
NATIONAL CASUALTY CO	WI	144.3
NATIONWIDE MUTUAL FIRE INS CO	OH	4,143.4
PACIFIC INDEMNITY CO	WI	5,651.8
STATE FARM MUTUAL AUTOMOBILE INS CO	IL	88,473.2
USAA GENERAL INDEMNITY CO	TX	452.4
WESTERN AGRICULTURAL INS CO	IA	309.2
WESTERN COMMUNITY INS CO	ID	30.0

Illinois

INSURANCE COMPANY NAME	DOM. STATE	TOTAL ASSETS ($MIL)
Rating: A+		
DAIRYLAND INS CO	WI	1,222.3
HASTINGS MUTUAL INS CO	MI	591.7
UNITED SERVICES AUTOMOBILE ASN	TX	19,904.8
USAA CASUALTY INS CO	TX	6,714.4
Rating: A		
AUTO-OWNERS INS CO	MI	8,899.8
CHURCH MUTUAL INS CO	WI	1,150.7
COUNTRY MUTUAL INS CO	IL	3,364.1
FRANKENMUTH MUTUAL INS CO	MI	955.3
HOME-OWNERS INS CO	MI	1,353.2
MERRIMACK MUTUAL FIRE INS CO	MA	883.0
PROTECTIVE INS CO	IN	529.3
SENTRY INS A MUTUAL CO	WI	5,330.6
TOKIO MARINE & NICHIDO FIRE INS LTD	NY	1,706.6
Rating: A-		
BITUMINOUS CASUALTY CORP	IL	725.4
BITUMINOUS FIRE & MARINE INS CO	IL	463.7
CINCINNATI INDEMNITY CO	OH	87.6
CINCINNATI INS CO	OH	8,454.0
FEDERATED MUTUAL INS CO	MN	3,817.8
GENERAL STAR NATIONAL INS CO	OH	340.1
GRANGE MUTUAL CAS CO	OH	1,525.7
GREAT WEST CASUALTY CO	NE	1,460.5
JEWELERS MUTUAL INS CO	WI	186.8
NATIONAL LIABILITY & FIRE INS CO	CT	1,040.7
OLD REPUBLIC GENERAL INS CORP	IL	985.4
OLD REPUBLIC INS CO	PA	2,301.6
OLD REPUBLIC SURETY CO	WI	94.2
OWNERS INS CO	OH	2,535.6
PROPERTY-OWNERS INS CO	IN	147.1
TRAVELERS INDEMNITY CO	CT	20,531.8
Rating: B+		
ALLSTATE INS CO	IL	39,333.3
AMERICAN FAMILY HOME INS CO	FL	443.6
AMERICAN MERCURY INS CO	OK	334.3
AMERICAN MODERN HOME INS CO	OH	888.8
AMERICAN NATIONAL GENERAL INS CO	MO	99.8
AMERICAN NATIONAL PROPERTY & CAS CO	MO	1,068.4
AMERICAN STANDARD INS CO OF WI	WI	394.2
ARCH SPECIALTY INS CO	NE	437.3
BAY STATE INS CO	MA	285.6
CANAL INS CO	SC	1,010.6
CENTRAL MUTUAL INS CO	OH	1,238.6
CENTRAL STATES INDEMNITY CO OF OMAHA	NE	209.1
COUNTRY CASUALTY INS CO	IL	75.7
CUMIS INS SOCIETY INC	IA	1,228.8
ERIE INS CO OF NY	NY	58.4
FARMERS AUTOMOBILE INS ASN	IL	852.7
FARMLAND MUTUAL INS CO	IA	371.1
FEDERAL INS CO	IN	28,842.9
FEDERATED SERVICE INS CO	MN	358.9
FOREMOST INS CO	MI	2,024.3
GEICO GENERAL INS CO	MD	175.2
GEICO INDEMNITY CO	MD	5,117.3
GOVERNMENT EMPLOYEES INS CO	MD	12,473.2
GREAT NORTHERN INS CO	IN	1,518.9
HARTFORD FIRE INS CO	CT	23,864.9
HARTFORD INS CO OF THE MIDWEST	IN	359.6
HARTFORD UNDERWRITERS INS CO	CT	1,564.1
METROPOLITAN PROPERTY & CAS INS CO	RI	4,771.4
MIDWEST MEDICAL INS CO	MN	490.6
NATIONAL CASUALTY CO	WI	144.3
NATIONWIDE MUTUAL FIRE INS CO	OH	4,143.4
PACIFIC INDEMNITY CO	WI	5,651.8
PEKIN INS CO	IL	195.5
SOUTHERN-OWNERS INS CO	MI	377.7
STATE FARM MUTUAL AUTOMOBILE INS CO	IL	88,473.2
TRUSTGARD INS CO	OH	66.4
USAA GENERAL INDEMNITY CO	TX	452.4
WEST BEND MUTUAL INS CO	WI	1,438.7
WESTERN AGRICULTURAL INS CO	IA	309.2
WESTFIELD NATIONAL INS CO	OH	437.0

Indiana

INSURANCE COMPANY NAME	DOM. STATE	TOTAL ASSETS ($MIL)
Rating: A+		
DAIRYLAND INS CO	WI	1,222.3
HASTINGS MUTUAL INS CO	MI	591.7
UNITED SERVICES AUTOMOBILE ASN	TX	19,904.8
USAA CASUALTY INS CO	TX	6,714.4
Rating: A		
AUTO-OWNERS INS CO	MI	8,899.8
CHURCH MUTUAL INS CO	WI	1,150.7
COUNTRY MUTUAL INS CO	IL	3,364.1
FRANKENMUTH MUTUAL INS CO	MI	955.3
HOME-OWNERS INS CO	MI	1,353.2
PIONEER STATE MUTUAL INS CO	MI	294.4
PROTECTIVE INS CO	IN	529.3
SENTRY INS A MUTUAL CO	WI	5,330.6
TOKIO MARINE & NICHIDO FIRE INS LTD	NY	1,706.6
Rating: A-		
BITUMINOUS CASUALTY CORP	IL	725.4
BITUMINOUS FIRE & MARINE INS CO	IL	463.7
CINCINNATI INDEMNITY CO	OH	87.6
CINCINNATI INS CO	OH	8,454.0
FEDERATED MUTUAL INS CO	MN	3,817.8
GENERAL STAR NATIONAL INS CO	OH	340.1
GRANGE MUTUAL CAS CO	OH	1,525.7
GREAT WEST CASUALTY CO	NE	1,460.5
JEWELERS MUTUAL INS CO	WI	186.8
NATIONAL LIABILITY & FIRE INS CO	CT	1,040.7
OLD REPUBLIC GENERAL INS CORP	IL	985.4
OLD REPUBLIC INS CO	PA	2,301.6
OLD REPUBLIC SURETY CO	WI	94.2
OWNERS INS CO	OH	2,535.6
PROPERTY-OWNERS INS CO	IN	147.1
STATE VOLUNTEER MUTUAL INS CO	TN	996.2
TRAVELERS INDEMNITY CO	CT	20,531.8
Rating: B+		
ALLSTATE INS CO	IL	39,333.3
AMERICAN FAMILY HOME INS CO	FL	443.6
AMERICAN MERCURY INS CO	OK	334.3
AMERICAN MODERN HOME INS CO	OH	888.8
AMERICAN NATIONAL GENERAL INS CO	MO	99.8
AMERICAN NATIONAL PROPERTY & CAS CO	MO	1,068.4
AMERICAN STANDARD INS CO OF WI	WI	394.2
CANAL INS CO	SC	1,010.6
CENTRAL MUTUAL INS CO	OH	1,238.6
CENTRAL STATES INDEMNITY CO OF OMAHA	NE	209.1
COUNTRY CASUALTY INS CO	IL	75.7
CUMIS INS SOCIETY INC	IA	1,228.8
FARMERS AUTOMOBILE INS ASN	IL	852.7
FARMLAND MUTUAL INS CO	IA	371.1
FEDERAL INS CO	IN	28,842.9
FEDERATED SERVICE INS CO	MN	358.9
FOREMOST INS CO	MI	2,024.3
GEICO GENERAL INS CO	MD	175.2
GEICO INDEMNITY CO	MD	5,117.3
GOVERNMENT EMPLOYEES INS CO	MD	12,473.2
GREAT NORTHERN INS CO	IN	1,518.9
HARTFORD FIRE INS CO	CT	23,864.9
HARTFORD INS CO OF THE MIDWEST	IN	359.6
HARTFORD UNDERWRITERS INS CO	CT	1,564.1
METROPOLITAN PROPERTY & CAS INS CO	RI	4,771.4
MOTORISTS MUTUAL INS CO	OH	1,212.1
NATIONAL CASUALTY CO	WI	144.3
NATIONWIDE MUTUAL FIRE INS CO	OH	4,143.4
PACIFIC INDEMNITY CO	WI	5,651.8
PEKIN INS CO	IL	195.5
SOUTHERN-OWNERS INS CO	MI	377.7
STATE FARM MUTUAL AUTOMOBILE INS CO	IL	88,473.2
TRUSTGARD INS CO	OH	66.4
UNITED FARM FAMILY MUTUAL INS CO	IN	787.9
USAA GENERAL INDEMNITY CO	TX	452.4
WEST BEND MUTUAL INS CO	WI	1,438.7
WESTERN AGRICULTURAL INS CO	IA	309.2
WESTFIELD NATIONAL INS CO	OH	437.0

Iowa

INSURANCE COMPANY NAME	DOM. STATE	TOTAL ASSETS ($MIL)
Rating: A+		
DAIRYLAND INS CO	WI	1,222.3
UNITED SERVICES AUTOMOBILE ASN	TX	19,904.8
USAA CASUALTY INS CO	TX	6,714.4
Rating: A		
AUTO-OWNERS INS CO	MI	8,899.8
CHURCH MUTUAL INS CO	WI	1,150.7
COUNTRY MUTUAL INS CO	IL	3,364.1
FRANKENMUTH MUTUAL INS CO	MI	955.3
HOME-OWNERS INS CO	MI	1,353.2
PROTECTIVE INS CO	IN	529.3
SENTRY INS A MUTUAL CO	WI	5,330.6
TOKIO MARINE & NICHIDO FIRE INS LTD	NY	1,706.6
Rating: A-		
BITUMINOUS CASUALTY CORP	IL	725.4
BITUMINOUS FIRE & MARINE INS CO	IL	463.7
CINCINNATI INDEMNITY CO	OH	87.6
CINCINNATI INS CO	OH	8,454.0
FARM BUREAU MUTUAL INS CO	IA	1,586.9
FEDERATED MUTUAL INS CO	MN	3,817.8
GENERAL STAR NATIONAL INS CO	OH	340.1
GRANGE MUTUAL CAS CO	OH	1,525.7
GREAT WEST CASUALTY CO	NE	1,460.5
JEWELERS MUTUAL INS CO	WI	186.8
NATIONAL LIABILITY & FIRE INS CO	CT	1,040.7
OLD REPUBLIC GENERAL INS CORP	IL	985.4
OLD REPUBLIC INS CO	PA	2,301.6
OLD REPUBLIC SURETY CO	WI	94.2
OWNERS INS CO	OH	2,535.6
PROPERTY-OWNERS INS CO	IN	147.1
TRAVELERS INDEMNITY CO	CT	20,531.8
Rating: B+		
ALLSTATE INS CO	IL	39,333.3
AMERICAN FAMILY HOME INS CO	FL	443.6
AMERICAN MERCURY INS CO	OK	334.3
AMERICAN MODERN HOME INS CO	OH	888.8
AMERICAN NATIONAL GENERAL INS CO	MO	99.8
AMERICAN NATIONAL PROPERTY & CAS CO	MO	1,068.4
AMERICAN STANDARD INS CO OF WI	WI	394.2
CANAL INS CO	SC	1,010.6
CENTRAL MUTUAL INS CO	OH	1,238.6
CENTRAL STATES INDEMNITY CO OF OMAHA	NE	209.1
COPIC INS CO	CO	435.6
CORNHUSKER CASUALTY CO	NE	533.2
COUNTRY CASUALTY INS CO	IL	75.7
CUMIS INS SOCIETY INC	IA	1,228.8
FARMERS AUTOMOBILE INS ASN	IL	852.7
FARMLAND MUTUAL INS CO	IA	371.1
FEDERAL INS CO	IN	28,842.9
FEDERATED SERVICE INS CO	MN	358.9
FOREMOST INS CO	MI	2,024.3
GEICO GENERAL INS CO	MD	175.2
GEICO INDEMNITY CO	MD	5,117.3
GOVERNMENT EMPLOYEES INS CO	MD	12,473.2
GREAT NORTHERN INS CO	IN	1,518.9
HARTFORD FIRE INS CO	CT	23,864.9
HARTFORD INS CO OF THE MIDWEST	IN	359.6
HARTFORD UNDERWRITERS INS CO	CT	1,564.1
METROPOLITAN PROPERTY & CAS INS CO	RI	4,771.4
MIDWEST MEDICAL INS CO	MN	490.6
NATIONAL CASUALTY CO	WI	144.3
NATIONWIDE MUTUAL FIRE INS CO	OH	4,143.4
PACIFIC INDEMNITY CO	WI	5,651.8
PEKIN INS CO	IL	195.5
SOUTHERN-OWNERS INS CO	MI	377.7
STATE FARM MUTUAL AUTOMOBILE INS CO	IL	88,473.2
TRUSTGARD INS CO	OH	66.4
USAA GENERAL INDEMNITY CO	TX	452.4
WESCO-FINANCIAL INS CO	NE	2,526.8
WEST BEND MUTUAL INS CO	WI	1,438.7
WESTERN AGRICULTURAL INS CO	IA	309.2
WESTFIELD NATIONAL INS CO	OH	437.0

Kansas

INSURANCE COMPANY NAME	DOM. STATE	TOTAL ASSETS ($MIL)
Rating: A+		
DAIRYLAND INS CO	WI	1,222.3
UNITED SERVICES AUTOMOBILE ASN	TX	19,904.8
USAA CASUALTY INS CO	TX	6,714.4
Rating: A		
AUTO-OWNERS INS CO	MI	8,899.8
CHURCH MUTUAL INS CO	WI	1,150.7
COUNTRY MUTUAL INS CO	IL	3,364.1
FRANKENMUTH MUTUAL INS CO	MI	955.3
PROTECTIVE INS CO	IN	529.3
SENTRY INS A MUTUAL CO	WI	5,330.6
TOKIO MARINE & NICHIDO FIRE INS LTD	NY	1,706.6
Rating: A-		
BITUMINOUS CASUALTY CORP	IL	725.4
BITUMINOUS FIRE & MARINE INS CO	IL	463.7
CINCINNATI INDEMNITY CO	OH	87.6
CINCINNATI INS CO	OH	8,454.0
FARM BUREAU MUTUAL INS CO	IA	1,586.9
FEDERATED MUTUAL INS CO	MN	3,817.8
GENERAL STAR NATIONAL INS CO	OH	340.1
GRANGE MUTUAL CAS CO	OH	1,525.7
GREAT WEST CASUALTY CO	NE	1,460.5
JEWELERS MUTUAL INS CO	WI	186.8
NATIONAL LIABILITY & FIRE INS CO	CT	1,040.7
OLD REPUBLIC GENERAL INS CORP	IL	985.4
OLD REPUBLIC INS CO	PA	2,301.6
OLD REPUBLIC SURETY CO	WI	94.2
OWNERS INS CO	OH	2,535.6
TRAVELERS INDEMNITY CO	CT	20,531.8
Rating: B+		
ALLSTATE INS CO	IL	39,333.3
AMERICAN FAMILY HOME INS CO	FL	443.6
AMERICAN MERCURY INS CO	OK	334.3
AMERICAN MODERN HOME INS CO	OH	888.8
AMERICAN NATIONAL GENERAL INS CO	MO	99.8
AMERICAN NATIONAL PROPERTY & CAS CO	MO	1,068.4
AMERICAN STANDARD INS CO OF WI	WI	394.2
CANAL INS CO	SC	1,010.6
CENTRAL STATES INDEMNITY CO OF OMAHA	NE	209.1
COPIC INS CO	CO	435.6
CORNHUSKER CASUALTY CO	NE	533.2
COUNTRY CASUALTY INS CO	IL	75.7
CUMIS INS SOCIETY INC	IA	1,228.8
FARMLAND MUTUAL INS CO	IA	371.1
FEDERAL INS CO	IN	28,842.9
FEDERATED SERVICE INS CO	MN	358.9
FOREMOST INS CO	MI	2,024.3
GEICO GENERAL INS CO	MD	175.2
GEICO INDEMNITY CO	MD	5,117.3
GOVERNMENT EMPLOYEES INS CO	MD	12,473.2
GREAT NORTHERN INS CO	IN	1,518.9
HARTFORD FIRE INS CO	CT	23,864.9
HARTFORD INS CO OF THE MIDWEST	IN	359.6
HARTFORD UNDERWRITERS INS CO	CT	1,564.1
METROPOLITAN PROPERTY & CAS INS CO	RI	4,771.4
MIDWEST MEDICAL INS CO	MN	490.6
NATIONAL CASUALTY CO	WI	144.3
NATIONWIDE MUTUAL FIRE INS CO	OH	4,143.4
PACIFIC INDEMNITY CO	WI	5,651.8
STATE FARM MUTUAL AUTOMOBILE INS CO	IL	88,473.2
TRUSTGARD INS CO	OH	66.4
USAA GENERAL INDEMNITY CO	TX	452.4
WESTERN AGRICULTURAL INS CO	IA	309.2

Kentucky

INSURANCE COMPANY NAME	DOM. STATE	TOTAL ASSETS ($MIL)
Rating: A+		
DAIRYLAND INS CO	WI	1,222.3
HASTINGS MUTUAL INS CO	MI	591.7
UNITED SERVICES AUTOMOBILE ASN	TX	19,904.8
USAA CASUALTY INS CO	TX	6,714.4
Rating: A		
AUTO-OWNERS INS CO	MI	8,899.8
CHURCH MUTUAL INS CO	WI	1,150.7
COUNTRY MUTUAL INS CO	IL	3,364.1
FRANKENMUTH MUTUAL INS CO	MI	955.3
HOME-OWNERS INS CO	MI	1,353.2
KENTUCKY FARM BUREAU MUTUAL INS CO	KY	1,580.7
PROTECTIVE INS CO	IN	529.3
SENTRY INS A MUTUAL CO	WI	5,330.6
TOKIO MARINE & NICHIDO FIRE INS LTD	NY	1,706.6
Rating: A-		
BITUMINOUS CASUALTY CORP	IL	725.4
BITUMINOUS FIRE & MARINE INS CO	IL	463.7
CINCINNATI INDEMNITY CO	OH	87.6
CINCINNATI INS CO	OH	8,454.0
FEDERATED MUTUAL INS CO	MN	3,817.8
GENERAL STAR NATIONAL INS CO	OH	340.1
GRANGE MUTUAL CAS CO	OH	1,525.7
GREAT WEST CASUALTY CO	NE	1,460.5
JEWELERS MUTUAL INS CO	WI	186.8
NATIONAL LIABILITY & FIRE INS CO	CT	1,040.7
OLD REPUBLIC GENERAL INS CORP	IL	985.4
OLD REPUBLIC INS CO	PA	2,301.6
OWNERS INS CO	OH	2,535.6
PROPERTY-OWNERS INS CO	IN	147.1
STATE VOLUNTEER MUTUAL INS CO	TN	996.2
TRAVELERS INDEMNITY CO	CT	20,531.8
Rating: B+		
ALLSTATE INS CO	IL	39,333.3
AMERICAN FAMILY HOME INS CO	FL	443.6
AMERICAN MERCURY INS CO	OK	334.3
AMERICAN MODERN HOME INS CO	OH	888.8
AMERICAN NATIONAL GENERAL INS CO	MO	99.8
AMERICAN NATIONAL PROPERTY & CAS CO	MO	1,068.4
CANAL INS CO	SC	1,010.6
CENTRAL MUTUAL INS CO	OH	1,238.6
CENTRAL STATES INDEMNITY CO OF OMAHA	NE	209.1
COUNTRY CASUALTY INS CO	IL	75.7
CUMIS INS SOCIETY INC	IA	1,228.8
FARMLAND MUTUAL INS CO	IA	371.1
FEDERAL INS CO	IN	28,842.9
FEDERATED SERVICE INS CO	MN	358.9
FOREMOST INS CO	MI	2,024.3
GEICO GENERAL INS CO	MD	175.2
GEICO INDEMNITY CO	MD	5,117.3
GOVERNMENT EMPLOYEES INS CO	MD	12,473.2
GREAT NORTHERN INS CO	IN	1,518.9
HARTFORD FIRE INS CO	CT	23,864.9
HARTFORD INS CO OF THE MIDWEST	IN	359.6
HARTFORD UNDERWRITERS INS CO	CT	1,564.1
METROPOLITAN PROPERTY & CAS INS CO	RI	4,771.4
MOTORISTS MUTUAL INS CO	OH	1,212.1
NATIONAL CASUALTY CO	WI	144.3
NATIONWIDE MUTUAL FIRE INS CO	OH	4,143.4
PACIFIC INDEMNITY CO	WI	5,651.8
SOUTHERN-OWNERS INS CO	MI	377.7
STATE FARM MUTUAL AUTOMOBILE INS CO	IL	88,473.2
TRUSTGARD INS CO	OH	66.4
USAA GENERAL INDEMNITY CO	TX	452.4
WESTFIELD NATIONAL INS CO	OH	437.0

Louisiana

INSURANCE COMPANY NAME	DOM. STATE	TOTAL ASSETS ($MIL)
Rating: A+		
UNITED SERVICES AUTOMOBILE ASN	TX	19,904.8
USAA CASUALTY INS CO	TX	6,714.4
Rating: A		
CHURCH MUTUAL INS CO	WI	1,150.7
FRANKENMUTH MUTUAL INS CO	MI	955.3
PROTECTIVE INS CO	IN	529.3
SENTRY INS A MUTUAL CO	WI	5,330.6
TOKIO MARINE & NICHIDO FIRE INS LTD	NY	1,706.6
Rating: A-		
BITUMINOUS CASUALTY CORP	IL	725.4
BITUMINOUS FIRE & MARINE INS CO	IL	463.7
CINCINNATI INS CO	OH	8,454.0
FEDERATED MUTUAL INS CO	MN	3,817.8
GENERAL STAR NATIONAL INS CO	OH	340.1
GREAT WEST CASUALTY CO	NE	1,460.5
JEWELERS MUTUAL INS CO	WI	186.8
NATIONAL LIABILITY & FIRE INS CO	CT	1,040.7
OLD REPUBLIC GENERAL INS CORP	IL	985.4
OLD REPUBLIC INS CO	PA	2,301.6
TRAVELERS INDEMNITY CO	CT	20,531.8
Rating: B+		
ALLSTATE INS CO	IL	39,333.3
AMERICAN FAMILY HOME INS CO	FL	443.6
AMERICAN MERCURY INS CO	OK	334.3
AMERICAN MODERN HOME INS CO	OH	888.8
AMERICAN NATIONAL GENERAL INS CO	MO	99.8
AMERICAN NATIONAL PROPERTY & CAS CO	MO	1,068.4
CANAL INS CO	SC	1,010.6
CENTRAL STATES INDEMNITY CO OF OMAHA	NE	209.1
CUMIS INS SOCIETY INC	IA	1,228.8
FEDERAL INS CO	IN	28,842.9
FEDERATED SERVICE INS CO	MN	358.9
FOREMOST INS CO	MI	2,024.3
GEICO GENERAL INS CO	MD	175.2
GEICO INDEMNITY CO	MD	5,117.3
GOVERNMENT EMPLOYEES INS CO	MD	12,473.2
GREAT NORTHERN INS CO	IN	1,518.9
HARTFORD FIRE INS CO	CT	23,864.9
HARTFORD INS CO OF THE MIDWEST	IN	359.6
HARTFORD UNDERWRITERS INS CO	CT	1,564.1
METROPOLITAN PROPERTY & CAS INS CO	RI	4,771.4
NATIONAL CASUALTY CO	WI	144.3
NATIONWIDE MUTUAL FIRE INS CO	OH	4,143.4
PACIFIC INDEMNITY CO	WI	5,651.8
SOUTHERN FARM BUREAU CAS INS CO	MS	1,807.1
STATE FARM MUTUAL AUTOMOBILE INS CO	IL	88,473.2
USAA GENERAL INDEMNITY CO	TX	452.4

Maine

INSURANCE COMPANY NAME	DOM. STATE	TOTAL ASSETS ($MIL)
Rating: A+		
DAIRYLAND INS CO	WI	1,222.3
INTERINS EXCH OF THE AUTOMOBILE CLUB	CA	5,434.9
UNITED SERVICES AUTOMOBILE ASN	TX	19,904.8
USAA CASUALTY INS CO	TX	6,714.4
Rating: A		
CHURCH MUTUAL INS CO	WI	1,150.7
COUNTRY MUTUAL INS CO	IL	3,364.1
FRANKENMUTH MUTUAL INS CO	MI	955.3
MERRIMACK MUTUAL FIRE INS CO	MA	883.0
PROTECTIVE INS CO	IN	529.3
SENTRY INS A MUTUAL CO	WI	5,330.6
TOKIO MARINE & NICHIDO FIRE INS LTD	NY	1,706.6
Rating: A-		
BITUMINOUS CASUALTY CORP	IL	725.4
CINCINNATI INS CO	OH	8,454.0
FEDERATED MUTUAL INS CO	MN	3,817.8
GENERAL STAR NATIONAL INS CO	OH	340.1
GREAT WEST CASUALTY CO	NE	1,460.5
JEWELERS MUTUAL INS CO	WI	186.8
NATIONAL LIABILITY & FIRE INS CO	CT	1,040.7
OLD REPUBLIC GENERAL INS CORP	IL	985.4
OLD REPUBLIC INS CO	PA	2,301.6
TRAVELERS INDEMNITY CO	CT	20,531.8
Rating: B+		
ALLSTATE INS CO	IL	39,333.3
AMERICAN MODERN HOME INS CO	OH	888.8
AMERICAN NATIONAL PROPERTY & CAS CO	MO	1,068.4
BAY STATE INS CO	MA	285.6
CANAL INS CO	SC	1,010.6
CENTRAL STATES INDEMNITY CO OF OMAHA	NE	209.1
COMMERCE INS CO	MA	2,513.5
COUNTRY CASUALTY INS CO	IL	75.7
CUMIS INS SOCIETY INC	IA	1,228.8
FEDERAL INS CO	IN	28,842.9
FEDERATED SERVICE INS CO	MN	358.9
FOREMOST INS CO	MI	2,024.3
GEICO GENERAL INS CO	MD	175.2
GEICO INDEMNITY CO	MD	5,117.3
GOVERNMENT EMPLOYEES INS CO	MD	12,473.2
GREAT NORTHERN INS CO	IN	1,518.9
HARTFORD FIRE INS CO	CT	23,864.9
HARTFORD INS CO OF THE MIDWEST	IN	359.6
HARTFORD UNDERWRITERS INS CO	CT	1,564.1
METROPOLITAN PROPERTY & CAS INS CO	RI	4,771.4
NATIONAL CASUALTY CO	WI	144.3
NATIONWIDE MUTUAL FIRE INS CO	OH	4,143.4
PACIFIC INDEMNITY CO	WI	5,651.8
STATE FARM MUTUAL AUTOMOBILE INS CO	IL	88,473.2
USAA GENERAL INDEMNITY CO	TX	452.4

INSURANCE COMPANY NAME	DOM. STATE	TOTAL ASSETS ($MIL)

Maryland

INSURANCE COMPANY NAME	DOM. STATE	TOTAL ASSETS ($MIL)
Rating: A+		
DAIRYLAND INS CO	WI	1,222.3
UNITED SERVICES AUTOMOBILE ASN	TX	19,904.8
USAA CASUALTY INS CO	TX	6,714.4
Rating: A		
CHURCH MUTUAL INS CO	WI	1,150.7
FRANKENMUTH MUTUAL INS CO	MI	955.3
PROTECTIVE INS CO	IN	529.3
SENTRY INS A MUTUAL CO	WI	5,330.6
TOKIO MARINE & NICHIDO FIRE INS LTD	NY	1,706.6
Rating: A-		
BITUMINOUS CASUALTY CORP	IL	725.4
BITUMINOUS FIRE & MARINE INS CO	IL	463.7
CINCINNATI INDEMNITY CO	OH	87.6
CINCINNATI INS CO	OH	8,454.0
FEDERATED MUTUAL INS CO	MN	3,817.8
GENERAL STAR NATIONAL INS CO	OH	340.1
GREAT WEST CASUALTY CO	NE	1,460.5
JEWELERS MUTUAL INS CO	WI	186.8
NATIONAL LIABILITY & FIRE INS CO	CT	1,040.7
OLD REPUBLIC GENERAL INS CORP	IL	985.4
OLD REPUBLIC INS CO	PA	2,301.6
OLD REPUBLIC SURETY CO	WI	94.2
TRAVELERS INDEMNITY CO	CT	20,531.8
Rating: B+		
ALLSTATE INS CO	IL	39,333.3
AMERICAN FAMILY HOME INS CO	FL	443.6
AMERICAN MODERN HOME INS CO	OH	888.8
AMERICAN NATIONAL GENERAL INS CO	MO	99.8
AMERICAN NATIONAL PROPERTY & CAS CO	MO	1,068.4
CANAL INS CO	SC	1,010.6
CENTRAL STATES INDEMNITY CO OF OMAHA	NE	209.1
COUNTRY CASUALTY INS CO	IL	75.7
CUMBERLAND MUTUAL FIRE INS CO	NJ	245.0
CUMIS INS SOCIETY INC	IA	1,228.8
FARMLAND MUTUAL INS CO	IA	371.1
FEDERAL INS CO	IN	28,842.9
FEDERATED SERVICE INS CO	MN	358.9
FOREMOST INS CO	MI	2,024.3
GEICO GENERAL INS CO	MD	175.2
GEICO INDEMNITY CO	MD	5,117.3
GOVERNMENT EMPLOYEES INS CO	MD	12,473.2
GREAT NORTHERN INS CO	IN	1,518.9
HARTFORD FIRE INS CO	CT	23,864.9
HARTFORD INS CO OF THE MIDWEST	IN	359.6
HARTFORD UNDERWRITERS INS CO	CT	1,564.1
INS CO OF GREATER NY	NY	101.2
METROPOLITAN PROPERTY & CAS INS CO	RI	4,771.4
NATIONAL CASUALTY CO	WI	144.3
NATIONWIDE MUTUAL FIRE INS CO	OH	4,143.4
PACIFIC INDEMNITY CO	WI	5,651.8
STATE FARM MUTUAL AUTOMOBILE INS CO	IL	88,473.2
USAA GENERAL INDEMNITY CO	TX	452.4

Massachusetts

INSURANCE COMPANY NAME	DOM. STATE	TOTAL ASSETS ($MIL)
Rating: A+		
DAIRYLAND INS CO	WI	1,222.3
UNITED SERVICES AUTOMOBILE ASN	TX	19,904.8
USAA CASUALTY INS CO	TX	6,714.4
Rating: A		
CHURCH MUTUAL INS CO	WI	1,150.7
COUNTRY MUTUAL INS CO	IL	3,364.1
FRANKENMUTH MUTUAL INS CO	MI	955.3
MERRIMACK MUTUAL FIRE INS CO	MA	883.0
PROTECTIVE INS CO	IN	529.3
SENTRY INS A MUTUAL CO	WI	5,330.6
TOKIO MARINE & NICHIDO FIRE INS LTD	NY	1,706.6
Rating: A-		
BITUMINOUS CASUALTY CORP	IL	725.4
BITUMINOUS FIRE & MARINE INS CO	IL	463.7
CINCINNATI INS CO	OH	8,454.0
FEDERATED MUTUAL INS CO	MN	3,817.8
GENERAL STAR NATIONAL INS CO	OH	340.1
GREAT WEST CASUALTY CO	NE	1,460.5
JEWELERS MUTUAL INS CO	WI	186.8
OLD REPUBLIC GENERAL INS CORP	IL	985.4
OLD REPUBLIC INS CO	PA	2,301.6
TRAVELERS INDEMNITY CO	CT	20,531.8
Rating: B+		
ALLSTATE INS CO	IL	39,333.3
AMERICAN FAMILY HOME INS CO	FL	443.6
AMERICAN MODERN HOME INS CO	OH	888.8
BAY STATE INS CO	MA	285.6
CANAL INS CO	SC	1,010.6
CENTRAL MUTUAL INS CO	OH	1,238.6
CENTRAL STATES INDEMNITY CO OF OMAHA	NE	209.1
CITATION INS CO	MA	304.8
COMMERCE INS CO	MA	2,513.5
COUNTRY CASUALTY INS CO	IL	75.7
CUMIS INS SOCIETY INC	IA	1,228.8
FEDERAL INS CO	IN	28,842.9
FEDERATED SERVICE INS CO	MN	358.9
FOREMOST INS CO	MI	2,024.3
GEICO GENERAL INS CO	MD	175.2
GOVERNMENT EMPLOYEES INS CO	MD	12,473.2
GREAT NORTHERN INS CO	IN	1,518.9
HARTFORD FIRE INS CO	CT	23,864.9
HARTFORD INS CO OF THE MIDWEST	IN	359.6
HARTFORD UNDERWRITERS INS CO	CT	1,564.1
INS CO OF GREATER NY	NY	101.2
METROPOLITAN PROPERTY & CAS INS CO	RI	4,771.4
NATIONAL CASUALTY CO	WI	144.3
NATIONWIDE MUTUAL FIRE INS CO	OH	4,143.4
PACIFIC INDEMNITY CO	WI	5,651.8
SAFETY INS CO	MA	1,190.4
STATE FARM MUTUAL AUTOMOBILE INS CO	IL	88,473.2
USAA GENERAL INDEMNITY CO	TX	452.4

Michigan

INSURANCE COMPANY NAME	DOM. STATE	TOTAL ASSETS ($MIL)
Rating: A+		
DAIRYLAND INS CO	WI	1,222.3
HASTINGS MUTUAL INS CO	MI	591.7
UNITED SERVICES AUTOMOBILE ASN	TX	19,904.8
USAA CASUALTY INS CO	TX	6,714.4
Rating: A		
AUTO-OWNERS INS CO	MI	8,899.8
CHURCH MUTUAL INS CO	WI	1,150.7
COUNTRY MUTUAL INS CO	IL	3,364.1
FRANKENMUTH MUTUAL INS CO	MI	955.3
HOME-OWNERS INS CO	MI	1,353.2
PIONEER STATE MUTUAL INS CO	MI	294.4
PROTECTIVE INS CO	IN	529.3
SENTRY INS A MUTUAL CO	WI	5,330.6
TOKIO MARINE & NICHIDO FIRE INS LTD	NY	1,706.6
Rating: A-		
BITUMINOUS CASUALTY CORP	IL	725.4
BITUMINOUS FIRE & MARINE INS CO	IL	463.7
CINCINNATI INDEMNITY CO	OH	87.6
CINCINNATI INS CO	OH	8,454.0
FEDERATED MUTUAL INS CO	MN	3,817.8
GENERAL STAR NATIONAL INS CO	OH	340.1
GREAT WEST CASUALTY CO	NE	1,460.5
JEWELERS MUTUAL INS CO	WI	186.8
NATIONAL LIABILITY & FIRE INS CO	CT	1,040.7
OLD REPUBLIC GENERAL INS CORP	IL	985.4
OLD REPUBLIC INS CO	PA	2,301.6
OWNERS INS CO	OH	2,535.6
PROPERTY-OWNERS INS CO	IN	147.1
TRAVELERS INDEMNITY CO	CT	20,531.8
Rating: B+		
ALLSTATE INS CO	IL	39,333.3
AMERICAN FAMILY HOME INS CO	FL	443.6
AMERICAN MODERN HOME INS CO	OH	888.8
AMERICAN NATIONAL PROPERTY & CAS CO	MO	1,068.4
CANAL INS CO	SC	1,010.6
CENTRAL MUTUAL INS CO	OH	1,238.6
CENTRAL STATES INDEMNITY CO OF OMAHA	NE	209.1
COUNTRY CASUALTY INS CO	IL	75.7
CUMIS INS SOCIETY INC	IA	1,228.8
FARMERS AUTOMOBILE INS ASN	IL	852.7
FARMLAND MUTUAL INS CO	IA	371.1
FEDERAL INS CO	IN	28,842.9
FEDERATED SERVICE INS CO	MN	358.9
FOREMOST INS CO	MI	2,024.3
GEICO GENERAL INS CO	MD	175.2
GEICO INDEMNITY CO	MD	5,117.3
GOVERNMENT EMPLOYEES INS CO	MD	12,473.2
GREAT NORTHERN INS CO	IN	1,518.9
HARTFORD FIRE INS CO	CT	23,864.9
HARTFORD INS CO OF THE MIDWEST	IN	359.6
HARTFORD UNDERWRITERS INS CO	CT	1,564.1
METROPOLITAN PROPERTY & CAS INS CO	RI	4,771.4
MOTORISTS MUTUAL INS CO	OH	1,212.1
NATIONAL CASUALTY CO	WI	144.3
NATIONWIDE MUTUAL FIRE INS CO	OH	4,143.4
PACIFIC INDEMNITY CO	WI	5,651.8
PEKIN INS CO	IL	195.5
SOUTHERN-OWNERS INS CO	MI	377.7
STATE FARM MUTUAL AUTOMOBILE INS CO	IL	88,473.2
USAA GENERAL INDEMNITY CO	TX	452.4
WEST BEND MUTUAL INS CO	WI	1,438.7
WESTERN AGRICULTURAL INS CO	IA	309.2
WESTFIELD NATIONAL INS CO	OH	437.0

Minnesota

INSURANCE COMPANY NAME	DOM. STATE	TOTAL ASSETS ($MIL)
Rating: A+		
DAIRYLAND INS CO	WI	1,222.3
UNITED SERVICES AUTOMOBILE ASN	TX	19,904.8
USAA CASUALTY INS CO	TX	6,714.4
Rating: A		
AUTO-OWNERS INS CO	MI	8,899.8
CHURCH MUTUAL INS CO	WI	1,150.7
COUNTRY MUTUAL INS CO	IL	3,364.1
FRANKENMUTH MUTUAL INS CO	MI	955.3
PROTECTIVE INS CO	IN	529.3
SENTRY INS A MUTUAL CO	WI	5,330.6
TOKIO MARINE & NICHIDO FIRE INS LTD	NY	1,706.6
Rating: A-		
BITUMINOUS CASUALTY CORP	IL	725.4
BITUMINOUS FIRE & MARINE INS CO	IL	463.7
CINCINNATI INDEMNITY CO	OH	87.6
CINCINNATI INS CO	OH	8,454.0
FARM BUREAU MUTUAL INS CO	IA	1,586.9
FEDERATED MUTUAL INS CO	MN	3,817.8
GENERAL STAR NATIONAL INS CO	OH	340.1
GRANGE MUTUAL CAS CO	OH	1,525.7
GREAT WEST CASUALTY CO	NE	1,460.5
JEWELERS MUTUAL INS CO	WI	186.8
NATIONAL LIABILITY & FIRE INS CO	CT	1,040.7
OLD REPUBLIC GENERAL INS CORP	IL	985.4
OLD REPUBLIC INS CO	PA	2,301.6
OLD REPUBLIC SURETY CO	WI	94.2
OWNERS INS CO	OH	2,535.6
TRAVELERS INDEMNITY CO	CT	20,531.8
Rating: B+		
ALLSTATE INS CO	IL	39,333.3
AMERICAN FAMILY HOME INS CO	FL	443.6
AMERICAN MERCURY INS CO	OK	334.3
AMERICAN MODERN HOME INS CO	OH	888.8
AMERICAN NATIONAL GENERAL INS CO	MO	99.8
AMERICAN NATIONAL PROPERTY & CAS CO	MO	1,068.4
AMERICAN STANDARD INS CO OF WI	WI	394.2
CANAL INS CO	SC	1,010.6
CENTRAL STATES INDEMNITY CO OF OMAHA	NE	209.1
COUNTRY CASUALTY INS CO	IL	75.7
CUMIS INS SOCIETY INC	IA	1,228.8
ERIE INS CO OF NY	NY	58.4
FARMLAND MUTUAL INS CO	IA	371.1
FEDERAL INS CO	IN	28,842.9
FEDERATED SERVICE INS CO	MN	358.9
FOREMOST INS CO	MI	2,024.3
GEICO GENERAL INS CO	MD	175.2
GEICO INDEMNITY CO	MD	5,117.3
GOVERNMENT EMPLOYEES INS CO	MD	12,473.2
GREAT NORTHERN INS CO	IN	1,518.9
HARTFORD FIRE INS CO	CT	23,864.9
HARTFORD INS CO OF THE MIDWEST	IN	359.6
HARTFORD UNDERWRITERS INS CO	CT	1,564.1
METROPOLITAN PROPERTY & CAS INS CO	RI	4,771.4
MIDWEST MEDICAL INS CO	MN	490.6
NATIONAL CASUALTY CO	WI	144.3
NATIONWIDE MUTUAL FIRE INS CO	OH	4,143.4
NORTH STAR MUTUAL INS CO	MN	340.1
PACIFIC INDEMNITY CO	WI	5,651.8
STATE FARM MUTUAL AUTOMOBILE INS CO	IL	88,473.2
TRUSTGARD INS CO	OH	66.4
USAA GENERAL INDEMNITY CO	TX	452.4
WEST BEND MUTUAL INS CO	WI	1,438.7
WESTERN AGRICULTURAL INS CO	IA	309.2
WESTFIELD NATIONAL INS CO	OH	437.0

Mississippi

INSURANCE COMPANY NAME	DOM. STATE	TOTAL ASSETS ($MIL)
Rating: A+		
DAIRYLAND INS CO	WI	1,222.3
UNITED SERVICES AUTOMOBILE ASN	TX	19,904.8
USAA CASUALTY INS CO	TX	6,714.4
Rating: A		
AUTO-OWNERS INS CO	MI	8,899.8
CHURCH MUTUAL INS CO	WI	1,150.7
FRANKENMUTH MUTUAL INS CO	MI	955.3
PROTECTIVE INS CO	IN	529.3
SENTRY INS A MUTUAL CO	WI	5,330.6
TOKIO MARINE & NICHIDO FIRE INS LTD	NY	1,706.6
Rating: A-		
BITUMINOUS CASUALTY CORP	IL	725.4
BITUMINOUS FIRE & MARINE INS CO	IL	463.7
CINCINNATI INS CO	OH	8,454.0
FEDERATED MUTUAL INS CO	MN	3,817.8
GENERAL STAR NATIONAL INS CO	OH	340.1
GREAT WEST CASUALTY CO	NE	1,460.5
JEWELERS MUTUAL INS CO	WI	186.8
NATIONAL LIABILITY & FIRE INS CO	CT	1,040.7
OLD REPUBLIC GENERAL INS CORP	IL	985.4
OLD REPUBLIC INS CO	PA	2,301.6
OLD REPUBLIC SURETY CO	WI	94.2
OWNERS INS CO	OH	2,535.6
STATE VOLUNTEER MUTUAL INS CO	TN	996.2
TRAVELERS INDEMNITY CO	CT	20,531.8
Rating: B+		
ALLSTATE INS CO	IL	39,333.3
AMERICAN FAMILY HOME INS CO	FL	443.6
AMERICAN MERCURY INS CO	OK	334.3
AMERICAN MODERN HOME INS CO	OH	888.8
AMERICAN NATIONAL GENERAL INS CO	MO	99.8
AMERICAN NATIONAL PROPERTY & CAS CO	MO	1,068.4
CANAL INS CO	SC	1,010.6
CENTRAL STATES INDEMNITY CO OF OMAHA	NE	209.1
CORNHUSKER CASUALTY CO	NE	533.2
CUMIS INS SOCIETY INC	IA	1,228.8
FARMLAND MUTUAL INS CO	IA	371.1
FEDERAL INS CO	IN	28,842.9
FEDERATED SERVICE INS CO	MN	358.9
FOREMOST INS CO	MI	2,024.3
GEICO GENERAL INS CO	MD	175.2
GEICO INDEMNITY CO	MD	5,117.3
GOVERNMENT EMPLOYEES INS CO	MD	12,473.2
GREAT NORTHERN INS CO	IN	1,518.9
HARTFORD FIRE INS CO	CT	23,864.9
HARTFORD INS CO OF THE MIDWEST	IN	359.6
HARTFORD UNDERWRITERS INS CO	CT	1,564.1
METROPOLITAN PROPERTY & CAS INS CO	RI	4,771.4
NATIONAL CASUALTY CO	WI	144.3
NATIONWIDE MUTUAL FIRE INS CO	OH	4,143.4
PACIFIC INDEMNITY CO	WI	5,651.8
SOUTHERN FARM BUREAU CAS INS CO	MS	1,807.1
STATE FARM MUTUAL AUTOMOBILE INS CO	IL	88,473.2
USAA GENERAL INDEMNITY CO	TX	452.4

Missouri

INSURANCE COMPANY NAME	DOM. STATE	TOTAL ASSETS ($MIL)
Rating: A+		
DAIRYLAND INS CO	WI	1,222.3
UNITED SERVICES AUTOMOBILE ASN	TX	19,904.8
USAA CASUALTY INS CO	TX	6,714.4
Rating: A		
AUTO-OWNERS INS CO	MI	8,899.8
CHURCH MUTUAL INS CO	WI	1,150.7
COUNTRY MUTUAL INS CO	IL	3,364.1
FRANKENMUTH MUTUAL INS CO	MI	955.3
HOME-OWNERS INS CO	MI	1,353.2
PROTECTIVE INS CO	IN	529.3
SENTRY INS A MUTUAL CO	WI	5,330.6
TOKIO MARINE & NICHIDO FIRE INS LTD	NY	1,706.6
Rating: A-		
BITUMINOUS CASUALTY CORP	IL	725.4
BITUMINOUS FIRE & MARINE INS CO	IL	463.7
CINCINNATI INDEMNITY CO	OH	87.6
CINCINNATI INS CO	OH	8,454.0
FARM BUREAU MUTUAL INS CO	IA	1,586.9
FEDERATED MUTUAL INS CO	MN	3,817.8
GENERAL STAR NATIONAL INS CO	OH	340.1
GRANGE MUTUAL CAS CO	OH	1,525.7
GREAT WEST CASUALTY CO	NE	1,460.5
JEWELERS MUTUAL INS CO	WI	186.8
NATIONAL LIABILITY & FIRE INS CO	CT	1,040.7
OLD REPUBLIC GENERAL INS CORP	IL	985.4
OLD REPUBLIC INS CO	PA	2,301.6
OLD REPUBLIC SURETY CO	WI	94.2
OWNERS INS CO	OH	2,535.6
PROPERTY-OWNERS INS CO	IN	147.1
STATE VOLUNTEER MUTUAL INS CO	TN	996.2
TRAVELERS INDEMNITY CO	CT	20,531.8
Rating: B+		
ALLSTATE INS CO	IL	39,333.3
AMERICAN FAMILY HOME INS CO	FL	443.6
AMERICAN MERCURY INS CO	OK	334.3
AMERICAN MODERN HOME INS CO	OH	888.8
AMERICAN NATIONAL GENERAL INS CO	MO	99.8
AMERICAN NATIONAL PROPERTY & CAS CO	MO	1,068.4
AMERICAN STANDARD INS CO OF WI	WI	394.2
CANAL INS CO	SC	1,010.6
CENTRAL STATES INDEMNITY CO OF OMAHA	NE	209.1
COUNTRY CASUALTY INS CO	IL	75.7
CUMIS INS SOCIETY INC	IA	1,228.8
FARMLAND MUTUAL INS CO	IA	371.1
FEDERAL INS CO	IN	28,842.9
FEDERATED SERVICE INS CO	MN	358.9
FOREMOST INS CO	MI	2,024.3
GEICO GENERAL INS CO	MD	175.2
GEICO INDEMNITY CO	MD	5,117.3
GOVERNMENT EMPLOYEES INS CO	MD	12,473.2
GREAT NORTHERN INS CO	IN	1,518.9
HARTFORD FIRE INS CO	CT	23,864.9
HARTFORD INS CO OF THE MIDWEST	IN	359.6
HARTFORD UNDERWRITERS INS CO	CT	1,564.1
METROPOLITAN PROPERTY & CAS INS CO	RI	4,771.4
MIDWEST MEDICAL INS CO	MN	490.6
NATIONAL CASUALTY CO	WI	144.3
NATIONWIDE MUTUAL FIRE INS CO	OH	4,143.4
PACIFIC INDEMNITY CO	WI	5,651.8
SOUTHERN-OWNERS INS CO	MI	377.7
STATE FARM MUTUAL AUTOMOBILE INS CO	IL	88,473.2
TRUSTGARD INS CO	OH	66.4
USAA GENERAL INDEMNITY CO	TX	452.4
WESTERN AGRICULTURAL INS CO	IA	309.2

Montana

INSURANCE COMPANY NAME	DOM. STATE	TOTAL ASSETS ($MIL)
Rating: A+		
DAIRYLAND INS CO	WI	1,222.3
UNITED SERVICES AUTOMOBILE ASN	TX	19,904.8
USAA CASUALTY INS CO	TX	6,714.4
Rating: A		
CHURCH MUTUAL INS CO	WI	1,150.7
COUNTRY MUTUAL INS CO	IL	3,364.1
FRANKENMUTH MUTUAL INS CO	MI	955.3
MOUNTAIN WEST FARM BU MUTUAL INS CO	WY	339.7
PROTECTIVE INS CO	IN	529.3
SENTRY INS A MUTUAL CO	WI	5,330.6
TOKIO MARINE & NICHIDO FIRE INS LTD	NY	1,706.6
Rating: A-		
BITUMINOUS CASUALTY CORP	IL	725.4
BITUMINOUS FIRE & MARINE INS CO	IL	463.7
CINCINNATI INDEMNITY CO	OH	87.6
CINCINNATI INS CO	OH	8,454.0
FEDERATED MUTUAL INS CO	MN	3,817.8
GENERAL STAR NATIONAL INS CO	OH	340.1
GREAT WEST CASUALTY CO	NE	1,460.5
JEWELERS MUTUAL INS CO	WI	186.8
NATIONAL LIABILITY & FIRE INS CO	CT	1,040.7
OLD REPUBLIC GENERAL INS CORP	IL	985.4
OLD REPUBLIC INS CO	PA	2,301.6
OLD REPUBLIC SURETY CO	WI	94.2
TRAVELERS INDEMNITY CO	CT	20,531.8
Rating: B+		
ALLSTATE INS CO	IL	39,333.3
AMERICAN FAMILY HOME INS CO	FL	443.6
AMERICAN MERCURY INS CO	OK	334.3
AMERICAN MODERN HOME INS CO	OH	888.8
AMERICAN NATIONAL GENERAL INS CO	MO	99.8
AMERICAN NATIONAL PROPERTY & CAS CO	MO	1,068.4
AMERICAN STANDARD INS CO OF WI	WI	394.2
CANAL INS CO	SC	1,010.6
CENTRAL STATES INDEMNITY CO OF OMAHA	NE	209.1
COPIC INS CO	CO	435.6
COUNTRY CASUALTY INS CO	IL	75.7
CUMIS INS SOCIETY INC	IA	1,228.8
FARMLAND MUTUAL INS CO	IA	371.1
FEDERAL INS CO	IN	28,842.9
FEDERATED SERVICE INS CO	MN	358.9
FOREMOST INS CO	MI	2,024.3
GEICO GENERAL INS CO	MD	175.2
GEICO INDEMNITY CO	MD	5,117.3
GOVERNMENT EMPLOYEES INS CO	MD	12,473.2
GREAT NORTHERN INS CO	IN	1,518.9
HARTFORD FIRE INS CO	CT	23,864.9
HARTFORD INS CO OF THE MIDWEST	IN	359.6
HARTFORD UNDERWRITERS INS CO	CT	1,564.1
METROPOLITAN PROPERTY & CAS INS CO	RI	4,771.4
MIDWEST MEDICAL INS CO	MN	490.6
NATIONAL CASUALTY CO	WI	144.3
NATIONWIDE MUTUAL FIRE INS CO	OH	4,143.4
PACIFIC INDEMNITY CO	WI	5,651.8
STATE FARM MUTUAL AUTOMOBILE INS CO	IL	88,473.2
USAA GENERAL INDEMNITY CO	TX	452.4
WESTERN AGRICULTURAL INS CO	IA	309.2

Nebraska

INSURANCE COMPANY NAME	DOM. STATE	TOTAL ASSETS ($MIL)
Rating: A+		
DAIRYLAND INS CO	WI	1,222.3
UNITED SERVICES AUTOMOBILE ASN	TX	19,904.8
USAA CASUALTY INS CO	TX	6,714.4
Rating: A		
AUTO-OWNERS INS CO	MI	8,899.8
CHURCH MUTUAL INS CO	WI	1,150.7
COUNTRY MUTUAL INS CO	IL	3,364.1
FRANKENMUTH MUTUAL INS CO	MI	955.3
HOME-OWNERS INS CO	MI	1,353.2
PROTECTIVE INS CO	IN	529.3
SENTRY INS A MUTUAL CO	WI	5,330.6
TOKIO MARINE & NICHIDO FIRE INS LTD	NY	1,706.6
Rating: A-		
BITUMINOUS CASUALTY CORP	IL	725.4
BITUMINOUS FIRE & MARINE INS CO	IL	463.7
CINCINNATI INDEMNITY CO	OH	87.6
CINCINNATI INS CO	OH	8,454.0
FARM BUREAU MUTUAL INS CO	IA	1,586.9
FEDERATED MUTUAL INS CO	MN	3,817.8
GENERAL STAR NATIONAL INS CO	OH	340.1
GREAT WEST CASUALTY CO	NE	1,460.5
JEWELERS MUTUAL INS CO	WI	186.8
NATIONAL LIABILITY & FIRE INS CO	CT	1,040.7
OLD REPUBLIC GENERAL INS CORP	IL	985.4
OLD REPUBLIC INS CO	PA	2,301.6
OLD REPUBLIC SURETY CO	WI	94.2
OWNERS INS CO	OH	2,535.6
PROPERTY-OWNERS INS CO	IN	147.1
TRAVELERS INDEMNITY CO	CT	20,531.8
Rating: B+		
ALLSTATE INS CO	IL	39,333.3
AMERICAN FAMILY HOME INS CO	FL	443.6
AMERICAN MERCURY INS CO	OK	334.3
AMERICAN MODERN HOME INS CO	OH	888.8
AMERICAN NATIONAL GENERAL INS CO	MO	99.8
AMERICAN NATIONAL PROPERTY & CAS CO	MO	1,068.4
AMERICAN STANDARD INS CO OF WI	WI	394.2
ARCH SPECIALTY INS CO	NE	437.3
CANAL INS CO	SC	1,010.6
CENTRAL STATES INDEMNITY CO OF OMAHA	NE	209.1
COPIC INS CO	CO	435.6
CORNHUSKER CASUALTY CO	NE	533.2
COUNTRY CASUALTY INS CO	IL	75.7
CUMIS INS SOCIETY INC	IA	1,228.8
FARMLAND MUTUAL INS CO	IA	371.1
FEDERAL INS CO	IN	28,842.9
FEDERATED SERVICE INS CO	MN	358.9
FOREMOST INS CO	MI	2,024.3
GEICO GENERAL INS CO	MD	175.2
GEICO INDEMNITY CO	MD	5,117.3
GOVERNMENT EMPLOYEES INS CO	MD	12,473.2
GREAT NORTHERN INS CO	IN	1,518.9
HARTFORD FIRE INS CO	CT	23,864.9
HARTFORD INS CO OF THE MIDWEST	IN	359.6
HARTFORD UNDERWRITERS INS CO	CT	1,564.1
METROPOLITAN PROPERTY & CAS INS CO	RI	4,771.4
MIDWEST MEDICAL INS CO	MN	490.6
NATIONAL CASUALTY CO	WI	144.3
NATIONWIDE MUTUAL FIRE INS CO	OH	4,143.4
NORTH STAR MUTUAL INS CO	MN	340.1
PACIFIC INDEMNITY CO	WI	5,651.8
SOUTHERN-OWNERS INS CO	MI	377.7
STATE FARM MUTUAL AUTOMOBILE INS CO	IL	88,473.2
TRUSTGARD INS CO	OH	66.4
USAA GENERAL INDEMNITY CO	TX	452.4
WESCO-FINANCIAL INS CO	NE	2,526.8
WESTERN AGRICULTURAL INS CO	IA	309.2

Nevada

INSURANCE COMPANY NAME	DOM. STATE	TOTAL ASSETS ($MIL)
Rating: A+		
DAIRYLAND INS CO	WI	1,222.3
UNITED SERVICES AUTOMOBILE ASN	TX	19,904.8
USAA CASUALTY INS CO	TX	6,714.4
Rating: A		
AUTO-OWNERS INS CO	MI	8,899.8
CHURCH MUTUAL INS CO	WI	1,150.7
COUNTRY MUTUAL INS CO	IL	3,364.1
FRANKENMUTH MUTUAL INS CO	MI	955.3
HOME-OWNERS INS CO	MI	1,353.2
PROTECTIVE INS CO	IN	529.3
SENTRY INS A MUTUAL CO	WI	5,330.6
TOKIO MARINE & NICHIDO FIRE INS LTD	NY	1,706.6
Rating: A-		
BITUMINOUS CASUALTY CORP	IL	725.4
BITUMINOUS FIRE & MARINE INS CO	IL	463.7
CALIFORNIA STATE AUTO ASN INTER-INS	CA	5,291.7
CINCINNATI INS CO	OH	8,454.0
FEDERATED MUTUAL INS CO	MN	3,817.8
GENERAL STAR NATIONAL INS CO	OH	340.1
GREAT WEST CASUALTY CO	NE	1,460.5
JEWELERS MUTUAL INS CO	WI	186.8
MERCURY CASUALTY CO	CA	2,212.7
NATIONAL LIABILITY & FIRE INS CO	CT	1,040.7
OLD REPUBLIC GENERAL INS CORP	IL	985.4
OLD REPUBLIC INS CO	PA	2,301.6
OLD REPUBLIC SURETY CO	WI	94.2
OWNERS INS CO	OH	2,535.6
PROPERTY-OWNERS INS CO	IN	147.1
TRAVELERS INDEMNITY CO	CT	20,531.8
Rating: B+		
ALLSTATE INS CO	IL	39,333.3
AMERICAN FAMILY HOME INS CO	FL	443.6
AMERICAN MERCURY INS CO	OK	334.3
AMERICAN MODERN HOME INS CO	OH	888.8
AMERICAN NATIONAL GENERAL INS CO	MO	99.8
AMERICAN NATIONAL PROPERTY & CAS CO	MO	1,068.4
AMERICAN STANDARD INS CO OF WI	WI	394.2
CANAL INS CO	SC	1,010.6
CENTRAL MUTUAL INS CO	OH	1,238.6
CENTRAL STATES INDEMNITY CO OF OMAHA	NE	209.1
COUNTRY CASUALTY INS CO	IL	75.7
CUMIS INS SOCIETY INC	IA	1,228.8
FARMLAND MUTUAL INS CO	IA	371.1
FEDERAL INS CO	IN	28,842.9
FEDERATED SERVICE INS CO	MN	358.9
FOREMOST INS CO	MI	2,024.3
GEICO GENERAL INS CO	MD	175.2
GEICO INDEMNITY CO	MD	5,117.3
GOVERNMENT EMPLOYEES INS CO	MD	12,473.2
GREAT NORTHERN INS CO	IN	1,518.9
HARTFORD FIRE INS CO	CT	23,864.9
HARTFORD INS CO OF THE MIDWEST	IN	359.6
HARTFORD UNDERWRITERS INS CO	CT	1,564.1
METROPOLITAN PROPERTY & CAS INS CO	RI	4,771.4
NATIONAL CASUALTY CO	WI	144.3
NATIONWIDE MUTUAL FIRE INS CO	OH	4,143.4
PACIFIC INDEMNITY CO	WI	5,651.8
SOUTHERN-OWNERS INS CO	MI	377.7
STATE FARM MUTUAL AUTOMOBILE INS CO	IL	88,473.2
USAA GENERAL INDEMNITY CO	TX	452.4
WESTERN AGRICULTURAL INS CO	IA	309.2

New Hampshire

INSURANCE COMPANY NAME	DOM. STATE	TOTAL ASSETS ($MIL)
Rating: A+		
DAIRYLAND INS CO	WI	1,222.3
INTERINS EXCH OF THE AUTOMOBILE CLUB	CA	5,434.9
UNITED SERVICES AUTOMOBILE ASN	TX	19,904.8
USAA CASUALTY INS CO	TX	6,714.4
Rating: A		
CHURCH MUTUAL INS CO	WI	1,150.7
FRANKENMUTH MUTUAL INS CO	MI	955.3
MERRIMACK MUTUAL FIRE INS CO	MA	883.0
PROTECTIVE INS CO	IN	529.3
SENTRY INS A MUTUAL CO	WI	5,330.6
TOKIO MARINE & NICHIDO FIRE INS LTD	NY	1,706.6
Rating: A-		
CINCINNATI INS CO	OH	8,454.0
FEDERATED MUTUAL INS CO	MN	3,817.8
GENERAL STAR NATIONAL INS CO	OH	340.1
GREAT WEST CASUALTY CO	NE	1,460.5
JEWELERS MUTUAL INS CO	WI	186.8
OLD REPUBLIC GENERAL INS CORP	IL	985.4
OLD REPUBLIC INS CO	PA	2,301.6
TRAVELERS INDEMNITY CO	CT	20,531.8
Rating: B+		
ALLSTATE INS CO	IL	39,333.3
AMERICAN MODERN HOME INS CO	OH	888.8
AMERICAN NATIONAL PROPERTY & CAS CO	MO	1,068.4
BAY STATE INS CO	MA	285.6
CANAL INS CO	SC	1,010.6
CENTRAL MUTUAL INS CO	OH	1,238.6
CENTRAL STATES INDEMNITY CO OF OMAHA	NE	209.1
COMMERCE INS CO	MA	2,513.5
CUMIS INS SOCIETY INC	IA	1,228.8
FEDERAL INS CO	IN	28,842.9
FOREMOST INS CO	MI	2,024.3
GEICO GENERAL INS CO	MD	175.2
GEICO INDEMNITY CO	MD	5,117.3
GOVERNMENT EMPLOYEES INS CO	MD	12,473.2
GREAT NORTHERN INS CO	IN	1,518.9
HARTFORD FIRE INS CO	CT	23,864.9
HARTFORD INS CO OF THE MIDWEST	IN	359.6
HARTFORD UNDERWRITERS INS CO	CT	1,564.1
METROPOLITAN PROPERTY & CAS INS CO	RI	4,771.4
NATIONAL CASUALTY CO	WI	144.3
NATIONWIDE MUTUAL FIRE INS CO	OH	4,143.4
PACIFIC INDEMNITY CO	WI	5,651.8
STATE FARM MUTUAL AUTOMOBILE INS CO	IL	88,473.2
USAA GENERAL INDEMNITY CO	TX	452.4

New Jersey

INSURANCE COMPANY NAME	DOM. STATE	TOTAL ASSETS ($MIL)
Rating: A+		
UNITED SERVICES AUTOMOBILE ASN	TX	19,904.8
USAA CASUALTY INS CO	TX	6,714.4
Rating: A		
CHURCH MUTUAL INS CO	WI	1,150.7
FRANKENMUTH MUTUAL INS CO	MI	955.3
MERRIMACK MUTUAL FIRE INS CO	MA	883.0
PROTECTIVE INS CO	IN	529.3
SENTRY INS A MUTUAL CO	WI	5,330.6
TOKIO MARINE & NICHIDO FIRE INS LTD	NY	1,706.6
Rating: A-		
BITUMINOUS CASUALTY CORP	IL	725.4
BITUMINOUS FIRE & MARINE INS CO	IL	463.7
CINCINNATI INS CO	OH	8,454.0
FEDERATED MUTUAL INS CO	MN	3,817.8
GENERAL STAR NATIONAL INS CO	OH	340.1
GREAT WEST CASUALTY CO	NE	1,460.5
JEWELERS MUTUAL INS CO	WI	186.8
NATIONAL LIABILITY & FIRE INS CO	CT	1,040.7
OLD REPUBLIC GENERAL INS CORP	IL	985.4
OLD REPUBLIC INS CO	PA	2,301.6
TRAVELERS INDEMNITY CO	CT	20,531.8
Rating: B+		
AMERICAN FAMILY HOME INS CO	FL	443.6
AMERICAN MERCURY INS CO	OK	334.3
AMERICAN MODERN HOME INS CO	OH	888.8
AMERICAN NATIONAL PROPERTY & CAS CO	MO	1,068.4
BAY STATE INS CO	MA	285.6
CENTRAL MUTUAL INS CO	OH	1,238.6
CENTRAL STATES INDEMNITY CO OF OMAHA	NE	209.1
CUMBERLAND MUTUAL FIRE INS CO	NJ	245.0
CUMIS INS SOCIETY INC	IA	1,228.8
FEDERAL INS CO	IN	28,842.9
FOREMOST INS CO	MI	2,024.3
GEICO GENERAL INS CO	MD	175.2
GEICO INDEMNITY CO	MD	5,117.3
GOVERNMENT EMPLOYEES INS CO	MD	12,473.2
GREAT NORTHERN INS CO	IN	1,518.9
HARTFORD FIRE INS CO	CT	23,864.9
HARTFORD INS CO OF THE MIDWEST	IN	359.6
HARTFORD UNDERWRITERS INS CO	CT	1,564.1
INS CO OF GREATER NY	NY	101.2
METROPOLITAN PROPERTY & CAS INS CO	RI	4,771.4
NATIONAL CASUALTY CO	WI	144.3
NATIONWIDE MUTUAL FIRE INS CO	OH	4,143.4
PACIFIC INDEMNITY CO	WI	5,651.8
STATE FARM MUTUAL AUTOMOBILE INS CO	IL	88,473.2
USAA GENERAL INDEMNITY CO	TX	452.4

INSURANCE COMPANY NAME	DOM. STATE	TOTAL ASSETS ($MIL)

New Mexico

INSURANCE COMPANY NAME	DOM. STATE	TOTAL ASSETS ($MIL)
Rating: A+		
DAIRYLAND INS CO	WI	1,222.3
INTERINS EXCH OF THE AUTOMOBILE CLUB	CA	5,434.9
UNITED SERVICES AUTOMOBILE ASN	TX	19,904.8
USAA CASUALTY INS CO	TX	6,714.4
Rating: A		
AUTO-OWNERS INS CO	MI	8,899.8
CHURCH MUTUAL INS CO	WI	1,150.7
FRANKENMUTH MUTUAL INS CO	MI	955.3
PROTECTIVE INS CO	IN	529.3
SENTRY INS A MUTUAL CO	WI	5,330.6
TOKIO MARINE & NICHIDO FIRE INS LTD	NY	1,706.6
Rating: A-		
BITUMINOUS CASUALTY CORP	IL	725.4
BITUMINOUS FIRE & MARINE INS CO	IL	463.7
CINCINNATI INS CO	OH	8,454.0
FARM BUREAU MUTUAL INS CO	IA	1,586.9
FEDERATED MUTUAL INS CO	MN	3,817.8
GENERAL STAR NATIONAL INS CO	OH	340.1
GREAT WEST CASUALTY CO	NE	1,460.5
JEWELERS MUTUAL INS CO	WI	186.8
MUTUAL INS CO OF AZ	AZ	891.6
NATIONAL LIABILITY & FIRE INS CO	CT	1,040.7
OLD REPUBLIC GENERAL INS CORP	IL	985.4
OLD REPUBLIC INS CO	PA	2,301.6
OLD REPUBLIC SURETY CO	WI	94.2
OWNERS INS CO	OH	2,535.6
TRAVELERS INDEMNITY CO	CT	20,531.8
Rating: B+		
ALLSTATE INS CO	IL	39,333.3
AMERICAN FAMILY HOME INS CO	FL	443.6
AMERICAN MERCURY INS CO	OK	334.3
AMERICAN MODERN HOME INS CO	OH	888.8
AMERICAN NATIONAL GENERAL INS CO	MO	99.8
AMERICAN NATIONAL PROPERTY & CAS CO	MO	1,068.4
AMERICAN STANDARD INS CO OF WI	WI	394.2
CANAL INS CO	SC	1,010.6
CENTRAL MUTUAL INS CO	OH	1,238.6
CENTRAL STATES INDEMNITY CO OF OMAHA	NE	209.1
COUNTRY CASUALTY INS CO	IL	75.7
CUMIS INS SOCIETY INC	IA	1,228.8
FEDERAL INS CO	IN	28,842.9
FEDERATED SERVICE INS CO	MN	358.9
FOREMOST INS CO	MI	2,024.3
GEICO GENERAL INS CO	MD	175.2
GEICO INDEMNITY CO	MD	5,117.3
GOVERNMENT EMPLOYEES INS CO	MD	12,473.2
GREAT NORTHERN INS CO	IN	1,518.9
HARTFORD FIRE INS CO	CT	23,864.9
HARTFORD INS CO OF THE MIDWEST	IN	359.6
HARTFORD UNDERWRITERS INS CO	CT	1,564.1
METROPOLITAN PROPERTY & CAS INS CO	RI	4,771.4
NATIONAL CASUALTY CO	WI	144.3
NATIONWIDE MUTUAL FIRE INS CO	OH	4,143.4
PACIFIC INDEMNITY CO	WI	5,651.8
STATE FARM MUTUAL AUTOMOBILE INS CO	IL	88,473.2
USAA GENERAL INDEMNITY CO	TX	452.4
WESTERN AGRICULTURAL INS CO	IA	309.2
WESTFIELD NATIONAL INS CO	OH	437.0

New York

INSURANCE COMPANY NAME	DOM. STATE	TOTAL ASSETS ($MIL)
Rating: A+		
DAIRYLAND INS CO	WI	1,222.3
UNITED SERVICES AUTOMOBILE ASN	TX	19,904.8
USAA CASUALTY INS CO	TX	6,714.4
Rating: A		
CHURCH MUTUAL INS CO	WI	1,150.7
FRANKENMUTH MUTUAL INS CO	MI	955.3
MERRIMACK MUTUAL FIRE INS CO	MA	883.0
PROTECTIVE INS CO	IN	529.3
SENTRY INS A MUTUAL CO	WI	5,330.6
TOKIO MARINE & NICHIDO FIRE INS LTD	NY	1,706.6
Rating: A-		
BITUMINOUS CASUALTY CORP	IL	725.4
BITUMINOUS FIRE & MARINE INS CO	IL	463.7
CINCINNATI INDEMNITY CO	OH	87.6
CINCINNATI INS CO	OH	8,454.0
FEDERATED MUTUAL INS CO	MN	3,817.8
GENERAL STAR NATIONAL INS CO	OH	340.1
GREAT WEST CASUALTY CO	NE	1,460.5
JEWELERS MUTUAL INS CO	WI	186.8
MERCURY CASUALTY CO	CA	2,212.7
NATIONAL LIABILITY & FIRE INS CO	CT	1,040.7
OLD REPUBLIC GENERAL INS CORP	IL	985.4
OLD REPUBLIC INS CO	PA	2,301.6
OTSEGO MUTUAL FIRE INS CO	NY	70.8
TRAVELERS INDEMNITY CO	CT	20,531.8
Rating: B+		
ALLSTATE INS CO	IL	39,333.3
AMERICAN FAMILY HOME INS CO	FL	443.6
AMERICAN MODERN HOME INS CO	OH	888.8
BAY STATE INS CO	MA	285.6
CANAL INS CO	SC	1,010.6
CENTRAL MUTUAL INS CO	OH	1,238.6
CENTRAL STATES INDEMNITY CO OF OMAHA	NE	209.1
CUMIS INS SOCIETY INC	IA	1,228.8
ERIE INS CO OF NY	NY	58.4
FEDERAL INS CO	IN	28,842.9
FEDERATED SERVICE INS CO	MN	358.9
FOREMOST INS CO	MI	2,024.3
GEICO GENERAL INS CO	MD	175.2
GEICO INDEMNITY CO	MD	5,117.3
GOVERNMENT EMPLOYEES INS CO	MD	12,473.2
GREAT NORTHERN INS CO	IN	1,518.9
HARTFORD FIRE INS CO	CT	23,864.9
HARTFORD INS CO OF THE MIDWEST	IN	359.6
HARTFORD UNDERWRITERS INS CO	CT	1,564.1
INS CO OF GREATER NY	NY	101.2
METROPOLITAN PROPERTY & CAS INS CO	RI	4,771.4
NATIONAL CASUALTY CO	WI	144.3
NATIONWIDE MUTUAL FIRE INS CO	OH	4,143.4
PACIFIC INDEMNITY CO	WI	5,651.8
SAMSUNG FIRE & MARINE INS CO LTD US	NY	69.7
STATE FARM MUTUAL AUTOMOBILE INS CO	IL	88,473.2
USAA GENERAL INDEMNITY CO	TX	452.4

North Carolina

INSURANCE COMPANY NAME	DOM. STATE	TOTAL ASSETS ($MIL)
Rating: A+		
DAIRYLAND INS CO	WI	1,222.3
UNITED SERVICES AUTOMOBILE ASN	TX	19,904.8
USAA CASUALTY INS CO	TX	6,714.4
Rating: A		
AUTO-OWNERS INS CO	MI	8,899.8
CHURCH MUTUAL INS CO	WI	1,150.7
FRANKENMUTH MUTUAL INS CO	MI	955.3
NORTH CAROLINA FARM BU MUTUAL INS CO	NC	1,627.5
PROTECTIVE INS CO	IN	529.3
SENTRY INS A MUTUAL CO	WI	5,330.6
TOKIO MARINE & NICHIDO FIRE INS LTD	NY	1,706.6
Rating: A-		
BITUMINOUS CASUALTY CORP	IL	725.4
BITUMINOUS FIRE & MARINE INS CO	IL	463.7
CINCINNATI INDEMNITY CO	OH	87.6
CINCINNATI INS CO	OH	8,454.0
FEDERATED MUTUAL INS CO	MN	3,817.8
GENERAL STAR NATIONAL INS CO	OH	340.1
GREAT WEST CASUALTY CO	NE	1,460.5
JEWELERS MUTUAL INS CO	WI	186.8
NATIONAL LIABILITY & FIRE INS CO	CT	1,040.7
OLD REPUBLIC GENERAL INS CORP	IL	985.4
OLD REPUBLIC INS CO	PA	2,301.6
OLD REPUBLIC SURETY CO	WI	94.2
OWNERS INS CO	OH	2,535.6
STATE VOLUNTEER MUTUAL INS CO	TN	996.2
TRAVELERS INDEMNITY CO	CT	20,531.8
Rating: B+		
ALLSTATE INS CO	IL	39,333.3
AMERICAN FAMILY HOME INS CO	FL	443.6
AMERICAN MODERN HOME INS CO	OH	888.8
AMERICAN NATIONAL PROPERTY & CAS CO	MO	1,068.4
AMERICAN STANDARD INS CO OF WI	WI	394.2
CANAL INS CO	SC	1,010.6
CENTRAL MUTUAL INS CO	OH	1,238.6
CENTRAL STATES INDEMNITY CO OF OMAHA	NE	209.1
CORNHUSKER CASUALTY CO	NE	533.2
CUMIS INS SOCIETY INC	IA	1,228.8
FARMLAND MUTUAL INS CO	IA	371.1
FEDERAL INS CO	IN	28,842.9
FEDERATED SERVICE INS CO	MN	358.9
FOREMOST INS CO	MI	2,024.3
GEICO GENERAL INS CO	MD	175.2
GEICO INDEMNITY CO	MD	5,117.3
GOVERNMENT EMPLOYEES INS CO	MD	12,473.2
GREAT NORTHERN INS CO	IN	1,518.9
HARTFORD FIRE INS CO	CT	23,864.9
HARTFORD INS CO OF THE MIDWEST	IN	359.6
HARTFORD UNDERWRITERS INS CO	CT	1,564.1
METROPOLITAN PROPERTY & CAS INS CO	RI	4,771.4
NATIONAL CASUALTY CO	WI	144.3
NATIONWIDE MUTUAL FIRE INS CO	OH	4,143.4
PACIFIC INDEMNITY CO	WI	5,651.8
STATE FARM MUTUAL AUTOMOBILE INS CO	IL	88,473.2
USAA GENERAL INDEMNITY CO	TX	452.4

North Dakota

INSURANCE COMPANY NAME	DOM. STATE	TOTAL ASSETS ($MIL)
Rating: A+		
DAIRYLAND INS CO	WI	1,222.3
UNITED SERVICES AUTOMOBILE ASN	TX	19,904.8
USAA CASUALTY INS CO	TX	6,714.4
Rating: A		
AUTO-OWNERS INS CO	MI	8,899.8
CHURCH MUTUAL INS CO	WI	1,150.7
COUNTRY MUTUAL INS CO	IL	3,364.1
FRANKENMUTH MUTUAL INS CO	MI	955.3
HOME-OWNERS INS CO	MI	1,353.2
PROTECTIVE INS CO	IN	529.3
SENTRY INS A MUTUAL CO	WI	5,330.6
TOKIO MARINE & NICHIDO FIRE INS LTD	NY	1,706.6
Rating: A-		
BITUMINOUS CASUALTY CORP	IL	725.4
BITUMINOUS FIRE & MARINE INS CO	IL	463.7
CINCINNATI INDEMNITY CO	OH	87.6
CINCINNATI INS CO	OH	8,454.0
FEDERATED MUTUAL INS CO	MN	3,817.8
GENERAL STAR NATIONAL INS CO	OH	340.1
GREAT WEST CASUALTY CO	NE	1,460.5
JEWELERS MUTUAL INS CO	WI	186.8
NATIONAL LIABILITY & FIRE INS CO	CT	1,040.7
OLD REPUBLIC GENERAL INS CORP	IL	985.4
OLD REPUBLIC INS CO	PA	2,301.6
OLD REPUBLIC SURETY CO	WI	94.2
OWNERS INS CO	OH	2,535.6
PROPERTY-OWNERS INS CO	IN	147.1
TRAVELERS INDEMNITY CO	CT	20,531.8
Rating: B+		
ALLSTATE INS CO	IL	39,333.3
AMERICAN FAMILY HOME INS CO	FL	443.6
AMERICAN MERCURY INS CO	OK	334.3
AMERICAN MODERN HOME INS CO	OH	888.8
AMERICAN NATIONAL GENERAL INS CO	MO	99.8
AMERICAN NATIONAL PROPERTY & CAS CO	MO	1,068.4
AMERICAN STANDARD INS CO OF WI	WI	394.2
CANAL INS CO	SC	1,010.6
CENTRAL STATES INDEMNITY CO OF OMAHA	NE	209.1
COUNTRY CASUALTY INS CO	IL	75.7
CUMIS INS SOCIETY INC	IA	1,228.8
FARMLAND MUTUAL INS CO	IA	371.1
FEDERAL INS CO	IN	28,842.9
FEDERATED SERVICE INS CO	MN	358.9
FOREMOST INS CO	MI	2,024.3
GEICO GENERAL INS CO	MD	175.2
GEICO INDEMNITY CO	MD	5,117.3
GOVERNMENT EMPLOYEES INS CO	MD	12,473.2
GREAT NORTHERN INS CO	IN	1,518.9
HARTFORD FIRE INS CO	CT	23,864.9
HARTFORD INS CO OF THE MIDWEST	IN	359.6
HARTFORD UNDERWRITERS INS CO	CT	1,564.1
METROPOLITAN PROPERTY & CAS INS CO	RI	4,771.4
MIDWEST MEDICAL INS CO	MN	490.6
NATIONAL CASUALTY CO	WI	144.3
NATIONWIDE MUTUAL FIRE INS CO	OH	4,143.4
NORTH STAR MUTUAL INS CO	MN	340.1
PACIFIC INDEMNITY CO	WI	5,651.8
SOUTHERN-OWNERS INS CO	MI	377.7
STATE FARM MUTUAL AUTOMOBILE INS CO	IL	88,473.2
TRUSTGARD INS CO	OH	66.4
USAA GENERAL INDEMNITY CO	TX	452.4
WESTERN AGRICULTURAL INS CO	IA	309.2
WESTFIELD NATIONAL INS CO	OH	437.0

Ohio

INSURANCE COMPANY NAME	DOM. STATE	TOTAL ASSETS ($MIL)
Rating: A+		
DAIRYLAND INS CO	WI	1,222.3
HASTINGS MUTUAL INS CO	MI	591.7
INTERINS EXCH OF THE AUTOMOBILE CLUB	CA	5,434.9
UNITED SERVICES AUTOMOBILE ASN	TX	19,904.8
USAA CASUALTY INS CO	TX	6,714.4
Rating: A		
AUTO-OWNERS INS CO	MI	8,899.8
CHURCH MUTUAL INS CO	WI	1,150.7
FRANKENMUTH MUTUAL INS CO	MI	955.3
HOME-OWNERS INS CO	MI	1,353.2
PROTECTIVE INS CO	IN	529.3
SENTRY INS A MUTUAL CO	WI	5,330.6
TOKIO MARINE & NICHIDO FIRE INS LTD	NY	1,706.6
Rating: A-		
BITUMINOUS CASUALTY CORP	IL	725.4
BITUMINOUS FIRE & MARINE INS CO	IL	463.7
CINCINNATI INDEMNITY CO	OH	87.6
CINCINNATI INS CO	OH	8,454.0
FEDERATED MUTUAL INS CO	MN	3,817.8
GENERAL STAR NATIONAL INS CO	OH	340.1
GRANGE MUTUAL CAS CO	OH	1,525.7
GREAT WEST CASUALTY CO	NE	1,460.5
JEWELERS MUTUAL INS CO	WI	186.8
NATIONAL LIABILITY & FIRE INS CO	CT	1,040.7
OLD REPUBLIC GENERAL INS CORP	IL	985.4
OLD REPUBLIC INS CO	PA	2,301.6
OLD REPUBLIC SURETY CO	WI	94.2
OWNERS INS CO	OH	2,535.6
TRAVELERS INDEMNITY CO	CT	20,531.8
Rating: B+		
ALLSTATE INS CO	IL	39,333.3
AMERICAN FAMILY HOME INS CO	FL	443.6
AMERICAN MODERN HOME INS CO	OH	888.8
AMERICAN NATIONAL GENERAL INS CO	MO	99.8
AMERICAN NATIONAL PROPERTY & CAS CO	MO	1,068.4
AMERICAN STANDARD INS CO OF WI	WI	394.2
CANAL INS CO	SC	1,010.6
CENTRAL MUTUAL INS CO	OH	1,238.6
CENTRAL STATES INDEMNITY CO OF OMAHA	NE	209.1
COUNTRY CASUALTY INS CO	IL	75.7
CUMBERLAND MUTUAL FIRE INS CO	NJ	245.0
CUMIS INS SOCIETY INC	IA	1,228.8
FARMERS AUTOMOBILE INS ASN	IL	852.7
FARMLAND MUTUAL INS CO	IA	371.1
FEDERAL INS CO	IN	28,842.9
FEDERATED SERVICE INS CO	MN	358.9
FOREMOST INS CO	MI	2,024.3
GEICO GENERAL INS CO	MD	175.2
GEICO INDEMNITY CO	MD	5,117.3
GOVERNMENT EMPLOYEES INS CO	MD	12,473.2
GREAT NORTHERN INS CO	IN	1,518.9
HARTFORD FIRE INS CO	CT	23,864.9
HARTFORD INS CO OF THE MIDWEST	IN	359.6
HARTFORD UNDERWRITERS INS CO	CT	1,564.1
METROPOLITAN PROPERTY & CAS INS CO	RI	4,771.4
MOTORISTS MUTUAL INS CO	OH	1,212.1
NATIONAL CASUALTY CO	WI	144.3
NATIONWIDE MUTUAL FIRE INS CO	OH	4,143.4
PACIFIC INDEMNITY CO	WI	5,651.8
PEKIN INS CO	IL	195.5
STATE FARM MUTUAL AUTOMOBILE INS CO	IL	88,473.2
TRUSTGARD INS CO	OH	66.4
TUSCARORA WAYNE MUTUAL INS CO	PA	54.2
UNITED FARM FAMILY MUTUAL INS CO	IN	787.9
USAA GENERAL INDEMNITY CO	TX	452.4
WEST BEND MUTUAL INS CO	WI	1,438.7
WESTFIELD NATIONAL INS CO	OH	437.0

Oklahoma

INSURANCE COMPANY NAME	DOM. STATE	TOTAL ASSETS ($MIL)
Rating: A+		
UNITED SERVICES AUTOMOBILE ASN	TX	19,904.8
USAA CASUALTY INS CO	TX	6,714.4
Rating: A		
CHURCH MUTUAL INS CO	WI	1,150.7
COUNTRY MUTUAL INS CO	IL	3,364.1
FRANKENMUTH MUTUAL INS CO	MI	955.3
PROTECTIVE INS CO	IN	529.3
SENTRY INS A MUTUAL CO	WI	5,330.6
TOKIO MARINE & NICHIDO FIRE INS LTD	NY	1,706.6
Rating: A-		
BITUMINOUS CASUALTY CORP	IL	725.4
BITUMINOUS FIRE & MARINE INS CO	IL	463.7
CINCINNATI INS CO	OH	8,454.0
FEDERATED MUTUAL INS CO	MN	3,817.8
GENERAL STAR NATIONAL INS CO	OH	340.1
GREAT WEST CASUALTY CO	NE	1,460.5
JEWELERS MUTUAL INS CO	WI	186.8
NATIONAL LIABILITY & FIRE INS CO	CT	1,040.7
OLD REPUBLIC GENERAL INS CORP	IL	985.4
OLD REPUBLIC INS CO	PA	2,301.6
OLD REPUBLIC SURETY CO	WI	94.2
TRAVELERS INDEMNITY CO	CT	20,531.8
Rating: B+		
ALLSTATE INS CO	IL	39,333.3
AMERICAN FAMILY HOME INS CO	FL	443.6
AMERICAN MERCURY INS CO	OK	334.3
AMERICAN MODERN HOME INS CO	OH	888.8
AMERICAN NATIONAL GENERAL INS CO	MO	99.8
AMERICAN NATIONAL PROPERTY & CAS CO	MO	1,068.4
CANAL INS CO	SC	1,010.6
CENTRAL MUTUAL INS CO	OH	1,238.6
CENTRAL STATES INDEMNITY CO OF OMAHA	NE	209.1
COUNTRY CASUALTY INS CO	IL	75.7
CUMIS INS SOCIETY INC	IA	1,228.8
FARMLAND MUTUAL INS CO	IA	371.1
FEDERAL INS CO	IN	28,842.9
FEDERATED SERVICE INS CO	MN	358.9
FOREMOST INS CO	MI	2,024.3
GEICO GENERAL INS CO	MD	175.2
GEICO INDEMNITY CO	MD	5,117.3
GOVERNMENT EMPLOYEES INS CO	MD	12,473.2
GREAT NORTHERN INS CO	IN	1,518.9
HARTFORD FIRE INS CO	CT	23,864.9
HARTFORD INS CO OF THE MIDWEST	IN	359.6
HARTFORD UNDERWRITERS INS CO	CT	1,564.1
METROPOLITAN PROPERTY & CAS INS CO	RI	4,771.4
NATIONAL CASUALTY CO	WI	144.3
NATIONWIDE MUTUAL FIRE INS CO	OH	4,143.4
NORTH STAR MUTUAL INS CO	MN	340.1
PACIFIC INDEMNITY CO	WI	5,651.8
STATE FARM MUTUAL AUTOMOBILE INS CO	IL	88,473.2
USAA GENERAL INDEMNITY CO	TX	452.4
WESTERN AGRICULTURAL INS CO	IA	309.2

Oregon

INSURANCE COMPANY NAME	DOM. STATE	TOTAL ASSETS ($MIL)
Rating: A+		
DAIRYLAND INS CO	WI	1,222.3
UNITED SERVICES AUTOMOBILE ASN	TX	19,904.8
USAA CASUALTY INS CO	TX	6,714.4
Rating: A		
AUTO-OWNERS INS CO	MI	8,899.8
CHURCH MUTUAL INS CO	WI	1,150.7
COUNTRY MUTUAL INS CO	IL	3,364.1
FRANKENMUTH MUTUAL INS CO	MI	955.3
PROTECTIVE INS CO	IN	529.3
SENTRY INS A MUTUAL CO	WI	5,330.6
TOKIO MARINE & NICHIDO FIRE INS LTD	NY	1,706.6
Rating: A-		
BITUMINOUS CASUALTY CORP	IL	725.4
BITUMINOUS FIRE & MARINE INS CO	IL	463.7
CINCINNATI INDEMNITY CO	OH	87.6
CINCINNATI INS CO	OH	8,454.0
FEDERATED MUTUAL INS CO	MN	3,817.8
GENERAL STAR NATIONAL INS CO	OH	340.1
GREAT WEST CASUALTY CO	NE	1,460.5
JEWELERS MUTUAL INS CO	WI	186.8
NATIONAL LIABILITY & FIRE INS CO	CT	1,040.7
OLD REPUBLIC GENERAL INS CORP	IL	985.4
OLD REPUBLIC INS CO	PA	2,301.6
OLD REPUBLIC SURETY CO	WI	94.2
OWNERS INS CO	OH	2,535.6
TRAVELERS INDEMNITY CO	CT	20,531.8
Rating: B+		
ALLSTATE INS CO	IL	39,333.3
AMERICAN FAMILY HOME INS CO	FL	443.6
AMERICAN MERCURY INS CO	OK	334.3
AMERICAN MODERN HOME INS CO	OH	888.8
AMERICAN NATIONAL GENERAL INS CO	MO	99.8
AMERICAN NATIONAL PROPERTY & CAS CO	MO	1,068.4
AMERICAN STANDARD INS CO OF WI	WI	394.2
CANAL INS CO	SC	1,010.6
CENTRAL STATES INDEMNITY CO OF OMAHA	NE	209.1
CORNHUSKER CASUALTY CO	NE	533.2
COUNTRY CASUALTY INS CO	IL	75.7
CUMIS INS SOCIETY INC	IA	1,228.8
FARMLAND MUTUAL INS CO	IA	371.1
FEDERAL INS CO	IN	28,842.9
FEDERATED SERVICE INS CO	MN	358.9
FOREMOST INS CO	MI	2,024.3
GEICO GENERAL INS CO	MD	175.2
GEICO INDEMNITY CO	MD	5,117.3
GOVERNMENT EMPLOYEES INS CO	MD	12,473.2
GREAT NORTHERN INS CO	IN	1,518.9
HARTFORD FIRE INS CO	CT	23,864.9
HARTFORD INS CO OF THE MIDWEST	IN	359.6
HARTFORD UNDERWRITERS INS CO	CT	1,564.1
METROPOLITAN PROPERTY & CAS INS CO	RI	4,771.4
NATIONAL CASUALTY CO	WI	144.3
NATIONWIDE MUTUAL FIRE INS CO	OH	4,143.4
PACIFIC INDEMNITY CO	WI	5,651.8
STATE FARM MUTUAL AUTOMOBILE INS CO	IL	88,473.2
TRUSTGARD INS CO	OH	66.4
USAA GENERAL INDEMNITY CO	TX	452.4
WESTERN AGRICULTURAL INS CO	IA	309.2
WESTERN COMMUNITY INS CO	ID	30.0

Pennsylvania

INSURANCE COMPANY NAME	DOM. STATE	TOTAL ASSETS ($MIL)
Rating: A+		
DAIRYLAND INS CO	WI	1,222.3
INTERINS EXCH OF THE AUTOMOBILE CLUB	CA	5,434.9
UNITED SERVICES AUTOMOBILE ASN	TX	19,904.8
USAA CASUALTY INS CO	TX	6,714.4
Rating: A		
AUTO-OWNERS INS CO	MI	8,899.8
CHURCH MUTUAL INS CO	WI	1,150.7
COUNTRY MUTUAL INS CO	IL	3,364.1
FRANKENMUTH MUTUAL INS CO	MI	955.3
HOME-OWNERS INS CO	MI	1,353.2
PROTECTIVE INS CO	IN	529.3
SENTRY INS A MUTUAL CO	WI	5,330.6
TOKIO MARINE & NICHIDO FIRE INS LTD	NY	1,706.6
Rating: A-		
BITUMINOUS CASUALTY CORP	IL	725.4
BITUMINOUS FIRE & MARINE INS CO	IL	463.7
CINCINNATI INDEMNITY CO	OH	87.6
CINCINNATI INS CO	OH	8,454.0
FEDERATED MUTUAL INS CO	MN	3,817.8
GENERAL STAR NATIONAL INS CO	OH	340.1
GRANGE MUTUAL CAS CO	OH	1,525.7
GREAT WEST CASUALTY CO	NE	1,460.5
JEWELERS MUTUAL INS CO	WI	186.8
NATIONAL LIABILITY & FIRE INS CO	CT	1,040.7
OLD REPUBLIC GENERAL INS CORP	IL	985.4
OLD REPUBLIC INS CO	PA	2,301.6
OLD REPUBLIC SURETY CO	WI	94.2
OWNERS INS CO	OH	2,535.6
TRAVELERS INDEMNITY CO	CT	20,531.8
Rating: B+		
ALLSTATE INS CO	IL	39,333.3
AMERICAN FAMILY HOME INS CO	FL	443.6
AMERICAN MERCURY INS CO	OK	334.3
AMERICAN MODERN HOME INS CO	OH	888.8
AMERICAN NATIONAL GENERAL INS CO	MO	99.8
AMERICAN NATIONAL PROPERTY & CAS CO	MO	1,068.4
CANAL INS CO	SC	1,010.6
CENTRAL MUTUAL INS CO	OH	1,238.6
CENTRAL STATES INDEMNITY CO OF OMAHA	NE	209.1
COUNTRY CASUALTY INS CO	IL	75.7
CUMBERLAND MUTUAL FIRE INS CO	NJ	245.0
CUMIS INS SOCIETY INC	IA	1,228.8
ERIE INS CO OF NY	NY	58.4
FARMLAND MUTUAL INS CO	IA	371.1
FEDERAL INS CO	IN	28,842.9
FEDERATED SERVICE INS CO	MN	358.9
FOREMOST INS CO	MI	2,024.3
GEICO GENERAL INS CO	MD	175.2
GEICO INDEMNITY CO	MD	5,117.3
GOVERNMENT EMPLOYEES INS CO	MD	12,473.2
GREAT NORTHERN INS CO	IN	1,518.9
HARTFORD FIRE INS CO	CT	23,864.9
HARTFORD INS CO OF THE MIDWEST	IN	359.6
HARTFORD UNDERWRITERS INS CO	CT	1,564.1
INS CO OF GREATER NY	NY	101.2
METROPOLITAN PROPERTY & CAS INS CO	RI	4,771.4
MOTORISTS MUTUAL INS CO	OH	1,212.1
NATIONAL CASUALTY CO	WI	144.3
NATIONWIDE MUTUAL FIRE INS CO	OH	4,143.4
PACIFIC INDEMNITY CO	WI	5,651.8
STATE FARM MUTUAL AUTOMOBILE INS CO	IL	88,473.2
TRUSTGARD INS CO	OH	66.4
TUSCARORA WAYNE MUTUAL INS CO	PA	54.2
USAA GENERAL INDEMNITY CO	TX	452.4
WESTFIELD NATIONAL INS CO	OH	437.0

Rhode Island

INSURANCE COMPANY NAME	DOM. STATE	TOTAL ASSETS ($MIL)
Rating: A+		
DAIRYLAND INS CO	WI	1,222.3
UNITED SERVICES AUTOMOBILE ASN	TX	19,904.8
USAA CASUALTY INS CO	TX	6,714.4
Rating: A		
CHURCH MUTUAL INS CO	WI	1,150.7
COUNTRY MUTUAL INS CO	IL	3,364.1
FRANKENMUTH MUTUAL INS CO	MI	955.3
MERRIMACK MUTUAL FIRE INS CO	MA	883.0
PROTECTIVE INS CO	IN	529.3
SENTRY INS A MUTUAL CO	WI	5,330.6
TOKIO MARINE & NICHIDO FIRE INS LTD	NY	1,706.6
Rating: A-		
BITUMINOUS CASUALTY CORP	IL	725.4
CINCINNATI INS CO	OH	8,454.0
FEDERATED MUTUAL INS CO	MN	3,817.8
GENERAL STAR NATIONAL INS CO	OH	340.1
GREAT WEST CASUALTY CO	NE	1,460.5
JEWELERS MUTUAL INS CO	WI	186.8
NATIONAL LIABILITY & FIRE INS CO	CT	1,040.7
OLD REPUBLIC GENERAL INS CORP	IL	985.4
OLD REPUBLIC INS CO	PA	2,301.6
TRAVELERS INDEMNITY CO	CT	20,531.8
Rating: B+		
ALLSTATE INS CO	IL	39,333.3
AMERICAN FAMILY HOME INS CO	FL	443.6
AMERICAN MODERN HOME INS CO	OH	888.8
AMERICAN NATIONAL PROPERTY & CAS CO	MO	1,068.4
BAY STATE INS CO	MA	285.6
CANAL INS CO	SC	1,010.6
CENTRAL STATES INDEMNITY CO OF OMAHA	NE	209.1
COMMERCE INS CO	MA	2,513.5
COUNTRY CASUALTY INS CO	IL	75.7
CUMIS INS SOCIETY INC	IA	1,228.8
FEDERAL INS CO	IN	28,842.9
FOREMOST INS CO	MI	2,024.3
GEICO GENERAL INS CO	MD	175.2
GEICO INDEMNITY CO	MD	5,117.3
GOVERNMENT EMPLOYEES INS CO	MD	12,473.2
GREAT NORTHERN INS CO	IN	1,518.9
HARTFORD FIRE INS CO	CT	23,864.9
HARTFORD INS CO OF THE MIDWEST	IN	359.6
HARTFORD UNDERWRITERS INS CO	CT	1,564.1
METROPOLITAN PROPERTY & CAS INS CO	RI	4,771.4
NATIONAL CASUALTY CO	WI	144.3
NATIONWIDE MUTUAL FIRE INS CO	OH	4,143.4
PACIFIC INDEMNITY CO	WI	5,651.8
STATE FARM MUTUAL AUTOMOBILE INS CO	IL	88,473.2
USAA GENERAL INDEMNITY CO	TX	452.4

South Carolina

INSURANCE COMPANY NAME	DOM. STATE	TOTAL ASSETS ($MIL)
Rating: A+		
DAIRYLAND INS CO	WI	1,222.3
UNITED SERVICES AUTOMOBILE ASN	TX	19,904.8
USAA CASUALTY INS CO	TX	6,714.4
Rating: A		
AUTO-OWNERS INS CO	MI	8,899.8
CHURCH MUTUAL INS CO	WI	1,150.7
FRANKENMUTH MUTUAL INS CO	MI	955.3
HOME-OWNERS INS CO	MI	1,353.2
PROTECTIVE INS CO	IN	529.3
SENTRY INS A MUTUAL CO	WI	5,330.6
TOKIO MARINE & NICHIDO FIRE INS LTD	NY	1,706.6
Rating: A-		
BITUMINOUS CASUALTY CORP	IL	725.4
BITUMINOUS FIRE & MARINE INS CO	IL	463.7
CINCINNATI INDEMNITY CO	OH	87.6
CINCINNATI INS CO	OH	8,454.0
FEDERATED MUTUAL INS CO	MN	3,817.8
GENERAL STAR NATIONAL INS CO	OH	340.1
GREAT WEST CASUALTY CO	NE	1,460.5
JEWELERS MUTUAL INS CO	WI	186.8
NATIONAL LIABILITY & FIRE INS CO	CT	1,040.7
OLD REPUBLIC GENERAL INS CORP	IL	985.4
OLD REPUBLIC INS CO	PA	2,301.6
OLD REPUBLIC SURETY CO	WI	94.2
OWNERS INS CO	OH	2,535.6
PROPERTY-OWNERS INS CO	IN	147.1
TRAVELERS INDEMNITY CO	CT	20,531.8
Rating: B+		
ALLSTATE INS CO	IL	39,333.3
AMERICAN FAMILY HOME INS CO	FL	443.6
AMERICAN MODERN HOME INS CO	OH	888.8
AMERICAN NATIONAL GENERAL INS CO	MO	99.8
AMERICAN NATIONAL PROPERTY & CAS CO	MO	1,068.4
AMERICAN STANDARD INS CO OF WI	WI	394.2
CANAL INS CO	SC	1,010.6
CENTRAL MUTUAL INS CO	OH	1,238.6
CENTRAL STATES INDEMNITY CO OF OMAHA	NE	209.1
CORNHUSKER CASUALTY CO	NE	533.2
CUMIS INS SOCIETY INC	IA	1,228.8
FARMLAND MUTUAL INS CO	IA	371.1
FEDERAL INS CO	IN	28,842.9
FEDERATED SERVICE INS CO	MN	358.9
FOREMOST INS CO	MI	2,024.3
GEICO GENERAL INS CO	MD	175.2
GEICO INDEMNITY CO	MD	5,117.3
GOVERNMENT EMPLOYEES INS CO	MD	12,473.2
GREAT NORTHERN INS CO	IN	1,518.9
HARTFORD FIRE INS CO	CT	23,864.9
HARTFORD INS CO OF THE MIDWEST	IN	359.6
HARTFORD UNDERWRITERS INS CO	CT	1,564.1
METROPOLITAN PROPERTY & CAS INS CO	RI	4,771.4
NATIONAL CASUALTY CO	WI	144.3
NATIONWIDE MUTUAL FIRE INS CO	OH	4,143.4
PACIFIC INDEMNITY CO	WI	5,651.8
SOUTHERN FARM BUREAU CAS INS CO	MS	1,807.1
SOUTHERN-OWNERS INS CO	MI	377.7
STATE FARM MUTUAL AUTOMOBILE INS CO	IL	88,473.2
TRUSTGARD INS CO	OH	66.4
USAA GENERAL INDEMNITY CO	TX	452.4

South Dakota

INSURANCE COMPANY NAME	DOM. STATE	TOTAL ASSETS ($MIL)
Rating: A+		
DAIRYLAND INS CO	WI	1,222.3
UNITED SERVICES AUTOMOBILE ASN	TX	19,904.8
USAA CASUALTY INS CO	TX	6,714.4
Rating: A		
AUTO-OWNERS INS CO	MI	8,899.8
CHURCH MUTUAL INS CO	WI	1,150.7
COUNTRY MUTUAL INS CO	IL	3,364.1
FRANKENMUTH MUTUAL INS CO	MI	955.3
HOME-OWNERS INS CO	MI	1,353.2
PROTECTIVE INS CO	IN	529.3
SENTRY INS A MUTUAL CO	WI	5,330.6
TOKIO MARINE & NICHIDO FIRE INS LTD	NY	1,706.6
Rating: A-		
BITUMINOUS CASUALTY CORP	IL	725.4
BITUMINOUS FIRE & MARINE INS CO	IL	463.7
CINCINNATI INDEMNITY CO	OH	87.6
CINCINNATI INS CO	OH	8,454.0
FARM BUREAU MUTUAL INS CO	IA	1,586.9
FEDERATED MUTUAL INS CO	MN	3,817.8
GENERAL STAR NATIONAL INS CO	OH	340.1
GREAT WEST CASUALTY CO	NE	1,460.5
JEWELERS MUTUAL INS CO	WI	186.8
NATIONAL LIABILITY & FIRE INS CO	CT	1,040.7
OLD REPUBLIC GENERAL INS CORP	IL	985.4
OLD REPUBLIC INS CO	PA	2,301.6
OLD REPUBLIC SURETY CO	WI	94.2
OWNERS INS CO	OH	2,535.6
PROPERTY-OWNERS INS CO	IN	147.1
TRAVELERS INDEMNITY CO	CT	20,531.8
Rating: B+		
ALLSTATE INS CO	IL	39,333.3
AMERICAN FAMILY HOME INS CO	FL	443.6
AMERICAN MERCURY INS CO	OK	334.3
AMERICAN MODERN HOME INS CO	OH	888.8
AMERICAN NATIONAL GENERAL INS CO	MO	99.8
AMERICAN NATIONAL PROPERTY & CAS CO	MO	1,068.4
AMERICAN STANDARD INS CO OF WI	WI	394.2
CANAL INS CO	SC	1,010.6
CENTRAL STATES INDEMNITY CO OF OMAHA	NE	209.1
CORNHUSKER CASUALTY CO	NE	533.2
COUNTRY CASUALTY INS CO	IL	75.7
CUMIS INS SOCIETY INC	IA	1,228.8
FARMLAND MUTUAL INS CO	IA	371.1
FEDERAL INS CO	IN	28,842.9
FEDERATED SERVICE INS CO	MN	358.9
FOREMOST INS CO	MI	2,024.3
GEICO GENERAL INS CO	MD	175.2
GEICO INDEMNITY CO	MD	5,117.3
GOVERNMENT EMPLOYEES INS CO	MD	12,473.2
GREAT NORTHERN INS CO	IN	1,518.9
HARTFORD FIRE INS CO	CT	23,864.9
HARTFORD INS CO OF THE MIDWEST	IN	359.6
HARTFORD UNDERWRITERS INS CO	CT	1,564.1
METROPOLITAN PROPERTY & CAS INS CO	RI	4,771.4
MIDWEST MEDICAL INS CO	MN	490.6
NATIONAL CASUALTY CO	WI	144.3
NATIONWIDE MUTUAL FIRE INS CO	OH	4,143.4
NORTH STAR MUTUAL INS CO	MN	340.1
PACIFIC INDEMNITY CO	WI	5,651.8
SOUTHERN-OWNERS INS CO	MI	377.7
STATE FARM MUTUAL AUTOMOBILE INS CO	IL	88,473.2
TRUSTGARD INS CO	OH	66.4
USAA GENERAL INDEMNITY CO	TX	452.4
WESTERN AGRICULTURAL INS CO	IA	309.2
WESTFIELD NATIONAL INS CO	OH	437.0

Tennessee

INSURANCE COMPANY NAME	DOM. STATE	TOTAL ASSETS ($MIL)
Rating: A+		
DAIRYLAND INS CO	WI	1,222.3
UNITED SERVICES AUTOMOBILE ASN	TX	19,904.8
USAA CASUALTY INS CO	TX	6,714.4
Rating: A		
AUTO-OWNERS INS CO	MI	8,899.8
CHURCH MUTUAL INS CO	WI	1,150.7
COUNTRY MUTUAL INS CO	IL	3,364.1
FRANKENMUTH MUTUAL INS CO	MI	955.3
PROTECTIVE INS CO	IN	529.3
SENTRY INS A MUTUAL CO	WI	5,330.6
TENNESSEE FARMERS ASR CO	TN	879.3
TENNESSEE FARMERS MUTUAL INS CO	TN	1,948.5
TOKIO MARINE & NICHIDO FIRE INS LTD	NY	1,706.6
Rating: A-		
BITUMINOUS CASUALTY CORP	IL	725.4
BITUMINOUS FIRE & MARINE INS CO	IL	463.7
CINCINNATI INDEMNITY CO	OH	87.6
CINCINNATI INS CO	OH	8,454.0
FEDERATED MUTUAL INS CO	MN	3,817.8
GENERAL STAR NATIONAL INS CO	OH	340.1
GRANGE MUTUAL CAS CO	OH	1,525.7
GREAT WEST CASUALTY CO	NE	1,460.5
JEWELERS MUTUAL INS CO	WI	186.8
NATIONAL LIABILITY & FIRE INS CO	CT	1,040.7
OLD REPUBLIC GENERAL INS CORP	IL	985.4
OLD REPUBLIC INS CO	PA	2,301.6
OLD REPUBLIC SURETY CO	WI	94.2
OWNERS INS CO	OH	2,535.6
STATE VOLUNTEER MUTUAL INS CO	TN	996.2
TRAVELERS INDEMNITY CO	CT	20,531.8
Rating: B+		
ALLSTATE INS CO	IL	39,333.3
AMERICAN FAMILY HOME INS CO	FL	443.6
AMERICAN MERCURY INS CO	OK	334.3
AMERICAN MODERN HOME INS CO	OH	888.8
AMERICAN NATIONAL GENERAL INS CO	MO	99.8
AMERICAN NATIONAL PROPERTY & CAS CO	MO	1,068.4
CANAL INS CO	SC	1,010.6
CENTRAL MUTUAL INS CO	OH	1,238.6
CENTRAL STATES INDEMNITY CO OF OMAHA	NE	209.1
COUNTRY CASUALTY INS CO	IL	75.7
CUMIS INS SOCIETY INC	IA	1,228.8
ERIE INS CO OF NY	NY	58.4
FARMLAND MUTUAL INS CO	IA	371.1
FEDERAL INS CO	IN	28,842.9
FEDERATED SERVICE INS CO	MN	358.9
FOREMOST INS CO	MI	2,024.3
GEICO GENERAL INS CO	MD	175.2
GEICO INDEMNITY CO	MD	5,117.3
GOVERNMENT EMPLOYEES INS CO	MD	12,473.2
GREAT NORTHERN INS CO	IN	1,518.9
HARTFORD FIRE INS CO	CT	23,864.9
HARTFORD INS CO OF THE MIDWEST	IN	359.6
HARTFORD UNDERWRITERS INS CO	CT	1,564.1
METROPOLITAN PROPERTY & CAS INS CO	RI	4,771.4
NATIONAL CASUALTY CO	WI	144.3
NATIONWIDE MUTUAL FIRE INS CO	OH	4,143.4
PACIFIC INDEMNITY CO	WI	5,651.8
STATE FARM MUTUAL AUTOMOBILE INS CO	IL	88,473.2
TRUSTGARD INS CO	OH	66.4
USAA GENERAL INDEMNITY CO	TX	452.4
WESTERN AGRICULTURAL INS CO	IA	309.2
WESTFIELD NATIONAL INS CO	OH	437.0

Texas

INSURANCE COMPANY NAME	DOM. STATE	TOTAL ASSETS ($MIL)
Rating: A+		
DAIRYLAND INS CO	WI	1,222.3
INTERINS EXCH OF THE AUTOMOBILE CLUB	CA	5,434.9
UNITED SERVICES AUTOMOBILE ASN	TX	19,904.8
USAA CASUALTY INS CO	TX	6,714.4
Rating: A		
CHURCH MUTUAL INS CO	WI	1,150.7
COUNTRY MUTUAL INS CO	IL	3,364.1
FRANKENMUTH MUTUAL INS CO	MI	955.3
PROTECTIVE INS CO	IN	529.3
SENTRY INS A MUTUAL CO	WI	5,330.6
TOKIO MARINE & NICHIDO FIRE INS LTD	NY	1,706.6
Rating: A-		
BITUMINOUS CASUALTY CORP	IL	725.4
BITUMINOUS FIRE & MARINE INS CO	IL	463.7
CINCINNATI INS CO	OH	8,454.0
FEDERATED MUTUAL INS CO	MN	3,817.8
GENERAL STAR NATIONAL INS CO	OH	340.1
GREAT WEST CASUALTY CO	NE	1,460.5
JEWELERS MUTUAL INS CO	WI	186.8
MERCURY CASUALTY CO	CA	2,212.7
NATIONAL LIABILITY & FIRE INS CO	CT	1,040.7
OLD REPUBLIC GENERAL INS CORP	IL	985.4
OLD REPUBLIC INS CO	PA	2,301.6
OLD REPUBLIC SURETY CO	WI	94.2
STATE FARM CTY MUTUAL INS CO OF TX	TX	99.4
TRAVELERS INDEMNITY CO	CT	20,531.8
Rating: B+		
ALLSTATE INS CO	IL	39,333.3
AMERICAN MERCURY INS CO	OK	334.3
AMERICAN MODERN HOME INS CO	OH	888.8
AMERICAN NATIONAL GENERAL INS CO	MO	99.8
AMERICAN NATIONAL PROPERTY & CAS CO	MO	1,068.4
AMICA LLOYDS OF TEXAS	TX	70.2
AUTO CLUB CASUALTY CO	TX	2.8
AUTO CLUB INDEMNITY CO	TX	8.7
CANAL INS CO	SC	1,010.6
CENTRAL MUTUAL INS CO	OH	1,238.6
CENTRAL STATES INDEMNITY CO OF OMAHA	NE	209.1
COUNTRY CASUALTY INS CO	IL	75.7
CUMIS INS SOCIETY INC	IA	1,228.8
FARMLAND MUTUAL INS CO	IA	371.1
FEDERAL INS CO	IN	28,842.9
FEDERATED SERVICE INS CO	MN	358.9
FOREMOST INS CO	MI	2,024.3
GEICO GENERAL INS CO	MD	175.2
GEICO INDEMNITY CO	MD	5,117.3
GOVERNMENT EMPLOYEES INS CO	MD	12,473.2
GREAT NORTHERN INS CO	IN	1,518.9
HARTFORD FIRE INS CO	CT	23,864.9
HARTFORD INS CO OF THE MIDWEST	IN	359.6
HARTFORD UNDERWRITERS INS CO	CT	1,564.1
METROPOLITAN PROPERTY & CAS INS CO	RI	4,771.4
NATIONAL CASUALTY CO	WI	144.3
NATIONWIDE MUTUAL FIRE INS CO	OH	4,143.4
PACIFIC INDEMNITY CO	WI	5,651.8
SOUTHERN FARM BUREAU CAS INS CO	MS	1,807.1
STATE FARM MUTUAL AUTOMOBILE INS CO	IL	88,473.2
TRUSTGARD INS CO	OH	66.4
USAA GENERAL INDEMNITY CO	TX	452.4
WESTFIELD NATIONAL INS CO	OH	437.0

Utah

INSURANCE COMPANY NAME	DOM. STATE	TOTAL ASSETS ($MIL)
Rating: A+		
DAIRYLAND INS CO	WI	1,222.3
UNITED SERVICES AUTOMOBILE ASN	TX	19,904.8
USAA CASUALTY INS CO	TX	6,714.4
Rating: A		
AUTO-OWNERS INS CO	MI	8,899.8
CHURCH MUTUAL INS CO	WI	1,150.7
FRANKENMUTH MUTUAL INS CO	MI	955.3
HOME-OWNERS INS CO	MI	1,353.2
PROTECTIVE INS CO	IN	529.3
SENTRY INS A MUTUAL CO	WI	5,330.6
TOKIO MARINE & NICHIDO FIRE INS LTD	NY	1,706.6
Rating: A-		
BITUMINOUS CASUALTY CORP	IL	725.4
BITUMINOUS FIRE & MARINE INS CO	IL	463.7
CALIFORNIA STATE AUTO ASN INTER-INS	CA	5,291.7
CINCINNATI INS CO	OH	8,454.0
FARM BUREAU MUTUAL INS CO	IA	1,586.9
FEDERATED MUTUAL INS CO	MN	3,817.8
GENERAL STAR NATIONAL INS CO	OH	340.1
GREAT WEST CASUALTY CO	NE	1,460.5
JEWELERS MUTUAL INS CO	WI	186.8
MUTUAL INS CO OF AZ	AZ	891.6
NATIONAL LIABILITY & FIRE INS CO	CT	1,040.7
OLD REPUBLIC GENERAL INS CORP	IL	985.4
OLD REPUBLIC INS CO	PA	2,301.6
OLD REPUBLIC SURETY CO	WI	94.2
OWNERS INS CO	OH	2,535.6
PROPERTY-OWNERS INS CO	IN	147.1
TRAVELERS INDEMNITY CO	CT	20,531.8
Rating: B+		
ALLSTATE INS CO	IL	39,333.3
AMERICAN FAMILY HOME INS CO	FL	443.6
AMERICAN MERCURY INS CO	OK	334.3
AMERICAN MODERN HOME INS CO	OH	888.8
AMERICAN NATIONAL GENERAL INS CO	MO	99.8
AMERICAN NATIONAL PROPERTY & CAS CO	MO	1,068.4
AMERICAN STANDARD INS CO OF WI	WI	394.2
CANAL INS CO	SC	1,010.6
CENTRAL STATES INDEMNITY CO OF OMAHA	NE	209.1
COPIC INS CO	CO	435.6
CUMIS INS SOCIETY INC	IA	1,228.8
FARMLAND MUTUAL INS CO	IA	371.1
FEDERAL INS CO	IN	28,842.9
FEDERATED SERVICE INS CO	MN	358.9
FOREMOST INS CO	MI	2,024.3
GEICO GENERAL INS CO	MD	175.2
GEICO INDEMNITY CO	MD	5,117.3
GOVERNMENT EMPLOYEES INS CO	MD	12,473.2
GREAT NORTHERN INS CO	IN	1,518.9
HARTFORD FIRE INS CO	CT	23,864.9
HARTFORD INS CO OF THE MIDWEST	IN	359.6
HARTFORD UNDERWRITERS INS CO	CT	1,564.1
METROPOLITAN PROPERTY & CAS INS CO	RI	4,771.4
NATIONAL CASUALTY CO	WI	144.3
NATIONWIDE MUTUAL FIRE INS CO	OH	4,143.4
PACIFIC INDEMNITY CO	WI	5,651.8
SOUTHERN-OWNERS INS CO	MI	377.7
STATE FARM MUTUAL AUTOMOBILE INS CO	IL	88,473.2
USAA GENERAL INDEMNITY CO	TX	452.4
WESCO-FINANCIAL INS CO	NE	2,526.8
WESTERN AGRICULTURAL INS CO	IA	309.2

Vermont

INSURANCE COMPANY NAME	DOM. STATE	TOTAL ASSETS ($MIL)
Rating: A+		
DAIRYLAND INS CO	WI	1,222.3
INTERINS EXCH OF THE AUTOMOBILE CLUB	CA	5,434.9
UNITED SERVICES AUTOMOBILE ASN	TX	19,904.8
USAA CASUALTY INS CO	TX	6,714.4
Rating: A		
CHURCH MUTUAL INS CO	WI	1,150.7
FRANKENMUTH MUTUAL INS CO	MI	955.3
MERRIMACK MUTUAL FIRE INS CO	MA	883.0
PROTECTIVE INS CO	IN	529.3
SENTRY INS A MUTUAL CO	WI	5,330.6
TOKIO MARINE & NICHIDO FIRE INS LTD	NY	1,706.6
Rating: A-		
BITUMINOUS CASUALTY CORP	IL	725.4
CINCINNATI INS CO	OH	8,454.0
FEDERATED MUTUAL INS CO	MN	3,817.8
GENERAL STAR NATIONAL INS CO	OH	340.1
GREAT WEST CASUALTY CO	NE	1,460.5
JEWELERS MUTUAL INS CO	WI	186.8
NATIONAL LIABILITY & FIRE INS CO	CT	1,040.7
OLD REPUBLIC GENERAL INS CORP	IL	985.4
OLD REPUBLIC INS CO	PA	2,301.6
TRAVELERS INDEMNITY CO	CT	20,531.8
Rating: B+		
ALLSTATE INS CO	IL	39,333.3
AMERICAN FAMILY HOME INS CO	FL	443.6
AMERICAN MODERN HOME INS CO	OH	888.8
AMERICAN NATIONAL PROPERTY & CAS CO	MO	1,068.4
CANAL INS CO	SC	1,010.6
CENTRAL STATES INDEMNITY CO OF OMAHA	NE	209.1
COMMERCE INS CO	MA	2,513.5
CUMIS INS SOCIETY INC	IA	1,228.8
FEDERAL INS CO	IN	28,842.9
FOREMOST INS CO	MI	2,024.3
GEICO GENERAL INS CO	MD	175.2
GEICO INDEMNITY CO	MD	5,117.3
GOVERNMENT EMPLOYEES INS CO	MD	12,473.2
GREAT NORTHERN INS CO	IN	1,518.9
HARTFORD FIRE INS CO	CT	23,864.9
HARTFORD INS CO OF THE MIDWEST	IN	359.6
HARTFORD UNDERWRITERS INS CO	CT	1,564.1
HOUSING ENTERPRISE INS CO	VT	36.4
METROPOLITAN PROPERTY & CAS INS CO	RI	4,771.4
NATIONAL CASUALTY CO	WI	144.3
NATIONWIDE MUTUAL FIRE INS CO	OH	4,143.4
PACIFIC INDEMNITY CO	WI	5,651.8
STATE FARM MUTUAL AUTOMOBILE INS CO	IL	88,473.2
USAA GENERAL INDEMNITY CO	TX	452.4

Virginia

INSURANCE COMPANY NAME	DOM. STATE	TOTAL ASSETS ($MIL)
Rating: A+		
DAIRYLAND INS CO	WI	1,222.3
UNITED SERVICES AUTOMOBILE ASN	TX	19,904.8
USAA CASUALTY INS CO	TX	6,714.4
Rating: A		
AUTO-OWNERS INS CO	MI	8,899.8
CHURCH MUTUAL INS CO	WI	1,150.7
FRANKENMUTH MUTUAL INS CO	MI	955.3
HOME-OWNERS INS CO	MI	1,353.2
PROTECTIVE INS CO	IN	529.3
SENTRY INS A MUTUAL CO	WI	5,330.6
TOKIO MARINE & NICHIDO FIRE INS LTD	NY	1,706.6
Rating: A-		
BITUMINOUS CASUALTY CORP	IL	725.4
BITUMINOUS FIRE & MARINE INS CO	IL	463.7
CINCINNATI INDEMNITY CO	OH	87.6
CINCINNATI INS CO	OH	8,454.0
FEDERATED MUTUAL INS CO	MN	3,817.8
GENERAL STAR NATIONAL INS CO	OH	340.1
GREAT WEST CASUALTY CO	NE	1,460.5
JEWELERS MUTUAL INS CO	WI	186.8
MERCURY CASUALTY CO	CA	2,212.7
NATIONAL LIABILITY & FIRE INS CO	CT	1,040.7
OLD REPUBLIC GENERAL INS CORP	IL	985.4
OLD REPUBLIC INS CO	PA	2,301.6
OLD REPUBLIC SURETY CO	WI	94.2
OWNERS INS CO	OH	2,535.6
PROPERTY-OWNERS INS CO	IN	147.1
STATE VOLUNTEER MUTUAL INS CO	TN	996.2
TRAVELERS INDEMNITY CO	CT	20,531.8
Rating: B+		
ALLSTATE INS CO	IL	39,333.3
AMERICAN FAMILY HOME INS CO	FL	443.6
AMERICAN MERCURY INS CO	OK	334.3
AMERICAN MODERN HOME INS CO	OH	888.8
AMERICAN NATIONAL GENERAL INS CO	MO	99.8
AMERICAN NATIONAL PROPERTY & CAS CO	MO	1,068.4
CANAL INS CO	SC	1,010.6
CENTRAL MUTUAL INS CO	OH	1,238.6
CENTRAL STATES INDEMNITY CO OF OMAHA	NE	209.1
CORNHUSKER CASUALTY CO	NE	533.2
CUMIS INS SOCIETY INC	IA	1,228.8
FARMLAND MUTUAL INS CO	IA	371.1
FEDERAL INS CO	IN	28,842.9
FEDERATED SERVICE INS CO	MN	358.9
FOREMOST INS CO	MI	2,024.3
GEICO GENERAL INS CO	MD	175.2
GEICO INDEMNITY CO	MD	5,117.3
GOVERNMENT EMPLOYEES INS CO	MD	12,473.2
GREAT NORTHERN INS CO	IN	1,518.9
HARTFORD FIRE INS CO	CT	23,864.9
HARTFORD INS CO OF THE MIDWEST	IN	359.6
HARTFORD UNDERWRITERS INS CO	CT	1,564.1
METROPOLITAN PROPERTY & CAS INS CO	RI	4,771.4
NATIONAL CASUALTY CO	WI	144.3
NATIONWIDE MUTUAL FIRE INS CO	OH	4,143.4
PACIFIC INDEMNITY CO	WI	5,651.8
SOUTHERN-OWNERS INS CO	MI	377.7
STATE FARM MUTUAL AUTOMOBILE INS CO	IL	88,473.2
TRUSTGARD INS CO	OH	66.4
USAA GENERAL INDEMNITY CO	TX	452.4
WESTERN AGRICULTURAL INS CO	IA	309.2

Washington

INSURANCE COMPANY NAME	DOM. STATE	TOTAL ASSETS ($MIL)
Rating: A+		
DAIRYLAND INS CO	WI	1,222.3
UNITED SERVICES AUTOMOBILE ASN	TX	19,904.8
USAA CASUALTY INS CO	TX	6,714.4
Rating: A		
AUTO-OWNERS INS CO	MI	8,899.8
CHURCH MUTUAL INS CO	WI	1,150.7
COUNTRY MUTUAL INS CO	IL	3,364.1
FRANKENMUTH MUTUAL INS CO	MI	955.3
PROTECTIVE INS CO	IN	529.3
SENTRY INS A MUTUAL CO	WI	5,330.6
TOKIO MARINE & NICHIDO FIRE INS LTD	NY	1,706.6
Rating: A-		
BITUMINOUS CASUALTY CORP	IL	725.4
BITUMINOUS FIRE & MARINE INS CO	IL	463.7
CINCINNATI INDEMNITY CO	OH	87.6
CINCINNATI INS CO	OH	8,454.0
FEDERATED MUTUAL INS CO	MN	3,817.8
GENERAL STAR NATIONAL INS CO	OH	340.1
GREAT WEST CASUALTY CO	NE	1,460.5
JEWELERS MUTUAL INS CO	WI	186.8
MERCURY CASUALTY CO	CA	2,212.7
NATIONAL LIABILITY & FIRE INS CO	CT	1,040.7
OLD REPUBLIC GENERAL INS CORP	IL	985.4
OLD REPUBLIC INS CO	PA	2,301.6
OLD REPUBLIC SURETY CO	WI	94.2
OWNERS INS CO	OH	2,535.6
TRAVELERS INDEMNITY CO	CT	20,531.8
Rating: B+		
ALLSTATE INS CO	IL	39,333.3
AMERICAN FAMILY HOME INS CO	FL	443.6
AMERICAN MERCURY INS CO	OK	334.3
AMERICAN MODERN HOME INS CO	OH	888.8
AMERICAN NATIONAL GENERAL INS CO	MO	99.8
AMERICAN NATIONAL PROPERTY & CAS CO	MO	1,068.4
AMERICAN STANDARD INS CO OF WI	WI	394.2
CANAL INS CO	SC	1,010.6
CENTRAL STATES INDEMNITY CO OF OMAHA	NE	209.1
CORNHUSKER CASUALTY CO	NE	533.2
COUNTRY CASUALTY INS CO	IL	75.7
CUMIS INS SOCIETY INC	IA	1,228.8
FARMLAND MUTUAL INS CO	IA	371.1
FEDERAL INS CO	IN	28,842.9
FEDERATED SERVICE INS CO	MN	358.9
FOREMOST INS CO	MI	2,024.3
GEICO GENERAL INS CO	MD	175.2
GEICO INDEMNITY CO	MD	5,117.3
GOVERNMENT EMPLOYEES INS CO	MD	12,473.2
GREAT NORTHERN INS CO	IN	1,518.9
HARTFORD FIRE INS CO	CT	23,864.9
HARTFORD INS CO OF THE MIDWEST	IN	359.6
HARTFORD UNDERWRITERS INS CO	CT	1,564.1
METROPOLITAN PROPERTY & CAS INS CO	RI	4,771.4
NATIONAL CASUALTY CO	WI	144.3
NATIONWIDE MUTUAL FIRE INS CO	OH	4,143.4
PACIFIC INDEMNITY CO	WI	5,651.8
STATE FARM MUTUAL AUTOMOBILE INS CO	IL	88,473.2
TRUSTGARD INS CO	OH	66.4
USAA GENERAL INDEMNITY CO	TX	452.4
WESTERN AGRICULTURAL INS CO	IA	309.2
WESTERN COMMUNITY INS CO	ID	30.0

West Virginia

INSURANCE COMPANY NAME	DOM. STATE	TOTAL ASSETS ($MIL)
Rating: A+		
DAIRYLAND INS CO	WI	1,222.3
UNITED SERVICES AUTOMOBILE ASN	TX	19,904.8
USAA CASUALTY INS CO	TX	6,714.4
Rating: A		
CHURCH MUTUAL INS CO	WI	1,150.7
FRANKENMUTH MUTUAL INS CO	MI	955.3
PROTECTIVE INS CO	IN	529.3
SENTRY INS A MUTUAL CO	WI	5,330.6
TOKIO MARINE & NICHIDO FIRE INS LTD	NY	1,706.6
Rating: A-		
BITUMINOUS CASUALTY CORP	IL	725.4
BITUMINOUS FIRE & MARINE INS CO	IL	463.7
CINCINNATI INDEMNITY CO	OH	87.6
CINCINNATI INS CO	OH	8,454.0
FEDERATED MUTUAL INS CO	MN	3,817.8
GENERAL STAR NATIONAL INS CO	OH	340.1
GREAT WEST CASUALTY CO	NE	1,460.5
JEWELERS MUTUAL INS CO	WI	186.8
NATIONAL LIABILITY & FIRE INS CO	CT	1,040.7
OLD REPUBLIC GENERAL INS CORP	IL	985.4
OLD REPUBLIC INS CO	PA	2,301.6
OLD REPUBLIC SURETY CO	WI	94.2
TRAVELERS INDEMNITY CO	CT	20,531.8
Rating: B+		
ALLSTATE INS CO	IL	39,333.3
AMERICAN FAMILY HOME INS CO	FL	443.6
AMERICAN MODERN HOME INS CO	OH	888.8
AMERICAN NATIONAL GENERAL INS CO	MO	99.8
AMERICAN NATIONAL PROPERTY & CAS CO	MO	1,068.4
CANAL INS CO	SC	1,010.6
CENTRAL STATES INDEMNITY CO OF OMAHA	NE	209.1
CUMIS INS SOCIETY INC	IA	1,228.8
FARMLAND MUTUAL INS CO	IA	371.1
FEDERAL INS CO	IN	28,842.9
FEDERATED SERVICE INS CO	MN	358.9
FOREMOST INS CO	MI	2,024.3
GEICO GENERAL INS CO	MD	175.2
GEICO INDEMNITY CO	MD	5,117.3
GOVERNMENT EMPLOYEES INS CO	MD	12,473.2
GREAT NORTHERN INS CO	IN	1,518.9
HARTFORD FIRE INS CO	CT	23,864.9
HARTFORD INS CO OF THE MIDWEST	IN	359.6
HARTFORD UNDERWRITERS INS CO	CT	1,564.1
METROPOLITAN PROPERTY & CAS INS CO	RI	4,771.4
MOTORISTS MUTUAL INS CO	OH	1,212.1
NATIONAL CASUALTY CO	WI	144.3
NATIONWIDE MUTUAL FIRE INS CO	OH	4,143.4
PACIFIC INDEMNITY CO	WI	5,651.8
STATE FARM MUTUAL AUTOMOBILE INS CO	IL	88,473.2
USAA GENERAL INDEMNITY CO	TX	452.4
WESTFIELD NATIONAL INS CO	OH	437.0

Wisconsin

INSURANCE COMPANY NAME	DOM. STATE	TOTAL ASSETS ($MIL)
Rating: A+		
DAIRYLAND INS CO	WI	1,222.3
HASTINGS MUTUAL INS CO	MI	591.7
UNITED SERVICES AUTOMOBILE ASN	TX	19,904.8
USAA CASUALTY INS CO	TX	6,714.4
Rating: A		
AUTO-OWNERS INS CO	MI	8,899.8
CHURCH MUTUAL INS CO	WI	1,150.7
COUNTRY MUTUAL INS CO	IL	3,364.1
FRANKENMUTH MUTUAL INS CO	MI	955.3
HOME-OWNERS INS CO	MI	1,353.2
PROTECTIVE INS CO	IN	529.3
SENTRY INS A MUTUAL CO	WI	5,330.6
TOKIO MARINE & NICHIDO FIRE INS LTD	NY	1,706.6
Rating: A-		
BITUMINOUS CASUALTY CORP	IL	725.4
BITUMINOUS FIRE & MARINE INS CO	IL	463.7
CINCINNATI INDEMNITY CO	OH	87.6
CINCINNATI INS CO	OH	8,454.0
FEDERATED MUTUAL INS CO	MN	3,817.8
GENERAL STAR NATIONAL INS CO	OH	340.1
GRANGE MUTUAL CAS CO	OH	1,525.7
GREAT WEST CASUALTY CO	NE	1,460.5
JEWELERS MUTUAL INS CO	WI	186.8
NATIONAL LIABILITY & FIRE INS CO	CT	1,040.7
OLD REPUBLIC GENERAL INS CORP	IL	985.4
OLD REPUBLIC INS CO	PA	2,301.6
OLD REPUBLIC SURETY CO	WI	94.2
OWNERS INS CO	OH	2,535.6
PROPERTY-OWNERS INS CO	IN	147.1
TRAVELERS INDEMNITY CO	CT	20,531.8
Rating: B+		
ALLSTATE INS CO	IL	39,333.3
AMERICAN FAMILY HOME INS CO	FL	443.6
AMERICAN MERCURY INS CO	OK	334.3
AMERICAN MODERN HOME INS CO	OH	888.8
AMERICAN NATIONAL GENERAL INS CO	MO	99.8
AMERICAN NATIONAL PROPERTY & CAS CO	MO	1,068.4
AMERICAN STANDARD INS CO OF WI	WI	394.2
ARCH SPECIALTY INS CO	NE	437.3
CANAL INS CO	SC	1,010.6
CENTRAL MUTUAL INS CO	OH	1,238.6
CENTRAL STATES INDEMNITY CO OF OMAHA	NE	209.1
CORNHUSKER CASUALTY CO	NE	533.2
COUNTRY CASUALTY INS CO	IL	75.7
CUMIS INS SOCIETY INC	IA	1,228.8
FARMERS AUTOMOBILE INS ASN	IL	852.7
FARMLAND MUTUAL INS CO	IA	371.1
FEDERAL INS CO	IN	28,842.9
FEDERATED SERVICE INS CO	MN	358.9
FOREMOST INS CO	MI	2,024.3
GEICO GENERAL INS CO	MD	175.2
GEICO INDEMNITY CO	MD	5,117.3
GOVERNMENT EMPLOYEES INS CO	MD	12,473.2
GREAT NORTHERN INS CO	IN	1,518.9
HARTFORD FIRE INS CO	CT	23,864.9
HARTFORD INS CO OF THE MIDWEST	IN	359.6
HARTFORD UNDERWRITERS INS CO	CT	1,564.1
METROPOLITAN PROPERTY & CAS INS CO	RI	4,771.4
MIDWEST MEDICAL INS CO	MN	490.6
NATIONAL CASUALTY CO	WI	144.3
NATIONWIDE MUTUAL FIRE INS CO	OH	4,143.4
PACIFIC INDEMNITY CO	WI	5,651.8
PEKIN INS CO	IL	195.5
SOUTHERN-OWNERS INS CO	MI	377.7
STATE FARM MUTUAL AUTOMOBILE INS CO	IL	88,473.2
TRUSTGARD INS CO	OH	66.4
USAA GENERAL INDEMNITY CO	TX	452.4
WEST BEND MUTUAL INS CO	WI	1,438.7
WESTERN AGRICULTURAL INS CO	IA	309.2
WESTFIELD NATIONAL INS CO	OH	437.0

Wyoming

INSURANCE COMPANY NAME	DOM. STATE	TOTAL ASSETS ($MIL)
Rating: A+		
DAIRYLAND INS CO	WI	1,222.3
UNITED SERVICES AUTOMOBILE ASN	TX	19,904.8
USAA CASUALTY INS CO	TX	6,714.4
Rating: A		
CHURCH MUTUAL INS CO	WI	1,150.7
COUNTRY MUTUAL INS CO	IL	3,364.1
FRANKENMUTH MUTUAL INS CO	MI	955.3
MOUNTAIN WEST FARM BU MUTUAL INS CO	WY	339.7
PROTECTIVE INS CO	IN	529.3
SENTRY INS A MUTUAL CO	WI	5,330.6
TOKIO MARINE & NICHIDO FIRE INS LTD	NY	1,706.6
Rating: A-		
BITUMINOUS CASUALTY CORP	IL	725.4
BITUMINOUS FIRE & MARINE INS CO	IL	463.7
CALIFORNIA STATE AUTO ASN INTER-INS	CA	5,291.7
CINCINNATI INS CO	OH	8,454.0
FEDERATED MUTUAL INS CO	MN	3,817.8
GENERAL STAR NATIONAL INS CO	OH	340.1
GREAT WEST CASUALTY CO	NE	1,460.5
JEWELERS MUTUAL INS CO	WI	186.8
NATIONAL LIABILITY & FIRE INS CO	CT	1,040.7
OLD REPUBLIC GENERAL INS CORP	IL	985.4
OLD REPUBLIC INS CO	PA	2,301.6
OLD REPUBLIC SURETY CO	WI	94.2
TRAVELERS INDEMNITY CO	CT	20,531.8
Rating: B+		
ALLSTATE INS CO	IL	39,333.3
AMERICAN FAMILY HOME INS CO	FL	443.6
AMERICAN MERCURY INS CO	OK	334.3
AMERICAN MODERN HOME INS CO	OH	888.8
AMERICAN NATIONAL GENERAL INS CO	MO	99.8
AMERICAN NATIONAL PROPERTY & CAS CO	MO	1,068.4
AMERICAN STANDARD INS CO OF WI	WI	394.2
CANAL INS CO	SC	1,010.6
CENTRAL STATES INDEMNITY CO OF OMAHA	NE	209.1
COPIC INS CO	CO	435.6
CORNHUSKER CASUALTY CO	NE	533.2
COUNTRY CASUALTY INS CO	IL	75.7
CUMIS INS SOCIETY INC	IA	1,228.8
FARMLAND MUTUAL INS CO	IA	371.1
FEDERAL INS CO	IN	28,842.9
FEDERATED SERVICE INS CO	MN	358.9
FOREMOST INS CO	MI	2,024.3
GEICO GENERAL INS CO	MD	175.2
GEICO INDEMNITY CO	MD	5,117.3
GOVERNMENT EMPLOYEES INS CO	MD	12,473.2
GREAT NORTHERN INS CO	IN	1,518.9
HARTFORD FIRE INS CO	CT	23,864.9
HARTFORD INS CO OF THE MIDWEST	IN	359.6
HARTFORD UNDERWRITERS INS CO	CT	1,564.1
METROPOLITAN PROPERTY & CAS INS CO	RI	4,771.4
NATIONAL CASUALTY CO	WI	144.3
NATIONWIDE MUTUAL FIRE INS CO	OH	4,143.4
PACIFIC INDEMNITY CO	WI	5,651.8
STATE FARM MUTUAL AUTOMOBILE INS CO	IL	88,473.2
USAA GENERAL INDEMNITY CO	TX	452.4
WESTERN AGRICULTURAL INS CO	IA	309.2

Section VI

All Companies Listed by Rating

A list of all rated and unrated

U.S. Property and Casualty Insurers.

Companies are ranked by TheStreet.com Financial Strength Rating and then listed alphabetically within each rating category.

Section VI Contents

This section sorts all companies by their Financial Strength Rating and then lists them alphabetically within each rating category. The purpose of this section is to provide in one place all of those companies receiving a given rating. Companies with the same rating should be viewed as having the same relative financial strength regardless of their order in this table.

1. **Insurance Company Name** The legally registered name, which can sometimes differ from the name that the company uses for advertising. An insurer's name can be very similar to that of another, so verify the company's exact name and state of domicile to make sure you are looking at the correct company.

2. **Domicile State** The state which has primary regulatory responsibility for the company. It may differ from the location of the company's corporate headquarters. You do not have to be living in the domicile state to purchase insurance from this firm, provided it is licensed to do business in your state.

3. **Total Assets** All assets admitted by state insurance regulators in millions of dollars. This includes investments and current business assets such as receivables from agents and reinsurers.

INSURANCE COMPANY NAME	DOM. STATE	TOTAL ASSETS ($MIL)
Rating: A+		
DAIRYLAND INS CO	WI	1,222.3
HASTINGS MUTUAL INS CO	MI	591.7
INTERINS EXCH OF THE AUTOMOBILE CLUB	CA	5,434.9
UNITED SERVICES AUTOMOBILE ASN	TX	19,904.8
USAA CASUALTY INS CO	TX	6,714.4
Rating: A		
AUTO-OWNERS INS CO	MI	8,899.8
CHURCH MUTUAL INS CO	WI	1,150.7
COUNTRY MUTUAL INS CO	IL	3,364.1
FRANKENMUTH MUTUAL INS CO	MI	955.3
HOME-OWNERS INS CO	MI	1,353.2
KENTUCKY FARM BUREAU MUTUAL INS CO	KY	1,580.7
MERRIMACK MUTUAL FIRE INS CO	MA	883.0
MOUNTAIN WEST FARM BU MUTUAL INS CO	WY	339.7
NORTH CAROLINA FARM BU MUTUAL INS CO	NC	1,627.5
PIONEER STATE MUTUAL INS CO	MI	294.4
PROTECTIVE INS CO	IN	529.3
SENTRY INS A MUTUAL CO	WI	5,330.6
TENNESSEE FARMERS ASR CO	TN	879.3
TENNESSEE FARMERS MUTUAL INS CO	TN	1,948.5
TOKIO MARINE & NICHIDO FIRE INS LTD	NY	1,706.6
Rating: A-		
BITUMINOUS CASUALTY CORP	IL	725.4
BITUMINOUS FIRE & MARINE INS CO	IL	463.7
CALIFORNIA STATE AUTO ASN INTER-INS	CA	5,291.7
CINCINNATI INDEMNITY CO	OH	87.6
CINCINNATI INS CO	OH	8,454.0
COOPERATIVA D SEGUROS MULTIPLES D PR	PR	455.9
FARM BUREAU MUTUAL INS CO	IA	1,586.9
FEDERATED MUTUAL INS CO	MN	3,817.8
GENERAL STAR NATIONAL INS CO	OH	340.1
GRANGE MUTUAL CAS CO	OH	1,525.7
GREAT WEST CASUALTY CO	NE	1,460.5
JEWELERS MUTUAL INS CO	WI	186.8
MERCURY CASUALTY CO	CA	2,212.7
MERCURY INS CO	CA	1,373.9
MUTUAL INS CO OF AZ	AZ	891.6
NATIONAL LIABILITY & FIRE INS CO	CT	1,040.7
OLD REPUBLIC GENERAL INS CORP	IL	985.4
OLD REPUBLIC INS CO	PA	2,301.6
OLD REPUBLIC SURETY CO	WI	94.2
OTSEGO MUTUAL FIRE INS CO	NY	70.8
OWNERS INS CO	OH	2,535.6
PROPERTY-OWNERS INS CO	IN	147.1
STATE FARM CTY MUTUAL INS CO OF TX	TX	99.4
STATE VOLUNTEER MUTUAL INS CO	TN	996.2
TRAVELERS INDEMNITY CO	CT	20,531.8
Rating: B+		
ALLSTATE INS CO	IL	39,333.3
AMERICAN FAMILY HOME INS CO	FL	443.6
AMERICAN MERCURY INS CO	OK	334.3
AMERICAN MODERN HOME INS CO	OH	888.8
AMERICAN NATIONAL GENERAL INS CO	MO	99.8
AMERICAN NATIONAL PROPERTY & CAS CO	MO	1,068.4
AMERICAN STANDARD INS CO OF WI	WI	394.2
AMICA LLOYDS OF TEXAS	TX	70.2
ARCH SPECIALTY INS CO	NE	437.3
AUTO CLUB CASUALTY CO	TX	2.8
AUTO CLUB INDEMNITY CO	TX	8.7
BAY STATE INS CO	MA	285.6
CANAL INS CO	SC	1,010.6
CENTRAL MUTUAL INS CO	OH	1,238.6
CENTRAL STATES INDEMNITY CO OF OMAHA	NE	209.1
CITATION INS CO	MA	304.8
COMMERCE INS CO	MA	2,513.5
COPIC INS CO	CO	435.6
CORNHUSKER CASUALTY CO	NE	533.2
COUNTRY CASUALTY INS CO	IL	75.7
CUMBERLAND MUTUAL FIRE INS CO	NJ	245.0
CUMIS INS SOCIETY INC	IA	1,228.8
ERIE INS CO OF NY	NY	58.4
FARM BUREAU MUTUAL INS CO OF ID	ID	346.7
FARMERS AUTOMOBILE INS ASN	IL	852.7
FARMLAND MUTUAL INS CO	IA	371.1
FEDERAL INS CO	IN	28,842.9
FEDERATED SERVICE INS CO	MN	358.9
FOREMOST INS CO	MI	2,024.3
GEICO GENERAL INS CO	MD	175.2
GEICO INDEMNITY CO	MD	5,117.3
GOVERNMENT EMPLOYEES INS CO	MD	12,473.2
GREAT NORTHERN INS CO	IN	1,518.9
HARTFORD FIRE INS CO	CT	23,864.9
HARTFORD INS CO OF THE MIDWEST	IN	359.6
HARTFORD UNDERWRITERS INS CO	CT	1,564.1
HOUSING ENTERPRISE INS CO	VT	36.4
INS CO OF GREATER NY	NY	101.2
METROPOLITAN PROPERTY & CAS INS CO	RI	4,771.4
MIDWEST MEDICAL INS CO	MN	490.6
MOTORISTS MUTUAL INS CO	OH	1,212.1
NATIONAL CASUALTY CO	WI	144.3
NATIONWIDE MUTUAL FIRE INS CO	OH	4,143.4
NORTH STAR MUTUAL INS CO	MN	340.1
PACIFIC INDEMNITY CO	WI	5,651.8
PEKIN INS CO	IL	195.5
SAFETY INS CO	MA	1,190.4
SAMSUNG FIRE & MARINE INS CO LTD US	NY	69.7
SOUTHERN FARM BUREAU CAS INS CO	MS	1,807.1
SOUTHERN-OWNERS INS CO	MI	377.7
STATE FARM MUTUAL AUTOMOBILE INS CO	IL	88,473.2
TRUSTGARD INS CO	OH	66.4
TUSCARORA WAYNE MUTUAL INS CO	PA	54.2
UNITED FARM FAMILY MUTUAL INS CO	IN	787.9
USAA GENERAL INDEMNITY CO	TX	452.4
WESCO-FINANCIAL INS CO	NE	2,526.8
WEST BEND MUTUAL INS CO	WI	1,438.7
WESTERN AGRICULTURAL INS CO	IA	309.2
WESTERN COMMUNITY INS CO	ID	30.0
WESTFIELD NATIONAL INS CO	OH	437.0

Rating: B

INSURANCE COMPANY NAME	DOM. STATE	TOTAL ASSETS ($MIL)
21ST CENTURY CASUALTY CO	CA	18.3
21ST CENTURY INS CO	CA	1,260.1
ACUITY A MUTUAL INS CO	WI	1,817.0
AIG CENTENNIAL INS CO	PA	802.9
AIG HAWAII INS CO INC	HI	187.5
AIG INDEMNITY INS CO	PA	79.7
AIG PREFERRED INS CO	PA	93.5
ALASKA NATIONAL INS CO	AK	696.6
ALFA INS CORP	AL	111.6
ALFA MUTUAL FIRE INS CO	AL	571.5
ALFA MUTUAL GENERAL INS CO	AL	77.0
ALFA MUTUAL INS CO	AL	1,089.8
ALL AMERICA INS CO	OH	245.0
ALLIED PROPERTY & CASUALTY INS CO	IA	120.4
ALLSTATE COUNTY MUTUAL INS CO	TX	14.4
ALLSTATE FLORIDIAN INDEMNITY CORP	IL	14.6
ALLSTATE INDEMNITY CO	IL	159.1
ALLSTATE PROPERTY & CASUALTY INS CO	IL	164.3
ALLSTATE TEXAS LLOYDS	TX	25.2
ALPHA PROPERTY & CASUALTY INS CO	WI	37.0
AMCO INS CO	IA	2,453.5
AMERICAN AGRICULTURAL INS CO	IN	1,597.7
AMERICAN BUS & PERSONAL INS MUT INC	DE	42.5
AMERICAN EQUITY SPECIALTY INS CO	CT	78.5
AMERICAN FAMILY INS CO	OH	55.4
AMERICAN FEDERATION INS CO	FL	20.1
AMERICAN HARDWARE MUTUAL INS CO	OH	334.2
AMERICAN INTERNATIONAL INS CO	NY	1,612.1
AMERICAN INTERNATIONAL INS CO OF NJ	NJ	79.3
AMERICAN INTERNATIONAL SOUTH INS CO	PA	44.5
AMERICAN INTL INS CO OF PR	PR	253.1
AMERICAN MERCURY LLOYDS INS CO	TX	4.8
AMERICAN MODERN LLOYDS INS CO	TX	5.4
AMERICAN NATIONAL LLOYDS INS CO	TX	61.8
AMERICAN PACIFIC INS COMPANY	HI	24.8
AMERICAN SECURITY INS CO	DE	1,854.3
AMERICAN SOUTHERN HOME INS CO	FL	93.3
AMERICAN STANDARD INS CO OF OH	OH	11.3
AMERICAN STATES PREFERRED INS CO	IN	284.2
AMERICAN STRATEGIC INS CO	FL	286.4
AMICA MUTUAL INS CO	RI	3,433.2
ANTILLES INS CO	PR	68.7
ATLANTIC STATES INS CO	PA	451.2
AUTO CLUB INS ASSN	MI	2,905.4
AUTOMOBILE INS CO OF HARTFORD CT	CT	954.1
AVEMCO INS CO	MD	120.3
BALBOA INS CO	CA	2,605.2
BROTHERHOOD MUTUAL INS CO	IN	315.2
BUILDERS MUTUAL INS CO	NC	481.6
CALIFORNIA AUTOMOBILE INS CO	CA	216.3
CALIFORNIA GENERAL UNDERWRITERS I C	CA	16.1
CAMBRIDGE MUTUAL FIRE INS CO	MA	537.4
CANAL INDEMNITY CO	SC	43.5
CENTURION CASUALTY CO	IA	394.7
CHARTER OAK FIRE INS CO	CT	894.8
CHUBB CUSTOM INS CO	DE	306.0
CHUBB INDEMNITY INS CO	NY	261.0
CHUBB INS CO OF NEW JERSEY	NJ	42.0
CHUBB LLOYDS INS CO OF TX	TX	28.0
CHUBB NATIONAL INS CO	IN	200.7
CINCINNATI CASUALTY CO	OH	297.7
CITIZENS INS CO OF AMERICA	MI	1,489.6
CMG MORTGAGE ASR CO	WI	9.3
CMI LLOYDS	TX	12.9
COLONIAL COUNTY MUTUAL INS CO	TX	69.9
COLUMBIA MUTUAL INS CO	MO	343.2
COMPANION COMMERCIAL INS CO	SC	13.3
COMPANION PROPERTY & CASUALTY INS CO	SC	536.7
CONTINENTAL DIVIDE INS CO	CO	9.3
CONTRACTORS BONDING & INS CO	WA	214.7
COUNTRY PREFERRED INS CO	IL	97.2
DAIRYLAND COUNTY MUTUAL INS CO OF TX	TX	16.5
DEERBROOK INS CO	IL	22.2
EAGLE WEST INS CO	CA	85.7
ECONOMY PREFERRED INS CO	IL	8.8
ECONOMY PREMIER ASR CO	IL	35.9
EMC PROPERTY & CASUALTY CO	IA	130.8
ENCOMPASS INDEMNITY CO	IL	23.8
ERIE INS CO	PA	601.5
ERIE INS EXCHANGE	PA	8,719.4
ERIE INS PROPERTY & CASUALTY CO	PA	59.2
EXECUTIVE RISK INDEMNITY INC	DE	2,691.1
FARM BU TOWN & COUNTRY INS CO OF MO	MO	223.4
FARM BUREAU GENERAL INS CO OF MI	MI	312.6
FARM BUREAU INS OF NC INC	NC	9.2
FARM FAMILY CASUALTY INS CO	NY	954.1
FARMERS & MECH MUTUAL INS CO	PA	3.0
FARMINGTON CASUALTY CO	CT	976.9
FINANCIAL INDEMNITY CO	CA	143.5
FIRST FLORIDIAN AUTO & HOME INS CO	FL	410.3
FIRST LIBERTY INS CORP	IA	51.7
FIRST NATIONAL INS CO OF AMERICA	WA	658.5
FLAGSHIP CITY INS CO	PA	22.0
FLORIDA FARM BUREAU GENERAL INS CO	FL	5.4
FRANKLIN MUTUAL INS CO	NJ	462.1
FREDERICK MUTUAL INS CO	MD	43.4
GARRISON PROPERTY & CASUALTY INS CO	TX	215.0
GEICO CASUALTY CO	MD	283.4
GENERAL STAR INDEMNITY CO	CT	888.7
GENESIS INDEMNITY INS CO	ND	60.5
GEORGIA FARM BUREAU CASUALTY INS CO	GA	4.6
GEORGIA FARM BUREAU MUTUAL INS CO	GA	743.0
GERMANIA FARM MUTUAL INS ASN	TX	312.7
GLOBE AMERICAN CAS CO	OH	8.8
GNY CUSTOM INS CO	AZ	48.7
GOTHAM INS CO	NY	117.8
GREATER NEW YORK MUTUAL INS CO	NY	810.8
GREEN MOUNTAIN INS CO INC	VT	9.3
GRINNELL SELECT INS CO	IA	87.6

Rating: B (Continued)

INSURANCE COMPANY NAME	DOM. STATE	TOTAL ASSETS ($MIL)
GUIDEONE PROPERTY & CASUALTY INS CO	IA	376.0
HARBOR POINT REINS US INC	CT	793.7
HARCO NATIONAL INS CO	IL	301.2
HARLEYSVILLE-ATLANTIC INS CO	GA	204.9
HARTFORD CASUALTY INS CO	IN	2,124.5
HARTFORD INS CO OF IL	IL	3,683.3
HARTFORD INS CO OF THE SOUTHEAST	CT	170.0
HARTFORD LLOYDS INS CO	TX	55.1
HARTFORD SM BOIL INSPECTION IC OF CT	CT	101.1
HOLYOKE MUTUAL INS CO IN SALEM	MA	183.4
HORACE MANN INS CO	IL	362.0
HORACE MANN PROP & CAS INS CO	CA	171.8
INDIANA FARMERS MUTUAL INS CO	IN	246.6
IOWA MUTUAL INS CO	IA	80.8
IRONSHORE INDEMNITY INC	MN	76.4
KANSAS BANKERS SURETY CO	KS	156.2
LANDMARK INS CO	CA	449.5
LIBERTY LLOYDS OF TX INS CO	TX	6.4
LITITZ MUTUAL INS CO	PA	168.8
LOUISIANA FARM BUREAU CAS INS CO	LA	8.8
MAPFRE PRAICO INS CO	PR	444.6
MASSACHUSETTS HOMELAND INS CO	MA	9.1
MEDICAL PROTECTIVE CO	IN	1,922.5
MEMBERSELECT INS CO	MI	215.0
MENDAKOTA INS CO	MN	12.3
MERCURY INDEMNITY CO OF GEORGIA	GA	9.6
MERCURY INS CO OF GA	GA	14.4
MERCURY INS CO OF IL	IL	28.3
MERCURY NATIONAL INS CO	IL	13.2
METROPOLITAN CASUALTY INS CO	RI	51.0
METROPOLITAN DIRECT PROP & CAS INS	RI	26.6
METROPOLITAN GENERAL INS CO	RI	33.0
METROPOLITAN GROUP PROP & CAS INS CO	RI	414.3
METROPOLITAN LLOYDS INS CO TEXAS	TX	14.0
MHA INS CO	MI	427.5
MID AMERICAN FIRE & CAS CO	OH	8.1
MIDDLESEX INS CO	WI	660.8
MILWAUKEE CASUALTY INS CO	WI	26.9
MISSISSIPPI FARM BUREAU CAS INS CO	MS	293.8
MITSUI SUMITOMO INS CO OF AMER	NY	712.3
MODERN SERVICE INS CO	IL	26.4
MUTUAL OF ENUMCLAW INS CO	WA	533.6
NATIONAL UNION FIRE INS CO OF LA	LA	6.8
NATIONAL UNION FIRE INS CO OF PITTSB	PA	33,210.5
NATIONWIDE LLOYDS	TX	41.0
NATIONWIDE MUTUAL INS CO	OH	25,410.2
NAVIGATORS INS CO	NY	1,680.3
NEW HAMPSHIRE INDEMNITY CO INC	PA	343.0
NEW JERSEY MANUFACTURERS INS CO	NJ	4,941.6
NEW JERSEY RE-INS CO	NJ	1,506.3
NEW YORK MARINE & GENERAL INS CO	NY	598.4
NIPPONKOA INS CO LTD US BR	NY	241.9
NORTHLAND CASUALTY CO	MN	101.0
NORTHLAND INS CO	MN	1,176.4

INSURANCE COMPANY NAME	DOM. STATE	TOTAL ASSETS ($MIL)
NORTHWESTERN PACIFIC INDEMNITY CO	OR	15.6
OHIO FARMERS INS CO	OH	1,314.5
OLD REPUBLIC LLOYDS OF TX	TX	2.2
OLD REPUBLIC SECURITY ASR CO	AZ	107.3
OLD REPUBLIC UNION INS CO	IL	24.6
OMNI INS CO	IL	190.5
ONEBEACON LLOYDS OF TEXAS	TX	17.8
OPHTHALMIC MUTUAL INS CO RRG	VT	195.1
PACIFIC INS CO LTD	CT	622.5
PACIFIC PROPERTY & CASUALTY CO	CA	45.0
PATRIOT GENERAL INS CO	WI	25.8
PEAK PROP & CAS INS CORP	WI	38.0
PEMCO MUTUAL INS CO	WA	492.9
PHARMACISTS MUTUAL INS CO	IA	183.9
PHILADELPHIA CBSP FOR INS OF HOUSES	PA	235.6
PHILADELPHIA CONTRIBUTIONSHIP INS CO	PA	138.5
PHILADELPHIA INDEMNITY INS CO	PA	3,975.6
PHOENIX INS CO	CT	3,614.1
PROASSURANCE INDEMNTIY CO INC	AL	1,822.2
PROGRESSIVE GULF INS CO	OH	340.1
PROGRESSIVE MOUNTAIN INS CO	OH	176.0
PROGRESSIVE SPECIALTY INS CO	OH	1,061.2
PROPERTY & CASUALTY I CO OF HARTFORD	IN	226.5
QUINCY MUTUAL FIRE INS CO	MA	997.9
RADIAN ASSET ASR CO	NY	2,309.6
REDWOOD FIRE & CAS INS CO	NE	863.5
RLI INS CO	IL	1,266.2
SAFECO INS CO OF ILLINOIS	IL	1,767.4
SAFECO INS CO OF OREGON	OR	205.9
SAFECO LLOYDS INS CO	TX	103.6
SAFECO NATIONAL INS CO	MO	188.1
SAFECO SURPLUS LINES INS CO	WA	46.0
SAGAMORE INS CO	IN	148.6
SCOTTSDALE INDEMNITY CO	OH	25.9
SCOTTSDALE SURPLUS LINES INS CO	AZ	19.2
SECURIAN CASUALTY CO	MN	66.3
SELECTIVE INS CO OF AMERICA	NJ	2,215.7
SELECTIVE INS CO OF NEW YORK	NY	306.1
SELECTIVE WAY INS CO	NJ	932.9
SENTINEL INS CO LTD	CT	201.4
SENTRY CASUALTY CO	WI	168.6
SENTRY LLOYDS OF TX	TX	5.6
SENTRY SELECT INS CO	WI	676.3
SHELTER MUTUAL INS CO	MO	2,130.8
SONNENBERG MUTUAL INS ASSOC	OH	17.0
SOUTH CAROLINA FARM BU MUTUAL INS CO	SC	111.1
SPARTA INS CO	MA	306.0
ST PAUL FIRE & CAS INS CO	WI	16.6
ST PAUL FIRE & MARINE INS CO	MN	19,047.7
STANDARD FIRE INS CO	CT	3,656.8
STATE AUTO INS CO OF OHIO	OH	41.0
STATE AUTO INS CO OF WISCONSIN	WI	19.0
STATE AUTO PROPERTY & CASUALTY INS	IA	1,705.4
STATE AUTOMOBILE MUTUAL INS CO	OH	1,781.8
STATE FARM FIRE & CAS CO	IL	25,307.9
STATE FARM GENERAL INS CO	IL	4,555.6

INSURANCE COMPANY NAME	DOM. STATE	TOTAL ASSETS ($MIL)
Rating: B (Continued)		
STATE FARM INDEMNITY CO	IL	1,905.4
STRATHMORE INS CO	NY	46.3
SUNAPEE MUTUAL FIRE INS CO	NH	2.4
TEXAS PACIFIC INDEMNITY CO	TX	5.9
TM CASUALTY INS CO	NY	2.7
TM SPECIALTY INS CO	AZ	21.3
TRANS PACIFIC INS CO	NY	64.5
TRAVCO INS CO	CT	203.7
TRAVELERS AUTO INS CO OF NJ	NJ	90.0
TRAVELERS CASUALTY & SURETY CO	CT	15,135.9
TRAVELERS CASUALTY CO OF CONNECTICUT	CT	312.5
TRAVELERS CASUALTY INS CO OF AMERICA	CT	1,830.4
TRAVELERS COMMERCIAL CASUALTY CO	CT	330.5
TRAVELERS COMMERCIAL INS CO	CT	322.3
TRAVELERS EXCESS & SURPLUS LINES CO	CT	197.7
TRAVELERS HOME & MARINE INS CO	CT	261.7
TRAVELERS INDEMNITY CO OF AMERICA	CT	582.7
TRAVELERS INDEMNITY CO OF CT	CT	1,055.2
TRAVELERS LLOYDS OF TEXAS INS CO	TX	22.0
TRAVELERS PERSONAL INS CO	CT	194.4
TRAVELERS PERSONAL SECURITY INS CO	CT	197.5
TRAVELERS PROPERTY CAS OF AMERICA	CT	335.8
TRAVELERS PROPERTY CASUALTY INS CO	CT	218.3
TRIAD GUARANTY ASR CORP	IL	26.8
TRINITY LLOYDS INS CO	TX	3.1
TRINITY UNIVERSAL INS CO OF KS	KS	32.6
TRUMBULL INS CO	CT	200.1
TWIN CITY FIRE INS CO	IN	659.2
UFB CASUALTY INS CO	IN	7.8
UNION INS CO OF PROVIDENCE	IA	93.5
UNION NATIONAL FIRE INS CO	LA	15.5
UNITED CASUALTY INS CO OF AMERICA	IL	16.1
UNITED FARM FAMILY INS CO	NY	24.6
UNITED OHIO INS CO	OH	203.1
UNITRIN SAFEGUARD INS CO	WI	15.4
UNIVERSAL INS CO	PR	517.7
USAA COUNTY MUTUAL INS CO	TX	132.8
USAA TEXAS LLOYDS CO	TX	349.1
UTICA LLOYDS OF TX	TX	7.4
VALLEY INS CO	CA	27.7
VERMONT ACCIDENT INS CO INC	VT	5.6
VICTORIA AUTOMOBILE INS CO	IN	17.0
VIGILANT INS CO	NY	375.6
WAWANESA MUTUAL INS CO US BR	CA	250.3
WESTERN HERITAGE INS CO	AZ	117.6
WILSON MUTUAL INS CO	WI	76.3
Rating: B-		
AEGIS SECURITY INS CO	PA	67.9
AGRI GENERAL INS CO	IA	753.7
AIG ADVANTAGE INS CO	MN	73.2
AIG AUTO INS CO OF NEW JERSEY	NJ	48.4
AIG NATIONAL INS CO INC	NY	60.1
AIG PREMIER INS CO	PA	444.7
AIX SPECIALTY INS CO	DE	21.4
ALFA SPECIALTY INS CORP	AL	34.2
ALLSTATE FLORIDIAN INS CO	IL	363.6
ALLSTATE NJ INS CO	IL	2,258.5
AMERICA FIRST INS CO	NH	13.3
AMERICAN BANKERS INS CO OF FL	FL	1,253.6
AMERICAN COMMERCE INS CO	OH	340.1
AMERICAN ECONOMY INS CO	IN	1,774.2
AMERICAN FAMILY MUT INS CO	WI	10,575.6
AMERICAN FUJI FIRE & MARINE INS CO	IL	92.9
AMERICAN INS CO	OH	1,425.7
AMERICAN INTERNATIONAL INS CO OF CA	CA	74.2
AMERICAN INTERNATIONAL INS CO OF DE	DE	103.5
AMERICAN INTERNATIONAL PACIFIC INS	CO	89.1
AMERICAN MILLERS INS CO	PA	7.9
AMERICAN NATL COUNTY MUT INS CO	TX	12.5
AMERICAN SELECT INS CO	OH	160.2
AMERICAN STANDARD LLOYDS INS CO	TX	4.5
AMERICAN STATES INS CO	IN	3,359.1
AMERICAN STATES INS CO OF TX	TX	117.4
AMERICAN STATES LLOYDS INS CO	TX	4.5
AMERICAN ZURICH INS CO	IL	195.0
AMERIHEALTH CASUALTY INS CO	DE	187.2
AMERISURE INS CO	MI	647.9
AMEX ASSURANCE CO	IL	312.6
ANPAC LOUISIANA INS CO	LA	97.0
ANSUR AMERICA INS CO	MI	58.9
ARAG INS CO	IA	51.4
AUDUBON INDEMNITY CO	MS	33.1
AUTO CLUB GROUP INS CO	MI	185.6
BADGER MUTUAL INS CO	WI	162.4
BARNSTABLE COUNTY MUTUAL INS CO	MA	71.6
BCS INS CO	OH	236.3
BEAR RIVER MUTUAL INS CO	UT	140.5
BERKLEY REGIONAL INS CO	DE	2,639.6
BRETHREN MUTUAL INS CO	MD	187.6
BRIDGEFIELD EMPLOYERS INS CO	FL	163.9
BROOKWOOD INS CO	IA	9.4
CALIFORNIA CAPITAL INS CO	CA	425.3
CENTENNIAL CASUALTY CO	AL	59.9
CHARTER INDEMNITY CO	TX	13.1
CHICAGO INS CO	IL	293.7
CMG MORTGAGE INS CO	WI	399.8
CO-OPERATIVE INS COMPANIES	VT	81.3
COMMERCE WEST INS CO	CA	164.3
COMP OPTIONS INS CO INC	FL	60.0
COURTESY INS CO	FL	421.8
CYPRESS INS CO	CA	582.9
DENTISTS INS CO	CA	204.0
DEPOSITORS INS CO	IA	66.6
DIAMOND STATE INS CO	IN	188.6
DOCTORS CO AN INTERINSURANCE EXCH	CA	2,076.4
EASTERN AMERICA INS CO	PR	109.0
ECONOMY FIRE & CAS CO	IL	388.6
EMCASCO INS CO	IA	360.1
EMPLOYERS COMPENSATION INS CO	CA	1,296.7
EMPLOYERS INS OF WAUSAU	WI	4,009.7

INSURANCE COMPANY NAME	DOM. STATE	TOTAL ASSETS ($MIL)
Rating: B- (Continued)		
EMPLOYERS MUTUAL CAS CO	IA	2,009.8
ENCOMPASS HOME & AUTO INS CO	IL	6.6
ENCOMPASS INDEPENDENT INS CO	IL	6.6
EULER HERMES AMERICAN CREDIT IND CO	MD	444.7
EXCELSIOR INS CO	NH	52.4
EXECUTIVE RISK SPECIALTY INS CO	CT	203.1
FAIRMONT FARMERS MUTUAL INS CO	MN	16.1
FARM BUREAU MUTUAL INS CO OF MI	MI	559.9
FARMERS & MECHANICS MUTUAL IC OF WV	WV	35.4
FARMERS INS CO OF OR	OR	1,505.0
FARMERS MUTUAL INS CO OF NE	NE	431.3
FB INS CO	KY	41.5
FFVA MUTUAL INS CO	FL	276.7
FIREMANS FUND COUNTY MUTUAL INS CO	TX	3.0
FIREMANS FUND INDEMNITY CORP	NJ	15.5
FIREMANS FUND INS CO OF HI INC	HI	10.5
FIREMANS FUND INS CO OF OH	OH	57.1
FIRST COLONIAL INS CO	FL	363.8
FIRST MARINE INS CO	MO	9.6
FIRST TRENTON INDEMNITY CO	NJ	862.1
FLORIDA FARM BU CASUALTY INS CO	FL	424.6
GENERAL CASUALTY CO OF IL	WI	154.7
GENERAL CASUALTY CO OF WI	WI	1,150.7
GENERAL FIDELITY INS CO	SC	699.3
GENERAL INS CO OF AMERICA	WA	3,068.0
GENERAL REINSURANCE CORP	DE	13,285.1
GENWORTH RESIDENTIAL MTG INS CORP NC	NC	230.6
GOVERNMENTAL INTERINSURANCE EXCHANGE	IL	64.3
GRANGE INDEMNITY INS CO	OH	72.3
GRANITE STATE INS CO	PA	38.6
GRAY INS CO	LA	328.3
GRINNELL MUTUAL REINSURANCE CO	IA	725.2
GUIDEONE AMERICA INS CO	IA	14.0
GUIDEONE LLOYDS INS CO	TX	3.6
HANOVER INS CO	NH	4,742.8
HARFORD MUTUAL INS CO	MD	271.9
HARLEYSVILLE INS CO OF NJ	NJ	696.3
HARLEYSVILLE INS CO OF OHIO	OH	38.5
HARLEYSVILLE MUTUAL INS CO	PA	1,296.4
HARLEYSVILLE PREFERRED INS CO	PA	693.3
HARTFORD SM BOIL INSPECTION & INS	CT	1,164.7
HERITAGE CASUALTY INS CO	IL	113.3
HIGH POINT PROPERTY & CASUALTY INS	NJ	36.0
HISCOX INS CO INC	IL	57.7
HOUSTON CASUALTY CO	TX	2,917.5
HYUNDAI MARINE & FIRE INS CO LTD	CA	29.1
IDS PROPERTY CASUALTY INS CO	WI	972.4
ILLINOIS NATIONAL INS CO	IL	66.9
IMT INS CO	IA	212.4
INFINITY INS CO	IN	1,411.6
INTEGRITY MUTUAL INS CO	WI	63.3
INTREPID INS CO	MI	38.6
IOWA AMERICAN INS CO	IA	14.3
ISLAND INS CO LTD	HI	313.0
KEMPER INDEPENDENCE INS CO	IL	129.6
KNIGHTBROOK INS CO	DE	29.6
LACKAWANNA CASUALTY CO	PA	190.3
LAFAYETTE INS CO	LA	134.1
LIBERTY MUTUAL FIRE INS CO	WI	4,524.1
LIBERTY MUTUAL INS CO	MA	33,672.9
LIGHTNING ROD MUTUAL INS CO	OH	189.3
LIVINGSTON MUTUAL INS CO	PA	2.8
LOUISIANA FARM BUREAU MUTUAL INS CO	LA	139.7
LUBA CASUALTY INS CO	LA	190.7
MAG MUTUAL INS CO	GA	1,367.0
MAIN STREET AMERICA ASR CO	FL	118.3
MAPFRE PREFERRED RISK INS CO	PR	102.2
MAPLE VALLEY MUTUAL INS CO	WI	9.1
MEDICAL INS EXCHANGE OF CALIFORNIA	CA	371.4
MEDICAL MUTUAL INS CO OF NC	NC	445.8
MEDICAL MUTUAL LIAB INS SOC OF MD	MD	787.8
MENDOTA INS CO	MN	68.9
MERITPLAN INS CO	CA	195.3
MICHIGAN INS CO	MI	94.7
MICHIGAN MILLERS MUTUAL INS CO	MI	285.9
MICO INS CO	OH	18.8
MID-CENTURY INS CO OF TEXAS	TX	54.2
MIDDLESEX MUTUAL ASR CO	CT	238.2
MILBANK INS CO	SD	461.0
MILWAUKEE INS CO	WI	40.4
MOUNT VERNON FIRE INS CO	PA	283.4
MSA INS CO	SC	5.7
MUTUAL BENEFIT INS CO	PA	166.4
NATIONAL FARMERS UNION PROP & CAS CO	CO	319.7
NATIONAL GENERAL INS CO	MO	99.9
NATIONAL INDEMNITY CO OF MID-AMERICA	IA	125.3
NATIONAL INDEMNITY CO OF THE SOUTH	FL	169.8
NATIONAL LLOYDS INS CO	TX	166.0
NATIONWIDE AFFINITY INS CO OF AMER	OH	45.5
NATIONWIDE AGRIBUSINESS INS CO	IA	168.9
NATIONWIDE ASR CO	WI	62.4
NATIONWIDE GENERAL INS CO	OH	54.2
NATIONWIDE INS CO OF AMERICA	WI	189.5
NATIONWIDE PROPERTY & CAS INS CO	OH	152.8
NETHERLANDS INS CO	NH	488.3
NEW ENGLAND MUTUAL INS CO	MA	27.7
NEW LONDON COUNTY MUTUAL INS CO	CT	115.0
NEW YORK CENTRAL MUTUAL FIRE INS CO	NY	915.1
NEW YORK SCHOOLS INS RECIPROCAL	NY	205.9
NEWPORT INS CO	AZ	120.5
NGM INS CO	FL	1,790.2
NORCAL MUTUAL INS CO	CA	1,142.9
NORGUARD INS CO	PA	387.1
NORTHBROOK INDEMNITY CO	IL	39.6
NUTMEG INS CO	CT	349.9
OAK RIVER INS CO	NE	286.1
OHIO MUTUAL INS ASSOC	OH	159.9
OKLAHOMA FARM BUREAU MUTUAL INS CO	OK	297.9
OLD DOMINION INS CO	FL	28.0
OLD UNITED CAS CO	KS	376.9

INSURANCE COMPANY NAME	DOM. STATE	TOTAL ASSETS ($MIL)
Rating: B- (Continued)		
ONEBEACON INS CO	PA	2,859.8
OREGON MUTUAL INS CO	OR	199.6
PEMCO INS CO	WA	132.6
PENN MILLERS INS CO	PA	183.6
PENN-AMERICA INS CO	PA	350.9
PENN-STAR INS CO	PA	167.4
PENNSYLVANIA LUMBERMENS MUTUAL INS	PA	300.3
PENNSYLVANIA NTL MUTUAL CAS INS CO	PA	1,025.3
PHYSICIANS INS A MUTUAL CO	WA	406.6
PREFERRED PHYSICIANS MEDICAL RRG	MO	147.4
PREMIER INS CO OF MASSACHUSETTS	MA	447.7
PRIVILEGE UNDERWRITERS RECIP EXCH	FL	65.9
PROFESSIONALS ADVOCATE INS CO	MD	103.4
PROGRESSIVE AMERICAN INS CO	FL	323.6
PROGRESSIVE BAYSIDE INS CO	FL	101.0
PROGRESSIVE PREMIER INS CO OF IL	OH	126.6
PROGRESSIVE SOUTHEASTERN INS CO	IN	128.4
PROGRESSIVE WEST INS CO	OH	138.3
PROVIDENCE MUTUAL FIRE INS CO	RI	153.4
QBE INS CORP	PA	844.5
QBE REINSURANCE CORP	PA	1,129.0
RED SHIELD INS CO	WA	41.4
REGENT INS CO	WI	228.2
REPUBLIC INDEMNITY CO OF AMERICA	CA	862.6
REPUBLIC UNDERWRITERS INS CO	TX	694.4
REPUBLIC VANGUARD INS CO	AZ	22.1
RLI INDEMNITY CO	IL	41.0
RURAL COMMUNITY INS CO	MN	856.9
RVI AMERICA INS CO	CT	54.4
SAFECO INS CO OF AMERICA	WA	7,272.4
SAFECO INS CO OF INDIANA	IN	140.5
SAFETY INDEMNITY INS CO	MA	93.9
SAFEWAY INS CO	IL	334.5
SCOTTSDALE INS CO	OH	1,727.0
SECURA INS A MUTUAL CO	WI	600.5
SECURITY NATIONAL INS CO	TX	43.7
SELECT RISK INS CO	PA	35.3
SELECTIVE INS CO OF SC	IN	427.7
SELECTIVE INS CO OF THE SOUTHEAST	IN	321.5
SERVICE LLOYDS INS CO	TX	259.5
SHELTER GENERAL INS CO	MO	189.8
SHELTER REINSURANCE CO	MO	229.9
SOUTHERN INS CO OF VIRGINIA	VA	137.8
SOUTHERN VANGUARD INS CO	TX	7.8
SOUTHWEST MARINE & GEN INS CO	AZ	44.6
ST PAUL GUARDIAN INS CO	MN	78.2
ST PAUL MERCURY INS CO	MN	262.2
ST PAUL PROTECTIVE INS CO	IL	514.6
STANDARD GUARANTY INS CO	DE	182.8
STATE AUTO NATIONAL INS CO	OH	99.4
STRATFORD INS CO	NH	175.3
SUTTER INS CO	CA	44.4
TEACHERS INS CO	IL	280.2
TEXAS FARM BUREAU MUTUAL INS CO	TX	304.1
TITAN INDEMNITY CO	TX	293.4
TOA-RE INS CO OF AMERICA	DE	1,323.0
TRAVELERS CASUALTY & SURETY CO OF AM	CT	4,307.8
TRAVELERS LLOYDS INS CO	TX	25.0
TRINITY UNIVERSAL INS CO	TX	2,583.6
TRITON INS CO	TX	768.2
TUDOR INS CO	NH	440.5
UNDERWRITER FOR THE PROFESSIONS INC	CO	239.6
UNION MUTUAL FIRE INS CO	VT	152.9
UNITED FIRE & CAS CO	IA	1,194.1
UNITED GUARANTY CREDIT INS CO	NC	22.3
UNITED NATIONAL SPECIALTY INS CO	WI	90.0
UNITED STATES FIDELITY & GUARANTY CO	MD	4,250.9
UNITED SURETY & INDEMNITY CO	PR	101.8
UNITRIN DIRECT PROPERTY & CAS CO	IL	50.6
US SPECIALTY INS CO	TX	1,212.9
US UNDERWRITERS INS CO	ND	140.1
UTICA MUTUAL INS CO	NY	2,101.3
UTICA NATIONAL INS CO OF TX	TX	29.5
VALLEY PROPERTY & CASUALTY INS CO	OR	16.8
VEREX ASR INC	WI	28.8
VICTORIA FIRE & CASUALTY CO	OH	512.6
VICTORIA SELECT INS CO	OH	45.6
WAUSAU BUSINESS INS CO	WI	255.2
WAUSAU GENERAL INS CO	WI	36.1
WESTERN NATIONAL MUTUAL INS CO	MN	488.1
WESTERN RESERVE MUTUAL CAS CO	OH	139.4
WESTFIELD INS CO	OH	2,029.3
Rating: C+		
AAA MIDATLANTIC INS CO OF NJ	NJ	32.5
AAA SOUTHERN NEW ENGLAND INS CO	RI	60.0
ACA HOME INS CORP	FL	21.9
ACA INS CO	IN	50.7
ACCIDENT FUND GENERAL INS CO	MI	131.5
ACCIDENT FUND INS CO OF AMERICA	MI	2,092.9
ACE AMERICAN INS CO	PA	8,025.1
ADDISON INS CO	IL	80.2
ADVANTAGE WORKERS COMP INS CO	IN	118.9
AG SECURITY INS CO	OK	42.0
AIG CASUALTY CO	PA	4,051.5
AIG EXCESS LIABILITY INS CO LTD	DE	4,028.7
AIG GLOBAL TRADE & POL RISK INS CO	NJ	369.2
AIU INS CO	NY	2,824.7
ALLEGANY CO-OP INS CO	NY	31.3
ALLIANCE INDEMNITY CO	KS	8.9
ALLIANZ GLOBAL RISKS US INS CO	CA	5,045.2
ALLMERICA FINANCIAL ALLIANCE INS CO	NH	16.8
ALLMERICA FINANCIAL BENEFIT INS CO	MI	16.3
AMERICAN AGRI BUSINESS INS CO	TX	420.3
AMERICAN CAPITAL ASR CORP	FL	108.8
AMERICAN CONTRACTORS INDEMNITY CO	CA	256.6
AMERICAN EMPIRE INS CO	OH	44.8
AMERICAN EUROPEAN INS CO	NH	194.2
AMERICAN GENERAL INDEMNITY CO	IL	8.7
AMERICAN HOME ASR CO	NY	24,768.6

INSURANCE COMPANY NAME	DOM. STATE	TOTAL ASSETS ($MIL)
Rating: C+ (Continued)		
AMERICAN INTERSTATE INS CO	LA	934.9
AMERICAN MODERN SURPLUS LINES INS CO	OH	87.4
AMERICAN SENTINEL INS CO	PA	22.9
AMERICAN SOUTHERN INS CO	KS	89.3
AMERISURE MUTUAL INS CO	MI	1,645.4
ARBELLA MUTUAL INS CO	MA	920.8
ARBELLA PROTECTION INS CO	MA	268.6
ARCH EXCESS & SURPLUS INS CO	NE	32.6
ARCH INS CO	MO	1,680.7
ARECA INS EXCHANGE	AK	22.3
ASI ASR CORP	FL	87.7
ASI LLOYDS	TX	106.1
ASSOCIATED INDEMNITY CORP	CA	181.4
ASSURANCE COMPANY OF AMERICA	NY	32.1
ATHENA ASSURANCE CO	MN	198.1
AUDUBON INS CO	LA	76.4
AUTOMOBILE CLUB INTERINSURANCE EXCH	MO	280.9
AUTOONE INS CO	NY	71.3
AXIS REINS CO	NY	2,116.6
BENCHMARK INS CO	KS	90.8
BRITISH AMERICAN INS CO	TX	52.9
CALIFORNIA CAS COMPENSATION INS CO	CA	66.4
CALIFORNIA CAS GEN INS CO OF OREGON	OR	96.0
CALIFORNIA CASUALTY & FIRE INS CO	CA	53.2
CALIFORNIA CASUALTY INS CO	CA	122.3
CALIFORNIA INS CO	CA	288.9
CARIBBEAN ALLIANCE INS CO	PR	226.0
CARIBBEAN AMERICAN PROPERTY INS CO	PR	36.2
CATLIN SPECIALTY INS CO	DE	212.4
CENTURY-NATIONAL INS CO	CA	484.5
CIM INS CORP	MI	17.6
CINCINNATI SPECIALTY UNDERWRITER	DE	198.2
CITIZENS INS CO OF ILLINOIS	IL	4.4
CLUB INS CO	OH	13.7
COLONIAL AMERICAN CAS & SURETY CO	MD	25.9
COLORADO CASUALTY INS CO	CO	21.9
COLORADO FARM BUREAU MUTUAL INS CO	CO	89.0
COLUMBIA INS CO	NE	8,967.5
COLUMBIA LLOYDS INS CO	TX	32.1
COLUMBIA NATIONAL INS CO	NE	84.7
COMMERCE & INDUSTRY INS CO	NY	8,533.0
CONCORD GENERAL MUTUAL INS CO	NH	306.4
CONNECTICUT MEDICAL INS CO	CT	404.2
CONSOLIDATED INS CO	IN	24.4
CONTINENTAL INS CO	PA	3,668.1
CRUSADER INS CO	CA	147.9
DANBURY INS CO	MA	16.5
DEVELOPERS SURETY & INDEMNITY CO	IA	128.0
DIRECT GENERAL INS CO	IN	425.1
DIRECT NATIONAL INS CO	AR	23.8
DISCOVER PROPERTY & CASUALTY INS CO	IL	175.0
DISCOVER SPECIALTY INS CO	IL	110.8
DONEGAL MUTUAL INS CO	PA	302.1
DRIVE NEW JERSEY INS CO	NJ	115.4
DRYDEN MUTUAL INS CO	NY	104.9
EASTGUARD INS CO	PA	102.0
ELECTRIC INS CO	MA	1,423.1
EMC REINSURANCE CO	IA	251.7
EMPIRE INDEMNITY INS CO	OK	16.0
EMPLOYERS DIRECT INS CO	CA	366.4
ENDURANCE REINS CORP OF AMERICA	DE	1,884.9
EQUITY INS CO	TX	57.9
EXACT PROPERTY & CASUALTY CO INC	CA	211.8
FARM CREDIT SYS ASSOC CAPTIVE INS CO	CO	89.1
FARMERS FIRE INS CO	PA	25.1
FARMERS INS CO INC	KS	322.3
FARMERS INS CO OF AZ	AZ	70.7
FARMERS INS CO OF ID	ID	169.6
FARMERS INS CO OF WA	WA	501.2
FARMERS INS OF COLUMBUS INC	OH	231.6
FARMERS MUTUAL HAIL INS CO OF IA	IA	497.8
FARMERS NEW CENTURY INS CO	IL	173.7
FARMERS REINS CO	CA	1,536.5
FARMERS TEXAS COUNTY MUTUAL INS CO	TX	157.6
FCCI ADVANTAGE INS CO	FL	5.8
FCCI INS CO	FL	1,450.2
FIDELITY & DEPOSIT CO OF MARYLAND	MD	229.1
FIDELITY & GUARANTY INS CO	IA	23.2
FIDELITY & GUARANTY INS UDWRS INC	WI	83.4
FIDELITY MOHAWK INS CO	NJ	11.3
FIREMANS FUND INS CO OF LA	LA	6.3
FIRST INS CO OF HI LTD	HI	602.2
FIRST PROFESSIONALS INS CO INC	FL	615.6
FIRSTLINE NATIONAL INS CO	MD	59.3
FLORIDA HOSPITALITY MUTUAL INS CO	FL	123.5
FLORISTS MUTUAL INS CO	IL	154.2
FOREMOST LLOYDS OF TEXAS	TX	39.5
FOREMOST SIGNATURE INS CO	MI	57.0
GENWORTH MTG INS CORP OF NC	NC	601.6
GERMANIA FIRE & CASUALTY CO	TX	20.3
GERMANTOWN INS CO	PA	75.1
GERMANTOWN MUTUAL INS CO	WI	62.8
GOLDEN EAGLE INS CORP	CA	975.7
GOODVILLE MUTUAL CAS CO	PA	119.6
GRANGE INS ASN	WA	203.0
GRANITE MUTUAL INS CO	VT	4.0
GRAPHIC ARTS MUTUAL INS CO	NY	124.0
GREAT AMERICAN ASR CO	OH	16.9
GREAT AMERICAN CONTEMPORARY INS CO	OH	10.5
GREAT AMERICAN SPIRIT INS CO	OH	20.2
GUARDIAN INS CO INC	VI	26.5
GUIDEONE ELITE INS CO	IA	27.6
GUIDEONE MUTUAL INS CO	IA	1,000.8
GUIDEONE SPECIALTY MUTUAL INS CO	IA	222.1
HANOVER AMERICAN INS CO	NH	16.2
HANOVER LLOYDS INS CO	TX	5.0
HARLEYSVILLE INS CO OF NEW YORK	NY	80.0
HARLEYSVILLE LAKE STATES INS CO	MI	295.5
HARLEYSVILLE PENNLAND INS CO	PA	184.6
HARLEYSVILLE WORCESTER INS CO	PA	535.2

INSURANCE COMPANY NAME	DOM. STATE	TOTAL ASSETS ($MIL)
Rating: C+ (Continued)		
HARTFORD ACCIDENT & INDEMNITY CO	CT	10,829.4
HAWKEYE-SECURITY INS CO	WI	12.8
HCC INS CO	IN	29.0
HERITAGE INDEMNITY CO	CA	182.1
HIGH POINT PREFERRED INS CO	NJ	866.7
HIGH POINT SAFETY & INS CO	NJ	56.4
HOOSIER MOTOR MUTUAL INS CO	IN	12.4
HOUSING AUTHORITY PROP A MUTUAL CO	VT	157.1
IL STATE BAR ASSOC MUTUAL INS CO	IL	56.0
ILLINOIS EMCASCO INS CO	IA	268.8
ILLINOIS FARMERS INS CO	IL	253.4
INDEPENDENCE CASUALTY & SURETY CO	TX	28.2
INDEPENDENT MUTUAL FIRE INS CO	IL	25.3
INDIANA INS CO	IN	1,264.7
INS CO OF ILLINOIS	IL	37.3
INS CO OF THE STATE OF PA	PA	4,578.1
INTEGON CASUALTY INS CO	NC	44.2
INTEGON GENERAL INS CORP	NC	46.2
INTEGON INDEMNITY CORP	NC	98.8
INTEGON NATIONAL INS CO	NC	186.6
INTEGON PREFERRED INS CO	NC	30.1
INTERNATIONAL FIDELITY INS CO	NJ	200.1
ISMIE MUTUAL INS CO	IL	1,396.5
KANSAS MEDICAL MUTUAL INS CO	KS	177.6
KEYSTONE INS CO	PA	372.4
LA MEDICAL MUTUAL INS CO	LA	325.9
LANCER INS CO	IL	623.9
LEXINGTON INS CO	DE	15,208.1
LIBERTY INS CO OF AMERICA	IL	12.2
LYNDON PROPERTY INS CO	MO	422.9
MADISON MUTUAL INS CO	NY	11.1
MAPFRE PAN AMERICAN INS CO	PR	23.7
MARYLAND CASUALTY CO	MD	384.6
MASSACHUSETTS BAY INS CO	NH	46.9
MEDICAL MUTUAL INS CO OF MAINE	ME	212.6
MEDICAL PROFESSIONAL MUTUAL INS CO	MA	2,198.8
MEDICAL SECURITY INS CO	NC	8.1
MEDMARC MUTUAL INS CO	VT	238.3
MEEMIC INS CO	MI	118.0
MERASTAR INS CO	IN	32.8
MERCHANTS BONDING CO (MUTUAL)	IA	80.2
MERCHANTS MUTUAL INS CO	NY	351.7
MGIC MORTGAGE REINSURANCE CORP	WI	32.8
MGIC RESIDENTIAL REINSURANCE CORP	WI	32.1
MIC GENERAL INS CORP	MI	38.1
MILLERS CAPITAL INS CO	PA	119.6
MINNESOTA LAWYERS MUTUAL INS CO	MN	108.5
MISSOURI HOSPITAL PLAN	MO	137.2
MITSUI SUMITOMO INS USA INC	NY	105.6
MMG INS CO	ME	161.7
MONTEREY INS CO	CA	61.4
MOTORS INS CORP	MI	5,444.4
MOUNTAIN STATES MUTUAL CAS CO	NM	152.7
MT HAWLEY INS CO	IL	1,050.6
NAMIC INS CO INC	IN	43.8
NATIONAL GENERAL ASR CO	MO	39.8
NATIONAL INDEMNITY CO	NE	59,159.5
NATIONAL INTERSTATE INS CO	OH	740.4
NATIONWIDE INDEMNITY CO	OH	3,670.8
NATIONWIDE INS CO OF FLORIDA	OH	436.1
NAUTILUS INS CO	AZ	1,408.7
NAVIGATORS SPECIALTY INS CO	NY	125.9
NCMIC INS CO	IA	467.3
NEIGHBORHOOD SPIRIT PROP & CAS CO	CA	211.1
NEW HAMPSHIRE INS CO	PA	4,181.7
NEW JERSEY CASUALTY INS CO	NJ	236.1
NEW JERSEY INDEMNITY INS CO	NJ	101.9
NEW SOUTH INS CO	NC	71.5
NODAK MUTUAL INS CO	ND	122.6
NORTH PACIFIC INS CO	OR	62.9
NORTHERN INS CO OF NY	NY	31.6
NORTHFIELD INS CO	IA	373.0
OHIO BAR LIABILITY INS CO	OH	35.5
OHIO CASUALTY INS CO	OH	5,328.1
OKLAHOMA ATTORNEYS MUTUAL INS CO	OK	44.4
OMS NATIONAL INS CO RRG	IL	286.1
PACIFIC EMPLOYERS INS CO	PA	2,554.7
PEERLESS INS CO	NH	12,656.5
PENN NATIONAL SECURITY INS CO	PA	659.6
PERSONAL SERVICE INS CO	PA	44.2
PHILADELPHIA INS CO	PA	243.6
PIONEER GENERAL INS CO	CO	11.6
PLANS LIABILITY INS CO	OH	89.5
PMSLIC INS CO	PA	482.4
PRAETORIAN INS CO	IL	934.9
PREFERRED MUTUAL INS CO	NY	367.2
PREFERRED PROFESSIONAL INS CO	NE	320.0
PRINCETON EXCESS & SURPLUS LINES INS	DE	206.8
PRIORITY ONE INS CO	TX	17.7
PROASSURANCE CASUALTY CO	MI	1,108.5
PROASSURANCE SPECIALTY INS CO INC	AL	33.7
PROCENTURY INS CO	TX	130.4
PROFESSIONAL UNDRWTRS LIAB INS CO	UT	96.1
PROGRESSIVE CLASSIC INS CO	WI	301.0
PROGRESSIVE MAX INS CO	OH	252.9
PROGRESSIVE NORTHEASTERN INS CO	NY	183.1
PROGRESSIVE NORTHERN INS CO	WI	1,147.5
PROGRESSIVE NORTHWESTERN INS CO	OH	1,118.3
PROGRESSIVE SECURITY INS CO	LA	192.5
PROGRESSIVE UNIVERSAL INS CO	WI	172.4
PUBLIC SERVICE MUTUAL INS CO	NY	639.5
RADIAN MORTGAGE INS INC	AZ	65.2
RAINIER INS CO	AZ	27.9
REPUBLIC FIRE & CASUALTY INS CO	OK	5.7
REPUBLIC-FRANKLIN INS CO	OH	84.2
RIVERPORT INS CO	MN	84.7
RURAL MUTUAL INS CO	WI	259.6
RVOS FARM MUTUAL INS CO	TX	73.1
SAFEWAY INS CO OF AL	IL	51.1
SAFEWAY INS CO OF LA	LA	92.8

INSURANCE COMPANY NAME	DOM. STATE	TOTAL ASSETS ($MIL)
Rating: C+ (Continued)		
SECURA SUPREME INS CO	WI	82.8
SELECTIVE AUTO INS CO OF NJ	NJ	275.8
SEQUOIA INS CO	CA	178.9
SOCIETY INS	WI	272.4
SOMPO JAPAN INS CO OF AMERICA	NY	792.8
SOUTHERN FIRE & CASUALTY CO	WI	7.6
SOUTHERN INS CO	TX	25.8
SOUTHERN TRUST INS CO	GA	39.3
SOUTHERN UNDERWRITERS INS CO	OK	5.2
ST PAUL MEDICAL LIABILITY INS CO	MN	198.6
STARR INDEMNITY & LIABILITY CO	TX	298.5
STATE FARM LLOYDS	TX	2,667.7
STATE NATIONAL INS CO INC	TX	188.7
STONEBRIDGE CASUALTY INS CO	OH	296.6
SURETY BONDING CO OF AMERICA	SD	9.7
TERRA INS CO RRG	VT	36.3
TITAN INS CO	MI	116.2
TNUS INS CO	NY	58.6
TOPA INS CO	CA	188.4
TRANSATLANTIC REINSURANCE CO	NY	11,688.1
UNIGARD INS CO	WA	646.6
UNITED FINANCIAL CASUALTY CO	OH	1,839.0
UNITED FIRE & INDEMNITY CO	TX	39.0
UNITED NATIONAL CASUALTY INS CO	IN	52.9
UNITED NATIONAL INS CO	PA	643.6
UNITED WISCONSIN INS CO	WI	306.2
UNITRIN COUNTY MUTUAL INS CO	TX	37.4
UNITRIN DIRECT INS CO	IL	33.9
UNIVERSAL INS CO OF NORTH AMERICA	FL	105.5
UNIVERSAL UNDERWRITERS OF TX	TX	14.8
UTAH MEDICAL INS ASN	UT	271.0
UTICA FIRST INS CO	NY	179.8
UTICA SPECIALTY RISK INS CO	TX	26.0
VALIANT INS CO	DE	67.7
VANLINER INS CO	MO	475.9
VERMONT MUTUAL INS CO	VT	413.9
VIRGINIA SURETY CO INC	IL	1,015.5
VOYAGER INDEMNITY INS CO	GA	88.9
WASHINGTON INTERNATIONAL INS CO	NH	116.2
WAUSAU UNDERWRITERS INS CO	WI	385.2
WESCO INS CO	DE	205.3
WESTERN UNITED INS CO	IN	148.6
WESTERN WORLD INS CO	NH	1,019.6
XL SPECIALTY INS CO	DE	510.3
YORK INS CO OF MAINE	ME	15.9
YOSEMITE INS CO	IN	335.2
ZENITH INS CO	CA	2,089.6
ZNAT INS CO	CA	60.5
ZURICH AMERICAN INS CO OF IL	IL	54.3
Rating: C		
1ST AUTO & CASUALTY INS CO	WI	29.6
21ST CENTURY INS CO OF THE SW	TX	5.6
A CENTRAL INS CO	NY	37.6
AAA MID-ATLANTIC INS CO	PA	24.1

INSURANCE COMPANY NAME	DOM. STATE	TOTAL ASSETS ($MIL)
ACADIA INS CO	NH	134.6
ACCC INS CO	TX	135.5
ACCEPTANCE CASUALTY INS CO	NE	37.3
ACCEPTANCE INDEMNITY INS CO	NE	113.0
ACCIDENT FUND NATIONAL INS CO	MI	214.3
ACE FIRE UNDERWRITERS INS CO	PA	112.4
ACE PROPERTY & CASUALTY INS CO	PA	5,938.4
ACSTAR INS CO	IL	81.8
ADMIRAL INDEMNITY CO	DE	73.7
ADMIRAL INS CO	DE	2,494.8
ADRIATIC INS CO	ND	65.9
AETNA INS CO OF CT	CT	19.5
AFFILIATED FM INS CO	RI	1,486.6
AFFINITY MUTUAL INS CO	OH	13.3
AGCS MARINE INS CO	IL	188.5
AGENCY INS CO OF MARYLAND INC	MD	58.6
AGRICULTURAL WORKERS MUT AUTO INS CO	TX	54.0
AIOI INS CO OF AMERICA	NY	68.3
ALABAMA MUNICIPAL INS CORP	AL	83.9
ALASKA TIMBER INS EXCHANGE	AK	18.0
ALFA ALLIANCE INS CORP	VA	34.9
ALFA GENERAL INS CORP	AL	119.6
ALFA VISION INS CORP	AL	89.3
ALLIANCE INS CO INC	KS	22.6
ALLIANZ UNDERWRITERS INS CO	CA	94.3
ALLIED EASTERN INDEMNITY CO	PA	25.3
ALLIED WORLD NATL ASR CO	NH	198.4
ALLIED WORLD REINS CO	NJ	795.0
ALLSTATE FIRE & CASUALTY INS CO	IL	60.4
AMALGAMATED CASUALTY INS CO	DC	39.0
AMERICAN ACCESS CASUALTY CO	IL	122.6
AMERICAN ALTERNATIVE INS CORP	DE	527.0
AMERICAN AUTOMOBILE INS CO	MO	457.0
AMERICAN CASUALTY CO OF READING	PA	114.2
AMERICAN COMPENSATION INS CO	MN	89.9
AMERICAN EMPIRE SURPLUS LINES INS CO	DE	328.9
AMERICAN FEDERATED INS CO	MS	21.9
AMERICAN FEED INDUSTRY INS CO RRG	IA	14.9
AMERICAN GUARANTEE & LIABILITY INS	NY	212.0
AMERICAN GUARANTY INS CO	NC	8.5
AMERICAN INTER FIDELITY EXCHANGE RRG	IN	22.4
AMERICAN INTERSTATE INS CO OF TEXAS	TX	41.6
AMERICAN INTL SPECIALTY LINES INS CO	IL	2,497.8
AMERICAN MERCHANTS CASUALTY CO	DE	61.1
AMERICAN MINING INS CO INC	AL	35.4
AMERICAN MODERN SELECT INS CO	OH	120.9
AMERICAN RELIABLE INS CO	AZ	316.2
AMERICAN ROAD INS CO	MI	564.2
AMERICAN SAFETY INS CO	GA	19.1
AMERICAN SUMMIT INS CO	TX	39.7
AMERICAN SURETY CO	IN	13.3
AMERICAN VEHICLE INS CO	FL	72.2
AMERICAN WEST INS CO	ND	8.5
AMERICAN WESTERN HOME INS CO	OK	196.0
AMERICAS INS CO	LA	14.7
AMGUARD INS CO	PA	274.2

Rating: C (Continued)

INSURANCE COMPANY NAME	DOM. STATE	TOTAL ASSETS ($MIL)
AMICA PROPERTY & CASUALTY INS CO	RI	28.0
ANCHOR GENERAL INS CO	CA	47.7
ANESTHESIOLOGISTS PROF ASR CO	FL	80.8
APPALACHIAN INS CO	RI	193.2
ARBELLA INDEMNITY INS CO	MA	45.6
ARCH REINSURANCE CO	NE	1,212.8
ARGONAUT INS CO	IL	1,390.6
ARGONAUT-SOUTHWEST INS CO	LA	16.9
ARI MUTUAL INS CO	NJ	67.0
ARMED FORCES INS EXCHANGE	KS	133.8
ARROW MUTUAL LIABILITY INS CO	MA	47.1
ARTISAN & TRUCKERS CASUALTY CO	WI	82.7
ASPEN SPECIALTY INS CO	ND	184.1
ASSOCIATED EMPLOYERS INS CO	MA	4.4
ASSOCIATED INDUSTRIES OF MA MUT INS	MA	372.1
ASSURED GUARANTY CORP	MD	1,926.3
ASSURED GUARANTY MORTGAGE INS CO	NY	50.9
ATLANTIC CHARTER INS CO	MA	167.6
ATLANTIC EMPLOYERS INS CO	NJ	71.5
ATLANTIC SPECIALTY INS CO	NY	66.5
ATRADIUS TRADE CREDIT INS CO	MD	96.4
AUSTIN MUTUAL INS CO	MN	144.9
AUTO CLUB FAMILY INS CO	MO	70.9
AUTO CLUB PROPERTY & CASUALTY INS CO	IA	35.5
AUTO CLUB SOUTH INS CO	FL	71.7
AUTOONE SELECT INS CO	NY	83.4
AXA ART INS CORP	NY	53.9
AXIS INS CO	IL	621.6
BANKERS INDEPENDENT INS CO	PA	25.0
BANKERS STANDARD FIRE & MARINE CO	PA	155.7
BANKERS STANDARD INS CO	PA	349.2
BAR PLAN MUTUAL INS CO	MO	57.9
BAR PLAN SURETY & FIDELITY CO	MO	4.2
BARNSTABLE COUNTY INS CO	MA	16.0
BEACON LLOYDS INS CO	TX	4.3
BEACON NATIONAL INS CO	TX	25.0
BEAZLEY INS CO INC	CT	201.1
BELL UNITED INS CO	NV	32.2
BERKLEY INS CO	DE	6,918.5
BERKLEY REGIONAL SPECIALTY INS CO	DE	29.3
BLOOMINGTON COMPENSATION INS CO	MN	23.3
BLUE RIDGE INDEMNITY CO	WI	14.0
BLUE RIDGE INS CO	WI	46.0
BOND SAFEGUARD INS CO	IL	64.4
BREMEN FARMERS MUTUAL INS CO	KS	29.6
BRIDGEFIELD CASUALTY INS CO	FL	121.9
BRIERFIELD INS CO	MS	9.9
BUCKEYE STATE MUTUAL INS CO	OH	58.1
BUILDERS INS (A MUTUAL CAPTIVE CO)	GA	339.5
BUNKER HILL INS CO	MA	39.3
CALIFORNIA CASUALTY INDEMNITY EXCH	CA	539.9
CALIFORNIA HEALTHCARE INS CO INC RRG	HI	104.2
CALLICOON CO-OPERATIVE INS CO	NY	21.5
CAMDEN FIRE INS ASSN CO OF NJ	NJ	66.9
CAMERON MUTUAL INS CO	MO	89.6
CAMICO MUTUAL INS CO	CA	182.7
CAPITOL CASUALTY CO	NE	16.9
CAPITOL COUNTY MUTUAL FIRE INS CO	TX	27.8
CAPITOL INDEMNITY CORP	WI	379.0
CAPITOL SPECIALTY INS CORP	WI	75.9
CAROLINA CASUALTY INS CO	IA	786.5
CASTLEPOINT INS CO	NY	317.6
CATERPILLAR INS CO	MO	327.3
CATLIN INS CO	TX	71.1
CELINA MUTUAL INS CO	OH	47.8
CENTER MUTUAL INS CO	ND	32.9
CENTRE INS CO	DE	263.2
CHRYSLER INS CO	MI	227.3
CHURCH INS CO	NY	49.8
CITIZENS INS CO OF OH	OH	12.4
CITIZENS INS CO OF THE MIDWEST	IN	23.1
CIVIC PROPERTY & CASUALTY CO INC	CA	218.2
CIVIL SERVICE EMPLOYEES INS CO	CA	181.6
CLERMONT INS CO	IA	24.8
CNL/INS AMERICA INC	GA	29.0
COFACE NORTH AMERICA INS CO	MA	103.9
COLISEUM REINS CO	DE	430.9
COLOGNE REINSURANCE CO OF AMERICA	CT	109.0
COLONY INS CO	VA	1,390.5
COLONY NATIONAL INS CO	VA	328.1
COLUMBIA CASUALTY CO	IL	274.7
COMMERCIAL ALLIANCE INS CO	TX	25.1
COMMONWEALTH MORTGAGE ASR CO OF TX	TX	573.8
COMMUNITY INS CORP	WI	19.9
COMPUTER INS CO	RI	44.2
CONSUMERS INS USA INC	TN	60.6
CONTINENTAL CASUALTY CO	IL	38,541.1
CONTINENTAL HERITAGE INS CO	FL	7.7
CONTINENTAL INDEMNITY CO	IA	48.6
CONTINENTAL INS CO OF NJ	NJ	22.8
CONTINENTAL WESTERN INS CO	IA	252.6
CONTROLLED RISK INS CO OF VT RRG	VT	120.7
CONVENTUS INTER INS EXCHANGE	NJ	79.3
COOPERATIVE MUTUAL INS CO	NE	27.8
COTTON STATES MUTUAL INS CO	GA	245.5
COUNTRYWAY INS CO	NY	58.2
COVENANT INS CO	CT	66.6
CPA INS CO	MI	19.8
CRUM & FORSTER SPECIALTY INS CO	AZ	88.2
CSE SAFEGUARD INS CO	CA	73.1
DAILY UNDERWRITERS OF AMERICA	PA	29.4
DAKOTA FIRE INS CO	ND	174.6
DAKOTA TRUCK UNDERWRITERS	SD	77.7
DARWIN NATIONAL ASR CO	DE	687.3
DARWIN SELECT INS CO	AR	92.7
DE SMET FARM MUTUAL INS CO OF SD	SD	30.5
DEALERS ASR CO	OH	57.8
DIRECT GENERAL INS CO OF MS	MS	50.9
DIRECT INS CO	TN	81.0
DOCTORS DIRECT INS INC	IL	7.7

Rating: C (Continued)

INSURANCE COMPANY NAME	DOM. STATE	TOTAL ASSETS ($MIL)
DORCHESTER INS CO LTD	VI	19.9
DORCHESTER MUTUAL INS CO	MA	47.8
DTRIC INS CO LTD	HI	79.2
EASTERN MUTUAL INS CO	NY	15.8
ELECTRIC LLOYDS OF TX	TX	2.8
EMPIRE FIRE & MARINE INS CO	NE	121.1
EMPLOYERS ASSURANCE CO	FL	450.9
EMPLOYERS FIRE INS CO	MA	91.2
EMPLOYERS INS CO OF NEVADA INC	NV	1,999.2
EMPLOYERS PREFERRED INS CO	FL	442.9
ENCOMPASS INS CO	IL	24.6
ENCOMPASS INS CO OF AMERICA	IL	22.7
ENCOMPASS INS CO OF NJ	IL	26.9
ENCOMPASS PROPERTY & CASUALTY CO	IL	12.0
ENDEAVOUR INS CO	MA	4.8
ENDURANCE AMERICAN INS CO	DE	162.9
ENDURANCE AMERICAN SPECIALTY INS CO	DE	149.4
ERIE & NIAGARA INS ASSOC	NY	104.4
ESSENTIA INS CO	MO	48.6
ESSEX INS CO	DE	1,033.7
ESURANCE INS CO	WI	445.1
ESURANCE INS CO OF NEW JERSEY	WI	21.1
ESURANCE PROP & CAS INS CO	CA	106.5
EVANSTON INS CO	IL	2,108.9
EVER-GREENE MUTUAL INS CO	PA	3.4
EVEREST INDEMNITY INS CO	DE	173.7
EVEREST NATIONAL INS CO	DE	467.9
EVEREST SECURITY INS CO	GA	33.4
EVERETT CASH MUTUAL INS CO	PA	59.3
EVERGREEN NATIONAL INDEMNITY CO	OH	46.0
EXCESS SHARE INS CORP	OH	63.6
FACTORY MUTUAL INS CO	RI	8,433.0
FARM BUREAU CNTY MUTUAL INS CO OF TX	TX	17.3
FARM BUREAU MUTUAL INS CO OF AR	AR	257.8
FARMERS & MERCHANTS MUTUAL FIRE I C	MI	19.1
FARMERS ALLIANCE MUTUAL INS CO	KS	286.0
FARMERS CASUALTY INS CO	IA	85.1
FARMERS INS CO OF FLEMINGTON	NJ	52.9
FARMERS INS EXCHANGE	CA	13,763.9
FARMERS MUTUAL F I C OF OKARCHE OK	OK	12.4
FARMERS MUTUAL F I C OF SALEM CTY	NJ	86.3
FARMERS MUTUAL OF TENNESSEE	TN	18.7
FARMERS UNION COOPERATIVE INS CO	IA	8.0
FARMERS UNION MUTUAL INS CO	MT	44.8
FARMERS UNION MUTUAL INS CO	ND	62.7
FEDERATED RURAL ELECTRIC INS EXCH	KS	339.0
FFG INS CO	TX	140.2
FIDELITY FIRE & CASUALTY CO	FL	25.8
FIDELITY NATIONAL INS CO	CA	258.7
FIDELITY NATIONAL PROP & CAS INS	NY	153.6
FINANCIAL PACIFIC INS CO	CA	226.8
FINGER LAKES FIRE & CASUALTY CO	NY	21.6
FIRE INS EXCHANGE	CA	2,315.5
FIREMANS FUND INS CO	CA	9,398.7
FIREMENS INS CO OF WASHINGTON DC	DE	102.3
FIRST AMERICAN PROP & CAS INS CO	CA	74.1
FIRST AMERICAN SPECIALTY INS CO	CA	98.3
FIRST COMMUNITY INS CO	FL	59.8
FIRST FIRE & CASUALTY INS OF HI INC	HI	6.4
FIRST INDEMNITY INS OF HI INC	HI	6.6
FIRST NONPROFIT INS CO	IL	126.2
FIRST SEALORD SURETY INC	PA	13.4
FIRST SECURITY INS OF HI INC	HI	5.0
FIRST SPECIALTY INS CORP	MO	183.0
FIRSTCOMP INS CO	NE	248.8
FITCHBURG MUTUAL INS CO	MA	68.0
FLORIDA LAWYERS MUTUAL INS CO	FL	53.9
FLORISTS INS CO	IL	11.8
FMI INS CO	NJ	18.7
FOREMOST COUNTY MUTUAL INS CO	TX	44.2
FOREMOST PROPERTY & CASUALTY INS CO	MI	47.1
FORTRESS INS CO	IL	47.4
FOUNDERS INS CO	NJ	6.7
FOUNDERS INS CO	IL	209.8
FRANDISCO PROPERTY & CAS INS CO	GA	55.3
FRANKLIN HOMEOWNERS ASR CO	PA	13.7
FRANKLIN INS CO	PA	28.0
GEMINI INS CO	DE	81.7
GENESIS INS CO	CT	203.2
GENWORTH FINANCIAL ASR CORP	NC	24.4
GENWORTH MORTGAGE INS CORP	NC	3,060.0
GEOVERA INS CO	CA	96.8
GEOVERA SPECIALTY INS CO	CA	65.0
GERMAN MUTUAL INS CO	OH	31.0
GERMANIA SELECT INS CO	TX	111.4
GHS PROPERTY & CASUALTY INS CO	OK	44.5
GMAC INS CO ONLINE INC	MO	13.7
GRANGE INS CO OF MI	OH	49.6
GRANGE PROPERTY & CASUALTY INS CO	OH	37.2
GREAT AMERICAN ALLIANCE INS CO	OH	27.7
GREAT AMERICAN E & S INS CO	DE	26.1
GREAT AMERICAN FIDELITY INS CO	DE	25.9
GREAT AMERICAN INS CO	OH	5,206.4
GREAT AMERICAN INS CO OF NEW YORK	NY	58.9
GREAT AMERICAN LLOYDS INS CO	TX	1.4
GREAT AMERICAN SECURITY INS CO	OH	18.2
GREAT DIVIDE INS CO	ND	157.5
GREAT MIDWEST INS CO	MI	44.5
GUARANTEE CO OF NORTH AMERICA USA	MI	179.8
GULF GUARANTY INS CO	MS	4.9
HAMILTON MUTUAL INS CO	IA	63.9
HANOVER NJ INS CO	NH	26.2
HANYS MEMBER HOSP SELF INS TRUST	NY	62.0
HARLEYSVILLE INS CO	PA	133.8
HAULERS INS CO INC	TN	50.8
HAWAIIAN INS & GUARANTY CO LTD	HI	24.8
HCC SPECIALTY INS CO	OK	22.4
HEALTH CARE INDEMNITY INC	CO	1,637.6
HERMITAGE INS CO	NY	188.1
HIGHMARK CASUALTY INS CO	PA	221.7

INSURANCE COMPANY NAME	DOM. STATE	TOTAL ASSETS ($MIL)
Rating: C (Continued)		
HILLSTAR INS CO	IN	6.8
HINGHAM MUTUAL FIRE INS CO	MA	90.3
HOCHHEIM PRAIRIE FARM MUT INS ASN	TX	139.3
HOMELAND INS CO OF NEW YORK	NY	464.7
HOMESITE INS CO OF FL	FL	11.9
HOMESITE INS CO OF IL	IL	20.3
HOMESITE INS CO OF NY	NY	27.1
HOMESITE INS CO OF PA	PA	14.8
HOMEWISE INS CO	FL	11.8
HOOSIER INS CO	IN	99.7
HORACE MANN LLOYDS	TX	3.0
HOUSING AUTHORITY RISK RET GROUP INC	VT	275.4
HOUSTON GENERAL INS CO	TX	27.2
HOUSTON GENERAL INS EXCH	TX	24.0
HSBC INS CO OF DELAWARE	DE	370.0
IFA INS CO	NJ	88.7
ILLINOIS UNION INS CO	IL	393.3
IMPERIAL FIRE & CASUALTY INS CO	LA	71.8
INDEMNITY CO OF CA	CA	22.5
INDEMNITY INS CO OF NORTH AMERICA	PA	409.2
INDEMNITY NATIONAL INS CO	MS	13.0
INDEPENDENCE AMERICAN INS CO	DE	74.1
INDIANA LUMBERMENS MUTUAL INS CO	IN	108.0
INFINITY ASSURANCE INS CO	OH	6.9
INFINITY AUTO INS CO	OH	12.3
INFINITY CASUALTY INS CO	OH	8.5
INFINITY COUNTY MUTUAL INS CO	TX	30.7
INFINITY GENERAL INS CO	OH	5.1
INFINITY INDEMNITY INS CO	IN	7.1
INFINITY PREFERRED INS CO	OH	5.5
INFINITY PREMIER INS CO	IN	7.1
INFINITY RESERVE INS CO	OH	4.9
INFINITY SAFEGUARD INS CO	OH	7.2
INFINITY SECURITY INS CO	IN	8.1
INFINITY SELECT INS CO	IN	7.2
INFINITY SPECIALTY INS CO	OH	10.1
INFINITY STANDARD INS CO	IN	11.6
INLAND INS CO	NE	132.9
INS CO OF NORTH AMERICA	PA	764.4
INS CO OF THE WEST	CA	801.8
INTEGON SPECIALTY INS	NC	54.8
INTEGRAND ASR CO	PR	137.7
INTERMED INS CO	MO	139.1
INTERSTATE BANKERS CASUALTY CO	IL	18.3
INTERSTATE FIRE & CAS CO	IL	612.2
IRONSHORE SPECIALTY INS CO	AZ	128.3
JAMES RIVER INS CO	OH	471.3
JEFFERSON INS CO	NY	66.2
KENTUCKY EMPLOYERS MUTUAL INS	KY	626.3
KEY RISK INS CO	NC	74.8
KEYSTONE NATIONAL INS CO	PA	5.7
KODIAK INS CO	NJ	40.8
LACKAWANNA AMERICAN INS CO	PA	53.6
LACKAWANNA NATIONAL INS CO	PA	16.7
LANDMARK AMERICAN INS CO	OK	344.4
LAWYERS MUTUAL INS CO	CA	242.7
LAWYERS MUTUAL INS CO OF KENTUCKY	KY	21.6
LAWYERS MUTUAL LIAB INS CO OF NC	NC	72.6
LE MARS INS CO	IA	51.4
LEADING INS GROUP INS CO LTD US BR	NY	58.4
LEBANON MUTUAL INS CO	PA	23.7
LEXINGTON NATIONAL INS CORP	MD	54.0
LEXON INS CO	TX	92.7
LIBERTY AMERICAN INS CO	FL	32.0
LIBERTY AMERICAN SELECT INS CO	FL	29.2
LIBERTY INS CORP	IL	1,101.9
LIBERTY INS UNDERWRITERS INC	NY	154.8
LIBERTY MUTUAL MID ATLANTIC INS CO	PA	20.3
LIBERTY NORTHWEST INS CORP	OR	185.1
LIBERTY SURPLUS INS CORP	NH	114.1
LION INS CO	FL	362.7
LM INS CORP	IA	77.2
LUMBERMENS UNDERWRITING ALLIANCE	MO	331.7
LUTHERAN MUTUAL FIRE INS CO	IL	9.0
LYNDON SOUTHERN INS CO	LA	22.7
MADISON MUTUAL INS CO	IL	60.6
MANUFACTURERS ALLIANCE INS CO	PA	207.0
MARKEL AMERICAN INS CO	VA	448.8
MARYSVILLE MUTUAL INS CO	KS	23.9
MASSACHUSETTS EMPLOYERS INS CO	MA	4.0
MAX SPECIALTY INS CO	DE	199.0
MAXUM INDEMNITY CO	DE	173.3
MCMILLAN WARNER MUTUAL INS CO	WI	12.2
MEDAMERICA MUTUAL RRG INC	HI	54.4
MEDICAL LIABILITY ALLIANCE	MO	41.8
MEDMARC CASUALTY INS CO	VT	110.2
MEMIC INDEMNITY CO	NH	149.2
MERCED MUTUAL INS CO	CA	17.6
MERCER INS CO OF NJ INC	NJ	72.8
MERCHANTS NATIONAL INS CO	NH	59.3
MERCHANTS PREFERRED INS CO	NY	33.7
MERCURY COUNTY MUTUAL INS CO	TX	10.1
MERIDIAN CITIZENS MUTUAL INS CO	IN	24.4
MERIDIAN SECURITY INS CO	IN	64.8
MIAMI MUTUAL INS CO	OH	25.6
MIC PROPERTY & CASUALTY INS CORP	MI	133.5
MICHIGAN PROFESSIONAL INS EXCHANGE	MI	103.0
MID-CONTINENT INS CO	OH	32.1
MID-HUDSON CO-OPERTIVE INS CO	NY	12.6
MIDDLE GEORGIA MUTUAL INS CO	GA	14.8
MIDSTATE MUTUAL INS CO	NY	32.3
MIDWEST FAMILY MUTUAL INS CO	MN	109.5
MIDWESTERN INDEMNITY CO	OH	16.4
MILLERS CLASSIFIED INS CO	WI	23.0
MILLVILLE MUTUAL INS CO	PA	42.7
MLBA MUTUAL INS CO	MI	12.0
MO EMPLOYERS MUTUAL INS CO	MO	335.4
MODERN USA INS CO	FL	24.7
MONROE GUARANTY INS CO	IN	28.3
MONTGOMERY MUTUAL INS CO	MD	48.8

INSURANCE COMPANY NAME	DOM. STATE	TOTAL ASSETS ($MIL)
Rating: C (Continued)		
MOUNTAIN LAUREL ASR CO	OH	94.1
MOUNTAIN STATES INDEMNITY CO	NM	66.2
MT WASHINGTON ASR CORP	NH	5.1
MUNICH REINSURANCE AMERICA INC	DE	15,783.4
MUNICIPAL MUTUAL INS CO	WV	22.9
MUTUAL FIRE MARINE & INLAND INS CO	PA	127.3
MUTUALAID EXCHANGE	KS	30.0
NATIONAL BUILDING MATERIAL ASR CO	IN	3.1
NATIONAL FIRE & MARINE INS CO	NE	3,829.2
NATIONAL FIRE INS CO OF HARTFORD	IL	138.7
NATIONAL INS CO	PR	130.0
NATIONAL INS CO OF WISCONSIN INC	WI	44.9
NATIONAL MERIT INS CO	WA	33.4
NATIONAL MUTUAL INS CO	OH	51.6
NATIONAL SECURITY FIRE & CAS CO	AL	68.2
NATIONAL SERVICE CONTRACT INS CO RRG	DC	16.2
NATIONAL SPECIALTY INS CO	TX	29.0
NATIONAL SURETY CORP	IL	624.0
NEVADA CAPITAL INS CO	NV	65.3
NEVADA GENERAL INS CO	NV	28.0
NEW CENTURY INS CO	TX	3.6
NEW ENGLAND GUARANTY INS CO INC	VT	32.2
NEW JERSEY SKYLANDS INS ASSN	NJ	86.4
NEW MEXICO MUTUAL CASUALTY CO	NM	253.6
NEW YORK MUNICIPAL INS RECIPROCAL	NY	120.4
NOETIC SPECIALTY INS CO	IL	95.6
NORFOLK & DEDHAM MUTUAL FIRE INS CO	MA	244.0
NORTH AMERICAN CAPACITY INS CO	NH	66.1
NORTH AMERICAN ELITE INS CO	NH	42.3
NORTH AMERICAN SPECIALTY INS CO	NH	541.9
NORTH RIVER INS CO	NJ	1,011.9
NORTHERN ASR CO OF AMERICA	MA	281.5
NORTHERN MUTUAL INS CO	MI	21.7
NORTHERN SECURITY INS CO INC	VT	7.5
NORTHWEST DENTISTS INS CO	WA	16.9
NORTHWEST PHYSICIANS INS CO	OR	129.5
OAK BROOK COUNTY MUTUAL INS CO	TX	8.6
OCEANUS INS CO A RRG	SC	37.7
ODYSSEY AMERICA REINSURANCE CO	CT	6,880.8
OHIO INDEMNITY CO	OH	99.1
OKLAHOMA SURETY CO	OH	28.9
OLD GUARD INS CO	OH	289.3
OMEGA ONE INS CO	AL	10.6
OMNI INDEMNITY CO	IL	73.7
ONEBEACON AMERICA INS CO	MA	722.9
ONEBEACON MIDWEST INS CO	WI	21.8
OPTIMUM PROPERTY & CASUALTY INS CO	TX	3.5
OREGON AUTOMOBILE INS CO	OR	26.6
PACIFIC SELECT PROPERTY INS CO	CA	109.7
PACIFIC SPECIALTY INS CO	CA	227.0
PACIFIC STAR INS CO	WI	8.4
PACO ASR CO INC	IL	46.7
PALISADES SAFETY & INS ASSOC	NJ	754.6
PALMETTO CASUALTY INS CO	SC	6.0
PARAMOUNT INS CO	NY	62.5
PARIS RE AMERICA INS CO	DE	305.2
PARTNERRE INS CO OF NEW YORK	NY	117.1
PARTNERS MUTUAL INS CO	WI	39.5
PATRIOT INS CO	ME	59.0
PATRONS MUTUAL INS CO OF CT	CT	39.9
PATRONS-OXFORD INS CO	ME	15.5
PEERLESS INDEMNITY INS CO	IL	789.6
PENINSULA INDEMNITY CO	MD	9.6
PENINSULA INS CO	MD	72.9
PENN CHARTER MUTUAL INS CO	PA	6.1
PENN PATRIOT INS CO	VA	69.0
PENNSYLVANIA GENERAL INS CO	PA	387.4
PENNSYLVANIA MANUFACTURERS ASN INS	PA	717.6
PENNSYLVANIA MANUFACTURERS IND CO	PA	217.5
PERMANENT GEN ASR CORP OF OHIO	OH	96.5
PERMANENT GENERAL ASR CORP	TN	212.4
PERSONAL EXPRESS INS CO	CA	20.9
PHYSICIANS PROFESSIONAL LIABILTY RRG	VT	40.3
PILGRIM INS CO	MA	30.5
PLATEAU CASUALTY INS CO	TN	19.8
PLATINUM UNDERWRITERS REINS CO	MD	1,770.8
PLYMOUTH ROCK ASR CORP	MA	385.3
PODIATRY INS CO OF AMERICA A MUT CO	IL	262.4
PREFERRED EMPLOYERS INS CO	CA	95.4
PROASSURANCE NATIONAL CAPITAL INS CO	DC	258.2
PROASSURANCE WISCONSIN INS CO	WI	364.5
PRODUCERS AGRICULTURE INS CO	TX	153.0
PRODUCERS LLOYDS INS CO	TX	4.1
PROFESSIONAL SECURITY INS CO	AZ	19.0
PROGRESSIVE ADVANCED INS CO	OH	177.5
PROGRESSIVE CASUALTY INS CO	OH	5,072.6
PROGRESSIVE CHOICE INS CO	OH	195.8
PROGRESSIVE COUNTY MUTUAL INS CO	TX	310.1
PROGRESSIVE EXPRESS INS CO	FL	250.7
PROGRESSIVE FREEDOM INS CO	NJ	20.5
PROGRESSIVE GARDEN STATE INS CO	NJ	73.1
PROGRESSIVE HAWAII INS CORP	OH	101.5
PROGRESSIVE MARATHON INS CO	MI	248.1
PROGRESSIVE MICHIGAN INS CO	MI	390.7
PROGRESSIVE PALOVERDE INS CO	IN	66.2
PROGRESSIVE PREFERRED INS CO	OH	604.6
PROGRESSIVE SELECT INS CO	FL	256.3
PROSELECT INS CO	MA	72.1
PUTNAM REINSURANCE CO	NY	623.2
RAM MUTUAL INS CO	MN	64.0
REAL LEGACY ASR CO INC	PR	143.3
REDLAND INS CO	NJ	163.3
REPUBLIC INDEMNITY OF CA	CA	42.5
REPUBLIC LLOYDS	TX	7.0
REPUBLIC MORTGAGE INS CO OF FLORIDA	FL	49.3
REPUBLIC MORTGAGE INS CO OF NC	NC	687.3
RESIDENCE MUTUAL INS CO	CA	69.1
RESPONSE INS CO	CT	80.3
RESPONSE WORLDWIDE DIRECT AUTO INS	CT	45.5
RESPONSE WORLDWIDE INS CO	CT	86.3

Rating: C (Continued)

INSURANCE COMPANY NAME	DOM. STATE	TOTAL ASSETS ($MIL)
RIDER INS CO	NJ	39.7
ROCKFORD MUTUAL INS CO	IL	63.8
ROCKHILL INS CO	AZ	206.4
ROCKINGHAM CASUALTY CO	VA	42.0
ROCKINGHAM MUTUAL INS CO	VA	57.8
ROCKY MOUNTAIN FIRE & CAS CO	WA	25.5
RSUI INDEMNITY CO	NH	2,480.2
SAFE AUTO INS CO	OH	442.1
SAFETY FIRST INS CO	IL	15.8
SAFETY NATIONAL CASUALTY CORP	MO	1,969.0
SAFETY PROPERTY & CASUALTY INS CO	MA	33.7
SAFEWAY DIRECT INS CO	CA	15.0
SAFEWAY INS CO OF GEORGIA	GA	53.1
SAFEWAY PROPERTY INS CO	NE	34.9
SAVERS PROPERTY & CASUALTY INS CO	MO	179.2
SCF PREMIER INS CO	AZ	15.1
SCPIE INDEMNITY COMPANY	CA	478.4
SEAWORTHY INS CO	MD	48.3
SECURITY MUTUAL INS CO	NY	73.5
SENECA INS CO INC	NY	329.3
SENTRUITY CASUALTY CO	TX	23.1
SEQUOIA INDEMNITY CO	NV	15.0
SERVICE INS CO	FL	19.2
SEVEN SEAS INS CO INC	FL	16.3
SFM MUTUAL INS CO	MN	351.8
SHEBOYGAN FALLS INS CO	WI	20.5
SHIELD INS CO	GA	24.8
SILVER OAK CASUALTY INC	LA	144.6
SLAVONIC MUTUAL FIRE INS ASN	TX	22.8
SOMPO JAPAN FIRE & MAR INS CO AMER	NY	67.9
SOUTHERN COUNTY MUTUAL INS CO	TX	27.6
SOUTHERN GENERAL UNDERWRITERS INS CO	GA	33.4
SOUTHERN GUARANTY INS CO	WI	182.5
SOUTHERN MUTUAL CHURCH INS CO	SC	41.1
SOUTHERN PILOT INS CO	WI	13.2
SOUTHERN STATES INS EXCHANGE	VA	30.1
SOUTHWEST CASUALTY CO	NM	23.2
SPARTAN PROPERTY INS CO	SC	27.5
SPRINGFIELD FIRE & CASUALTY CO	IL	11.0
ST PAUL SURPLUS LINES INS CO	DE	610.7
STANDARD CASUALTY CO	TX	20.3
STANDARD MUTUAL INS CO	IL	63.3
STAR INS CO	MI	680.3
STARNET INS CO	DE	167.1
STATE & COUNTY MUTUAL FIRE INS CO	TX	2.7
STATE AUTO FLORIDA INS CO	IN	11.1
STATE FARM FLORIDA INS CO	FL	2,108.2
STATE MUTUAL INS CO	ME	1.7
STATE-WIDE INS CO	NY	120.3
STEADFAST INS CO	DE	552.0
STERLING INS CO	NY	104.5
STICO MUTUAL INS CO A RRG	VT	18.8
STONEWOOD INS CO	NC	103.0
SUA INS CO	IL	331.1
SUBLIMITY INS CO	OR	17.4
SURETEC INS CO	TX	98.1
SWISS REINSURANCE AMERICA CORP	NY	14,479.3
T H E INS CO	LA	172.9
TEACHERS AUTO INS CO	NJ	14.7
TECHNOLOGY INS CO INC	NH	577.1
TEXAS FARM BUREAU UNDERWRITERS	TX	16.7
TEXAS FARMERS INS CO	TX	242.3
THAMES INS CO INC	CT	34.6
TOWER INS CO OF NEW YORK	NY	872.6
TOYOTA MOTOR INS CO	IA	341.5
TRADEWIND INS CO LTD	HI	14.2
TRANS CITY CASUALTY INS CO	AZ	19.7
TRANSGUARD INS CO OF AMERICA INC	IL	193.1
TRANSPORTATION INS CO	IL	35.5
TRI STATE INS CO OF MINNESOTA	MN	33.0
TRI-STATE CONSUMER INS CO	NY	95.1
TRIANGLE INS CO INC	OK	36.9
TRIPLE S PROPIEDAD INC	PR	270.0
TRIUMPHE CASUALTY CO	PA	22.2
TRUCK INS EXCHANGE	CA	1,954.4
TUSCARORA WAYNE INS CO	PA	20.5
ULICO CASUALTY CO	DE	221.4
UMIALIK INS CO	AK	42.6
UNIGARD INDEMNITY CO	WA	77.8
UNION INS CO	IA	92.4
UNION STANDARD LLOYDS	TX	3.2
UNITED EDUCATORS INS A RECIP RRG	VT	500.6
UNITED FIRE LLOYDS	TX	16.3
UNITED GUARANTY INS CO	NC	242.1
UNITED GUARANTY MORTGAGE INDEM CO	NC	378.2
UNITED GUARANTY MORTGAGE INS CO	NC	242.0
UNITED GUARANTY MTG INS CO OF NC	NC	242.3
UNITED SECURITY INS CO	CO	11.7
UNITED STATES FIRE INS CO	DE	2,603.1
UNITED STATES LIABILITY INS CO	PA	406.1
UNITED STATES SURETY CO	MD	61.9
UNIVERSAL CASUALTY CO	IL	98.4
UNIVERSAL SURETY CO	NE	82.8
UNIVERSAL SURETY OF AMERICA	SD	25.5
UNIVERSAL UNDERWRITERS INS CO	KS	429.9
UPLAND MUTUAL INS INC	KS	17.6
US AGENCIES CASUALTY INS CO INC	LA	89.1
US SECURITY INS CO	FL	72.3
USF INS CO	MI	151.5
USPLATE GLASS INS CO	IL	17.1
UTICA NATIONAL ASR CO	NY	56.8
VA FARM BUREAU TOWN & COUNTRY INS CO	VA	48.2
VALLEY FORGE INS CO	PA	55.7
VERLAN FIRE INS CO	NH	23.2
VETERINARY PET INS CO	CA	152.7
VIKING COUNTY MUTUAL INS CO	TX	2.6
VIKING INS CO OF WI	WI	406.7
VININGS INS CO	SC	44.0
VIRGINIA FARM BUREAU FIRE & CAS INS	VA	40.7
VIRGINIA FARM BUREAU MUTUAL INS CO	VA	261.7

INSURANCE COMPANY NAME	DOM. STATE	TOTAL ASSETS ($MIL)
Rating: C (Continued)		
WADENA INS CO	IA	36.4
WAWANESA GENERAL INS CO	CA	334.8
WAYNE MUTUAL INS CO	OH	28.3
WEA PROPERTY & CASUALTY INS CO	WI	14.0
WEST AMERICAN INSURANCE CO	IN	404.3
WESTCHESTER SURPLUS LINES INS CO	GA	421.4
WESTERN GENERAL INS CO	CA	76.8
WESTERN NATIONAL ASR CO	MN	41.5
WESTERN PACIFIC MUT INS CO RISK RET	CO	122.1
WESTERN PROTECTORS INS CO	OR	13.5
WESTERN SURETY CO	SD	1,232.9
WESTERN UNDERWRITERS INS CO	CA	16.8
WESTPORT INS CORP	MO	7,822.1
WI LAWYERS MUTUAL INS CO	WI	25.6
WILSHIRE INS CO	NC	129.8
WINDSOR MOUNT JOY MUTUAL INS CO	PA	43.2
WISCONSIN AMERICAN MUTUAL INS CO	WI	4.8
WISCONSIN COUNTY MUTUAL INS CORP	WI	56.6
WISCONSIN MUTUAL INS CO	WI	86.7
WISCONSIN REINSURANCE CORP	WI	71.7
WOLVERINE MUTUAL INS CO	MI	41.6
WORTH CASUALTY CO	TX	4.7
XL REINS AMERICA INC	NY	5,090.1
YOUNG AMERICA INS CO	TX	39.8
ZALE INDEMNITY CO	TX	13.9
ZC SPECIALTY INS CO	TX	99.0
Rating: C-		
1ST CHOICE AUTO INS CO	PA	10.0
AAA TEXAS COUNTY MUTUAL INS CO	TX	62.2
ACCREDITED SURETY & CAS CO INC	FL	28.4
ACE INDEMNITY INS CO	PA	34.4
ACE INS CO	PR	94.0
AFFIRMATIVE INS CO	IL	476.9
AGRI INS EXCHANGE RISK RETENTION GRP	IN	10.1
ALAMANCE INS CO	IL	421.7
ALLEGHENY CASUALTY CO	PA	22.6
ALLIED WORLD ASR CO (US) INC	DE	239.3
ALLSTATE NJ PROPERTY & CASUALTY INS	IL	27.6
AMERICA FIRST LLOYD'S INS CO	TX	6.2
AMERICAN EQUITABLE INC	MI	9.9
AMERICAN FIRE & CASUALTY CO	OH	200.1
AMERICAN HALLMARK INS CO OF TX	TX	240.4
AMERICAN HEALTHCARE INDEMNITY CO	DE	124.7
AMERICAN KEYSTONE INS CO	FL	24.1
AMERICAN MODERN INS CO OF FLORIDA	FL	20.0
AMERICAN MUTUAL SHARE INS CORP	OH	184.2
AMERICAN RESOURCES INS CO INC	AL	37.5
AMERICAN SERVICE INS CO INC	IL	130.3
AMERITRUST INS CORP	MI	78.7
ANTHRACITE MUTUAL FIRE INS CO	PA	2.5
APOLLO CASUALTY CO OF FL	FL	14.8
ARCHITECTS & ENGINEERS INS CO RRG	DE	17.1
ARGONAUT GREAT CENTRAL INS CO	IL	143.6
ASSOCIATED INDUSTRIES INS CO INC	FL	174.2
ASSOCIATED INTERNATIONAL INS CO	IL	206.3
ASSOCIATED LOGGERS EXCHANGE	ID	28.0
ASSOCIATION CASUALTY INS CO	TX	47.2
ASSOCIATION INS CO	GA	66.1
ATTORNEYS INS MUTUAL OF ALABAMA INC	AL	16.0
AUTO CLUB INS CO OF FL	FL	23.1
AXA INS CO	NY	186.4
AXIS SPECIALTY INS CO	CT	224.1
BANCINSURE INC	OK	99.1
BANKERS INS CO	FL	112.4
BEDFORD GRANGE MUTUAL INS CO	PA	5.2
BRIAR CREEK MUTUAL INS CO	PA	9.2
BRISTOL WEST INS CO	OH	188.6
BUILDING INDUSTRY INS ASSN INC	VA	13.2
BURLINGTON INS CO	NC	387.1
BUSINESS ALLIANCE INS CO	CA	31.1
CALIFORNIA MEDICAL GROUP INS CO RRG	AZ	14.5
CAMERON NATIONAL INS CO	MO	11.4
CAPITAL CITY INS CO INC	SC	135.5
CARDIF PROPERTY & CASUALTY INS CO	TX	10.2
CAROLINA FARMERS MUTUAL INS CO	NC	8.6
CASCO INDEMNITY CO	ME	22.4
CATHOLIC RELIEF INS CO OF AMERICA	NE	79.0
CENTURY SURETY CO	OH	472.3
CHAUTAUQUA PATRONS INS CO	NY	14.9
CHEROKEE INS CO	MI	228.0
CLARENDON AMERICA INS CO	NJ	231.5
CLARENDON NATIONAL INS CO	NJ	748.2
CLEARFIELD CTY GRNGE MUT FIRE INS CO	PA	3.1
COASTAL CASUALTY INS CO	NC	3.8
COLONY SPECIALTY INS CO	OH	198.5
COMMERCIAL MUTUAL INS CO	NY	22.3
COMMONWEALTH REINS CO	MA	34.8
COMMUNITY BLOOD CENTERS EXCHANGE RRG	IN	19.7
CORNERSTONE NATIONAL INS CO	MO	56.2
CPA MUTUAL INS CO OF AMERICA RRG	VT	22.2
CRUM & FORSTER INS CO	NJ	37.6
CUMBERLAND INS CO INC	NJ	86.1
DALLAS NATIONAL INS CO	TX	262.6
DANIELSON NATIONAL INS CO	CA	15.2
DE SMET INS CO OF SD	SD	11.1
DEERFIELD INS CO	IL	53.8
DELTA FIRE & CAS INS CO	GA	7.8
DENTISTS BENEFITS INS CO	OR	15.3
DIRECT GENERAL INS CO OF LA	LA	44.1
DISTRIBUTORS INS CO	TN	16.4
DRIVERS INS CO	OK	16.1
DTRIC INS UNDERWRITERS LTD	HI	6.2
EASTERN ATLANTIC INS CO	PA	45.1
ELLINGTON MUTUAL INS CO	WI	5.4
ENCOMPASS FLORIDIAN INDEMNITY CO	IL	5.9
ENCOMPASS FLORIDIAN INS CO	IL	6.2
ENCOMPASS INS CO OF MA	MA	6.2
ENUMCLAW PROP & CAS INS CO	WA	7.7
EVEREADY INS CO	NY	20.4
EVEREST REINSURANCE CO	DE	8,311.4

INSURANCE COMPANY NAME	DOM. STATE	TOTAL ASSETS ($MIL)
Rating: C- (Continued)		
EXECUTIVE INS CO	NY	4.3
EXPLORER INS CO	CA	163.1
FACILITY INS CORP	TX	191.4
FAIRMONT PREMIER INS CO	CA	209.7
FARMERS MUTUAL F I C OF MCCANDLESS	PA	5.5
FARMERS MUTUAL FIRE INS CO OF MARBLE	PA	15.0
FCCI COMMERCIAL INS CO	FL	12.6
FIDELITY NATIONAL INDEMNITY INS CO	TX	20.3
FINANCIAL CASUALTY & SURETY INC	TX	18.8
FIRE DISTRICTS OF NY MUT INS CO INC	NY	47.4
FIRST ACCEPTANCE INS CO OF TN INC	TN	21.9
FIRST DAKOTA INDEMNITY CO	SD	32.9
FIRST FINANCIAL INS CO	IL	492.2
FIRST GUARD INS CO	AZ	13.6
FIRST MERCURY CASUALTY CO	MN	69.8
FLORIDA FAMILY INS CO	FL	65.1
FLORIDA PENINSULA INS CO	FL	193.0
FORESTRY MUTUAL INS CO	NC	50.3
FOUNDATION RESERVE INS CO INC	NM	17.3
FRIENDS COVE MUTUAL INS CO	PA	6.1
GATEWAY INS CO	MO	36.4
GEM STATE INS CO	ID	6.0
GENERALI - US BRANCH	NY	56.7
GENWORTH HOME EQUITY INS CORP	NC	12.4
GEORGIA MUTUAL INS CO	GA	8.6
GERMANIA INS CO	TX	56.8
GRAIN DEALERS MUTUAL INS CO	IN	49.1
GRAMERCY INS CO	TX	30.5
GRANITE RE INC	OK	26.3
GRAY CASUALTY & SURETY CO	LA	17.2
GREAT LAKES CASUALTY INS CO	MI	12.8
GROWERS AUTOMOBILE INS ASN	IN	4.3
GUILFORD INS CO	IL	356.4
HARTLAND MUT INS CO	ND	7.3
HEALTH PROVIDERS INS RECIPROCAL RRG	HI	60.7
HEALTHCARE PROVIDERS INS EXCH	PA	99.8
HILLCREST INS CO	FL	24.3
HOCHHEIM PRAIRIE CASUALTY INS CO	TX	43.0
HOME & FARM INS CO	IN	4.0
HOMESITE INDEMNITY CO	KS	58.8
HOMESITE INS CO	CT	133.8
ILLINOIS CASUALTY CO	IL	78.9
IMPERIAL CASUALTY & INDEMNITY CO	OK	39.6
INDIAN HARBOR INS CO	ND	201.0
INLAND MUTUAL INS CO	WV	5.3
INSURA PROPERTY & CAS INS CO INC	IL	35.4
INTERLEX INS CO	MO	35.4
ISLAND PREMIER INS CO LTD	HI	7.1
KANSAS MUTUAL INS CO	KS	9.7
LANDCAR CASUALTY CO	UT	8.9
LAUNDRY OWNERS MUTUAL LIAB INS ASN	PA	10.5
LEAGUE OF WI MUNICIPALITIES MUT INS	WI	44.9
LIBERTY COUNTY MUTUAL INS CO	TX	13.5
LIBERTY FIRST RRG INS CO	UT	2.4
LITCHFIELD MUTUAL FIRE INS CO	CT	7.0
MANUFACTURING TECHNOLOGY MUT INS CO	MI	28.2
MAPFRE INS CO OF FLORIDA	FL	45.4
MARKEL INS CO	IL	643.9
MDADVANTAGE INS CO OF NJ	NJ	301.1
MENNONITE MUTUAL INS CO	OH	16.2
MENTAL HEALTH RISK RETENTION GROUP	VT	19.8
MERCER INS CO	PA	227.0
MERCURY INS CO OF FL	FL	63.2
MFS MUTUAL INS CO	IA	3.6
MGA INS CO INC	TX	219.5
MGIC CREDIT ASR CORP	WI	44.3
MGIC REINSURANCE CORP	WI	384.4
MICHIGAN COMMERCIAL INS MUTUAL	MI	118.8
MID-CENTURY INS CO	CA	3,285.3
MID-CONTINENT CAS CO	OH	696.5
MIDWEST EMPLOYERS CAS CO	DE	371.2
MIDWEST INS CO	IL	53.9
NARRAGANSETT BAY INS CO	RI	33.4
NATIONAL FIRE & CASUALTY CO	IL	7.8
NATIONAL FIRE & INDEMNITY EXCHANGE	MO	10.7
NATIONAL HOME INS CO RRG	CO	72.6
NATIONAL TRUST INS CO	TN	25.7
NATIONAL UNITY INS CO	TX	37.4
NAU COUNTRY INS CO	MN	447.1
NEVADA MUTUAL INS CO INC	NV	55.0
NEW JERSEY HEALTHCARE PROVIDERS INS	NJ	14.6
NEW JERSEY PHYS UNITED RECIP EXCH	NJ	43.0
NEW JERSEY SKYLANDS INS CO	NJ	44.6
NLC MUTUAL INS CO	VT	235.6
NORTH CAROLINA GRANGE MUTUAL INS CO	NC	17.9
NORTH COUNTRY INS CO	NY	19.0
NORTH POINTE CASUALTY INS CO	FL	44.8
NORTH POINTE INS CO	MI	111.8
NORTH SEA INS CO	NY	11.9
NOVA CASUALTY CO	NY	96.9
OCCIDENTAL FIRE & CAS CO OF NC	NC	191.1
OCEAN HARBOR CASUALTY INS CO	FL	101.6
OCEAN MARINE INDEMNITY INS CO	LA	13.4
OHIC INS CO	OH	231.0
OHIO SECURITY INS CO	OH	20.5
OLD RELIABLE CAS CO	MO	10.7
OLYMPUS INS CO	FL	65.7
ONTARIO INS CO	NY	12.3
OSWEGO COUNTY MUTUAL INS CO	NY	14.2
PEACHTREE CASUALTY INS CO	FL	12.4
PEGASUS INS CO	OK	10.7
PETROLEUM CAS CO	TX	24.3
PHENIX MUTUAL FIRE INS CO	NH	43.3
PHP RRG LTD	AZ	10.1
PIONEER SPECIALTY INS CO	MN	33.7
PLATTE RIVER INS CO	NE	155.2
PLAZA INS CO	MO	32.7
PRE-PAID LEGAL CAS INC	OK	23.0
PREMIER GROUP INS CO INC	TN	61.0
PROFESSIONALS DIRECT INS CO	MI	20.7

Rating: C- (Continued)

INSURANCE COMPANY NAME	DOM. STATE	TOTAL ASSETS ($MIL)
PROGRESSIVE DIRECT INS CO	OH	3,169.5
PROVIDENCE PROPERTY & CAS INS CO	OK	92.0
QUANTA INDEMNITY CO	CO	173.8
QUANTA SPECIALTY LINES INS CO	IN	89.5
RADIAN INS INC	PA	769.7
REGIS INS CO	PA	16.9
REPUBLIC RRG	SC	2.4
REPUBLIC WESTERN INS CO	AZ	232.2
RESIDENTIAL INS CO INC RRG	HI	3.2
RESPONSE INDEMNITY CO OF CA	CA	7.9
RESTORATION RRG INC	AZ	25.9
ROAD CONTRACTORS MUTUAL INS CO	TN	11.1
ROCKWOOD CASUALTY INS CO	PA	256.8
SAUQUOIT VALLEY INS CO	NY	3.5
SECURITY FIRST INS CO	FL	43.2
SHEFFIELD INS CO	TN	13.1
SOUTHERN FIDELITY INS CO INC	FL	171.8
SOUTHERN GENERAL INS CO	GA	53.5
SOUTHERN GUARANTY INS CO OF GEORGIA	GA	6.1
SOUTHERN MUTUAL INS CO	GA	20.4
SOUTHERN PIONEER PROP & CAS INS CO	AR	22.1
STATE NATIONAL FIRE INS CO	LA	2.1
STONINGTON LLOYDS INS CO	TX	7.0
SU INS CO	WI	14.8
SYNERGY INS CO	NC	9.6
TORUS SPECIALTY INS CO	DE	61.1
TPA CAPTIVE INSURANCE CO INC	GA	9.5
TRADERS INS CO	MO	13.3
UNITED FRONTIER MUTUAL INS CO	NY	11.6
UNITED INS CO	UT	5.5
UNITED PROPERTY & CASUALTY INS CO	FL	157.5
UNITRIN AUTO & HOME INS CO	NY	171.1
UNITRIN PREFERRED INS CO	NY	47.1
UNIVERSAL FIRE & CASUALTY INS CO	IN	8.9
UNIVERSAL NORTH AMERICA INS CO	TX	44.5
USIC OF FLORIDA INC	FL	6.0
VERSANT CASUALTY INS CO	MS	15.1
WARNER INS CO	CT	25.4
WAYNE COOPERATIVE INS CO	NY	19.3
WELLINGTON INS CO	TX	31.7
WEST VIRGINIA FARMERS MUT INS ASSOC	WV	4.4
WESTCHESTER FIRE INS CO	NY	2,561.4
WESTERN HOME INS CO	MN	33.1
WESTERN MUTUAL INS CO	CA	45.6
WESTMINSTER AMERICAN INS CO	MD	11.1
WHITE MOUNTAINS REINS CO OF AMER	NY	2,449.0
WILLIAMSBURG NATIONAL INS CO	MI	99.5
XL INS AMERICA INC	DE	629.4
YEL CO INS	FL	13.7
ZURICH AMERICAN INS CO	NY	29,566.7

Rating: D+

INSURANCE COMPANY NAME	DOM. STATE	TOTAL ASSETS ($MIL)
ACCESS INS CO	TX	96.8
ACIG INS CO	IL	254.2
ADVANTA INS CO	AZ	18.1
AGENT ALLIANCE INS CO	NC	8.9
ALLIANCE MUTUAL INS CO	NC	10.7
ALLIED PROFESSIONALS INS CO RRG	AZ	17.4
AMERICAN FARMERS & RANCHERS MUTUAL	OK	96.9
AMERICAN FREEDOM INS CO	IL	28.2
AMERICAN HEALTHCARE SPECIALTY INS CO	AR	70.3
AMERICAN INDEPENDENT INS CO	PA	81.7
AMERICAN PHYSICIANS ASR CORP	MI	816.0
AMERICAN SAFETY CASUALTY INS CO	OK	156.8
AMERICAN TRADITIONS INS CO	FL	30.3
AMERICAN UNDERWRITERS INS CO	AR	6.2
APOLLO CASUALTY CO	IL	39.8
ARGONAUT-MIDWEST INS CO	IL	74.5
ARI CASUALTY CO	NJ	38.6
ARIZONA HOME INS CO	AZ	14.7
ASSOCIATED MUTUAL INS CO	NY	26.9
ATLAS RRG INC	DC	2.3
ATTORNEYS LIAB ASR SOCIETY INC RRG	VT	246.2
AXA RE PROP & CAS INS CO	DE	39.8
BLOOMFIELD MUTUAL INS CO	MN	5.9
CAMPMED CAS & INDEM CO INC OF MD	MD	36.2
CAPITAL MARKETS ASR CORP	NY	127.3
CAPITOL INS CO	PA	6.2
CENSTAT CASUALTY CO	NE	13.1
CENTRE COUNTY MUTUAL FIRE INS CO	PA	4.4
CENTURY CASUALTY CO	GA	7.6
CMG MORTGAGE REINS CO	WI	38.6
COAST NATIONAL INS CO	CA	559.1
COLONIAL MORTGAGE INS CO	TX	9.6
COLONIAL SURETY CO	PA	34.5
COMMONWEALTH INS CO OF AMERICA	WA	54.7
CONSOLIDATED INS ASN	TX	14.2
CONSOLIDATED LLOYDS	TX	2.3
CONTINUING CARE RRG INC	SC	9.2
CRUM & FORSTER INDEMNITY CO	DE	37.5
DANIELSON INS CO	CA	8.5
DELOS INS CO	DE	568.2
DRIVERS INS CO	NY	7.1
EASTERN DENTISTS INS CO RRG	VT	36.8
EVERGREEN USA RRG INC	VT	12.1
FAIRMONT INS CO	CA	38.2
FAIRMONT SPECIALTY INS CO	CA	210.0
FARM BUREAU NEW HORIZONS INS CO MO	MO	7.5
FARMERS & MECH MU I ASN OF CECIL CTY	MD	1.3
FARMERS MUTUAL INS CO	MI	2.7
FARMERS MUTUAL INS CO OF ELLINWOOD	KS	5.7
FARMERS UNION MUTUAL INS CO	AR	8.7
FINANCIAL SECURITY ASR INC	NY	4,298.5
FIRST HOME INS CO	FL	73.7
FIRST MERCURY INS CO	IL	579.6
FIRST SURETY CORP	WV	6.3
FLORIDA DOCTORS INS CO	FL	46.7
FREMONT INS CO	MI	78.7
GENERAL EASTERN SKI INS RRG INC	VT	4.9
GENERAL SECURITY IND CO OF AZ	AZ	86.2
GENEVA INS CO	IN	4.1

INSURANCE COMPANY NAME	DOM. STATE	TOTAL ASSETS ($MIL)
Rating: D+ (Continued)		
GEORGIA CASUALTY & SURETY CO	GA	36.7
GLOBAL INTL INS CO RRG	DC	16.7
GRANGE MUTUAL FIRE INS CO	PA	2.9
GREAT CENTRAL FIRE INS CO	LA	3.4
GREENWICH INS CO	DE	919.6
GUARANTEE INS CO	FL	139.2
GULFSTREAM PROP & CAS INS CO	FL	55.5
HALIFAX MUTUAL INS CO	NC	5.0
HANOVER FIRE & CASUALTY INS CO	PA	3.4
HARBOR INS CO	OK	12.8
HAWAII EMPLOYERS MUTUAL INS CO	HI	258.9
HEALTHCARE UNDERWRITERS GROUP OF KY	KY	28.0
HEALTHCARE UNDERWRITERS GRP MUT OH	OH	21.0
HEARTLAND MUTUAL INS CO	MN	3.4
HOMEOWNERS CHOICE PROP & CAS INS CO	FL	138.0
HOMESITE INS CO OF CA	CA	71.0
HOMESITE INS CO OF THE MIDWEST	ND	148.4
HUDSON SPECIALTY INS CO	NY	189.6
INSUREMAX INS CO	IN	17.0
INTEGRITY PROP & CAS INS CO	WI	13.2
JUNIATA MUTUAL INS CO	PA	6.4
KENTUCKY NATIONAL INS CO	KY	6.4
LANDMARK ONE INS CO	FL	29.7
LAURIER INDEMNITY CO	WI	24.6
LEATHERSTOCKING COOP INS CO	NY	11.5
LINCOLN MUTUAL INS CO	NC	3.0
MAJESTIC INS CO	CA	326.6
MBIA INS CORP	NY	6,123.8
MEDICAL LIABILITY MUTUAL INS CO	NY	4,915.9
MID-CONTINENT INS CO	PA	41.2
MIDDLE STATES INS CO INC	OK	5.3
MIDROX INS CO	NY	5.6
MIDWESTERN EQUITY TITLE INS CO	IN	2.8
MILLERS FIRST INS CO	IL	37.4
MISSOURI VALLEY MUTUAL INS CO	SD	6.0
MOUNTAIN VALLEY INDEMNITY CO	NH	36.9
MT MORRIS MUTUAL INS CO	WI	15.3
MUTUAL FIRE INS CO OF S BEND TOWNSHP	PA	2.8
NATIONAL AMERICAN INS CO	OK	146.3
NATIONAL BUILDERS & CONTRACTORS INS	NV	6.3
NATIONAL CONTINENTAL INS CO	NY	243.4
NATIONAL GROUP INS CO	FL	9.5
NATIONAL HERITAGE INS CO	IL	6.3
NATIONAL INDEPENDENT TRUCKERS IC RRG	SC	7.8
NATIONWELD RRG INC	DC	1.7
NAZARETH MUTUAL INS CO	PA	10.1
NEVADA CONTRACTORS INS CO INC	NV	47.4
NORTHERN CASUALTY CO (MUTUAL)	IA	2.4
OHA INS SOLUTIONS	OH	44.5
PACIFIC INDEMNITY INS CO	GU	15.2
PACIFIC PIONEER INSURANCE CO	CA	23.1
PACIFIC SPECIALTY PROPERTY & CAS CO	TX	3.3
PALISADES INS CO	NJ	25.9
PANHANDLE FARMERS MUT INS CO OF WV	WV	3.8
PATRONS MUTUAL FIRE INS CO OF IN PA	PA	2.6
PMA CAPITAL INS CO	PA	276.4
PMI MORTGAGE GUARANTY COMPANY	AZ	14.8
PRESERVER INS CO	NJ	114.1
PRIME INS SYNDICATE INC	IL	23.0
PRINCETON INS CO	NJ	976.8
PYMATUNING MUTUAL FIRE INS CO	PA	3.3
RANCHERS & FARMERS INS CO	TX	8.5
RANCHERS & FARMERS MUTUAL INS CO	TX	9.1
REINSURANCE CO OF AMERICA INC	IL	14.6
RELIABLE LLOYDS INS CO	TX	8.7
REPUBLIC MUTUAL INS CO	OH	15.3
RESIDENTIAL INS CO	AZ	8.5
ROCHE SURETY & CASUALTY INC	FL	16.8
RUTGERS CASUALTY INS CO	NJ	52.6
RVI NATIONAL INS CO	CT	13.6
SAFE HARBOR INS CO	FL	15.6
SAN ANTONIO INDEMNITY CO	TX	2.8
SANTA FE AUTO INS CO	TX	20.5
SEABRIGHT INS CO	IL	767.4
SECURITY NATIONAL INS CO	FL	135.0
SELECT MARKETS INS CO	IL	14.0
SOUTHERN EAGLE INS CO	FL	31.9
SOUTHERN UNITED FIRE INS CO	AL	26.7
SOUTHLAND LLOYDS INS CO	TX	3.1
STATE FARM GUARANTY INS CO	IL	13.9
STONINGTON INS CO	TX	335.0
SUNSHINE STATE INS CO	FL	38.2
TANK OWNER MEMBERS INS CO	TX	21.7
TEXAS BUILDERS INS CO	TX	14.6
TEXAS LAWYERS INS EXCHANGE	TX	71.4
TITLE REINSURANCE CO	VT	15.7
TOWN & COUNTRY MUTUAL INS CO	AR	2.9
TRI CENTURY INS CO	PA	28.4
TRIAD GUARANTY INS CORP	IL	1,036.4
UNDERWRITERS AT LLOYDS	KY	206.9
UNITED GUARANTY COML INS CO OF NC	NC	266.3
UNITED GUARANTY RESIDENTIAL INS CO	NC	2,518.8
UNITED HERITAGE PROP & CAS CO	ID	18.6
UPPER HUDSON NATIONAL INS CO	NY	6.1
US FIDELIS INS CO RRG INC	MT	0.7
VICTORE INS CO	OK	4.7
VISION INS CO	TX	13.3
WASHINGTON MUTUAL FIRE & STORM INS	PA	3.3
WESTGUARD INS CO	PA	29.7
WISCONSIN MUNICIPAL MUTUAL INS CO	WI	49.7
XL SELECT INS CO	DE	128.7
Rating: D		
ADIRONDACK INS EXCH	NY	239.3
ADVOCATE MD INS OF THE SW INC	TX	74.3
AEQUICAP PROPERTY & CASUALTY INS CO	FL	7.1
AFFIRMATIVE INS CO OF MI	MI	16.4
AGENTS MUTUAL INS CO	AR	1.8
ALEA NORTH AMERICA INS CO	NY	260.6
ALLEGHENY SURETY CO	PA	3.4

Rating: D (Continued)

INSURANCE COMPANY NAME	DOM. STATE	TOTAL ASSETS ($MIL)
ALLIANCE NATIONAL INS CO	NY	7.5
ALLIANCE OF NONPROFITS FOR INS RRG	VT	40.4
ALLIANCE UNITED INS CO	CA	44.9
AMBAC ASSURANCE CORP	WI	9,392.4
AMERICAN CONTRACTORS INS CO RISK RET	TX	9.6
AMERICAN COUNTRY INS CO	IL	87.2
AMERICAN EAGLE INS CO RRG	VT	9.4
AMERICAN FARMERS & RANCHERS INS CO	ID	24.9
AMERICAN FELLOWSHIP MUT INS CO	MI	7.6
AMERICAN INTEGRITY INS CO OF FL	FL	87.4
AMERICAN LIBERTY INS CO	UT	9.6
AMERICAN MILLENNIUM INS CO	NJ	10.6
AMERICAN MOTORISTS INS CO	IL	19.7
AMERICAN PHYSICIANS INS CO	TX	220.3
AMERICAN SAFETY INDEMNITY CO	OK	243.7
AMERICAN SAFETY RRG INC	VT	18.3
AMERICAN STERLING INS CO	CA	21.7
AMFED CAS INS CO	MS	2.3
APOLLO MUTUAL FIRE INS CO	PA	3.2
APPLIED MEDICO LEGAL SOLUTIONS RRG	AZ	50.9
AQUAGARDIAN INS CO INC	AZ	19.0
ARGUS FIRE & CASUALTY INS CO	FL	47.9
ARIZONA AUTOMOBILE INS CO	AZ	6.9
ARROWOOD INDEMNITY CO	DE	2,370.5
ATLANTIC BONDING CO	MD	9.1
ATLANTIC CASUALTY INS CO	NC	174.2
ATRADIUS TRADE CREDIT INS NJ	NJ	7.0
ATTORNEYS LIAB PROTECTION SOC RRG	MT	84.4
AVERA PROPERTY INS INC	SD	1.5
AXIS SURPLUS INS CO	IL	405.2
BEDFORD PHYSICIANS RRG INC	VT	13.4
BRISTOL WEST CASUALTY INS CO	OH	21.6
BUILDERS INS ASSN INC RRG	SC	2.2
BUILDERS INS CO INC	NV	29.7
BUSINESSFIRST INS CO	FL	35.5
CANONSBURG MUTUAL FIRE INS CO	PA	1.7
CAPACITY INS CO	FL	9.4
CASUALTY UNDERWRITERS INS CO	UT	4.1
CATAWBA INS CO	SC	15.6
CBIA COMP SERVICES INC	CT	18.3
CENTENNIAL INS CO	NY	94.2
CENTER VALLEY MUTUAL FIRE INS CO	PA	2.2
CENTRAL CO-OPERATIVE INS CO	NY	9.3
CENTRAL PA PHYSICIANS RRG INC	SC	40.1
CHARITABLE SERVICE PROVIDERS RRG	AZ	3.1
CHATTAHOCHEE RRG CAPTIVE INS CO	GA	5.3
CHERRY VALLEY COOPERATIVE INS CO	NY	1.3
CIMARRON INS EXCH RRG	VT	6.1
CITIES & VILLAGES MUTUAL INS CO	WI	39.2
CITIZENS UNITED RECIP EXCH	NJ	78.1
CLEARWATER INS CO	DE	1,242.4
COLLEGE LIAB INS CO LTD RRG	HI	9.3
COLONIAL LLOYDS	TX	29.6
COLUMBIA FEDERAL INS CO	DC	3.2
COLUMBIA NATIONAL RRG INC	VT	3.6
COMMERCE PROTECTIVE INS CO	PA	5.6
COMMONWEALTH MUTUAL INS CO	MA	6.3
COMMUNITIES OF FAITH RRG INC	SC	9.6
COMMUNITY HEALTH ALLIANCE RECIP RRG	VT	104.8
COMMUNITY HOSPITAL ALTERNATIVE RRG	VT	156.2
COMMUNITY MUTUAL INS CO	NY	4.1
COMPANION INC	VI	11.6
COMPWEST INS CO	CA	227.8
CONEMAUGH VALLEY MUTUAL INS CO	PA	4.0
CONSUMERS COUNTY MUTUAL INS CO	TX	117.7
CONSUMERS SPECIALTIES INS CO RRG	VT	6.9
CONTINENTAL MUTUAL INS CO	PA	1.1
CONTRACTORS INS CO OF NORTH AMER RRG	HI	39.6
CYPRESS PROPERTY & CASUALTY INS CO	FL	97.1
DELAWARE GRANGE MUTUAL FIRE INS CO	DE	1.1
DELPHI CASUALTY CO	IL	9.0
DELTA LLOYDS INS CO OF HOUSTON	TX	8.2
DISCOVERY INS CO	NC	29.4
DORINCO REINSURANCE CO	MI	1,545.7
DUBOIS MEDICAL RRG	DC	3.9
EASTERN ALLIANCE INS CO	PA	133.3
ELDERCARE MUTUAL CO RRG INC	AZ	1.8
ELITE TRANSPORTATION RRG INC	AZ	12.7
ESSEX BENEFITS INS CO INC	MO	2.7
EZ AUTO INC CO	UT	3.4
FARMERS & MECHANICS FIRE & CAS INS	WV	3.6
FARMERS MUTUAL F I C OF BRANCH CTY	MI	1.7
FARMERS MUTUAL F I C OF DUG HILL	MD	3.6
FARMERS MUTUAL INS CO	PA	4.0
FARMINGTON MUTUAL INS CO	WI	5.9
FINANCIAL ADVISORS ASR SELECT RRG	NV	1.4
FINIAL REINS CO	CT	1,278.3
FIRST ACCEPTANCE INS CO INC	TX	224.0
FIRST ACCEPTANCE INS CO OF GEORGIA	GA	72.0
FIRST CHICAGO INS CO	IL	21.5
FIRST FOUNDERS ASR CO	NJ	2.6
FIRST JERSEY CASUALTY INS CO INC	NJ	12.9
FIRST KEYSTONE RRG INC	SC	18.3
FIRST MEDICAL INS CO RRG	VT	66.6
FIRST MUTUAL INS CO	NC	4.2
FORT WAYNE MEDICAL ASR CO RRG	AZ	2.2
FREDERICKSBURG PROFESSIONAL RISK EXC	VT	25.3
FREEDOM ADVANTAGE INS CO	PA	10.8
FSA INS CO	OK	2,034.9
FULMONT MUTUAL INS CO	NY	4.8
GENERAL SECURITY NATIONAL INS CO	NY	291.5
GEORGIA TRANSPORTATION CAPTIVE INS	GA	1.4
GERLING AMERICA INS CO	NY	201.5
GLOBAL HAWK INS CO RRG	VT	4.9
GOLDEN BEAR INS CO	CA	96.8
GRACO RRG INC	SC	1.7
GREAT LAKES MUTUAL INS CO	MI	4.0
GREAT NORTHWEST INS CO	IN	25.8
GUTHRIE RRG	SC	32.7
HALLMARK INS CO	AZ	163.7

Rating: D (Continued)

INSURANCE COMPANY NAME	DOM. STATE	TOTAL ASSETS ($MIL)
HALLMARK SPECIALTY INS CO	OK	90.1
HANNAHSTOWN MUTUAL INS CO	PA	2.2
HEALTH CARE INS RECIPROCAL	MN	21.5
HEALTH CARE MUT CAPTIVE INS CO	GA	10.7
HEALTH NETWORK PROVIDERS MUT INS CO	DC	8.0
HEALTHCARE PROVIDERS INS CO RRG	SC	52.1
HEALTHCARE UNDERWRITERS GRP OF FL	FL	40.9
HEREFORD INS CO	NY	124.2
HIGH TECH SERVICES RRG INC	VT	33.6
HOME STATE COUNTY MUTUAL INS CO	TX	131.1
HOMESITE LLOYDS OF TEXAS	TX	16.0
HOMEWISE PREFERRED INS CO	FL	85.0
HOUSING & REDEVELOPMENT INS EXCH	PA	38.7
HUDSON INS CO	DE	431.0
ICAT SPECIALTY INS CO	FL	20.0
ICM INS CO	NY	10.9
ID COUNTIES RISK MGMT PROGRAM UNDW	ID	45.3
INDIANA OLD NATIONAL INS CO	VT	1,597.5
INNOVATIVE PHYSICIAN SOLUTIONS RRG	AZ	4.0
INSURORS INDEMNITY CO	TX	14.5
INSURORS INDEMNITY LLOYDS	TX	3.3
INTEGRA INS INC	MN	1.8
INTERNATIONAL CREDIT OF N AMER REIN	NY	2.3
INTERSTATE AUTO INS CO	MD	5.5
KENTUCKIANA MEDICAL RRG & INS CO INC	KY	41.6
LEMIC INS CO	LA	68.8
LENDERS PROTECTION ASR CO RRG	NE	2.5
LIFE SERVICES NETWORK RECIP INS RRG	DC	7.6
LINCOLN GENERAL INS CO	PA	386.7
LOUISIANA PEST CONTROL INS CO	LA	3.2
LOUISIANA RETAILERS MUTUAL INS CO	LA	53.5
LOYA INS CO	TX	226.6
MARATHON FINANCIAL INS INC RRG	SC	12.4
MAXUM CASUALTY INS CO	DE	11.5
MEDICAL ALLIANCE INS CO	IL	37.2
MEDICAL INS UNDERWRITERS RRG INC	AZ	0.9
MGIC REINSURANCE CORP OF WI	WI	982.7
MID-ATLANTIC INS CORP	VA	0.0
MIDWEST PROVIDER INS CO RRG INC	AZ	9.7
MINNESOTA SURETY & TRUST CO	MN	2.4
MONTOUR MUTUAL INS CO	PA	1.0
MONTPELIER US INS CO	OK	57.2
MORTGAGE GUARANTY INS CORP	WI	7,527.3
MOUND PRAIRIE MUTUAL INS CO	MN	3.7
MOUNT CARROLL MUTUAL FIRE INS CO	IL	3.2
MOWER COUNTY FARMERS MUT INS CO	MN	2.8
MUTUAL INS CO OF LEHIGH CTY	PA	3.8
MUTUAL SAVINGS FIRE INS CO	AL	6.1
NATIONAL AMERICAN INS CO OF CA	CA	38.5
NATIONAL ASSISTED LIVING RRG INC	DC	5.9
NATIONAL AUTOMOTIVE INS	LA	19.5
NATIONAL HOME WARRANTY INC	NV	3.5
NATIONAL MEDICAL PROFESSIONAL RRG	SC	7.3
NATIONS BONDING CO	TX	3.4
NATIONSBUILDERS INS CO	DC	153.7
NEVADA DIRECT INS CO	NV	3.5
NEW YORK HEALTHCARE INS CO INC RRG	DC	10.4
NEW YORK TRANSPORTATION INS CORP	NY	3.5
NORTH EAST INS CO	ME	62.7
NORTHWEST GF MUTUAL INS CO	SD	9.7
OLD GLORY INS CO	TX	11.6
OOIDA RISK RETENTION GROUP INC	VT	61.0
OPTIMA INS CO	PR	33.2
ORDINARY MUTUAL A RRG CORP	VT	38.8
OTSEGO COUNTY PATRONS CO-OP F R ASN	NY	1.8
PALISADES PROPERTY & CASUALTY INS	NJ	103.0
PARATRANSIT INS CO A MUTUAL RRG	TN	19.9
PARTNER REINSURANCE CO OF THE US	NY	3,410.2
PATRONS MUTUAL FIRE ASSOC OF NW PA	PA	1.2
PENNSYLVANIA SURFACE COAL MIN INS EX	PA	3.0
PETROLEUM MARKETERS MGMT INS CO	IA	20.9
PHYSICIANS INS CO	FL	17.1
PHYSICIANS INS PROGRAM RECIP EXCH	PA	23.5
PHYSICIANS PREFERRED INS	FL	42.4
PHYSICIANS PROACTIVE PROTECTION INC	SC	29.9
PIEDMONT MUTUAL INS CO	NC	2.7
PINNACLE CONSORTIUM OF HIGHER ED RRG	VT	5.3
PINNACLE RRG INC	DC	2.1
PMI INS CO	AZ	524.4
PONCE DE LEON LTC RRG INC	FL	17.9
PRIME INS CO	IL	35.3
PROFESSIONAL CASUALTY ASSN	PA	52.5
PROFESSIONAL QUALITY LIABILITY INS	VT	1.5
PROFESSIONAL SOLUTIONS INS CO	IA	12.3
PXRE REINSURANCE CO	CT	200.9
RADIAN GUARANTY INC	PA	4,318.0
REAMSTOWN MUTUAL INS CO	PA	5.5
REPUBLIC MORTGAGE INS CO	NC	1,998.0
ROCHDALE INS CO OF NEW YORK NY	NY	174.9
SAFECARD SERVICE INS CO	ND	2.1
SAINT LUKES HEALTH SYSTEM RRG	SC	14.6
SAMARITAN RRG INC	SC	14.5
SANILAC MUTUAL INS CO	MI	1.1
SCOR REINSURANCE CO	NY	1,450.6
SCRUBS MUTUAL ASR CO RRG	NV	5.1
SECURITY PLAN FIRE INS CO	LA	7.1
SELECTIVE INS CO OF NEW ENGLAND	ME	29.8
SEMINOLE CASUALTY INS CO	FL	54.8
SENECA SPECIALTY INS CO	AZ	27.3
SHARED SERVICE INS GROUP INC	PA	2.7
SIMED	PR	139.0
SOMERSET CASUALTY INS CO	PA	24.3
SOUTHWEST GENERAL INS CO	NM	5.2
SOUTHWEST PHYSICIANS RRG INC	SC	27.3
SPARTAN INS CO	TX	7.9
SPRINGFIELD INS CO INC	CA	80.3
STAR CASUALTY INS CO	FL	21.9
STONETRUST COMMERCIAL INS CO	LA	64.3
SUN SURETY INS CO	SD	12.2
SUNZ INS CO	FL	21.0

INSURANCE COMPANY NAME	DOM. STATE	TOTAL ASSETS ($MIL)
Rating: D (Continued)		
TEXAS HERITAGE INS CO	TX	35.3
TEXAS HOSPITAL INS EXCHANGE	TX	28.4
TIFT AREA CAPTIVE INS CO	GA	5.8
TITAN INS CO INC RRG	SC	22.8
TITLE INDUSTRY ASR CO RRG	VT	8.9
TOWER BONDING & SURETY CO	PR	3.2
TOWER HILL PREFERRED INS CO	FL	42.9
TOWER HILL SELECT INS CO	FL	47.5
TRANSIT MUTUAL INS CORP OF WI	WI	11.8
TWIN LIGHTS INS CO	NJ	11.8
U S LLOYDS INS CO	TX	16.9
UNIQUE INS CO	IL	33.6
UNITED CASUALTY & SURETY CO INC	MA	11.4
UNITED CENTRAL PA RRG	VT	24.1
UNITED CONTRACTORS INS CO INC RRG	DC	26.1
UNITED EQUITABLE INS CO	IL	14.9
UNITED GROUP CAPTIVE INS CO	GA	2.3
UNITED HOME INS CO	AR	12.6
UNITED MEDICAL LIABILITY INS CO RRG	HI	2.9
UNITRIN ADVANTAGE INS CO	NY	3.7
UNIVERSAL INS CO	NC	25.6
URGENT CARE ASR CO RRG INC	NV	1.4
US INS CO OF AMERICA	IL	3.0
US RAIL INS CO A RRG	VT	2.3
VICTORIA SPECIALTY INSURANCE CO	OH	23.5
VICTORY INS CO INC	MT	4.0
WACO FIRE & CAS INS CO	GA	39.8
WALLROSE MUTUAL INS CO	PA	1.0
WARRANTY UNDERWRITERS INS CO	TX	43.9
WASHINGTON MUT F I C OF LAWRENCE CTY	PA	1.6
WELLSPAN RRG	VT	27.9
WEST VIRGINIA NATIONAL AUTO INS CO	WV	9.2
WESTERN INS RRG INC	AZ	1.1
WILMINGTON INS CO	DE	4.5
WORK FIRST CASUALTY CO	DE	33.8
WORKMENS AUTO INS CO	CA	60.5
WVA INS CO	WV	36.3
X L INS CO OF NY	NY	210.5
Rating: D-		
ACA FINANCIAL GUARANTY CORP	MD	419.2
ALLIED SERVICES RRG	SC	4.2
AMERICAN ASSOC OF ORTHODONTIST RRG	VT	24.2
AMERICAN COASTAL INS CO	FL	130.4
AMERICAN EXCESS INS EXCHANGE RRG	VT	325.7
AMERICAN TRUCKING & TRANSP INS RRG	MT	10.4
AMERIGUARD RRG INC	VT	9.8
ARMOR INS CO	VT	22.9
ATLANTIC MUTUAL INS CO	NY	271.8
ATTORNEYS INS MUTUAL RRG	HI	27.8
AUTOMOTIVE UNDERWRITERS INS CO INC	NV	20.7
BALDWIN MUTUAL INS CO	AL	7.2
BAR VERMONT RRG INC	VT	16.1
BATTLE CREEK MUTUAL INS CO	NE	5.6
BRICKSTREET MUTUAL INS CO	WV	1,529.6
BRISTOL WEST PREFERRED INS CO	MI	34.3
CALIFORNIA MUTUAL INS CO	CA	12.5
CARDINAL SELECT RRG INC	SC	6.0
CARE RRG INC	DC	37.6
CARE WEST INS CO	CA	110.8
CAREGIVERS UNITED LIAB INS CO RRG	SC	25.5
CARING COMMUNITIES RECIP RRG	DC	61.2
CASSATT RISK RETENTION GROUP INC	VT	7.4
CEM INS CO	IL	10.1
CENTURION MEDICAL LIAB PROTECT RRG	AZ	8.9
CIRCLE STAR INS CO RRG	VT	5.2
CLAIM PROFESSIONALS LIAB INS CO RRG	VT	3.0
CLEARWATER SELECT INS CO	DE	103.3
COASTAL INS RRG INC	AL	49.4
COMCARE PRO INS RECIPROCAL RRG	VT	2.3
CONSTITUTIONAL CASUALTY CO	IL	18.3
COUNTRYWIDE INS CO	NY	135.9
CRANBROOK INS CO	TX	31.6
CYPRESS TEXAS LLOYDS	TX	47.6
DELAWARE PROFESSIONAL INS CO	DE	9.4
DONGBU INS CO LTD	HI	28.7
EMERGENCY MEDICINE PROFESSIONAL ASR	NV	13.6
EMERGENCY PHYSICIANS INS CO RRG	NV	31.7
EMPLOYERS SECURITY INS CO	IN	29.7
EQUITIBLE LIABILITY INS CO	DC	4.7
FEDERATED NATIONAL INS CO	FL	79.1
FINANCIAL GUARANTY INS CO	NY	3,301.3
FIRST INDEMNITY OF AMERICA INS CO	NJ	4.9
FIRST NET INS CO	GU	11.3
FIRST PROTECTIVE INS CO	FL	67.4
FRANK WINSTON CRUM INS INC	FL	74.0
GALEN INS CO	MO	6.2
GENESEE PATRONS COOP INS	NY	6.7
GLOBAL LIBERTY INS CO OF NY	NY	44.1
GLOBAL REINS CORP OF AMERICA	NY	504.8
GOOD SHEPHERD RECIPROCAL RRG	SC	2.7
GOVERNMENT ENTITIES MUTUAL INC	DC	45.6
GREEN HILLS INS CO RRG	VT	14.3
GREENVILLE CASUALTY INS CO INC	SC	11.9
HEALTH FACILITIES OF CA MUT I C RRG	NV	5.6
HOME CONSTRUCTION INS CO RRG	NV	5.9
HOMEOWNERS OF AMERICA INS CO	TX	7.7
INTERMODAL INS CO RRG	DC	7.5
JAMESTOWN INS CO RRG	SC	7.4
JM WOODWORTH RRG INC	NV	9.0
JOLIET AREA RRG CAPTIVE INS CO	GA	8.6
KEMPER CASUALTY INS CO	IL	20.2
KENSINGTON INS CO	NY	12.7
LAKE STREET RRG INC	VT	2.8
LEGAL MUTUAL LIAB INS SOCIETY OF MD	MD	3.6
LITTLE BLACK MUTUAL INS CO	WI	4.9
LONE STAR NATIONAL INS CO	IN	3.7
LOYA CASUALTY INS CO	CA	38.4
MACHINERY INS INC AN ASSESSABLE MUT	FL	2.2
MANITOWOC MUTUAL INS CO	WI	5.9
MAYA ASR CO	NY	19.9

INSURANCE COMPANY NAME	DOM. STATE	TOTAL ASSETS ($MIL)
Rating: D- (Continued)		
MCIC VERMONT INC RRG	VT	236.1
MD RRG INC	MT	8.4
MEDICUS INS CO	TX	59.7
MEDSTAR LIABILITY LTD INS CO INC RRG	DC	5.1
MERCURY INDEMNITY CO OF AMERICA	FL	46.6
NATIONAL GUARANTY INS CO	AZ	11.0
NATIONAL INTERSTATE INS CO OF HAWAII	OH	28.8
NEW STAR RRG INC	SC	5.4
NEWPORT E&S INS CO	TX	30.8
NHRMA MUTUAL INS CO	IL	23.9
OMEGA INS CO	FL	23.5
ONTARIO REINS CO LTD	GA	14.2
ORANGE COUNTY MEDICAL RECIP INS RRG	AZ	3.4
ORISKA INS CO	NY	9.8
PCH MUTUAL INS CO INC RRG	DC	10.3
PEACE CHURCH RRG INC	VT	19.2
PEDIATRICIANS INS RRG OF AMERICA	DC	2.8
PELICAN INS RRG	VT	16.6
PHOEBE RECIPROCAL RRG	SC	3.6
PHYSICIANS REIMBURSEMENT FUND RRG	VT	24.4
PHYSICIANS SPECIALTY LTD RRG	SC	8.1
PMI MORTGAGE INS CO	AZ	3,434.9
PREFERRED AUTO INS CO INC	TN	7.6
PREMIER PHYSICIANS INS CO INC A RRG	NV	9.3
PRIMERO INS CO	NV	16.8
PROFESSIONAL INS EXCHANGE	UT	6.4
PROFESSIONAL LIAB INS CO OF AMERICA	NY	40.9
QBE SPECIALTY INS CO	ND	318.7
RETAILERS MUTUAL INS CO	MI	14.1
SAFE INS CO	WV	6.6
SECURITY AMERICA RRG INC	VT	5.0
SENTINEL ASR RRG INC	HI	13.4
SERVICE INS CO INC	NJ	9.1
SFM SELECT INS CO	SD	5.4
SOPHIA PALMER NURSES RRG INC	NV	1.3
SOUTHERN OAK INS CO	FL	51.0
SPIRIT MOUNTAIN INS CO RRG INC	DC	5.6
ST JOHNS INS CO INC	FL	128.5
SUPERIOR INS CO RRG	SC	14.1
SYNERGY COMP INS CO	PA	12.3
SYSTEMS PROTECTION ASR RRG INC	MT	0.0
TAXISURE EXCHANGE	NJ	7.4
TEXAS MEDICAL INS CO	TX	21.1
TIG INS CO	CA	1,722.5
TOWER HILL PRIME INS CO	FL	72.3
TRUSTSTAR INS CO	MD	2.2
UNITED BUSINESS INS CO	GA	3.7
UNITED GUAR RESIDENTIAL INS CO OF NC	NC	1,106.8
VASA SPRING GARDEN MUTUAL INS CO	MN	2.7
VIRGINIA HEALTH SYSTEMS ALLIANCE RRG	VT	91.0
WEST VIRGINIA MUTUAL INS CO	WV	156.9
WHITECAP SURETY CO	MN	1.3
YELLOWSTONE INS EXCH RRG	VT	22.2

INSURANCE COMPANY NAME	DOM. STATE	TOTAL ASSETS ($MIL)
Rating: E+		
ACBG RRG INC	VT	3.4
AEQUICAP INS CO	FL	49.9
AMERICAN BUILDERS INS CO RRG INC	MT	1.6
AMERICAN FOREST CASUALTY CO RRG	SC	8.7
AMERICAN HEARTLAND INS CO	IL	13.1
AMERICAN MANUFACTURERS MUTUAL INS CO	IL	11.8
AMERICAN TRANSIT INS CO	NY	396.8
AMFED NATIONAL INS CO	MS	37.1
ASTRAEA RRG INC	AZ	3.7
ATRIUM INS CORP	NY	340.9
BUTTE MUTUAL INS CO	NM	1.0
CAPITOL PREFERRED INS CO	FL	30.4
CASUALTY CORP OF AMERICA	OK	4.4
CATASTROPHE REINS CO	TX	1,417.9
CHC CASUALTY RRG	VT	29.1
CLINICAL TRIALS RECIP INS CO RRG	AZ	2.3
COMMONWEALTH INS CO	PA	1.7
COMMONWEALTH MUTUAL INS CO	MD	1.1
CROWN CAPTIVE INS CO INC	DC	3.5
CRUDEN BAY RRG INC	VT	11.1
DISTRICTS MUTUAL INS	WI	12.9
ECHELON PROP & CAS INS CO	IL	5.7
EDISON INS CO	FL	28.8
EMERGENCY MEDICINE RRG INC	SC	29.5
ESSENTIAL RRG INC	SC	8.8
ETHIO AMERICAN INS CO	GA	6.9
FAIRWAY PHYSICIANS INS CO RRG	DC	17.4
FAITH AFFILIATED RRG INC	SC	6.6
FIDUCIARY INS CO OF AMERICA	NY	64.1
GIBRALTAR NATIONAL INS CO	AR	5.4
GRANADA INS CO	FL	28.1
GUARDIAN RRG INC	MT	4.9
HAY CREEK MUTUAL INS CO	MN	3.5
HEARTLAND HEALTHCARE RECIPROCAL RRG	VT	14.0
HERITAGE WARRANTY INS RRG INC	SC	4.4
INDEPENDENCE CASUALTY INS CO	MA	3.7
INDIANA HEALTHCARE RECIPROCAL RRG	VT	18.6
INS CO OF THE AMERICAS	FL	38.9
KENTUCKY HOSPITAL INS CO RRG	KY	23.7
LEWIS & CLARK LTC RRG INC	NV	16.4
MAKE TRANSPORTATION INS INC RRG	DE	3.6
MEMBERS INS CO	NC	5.9
MISSOURI PROFESSIONALS MUTUAL INS CO	MO	76.1
NATIONAL CATHOLIC RRG	VT	54.1
NATIONAL CONTRACTORS INS CO INC RRG	MT	21.6
NEVADA DOCS MEDICAL RRG INC	NV	3.6
NORTHEAST PHYSICIANS RRG INC	SC	8.2
NORTHERN CAPITAL INS CO	FL	68.6
NORTHWESTERN NATL INS CO SEG ACCNT	WI	57.5
NOVUS INS CO RRG	SC	17.5
NUCLEAR ELECTRIC INS LTD	DE	3,950.3
OBSTETRICIANS & GYNECOLOGISTS RRG	MT	2.8
OKLAHOMA PROPERTY & CAS INS CO	OK	4.4
OLD AMERICAN CTY MUTUAL FIRE INS CO	TX	86.9
PACE RRG INC	VT	22.2

INSURANCE COMPANY NAME	DOM. STATE	TOTAL ASSETS ($MIL)
Rating: E+ (Continued)		
PARAMOUNT INS CO	MD	7.5
PENNSYLVANIA PHYSICIANS RECIP INS	PA	57.2
PINELANDS INS CO RRG INC	DC	9.0
POSITIVE PHYSICIANS INS EXCHANGE	PA	31.0
PREFERRED CONTRACTORS INS CO RRG LLC	MT	29.3
REGIONAL HEALTH INS CO RRG	DC	3.8
ROYAL PALM INS CO	FL	180.2
SCAFFOLD INDUSTRY INS CO RRG INC	DC	3.3
SCHOOL BOARDS INS CO OF PA INC	PA	200.9
SCHUYLKILL CROSSING RECIPROCAL RRG	VT	25.1
STATES SELF-INSURERS RISK RET GROUP	VT	20.2
STERLING CAS INS CO	CA	26.9
SUNDERLAND MARINE MUTUAL CO LTD	AK	8.3
TRANSURANCE RRG INC	AZ	0.0
UNDERWRITERS AT LLOYDS LONDON	IL	687.7
UNION MUTUAL INS CO	OK	4.0
UNIVERSAL PROPERTY & CASUALTY INS	FL	374.8
UTAH BUILDERS INS CO INC	UT	10.7
VFH CAPTIVE INS CO	GA	5.7
WARREN RRG INC	VT	8.3
WASHINGTON COUNTY CO-OPERATIVE INS	NY	6.0
WINDHAVEN INS CO	FL	8.7
ZEPHYR INS CO INC	HI	57.2
Rating: E		
ACADEMIC HLTH PROFESSIONALS INS ASSO	NY	110.6
ACCIDENT INS CO INC	SC	41.0
AEGIS HEALTHCARE RRG INC	DC	3.9
AGRINATIONAL INS CO	VT	513.6
AIMCO MUTUAL INS CO	NC	16.7
ALLEGIANT INS CO INC A RRG	HI	11.2
AMERICAN LIFE INS CO	DE	95.6
AMERICAN STEAMSHIP O M PROT & IND AS	NY	353.0
ASSET PROTECTION PROGRAM RRG INC	SC	3.4
ASSURANCEAMERICA INS CO	SC	69.2
AUTO DEALERS RRG INC	MT	1.0
CLARIAN HEALTH RRG INC	SC	3.8
COLONIAL COOPERATIVE INS CO	NY	6.9
CTLIC RRG INC	DC	0.0
DIAMOND INS CO	IL	47.4
FEDERAL MOTOR CARRIERS RRG INC	DE	25.1
FRANKLIN CASUALTY INS CO RRG	VT	24.2
GEISINGER INS CORP RRG	VT	14.8
GEORGIA REST MUTUAL CAPTIVE INS CO	GA	2.5
HEALTH CARE CASUALTY RRG INC	DC	31.3
HEALTH CARE INDUSTRY LIAB RECIP INS	DC	130.0
HEALTH FUTURE INS EXCHANGE RRG	NV	3.2
HEALTHCARE PROFESSIONAL INS CO INC	NY	177.4
HOSPITALS INS CO INC	NY	800.3
INDEMNITY INS CORP OF DC RRG	DC	15.9
INDEPENDENT NEVADA DOCTORS INS EXCH	NV	44.3
LONG ISLAND INS CO	NY	6.3
LUMBERMENS MUTUAL CAS CO	IL	1,346.1
MIDWEST INS GROUP INC RRG	AZ	10.6
MISSOURI DOCTORS MUTUAL INS CO	MO	6.2
MOUNTAIN LAUREL RRG INC	VT	15.6
MOUNTAIN STATES HEALTHCARE RECIP RRG	MT	64.8
MOUNTAINEER FREEDOM RRG INC	WV	18.1
N A D A INDEMNITY INC	CO	1.2
NATIONAL GUARDIAN RRG INC	HI	20.8
NEW MEXICO PROPERTY & CASUALTY CO	NM	5.3
OCEAN RRG INC	DC	16.6
PEOPLES TRUST INS CO	FL	38.0
PHYSICIANS IND RRG INC	NV	6.8
PHYSICIANS LIABILITY INS CO	OK	176.2
PHYSICIANS PROFESSIONAL IND ASSN	MO	17.2
PINE TREE INS RECIPROCAL RRG	VT	16.1
PROBUILDERS SPECIALTY INS CO RRG	DC	208.2
PUBLIC UTILITY MUTUAL INS CO RRG	VT	4.9
QUALITY CASUALTY INS CO INC	AL	2.8
R&Q REINS CO	PA	265.6
RELIAMAX INS CO	SD	6.4
SOUTHEASTERN US INS INC	GA	42.5
SPRING VALLEY MUTUAL INS CO	MN	8.0
ST CHARLES INS CO RRG	SC	10.0
ST LUKES HEALTH NETWORK INS CO RRG	VT	41.4
SYSTEM & AFFILIATE MEMBERS RECIP	VT	2.7
UNITED AUTOMOBILE INS CO	FL	517.2
USA INS CO	MS	8.2
WORKERS COMPENSATION EXCHANGE	ID	8.5
Rating: E-		
AMERIN GUARANTY CORP	IL	38.9
CIFG ASR NORTH AMERICA INC	NY	267.2
PHYSICIANS RECIPROCAL INSURERS	NY	1,423.9
SYNCORA GUARANTEE INC	NY	3,409.9
TRANSPORTATION LIABILITY INS CO RRG	SC	0.8
Rating: F		
ACCEPTANCE INS CO	NE	35.3
AUSTIN INDEMNITY LLOYDS INS CO	TX	5.5
BEST AMERICAN INS CO	PR	0.0
CENTRAL NATIONAL INS CO OF OMAHA	NE	31.9
COLONIAL INDEMNITY INS CO	NY	0.0
COMMERCIAL MUT INS CO	GA	0.0
CONSUMER FIRST INS CO	NJ	10.7
CORAL INS CO	FL	13.9
CUMBERLAND CASUALTY & SURETY CO	FL	5.7
EMPIRE INS CO	NY	70.6
FARMERS MUTUAL INS CO	WV	9.0
FIRST COMMERCIAL INS CO	FL	79.7
FIRST COMMERCIAL TRANSPORTATION	FL	18.5
FLORIDA SELECT INS CO	FL	11.8
FRONTIER INS CO	NY	95.9
HIG LTD	HI	0.0
INSURANCE CORP OF NY	NY	62.2
INTERBORO MUTUAL INDEMNITY INS CO	NY	67.8
LION INS CO	NY	0.0
LUMBER MUTUAL INS CO	MA	38.5
NEW AMERICA INS CO INC	FL	0.7
NEWARK INS CO	NJ	0.0
NORTHWESTERN NTL INS CO MILWAUKEE	WI	60.1

INSURANCE COMPANY NAME	DOM. STATE	TOTAL ASSETS ($MIL)
Rating: F (Continued)		
NSA RRG INC	VT	19.6
PAWTUCKET INS CO	RI	12.0
SHELBY CASUALTY INS CO	TX	0.0
SHELBY INS CO	TX	0.0
TEXAS SELECT LLOYDS INS CO	TX	0.0
TOWER NATIONAL INS CO	MA	63.7
TRENWICK AMERICA REINSURANCE CORP	CT	158.3
UNION AMERICAN INS CO	FL	2.1
VESTA FIRE INS CO	TX	0.0
VESTA INS CORP	TX	0.0
WASHINGTON CASUALTY CO	WA	38.1
Rating: U		
2-10 HOME BUYERS WARRANTY OF VA	VA	0.0
ABBA INDEMNITY CO	TX	1.7
ACE INS CO OF THE MIDWEST	IN	51.1
ADVANCED PHYSICIANS INS RRG INC	AZ	0.7
ALICOT INS CO	TX	2.6
ALLIANCE HOME WARRANTY INC	UT	0.0
AMERICAN AMBASSADOR CASUALTY CO	IL	9.5
AMERICAN CENTENNIAL INS CO	DE	29.0
AMERICAN COLONIAL INS CO INC	FL	4.6
AMERICAN CONCEPT INS CO	RI	7.3
AMERICAN EQUITY INS CO	AZ	104.6
AMERICAN GENERAL PROP INS CO OF FL	FL	12.9
AMERICAN GENERAL PROPERTY INS CO	TN	56.9
AMERICAN HOME SHIELD OF NV INC	NV	0.0
AMERICAN HOME SHIELD OF VA INC	VA	0.0
AMERICAN MEDICAL ASR CO	IL	4.1
AMERICAN MEDICAL INS EXCHANGE	IN	0.6
AMERICAN PET INS CO INC	NY	10.1
AMERICAN PROFESSIONALS INS CO	IN	0.0
AMERICAN SPECIAL RISK INS CO	DE	5.4
AMERICAN UNION INS CO	IL	122.0
AMERISURE PARTNERS INS CO	MI	11.2
AMSTAR INS CO	FL	6.0
APEX LLOYDS INS CO	TX	2.8
APPLIANCE MANUFACTURERS ASR CO RRG	IA	0.0
APSPECIALTY INS CORP	MI	26.8
ARA CASUALTY INS CO	FL	3.7
ARCH INDEMNITY INS CO	NE	21.6
ARGONAUT LIMITED RISK INS CO	IL	20.0
ARROWOOD SURPLUS LINES INS CO	DE	256.5
ASHLAND MUTUAL FIRE INS CO OF PA	PA	0.6
ASOC DE SUSCRIPCION CONJUNTA DEL SEG	PR	347.2
ASSURECARE RRG	DC	31.1
ASURE WORLDWIDE INS CO	MI	12.5
ATLANTA INTERNATIONAL INS CO	NY	36.0
ATLANTIC FLORIDIAN INS CO	OH	5.5
ATLANTIC INS CO	TX	8.7
AUTOGLASS INS CO	NY	0.3
AVIVA INS CO OF CANADA (US BR)	NY	18.5
AVOMARK INS CO	IN	11.2
AZTEC INS CO	FL	8.6
BALTIMORE EQUITABLE SOCIETY	MD	108.6
BEACON MUTUAL INS CO	RI	435.5
BRENTWOOD NATIONAL INS CO	TN	10.0
BROWARD FACTORY SERVICE INC	NV	0.9
BUCKS COUNTY CONTRIBUTIONSHIP	PA	5.0
CAMBRIA COUNTY MUTUAL INS CO	PA	0.6
CAPITAL ASSURANCE CO INC	FL	30.6
CASTLE HILL INS CO	RI	22.6
CENTURY INDEMNITY CO	PA	1,111.1
CENTURY REINSURANCE CO	PA	104.8
CINCINNATI EQUITABLE INS CO	OH	6.7
CITADEL INS CO	TX	2.9
CITATION INS CO	CA	26.5
CITIZENS INS CO INC	KY	2.8
CITIZENS PROPERTY INS CORP	FL	8,209.6
CLAREMONT LIABILITY INS CO	CA	22.0
CLARENDON SELECT INS CO	FL	17.2
CLINIC MUTUAL INS CO RRG	HI	4.7
CLOISTER MUTUAL CASUALTY INS CO	PA	4.3
COMBINED BENEFITS INS CO	MT	0.0
COMMERCIAL CASUALTY INS CO	CA	182.2
COMMERCIAL GUARANTY INS CO	DE	34.9
COMMERCIAL LOAN INS CORP	WI	12.1
COMMERCIAL RISK RE-INSURANCE CO	VT	36.9
COMPASS INS CO	NY	13.2
CONNIE LEE INS CO	WI	184.2
CONSORTIUM (A RRG)	VT	16.4
CONSTELLATION REINSURANCE CO	NY	17.4
CONSTITUTION INS CO	NY	42.7
CONTRACTORS LIABILITY INS CO RRG	NV	4.2
CORNERSTONE MUTUAL INS CO	GA	0.0
COVENTRY INSURANCE CO	RI	1.5
CRESTBROOK INS CO	OH	90.4
CROWN CAPTIVE INS CO	GA	0.8
EASTERN CASUALTY INS CO	MA	28.2
FAIRFIELD INS CO	CT	26.4
FIDELITY FIRST INS CO	TX	7.6
FINANCIAL BENEFITS INS CO	IL	5.1
FINANCIAL INSTITUTIONS RESERVE RRG	VT	36.9
FIRST AMERICAN HOME BUYERS PRO CORP	CA	0.0
FIRST AUTOMOTIVE INS RRG INC	HI	5.5
FIRST STATE INS CO	CT	914.7
FIRST WASHINGTON INS CO INC	DC	3.7
FLEET INS CO	AZ	63.1
FORTUITY INS CO	MI	13.3
FOUNDERS INS CO OF MICHIGAN	MI	6.9
GA TIMBER HARVESTERS MUTL CAPTIVE IC	GA	1.2
GARDEN STATE INDEMNITY CO INC	NJ	2.7
GENWORTH MORTGAGE REINS CORP	NC	1.5
GLOBAL INS CO	GA	3.1
GLOBAL REINSURANCE CORP	NY	266.6
GLOBAL SURETY & INS CO	NE	74.2
GOLDSTREET INS CO	NY	18.4
GREAT AMERICAN CASUALTY INS CO	OH	11.8
GREAT AMERICAN PROTECTION INS CO	OH	24.5
GREEN TREE PERPETUAL ASR CO	PA	1.2
GSA INS CO	NJ	0.0

INSURANCE COMPANY NAME	DOM. STATE	TOTAL ASSETS ($MIL)
Rating: U (Continued)		
GUILDERLAND REINSURANCE CO	NY	13.7
GULF BUILDERS RRG INC	SC	0.9
GULF UNDERWRITERS INS CO	CT	60.7
HARBOR SPECIALTY INS CO	NJ	131.8
HEARTLAND LLOYDS INS CO	TX	7.3
HOMESHIELD FIRE & CASUALTY INS CO	OK	0.9
HOMESTEAD INS CO	PA	6.4
HOMESURE OF VIRGINIA INC	VA	0.0
HOSPITAL UNDERWRITING GROUP INC	TN	34.5
HOSPITALITY MUT CAPT INS CO	GA	0.0
HOW INS CO A RRG	VA	131.2
INSURANCE CORP OF AMERICA	MI	33.0
INVERNESS INS CO	AZ	1.7
ISMIE INDEMNITY CO	IL	16.5
KEMPER INS CO OF TEXAS	TX	2.8
LIBERTY PERSONAL INS CO	MI	22.4
LILLIAN ASR GROUP INC	FL	5.6
LM GENERAL INS CO	DE	9.6
LM PERSONAL INS CO	DE	8.0
LM PROPERTY & CASUALTY INS CO	IN	128.8
LOCUST MUTUAL FIRE INS CO	PA	1.4
LONE STAR RRG INC	TX	2.7
LOUISIANA WORKERS COMPENSATION CORP	LA	1,269.3
LR INS INC	DE	2.6
LUMBERMENS UNDERWRITERS	TX	0.7
LVHN RRG	SC	30.2
MADA INS EXCHANGE	MN	1.0
MADISON INS CO	GA	9.1
MAIDEN REINS CO	MO	8.3
MAINE BONDING & CAS CO	ME	6.5
MAINE EMPLOYERS MUTUAL INS CO	ME	649.5
MAINLAND INS CO	PA	4.9
MANHATTAN RE-INS CO	DE	0.0
MAPFRE INSURANCE CO	NJ	38.4
MARTINGALE NATIONAL INS CO	IL	3.1
MARYLAND INS CO	TX	18.9
MAX AMERICA INS CO	IN	20.0
MEDILINK RRG INC	SC	0.8
MERCHANTS PROPERTY INS CO OF IN	IN	43.4
MGIC ASSURANCE CORP	WI	9.8
MGIC INDEMNITY CORP	WI	24.3
MIDSTATES REINSURANCE CORP	IL	140.6
MIDWEST TRUCKERS INS EXCHANGE	IN	0.0
MISSISSIPPI FARM BU MUTUAL INS CO	MS	25.5
MISSOURI PHYSICIANS ASSOCIATES	MO	3.4
MSI PREFERRED INS CO	IL	22.7
MT MCKINLEY INS CO	DE	49.9
NATIONAL CONSUMER INS CO	NJ	0.0
NATIONAL INS ASN	IN	11.5
NATIONAL PUBLIC FINANCE GUAR CORP	IL	187.4
NATIONAL REINSURANCE CORP	DE	699.9
NATIONAL STANDARD INS CO	TX	7.8
NEW ENGLAND INS CO	CT	298.9
NEW ENGLAND REINSURANCE CORP	CT	137.6
NEW JERSEY CAR RRG	DC	0.8
NEWPORT BONDING & SURETY CO	PR	6.6
NEWPORT MUT INS RRG INC	HI	0.7
NEWSTEAD INS CO	DE	1.3
NISSAY DOWA GENERAL INS CO LTD US BR	NY	18.7
NORTH AMERICAN FIRE & CAS INS CO	LA	3.1
NORTH AMERICAN INDEMNITY CO	TN	1.3
NORTH STAR GENERAL INS CO	MN	4.5
NORTH STAR REINSURANCE CORP	DE	22.4
OHIO CASUALTY OF NEW JERSEY INC	OH	76.3
OKLAHOMA TRANSIT INS CO	OK	1.0
OLD ELIZABETH MUTUAL FIRE INS CO	PA	0.7
OLD LYME INS CO OF RI INC	RI	27.3
OLD REPUBLIC MERCANTILE INS CO	IL	3.2
OMAHA INDEMNITY CO	WI	20.9
ONECIS INS CO	IL	10.2
PADDINGTON LIABILITY RRG	NV	1.3
PALADIN REINSURANCE CORP	NY	8.4
PASSPORT INS CO	ND	2.0
PATHFINDER INS CO	CO	8.8
PHILADELPHIA REINSURANCE CORP	PA	151.3
PHILADELPHIA UNITED FIRE INS CO	PA	0.9
PHYSICIANS INS CO OF OHIO	OH	55.6
POLICYHOLDERS MUTUAL INS CO	WI	0.2
POTOMAC INS CO	PA	10.3
PREFERRED MANAGED RISK LTD	DC	0.0
PREMIER INS EXCHANGE RRG	VT	24.4
PRIDE NATIONAL INS CO	OK	6.7
PROFESSIONAL LIABILITY INS CO	TN	3.7
PROFESSIONAL MEDICAL INS RRG	HI	0.3
PROGRESSIVE COMMERCIAL CASUALTY CO	OH	8.4
PROSELECT NATIONAL INS CO INC	AZ	11.8
PROTECTION MUT INS CO OF LITTLESTOWN	PA	0.7
PROVIDENCE PLANTATIONS INS CO	RI	1.3
PROVIDENCE WASHINGTON INS CO	RI	165.4
RAMPART INS CO	NY	77.9
RED VIKING INS CO	CA	10.1
RESPONSE INDEMNITY CO	NY	4.1
RICHPORT INS CO	PR	2.5
RISK MGMT INDEMNITY INC	DE	0.0
RUTGERS ENHANCED INS CO	NJ	3.7
SAIF CORP	OR	3,879.9
SALEM COUNTY MUTUAL FIRE INS CO	NJ	2.2
SAN DIEGO INS CO	CA	75.1
SAN FRANCISCO REINSURANCE CO	CA	107.8
SAUCON MUTUAL INS CO	PA	14.1
SEATON INS CO	RI	77.1
SELECT INS CO	TX	67.9
SHAMOKIN TOWNSHIP MUTUAL FIRE INS CO	PA	0.1
SLAVONIC INS CO OF TX	TX	2.5
SOUTHEAST EMPLOYERS MUT CAP INS CO	GA	0.0
SOUTHERN FARM BUREAU PROPERTY	MS	50.7
SOUTHERN MICHIGAN INS CO	MI	6.1
SPECIALTY SURPLUS INS CO	IL	35.1
STEWARD RRG	DC	0.0
STONE VALLEY MUTUAL FIRE INS CO	PA	0.6

INSURANCE COMPANY NAME	DOM. STATE	TOTAL ASSETS ($MIL)
Rating: U (Continued)		
STONEWALL INS CO	RI	88.5
SUECIA INS CO	NY	58.8
SUNBELT INS CO	TX	4.7
SUPERIOR GUARANTY INS CO	FL	6.9
SUPERIOR INS CO	FL	5.7
TENNESSEE INS CO	TN	10.7
TEXAS CONSTRUCTION INS CO RRG INC	NV	0.5
TEXAS GENERAL INDEMNITY CO	CO	30.7
TEXAS MUTUAL INS CO	TX	3,385.7
THIRD COAST INS CO	IL	13.9
THOMSON SECURITY INS CO	DE	0.0
TIG INDEMNITY CO	CA	27.2
TRADERS & GENERAL INS CO	TX	46.9
TRANSPORT INS CO	OH	40.3
TRAVEL AIR INS CO KANSAS	KS	6.1
TRISTATE MEDICAL INS CO RRG	NV	3.4
TRYGG-HANSA INS CO LTD US BR	NY	4.0
ULICO STANDARD OF AMER CAS CO	CA	20.6
UNION STANDARD INS CO	OK	24.6
UNIONE ITALIANA REINS CO OF AMERICA	NY	77.6
UNITED AMERICAS INS CO	NY	8.3
UNITED HOME INS CO A RRG	VT	9.2
UNITED INTERNATIONAL INS CO	NY	4.4
UNIVERSAL INS EXCHANGE	TX	0.0
USAGENCIES DIRECT INS CO	NY	7.7
VANTAGE CASUALTY INS CO	IN	128.7
VANTAPRO SPECIALTY INS CO	AR	3.2
VEHICULAR SERVICE INS CO RRG	OK	1.8
VICTORIA NATIONAL INS CO	OH	3.3
VINTAGE INS CO	CA	20.5
WEST BRANCH MUTUAL INS CO	PA	0.5
WESTERN PROFESSIONAL INS CO	WA	12.4
WESTERN SELECT INS CO	CA	13.9
WESTWARD INS CO	CA	2.4
WMAC CREDIT INS CORP	WI	6.2
WORKCOMP HAWAII INS CO INC	HI	19.8
WORKCOMP HAWAII SELECT INS CO INC	HI	13.3
WORKERS COMPENSATION FUND OF UTAH	UT	1,379.4
WRM AMERICA INDEMNITY CO INC	NY	61.9
XL LLOYDS INS CO	TX	3.3
YORK INS CO	RI	23.4
ZURICH INS (GUAM) INC	GU	0.0

Section VII

Rating Upgrades and Downgrades

A list of all

U.S. Property and Casualty Insurers

receiving a rating upgrade or downgrade during the current quarter.

Section VII Contents

This section identifies those companies receiving a rating change since the previous edition of this publication, whether it is a rating upgrade, rating downgrade, newly rated company or the withdrawal of a rating. A rating may be withdrawn due to a merger, dissolution, or liquidation. A rating upgrade or downgrade may entail a change from one letter grade to another, or it may mean the addition or deletion of a plus or minus sign within the same letter grade previously assigned to the company. Ratings are normally updated once each quarter of the year. In some instances, however, a company's rating may be downgraded outside of the normal updates due to overriding circumstances.

Unlike other rating agencies, TheStreet.com ratings are reviewed each and every quarter to ensure that the company's current rating reflects the most recent information available. This allows us to react more promptly and with greater flexibility to changing conditions as they occur. In addition, we are not inhibited to upgrade or downgrade a company as soon as its financial condition warrants the change. You should therefore consider the magnitude of the rating change along with the meaning of the new rating when evaluating the significance of a rating upgrade or downgrade.

1. **Insurance Company Name** The legally-registered name, which can sometimes differ from the name that the company uses for advertising. An insurer's name can be very similar to that of another, so verify the company's exact name and state of domicile to make sure you are looking at the correct company.

2. **Domicile State** The state which has primary regulatory responsibility for the company. It may differ from the location of the company's corporate headquarters. You do not have to be living in the domicile state to purchase insurance from this firm, provided it is licensed to do business in your state.

3. **Total Assets** All assets admitted by state insurance regulators in millions of dollars. This includes investments and current business assets such as receivables from agents and reinsurers.

4. **New Financial Strength Rating** The rating assigned to the company as of the date of this Guide's publication. Our rating is measured on a scale from A to F and considers a wide range of factors. Highly-rated companies are, in our opinion, less likely to experience financial difficulties than lower-rated firms. See *About TheStreet.com Financial Strength Ratings* on page 9 for more information.

5. **Previous Financial Strength Rating** The rating assigned to the company prior to its most recent change.

6. **Date of Change** The date that the rating upgrade or downgrade officially occurred. Normally, all rating changes are put into effect on a single day each quarter of the year. In some instances, however, a rating may have been changed outside of this normal update.

Withdrawn Ratings

INSURANCE COMPANY NAME	DOM. STATE	TOTAL ASSETS ($MIL)	NEW RATING	PREVIOUS RATING	DATE OF CHANGE
ABBA INDEMNITY CO	TX	1.7	U	D	06/09/09
ACE INS CO OF THE MIDWEST	IN	51.1	U	C	06/09/09
AMERICAN EQUITY INS CO	AZ	104.6	U	B-	06/09/09
AMERICAN GENERAL PROP INS CO OF FL	FL	12.9	U	B	06/09/09
AMERICAN GENERAL PROPERTY INS CO	TN	56.9	U	C+	06/09/09
APEX LLOYDS INS CO	TX	2.8	U	D+	06/09/09
APEX LLOYDS INS CO	TX	2.8	U	D+	06/09/09
ARA CASUALTY INS CO	FL	3.7	U	E+	06/09/09
ASOC DE SUSCRIPCION CONJUNTA DEL SEG	PR	347.2	U	E	06/09/09
ASSURECARE RRG	DC	31.1	U	E	06/09/09
ATLANTIC INS CO	TX	8.7	U	B-	06/09/09
AVOMARK INS CO	IN	11.2	U	B-	06/09/09
CAPITAL ASR RRG INC	SC	0.0	U	D+	06/09/09
CENTURY INDEMNITY CO	PA	1,111.1	U	C-	06/09/09
CINCINNATI EQUITABLE INS CO	OH	6.7	U	D+	06/09/09
CITADEL INS CO	TX	2.9	U	C+	06/09/09
CLAREMONT LIABILITY INS CO	CA	22.0	U	C	06/09/09
COMMERCIAL CASUALTY INS CO	CA	182.2	U	D	06/09/09
COMMERCIAL RISK RE-INSURANCE CO	VT	36.9	U	D	06/09/09
CONNECTICUT HEALTH CARE PARTNERS RRG	VT	0.0	U	E+	06/09/09
CONNECTICUT LIFE & CASUALTY INS CO	CT	25.4	U	C-	06/09/09
CONSORTIUM (A RRG)	VT	16.4	U	D-	06/09/09
CONTRACTORS LIABILITY INS CO RRG	NV	4.2	U	D-	06/09/09
FAIRFIELD INS CO	CT	26.4	U	C	06/09/09
FINANCIAL BENEFITS INS CO	IL	5.1	U	C-	06/09/09
FIRST AUTOMOTIVE INS RRG INC	HI	5.5	U	E+	06/09/09
FIRST STATE INS CO	CT	914.7	U	E	06/09/09
GA TIMBER HARVESTERS MUTL CAPTIVE IC	GA	1.2	U	E	06/09/09
GLOBAL SURETY & INS CO	NE	74.2	U	C	06/09/09
GOLD MEDAL INS CO	MN	0.0	U	E-	06/09/09
GULF UNDERWRITERS INS CO	CT	60.7	U	B-	06/09/09
HANOVER FIRE & CASUALTY INS CO	PA	2.5	U	D	06/09/09
HARBOR SPECIALTY INS CO	NJ	131.8	U	D+	06/09/09
ISMIE INDEMNITY CO	IL	16.5	U	C	06/09/09
LIBERTY PERSONAL INS CO	MI	22.4	U	C	06/09/09
LM PROPERTY & CASUALTY INS CO	IN	128.8	U	C+	06/09/09
LONE STAR RRG INC	TX	2.7	U	D+	06/09/09
LUMBERMENS UNDERWRITERS	TX	0.7	U	D	06/09/09
MADISON INS CO	GA	9.1	U	C-	06/09/09
MAIDEN REINS CO	MO	8.3	U	B-	06/09/09
MAPFRE INSURANCE CO	NJ	38.4	U	C-	06/09/09
MARYLAND HLTHCARE PROVIDERS INS EXCH	MD	8.0	U	E+	06/09/09
MEDILINK RRG INC	SC	0.8	U	E+	06/09/09
MILLENNIUM INS CO	PA	7.9	U	E+	06/09/09
NATIONAL INS ASN	IN	11.5	U	C	06/09/09
NATIONAL REINSURANCE CORP	DE	699.9	U	C+	06/09/09
NORTH STAR REINSURANCE CORP	DE	22.4	U	B	06/09/09
OLD LYME INS CO OF RI INC	RI	27.3	U	C	06/09/09

Withdrawn Ratings (Continued)

INSURANCE COMPANY NAME	DOM. STATE	TOTAL ASSETS ($MIL)	NEW RATING	PREVIOUS RATING	DATE OF CHANGE
OLD REPUBLIC MERCANTILE INS CO	IL	3.2	**U**	C+	06/09/09
OMAHA INDEMNITY CO	WI	20.9	**U**	C	06/09/09
PADDINGTON LIABILITY RRG	NV	1.3	**U**	E	06/09/09
PATHFINDER INS CO	CO	8.8	**U**	C	06/09/09
PENNSYLVANIA MEDICAL REINS CO	PA	46.7	**U**	E+	06/09/09
PINE CREEK MUTUAL FIRE INS CO	PA	1.8	**U**	D	06/09/09
PREMIER INS EXCHANGE RRG	VT	24.4	**U**	C-	06/09/09
PROVIDENCE WASHINGTON INS CO	RI	165.4	**U**	D	06/09/09
RUTGERS ENHANCED INS CO	NJ	3.7	**U**	D+	06/09/09
SEABOARD SURETY CO	NY	159.2	**U**	B-	06/09/09
SOUTHERN FARM BUREAU PROPERTY	MS	50.7	**U**	C-	06/09/09
SOUTHERN MICHIGAN INS CO	MI	6.1	**U**	C-	06/09/09
TENNESSEE INS CO	TN	10.7	**U**	D	06/09/09
TRISTATE MEDICAL INS CO RRG	NV	3.4	**U**	D-	06/09/09
USAGENCIES DIRECT INS CO	NY	7.7	**U**	D	06/09/09
VANTAGE CASUALTY INS CO	IN	128.7	**U**	C-	06/09/09
VICTORIA NATIONAL INS CO	OH	3.3	**U**	B	06/09/09
VOYAGER PROPERTY & CAS INS CO	SC	62.2	**U**	C+	06/09/09
WOODBROOK CASUALTY INS INC	AL	34.7	**U**	C	06/09/09
XL LLOYDS INS CO	TX	3.3	**U**	D-	06/09/09

Rating Upgrades

ACA HOME INS CORP was upgraded to C+ from D+ in August 2009 based on an increase in the stability index from a 2.50(weak) to 3.10(fair). Other factors: The company's net asset base increased during the period by 20.4%, from $18.2 million to $21.9 million.

AMERICAN CAPITAL ASR CORP was upgraded to C+ from D+ in August 2009 based on an increase in the stability index from a 2.40(weak) to 3.60(fair). Other factors: The company's net asset base increased during the period by 5.3%, from $103.3 million to $108.8 million.

EMPLOYERS SECURITY INS CO was upgraded to D- from E+ in August 2009 based on an increase in the capitalization index from a 4.50(fair) to 6.30(good) and stability index from a 0.50(weak) to 1.00(weak). Other factors: The company's net asset base increased during the period by 24.1%, from $23.9 million to $29.7 million.

FIRST MERCURY CASUALTY CO was upgraded to C- from D+ in August 2009 based on an increase in the capitalization index from a 2.70(weak) to 3.30(fair) and stability index from a 2.50(weak) to 3.00(fair).

GREAT LAKES CASUALTY INS CO was upgraded to C- from D+ in August 2009 based on an increase in the capitalization index from a 8.70(excellent) to 9.90(excellent) and stability index from a 2.20(weak) to 3.20(fair).

HEALTHCARE PROVIDERS INS EXCH was upgraded to C- from D+ in August 2009 based on an increase in the capitalization index from a 4.40(fair) to 5.20(good) and stability index from a 2.40(weak) to 2.90(fair).

MGA INS CO INC was upgraded to C- from D+ in August 2009 based on an increase in the capitalization index from a 4.50(fair) to 7.30(excellent), profitability index from a 4.60(fair) to 4.90(good), and stability index from a 2.70(weak) to 2.90(fair).

NOVA CASUALTY CO was upgraded to C- from D+ in August 2009 based on an increase in the capitalization index from a 5.60(good) to 7.00(excellent), profitability index from a 3.80(fair) to 4.40(fair), and stability index from a 2.40(weak) to 2.90(fair). Other factors: Capital and surplus increased during the period by 46.5%, from $58.7 million to $86.0 million.

PEAK PROP & CAS INS CORP was upgraded to B from C+ in August 2009 based on an increase in the stability index from a 2.90(fair) to 4.00(fair). Other factors: The company's net asset base increased during the period by 5.7%, from $36.0 million to $38.0 million. Capital and surplus increased during the period by 5.4%, from $16.2 million to $17.1 million.

SELECTIVE AUTO INS CO OF NJ was upgraded to C+ from C in July 2009 due to an improvement in its reserve adequacy index following favorable reserve development in 2008. The company has excellent capitalization; however, it suffered a $236,000 underwriting loss during the first quarter.

SELECTIVE INS CO OF NEW ENGLAND was upgraded to D from D- in August 2009 based on an increase in the stability index from a 1.00(weak) to 1.40(weak).

SIMED was upgraded to D from E in August 2009 based on an increase in the capitalization index from a 0.00(weak) to 1.80(weak) and stability index from a 0.00(weak) to 1.40(weak). Other factors: Capital and surplus increased during the period by 10.2%, from $33.5 million to $37.0 million.

TRINITY LLOYDS INS CO was upgraded to B from B- in August 2009 based on an increase in the capitalization index from a 8.60(excellent) to 10.00(excellent) and stability index from a 3.50(fair) to 4.00(fair).

WESTMINSTER AMERICAN INS CO was upgraded to C- from D+ in August 2009 based on an increase in the stability index from a 1.20(weak) to 2.20(weak). Other factors: Capital and surplus increased during the period by 8.0%, from $6.7 million to $7.2 million.

Rating Downgrades

21ST CENTURY INS CO OF THE SW was downgraded to C from C+ in August 2009 based on a decrease in the stability index from a 3.30(fair) to 3.20(fair).

ADMIRAL INS CO was downgraded to C from C+ in August 2009 based on a decrease in the capitalization index from a 5.20(good) to 4.30(fair), profitability index from a 7.20(excellent) to 6.50(good), and stability index from a 4.40(fair) to 4.10(fair).

AIU INS CO was downgraded to C+ from B- in August 2009 based on a decrease in the stability index from a 3.90(fair) to 3.70(fair). Other factors: The company's net asset base decreased during the period by 11.8%, from $3156.8 million to $2824.7 million. Capital and surplus decreased during the period by 9.0%, from $725.7 million to $665.9 million.

ATLANTIC CASUALTY INS CO was downgraded to D from D+ in August 2009 based on a decrease in the stability index from a 2.50(weak) to 2.20(weak) and capitalization index from a 1.40(weak) to 1.10(weak).

BATTLE CREEK MUTUAL INS CO was downgraded to D- from D in August 2009 based on a decrease in the stability index from a 1.70(weak) to 0.50(weak), capitalization index from a 7.00(excellent) to 6.60(good), and profitability index from a 1.90(weak) to 1.60(weak). Other factors: The company's net asset base decreased during the period by 19.9%, from $6.7 million to $5.6 million. Capital and surplus decreased during the period by 56.6%, from $2.9 million to $1.9 million.

BEST AMERICAN INS CO was downgraded to F from E+ as the Comisionado de Seguros de Puerto Rico place the company in liquidation in March 2008.

COLUMBIA INS CO was downgraded to C+ from B- in August 2009 based on a decrease in the capitalization index from a 7.20(excellent) to 6.70(good) and stability index from a 4.80(fair) to 4.50(fair). Other factors: The company's net asset base decreased during the period by 23.2%, from $11050.0 million to $8967.5 million. Capital and surplus decreased during the period by 22.1%, from $7370.6 million to $6038.8 million.

COMCARE PRO INS RECIPROCAL RRG was downgraded to D- from D in August 2009 based on a decrease in the stability index from a 1.00(weak) to 0.60(weak), profitability index from a 1.60(weak) to 1.40(weak), and capitalization index from a 1.50(weak) to 1.30(weak). Other factors: Capital and surplus decreased during the period by 15.8%, from $1.3 million to $1.1 million.

CONTINENTAL INDEMNITY CO was downgraded to C from C+ in August 2009 based on a decrease in the profitability index from a 7.40(excellent) to 6.20(good) and capitalization index from a 4.40(fair) to 3.20(fair).

CYPRESS INS CO was downgraded to B- from B in August 2009 based on a decrease in the profitability index from a 6.10(good) to 5.50(good) and capitalization index from a 7.50(excellent) to 7.40(excellent). Other factors: Capital and surplus decreased during the period by 14.6%, from $239.1 million to $208.6 million.

DONEGAL MUTUAL INS CO was downgraded to C+ from B- in August 2009 based on a decrease in the capitalization index from a 5.70(good) to 3.70(fair), stability index from a 4.70(fair) to 4.30(fair), and profitability index from a 8.70(excellent) to 8.40(excellent).

EASTERN ALLIANCE INS CO was downgraded to D from D+ in August 2009 based on a decrease in the profitability index from a 7.20(excellent) to 5.90(good) and capitalization index from a 6.90(excellent) to 6.40(good). Other factors: Capital and surplus decreased during the period by 33.9%, from $41.7 million to $31.1 million.

FIRST COLONIAL INS CO was downgraded to B- from B in August 2009 based on a decrease in the capitalization index from a 6.00(good) to 5.20(good) and stability index from a 5.50(good) to 5.30(good). Other factors: The company's net asset base decreased during the period by 5.2%, from $382.7 million to $363.8 million.

FIRST COMMERCIAL INS CO was downgraded to F from E+ in July 2009 when the Department of Financial Services of the State of Florida placed the company in rehabilitation.

FIRST COMMERCIAL TRANSPORTATION was downgraded to F from E+ in July 2009 when the Department of Financial Services of the State of Florida placed the company in rehabilitation.

FSA INS CO was downgraded to D from D+ in August 2009 based on a decrease in the stability index from a 1.00(weak) to 0.80(weak) and capitalization index from a 4.90(good) to 4.80(fair).

Rating Downgrades (Continued)

GEORGIA FARM BUREAU MUTUAL INS CO was downgraded to B from B+ in August 2009 based on a decrease in the stability index from a 5.00(good) to 4.80(fair) and profitability index from a 2.40(weak) to 2.20(weak). Other factors: Capital and surplus decreased during the period by 8.9%, from $307.0 million to $282.0 million.

GERMANIA FIRE & CASUALTY CO was downgraded to C+ from B- in August 2009 based on a decrease in the stability index from a 4.70(fair) to 4.10(fair), capitalization index from a 7.90(excellent) to 7.80(excellent), and profitability index from a 2.50(weak) to 2.40(weak).

HOMESITE LLOYDS OF TEXAS was downgraded to D from D+ in August 2009 based on a decrease in the stability index from a 1.00(weak) to 0.40(weak), capitalization index from a 3.90(fair) to 3.50(fair), and profitability index from a 2.80(weak) to 2.60(weak). Other factors: Capital and surplus decreased during the period by 29.0%, from $4.8 million to $3.8 million.

LANDMARK ONE INS CO was downgraded to D+ from C- in August 2009 based on a decrease in the profitability index from a 3.50(fair) to 2.80(weak) and stability index from a 2.70(weak) to 2.40(weak). Other factors: Capital and surplus decreased during the period by 23.3%, from $9.7 million to $7.9 million.

LINCOLN MUTUAL INS CO was downgraded to D+ from C- in August 2009 based on a decrease in the stability index from a 2.00(weak) to 1.80(weak), capitalization index from a 7.70(excellent) to 7.60(excellent), and profitability index from a 1.50(weak) to 1.40(weak). Other factors: The company's net asset base decreased during the period by 7.3%, from $3.2 million to $3.0 million. Capital and surplus decreased during the period by 20.0%, from $2.2 million to $1.9 million.

MGIC CREDIT ASR CORP was downgraded to C- from C in August 2009 based on a decrease in the stability index from a 3.70(fair) to 2.90(fair) and profitability index from a 5.20(good) to 5.10(good).

MGIC MORTGAGE REINSURANCE CORP was downgraded to C+ from B- in August 2009 based on a decrease in the profitability index from a 7.90(excellent) to 6.90(excellent) and capitalization index from a 8.40(excellent) to 7.70(excellent).

MGIC REINSURANCE CORP was downgraded to C- from C in August 2009 based on a decrease in the stability index from a 3.40(fair) to 2.90(fair) and capitalization index from a 3.50(fair) to 3.10(fair).

MGIC REINSURANCE CORP OF WI was downgraded to D from C in August 2009 based on a decrease in the stability index from a 3.40(fair) to 1.40(weak), profitability index from a 0.70(weak) to 0.50(weak), and capitalization index from a 2.30(weak) to 2.20(weak).

MGIC RESIDENTIAL REINSURANCE CORP was downgraded to C+ from B- in August 2009 based on a decrease in the profitability index from a 7.80(excellent) to 6.90(excellent) and capitalization index from a 8.30(excellent) to 7.60(excellent).

MICHIGAN MILLERS MUTUAL INS CO was downgraded to B- from B in August 2009 based on a decrease in the stability index from a 5.40(good) to 4.90(good), profitability index from a 2.10(weak) to 1.90(weak), and capitalization index from a 8.10(excellent) to 8.00(excellent). Other factors: The company's net asset base decreased during the period by 7.2%, from $306.7 million to $285.9 million. Capital and surplus decreased during the period by 14.6%, from $95.4 million to $83.2 million.

MORTGAGE GUARANTY INS CORP was downgraded to D from D+ in August 2009 based on a decrease in the profitability index from a 6.80(good) to 4.70(fair), stability index from a 2.40(weak) to 1.40(weak), and capitalization index from a 3.40(fair) to 3.20(fair). Other factors: Capital and surplus decreased during the period by 13.3%, from $1529.0 million to $1350.0 million.

NATIONAL INDEMNITY CO was downgraded to C+ from B- in August 2009 based on a decrease in the stability index from a 4.80(fair) to 4.30(fair) and capitalization index from a 3.50(fair) to 3.00(fair). Other factors: Capital and surplus decreased during the period by 14.5%, from $27613.1 million to $24111.0 million.

NAZARETH MUTUAL INS CO was downgraded to D+ from C- in August 2009 based on a decrease in the profitability index from a 2.00(weak) to 1.60(weak), capitalization index from a 4.10(fair) to 3.80(fair), and stability index from a 2.30(weak) to 2.10(weak). Other factors: The company's net asset base decreased during the period by 6.6%, from $10.8 million to $10.1 million. Capital and surplus decreased during the period by 24.6%, from $3.1 million to $2.5 million.

NOVUS INS CO RRG was downgraded to E+ from D- in August 2009 based on a decrease in the profitability index from a 2.80(weak) to 2.30(weak). Other factors: The company's net asset base decreased during the period by 17.2%, from $20.6 million to $17.5 million. Capital and surplus decreased during the period by 28.0%, from $4.6 million to $3.6 million.

Rating Downgrades (Continued)

NSA RRG INC was downgraded to F from E- as the Vermont Commissioner of Banking, Insurance, Securities and Health Care Administration placed the company in rehabilitation in March 2009.

RADIAN MORTGAGE INS INC was downgraded to C+ from B in August 2009 based on a decrease in the profitability index from a 4.90(good) to 2.90(fair), stability index from a 4.60(fair) to 3.70(fair), and capitalization index from a 8.80(excellent) to 8.10(excellent). Other factors: Capital and surplus decreased during the period by 19.3%, from $26.7 million to $22.4 million.

SOPHIA PALMER NURSES RRG INC was downgraded to D- from D in August 2009 based on a decrease in the stability index from a 0.60(weak) to 0.00(weak) and capitalization index from a 1.70(weak) to 1.60(weak). Other factors: Capital and surplus decreased during the period by 10.4%, from $0.6 million to $0.5 million.

SOUTHERN GENERAL INS CO was downgraded to C- from C in August 2009 based on a decrease in the stability index from a 3.40(fair) to 2.90(fair), profitability index from a 1.60(weak) to 1.40(weak), and capitalization index from a 7.30(excellent) to 7.20(excellent). Other factors: Capital and surplus decreased during the period by 21.5%, from $21.4 million to $17.6 million.

UNITED STATES LIABILITY INS CO was downgraded to C from C+ in August 2009 based on a decrease in the stability index from a 4.70(fair) to 4.30(fair). Other factors: The company's net asset base decreased during the period by 17.4%, from $476.9 million to $406.1 million. Capital and surplus decreased during the period by 38.1%, from $281.5 million to $203.8 million.

US FIDELIS INS CO RRG INC was downgraded to D+ from C- in August 2009 based on a decrease in the stability index from a 1.80(weak) to 1.00(weak) and profitability index from a 1.90(weak) to 1.50(weak). Other factors: The company's net asset base decreased during the period by 66.5%, from $1.2 million to $0.7 million. Capital and surplus decreased during the period by 102.0%, from $1.0 million to $0.5 million.

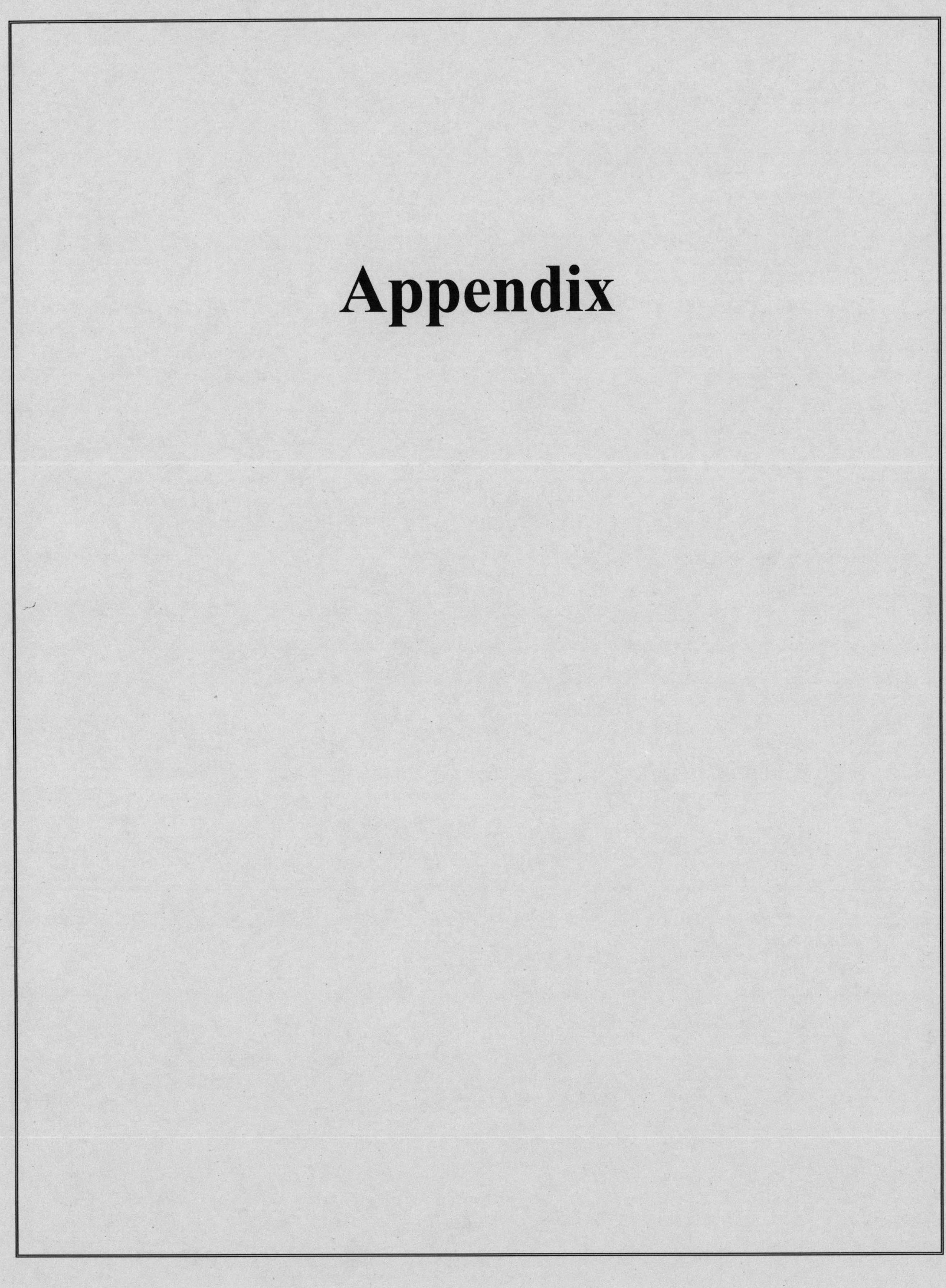

Appendix

State Guaranty Associations

The states have established insurance guaranty associations to help pay claims to policyholders of failed insurance companies. However, there are several cautions which you must be aware of with respect to this coverage:

1. Most of the guaranty associations do not set aside funds in advance. Rather, states assess contributions from other insurance companies after an insolvency occurs.

2. There can be an unacceptably long delay before claims are paid.

3. Each state has different levels and types of coverage, often governed by legislation unique to that state that can sometimes conflict with coverage of other states. Generally speaking, most property and casualty lines of business written by licensed insurers are covered by guaranty associations subject to the conditions and limitations set forth in the various acts. The Guaranty Funds do not cover non-admitted carriers (except in the state of New Jersey). Most state guaranty funds will not cover title, surety, credit, mortgage guarantee or ocean marine insurance.

The table on the following page is designed to help you sort out these issues. However, it is not intended to handle all of them. If your carrier has failed and you need a complete answer, we recommend you contact your State Insurance Official (see page 420 for phone numbers).

Following is a brief explanation of each of the columns in the table.

1. **Maximum Per Claim** — The maximum amount payable by the State Guaranty Fund on a single covered claim, with the exception of workers' compensation claims, which are paid in full in most states.

2. **Workers' Comp. Paid in Full** — "Yes" indicates that there is no cap on the amount paid for workers' compensation claims.

3. **Net Worth Provision** — A net worth provision gives the association the right to seek reimbursement from an insured if the insured's net worth exceeds $50 million, essentially excluding certain large organizations from coverage by the guaranty association. Roughly half of the states have a net worth provision. If a state has a provision, marked "yes", there are other conditions applicable; contact your local department of insurance for further information, (phone numbers on page 420).

4. **Guaranty Fund Trigger** — The action that triggers the guaranty fund process.

See the notes on page 419 regarding peculiarities in state coverages.

COVERAGE OF STATE GUARANTY FUNDS

STATE	MAXIMUM PER CLAIM	WORKERS' COMP. PAID IN FULL	NET WORTH PROVISION	GUARANTY FUND TRIGGER		
				FINAL ORDER OF LIQUIDATION WITH FINDING OF INSOLVENCY	FINDING OF INSOLVENCY ONLY	OTHER
Alabama	$150,000	yes	yes	X		
Alaska	$500,000	yes	none	X		
Arizona	$100,000	(8)	none		X	
Arkansas	$300,000	(9)	yes		X	
California	$500,000	yes	none			(14)
Colorado	$100,000	yes	yes	X		
Connecticut	$400,000	yes	yes		X	
Delaware	$300,000	yes	yes	X		
Dist. of Colombia	$300,000	yes	yes	X		
Florida	$300,000 (1)	(10)	none	X		(16)
Georgia	$300,000	yes	yes	X		
Hawaii	$300,000	yes	yes	X		
Idaho	$300,000	yes	none	X		
Illinois	$300,000	yes	yes	X		
Indiana	$100,000 (2)	(9)	yes	X		(16)
Iowa	$300,000	yes	none (13)	X		
Kansas	$300,000	yes	none		X	
Kentucky	$300,000	yes	yes	X		
Louisiana	$150,000 (2)	yes	yes	X		(15)
Maine	$300,000	yes	yes	X		
Maryland	$300,000	yes	yes	X		
Massachusetts	$300,000	yes	yes		X	
Michigan	(3)	(11)	yes			(19)
Minnesota	$300,000	yes	yes	X		
Mississippi	$300,000	yes	none	X		
Missouri	$300,000	yes	yes	X		
Montana	$300,000	yes	yes	X		
Nebraska	$300,000	yes	none	X		
Nevada	$300,000	yes	yes	X		(17)
New Hampshire	$300,000	yes	yes (21)		X	(22)
New Jersey	$300,000 (4)	(10)	none		X	
New Mexico	$100,000	yes	none	X		
New York	$1,000,000 (5)	(10)	none			(20)
North Carolina	$300,000	yes	yes	X		
North Dakota	$300,000	(12)	yes	X		
Ohio	$300,000	(12)	yes			(14)
Oklahoma	$150,000	yes	yes			(14)
Oregon	$300,000	yes	yes	X		
Pennsylvania	$300,000	(10)	yes	X		
Puerto Rico	$150,000	yes	none	X		
Rhode Island	$00,000	yes	yes	X		
South Carolina	$300,000	yes	yes		X	
South Dakota	$300,000	yes	yes	X		
Tennessee	$100,000	yes	yes	X		
Texas	$300,000	yes	yes		X	(18)
Utah	$300,000	yes	yes	X		
Vermont	$300,000	yes	none	X		
Virgin Island	$50,000	(9)	none		X	
Virginia	$300,000	yes	yes	X		
Washington	$300,000	(12)	none			(14)
West Virginia	$300,000	(12)	none			(14)
Wisconsin	$300,000 (6)	(11)	yes			(19)
Wyoming	$150,000 (7)	yes	none	X		

NOTES

1. Limit of $100,000 per residential unit for policies covering condominium associations or homeowners' associations.
2. Maximum claim per occurrence is $300,000.
3. All claims, except for workers' compensation claims, that exceed .05% of the aggregate premiums written by association member in the previous calendar year are not covered.
4. Maximum per auto claim is $75,000. This applies only to No Fault Personal Injury Protection Claims. The difference between the Maximum Per Claim and the $75,000 is covered by the Unsatisfied Claim & Judgement Fund.
5. Maximum of $5,000,000 for all claims arising out of any one policy, for policies issued to residents insuring property or risks located outside the state.
6. $300,000 is the limit on a single risk, loss or life.
7. $150,000 limit per claimant for each covered claim.
8. Workers' compensation claims of insolvent insurers paid by Arizona's state fund.
9. Workers' compensation payments limited to the maximum claim amount.
10. Workers' compensation claims covered by a separate workers' compensation security fund that is not intermingled with any other state funds and is administered by the state insurance commissioner.
11. Workers Compensation payments subject only to deductible.
12. Only a state fund is permitted to write workers' compensation insurance.
13. Iowa does not cover claims of a person whose net worth is greater than that allowed by guaranty fund law of his or her state of residence.
14. Triggered by finding of insolvency and liquidation order.
15. The State Guaranty Association is also obligated to pay claims of an insurer that is in rehabilitation upon joint motion of association and receiver.
16. Liquidation order not final until there is no further right of appeal.
17. Also triggered if the insolvent insurer is involved in a court proceeding to determine its status of solvency, rehabilitation or liquidation, and the court has prohibited the insurer from paying claims for more than thirty days.
18. Triggered if (1) insurer is placed in receivership based on finding of insolvency, or (2) conservatorship after being deemed by commissioner to be insolvent and an impared insurer.
19. Final Order of Liquidation.
20. Insolvency of Insurer.
21. A new act (NH Act of 2004) was enacted for insolvencies occurring after 8-6-2004 and gives the association the right to recover from the following persons the amount of any covered claim paid, whether for defense, indemnity, or otherwise, on behalf of such person, any insured whose net worth exceeds $25 million, provided the insured's net worth shall be deemed to include the net worth of the insured and all of its affiliates on a consolidated basis. The prior act does not cover a claim of an insured or third party liability claimant whose net worth exceeds $25 million.
22. A new act (NH Act of 2004) was enacted for insolvencies occurring after 8-6-2004 and defines an insolvent insurer as a licensed insurer against whom a final order of liquidation has been entered with a finding of insolvency by a court of competent jurisdiction in the insurer's state of domicile. The prior act requires a finding of insolvency only.

Information provided in the Coverage of State Guaranty Funds chart was obtained from the National Conference of Insurance Guaranty Funds (NCIGF).

State Insurance Commissioners' Departmental Contact Information

State	*Official's Title*	*Website Address*	*Phone Number*
Alabama	Commissioner	www.aldoi.org	(334) 269-3550
Alaska	Director	www.dced.state.ak.us/insurance/	(907) 465-2515
Arizona	Director	www.id.state.az.us	(800) 325-2548
Arkansas	Commissioner	www.insurance.arkansas.gov	(800) 282-9134
California	Commissioner	www.insurance.ca.gov	(800) 927-4357
Colorado	Commissioner	www.dora.state.co.us/insurance/	(800) 930-3745
Connecticut	Commissioner	www.ct.gov/cid/	(860) 297-3800
Delaware	Commissioner	www.state.de.us/inscom/	(302) 674-7300
Dist. of Columbia	Commissioner	disr.dc.gov/disr/	(202) 727-8000
Florida	Commissioner	www.fldfs.com	(800) 342-2762
Georgia	Commissioner	www.gainsurance.org	(800) 656-2298
Hawaii	Commissioner	www.hawaii.gov/dcca/areas/ins/	(808) 586-2790
Idaho	Director	www.doi.idaho.gov	(800) 721-3272
Illinois	Director	www.idfpr.com/doi/	(217) 782-4515
Indiana	Commissioner	www.ia.org/idoi/	(317) 232-2385
Iowa	Commissioner	www.iid.state.ia.us	(877) 955-1212
Kansas	Commissioner	www.ksinsurance.org	(800) 432-2484
Kentucky	Executive Director	www.doi.ppr.ky.gov/kentucky/	(800) 595-6053
Louisiana	Commissioner	www.ldi.state.la.us	(800) 259-5300
Maine	Superintendent	www.maine.gov/pfr/insurance/	(800) 300-5000
Maryland	Commissioner	www.mdinsurance.state.md.us	(800) 492-6116
Massachusetts	Commissioner	www.mass.gov/doi/	(617) 521-7794
Michigan	Commissioner	www.michigan.gov/cis/	(877) 999-6442
Minnesota	Commissioner	www.commerce.state.mn.us	(651) 296-4026
Mississippi	Commissioner	www.doi.state.ms.us	(800) 562-2957
Missouri	Director	www.insurance.mo.gov/	(800) 726-7390
Montana	Commissioner	www.sao.state.mt.us	(800) 332-6148
Nebraska	Director	www.nebraska.gov	(402) 471-2306
Nevada	Commissioner	doi.state.nv.us	(775) 687-4270
New Hampshire	Commissioner	www.nh.gov/insurance/	(800) 852-3416
New Jersey	Commissioner	www.state.nj.us/dobi/	(800) 446-7467
New Mexico	Superintendent	www.nmprc.state.nm.us/id.htm	(888) 427-5772
New York	Superintendent	www.ins.state.ny.us	(800) 342-3736
North Carolina	Commissioner	www.ncdoi.com	(800) 546-5664
North Dakota	Commissioner	www.nd.gov/ndins/	(800) 247-0560
Ohio	Director	www.ohioinsurance.gov	(800) 686-1526
Oklahoma	Commissioner	www.oid.state.ok.us	(800) 522-0071
Oregon	Insurance Administrator	www.cbs.state.or.us/ins/	(503) 947-7980
Pennsylvania	Commissioner	www.ins.state.pa.us/ins/	(877) 881-6388
Puerto Rico	Commissioner	www.ocs.gobierno.pr	(787) 722-8686
Rhode Island	Superintendent	www.dbr.state.ri.us	(401) 222-2223
South Carolina	Director	www.doi.sc.gov	(800) 768-3467
South Dakota	Director	www.state.sd.us/drr2/reg/insurance/	(605) 773-3563
Tennessee	Commissioner	www.state.tn.us/commerce/insurance/	(800) 342-4029
Texas	Commissioner	www.tdi.state.tx.us	(800) 252-3439
Utah	Commissioner	www.insurance.utah.gov	(800) 439-3805
Vermont	Commissioner	www.bishca.state.vt.us	(802) 828-3301
Virgin Islands	Lieutenant Governor	www.ltg.gov.vi	(340) 774-7166
Virginia	Commissioner	www.scc.virginia.gov/division/boi/	(877) 310-6560
Washington	Commissioner	www.insurance.wa.gov	(800) 562-6900
West Virginia	Commissioner	www.wvinsurance.gov	(304) 558-3386
Wisconsin	Commissioner	oci.wi.gov	(800) 236-8517
Wyoming	Commissioner	insurance.state.wy.us	(800) 438-5768

Risk-Adjusted Capital for Property and Casualty Insurers in TheStreet.com Rating Model

Among the most important indicators used in the analysis of an individual company are our two risk-adjusted capital ratios, which are useful tools in determining exposure to investment, liquidity and insurance risk in relation to the capital the company has to cover those risks.

The first risk-adjusted capital ratio evaluates the company's ability to withstand a moderate loss scenario. The second ratio evaluates the company's ability to withstand a severe loss scenario.

In order to calculate these Risk-Adjusted Capital Ratios, we follow these steps:

1. **Capital Resources** First, we find out how much capital a company actually has by adding the company's resources which could be used to cover unexpected losses. These resources are primarily composed of stock issued by the company (capital) and accumulated funds from prior year profits (retained earnings or surplus). Additional credit can also be given for conservative reserving practices and other "hidden capital" where applicable.

   Conservative policy reserves can be an important source of capital and can contribute significantly to the financial strength of a company. Companies that set aside more than is necessary in their reserves year after year are less likely to be over run with claims and forced to dip into capital to pay them. Conversely, a company that understates its reserves year after year will be forced to routinely withdraw from capital to pay claims. Accordingly, we give companies credit for consistent over- reserving and penalize companies for consistent under-reserving.

2. **Target Capital** Next, we determine how much capital the company should have to cover moderate losses based upon the company's level of risk in both its insurance business and its investment portfolio. We examine each of the company's risk areas and determine how much capital is needed for each area, based on how risky it is and how much exposure it has in that area. Then we combine these amounts to arrive at a total risk figure.

   Credit is given for the company's diversification, since it is unlikely that "the worst" will happen in all areas at once.

3. **Risk-Adjusted Capital Ratio #1** We compare the results of Step 1 with those of Step 2. Specifically, we divide the "capital resources" by the "target capital" and express it in terms of a ratio. This ratio is called RACR #1.

   If a company has a Risk-Adjusted Capital Ratio of 1.0 or more, it means the company has all of the capital we believe it requires to withstand potential losses which could be inflicted by a moderate economic decline. If the company has a ratio of less than 1.0, it does not currently have all of the capital resources we think it needs. During times of financial distress, companies often have access to additional capital through contributions from a parent or holding company, current profits or reductions in dividends. Therefore, we make an allowance for firms with Risk-Adjusted Capital Ratios of somewhat less than 1.0.

4. **Risk-Adjusted Capital Ratio #2** We repeat Steps 2 and 3 but now assume a severe loss scenario. This ratio is called RACR #2.

5. **Risk-Adjusted Capital Index** We convert RACR #1 and #2 into an index. It is measured on a scale of zero to ten, with ten being the best and seven or better considered strong. A company whose capital resources exactly equal its target capital will have a Risk-Adjusted Capital Ratio of 1.0 and a Risk-Adjusted Capital Index of 7.0.

How We Determine Target Capital

The basic procedure for determining target capital is to identify the risk areas where the company is exposed to loss such as: (1) the risk of receiving more claims than expected; (2) the risk of not being able to collect from reinsurers or others who owe the company money; (3) the risk of losses on investments and (4) the risk of having inadequate reserves. Then we ask questions, such as:

- What is the breakdown of the company's investment portfolio? What types of policies does the company offer? Who owes the company money and how likely are they to pay? What losses has the company experienced on its underwriting (when claims and expenses exceeded premiums)? How accurate have reserve estimates been? What exposure does the company have to catastrophic property losses, such as Hurricane Andrew or the Los Angeles earthquake? What exposure does the company have to catastrophic liability losses such as asbestos pollution?
- For each category, what are the potential losses which could be incurred in both a moderate loss and a severe loss scenario?
- In order to cover those potential losses, how much in capital resources does the company need? It stands to reason that more capital is needed as a cushion for losses on high-risk investments, such as junk bonds, than on low-risk investments, such as AAA-rated utility bonds.

Amounts from each separate risk area are added together and adjustments are made to take into account the low likelihood that all risk areas would suffer severe losses at the same time. Finally, target capital is adjusted for the company's spread of risk in the diversification of its investment portfolio, the size and number of the policies it writes and the diversification of its business.

Table 1 on the next page shows target capital percentages used by the National Association of Insurance Commissioners (NAIC) in relation to TheStreet.com Ratings Risk-Adjusted Capital Ratios #1 and #2 (RACR #1 and RACR #2).

The percentages shown in the table answer the question: How much should the firm hold in capital resources for every $100 it has committed to each category? Several of the items in Table 1 are expressed as ranges. The actual percentages used in the calculation of target capital for an individual company are determined by the levels of risk in the operations, investments or policy obligations of that specific company.

Table 1. Target Capital Percentages

	TheStreet.com Ratings		
Invested Asset Risk	**RACR#1**	**RACR#2**	**NAIC**
Bonds	**(%)**	**(%)**	**(%)**
Government guaranteed bonds	0	0	0
Class 1	.5-.75	1-1.5	0.3
Class 2	2	5	1
Class 3	5	15	2
Class 4	10	30	4.5
Class 5	20	60	10
Class 6	20	60	30
Preferred Stock	7	9.1	2.3-30
Common Stock			
Unaffiliated	25	33	15
Affiliated	25-100	33-100	N/A
Mortgages	5	15	5
Real Estate	10	33	10
Short-term investment	0.5	1	0.3
Collateral loans	2	5	5
Other invested assets	5	10	20
Credit Risk			
Agents' Balances	0.5	1	
Premium Notes	2	5	
Receivable Investment Income	2	3	5
Misc. Non-invested Assets	5	10	5
Reinsurance Recov. Current	1	1.5	10
30 to 90 Days Overdue	2	3	10
90 to 180 Days Overdue	5	7.5	10
More Than 180 Days Overdue	10	15	10
Rein Recov on Unpaid Losses	5	7.5	10
Rein Recov on IBNR	10	15	10
Rein Recov on UEP	5	7.5	10
Off Balance Sheet RBC			
Noncontrolled assets	1	2	1
Guarantee for affiliates	2	5	1
Contingent Liabilities	2	5	1
Reserve Risk*			
Homeowner Reserves	19-152	22-176	19-154
Private Auto Reserves	10-80	14-108	13-107
Commercial Auto Reserves	11-88	14-108	14-108
Worker's Comp Reserves	8-60	21-168	6-48
Commercial Multiple Peril Res.	19-152	22-176	19-153
Medical Malpractice Res.	26-208	39-312	26-201
Special Liability Res.	13-100	15-120	13-102
Other Liability Res.	24-192	26-208	24-190
International Reserves	16-128	19-152	16-127
Product Liability Reserves	24-192	39-312	24-192
Health Lines Reserves	15-116	23-180	20-157
Other Lines Reserves	20-156	25-196	20-157
Premium Risk*			
Homeowners NPW	29-260	43-260	43-260
Auto Liability NPW	34-304	35-319	52-304
Worker's Comp NPW	34-303	40-363	50-303
Commercial Multiperil NPW	30-272	39-347	45-272
Medical Malpractice NPW	53-478	79-478	80-478
Special Liabilities NPW	29-266	32-281	44-266
Other Liabilities NPW	38-342	49-441	57-342
International NPW	41-373	43-388	62-373
Product Liabilities NPW	41-365	52-464	61-365
Other Lines NPW	24-220	26-234	27-220

* All numbers are shown for illustrative purposes. Figures actually used in the formula vary annually based on industry experience.

Investment Class		**Description**
Government guaranteed bonds		Guaranteed bonds issued by U.S. and other governments which receive the top rating of state insurance commissioners
Bonds	Class 1	Investment grade bonds rated AAA, AA or A by Moody's or Standard & Poor's or deemed AAA - A equivalent by state insurance regulators
	Class 2	Investment grade bonds with some speculative elements rated BBB or equivalent
	Class 3	Noninvestment grade bonds, rated BB or equivalent
	Class 4	Noninvestment grade bonds, rated B or equivalent
	Class 5	Noninvestment grade bonds, rated CCC, C, C- or equivalent
	Class 6	Noninvestment grade bonds, in or near default
Preferred Stock		
Common Stock		
		Unaffiliated common stock
		Affiliated common stock
Mortgages		
Real Estate		Company occupied and other investment properties
Short-term Investments		All investments whose maturities at the time of acquisition were one year or less
Collateral Loans		Loans made to a company or individual where the underlying security is in the form of bonds, stocks or other marketable securities
Other Invested Assets		Any invested assets that do not fit under the main categories above
Credit Risk		
Agents' Balances		Amounts which have been booked as written and billed to agents
Premium Notes		Loans to policyholders for payments of premiums
Receivable Interest Income		Interest income due but not yet received
Misc. Noninvested Income		Misc. income that is not related to invested assets
Reinsurance Recov. Current		Current receivables from reinsurers for their portion of the recorded losses
30 to 90 Days Overdue		Receivables from reinsurers 30 - 90 days overdue
90 to 180 Days Overdue		Receivables from reinsurers 90 - 180 days overdue
More Than 180 Days Overdue		Receivables from reinsurers more than 180 days overdue
Rein. Recov. on Unpaid Losses		Receivables from reinsurers for unpaid losses
Rein. Recov. on IBNR		Receivables from reinsurers for incurred but not reported losses
Rein. Recov. on UEP		Receivables from reinsurers for unearned premium
Off Balance Sheet Risk		
Noncontrolled Assets		Assets not subject to complete insurer control
Guarantee for Affiliates		Guarantees on behalf of affiliates
Contingent Liabilities		Liabilities that are likely to happen but are not certain

Table 2. Bond Default Rates - potential losses as a percent of bond portfolio

Bond Rating	(1) Moody's 15 Yr Rate (%)	(2) Moody's 12 Yr Rate (%)	(3) Worst Year (%)	(4) 3 Cum. Recession Years (%)	(5) TheStreet.com Ratings 15 Year Rate (%)	(6) Assumed Loss Rate (%)	(7) Losses as % of Holdings (%)	(8) RACR #2 Rate (%)
Aaa	2.80	1.60	0.10	0.30	1.89	50	0.95	1.00
Aa	2.00	1.60	0.20	0.60	2.19	50	1.09	1.00
A	3.30	2.50	0.40	1.20	3.67	55	2.02	1.00
Baa	7.20	5.50	1.10	3.26	8.58	60	5.15	5.00
Ba	20.10	17.90	8.40	23.08	36.47	65	23.71	15.00
B	33.70	32.50	21.60	50.80	62.24	70	43.57	30.00

Comments on Target Capital Percentages

The factors in the RACR calculations can be grouped into five categories: (1) Investment Risks; (2) Credit Risks; (3) Off Balance Sheet Risks; (4) Reserve Risks and (5) Premium Risks. Each of these has numerous subcomponents. The five categories are discussed below along with specific comments on some of the most important subcomponents.

Investment Risks:

Bonds

Target capital percentages for bonds are derived from a model that factors in historical cumulative bond default rates from the last twenty years and the additional loss potential during a prolonged economic decline. The continuance of post-World War II prosperity is by no means certain. Realistic analysis of potential losses must factor in the possibility of a severe economic recession.

Table 2 shows how this was done for each bond rating classification. A 15-year cumulative default rate is used (column 1). These are historical default rates for 1970-1990 for each bond class, taken from Moody's Studies of Loss Potential of Life Insurance Assets.

To factor in the additional loss potential of a severe three-year-long economic decline, we reduced the base to Moody's 12-year rate (column 2), determined the worst single year experience (column 3), spread that experience over three years (column 4) and added the historical 12-year rate to the 3-year projection to derive TheStreet.com Ratings 15-year default rate (column 5). Note: Due to the shrinking base of nondefaulted bonds in each year, column 4 may be somewhat less than three times column 3; and column 5 may be somewhat less than the sum of column 2 and column 4.

The next step was to determine the losses that could be expected from these defaults. This would be equivalent to the capital a company should have to cover those losses. Loss rates were assigned for each bond class (column 6), based on the fact that higher rated issues generally carry less debt and the fact that the debt is also better secured, leading to higher recovery rates upon default.

Column 7 shows losses as a percent of holdings for each bond class. Column 8 shows the target capital percentages that are used in RACR #2 (Table 1, RACR #2 column, Bonds -classes 1 to 6).

Regulations limiting junk bond holdings of insurers to a set percent of assets are a tacit acknowledgement that the maximum reserve requirements used by State Insurance Commissioners (Table 1, NAIC column, Bonds — classes 4, 5 and 6) are inadequate. If the figure adequately represented full loss potential, there would be no need to limit holdings through legislation since an adequate loss reserve would provide sufficient capital to absorb potential losses.

Affiliate Common Stock These stocks are often only "paper" assets, difficult to sell, and not truly available to pay insurance claims. The appropriate value of the stock may also be difficult to determine unless the stock is publicly traded.

The target capital rate on affiliate common stock for RACR #2 can vary between 33% and 100% (Table 1, RACR #2 column, Common stock — Affiliated), depending on the financial strength of the affiliate and the prospects for obtaining capital from the affiliate should the need arise.

Credit Risk This category refers to the financial risk faced if the company cannot collect funds it is owed. These include funds owed to the company by its agents and funds owed to the company by its reinsurers.

Off Balance Sheet Risk A miscellaneous category of risk that is developed from data not found on the company's balance sheet. It includes risks associated with rapid premium growth, unsettled lawsuits against the company, guarantees to affiliates and investment risks such as interest rate swaps.

Reserve Risk The risk that reserve estimates are too low to pay all outstanding claims. Target capital percentages used for each line of business are based on the historical experience of both the company and industry, for that line.

Rather than basing our figures solely on the company's average experience over the last nine years, as is done in the NAIC formula, we factor in the company's worst results over the same period. We believe that this gives a more realistic appraisal of the company's loss potential. Of two companies with identical averages, one may have greater ups and downs than the other. Under the NAIC formula, the companies would have the same target capital, while our formula would require more target capital from the company with the more volatile history.

Target capital requirements have been reduced for each line of business in order to reflect the time value of money. As claims are generally paid months or years after premiums are received, insurers invest those premium funds, accumulating investment income until the claims must be paid. The discount given varies from 9% for private auto liability, a "short-tail" line where claims are paid shortly after receipt of premiums, to 21% for medical malpractice, a "long-tail" line where claims are generally paid many years after receipt of premiums.

Premium Risk The risk that premium levels are not sufficient to pay claims and related expenses. Individual target capital percentages are used for each line of business based on the riskiness of the line and the company's own experience with reserve risk. Target capital requirements are reduced to account for the time value of money, using a technique similar to that used for reserve risk.

Risky Lines of Business and Catastrophic Losses

These include fire, earthquake, multiple peril (including storm damage) and similar personal and commercial property coverages. Even excluding Hurricane Andrew, the insured losses from natural disasters since 1989 have been far greater than in previous decades. Yet, too many insurance companies are basing their risk calculations on the assumption that losses will return to more normal levels. They are not ready for the possibility that the pattern of increasing disasters might be a real, continuing trend.

Also considered high risk lines are medical malpractice, general liability, product liability and other similar liability coverages. Court awards for damages often run into the millions. These settlement amounts can be very difficult to predict. This uncertainty hinders an insurer's ability to accurately assess how much to charge policyholders and how much to set aside to pay claims. Of special concern are large, unexpected liabilities related to environmental damages such as asbestos. Similar risk may lie hidden in coverage for medical equipment and procedures, industrial wastes, carcinogens and other substances found in products previously viewed as benign.

RECENT INDUSTRY FAILURES

2009

Institution	Headquarters	Industry	Date of Failure	At Date of Failure	
				Total Assets ($Mil)	Financial Strength Rating
American Network Ins Co	Pennsylvania	L&H	01/06/09	125.8	D+ (Weak)
Consumer First Ins Co	New Jersey	P&C	04/22/09	10.7	D- (Weak)
Coral Ins Co	Florida	P&C	04/09/09	15.4	E+ (Very Weak)
Escude Life Ins Co	Louisiana	L&H	04/27/09	3.0	E- (Very Weak)
First Commercial Ins Co.	Florida	P&C	07/10/09	87.1	E+ (Very Weak)
First Comm. Transp. & Prop Ins Co.	Florida	P&C	07/10/09	19.6	E+ (Very Weak)
Insurance Corp of New York	New York	P&C	06/29/09	87.3	
NSA Rrg Inc.	Vermont	P&C	03/09/09	23.4	
Penn Treaty Network Am.Ins Co	Pennsylvania	L&H	01/06/09	1037.6	C- (Fair)
Preferred Health	Puerto Rico	HMO	07/30/09	16.2	D- (Weak)
Scottish RE US Inc	Delaware	L&H	01/05/09	2950.6	D (Weak)
Shenandoah Life Ins Co	Virginia	L&H	02/12/09	1735.0	B (Good)
Texas Memorial Life Ins Co	Texas	L&H	06/10/09	3.80	E- (Very Weak)
Universal Life Ins. Co.	Alabama	L&H	04/24/09		E (Very Weak)

2008

Institution	Headquarters	Industry	Date of Failure	At Date of Failure	
				Total Assets ($Mil)	Financial Strength Rating
Americas Health Choice Medical Plans Inc.	Florida	Health	08/06/08	N/A	U
Austin Indemnity Lloyds Ins Co	Texas	P&C	12/29/08	5.5	E+(Very Weak)
Fremont Life Ins Co.	California	L&H	06/05/08	6.1	E+ (Very Weak)
Jordan Funeral and Ins Co, Inc	Alabama	L&H	09/12/08		U
Lincoln Memorial Life Ins Co.	Texas	L&H	05/14/08	124.0	C (Fair)
MD Medicare Choice, Inc.	Florida	HMO	09/29/08	N/A	U

MDNY HealthCare, Inc.	New York	HMO	07/31/08	10.3	E (Very Weak)
Medical Savings Ins Co	Indiana	HMO	12/01/08	43.5	D+ (Weak)
Memorial Service Life Ins Co.	Texas	L&H	05/14/08	23.4	D+ (Weak)
Standard Life Insurance Co	Indiana	L&H	12/18/08	2021.1	C (Fair)

2007

Institution	Headquarters	Industry	Date of Failure	At Date of Failure	
				Total Assets ($Mil)	Financial Strength Rating
Benicorp Insurance Co	Indiana	L&H	06/05/07	53.4	D (Weak)
Colonial Indemnity Ins. Co	New York	P&C	9/6/2007	0	U
Community Health Plan Inc	New York	HMO	08/30/07		U
Lincoln Memorial Life Ins Co	Texas	L&H	10/24/07		C+ (Fair)
Lion Ins. Co	New York	P&C	09/06/07	0.0	U
Memorial Service Life Ins Co	Texas	L&H	10/24/07		D+ (Weak)
Municipal Ins. Co of America	Illinois	L&H	10/24/07	12.6	D (Weak)
National Annuity Co	Utah	L&H	03/23/07		E (Very Weak)
Northwestern National Ins Co of Milwaukee, WI	Wisconsin	P&C	03/08/07		U
Patriot Health Ins Co Inc	New Hampshire	HMO	12/12/07		U
Suncoast Physicians Health Plan, Inc	Florida	HMO	08/10/07	2.1	U
Vanguard Fire & Casualty	Florida	P&C	1/19/2007	47.8	E (Very Weak)
Universal Health Care Ins Co Inc	Florida	HMO	02/21/07	N/A	U

2006

Institution	Headquarters	Industry	Date of Failure	At Date of Failure	
				Total Assets ($Mil)	Financial Strength Rating
Atlantic Preferred	Florida	P&C	05/01/06	63.4	D (Weak)
Booker T Washington Ins	Alabama	L&H	03/02/06	54.3	E (Very Weak)
DoctorCare Inc	Florida	Health	11/20/06	11.4	U
Family Life Ins Co of Am	Texas	L&H	08/24/06	n/a	U
Florida Preferred Prop Ins	Florida	P&C	05/25/06	63.4	E+ (Very Weak)
Florida Select Ins Co	Florida	P&C	06/30/06	38.6	D (Weak)
Hawaiian Ins & Guaranty	Hawaii	P&C	06/30/06	26.4	D (Weak)
Municipal Mutual Ins Co	California	P&C	10/24/06	n/a	E (Very Weak)
NJ Exchange	New Jersey	P&C	07/10/06	3.6	E+ (Very Weak)
Phoenix Fund Inc	No Carolina	P&C	10/17/06	29.0	E (Very Weak)
Security General Life Ins	Oklahoma	L&H	09/29/06	6.2	B- (Good)
Shelby Casualty Ins Co	Illinois	P&C	06/30/06	29.3	D (Weak)
Southern Family Ins Co	Florida	P&C	04/25/06	56.1	D (Weak)
Texas Select Lloyds Ins	Texas	P&C	06/30/06	47.5	D (Weak)
The Shelby Ins Co	Illinois	P&C	06/30/06	29.0	D (Weak)
Ultimed HMO	Michigan	Health	01/25/06	2.7	D- (Weak)
Universal Ins Exchange	Texas	P&C	01/26/06	10.0	D (Weak)
Valor Ins Co	Montana	P&C	08/03/06	3.8	U
Vesta Fire Ins Co	Illinois	P&C	06/30/06	344.1	D (Weak)
Vesta Ins Corp	Illinois	P&C	06/30/06	19.4	D (Weak)

2005

Institution	Headquarters	Industry	Date of Failure	At Date of Failure	
				Total Assets ($Mil)	Financial Strength Rating
Amil Int'l (Texas), Inc	Texas	Health	03/07/05	9.9	E (Very Weak)
Benton Life Ins Co, Inc	Louisiana	L&H	06/23/05	n/a	U
Commercial Mutual Ins	Georgia	P&C	06/15/05	18.7	E (Very Weak)
Consolidated Amer Ins Co	So Carolina	P&C	03/08/05	4.0	D (Weak)
Cornerstone Mutual Ins	Georgia	P&C	06/15/05	28.5	D- (Weak)
Employers Life Ins Corp	So Carolina	L&H	07/24/05	12.1	E- (Very Weak)
Financial Life & Acc Ins	Florida	L&H	04/18/05	10.6	U
Hospitality Mut Capt Ins	Georgia	P&C	08/24/05	4.1	E+ (Very Weak)
MagnaHealth of NY Inc	New York	Health	08/24/05	2.4	D (Weak)
North America Life Ins	Texas	L&H	06/30/05	n/a	E (Very Weak)
Old American Cnty Mutual Fire	Texas	P&C	11/07/05	n/a	E+ (Very Weak)
Omnicare Health Plan	Tennessee	Health	04/21/05	12.3	C+ (Fair)
PrimeGuard Ins Co RRG	Hawaii	P&C	12/19/05	3.3	D- (Weak)
Realm National Ins Co	New York	P&C	06/15/05	31.2	U
Reliant American Ins Co	Texas	P&C	05/06/05	21.5	E- (Very Weak)
Senior Citizens Mutual	Florida	P&C	05/09/05	21.9	C- (Fair)
South Carolina Ins Co	So Carolina	P&C	03/08/05	19.3	E+ (Very Weak)
States General Life Inc Co	Texas	L&H	03/09/05	7.5	D- (Weak)
Texas International Life	Texas	L&H	06/29/05	n/a	E (Very Weak)
Top Flight	Oklahoma	P&C	05/10/05	5.9	E+ (Very Weak)
Union American Ins Co	Florida	P&C	02/09/05	11.0	D (Weak)

2004

Institution	Headquarters	Industry	Date of Failure	At Date of Failure	
				Total Assets ($Mil)	Financial Strength Rating
Acadian Life Ins	Louisiana	L&H	08/31/04	16.0	E- (Very Weak)
American Superior Ins Co	Florida	P&C	09/29/04	13.5	D (Weak)
American Skyline Ins Co	Maryland	P&C	11/30/04	6	E+ (Very Weak)
Assoc Trial Lawyers Asr	Illinois	P&C	10/14/04	1.5	U
Capitol Life Ins Co	Texas	L&H	03/03/04	304.8	D (Weak)
Cascade National Ins Co	Washington	P&C	11/30/04	27.3	D (Weak)
Colorado Western Ins Co	Colorado	P&C	05/27/04	17.2	D- (Weak)
Cumberland Cas & Surety	Florida	P&C	02/26/04	12.1	D (Weak)
Family Health Care Plus	Mississippi	Health	07/15/04	25.3	U
Financial Ins Co	Texas	P&C	05/03/04	10.6	D (Weak)
Foundation Ins Co	S Carolina	P& C	05/17/04	25.5	E (Very Weak)
Hospital Casualty Co	Oklahoma	P&C	03/31/04	6.5	E (Very Weak)
Interboro Mutual Indem	New York	P&C	04/06/04	58.4	E- (Very Weak)
L&H Ins Co of America	Pennsylvania	L&H	07/02/04	47.9	E- (Very Weak)
Mack H Hannah Life Ins	Texas	L&H	07/23/04	n/a	U
Metrowest Health Plan	Texas	Health	06/10/04	7.2	B (Good)
MIIX Insurance Co	New Jersey	P&C	08/27/04	813.0	U
Mutual Fire Ins Co of Carrol Cnty	Maryland	P&C	04/12/04	n/a	D (Weak)
National Health Ins Co	Texas	L&H	03/03/04	873.8	E (Very Weak)
New America Ins Co	Florida	P&C	07/01/04	10.9	C- (Fair)
Physicians Liability Ins	Oklahoma	P&C	03/31/04	1.5	E+ (Very Weak)
Pinnacle Cas Assur Corp	Alabama	P&C	02/02/04	3.4	E (Very Weak)
PrimeHealth of Alabama	Alabama	Health	02/13/04	3.7	E (Very Weak)
State Capital Ins Co	No Carolina	P&C	06/21/04	8.7	D- (Weak)
Statewide Insurance Co	Illinois	P&C	01/06/04	33.1	D- (Weak)
Twin Falls Mutual Ins Co	Idaho	P&C	10/29/04	2.1	D- (Weak)

Glossary

This glossary contains the most important terms used in this publication.

Admitted Assets — The total of all investments and business interests which are acceptable under statutory accounting rules.

Asset/Liability Matching — Management of cash flows so that investments pay interest or mature at just the right time to meet the need for cash to pay claims and expenses.

Average Recession — A recession involving a decline in real GDP which is approximately equivalent to the average of the postwar recessions of 1957-58, 1960, 1970, 1974-75, 1980 and 1981-82. It is assumed, however, that in today's market, the financial losses suffered from a recession of that magnitude would be greater than those experienced in previous decades. (See also "Severe Recession.")

Capital — Strictly speaking, capital refers to funds raised through the sale of common and preferred stock. Mutual companies have capital in the form of retained earnings. In a more general sense, the term capital is commonly used to refer to a company's equity or net worth, that is, the difference between assets and liabilities (i.e., capital and surplus as shown on the balance sheet).

Capital Resources — The sum of various resources which serve as a capital cushion to losses, including capital and surplus.

Cash and Demand Deposits — Includes cash on hand and on deposit. A negative figure indicates that the company has more checks outstanding than current funds to cover those checks. This is not an unusual situation for an insurance company.

Common and Preferred Stocks — See "Stocks".

Direct Premiums Written — Premiums derived from policies issued directly by the company. This figure excludes the impact of reinsurance.

Financial Strength Rating — TheStreet.com Financial Strength Ratings grade insurers on a scale from A (Excellent) to F (Failed). Ratings for property and casualty insurers are based on five major factors: liquidity, reserve adequacy, capitalization, profitability, and stability of operations.

Five-Year Profitability Index — See "Profitability Index".

Government Securities — Securities issued and/or guaranteed by U.S. and foreign governments which are rated as highest quality (class 1) by state insurance commissioners. Included in this category are bonds issued by governmental agencies and guaranteed with the full faith and credit of the government. Regardless of the issuing entity, they are viewed as being relatively safer than the other investment categories.

Interest Rate Risk
The risk that, due to changes in interest rates, investment income will not meet the needs of policy commitments. This risk can be reduced by effective asset/liability matching.

Invested Assets
The total size of the firm's investment portfolio.

Investments in Affiliates
Includes bonds, preferred stocks and common stocks, as well as other vehicles which many insurance companies use to invest in—and establish a corporate link with—affiliated companies.

Line of Business
Types of insurance coverage such as fire, inland marine, group accident and health, auto physical damage and auto liability. Statutory accounting uses over 30 different lines of business. A particular insurer may write coverage in any or all of these lines.

Liquidity Index
An index, expressed on a scale of zero to ten, with seven or higher considered excellent, that measures a company's ability to raise the necessary cash to settle claims. It is possible for a company to have the resources to pay claims on paper, but be unable to raise the cash. This can occur when a company is owed a great deal of money by its agents or reinsurers, or when it cannot sell its investments at the anticipated price.

Our liquidity tests examine how the company might fare under various cash flow scenarios.

Long/Short-Tail Lines
Time periods over which claims are paid out. For example, auto physical damage is considered a short-tail line, since claims are generally paid within one year of an accident. On the other hand, medical malpractice is considered a long-tail line as claims are typically paid five years or more after the occurrence of the incident giving rise to the claim.

For the insurer, the risks associated with long-tail lines are greater than with short-tail lines because the period of uncertainty in which unexpected claims can arise is longer.

Moderate Loss Scenario
Possible future events that would result in loss levels comparable to those experienced in recent history. (Compare with "Severe Loss Scenario.")

Net Premiums Written
The dollar volume of premiums retained by the company. This figure is equal to direct premiums written, plus reinsurance assumed, less reinsurance ceded to other companies.

Noninvestment Grade Bonds
Low-rated issues, commonly known as "junk bonds," which carry a high risk as defined by the state insurance commissioners. These include bond classes 3 - 6.

Other Investments	Items not included in any of the other categories, such as premium notes, collateral loans, short-term investments and other miscellaneous items.
Premium Risk	The risk that, for a particular group of policies, premiums will not be sufficient to meet the level of claims and related expenses.
Profitability Index	An index, expressed on a scale of zero to ten, with seven or higher considered excellent, that measures the soundness of the company's operations and the contribution of profits to the company's fiscal strength. The Profitability Index is a composite of five factors: (1) gain or loss on underwriting (core insurance business); (2) gain or loss on overall operations; (3) consistency of operating results; (4) impact of operating results on surplus and (5) expenses in relation to industry averages for the types of policies that the company offers.
Real Estate	Direct real estate investments, including property (a) occupied by the company; (b) acquired through foreclosure of a mortgage and (c) purchased as an investment.
Reinsurance Assumed	Insurance risk acquired by taking on partial or full responsibility for claims on policies written by other companies. (See "Reinsurance Ceded.")
Reinsurance Ceded	Insurance risk sold to another company. When there is a claim on a reinsured policy, the original company generally pays the claim and then is reimbursed by its reinsurer.
Reserve Adequacy Index	An index, expressed on a scale of zero to ten with seven or higher considered excellent, that measures the adequacy of the company's reserves over the last five years. Companies that have a history of inadequate reserves will receive a low score. Reserves are company estimates of unsettled claims in each year, including both claims that have been received but not yet settled, as well as claims that the company expects to receive. A company that underestimates its claims inflates profits and capital. Additionally, chronically deficient reserves call into question the company's ability to manage its policy risk effectively.
Risk-Adjusted Capital	The capital resources that would be needed to deal with unexpected claims or other adverse developments (same as "Target Capital").
Risk-Adjusted Capital Ratio #1	The capital resources which a company currently has, expressed as a ratio, to the resources that would be needed to deal with a moderate loss scenario. (See "Moderate Loss Scenario.")
Risk-Adjusted Capital Ratio #2	The capital resources which a company currently has, expressed as a ratio, to the resources that would be needed to

deal with a severe loss scenario. (See "Severe Loss Scenario.")

Severe Loss Scenario Possible future events that could result in loss levels that are somewhat higher than recent experience. These levels are developed from examination of current trends. (Compare with "Moderate Loss Scenario.")

Severe Recession A prolonged economic slowdown in which the single worst year of the postwar period is extended for a period of three years. (See also "Average Recession.")

Short-Tail Lines See "Long/Short-Tail Lines".

Stability Index An index, measured on a scale of zero to ten, integrating a wide variety of factors that reflect the company's stability and diversification of risk.

State of Domicile Although most insurance companies are licensed to do business in many states, they have only one state of domicile. This is the state which has primary regulatory responsibility for the company. Use the state of domicile to make absolutely sure that you have the correct company. Bear in mind, however, that this need not be the state where the company's main offices are located.

State Guaranty Funds Funds that are designed to raise cash from existing insurance carriers to cover policy claims of bankrupt insurance companies.

Stocks Common and preferred equities, including stocks in affiliates.

Surplus Accumulated funds from prior years' profits (retained earnings) plus additional amounts paid-in by a parent or other corporation. The term "surplus" is also sometimes used broadly to include capital such as common stock.

Target Capital See "Risk-Adjusted Capital."

Total Assets Total admitted assets, including investments and other business assets. (See "Admitted Assets.")

TheStreet.com Ratings'

THESTREET.COM RATINGS' FINANCIAL STRENGTH GUIDES

TheStreet.com Ratings' comprehensive industry-wide guides provide the most accurate, complete source of financial strength ratings on more than 15,000 financial institutions including banks and insurance companies.

Issued Quarterly. Price: $499 + $19.95 s/h for 4 quarterly issues, or $249 + $8.95 s/h for a single edition.

Guide to Life and Annuity Insurers covers more than 1,500 U.S. life, health and annuity insurers.

Guide to Property and Casualty Insurers covers more than 2,500 property and casualty insurers in the U.S.

Guide to Health Insurers is the only source covering more than 1,200 U.S. health insurers including all Blue Cross/Blue Shield plans.

Guide to Banks and Thrifts covers more than 9,000 banks and thrifts in the U.S.

THESTREET.COM RATINGS' INVESTMENT GUIDES

TheStreet.com Ratings' comprehensive investment guides provide the most accurate, complete information for more than 20,000 investment choices.

Issued Quarterly. Price: $499 + $19.95 s/h for 4 quarterly issues, or $249 + $8.95 s/h for a single edition.

Ultimate Guided Tour of Stock Investing is a must-have, easy-to-understand guide presented in a friendly, fun format complete with our "Wise Guide" who leads you on an informative safari through the stock market jungle. Complete with how-to information on stock investing, useful worksheets, examples on common topics such as diversification, TheStreet.com Performance and Risk Ratings, and much more! This guide will help you learn to invest and successfully manage your stock portfolio. Covers every stock on the American Stock Exchange, New York Stock Exchange, and the NASDAQ.

Guide to Stock Mutual Funds covers more than 7,000 equity mutual funds, including balanced funds, international funds, and individual sector funds.

Guide to Bond and Money Market Mutual Funds covers more than 4,200 fixed-income mutual funds, including government bond funds, municipal bond funds, and corporate bond funds.

Guide to Exchange-Traded Funds covers more than 600 closed-end mutual funds, including growth funds, sector funds, international funds, municipal bond funds and other closed-end funds.

Guide to Common Stocks covers stocks on the American Stock Exchange, New York Stock Exchange, and the NASDAQ, plus more.

To Place your Print Guide Order

➊ Call Grey House Publishing at (800) 562-2139

➋ Order Online at www.greyhouse.com

THESTREET.COM RATINGS' REPORTS AND SERVICES

See pricing below for each report and service.

Ratings Online — An on-line summary covering an individual company's TheStreet.com Financial Strength Rating or an investment's unique TheStreet.com Investment Rating with the factors contributing to that rating; available 24 hours a day by visiting www.thestreet.com/tscratings/.

Unlimited Ratings Research — The ultimate research tool providing fast, easy online access to the very latest TheStreet.com Financial Strength Ratings and Investment Ratings. Price: $559 per industry.

THESTREET.COM RATINGS' CUSTOM REPORTS

TheStreet.com Ratings is pleased to offer two customized options for receiving our data. Each taps into our vast data repositories and is designed to provide exactly the data you need. Choose from a variety of industries, companies, data variables, and delivery formats including print, Excel, SQL, Text or Access.

Customized Reports - get right to the heart of your company's research and data needs with a report customized with just the data you need.

Complete Database Download - we design and deliver the database; you're then free to sort it, recalculate it, and format your results to suit your specific needs.

To Place your Reports Order

➊ Call TheStreet.com at (800) 289-9222

➋ Order Online at www.thestreet.com/ratings

TheStreet.com Ratings Guide to Health Insurers

TheStreet.com Ratings Guide to Health Insurers is the first and only source to cover the financial stability of the nation's health care system, rating the financial safety of more than 6,000 health insurance providers, health maintenance organizations (HMOs) and all of the Blue Cross Blue Shield plans – updated quarterly to ensure the most accurate information. The Guide also provides a complete listing of all the major health insurers, including all Long-Term Care and Medigap insurers. Our *Guide to Health Insurers* includes comprehensive, timely coverage on the financial stability of HMOs and health insurers; the most accurate insurance company ratings available–the same quality ratings heralded by the U.S. General Accounting Office; separate listings for those companies offering Medigap and long-term care policies; the number of serious consumer complaints filed against most HMOs so you can see who is actually providing the best (or worst) service and more. The easy-to-use layout gives you a one-line summary analysis for each company that we track, followed by an in-depth, detailed analysis of all HMOs and the largest health insurers. The guide also includes a list of TheStreet.com Ratings Recommended Companies with information on how to contact them, and the reasoning behind any rating upgrades or downgrades.

"With 20 years behind its insurance-advocacy research [the rating guide] continues to offer a wealth of information that helps consumers weigh their healthcare options now and in the future." -Today's Librarian

Issues published quarterly, Softcover, 550 pages, $499.00 for four quarterly issues, $249.00 for a single issue

TheStreet.com Ratings Guide to Life & Annuity Insurers

TheStreet.com Safety Ratings are the most reliable source for evaluating an insurer's financial solvency risk. Consequently, policy-holders have come to rely on TheStreet.com's flagship publication, *TheStreet.com Ratings Guide to Life & Annuity Insurers*, to help them identify the safest companies to do business with. Each easy-to-use edition delivers TheStreet.com's independent ratings and analyses on more than 1,100 insurers, updated every quarter. Plus, your patrons will find a complete list of TheStreet.com Recommended Companies, including contact information, and the reasoning behind any rating upgrades or downgrades. This guide is perfect for those who are considering the purchase of a life insurance policy, placing money in an annuity, or advising clients about insurance and annuities. A life or health insurance policy or annuity is only as secure as the insurance company issuing it. Therefore, make sure your patrons have what they need to periodically monitor the financial condition of the companies with whom they have an investment. The TheStreet.com Ratings product line is designed to help them in their evaluations.

"Weiss has an excellent reputation and this title is held by hundreds of libraries. This guide is recommended for public and academic libraries." -ARBA

Issues published quarterly, Softcover, 360 pages, $499.00 for four quarterly issues, $249.00 for a single issue

TheStreet.com Ratings Guide to Property & Casualty Insurers

TheStreet.com Ratings Guide to Property and Casualty Insurers provides the most extensive coverage of insurers writing policies, helping consumers and businesses avoid financial headaches. Updated quarterly, this easy-to-use publication delivers the independent, unbiased TheStreet.com Safety Ratings and supporting analyses on more than 2,800 U.S. insurance companies, offering auto & homeowners insurance, business insurance, worker's compensation insurance, product liability insurance, medical malpractice and other professional liability insurance. Each edition includes a list of TheStreet.com Recommended Companies by type of insurance, including a contact number, plus helpful information about the coverage provided by the State Guarantee Associations.

"In contrast to the other major insurance rating agencies...Weiss does not have a financial relationship worth the companies it rates. A GAO study found that Weiss identified financial vulnerability earlier than the other rating agencies." -ARBA

Issues published quarterly, Softcover, 455 pages, $499.00 for four quarterly issues, $249.00 for a single issue

TheStreet.com Ratings Consumer Box Set

Deliver the critical information your patrons need to safeguard their personal finances with *TheStreet.com Ratings' Consumer Guide Box Set*. Each of the eight guides is packed with accurate, unbiased information and recommendations to help your patrons make sound financial decisions. TheStreet.com Ratings Consumer Guide Box Set provides your patrons with easy to understand guidance on important personal finance topics, including: *Consumer Guide to Variable Annuities, Consumer Guide to Medicare Supplement Insurance, Consumer Guide to Elder Care Choices, Consumer Guide to Automobile Insurance, Consumer Guide to Long-Term Care Insurance, Consumer Guide to Homeowners Insurance, Consumer Guide to Term Life Insurance, and Consumer Guide to Medicare Prescription Drug Coverage*. Each guide provides an easy-to-read overview of the topic, what to look out for when selecting a company or insurance plan to do business with, who are the recommended companies to work with and how to navigate through these often-times difficult decisions. Custom worksheets and step-by-step directions make these resources accessible to all types of users. Packaged in a handy custom display box, these helpful guides will prove to be a much-used addition to any reference collection.

Issues published twice per year, Softcover, 600 pages, $499.00 for two biennial issues

TheStreet.com Ratings Guide to Stock Mutual Funds

TheStreet.com Ratings Guide to Stock Mutual Funds offers ratings and analyses on more than 8,800 equity mutual funds – more than any other publication. The exclusive TheStreet.com Investment Ratings combine an objective evaluation of each fund's performance and risk to provide a single, user-friendly, composite rating, giving your patrons a better handle on a mutual fund's risk-adjusted performance. Each edition identifies the top-performing mutual funds based on risk category, type of fund, and overall risk-adjusted performance. TheStreet.com's unique investment rating system makes it easy to see exactly which stocks are on the rise and which ones should be avoided. For those investors looking to tailor their mutual fund selections based on age, income, and tolerance for risk, we've also assigned two component ratings to each fund: a performance rating and a risk rating. With these, you can identify those funds that are best suited to meet your - or your client's – individual needs and goals. Plus, we include a handy Risk Profile Quiz to help you assess your personal tolerance for risk. So whether you're an investing novice or professional, the *Guide to Stock Mutual Funds* gives you everything you need to find a mutual fund that is right for you.

"There is tremendous need for information such as that provided by this Weiss publication. This reasonably priced guide is recommended for public and academic libraries serving investors." -ARBA

Issues published quarterly, Softcover, 655 pages, $499 for four quarterly issues, $249 for a single issue

TheStreet.com Ratings Guide to Exchange-Traded Funds

TheStreet.com Ratings editors analyze hundreds of mutual funds each quarter, condensing all of the available data into a single composite opinion of each fund's risk-adjusted performance. The intuitive, consumer-friendly ratings allow investors to instantly identify those funds that have historically done well and those that have under-performed the market. Each quarterly edition identifies the top-performing exchange-traded funds based on risk category, type of fund, and overall risk-adjusted performance. The rating scale, A through F, gives you a better handle on an exchange-traded fund's risk-adjusted performance. Other features include Top & Bottom 200 Exchange-Traded Funds; Performance and Risk: 100 Best and Worst Exchange- Traded Funds; Investor Profile Quiz; Performance Benchmarks and Fund Type Descriptions. With the growing popularity of mutual fund investing, consumers need a reliable source to help them track and evaluate the performance of their mutual fund holdings. Plus, they need a way of identifying and monitoring other funds as potential new investments. Unfortunately, the hundreds of performance and risk measures available, multiplied by the vast number of mutual fund investments on the market today, can make this a daunting task for even the most sophisticated investor. This Guide will serve as a useful tool for both the first-time and seasoned investor.

Editions published quarterly, Softcover, 440 pages, $499.00 for four quarterly issues, $249.00 for a single issue

TheStreet.com Ratings Guide to Bond & Money Market Mutual Funds

TheStreet.com Ratings Guide to Bond & Money Market Mutual Funds has everything your patrons need to easily identify the top-performing fixed income funds on the market today. Each quarterly edition contains TheStreet.com's independent ratings and analyses on more than 4,600 fixed income funds – more than any other publication, including corporate bond funds, high-yield bond funds, municipal bond funds, mortgage security funds, money market funds, global bond funds and government bond funds. In addition, the fund's risk rating is combined with its three-year performance rating to get an overall picture of the fund's risk-adjusted performance. The resulting TheStreet.com Investment Rating gives a single, user-friendly, objective evaluation that makes it easy to compare one fund to another and select the right fund based on the level of risk tolerance. Most investors think of fixed income mutual funds as "safe" investments. That's not always the case, however, depending on the credit risk, interest rate risk, and prepayment risk of the securities owned by the fund. TheStreet.com Ratings assesses each of these risks and assigns each fund a risk rating to help investors quickly evaluate the fund's risk component. Plus, we include a handy Risk Profile Quiz to help you assess your personal tolerance for risk. So whether you're an investing novice or professional, the *Guide to Bond and Money Market Mutual Funds* gives you everything you need to find a mutual fund that is right for you.

"Comprehensive... It is easy to use and consumer-oriented, and can be recommended for larger public and academic libraries." -ARBA

Issues published quarterly, Softcover, 470 pages, $499.00 for four quarterly issues, $249.00 for a single issue

TheStreet.com Ratings Guide to Banks & Thrifts

Updated quarterly, for the most up-to-date information, *TheStreet.com Ratings Guide to Banks and Thrifts* offers accurate, intuitive safety ratings your patrons can trust; supporting ratios and analyses that show an institution's strong & weak points; identification of the TheStreet.com Recommended Companies with branches in your area; a complete list of institutions receiving upgrades/downgrades; and comprehensive coverage of every bank and thrift in the nation – more than 9,000. TheStreet.com Safety Ratings are then based on the analysts' review of publicly available information collected by the federal banking regulators. The easy-to-use layout gives you: the institution's TheStreet.com Safety Rating for the last 3 years; the five key indexes used to evaluate each institution; along with the primary ratios and statistics used in determining the company's rating. *TheStreet.com Ratings Guide to Banks & Thrifts* will be a must for individuals who are concerned about the safety of their CD or savings account; need to be sure that an existing line of credit will be there when they need it; or simply want to avoid the hassles of dealing with a failing or troubled institution.

"Large public and academic libraries most definitely need to acquire the work. Likewise, special libraries in large corporations will find this title indispensable." -ARBA

Issues published quarterly, Softcover, 370 pages, $499.00 for four quarterly issues, $249.00 for a single issue

TheStreet.com Ratings Guide to Common Stocks

TheStreet.com Ratings Guide to Common Stocks gives your patrons reliable insight into the risk-adjusted performance of common stocks listed on the NYSE, AMEX, and Nasdaq – over 5,800 stocks in all – more than any other publication. TheStreet.com's unique investment rating system makes it easy to see exactly which stocks are on the rise and which ones should be avoided. In addition, your patrons also get supporting analysis showing growth trends, profitability, debt levels, valuation levels, the top-rated stocks within each industry, and more. Plus, each stock is ranked with the easy-to-use buy-hold-sell equivalents commonly used by Wall Street. Whether they're selecting their own investments or checking up on a broker's recommendation, TheStreet.com Ratings can help them in their evaluations.

"Users... will find the information succinct and the explanations readable, easy to understand, and helpful to a novice." -Library Journal

Issues published quarterly, Softcover, 440 pages, $499.00 for four quarterly issues, $249.00 for a single issue

TheStreet.com Ratings Ultimate Guided Tour of Stock Investing

This important reference guide from TheStreet.com Ratings is just what librarians around the country have asked for: a step-by-step introduction to stock investing for the beginning to intermediate investor. This easy-to-navigate guide explores the basics of stock investing and includes the intuitive TheStreet.com Investment Rating on more than 5,800 stocks, complete with real-world investing information that can be put to use immediately with stocks that fit the concepts discussed in the guide; informative charts, graphs and worksheets; easy-to-understand explanations on topics like P/E, compound interest, marked indices, diversifications, brokers, and much more; along with financial safety ratings for every stock on the NYSE, American Stock Exchange and the Nasdaq. This consumer-friendly guide offers complete how-to information on stock investing that can be put to use right away; a friendly format complete with our "Wise Guide" who leads the reader on a safari to learn about the investing jungle; helpful charts, graphs and simple worksheets; the intuitive TheStreet.com Investment rating on over 6,000 stocks — every stock found on the NYSE, American Stock Exchange and the NASDAQ; and much more.

"Provides investors with an alternative to stock broker recommendations, which recently have been tarnished by conflicts of interest. In summary, the guide serves as a welcome addition for all public library collections." -ARBA

Issues published quarterly, Softcover, 370 pages, $499.00 for four quarterly issues, $249.00 for a single issue

TheStreet.com Ratings' Reports & Services

- Ratings Online — An on-line summary covering an individual company's TheStreet.com Financial Strength Rating or an investment's unique TheStreet.com Investment Rating with the factors contributing to that rating; available 24 hours a day by visiting www.thestreet.com/tscratings or calling (800) 289-9222.
- Unlimited Ratings Research — The ultimate research tool providing fast, easy online access to the very latest TheStreet.com Financial Strength Ratings and Investment Ratings. Price: $559 per industry.

Contact TheStreet.com for more information about Reports & Services at www.thestreet.com/tscratings or call (800) 289-9222

TheStreet.com Ratings' Custom Reports

TheStreet.com Ratings is pleased to offer two customized options for receiving ratings data. Each taps into TheStreet.com's vast data repositories and is designed to provide exactly the data you need. Choose from a variety of industries, companies, data variables, and delivery formats including print, Excel, SQL, Text or Access.

- Customized Reports - get right to the heart of your company's research and data needs with a report customized to your specifications.
- Complete Database Download – TheStreet.com will design and deliver the database; from there you can sort it, recalculate it, and format your results to suit your specific needs.

Contact TheStreet.com for more information about Reports & Services at www.thestreet.com/tscratings or call (800) 289-9222

The Directory of Business Information Resources, 2009

With 100% verification, over 1,000 new listings and more than 12,000 updates, *The Directory of Business Information Resources* is the most up-to-date source for contacts in over 98 business areas – from advertising and agriculture to utilities and wholesalers. This carefully researched volume details: the Associations representing each industry; the Newsletters that keep members current; the Magazines and Journals - with their "Special Issues" - that are important to the trade, the Conventions that are "must attends," Databases, Directories and Industry Web Sites that provide access to must-have marketing resources. Includes contact names, phone & fax numbers, web sites and e-mail addresses. This one-volume resource is a gold mine of information and would be a welcome addition to any reference collection.

"This is a most useful and easy-to-use addition to any researcher's library." –The Information Professionals Institute

Softcover ISBN 978-1-59237-399-4, 2,500 pages, $195.00 | Online Database: http://gold.greyhouse.com Call (800) 562-2139 for quote

Hudson's Washington News Media Contacts Directory, 2009

With 100% verification of data, *Hudson's Washington News Media Contacts Directory* is the most accurate, most up-to-date source for media contacts in our nation's capital. With the largest concentration of news media in the world, having access to Washington's news media will get your message heard by these key media outlets. Published for over 40 years, Hudson's Washington News Media Contacts Directory brings you immediate access to: News Services & Newspapers, News Service Syndicates, DC Newspapers, Foreign Newspapers, Radio & TV, Magazines & Newsletters, and Freelance Writers & Photographers. The easy-to-read entries include contact names, phone & fax numbers, web sites and e-mail and more. For easy navigation, Hudson's Washington News Media Contacts Directory contains two indexes: Entry Index and Executive Index. This kind of comprehensive and up-to-date information would cost thousands of dollars to replicate or countless hours of searching to find. Don't miss this opportunity to have this important resource in your collection, and start saving time and money today. Hudson's Washington News Media Contacts Directory is the perfect research tool for Public Relations, Marketing, Networking and so much more. This resource is a gold mine of information and would be a welcome addition to any reference collection.

Softcover ISBN 978-1-59237-407-6, 800 pages, $289.00 | Online Database: http://gold.greyhouse.com Call (800) 562-2139 for quote

Nations of the World, 2009 A Political, Economic and Business Handbook

This completely revised edition covers all the nations of the world in an easy-to-use, single volume. Each nation is profiled in a single chapter that includes Key Facts, Political & Economic Issues, a Country Profile and Business Information. In this fast-changing world, it is extremely important to make sure that the most up-to-date information is included in your reference collection. This edition is just the answer. Each of the 200+ country chapters have been carefully reviewed by a political expert to make sure that the text reflects the most current information on Politics, Travel Advisories, Economics and more. You'll find such vital information as a Country Map, Population Characteristics, Inflation, Agricultural Production, Foreign Debt, Political History, Foreign Policy, Regional Insecurity, Economics, Trade & Tourism, Historical Profile, Political Systems, Ethnicity, Languages, Media, Climate, Hotels, Chambers of Commerce, Banking, Travel Information and more. Five Regional Chapters follow the main text and include a Regional Map, an Introductory Article, Key Indicators and Currencies for the Region. As an added bonus, an all-inclusive CD-ROM is available as a companion to the printed text. Noted for its sophisticated, up-to-date and reliable compilation of political, economic and business information, this brand new edition will be an important acquisition to any public, academic or special library reference collection.

"A useful addition to both general reference collections and business collections." –RUSQ

Softcover ISBN 978-1-59237-273-7, 1,700 pages, $180.00

The Directory of Venture Capital & Private Equity Firms, 2009

This edition has been extensively updated and broadly expanded to offer direct access to over 2,800 Domestic and International Venture Capital Firms, including address, phone & fax numbers, e-mail addresses and web sites for both primary and branch locations. Entries include details on the firm's Mission Statement, Industry Group Preferences, Geographic Preferences, Average and Minimum Investments and Investment Criteria. You'll also find details that are available nowhere else, including the Firm's Portfolio Companies and extensive information on each of the firm's Managing Partners, such as Education, Professional Background and Directorships held, along with the Partner's E-mail Address. *The Directory of Venture Capital & Private Equity Firms* offers five important indexes: Geographic Index, Executive Name Index, Portfolio Company Index, Industry Preference Index and College & University Index. With its comprehensive coverage and detailed, extensive information on each company, The Directory of Venture Capital & Private Equity Firms is an important addition to any finance collection.

"The sheer number of listings, the descriptive information and the outstanding indexing make this directory a better value than ...Pratt's Guide to Venture Capital Sources. Recommended for business collections in large public, academic and business libraries." –Choice

Softcover ISBN 978-1-59237-398-7, 1,300 pages, $565/$450 Lib | Online DB: http://gold.greyhouse.com Call (800) 562-2139 for quote

The Encyclopedia of Emerging Industries

*Published under an exclusive license from the Gale Group, Inc.
The fifth edition of the *Encyclopedia of Emerging Industries* details the inception, emergence, and current status of nearly 120 flourishing U.S. industries and industry segments. These focused essays unearth for users a wealth of relevant, current, factual data previously accessible only through a diverse variety of sources. This volume provides broad-based, highly-readable, industry information under such headings as Industry Snapshot, Organization & Structure, Background & Development, Industry Leaders, Current Conditions, America and the World, Pioneers, and Research & Technology. Essays in this new edition, arranged alphabetically for easy use, have been completely revised, with updated statistics and the most current information on industry trends and developments. In addition, there are new essays on some of the most interesting and influential new business fields, including Application Service Providers, Concierge Services, Entrepreneurial Training, Fuel Cells, Logistics Outsourcing Services, Pharmacogenomics, and Tissue Engineering. Two indexes, General and Industry, provide immediate access to this wealth of information. Plus, two conversion tables for SIC and NAICS codes, along with Suggested Further Readings, are provided to aid the user. *The Encyclopedia of Emerging Industries* pinpoints emerging industries while they are still in the spotlight. This important resource will be an important acquisition to any business reference collection.

"This well-designed source…should become another standard business source, nicely complementing Standard & Poor's Industry Surveys. It contains more information on each industry than Hoover's Handbook of Emerging Companies, is broader in scope than The Almanac of American Employers 1998-1999, but is less expansive than the Encyclopedia of Careers & Vocational Guidance. Highly recommended for all academic libraries and specialized business collections." –Library Journal

Hardcover ISBN 978-1-59237-242-3, 1,400 pages, $495.00

Encyclopedia of American Industries

*Published under an exclusive license from the Gale Group, Inc.
The Encyclopedia of American Industries is a major business reference tool that provides detailed, comprehensive information on a wide range of industries in every realm of American business. A two volume set, Volume I provides separate coverage of nearly 500 manufacturing industries, while Volume II presents nearly 600 essays covering the vast array of services and other non-manufacturing industries in the United States. Combined, these two volumes provide individual essays on every industry recognized by the U.S. Standard Industrial Classification (SIC) system. Both volumes are arranged numerically by SIC code, for easy use. Additionally, each entry includes the corresponding NAICS code(s). The *Encyclopedia's* business coverage includes information on historical events of consequence, as well as current trends and statistics. Essays include an Industry Snapshot, Organization & Structure, Background & Development, Current Conditions, Industry Leaders, Workforce, America and the World, Research & Technology along with Suggested Further Readings. Both SIC and NAICS code conversion tables and an all-encompassing Subject Index, with cross-references, complete the text. With its detailed, comprehensive information on a wide range of industries, this resource will be an important tool for both the industry newcomer and the seasoned professional.

"Encyclopedia of American Industries contains detailed, signed essays on virtually every industry in contemporary society. ... Highly recommended for all but the smallest libraries." -American Reference Books Annual

Two Volumes, Hardcover ISBN 978-1-59237-244-7, 3,000 pages, $650.00

Encyclopedia of Global Industries

*Published under an exclusive license from the Gale Group, Inc.
This fourth edition of the acclaimed *Encyclopedia of Global Industries* presents a thoroughly revised and expanded look at more than 125 business sectors of global significance. Detailed, insightful articles discuss the origins, development, trends, key statistics and current international character of the world's most lucrative, dynamic and widely researched industries – including hundreds of profiles of leading international corporations. Beginning researchers will gain from this book a solid understanding of how each industry operates and which countries and companies are significant participants, while experienced researchers will glean current and historical figures for comparison and analysis. The industries profiled in previous editions have been updated, and in some cases, expanded to reflect recent industry trends. Additionally, this edition provides both SIC and NAICS codes for all industries profiled. As in the original volumes, *The Encyclopedia of Global Industries* offers thorough studies of some of the biggest and most frequently researched industry sectors, including Aircraft, Biotechnology, Computers, Internet Services, Motor Vehicles, Pharmaceuticals, Semiconductors, Software and Telecommunications. An SIC and NAICS conversion table and an all-encompassing Subject Index, with cross-references, are provided to ensure easy access to this wealth of information. These and many others make the *Encyclopedia of Global Industries* the authoritative reference for studies of international industries.

"Provides detailed coverage of the history, development, and current status of 115 of "the world's most lucrative and high-profile industries." It far surpasses the Department of Commerce's U.S. Global Trade Outlook 1995-2000 (GPO, 1995) in scope and coverage. Recommended for comprehensive public and academic library business collections." -Booklist

Hardcover ISBN 978-1-59237-243-0, 1,400 pages, $495.00

The Directory of Mail Order Catalogs, 2009

Published since 1981, *The Directory of Mail Order Catalogs* is the premier source of information on the mail order catalog industry. It is the source that business professionals and librarians have come to rely on for the thousands of catalog companies in the US. Since the 2007 edition, *The Directory of Mail Order Catalogs* has been combined with its companion volume, *The Directory of Business to Business Catalogs*, to offer all 13,000 catalog companies in one easy-to-use volume. Section I: Consumer Catalogs, covers over 9,000 consumer catalog companies in 44 different product chapters from Animals to Toys & Games. Section II: Business to Business Catalogs, details 5,000 business catalogs, everything from computers to laboratory supplies, building construction and much more. Listings contain detailed contact information including mailing address, phone & fax numbers, web sites, e-mail addresses and key contacts along with important business details such as product descriptions, employee size, years in business, sales volume, catalog size, number of catalogs mailed and more. *The Directory of Mail Order Catalogs*, now with its expanded business to business catalogs, is the largest and most comprehensive resource covering this billion-dollar industry. It is the standard in its field. This important resource is a useful tool for entrepreneurs searching for catalogs to pick up their product, vendors looking to expand their customer base in the catalog industry, market researchers, small businesses investigating new supply vendors, along with the library patron who is exploring the available catalogs in their areas of interest.

"This is a godsend for those looking for information." –Reference Book Review

Softcover ISBN 978-1-59237-396-3, 1,700 pages, $350/$250 Lib | Online DB: http://gold.greyhouse.com Call (800) 562-2139 for quote

Sports Market Place Directory, 2009

For over 20 years, this comprehensive, up-to-date directory has offered direct access to the Who, What, When & Where of the Sports Industry. With over 20,000 updates and enhancements, the *Sports Market Place Directory* is the most detailed, comprehensive and current sports business reference source available. In 1,800 information-packed pages, *Sports Market Place Directory* profiles contact information and key executives for: Single Sport Organizations, Professional Leagues, Multi-Sport Organizations, Disabled Sports, High School & Youth Sports, Military Sports, Olympic Organizations, Media, Sponsors, Sponsorship & Marketing Event Agencies, Event & Meeting Calendars, Professional Services, College Sports, Manufacturers & Retailers, Facilities and much more. The Sports Market Place Directory provides organization's contact information with detailed descriptions including: Key Contacts, physical, mailing, email and web addresses plus phone and fax numbers. *Sports Market Place Directory* provides a one-stop resources for this billion-dollar industry. This will be an important resource for large public libraries, university libraries, university athletic programs, career services or job placement organizations, and is a must for anyone doing research on or marketing to the US and Canadian sports industry.

"Grey House is the new publisher and has produced an excellent edition...highly recommended for public libraries and academic libraries with sports management programs or strong interest in athletics." -Booklist

Softcover ISBN 978-1-59237-418-2, 1,800 pages, $225.00 | Online Database: http://gold.greyhouse.com Call (800) 562-2139 for quote

Food and Beverage Market Place, 2009

Food and Beverage Market Place is bigger and better than ever with thousands of new companies, thousands of updates to existing companies and two revised and enhanced product category indexes. This comprehensive directory profiles over 18,000 Food & Beverage Manufacturers, 12,000 Equipment & Supply Companies, 2,200 Transportation & Warehouse Companies, 2,000 Brokers & Wholesalers, 8,000 Importers & Exporters, 900 Industry Resources and hundreds of Mail Order Catalogs. Listings include detailed Contact Information, Sales Volumes, Key Contacts, Brand & Product Information, Packaging Details and much more. *Food and Beverage Market Place* is available as a three-volume printed set, a subscription-based Online Database via the Internet, on CD-ROM, as well as mailing lists and a licensable database.

"An essential purchase for those in the food industry but will also be useful in public libraries where needed. Much of the information will be difficult and time consuming to locate without this handy three-volume ready-reference source." –ARBA

3 Vol Set, Softcover ISBN 978-1-59237-361-1, 8,500 pages, $595 | Online DB: http://gold.greyhouse.com Call (800) 562-2139 for quote

The Grey House Performing Arts Directory, 2009

The Grey House Performing Arts Directory is the most comprehensive resource covering the Performing Arts. This important directory provides current information on over 8,500 Dance Companies, Instrumental Music Programs, Opera Companies, Choral Groups, Theater Companies, Performing Arts Series and Performing Arts Facilities. Plus, this edition now contains a brand new section on Artist Management Groups. In addition to mailing address, phone & fax numbers, e-mail addresses and web sites, dozens of other fields of available information include mission statement, key contacts, facilities, seating capacity, season, attendance and more. This directory also provides an important Information Resources section that covers hundreds of Performing Arts Associations, Magazines, Newsletters, Trade Shows, Directories, Databases and Industry Web Sites. Five indexes provide immediate access to this wealth of information: Entry Name, Executive Name, Performance Facilities, Geographic and Information Resources. *The Grey House Performing Arts Directory* pulls together thousands of Performing Arts Organizations, Facilities and Information Resources into an easy-to-use source – this kind of comprehensiveness and extensive detail is not available in any resource on the market place today.

"Immensely useful and user-friendly … recommended for public, academic and certain special library reference collections." –Booklist

Softcover ISBN 978-1-59237-376-5, 1,500 pages, $185.00 | Online Database: http://gold.greyhouse.com Call (800) 562-2139 for quote

The Environmental Resource Handbook, 2009/10

The Environmental Resource Handbook is the most up-to-date and comprehensive source for Environmental Resources and Statistics. Section I: Resources provides detailed contact information for thousands of information sources, including Associations & Organizations, Awards & Honors, Conferences, Foundations & Grants, Environmental Health, Government Agencies, National Parks & Wildlife Refuges, Publications, Research Centers, Educational Programs, Green Product Catalogs, Consultants and much more. Section II: Statistics, provides statistics and rankings on hundreds of important topics, including Children's Environmental Index, Municipal Finances, Toxic Chemicals, Recycling, Climate, Air & Water Quality and more. This kind of up-to-date environmental data, all in one place, is not available anywhere else on the market place today. This vast compilation of resources and statistics is a must-have for all public and academic libraries as well as any organization with a primary focus on the environment.

"…the intrinsic value of the information make it worth consideration by libraries with environmental collections and environmentally concerned users." –Booklist

Softcover ISBN 978-1-59237-433-5, 1,000 pages, $155.00 | Online Database: http://gold.greyhouse.com Call (800) 562-2139 for quote

New York State Directory, 2009/10

The New York State Directory, published annually since 1983, is a comprehensive and easy-to-use guide to accessing public officials and private sector organizations and individuals who influence public policy in the state of New York. *The New York State Directory* includes important information on all New York state legislators and congressional representatives, including biographies and key committee assignments. It also includes staff rosters for all branches of New York state government and for federal agencies and departments that impact the state policy process. Following the state government section are 25 chapters covering policy areas from agriculture through veterans' affairs. Each chapter identifies the state, local and federal agencies and officials that formulate or implement policy. In addition, each chapter contains a roster of private sector experts and advocates who influence the policy process. The directory also offers appendices that include statewide party officials; chambers of commerce; lobbying organizations; public and private universities and colleges; television, radio and print media; and local government agencies and officials.

"This comprehensive directory covers not only New York State government offices and key personnel but pertinent U.S. government agencies and non-governmental entities. This directory is all encompassing... recommended." -Choice

New York State Directory - Softcover ISBN 978-1-59237-420-5, 800 pages, $145.00
Online Database: http://gold.greyhouse.com Call (800) 562-2139 for quote
New York State Directory with *Profiles of New York* – 2 Volumes, Softcover ISBN 978-1-59237-421-2, 1,600 pages, $225.00

The Grey House Homeland Security Directory, 2010

This updated edition features the latest contact information for government and private organizations involved with Homeland Security along with the latest product information and provides detailed profiles of nearly 1,000 Federal & State Organizations & Agencies and over 3,000 Officials and Key Executives involved with Homeland Security. These listings are incredibly detailed and include Mailing Address, Phone & Fax Numbers, Email Addresses & Web Sites, a complete Description of the Agency and a complete list of the Officials and Key Executives associated with the Agency. Next, *The Grey House Homeland Security Directory* provides the go-to source for Homeland Security Products & Services. This section features over 2,000 Companies that provide Consulting, Products or Services. With this Buyer's Guide at their fingertips, users can locate suppliers of everything from Training Materials to Access Controls, from Perimeter Security to BioTerrorism Countermeasures and everything in between – complete with contact information and product descriptions. A handy Product Locator Index is provided to quickly and easily locate suppliers of a particular product. This comprehensive, information-packed resource will be a welcome tool for any company or agency that is in need of Homeland Security information and will be a necessary acquisition for the reference collection of all public libraries and large school districts.

"Compiles this information in one place and is discerning in content. A useful purchase for public and academic libraries." –Booklist

Softcover ISBN 978-1-59237-365-9, 800 pages, $195.00 | Online Database: http://gold.greyhouse.com Call (800) 562-2139 for quote

The Grey House Safety & Security Directory, 2009

The Grey House Safety & Security Directory is the most comprehensive reference tool and buyer's guide for the safety and security industry. Arranged by safety topic, each chapter begins with OSHA regulations for the topic, followed by Training Articles written by top professionals in the field and Self-Inspection Checklists. Next, each topic contains Buyer's Guide sections that feature related products and services. Topics include Administration, Insurance, Loss Control & Consulting, Protective Equipment & Apparel, Noise & Vibration, Facilities Monitoring & Maintenance, Employee Health Maintenance & Ergonomics, Retail Food Services, Machine Guards, Process Guidelines & Tool Handling, Ordinary Materials Handling, Hazardous Materials Handling, Workplace Preparation & Maintenance, Electrical Lighting & Safety, Fire & Rescue and Security. Six important indexes make finding information and product manufacturers quick and easy: Geographical Index of Manufacturers and Distributors, Company Profile Index, Brand Name Index, Product Index, Index of Web Sites and Index of Advertisers. This comprehensive, up-to-date reference will provide every tool necessary to make sure a business is in compliance with OSHA regulations and locate the products and services needed to meet those regulations.

"Presents industrial safety information for engineers, plant managers, risk managers, and construction site supervisors…" –Choice

Softcover ISBN 978-1-59237-375-8, 1,500 pages, $165.00

The Grey House Transportation Security Directory & Handbook

This is the only reference of its kind that brings together current data on Transportation Security. With information on everything from Regulatory Authorities to Security Equipment, this top-flight database brings together the relevant information necessary for creating and maintaining a security plan for a wide range of transportation facilities. With this current, comprehensive directory at the ready you'll have immediate access to: Regulatory Authorities & Legislation; Information Resources; Sample Security Plans & Checklists; Contact Data for Major Airports, Seaports, Railroads, Trucking Companies and Oil Pipelines; Security Service Providers; Recommended Equipment & Product Information and more. Using the *Grey House Transportation Security Directory & Handbook*, managers will be able to quickly and easily assess their current security plans; develop contacts to create and maintain new security procedures; and source the products and services necessary to adequately maintain a secure environment. This valuable resource is a must for all Security Managers at Airports, Seaports, Railroads, Trucking Companies and Oil Pipelines.

"Highly recommended. Library collections that support all levels of readers, including professionals/practitioners; and schools/organizations offering education and training in transportation security." -Choice

Softcover ISBN 978-1-59237-075-7, 800 pages, $195.00

The Grey House Biometric Information Directory

This edition offers a complete, current overview of biometric companies and products – one of the fastest growing industries in today's economy. Detailed profiles of manufacturers of the latest biometric technology, including Finger, Voice, Face, Hand, Signature, Iris, Vein and Palm Identification systems. Data on the companies include key executives, company size and a detailed, indexed description of their product line. Information in the directory includes: Editorial on Advancements in Biometrics; Profiles of 700+ companies listed with contact information; Organizations, Trade & Educational Associations, Publications, Conferences, Trade Shows and Expositions Worldwide; Web Site Index; Biometric & Vendors Services Index by Types of Biometrics; and a Glossary of Biometric Terms. This resource will be an important source for anyone who is considering the use of a biometric product, investing in the development of biometric technology, support existing marketing and sales efforts and will be an important acquisition for the business reference collection for large public and business libraries.

"This book should prove useful to agencies or businesses seeking companies that deal with biometric technology. Summing Up: Recommended. Specialized collections serving researchers/faculty and professionals/practitioners." -Choice

Softcover ISBN 978-1-59237-121-1, 800 pages, $225.00

The Rauch Guide to the US Adhesives & Sealants, Cosmetics & Toiletries, Ink, Paint, Plastics, Pulp & Paper and Rubber Industries

The Rauch Guides save time and money by organizing widely scattered information and providing estimates for important business decisions, some of which are available nowhere else. Within each Guide, after a brief introduction, the ECONOMICS section provides data on industry shipments; long-term growth and forecasts; prices; company performance; employment, expenditures, and productivity; transportation and geographical patterns; packaging; foreign trade; and government regulations. Next, TECHNOLOGY & RAW MATERIALS provide market, technical, and raw material information for chemicals, equipment and related materials, including market size and leading suppliers, prices, end uses, and trends. PRODUCTS & MARKETS provide information for each major industry product, including market size and historical trends, leading suppliers, five-year forecasts, industry structure, and major end uses. Next, the COMPANY DIRECTORY profiles major industry companies, both public and private. Information includes complete contact information, web address, estimated total and domestic sales, product description, and recent mergers and acquisitions. *The Rauch Guides* will prove to be an invaluable source of market information, company data, trends and forecasts that anyone in these fast-paced industries.

"An invaluable and affordable publication. The comprehensive nature of the data and text offers considerable insights into the industry, market sizes, company activities, and applications of the products of the industry. The additions that have been made have certainly enhanced the value of the Guide." –Adhesives & Sealants Newsletter of the Rauch Guide to the US Adhesives & Sealants Industry

Paint Industry: Softcover ISBN 978-1-59237-428-1 $595 | Plastics Industry: Softcover ISBN 978-1-59237-445-8 $595 | Adhesives and Sealants Industry: Softcover ISBN 978-1-59237-440-3 $595 | Ink Industry: Softcover ISBN 978-1-59237-126-6 $595 | Rubber Industry: Softcover ISBN 978-1-59237-130-3 $595 | Pulp and Paper Industry: Softcover ISBN 978-1-59237-131-0 $595 | Cosmetic & Toiletries Industry: Softcover ISBN 978-1-59237-132-7 $895

Research Services Directory: Commercial & Corporate Research Centers

This ninth edition provides access to well over 8,000 independent Commercial Research Firms, Corporate Research Centers and Laboratories offering contract services for hands-on, basic or applied research. Research Services Directory covers the thousands of types of research companies, including Biotechnology & Pharmaceutical Developers, Consumer Product Research, Defense Contractors, Electronics & Software Engineers, Think Tanks, Forensic Investigators, Independent Commercial Laboratories, Information Brokers, Market & Survey Research Companies, Medical Diagnostic Facilities, Product Research & Development Firms and more. Each entry provides the company's name, mailing address, phone & fax numbers, key contacts, web site, e-mail address, as well as a company description and research and technical fields served. Four indexes provide immediate access to this wealth of information: Research Firms Index, Geographic Index, Personnel Name Index and Subject Index.

"An important source for organizations in need of information about laboratories, individuals and other facilities." –ARBA

Softcover ISBN 978-1-59237-003-0, 1,400 pages, $465.00

International Business and Trade Directories

Completely updated, the Third Edition of *International Business and Trade Directories* now contains more than 10,000 entries, over 2,000 more than the last edition, making this directory the most comprehensive resource of the worlds business and trade directories. Entries include content descriptions, price, publisher's name and address, web site and e-mail addresses, phone and fax numbers and editorial staff. Organized by industry group, and then by region, this resource puts over 10,000 industry-specific business and trade directories at the reader's fingertips. Three indexes are included for quick access to information: Geographic Index, Publisher Index and Title Index. Public, college and corporate libraries, as well as individuals and corporations seeking critical market information will want to add this directory to their marketing collection.

"Reasonably priced for a work of this type, this directory should appeal to larger academic, public and corporate libraries with an international focus." –Library Journal

Softcover ISBN 978-1-930956-63-6, 1,800 pages, $225.00

The Value of a Dollar 1860-2009, Fourth Edition

A guide to practical economy, *The Value of a Dollar* records the actual prices of thousands of items that consumers purchased from the Civil War to the present, along with facts about investment options and income opportunities. This brand new Third Edition boasts a brand new addition to each five-year chapter, a section on Trends. This informative section charts the change in price over time and provides added detail on the reasons prices changed within the time period, including industry developments, changes in consumer attitudes and important historical facts. Plus, a brand new chapter for 2005-2009 has been added. Each 5-year chapter includes a Historical Snapshot, Consumer Expenditures, Investments, Selected Income, Income/Standard Jobs, Food Basket, Standard Prices and Miscellany. This interesting and useful publication will be widely used in any reference collection.

"Business historians, reporters, writers and students will find this source... very helpful for historical research. Libraries will want to purchase it." –ARBA

Hardcover ISBN 978-1-59237-403-8, 600 pages, $145.00 | Ebook ISBN 978-1-59237-173-0 www.greyhouse.com/ebooks.htm

The Value of a Dollar 1600-1859, The Colonial Era to The Civil War

Following the format of the widely acclaimed, *The Value of a Dollar, 1860-2004, The Value of a Dollar 1600-1859, The Colonial Era to The Civil War* records the actual prices of thousands of items that consumers purchased from the Colonial Era to the Civil War. Our editorial department had been flooded with requests from users of our *Value of a Dollar* for the same type of information, just from an earlier time period. This new volume is just the answer – with pricing data from 1600 to 1859. Arranged into five-year chapters, each 5-year chapter includes a Historical Snapshot, Consumer Expenditures, Investments, Selected Income, Income/Standard Jobs, Food Basket, Standard Prices and Miscellany. There is also a section on Trends. This informative section charts the change in price over time and provides added detail on the reasons prices changed within the time period, including industry developments, changes in consumer attitudes and important historical facts. This fascinating survey will serve a wide range of research needs and will be useful in all high school, public and academic library reference collections.

"The Value of a Dollar: Colonial Era to the Civil War, 1600-1865 will find a happy audience among students, researchers, and general browsers. It offers a fascinating and detailed look at early American history from the viewpoint of everyday people trying to make ends meet. This title and the earlier publication, The Value of a Dollar, 1860-2004, complement each other very well, and readers will appreciate finding them side-by-side on the shelf." -Booklist

Hardcover ISBN 978-1-59237-094-8, 600 pages, $145.00 | Ebook ISBN 978-1-59237-169-3 www.greyhouse.com/ebooks.htm

Working Americans 1880-1999
Volume I: The Working Class, Volume II: The Middle Class, Volume III: The Upper Class

Each of the volumes in the *Working Americans* series focuses on a particular class of Americans, The Working Class, The Middle Class and The Upper Class over the last 120 years. Chapters in each volume focus on one decade and profile three to five families. Family Profiles include real data on Income & Job Descriptions, Selected Prices of the Times, Annual Income, Annual Budgets, Family Finances, Life at Work, Life at Home, Life in the Community, Working Conditions, Cost of Living, Amusements and much more. Each chapter also contains an Economic Profile with Average Wages of other Professions, a selection of Typical Pricing, Key Events & Inventions, News Profiles, Articles from Local Media and Illustrations. The *Working Americans* series captures the lifestyles of each of the classes from the last twelve decades, covers a vast array of occupations and ethnic backgrounds and travels the entire nation. These interesting and useful compilations of portraits of the American Working, Middle and Upper Classes during the last 120 years will be an important addition to any high school, public or academic library reference collection.

"These interesting, unique compilations of economic and social facts, figures and graphs will support multiple research needs. They will engage and enlighten patrons in high school, public and academic library collections." –Booklist

Volume I: The Working Class Hardcover ISBN 978-1-891482-81-6, 558 pages, $150.00 | Volume II: The Middle Class Hardcover ISBN 978-1-891482-72-4, 591 pages, $150.00 | Volume III: The Upper Class Hardcover ISBN 978-1-930956-38-4, 567 pages, $150.00 | www.greyhouse.com/ebooks.htm

Working Americans 1880-1999 Volume IV: Their Children

This Fourth Volume in the highly successful *Working Americans* series focuses on American children, decade by decade from 1880 to 1999. This interesting and useful volume introduces the reader to three children in each decade, one from each of the Working, Middle and Upper classes. Like the first three volumes in the series, the individual profiles are created from interviews, diaries, statistical studies, biographies and news reports. Profiles cover a broad range of ethnic backgrounds, geographic area and lifestyles – everything from an orphan in Memphis in 1882, following the Yellow Fever epidemic of 1878 to an eleven-year-old nephew of a beer baron and owner of the New York Yankees in New York City in 1921. Chapters also contain important supplementary materials including News Features as well as information on everything from Schools to Parks, Infectious Diseases to Childhood Fears along with Entertainment, Family Life and much more to provide an informative overview of the lifestyles of children from each decade. This interesting account of what life was like for Children in the Working, Middle and Upper Classes will be a welcome addition to the reference collection of any high school, public or academic library.

Hardcover ISBN 978-1-930956-35-3, 600 pages, $150.00 | Ebook ISBN 978-1-59237-166-2 www.greyhouse.com/ebooks.htm

Working Americans 1880-2003 Volume V: Americans At War

Working Americans 1880-2003 Volume V: Americans At War is divided into 11 chapters, each covering a decade from 1880-2003 and examines the lives of Americans during the time of war, including declared conflicts, one-time military actions, protests, and preparations for war. Each decade includes several personal profiles, whether on the battlefield or on the homefront, that tell the stories of civilians, soldiers, and officers during the decade. The profiles examine: Life at Home; Life at Work; and Life in the Community. Each decade also includes an Economic Profile with statistical comparisons, a Historical Snapshot, News Profiles, local News Articles, and Illustrations that provide a solid historical background to the decade being examined. Profiles range widely not only geographically, but also emotionally, from that of a girl whose leg was torn off in a blast during WWI, to the boredom of being stationed in the Dakotas as the Indian Wars were drawing to a close. As in previous volumes of the *Working Americans* series, information is presented in narrative form, but hard facts and real-life situations back up each story. The basis of the profiles come from diaries, private print books, personal interviews, family histories, estate documents and magazine articles. For easy reference, *Working Americans 1880-2003 Volume V: Americans At War* includes an in-depth Subject Index. The Working Americans series has become an important reference for public libraries, academic libraries and high school libraries. This fifth volume will be a welcome addition to all of these types of reference collections.

Hardcover ISBN 978-1-59237-024-5, 600 pages, $150.00 | Ebook ISBN 978-1-59237-167-9 www.greyhouse.com/ebooks.htm

Working Americans 1880-2005 Volume VI: Women at Work

Unlike any other volume in the *Working Americans* series, this Sixth Volume, is the first to focus on a particular gender of Americans. *Volume VI: Women at Work*, traces what life was like for working women from the 1860's to the present time. Beginning with the life of a maid in 1890 and a store clerk in 1900 and ending with the life and times of the modern working women, this text captures the struggle, strengths and changing perception of the American woman at work. Each chapter focuses on one decade and profiles three to five women with real data on Income & Job Descriptions, Selected Prices of the Times, Annual Income, Annual Budgets, Family Finances, Life at Work, Life at Home, Life in the Community, Working Conditions, Cost of Living, Amusements and much more. For even broader access to the events, economics and attitude towards women throughout the past 130 years, each chapter is supplemented with News Profiles, Articles from Local Media, Illustrations, Economic Profiles, Typical Pricing, Key Events, Inventions and more. This important volume illustrates what life was like for working women over time and allows the reader to develop an understanding of the changing role of women at work. These interesting and useful compilations of portraits of women at work will be an important addition to any high school, public or academic library reference collection.

Hardcover ISBN 978-1-59237-063-4, 600 pages, $145.00 | Ebook ISBN 978-1-59237-168-6 www.greyhouse.com/ebooks.htm

Working Americans 1880-2005 Volume VII: Social Movements

Working Americans series, Volume VII: Social Movements explores how Americans sought and fought for change from the 1880s to the present time. Following the format of previous volumes in the Working Americans series, the text examines the lives of 34 individuals who have worked -- often behind the scenes --- to bring about change. Issues include topics as diverse as the Anti-smoking movement of 1901 to efforts by Native Americans to reassert their long lost rights. Along the way, the book will profile individuals brave enough to demand suffrage for Kansas women in 1912 or demand an end to lynching during a March on Washington in 1923. Each profile is enriched with real data on Income & Job Descriptions, Selected Prices of the Times, Annual Incomes & Budgets, Life at Work, Life at Home, Life in the Community, along with News Features, Key Events, and Illustrations. The depth of information contained in each profile allow the user to explore the private, financial and public lives of these subjects, deepening our understanding of how calls for change took place in our society. A must-purchase for the reference collections of high school libraries, public libraries and academic libraries.

Hardcover ISBN 978-1-59237-101-3, 600 pages, $145.00 | Ebook ISBN 978-1-59237-174-7 www.greyhouse.com/ebooks.htm

Working Americans 1880-2005 Volume VIII: Immigrants

Working Americans 1880-2007 Volume VIII: Immigrants illustrates what life was like for families leaving their homeland and creating a new life in the United States. Each chapter covers one decade and introduces the reader to three immigrant families. Family profiles cover what life was like in their homeland, in their community in the United States, their home life, working conditions and so much more. As the reader moves through these pages, the families and individuals come to life, painting a picture of why they left their homeland, their experiences in setting roots in a new country, their struggles and triumphs, stretching from the 1800s to the present time. Profiles include a seven-year-old Swedish girl who meets her father for the first time at Ellis Island; a Chinese photographer's assistant; an Armenian who flees the genocide of his country to build Ford automobiles in Detroit; a 38-year-old German bachelor cigar maker who settles in Newark NJ, but contemplates tobacco farming in Virginia; a 19-year-old Irish domestic servant who is amazed at the easy life of American dogs; a 19-year-old Filipino who came to Hawaii against his parent's wishes to farm sugar cane; a French-Canadian who finds success as a boxer in Maine and many more. As in previous volumes, information is presented in narrative form, but hard facts and real-life situations back up each story. With the topic of immigration being so hotly debated in this country, this timely resource will prove to be a useful source for students, researchers, historians and library patrons to discover the issues facing immigrants in the United States. This title will be a useful addition to reference collections of public libraries, university libraries and high schools.

Hardcover ISBN 978-1-59237-197-6, 600 pages, $145.00 | Ebook ISBN 978-1-59237-232-4 www.greyhouse.com/ebooks.htm

Working Americans 1770-1896 Volume IX: From the Revolutionary War to the Civil War

Working Americans 1770-1869: From the Revolutionary War to the Civil War examines what life was like for the earliest of Americans. Like previous volumes in the successful Working Americans series, each chapter introduces the reader to three individuals or families. These profiles illustrate what life was like for that individual, at home, in the community and at work. The profiles are supplemented with information on current events, community issues, pricing of the times and news articles to give the reader a broader understanding of what was happening in that individual's world and how it shaped their life. Profiles extend through all walks of life, from farmers to merchants, the rich and poor, men, women and children. In these information-packed, fun-to-explore pages, the reader will be introduced to Ezra Stiles, a preacher and college president from 1776; Colonel Israel Angell, a continental officer from 1778; Thomas Vernon, a loyalist in 1776, Anna Green Winslow, a school girl in 1771; Sarah Pierce, a school teacher in 1792; Edward Hooker, an attorney in 1805; Jeremiah Greenman, a common soldier in 1775 and many others. Using these information-filled profiles, the reader can develop an understanding of what life was like for all types of Americans in these interesting and changing times. This new edition will be an important acquisition for high school, public and academic libraries as well as history reference collections.

Hardcover ISBN 978-1-59237-371-0, 660 pages, $145.00

Working Americans 1880-2009 Volume X: Sports & Recreation

Working Americans 1880-2009 Volume X: Sports & Recreation focuses on the lighter side of life in America. Examining professional sports to amateur sports to leisure time and recreation, this interesting volume illustrates how Americans had fun from the Civil War to the present time. Intriguing profiles in each decade-long chapter are supplemented with information on current events, community issues, pricing of the times and news articles to give the reader a broader understanding of what was happening in that individual's world and how it shaped their life. To further explore the life and times of these individuals, each chapter includes several other helpful elements: Historical Snapshots, Timelines, News Features, Selected Prices, and Illustrations. Readers will be able to examine the growth of professional sports and how ticket prices changed over the years, look at what games were popular, find out how early Americans spent their leisure time and get and understanding of the importance of recreation in any time period.

Hardcover ISBN 978-1-59237-441-0, 600 pages, $145.00

The Encyclopedia of Warrior Peoples & Fighting Groups

Many military groups throughout the world have excelled in their craft either by fortuitous circumstances, outstanding leadership, or intense training. This new second edition of *The Encyclopedia of Warrior Peoples and Fighting Groups* explores the origins and leadership of these outstanding combat forces, chronicles their conquests and accomplishments, examines the circumstances surrounding their decline or disbanding, and assesses their influence on the groups and methods of warfare that followed. Readers will encounter ferocious tribes, charismatic leaders, and daring militias, from ancient times to the present, including Amazons, Buffalo Soldiers, Green Berets, Iron Brigade, Kamikazes, Peoples of the Sea, Polish Winged Hussars, Teutonic Knights, and Texas Rangers. With over 100 alphabetical entries, numerous cross-references and illustrations, a comprehensive bibliography, and index, the *Encyclopedia of Warrior Peoples and Fighting Groups* is a valuable resource for readers seeking insight into the bold history of distinguished fighting forces.

"Especially useful for high school students, undergraduates, and general readers with an interest in military history." –*Library Journal*

Hardcover ISBN 978-1-59237-116-7, 660 pages, $165.00 | Ebook ISBN 978-1-59237-172-3 www.greyhouse.com/ebooks.htm

Speakers of the House of Representatives, 1789-2009

Beginning with Frederick Muhlenberg in 1789 and stretching to Nancy Pelosi, the first female Speaker of the House, this new reference work provides unique coverage of this important political position. Presiding over the House of Representatives and second the United States presidential line of succession, this position has particular influence over US politics. Features include: thoughtfully-written Biographies of each of the 52 Speakers of the House, all with photos; several full-length Essays, each covering an interesting and thought-provoking topic pertinent to the formation, history and current events surrounding the Speaker; Primary Documents, for added sources of research, include important articles, resignation letters, speeches and letters; several helpful Appendices: Years Served in Congress before Becoming Speaker, Speakers & Party Control of the Presidency, Dates of Election & States Represented, Speaker Firsts; a Chronology of Elections and Important Events, a comprehensive Bibliography and a cumulative Index. This new resource brings together a wealth of information on individual Speakers, the history of the position and its changing role in US politics. This resource will be a valuable addition to public libraries, high schools, university libraries along with history and political science collections.

Hardcover ISBN 978-1-59237-404-5, 500 pages, $135.00 | Ebook ISBN 978-1-59237-483-0 www.greyhouse.com/ebooks.htm

The Encyclopedia of Rural America: the Land & People

History, sociology, anthropology, and public policy are combined to deliver the encyclopedia destined to become the standard reference work in American rural studies. From irrigation and marriage to games and mental health, this encyclopedia is the first to explore the contemporary landscape of rural America, placed in historical perspective. With over 300 articles prepared by leading experts from across the nation, this timely encyclopedia documents and explains the major themes, concepts, industries, concerns, and everyday life of the people and land who make up rural America. Entries range from the industrial sector and government policy to arts and humanities and social and family concerns. Articles explore every aspect of life in rural America. *Encyclopedia of Rural America*, with its broad range of coverage, will appeal to high school and college students as well as graduate students, faculty, scholars, and people whose work pertains to rural areas.

"This exemplary encyclopedia is guaranteed to educate our highly urban society about the uniqueness of rural America. Recommended for public and academic libraries." -Library Journal

Two Volumes, Hardcover, ISBN 978-1-59237-115-0, 800 pages, $250.00

The Encyclopedia of Invasions & Conquests, From the Ancient Times to the Present

This second edition of the popular *Encyclopedia of Invasions & Conquests*, a comprehensive guide to over 150 invasions, conquests, battles and occupations from ancient times to the present, takes readers on a journey that includes the Roman conquest of Britain, the Portuguese colonization of Brazil, and the Iraqi invasion of Kuwait, to name a few. New articles will explore the late 20th and 21st centuries, with a specific focus on recent conflicts in Afghanistan, Kuwait, Iraq, Yugoslavia, Grenada and Chechnya. In addition to covering the military aspects of invasions and conquests, entries cover some of the political, economic, and cultural aspects, for example, the effects of a conquest on the invade country's political and monetary system and in its language and religion. The entries on leaders – among them Sargon, Alexander the Great, William the Conqueror, and Adolf Hitler – deal with the people who sought to gain control, expand power, or exert religious or political influence over others through military means. Revised and updated for this second edition, entries are arranged alphabetically within historical periods. Each chapter provides a map to help readers locate key areas and geographical features, and bibliographical references appear at the end of each entry. Other useful features include cross-references, a cumulative bibliography and a comprehensive subject index. This authoritative, well-organized, lucidly written volume will prove invaluable for a variety of readers, including high school students, military historians, members of the armed forces, history buffs and hobbyists.

"Engaging writing, sensible organization, nice illustrations, interesting and obscure facts, and useful maps make this book a pleasure to read." –ARBA

Hardcover ISBN 978-1-59237-114-3, 598 pages, $165.00 | Ebook ISBN 978-1-59237-171-6 www.greyhouse.com/ebooks.htm

Encyclopedia of Prisoners of War & Internment

This authoritative second edition provides a valuable overview of the history of prisoners of war and interned civilians, from earliest times to the present. Written by an international team of experts in the field of POW studies, this fascinating and thought-provoking volume includes entries on a wide range of subjects including the Crusades, Plains Indian Warfare, concentration camps, the two world wars, and famous POWs throughout history, as well as atrocities, escapes, and much more. Written in a clear and easily understandable style, this informative reference details over 350 entries, 30% larger than the first edition, that survey the history of prisoners of war and interned civilians from the earliest times to the present, with emphasis on the 19th and 20th centuries. Medical conditions, international law, exchanges of prisoners, organizations working on behalf of POWs, and trials associated with the treatment of captives are just some of the themes explored. Entries are arranged alphabetically, plus illustrations and maps are provided for easy reference. The text also includes an introduction, bibliography, appendix of selected documents, and end-of-entry reading suggestions. This one-of-a-kind reference will be a helpful addition to the reference collections of all public libraries, high schools, and university libraries and will prove invaluable to historians and military enthusiasts.

"Thorough and detailed yet accessible to the lay reader. Of special interest to subject specialists and historians; recommended for public and academic libraries." - Library Journal

Hardcover ISBN 978-1-59237-120-4, 676 pages, $165.00 | Ebook ISBN 978-1-59237-170-9 www.greyhouse.com/ebooks.htm

From Suffrage to the Senate, America's Political Women

From Suffrage to the Senate is a comprehensive and valuable compendium of biographies of leading women in U.S. politics, past and present, and an examination of the wide range of women's movements. This reference work explores American women's path to political power and social equality from the struggle for the right to vote and the abolition of slavery to the first African American woman in the U.S. Senate and beyond. The in-depth coverage also traces the political heritage of the abolition, labor, suffrage, temperance, and reproductive rights movements. The alphabetically arranged entries include biographies of every woman from across the political spectrum who has served in the U.S. House and Senate, along with women in the Judiciary and the U.S. Cabinet and, new to this edition, biographies of activists and political consultants. Bibliographical references follow each entry. For easy reference, a handy chronology is provided detailing 150 years of women's history. This up-to-date reference will be a must-purchase for women's studies departments, high schools and public libraries and will be a handy resource for those researching the key players in women's politics, past and present.

"An engaging tool that would be useful in high school, public, and academic libraries looking for an overview of the political history of women in the US." –Booklist

Two Volumes, Hardcover ISBN 978-1-59237-117-4, 1,160 pages, $199.00 | Ebook ISBN 978-1-59237-227-0
www.greyhouse.com/ebooks.htm

An African Biographical Dictionary

This landmark second edition is the only biographical dictionary to bring together, in one volume, cultural, social and political leaders – both historical and contemporary – of the sub-Saharan region. Over 800 biographical sketches of prominent Africans, as well as foreigners who have affected the continent's history, are featured, 150 more than the previous edition. The wide spectrum of leaders includes religious figures, writers, politicians, scientists, entertainers, sports personalities and more. Access to these fascinating individuals is provided in a user-friendly format. The biographies are arranged alphabetically, cross-referenced and indexed. Entries include the country or countries in which the person was significant and the commonly accepted dates of birth and death. Each biographical sketch is chronologically written; entries for cultural personalities add an evaluation of their work. This information is followed by a selection of references often found in university and public libraries, including autobiographies and principal biographical works. Appendixes list each individual by country and by field of accomplishment – rulers, musicians, explorers, missionaries, businessmen, physicists – nearly thirty categories in all. Another convenient appendix lists heads of state since independence by country. Up-to-date and representative of African societies as a whole, An African Biographical Dictionary provides a wealth of vital information for students of African culture and is an indispensable reference guide for anyone interested in African affairs.

"An unquestionable convenience to have these concise, informative biographies gathered into one source, indexed, and analyzed by appendixes listing entrants by nation and occupational field." –Wilson Library Bulletin

Hardcover ISBN 978-1-59237-112-9, 667 pages, $165.00 | Ebook ISBN 978-1-59237-229-4 www.greyhouse.com/ebooks.htm

African American Writers

A timely survey of an important sector of American letters, *African American Writers* covers the role and influence of African American cultural leaders, from all walks of life, from the 18th century to the present. Readers will explore what inspired various African-American writers to create poems, plays, short stories, novels, essays, opinion pieces and numerous other works, and how those writings contributed to culture in America today. With 200 new entries, over 35% larger than the previous edition, this edition features over 100 new Author biographies, for a total of 500, with illustrations, cover the important events in a writer's life, education, major works, honors and awards, and family and important associates; more Genre Tables, covering newspapers, journals, book publishers, online resources, illustrators and more, each with an introduction and listings of top authors in each genre, their pen names, key publications and awards; new Topical entries, including writing collaboratives, book clubs, celebrity authors and self-publishing; new Author Tables, covering additional authors in multiple genres, with author name, pen name, birth year, genre and more; an Appendix of Writers by Genre; a Chronology of Writers; a Chronology of Firsts, with interesting facts, from the first narrative written by an African-American slave, to the first African-American to receive the Nobel prize for literature; a list of Abbreviations and a Cumulative Index. More than a collection of biographies, this important work traces the evolution of African-American writers, their struggles, triumphs, and legacy, this volume is not to be missed. A comprehensive, easy to use source that will complement the reference collection of any public, high school or university library, and will prove useful to all university humanities and African American studies reference collections.

"No other single work seeks to include all past and present African American writers of significance in such an affordable format ... an appealing choice for all public and academic libraries." –Library Journal

Hardcover ISBN 978-1-59237-291-1, 667 pages, $165.00 | Ebook ISBN 978-1-59237-302-4 www.greyhouse.com/ebooks.htm

American Environmental Leaders, From Colonial Times to the Present

A comprehensive and diverse award winning collection of biographies of the most important figures in American environmentalism. Few subjects arouse the passions the way the environment does. How will we feed an ever-increasing population and how can that food be made safe for consumption? Who decides how land is developed? How can environmental policies be made fair for everyone, including multiethnic groups, women, children, and the poor? *American Environmental Leaders* presents more than 350 biographies of men and women who have devoted their lives to studying, debating, and organizing these and other controversial issues over the last 200 years. In addition to the scientists who have analyzed how human actions affect nature, we are introduced to poets, landscape architects, presidents, painters, activists, even sanitation engineers, and others who have forever altered how we think about the environment. The easy to use A–Z format provides instant access to these fascinating individuals, and frequent cross references indicate others with whom individuals worked (and sometimes clashed). End of entry references provide users with a starting point for further research.

"Highly recommended for high school, academic, and public libraries needing environmental biographical information." –Library Journal/Starred Review

Two Volumes, Hardcover ISBN 978-1-59237-119-8, 900 pages $195.00 | Ebook ISBN 978-1-59237-230-0
www.greyhouse.com/ebooks.htm

World Cultural Leaders of the Twentieth & Twenty-First Centuries

World Cultural Leaders of the Twentieth & Twenty-First Centuries is a window into the arts, performances, movements, and music that shaped the world's cultural development since 1900. A remarkable around-the-world look at one-hundred-plus years of cultural development through the eyes of those that set the stage and stayed to play. This second edition offers over 120 new biographies along with a complete update of existing biographies. To further aid the reader, a handy fold-out timeline traces important events in all six cultural categories from 1900 through the present time. Plus, a new section of detailed material and resources for 100 selected individuals is also new to this edition, with further data on museums, homesteads, websites, artwork and more. This remarkable compilation will answer a wide range of questions. Who was the originator of the term "documentary"? Which poet married the daughter of the famed novelist Thomas Mann in order to help her escape Nazi Germany? Which British writer served as an agent in Russia against the Bolsheviks before the 1917 revolution? A handy two-volume set that makes it easy to look up 450 worldwide cultural icons: novelists, poets, playwrights, painters, sculptors, architects, dancers, choreographers, actors, directors, filmmakers, singers, composers, and musicians. *World Cultural Leaders of the Twentieth & Twenty-First Centuries* provides entries (many of them illustrated) covering the person's works, achievements, and professional career in a thorough essay and offers interesting facts and statistics. Entries are fully cross-referenced so that readers can learn how various individuals influenced others. An index of leaders by occupation, a useful glossary and a thorough general index complete the coverage. This remarkable resource will be an important acquisition for the reference collections of public libraries, university libraries and high schools.

"Fills a need for handy, concise information on a wide array of international cultural figures."-ARBA

Two Volumes, Hardcover ISBN 978-1-59237-118-1, 900 pages, $199.00 | Ebook ISBN 978-1-59237-231-7
www.greyhouse.com/ebooks.htm

Political Corruption in America: An Encyclopedia of Scandals, Power, and Greed

The complete scandal-filled history of American political corruption, focusing on the infamous people and cases, as well as society's electoral and judicial reactions. Since colonial times, there has been no shortage of politicians willing to take a bribe, skirt campaign finance laws, or act in their own interests. Corruption like the Whiskey Ring, Watergate, and Whitewater cases dominate American life, making political scandal a leading U.S. industry. From judges to senators, presidents to mayors, *Political Corruption in America* discusses the infamous people throughout history who have been accused of and implicated in crooked behavior. In this new second edition, more than 250 A–Z entries explore the people, crimes, investigations, and court cases behind 200 years of American political scandals. This unbiased volume also delves into the issues surrounding Koreagate, the Chinese campaign scandal, and other ethical lapses. Relevant statutes and terms, including the Independent Counsel Statute and impeachment as a tool of political punishment, are examined as well. Students, scholars, and other readers interested in American history, political science, and ethics will appreciate this survey of a wide range of corrupting influences. This title focuses on how politicians from all parties have fallen because of their greed and hubris, and how society has used electoral and judicial means against those who tested the accepted standards of political conduct. A full range of illustrations including political cartoons, photos of key figures such as Abe Fortas and Archibald Cox, graphs of presidential pardons, and tables showing the number of expulsions and censures in both the House and Senate round out the text. In addition, a comprehensive chronology of major political scandals in U.S. history from colonial times until the present. For further reading, an extensive bibliography lists sources including archival letters, newspapers, and private manuscript collections from the United States and Great Britain. With its comprehensive coverage of this interesting topic, *Political Corruption in America: An Encyclopedia of Scandals, Power, and Greed* will prove to be a useful addition to the reference collections of all public libraries, university libraries, history collections, political science collections and high schools.

"...this encyclopedia is a useful contribution to the field. Highly recommended." - CHOICE
"Political Corruption should be useful in most academic, high school, and public libraries." Booklist

Two Volumes, Hardcover ISBN 978-1-59237-297-3, 500 pages, $195.00 | Ebook ISBN 978-1-59237-308-6
www.greyhouse.com/ebooks.htm

Encyclopedia of Religion & the Law in America

This informative, easy-to-use reference work covers a wide range of legal issues that affect the roles of religion and law in American society. Extensive A–Z entries provide coverage of key court decisions, case studies, concepts, individuals, religious groups, organizations, and agencies shaping religion and law in today's society. This *Encyclopedia* focuses on topics involved with the constitutional theory and interpretation of religion and the law; terms providing a historical explanation of the ways in which America's ever increasing ethnic and religious diversity contributed to our current understanding of the mandates of the First and Fourteenth Amendments; terms and concepts describing the development of religion clause jurisprudence; an analytical examination of the distinct vocabulary used in this area of the law; the means by which American courts have attempted to balance religious liberty against other important individual and social interests in a wide variety of physical and regulatory environments, including the classroom, the workplace, the courtroom, religious group organization and structure, taxation, the clash of "secular" and "religious" values, and the relationship of the generalized idea of individual autonomy of the specific concept of religious liberty. Important legislation and legal cases affecting religion and society are thoroughly covered in this timely volume, including a detailed Table of Cases and Table of Statutes for more detailed research. A guide to further reading and an index are also included. This useful resource will be an important acquisition for the reference collections of all public libraries, university libraries, religion reference collections and high schools.

Hardcover ISBN 978-1-59237-298-0, 500 pages, $135.00 | Ebook ISBN 978-1-59237-309-3 www.greyhouse.com/ebooks.htm

The Religious Right, A Reference Handbook

Timely and unbiased, this third edition updates and expands its examination of the religious right and its influence on our government, citizens, society, and politics. This text explores the influence of religion on legislation and society, while examining the alignment of the religious right with the political right. The coverage offers a critical historical survey of the religious right movement, focusing on its increased involvement in the political arena, attempts to forge coalitions, and notable successes and failures. The text offers complete coverage of biographies of the men and women who have advanced the cause and an up to date chronology illuminate the movement's goals, including their accomplishments and failures. Two new sections complement this third edition, a chapter on legal issues and court decisions and a chapter on demographic statistics and electoral patterns. To aid in further research, *The Religious Right*, offers an entire section of annotated listings of print and non-print resources, as well as of organizations affiliated with the religious right, and those opposing it. Comprehensive in its scope, this work offers easy-to-read, pertinent information for those seeking to understand the religious right and its evolving role in American society. A must for libraries of all sizes, university religion departments, activists, high schools and for those interested in the evolving role of the religious right.

" Recommended for all public and academic libraries." - Library Journal

Hardcover ISBN 978-1-59237-113-6, 600 pages, $165.00 | Ebook ISBN 978-1-59237-226-3 www.greyhouse.com/ebooks.htm

Human Rights in the United States: A Dictionary and Documents

This two volume set offers easy to grasp explanations of the basic concepts, laws, and case law in the field, with emphasis on human rights in the historical, political, and legal experience of the United States. Human rights is a term not fully understood by many Americans. Addressing this gap, the new second edition of *Human Rights in the United States: A Dictionary and Documents* offers a comprehensive introduction that places the history of human rights in the United States in an international context. It surveys the legal protection of human dignity in the United States, examines the sources of human rights norms, cites key legal cases, explains the role of international governmental and non-governmental organizations, and charts global, regional, and U.N. human rights measures. Over 240 dictionary entries of human rights terms are detailed—ranging from asylum and cultural relativism to hate crimes and torture. Each entry discusses the significance of the term, gives examples, and cites appropriate documents and court decisions. In addition, a Documents section is provided that contains 59 conventions, treaties, and protocols related to the most up to date international action on ethnic cleansing; freedom of expression and religion; violence against women; and much more. A bibliography, extensive glossary, and comprehensive index round out this indispensable volume. This comprehensive, timely volume is a must for large public libraries, university libraries and social science departments, along with high school libraries.

"...invaluable for anyone interested in human rights issues ... highly recommended for all reference collections."
- American Reference Books Annual

Two Volumes, Hardcover ISBN 978-1-59237-290-4, 750 pages, $225.00 | Ebook ISBN 978-1-59237-301-7 www.greyhouse.com/ebooks.htm

The Comparative Guide to American Elementary & Secondary Schools, 2009/10

The only guide of its kind, this award winning compilation offers a snapshot profile of every public school district in the United States serving 1,500 or more students – more than 5,900 districts are covered. Organized alphabetically by district within state, each chapter begins with a Statistical Overview of the state. Each district listing includes contact information (name, address, phone number and web site) plus Grades Served, the Numbers of Students and Teachers and the Number of Regular, Special Education, Alternative and Vocational Schools in the district along with statistics on Student/Classroom Teacher Ratios, Drop Out Rates, Ethnicity, the Numbers of Librarians and Guidance Counselors and District Expenditures per student. As an added bonus, *The Comparative Guide to American Elementary and Secondary Schools* provides important ranking tables, both by state and nationally, for each data element. For easy navigation through this wealth of information, this handbook contains a useful City Index that lists all districts that operate schools within a city. These important comparative statistics are necessary for anyone considering relocation or doing comparative research on their own district and would be a perfect acquisition for any public library or school district library.

"This straightforward guide is an easy way to find general information. Valuable for academic and large public library collections." –ARBA

Softcover ISBN 978-1-59237-436-6, 2,400 pages, $125.00 | Ebook ISBN 978-1-59237-238-6 www.greyhouse.com/ebooks.htm

The Complete Learning Disabilities Directory, 2009

The Complete Learning Disabilities Directory is the most comprehensive database of Programs, Services, Curriculum Materials, Professional Meetings & Resources, Camps, Newsletters and Support Groups for teachers, students and families concerned with learning disabilities. This information-packed directory includes information about Associations & Organizations, Schools, Colleges & Testing Materials, Government Agencies, Legal Resources and much more. For quick, easy access to information, this directory contains four indexes: Entry Name Index, Subject Index and Geographic Index. With every passing year, the field of learning disabilities attracts more attention and the network of caring, committed and knowledgeable professionals grows every day. This directory is an invaluable research tool for these parents, students and professionals.

"Due to its wealth and depth of coverage, parents, teachers and others… should find this an invaluable resource." -Booklist

Softcover ISBN 978-1-59237-368-0, 900 pages, $150.00 | Online Database: http://gold.greyhouse.com Call (800) 562-2139 for quote

Educators Resource Directory, 2009/10

Educators Resource Directory is a comprehensive resource that provides the educational professional with thousands of resources and statistical data for professional development. This directory saves hours of research time by providing immediate access to Associations & Organizations, Conferences & Trade Shows, Educational Research Centers, Employment Opportunities & Teaching Abroad, School Library Services, Scholarships, Financial Resources, Professional Consultants, Computer Software & Testing Resources and much more. Plus, this comprehensive directory also includes a section on Statistics and Rankings with over 100 tables, including statistics on Average Teacher Salaries, SAT/ACT scores, Revenues & Expenditures and more. These important statistics will allow the user to see how their school rates among others, make relocation decisions and so much more. For quick access to information, this directory contains four indexes: Entry & Publisher Index, Geographic Index, a Subject & Grade Index and Web Sites Index. *Educators Resource Directory* will be a well-used addition to the reference collection of any school district, education department or public library.

"Recommended for all collections that serve elementary and secondary school professionals." –Choice

Softcover ISBN 978-1-59237-397-0, 800 pages, $145.00 | Online Database: http://gold.greyhouse.com Call (800) 562-2139 for quote

Profiles of New York | Profiles of Florida | Profiles of Texas | Profiles of Illinois | Profiles of Michigan | Profiles of Ohio | Profiles of New Jersey | Profiles of Massachusetts | Profiles of Pennsylvania | Profiles of Wisconsin | Profiles of Connecticut & Rhode Island | Profiles of Indiana | Profiles of North Carolina & South Carolina | Profiles of Virginia | Profiles of California

The careful layout gives the user an easy-to-read snapshot of every single place and county in the state, from the biggest metropolis to the smallest unincorporated hamlet. The richness of each place or county profile is astounding in its depth, from history to weather, all packed in an easy-to-navigate, compact format. Each profile contains data on History, Geography, Climate, Population, Vital Statistics, Economy, Income, Taxes, Education, Housing, Health & Environment, Public Safety, Newspapers, Transportation, Presidential Election Results, Information Contacts and Chambers of Commerce. As an added bonus, there is a section on Selected Statistics, where data from the 100 largest towns and cities is arranged into easy-to-use charts. Each of 22 different data points has its own two-page spread with the cities listed in alpha order so researchers can easily compare and rank cities. A remarkable compilation that offers overviews and insights into each corner of the state, each volume goes beyond Census statistics, beyond metro area coverage, beyond the 100 best places to live. Drawn from official census information, other government statistics and original research, you will have at your fingertips data that's available nowhere else in one single source.

"The publisher claims that this is the 'most comprehensive portrait of the state of Florida ever published,' and this reviewer is inclined to believe it...Recommended. All levels." –Choice on Profiles of Florida

Each Profiles of... title ranges from 400-800 pages, priced at $149.00 each

America's Top-Rated Cities, 2009

America's Top-Rated Cities provides current, comprehensive statistical information and other essential data in one easy-to-use source on the 100 "top" cities that have been cited as the best for business and living in the U.S. This handbook allows readers to see, at a glance, a concise social, business, economic, demographic and environmental profile of each city, including brief evaluative comments. In addition to detailed data on Cost of Living, Finances, Real Estate, Education, Major Employers, Media, Crime and Climate, city reports now include Housing Vacancies, Tax Audits, Bankruptcy, Presidential Election Results and more. This outstanding source of information will be widely used in any reference collection.

"The only source of its kind that brings together all of this information into one easy-to-use source. It will be beneficial to many business and public libraries." –ARBA

Four Volumes, Softcover ISBN 978-1-59237-410-6, 2,500 pages, $195.00 | Ebook ISBN 978-1-59237-233-1
www.greyhouse.com/ebooks.htm

America's Top-Rated Smaller Cities, 2008/09

A perfect companion to *America's Top-Rated Cities*, *America's Top-Rated Smaller Cities* provides current, comprehensive business and living profiles of smaller cities (population 25,000-99,999) that have been cited as the best for business and living in the United States. Sixty cities make up this 2004 edition of America's Top-Rated Smaller Cities, all are top-ranked by Population Growth, Median Income, Unemployment Rate and Crime Rate. City reports reflect the most current data available on a wide-range of statistics, including Employment & Earnings, Household Income, Unemployment Rate, Population Characteristics, Taxes, Cost of Living, Education, Health Care, Public Safety, Recreation, Media, Air & Water Quality and much more. Plus, each city report contains a Background of the City, and an Overview of the State Finances. *America's Top-Rated Smaller Cities* offers a reliable, one-stop source for statistical data that, before now, could only be found scattered in hundreds of sources. This volume is designed for a wide range of readers: individuals considering relocating a residence or business; professionals considering expanding their business or changing careers; general and market researchers; real estate consultants; human resource personnel; urban planners and investors.

"Provides current, comprehensive statistical information in one easy-to-use source... Recommended for public and academic libraries and specialized collections." –Library Journal

Two Volumes, Softcover ISBN 978-1-59237-284-3, 1,100 pages, $195.00 | Ebook ISBN 978-1-59237-234-8
www.greyhouse.com/ebooks.htm

Profiles of America: Facts, Figures & Statistics for Every Populated Place in the United States

Profiles of America is the only source that pulls together, in one place, statistical, historical and descriptive information about every place in the United States in an easy-to-use format. This award winning reference set, now in its second edition, compiles statistics and data from over 20 different sources – the latest census information has been included along with more than nine brand new statistical topics. This Four-Volume Set details over 40,000 places, from the biggest metropolis to the smallest unincorporated hamlet, and provides statistical details and information on over 50 different topics including Geography, Climate, Population, Vital Statistics, Economy, Income, Taxes, Education, Housing, Health & Environment, Public Safety, Newspapers, Transportation, Presidential Election Results and Information Contacts or Chambers of Commerce. Profiles are arranged, for ease-of-use, by state and then by county. Each county begins with a County-Wide Overview and is followed by information for each Community in that particular county. The Community Profiles within the county are arranged alphabetically. *Profiles of America* is a virtual snapshot of America at your fingertips and a unique compilation of information that will be widely used in any reference collection.

A Library Journal Best Reference Book "An outstanding compilation." –Library Journal

Four Volumes, Softcover ISBN 978-1-891482-80-9, 10,000 pages, $595.00

The Comparative Guide to American Suburbs, 2009/10

The Comparative Guide to American Suburbs is a one-stop source for Statistics on the 2,000+ suburban communities surrounding the 50 largest metropolitan areas – their population characteristics, income levels, economy, school system and important data on how they compare to one another. Organized into 50 Metropolitan Area chapters, each chapter contains an overview of the Metropolitan Area, a detailed Map followed by a comprehensive Statistical Profile of each Suburban Community, including Contact Information, Physical Characteristics, Population Characteristics, Income, Economy, Unemployment Rate, Cost of Living, Education, Chambers of Commerce and more. Next, statistical data is sorted into Ranking Tables that rank the suburbs by twenty different criteria, including Population, Per Capita Income, Unemployment Rate, Crime Rate, Cost of Living and more. *The Comparative Guide to American Suburbs* is the best source for locating data on suburbs. Those looking to relocate, as well as those doing preliminary market research, will find this an invaluable timesaving resource.

"Public and academic libraries will find this compilation useful…The work draws together figures from many sources and will be especially helpful for job relocation decisions." – Booklist

Softcover ISBN 978-1-59237-432-8 1,700 pages, $130.00 | Ebook ISBN 978-1-59237-235-5 www.greyhouse.com/ebooks.htm

The American Tally: Statistics & Comparative Rankings for U.S. Cities with Populations over 10,000

This important statistical handbook compiles, all in one place, comparative statistics on all U.S. cities and towns with a 10,000+ population. *The American Tally* provides statistical details on over 4,000 cities and towns and profiles how they compare with one another in Population Characteristics, Education, Language & Immigration, Income & Employment and Housing. Each section begins with an alphabetical listing of cities by state, allowing for quick access to both the statistics and relative rankings of any city. Next, the highest and lowest cities are listed in each statistic. These important, informative lists provide quick reference to which cities are at both extremes of the spectrum for each statistic. Unlike any other reference, *The American Tally* provides quick, easy access to comparative statistics – a must-have for any reference collection.

"A solid library reference." -Bookwatch

Softcover ISBN 978-1-930956-29-2, 500 pages, $125.00 | Ebook ISBN 978-1-59237-241-6 www.greyhouse.com/ebooks.htm

The Asian Databook: Statistics for all US Counties & Cities with Over 10,000 Population

This is the first-ever resource that compiles statistics and rankings on the US Asian population. *The Asian Databook* presents over 20 statistical data points for each city and county, arranged alphabetically by state, then alphabetically by place name. Data reported for each place includes Population, Languages Spoken at Home, Foreign-Born, Educational Attainment, Income Figures, Poverty Status, Homeownership, Home Values & Rent, and more. Next, in the Rankings Section, the top 75 places are listed for each data element. These easy-to-access ranking tables allow the user to quickly determine trends and population characteristics. This kind of comparative data can not be found elsewhere, in print or on the web, in a format that's as easy-to-use or more concise. A useful resource for those searching for demographics data, career search and relocation information and also for market research. With data ranging from Ancestry to Education, *The Asian Databook* presents a useful compilation of information that will be a much-needed resource in the reference collection of any public or academic library along with the marketing collection of any company whose primary focus in on the Asian population.

"This useful resource will help those searching for demographics data, and market research or relocation information… Accurate and clearly laid out, the publication is recommended for large public library and research collections." -Booklist

Softcover ISBN 978-1-59237-044-3, 1,000 pages, $150.00

The Hispanic Databook: Statistics for all US Counties & Cities with Over 10,000 Population

Previously published by Toucan Valley Publications, this second edition has been completely updated with figures from the latest census and has been broadly expanded to include dozens of new data elements and a brand new Rankings section. The Hispanic population in the United States has increased over 42% in the last 10 years and accounts for 12.5% of the total US population. For ease-of-use, *The Hispanic Databook* presents over 20 statistical data points for each city and county, arranged alphabetically by state, then alphabetically by place name. Data reported for each place includes Population, Languages Spoken at Home, Foreign-Born, Educational Attainment, Income Figures, Poverty Status, Homeownership, Home Values & Rent, and more. Next, in the Rankings Section, the top 75 places are listed for each data element. These easy-to-access ranking tables allow the user to quickly determine trends and population characteristics. This kind of comparative data can not be found elsewhere, in print or on the web, in a format that's as easy-to-use or more concise. A useful resource for those searching for demographics data, career search and relocation information and also for market research. With data ranging from Ancestry to Education, *The Hispanic Databook* presents a useful compilation of information that will be a much-needed resource in the reference collection of any public or academic library along with the marketing collection of any company whose primary focus in on the Hispanic population.

"This accurate, clearly presented volume of selected Hispanic demographics is recommended for large public libraries and research collections."-Library Journal

Softcover ISBN 978-1-59237-008-5, 1,000 pages, $150.00

Ancestry in America: A Comparative Guide to Over 200 Ethnic Backgrounds

This brand new reference work pulls together thousands of comparative statistics on the Ethnic Backgrounds of all populated places in the United States with populations over 10,000. Never before has this kind of information been reported in a single volume. Section One, Statistics by Place, is made up of a list of over 200 ancestry and race categories arranged alphabetically by each of the 5,000 different places with populations over 10,000. The population number of the ancestry group in that city or town is provided along with the percent that group represents of the total population. This informative city-by-city section allows the user to quickly and easily explore the ethnic makeup of all major population bases in the United States. Section Two, Comparative Rankings, contains three tables for each ethnicity and race. In the first table, the top 150 populated places are ranked by population number for that particular ancestry group, regardless of population. In the second table, the top 150 populated places are ranked by the percent of the total population for that ancestry group. In the third table, those top 150 populated places with 10,000 population are ranked by population number for each ancestry group. These easy-to-navigate tables allow users to see ancestry population patterns and make city-by-city comparisons as well. This brand new, information-packed resource will serve a wide-range or research requests for demographics, population characteristics, relocation information and much more. *Ancestry in America: A Comparative Guide to Over 200 Ethnic Backgrounds* will be an important acquisition to all reference collections.

"This compilation will serve a wide range of research requests for population characteristics ... it offers much more detail than other sources." –Booklist

Softcover ISBN 978-1-59237-029-0, 1,500 pages, $225.00

Weather America, A Thirty-Year Summary of Statistical Weather Data and Rankings

This valuable resource provides extensive climatological data for over 4,000 National and Cooperative Weather Stations throughout the United States. Weather America begins with a new Major Storms section that details major storm events of the nation and a National Rankings section that details rankings for several data elements, such as Maximum Temperature and Precipitation. The main body of Weather America is organized into 50 state sections. Each section provides a Data Table on each Weather Station, organized alphabetically, that provides statistics on Maximum and Minimum Temperatures, Precipitation, Snowfall, Extreme Temperatures, Foggy Days, Humidity and more. State sections contain two brand new features in this edition – a City Index and a narrative Description of the climatic conditions of the state. Each section also includes a revised Map of the State that includes not only weather stations, but cities and towns.

"Best Reference Book of the Year." –Library Journal

Softcover ISBN 978-1-891482-29-8, 2,013 pages, $175.00 | Ebook ISBN 978-1-59237-237-9 www.greyhouse.com/ebooks.htm

Crime in America's Top-Rated Cities

This volume includes over 20 years of crime statistics in all major crime categories: violent crimes, property crimes and total crime. *Crime in America's Top-Rated Cities* is conveniently arranged by city and covers 76 top-rated cities. Crime in America's Top-Rated Cities offers details that compare the number of crimes and crime rates for the city, suburbs and metro area along with national crime trends for violent, property and total crimes. Also, this handbook contains important information and statistics on Anti-Crime Programs, Crime Risk, Hate Crimes, Illegal Drugs, Law Enforcement, Correctional Facilities, Death Penalty Laws and much more. A much-needed resource for people who are relocating, business professionals, general researchers, the press, law enforcement officials and students of criminal justice.

"Data is easy to access and will save hours of searching." –Global Enforcement Review

Softcover ISBN 978-1-891482-84-7, 832 pages, $155.00

The Complete Directory for People with Disabilities, 2009

A wealth of information, now in one comprehensive sourcebook. Completely updated, this edition contains more information than ever before, including thousands of new entries and enhancements to existing entries and thousands of additional web sites and e-mail addresses. This up-to-date directory is the most comprehensive resource available for people with disabilities, detailing Independent Living Centers, Rehabilitation Facilities, State & Federal Agencies, Associations, Support Groups, Periodicals & Books, Assistive Devices, Employment & Education Programs, Camps and Travel Groups. Each year, more libraries, schools, colleges, hospitals, rehabilitation centers and individuals add *The Complete Directory for People with Disabilities* to their collections, making sure that this information is readily available to the families, individuals and professionals who can benefit most from the amazing wealth of resources cataloged here.

"No other reference tool exists to meet the special needs of the disabled in one convenient resource for information." –Library Journal

Softcover ISBN 978-1-59237-367-3, 1,200 pages, $165.00 | Online Database: http://gold.greyhouse.com Call (800) 562-2139 for quote

The Complete Learning Disabilities Directory, 2009

The Complete Learning Disabilities Directory is the most comprehensive database of Programs, Services, Curriculum Materials, Professional Meetings & Resources, Camps, Newsletters and Support Groups for teachers, students and families concerned with learning disabilities. This information-packed directory includes information about Associations & Organizations, Schools, Colleges & Testing Materials, Government Agencies, Legal Resources and much more. For quick, easy access to information, this directory contains four indexes: Entry Name Index, Subject Index and Geographic Index. With every passing year, the field of learning disabilities attracts more attention and the network of caring, committed and knowledgeable professionals grows every day. This directory is an invaluable research tool for these parents, students and professionals.

"Due to its wealth and depth of coverage, parents, teachers and others… should find this an invaluable resource." -Booklist

Softcover ISBN 978-1-59237-368-0, 900 pages, $150.00 | Online Database: http://gold.greyhouse.com Call (800) 562-2139 for quote

The Complete Directory for People with Chronic Illness, 2009/10

Thousands of hours of research have gone into this completely updated edition – several new chapters have been added along with thousands of new entries and enhancements to existing entries. Plus, each chronic illness chapter has been reviewed by a medical expert in the field. This widely-hailed directory is structured around the 90 most prevalent chronic illnesses – from Asthma to Cancer to Wilson's Disease – and provides a comprehensive overview of the support services and information resources available for people diagnosed with a chronic illness. Each chronic illness has its own chapter and contains a brief description in layman's language, followed by important resources for National & Local Organizations, State Agencies, Newsletters, Books & Periodicals, Libraries & Research Centers, Support Groups & Hotlines, Web Sites and much more. This directory is an important resource for health care professionals, the collections of hospital and health care libraries, as well as an invaluable tool for people with a chronic illness and their support network.

"A must purchase for all hospital and health care libraries and is strongly recommended for all public library reference departments." –ARBA

Softcover ISBN 978-1-59237-415-1, 1,200 pages, $165.00 | Online Database: http://gold.greyhouse.com Call (800) 562-2139 for quote

The Complete Mental Health Directory, 2008/09

This is the most comprehensive resource covering the field of behavioral health, with critical information for both the layman and the mental health professional. For the layman, this directory offers understandable descriptions of 25 Mental Health Disorders as well as detailed information on Associations, Media, Support Groups and Mental Health Facilities. For the professional, The Complete Mental Health Directory offers critical and comprehensive information on Managed Care Organizations, Information Systems, Government Agencies and Provider Organizations. This comprehensive volume of needed information will be widely used in any reference collection.

"… the strength of this directory is that it consolidates widely dispersed information into a single volume." –Booklist

Softcover ISBN 978-1-59237-285-0, 800 pages, $165.00 | Online Database: http://gold.greyhouse.com Call (800) 562-2139 for quote

The Comparative Guide to American Hospitals, Second Edition

This new second edition compares all of the nation's hospitals by 24 measures of quality in the treatment of heart attack, heart failure, pneumonia, and, new to this edition, surgical procedures and pregnancy care. Plus, this second edition is now available in regional volumes, to make locating information about hospitals in your area quicker and easier than ever before. The Comparative Guide to American Hospitals provides a snapshot profile of each of the nations 4,200+ hospitals. These informative profiles illustrate how the hospital rates when providing 24 different treatments within four broad categories: Heart Attack Care, Heart Failure Care, Surgical Infection Prevention (NEW), and Pregnancy Care measures (NEW). Each profile includes the raw percentage for that hospital, the state average, the US average and data on the top hospital. For easy access to contact information, each profile includes the hospital's address, phone and fax numbers, email and web addresses, type and accreditation along with 5 top key administrations. These profiles will allow the user to quickly identify the quality of the hospital and have the necessary information at their fingertips to make contact with that hospital. Most importantly, *The Comparative Guide to American Hospitals* provides easy-to-use Regional State by State Statistical Summary Tables for each of the data elements to allow the user to quickly locate hospitals with the best level of service. Plus, a new 30-Day Mortality Chart, Glossary of Terms and Regional Hospital Profile Index make this a must-have source. This new, expanded edition will be a must for the reference collection at all public, medical and academic libraries.

"These data will help those with heart conditions and pneumonia make informed decisions about their healthcare and encourage hospitals to improve the quality of care they provide. Large medical, hospital, and public libraries are most likely to benefit from this weighty resource."-Library Journal

Four Volumes Softcover ISBN 978-1-59237-182-2, 3,500 pages, $325.00 | Regional Volumes $135.00 |
Ebook ISBN 978-1-59237-239-3 www.greyhouse.com/ebooks.htm

Older Americans Information Directory, 2008

Completely updated for 2008, this sixth edition has been completely revised and now contains 1,000 new listings, over 8,000 updates to existing listings and over 3,000 brand new e-mail addresses and web sites. You'll find important resources for Older Americans including National, Regional, State & Local Organizations, Government Agencies, Research Centers, Libraries & Information Centers, Legal Resources, Discount Travel Information, Continuing Education Programs, Disability Aids & Assistive Devices, Health, Print Media and Electronic Media. Three indexes: Entry Index, Subject Index and Geographic Index make it easy to find just the right source of information. This comprehensive guide to resources for Older Americans will be a welcome addition to any reference collection.

"Highly recommended for academic, public, health science and consumer libraries…" –Choice

1,200 pages; Softcover ISBN 978-1-59237-357-4, $165.00 | Online Database: http://gold.greyhouse.com Call (800) 562-2139 for quote

The Complete Directory for Pediatric Disorders, 2009/10

This important directory provides parents and caregivers with information about Pediatric Conditions, Disorders, Diseases and Disabilities, including Blood Disorders, Bone & Spinal Disorders, Brain Defects & Abnormalities, Chromosomal Disorders, Congenital Heart Defects, Movement Disorders, Neuromuscular Disorders and Pediatric Tumors & Cancers. This carefully written directory offers: understandable Descriptions of 15 major bodily systems; Descriptions of more than 200 Disorders and a Resources Section, detailing National Agencies & Associations, State Associations, Online Services, Libraries & Resource Centers, Research Centers, Support Groups & Hotlines, Camps, Books and Periodicals. This resource will provide immediate access to information crucial to families and caregivers when coping with children's illnesses.

"Recommended for public and consumer health libraries." –Library Journal

Softcover ISBN 978-1-59237-430-4, 1,200 pages, $165.00 | Online Database: http://gold.greyhouse.com Call (800) 562-2139 for quote

The Directory of Drug & Alcohol Residential Rehabilitation Facilities

This brand new directory is the first-ever resource to bring together, all in one place, data on the thousands of drug and alcohol residential rehabilitation facilities in the United States. The Directory of Drug & Alcohol Residential Rehabilitation Facilities covers over 1,000 facilities, with detailed contact information for each one, including mailing address, phone and fax numbers, email addresses and web sites, mission statement, type of treatment programs, cost, average length of stay, numbers of residents and counselors, accreditation, insurance plans accepted, type of environment, religious affiliation, education components and much more. It also contains a helpful chapter on General Resources that provides contact information for Associations, Print & Electronic Media, Support Groups and Conferences. Multiple indexes allow the user to pinpoint the facilities that meet very specific criteria. This time-saving tool is what so many counselors, parents and medical professionals have been asking for. *The Directory of Drug & Alcohol Residential Rehabilitation Facilities* will be a helpful tool in locating the right source for treatment for a wide range of individuals. This comprehensive directory will be an important acquisition for all reference collections: public and academic libraries, case managers, social workers, state agencies and many more.

"This is an excellent, much needed directory that fills an important gap…" –Booklist

Softcover ISBN 978-1-59237-031-3, 300 pages, $135.00

The Directory of Hospital Personnel, 2009

The Directory of Hospital Personnel is the best resource you can have at your fingertips when researching or marketing a product or service to the hospital market. A "Who's Who" of the hospital universe, this directory puts you in touch with over 150,000 key decision-makers. With 100% verification of data you can rest assured that you will reach the right person with just one call. Every hospital in the U.S. is profiled, listed alphabetically by city within state. Plus, three easy-to-use, cross-referenced indexes put the facts at your fingertips faster and more easily than any other directory: Hospital Name Index, Bed Size Index and Personnel Index. *The Directory of Hospital Personnel* is the only complete source for key hospital decision-makers by name. Whether you want to define or restructure sales territories… locate hospitals with the purchasing power to accept your proposals… keep track of important contacts or colleagues… or find information on which insurance plans are accepted, *The Directory of Hospital Personnel* gives you the information you need – easily, efficiently, effectively and accurately.

"Recommended for college, university and medical libraries." -ARBA

Softcover ISBN 978-1-59237-402-1, 2,500 pages, $325.00 | Online Database: http://gold.greyhouse.com Call (800) 562-2139 for quote

The HMO/PPO Directory, 2009

The HMO/PPO Directory is a comprehensive source that provides detailed information about Health Maintenance Organizations and Preferred Provider Organizations nationwide. This comprehensive directory details more information about more managed health care organizations than ever before. Over 1,100 HMOs, PPOs, Medicare Advantage Plans and affiliated companies are listed, arranged alphabetically by state. Detailed listings include Key Contact Information, Prescription Drug Benefits, Enrollment, Geographical Areas served, Affiliated Physicians & Hospitals, Federal Qualifications, Status, Year Founded, Managed Care Partners, Employer References, Fees & Payment Information and more. Plus, five years of historical information is included related to Revenues, Net Income, Medical Loss Ratios, Membership Enrollment and Number of Patient Complaints. Five easy-to-use, cross-referenced indexes will put this vast array of information at your fingertips immediately: HMO Index, PPO Index, Other Providers Index, Personnel Index and Enrollment Index. *The HMO/PPO Directory* provides the most comprehensive data on the most companies available on the market place today.

"Helpful to individuals requesting certain HMO/PPO issues such as co-payment costs, subscription costs and patient complaints. Individuals concerned (or those with questions) about their insurance may find this text to be of use to them." -ARBA

Softcover ISBN 978-1-59237-369-7, 600 pages, $325.00 | Online Database: http://gold.greyhouse.com Call (800) 562-2139 for quote

Medical Device Register, 2009

The only one-stop resource of every medical supplier licensed to sell products in the US. This award-winning directory offers immediate access to over 13,000 companies - and more than 65,000 products – in two information-packed volumes. This comprehensive resource saves hours of time and trouble when searching for medical equipment and supplies and the manufacturers who provide them. Volume I: The Product Directory, provides essential information for purchasing or specifying medical supplies for every medical device, supply, and diagnostic available in the US. Listings provide FDA codes & Federal Procurement Eligibility, Contact information for every manufacturer of the product along with Prices and Product Specifications. Volume 2 - Supplier Profiles, offers the most complete and important data about Suppliers, Manufacturers and Distributors. Company Profiles detail the number of employees, ownership, method of distribution, sales volume, net income, key executives detailed contact information medical products the company supplies, plus the medical specialties they cover. Four indexes provide immediate access to this wealth of information: Keyword Index, Trade Name Index, Supplier Geographical Index and OEM (Original Equipment Manufacturer) Index. *Medical Device Register* is the only one-stop source for locating suppliers and products; looking for new manufacturers or hard-to-find medical devices; comparing products and companies; know who's selling what and who to buy from cost effectively. This directory has become the standard in its field and will be a welcome addition to the reference collection of any medical library, large public library, university library along with the collections that serve the medical community.

"A wealth of information on medical devices, medical device companies… and key personnel in the industry is provide in this comprehensive reference work... A valuable reference work, one of the best hardcopy compilations available." -Doody Publishing

Two Volumes, Hardcover ISBN 978-1-59237-373-4, 3,000 pages, $325.00

The Directory of Health Care Group Purchasing Organizations, 2008

This comprehensive directory provides the important data you need to get in touch with over 800 Group Purchasing Organizations. By providing in-depth information on this growing market and its members, *The Directory of Health Care Group Purchasing Organizations* fills a major need for the most accurate and comprehensive information on over 800 GPOs – Mailing Address, Phone & Fax Numbers, E-mail Addresses, Key Contacts, Purchasing Agents, Group Descriptions, Membership Categorization, Standard Vendor Proposal Requirements, Membership Fees & Terms, Expanded Services, Total Member Beds & Outpatient Visits represented and more. Five Indexes provide a number of ways to locate the right GPO: Alphabetical Index, Expanded Services Index, Organization Type Index, Geographic Index and Member Institution Index. With its comprehensive and detailed information on each purchasing organization, *The Directory of Health Care Group Purchasing Organizations* is the go-to source for anyone looking to target this market.

"The information is clearly arranged and easy to access…recommended for those needing this very specialized information." –ARBA

1,000 pages; Softcover ISBN 978-1-59237-287-4, $325.00 | Online Database: http://gold.greyhouse.com Call (800) 562-2139 for quote

Canadian Almanac & Directory, 2009

The Canadian Almanac & Directory contains sixteen directories in one – giving you all the facts and figures you will ever need about Canada. No other single source provides users with the quality and depth of up-to-date information for all types of research. This national directory and guide gives you access to statistics, images and over 100,000 names and addresses for everything from Airlines to Zoos - updated every year. It's Ten Directories in One! Each section is a directory in itself, providing robust information on business and finance, communications, government, associations, arts and culture (museums, zoos, libraries, etc.), health, transportation, law, education, and more. Government information includes federal, provincial and territorial - and includes an easy-to-use quick index to find key information. A separate municipal government section includes every municipality in Canada, with full profiles of Canada's largest urban centers. A complete legal directory lists judges and judicial officials, court locations and law firms across the country. A wealth of general information, the *Canadian Almanac & Directory* also includes national statistics on population, employment, imports and exports, and more. National awards and honors are presented, along with forms of address, Commonwealth information and full color photos of Canadian symbols. Postal information, weights, measures, distances and other useful charts are also incorporated. Complete almanac information includes perpetual calendars, five-year holiday planners and astronomical information. Published continuously for 160 years, *The Canadian Almanac & Directory* is the best single reference source for business executives, managers and assistants; government and public affairs executives; lawyers; marketing, sales and advertising executives; researchers, editors and journalists.

Hardcover ISBN 978-1-59237-370-3, 1,600 pages, $325.00

Associations Canada, 2009

The Most Powerful Fact-Finder to Business, Trade, Professional and Consumer Organizations
Associations Canada covers Canadian organizations and international groups including industry, commercial and professional associations, registered charities, special interest and common interest organizations. This annually revised compendium provides detailed listings and abstracts for nearly 20,000 regional, national and international organizations. This popular volume provides the most comprehensive picture of Canada's non-profit sector. Detailed listings enable users to identify an organization's budget, founding date, scope of activity, licensing body, sources of funding, executive information, full address and complete contact information, just to name a few. Powerful indexes help researchers find information quickly and easily. The following indexes are included: subject, acronym, geographic, budget, executive name, conferences & conventions, mailing list, defunct and unreachable associations and registered charitable organizations. In addition to annual spending of over $1 billion on transportation and conventions alone, Canadian associations account for many millions more in pursuit of membership interests. *Associations Canada* provides complete access to this highly lucrative market. *Associations Canada* is a strong source of prospects for sales and marketing executives, tourism and convention officials, researchers, government officials - anyone who wants to locate non-profit interest groups and trade associations.

Hardcover ISBN 978-1-59237-401-4, 1,600 pages, $325.00

Financial Services Canada, 2009/10

Financial Services Canada is the only master file of current contacts and information that serves the needs of the entire financial services industry in Canada. With over 18,000 organizations and hard-to-find business information, Financial Services Canada is the most up-to-date source for names and contact numbers of industry professionals, senior executives, portfolio managers, financial advisors, agency bureaucrats and elected representatives. Financial Services Canada incorporates the latest changes in the industry to provide you with the most current details on each company, including: name, title, organization, telephone and fax numbers, e-mail and web addresses. *Financial Services Canada* also includes private company listings never before compiled, government agencies, association and consultant services - to ensure that you'll never miss a client or a contact. Current listings include: banks and branches, non-depository institutions, stock exchanges and brokers, investment management firms, insurance companies, major accounting and law firms, government agencies and financial associations. Powerful indexes assist researchers with locating the vital financial information they need. The following indexes are included: alphabetic, geographic, executive name, corporate web site/e-mail, government quick reference and subject. *Financial Services Canada* is a valuable resource for financial executives, bankers, financial planners, sales and marketing professionals, lawyers and chartered accountants, government officials, investment dealers, journalists, librarians and reference specialists.

Hardcover ISBN 978-1-59237-416-8, 900 pages, $325.00

Directory of Libraries in Canada, 2009/10

The Directory of Libraries in Canada brings together almost 7,000 listings including libraries and their branches, information resource centers, archives and library associations and learning centers. The directory offers complete and comprehensive information on Canadian libraries, resource centers, business information centers, professional associations, regional library systems, archives, library schools and library technical programs. *The Directory of Libraries in Canada* includes important features of each library and service, including library information; personnel details, including contact names and e-mail addresses; collection information; services available to users; acquisitions budgets; and computers and automated systems. Useful information on each library's electronic access is also included, such as Internet browser, connectivity and public Internet/CD-ROM/subscription database access. The directory also provides powerful indexes for subject, location, personal name and Web site/e-mail to assist researchers with locating the crucial information they need. *The Directory of Libraries in Canada* is a vital reference tool for publishers, advocacy groups, students, research institutions, computer hardware suppliers, and other diverse groups that provide products and services to this unique market.

Hardcover ISBN 978-1-59237-427-4, 850 pages, $325.00

Canadian Environmental Directory, 2009

The Canadian Environmental Directory is Canada's most complete and only national listing of environmental associations and organizations, government regulators and purchasing groups, product and service companies, special libraries, and more! The extensive Products and Services section provides detailed listings enabling users to identify the company name, address, phone, fax, e-mail, Web address, firm type, contact names (and titles), product and service information, affiliations, trade information, branch and affiliate data. The Government section gives you all the contact information you need at every government level – federal, provincial and municipal. We also include descriptions of current environmental initiatives, programs and agreements, names of environment-related acts administered by each ministry or department PLUS information and tips on who to contact and how to sell to governments in Canada. The Associations section provides complete contact information and a brief description of activities. Included are Canadian environmental organizations and international groups including industry, commercial and professional associations, registered charities, special interest and common interest organizations. All the Information you need about the Canadian environmental industry: directory of products and services, special libraries and resource, conferences, seminars and tradeshows, chronology of environmental events, law firms and major Canadian companies, *The Canadian Environmental Directory* is ideal for business, government, engineers and anyone conducting research on the environment.

Softcover ISBN 978-1-59237-374-1, 900 pages, $325.00

Canadian Parliamentary Guide, 2009

An indispensable guide to government in Canada, the annual *Canadian Parliamentary Guide* provides information on both federal and provincial governments, courts, and their elected and appointed members. The Guide is completely bilingual, with each record appearing both in English and then in French. The Guide contains biographical sketches of members of the Governor General's Household, the Privy Council, members of Canadian legislatures (federal, including both the House of Commons and the Senate, provincial and territorial), members of the federal superior courts (Supreme, Federal, Federal Appeal, Court Martial Appeal and Tax Courts) and the senior staff for these institutions. Biographies cover personal data, political career, private career and contact information. In addition, the Guide provides descriptions of each of the institutions, including brief historical information in text and chart format and significant facts (i.e. number of members and their salaries). The Guide covers the results of all federal general elections and by-elections from Confederations to the present and the results of the most recent provincial elections. A complete name index rounds out the text, making information easy to find. No other resources presents a more up-to-date, more complete picture of Canadian government and her political leaders. A must-have resource for all Canadian reference collections.

Hardcover ISBN 978-1-59237-417-5, 800 pages, $184.00